ISBN 978-0-332-31242-2
PIBN 10991717

This book is a reproduction of an important historical work. Forgotten Books uses
state-of-the-art technology to digitally reconstruct the work, preserving the original format
whilst repairing imperfections present in the aged copy. In rare cases, an imperfection in
the original, such as a blemish or missing page, may be replicated in our edition. We do,
however, repair the vast majority of imperfections successfully; any imperfections that
remain are intentionally left to preserve the state of such historical works.

The Encyclopedic Digest of Virginia and West Virginia Reports

BEING A COMPLETE

Encyclopedia and Digest of all the Virginia and West Virginia Case Law up to and including Vol. 103 Virginia Reports and Vol. 55 West Virginia Reports

---

UNDER THE EDITORIAL SUPERVISION OF

THOMAS JOHNSON MICHIE

VOLUME VIII

THE MICHIE COMPANY, LAW PUBLISHERS
CHARLOTTESVILLE, VA.
1907

Table of Titles

Cross references only are in lower case (small letters).

Table of Words and Phrases

Cross references only are in lower case (small letters).

The Encyclopedic Digest of Virginia and West Virginia Reports.

INTOXICATING LIQUORS.

CROSS REFERENCES.

See the titles AGENCY, vol. 1, p. 240; ASSOCIATIONS, vol. 1, p. 843; CONSTITUTIONAL LAW, vol. 3, p. 140; CRIMINAL LAW, vol. 4, p. 1; DRUGGISTS, vol. 4, p. 830; DRUNKENNESS, vol. 4, p. 834; EVIDENCE, vol. 5, p. 295; INNS AND INNKEEPERS, vol. 7, p. 654; INTERSTATE COMMERCE, vol. 7, p. 864; JUDICIAL NOTICE; PHYSICIANS AND SURGEONS; SALES; SUNDAYS AND HOLIDAYS.

I. Definitions and Distinctions.

A. DEFINITIONS.

1. In General.

The words "spirituous liquors," do not include wine, or other fermented liquor, for they imply that the beverage is composed in part or fully of alcohol extracted by distillation. Bishop on Statutory Crimes, § 1009. Wines may or may not be spirituous—depending upon the absence or presence of alcohol in each evolved in the process of the fermentation of the juice of the grape or other fruit out of which it is made. Ale, porter and beer are neither the result of distillation, nor the fermentation of the juice of any kind of fruit. State v. Oliver, 26 W. Va. 422.

"The word 'intoxicating' includes a larger class of cases than 'spirituous'. They bear the relation to each other of genus and species; all spirituous liquors are intoxicating, but all intoxicating liquors are not spirituous." Com. v. Josiah Herrick, 6 Cush. (Mass.) 465, quoted with approval in State v. Cain, 8 W. Va. 720.

The legislative declaration that intoxicating mixtures "shall be deemed spirituous liquors" is equivalent to a declaration that they are spirituous liquors for the purposes of the act. An unlicensed sale of spirituous liquors is made an offense, and as an intoxicating mixture, preparation, or liquid is, by force of the statute, such a liquor, an unlicensed sale thereof constitutes the offense. State v. Good (W. Va.), 49 S. E. 121.

2. Ale.

Webster defines ale to be a liquor made from an infusion of malt by fermentation, differing from beer in having a smaller proportion of hops. State v. Oliver, 26 W. Va. 422.

3. Beer.

Webster defines beer—"a fermented liquor made from any kind of malted grain, with hops or other flavoring matters; also as a fermented extract of the roots and other parts of various plants, as spruce, ginger, sassafras." State v. Oliver, 26 W. Va. 422.

In State v. Thompson, 20 W. Va. 674, it was held, that the words "spirituous liquors or wine," as used in the 4th section of chapter 107, acts, 1877, do not embrace beer, and consequently a druggist is not authorized by said section to sell lager beer, but must have a state license as provided under the first section of the act above referred to.

4. Brandy.

The court will take judicial notice that apple brandy is intoxicating. Thomas v. Com., 90 Va. 92, 17 S. E. 788.

5. Cider.

According to the true intent and meaning of the first section of ch. 107 of the acts of the West Virginia legislature of 1877, which prohibits the sale without license of spirituous liquors, wine, ale, porter, beer, or any drink of like nature, neither cider nor crab cider is included in those terms. State v. Oliver, 26 W. Va. 422.

6. Porter.

Webster defines "porter" to be a "malt liquor of a dark brown color, moderately bitter and possessing tonic and intoxicating qualities." State v. Oliver, 26 W. Va. 422.

B. DISTINCTIONS BETWEEN INTOXICATING LIQUORS AND MEDICINE.

1. In General.

"The question will always be, whether it is a sale of medicine or of liquor. If an apothecary sell brandy as such, it would be a violation of the law; if brandy made up into laudanum or other medicines, it is not a violation of a law prohibiting the sale of spirituous liquor. It will never be difficult to distinguish common store cordial in sweetened whiskey sold as spirituous liquor. Godfrey's cordial is a very different thing, known for and sold as medicine; and there can be no danger by the sale of it of promoting tippling, which is the evil designed to be provided for by our act of Assembly." State v. Haymond, 20 W. Va. 18.

2. Essence of Cinnamon.

Under § 1, ch. 32, W. Va. Amended Code providing that all mixtures or preparations known as "bitters" or otherwise, which will produce intoxication, shall be deemed spirituous liquors, the sale of the essence of cinnamon is prohibited. State v. Muncey, 28 W. Va. 494.

3. Gum Camphor.

The sale of gum camphor and alcohol mixed by the seller before delivery and sold as a medicine is not embraced by § 1 of ch. 107 of the acts of the legislature of 1877, which provides, that "No person without a state license therefor shall sell, offer or expose for sale spirituous liquors, wine, porter, ale or beer, or any drink of a like nature," etc. State v. Haymond, 20 W. Va. 18.

II. Regulation and Control.

A. REASONABLENESS OF REGULATION.

The grant by the legislature to the council of the city of Danville of the right to grant or refuse licenses to all sellers of wine, or spirituous, or fermented liquors, under such regulations as it may prescribe, confers upon the council absolute control of the subject, and power to wholly suppress the privilege or to grant it under such restrictions as it may deem proper. Whether the regulations are reasonable or not is not the subject of judicial investigation or inquiry. The subject rests wholly in the discretion of the council. Danville v. Hatcher, 101 Va. 523, 44 S. E. 723.

B. REGULATION AS TO PLACE OF SALE.

See post, "Regulation as to Place of Sale," IV, D.

C. CONSTITUTIONALITY OF STATUTES AND ORDINANCES.

1. Police Power.

In General.—To traffic in liquor is not an absolute right but a business which the state, under its police power, may regulate and control. Morganstern v. Com., 94 Va. 787, 26 S. E. 402; Danville v. Hatcher, 101 Va. 523, 533, 44 S. E. 723.

Establishment of Dispensary.—The regulation of the sale of intoxicating liquor is within the police power of the state, and it may authorize a municipal corporation to establish a dispensary for the sale of such liquor, although in doing so it may render necessary the expenditure of money, and ultimately the imposition of a tax. The object is a public one, in the promotion of which public money may be expended. The act of 1901, ch. 113, conferring such power on a municipal corporation, is not contrary to the constitution in force when it was passed. It is not a tax law, but a police regulation. Farmville v. Walker, 101 Va. 323, 43 S. E. 558.

Not Solely for Revenue.—Notwithstanding the fact that the power conferred on the council of the city of Danville to grant or refuse liquor licenses occurs in a chapter of the charter entitled, "Taxes, taxation, etc.," and

is found in a section which confers power on the city "to grant or refuse license" to insurance companies and other lawful businesses, still the provisions relating to the sale of intoxicating liquors are police regulations, and are not for the sole purpose of raising revenue. Danville v. Hatcher, 101 Va. 523, 44 S. E. 723.

2. Impairment of Obligation of Contract.

In General.—"These licenses to sell liquors," said the court in Metropolitan Board of Excise v. Barrie, 34 N. Y. 657, "are not contracts between the state and the person licensed, giving the latter vested rights, protected on general principles, and by the constitution of the United States against subsequent legislation; nor are they property in any legal or constitutional sense. * * * If the act had declared that licenses under it should be irrevocable, the legislatures of subsequent years would not have been bound by the declaration. The necessary powers of the legislature over all subjects of internal police, being a part of the general grant of legislative power given by the constitution, can not be sold, given away, or relinquished. Irrevocable grants of property and franchises may be made, if they do not impair the supreme authority to make laws for the right government of the state; but no one legislature can curtail the power of its successors to make such laws as they may deem proper in matters of police." Justice v. Com., 81 Va. 209.

Statute Prohibiting Sale of Liquors.—Whether a statute that prohibits the sale of intoxicating liquors—property in existence wherein the owner has vested rights at the time of its passage—is repugnant to the United States constitution, quære. Savage v. Com., 84 Va. 582, 5 S. E. 563, 565.

3. Abridgment of Privileges and Immunities of Citizens.

In General.—The regulation of the sale of intoxicating liquors is completely within the police power of the state, and may be exercised in such manner as the legislature deems proper. It may be entirely prohibited, or such restraints may be placed upon it as the legislature thinks wise, without supervision or control by the courts. The traffic is not one of the privileges or immunities of citizenship guaranteed by the constitution of the United States, or the fourteenth amendment thereof. Danville *v.* Hatcher, 101 Va. 523, 44 S. E. 723.

Statute Prohibiting the Keeping of Liquors in Possession.—The keeping of liquors in his possession by a person, whether for himself or for another, unless he does so for the illegal sale of it, or for some other improper purpose, can by no possibility injure or affect the health, morals, or safety of the public; and, therefore, the statute prohibiting such keeping in possession is not a legitimate exercise of the police power. It is an abridgment of the privileges and immunities of the citizen without any legal justification, and therefore void, being in conflict with that provision of the fourteenth amendment to the United States constitution, which declares: "No state shall make or enforce any law which shall abridge the privileges or immunities of citizens of the United States." It is also in violation of the state constitution, which declares that "laws may be passed regulating or prohibiting the sale of intoxicating liquors within the limits of this state," since by specifying the sale of intoxicating liquors, it ipso facto excludes the power of the legislature to regulate or prohibit the keeping in possession. State *v.* Gilman, 33 W. Va. 146, 10 S. E. 283, 285.

4. Due Process of Law.

Imposition of Fine and Imprisonment.—An ordinance of the town of Beckley, which provides, "that no person shall sell, offer or expose for sale any spirituous liquors, wine, porter, ale, beer or drinks of like nature within the town of Beckley without first obtaining authority therefor from the council of the town of Beckley, as prescribed in § 23, ch. 47, of the Code of West Virginia and subsequent acts pertaining thereto," and providing further, "that any person violating said ordinance shall for every offense forfeit not less than $10.00 nor more than $50.00—and be imprisoned not exceeding thirty days," is constitutional. Beasley *v.* Beckley, 28 W. Va. 81.

By Mayor.—The provisions of the statute law conferring on the town of Moundsville the power to require a license of any person selling spirituous liquors in the town, and to pass an ordinance forbidding the sale of spirituous liquors in the town without such license being obtained, and for a violation of such ordinance to impose a reasonable fine and imprisonment not exceeding thirty days; and that punishment may be imposed by the mayor of the town by a summary proceeding, but from his judgment an appeal lies to the circuit court, where the case may be tried de novo before a jury, do not violate any of the provisions of the constitution. Moundsville *v.* Fountain, 27 W. Va. 182.

By Recorder.—The ordinance of the city of Parkersburg, requiring a city license to sell spirituous liquors within the city, is constitutional, as also is the ordinance imposing a fine of from $1 to $20 on any person selling spirituous liquors in said city without such city license, to be imposed by the recorder of said city, and subjecting the offender to imprisonment by order of the recorder for not exceeding thirty days, if such fine and the costs of the proceedings are not paid, as the legislature by act of February 7, 1870, has granted an appeal in such case to the circuit court of Wood upon terms and conditions deemed not unreasonable, and the defendant can then have his case tried by a jury of twelve men, if he wishes. Jelly *v.* Dils, 27 W. Va. 267.

III. License or Tax Laws.

A. NECESSITY OF LICENSE.

1. For Persons Soliciting Orders.

From Points without to Points within the State.—So much of § 1, ch. 32, W. Va. Code, 1891, as requires a license to solicit or receive orders for spirituous liquors, is unconstitutional and void, as applied to those soliciting orders for the sale of goods to be shipped from points outside this state to points within this state. State v. Lichtenstein, 44 W. Va. 99, 28 S. E. 753. See generally, the title INTERSTATE COMMERCE, vol. 8, p. 864.

Where No Order Given.—The provision of W. Va. Code, 1891, § 1, ch. 32, prohibiting any person without license from soliciting or receiving orders for liquor, applies to one merely soliciting orders for liquor, though no such order be given. State v. Wheat, 48 W. Va. 259, 37 S. E. 544.

2. For Social Clubs.

See the title ASSOCIATIONS, vol. 1, p. 843.

Liquors kept by a club in its rooms, and served only to its members and their invited guests—the members alone paying therefor—and the money being used to replenish the stock, but insufficient for the purpose; held, not such sale of liquors as requires a license under Virginia acts, 1889-90, p. 242. Piedmont Club v. Com., 87 Va. 540, 12 S. E. 963.

The defendant club, in dispensing liquors to or at the expense of its own members, was not engaged in carrying on the business of selling liquor, and a liquor license is required of those persons only who sell or offer to sell liquor as a business. Piedmont Club v. Com., 87 Va. 540, 12 S. E. 963.

But see cl. 142 of the tax bill, p. 2262, of Pollards' Va. Code, for the law as to license for social clubs, requiring that they shall pay a tax to the state.

Under § 1, ch. 32, W. Va. Code, it is unlawful for a literary and social club, without first obtaining a state license therefor, to sell, offer, or expose for sale, to its members, spirituous liquors, wine, porter, ale, or beer, or any drink of a like nature. State v. Shumate, 44 W. Va. 490, 29 S. E. 1001.

3. For Brewers.

A brewery which has paid the license tax required by §§ 54, 55, ch. 32, of the West Virginia Code of 1899, must have a license under § 62 of said chapter, to entitle it to sell its product at wholesale. State v. Schmulbach Brewing Co. (W. Va.), 49 S. E. 249.

4. For One Keeping in Possession for Another.

Abridgment of Privileges or Immunities.—That portion of § 1, ch. 32, W. Va. Code, 1887, which provides that no person, without a state license therefor, shall "keep in his possession, for another, spirituous liquors," etc., is unconstitutional and void, as being an abridgment of the privileges and immunities of the citizen, and also in violation of that provision of the West Virginia constitution which declares that "laws may be passed regulating or prohibiting the sale of intoxicating liquors within the limits of this state." State v. Gilman, 33 W. Va. 146, 10 S. E. 283.

B. RIGHT TO LICENSE.

See post, "Discretion as to Granting or Refusing License," III, C, 3.

C. GRANT OR ISSUANCE OF LICENSE.

1. Who Is Applicant.

The applicant is a party directly in interest in the decision refusing the license, and comes within the letter of Va. Code, 1873, ch. 178, § 2. Not so with contestant. Ex parte Lester, 77 Va. 663.

The applicant is a party directly in interest in the decision refusing the license, and comes within the letter of Va. Code, 1873, ch. 178, § 2, and might have applied to the circuit court, or judge thereof in vacation, upon bill of exceptions taken at the trial in the county court, for a writ of error. Ex parte Lester, 77 Va. 663.

The contestant is not a party directly in interest in the decision refusing the license, and does not come within the letter of Va. Code, 1873, ch. 178, § 2, and so has no right to apply to the circuit court, or judge thereof in vacation, upon bill of exceptions taken at the time of the trial in the county court, for a writ of error. Ex parte Lester, 77 Va. 663.

2. Power of City Council to Grant.

Constitutionality.—The act of February 24, 1869, amending the charter of the town of Ceredo, confers upon the council of that town the sole power to grant or not grant a state license for the sale of intoxicating liquors within the limits of said town. Wilson v. Ross, 40 W. Va. 278, 21 S. E. 868.

Such act is not repugnant to the constitution of the state (see § 46 of article 6, and § 24 of article 8, of the state constitution), and such sole power to grant such license or not is recognized by § 11 of chapter 32 of the West Virginia Code as vested in the municipal authorities of such town. Wilson v. Ross, 40 W. Va. 278, 21 S. E. 868.

The provisions of chapter 44, acts, 1899, W. Va., that the council of the city of Grafton shall have exclusive power to grant liquor licenses within it, is not repugnant to § 24, art. 8, of the constitution, or any other clause therein. Ward v. County Court, 51 W. Va. 102, 41 S. E. 154.

Power of City Council as Distinguished from That of Corporation Court.—Under the provisions of the charter of the city of Danville, the power to adopt the policy of granting or refusing licenses to sell intoxicating liquors within the city limits is vested in the city council, but the power to grant or refuse licenses to individual applicants is vested in the corporation court of the city. The two provisions are not in conflict. Danville v. Hatcher, 101 Va. 523, 44 S. E. 723.

3. Discretion as to Granting or Refusing License.

a. Rule in Virginia.

Review of Case.—Ex parte Yeager, 11 Gratt. 655, construing the statute of 1849, and French v. Noel, 22 Gratt. 454, construing the similar statute of 1870, held that the discretion of county courts as to the granting or refusing of licenses was absolute, and not subject to appeal or review. Construing the statute, 1880, Leigton v. Maury, 76 Va. 865, held that the county courts had discretion in the matter of granting or refusing licenses, not an arbitrary discretion, but a sound judicial discretion, reviewable upon appeal and error upon petition of either applicant or contestant. Ailstock v. Page, 77 Va. 386, however, construing the law of 1880, as amended by act of March 6, 1882, overruled, Leigton v. Maury, so far as the latter allowed right of appeal or error to the contestant, but decided nothing concerning the applicant. Ex parte Lester, 77 Va. 663, construing act of March 6, 1882, held that to applicant denied liquor license by county court, there was given an appeal of right to the circuit court, and that upon bill of exceptions taken at the trial, he might apply to the circuit court for a writ of error and supersedeas. But in the latest case, Lester v. Price, 83 Va. 648, 3 S. E. 529, construing the act of 1883-84, it was held, that the application for license to retail liquor must be made to the county court, and either applicant or defendant might appeal of right from the decision to the circuit court, when the application would be heard de novo, and no appeal would lie from the decision of the latter court.

Present Statutory Law.—The law on the subject at present is substantially as follows, though there is no adjudged case on the subject: "Licenses to retail spirituous liquors shall be obtained from the circuit or corporation court of the county court or city in which the business is to be conducted. It shall be lawful for any person who may consider that he would be aggrieved by granting such license to have himself entered and made a party defendant to said application and to defend and contest the same. If the court be fully satisfied, upon the hearing of the testimony for and against the application, that the applicant is a fit person to conduct such business * * * the court may grant such license. * * * And after February 1st, 1904, there shall be no appeal by either party to such application from the order of the circuit court on such application." Acts, 1902, 1903, cl. 141, of Tax Bill.

b. Rule in West Virginia.

Early Rule.—The constitution and statutes are mandatory on the county court; and it is very wrong in that court to not strictly follow the requirements of the law, in the matter of granting, or refusing license to sell spirituous liquors, etc.; yet the sole power (except when by special law it is placed elsewhere), is lodged with that court to act in such matters; and the law certainly has not conferred upon the circuit court the power, by supersedeas, to review such action of the county court. Hein v. Smith, 13 W. Va. 358, 368.

The court is therefore of opinion, that the order of the defendant, Joseph Smith, judge of the circuit court of Mason county, dated the 8th day of April, 1878, awarding, on the petition of William Smith, a supersedeas to the said order of the county court of Mason county, and all the proceedings, which were afterwards had upon the said supersedeas, and especially the judgment, rendered upon the same by a circuit court held for said county on the 20th day of April, 1878, pronouncing the said orders of the county court to be erroneous, and considering that the same be reversed and annulled, and that the said Smith recover against the said Hein his costs, by him expended in prosecuting the said supersedeas, were all coram non judice and null and void; the said judge having no author-

ity to award the said supersedeas, and the said circuit court having no authority to entertain jurisdiction of the same. Hein v. Smith, 13 W. Va. 358.

Later Rule.—Section 28, W. Va. Code, acts, 1899, provides that "Whenever anything for which a state license is required is to be done in said city the council may require a city license therefor, and may impose a tax thereon for the use of said city, and whenever said city license is granted by the council for the sale of brandy, whisky, rum, gin, porter, ale or beer, or any other spirituous, vinous or malt liquors, or drinks of like nature, the county court shall grant a state license for the sale thereof within the corporate limits of said city." In an action of mandamus to compel a county court to issue a license to one licensed by the city council of Grafton, it was held, that the provision that the county court shall issue a license is mandatory. Ward v. County Court, 51 W. Va. 102, 41 S. E. 154.

c. Particular Forms of Review.

(1) In General.

To applicant denied liquor license, by the act of March 6, 1882, there is given an appeal of right to the circuit court. Under Code, 1873, ch. 178, § 2, he may upon bill of exceptions taken at the trial, apply to the circuit court for a writ of error and supersedeas. Of his two remedies he may resort to either. And if the circuit court also erroneously refuse the license, its decision is reviewable by this court upon appeal, or writ of error and supersedeas, as in other cases. Ex parte Lester, 77 Va. 663.

Where, under acts 1879-80, p. 148, application for liquor license is refused by county court, and during the same term the applicant appeals to circuit judge or court (not upon bill of exceptions to rulings of county court), the appeal is but a transfer of the application to another tribunal, where it is heard de novo. Leigton v. Maury, 76 Va. 865, 869; Ex parte Lester, 77 Va.

663; Haddox *v.* County of Clarke, 79 Va. 677.

(2) Mandamus.

The act, Va. Code, ch. 96, § 3, p. 443, vests in the county courts a discretion to grant or refuse a license to keep a tavern; in the exercise of which discretion they can not be controlled by the circuit court and by mandamus. Ex parte Yeager, 11 Gratt. 655.

(3) Certiorari.

The act, Va. Code, ch. 96, § 3, p. 443, vests in the county court a discretion to grant or refuse a license to keep a tavern; in the exercise of which discretion they can not be controlled by the circuit courts by certiorari. Ex parte Yeager, 11 Gratt. 655.

(4) Writ of Error.

The act, Va. Code, ch. 96, § 3, p. 443, vests in the county court a discretion to grant or refuse a license to keep a tavern; in the exercise of which discretion they can not be controlled by the circuit courts by writ of error. Ex parte Yeager, 11 Gratt. 655.

(5) Prohibition.

Against Circuit Court.—After the judgment of the circuit court annulling a certificate for obtaining a license to sell spirituous liquors, etc., granted by a county court, has been rendered, as well as before, the person injured by the judgment may obtain from the supreme court of appeals a writ of prohibition, to restrain the appellant and the judge from proceeding to enforce such judgment. Hein *v.* Smith, 13 W. Va. 358.

After the judgment of the circuit court has been rendered, reversing and annulling an order of the county court, which has granted a license to sell liquor by retail, as well as before, the person injured by the judgment may apply to the court of appeals for a writ of prohibition, to restrain the appellant and the judge from proceeding to enforce said judgment. French *v.* Noel, 22 Gratt. 454.

A. applied to county court of R. for license to sell, by retail, liquor at G. P. opposed. By the evidence the court was fully satisfied that A. brought his case within the requirements of the law, and granted the license. P. excepted. The court certified the evidence. P. obtained from the circuit judge a writ of error and supersedeas. On petition of A. to this court for a writ of prohibition to the circuit court; held, the circuit court had no jurisdiction to award a writ of error and supersedeas in this case. The writ of prohibition must be awarded, so that the judgment of the county court will remain as if no writ of error and supersedeas had been awarded. Ailstock *v.* Page, 77 Va. 386.

Against County Assessor.—Prohibition will not lie to prohibit a county assessor from issuing a license to sell liquor, as he is not a court, nor his action judicial, and this writ goes only against a judicial tribunal and judicial action. Hawk's Nest *v.* County Court, 55 W. Va. 689, 48 S. E. 205.

When Prohibition Will Lie.—Prohibition does not lie to prevent the issuance of a license to sell spirituous liquors, when the act complained of has been already done. Hawk's Nest *v.* County Court, 55 W. Va. 689, 48 S. E. 205.

D. WHEN LICENSE TAKES EFFECT.

In Sights *v.* Yarnalls, 12 Gratt. 292, the case was as follows: By an ordinance of the city of Wheeling, a license to keep a house of entertainment was to expire on May 1st next succeeding the date thereof. The council having in April granted such a license for the succeeding year, held such grant did not vest in the party to whom it was granted any absolute or vested right to such license; but the right did not become perfect until the actual emanation of the license, or until May 1st following.

Payment of Tax—Condition Precedent.—In Sights *v.* Yarnalls, 12 Gratt.

292, it was held that, the charter of the city of Wheeling authorizing it to levy a tax on innkeepers, the payment of the tax may be made a condition precedent to the issuing of the license. And, further, that where in such case a license had been ordered, though upon payment of a tax unequal, oppressive and illegal, the payment was notwithstanding a condition precedent and must be made before any right to the license will vest. Nor can the grant be considered as absolute, the condition being inseparable from it. The innkeeper must accept the whole or reject the whole.

E. LICENSE TO PARTNERS.

While a license may be granted to two persons jointly, it was held in Com. v. Hall, 8 Gratt. 588, that a license to one man to keep a tavern at his house in a village does not authorize another who formed a partnership with the first for the sale of spirituous liquors which the first was authorized to sell under his license, to sell liquor at a house on the same lot and within the same inclosure as that of the tavern.

F. HOW PAYMENT OF LICENSE ENFORCED.

Section 63, ch. 57, acts, 1866-67, p. 849, in relation to the assessment of taxes on licenses, which gives a sheriff power, if the taxes be not paid, to distrain and sell so much of the personal property of the person not paying taxes as may be necessary to pay the taxes so assessed, and if he shall be unable to find sufficient property to satisfy the property so assessed, and the same shall not be immediately paid, to arrest the person and hold him in custody until the payment is made, or until he enter into bond, with sufficient security, is not in conflict with that part of the Virginia bill of rights, which declares that no man shall "be deprived of his liberty, except by the law of the land or the judgment of his peers." Com. v. Byrne, 20 Gratt. 165.

G. REVOCATION OF LICENSE.

1. Nature of Revocation.

The revocation of a license to sell liquor is not a punishment for any special offense, but is simply the withdrawal of a privilege which the state grants to carry on legitimate business. Davis v. Com., 75 Va. 944.

2. Who May Revoke.

Section 106, ch. 206, of the acts of 1874-75, is not repealed by the acts of March 30th, 1877, in relation to the sale of wine, etc., as there is no repugnancy between the provision of the old act and the new, and therefore the judge of the hustings court of the city of Richmond has authority to revoke a license given for keeping a bar for the sale of wine, etc. Hogan v. Guigon, 29 Gratt. 705.

The court which grants a license to keep a barroom has the power to revoke the same for cause. Davis v. Com., 75 Va. 944.

3. Cause for Revocation.

The fact that the person to whom the license was granted has been convicted in another court of a violation of the law against selling liquor on Sunday, is a sufficient cause to warrant such revocation of the license. Davis v. Com., 75 Va. 944.

4. Proceedings to Revoke.

a. On Whose Motion.

Proceedings to revoke liquor licenses under § 106, ch. 206, acts of assembly, 1874-75, may be on the motion of any other person, as well as of the commonwealth's attorney. Cherry v. Com., 78 Va. 375.

b. Former Conviction in Bar.

In proceedings under § 106, ch. 206, acts of assembly, 1874-75, the defendant is not entitled to a trial by jury. The object is not punishment, but revocation of privilege. It is no bar to the proceeding that it is founded on some act or offense wherefor the defendant has been formerly convicted. Cherry v. Com., 78 Va. 375, citing Davis v. Com., 75 Va. 944.

c. **Defendant Competent to Testify.**

In proceedings to revoke liquor licenses under § 106, ch. 206, acts of assembly 1874-75, the defendants are competent to testify in their own behalf, those proceedings being not criminal in their nature. Cherry v. Com., 78 Va. 375.

d. **Writ of Prohibition.**

Prohibition does not lie to prevent a county court from granting license to sell liquor or compel it to revoke a license granted without the consent of a town counsel. Hawk's Nest v. County Court, 55 W. Va. 689, 48 S. E. 205.

e. **Application of Rules.**

It was not the intention of the legislature to require in proceedings under § 106, ch. 206, acts of assembly, 1874-75, p. 244, concerning the proceedings to revoke licenses, the application of the strict and technical rules applicable to indictments. Cherry v. Com., 78 Va. 375.

In a proceeding under § 560 of the Virginia Code, to revoke a license to sell liquor, the notice is sufficient if it states the charges in general terms; provided they are stated with sufficient certainty to enable the person whose license is sought to be revoked to understand the ground upon which the revocation will be asked. The proceeding is a summary one, and such strict and technical rules as are applied to indictments and other forms of accusation in criminal prosecutions will not be required. A notice is sufficient which states the charge as "selling, and causing to be sold, to minors, whiskey, wine and beer." Lillienfeld v. Com., 92 Va. 818, 23 S. E. 882.

H. **CONSTITUTIONALITY OF LAWS RELATING TO LICENSE.**

Equality and Uniformity of Taxation.—The provision of the act of the general assembly of March 30th, 1877, known as the Moffett register law, which directs that the cities of the commonwealth shall be first supplied with the registers, is not unconstitutional as being an unjust and partial discrimination against liquor dealers in the cities. Helfrick v. Com., 29 Gratt. 844.

I. **APPLICATION TO CHANGE BARROOM.**

Application to county court under Va. Code, 1873, ch. 34, § 7, to change barroom to some other place in the county, is an application for license to sell liquor by retail for which the applicant has no license, and comes under the provisions of acts, 1883-84, p. 605, and is subject to its provisions as to appeal; and applicant, refused license on appeal, by circuit court, is not entitled to an appeal to this court as provided by Code, 1873, ch. 178, § 2. Lester v. Price, 83 Va. 648, 3 S. E. 529.

J. **LICENSE BOND—SURETIES.**

Law Part of Sureties Contract.—Sureties on the bond of one who has given bond not to sell liquor to minors, stand on the letter of their contract, which is not to be extended by mere implication. But the law at the time of 'their contract is part of it, and, if it give to the contract a certain legal effect, it is as much part of it as if in terms incorporated therein, unless the law requires its insertion, and sureties are bound according to such law. State v. Nutter, 44 W. Va. 385, 30 S. E. 67.

Judgment against Principal Conclusive against Sureties.—A judgment against a principal for unlawfully selling intoxicating liquors to a minor does not bind the surety on his bond conclusively, as a general rule, but it is prima facie evidence of liability and its extent. If, however, the instrument binds its makers to abide the result of certain litigation, or to satisfy any judgment therein, or to indemnify against it, a judgment against the principal is conclusive upon the sureties, so that they can not contest the liability, in the absence of fraud or collusion. State v. Nutter, 44 W. Va. 385, 30 S. E. 67.

IV. Local Option.

A. PROSECUTION UNDER GENERAL LAW.

In a county where the "local option law" (Va. Code, 1887, ch. 25), has been adopted, the sale of liquor without license is none the less liable to prosecution as a violation of the general revenue laws. Webster *v.* Com., 89 Va. 154, 15 S. E. 513.

B. ELECTION.

1. Necessity of Notice.

Where, as under acts, 1879-80, p. 271, a question is submitted to the qualified voters of a county and of each magisterial district, and it is made the duty of the sheriff of the county to post notices of the election at every voting place in the county within a prescribed period preceding the election, the failure so to post said notices invalidates the election. Haddox *v.* County of Clarke, 79 Va. 677.

How Want of Notice May Be Proved. —On application for liquor license in a county where such an election has taken place, either in the first case before the county court, or in the second case before the circuit court or judge in vacation, parol evidence is admissible to prove that notices of the election had not been posted, or that any other plain and express provision of the statute, providing for the election, had not been complied with. Chalmers *v.* Funk, 76 Va. 717; Haddox *v.* County of Clarke, 79 Va. 677.

2. Number of Votes Necessary.

Under an act approved February 14th, 1882, entitled "An act authorizing the voters of Roanoke county to vote upon the question of granting license for the sale of liquors therein, or in any magisterial district thereof," an election was held on April 13th, 1882, at which 591 votes were cast, whereof 101 were for, and 339 were against granting license in the county. A majority of the votes cast in each magisterial district were also against the granting of the licenses. The number of registered voters in the county exceeded two thousand. F. & Son applied to the county court of said county for license to sell liquors therein. Of said act § 4 declares: "If it appear from the abstracts and returns of any such election that in the said county a majority of the registered votes have been cast against license for the sale of intoxicating liquors, then no license shall be granted to any person for the sale of such liquors." And § 5 declares: "But if it appears from the abstracts and returns of any such election, that in the said county a majority of votes have been cast in favor of license, and that a majority of votes have been cast against licenses in any district or districts of said county, then no license for such sale in any of the districts so voting shall be granted." When the act passed the house of delegates, the word "registered" was not in it. When it went to the senate, it was there amended by the insertion of the word "registered," before the word "votes," in the second line of § 4; and so amended, it passed the house and became a law. The county court denied the license on the ground that by the result of the said election it was forbidden to grant it. On appeal, the circuit court granted the license, and to its judgment the appellants sought a writ of supersedeas. Held: Applying the rules of construction without doing violence to the language used, or resorting to any strange interpretation, but looking to all the parts of the act and to the history of its passage, it is plain that the intent of the legislature was to require a majority of the registered voters of the county, instead of a majority of the votes cast, to be given against license in order to inhibit the granting of license to sell liquor in the said county, or in any magisterial district thereof. Chalmers *v.* Funk, 76 Va. 717.

3. Effect of Repeal of Act.

A local option election held July 1st, 1886, under act of February 26, 1886, was not invalidated by repeal of that act after May 1, 1888, by the adoption of Va. Code, § 4202, for even though the act itself were repealed, yet it does not follow that what was done under the said act, prior to the going into effect of the Code, was thereby undone or set aside. Thomas *v.* Com., 90 Va. 92, 17 S. E. 788.

4. Judicial Notice.

See the title INDICTMENTS, IN-FORMATIONS AND PRESENT-MENTS, vol. 7, p. 371.

The court will take notice judicially that at an election held under act of February 26, 1886, in the magisterial district wherein the offense is laid, the vote against license prevailed, and no allegation to that effect is necessary in the indictment. (Savage's Case, 84 Va 582, 5 S. E. 563. Thomas *v.* Com., 90 Va. 92, 17 S. E. 788.

Under Va. acts, 1885-86, p. 259, § 5, it is not necessary that indictment allege that the magisterial district wherein the sale occurred, voted against license, the court taking judicial notice of such vote; nor that the liquor sold was the subject of license before the vote was taken; nor the time when the sale was made, the time of sale not being of the essence of the offense. Acts, 1877-88, p. 335, §§ 11, 12. Savage *v.* Com., 84 Va. 582, 5 S. E. 563.

An indictment under Va. Code, 1887, § 587, for a violation of the local option law, reciting that the defendant at a certain time and place, "did unlawfully sell wine, spirituous liquors, etc.," is not bad because it fails to state that the magisterial district had voted against the sale of liquor therein, as the court will take judicial notice of such fact. Hargrave *v.* Com., 2 Va. Dec. 139, citing Savage *v.* Com., 84 Va. 582, 5 S. E. 563, and Thomas *v.* Com., 90 Va. 92, 17 S. E. 788.

An indictment under Va. Code, 1887, for a violation of the local option law, reciting that the defendant, at a certain time and place, "did unlawfully sell wine, spirituous liquors, etc.," is not bad because it fails to allege that the sale was without a license; or because it is not stated whether the sale was by wholesale or retail; or because it fails to state that the magisterial district had voted against the sale of liquors therein, as the court would take judicial notice of these facts. Hargrave *v.* Com., 2 Va. Dec. 139, citing Savage *v.* Com., 84 Va. 582, 5 S. E. 563, and Savage *v.* Com., 84 Va. 619, 5 S. E. 565, and Thomas *v.* Com., 90 Va. 92, 17 S. E. 788.

C. CONSTITUTIONALITY.

Delegation of Power.—In Savage *v.* Com., 84 Va. 619, 5 S. E. 565, it was held, that the statute providing for the submission of the question of liquor license to the qualified voters of the several counties, etc., of the state, was not unconstitutional as delegating a portion of the legislative power of the general assembly.

D. REGULATION AS TO PLACE OF SALE.

The provision in the act of February 13, 1871, amending the charter of the town of New Martinsville, in Wetzel county, that no license to sell spirituous liquors within one mile of said town shall be granted by the board of supervisors of said county, without the consent of said town, will not prevent the granting of license to sell spirituous liquors at a place within the town of Brooklyn, with the consent of said town of Brooklyn, and against the objection of said town of New Martinsville, though the place at which such liquors are to be sold be within one mile of the corporate limits of the town of New Martinsville. New Martinsville *v.* Dunlap, 33 W. Va. 457, 10 S. E. 803.

V. Violation of Liquor Laws.

A. WHAT ACT CONSTITUTES UNLAWFUL SALE.

Proof of procurement and delivery of a bottle of whiskey by one person to another, at the request of the latter, is not, without more, sufficient to establish an unlawful sale. State *v.* Thomas, 13 W. Va. 848.

Sale in County Other than That in Which Indictment Brought—Executory Contract of Sale.—A partner of a wholesale and retail licensed dealer in spirituous liquors in Wood county visits Taylor county, and there solicits orders on his firm for whiskey. The whiskey to fill these orders is shipped in jugs by the Baltimore & Ohio Railroad, being delivered by the firm to an express agent in Wood county for transportation to the purchasers in Taylor county. They receive the whiskey in Taylor county and pay the express charges, and subsequently, when on a visit to said county of Taylor, this partner collects in Taylor county of these parties the price, which had been agreed upon for the whiskey. Held, this partner can not be indicted in Taylor county for selling spirituous liquors without license, as on this state of facts the sales were made in Wood county, when the jugs of whiskey were delivered to the express agent. Until then there was only an executory contract for the sale of the whiskey, and the sale became complete and the property in the whiskey was transferred to the purchasers when it was delivered to the express agent for transportation, and not when it was received of the express agent by the purchasers. State *v.* Hughes, 22 W. Va. 743.

Sale C. O. D.—A party residing in Doddridge county sends a postal card through the mail to a licensed wholesale liquor dealer doing business as such in Wood county, directing a package of whiskey to be sent him by express C. O. D. The order thus sent having been received in Wood county, and having been complied with by delivering the package, marked "C. O. D.," addressed to the purchaser in Doddridge county, held, that under the circumstances the sale was made in Wood county, and said wholesale mer-

chant was not liable, under indictment in Doddridge county, for retailing liquors without license in Doddridge county. State *v.* Flanagan, 38 W. Va. 53, 17 S. E. 792.

B. PURCHASE AS DISTINGUISHED FROM SALE.

Under the West Virginia statute a man can not be subject to any penalty for the purchase of whiskey or other intoxicants, but only for the sale thereof without license. State *v.* Miller, 26 W. Va. 106.

C. SELLING WITHOUT LICENSE.
1. Definition.

"The offense of selling ardent spirits without license is not an offense against third persons, but an offense against the revenue laws, and it may be against social order and public morals. The offense is the selling without license. It matters not to whom or to what person it is sold; and therefore the name of the person is immaterial to be stated. But under the statute upon which the indictments before us are found, the offense is not the mere selling of ardent spirits; but selling or furnishing the same to a minor without the consent of the parent or guardian. In such a case the act constituting the offense, is an injury to third persons." Morganstern *v.* Com., 27 Gratt. 1018.

2. Single Sale a Violation.

Under § 534, Va. Code, forbidding the sale of wine, ardent spirits, etc., without a license, a single sale of liquor without a license is a violation, as the law is not limited to persons engaged in carrying on the traffic. Lewis *v.* Com., 90 Va. 843, 20 S. E. 777.

3. Sales by Physicians or Druggists.
a. Construction of Statute.

Under the West Virginia statute (§ 6, ch. 32, W. Va. Code, 1887) which declares that a prescription to authorize a druggist to sell spirituous liquors must specify that the liquors are absolutely necessary, it is held, that a prescription which omits the word "absolutely" is insufficient, as it is only in extreme cases that the sale of spirituous liquors was intended to be legally permitted by druggists, and, besides, it is a canon of construction that effect must be given to every word in a statute if that be possible. State *v.* Tetrick, 34 W. Va. 137, 11 S. E. 1002.

b. Necessity for Good Faith.

Under W. Va. Code, ch. 32, § 7, if a physician gives a prescription to enable one to obtain liquor from a druggist as medicine, either stating that it is, or that he believes it is, absolutely necessary as a medicine, and not as a beverage, when he either knows, or believes, or has reason to believe it is not so necessary, or when he does not know it to be so necessary, he violates said statute, and is guilty of the offense it creates. The physician must act in entire good faith. It is his duty to examine and ascertain whether the liquor is absolutely necessary as a medicine. State *v.* Berkeley, 41 W. Va. 455, 23 S. E. 608.

c. Prescription Must Name Person for Whom Prescribed.

A prescription to enable one to obtain liquor from a druggist as medicine, names A as the person needing such liquor, when he does not need it, and the physician knows he does not need it; but A is getting it for the use of another. The statute is violated, though that other person may so need the liquor as a medicine. The prescription must name the person for whom the liquor is prescribed. State *v.* Berkeley, 41 W. Va. 455, 23 S. E. 608.

In a prosecution against a druggist for selling alcohol, spirituous liquors, etc., where in a prescription by a physician the name "Mr. Gibson" only appears on the face of the prescription, and it is endorsed, "Taylor Gibson," and it is agreed that the Mr. Gibson referred to in said prescription is the same Gibson who got the spirits, this fixes the identity of the party to whom the prescription was given, and who made the purchase, and the prescription is sufficient so far as the name of the party for whom the spirits were prescribed is concerned. State *v.* Bluefield Drug Co., 43 W. Va. 144, 27 S. E. 350.

d. Presumption of Unlawful Sale.

In any prosecution against a druggist for selling alcohol, spirituous liquors, or wine, if the sale be proven, it shall be presumed that the sale was unlawful, in the absence of satisfactory proof to the contrary; but this presumption may be rebutted by the production of the written prescription of a practicing physician in good standing in his profession, and not of intemperate habits, complying with the requirements of § 6 of chapter 32 of the West Virginia Code. State *v.* Bluefield Drug Co., 43 W. Va. 144, 27 S. E. 350.

Sufficiency of Prescription to Rebut Presumption.—Where the statute (W. Va. Code, § 6, ch. 32) provides that "in any prosecution against a druggist for selling alcohol, etc., without a license therefor, if the sale be proven, it shall be presumed that the sale was unlawful in the absence of satisfactory proof to the contrary," and the prescription relied on to rebut the presumption stated that the liquor was for "Mr. Gibson," and it was agreed that the "Taylor Gibson" who got the liquor was the same as the one named in the prescription, and that the prescription otherwise complied with the statute; it was held, that under the circumstances of the case, it constituted a sufficient defense to the indictment. State *v.* Bluefield Drug Co., 43 W. Va. 144, 27 S. E. 350.

e. Sales by Clerk.

When a druggist · has spirituous liquors in his store, and a sale thereof is made in violation of the statute (ch. 107, W. Va. acts, 1877) by his clerk, he will be responsible for the sale, and may be fined therefor, notwithstanding the sale may have been without his knowledge and contrary to his instructions to his clerk. State *v.* Denoon, 31 W. Va. 122, 5 S. E. 315.

f. For What Purpose a Druggist May Sell Liquors.

By § 4, ch. 107, acts of the legislature of 1877, it is clearly manifested, that the legislative intent was to prohibit a druggist, unless he had the license mentioned in the first section, from selling spirituous liquors, wine, etc., except only in case he sold alcohol in good faith for medical purposes, or mechanical alcohol or other spirituous liquors, or wine upon the written prescription of a practicing physician, which prescription must have all the requisites prescribed in said section. State *v.* Cox, 23 W. Va. 797.

g. Necessity of State License to Sell Beer.

The words "spirituous liquors or wine," as used in the fourth section of chapter 107, acts of 1877, do not embrace beer; and therefore a druggist either with or without a proper prescription therefor is not authorized by said section to sell lager beer; but to do so, he must have a state license as provided under the first section of said act. State *v.* Thompson, 20 W. Va. 674.

4. Sales by Clubs.

See ante, "License or Tax Laws," III; "For Social Clubs," III, A, 2.

A corporation claiming to be a social and literary club, which requires no qualifications for membership except the payment of an initiation fee of one dollar, for which fee there is issued to the applicant a membership card and a coupon with twenty tickets attached each, "good for five cents for games and supplies," which tickets are received by the general manager of the club in exchange for drinks, one ticket for a glass of beer, and two tickets for a drink of whiskey, and the members are permitted to buy such coupons with five, ten, or twenty tickets attached at twenty-five cents, fifty cents, and one dollar each, respectively, to be so exchanged for such drinks at such club; held, to be a fraudulent devise to evade the revenue laws of the state. Cohen *v.* King Knob Club, 55 W. Va. 108, 46 S. E. 799. And see generally, the title ASSOCIATIONS, vol. 1, p. 843.

5. Sales by Keeper of House of Private Entertainment.

A person licensed to keep a house of private entertainment may be convicted of the offense of retailing intoxicating liquors without license. But such person, licensed as aforesaid, is not guilty of keeping an unlicensed ordinary merely because he sells liquor to be drunk at his place of entertainment in addition to furnish lodgings at that place. Burner *v.* Com., 13 Gratt. 778.

6. Sales by Wholesale Liquor Dealer.

One licensed as a wholesale liquor dealer in one county is not liable to prosecution under § 1, ch. 32, W. Va. Code, 1891, prohibiting any person without license from soliciting or receiving orders for liquor, for merely mailing circulars soliciting such orders, addressed to persons in another county. State *v.* Wheat, 48 W. Va. 259, 37 S. E. 544.

7. Sales after Passage of Moffett Register Act.

A person selling liquor without a license at a time after the passage of the Moffett register act, but before the registers provided for in that act were supplied, is not liable to the punishment of imprisonment imposed by that act, but only to that punishment by fine imposed by former revenue laws. Marxhausen *v.* Com., 29 Gratt. 853.

8. Sales on Board Vessel.

Liquor can not, without license obtained in accordance with the laws of this state, be lawfully sold therein, either on land or on board of a vessel, although the seller may have obtained from the United States government a special tax stamp therefor, it being expressly provided by § 3243 of the United States Revised Statutes that persons holding such stamps shall not be exempt from any penalty imposed by the laws of any state for carrying on the trade within its limits. Com. v. Sheckels, 78 Va. 36.

9. Sales by Wholesale Druggist.

An agent and commercial traveler for a wholesale druggist, who is doing business in the city of Parkersburg, Wood County, W. Va., who receives an order in Roane county, W. Va., on the firm he represents, for two gallons of alcohol, is liable to indictment and conviction under § 1, ch. 32, W. Va. Code, in the county where the order was received, unless he shows, by way of defense, that he was acting under a state license at the time and place of receiving said order. State v. Swift, 35 W. Va. 542, 14 S. E. 135.

10. Penalty for Violation of Law.

A person, although a druggist, may be convicted on an indictment found under the first section of ch. 107, acts, 1877, unless he can show, that as such druggist he had complied with all the requirements as to the sale of spirituous liquors, etc., provided by the fourth section; but if convicted on such indictment, only the penalty prescribed for a sale without a state license could be inflicted, and not the heavier penalty prescribed for the unlawful sale by a druggist as such. State v. Cox, 23 W. Va. 797.

D. SALES OF PROHIBITED LIQUOR.

The sale of cider or crab cider without a state license therefor is not prohibited by the first section of ch. 107 of the acts of the legislature of 1877, because according to the true intent and meaning of said statute, neither cider nor crab cider is included in the terms "spirituous liquors, wine, ale, porter, beer, or any drink of like nature." State v. Oliver, 26 W. Va. 422.

E. SALES TO PROHIBITED PERSONS.

1. Sales to Minors.

Knowledge of Minority Unnecessary to Constitute Offense.—It was error for the court, on the trial of an indictment founded upon the third section of chapter ninety-nine of the acts of the legislature of 1872-73, to instruct the jury that "unless the jury believe from the evidence that the defendant sold to one Toole intoxicating liquor, and that Toole was then a minor, and the defendant knew he was a minor, or had good cause to believe that he was a minor from reasonable inquiry by him made, they must find the defendant not guilty," because where a statute commands that an act be done or omitted, which, in the absence of such statute might have been done or omitted without culpability, ignorance of the fact or state of things contemplated by the statute, will not excuse the violation. State v. Cain, 9 W. Va. 559.

The sale of intoxicating liquors to a minor is an offense under the third section of chapter ninety-nine of the acts of the legislature of 1872-73, unless upon the written order, etc., of the parent, etc., specified in said section, though the vendor does not know that the purchaser is a minor. State v. Cain, 9 W. Va. 559.

Mitigation of Punishment.—In an indictment for selling intoxicating liquor to a minor under a statute which declared "it shall be unlawful for any person by agent or otherwise to sell intoxicating liquors to minors, unless upon the written order of their parents," this court decided that it was not necessary to prove that the person who sold liquor to a minor knew at the time of the sale that the purchaser was a minor. State v. Cain, 9 W. Va. 559. In that case the court expressly holds that the statute must be construed as remedial, and not penal. And in respect to motive or intent it says: "As to whether the seller intended to violate the law or not at the time of selling to the minor is, under the authorities above cited, immaterial, except in mitigation of the punishment." State v. Cain, 9 W. Va. 559, 576; State v. Denoon, 31 W. Va. 122, 5 S. E. 315.

Written Order as Defense.—Query, would a written order from the parent of the minor to a dealer, if produced and proved, be a defense to an indictment against the dealer for selling spirituous liquors to the minor? State v. Gillaspie, 47 W. Va. 336, 34 S. E. 733.

2. Sales to Persons in the Habit of Drinking to Intoxication.

In General.—The law is well settled in West Virginia and elsewhere that, where a statute commands an act to be done or omitted, which, in the absence of such statute, might have been done or omitted without culpability, ignorance of the fact or state of things contemplated by the statute will not excuse its violation. State v. Farr, 34 W. Va. 84, 11 S. E. 737, citing State v. Cain, 9 W. Va. 559; State v. Denoon, 31 W. Va. 122, 5 S. E. 315.

Knowledge Not Essential.—To make a saloon keeper liable to punishment under the provisions of § 16, ch. 32, W. Va. Code, for selling spirituous liquor to a person in the habit of drinking to intoxication, it is not necessary that he should know, or have reason to believe, that such person was in the habit of drinking to intoxication. State v. Farr, 34 W. Va. 84, 11 S. E. 737.

Permitting to Drink on Premises.—In order to constitute the offense of permitting a person who is in the habit of drinking to intoxication, to drink on his premises, a saloon keeper must do so knowing, or having reason to believe, that the person belongs to the class of those who drink to. intoxication. State v. Farr, 34 W. Va. 84, 11 S. E. 737.

3. Sales to Slaves.

A master may give a general written consent to the purchase by his slave of ardent spirits of a particular person; which will be valid to protect the seller from incurring the penalties prescribed in the Virginia Code, ch. 104, § 1, p. 459. Johnson v. Com., 12 Gratt. 714. See generally, the title SUNDAYS AND HOLIDAYS.

F. SELLING OR KEEPING OPEN ON SUNDAY.

1. Where Statute and City Ordinance Not the Same.

Chapter 44, § 13, of an ordinance of the city of Richmond provides that every hotel keeper, and keeper of a restaurant, lager beer saloon, or other place where ardent spirits, beer, cider or other drinks are sold or given away, shall close the bar where such drinks are sold or given away every Sunday during the whole day, and any person violating any provision of this section shall be fined not less than ten nor more than $500. The act of March 6, 1874, ch. 83, p. 76, enacts "that no intoxicating drinks shall be sold in any barroom, restaurant, saloon, store or other place within the limits of this commonwealth from 12 o'clock on each and every Saturday night of the week, until sunrise of the succeeding Monday morning." And the penalty for a violation of this act is a fine of not less than ten nor more than $500, and at the discretion of the court a forfeiture of his license: "Provided that this law shall not apply to any city having police regulations on this subject, and an ordinance inflicting a penalty equal to the penalty inflicted by this statute." Held, that the ordinance is not the same as the statute, either in the specification of the offense or in the penalty, so as to bring it within the proviso of the statute; and therefore a prosecution for a violation of the act may be sustained. Thon v. Com., 31 Gratt. 887.

On the trial for violation of the Virginia statute forbidding the opening of a barroom and selling liquor within certain hours (§ 3804, of the Code), the police regulations and ordinances of the city must define the same offense and prescribe substantially the same punishment as has been done by statute. The city of Richmond is not exempt from the operation of the statute, because its ordinances on the subject are less comprehensive than the statute, in that the time during which the barroom, etc., is to be kept closed is, under the ordinance, "Every Sunday, during the whole day," while under the statute it is from 12 o'clock Saturday night until sunrise the succeeding Monday morning, and the ordinance forbids only the opening of the barroom, etc., and not the sale of liquor, and prescribes only one penalty for keeping open the whole day, while the statute not only forbids the opening during the designated hours, but also the sale of liquor during those hours, and affixes a separate penalty for each sale of liquor during the prohibited time. Morganstern v. Com., 94 Va. 787, 26 S. E. 402.

What Constitutes Closing.—The mere enclosure of the bar counter, while free access is permitted into the room in which liquors are dispensed, is not a compliance with § 3804 of the Code, which requires the barroom to be closed within certain hours. The barroom must be faithfully closed and all access to it cut off during the prohibited hours, except, perhaps, to the casual entrance of the owner or his employee for some innocent and necessary purpose. The mere fact that no one is in attendance on the bar makes no difference. The sale of liquor is not an absolute right, but one which the state has the right to regulate and supervise. Morganstern v. Com., 94 Va. 787, 26 S. E. 402.

2. Where One Act Violates Two Different Statutes.

Prosecution for selling liquor on Sunday contrary to Va. Code, § 3804, is no bar to prosecution for selling same liquor without license, contrary to acts, 1889-90, p. 242, § 1. Arrington v. Com., 87 Va. 96, 12 S. E. 224. See post, "Former Jeopardy," VI, E.

3. Unconstitutionality of Statute Conferring Sole Jurisdiction of Cases Involving Violation of Liquor Laws on Sunday on Municipal Court of Wheeling.

The act of February 27th, 1871, in relation to the municipal court of Wheeling, is unconstitutional as being in violation of § 6, art. 6, of the state constitution, which provides that the circuit court shall have original jurisdiction of all crimes and misdemeanors, so far as it attempts to confer sole jurisdiction on that court for the trial of cases involving a violation of the revenue laws by selling ardent spirits on the Sabbath; where the party charged had given bond according to the provisions of ch. 32 of the West Virginia Code. Eckhart v. State, 5 W. Va. 515.

The sixth section of the act of February 27th, 1871, in relation to the municipal court of Wheeling, purports to repeal all acts and parts of acts, inconsistent with it, but it does not take away any jurisdiction from the circuit court in cases involving the violation of the revenue laws by selling ardent spirits on the Sabbath. Eckhart v. State, 5 W. Va. 515.

G. SALES BY DISTILLERS.

1. Sales of Less than One Gallon.

On trial of indictment for selling liquor by retail in quantities less than one gallon, under acts, 1879-80, ch. 155, § 12, p. 151, the jury asked of the court the question—"As a distiller has the defendant a right to sell one gallon of liquor, and receive pay therefor, and deliver it in less quantities at different times?" To which the jury received for answer—"The court doth instruct the jury that to constitute a sale by the gallon, there must be a sale and delivery to the buyer of an entire gallon; that a contract for a gallon, and the delivery of the same in parcels at different times, is a violation of the law." Held, the instruction correctly expounds the law. Sales of liquor in the mode suggested in the question of the jury, would be mere shifts to violate the statute. Richardson v. Com., 76 Va. 1007.

A licensed distiller, having no license to sell liquor in quantities of less than a gallon, violates the laws by selling a gallon or more, to be left in his custody, and taken away by the purchaser in quantities of less than a gallon. McKeever *v.* Com., 98 Va. 862, 36 S. E. 995.

2. Sales to Be Drunk at Place Where Sold.

The thirteenth section of the act for regulation of ordinaries, etc. (2 Rev. Va. Code, 1819, §§ 8, 13), is not to be construed as permitting persons, from the produce of whose estate ardent spirits are made, or distillers, to retail them, to be drank at the place where sold. Clemmons *v.* Com., 6 Rand. 681.

H. SALES TO TWO PERSONS AT SAME TIME.

The retailing to two distinct persons, at the same time and place, constitutes two separate and distinct offenses, and not one offense only. Com. *v.* Dove, 2 Va. Cas. 26.

I. INJUNCTION TO RESTRAIN UNLAWFUL SALE.

Conviction Necessary before Injunction Issues.—Under § 18 of ch. 32 of the West Virginia Code, a court of equity can not restrain by injunction a party charged with selling intoxicating liquor contrary to law until the owner or keeper of the house, building or place where such intoxicating liquors are alleged to be sold contrary to the law has been convicted of such unlawful selling at the place named in the bill. Hartley *v.* Henrietta, 35 W. Va. 222, 13 S. E. 375.

State Must Promptly Prove Its Case. —If an injunction is awarded under § 18, ch. 32, W. Va. Code, as amended by ch. 40, acts, 1897, enjoining and restraining the defendant from selling, offering, or exposing for sale, spirituous liquors, etc., in a certain building alleged to belong to them, the state must promptly prove its case, or, on answer filed, plainly and positively denying all the material allegations of the bill, a motion to dissolve must be sustained, unless good and sufficient cause is shown for further delay. State

v. Reymann, 48 W. Va. 307, 37 S. E. 591.

J. EFFECT OF REPEAL OF STATUTE.

The first section of chapter ninety-nine of the acts of the legislature, of 1872, in connection with § 7 of said chapter, so far as it prescribes the penalty for violating said first section of the said act of the legislature, and so far as it forbids the sale, without a license, of intoxicating liquors to be drank in, upon, or about, the building or premises where sold, or to be drank in any adjoining room, building or premises, or other place of public resort connected with said building, that far and to that extent operates a repeal of the provisions of said first section of chapter thirty-two of the Code, of 1868, and no further; and that as to all sales of spirituous liquors or other liquors or drinks whether by wholesale or retail, which are forbidden to be made by the first section of said chapter thirty-two, without a license for the purpose or uses not specified in the first section of said chapter ninety-nine of the acts of the legislature of 1872-73, the first section of said chapter thirty-two of the Code, still remains in force. State *v.* Cain, 8 W. Va. 720.

VI. Pleading and Practice.

A. VENUE.

Venue in County of Sale.—In an indictment for the unlawful sale of intoxicating liquor, the venue should be laid in the county where the sale was made. State *v.* Hughes, 22 W. Va. 743.

Offense Must Be Committed Where Venue Laid.—No conviction can be had where the evidence fails to show that the offense was committed in the county and magisterial district wherein the indictment laid the venue. Savage *v.* Com., 84 Va. 582, 5 S. E. 563.

B. JURISDICTION.

Sale on Boat on Ohio River.—P., opposite to Ravenswood, in Jackson county, West Virginia, on the Ohio side of the Ohio river, sold spirituous liquors in a boat, which was afloat on the river beyond low water mark but fastened by a rope to the bank. Held, the offense, if one, was committed within the jurisdiction of West Virginia. State v. Plants, 25 W. Va. 119.

Requiring Sureties.—The simple selling of intoxicating liquors is a statutory offense; hence, jurisdiction does not exist in courts of record to require sureties of the defendant for his good behavior. State v. Gilliland, 51 W. Va. 278, 41 S. E. 131.

Sale on Sunday.—The act of February 27th, 1871, in relation to the municipal court of Wheeling, is unconstitutional as being in violation of § 6, art. 6, of the West Virginia constitution, which provides that the circuit court shall have original jurisdiction of all crimes and misdemeanors, so far as it attempts to confer sole jurisdiction on that court for the trial of cases involving a violation of the revenue laws by selling ardent spirits on the Sabbath; where the party charged had given bond according to the provisions of ch. 32 of the Code. Eckhard v. State, 5 W. Va. 515.

C. JURY AND JURY TRIAL.

Right to Special Jury.—Where one was indicted for giving intoxicating drinks to a voter on election day, the offense charged being a misdemeanor, is not within the meaning of the term "civil case," as used in § 21, ch. 116, W. Va. Code, and therefore the accused was not entitled to a special jury. State v. Pearis, 35 W. Va. 320, 13 S. E. 1006.

Province of Jury.—Where a physician is indicted for giving false prescriptions as a physician to a druggist to enable a person to purchase spirituous liquors, it is a question for the jury to say, under all the circumstances, whether the word "believing" in the physician's prescription was intended as a mere expression of opinion, or as an affirmation of fact. State v. Berkeley, 41 W. Va. 455, 23 S. E. 608.

Instructions to Jury.—Where, under an indictment for selling liquors in violation of § 1, ch. 32, W. Va. Code, 1891, there is evidence before the jury tending to prove two different sales, it is error for the court to instruct the jury, against objection, that if either sale is proven it should convict. State v. Chisnell, 36 W. Va. 659, 15 S. E. 412.

Upon the trial of an indictment founded upon the third section of chapter ninety-nine of the acts of the legislature of 1872-73, it is not error in the court to refuse to instruct the jury that "Unless the jury believe from the evidence that the defendant, C., before (supposed to be intended to mean after) the fourth day of April, 1873, and before the finding of the indictment, sold to the said Michael Toole intoxicating liquor, and that the said Toole was a minor, and that the defendant knew he was a minor, they must find the defendant not guilty." Nor was it error in the court to refuse to instruct the jury that "In weighing the testimony in the case, the jury should consider all the circumstances of the case, and the declaration of the witness (the minor) as to the motives that prompted the prosecution, and if, from all the circumstances of the case, the jury have any reasonable doubt that the defendant sold the liquor; that the liquor was intoxicating; that the said Michael Toole was a minor, and that the defendant Cain knew he was a minor, they must find him not guilty." State v. Cain, 9 W. Va. 559.

D. INDICTMENTS, INFORMATIONS, AND PRESENTMENTS.

1. Duplicity.

Charging Sale to Two Persons.—An indictment for selling spirituous liquor may properly charge the sale to two persons. Peer v. Com., 5 Gratt. 674.

Where There Are Ten Counts, Each Charging Sale to Different Person.—Where there was an indictment against defendant for the unlawful sale of wine, etc., without license, containing ten counts, each charging a sale to a different person, which constitutes separate and distinct offenses, it was held, that a demurrer to the indictment was properly overruled, as there was no duplicity. Lewis v. Com., 90 Va. 843, 20 S. E. 777.

Charging Sale at "Storehouse and Dwelling House."—An indictment for selling spirituous liquors without a license, charges that the defendant, at his storehouse and dwelling house in Pennsboro, in said county, did sell, etc., and it is held, on motion to quash, that it was not intended to charge two distinct sales at different places, but rather to describe the store and dwelling house as constituting one building and one and the same place; and, therefore, there were not two distinct offenses charged in the same count. Conley v. State, 5 W. Va. 522.

2. Negative Averments.

Negativing Provisos in Statute Not Necessary.—What comes by way of proviso in a statute must be insisted on for the purpose of defense by the party accused. But where exceptions are in the enacting part of a law, it must be charged that the defendant is not within any of them. Hence it is not necessary to allege, in an indictment for selling, by retail, wine, etc., not to be drank where sold, that the defendant is not within the benefit of the provisos of the statute, that nothing in the act shall be construed to prohibit any person from retailing such liquors as shall have actually been made from the produce of his own estate, etc., though the purview should expressly notice them. Com. v. Hill, 5 Gratt. 682.

An indictment under the third section of the act of 1839-40, sess. acts, ch. 2, p. 5, is good, though it does not negative the exceptions and provisos contained in the fourth section. Com. v. Hill, 5 Gratt. 682.

Not Necessary When District Has Voted against License.—Where an act is made unlawful without regard to whether the wrongdoer had or had not a license and none could be granted authorizing such act, the indictment need not negative license; thus where by the terms of a local option law, no license could be granted in the local option district, an indictment for the violation of such law need not negative license. Hargrave v. Com., 2 Va. Dec. 139.

3. Averments of Knowledge and Intent.

a. General Criminal Intent Sufficient.

The latter clause of § 10, ch. 5, W. Va. Code, reads: "And if any person, whether a candidate or not, offer, give, or distribute any intoxicating drink to any voter on the day of an election, he shall forfeit not less than ten, nor more than fifty dollars." Held, that, in an indictment based on this section of the statute, it being charged that the person to whom the intoxicating drink was given was a legally qualified voter, it is not necessary to state the facts constituting such person a qualified voter, nor is it necessary to allege any special criminal intent, but the scienter, or general criminal intent, that is, that the accused knowingly and willfully did the unlawful act, is sufficient. State v. Pearis, 35 W. Va. 320, 13 S. E. 1006.

b. Averment of Knowledge of Minority Not Necessary.

To make a licensed seller of liquors liable under § 16, ch. 32, W. Va. Code, 1887, for selling to a minor, it is not necessary to aver in the indictment that he knew, or had reason to believe, the person to be a minor. State v. Bear, 37 W. Va. 1, 16 S. E. 368.

4. Description of Offenses.

a. Place.

Where Place Is of Essence of Offense.—It is not error to sustain a demurrer to an indictment for a violation of the conditions of a bond insuring that the seller will not permit any person to drink to intoxication on any premises under his control, etc., when the indictment does not allege that the violations occurred at the place where the liquors were to be sold under the license. State v. Church, 4 W. Va. 745.

An indictment for selling by retail, without a license, ardent spirits, to be drunk where sold, must set out the place in the county where the sale is made. It is not sufficient to state the sale in the county. Com. v. Head, 11 Gratt. 819.

Indictment under acts, 1889-90, p. 242, § 1, for selling liquor without license, must definitely state the place where sold, but the exact time of the sale need not be stated, nor need it be stated that the sale was "by sample, representation, or otherwise." Arrington v. Com., 87 Va. 96, 12 S. E. 224.

When Place Not of Essence of Offense.—An indictment under § 16, ch. 32, W. Va. Code, 1887, against a person having a license to sell spirituous liquors, for a sale to a minor, need not specify the particular place where the sale was made, or allege that the place where the sale was made was the place designated in the license as the place at which the license was to be exercised. State v. Boggess, 36 W. Va. 713, 15 S. E. 423.

An indictment founded upon the third section of chapter ninety-nine of the acts of the legislature of 1872-73, charging that C., on the first day of December, A. D., 1873, in Wood county, unlawfully did sell intoxicating liquors to one Michael Toole, a minor, under the age of twenty-one years, he, the said C., knowing the said Michael Toole to be a minor, and not having the written order of his parents, guardians, or family physician therefor, contrary to the form of the statute in such case, made and provided, and against the peace and dignity of the state; held, good after verdict, upon a motion in arrest of judgment, although place of sale in county is not mentioned. State v. Cain, 9 W. Va. 559.

In an indictment for selling spirituous liquors without a license, it is not necessary to allege in the indictment the place where the liquor was sold

State v. Cottrill, 31 W. Va. 162, 6 S. E. 428.

Where Place Charged in Disjunctive.—An indictment for selling without license intoxicating liquors to be drank where sold, uses the language of the first section of chapter 99, of acts, 1872-73, creating the offense, charging that the defendant, at a given place in the county, on a given day, did sell to a certain person, naming him, intoxicating liquors to be drank in, upon or about the building or premises where sold, without first obtaining a state license therefor according to law. Held, upon demurrer this indictment is fatally defective, for uncertainty in charging that the liquor was to be drank either in the building or upon the premises, because where a statute, on which an indictment is founded, enumerates the offenses or intent necessary to constitute the offenses disjunctively, the indictment is fatally defective, which uses the words of the statute charging them disjunctively. This case overrules Morgan's Case, 7 Gratt. 592, so far as in conflict with it. State v. Charlton, 11 W. Va. 332.

Name of County.—In a proceeding before the mayor of a city, town, or village to recover the fine or penalty imposed for the violation of its ordinance against selling spirituous liquors, etc., without having obtained a license therefor from the town council, it is not necessary that the warrant should allege that the offense was committed in the county, within which such city, town, or village is situated; it will be sufficient, if it appears that the offense was committed in such city, town, or village. Beasley v. Beckley, 28 W. Va. 81.

Stating Name of County in Body of Indictment Sufficient.—Though the name of the county be left blank in the margin of an indictment for retailing ardent spirits without license, it is enough if the county be stated in the body of the indictment. Tefft v. Com., 8 Leigh 721.

b. Time.

An indictment for selling spirituous liquors, which fails to aver the date of the sale or that the sale was made within one year from the time the indictment was found by the grand jury, is fatally defective and will be held bad on demurrer. State *v.* Bruce, 26 W. Va. 153.

Indictment under acts, 1889-90, p. 242, § 1, for selling liquor without license, need not state the exact time of the sale. Arrington *v.* Com., 87 Va. 96, 12 S. E. 224.

It is not necessary to prove the selling of liquor on the day alleged in the indictment; it is sufficient it was sold within one year prior to the finding of the indictment. State *v.* Ferrell, 22 W. Va. 759.

c. As to Kinds of Liquor.

The offense of retailing ardent spirits without license is sufficiently charged in an indictment alleging that the defendant sold by retail, without license, whiskey, brandy and other liquors to the jurors unknown, to be drunk at the place where sold. Tefft *v.* Com., 8 Leigh 721.

d. As to License.

In General.—In an indictment under § 18, ch. 38, of the Virginia Code, the words "without having a license therefor according to law," are not equivalent to the words "without paying such tax and obtaining such certificate as is prescribed by the fourteenth section," which are the words used in the statute; and the indictment is defective. Com. *v.* Young, 15 Gratt. 664.

An indictment, for that H., late of, etc., without having a license therefor according to law, did, on, etc., at, etc., in said county, sell by retail, wine, etc., not to be drank where sold, against the statute, etc., and against the peace and dignity of the commonwealth, is a good indictment. Com. *v.* Hatcher, 6 Gratt. 667.

Moffett Liquor Law.—In a prosecution under § 5 and § 10 of the "Moffett Liquor Law," the indictment alleges that the principal was a "barroom keeper," and a "barroom liquor dealer," but does not allege that he was licensed as such. On motion in arrest of judgment, held, that the indictment is fatally defective, as the requirements of that law apply only to licensed dealers. Glass *v.* Com., 33 Gratt. 827.

State License.—In an indictment for a violation of § 12, ch. 107, acts of 1877, it is necessary to allege and prove, that the defendant had a state license to sell spirituous liquors, etc. State *v.* Whitter, 18 W. Va. 306.

Keeping Ordinary.—An indictment which charges that the defendant, on a day and time specified, kept an ordinary without obtaining a license to do so, is sufficient, without setting out the facts of his furnishing for compensation, lodging or diet, etc. Burner *v.* Com., 13 Gratt. 778.

License and Certificate.—An information under the third section of the act of March 3d, 1840, must contain an averment that the person selling had not a license and certificate to sell spirituous liquors, because it only becomes an offense when committed without an ordinary license and certificate. So as to an indictment under the seventeenth section of the act. Com. *v.* Hampton, 3 Gratt. 590.

e. As to Manner of Sale.

Particulars of Sale.—An indictment under § 19, ch. 32, W. Va. Code, which, as a specification of the offense, alleges merely, that the defendant, "in the house and building in said county, knowingly and unlawfully permitted intoxicating liquors to be sold and vended contrary to law," is insufficient, as it should have charged specifically in what particular the sale or sales knowingly permitted by the defendant were unlawful, and should be quashed by the court on motion. State *v.* Parkersburg Brewing Co., 53 W. Va. 591, 45 S. E. 924.

The gist of the alleged offense, the

criminal fact to be found in the case where a corporation is indicted under § 19 of ch. 32 of the Code of West Virginia, is that defendant knowingly permitted intoxicating liquors to be sold in its property contrary to law, and the indictment should have charged specifically in what particular the sale or sales, knowingly permitted by defendant, were unlawful. State v. Parkersburg Brewing Co., 53 W. Va. 591, 45 S. E. 924.

Under § 18, ch. 32, W. Va. Code, an allegation in a bill in equity charging that intoxicating liquors are sold and vended by the defendant, at a certain described house, building or place "contrary to law" is insufficient for uncertainty. It should further allege in what manner such liquors are sold and vended contrary to law; as, without having a state license therefor. Cohen v. King Knob Club, 55 W. Va. 108, 46 S. E. 799. See generally, the title ASSOCIATIONS, vol. 1, p. 843.

Sale Without License.—An indictment for selling ardent spirits without a license, to be drunk where sold, must allege that the selling was by retail where the statute makes the selling by retail an ingredient of the offense. Boyle v. Com., 14 Gratt. 674.

Under Local Option Law.—An indictment under Va. Code, 1887, § 587, for a violation of the local option law, reciting that the defendant, at a certain time and place, "did unlawfully sell wine, spirituous liquors, etc.," is not bad because it does not state whether the sale was by wholesale or retail. Hargrave v. Com., 2 Va. Dec. 139.

f. As to Selling by Agent.

The language of the statute is: "It shall be unlawful for any person, or persons, by agent or otherwise, to sell, etc., intoxicating liquors. The indictment charges that Michael Gilmore on the tenth day of May, 1873, in said county of Mineral, did unlawfully sell, etc. Held, that the indictment is a sufficient finding within the statute, without alleging whether it was sold in person or by agent, as the words of the statute specify. State v. Gilmore, 9 W. Va. 641.

g. Names of Owners of Slaves.

In an indictment for selling ardent spirits to slaves, it is not necessary to state the names of the owners of the slaves to whom the liquor was sold. Com. v. Smith, 1 Gratt. 553.

h. Indictment under Form No. 646, Hutchinson's Treatise for Justices.

In an indictment against a person having a license to sell spirituous liquors, for selling liquor to a minor, the form of indictment No. 646, in Hutchinson's Treatise for Justices, was held good. State v. Boggess, 36 W. Va. 713, 15 S. E. 423.

5. Indictment in Language of Statute.

In General.—In an indictment for selling spirituous liquors without license, it is generally proper and safest to describe the offense in the very terms used by the statute for that purpose. State v. Riffe, 10 W. Va. 794.

It is generally sufficient, in an indictment, to allege a staututory offense in the language of the statute. State v. Boggess, 36 W. Va. 713, 15 S. E. 423.

An indictment upon a statute must state all the circumstances which constitute the definition of the offense in the act so as to bring the defendant precisely within it. Com. v. Hampton, 3 Gratt. 590.

Under §§ 6, 7, ch. 32, W. Va. Code.—An indictment against physician for issuing prescription under §§ 6, 7, ch. 32, of the Code of West Virginia, to aid druggists in violation of provisions of said chapter, in the language of the statute, is held sufficient. State v. Watts, 43 W. Va. 182, 27 S. E. 302.

Not to Be Drank Where Sold.—In an indictment under § 18, ch. 38, of the Virginia Code, p. 209, for retailing ardent spirits, the words "not to be drank where sold," not being in the statute, need not be in the indictment. Com. v. Young, 15 Gratt. 664.

6. Surplusage.

Statutory Language.—An indictment for selling spirituous liquors, etc., which charges the offense in the language of the statute, will not be held bad because it contains surplus matter. State v. Hall, 26 W. Va. 236.

Continuando.—An indictment against the defendant which charges that he, on a day and time specified, kept an ordinary without obtaining a license to do so, with the addition that he continued to keep the ordinary from the day stated to another subsequent day, is not defective; the continuando is mere surplusage. Burner v. Com., 13 Gratt. 778.

Omissions.—On an indictment for selling ardent spirits without a license, the omission in the counts of the words "and certificates of the statute," does not make them defective. Peer v. Com., 5 Gratt. 674.

Word "State" in Describing a License.—It was error to quash an indictment upon the ground that it used the language, "without a license so to do," instead of the statutory language used in ch. 32, § 1, W. Va. Code, 1869, viz.: "Without a state license therefor," the terms used being equivalent to those of the statute, the word "state" not being essential as descriptive. State v. Riffe, 10 W. Va. 794.

Words Rejected Must Not Change Offense.—Where one is charged in an indictment with retailing intoxicating liquors without license "to be drunk at the place where sold" the proof must sustain the averment and the words in quotations can not be rejected as surplusage and conviction had under the indictment in that form, the offense charged in the modified indictment being essentially different from that charged in the indictment in its original form. Com. v. Coe, 9 Leigh 620.

Where a defendant is indicted upon the statute of March 7, 1834 (acts of 1833-34, ch. 3), for retailing ardent spirits without license, the charge that the spirits were to be drunk at the place where sold, shows that the indictment is upon the seventeenth, not the third section of that statute, and such charge can not be rejected as surplusage, but must be proved. Com v. Coe, 9 Leigh 620.

7. Record of Finding of Indictments.

"Unlawful Retailing."—When, in an indictment, it is alleged that a person without having a state license therefor, sold, and offered and exposed for sale, at retail, spirituous liquors and other drinks, and it appears by the record that an indictment for "unlawful retailing" was presented, the record of the finding of the indictment is sufficient. State v. Fitzpatrick, 8 W. Va. 707.

Upon an indictment under § 1, ch. 107, acts, 1877, for selling spirituous liquors without a state license therefor, if the record shows that an "indictment for unlawful retailing" was found, such record is sufficient to show the finding of such indictment by the grand jury. State v. Chapman, 25 W. Va. 408.

Retailing Liquors.—The record of the finding of an indictment for retailing ardent spirits without license, states that the grand jury presented an indictment against W. T. for retailing liquors, a true bill. Held, this is sufficient. Tefft v. Com., 8 Leigh 721.

8. Variance.

a. As to Place.

In an indictment for selling spirituous liquor, etc., without a license, where the indictment alleges that the sale was at the "grocery" of defendant, and the proof shows that it was made in a room adjoining the "grocery," the jury had the right to infer, that it connected with the grocery and was a part thereof, and there was no variance between allegation and proof. State v. Ferrell, 22 W. Va. 759

b. As to Persons and Offenses.

Charge of Joint Sale and Proof of Separate Sale.—On an indictment charging the unlawful sale of liquors to two persons jointly, where the proof showed a separate sale to each of them, it was held, that there was no such variance between the averment and proof as would justify a reversal of the judgment. McKeever v. Com., 98 Va. 862, 36 S. E. 995.

Charge of Sale to "Persons Unknown" and Proof to Persons Known. —At the trial of an indictment for retailing ardent spirits without license, "to persons to the jurors unknown," defendant offers proof that the persons to whom he sold the same were known to the grand jury at the time the indictment was found. Held, this is not a material variance between the proof and the charge in the indictment; for it is not necessary in indictments for such offense to name the person to whom the liquor was sold, and so the words "to persons to the jurors unknown" are surplusage. Hulstead v. Com., 5 Leigh 724.

Misdescription of Defendant.—A presentment for selling ardent spirits by retail to be drank at the place where sold, without having first obtained a license to keep an ordinary, described the defendant as a free negro. For this offense, white persons, Indians, and free negroes were prosecuted and punished in the same manner. Held, a plea that defendant is an Indian and not a free negro, is an immaterial plea, and was properly excluded. Com. v. Scott, 10 Gratt. 749.

And such a plea if good, would be too late after pleading to issue. Com. v. Scott, 10 Gratt. 749.

c. Between Presentment and Information or Indictment.

Omission.—In Com. v. Chalmers, 2 Va. Cas. 76, it was held, that a motion in arrest of judgment should be overruled where the information made the averment of "without license" though the presentment omitted to do so, the defendant having pleaded "not guilty" to the information and a verdict having been rendered against him after trial.

Failure to Take Advantage of Variance.—If one be presented "for retailing spirituous liquors without license," and information be thereafter filed against him for a breach of another law, viz.: "for selling by retail divers articles of merchandise, of foreign growth and manufacture," to which information the defendant pleaded "not guilty;" and a trial was had, and a verdict and judgment; he, having failed to take advantage of the variance in due time, can not have the judgment reversed by the appellate court. Wells v. Com., 2 Va. Cas. 333.

Defective Presentment.—Where an information for selling spirituous liquors without a license is filed on a defective presentment, but the defendant pleads to the information, and there is a verdict against him, he can not arrest the judgment because the presentment charged no offense, or because there was a variance between the presentment and information. Com. v. Chalmers, 2 Va. Cas. 76.

d. As to Venue.

Under an indictment for selling intoxicating liquor contrary to law, no conviction can be had where the evidence fails to show that the offense was committed in the county and magisterial district wherein the indictment laid the venue. Savage v. Com., 84 Va. 582, 5 S. E. 563. See ante, "Venue," VI, A.

e. As to Prescription.

An indictment describes a prescription as stating that the liquor is absolutely necessary as a medicine, whereas the prescription states that the physician believes it to be so necessary. There is no variance between indictment and evidence because of the word "believe" in the prescription. State v. Berkeley, 41 W. Va. 455, 23 S. E. 608.

9. Names of Purchasers.

It is not necessary in an information for retailing spirituous liquors without a license, to name the person to whom the liquors were sold. Com. v. Dove, 2 Va. Cas. 26.

In an indictment under the provisions of § 1, ch. 107, acts of 1877, for selling spirituous liquors, wine, etc., it is not necessary to aver the name of the person, to whom the liquor was sold. State v. Pendergast, 20 W. Va. 672.

An indictment for selling liquors in violation of § 1, ch. 32, W. Va. Code, 1891, is good, though it does not name the purchaser. State v. Chisnell, 36 W. Va. 659, 15 S. E. 412.

In an indictment against a druggist under W. Va. Code, ch. 32, § 5, as amended by acts, 1887, ch. 29, it is unnecessary to insert the name of the person to whom the liquor was sold. State v. Ferrell, 30 W. Va. 683, 5 S. E. 155.

10. Joinder and Election.

a. Joinder.

Of Offenses.—Where a statute, in defining one offense, has specified a series of acts, any one of which separately or all together may constitute the offense, and has prescribed the same penalty for the commission of one or all the acts, the commission of any two or more of them may be alleged conjunctively in the same count of an indictment, and although each act may in itself constitute an offense under the statute, yet if they are all committed by the same person, at the same time and place, they are all to be considered as parts of the same transaction and collectively constitute a single offense, and hence an indictment which charges the defendant with keeping open a barroom and selling liquors therein at the same time charges but one offense. Morganstern v. Com., 94 Va. 787, 26 S. E. 402.

Where the several acts specified in the statute are conjunctively charged in the same count of an indictment, the proof of any one of them is sufficient to authorize a conviction, and where one or more of the acts are committed at one time, and other or the same acts are committed at another time, they may be charged in different counts

of an indictment, and if proved, the defendant may be convicted of the several offenses so committed on different occasions and punished for each offense. Morganstern v. Com., 94 Va. 787, 26 S. E. 402.

A count under the 17th section of the act of March 7th, 1834, sess. Acts, 1833-34, p. 7, and a count under the 3d section of the same act may be joined in the same indictment. Peer v. Com., 5 Gratt. 674.

Several misdemeanors of the same nature, and upon which the same or similar judgment may be rendered, may be united in the same indictment under separate counts. Mitchell v. Com., 93 Va. 775, 20 S. E. 892.

Of Persons.

Two Persons.—Two persons may be jointly indicted or proceeded against by information, for retailing ardent spirits without license. Com. v. Harris, 7 Gratt. 600.

Husband and Wife.—Husband and wife may be jointly indicted for a single act of retailing ardent spirits. Com. v. Hamor, 8 Gratt. 698.

b. Election.

Under an indictment of one count for selling liquors in violation of § 1, ch. 32, W. Va. Code, 1891, by giving evidence tending to show one sale, the state has not made a final election to rely on that sale which will preclude it from proving another to sustain its indictment; and it is not error for the court, in its discretion, to allow evidence of another sale. State v. Chisnell, 36 W. Va. 659, 15 S. E. 412.

When, under an indictment for selling liquors in violation of § 1, ch. 32, W. Va. Code, 1891, evidence of more than one sale is given, on the request of defendants, at the close of the state's evidence, the court should compel the state to elect the particular sale on which it will rely for conviction, and then exclude evidence of other sales. State v. Chisnell, 36 W. Va. 659, 15 S. E. 412.

In cases of indictments charging several misdemeanors of the same general character in separate counts, the prosecuting attorney will not be compelled to elect between them. Mitchell v. Com., 93 Va. 775, 20 S. E. 892.

11. Indictment in Disjunctive.

In an indictment for retailing ardent spirits without a license, where the indictment charges the selling of rum, wine, brandy, or other spirituous liquors, it was held, not to be error to use the word "or" in speaking of the various kinds of spirituous liquors charged to have been sold. Morgan v. Com., 7 Gratt. 592.

It is not error to charge the offense of selling spirituous liquors, wines, etc., without a license, in the disjunctive, instead of the conjunctive, by using the word "or" in lieu of "and," in describing the various kinds of liquors and drinks charged in the indictment to have been sold without a license. Cunningham v. State, 5 W. Va. 508, citing Morgan v. Com., 7 Gratt. 592.

Indictment laying the charges of unlawfully selling different kinds of intoxicating liquors in the disjunctive, is sufficient. Morgan's Case, 7 Gratt. 592; Thomas v. Com., 90 Va. 92, 17 S. E. 788.

12. Allegation of Former Offense.

Under the act of 1 Rev. Va. Code, 1792, which provides that persons having been convicted of retailing liquors who shall afterwards be guilty of the same offense and convicted thereof shall receive an increased punishment, a judgment as upon a second conviction should not be rendered in a case where a defendant is convicted on the same day under each of two informations for retailing spirituous liquor, the second information not alleging that it is for a second offense, after a conviction for a similar offense. Com. v. Welsh, 2 Va. Cas. 57.

13. Effect of Repeal of Statute.

An indictment was found by the grand jury attending the circuit court of Wood County, on the 10th day of June, 1874, against John Cain, in these words, to wit: "State of West Virginia, Wood County, to wit: In the circuit court of said county. The jurors of the state of West Virginia, in and for the body of the county of Wood, and now attending the said court, upon their oaths present, that John Cain, on the first day of December, A. D., one thousand, eight hundred and seventy-three, in the said county, unlawfully did sell and furnish to Michael Toole, spirituous liquors, wine, porter, ale, beer, and drinks of like nature, on Sunday, contrary to the form of the statute, in such cases, made and provided, and against the peace and dignity of the State." Held, that said indictment is not good, after verdict, upon a motion in arrest of judgment, under any statute of West Virginia, because § 1, ch. 32, W. Va. Code, 1868, under which the indictment was brought, was repealed by the provisions of ch. 99 of the acts of Legislature of 1872-73. State v. Cain, 8 W. Va. 720.

E. FORMER JEOPARDY.

Prosecution for selling liquor on Sunday contrary to Va. Code, § 3804, is no bar to prosecution for selling same liquor without license contrary to acts, 1889-90, p. 242, § 1. Arrington v. Com., 87 Va. 96, 12 S. E. 224.

F. WITHDRAWAL OF PLEA.

Discretion of Court.—On an indictment against selling spirituous liquors without license, the proper course is to move to quash before pleading, but the court may, at any time before the trial upon the plea, permit the plea to be withdrawn, and enter the motion to quash at the instance of the defendant. State v. Riffe, 10 W. Va. 794.

On an indictment for selling spirituous liquors without license, the court may permit the plea of guilty to be withdrawn, and another plea to be entered in its place, in the exercise of a sound discretion, if justice and a fair trial on the merits require it; but it must be in time, and the reason for it must be made to appear clearly and distinctly. State *v.* Shanley, 38 W. Va. 516, 18 S. E. 734.

Plea of "Guilty" May Be Entered without Formally Withdrawing Plea of "Not Guilty."—On an indictment for a violation of .the state revenue law in selling spirituous liquors without a license, the plea of guilty may be entered without formally and expressly withdrawing a plea of not guilty theretofore entered. State *v.* Shanley, 38 W. Va. 516, 18 S. E. 734.

G. Argument of Counsel.

On an indictment for selling liquors in violation of § 1, ch. 32, W. Va. Code, 1891, the prosecuting attorney, in argument before the jury, alludes to the failure of the accused to testify in his own behalf, but on exception he withdraws, and asks the jury not to consider his remarks in that respect, and the court declares the remarks improper, and directs the jury to disregard and not consider them. This is no ground for new trial. State *v.* Chisnell, 36 W. Va. 659, 15 S. E. 412.

H. APPEAL AND ERROR.

See generally, the title APPEAL AND ERROR, vol. 1, p. 418.

1. By the Accused.

Motion for New Trial Must Have Been Overruled in Trial Court.—A new trial for errors committed during the former trial of one convicted for selling spirituous liquors, etc., without a license, can only be had after motion made in the trial court and overruled, as this court will not ex mero motu grant a new trial. State *v.* Hall, 26 W. Va. 236.

Record of Judgment.—In a case where the defendant is convicted on an indictment for selling spirituous liquors, etc., without a license, by the court in lieu of a jury, while it is the usual practice, where a jury is waived, and the case submitted to the court in lieu of a jury, if the party, against whom the judgment is ren-

dered, is dissatisfied therewith, to except to the judgment and have the court certify the facts proved, yet it is not necessary for the record to show that the judgment was excepted to. It is sufficient, if the facts appear upon the record either by the certificate of the court or otherwise. State *v.* Miller, 26 W. Va. 106.

Practice on Appeal.—S. was indicted for selling spirituous liquors, and the summons was served on his wife. He did not appear, and judgment was rendered against him for a fine. He made no motion under ch. 134, to reverse the judgment but obtained a writ of error from the appellate court. His writ of error was dismissed as improvidently awarded. State *v.* Slack, 28 W. Va. 372.

Manner of Review.—On a conviction before a mayor of selling spirituous liquors, etc., without having obtained a license, where a party aggrieved can obtain redress by appeal or writ of error, he will not be allowed the extraordinary writ of certiorari. And in case where he has permitted the time for appeal to expire, certiorari will not issue for relief, unless upon special showing, unmixed with any blame or negligence on his part. Beasley *v.* Beckley, 28 W. Va. 81, citing Poe *v.* Machine Works, 24 W. Va. 517.

2. By the State.

As to right of appeal by the state in revenue cases, see the title APPEAL AND ERROR, vol. 1, p. 418.

I. SENTENCE AND PUNISHMENT.

Separate Fine upon Conviction on Joint Indictment.—Where husband and wife are jointly indicted for a single act of retailing ardent spirits, if they are convicted, a fine must be assessed, and a judgment rendered against each separately. Com. *v.* Hamor, 8 Gratt. 698.

Where two persons are jointly indicted or proceeded against, by information, for retailing ardent spirits without license, upon their conviction there should be a separate fine against each. Com. *v.* Harris, 7 Gratt. 600.

Judgment by Default.—Where one was indicted for selling spirituous liquors contrary to law, and, on his non-appearance, judgment was rendered against him by default, it was held, that § 5 of ch. 134 of the West Virginia Code includes judgments for fines in misdemeanor cases, as well as judgments in civil cases, where such judgments are entered by default. State *v.* Slack, 28 W. Va. 372.

J. ACTION AGAINST SURETIES ON LIQUOR BOND.

In an action against sureties on the bond of one who has been convicted of unlawfully selling liquor to a minor, it is not necessary to allege and prove that such sale was made, but it is enough to allege that fines were recovered for that offense by judgment. State *v.* Nutter, 44 W. Va. 385. 30 S. E. 67.

K. DECLARATION IN ACTION UNDER CIVIL DAMAGE ACT.

It is sufficient, in a declaration in a case of action brought by a wife against a saloon keeper, under ch. 107, § 16, acts, 877, p. 144, to allege generally that the plaintiff was injured in her means of support in consequence of such intoxication; but under such declaration the plaintiff could prove only the extent of the injury to her means of support which she had sustained as the necessary consequence of her husband's intoxication, as that resulting from his inability to labor while so intoxicated. Pegram *v.* Stortz, 31 W. Va. 220, 6 S. E. 485.

When the plaintiff wishes to prove that she has suffered damages in her means of support, the natural, but not the necessary result of her husband's intoxication—as when he, when drunk, expended his money with reckless prodigality, whereby she was injured in her means of support—she must allege that in her declaration. Pegram *v.* Stortz, 31 W. Va. 220, 6 S. E. 485.

VII. Evidence.

A. BURDEN OF PROOF.

Druggist Must Show Bona Fides after Sale Proven.—After the fact of sale of spirituous liquors by a druggist is proven, it devolves on him to show the bona fides of the transaction, he not having license to sell spirituous liquors. Chapter 32, § 4, W. Va. Code, 1868. Miles *v.* State, 5 W. Va. 524.

State Must Prove Knowledge of Habit in Sale to Inebriate.—On the trial of a licensee for selling or giving intoxicating liquors to a person in the habit of drinking to intoxication, it devolves upon the state to show beyond a reasonable doubt that such licensee knew, or had reason to believe, that such person was in the habit of drinking to intoxication. State *v.* Alderton, 50 W Va. 101, 40 S. E. 350.

B. BEST EVIDENCE.

On the trial of an indictment founded upon the third section of chapter ninety-nine of the acts of the legislature of 1872-73, it is competent and not improper for the minor to state on his examination as a witness on behalf of the state, upon his oath, his age to the jury, with the view of proving that he was a minor at the time of the sale of the intoxicating liquors in the indictment mentioned, to him by the defendant, and such statement may go to the jury as evidence to be considered by them, notwithstanding there is evidence given to the jury tending to show that his father and mother are living. And in such case, it is not error for the court to refuse to instruct the jury that "Unless it is proved beyond reasonable doubt, by the best evidence of which the case will admit, and the evidence of the minor himself is not such evidence, that the minor was at the time of the alleged selling to him of intoxicating liquor by defendant, under the age of twenty-one years, they must find the defendant not guilty." State *v.* Cain, 9 W. Va. 559.

C. WEIGHT AND SUFFICIENCY.

1. In General.

Upon review of a case tried by the court in lieu of a jury, where the defendant was indicted and convicted on a charge of selling spirituous liquors, etc., without a license, if the evidence was plainly insufficient to warrant the judgment, the appellate court will reverse the judgment and render judgment for defendant. State v. Miller, 26 W. Va. 106.

2. As to Sale.

Proof of Purchasing Will Not Warrant Conviction of Selling.—Where the defendant has been indicted for selling spirituous liquors, etc., and the proof shows that he was a purchaser, not a seller, the case was reversed because the facts proved were plainly insufficient to warrant the judgment. State v. Miller, 26 W. Va. 106.

When No Proof That Pay Was Received.—Where T. is indicted for unlawful retailing, the evidence is, that he with two others upon a street, was drinking, and when the supply was out, one of them asked T. to get some more whisky. He replied: "I don't know, I will do the best I can;" he went away, and soon returned with a bottle of whiskey, and handed it to one of them; there was no proof, that he received any pay for it. T. was found guilty, and fined $10. His motion to set aside the verdict, because it was contrary to the evidence, and to grant him a new trial, was overruled by the court and judgment rendered against him. Held, that the verdict should have been set aside, because there was no evidence to sustain it. State v. Thomas, 13 W. Va. 848.

It is proved that witness went into defendant's room attached to his grocery, found some whiskey in a bottle in a box, took a drink from the bottle, laid down ten cents and went out. It is the only time, according to the proof, that this was done; there is no evidence that the defendant knew it, or that he received the money; the jury found him guilty of selling the whiskey. Held, the evidence fails to sustain the verdict. State v. Ferrell, 22 W. Va. 759.

3. As to State License.

In an indictment for a violation of § 12, ch. 107, acts of 1877, proof on the trial, that the defendant "kept a hotel and public barroom," is not in itself sufficient evidence, that he had a state license to sell spirituous liquors, etc. State v. Whitter, 18 W. Va. 306.

4. As to Intoxicating Quality of Liquor.

Liquor Must Be Proved Intoxicating.—On an indictment for unlawfully selling intoxicating liquors without license, where the witnesses could not say positively whether or not the liquor was intoxicating, or whether it had been sold to the man named in the indictment, held, that the evidence was insufficient to sustain the conviction. Savage v. Com., 84 Va. 619, 5 S. E. 565.

Where at trial of such indictment, witness testifies that he in the former barroom of defendant's hotel, bought and drank something called "ginger," that looked and tasted like whisky, but he would not swear it was intoxicating, because he did not drink enough of it to make him drunk, though he thought that had he done so, it would have had that effect; held, there was insufficient proof that the liquor sold was intoxicating. Savage v. Com., 84 Va. 582, 5 S. E. 563.

Sale of So-Called Ginger by Defendant's Clerk.—In Savage v. Com., 84 Va. 582, 5 S. E. 563, it was held, that on proof that persons had bought from the clerk at defendant's hotel, liquor called ginger which, some witnesses said tasted like whisky, but could not say whether or not it was intoxicating, a conviction could not be had as the evidence neither shows that the liquor was intoxicating nor that the clerk was authorized by the defendant to sell it.

Facts from Which Intoxication May Be Inferred.—Upon an indictment for selling spirituous liquors, wine, etc., the jury found the defendant guilty, and the court entered judgment against him on proof that the defendant had sold a bottle of the "essence of cinnamon" to the state's witness; that before the sale the defendant said to witness, if he wanted to drink it he could not get it, but if he wanted it for cooking purposes he could have it, and the witness having answered he did not want to drink it, the defendant sold it to him, and that witness drank part of it and it affected him so he could not see after night. On writ of error the supreme court affirmed said judgment by a divided court. State v. Muncey, 28 W. Va. 494.

It is not necessary that it should have been proved as a fact that a liquor was intoxicating, but it is sufficient if facts were proved from which the jury might properly infer that it was intoxicating or that it produced intoxication. State v. Muncey, 28 W. Va. 494.

Mixture, Preparation, or Liquid "Which Will Produce Intoxication."—Proof of an unlawful sale of a mixture, preparation, or liquid, "which will produce intoxication" will sustain a conviction upon an indictment charging the unlawful sale of "spirituous liquors, wine, porter, ale, beer, and drinks of l:ke nature," without a state license therefor. For the purposes of ch. 32, § 1, of the West Virginia Code of 1899, such mixture, preparation, or liquid is, in law, spirituous liquor, whether it be such, in fact, or not. State v. Good (W. Va.), 49 S. E. 121.

Charge of Sale of "Spirituous Liquor" and Proof of Sale of "Glass of Liquor."—A verdict of guilty, found upon an indictment, under § 1 of chapter 107, W. Va. acts, 1877, which charges a sale of "spirituous liquors, wine, beer," etc., in which the proof was that the defendant sold "a glass of liquor" for "ten cents," will not be set aside by the appellate court upon the ground that the proof was insufficient to warrant such verdict. State v. Beasley, 21 W. Va. 777.

5. As to Place.

Where Proof of Sale in County, but Not in District Alleged.—Indictment for unlawful sale of ardent spirits charged that the offense was committed in a certain district where, under the local option law, "no license" prevailed. The evidence was that the defendant sold ardent spirits to witness in the county, but did not designate the district. Defendant moved to set aside the verdict of "guilty as charged in the indictment," and for a new trial; which motion was overruled. Held, the motion should have been sustained. Morgan v. Com., 90 Va. 80, 21 S. E. 826.

Where Liquor Sold Some Distance from House.—M. was indicted for selling liquor at Prillman's precinct, in the county of Franklin, without a license. The jury found him guilty, and he moved to arrest the judgment because the proof was not that he sold at the house or within the curtilage at Prillman's precinct, but in the woods some three or four hundred yards from the house. The court overruled the motion and rendered judgment on the verdict. It not appearing that the bill of exceptions contains all the evidence, this court must presume that there was proof that the sale of liquor was at Prillman's precinct, and that it was in the county of Franklin. Massie v. Com., 30 Gratt. 841.

Charge of Manufacturing Not Sustained by Proof of Selling.—Under a warrant charging one with carrying on the business of a manufacturer of malt liquors within a city, without license, the defendant can not be convicted of selling malt liquors within the city which were manufactured by him out of the city. The business of manufacturing is essentially different from that of selling. The allegation and proof must correspond in both civil and criminal cases. Consumers' Brewing Co. *v.* Norfolk, 101 Va. 171, 43 S. E. 336.

6. As to Sale on Sunday.

Where under § 3804 of the Code of Virginia the defendant was indicted for keeping his barroom open and selling liquor on Sunday, proof of either act was sufficient to authorize a conviction. Morganstern *v.* Com., 94 Va. 787, 26 S. E. 402.

7. As to Quantity.

Upon an indictment for retailing ardent spirits, specifying the precise quantity and the kind, to be drunk where sold, without license, proof of retailing any quantity of any kind of ardent spirits to be drunk where sold, is sufficient. Brock *v.* Com., 6 Leigh 634.

Averments of Quantity of Liquor Sold—The Precision Necessary.—The quantity of liquor need not be proved precisely as charged in the indictment. In Brock *v.* Com., 6 Leigh 634, the indictment states that the liquor sold was one and one-half pints of whisky and it was held, that proof of selling any quantity and any kind of intoxicating liquor was sufficient to support the indictment.

8. As to Persons.

Sale Must Be to Persons Charged.—An indictment for unlawfully selling ardent spirits to W. will not be sustained by proof of selling to C. Com. *v.* Taggart, 8 Gratt. 697.

Where Names of Persons Known.—On an indictment under the statute for selling liquor to minors without the consent of their parents or guardian, where the indictment is for selling to minors whose names are unknown, if it appear from the evidence that in fact the name of the minor, to whom the liquor was sold, was known to the grand jury, the evidence does not sustain the indictment. Morganstern *v.* Com., 27 Gratt. 1018.

9. As to Whisky Mixed with Medicine.

On the trial of an indictment against a druggist for selling spirituous liquors without license, it is proved that "witness went to defendant's drug store, and stated to defendant, who was a regular druggist, that he, witness, was sick and wanted some whisky. The defendant asked witness what was the matter; witness replied that he had the belly ache; whereupon the defendant mixed some whisky and ginger together in a glass and gave it to the witness, who drank it and paid defendant for it; witness said the drink was very hot with ginger, at which time above mentioned the whisky shops were all closed and not selling whisky. That he had got whisky there several times before, but it was always mixed with medicine, and he always got it for medicinal purposes. And on the part of the defendant it was proved by one other witness that defendant was a regular druggist and made it a part of his business to fill prescriptions for physicians, and in the course of his business frequently prescribed for acute diseases, and his judgment therein was relied upon." Held, that a verdict for the state is not unsupported by evidence, and it was not error to refuse to set it aside on such ground. Miles *v.* State, 5 W. Va. 524.

D. ADMISSIBILITY AND MATERIALITY.

Evidence of Purchasers.—When an intoxicating mixture called Rikk is sold in labeled bottles, as put up by the manufacturer, and has a commercial name or designation, the evidence of persons who have purchased it from the defendant and drunk it, whether at the same time or on different days and occasions, as to whether it is intoxicating, is admissible both for the state and the defendant. State *v.* Good (W. Va.), 49 S. E. 121.

Commonwealth Not Confined to Proof of Particular Offense upon Which the Indictment Was Found.—Under an indictment for selling spirituous liquors without a license, the commonwealth may prove any offense against the act by the defendant, within the prescribed time; and is not confined to proof of the particular offense which was brought to the notice of the grand jury, and upon proof of which they found the indictment. Loftus v. Com., 3 Gratt. 631.

Previous Indictments.—In a proceeding under § 560 of the Virginia Code, to revoke a license to sell whisky on the charge that defendant had been guilty of selling liquor to minors, it is competent to offer in evidence a number of indictments found in the same court against the same defendant for selling liquor to minors and also to receive the evidence of a minor that, within twelve months prior to the time when the license sought to be revoked took effect the said minor had purchased intoxicating liquor of the defendant. The whole matter being heard and determined by the court it is not confined to the strict rules of evidence which obtain upon the trial of an issue before a jury, but great latitude is allowed the court that it may be satisfied whether or not it had intrusted the sale of liquor to an unfit person or whether the privilege granted has been abused. Lillienfeld v. Com., 92 Va. 818, 23 S. E. 882.

Testimony as to Written Order.—On trial of an indictment for selling spirituous liquors to a minor, it is not error to exclude testimony relative to a written order from the parent of the minor to the dealer, for the liquor, in the absence of such order, and its non-production not accounted for. State v. Gillaspie, 47 W. Va. 336, 34 S. E. 733.

VIII. Abatement.

Fraudulent Club. — A corporation claiming to be a social and literary club, which requires no qualifications for membership except the payment of an initiation fee of one dollar, for which fee there is issued to the applicant a membership card and a coupon with twenty tickets attached each, "good for five cents for games and supplies" which tickets are received by the general manager of the club in exchange for drinks, one ticket for a glass of beer, and two tickets for a drink of whisky, and the members are permitted to buy such coupons with five, ten, or twenty tickets attached at twenty-five cents, fifty cents, and one dollar each, respectively, to be so exchanged for such drinks at such club; held, to be a fraudulent device to evade the revenue laws of the state, and the house, building or place where such sales are made will be held taken and deemed to be a common public nuisance, and will be abated as such. Cohen v. King Knob Club, 55 W. Va. 108, 46 S. E. 799.

Conviction First Necessary.—Under § 18 of ch. 32 of the West Virginia Code, a court of equity can not abate the house, buildings, or place where intoxicating liquors are alleged to be sold contrary to law, until the owner or keeper of such house or place has been convicted of such unlawful selling at the place named in the bill. Hartley v. Henretta, 35 W. Va. 222, 13 S. E. 375.

IX. Civil Damage Acts.

A. EFFECT OF REPEAL OF STATUTE.

Where, under W. Va. statute, a person had a right of action against one for selling, giving, etc., intoxicating liquors to husband, wife, child, etc., and this act was repealed by another of different import, held, that unless the repealing statute is the same in substance as that repealed, a pending suit would fall, unless it had been carried into judgment. Curran v. Owens, 15 W. Va. 208.

B. NOTICE BY PLAINTIFF.

Under chapter 107, § 16, W. Va. acts, 1877, giving a right of action after written notice served on the defendant by some member of the family, other than a brother or sister, the written notice required must be served on the defendant while he is engaged in the sale of intoxicating liquors for himself or for another as a business, or the plaintiff can not recover in a suit under this statute. Pegram v. Stortz, 31 W. Va. 220, 6 S. E. 485.

Under ch. 107, § 16, W. Va. acts, 1877, it is essential, to sustain an action, that when the defendant was served with notice, the husband named in the notice was in the habit of drinking to intoxication. Pegram v. Stortz, 31 W. Va. 220, 6 S. E. 485.

C. EXEMPLARY DAMAGES.

Common-Law Definition.—In a civil action for damages under the West Virginia statute giving a right of action to a third person for a wrongful sale of liquor in violation of the statute, the common-law definition of the term "exemplary damages," is damages inflicted by way of punishment upon a wrongdoer as a warning to him and others to prevent a repetition or commission of similar wrongs. Mayer v. Frobe, 40 W. Va. 246, 22 S. E. 58. But see Pegram v. Stortz, 31 W. Va. 220, 6 S. E. 485, which is overruled by the case.

By chapter 107, § 16, W. Va. acts, 1877, p. 144, it is provided: "An action may be maintained (under specified circumstances) by the wife against the person selling or furnishing such spirituous liquors, as well for all such damages as the plaintiff has sustained by reason of the selling or giving such liquors, as for exemplary damages." By exemplary damages is meant, not additional damages given as a punishment of the defendant for selling intoxicating liquors to her husband illegally, but damages which shall not only compensate her for injury to her means of support, but also, in a proper case, damages which shall compensate her for her mental anguish. Pegram v. Stortz, 31 W. Va. 220, 6 S. E. 485.

The first and second syllabi of Pegram v. Stortz, 31 W. Va. 220, 6 S. E. 485, in so far as they hold that exem-plary damages, in a proper case, can not be inflicted by way of punishment in a civil suit upon a wrongdoer, are hereby disapproved and overruled, in regard to an action for damages for injury to third person by reason of the wrongful sale of intoxicating liquors in violation of the West Virginia statute. Mayer v. Frobe, 40 W. Va. 246, 22 S. E. 58.

The case of Mayer v. Frobe, 40 W. Va. 246, 22 S. E. 58, determined that the rule as to exemplary damages propounded in the case of Pegram v. Stortz, 31 W. Va. 220, 6 S. E. 485, was not the law of this state. McMaster v. Dyer, 44 W. Va. 644, 29 S. E. 1016.

Where Fraud, Malice, etc., Shown.— Such exemplary damages can not be given to recompense her for her anxiety of mind, mortification, social degradation, and loss of her husband's society, by reason of his drunkenness and misconduct; but they can only be given where the defendant has not simply committed against her the tort of selling illegally intoxicating liquors to her husband, whereby she was injured in her means of support, but where the defendant made such sale under circumstances which showed actual malice, or wanton, deliberate, and willful disregard of her rights and known wishes. Pegram v. Stortz, 31 W. Va. 220, 6 S. E. 485.

In actions of tort, where gross fraud, malice, oppression, or wanton, willful, or reckless conduct or criminal indifference to civil obligations affecting the rights of others appear, or where legislative enactment authorizes it, the jury may assess exemplary, punitive, or vindictive damages; these terms being synonymous. Mayer v. Frobe, 40 W. Va. 246, 22 S. E. 58.

Where Court Will Set Aside Verdict. —Where it is clear, upon the facts proven by the evidence introduced before the jury, that it is not a case, under the rule above laid down, where the jury could legally award such exemplary damages, and it is obvious from their verdict that the damages must have included exemplary damages, it is the duty of the court, on the motion of the plaintiff, to set aside such verdict, and award a new trial. Pegram *v.* Stortz, 31 W. Va. 220, 6 S. E. 485.

Where the case is one in which a jury might properly and legally award to the plaintiff exemplary damages, the verdict will not be set aside on the grounds that the damages are excessive, unless they are so enormous as to furnish evidence of partiality, passion, corruption, or prejudice on the part of the jury. Pegram *v.* Stortz, 31 W. Va. 220, 6 S. E. 485.

D. DEATH OF HUSBAND.

In an action under ch. 107, § 16, W. Va. acts, 1877, p. 144, by a wife against the person selling or furnishing spirituous liquors to her husband, no damages can be given the plaintiff because of injury to her means of support by the death of her husband caused by his intoxication, the consequence of liquors illegally furnished or sold to him by the defendant. Pegram *v.* Stortz, 31 W. Va. 220, 6 S. E. 485.

E. ACTION BY MOTHER WHILE FATHER LIVING.

Under § 20, ch. 32, W. Va. Code, a married woman, injured in person, property, or means of support, by reason of unlawful sales of intoxicating liquors to a son, may maintain a suit for damages, notwithstanding her husband, father of such son, be living. McMaster *v.* Dyer, 44 W. Va. 644, 29 S. E. 1016.

Intoxication.

See the titles DRUNKENNESS, vol. 4, p. 834, and the references given; NEGLIGENCE.

In Transitu.

See the title SALES.

INTRUSION.—In Birthright *v.* Hall, 3 Munf. 536, 540, it is said: "An intrusion, 3 Bl. 168, is the entry of a stranger, after a particular estate of freehold is determined, before him, in remainder or reversion. The reversioner, or mainderman, by this act, is ousted (if I may use the expression), and the intruder becomes tenant to the lord. The reversioner or remainderman, however, may purge this intrusion by summary proceeding, without suit, to-wit, by a formal and peaceable entry, Ibid. 174, 175, such as is found in this verdict; which notorious act of ownership is equivalent to a feudal investiture by the lord, and gives him that hath right of entry a seisin; making him complete owner, and capable of conveying from himself either by descent or purchase. This is called his right of entry; and if he lies by until the death of the intruder, when the land descends to his heir, then his right of entry is tolled or taken away, and he has only a right of action." See also, Hall *v.* Hall, 3 Call. 488, 490. And see generally, the title REMAINDERS, REVERSIONS AND EXECUTORY INTERESTS.

INVALID.—In Fant *v.* Miller, 17 Gratt. 47, 65, it is said: "I need not, therefore, enter into the disquisition seeking to establish a difference between the terms 'invalid and unavailable for any purpose,' on the one hand, and the epithet 'void' on the other. I regard them as tantamount."

In Kanawha, etc., R. Co. *v.* Ryan, 31 W. Va. 364, 6 S. E. 924, 925, it is said: "The statute expressly commands that the return shall state that the service was in the county in which the person served resides; and declares that, unless this is done, 'the service shall be **invalid**.' The service being thus **invalid**, and there having been no appearance by the corporation before the justice, the judgment, under such circumstances, is an absolute nullity. An **invalid** service is the same as no service whatever; and the law is well settled that a judgment rendered without an appearance by or service upon the defendant is void for the want of jurisdiction in the court to pronounce judgment. Freem. Judgm., §§ 495, 521." See also, the titles JUDGMENTS AND DECREES; SERVICE OF PROCESS.

INVALIDATE.—In Ex parte Ellyson, 20 Gratt. 10, 25, it is said: "It is provided that the court, 'in judging of said election, shall proceed· upon the merits thereof, and determine finally concerning the same.' Depositions may be taken 'to sustain or **invalidate** said election.' We are not called upon, in this case, to define the scope of investigation and inquiry authorized by those provisions. But it seems to be very clear, that it is not restricted to a mere examination of the returns; and, moreover, that it may be such as to **invalidate** the election; in other words, such as to show that there has been no legal and valid election. The election which is contested, may be **invalidated** for the reason that the entire election was illegal and void; if the inquiry may take that scope, does it not follow that the judgment of the court may respond to the inquiry? Why authorize the court to inquire into what it can not determine?"

Inventions.
See the title PATENTS AND TRADE MARKS.

Inventory and Appraisal.
See the titles ASSIGNMENTS FOR THE BENEFIT OF CREDITORS, vol. 1, p. 808; BANKRUPTCY AND INSOLVENCY, vol. 2, p. 234; EXECUTORS AND ADMINISTRATORS, vol. 5, p. 526; FIRE INSURANCE, vol. 6, p. 106; PARTNERSHIP.

Inverse Order of Alienation.
See the title MARSHALING ASSETS AND SECURITIES.

Investments.
See the titles BANKS AND BANKING, vol. 2, p. 310; EXECUTORS AND ADMINISTRATORS, vol. 5, p. 529; GUARDIAN AND WARD, vol. 6, pp. 808, 810, 826; TRUSTS AND TRUSTEES.

INVOLUNTARY.—It has been said that this term can only apply to human beings. State *v.* Strauder, 11 W. Va. 745, 811.

Involuntary Bankruptcy.
See the title BANKRUPTCY AND INSOLVENCY, vol. 2, p. 232.

Involuntary Dismissal and Nonsuit.
See the title DISMISSAL, DISCONTINUANCE AND NONSUIT, vol. 4, p. 692.

Involuntary Manslaughter.
See the title HOMICIDE, vol. 7, p. 104.

Involuntary Payment.
See the title PAYMENT.

Iron Safe Clause.
See the title FIRE INSURANCE, vol. 6, p. 85.

IRREGULARITY.—In Ex parte Mooney, 26 W. Va. 36, 40, it is said: "An irregularity is defined to be a want of adherence to some prescribed rule or mode of proceeding; and it consists, either in omitting to do something that is necessary for the due and orderly conducting of a suit, or doing it in an unreasonable time or improper manner. Tidd's Pr. 434. It is the technical term for every defect in practical proceedings or the mode of conducting an action or defense, as distinguishable from defects in pleadings. 3 Chitty's Gen. Pr. 509."

A statute providing for tax sales enacted that no **irregularity**, error, or mistake in the delinquent list, or in the return thereof, or in the affidavit thereto, or in the list of sales filed with the clerk of the county court, or in the recordation of such list or affidavit, should prejudice the sale. In construing this provision, it is said: "It has been said that all those things which the statute requires to be done are essentials, and not mere **irregularities**, and that the statute intends to cure mere **irregularities**; but I would say that an **irregularity** is the erroneous doing of something required by the statute, for surely those things that are required by the statute are necessary, and things not required by it need not be done; and hence, when the statute cures what is called an **irregularity**, it must refer to something which, under the statute, ought to have been, but was not, done. It can not possibly refer to something that the statute did not require to be done. Hence 'irregularity, error, or mistake' means something omitted or misdone required by the statute, making the act one badly done. Note that the statute uses all three words in its struggle to cure these defects." Winning v. Eakin, 44 W. Va. 19, 28 S. E. 757, 758. Compare Hays v. Heatherly, 36 W. Va. 613, 15 S. E. 223; Baxter v. Wade, 39 W. Va. 281, 19 S. E. 404; Phillips v. Minear, 40 W. Va. 58, 20 S. E. 924; Jackson v. Kittle, 34 W. Va. 207, 12 S. E. 484. And see the title TAXATION.

Irrelevancy.
See the title EVIDENCE, vol. 5, p. 299.

IRREPARABLE.—The word irreparable means that which can not be repared, restored, or adequately compensated for in money, or where the compensation can not be safely measured. Bettman v. Harness, 42 W. Va. 437, 26 S. E. 271.

Irreparable Injury.
See the title INJUNCTIONS, vol. 7, p. 512.

IRRESISTIBLE IMPULSE.—See the titles HOMICIDE, vol. 7, p. 104; INSANITY, vol. 7, p. 688. And see State v. Harrison, 36 W. Va. 729, 15 S. E. 982, 990.

Irrigation.

See the title WATERS AND WATERCOURSES.

Islands.

See the titles NAVIGABLE WATERS; PUBLIC LANDS; WATERS AND WATERCOURSES.

ISSUE (DESCENDANTS).—See the titles HEIR, HEIRS AND THE LIKE, vol. 7, p. 62; SHELLEY'S CASE (RULE IN); WILLS.

Issue in its technical sense comprehends the whole generation as well as the word heirs and is therefore more properly, in its natural signification, a word of limitation than of purchase. Birthright *v.* Hall, 3 Munf. 536, 544.

In Pryor *v.* Duncan, 6 Gratt. 27, 37, it is said: "In 2 Jarman on Wills 353, it s said: 'If the testator annex to the gift to the issue, words of explanation, indicating that he uses the term "issue," in a special and limited sense it is, of course, restricted to that sense.'"

As words of limitation, see Atkinson *v.* McCormick, 76 Va. 791, 799. And see the title WILLS.

Although the term children is not to be taken as synonymous with issue, except to effectuate the manifest intention of the testator, yet to effectuate such intention it may be taken in that sense. Merryman *v.* Merryman, 5 Munf. 440, 442; Smith *v.* Fox, 82 Va. 763, 767, 1 S. E. 200.

Children in the sense of issue. See Mosby *v.* Paul, 88 Va. 533, 537, 14 S. E. 336; East *v.* Garrett, 84 Va. 523, 9 S. E. 1112; Bain *v.* Buff, 76 Va. 371; Smith *v.* Fox, 82 Va. 763, 1 S. E. 200. See also, the title WILLS.

Heirs.—In Smith *v.* Chapman, 1 Hen. & M. 240, 249, it is said: "The idea, that A. an illiterate testator, using the word 'issue' or 'children' in a will, would turn his estate into a different channel from his neighbor, B., who should chance to use 'heirs,' when both words meant the same thing, as well in law as in common parlance, would be making the system of testaments, with those not learned in the law, a system of chance and uncertainty, and more a system of frustrating the will than of publishing the will."

Dying without Issue.—See the titles REMAINDERS, REVERSIONS AND EXECUTORY INTERESTS; WILLS.

Issue Out of Chancery.

See the tittle ISSUES TO THE JURY.

ISSUE (PLEADING).—See also, the title PLEADING.

In Tinsley *v.* Jones, 13 Gratt. 289, 292, it is said: " 'Issue' is nomen collectivum, and a word of very extensive import, embracing the whole line of lineal descendants. It is used in the statute de bonis, in some instances, at least, synonymously with heirs of the body; and a devise to A. and his issue has even been stated by an eminent judge (Lord Thurlow), as 'the aptest way of describing an estate tail, according to the statute.' 2 Jarm. on Wills 329, 331. It is a technical word of established meaning, and must always have its effect accordingly, unless there be a clear manifestation of intention in the context to use it in the restricted sense of issue living at the death."

In White *v.* Emblem, 43 W. Va. 819, 28 S. E. 761, 762, it is said: "See, also, Baltimore, etc., R. Co. *v.* Christie, 5 W. Va. 325, where it is held, that 'it is error to swear a jury to try the issue joined when there is no issue.' To the same effect, see Baltimore, etc., Co. *v.* Gettle, 3 W. Va. 377; also, Williams *v.* Knights, 7 W. Va. 335. Sir Mathew Hale, followed by Mr. Justice Blackstone, in defining an issue, says: 'When, in the course of pleading, they come to a point which is affirmed on one side and denied on the other, they are then said to be at issue.' And in 3 Bl. Comm. 313, it is said: "An issue is, when both the parties join upon somewhat that they refer unto a trial to make an end of the plea.'"

In Hickman *v.* Baltimore, etc., R. Co., 30 W. Va. 296, 7 S. E. 455, 462, it is said: "The term verdict, at common law, necessarily imports that there has been an 'issue' between the parties; for without an issue there could be no verdict, for by every verdict the jury declares that they have 'found the issue' for the plaintiff or for defendant (2 Bl. Comm. 377); so that whether it be called an 'issue,' or the 'matter in difference,' or the 'matter in variance,' between the parties, it is wholly immaterial. Without an issue of fact, it would be an absurdity for the jury to declare that they have found for the plaintiff or defendant what in fact never existed."

There being two issues joined in an action, the jury is sworn to try the issue; but they find a verdict responsive to both issues; the misprison of charging the jury to try the issue, is immaterial. White *v.* Clay, 7 Leigh 68.

Issue in Fact.—In Bias *v.* Vickers, 27 W. Va. 456, 463, it is said: "The words issue in fact, are not necessarily the same as the phrase 'issue of fact.' An issue in fact may be either an issue of law raised by a demurrer or of fact raised by a plea; but an issue of fact can only be on a plea presenting an issue to be decided by a jury or the court. The meaning is doubtful, to say the least; and in that case it is the duty of courts to so interpret the statute as not to affect the general law."

Issue in Law.—In Hays *v.* Heatherly, 36 W. Va. 613, 15 S. E. 223, 225, it is said: "A demurrer, though frequently called an issue in law, may, with more propriety, be said to tender such issue; for the issue is not formed until there is a joinder in demurrer, which affirms the legal sufficiency of the allegations demurred to—see Gould, Pl. (4th Ed. 1861), c. 9, passim; ch. 125, §§ 28-30; Code (Ed. 1891), p. 801—which has been held to apply to demurrers in equity as well as at common law." See also, the title DEMURRERS, vol. 4, p. 456.

ISSUES TO THE JURY.

VIII. Direction of Action at Law, 85.

CROSS REFERENCES.

See the titles ANSWERS, vol. 1, p. 389; APPEAL AND ERROR, vol. 1, p. 418; EVIDENCE, vol. 5, p. 295; EXCEPTIONS, BILL OF, vol. 5, p. 357; INSTRUCTIONS, vol. 7, p. 701; JURY; NEW TRIALS; RECEIVERS; USURY; VERDICT; WILLS.

As to special interrogatories to the jury, see the title VERDICT.

I. Nature and Object.

Object.—"The object of an issue to be tried by a jury is to satisfy the conscience of the chancellor when the evidence is contradictory and it is difficult to decide upon it." Crebs v. Jones, 79 Va. 381, 385. See, to the same effect, Slaughter v. Danner, 102 Va. 270, 41 S. E. 289; Hull v. Watts, 95 Va. 10, 27 S. E. 829; Miller v. Wills, 95 Va. 337, 28 S. E. 337; Loftus v. Maloney, 89 Va. 576, 16 S. E. 749; Keagy v. Trout, 85 Va. 390, 7 S. E. 329; Reed v. Axtell, 84 Va. 231, 4 S. E. 587; Fishburne v. Ferguson, 84 Va. 87, 4 S. E. 575; M'Cully v. M'Cully, 78 Va. 159; Moseley v. Brown, 76 Va. 419; Almond v. Wilson, 75 Va. 613, 626; Hurley v. Oakley Land, etc., Co., 2 Va. Dec. 319; Steptoe v. Flood, 31 Gratt. 323; Steptoe v. Pollard, 30 Gratt. 689; Hord v. Colbert, 28 Gratt. 49, saying, "the issue is directed exclusively for the information of the court;" Lamberts v. Cooper, 29 Gratt. 61, 64; Powell v. Manson, 22 Gratt. 177; Brockenbrough v. Spindle, 17 Gratt. 21; Lee v. Boak, 11 Gratt. 182; Fitzhugh v. Fitzhugh, 11 Gratt. 210; Watkins v. Carlton, 10 Leigh 560; Whitworth v. Adams, 5 Rand. 333, 397; Douglass v. McChesney, 2 Rand. 109; Carter v. Campbell, Gilmer 159; Pleasants v. Ross, 1 Wash. 156; Rowton v. Rowton, 1 Hen. & M. 92; Hickman v. Baltimore, etc., R. Co., 30 W. Va. 296, 301, 4 S. E. 654, 657; Nease v. Capehart, 15 W. Va. 299, 300; Tompkins v. Stephens, 10 W. Va. 156; Henry v. Davis, 7 W. Va. 715. See also, Ogle v. Adams, 12 W. Va. 213.

Refers Doubtful Question of Fact.—"An issue directed by a court of chancery in an ordinary suit refers a doubtful question of fact to the decision of a jury, to which such question properly belongs." Brockenbrough v. Spindle, 17 Gratt. 21; Rowton v. Rowton, 1 Hen. & M. 92. See post, "Where Evidence Conflicting," II, C, 2.

Incident to Suit.—"The issue, except where it is directed by statute, is a mere incident to the suit in chancery." Miller v. Wills, 95 Va. 337, 28 S. E. 337; Hull v. Watts, 95 Va. 10, 27 S. E. 829; Reed v. Axtell, 84 Va. 231, 4 S. E. 587; Brockenbrough v. Spindle, 17 Gratt. 21. See also, McCully v. McCully, 78 Va. 159 and Almond v. Wilson, 75 Va. 613, 626, where it is said: "An issue out of chancery, except in cases of contested wills, is a mere incident to the suit." And see, to the same effect. Lamberts v. Cooper, 29 Gratt. 61, 65, citing Watkins v. Carlton, 10 Leigh 560; Brockenbrough v. Spindle, 17 Gratt. 21; Powell v. Manson, 22 Gratt. 177.

Substitute for Omitted Evidence.— See post, "General Rule," II, C, 1, b, (1).

Distinguished from Verdict in Action at Common Law.—The verdict rendered upon the trial of an issue at chancery differs from a verdict in an action at common law in that in the former case the issue is a mere incident of the proceedings and may be disregarded or approved by the chancellor according to what, in his judgment, the law and the evidence in the particular case may require, while in the latter case the verdict is conclusive until set aside or reversed. Hull *v.* Watts, 95 Va. 10, 27 S. E. 829; Henry *v.* Davis, 7 W. Va. 715. See also, Reed *v.* Axtell, 84 Va. 231, 4 S. E. 587. See post, "Conclusiveness of Verdict," V. See also, the titles NEW TRIALS; VERDICT.

Distinguished from an Issue Devisavit Vel Non.—The rules which govern upon an issue out of chancery for the trial of a disputed fact to satisfy the conscience of the chancellor, are very different from those which govern upon an issue devisavit vel non. "The issue devisavit vel non is a statutory proceeding. 'It is the sole object, and not the mere incident of the suit.' It is not intended to inform the conscience of the court, which is bound to decree according to the verdict, unless for good cause shown a new trial is granted. It is probate jurisdiction exercised by the jury in order to the final probate of the will." Lamberts *v.* Cooper, 29 Gratt. 61, 65. See also, Reed *v.* Axtell, 84 Va. 231, 4 S. E. 587; Hull *v.* Watts, 95 Va. 10, 27 S. E. 829; Coalter *v.* Bryan, 1 Gratt. 18; Malone *v.* Hobbs, 1 Rob. 346. See the title WILLS.

Distinguished from Issue, "Whether or No the Transaction Be Usurious." —The issue, "whether or no the transaction be usurious," directed by the 10th section of chapter 141, Code of 1860, to be made by the court and tried at its bar by a jury, is the sole object and not an incident of the suit. Its purpose is, not to inform the conscience of the court, but to conclude the question of fact; and the court is bound to decree in accordance with the verdict, unless for good cause a new trial be granted. Brockenbrough *v.*

Spindle, 17 Gratt. 21. See the title USURY.

II. Discretion of Court.

A. GENERAL RULE.

Whether or not an issue out of chancery is desirable rests always in the sound discretion of the court. The chancellor may in the exercise of his discretion, either direct an issue or refuse to do so, and decide the question of fact for himself. Slaughter *v.* Danner, 102 Va. 270, 41 S. E. 289. See, to the same effect, Miller *v.* Wills, 95 Va. 337, 28 S. E. 337; Robinson *v.* Allen, 85 Va. 721, 8 S. E. 835; Keagy *v.* Trout, 85 Va. 390, 7 S. E. 329; Fishburne *v.* Ferguson, 84 Va. 87, 4 S. E. 575; Carter *v.* Carter, 82 Va. 624, 636; Beverly *v.* Walden, 20 Gratt. 147; Mettert *v.* Hagan, 18 Gratt. 231; Reed *v.* Cline, 9 Gratt. 136; Wise *v.* Lamb, 9 Gratt. 294; Grigsby *v.* Weaver, 5 Leigh 197; Samuel *v.* Marshall, 3 Leigh 567; Rowton *v.* Rowton, 1 Hen. & M. 92; Stannard *v.* Graves, 2 Call 369; Pryor *v.* Adams, 1 Call 382; West Virginia Bldg. Co. *v.* Saucer, 45 W. Va. 483, 31 S. E. 965; Alexander *v.* Davis, 42 W. Va. 465, 26 S. E. 291; Mahnke *v.* Neale, 23 W. Va. 57; Setzer *v.* Beale, 19 W. Va. 274; Jarrett *v.* Jarrett, 11 W. Va. 584; Anderson *v.* Cranmer, 11 W. Va. 562; Rohrer *v.* Travers, 11 W. Va. 146, 154; Arnold *v.* Arnold, 11 W. Va. 449; Nease *v.* Capehart, 8 W. Va. 95; Henry *v.* Davis, 7 W. Va. 715; Powell *v.* Batson, 4 W. Va. 610. See also, Hord *v.* Colbert, 28 Gratt. 49; Lavell *v.* Gold, 25 Gratt. 473; New York Life Ins. Co. *v.* Davis, 94 Va. 427, 26 S. E. 941.

A chancellor has a discretionary authority to direct or to decline to direct an issue to try any material fact put in issue by the pleadings in the cause. Powell *v.* Batson, 4 W. Va. 610. See post, "Necessity for Allegation and Prima Facie Proof," II, C, 1.

A Judicial Discretion.—"While directing an issue to be tried by a jury is a matter of discretion in a court of equity, it is not, however, a mere arbitrary discretion, but such discretion must be exercised upon sound principles of reason and justice. A mistake in its exercise is a just ground of appeal, and the appellate court will judge whether such discretion has been soundly exercised in a given case. Stannard v. Graves, 2 Call 369; Reed v. Cline, 9 Gratt. 136; Wise v. Lamb, 9 Gratt. 294; and Beverley v. Walden, 20 Gratt. 147." Miller v. Wills, 95 Va. 337, 28 S. E. 337. See, to the same effect, Robinson v. Allen, 85 Va. 721, 8 S. E. 835; Fishburne v. Ferguson, 84 Va. 87, 4 S. E. 575; Carter v. Carter, 82 Va. 624, 636; Magill v. Manson, 20 Gratt. 527; Mettert v. Hagan, 18 Gratt. 231; Grigsby v. Weaver, 5 Leigh 197; Pryor v. Adams, 1 Call 382; West Virginia Bldg. Co. v. Saucer, 45 W. Va. 483, 31 S. E. 965; Alexander v. Davis, 42 W. Va. 465, 26 S. E. 291; Mahnke v. Neale, 23 W. Va. 57; Setzer v. Beale, 19 W. Va. 274; Jarrett v. Jarrett, 11 W. Va. 584; Arnold v. Arnold, 11 W. Va. 449; Tompkins v. Stephens, 10 W. Va. 156; Nease v. Capehart, 8 W. Va. 95; Henry v. Davis, 7 W. Va. 715; Powell v. Batson, 4 W. Va. 610. See also, Keagy v. Trout, 85 Va. 390, 7 S. E. 329; Reed v. Axtell, 84 Va. 231, 4 S. E. 587; Hord v. Colbert, 28 Gratt. 49; Lavell v. Gold, 25 Gratt. 473; Ogle v. Adams, 12 W. Va. 213. See post, "General Rule," VII, A.

Ex Mero Motu.—Of its own motion the court may direct an issue out of chancery, to be tried at the bar, on the common-law side of the court when the evidence in the depositions is conflicting. Meek v. Spracher, 87 Va. 162, 12 S. E. 397, citing Snouffer v. Hansbrough, 79 Va. 166. See also, Hull v. Watts, 95 Va. 10, 14, 27 S. E. 829. See post, "Where Evidence Conflicting," II, C, 2; "In What Court Tried," IV, A.

B. WHEN MATTER OF RIGHT.

In General.—See post, "When Matter of Right," II, C, 2, b.

Devisavit Vel Non.—See the title WILLS.

Whether or No Transaction Usurious.—See the title USURY. See also, the title JURY.

Policy of Insurance Subject of Litigation.—See post, "Policy of Insurance Subject of Litigation." II, C, 2, a, (6).

C. PRINCIPLES AND RULES CONTROLLING AWARD OF ISSUE.

1. Necessity for Allegation and Prima Facie Proof.

a. In General.

The fact as to which an issue was directed must be a material fact put in issue by the pleadings in the cause. Powell v. Batson, 4 W. Va. 610, 617, citing Wise v. Lamb, 9 Gratt. 294; Mettert v. Hagan, 18 Gratt. 231; Mahnke v. Neale, 23 W. Va. 57. See ante, "General Rule," II, A.

Inquiries Outside of Pleadings.—It is a sufficient objection to an issue ordered to be tried by a jury that the principal inquires thereby directed are outside of the pleadings. Mahnke v. Neale, 23 W. Va. 57, 83.

Title Not Alleged in Bill.—An issue ought not to be directed to try a title not alleged in the plaintiff's bill, but it is said by way of exception, "that if a matter does appear to the court, at the hearing, which goes to the very right, the court will sometimes order an issue to try it." Paynes v. Coles, 1 Munf. 373.

Claim Unsupported by Testimony.—An issue out of chancery ought not to be directed to try a claim altogether unsupported by testimony, or a title not alleged in the bill, but suggested in the answer, without proof. Neither is this rule to be varied by the circumstance that infants are interested. Paynes v. Coles, 1 Munf. 373.

Where, in order to sustain a bill of injunction, a jurisdictional fact is necessary to be established, such fact must be not only alleged in the bill, but it should be sustained by sufficient evidence to at least make a prima facie case before the court proceeds to order an issue out of chancery. Ohio River R. Co. *v.* Ward, 35 W. Va. 481, 14 S. E. 142.

Where an injunction is obtained upon a bill alleging a parol contract for the extension of the time for the collection of a debt secured by trust deed, and the proof does not, in the opinion of the appellate court, establish such a contract as would be specifically enforced by a court of equity, it will not be held, that the circuit court erred in refusing to direct an issue to be tried by a jury to ascertain, whether such contract was in fact made. Craig *v.* McCulloch, 20 W. Va. 148. See also, the title INJUNCTIONS, vol. 7, p. 512.

b. **Burden of Proof Must Be Thrown on Defendant.**

(1) **In General.**

" 'No issue should be ordered until the plaintiff has thrown the burden of proof on the defendant.' Beverley *v.* Walden, 20 Gratt. 147." Vangilder *v.* Hoffman, 22 W. Va. 1; Jarrett *v.* Jarrett. 11 W. Va. 584; Sands *v.* Beardsley, 32 W. Va. 594, 9 S. E. 925; Jones *v.* Christian, 86 Va. 1017, 11 S. E. 984; Keagy *v.* Trout, 85 Va. 390, 7 S. E. 329: Carter *v.* Carter, 82 Va. 624; Wise *v.* Lamb, 9 Gratt. 294; Smith *v.* Betty, 11 Gratt. 752: Grigsby *v.* Weaver, 5 Leigh 197; Pryor *v.* Adams, 1 Call 382.

Until the onus is shifted, and the case rendered doubtful by the conflicting evidence of the opposing parties, the defendant can not be deprived, by an order for an issue, of his right to a decision by the court on the case as made by the pleadings and proofs. Keagy *v.* Trout, 85 Va. 390, 7 S. E. 329, quoting Beverley *v.* Walden, 20 Gratt. 147; Carter *v.* Carter, 82 Va. 624; Jones *v.* Christian, 86 Va. 1017, 11 S. E. 984; Smith *v.* Betty, 11 Gratt. 752; Wise *v.* Lamb, 9 Gratt. 294; Grigsby *v.* Weaver, 5 Leigh 197; Pryor *v.* Adams, 1 Call 382; Jarrett *v.* Jarrett, 11 W. Va. 584.

In Grigsby *v.* Weaver, 5 Leigh 197, Judge Carr says: "It is the bounden duty of the plaintiff, who calls for the solemn judgment of the court, to furnish that court with something like certainty on which to rest that judgment; he may draw this from the defendant if he can; he may prove it by witnesses; he may establish it by documents; but in some way he must shew it, or he fails, and his bill must be dismissed." Beverley *v.* Walden, 20 Gratt. 147.

Not to Enable Party to Obtain Additional Evidence.—It seems to be well settled that in no case ought an issue to be ordered to enable a party to obtain evidence to make out his case; they are not directed to enable the party to obtain additional evidence. Vangilder *v.* Hoffman, 22 W. Va. 1; Sands *v.* Beardsley, 32 W. Va. 594, 9 S. E. 925; Anderson *v.* Cranmer, 11 W. Va. 562; Jarrett *v.* Jarrett, 11 W. Va. 584; Carter *v.* Carter, 82 Va . 624; Jones *v.* Christian, 86 Va. 1017, 11 S. E. 984; Elder *v.* Harris, 75 Va. 68; Beverley *v.* Walden, 20 Gratt. 147, 154; Smith *v.* Betty, 11 Gratt. 752; Wise *v.* Lamb, 9 Gratt. 294; Grigsby *v.* Weaver, 5 Leigh 197; Pryor *v.* Adams, 1 Call 382.

Substitute for Omitted Evidence.— An issue out of chancery is not adopted as a substitute for omitted evidence, but in cases of doubt and difficulty produced by a conflict of testimony. In such cases, the chancellor considers the purposes of justice will be better attained by an investigation before a jury, where the witnesses may be seen by the triers of the fact, their capacity, deportment, accuracy and sources of information, subjected to the tests of a public cross-examination, and the whole merits of the controversy more satisfactorily investigated, than by an examination on paper in the county. Powell *v.* Manson, 22 Gratt. 177; Fishburne *v.* Ferguson, 84 Va. 87, 4 S. E. 575; Steptoe *v.* Pollard, 30 Gratt. 689; Hord *v.* Colbert, 28 Gratt. 49; Mettert *v.* Hagan, 18 Gratt. 231; Wise *v.* Lamb, 9 Gratt. 294; Grigsby *v.* Weaver, 5 Leigh 197; Samuel *v.* Marshall, 3 Leigh

567; Stannard *v.* Graves, 2 Call 369;
Henry *v.* Davis, 7 W. Va. 715.

Simple Failure to Prove Material Facts.—"If there be no conflict between different portions of the evidence, no ambiguity or uncertainty in it, but a simply failure to prove material facts, it is improper to direct an issue. Pryor *v.* Adams, 1 Call 382; Reed *v.* Cline, 9 Gratt. 136." Rohrer *v.* Travers, 11 W. Va. 146. See also, Beverley *v.* Rhodes, 86 Va. 415, 419, 10 S. E. 572; Noble *v.* Davies, 1 Va. Dec. 633; Wise *v.* Lamb, 9 Gratt. 294.

(2) Determined by Proofs at Time Issue Ordered.

(a) In General.

The question whether it was proper, or improper in any particular case to direct an issue of fact therein, to be tried by a jury, must be determined by the proofs in the cause at the time such issue was directed. Mahnke *v.* Neale, 23 W. Va. 57; Vangilder *v.* Hoffman, 22 W. Va. 1; Sands *v.* Beardsley, 32 W. Va. 594, 9 S. E. 925; Setzer *v.* Beale, 19 W. Va. 274; Anderson *v.* Cranmer, 11 W. Va. 562; Jarrett *v.* Jarrett, 11 W. Va. 584; McFarland *v.* Douglass, 11 W. Va. 637; Elder *v.* Harris, 75 Va. 68; Beverley *v.* Walden, 20 Gratt. 147; Reed *v.* Cline, 9 Gratt. 136; Wise *v.* Lamb, 9 Gratt. 294; Ohio River R. Co. *v.* Sehon, 33 W. Va. 559, 11 S. E. 18. See post, "Looks to State of Proofs When Issue Ordered," VII, E, 3.

Facts Sufficiently Established by Evidence in Record.—It is error to award an issue out of chancery to establish a fact already sufficiently established by the evidence in the record; but, the issue not having been tried before the appeal, the appellate court will set aside the issue, and enter such decree as the circuit court ought to have entered. Jackson *v.* Pleasanton, 95 Va. 654, 29 S. E. 680. See post, "Disposition of Cause and Remand," VII, F.

Decree against Complainant Improper.—Where the record contains nothing which warrants a decree against the complainant, the court does not err in deciding the case without the aid of a jury. Beverly *v.* Rhodes, 86 Va. 415, 10 S. E. 572, citing Beverley *v.* Walden, 20 Gratt. 147; Keagy *v.* Trout, 85 Va. 390, 7 S. E. 329. See post, "When Bill Should Be Dismissed upon Pleadings and Proof," II, C, 1, b, (2), (b).

(b) When Bill Should Be Dismissed upon Pleadings and Proof.

See post, "When Merits of Cause Clear," II, C, 2, a, (2).

aa. In General.

If upon the state of the proofs at the time the issue is directed the bill should be dismissed, it is error to direct the issue; and though the issue be found in favor of the plaintiff, the bill should notwithstanding be dismissed at the hearing; and in such case, if the bill is not dismissed by the circuit court, it will be dismissed by the appellate court. Vangilder *v.* Hoffman, 22 W. Va. 1; Mahnke *v.* Neale, 23 W. Va. 57; Setzer *v.* Beale, 19 W. Va. 274; Jarrett *v.* Jarrett, 11 W. Va. 584; McFarland *v.* Douglass, 11 W. Va. 637; Anderson *v.* Cranmer, 11 W. Va. 562; Elder *v.* Harris, 75 Va. 68; Beverley *v.* Walden, 20 Gratt. 147; Smith *v.* Betty, 11 Gratt. 752; Hudson *v.* Cline, 9 Gratt. 379, 384; Wise *v.* Lamb, 9 Gratt. 294; Reed *v.* Cline, 9 Gratt. 136; Collins *v.* Jones, 6 Leigh 530; Pryor *v.* Adams, 1 Call 382. See, to the same effect, McCully *v.* McCully, 78 Va. 159; Almond *v.* Wilson, 75 Va. 613; DeVaugh *v.* Hustead, 27 W. Va. 773; Jones *v.* Christian, 86 Va. 1017, 11 S. E. 984; Carter *v.* Carter, 82 Va. 624; Grigsby *v.* Weaver, 5 Leigh 197. See ante, "In General," II, C, 1, b, (2), (a); post, "When Issue Erroneously Ordered," V, C.

Therefore, where there is a direct conflict between two witnesses, the one affirming and the other denying the fact to be proved, no issue should be directed; and if one is directed, upon which the jury render an affirmative verdict, and a decree is made accordingly, the appellate court will reverse the decree, because the issue was improperly ordered. Sands v. Beardsley, 32 W. Va. 594, 9 S. E. 925. See post, "Looks to State of Proofs When Issue Ordered," VII, E, 3.

"No injury can result to the defendant certainly in awarding it, unless it be a case in which the bill ought to be dismissed at the hearing. Almond v. Wilson, 75 Va. 613, 626." McCully v. McCully, 78 Va. 159.

Mahnke v. Neale, 23 W. Va. 57, is a case wherein a decree of the circuit court, directed certain issues of fact to be tried by a jury, when the proofs in the cause at that time, clearly preponderated against the facts as to which such issues were directed, and where the said decree and all proceedings subsequent thereto were set aside, and the bill dismissed.

The case of Ohio River R. Co. v. Sehon, 33 W. Va. 559, 11 S. E. 18, is a cause in which it was held, that upon the facts and circumstances appearing in the record, the circuit court improperly directed an issue out of chancery.

bb. Allegations of Bill Expressly Denied by Answer.

(aa) Former Doctrine.

In Beverley v. Walden, 20 Gratt. 147, it was decided "that when the allegations of the bill are positively denied by the answer, and the plaintiff has failed to furnish two witnesses, or one witness and strong corroborating circumstances, in support of the bill, it is error in the chancellor to order an issue." Keagy v. Trout, 85 Va. 390, 7 S. E. 329; Loftus v. Maloney, 89 Va. 576, 16 S. E. 749; Carter v. Carter, 82 Va. 624; Jones v. Christian, 86 Va. 1017, 11 S. E. 984; Beverly v. Rhodes, 86 Va. 415, 10 S. E. 572; Snouffer v. Hansbrough, 79 Va. 166; Elder v. Harris, 75 Va. 68, 73; Smith v. Betty, 11 Gratt. 752; Wise v. Lamb, 9 Gratt. 305, holding that where the allegations of the bill are expressly and directly denied in the answer, and are supported by the

evidence of one witness only, the court should not direct an issue, but should dismiss the bill. And see, to the same effect, Grigsby v. Weaver, 5 Leigh 197; Paynes v. Coles, 1 Munf. 373, 396; Bullock v. Gordon, 4 Munf. 450; Galt v. Carter, 6 Munf. 245. Pryor v. Adams, 1 Call 382; Vangilder v. Hoffman, 22 W. Va. 1, 8; Sands v. Beardsley, 32 W. Va. 594, 9 S. E. 925; Devaugh v. Hustead, 27 W. Va. 773. See post, "Answer," IV, D, 2, c; "Looks to State of Proofs When Issue Ordered," VII, E, 3.

Whether Deeds Procured by Fraud. —When plaintiff avers that certain deeds were procured by the fraud of the prior grantee from their common grantor, when she was mentally incapable of conveying, and both the grantor and the prior grantee, by their answers, positively deny every material averment, and plaintiff fails to furnish two witnesses, or one, and corroborating circumstances in support of the bill, or even to throw the burden of proof on the defendant, and to render the case doubtful by conflicting evidence, no issue should be directed. Carter v. Carter, 82 Va. 624.

To Try Question of Usury.—L. files a bill against W. and his assignees, to enjoin two judgments, one for $1,200 and the other for $300, recovered upon bonds executed by L. to his son, and by his son assigned to W., on the ground of usury. The usury as stated in the bill, amounted to $300, for which the small bond was given. W. answered the bill, meeting and denying explicitly all its allegations in relation to the usury. The son was examined as a witness by L. and proved the usury as stated in the bill, but his testimony was excepted to by the defendants. No other witness speaks as to the usury. On filing his answer W. gave notice that he would move for a dissolution of the injunction at the next term; and accordingly at the next term of the court the motion was made, and the injunction was dissolved as to the principal of the judgment for $1,200, but was continued as to the residue. At the next term of the court a motion was made to dissolve the injunction in toto, but the court overruled the motion, and directed an issue to try the question of usury; and upon the trial of the issue the verdict of the jury was that the bonds were in fact executed upon a usurious consideration as stated in the bill; and the court thereupon perpetuated the injunction. It was held, as the testimony of the son, the obligee in the bonds, was not competent evidence to prove the usury in a controversy between the obligor and assignee; and as the answer fully and explicitly denied the allegations of the bill as to the usury, and there being no competent evidence to prove it, the court should, when the motion was first made, have dissolved the injunction in toto, and not have directed an issue to try the question. Wise v. Lamb, 9 Gratt. 294.

The issue having been improperly directed, the injunction should have been dissolved and the bill dismissed upon the final hearing, notwithstanding the verdict of the jury finding the usury as charged in the bill. Wise v. Lamb, 9 Gratt. 294. See post, "When Issue Erroneously Ordered," V, C.

So when the second motion to dissolve was made, it should for the same reason have been sustained, and if the cause was ready for a final hearing, the bill should have been dismissed; and it was error to direct an issue. Wise v. Lamb, 9 Gratt. 294. See also, the title INJUNCTIONS, vol. 7, p. 512.

(bb) Modification of Doctrine.

The act of 1883-84 (Code, 1887, § 3281) authorizing a plaintiff in equity in his bill to waive an answer under oath, etc., modifies the rule above stated as respects the effect of an answer where such waiver is made in the bill. "Subject to such modification, in this and like cases, the rule, as above stated, remains unchanged; and now, as formerly, it is incumbent upon the plaintiff, though answer under oath be waived, to uphold the case made in his bill by competent and sufficient evidence, the answer in such case being equivalent to a traverse." Though answer under oath be waived, yet where the case made by the bill is not sustained by proof, an issue out of chancery should not be awarded. Jones v. Christian, 86 Va. 1017, 11 S. E. 984.

Under § 3281, Va. Code, 1887.—It is provided by statute in Virginia that the court may, in its discretion, direct an issue to be tried before any proof has been taken by either the plaintiff or defendant if it shall be shown by affidavit or affidavits after reasonable notice that the case will be rendered doubtful by the conflicting evidence of the opposing party. See Va. Code, 1887, § 3281, as amended in acts, 1897-98, p. 942; same section, Va. Code, 1904.

Under the West Virginia Code, ch. 125, § 59, the effect of a full, direct and explicit denial of the material allegations of the bill, shall only be to put the plaintiff on satisfactory proof of the truth of such allegation, and any evidence which satisfies the court or jury of the truth thereof shall be sufficient to establish the same. McFarland v. Douglass, 11 W. Va. 637. See post, "Answer," IV, D, 2, c.

2. Where Evidence Conflicting.

See post, "Instances Where Issue Held Proper," II, C, 2, a, (7).

a. Issue Discretionary with Chancellor.

(1) General Rule.

Where there is a conflict of evidence, and it is so nearly balanced as to make it doubtful on which side is the preponderance, an issue ought to be directed; but where, though there be a conflict but not of such a character, no issue should be ordered. Pickens v. McCoy, 24 W. Va. 344; Mahnke v. Neale, 23 W. Va. 57; Jarrett v. Jarrett, 11 W. Va. 584; Setzer v. Beale, 19 W. Va. 274; Anderson v. Cranmer, 11 W.

Va. 562; McFarland v. Douglass, 11 W. Va. 637; Arnold v. Arnold, 11 W. Va. 449; Rohrer v. Travers, 11 W. Va. 146. See, to the same effect, West Virginia Bldg. Co. v. Saucer, 45 W. Va. 483, 31 S. E. 965; Alexander v. Davis, 42 W. Va. 465, 26 S. E. 291. See also, Vangilder v. Hoffman, 22 W. Va. 1; Nease v. Capehart, 15 W. Va. 299; Ogle v. Adams, 12 W. Va. 213; Nease v. Capehart, 8 W. Va. 95; Henry v. Davis, 7 W. Va. 715; Powell v. Batson, 4 W. Va. 610; Randolph v. Adams, 2 W. Va. 519; Loftus v. Maloney, 89 Va. 576, 16 S. E. 749; Keagy v. Trout, 85 Va. 390, 7 S. E. 329; Fishburne v. Ferguson, 84 Va. 87, 4 S. E. 575; Crebs v. Jones, 79 Va. 381; McCully v. McCully, 78 Va. 159; Hurley v. Oakley Land, etc., Co., 2 Va. Dec. 319; Hord v. Colbert, 28 Gratt. 49; Grigsby v. Weaver, 5 Leigh 197. See ante, "General Rule," II, A; post, "Where Evidence Conflicting," V, B, 2.

An issue ought to be directed where the credit and accuracy of the witnesses are impeached, or where the evidence is so clashing as to render it necessary to weigh the character and credibility of the witnesses, or where the evidence is so equally balanced on both sides that it is doubtful which scale preponderates. Williams v. Blakely, 76 Va. 254, citing Hord v. Colbert, 28 Gratt. 49; and Wise v. Lamb, 9 Gratt. 294; Meek v. Spracher, 87 Va. 162, 12 S. E. 397; Robinson v. Allen, 85 Va. 721, 725, 8 S. E. 835; Keagy v. Trout, 85 Va. 390, 7 S. E. 329; Carter v. Carter, 82 Va. 624; Snouffer v. Hansbrough, 79 Va. 166, 177; McCully v. McCully, 78 Va. 159; Pairo v. Bethell, 75 Va. 825; Steptoe v. Flood, 31 Gratt. 323; Powell v. Manson, 22 Gratt. 177; Beverley v. Walden, 20 Gratt. 147, 154; Kraker v. Shields, 20 Gratt. 377; Mettert v. Hagan, 18 Gratt. 231; Smith v. Betty, 11 Gratt. 752; Isler v. Grove, 8 Gratt. 257; Beale v. Digges, 6 Gratt. 582; Nelson v. Armstrong, 5 Gratt. 354; Cocke v. Upshaw, 6 Munf. 464; Boyd v. Hamilton, 6 Munf. 459; Rowton v. Rowton, 1 Hen. & M. 92, 93; Nice v. Purcell, 1 Hen. & M. 372; Ford v. Gardner, 1 Hen. & M. 72; Bullock v. Gordon, 4 Munf. 450; Marshall v. Thompson, 2 Munf. 412; Douglass v. McChesney, 2 Rand. 109; Knibb v. Dixon, 1 Rand. 249; Love v. Braxton, 5 Call 536, 542; Chapman v. Chapman, 4 Call 430, 440; Stannard v. Graves, 2 Call 369; Brent v. Dold, Gilmer 211; Vangilder v. Hoffman, 22 W. Va. 1; Jarrett v. Jarrett, 11 W. Va. 584.

Where the testimony to an important fact is such as to leave it doubtful, the court of equity ought to direct an issue to ascertain it. Wise v. Lamb, 9 Gratt. 294, 303; Marshall v. Thompson, 2 Munf. 412; Steptoe v. Pollard, 30 Gratt. 689, citing Isler v. Grove, 8 Gratt. 257; Mettert v. Hagan, 18 Gratt. 231; and Hord v. Colbert, 28 Gratt. 49; Steptoe v. Flood 31 Gratt. 323; Bullock v. Gordon, 4 Munf. 450; Johnson v. Hendley, 5 Munf. 219; Galt v. Carter, 6 Munf. 245; Banks v. Booth, 6 Munf. 385; Knibb v. Dixon, 1 Rand. 249; Douglass v. McChesney, 2 Rand. 109; Magill v. Manson, 20 Gratt. 527; Nelson v. Armstrong, 5 Gratt. 354; Love v. Braxton, 5 Call 537, 542; Hooe v. Marquess, 4 Call 416; Chapman v. Chapman, 4 Call 440.

When the evidence in behalf of a plaintiff in equity is sufficient to establish his claim, but the counter evidence adduced by the defendant impeaches and contradicts it, and there is such conflict that the court can not decide the question of fact satisfactorily, it directs an issue. Nease v. Capehart, 8 W. Va. 95.

Necessity for Reasonable Doubt.— Such doubt in the mind of the chancellor must not be a factitious but a reasonable one, justified by such conflict of the evidence. Anderson v. Cranmer, 11 W. Va. 562; Jarrett v. Jarrett, 11 W. Va. 584; Setzer v. Beale, 19 W. Va. 274.

On Demand of Parties.— In any pending chancery case, where an issue of fact is raised depending on a conflict of evidence on the demand of the parties in interest, it is proper for the court to direct such issue to be tried by a jury. Alexander v. Davis, 42 W. Va. 465, 26 S. E. 291; Anderson v. Cranmer, 11 W. Va. 562; Nease v. Capehart, 8 W. Va. 95; Griffith v. Blackwater Boom, etc., Co., 46 W. Va. 56, 33 S. E. 125.

Defendant's Conceding That There Is Conflict.—"But where the defendant himself concedes there is such a conflict of testimony as to call for a jury, the court ought to feel less difficulty in directing it." Almond v. Wilson, 75 Va. 613, 626. See also, McCully v. McCully, 78 Va. 159; Barnun v. Barnun, 83 Va. 365, 5 S. E. 372; Fishburne v. Ferguson, 84 Va. 87, 4 S. E. 575.

(2) When Merits of Cause Clear.

(a) In General.

When the merits of the cause are clear, there being no occasion for an issue, none should be directed. The court should judge on the proofs before it. Pryor v. Adams, 1 Call 382; Paynes v. Coles, 1 Munf. 373; Samuel v. Marshall, 3 Leigh 567; Reed v. Cline, 9 Gratt. 136; Wise v. Lamb, 9 Gratt. 294; Greer v. Greers, 9 Gratt. 330, 333; Love v. Braxton, 5 Call 537; Smith v. Betty, 11 Gratt. 752; Kraker v. Shields, 20 Gratt. 377; Setzer v. Beale, 19 W. Va. 274, 289; Nice v. Purcell, 1 Hen. & M. 372; Watkins v. Young, 31 Gratt. 84; Beverly v. Rhodes, 86 Va. 415, 419, 10 S. E. 572; Jones v. Christian, 86 Va. 1017, 11 S. E. 984; Keagy v. Trout, 85 Va. 390, 7 S. E. 329; Loftus v. Maloney, 89 Va. 576, 16 S. E. 749; Hurley v. Oakley Land, etc., Co., 2 Va. Dec. 319; McFarland v. Douglass, 11 W. Va. 637; Arnold v. Arnold, 11 W. Va. 449; Anderson v. Cranmer, 11 W. Va. 562; Jarrett v. Jarrett, 11 W. Va. 584. See also, Stannard v. Graves, 2 Call 369. See ante, "When Bill Should Be Dismissed upon Pleadings and Proof," II, C, 1, b, (2), (b).

An issue is not necessary and proper in every case where the evidence happens to be conflicting. If this was the rule the chief time of the chancery courts would be occupied with trials before juries, or in considering their verdicts. Hord v. Colbert, 28 Gratt. 49; Setzer v. Beale, 19 W. Va. 274.

On the contrary, if the evidence in the case be such as ought fairly to satisfy the conscience, of the chancellor though various and conflicting an issue, with its attendant delay and expense, ought not to be directed except in certain particular cases in which, by statute or practice, it is made a matter of right. Crebs v. Jones, 79 Va. 381, 385; Robinson v. Allen, 85 Va. 721, 8 S. E. 835; Keagy v. Trout, 85 Va. 390, 7 S. E. 329; Hord v. Colbert, 28 Gratt. 49; Smith v. Betty, 11 Gratt. 752; Wise v. Lamb, 9 Gratt. 294; Samuel v. Marshall, 3 Leigh 567; Jarrett v. Jarrett, 11 W. Va. 584; Arnold v. Arnold, 11 W. Va. 449.

"A court can and should itself decide matters of fact, and even state an account, and save the cost and time of a protracted jury trial, if it have such data and evidence to enable it to do so properly. Darby v. Gilligan, 43 W. Va. 755, 28 S. E. 737; Bart. Ch. Prac. 848." West Virginia Bldg. Co. v. Saucer, 45 W. Va. 483, 31 S. E. 965. See also, Slaughter v. Danner, 102 Va. 270, 41 S. E. 289; Rowton v. Rowton, 1 Hen. & M. 92; Mahnke v. Neale, 23 W. Va. 57; Henry v. Davis, 7 W. Va. 715, 716.

In Nice v. Purcell, 1 Hen. & M. 372, it was held, that no court of equity is bound to direct an issue on the mere ground that the evidence is contradictory; but it may judge of the weight of evidence; and if its conscience is satisfied, decide without a jury. Hord v. Colbert, 28 Gratt. 49; Miller v. Wills, 95 Va. 337, 350, 28 S. E. 337; Hull v. Watts, 95 Va. 10, 27 S. E. 829; Robinson v. Allen, 85 Va. 721, 8 S. E. 835; Keagy v. Trout, 85 Va. 390, 7 S. E. 329; Crebs v. Jones, 79 Va. 381, 385; Williams v. Blakely, 76 Va. 254; Kraker v. Shields, 20 Gratt. 377, 394; Wise v.

Lamb, 9 Gratt. 294; Smith *v.* Betty, 11 Gratt. 752; Samuel *v.* Marshall, 3 Leigh 567; Rowton *v.* Rowton, 1 Hen. & M. 92, 93; Stannard *v.* Graves, 2 Call 369; Carter *v.* Campbell, Gilmer 159, 170; Setzer *v.* Beale, 19 W. Va. 274; Nease *v.* Capehart, 15 W. Va. 299; Jarrett *v.* Jarrett, 11 W. Va. 584; Rohrer *v.* Travers, 11 W. Va. 146; Arnold *v.* Arnold, 11 W. Va. 449; Anderson *v.* Cranmer, 11 W. Va. 562; Jarrett *v.* Jarrett, 11 W. Va. 584. See ante, "Nature and Object," I.

Whether Debts Are Bona Fide.—H. recovers a judgment against M., and dies. Subsequently M. conveys land, etc., to C., to secure two bonds held by W., and this deed is recorded. The administrator of H. files a bill against C. and W., in which he charges that C. and W. had notice of the judgment of H. when the deed was executed, and that the debts secured by the deed are not bona fide. C. and W. are examined as witnesses in their own behalf, and C. is cross-examined on all the issues by the plaintiff, with a knowledge at the time of the objection to his competency; and after the testimony of C. and W. is ended, plaintiff excepts to the competence of each of them, on the ground that H. was dead. Held, though the evidence is contradictory, if the chancellor is satisfied that the weight of evidence is on one side, he is not bound to direct an issue. Hord *v.* Colbert, 28 Gratt. 49.

(b) Evidence All in Record.

The court of chancery, when the evidence is all in the record, may decide the cause, without directing an issue. Love *v.* Braxton, 5 Call 537; Paynes *v.* Coles, 1 Munf. 373.

(c) Where Evidence Clearly Preponderates.

Where the evidence clearly preponderates in favor of, or against any material fact at issue in the cause, the court should not direct an issue as to such facts, to be tried by a jury. If in such case an issue is directed, the decree directing such issue will be reversed, although the evidence in regard to such facts may have been conflicting. Mahnke *v.* Neale, 23 W. Va. 57. See post, "General Rule," VII, A.

Rescission on Ground of Fraud and Misrepresentation.—In a bill for the rescission of a contract of purchase of real property on the ground of fraud and misrepresentation, the court will not direct the issue to a jury, where the evidence clearly determines it. Hurley *v.* Oakley Land, etc., Co., 2 Va. Dec. 319.

Upon a bill filed to set aside a written contract for the purchase of land or to obtain an abatement of the purchase money on account of deceit and false and fraudulent representations by the vendor, when the answer positively denies the allegations of fraud and deceit, and the testimony greatly preponderates in favor of the defendant, it is error to direct an issue out of chancery to a jury to determine whether or not there were such deceit and fraudulent representations. DeVaugh *v.* Hustead, 27 W. Va. 773.

Question of Laches.—Where bond fell due in 1875; suit brought ten years afterwards when all the obligors were dead; and bond having been assigned as collateral and the interest regularly paid; held, not laches, and not a case for an issue out of chancery. Beverly *v.* Rhodes, 86 Va. 415, 10 S. E. 572.

Imbecility from Habitual Drunkenness.—In Samuel *v.* Marshall, 3 Leigh 567, "a question of imbecility, from habitual drunkenness, in the execution of a deed was involved; it was a deed of gift; and this deed was set aside upon the hearing [the question being determined by the court]. Tucker, president, observed: 'Had there been a quid pro quo, we might have hesitated; but surely the question is very different between a contract for valuable consideration, and this gift by an habitual sot, of his whole estate; to take effect at his death, to the disherison of his sisters and natural heirs.'" Jarrett v. Jarrett, 11 W. Va. 584.

(3) Questions as to Partnerships.

"The fact that a question of partnership arises in the case, does not affect the general rule in relation to an issue in chancery causes." Robinson v. Allen, 85 Va. 721, 8 S. E. 835. See also, McCully v. McCully, 78 Va. 159; Slaughter v. Danner, 102 Va. 270, 41 S. E. 289.

In cases of partnership, where there is an application for a receiver, and upon the evidence there is doubt whether there was a subsisting partnership between the parties, or as to the share of the profits to which the plaintiff is entitled, or as to the dissolution of the partnership by mutual consent at a particular time, the court should direct an issue or issues at law to determine these questions. Satterlee v. Cameron, 1 Va. Dec. 517.

The supreme court of appeals will not reverse the action of the trial court in refusing to order an issue out of chancery to settle the partnership accounts, it being one of the peculiar functions of a court of equity to settle the partnership accounts. Slaughter v. Danner, 102 Va. 270, 41 S. E. 289. See also, the titles JURISDICTION; PARTNERSHIP.

An issue is properly awarded to try the question of the existence of a partnership between parties if the chancellor feels the necessity of a trial by jury to satisfy his conscience upon the question and the evidence is conflicting, and the credibility of witnesses involved. McCully v. McCully, 78 Va. 159. See ante, "Nature and Object," I; "Where Evidence Conflicting," II, C, 2.

If, upon a bill in equity to subject the estate of a secret partner in trade to the payment of a debt contracted by the ostensible members of the firm, the fact of the secret partnership be doubtful on the testimony, the court should direct an issue to ascertain it. Cock v. Upshaw, 6 Munf. 464.

(4) Issue Quantum Damnificatus.
(a) In General.

It is not consistent with equity practice to order an issue quantum damnificatus in any case in which the court can lay hold of a simple, equitable and precise rule to ascertain the amount, which it ought to decree. Mason v. Harper's Ferry Bridge Co., 17 W. Va. 396, 422.

(b) Subject Matter in Nature of Unliquidated Damages.

Where the subject matter in controversy is of the nature of estimated and unliquidated damages, and the accuracy and credit of the witnesses is impeached, an issue should be directed. Isler v. Grove, 8 Gratt. 257; Nagle v. Newton, 22 Gratt. 814; Braxton v. Willing, 4 Call 288. Mason v. Harper's Ferry Bridge Co., 17 W. Va. 396, 422. See ante, "Where Evidence Conflicting," II. C, 2.

Damage to Property Owner by Internal Improvement Company.—In Mason v. Harper's Ferry Bridge Co., 17 W. Va. 396, 422, an issue of quantum damnificatus to assess the damages, which the plaintiff has sustained by the entry and acts of the commissioners and by his own act in lowering his dam, which was a consequence of their directions, was awarded. There being as yet no legislation prescribing the manner in which an internal improvement company can acquire the legal right to damage private property for the use of such corporation, and the plaintiff having the right, as was done in this cause, to restrain the defendant from constructing and operating its bridge, and thus damaging his private property, until just compensation should be paid or secured to be paid to him, equity will in this cause award an issue quantum damnificatus, to assess the damage to the plaintiff's ferry franchise by the erection and use for public travel of the toll bridge of the defendant across the Shenandoah river at Harper's Ferry; in which issue said Mason shall be plaintiff, and the Harper's Ferry Bridge company defendant; and after said damage is so ascertained the injunction shall continue in force until compensation for the same is paid; but when paid the injunction shall be wholly dissolved. See also, the title EMINENT DOMAIN, vol. 5, p. 66.

Value of Timber Taken by Guardian from Ward's Land.—"In Isler *v.* Grove (8 Gratt. 257), the question was whether any timber unaccounted for had been taken by the guardian from his ward's lands, and if so, what sum would be a proper charge for the timber so taken and sold or converted to the use of said guardian. Allen, Judge, said the case from the character of the claim was peculiarly proper for issue; for although it was competent for the appellees to make the alleged profits received and made by the guardian from the use and sale of the timber taken from the ward's estate a matter of account, yet the extent of the charge on this account, if any was proper, depends upon estimate. and is in the nature of unliquidated damages, and therefore should have been submitted to a jury." Mason *v.* Harper's Ferry Bridge Co., 17 W. Va. 396, 422.

Negligent Killing of Horse—Railroad in Receiver's Hands.—Where upon petition filed in suit wherein a railway company had been put into a receiver's hands, for damages sustained by petitioner by the negligent killing of the petitioner's horse, alleged to have been of the value of $50,000, a reference had been made to ascertain and report the value of the horse, the commissioner, having taken all the evidence procurable, reported the horse to have been worth $40,000; but the court recommitted the report, and the commissioner took additional evidence, and reported the horse to have been worth only $1,000; the additional evidence does not warrant the last report, yet the evidence offered by petitioner as to the speed and celebrity of the horse does not sustain his claim to have the

first report confirmed. It was held, that both reports should be set aside and an issue directed to be tried by a jury at the bar of the court below to ascertain the amount of the damages sustained by the petitioner. Melendy *v.* Barbour, 78 Va. 544.

Suit for Specific Performance.—"It is the settled doctrine that when a court of chancery has jurisdiction of the case, and it is a case proper for specific performance, such court may, as ancillary to specific performance, decree compensation or damages; and where the ascertainment of damages is asserted in the case before it, the court ought not to send the parties to another forum to litigate their rights, but should refer the matter to one of its commissioners, or direct an issue quantum damnificatus to be tried at its own bar. Nagle *v.* Newton, 22 Gratt. 814." Campbell *v.* Rust, 85 Va. 653, 8 S. E. 664; Witz *v.* Mullin, 90 Va. 805, 806, 20 S. E. 783; Ewing *v.* Litchfield, 91 Va. 575, 580, 22 S. E. 362; Ayres *v.* Robins, 30 Gratt. 105, 118.

N. sues J. in equity to rescind specific execution of a contract, for the sale of land by N. to J. J. answers, not objecting to specific execution, but insisting that he shall be compensated for injuries to which he has been subjected by the failure of N. to comply with his contract, and by the intermeddling of N. and his agents with J.'s possession of the land and the property upon it. Held, the damages may be ascertained either by a commissioner, or by an issue of quantum damnificatus to be tried at the bar of the court. Nagle *v.* Newton, 22 Gratt. 814. See the title SPECIFIC PERFORMANCE.

Whether Vendee Has Performed Covenant and to Ascertain Damages. —On the 31st of July, 1866, R. and A. enter into a contract by which R. sells to A. a tract of land on Cherrystone creek, and covenants that by the 1st of January, 1867, he will convey the land to A. by deed, with general warrants at the cost of the vendee by proper deed tendered by A., and will deliver possession free of incumbrance. And A. covenants to pay to R. $9,000, of which $5,000 by the 1st of January, 1867, and sooner if R. shall have made the conveyance and delivered possession, and for the balance in one and two years, with lien on the land from the day the conveyance is made and possession given. And R. covenanted that he would on or before the 1st of May, 1867, remove or cause to be removed the stakes marking the oyster grounds of S. and D., so that these grounds shall be left unencumbered by the latter, and remain to the use of A. A. was put into possession and paid the $5,000 and the first and a part of the second deferred payments; but had not tendered to R. a deed to be executed. In October, 1870, R. files his bill for the specific performance of the contract, and averring his performance or willingness to perform. A. answers and says that R. has not complied with his covenant to remove the stakes of S. and D., whereby he lost an important part of his inducement to purchase the land, and that the damage thus sustained was fully equal to the balance of the purchase money unpaid, and without asking for a rescission of the contract, claimed an abatement of the price. The court directs an issue to be tried at its bar to ascertain whether R. has complied with his covenant to remove the stakes of S. and D., and if he has not, what damage A. has sustained by his failure to do so. The first jury return a verdict that all the stakes have not been removed, and ascertain its damage at $2,137.50. This verdict is set aside by the court on the motion of the plaintiff, and no exception is taken. The second jury did not agree, and the third found, as did the first, as to the removal of the stakes, but found a verdict for only $350 damages. A. moved the court to set aside this verdict, but the court overruled the motion, and A. excepted; but the

exception does not contain the facts or the evidence. The court makes a decree for the amount of the purchase money due, after crediting the $350, and A. appeals. It was held, that an issue was the proper mode of ascertaining the damages. Ayres *v.* Robins, 30 Gratt. 105.

Breach of Promise to Pay Debt of Another.—If A promise B to pay a debt, which the latter owes to C, but fails to do so; whereby B sustains an injury; equity will direct an issue to ascertain the damages sustained by B. Braxton *v.* Willing, 4 Call 288.

(c) Amount of Damages Fixed and Certain.

Measure of Damages against Heirs on Warranty of Ancestor.—In order to secure the accommodation indorsers of a note due at bank, the maker conveys land to trustees by a deed in which he covenants for himself and his heirs, with the trustees and the bank respectively, that he is possessed of an absolute estate of inheritance in the premises, and that he will warrant and defend the same against all persons. After the death of the grantor, the indorsers pay the debt to the bank, and the trust property having been sold to satisfy a debt secured by a prior deed of trust thereon, they file a bill to be subrogated to the rights of the bank under the second trust deed, and to have satisfaction out of other lands of the grantor descended to his heirs. The complainants came into equity for satisfaction out of the real assets in the hands of the heirs, to the extent of the damages accruing from the breach of the ancestor's covenant. It was held, that the amount of those damages being the sum paid in discharge of the first encumbrance, and so fixed and certain, an issue for the purpose of assessing them is unnecessary. Haffey *v.* Birchetts, 11 Leigh 83. See the title COVENANTS, vol. 3, p. 741.

(5) When Case Proper for Reference.

If the court considers an issue unnecessary, and deems it proper that the case ought to go to a commissioner instead of a jury, it should so direct. This rule is fairly deducible from Grigsby *v.* Weaver, 5 Leigh 197; and Samuel *v.* Marshall, 3 Leigh 567; Rohrer *v.* Travers, 11 W. Va. 146. See the title REFERENCE.

An account of rents and profits may be taken by a commissioner, as well as be ascertained by a jury; and the former is the most usual course. Newman *v.* Chapman, 2 Rand. 93.

"It is not necessary or proper in an attachment suit in equity, to direct an inquiry whether the rents and profits of the real estate attached will pay the debt within a reasonable time." Curry *v.* Hale, 15 W. Va. 867, 879.

To Try Question of Usury.—R. filed his bill in equity, alleging that he borrowed of P. $7,650, and executed his note to P. therefor March 25, 1875, payable April 1, 1874, for $8,500, he, P., being allowed and retaining $850, as interest on this loan in advance, for one year and six days use of said money; and he, R., therefore claimed a credit on the principal of said note, of the excess of interest so paid over six per cent. of $383; that R., to secure the $8,500, conveyed to T. as trustee certain real estate; that in making that conveyance to T. he, R., omitted by mistake to except two parcels of real estate that he had before conveyed respectively to B. and F. in fee; and also, to except a prior lien in favor of the estate of L., deceased, a balance of said lien of about $2,000, remaining unpaid; that T. as trustee had advertised the whole of said real estate to be sold for the payment of said $8,500 and interest for the benefit of P.'s estate, he having since died; and prayed that said trustee be enjoined from making said sale, and that an account be taken ascertaining said liens, also the just amount due the estate of said P., and for general relief. The executors of P. and the executors of L. answered the bill, admitting the prior

conveyance of said two parcels to B. and F., and the balance unpaid on the prior lien of L.'s estate, but denied any knowledge of the alleged usury. The deposition of one witness was taken, that P. had told him, he had loaned R. $8,500 at ten per cent., as the witness understood him. The note said nothing about interest, and was for $8,500, dated March 25, 1873, payable April 1, 1874. The court decreed the sale of the land conveyed to said trustee, or so much thereof as should be required, excluding the parts conveyed to B. and F. by R., the plaintiff, "to pay the following sums which are liens thereon;" $2,000, with interest from November 1, 1873, less $300 paid February 3, 1874, due the executors of L.; and $8,500 with interest from April 1, 1874, due the executors of P., etc. The court further ordered, that the cause be referred to a commissioner, to inquire and report what amounts have been paid as interest on said debts, and whether said payment was in excess of legal interest, stating the amount of said excess, etc. Held, that it is in the sound discretion of the court, under the circumstances of this cause, to refer the question of usury to a commissioner, instead of directing an issue out of chancery to try it. "But if the testimony is of so vague and indefinite a character, or so conflicting and contradictory that the court can not satisfactorily determine the question of usury, it of course should exercise the wise discretion of directing an issue out of chancery to determine the question, instead of referring it to a commissioner." Rohrer *v.* Travers, 11 W. Va. 146. See ante, "Where Evidence Conflicting," II, C, 2. See also, the title USURY.

Whether Contract Made with Reference to Confederate Currency.—In November, 1862, S. sells to K. a house and lot in Richmond, for $14,500, of which $4,500 is paid in cash, and notes with interest for the balance are given, payable in one, two, three and four years, with a deed of trust to secure them. The cash payment, and first and second notes, are paid in confederate money, the third is paid four months before it fell due by a compromise, S. taking for it $2,000 in United States currency. Bill to enjoin the sale of the house and lot for the payment of the fourth note, alleges that it was given with reference to confederate currency as the standard of value, and prays that S. might be required to receive payment according to the value of that money at the time the note fell due, and asks the court to adjudicate the question. It was held, that it is not a case in which the court should have directed an issue. And this especially as there was no conflict of testimony when the case was referred to a commissioner. Kraker *v.* Shields, 20 Gratt. 377.

Difference between Purchase Price and Price Land Should Have Brought. —Testator directs that his land should be sold on such credit as his executors shall think best for the interest of his children, to whom he bequeaths the proceeds; the executor advertises land for sale at auction in 1825, without specifying the terms of sale; offers it for sale, and at the sale requires near one-half of purchase money to be paid in cash, and residue in two equal annual installments; and purchases at his own sale; as executor's sale and purchase not being a due performance of his trust; he may, at election of cestuis que trust, be rightly required to keep the land, and pay the purchase money for which he bought it, and as much more as the land would have sold for, if it had been offered for sale on the usual terms of one, two and three years credit; it was held, that the difference between the price the land would have brought on a sale on such credit in 1825, and that which it brought on the terms on which it was then sold and purchased, should rather be referred to a commissioner to be by him ascertained, than to a jury upon an issue directed for the purpose. Moore

v. Hilton, 12 Leigh 1. See also, the title EXECUTORS AND ADMINISTRATORS, vol. 5, p. 483.

(6) Policy of Insurance Subject of Litigation.

If an insurance company is properly before the court in a chancery suit where its policy is the subject of litigation, any issue or issues raised by the pleadings as to its liability on the policy must be tried according to the rules and principles governing courts of equity in such cases. It is not entitled to a jury trial as matter or right, but only in the event that the case made shows that a jury trial is proper. New York Life Ins. Co. *v.* Davis, 94 Va. 427, 26 S. E. 941. See the titles INSURANCE, vol. 7, p. 746; JURY.

(7) Instances Where Issue Held Proper.

See ante, "Where Evidence Conflicting," II, C, 2.

Payment of Bond.—W., in 1853, at sale made by B., as commissioner under decree of court, purchased house and lot in F., and gave four bonds, each for $720, payable in one, two, three, and four years thereafter. Payment of all but the second bond is admitted. As far back as 1869, W. insisted he had paid all, and was entitled to his deed. B. insisted that the second was unpaid; but finally, in 1872, executed a deed acknowledging receipt of all the purchase money, and conveying the property to W. In 1874, the bond was found in possession of H., a lawyer to whom, in 1855, it had been entrusted for collection. In 1877, B. filed his petition in the suit wherein the decree of sale was rendered, praying for a rule against W. to show cause why he should not pay this bond, etc. W. filed his answer, insisting the bond had been paid. Much documentary evidence and many depositions of conflicting nature were in the case. It was held, that in view of the conflicting evidence, and the nature of the issue involved, W. is entitled to an issue out of chancery. Williams *v.* Blakely, 76 Va. 254.

Nature and Validity of Written Instrument.—An issue may be directed to try the validity of a paper writing. Powell *v.* Batson, 4 W. Va. 610; Brent *v.* Dold, Gilmer 211; Bank *v.* Booth, 6 Munf. 385.

An issue will be directed, on satisfactory proof adduced, to try whether a will said to be lost, was ever in fact executed, and what were its provisions. Brent *v.* Dold, Gilmer 211.

Notwithstanding a paper purporting to be a will be proved in a suit in chancery, to have been wholly written and subscribed by the supposed testator; yet if upon the evidence (there being no attesting witness), it be doubtful whether, at the time he wrote it, he was in a proper state of mind to make a testament; whether it was seriously intended by him as such; or, if so, whether it has not been subsequently nullified, by the republication of a former will, a revocation of it, or otherwise; the court ought to direct issues to ascertain such facts, before any decision of the cause. Banks *v.* Booth, 6 Munf. 385. See the titles TESTAMENTARY CAPACITY; WILLS.

Interlock.—Where the evidence fails to show that an elder grant under which a complainant in the court below claimed, covered the land embraced by a junior patent sought to be repealed, and yet was sufficient to make it probable that such is the fact, the court below should direct an issue to be tried by a jury to ascertain that fact. Randolph *v.* Adams, 2 W. Va. 519.

Location of Boundary Lines.—Where it is necessary to ascertain the quantity of deficiency in the sale of a tract of land, and it becomes necessary to establish the boundary lines of the tract conveyed, the evidence being conflicting in regard to the location of the lines, it is proper for the court in determining their location to call a jury to its aid. Hull *v.* Watts, 95 Va. 10, 27 S. E. 829.

Proportionate Value of Dower to Estate in Remainder.—In Pollard *v.* Underwood, 4 Hen. & M. 459, an issue out of chancery was directed to ascertain what proportion the value of a dower estate bore to that in remainder (where the land had been sold upon a decree to foreclose a mortgage); and the sum found by the jury decreed to the tenent in dower. See also, the title DOWER, vol. 4, p. 782.

Breach of Contract to Make Good Title.—If a purchaser of land, suing for breach of a contract to make a good title, come into a court of equity for a pecuniary compensation, instead of proceeding at law in the first instance, the court has the power to direct the justice of the plaintiff's claim tried by an issue out of chancery. Sims *v.* Lewis, 5 Munf. 29.

Adverse Possession of Chattels.—On a bill of injunction to prevent the sale of chattels if defendant alleges adverse possession for five years, and the evidence on this point is doubtful, an issue should be directed to ascertain the truth of the allegation. Galt *v.* Carter, 6 Munf. 245; Marshall *v.* Thompson, 2 Munf. 412.

Whether Bill of Sale Intended as Security.—On a question whether an absolute bill of sale was intended only as a security, the evidence being contradictory, a court of chancery ought to direct an issue to try that point. Knibb *v.* Dixon, 1 Rand. 249.

Question of Fraud.—Where fraud is charged in a bill, but denied in the answer, and the testimony is conflicting and unsatisfactory, an issue out of chancery ought to be directed. Hooe *v.* Marquess, 4 Call 416; Chapman *v.* Chapman, 4 Call 430; Bullock *v.* Gordon, 4 Munf. 450; Knibb *v.* Dixon, 1 Rand. 249; West *v.* Logwood, 6 Munf. 491; Marshall *v.* Thompson, 2 Munf. 412; Magill *v.* Manson, 20 Gratt. 527; Mettert *v.* Hagan, 18 Gratt. 231.

A contract was clearly fraudulent by reason of misrepresentations. A second contract intended to be a distinct transaction of confirmation was made. It was claimed that the second contract was made while under the influence of such misrepresentations and a repetition thereof. The testimony was not entirely satisfactory, but vague and indefinite as to the fact whether the party was fully informed at the time of making the second contract, that he had been defrauded, and that he intended the second contract to be a distinct transaction of confirmation. It was held, that it would be eminently proper to settle the question, by an issue out of chancery. Davis *v.* Henry, 4 W. Va. 571.

Deed Charged to Be Fraudulent.— When a deed is charged to be fraudulent and the answer does not confess the fraud, if the testimony be conflicting and unsatisfactory, an issue should be directed. Hooe *v.* Marquess, 4 Call 416; Chapman *v.* Chapman, 4 Call 430; Bullock *v.* Gordon, 4 Munf. 450; Knibb *v.* Dixon, 1 Rand. 249; West *v.* Logwood, 6 Munf. 491; Marshall *v.* Thompson, 2 Munf. 412.

Whether Bond Obtained by Misrepresentations.—M. sues O. in equity, to set aside her bond, as having been fraudulently obtained. Upon the question whether the bond of M. was obtained by the misrepresentations of O., the evidence being conflicting, an issue should be directed. Magill *v.* Manson, 20 Gratt. 527.

Whether Deed Was Substituted.— Where a son had obtained a deed from his father for ninety acres of land and five slaves, in consideration of £1, 16, and maintenance for life; after which he sold the land to a third person; who filed a bill alleging that deed to have been recorded, but to have been afterwards destroyed; another substituted in its room, and the land sold again by the first doner to a purchaser with notice of the plaintiff's title, whose deed had been recorded; the court of appeals directed an issue to try whether there was such substitution, and, if so,

what were the terms of the first deed? Hooe *v.* Marquess, 4 Call 416

Whether Conveyance Is Fraudulent. —Where a charge of fraud is made in the bill, to set aside a fraudulent conveyance, but denied in the answer, and the testimony is such as to leave it doubtful, the court of equity ought to direct an issue to ascertain it. Bullock *v.* Gordon, 4 Munf. 450.

Whether Deed Obtained by Fraud— Whether Afterwards Confirmed.—M., in his lifetime, conveyed by deed to H., M.'s interest in the estate of J., deceased, upon the consideration, as expressed in the deed, of $1,000. After the death of M., H. files his bill to recover the said interest; and M.'s administrator resists it, on the ground that M. was incapable from drink of making a contract, and that the deed was obtained by the fraud of H., and that H. gave no consideration for it. The evidence touching M.'s competency being contradictory, and there being some proof that M. had confirmed the deed after its execution; it was held, that an issue should be directed to ascertain: 1st. Whether the deed had been procured by fraud; and, 2d. If procured by fraud, whether it had afterwards been confirmed by M., without coercion or restraint, when he was competent to act. Mettert *v.* Hagan, 18 Gratt. 231.

Whether Creditor's Claim Bona Fide.—B. remained in possession of slaves for five years under parol loan. The possession of them was resumed by the lender before executions were levied upon them to satisfy a creditor of B. It was held, that under the circumstances an issue directed for the purpose of ascertaining whether the claim of the creditors for which he was attempting to subject the slaves, was fair and bona fide, or fictitious and fraudulent was proper. Beale *v.* Digges, 6 Gratt. 582.

Whether Consideration of Debt Good and Lawful.—On bill filed to enjoin a judgment on the ground that the debt on which it was founded was for money won at cards, it being doubtful on the evidence, whether such was the consideration; or if it was, whether the plaintiff in the judgment, who was a transferee of the debt, had not been induced to take the transfer of the debt under the belief, induced by the concealment or misrepresentation of the debtor, that the consideration of said debt was good and lawful; the court should continue the injunction, and direct an issue to ascertain the facts. Nelson v. Armstrong, 5 Gratt. 354.

Shift to Evade Statute against Usury. —Where a court of chancery had doubts, whether the sale of a horse or other property is really intended as a shift to evade the statute against usury, it ought to direct an issue to be tried upon viva voce testimony, if to be had. Douglass v. McChesney, 2 Rand. 109. See the title USURY.

Whether Cestui Que Trust Entitled to Slaves by Possession.—Upon a bill of injunction to prevent the sale, under execution, of slaves devised in trust, if the defendants allege that the cestui que trust was entitled to the slaves by five years' possession before the death of the devisor; and the truth of such allegation be doubtful on the evidence; the chancellor ought to direct an issue to ascertain that fact. Galt v. Carter, 6 Munf. 245. See also, Marshall v. Thompson, 2 Munf. 412; Bullock v. Gordon. 4 Munf. 450.

Whether J. O. Alive within Seven Years Next before Bringing Suit.— When in a cause in equity, the plaintiff by evidence in the cause has made out a prima facie case of the death of her husband from his absence and from not being heard from for twelve or fifteen years prior to the bringing of her suit, and the defendant, by the deposition of a witness or witnesses, filed in the cause, undertakes to prove that such witness or witnesses heard from the plaintiff's absent husband by letter or letters, written by him from another and adjoining state, and from the dep-

ositions of the witness or witnesses themselves, and other circumstances, the appellate court sees that there is such doubt of the truth of the testimony of such witness or witnesses, or as to the genuineness or falsity of such letters as that the conscience and judgment of the chancellor might well be in doubt as to the truth or falsity of the testimony of such witness or witnesses, or as to the genuineness or falsity of such letters, the appellate court will not in such a case reverse an order of the court directing an issue to be tried at the bar of the court, to ascertain and determine whether the plaintiff's husband (J. O.) was alive at any time within seven years next before the bringing of the suit. Ogle v. Adams, 12 W. Va. 213.

b. When Matter of Right.

In particular cases wherein by statute or practice it is made a matter of right, an issue out of chancery may be awarded, although the case has not been rendered doubtful by the conflicting evidence of the opposing parties. Beverly v. Rhodes, 86 Va. 415, 10 S. E. 572; Beverly v. Walden, 20 Gratt. 147; Keagy v. Trout, 85 Va. 390, 7 S. E. 329; Meem v. Dulaney, 88 Va. 674, 14 S. E. 363. See also, Jarrett v. Jarrett, 11 W. Va. 584; Vangilder v. Hoffman, 22 W. Va. 1, 6, citing Davis v. Demming, 12 W. Va. 246; Brockenbrough v. Spindle, 17 Gratt. 21; Moseley v. Brown, 76 Va. 419. See also, the titles USURY; WILLS.

D. PROCEEDINGS BY MOTION UNDER STATUTE.

On a proceeding by motion under the statute a court of equity might, perhaps, in the exercise of a sound discretion, direct an issue or issues under circumstances which would warrant such direction in a regular chancery suit; and so, if the case required it, there seems to be no good reason why there might not be a reference to a commissioner to make inquiries and to take and state accounts. Pairo v. Bethell, 75 Va. 825. See also, the title REFERENCE.

A party has no absolute right to a trial by jury of an issue joined in a motion, it being in the nature of an equitable remedy, and the statute (ch. 163, § 8, Va. Code, 1873) not applying to motions which partake of the nature of an equitable proceeding to enforce a charge on real estate. Pairo v. Bethell, 75 Va. 825. See the title JURY.

E. ON BILL IN EQUITY FOR RELIEF AGAINST JUDGMENT.

On a bill in equity for relief against a judgment at law, where a temporary injunction has been granted, "the regular course would seem to be for the chancery court to order such issue or issues as may be proper, and to base its decree on the finding of the jury at the hearing, either dissolving or perpetuating the injunction, in whole or in part, according to circumstances. Such was the course pursued by this court in Knifong v. Hendricks, 2 Gratt. 212, 213. In the present case, if a new trial was proper, the court should have ordered an issue, the same as in the action at law, to be tried as other issues out of chancery are tried, the verdict of the jury, if the trial was in the law court, to be certified to the chancery court, and in the meantime continue the injunction till the hearing of the cause; and if the finding was for the defendant and affirmed, dissolve the injunction; if for the plaintiff, perpetuate the injunction and decree for the complainant according to the verdict." Wynne v. Newman, 75 Va. 811, 815. See post, "Certification of Verdict and Proceedings," IV, H. See the title JUDGMENTS AND DECREES.

F. CASE NOT PROPER FOR RELIEF IN EQUITY.

Bill for relief in equity against a judgment at law, on grounds which would have been a good defense at law, without showing any reason why the defense was not made at law; defendants object to the jurisdiction in their answers; the court directs an issue to try the facts on which the relief is asked, and a verdict is found for the plaintiff; and then the court decrees relief. Held, the case was not proper for relief in equity, and notwithstanding the verdict for the plaintiff on the issue, the bill should have been dismissed. Colloins v. Jones, 6 Leigh 530.

Whether Creditors Injured by Fraudulent Misrepresentations in Deed.—A, residing in Virginia, owns certain slaves in Florida, and wishes to bring them to Virginia, but fearing lest his creditors should seize them under execution, on their arrival, he persuades B to assume to be the owner of them, and convey them, by deed, to a trustee for the benefit of his wife and children. This is done, and the negroes are brought to Virginia, are kept here in the possession of A for several years, and are then carried by A, with his family, beyond the limits of the state. Certain judgment creditors of A then seek to hold B liable in equity for the value of the negroes. B never had the title to the negroes, nor possession or control of them, but merely lent himself to the scheme of A, as above stated. It was held, that if any creditor has suffered actual damage by the fraudulent misrepresentation, his remedy is at law. It is, therefore, error in such a case to direct an issue out of chancery to try the question whether the creditors were injured by the act of B. Bolling v. Harrison, 2 Pat. & H. 532.

III. Proceedings to Obtain Award of Issue.

A. APPLICATION.

It seems that where it is desired that the court direct an issue to try a question in dispute, that application should be made to the court to direct an issue. See Robinson v. Allen, 85 Va. 721, 725, 8 S. E. 835; Powell v. Batson, 4 W. Va. 610.

B. EFFECT OF FAILURE TO DEMAND.

"When a court has used its discretion, and gone on without an issue, it can not be reversed for omission to direct one, unless it be asked. This is sustained by Dorr *v.* Dewing, 36 W. Va. 466, 15 S. E. 93, holding that, if a cause has been heard without order of reference asked or suggested, a party can not, for the first time in the appellate court, assign the failure to direct a reference, unless it appear that manifest injustice has been done him thereby. I should think it would be much more so in the case of failure to direct an issue than as to a failure to direct a reference to commissioner. Judge Snyder says, in McKinsey *v.* Squires, 32 W. Va. 41, 43, 9 S. E. 55, that the party should ask an issue if he wants it." West Virginia Bldg. Co. *v.* Saucer, 45 W. Va. 483, 31 S. E. 965. See also, the title APPEAL AND ERROR, vol. 1, p. 547.

In the case at bar neither party demanded an issue, and as the decree was justified by the evidence. it was not error in omitting to direct an issue to try the validity of a paper writing in question. Powell *v.* Batson, 4 W. Va. 610.

C. FRAMING OF ISSUE.

The issue must be so framed as to embrace the contemplated object. It must not be materially varied from, and misapplicable to, the question controverted between the parties. Braxton *v.* Willing, 4 Call 288; Carter *v.* Campbell, Gilmer 159. If the issue be so framed as not to embrace the contemplated object, and be found for the defendant, the appellate court will direct another issue more appropriate to the case. Braxton *v.* Willing, 4 Call 288. See post, "Disposition of Cause and Remand," VII, F.

D. EFFECT OF FAILURE TO OBJECT TO AWARD.

Not Waiver of Objections.—"It may be argued that the defendant, not having formally and expressly objected to the order directing the issue, nor taken an appeal from it at the time to this court, but having gone to trial of the issue before the jury, may be regarded as having waived all objection to the order for the issue, and that the irregularity, if any, in its direction, has been thus fully cured; that the error of the court, if it did err in directing the issue, was but in the exercise of the discretion with which it was invested, and that the decree granting relief conformable to the verdict should not for this cause be now disturbed. Factum valet, fieri non debet. But I do not concur in this reasoning. The defendant asked for the dissolution of the injunction, to which, as I think, upon the case before the court, he was justly entitled. The court overruled his motion, and proceeded not upon his motion nor that of the complainant, but because it thought it was proper so to do, to direct an issue to try the question of usury. The defendant could but submit to the order. He was not required to express any objection, and although he might have appealed from it to this court as an order to a certain extent settling the principles of the case, and if erroneous, improperly involving him in the delay, trouble and expense necessarily incident to a trial by jury (as held by this court in the case of Reed *v.* Cline's heirs); yet he was not bound to take his appeal at that time. He had a right, if he chose to await the final hearing of the ause, to take a part in the trial before the jury, or, if he pleased, wholly to abstain from doing so, and take his chance, if the verdict should prove adverse, to obtain redress non obstante veredicto, upon the final hearing of the cause; or, if he failed in the circuit court, by an appeal to the court of appellate jurisdiction. Whether he took a part or not in the trial of the issue before the jury, does not appear, as the record of that trial is not embraced in the record before us; but whether he did or did not I think immaterial, as either way, I conceive, he lost no right which he could otherwise claim, nor is to be held as acquiescing in the irregular order directing the issue." Wise v. Lamb, 9 Gratt. 294.

IV. Trial of Issue and Certification of Verdict and Proceedings.

A. IN WHAT COURT TRIED.

"A court of equity has the right to order in a proper case one or more issues to be tried by a jury, either in a court of common law, or at its own bar." Miller v. Wills, 95 Va. 337, 28 S. E. 337; Lavell v. Gold, 25 Gratt. 473; Ayres v. Robins, 30 Gratt. 105; Coalter v. Bryan, 1 Gratt. 18. See also, Brockenbrough v. Spindle, 17 Gratt. 21; Meek v. Spracher, 87 Va. 162, 12 S. E. 397; Snouffer v. Hansbrough, 79 Va. 166; Hull v. Watts, 95 Va. 10, 27 S. E. 829.

Under § 4, Ch. 131, W. Va. Code.—In a pending chancery case, in which in the opinion of the court, it is proper, such court may direct an issue to be tried in such court, or in any other circuit court. Alexander v. Davis, 42 W. Va. 465, 26 S. E. 291; Jarrett v. Jarrett, 11 W. Va. 584; Ogle v. Adams, 12 W. Va. 213. See ante, "Where Evidence Conflicting," II, C, 2.

Section 4 of chapter 131 of the Code of West Virginia does not change the general chancery practice as to the ordering of issues; it only specifies where the issue may be tried. Jarrett v. Jarrett, 11 W. Va. 584. See also, Ogle v. Adams, 12 W. Va. 213.

"At the Bar of This Court."—"If there were sufficient reasons appearing in the cause at the time the decree was rendered, to authorize the court to order an issue to be tried by jury, it was not error in the circuit court to direct the issue to be tried 'at the bar of this court.' This was substantially the language used in the case of Smith v. Beatty, 11 Gratt. 752, 757. The objection is more technical than substan-

tial, and the order should be construed as directing the issue to be tried in the circuit court as authorized by the statute, and whether at the bar of this court or on the law side of the court, is undecided." Ogle v. Adams, 12 W. Va. 213.

B. JURISDICTION ANCILLARY.

If an issue out of chancery is tried before a court of common law, the latter court is but ancillary to the court of chancery. It has no jurisdiction except what is conferred by the chancellor. Lamberts v. Cooper, 29 Gratt. 61, citing Watkins v. Carlton, 10 Leigh 560; Brockenbrough v. Spindle, 17 Gratt. 21; Powell v. Manson, 22 Gratt. 117; Henry v. Davis, 7 W. Va. 715. See post, "Power of Trial Court as to Verdict," IV, I.

C. DUTIES OF TRIAL JUDGE.

1. Superintendence of Trial.

When an issue is tried, it is under the superintendence of the court which will prevent the introduction of improper testimony. Henry v. Davis, 7 W. Va. 715, citing Pleasants v. Ross, 1 Wash. 156; Southall v. M'Keand, 1 Wash. 336. See post, "Evidence—Admissibility and Weight," IV, D.

2. Decides Question of Law.

The court before which an issue out of chancery is tried decides questions of law arising in the progress of the trial. Brockenbrough v. Spindle, 17 Gratt. 21.

D. EVIDENCE — ADMISSIBILITY AND WEIGHT.

1. Viva Voce Testimony.

a. In General.

Viva voce testimony as well as written is admissible in the trial of an issue out of chancery. It is the right and usual course in the trial of such issue, to examine the witnesses viva voce. Paul v. Paul, 2 Hen. & M. 525; Ford v. Gardner, 1 Hen. & M. 72; Douglass v. McChesney, 2 Rand. 109. See also, the title EVIDENCE, vol. 5, p. 295.

b. Illustrations.

To Disprove Imposition.—At trial of issue, whether vendee was induced to buy by vendor's misrepresentation as to boundaries, evidence of the value of the land at time of sale and since, is admissible, as tending to disprove imposition. Snouffer v. Hansbrough, 79 Va. 166.

Proof of Handwriting.—On the trial of an issue out of chancery the plaintiff in the issue relies upon a receipt to which there is an attesting witness, but both the witness and the principal are dead. The plaintiff having proved the handwriting of the witness, the defendant may introduce the testimony of witnesses to prove that the name of the principal to the receipt is not in his handwriting. Steptoe v. Flood, 31 Gratt. 323. See also, the title HANDWRITING, vol 7, p. 29.

Nonprofessional Witnesses as to Mental Capacity.—At trial of an issue, whether or not at the time the deed in question was executed, the grantor was incapable, by reason of disease, old age, or other cause, of clearly understanding its purport and object, the evidence of nonprofessional witnesses who approached grantor on business, that they found him non compos mentis, giving the grounds of their opinions, is admissible. Fishburne v. Ferguson, 84 Va. 87, 4 S. E. 575.

Legitimacy—Mulatto Vel Non.—J. C., and S., his wife, being both white persons, a child is born of the wife during their wedlock and cohabitation; upon the trial of an issue, whether this child is the legitimate child of the husband, evidence that the child is a mulatto, and that in the course of nature a white man and white woman can not procreate a mulatto, is admissible and proper. Watkins v. Carlton, 10 Leigh 560.

2. Papers to Be Read at Trial.

a. In General.

Where an issue is directed by the court of chancery to be tried at law, any papers may be read at the trial of such issue, which were read upon the hearing of the cause, or at a former trial. M'Call v. Graham, 1 Hen. & M. 13. See also, Fant v. Miller, 17 Gratt. 187, 227; Paul v. Paul, 2 Hen. & M. 525, 533; Ford v. Gardner, 1 Hen. & M. 72.

Papers Ordered by Chancellor to Be Read.—The court of law must pursue the chancellor's directions, admitting papers to be read which he orders to be read. Henry v. Davis, 7 W. Va. 715; Watkins v. Carlton, 10 Leigh 560.

Failure to Direct Papers to Be Read.—Upon an issue from a court of chancery to try the validity of a will, the court ought to give directions respecting the reading of the papers filed in the cause; otherwise the omission to read any of them on the trial of such issue will not be a ground for reversing the proceedings, if the court of chancery refuses to grant a new trial. Ford v. Gardner, 1 Hen. & M. 72. See also, Paul v. Paul, 2 Hen. & M. 525; Joslyn v. Bank, 86 Va. 289, 10 S. E. 166; Fant v. Miller, 17 Gratt. 187, 227.

b. Depositions.

Upon the trial of an issue out of chancery, depositions taken in the cause in the chancery court are not to be read to the jury, unless proof be given that the witnesses are dead, or abroad, or otherwise unable to attend the trial. Powell v. Manson, 22 Gratt. 177.

Depositions can not be regularly read on the trial of an issue directed by the chancellor himself, unless by his special order. Joslyn v. Bank, 86 Va. 289, 10 S. E. 166; Paul v. Paul, 2 Hen. & M. 525; Powell v. Manson, 22 Gratt. 177. See also, Ford v. Gardner, 1 Hen. & M. 72.

c. Answer.

Former Doctrine.—Prior to the passage of the Code of West Virginia, on the trial of an issue out of chancery, a defendant has a right to have his answer read, as evidence to the jury.

And allegations of fact, positively stated in the answer, responsive to the bill, should have had, before the jury, the same effect as such answer then should have had, when read on the hearing in the chancery cause. Tompkins v. Stephens, 10 W. Va. 156. See ante, "Former Doctrine," II, C, 1, b, (2), (b), bb, (aa).

On the trial of an issue out of chancery, the allegations of the answer responsive to the bill must be taken as true, unless contradicted by two witnesses, or one witness and corroborating circumstances. The rule of evidence is the same as on the hearing in the chancery court. Powell v. Manson, 22 Gratt. 177. See also, Thornton v. Gordon, 2 Rob. 719. See post, "Evidence Erroneously Admitted or Rejected." VI, E, 1, b.

Upon the trial of an issue out of chancery, the answer is not proof of the allegations therein contained, unless the allegations in the answer, as to facts, be positive, and responsive to some allegations of the bill. And to be responsive, such allegations of the answer must not be either evasive or contradictory. Powell v. Manson, 22 Gratt. 177.

"If the jury may disregard this rule when the case is before them; if they may find a verdict upon the testimony of a single witness in opposition to the answer, the plaintiff will often succeed upon testimony insufficient to justify even the ordering of an issue." Powell v. Manson, 22 Gratt. 177.

The plaintiff can not destroy the weight of the whole answer by proving that the defendant is unworthy of credit; nor can he do so by proving, directly or indirectly, that the answer is false in one respect, or several respects. The only effect of such proof being to destroy the weight of the answer to the extent to which it is disproved by that amount of evidence which is required by the rule in chancery. Powell v. Manson, 22 Gratt. 177.

The positive denials or statements of an answer, responsive to the bill, can not be overthrown by the admissions, evasions and contradictions, if any, which may be found in the answer. Powell v. Manson, 22 Gratt. 177.

At the trial of an issue out of chancery, instruction that jury shall weigh defendant's answer instead of merely the parts responsive to the bill, though rather broad, is not error for which the verdict will be set aside. Snouffer v. Hansbrough, 79 Va. 166, citing Danville Bank v. Waddill, 27 Gratt. 448; Powell v. Manson, 22 Gratt. 177, 192. See also, the title ANSWERS, vol. 1. p. 404, et seq.

Present Doctrine.—See ante, "Modification of Doctrine," II, C, 1, b, (2), (b), bb, (bb); post, "Looks to State of Proofs When Issue Ordered," VII, E, 3. See also, the title ANSWERS, vol. 1, p. 404, et seq.

In West Virginia, however, this rule does not apply, having been changed by statute, for which, see Tompkins v. Stephens, 10 W. Va. 156, 163.

3. Weight of Bill.

Upon the trial of an issue out of chancery, the bill is not proof of its allegations, except so far as these allegations are admitted to be true by the answer. Powell v. Manson, 22 Gratt. 177.

E. INSTRUCTIONS.

Instructions to the jury should be pertinent to the issue, and not addressed to a different inquiry than that contained therein; and should not be couched in ambiguous language, or be of doubtful meaning, and if otherwise, they should be refused. Henry v. Davis, 7 W. Va. 715. See the title INSTRUCTIONS, vol. 7, p. 701.

F. OPEN AND CLOSE.

The party holding the affirmative of the issue is entitled to open and conclude before the jury. Satterlee v. Cameron, 1 Va. Dec. 517; Ogle v. Adams, 12 W. Va. 213. See the title OPEN AND CLOSE.

As a general rule, the party entitled

to begin is he who would have a verdict against him if no evidence were given on either side. It seems that this rule may not be universal in issues out of chancery, or at least a departure from it would not in all cases, if any, be error of which the party given the affirmative could be heard to complain in an appellate court, especially if the court can see that such party could not possibly have been prejudiced thereby. Ogle v. Adams, 12 W. Va. 213.

G. VERDICT.

Must Respond to Issue.—"In Nease v. Capehart, 15 W. Va. 299, it was held, that after a verdict is rendered upon an issue properly directed, the court can not look at the record for the facts submitted in the issue, nor to the facts or evidence certified upon the trial of the issue, but must accept the verdict of the jury for such facts, unless under the rule governing courts of equity in such cases it should set aside the verdict and grant a new trial. This being true, the verdict must be responsive to the issue directed, otherwise the court has not before it the very facts, to ascertain which the issues were directed." Marshall v. Marshall, 18 W. Va. 395. See also, Watkins v. Carlton, 10 Leigh 560. See also, the title VERDICT.

H. CERTIFICATE OF VERDICT AND PROCEEDINGS.
1. In General.

The verdict and all the proceedings on the issue are certified by the court of law to the court of chancery. Brockenbrough v. Spindle. 17 Gratt. 21; Henry v. Davis, 7 W. Va. 715. See also, Wynn v. Newman, 75 Va. 811, 815; Repass v. Richmond, 99 Va. 508, 516, 39 S. E. 160. See post. "Power of Trial Court as to Verdict," IV, I.

Since the union of the jurisdictions of the law and chancery court "the verdict and proceedings are certified as heretofore, or at least supposed to be, to the chancellor; they still become a part of the chancery case, in reference to them." Henry v. Davis, 7 W. Va. 715. See also, Repass v. Richmond, 99 Va. 508, 516, 39 S. E. 160, where the verdict was certified from the law side to the chancery side of the court.

What Constitutes.—"Upon all trials at law of issues out of chancery, all the proceedings upon the trial of the issues as spread upon the record thereof, constitute part of the certificate of the verdict, and with it become part of the chancery record. Watkins v. Carlton, 10 Leigh 560. Judge Tucker delivering the opinion of the court says: 'And upon this point, I observe that I shall take the whole proceedings in the court of law upon an issue directed out of chancery for the purpose of ascertaining a particular fact, to be part and parcel of the chancery cause.'" Henry v. Davis, 7 W. Va. 715.

The certificate of the verdict to the chancellor might or might not be accompanied with a certificate of the facts proved, or of the evidence, or of the opinion of the judge who presided at the trial, or of any of the proceedings which attended it. Henry v. Davis, 7 W. Va. 715, 716.

As to Instruction Given.—The court of law, if required, must certify any instructions which are given to the jury, that the chancellor may decide whether they were rightly given or not. Henry v. Davis, 7 W. Va. 715; Watkins v. Carlton, 10 Leigh 560.

2. Certification against Verdict.

The court before which an issue out of chancery is tried certifies against the verdict if that is, in its opinion, contrary to the evidence. Brockenbrough v. Spindle, 17 Gratt. 21; Lamberts v. Cooper, 29 Gratt. 61, 64, citing Watkins v. Carlton, 10 Leigh 560; Powell v. Manson, 22 Gratt. 177; Henry v. Davis, 7 W. Va. 715, citing Pleasants v. Ross, 1 Wash. 156; Southall v. McKeand, 1 Wash. 336.

Necessity.—In a chancery cause, the

court directs an issue to be tried at its bar. This is tried on the common-law side of the court and the verdict is certified to the chancery side of the court; and there is a motion to set it aside and for a new trial. The court sets aside the verdict and directs a new trial of the issue as amended by him, he being the same judge who presided at the trial of the issue. It was held, that it is not necessary for the judge sitting on the common-law side of the court to certify to himself on the chancery side, that he is dissatisfied with the verdict; but he may set it aside without such certificate. Lavell *v.* Gold, 25 Gratt. 473; Ayres *v.* Robins, 30 Gratt. 105, where it is said: "When the trial takes place on the law side, it would be more regular if the proceedings were certified to the court on the chancery side."

I. POWER OF TRIAL COURT AS TO VERDICT.

See ante, "Jurisdiction Ancillary," IV, B.

1. To Give Judgment.

The common-law court can give no judgment on the verdict, but must certify it to the court of chancery to avail there as it may. Henry *v.* Davis, 7 W. Va. 715; Watkins *v.* Carlton, 10 Leigh 560. See ante, "Certification of Verdict and Proceedings," IV, H.

2. Grant New Trial.

It was a well-established rule of practice, before the common law and chancery jurisdiction were united in the same judge, that a court of common law before which an issue out of chancery is tried can not set aside the verdict or grant a new trial. Brockenbrough *v.* Spindle, 17 Gratt. 21; Lamberts *v.* Cooper, 29 Gratt. 61, 65; Watkins *v.* Carlton, 10 Leigh 560; Powell *v.* Manson, 22 Gratt. 177; Lavell *v.* Gold, 25 Gratt. 473. See post, "New Trial," VI.

V. Conclusiveness of Verdict.

A. GENERAL RULE.

A court of chancery which has di-

rected an issue to be tried, "may approve the verdict and act upon it, when rendered, or, if dissatisfied with it, he may set it aside and direct another trial of the issue, or he may decide the cause contrary to the verdict, without the aid of another jury, if in his judgment the law and the evidence requires it, for the verdict is merely advisory." Fishburne *v.* Ferguson, 84 Va. 87, 4 S. E. 575; Hull *v.* Watts, 95 Va. 10, 27 S. E. 829; Miller *v.* Wills, 95 Va. 337, 28 S. E. 337; McCully *v.* McCully, 78 Va. 159; Almond *v.* Wilson, 75 Va. 613, 626; Snouffer *v.* Hansbrough, 79 Va. 166; Reed *v.* Axtell, 84 Va. 231, 4 S. E. 587; Steptoe *v.* Flood, 31 Gratt. 323; Steptoe *v.* Pollard, 30 Gratt. 689; Lamberts *v.* Cooper, 29 Gratt. 61, 65; Powell *v.* Manson, 22 Gratt. 177; Brockenbrough *v.* Spindle, 17 Gratt. 21; Wise *v.* Lamb, 9 Gratt. 294; Watkins *v.* Carlton, 10 Leigh 560; Love *v.* Braxton, 5 Call 537; Wood *v.* Boughan, 1 Call 329; Vangilder *v.* Hoffman, 22 W. Va. 1; Jarrett *v.* Jarrett, 11 W. Va. 584; Anderson *v.* Cranmer, 11 W. Va. 562; Henry *v.* Davis, 7 W. Va. 715.

The court decided the case not upon the verdict only, but also upon the pleadings and proof. It may decree upon the proper pleadings and proof in the case without regard to the verdict. Brockenbrough *v.* Spindle, 17 Gratt. 21; Steptoe *v.* Pollard, 30 Gratt. 689. See post, "New Trial," VI.

B. IN ABSENCE OF GROUNDS FOR SETTING ASIDE VERDICT.

1. In General.

When an issue out of chancery is properly directed and regularly tried, when directed by an appellate or inferior court and a verdict is rendered by a jury, unless there is some sufficient ground for setting it aside, it must be held to be conclusive of the facts submitted, and the chancellor must render a decree in accordance therewith. Setzer *v.* Beale, 19 W. Va. 274; Nease *v.* Capehart, 15 W. Va. 299;

Marshall v. Marshall, 18 W. Va. 395; Hickman v. Baltimore, etc., R. Co., 30 W. Va. 296, 301, 4 S. E. 654, 657; Fishburne v. Ferguson, 84 Va. 87, 4 S. E. 575; McCully v. McCully, 78 Va. 159; Paul v. Paul, 2 Hen. & M. 525; Carter v. Campbell, Gilmer 159; Pleasants v. Ross, 1 Wash. 156; Southall v. M'Keand, 1 Wash. 336.

"It is true that the object of directing the issues is to satisfy the conscience of the chancellor; but that conscience must be satisfied with the verdict of the jury upon an issue properly directed, where no errors have been committed during the trial thereof, either by the court or jury to the prejudice of either party. Henry v. Davis, 7 W. Va. 715; S. C., 13 W. Va. 230." Nease v. Capehart, 15 W. Va. 299; Hickman v. Baltimore, etc., R. Co., 30 W. Va. 296, 301, 4 S. E. 654, 657, citing Carter v. Campbell, Gilmer 159; Lee v. Boak, 11 Gratt. 182; and Fitzhugh v. Fitzhugh, 11 Gratt. 210; Setzer v. Beale, 19 W. Va. 274. See ante, "Nature and Object," I.

"It would be absurd to say that in a certain cause it was error not to direct an issue; and when that issue had been directed and regularly tried, and no errors committed in the trial thereof, and the verdict of the jury rendered thereon and properly not set aside by the court, that the court below erred in accepting the verdict of the jury as conclusive of the facts submitted, and in decreeing accordingly." Nease v. Capehart, 15 W. Va. 299.

After the verdict is rendered upon an issue properly directed, the court can not look at the record for the facts submitted in the issue, nor to the facts or evidence certified upon the trial of the issue, but must accept the verdict of the jury for such facts, unless under the rules governing courts of equity in such cases it should set aside the verdict and grant a new trial. Nease v. Capehart, 15 W. Va. 299. See post, "New Trial," VI.

Admissibility of Deposition Taken after Verdict.—"Generally, the depositions of witnesses taken after the verdict, to which there is no sufficient objection, and before the decree, can not be read upon the final hearing of the cause, because if that principle were admitted, it would be a needless waste of time to try the issue, and would be a premium put upon the grossest negligence. There is nothing in the record to take this cause out of the general rule." Nease v. Capehart, 15 W. Va. 299.

2. Where Evidence Conflicting.

"Where a court of equity, in the exercise of a sound judicial discretion, has, in a proper case, where the evidence relating to a particular fact in dispute is contradictory and evenly balanced, directed an issue to be tried by a jury, it is the practice, without good cause for the contrary course, for the chancellor to abide by the verdict, since it is the peculiar province of a jury to decide a question of fact arising in a cause, and upon the weight of the testimony on which it depends." Under such circumstances, it is error for the chancellor to set aside the verdict. Miller v. Wills, 95 Va. 337, 28 S. E. 337; Carter v. Campbell, Gilmer 159, holding, in a case proper for an issue, the verdict is conclusive, where the evidence is conflicting. See, to the same effect, Lee v. Boak, 11 Gratt. 182; Fitzhugh v. Fitzhugh, 11 Gratt. 210; Hickman v. Baltimore, etc., R. Co., 30 W. Va. 296, 301, 4 S. E. 654, 657; Nease v. Capehart, 15 W. Va. 299, 305; Mahnke v. Neale, 23 W. Va. 57; Henry v. Davis, 7 W. Va. 715. See also, Lamberts v. Cooper, 29 Gratt. 61; Watkins v. Carlton, 10 Leigh 560; Brockenbrough v. Spindle, 17 Gratt. 21; Powell v. Manson, 22 Gratt. 177; Henry v. Davis, 7 W. Va. 715. See ante, "Where Evidence Conflicting," II, C, 2.

Issue Variant from Question Controverted.—The verdict upon the issue in such case is conclusive, unless that issue were materially variant from, and inapplicable to, the question controverted between the parties. Carter *v.* Campbell, Gilmer 159.

Certificate That Testimony Conflicting.—"In Foushee *v.* Lea, 4 Call 279, the court of law, which tried the issue out of chancery, having certified to the chancellor 'that strong testimony was offered on both sides sufficient to have established a verdict in a court of law in favor of either plaintiff or defendant,' this court held, upon an appeal, that 'the chancellor did right, therefore, in declaring himself satisfied, as the jury were the proper judges of the facts.' See also, McRea *v.* Woods, 1 Hen. & M. 548; and Steptoe *v.* Flood, 31 Gratt. 323, 342." Miller *v.* Wills, 95 Va. 337, 28 S. E. 337.

Whether Misrepresentations Made.—Where an issue out of chancery ascertains that the defendant did not make any representation, or induce the plaintiff to believe that certain improvements were included in the purchase, although the plaintiff did not know this, and purchased under the bona fide belief that they were included, the bill should be dismissed. DeVaugh *v.* Hustead, 27 W. Va. 773.

C. WHEN ISSUE ERRONEOUSLY ORDERED.

Even after a verdict is rendered by a jury on an issue out of chancery, if, upon the proofs, as they stood at the hearing, an issue ought not to have been ordered, it is the duty of the chancellor, notwithstanding the verdict, to set aside the order directing the issue, and enter a decree on the merits, as disclosed by the proofs on the hearing, when the issue was directed. Jarrett *v.* Jarrett, 11 W. Va. 584; Setzer *v.* Beale, 19 W. Va. 274; McFarland *v.* Douglass, 11 W. Va. 637. See, to the same effect, Mahnke *v.* Neale, 23 W. Va. 57; Sands *v.* Beardsley, 32 W. Va. 594, 9 S. E. 925; Anderson *v.* Cranmer, 11 W. Va. 562; Vangilder *v.* Hoffman, 21 W. Va. 1; Miller *v.* Wills, 95 Va.

337, 351, 28 S. E. 337; Elder *v.* Harris, 75 Va. 68; Beverly *v.* Walden, 20 Gratt. 147; Reed *v.* Cline, 9 Gratt. 136; Wise *v.* Lamb, 9 Gratt. 294; Smith *v.* Betty, 11 Gratt. 752, 760; Collins *v.* Jones, 6 Gratt. 530; Pryor *v.* Adams, 1 Call 382. See also, Fant *v.* Miller, 17 Gratt. 187, 205. See ante, "When Bill Should Be Dismissed upon Pleadings and Proof," II, C, 1, b, (2), (b); post, "Looks to State of Proofs When Issue Ordered," VII, E, 3.

Instances.—In Love *v.* Braxton, 5 Call 537, 542, it is said: There was no occasion for directing the issue, as the evidence all stood in the record, and there was neither conflict among the witnesses, nor imputation upon their credit. Therefore, as the chancellor was justly dissatisfied with the verdict, he was at liberty to set it aside, and decide the cause himself, especially as it does not appear that the former witnesses were examined again, or any new evidence introduced, upon the trial. Southall *v.* M'Keand, 1 Wash. 336, 337; S. C., Wythe 95. See ante, "Where Evidence Conflicting," II, C, 2.

D. REPORT OF ARBITRATORS CERTIFIED IN LIEU OF VERDICT.

The court of chancery having directed an issue, the parties agreed to waive the trial by jury, and to submit the question to certain persons mutually chosen by them, whose report should be certified to the chancellor, in lieu of a verdict. The court must consider the report as an award, to be governed by the same rules and principles which prevail in cases of awards. Pleasants *v.* Ross, 1 Wash. 156. See the title ARBITRATION AND AWARD, vol. 1, p. 687.

VI. New Trial.

See ante, "Conclusiveness of Verdict," V.

A. IN WHAT COURT MOTION MADE.

A motion for a new trial of an issue,

if devised, must be made to the court of chancery. Lavell *v.* Gold, 25 Gratt. 473; Brockenbrough *v.* Spindle, 17 Gratt. 21; Watkins *v.* Carlton, 10 Leigh 560; Reed *v.* Axtell, 84 Va. 231, 236, 4 S. E. 587.

B. PRINCIPLES DIFFER FROM THOSE GOVERNING COURTS OF LAW.

"The principles upon which a court of equity directs a new trial of an issue are somewhat different from those which govern courts of law in granting new trials. In Barker *v.* Ray, 2 Russell 63, 3 Eng. Cond. Chy. R., 31, the Lord Chancellor says: 'Issues are directed to satisfy the judge, which judge is supposed, after he is in possession of all that transpired at the trial, to know all that passed here; and looking at the depositions in the cause, and the proceedings both here and at law, he is to see whether, on the whole, they do or do not satisfy him.'" Tompkins *v.* Stephens, 10 W. Va. 156; Repass *v.* Richmond, 99 Va. 508, 39 S. E. 160, 516, citing Miller *v.* Wills, 95 Va. 337, 28 S. E. 337; Powell *v.* Manson, 22 Gratt. 117, 192; Brockenbrough *v.* Spindle, 17 Gratt. 21, 28; Watkins *v.* Carlton, 10 Leigh 560. See ante, "Nature and Object," I.

C. MATTER OF SOUND DISCRETION.

In General.—It is a matter of sound discretion whether a chancellor should set aside the verdict on the issue and award a new trial or not. Henry *v.* Davis, 7 W. Va. 715, 716; Grigsby *v.* Weaver, 5 Leigh 197. See ante, "In Absence of Grounds for Setting Aside Verdict," V, B.

Review on Appeal.—See post, "General Rule," VII, A.

D. WHERE TRIAL JUDGE CERTIFIES IN FAVOR OF VERDICT.

When the judge before whom the issue is tried certifies in favor of the verdict, no new trial ought to be granted. In determining the weight of the evidence it should be remembered that viva voce testimony as well as written was admissible in the trial of the issue, and though the verdict be against the documentary testimony, it may not be contrary to the weight of the evidence. Paul *v.* Paul, 2 Hen. & M. 525, 533; Ford *v.* Gardner, 1 Hen. & M. 72. See also, Douglass *v.* McChesney, 2 Rand. 109.

E. GROUNDS.

1. Mere Errors in Trial of Issue.

a. In General.

The chancellor does not sit as an appellate court to revise or review the action of the court of law, and does not grant new trials merely because there were errors in the proceeding. These are considered matters of indifference in themselves as it is in the power of the chancellor, in a review of the whole case, to prevent their operating any prejudice to the rights of the parties. Henry *v.* Davis, 7 W. Va. 715.

If the chancellor is satisfied, upon a consideration of the whole case, that the result ought not to have been different had there been no error on the trial of the issue, he may refuse to order a new trial, and enter a decree in accordance with the finding of the jury. Repass *v.* Richmond, 99 Va. 508, 39 S. E. 160.

b. Evidence Erroneously Admitted or Rejected.

It has been ruled over and over again, that if, on the trial of an issue, a judge reject evidence which ought to have been received, or receive evidence which ought to have been refused. though in that case a court of law would grant a new trial, yet if this court is satisfied that, if the evidence improperly received had been rejected, or the evidence improperly rejected had been received, the verdict ought not to have been different, it will not grant a new trial merely upon such grounds. Tompkins *v.* Stephens, 10 W. Va. 156; Nease *v.* Capehart. 15 W. Va. 299; Corder *v.* Talbott. 14 W. Va. 277;

Henry *v.* Davis, 7 W. Va. 715; Brockenbrough *v.* Spindle, 17 Gratt. 21; Lamberts *v.* Cooper, 29 Gratt. 61, 65; Powell *v.* Manson, 22 Gratt. 177; Watkins *v.* Carlton, 10 Leigh 560; Repass *v.* Richmond, 99 Va. 508, 516, 39 S. E. 160; Miller *v.* Wills, 95 Va. 337, 28 S. E. 337. See also, Fant *v.* Miller, 17 Gratt. 187, 227; Paul *v.* Paul, 2 Hen. & M. 525, 535; Ford *v.* Gardner, 1 Hen. & M. 72.

Decree Regardless of Improper Evidence.—The court may render a decree upon the proper pleadings and proofs in the case, without regard to any improper evidence introduced on the trial of the issue. And if the competent evidence justifies the decree, it will not be reversed because incompetent evidence was admitted before the jury. Steptoe *v.* Pollard, 30 Gratt. 689; Brockenbrough *v.* Spindle, 17 Gratt. 21; Repass *v.* Richmond, 99 Va. 508, 516; Miller *v.* Wills, 95 Va. 337, 28 S. E. 337; Powell *v.* Manson, 22 Gratt. 177, 192; Watkins *v.* Carlton, 10 Leigh 560; Lamberts *v.* Cooper, 29 Gratt. 61; Henry *v.* Davis, 7 W. Va. 715.

Issue Directed in Improper Manner.—If a court of chancery directs an issue to be taken in an improper manner and evidence not regularly taken is introduced, the appellate court will set aside the issues and order a new trial. Watkins *v.* Carlton, 10 Leigh 560, 573.

Failure to Read Defendant's Answer.—Prior to the passage of the West Virginia Code, if the defendant's answer was not permitted to be read to the jury as evidence, and allegations of fact, positively stated in such answer, responsive to the bill, to have, before the jury, the same effect as such answer should have had, when read on the hearing in the chancery cause, a new trial of the issue should have been awarded by the chancellor, unless he was satisfied that if such answer had been read as such evidence, the verdict of the jury ought not, on that account, to have been different. Tompkins *v.*

Stephens, 10 W. Va. 156. See ante, "Answer," IV, D, 2, c.

c. Erroneous Instructions.

The chancery court may refuse to order a new trial, notwithstanding any errors committed by the court of law in instructing or refusing to instruct the jury, provided the verdict, in the opinion of the court of chancery, was unaffected by such errors. Brockenbrough *v.* Spindle, 17 Gratt. 21; Lamberts *v.* Cooper, 29 Gratt. 61, 65; Powell *v.* Manson, 22 Gratt. 177; Watkins *v.* Carlton, 10 Leigh 560; Repass *v.* Richmond, 99 Va. 508, 516, 39 S. E. 160; Miller *v.* Wills, 95 Va. 337, 28 S. E. 337; Henry *v.* Davis, 7 W. Va. 715. But see Watkins *v.* Carlton, 10 Leigh 560, where it is said there should be a new trial of the issue where the verdict was found under a misdirection of the judge.

Where at such trial, impartially had, the verdict could not have been different, had a certain instruction been given, the refusal to give the instruction is not error, for which the verdict will be set aside. And the rule is the same where the court gives, in lieu of instructions asked for by a party, others substantially embodying the same ideas. Snouffer *v.* Hansbrough, 79 Va. 166.

Illustration.—At such trial, though instructions that vendee must be held to have had notice from the written contract or sale and the title papers therein referred to, that the purchased tract included 135 acres of mountain land, might not have been directed relevant to the issue, the solution whereof depended on the credit the jury attached to the witnesses, yet the instruction could not affect the verdict, and even if erroneous is no ground of reversal. Snouffer *v.* Hansbrough, 79 Va. 166, citing Powell *v.* Manson, 22 Gratt. 177, 192; Bell *v.* Alexander, 21 Gratt. 1; Kincheloe *v.* Tracewell, 11 Gratt. 587; Colvin *v.* Menefee, 11 Gratt. 87.

2. After-Discovered Evidence.

"If, after verdict has been rendered, there be after-discovered evidence, the chancellor may set aside the verdict for such cause under the rules applicable in such cases." Nease v. Capehart, 15 W. Va. 299.

3. Verdict Not Responsive to Issue.

Where an issue has been properly directed, and the verdict is not responsive thereto, it must be set aside and a new trial granted. Marshall v. Marshall, 18 W. Va. 395. See also, Nease v. Capehart, 15 W. Va. 299; Com. v. Mister, 79 Va. 5; Watkins v. Carlton, 10 Leigh 560. See ante, "Verdict," IV, G.

4. Verdict Contrary to Law and Evidence.

In Powell v. Manson, 22 Gratt. 177, one of the questions was whether the court below erred in refusing to grant a new trial of an issue out of chancery, upon the ground that the verdict was contrary to law and the evidence, which was set out in a bill of exceptions. Steptoe v. Pollard, 30 Gratt. 689. See post, "Necessity," VII, D, 2.

In the absence of a certificate against the verdict by the trial judge, the chancellor will not direct a new trial upon affidavits tending to prove that the verdict is contrary to the evidence. Pleasants v. Ross, 1 Wash. 156.

5. Verdict Unsatisfactory because of Circumstances Occasioned by War.

If an issue out of chancery was tried during the late war under circumstances occasioned by the war that rendered the trial unsatisfactory, the chancellor ought to have set it aside; but though the trial was during the war and unsatisfactory in its character, yet if this unsatisfactory character of the trial was not occasioned by the war, but by the fact that one of the parties to the issue had, at the time of the trial, abandoned the case or become utterly indifferent to the result of the trial, the chancellor, on his application made two years after the close of the war, ought not to have set aside such verdict. Tompkins v. Stephens, 10 W. Va. 156.

6. Abandonment of Case by Party to Cause.

See ante, "Verdict Unsatisfactory because of Circumstances Occasioned by War," VI, E, 5.

7. Certificate of Trial-Judge against Verdict.

a. In General.

The general rule is that where the judge before whom the issue is tried certifies to the chancellor against the verdict, it is the duty of the chancellor to set it aside, unless it appears from the evidence certified, or circumstances varying the case, that the verdict was right. Lavell v. Gold, 25 Gratt. 473; Fishburne v. Ferguson, 84 Va. 87, 101, 4 S. E. 575; Grigsby v. Weaver, 5 Leigh 197; Love v. Braxton, 5 Call 537, 542; Southall v. M'Keand, 1 Wash. 336; Southall v. M'Keand, Wythe 95, 96; Henry v. Davis, 7 W. Va. 715.

In Grigsby v. Weaver, 5 Leigh 197, "Judge Carr, referring to Pleasants v. Ross, 1 Wash. 156, and Southall v. Mc-Keand, 1 Wash. 336, says, the farthest they go, is to hold, that as a general rule the chancellor ought not to be satisfied, where the certificate is against the verdict; admitting at the same time that the rule only holds where there is no circumstance appearing to vary the case." Lavell v Gold, 25 Gratt. 473.

A chancellor is not bound to set aside the verdict and direct a new trial of an issue out of chancery in deference to the certificate of the judge of the court of law against it. If the chancellor's conscience is satisfied he may refuse a new trial, but this exercise of his discretion is subject to review in the appellate court. Henry v. Davis, 7 W. Va. 715; Miller v. Wills, 95 Va. 337, 28 S. E. 337; Snouffer v. Hansbrough, 79 Va. 166; Lavell v. Gold, 25 Gratt. 473; Grigsby v. Weaver, 5 Leigh 197; Ross v. Pynes, 3 Call 568;

Southall *v.* M'Keand, Wythe 95, 96.
See ante, "Nature and Object," I; post,
"Appellate Review," VII.

"In Grigsby *v.* Weaver, 5 Leigh 197,
the judge before whom the issue was
tried certified not only that the verdict
was against evidence, but also the facts
proved. The chancellor not only refused to direct a new trial, but entered
a decree, founded upon the verdict,
dismissing the bill. And the court of
appeals—only three judges sitting—
affirmed the decree; Brockenbrough, J.,
dissenting." Lavell *v.* Gold, 25 Gratt.
473; Henry *v.* Davis, 7 W. Va. 715. In
Grigsby *v.* Weaver, 5 Leigh 197,
Brooke, J., says that "'if the judge
had certified the verdict was contrary
to the evidence, and no more,' he (the
chancellor) would have been bound to
direct a new trial. Judge Brockenbrough did not think it clear that the
judge had no other evidence than what
he certified. And he thought the chancellor erred in confirming the verdict
and decreeing upon it. He says no
case has been produced in which, after
a single trial, the certificate of the
judge against the verdict has been entirely disregarded." Lavell *v.* Gold, 25
Gratt. 473.

b. Concurring Verdicts.

After two concurring verdicts for the
same party, on an issue directed by the
chancellor to be tried at common law,
he is not bound to direct a new trial,
notwithstanding both verdicts were in
opposition to the opinions of the judges
before whom the issues were tried, and
a verdict had originally been rendered
in favor of the other party. M'Rae *v.*
Woods, 1 Hen. & M. 548; Ross *v.*
Pynes, 3 Call 568; Grigsby *v.* Weaver,
5 Leigh 197; Lavell *v.* Gold, 25 Gratt.
473; Henry *v.* Davis, 7 W. Va. 715.

After three verdicts, the court of
chancery did right in decreeing according to the opinions of the juries.
Stannard *v.* Graves, 2 Call 369.

In Ross *v.* Pynes, 3 Call 568, and in
M'Rae *v.* Woods, 1 Hen. & M. 548,

there were two verdicts of the jury
one way, and two certificates of the
judges against them; and in each case
the court said, that the chancellor
ought to be satisfied with the finding,
notwithstanding the opinion of the
judge. Grigsby *v.* Weaver, 5 Leigh
197. See also, Henry *v.* Davis, 7 W.
Va. 715.

The chancellor is not to wait and
endeavor, by repeated trials, to secure
an agreement between the court and
jury which tried the case, as to the
weight of the evidence; he is at liberty, to inspect the whole record of
the proceedings, and render his decision, according to the best dictates of
his own judgment, as informed or enlightened by the means thus employed.
Henry *v.* Davis, 7 W. Va. 715; Ross *v.*
Pynes, 3 Call 568. See also, Grigsby
v. Weaver, 5 Leigh 197.

8. Misbehavior of Jury.

The chancellor will in some instances
direct a new trial, on affidavits proving
misbehavior in the jury, afterwards
discovered. Pleasants *v.* Ross, 1 Wash.
156.

9. Verdict Impeached by Affidavit of
   Jurors.

It is the general rule that a verdict
on an issue out of chancery will not
be disturbed upon the affidavit of jurors. Steptoe *v.* Flood, 31 Gratt. 323;
Steptoe *v.* Pollard, 30 Gratt. 689.

The court will not set aside the verdict of the jury on the certificate or
affidavit of two of the jurors, that they
thought the receipt proved and ought
to be considered; but the other members of the jury insisted that the receipt had nothing to do with the case,
and they were persuaded against their
judgment to consent to the verdict,
and that it is now against their judgment. Steptoe *v.* Flood, 31 Gratt. 323.

"And especially if the issue be tried
before the same court, which sees and
hears the witnesses testify on its trial,
and concurs as to the correctness of
the verdict found by the jury upon the

issue, the said court will not set aside the verdict and order a new trial of the issue because one or more of the jury may certify, or even swear, to the effect of the certificate of the two jurors in this case." Steptoe *v.* Flood, 31 Gratt. 323. See the title VERDICT.

F. REINSTATEMENT OF VERDICT AFTER NEW TRIAL DIRECTED.

Another judge holding a subsequent term can not set aside the order of the judge setting aside the verdict and directing a new trial entered, at the previous term, and reinstate the verdict. Lavell *v.* Gold, 25 Gratt. 473.

VII. Appellate Review.

A. GENERAL RULE.

If an issue is improperly directed in the one case or refused in the other, the mistake of the chancellor will be corrected on appeal. See, to the same effect, Miller *v.* Wills, 95 Va. 337, 28 S. E. 337; Reed *v.* Axtell, 84 Va. 231, 4 S. E. 587; Robinson *v.* Allen, 85 Va. 721, 8 S. E. 835; Carter *v.* Carter, 82 Va. 624, 636; Hord *v.* Colbert, 28 Gratt. 49; Magill *v.* Manson, 20 Gratt. 527; Bevere *v.* Walden, 20 Gratt. 147; Mettert *v.* Hagan, 18 Gratt. 231; Lavell *v.* Gold, 25 Gratt. 473; Reed *v.* Cline, 9 Gratt. 136; Wise *v.* Lamb, 9 Gratt. 294; Pleasants *v.* Ross, 1 Wash. 156; Stannard *v.* Graves, 2 Call 369; Pryor *v.* Adams, 1 Call 382; West Virginia Bldg. Co. *v.* Saucer, 45 W. Va. 483, 31 S. E. 965; Alexander *v.* Davis, 42 W. Va. 465, 26 S. E. 291; Devaugh *v.* Hustead, 27 W. Va. 773; Mahnke *v.* Neale, 23 W. Va. 57; Setzer *v.* Beale, 19 W. Va. 274; Jarrett *v.* Jarrett, 11 W. Va. 584; Anderson *v.* Cranmer, 11 W. Va. 562; Rohrer *v.* Travers, 11 W. Va. 146, 154; Arnold *v.* Arnold, 11 W. Va. 449; Tompkins *v.* Stephens, 10 W. Va. 156; Nease *v.* Capehart, 8 W. Va. 95; Henry *v.* Davis, 7 W. Va. 715; Powell *v.* Batson, 4 W. Va. 610. See also, Keagy *v.* Trout, 85 Va. 390, 7 S. E. 329; Grigsby *v.* Weaver, 5 Leigh 197; Ogle *v.* Adams,

12 W. Va. 213; Sands *v.* Beardsley, 32 W. Va. 594, 9 S. E. 925, where it is said: "The law is well settled in this state that, if the circuit court improperly directs an issue, its action will be reviewed and reversed by the appellate court, regardless of the verdict of the jury." Sands *v.* Beardsley, 32 W. Va. 594, 9 S. E. 925. See ante, "General Rule," II, A.

The action of a court of equity, in approving the verdict of a jury upon an issue and decreeing in accordance with it, or in disregarding it and decreeing against it, is a subject of review by the appellate tribunal. Miller *v.* Wills, 95 Va. 337, 28 S. E. 337; Reed *v.* Axtell, 84 Va. 231, 4 S. E. 587; Southall *v.* McKeand, 1 Wash. 336; Pleasants *v.* Ross, 1 Wash. 156; Pryor *v.* Adams, 1 Call 382; Grigsby *v.* Weaver, 5 Leigh 197; Tompkins *v.* Stephens, 10 W. Va. 156; Powell *v.* Manson, 22 Gratt. 177; Steptoe *v.* Pollard, 30 Gratt. 689.

B. NECESSITY THAT DECREE SETTLE PRINCIPLES OF CAUSE.

General Rule.—When the ruling of the chancellor, directing or refusing to direct an issue to be tried by a jury, impliedly involves a settlement of the principles of the cause, it is liable to be reversed by the appellate tribunal. Carter *v.* Carter, 82 Va. 624; Elder *v.* Harris, 75 Va. 68; Beverly *v.* Walden, 20 Gratt. 147, 154; Reed *v.* Cline, 9 Gratt. 136; Wise *v.* Lamb, 9 Gratt. 294, 302. See also, Alexander *v.* Byrd, 85 Va. 690, 696, 8 S. E. 577; Wood *v.* Harmison, 41 W. Va. 376, 381, 23 S. E. 562; Wood *v.* Boughan, 1 Call 329.

Instances.—In Carter *v.* Carter, 82 Va. 624, "by overruling the demurrer and directing the issue, the chancellor in effect decided that if the facts alleged be found to be true, there should be a change of property from the defendant, B. G. Carter, to the complainant, George Carter. And so the principles of the cause were settled by the decree which entitles the plaintiff to appeal therefrom."

"Reed v. Cline, 9 Gratt. 136, was an appeal from an order directing an issue out of chancery, and it was objected by the appellee that the order was interlocutory, and that the appeal was prematurely taken to this court. But the court holding that the decree of the circuit court directing the issues, settles the principles of the case erroneously in deciding that the statute of limitations and the staleness of the demand are not sufficient defenses against the complainant's demand, was of opinion that this court may take cognizance of the appeal, and reversed the decree and dismissed the bill with costs. This decision seems to have been upon the ground that upon the case made by the record the statute of limitations and the staleness of the plaintiff's demand were a sufficient defense to the plaintiff's demand, and that his bill ought to have been dismissed; and that the circuit court, by directing other issues to be tried by a jury, had settled the principles of the case to the contrary —to wit, that the statute of limitations and the staleness of the plaintiff's demand were not a sufficient defense; and upon that ground it took cognizance of the case and reversed the decree and dismissed complainant's bill." Elder v. Harris, 75 Va. 68. See also, the title LIMITATION OF ACTIONS.

"In Beverley v. Walden, 20 Gratt. 147, which was an appeal from an interlocutory order, directing issues to be tried by a jury, the question of jurisdiction was not raised, nor expressly passed on by the court. But the court held, that upon the case made by the record, all the material allegations of the bill were positively denied by the answer, and were not supported by two witnesses, or one witness and corroborating circumstances; that consequently the plaintiff had failed to make out his case, and his bill ought to have been dismissed;

that it was error to direct issues to be tried by a jury to enable him to make out his case by new testimony, and that the circuit court, by directing the issues to be tried by a jury, must have held either that the plaintiff had not failed to make out his case by the proofs, or that if he had, his bill should not be dismissed, but an issue should be directed to enable him by new and additional testimony to maintain the allegations of his bill; and that upon either ground the decision was erroneous, and settled the principles of the case adversely to the defendant and erroneously, as upon the face of the record he was entitled to the dismission of the plaintiff's bill. And this decision is in accord with the decision in Reed v. Cline (9 Gratt. 136), and we think both are consonant with the plain declarations of the statute." Elder v. Harris, 75 Va. 68.

Decree Deciding No Principle.—In a pending cause a commissioner is directed to take an account of certain personal property and rents of land. The report is returned and excepted to; and the court, without deciding upon any question upon the report, directs a jury to try an issue of fact as to what was the value of the personal property. Held, the decree decides no principle in the cause, and an appeal allowed from it will be dismissed as improvidently awarded. Elder v. Harris, 75 Va. 68.

C. NECESSITY OF MOTION FOR NEW TRIAL.

Errors committed on the trial of the issue can not be reached directly by an appellate forum, but must form the subject of a motion to the chancellor, in the chancery cause, for a new trial; and if improperly refused by him, an appeal lies from his decree. Coalter v. Bryan, 1 Gratt. 18; Lamberts v. Cooper, 29 Gratt. 61, 65.

D. BILL OF EXCEPTIONS.
1. Propriety.

"Whatever has been the rule in other

states, it seems to have been recognized as proper and right for courts in Virginia and this state to sign bills of exceptions to their rulings on trials of issues out of chancery. Stannard v. Graves, 2 Call 369; Ford v. Gardner, 1 Hen. & M. 72; Fitzhugh v. Fitzhugh, 11 Gratt. 210." Henry v. Davis, 13 W. Va. 230; Brockenbrough v. Spindle, 17 Gratt. 21.

Where the trial is at the chancery bar, the mode of saving questions decided by the judge during the trial, is the same as in common-law actions; to wit, by bill of exceptions. Coalter v. Bryan, 1 Gratt. 18; Lamberts v. Cooper, 29 Gratt. 61, 65.

2. Necessity.

Upon an issue directed out of chancery, the verdict of the jury is conclusive, where there is no exception spreading the facts proved upon the record. Fitzhugh v. Fitzhugh, 11 Gratt. 210; Paul v. Paul, 2 Hen. & M. 525; Lamberts v. Cooper, 29 Gratt. 61, 65; Joslyn v. Bank, 86 Va. 289, 10 S. E. 166, where it is said: On an issue out of chancery the judgment of the court is conclusive, unless there be a bill of exceptions spreading the evidence in the record and showing the exact ground of complaint. "And in this respect there can be no difference between the case where there has been a verdict and the case where the whole matter of law and fact has been submitted to the court; for properly speaking, the appeal is always from the judgment of the court and not from the verdict of the jury. Wickham v. Martin, 13 Gratt. 427, 446. In each case there must be a bill of exceptions pointing out the alleged error, and a certificate of evidence showing what testimony was before the court or jury. Paul v. Paul, 2 Hen. & M. 525; Lee v. Boak, 11 Gratt. 182; Bart. Chy. 857, et seq." Henry v. Davis, 13 W. Va. 230; Henry v. Davis, 7 W. Va. 715.

Where an issue is directed in a chancery cause, and a verdict is found to which no exception is taken, and a decree is rendered thereon, the facts found in the verdict must be regarded in the appellate court, as the established facts of the case. Fitzhugh v. Fitzhugh, 11 Gratt. 210; Lee v. Boak, 11 Gratt. 182; Nease v. Capehart, 15 W. Va. 299; Henry v. Davis, 7 W. Va. 715.

If the party objecting to setting aside the verdict is dissatisfied with the order, he should except to it, and have the facts proved on trial, or the evidence spread upon the record, and thus the order may be reviewed. Lavell v. Gold, 25 Gratt. 473.

The case of Watkins v. Carlton, 10 Leigh 560, does not decide that a bill of exceptions is not necessary upon the trial of an issue out of chancery. "It merely decides that when exceptions are filed to opinions of the court and made a part of the record, and the court of law certifies the verdict, although it does not expressly certify the exceptions, yet all the proceedings upon the trial of the issues spread upon the record thereof, constitute part of the certificate of the verdict, and with it becomes part of the chancery record." Under such circumstances it is not necessary to expressly certify the exceptions. Lamberts v. Cooper, 29 Gratt. 61, 65.

Principles Same as in Action at Law. —"If in an action at common law a party is held to have waived his objection by his failure to save the point in due season, it is difficult to see why he should not be held equally to have done so in a like case upon the trial of an issue out of chancery. The very same principles, it would seem, must apply in both cases." Lamberts v. Cooper, 29 Gratt. 61, 65, citing Fitzhugh v. Fitzhugh, 11 Gratt. 210. See also, Lavell v. Gold, 25 Gratt. 473.

Where Error Appears upon Record. —"Of course it must be understood that in such a case the issue was properly directed, and there were no erroneous rulings, saved upon the record, which would show that the verdict ought to be set aside." Henry v. Davis, 13 W. Va. 230, citing Fitzhugh v. Fitzhugh, 11 Gratt. 210. See post, "Looks to State of Proofs When Issue Ordered," VII, E, 3.

Can Not Be Supplied by Affidavit of Counsel.—If the judge who tried the cause is dissatisfied with the verdict it ought to be certified or a bill of exceptions taken; else the omission can not be supplied by affidavits, especially of the counsel, for it would be a most dangerous precedent. Stannard v. Graves, 2 Call 369.

3. Form and Requisites.

a. Necessity for Showing Evidence Introduced—Presumption.

Where the bill of exceptions does not give the evidence before the jury, the appellate court must presume, in the absence of the evidence, that the verdict was correct. In this case there were depositions in the record, which were taken before the trial of the issue, but it did not appear that they were read before the jury, or if read that they were the only evidence. Ayres v. Robins, 30 Gratt. 105.

"In George v. Pilcher, 28 Gratt. 299, this court reversed the decree of the court below on the ground that the court erred in not ordering a new trial of the issue which had been directed and tried in the case, on the ground of the improper exclusion of evidence offered on the said trial. But in that case the evidence introduced on the trial was not certified in the record, and it was impossible for this court to say that the party complaining was not injured by the exclusion of evidence aforesaid." Steptoe v. Pollard, 30 Gratt. 689.

Presumption as to Evidence Exhibited.—It can not properly be inferred that the answer and depositions, were the only evidence exhibited on the trial of an issue out of chancery; on the contrary, it ought rather to appear that such written evidence was actually made use of, since the court of chancery ought to give directions respecting

the reading of the papers filed in the cause. Paul v. Paul, 2 Hen. & M. 525. See also, Ford v. Gardner, 1 Hen. & M. 72; Joslyn v. Bank, 86 Va. 289, 10 S. E. 166; Fant v. Miller, 17 Gratt. 187, 227.

"Inasmuch as depositions can not be regularly read even on the trial of an issue directed by the chancellor himself, unless by his special order, it can not be assumed that such depositions were read, although they may appear as a part of the printed record of the chancery cause." Joslyn v. Bank, 86 Va. 289, 10 S. E. 166; Paul v. Paul, 2 Hen. & M. 525.

b. Necessity for Showing Relevancy of Evidence Excluded.

If on the trial of an issue out of chancery an exception is taken to the opinion of the court, excluding evidence, the exception must show the relevancy of the evidence, or it is no ground for reversing the judgment. Nease v. Capehart, 15 W. Va. 299.

Where on the trial of an issue out of chancery a question is propounded to a witness which is objected to, and the objection is overruled and an exception taken, but the exception does not state the answer of the witness, or that he answered the question, the appellate court will not on such an exception reverse the judgment. Nease v. Capehart, 15 W. Va. 299.

c. Certificate of Exceptions.

(1) Duty of Judge.

(a) General Rule.

In a trial of an issue out of chancery it is the duty of the court presiding at the trial of such issue, to sign bills of exceptions to its opinion, as in trials of law issues before a jury. Henry v. Davis, 13 W. Va. 230.

(b) Compelling Certification.

In General.—A judge, by mandamus, may be compelled by the supreme court of appeals to sign a bill of exceptions to his opinion in the trial of an issue out of chancery, where such bill of exceptions states fairly the truth of the case involved therein. Henry v. Davis, 13 W. Va. 230. See the titles EXCEPTIONS, BILL OF, vol. 5, p. 385; MANDAMUS.

Where the trial is at the chancery bar there is no statutory remedy in case the judge should refuse to allow an exception. This, however, is equally true, whether the issue be tried in a court, of common law, or a court of chancery; for the statute of Westm. 2, 13 Edw. 1, ch. 31, adopted into our Code, applies only to common-law actions, and not to mere issues directed by a chancellor, in which no judgment is rendered upon the verdict, but the verdict merely certified for the action of the chancellor thereupon in the chancery cause. Coalter v. Bryan, 1 Gratt. 18; Lamberts v. Cooper, 29 Gratt. 61, 65.

"In common-law actions, if the judge should refuse to seal a true bill of exceptions, the remedy is by complaint to a higher court, and a writ founded on the statute. But such refusal on the trial of an issue out of chancery would be matter for a motion to the chancellor for a new trial, and if refused, for an appeal from his decision." Coalter v. Bryan, 1 Gratt. 18.

Certification of Facts Proved.—On the trial of an issue out of chancery, a court can not be required to certify the facts proved, where the evidence is conflicting. Nease v. Capehart, 15 W. Va. 299. See also, the title EXCEPTIONS, BILL OF, vol. 5, p. 382.

(2) Necessity.

Where an issue out of chancery has been tried in the court below, and verdict rendered, which is satisfactory to the court; and a decree rendered, based on such verdict, and, pending the trial of the issue, the defendant therein excepts to an opinion of the court, refusing to permit evidence to be introduced to the jury by such defendant, and the judge refuses to sign a bill of exceptions to such opinion, and the defendant appeals from the de-

cree to the supreme court of appeals, and does not apply to that court for a mandamus, to compel the judge to sign a bill of exceptions, but proceeds to have his cause heard and determined by the supreme court of appeals on the record, without such bill of exceptions, and the decree is affirmed; the defendant has waived the benefit of such exceptions, and can not afterwards be heard to complain of the action of the judge in refusing to sign such bill of exceptions. Henry v. Davis, 13 W. Va. 230.

When Express Certification Unnecessary.—See ante, "Necessity," VII, D, 3, c, (2).

(3) Time of.

"There was no motion to set aside the verdict at the time of the trial, which was April, 1879, and no certificate of the facts or of the evidence asked for until 1881, when it was too late to certify the evidence which was given orally nearly two years before.' McCully v. McCully, 78 Va. 159.

(4) Effect as Admitting Allegations Relative to Trial.

When the verdict, in such a case, is certified to the court sitting in chancery, and a new trial refused, the allegations relative to what passed at the trial stated in a bill of exceptions to the opinion of the court in refusing the new trial, if not proof of the truth of these allegations, appear on the record, are not to be taken as admitted to be true by the court's signing and sealing. Ford v. Gardner, 1 Hen. & M. 72.

E. RULES OF DECISION.

1. Proper Criterion by Which to Test Propriety of Issue.

The proper criterion by which to test the propriety or impropriety of such an issue, is that, where in a given case the decree rendered is sustained with reasonable certainty by the facts and circumstances disclosed by the record, there would be no error in omitting or refusing to direct an issue to try any material matters of fact put in issue by the pleadings. But if the correctness of the decree is made to depend on the existence or nonexistence of such material facts, and the evidence and circumstances of the case are so equally balanced as to make their existence or nonexistence doubtful, then it would be error to fail or refuse to direct an issue to be tried by a jury. Powell v. Batson, 4 W. Va. 610; West Virginia Bldg. Co. v. Saucer, 45 W. Va. 483, 31 S. E. 965.

2. Where Evidence Certified—Motion for New Trial Overruled.

"Where, because of a conflict of testimony, an issue is directed, the solution of which depends on the credibility of witnesses, and the verdict is sanctioned by the trial court (all the oral testimony being certified and not the facts proved), the settled rule is, that the appellate court will consider not merely whether the evidence warrants the verdict, but, also, whether, upon the whole, further investigation is necessary to justice; and though there may have been misdirection, or improper rejection of evidence, it will not grant a new trial, if, on considering the evidence, including that rejected, the verdict appears right." Meek v. Spracher, 87 Va. 162, 12 S. E. 397; Barnum v. Barnum, 83 Va. 365, 5 S. E. 372; Almond v. Wilson, 75 Va. 613; Fishburne v. Ferguson, 84 Va. 87, 4 S. E. 575; Snouffer v. Hansbrough, 79 Va. 166; Barbour v. Meledy, 88 Va. 595, 14 S. E. 326; Magarity v. Shipman, 82 Va. 784; Powell v. Manson, 22 Gratt. 117; Steptoe v. Pollard, 30 Gratt. 689; Lamberts v. Cooper, 29 Gratt. 61; George v. Pilcher, 28 Gratt. 299; Brockenbrough v. Spindle, 17 Gratt. 21; Borwell v. Corbin, 1 Rand. 153; Watkins v. Carlton, 10 Leigh 560. See also, Henry v. Davis, 7 W. Va. 715.

This is true, though there have been two new trials of the issue in the lower court. Ruffners v. Barrett, 6 Munf. 207; Ross v. Pynes, 3 Call 568; M'Rae v. Woods, 1 Hen. & M. 548.

If on the trial of an issue a court rejects evidence which ought to have been received, or receives evidence which ought to have been refused, though in that case a court of law would grant a new trial, yet if the appellate court is satisfied that, if the evidence improperly received had been rejected, or the evidence improperly rejected had been received, the verdict ought not to have been different, it will not grant a new trial merely upon such grounds. Nease v. Capehart, 15 W. Va. 299.

If improper evidence was received, and it can not be seen or said that the improper evidence did not affect the verdict, a decree based solely upon the verdict, rendered upon conflicting evidence, and not upon a consideration of the whole case, should be reversed. Repass v. Richmond, 99 Va. 508, 39 S. E. 160.

Demurrer to Evidence Rule Applied. —Where a motion is made to set aside the verdict, and grant a new trial of an issue out of chancery, and the motion is overruled by the court, and the bill of exceptions certifies the evidence and not the facts proved on the trial, the appellate court will not reverse the decree and grant a new trial of the issue, unless by rejecting all the parol evidence of the exceptor, and giving full force and credit to that of the adverse party, the decision of the court in overruling the motion for a new trial still appears to be wrong. Nease v. Capehart, 15 W. Va. 299; Henry v. Davis, 7 W. Va. 715.

"When a question of fact is referred to a jury, depending upon the testimony of witnesses conflicting in their statements, and is passed upon by them, and approved by the trial court, unless there be palpable error, the court must affirm, as when conflicting statements are made there is no safe method by which this court can decide between them, seen on paper. We can not pass upon the credibility of witnesses, or the weight of conflicting testimony, and reverse the trial court, except when the error is palpable and obvious, and the result is without evidence to support it, or plainly against the evidence. See Snouffer *v.* Hansbrough, 79 Va. 166; Magarity *v.* Shipman, 82 Va. 784, 1 S. E. 109." Barbour *v.* Melendy, 88 Va. 595, 14 S. E. 326.

Jury, Master and Chancellor Concurring in Opinion.—Where the issue has been properly awarded, and the verdict of the jury, the report of the master, and the opinion of the chancellor, before each of whom the witnesses testified, all concur, it would be an unusual exercise of jurisdiction for the appellate court to reverse the decree. McCully *v.* McCully, 78 Va. 159; Almond *v.* Wilson, 75 Va. 613; Barnum *v.* Barnum, 83 Va. 365, 5 S. E. 372; Fishburne *v.* Ferguson, 84 Va. 87, 4 S. E. 575.

Judges in Appellate Court Divided in Opinion.—The conflict of evidence must be regarded as of such character as justifies the direction of an issue by the circuit court, whenever on appeal the appellate court is so divided in opinion as to the weight of the evidence, that one or more of the judges thinks the issue ought not to have been ordered, because the evidence established clearly a certain state of facts, while the other judge or judges think the issue ought not to have been directed, because in his or their opinion the evidence establishes an opposite state of facts. This marked diversity of opinion as to the weight of the evidence is itself sufficient to show that it is doubtful on which side is the preponderance. In such case therefore the order of the circuit court directing the issue can not be reversed but must be affirmed. Pickens *v.* McCoy, 24 W. Va. 344; Vangilder *v.* Hoffman, 22 W. Va. 1. See ante, "Where Evidence Conflicting," II, C, 2.

Illustrations.—An issue was directed to try whether the signature, of "W. J. Read," to receipt No. 1, filed with the bill, is in the handwriting of W. J. Read, the assignor of Henry D. Flood,

the intestate of Thomas J. Kirkpatrick, the appeller in the cause. A motion for a new trial on the ground that the verdict was contrary to the evidence was overruled. There was certainly a great conflict in the evidence as to this question. It was held, that the mere fact of the existence of such a conflict seems of itself to be a sufficient and unanswerable ground for affirming the action of the court below in overruling the motion of the plaintiff to set aside the verdict and grant a new trial of the said issue. Steptoe *v.* Flood, 31 Gratt. 323.

Barnum *v.* Barnum, 83 Va. 365, 5 S. E. 372, is a case where the circumstances established by the evidence fully warrants the verdict found on the issues that were directed, in effect that there was fraud in the deed in controversy which was set up by the appellant.

Where at trial of an issue out of chancery directed to ascertain the value of a race horse killed by carrier's negligence, there is a conflict in the evidence, the verdict of the jury, assessing his value at $17,000, will not be disturbed. Barbour *v.* Melendy, 88 Va. 595, 14 S. E. 326.

3. Looks to State of Proofs When Issue Ordered.

The appellate court, in reviewing a decree founded on the verdict of a jury rendered on an issue out of chancery, will look to the state of the proofs at the time the issue was ordered; and if satisfied that the chancellor had improperly exercised his discretion in directing the issue, it will reverse the decree directing such issue, and set aside all subsequent proceedings thereon and enter such decree as the circuit court ought to have entered notwithstanding said verdict. Mahnke *v.* Neale, 23 W. Va. 57; Jarrett *v.* Jarrett, 11 W. Va. 584; Anderson *v.* Cranmer, 11 W. Va. 562; McFarland *v.* Douglass, 11 W. Va. 637; Setzer *v.* Beale, 19 W. Va. 274; Vangilder *v.* Hoffman, 22 W. Va. 1; Sands *v.* Beardsley, 32 W. Va. 594, 9 S. E. 925; Miller *v.* Wills, 95 Va. 337, 28 S. E. 337; Elder *v.* Harris, 75 Va. 68; Beverley *v.* Walden, 20 Gratt. 147; Reed *v.* Cline, 9 Gratt. 136; Wise *v.* Lamb, 9 Gratt. 294; Collins *v.* Jones, 6 Gratt. 530; Pryor *v.* Adams, 1 Call 382. See also, Fant *v.* Miller, 17 Gratt. 189, 205. See ante, "Determined by Proofs at Time Issue Ordered," II, C, 1, b, (2); "Necessity," VII, D, 2.

"In the case of Pryor *v.* Adams, 1 Call 382' the bill was filed to compel payment of the amount of depreciation on a bond which the complainant had held on the defendant, and of which he had consented to receive and had received payment in depreciated paper money, and had surrendered up the bond upon an express promise which he alleged the defendant made at the time, to pay the depreciation. The defendant in his answer denied the alleged promise. The chancellor held that the allegations of the bill which were denied by the answer had not been proved by the evidence, and dismissed the bill with costs; but that (he) afterwards, during the same term, set aside that decree and directed an issue to determine whether the defendant, at the time the money paid in discharge of the bond in the bill mentioned was received or after, agreed to allow the depreciation. The issue was tried, and the jury found that the defendant had agreed to allow it. The court thereupon decreed that the defendant should pay the amount of the depreciation and the costs, and the defendant appealed. And it was held in the court of appeals that the complainant having failed to overcome the defendant's denial in his answer and to support the allegations of his bill by proof, the first decree dismissing the bill was right and should be affirmed; and that notwithstanding the verdict for the plaintiff, the order directing the issue and all the subsequent proceedings should be reversed; and it was so decreed accordingly." Wise *v.* Lamb, 9 Gratt. 294.

"In the case of Collins *v.* Jones, 6 Leigh 530, an issue was directed and a verdict was found in favor of the complainants, and relief thereupon decreed. This court held, that the issue was improperly directed; and that notwithstanding the verdict in favor of the complainant, the decree should be reversed, the injunction dissolved, and the bill dismissed; and it was so decreed accordingly." Wise *v.* Lamb, 9 Gratt. 294.

F. DISPOSITION OF CAUSE AND REMAND.

The appellate court upon a review of the whole case, may simply affirm, or reverse the decree of the chancellor, and itself make a final disposition of the cause. Henry *v.* Davis, 7 W. Va. 715; Jackson *v.* Pleasanton, 95 Va. 654, 29 S. E. 680.

If, however, the case does not seem satisfactory to the appellate court, and there is reason to believe that fuller and more satisfactory information touching the fact in question may be obtained, that court may direct another trial by jury, upon its own motion, its powers and those of the chancellor being the same. Henry *v.* Davis, 7 W. Va. 715. See ante, "Framing of Issue," III, C.

Remand.—A court of chancery directs issues of fact to be tried at law, without evidence regularly taken before the court, touching the facts to which the issues relate; but there was evidence, which, if regular, would have rendered the order for the issues proper. Held, that if the appellate court should set aside the issues, for being, in the actual state of the case, improperly ordered, it should, under such circumstances, remand the cause to the court of chancery, where the evidence may be regularly taken, and thereupon the issues ordered new. Watkins *v.* Carlton, 10 Leigh 560. See also, Henry *v.* Davis, 7 W. Va. 715;

New York Life Ins. Co. *v.* Davis, 94 Va. 427, 26 S. E. 941. See ante, "In General," II, C, 1, b, (2), (b), aa.

VIII. Direction of Action at Law.

Direction of Suit by Receiver.—See the title RECEIVERS.

Suits against Receivers.—"Barton *v.* Barbour, Receiver, 14 Otto 126. In the last-named case it is distinctly held that the rule that a receiver can not be sued without leave of the court of equity which appointed him, applies to suits against him on a money demand, or for damages, as well as to those the object of which is to recover property which he holds by order of that court; and that in a case before such court involving disputed facts, that court may, in a proper case, either of its own motion or on the prayer of the parties injured, allow its receiver to be sued at law, or direct the trial of a feigned issue to settle the facts; and that the determination by a court of equity, according to its own course and practice, of issues of fact growing out of the administration of trust property in its possession, does not impair the constitutional right of trial by jury." Melendy *v.* Barbour, 78 Va. 544. See the title RECEIVERS.

Partition—Title of Plaintiffs.—Upon a bill for a partition of land, if the title of the plaintiffs is doubtful, the court prior to the act, Va. Code, ch. 124, § 1, p. 526, should have sent the parties to law to try their title. Currin *v.* Spraull, 10 Gratt. 145. See also, the title PARTITION.

Itinerant Physicians.

See the title PHYSICIANS AND SURGEONS.

Itinerant Vendors.

See the title HAWKERS AND PEDDLERS, vol. 7, p. 36.

Jailer.

See the titles BANKRUPTCY AND INSOLVENCY, vol. 2, p. 250; EXECUTIONS AGAINST THE BODY AND ARREST IN CIVIL CASES, vol. 5, p. 474; PRISONS AND PRISONERS; SHERIFFS AND CONSTABLES.

Jail Fees and Prisons Bounds.

See the title EXECUTIONS AGAINST THE BODY AND ARREST IN CIVIL CASES, vol. 5, p. 477.

Jails.

See the titles ESCAPE, vol. 5, p. 137; PRISONS AND PRISONERS.

James River and Kanawha Canal Co.

See the titles CANALS, vol. 2, p. 666; INTERNAL IMPROVEMENT COMPANIES, vol. 7, p. 844.

JEALOUS EYE.—"It is, however, assigned as error in this cause that the court below corrected the second instruction asked for by the contestants by striking out the words 'jealous eye,' and inserting 'careful scrutiny,' but the words, taken in connection with the language used in the instruction, are so nearly synonymous that either expression might have been used without creating a different impression on the minds of the jury. I do not, therefore, regard the correction as material. See Cheatham *v.* Hatcher, 30 Gratt. 56; sixth section of syllabus." Coffman *v.* Hedrick, 32 W. Va. 119, 9 S. E. 65, 70.

Jeofails.

See the title AMENDMENTS, vol. 1, p. 359.

Jeopardy.

See the title AUTREFOIS, ACQUIT AND CONVICT, vol. 2, p. 181.

Jettison.

See the title GENERAL AVERAGE, vol. 6, p. 710.

Joinder.

As to plea in abatement, see the title ABATEMENT, REVIVAL AND SURVIVAL, vol. 1, p. 6.

Joinder in Demurrer.

See the titles DEMURRERS, vol. 4, p. 513; DEMURRER TO THE EVIDENCE, vol. 4, p. 528.

Joinder of Causes of Action.

See the title ACTIONS, vol. 1, p. 135.

Joinder of Counts.

See the titles ACTIONS, vol. 1, p. 135; INDICTMENTS, INFORMATIONS AND PRESENTMENTS, vol. 7, p. 440.

Joinder of Issue.

See the titles JUDGMENTS AND DECREES; PLEADING.

Joinder of Parties.

See generally, the title PARTIES.

JOINT ADVENTURES.

CROSS REFERENCES.

See the titles CONTRACTS, vol. 3, p. 438; CONTRIBUTION AND EX-ONERATION, vol 3, p. 461; NOTICE; PARTNERSHIP; SET-OFF, RECOUPMENT AND COUNTERCLAIM; SURETYSHIP.

Liability of Parties.—T., as agent of F. & C., presented to R. a written contract for the purchase of a stallion at the price of $1,800, which specified that those who should execute the contract and join in the purchase of the horse should, after the purchase, own interests therein by shares of $100 each, the interest of each party to be determined by the number of shares for which he should subscribe. R. signed it, subscribing for two shares, and delivered it to T., upon the verbally expressed condition that it should not be effective as to him unless M. and W. should sign it, and, they refusing to join in the enterprise, T. obtained the signatures of fifteen other persons who took the remaining sixteen shares, and executed and delivered to T. two negotiable notes for the sum of $900 each, without notice of the condition upon which R. had signed, and F. & C. delivered the horse at R.'s stable, and indorsed and delivered one of the notes to a stranger, without having obtained R.'s signature thereto, and without the knowledge of the other parties to the contract, who afterwards paid it, and then instituted an action to recover from R. one-ninth of the sum so paid, proving the additional fact that, after the contract had been completed and shown to R., he expressed approval thereof. Held, that they may recover in an action at law. Newman v. Ruby, 54 W. Va. 381, 46 S. E. 172.

C. and B. agree in writing to pay equally for a tract of land, sell it, and divide the proceeds between them. On the cash payment C. and B. pay unequally, but from sales of part of the land and of the timber C. received $54 more than enough to pay the balance and refund what he had paid, leaving unsold 426 acres of the land which cost $1,772.16. B. has not been refunded what he paid, and is entitled also to his moiety of the net profits. He files his bill for settlement. Held, the proper course is to direct sale of the partnership effects, and apply the proceeds to the payment of the amount to which B. is entitled, and to enter a personal decree against C. for one-half of such balance as may remain due B., or else to divide those effects equally between B. and C. and enter a personal decree against the latter for one-half of the amount due B. Canada v. Barksdale, 76 Va. 899.

What Sum Included.—S. gave N. a sum of money, in the presence of a witness, and stated that it was to purchase sheep with, and that if losses occurred he was not to have any interest for his money, but if profits accrued he was to have one-half thereof; and subsequently stated that he and N. were partners, and that the interest of his money was to offset the labor of N. in the enterprise. Held, that this was a partnership as to the whole sum, and that it was not limited to the profits or any portion of the adventure only. Newbrau v. Snider, 1 W. Va. 153.

Security in Name of One of Several Beneficiaries.—In a transaction for the benefit of several, a security taken by one of them inures to the benefit of all as fully as if each was named., Armstrong v. Henderson, 99 Va. 234, 37 S. E. 839.

Joint and Joint and Several Bonds.

See the title BONDS, vol. 2, pp. 531, 533.

Joint and Joint and Several Obligations.

See the title FORMER ADJUDICATION OR RES ADJUDICATA, vol. 6, p. 325.

Joint and Several Contracts.

See the titles CONTRACTS, vol. 3, p. 388, and references given; EXECUTORS AND ADMINISTRATORS, vol. 5, p. 582.

Joint Appeals.

See the title APPEAL AND ERROR, vol. 1, p. 474.

Joint Debtors or Obligors.

See the titles COMPROMISE, vol. 3, p. 45; CONTRIBUTION AND EXONERATION, vol. 3, p. 469; FORMER ADJUDICATION OR RES ADJUDICATA, vol. 6, p. 325; JUSTICES OF THE PEACE; MOTIONS; WITNESSES.

Joint Executors and Administrators.

See the title EXECUTORS AND ADMINISTRATORS, vol. 5, p. 524.

Joint Indictments.

See the title INDICTMENTS, INFORMATIONS AND PRESENTMENTS, vol. 7, p. 422.

Joint Judgments.

See the title FORMER ADJUDICATION OR RES ADJUDICATA, vol. 6, p. 325 et seq.

JOINT LIVES.—In Lazier *v.* Lazier, 35 W. Va. 567, 14 S. E. 148, 151, it is said: "In the case of Smith *v.* Oakes, 14 Sim., 122, it was held 'the words during their joint and natural lives in a settlement meant during their joint lives and the lives of each of them." See also, the titles JOINT TENANTS AND TENANTS IN COMMON; WILLS.

Joint Owners.

See the title JOINT TENANTS AND TENANTS IN COMMON.

Joint Parties.

See the title PARTIES.

JOINT STOCK COMPANIES.

CROSS REFERENCES.

See the titles ASSOCIATIONS, vol. 1, p. 843; BENEFICIAL AND BENEVOLENT ASSOCIATIONS, vol. 2, p. 344; BUILDING AND LOAN ASSOCIATIONS, vol. 2, p. 645; CORPORATIONS, vol. 3, p. 510; PARTNERSHIP; STOCK AND STOCKHOLDERS.

Definition.—The words "joint-stock company," include every corporation having a joint stock or capital divided into shares owned by the stockholders respectively. W. Va. Code, ch. 53, § 2230.

Effect of Agreement to Become Stockholders.—When an agreement to become stockholders in specified shares, in a partnership, and to pay the amounts subscribed, is signed by a number of persons, with the number of shares and the aggregate amount thereof annexed to their names, though no promise is named in the agreement, in effect, each party promises to the others, to pay the amount, and the promises of the others are a consideration for the promise of each, and the parties are sufficiently definite. Kimmins *v.* Wilson, 8 W. Va. 584.

JOINT TENANTS AND TENANTS IN COMMON.

CROSS REFERENCES.

See the titles CORPORATIONS, vol. 3, p. 510; HUSBAND AND WIFE, vol. 7, p. 178; PARCENARY, ESTATES IN; PARTITION; PARTNERSHIP.

As to sale of undivided interest under attachment, see the title ATTACHMENT AND GARNISHMENT, vol. 2, p. 85. As to ejectment between joint tenants and tenants in common, see the title EJECTMENT, vol. 4, pp. 887, 900. As to suit for partition and for rents and profits, see the title PARTITION.

1. Definitions and Distinctions.

A. DEFINITIONS.

1. Joint Tenants.

See post, "Character of Possession," II, A, 1.

A widow entitled to dower is not a joint tenant with the heirs at law. Hull v. Hull, 26 W. Va. 1.

2. Tenancy in Common.

"A tenancy in common is where two or more hold the same land, with interests accruing under different titles; or accruing under the same title, but at different periods; or conferred by words of limitation importing that the grantees are to take any distinguished shares." 2 Min. Inst. (4th Ed.) 494; Carneal *v.* Lynch, 91 Va. 114, 20 S. E. 959; Patton *v.* Hoge, 22 Gratt. 443, 450.

"A tenancy in common is where two or more persons hold lands or tenements in fee simple, fee tail, or for term of life, or years, by several titles, not by a joint title, and occupy the same lands or tenements in common; from which circumstance, they are called tenants in common, and their estate a tenancy in common." 1 Lomax Digest 641; Carneal *v.* Lynch, 91 Va. 114, 20 S. E. 959.

But a doweress is not a cotenant with the heirs under the partition statute. Hull *v.* Hull, 26 W. Va. 1.

3. Parceners.

The term "parceners" applies only to owners of lands descended by inheritance. They are seized of their shares by descent from a common ancestor. 2 Bl. Comm. 187; Ward *v.* Ward, 40 W. Va. 611, 21 S. E. 746, 52 Am. St. Rep. 911; Bolling *v.* Teel, 76 Va. 487.

A widow entitled to dower is not a coparcener with the heirs at law under the statute concerning partition. Hull *v.* Hull, 26 W. Va. 1.

B. DISTINCTIONS.

1. Distinguished from Parceners.

In 21 Am. & Eng. Ency. Law, it is said: Parceners hold a position intermediate between joint tenants and tenants in common. Like joint tenants, they have among them only one single freehold, so long as no partition is made. Like tenants in common, they have among them no jus accrescendi; but upon the death of one parcener, a descent takes the place of her aliquot share. And one parcener may at common law convey to another by an assurance proper to convey a several estate, as a feoffment. But such conveyance might also be made by release. The properties of the estates of ,parceners are in some respects like those of joint tenants. They have the same unities of interest, title, and possession, but no unity of time is necessary to create an estate in coparcenary, nor have coparceners that entirety of interest which belongs to joint tenants. They constitute but one heir, how many soever they be, but are properly entitled each to the whole of a distinct moiety and not as joint tenants are, per nihil et per totum to the whole jointly, and to nothing separately. Of course, therefore, there is no jus accrescendi, or survivorship, between them, for each part descends severally to their respective heirs, though the unity of possession may be continued. At common law coparceners were not liable one to the other for trespass. So at common law coparceners were not liable for waste; but this, it would seem, has been changed by statute, and with other cotenants they are liable for waste in most jurisdictions. And at common law a coparcener was not accountable where he had received more than his share of the profits from the common property, but as joint tenants and tenants in common have been made expressly accountable for such excess of profits, it would seem that coparceners would also be liable. Citing 2 Min. Inst. 434, 436, 437; O'Bannon *v.* Roberts, 2 Dana (Ky.) 55.

In the case of Ward *v.* Ward, 40 W. Va. 611, 21 S. E. 746, 52 Am. St. Rep. 911, Judge Brannon, in a well-considered opinion, held, in construing that statute providing that an action of account may be maintained by one joint tenant or tenant in common against the other for receiving more than his just share, that there was a distinction between joint tenants and tenants in common on the one hand, and coparceners on the other. He reviewed and disapproved the language of Prof. Minor. 2 Minor's Inst. 437, and said that the case of O'Bannon *v.* Roberts, 2 Dana 54, was dictum as to this point. This would seem to be the only American case in which it has been held that any distinction remains as to these parties. In 4 Kent's Com. 367, it is said that the technical distinction between coparcenary and estates in common may be considered as essentially extinguished in the United States.

"If there is a case in either state pointedly holding that a mere sole use by a coparcener subjects him to account, I have not seen it, except Fry v. Payne, 82 Va. 759, 1 S. E. 197, holding, by a mere remark, a parcener liable to account for sole use; but there was no consideration of the point whether the statute applied to parceners, but it was assumed it did. The distinction between parceners and joint tenants or tenants in common was not thought of. So, I do not think these parceners could by law demand an account of use and occupation." Ward v. Ward, 40 W. Va. 611, 21 S. E. 746, 52 Am. St. 911.

2. Distinguished from Partnerships.

When real estate is purchased with partnership funds for partnership purposes, and so used, and the conveyance is made to the partners individually as tenants in common, or joint tenants, but it appears on the face of the deed that they are partners, and as such have bought the property, the individual partners hold the legal estate subject to the debts and equities of the partnership. Cunningham v. Ward, 30 W. Va. 572, 5 S. E. 646.

And where tenants in common or joint tenants of an oil lease or mine unite and co-operate in working it, they constitute a mining partnership. Childers v. Neely, 47 W. Va. 70, 34 S. E. 828, saying: "'Partnership must be distinguished from joint management of property owned in common. Where two partners own a chattel, and make a profit by the use of it, they are not partners, without some special agreement which makes them so.' T. Pars. Partn., § 76. Two heirs or other co-owners of a farm, jointly farming it for profit, are not partners. There is a peculiar partnership, called a 'mining partnership,' partaking partly of the nature of an ordinary trading or general partnership, on the one hand, and

partly of a tenancy in common, on the other. It is an important question to those engaged in the oil and other mining business whether each one is jointly and severally liable for all the doings of every or any other of the associates in the venture, as in ordinary trading partnerships. What is a mining partnership? 15 Am. & Eng. Ency. Law, p. 609, says: 'When tenants in common of a mine unite and co-operate in working it, they constitute a mining partnership.' Many authorities there cited thus define it. See the California case of Skillman v. Lachman, 83 Am. Dec. 96, and note discussing it fully; Lamar's Ex'r v. Hale, 79 Va. 147. Mere coworking makes them partners, without special contract. Barring. & A. Mines & M. Courts of equity take jurisdiction of them as if general partnerships. 2 Colly. Partn., ch. 35. Of course, owners of mines, oil leases, or farms can by agreement make an ordinary partnership therein; but 'where tenants in common of mines or oil leases or lands actually engage in working the same, and share, according to the interest of each, the profit and loss, the partnership relation subsists between them, though there is no express agreement between them to be partners or to share profits and loss.' Duryea v. Burt, 28 Cal. 569." Childers v. Neely, 47 W. Va. 70, 34 S. E. 828.

3. Tenancy in Common and Joint Tenancy.

"A tenancy in common differs from a joint tenancy in this respect; joint tenants have one estate in the whole and no estate in any particular part; they have the power of alienation over their respective aliquot parts, and by exercising that power may give a separate and distinct right to their particular parts. Tenants in common have several and distinct estates in their respective parts. Hence the difference in the several modes of assurance by them. Each tenant in common has, in contemplation of law, a

distinct tenement, a distinct freehold."
Patton *v.* Hoge, 22 Gratt. 443, 450.

4. Owners of Surface and Mineral Interests.

The owner of the surface of land and the owner of the minerals under it, where each holds a separate and distinct title, are neither joint tenants nor tenants in common. They are not the owners of undivided interests of the same subject but are the owners of distinct subjects of entirely different natures. Virginia Coal, etc., Co. *v.* Kelly, 93 Va. 332, 24 S. E. 1020.

II. Nature and Incidents of Estate.

A. JOINT TENANCIES.

1. Character of Possession.

"With respect to unity of possession, joint tenants are said to be seized, per mi et per tout—that is, each of them has the entire possession as well of every part as of the whole. They have not, one of them a seizin of one-half, and the other of the remaining half; neither can one be exclusively seized of one acre and his companion of another; but each has an undivided moiety of the whole, not the whole of an undivided moiety. From which it follows that the possession and seizin of one joint tenant is the possession and seizin of the other." Patton *v.* Hoge, 22 Gratt. 443, 450; McNeeley *v.* South Penn Oil Co., 52 W. Va. 616, 44 S. E. 508.

Mr. William Green, in his learned note on the "True Nature of a Joint Tenancy," explains this unity in the following manner: "Bracton says: 'Quilibet cohæredum tantundem juris habet tenendi hæreditatem, quantum et alii; sed tamen non per se ante divisionem, sed pro se in communi cum aliis; et sic totum tenet et nihil tenet, scilicet, totum in communi et nihil separatim per se.' The words of this quotation extend only to coparceners; but in exact accordance with the author's meaning, as that is apparent from the context, the concluding expression has been quoted by Sir Edward Coke, and after him repeatedly by others, as descriptive of joint tenants; of whom, as they existed by the common law, the wit of man can not devise a more accurate, nor perhaps a more felicitous, representation. And Bracton elsewhere, in speaking of them, uses an expression, in words almost, in effect altogether, identical. The same thing is declared also, not indeed so obviously, nor near so strikingly, but yet with equal certainty, by the phrase (long ago become, from continual use, a decantatum), that every joint tenant is seized per my et per tout. To make this manifest, let us suppose that A. and B. are thus seized of an estate in land, and let us designate the moieties of their estate (as contradistinguished from both the land which is the subject of it, and the mere possession or occupation thereof), by numbers 1 and 2. Now A. is seized of moiety, 1, and B. is seized of moiety 2, because each is seized per my; were this all, each would have the whole of an undivided moiety, and neither would have more, of the estate; but that result, in both its aspects, is prevented by the remainder of the description, according to which each is also seized per tout, the consequence whereof is, that A. is seized of moiety 2 as much as he is of moiety 1, and B. is seized of moiety 1 not less than he is of moiety 2; each is seized of both moieties (per tout), and both are seized of each moiety (per my), at one and the same time—which can not be, otherwise than by each being seized, of the whole conjointly with the other, and of nothing whatever separately. Hence Blackstone is right in saying, that of two joint tenants neither (that is neither separately) has the whole of an undivided moiety; but when he says, that 'each has an undivided moiety of the whole,' he uses language that can hardly fail to mislead. In a certain sense each has an undivided moiety, because what he has in a moiety is conjoint; but he has not (what the expression easily may be, and perhaps generally is understood to mean) either separately or only such moiety; for in the same manner, that is to say conjointly with his companion, he has both it and the residue of the estate. * * * When it is affirmed, that each joint tenant owns conjointly with the rest the entire estate, and separately nothing, no more is asserted than that this is so while the joint estate endures. Whenever it is destroyed, in that instant it is transmuted into the estates which succeed it. And what is necessary to a perfect comprehension of the subject, in all its aspects, is (as it seems to me, to keep in view steadily the nature of this transmutation, with a reference to the distinctive principles of the estate, which simultaneously it annihilates on the one hand, and brings into existence, on the other. Until then, to all intents and purposes, whether as among the joint tenants themselves, or as between all or any of them, on the one hand, and the rest of mankind, collectively or individually, on the other, each joint tenant, both in point of seisin and in point of right, has, in the words and meaning of Bracton, totum et, or nihil; to vary the phrase, and adopt the words, less elegant but quite as significant, of Fleta, on the like occasion, joint tenants are proprietors, 'quorum nullus jus habet separatim, cum jus commune sit in personis omnium simul.'" Appendix, Wythe 391, et seq.

And though the common-law right of survivorship in estates of joint tenancy has been abolished in Virginia by statute, yet many of the common-law incidents of the estate still remain, and especially the entirety of possession of each tenant, as well of every part as of the whole. Patton v. Hoge, 22 Gratt. 443, 451.

2. Survivorship.

In General.—Formerly, the jus accrescendi carried the whole estate upon the death of one of the joint tenants,

to the survivors. Appendix, Wythe 301.

Surplus of Fund Set Apart for Suit Rents.—Where a testator devised a tract of land jointly to his four daughters, who were his only children, and provided a fund to be applied by his executors to pay the quit rents, which they accordingly paid annually; and a surplus remained in their hands; it was held, that the surviving daughter was not entitled to the whole of that surplus, but each of the daughters to one-fourth. Jones v. Williams, 2 Call 102.

The statute in Virginia now provides that: "When any joint tenant shall die, whether the estate be real or personal, or whether partition could have been compelled or not, his part shall descend to his heirs, or pass by devise, or go to his personal representative, subject to debts, curtesy, dower or distribution, as if he had been a tenant in common." Va. Code 1887, § 2430. The West Virginia Code contains a similar provision. W. Va. Code, 1899, ch. 71, § 18, p. 681. See Patton v. Hoge, 22 Gratt. 443, 451.

Estates by Entireties.—Survivorship in estates by entirety was abolished July 1st, 1850, by § 18, ch. 116, Virginia Code of 1849, continued in the West Virginia Code of 1868, ch. 71, § 18. McNeeley v. South Penn Oil Co., 52 W. Va. 616, 44 S. E. 508.

The provision that, "if hereafter an estate of inheritance be conveyed or devised to a husband and his wife, one moiety of such estate shall, on the death of either, descend to his or her heirs subject to debts, curtesy or dower, as the case may be" was first introduced into the Virginia Code by the revisal of 1849. Previous thereto survivorship was abolished only as between joint tenants, which was held not to extend to tenants by entireties. Thornton v. Thornton, 3 Rand. 179; Norman v. Cunningham, 5 Gratt. 64, 70; 2 Min. Inst. (4th Ed.) 477. See Dooley v. Baynes, 86 Va. 644, 10 S. E. 974. See the title HUSBAND AND WIFE, vol. 7, p. 178.

Might Have Been Waived.—Before the Revolution, two brothers, British subjects, purchased jointly lands in Virginia and North Carolina. One, who had acted as agent in said purchases, and was also appointed executor of the decedent, became entitled to the legal right by survivorship; but he repeatedly declared it unconscientious to avail himself of said survivorship and made efforts during his life to confer his brother's interest upon said brother's heirs. So that it was plainly known to be his intention not to take the benefit of his survivorship. After his death, the children of the other brother claimed their father's interest. Held, that the survivor was a trustee for the plaintiffs, who were entitled to their father's rights and interests in the lands even against the survivor's devisees. Farley v. Shippen, Wythe 254.

Separate Estate of Married Women. —The conveyance of land to husband and wife since April 1st, 1869, does not create an estate by entirety, but a joint tenancy, and the wife's interest is separate estate. The joint effect of § 18, ch. 71, abolishing survivorship in estates by entirety, and of ch. 66, relating to separate estate of married women, of the West Virginia Code of 1868, is to abolish estates by entirety. The husband is not entitled to sole possession during coverture, but has curtesy in his wife's half after her death. McNeeley v. South Penn Oil Co., 52 W. Va. 616, 617, 44 S. E. 508. See the title SEPARATE ESTATE OF MARRIED WOMEN.

Statutory Exceptions.—The preceding section shall not apply to any estate which joint tenants have as executors or trustees, nor to an estate conveyed or devised to persons in their own right, when it manifestly appears from the tenor of the instrument that it was intended the part of the one dying should then belong to the others. Neither shall it affect the mode of proceeding on any joint judgment or decree in favor of or on any contract with two or more, one of whom dies." Va. Code, 1887, § 2431; W. Va. Code, 1899, ch. 71, § 19, p. 681.

Survivorship Provided for in Conveyance.—Two persons unite in a joint deed giving to a third person all their personal property "that they may have at the time of their death," and reserving the "use and control" thereof "so long as they both shall live;" they thereby create a joint tenancy survivorship in such personal property, the manifest intention of which is that on the death of one, the residue vests in the survivor, and such third person is not entitled to any of their property until the death of both the grantors. Bank v. Effingham, 51 W. Va. 267, 41 S. E. 143. For the common-law rule of survivorship was changed by the above statute in this respect.

Gift Over in Event of Death—Only Original Shares Survive.—In the absence of a positive and distinct indication of a contrary intention, only original, and not accrued, shares survive in case of a gift over in event of death. Armistead v. Hartt, 97 Va. 316, 33 S. E. 616, 5 Va. Law Reg. 387.

Statutes Does Not Apply Where One Joint Tenant Dies before Estate Vests. —The Virginia statute abolishing survivorship among joint tenants has no application where the estate in joint tenancy has not vested, and hence upon the death of one of two joint devisees in the lifetime of the testator the whole estate passes to the survivor. Lockhart v. Vandyke, 97 Va. 356, 33 S. E. 613, 5 Va. Law Reg. 303, and note, p. 309.

A testator gave "all the residuum of his estate to be equally divided between the children of his uncle and his cousin, and their heirs forever, share and share alike." Between the date of the will and the testator's death, one of the children of the uncle died. Held, that her share did not lapse, so that the heir at law would take it, but survived to the legatees or their assignees just as if the deceased child had never existed. Pendleton *v.* Hoomes, Wythe 94.

But upon a devise to four children, share and share alike, and in the event of the death of one or more of them, his or their share to go to the survivors, the event which is to fix the rights of the children is the death of the testator. If all survive the testator, each takes his or her share of the real estate devised free from any right of survivorship. Armistead *v.* Hartt, 97 Va. 316, 33 S. E. 616, 5 Va. Law Reg. 387.

B. TENANCIES IN COMMON.

1. In General.

Distinguished from Joint Tenancy.— See ante, "Tenancy in Common and Joint Tenancy," I, B, 3.

Unity of Possession Alone Required. —Neither unity of interest, time nor title is necessary to constitute a tenancy in common, but only unity in possession. As tenants in common they may hold by several seizures. Johnson *v.* National Exchange Bank, 33 Gratt. 473, 481.

Unity of Fine Unnecessary.—One of the conditions creating a tenancy in common is where two or more persons hold the same land, with interests accruing under the same title, but at different times. Carneal *v.* Lynch, 91 Va. 114, 117, 20 S. E. 959.

Cotenancy is a question of possession entirely, without regard to the source of title. Davis *v.* Settle, 43 W. Va. 17, 26 S. E. 557.

2. Shares or Interests of Tenants in Common.

Equality of Interest.—Where there is no evidence as to the shares of the several tenants in common, they are presumed to be equal. Jarrett *v.* Johnson, 11 Gratt. 327. See also, Livesay *v.* Beard, 22 W. Va. 585, 595.

Devise to Five Children to Be Divided between Them.—The provisions of testatrix's will giving to one daughter one-half the land, her half to be taken off the entire tract next to a certain creek, and to include timber suffi- cient for said half next to certain lands, and giving the remaining half to be divided equally among the other four children except that one should have $500 more in the half to be divided among the four, constituted the five children tenants in common in the lands, giving one a half interest in value to be laid off when partitioned as directed, and giving to the other four the other half in value, to be so divided that one's share should be greater by $500 in value than that of any of the other three, whose shares should be equal. McCamant *v.* Nuckolls, 85 Va. 331, 12 S. E. 160.

III. Creation of Estates in Cotenancy.

A. JOINT TENANCIES.

1. In General.

By Act of Parties Only.—"A joint tenancy arises by act of the parties, and never by act of law. It may be created by the devise, or by any conveyance inter vivos, by words which give an estate to a plurality of persons, without adding any restrictive, exclusive, or explanatory words. Thus, if an estate be granted to A and B and their heirs, this makes them joint tenants in fee of the lands. For the law interprets the grant so as to make all parts of it take effect, which can only be done by creating an equal estate in them both." 2 Min. Inst. (4th Ed.) 467; Lockhart *v.* Vandyke, 97 Va. 356, 33 S. E. 613, 5 Va. Law Reg. 303.

Construction as Tenancies in Common Favored.—The present tendency of the courts, is to lay hold of every available expression to construe estates given to a plurality of tenants as tenancies in common. And although this innovation began in equity, and in reference to wills, yet it has long prevailed in the courts of common law as well, and the doctrine extends to deeds as uniformly as to wills. Hence, such expressions as "equally to be divided," "share and share alike," "respectively between and amongst them," will, according to this modern construction, convert into a tenancy in common what would once have been a joint tenancy. 2 Min. Inst. (4th Ed.) 467; Lockhart v. Vandyke, 97 Va. 356, 33 S. E. 613, 5 Va. Law Reg. 303.

2. By Patent or Deed.

An inclusive patent to three creates a joint tenancy. Jones v. Jones, 1 Call 458.

A father and his two sons obtained separate patents for 400 acres of land, the three tracts adjoining each other, and the father obtained a patent for another 400 acres. Afterwards, the three took one inclusive patent for the tracts mentioned and another tract of 1162 acres. Held, that this destroyed the separate estates in the first tracts, and created a joint tenancy in the whole 2762 acres. Jones v. Jones, 1 Call 458.

Under Statutes Abolishing Survivorship.—Where two persons unite in a joint deed, giving to a third person all their personal property, "that they may have at the time of their death, the party of the first part to have full use and control of all their personal property so long as they both shall live," this language creates a joint tenancy pure and simple, not only at common law, but under the provision of the statute changing the rule of joint tenancy at common law and providing that such change shall not apply when it manifestly appears from the tenor of the instrument that it was intended that the part of the one dying should then belong to the survivor. Bank v. Effingham, 51 W. Va. 267, 41 S. E. 143.

3. Farming on Shares.

An agreement between two persons for the raising of a crop on the lands of a third, by his license and permission, and for a division of the crop between such two persons, constitutes them joint tenants of the crop, and neither can defeat the interests of the other by taking a conveyance of the lands from the owner. Lowe v. Miller, 3 Gratt. 205, 46 Am. Dec. 188.

4. Agreement for Purchase.

A contract between the plaintiff and the defendant that the defendant should purchase for them jointly, at an auction, certain property, it to be divided between them, and the plaintiff to pay the defendant half the purchase price, is not an agreement between them as joint tenants, but as individuals, so that an action for damages will lie for breach thereof. Barnes v. Morrison, 97 Va. 372, 34 S. E. 93.

5. By Will.

a. In General.

A devise "unto my two sons, to wit, Charles and Henry, of all the lands I now reside on," makes them joint tenants. Lockhart v. Vandyke, 97 Va. 356, 33 S. E. 613, 5 Va. Law Reg. 303.

b. Gift to Wife and Children.

As to the effect of a gift "to wife and children," there has been some conflict in Virginia.

Grant to a Woman and Her Children.—In Nye v. Lovitt, 92 Va. 710, 24 S. E. 345, 2 Va. Law Reg. 29, Judge Buchanan said: "This court, in a line of decisions beginning with Wallace v. Dold, 3 Leigh 258, and coming down to the case of Stace v. Bumgardner, 89 Va. 418, has held, that a grant or gift to a woman and her children or to a trustee for the benefit of herself and children, passed to the mother, and that the mention of the word 'children' in the deed or will merely indicated the motive for the conveyance or gift, without investing them with any interest therein." See Stinson v. Day, 1 Rob. 435; Leake v. Benson, 29 Gratt. 153.

"The late Judge Burks, in his excellent note to the opinion in Nye v. Lovitt, 92 Va. 710, 24 S. E. 345, 2 Va. Law Reg. 29, referring to the class of cases beginning with Wallace v. Dold, supra, shows that in no one of them is the decision, that the children took no interest, rested alone on the language that the gift is to 'the mother and her children' but that 'the intention to give exclusively to the woman is deduced from the context and the language of the instrument taken as a whole;' and in conclusion he says: 'The decisions only show that when the gift is to the woman and her child or children, or is in trust for them, or like phraseology is used, the children are excluded only when it appears from the context, or the whole instrument taken together, that it was the intention to exclude them.'" Lindsey v. Eckels, 99 Va. 668, 40 S. E. 23.

In Vaughan v. Vaughan, 97 Va. 322, 33 S. E. 603, 5 Va. Law Reg. 443, Judge Riley, in a dictum, said that such words standing alone would undoubtedly convey a joint estate to the wife and children. See criticism of this dictum, 5 Va. Law Reg. 427. See article approving dictum, 5 Va. Law Reg. 491. See also, Rhett v. Mason, 18 Gratt. 541.

Deed to Trustee for Maintenance and Support.—In Lindsey v. Eckels, 99 Va. 668, 40 S. E. 23, where a deed conveyed property to a trustee for the use, maintenance and support of a mother, and for the use, maintenance and support of her issue, and the grantor further declared that it was the intention of the deed that the mother should be supported from said property, or the proceeds thereof, during her life, and that the issue, during the life of the mother, should be supported and educated from the proceeds of said property, and, at the death of the mother, all of the property and its proceeds should be divided equally among such issue, it was held that the mother and her issue each take an equal interest in the proceeds of the property during the life of the mother and, at her death, the issue take the property in fee simple.

Gift to Wife and Children without More.—It seems that the question has been settled in Virginia by the decision in Fitzpatrick v. Fitzpatrick, 100 Va. 552, 42 S. E. 306, where it is held, that a gift to a wife and children, without

more, vests a joint estate in the wife and children, in equal portions.

6. Tenant by Dower.

A widow entitled to dower in the real estate of her deceased husband is neither a joint tenant, tenant in common nor coparcener with the heirs at law within the meaning of the statute concerning partition (W. Va. Code, ch. 79), so as to authorize a court of equity to sell the legal estate of the heirs descended to them, and to have her dower assigned to her out of the proceeds, and the residue divided among the heirs and those having vendor's liens on the lands, if any one heir refuses to give his assent thereto, or if any one heir be an infant defendant, the widow being the plaintiff in the suit. Hull v. Hull, 26 W. Va. 1.

"And therefore no power is conferred by that statute upon a court of equity to sell the whole estate against her will and without her consent, and to compel her to receive a monied compensation out of the proceeds in lieu of dower." Hull v. Hull, 26 W. Va. 1, 19.

B. TENANCIES IN COMMON.

1. In General.

"Formerly, joint tenancy was much favored; but for more than a century past the courts have laid hold of every available expression to construe estates given to a plurality of tenants as tenancies in common. And although this innovation began in equity, and in reference to wills, yet it has long prevailed in the courts of common law as well, and the doctrine extends to deeds as uniformly as to wills. Hence, such expressions as 'equally to be divided,' 'share and share alike,' 'respectively between and amongst them,' will, according to this modern construction, convert into a tenancy in common, what would once have been a joint tenancy." 2 Min. Inst. (4th Ed.) 467; Lockhart v. Vandyke, 97 Va. 356, 33 S. E. 613.

One of the conditions creating a tenancy in common is where two or more persons hold the same land, with interests accruing under the same title but at different times. Carneal v. Lynch, 91 Va. 114, 20 S. E. 959.

Common seisin in fact or law, without regard to source of title, creates cotenancy. Davis v. Settle, 43 W. Va. 17, 26 S. E. 557.

2. Tenant by Dower.

See ante, "Tenant by Dower," III, A, 6.

Assignment of Dower in Common Property.—Where a husband holds lands as tenant in common or (now that the jus accrescendi is abolished) as joint tenant, dower may be assigned his widow to be held in common with the other tenants. Parrish v. Parrish, 88 Va. 529, 14 S. E. 325.

3. Conveyance by One of Common Property.

It is well settled that a conveyance by metes and bounds of part of an estate held in common, though valid against the grantor, can not prejudice the rights of the cotenant, unless followed by entry and adversary possession. The grantee becomes thereby merely a tenant in common with the cotenants of his grantor; his possession is in presumption of law, the possession of all, and is to be deemed in support and not in derogation of the common title. Robinett v. Preston, 2 Rob. 272; Hannon v. Hannah, 9 Gratt. 146; Buchanan v. King, 22 Gratt. 414, 422. In the last case one of two joint tenants of land purchased a large tract including the land held jointly and took the conveyance to himself, and then conveyed part of the large tract including the land held jointly.

A deed by one of two cotenants purporting to convey a particular tract of the land held in common, though ineffectual to pass the particular tract as against the cotenant, will, as against the grantor and strangers, be effectual to pass the interest of the grantor. Possession under such deed will support a release from the cotenant; and if the part conveyed be assigned the alienee

on partition, the title will be absolute in law. The deed being good against the grantor, the entry of the tenant under it would be lawful, and though it might be inoperative as far as the rights of the cotenant were thereby prejudiced, yet as it would invest the grantee with the estate of the grantor so far as he could lawfully convey, the grantee would be tenant in common with the cotenant of his grantor, to the extent of the interest conveyed. His possession and seisin would be the possession and seisin of both, because such possession and seisin would not be adverse to the right of his companion, but in support of their common title. Robinett v. Preston, 2 Rob. 272.

And where a cotenant conveys his undivided interest in the lands held in common, without the knowledge or consent of his companions in interest, the grantee in the deed is a tenant in common in the land with all the rights and obligations of his grantor with reference thereto. Worthington v. Staunton, 16 W. Va. 208.

Where the title to the land held in common is conveyed to one of the joint owners and he, reciting that he owns the whole, conveys one-half of it to a third person, and purports to convey the upper moiety, it will be held, that the deed passes only an equal undivided moiety of the common subject, and that the other joint owner and the grantee hold in common the whole subject and every part thereof. Cox v. McMullin, 14 Gratt. 82.

One joint tenant may alien to a stranger, and his alienee, and the other joint tenant, will be tenants in common. Johnson v. National Exchange Bank, 33 Gratt. 473, 481.

If one tenant in common sells and conveys to a stranger, without the knowledge or consent of his cotenant, the entirety or an undivided moiety of a portion of the land defined by boundaries, such sale and conveyance does not make such stranger a cotenant in the lot purchased with the other co-tenant of the entire tract, so as to give an absolute right to have a portion of it assigned to him, but under such circumstances a court of equity ought in making the partition of the entire land to require as parties in the suit, not only the original cotenants of the entire tract, but also the purchaser of a part of the land from one of these co-tenants, and ought to assign to this purchaser the parcel of land bought by him, if he purchased the entirety, or a moiety of it, if he purchased but a moiety, and consider the part so assigned as a portion of the share of the cotenant who sold the land, if this can be done with justice to the other cotenant, or if he assents thereto; and the whole residue of the tract not so assigned to the purchaser should be partitioned according to their respective rights among the cotenants of the entire tract. Boggess v. Meredith, 16 W. Va. 1, 2.

Authority of Executor.—"As tenant in common he was already seized of the title, and held the possession promiscuously with Johnson's devisees, and when he acquired the title of his cotenants to their individual moiety, he was seized of the whole in severalty. A sale and conveyance to him of his moiety was unnecessary to invest him with the title and possession, and Johnson's executor was invested with no power or authority to sell it or convey it to him. He had only authority under the will of Johnson to sell and convey the Johnson moiety, and he and White had mutually agreed to unite in the sale of their respective moieties. If they had sold to a third party Johnson's executor and White would have been bound upon his compliance with the terms of the sale, to convey to him their respective interests; that is each of them to convey an undivided moiety in the whole. Johnson's executor could only have conveyed his interest, and White could only have conveyed his interest."

Johnson v. National Exchange Bank, 33 Gratt. 473, 483.

Possession of Common Tenant as Notice to Purchaser.—Where a tenant is put in possession by a party having title to land and in fact the rightful owner of it, and remains on it setting up no title in himself, his possession is, in law, that of the party so putting him on the land. Genin v. Ingersoll, 2 W. Va. 558.

4. Personal Representative of Life Tenant and Remainderman.

The personal representative of one or more remaindermen, dying during the lifetime of the life tenant, is tenant in common with the surviving remaindermen. Clarkson v. Booth, 17 Gratt. 490.

The personal representatives of one or more remaindermen, dying during the lifetime of the life tenants, are tenants in common with the surviving remaindermen and must be joined with them in an action to recover the property. Clarkson v. Booth, 17 Gratt. 490.

5. Purchase of Property for Partnership Purposes.

Where parties purchase an estate jointly for the purposes of their trade, it is considered in equity as an estate in common, in England, and in Virginia, where the jus accrescendi is abolished, it is so considered in law as well as in equity. Therefore, a surviving partner can have no other claim against real estate held in partnership than any other creditor has. Deloney v. Hutcheson, 2 Rand. 183.

Where real estate is purchased for partnership purposes and a conveyance is made to the partners in the name of the firm, the partners are tenants in common of the estate, and hold the legal estate subject to the equities of the partnership. Jones v. Neale. 2 Pat. & H. 339. See Hancock v. Talley, 1 Va. Dec. 433.

6. Life Tenant and Fee Simple Owner.

A life tenant of one undivided moiety cf a parcel of land and the fee simple owners of the other undivided moiety, whose estates accrue under the same title, but at different times, are tenants in common of the land. Carneal *v.* Lynch, 91 Va. 114, 20 S. E. 959.

7. Derivation of Title from One Cotenant.

"Persons deriving title from one cotenant will be regarded as tenants in common with the other cotenant. Dain *v.* Cowing, 39 Am. Dec. 585." Cecil *v.* Clark, 44 W. Va. 659, 30 S. E. 216, 225.

A tenant of land claiming under a tenant in common, adversely to other tenants in common, will, as to rents and profits, be treated as a tenant in common with the latter. Ruffners *v.* Lewis, 7 Leigh 720, 30 Am. Dec. 513.

8. Joint Adventures.

T., as agent of F. & C., presented to R. a written contract for the purchase of a stallion at the price of eighteen hundred dollars, which specified that those who should execute the contract and join in the purchase of the horse should, after the purchase, own interest therein by shares of one hundred dollars each, the interest of each party to be determined by the number of shares for which he should subscribe. R. signed it, subscribing for two shares, and delivered it to T., upon the verbally expressed condition that it should not be effective as to him, unless M. & W. should sign it, and, they refusing to join in the enterprise, T. obtained the signatures of fifteen other persons who took the remaining sixteen shares, and executed and delivered to T. two negotiable notes for the sum of nine hundred dollars each, without notice of the condition upon which R. had signed, and F. & C. delivered the horse at R.'s stable, and endorsed and delivered one of the notes to a stranger, without having obtained R.'s signature thereto, and without the knowledge of the other parties to the contract, who afterwards paid it and then instituted an action to recover from R. one-ninth of the sum so paid, proving the additional fact that, after the contract had been completed and shown to R., he expressed approval therefor. Held, that they may recover in an action at law. Newman *v.* Ruby, 54 W. Va. 381, 46 S. E. 172.

9. Creation by Will.

Mrs. C., an old and very wealthy lady, after disposing by her will and two codicils, of a large amount of her property, at the close of the second codicil says: In case of a sudden and unexpected death, I give the remainder of my property to be equally divided between my cousin, Dr. C., of Philadelphia, and my cousin, P. S., of New Orleans, one-half of which each must hold in trust for the benefit of their children. This is not a conditional legacy dependent upon the sudden and unexpected death of the testatrix. C. and S. took under the residuary clause of the will each one-half as tenants in common, and upon the revocation of the bequest to Dr. C., the half given to him does not pass to S. but is undisposed of by the will and goes to the next of kin. Skipwith *v.* Cabell, 19 Gratt. 758.

A testator devised as follows: "I loan to my two grandsons, Willis and Thomas Wootten, children of my deceased son, William Wootten, the tract of land in York county, I purchased from J. M. & P. M.; also one-third part of my negro slaves not otherwise disposed of, during their natural lives; and in case they should die, leaving lawfully begotten heir or heirs of their body, I give the property loaned them to such heir or heirs; but in case they or either of them should die leaving no such heir, I give the property loaned them to my grandson, Benjamin Wootten, to him and his heirs forever. The property loaned to my two grandsons as above to be equally divided between them." Held, that Willis and Thomas Wootten were tenants in common for life of the slaves bequeathed to them, and that on the death of either of them, leaving no issue at his death, his share of the slaves vested in Benjamin Wootten. Wootten *v.* Wootten, 2 Pat. & H. 494.

10. Lapse of Legacy or Devise.

"In 2 Minor (4th Ed.) at page 1049, it is said: 'The general doctrine at common law is that a devise lapses in all cases where the devisee dies before the testator. And if the devise be to several, as tenants in common, and one of them dies in the testator's lifetime, his share lapses. (See Frazier *v.* Frazier, 2 Leigh 642.) Where, however, the devise is to several jointly, and one of them dies in the testator's lifetime, his share does not lapse, but survives; for although such joint devisees are not joint tenants until the testator's death, yet the gift to them is a gift per mie et per tout, and so, if one should die, whereby, as he has nothing separately, his interest ceases to exist, the other or others are entitled to the whole as at first, but with no one to share it with them. And as the parties have not become joint tenants, the statute abolishing survivorship does not apply.' The law touching the lapse of devises is to be found in § 2523 of the Code, and is as follows: 'If a devisee or legatee die before the testator, leaving issue who survive the testator, such issue shall take the estate devised or bequeathed, as the devisee or legatee would have done if he had survived the testator, unless a different disposition thereof be made or required by the will;' but, as is justly observed by Mr. Minor, this statute is not applicable where independently of it no lapse could occur, and therefore can not be invoked in a case such as this, 'for by the force and effect of the joint taking, the share of the party deceased would survive to the survivor or survivors.' 2 Minor, supra. See, also, Pendleton *v.* Hoomes, Wythe 94. The law of the subject under consideration is discussed with a great wealth of learning by Mr. William Green in an appendix to the volume just cited, which is quoted in terms of high and deserved approbation in Freeman on Cotenancy and Partition, §§ 28, 40. He reaches the conclusion arrived at by Mr. Minor, and shows that the common-law doctrine is still the law, notwithstanding our statute which abolishes the survivorship among joint tenants. With respect to that statute, he observes that, while it does away with the right of survivorship, it does not destroy joint tenancy. To use his own language: 'It does not annihilate the legal entity called a joint estate, so as to prevent any such estate from vesting, nor does it destroy the joint estate forthwith after it has vested. On the contrary, it permits the estate to subsist as joint, with all its former incidents, during the joint lives of all its owners; and if, in that time, partition be made, or a severance effected without partition, it is quiescent as a deadletter. It begins to operate at all, only when one of the joint tenants has died before partition or severance. And on the happening of that event, and from thenceforth, it directs that the part of the deceased shall be considered as if he had been a tenant in common, not from the beginning, but only when the event to which it refers happened. Where it applies, and to the extent of its application, it operates, in articulo mortis, a statutory severance; and that is all. It does not extirpate the quality of a joint estate, which made it produce, among other fruits, the jus accrescendi, but only destroys in the moment of production, or blights by anticipation in the bloom, that particular fruit. In this manner it modifies the nature of a joint tenancy by the common law, so far as to take away one of the incidents which the law has annexed to it, but leaves it in all other respects as it was. In short, since the statute, joint tenants seem to have an estate that is to all purposes joint, both in its inception and also in its continuance, until a destruction or severance thereof takes place; which latter, where an interest has become vested, is effectuated by the statute at the moment any of them dies, to the extent of his part; and henceforth that part is to be regarded as it would have been (though the statute had never been enacted) if the joint estate had been to the same extent dissevered by any of the means which theretofore existed. And, if this be the sum of its efficacy, the consequence seems to be, that in regard to the lapsing of devises and legacies, and also in regard to the vesting of estates created or transferred by conveyances inter vivos, it has been productive of no change whatever.' He shows that in a case like that under discussion the doctrine of survivorship has no place, as it applies only where the estate in joint tenancy has been created and has vested; and, therefore, the abolition of the doctrine of survivorship does not affect the common-law rule with respect to the death of one or more devisees during the lifetime of the testator, for it is still true, notwithstanding the statute, 'that each joint tenant takes conjointly with the rest the entire estate—separately nothing,' from which it follows that 'if one should die, whereby, as he has nothing separately, his interest ceases to exist, the other or others are entitled to the whole as at first, but with no one to share it with them.' 2 Minor 1049. This subject was considered by the Supreme Court of West Virginia in the case of Hoke v. Hoke, 12 W. Va. 427, and a decision rendered in accordance with the views of the text writers above quoted. See also, 2 Redfield on Wills 169. 3 Lomax Digest 185; 2 Williams on Executors (with Perkins' notes), p. 1311; 2 Jarman on Wills, 265." Lockhart v. Vandyke, 97 Va. 356, 33 S. E. 613, 5 Va. Law Reg. 303.

"A release, and not a foefment is the proper form of conveyance by one joint tenant to another. 'A foefment, and not a release, is the proper assurance between tenants in common.'" Patton v. Hoge, 22 Gratt. 443, 450.

IV. Rights, Duties and Liabilities.

A. IN GENERAL.

Dealings between Each Other.—"The relation of trust and confidence is such between cotenants that it would be inequitable to permit one of them to do anything to the prejudice of the others in reference to the common property. For one cotenant in any way but the most open and avowed, with the full knowledge of those in common interest with him, to try and obtain the common title, has been held to be a breach of trust, amounting to a fraud against the rights of the cotenancy." Parker v. Brast, 45 W. Va. 399, 32 S. E. 269, 271.

As every joint tenant, or tenant in common, occupies a position of trust and confidence towards his companions, he who seeks to change these relations, and to expel the others from the enjoyment of the common property, must establish the facts which make such expulsion just and equitable. Buchanan v. King, 22 Gratt. 414, 420.

Co-ownership requires open dealing with each other. Neither may deceive and defraud the other, either by silence, acts or words. Weaver v. Akin, 48 W. Va. 456, 37 S. E. 600; Gilchrist v. Beswick, 33 W. Va. 168, 10 S. E. 371.

One cotenant or joint owner of land can not clandestinely, or without fair notice to his cotenants, stipulate with third persons for any private or selfish advantage and benefit to himself in respect to the joint property; and if he does so, a court of equity will, at the option of the co-owners, compel him to divide such benefits. Gilchrist v. Beswick, 33 W. Va. 168, 10 S. E. 371.

If one of several joint owners of a lease, to cure a defect therein, takes an additional lease in his own name, he will be presumed to be acting for the common benefit of all the owners and that such additional lease is a confirmation of the original lease. Weaver v. Akin, 48 W. Va. 456, 37 S. E. 600.

To oust his co-owners of such benefit, the second lessor, must show that, after they had notice by his act or words that he intended to hold his lease adversely to them, they delayed for an unreasonable time in accepting the terms thereof. Weaver v. Akin, 48 W. Va. 456, 37 S. E. 600.

If for eleven months, by his conduct, letters, and words, he leads his co-owners to believe that he has no intention of asserting the second lease in avoidance of the first, but during this period they continue mutually enjoying and developing the common property, he can not suddenly, and without reasonable notice to them, set up sole ownership under the second lease, and in this manner destroy the common ownership under the first. The dealings between co-owners must be fair and open, and free from deception and evil appearances. Weaver v. Akin, 48 W. Va. 456, 37 S. E. 600.

Presumption That Act Is for the Common Benefit.—"It is a principle of law that the acts of one joint tenant in relation to the joint property is the act of and for the benefit of all his cotenants, unless specially shown or stipulated to the contrary or repudiated." Elbon v. Adams, 44 W. Va. 237, 30 S. E. 150, 151. See also, Weaver v. Akin, 48 W. Va. 456, 37 S. E. 600.

B. USE AND ENJOYMENT BY ONE TENANT.

1. In General.

As against all others than his companions, a joint tenant, tenant in common, or coparcener, is entitled to the possession of the whole. One parcener or tenant in common may enter for all; and if he enters generally, it is in point of law an entry for all. 9 Vin. Abr. 456; Entry, F. pl. 1, 2, 3; and one parcener could, in assise, recover the whole against an abator; for she had right against all who had no right. Allen v. Gibson, 4 Rand. 468, 477.

Destruction of Property.—A tenant in common occupying and using the common property separately, will be responsible to his cotenants, if he willfully or by gross negligence destroys or wastes the common property. Graham v. Pierce, 19 Gratt. 28, 100 Am. Dec. 658.

But he can not be held responsible for such destruction or waste in a case in which the bill does not charge it. Graham v. Pierce, 19 Gratt. 28, 100 Am. Dec. 658.

Easement on Common Property.—One joint tenant can not create an easement or servitude upon the common estate injurious to the interests of his cotenant, but if such cotenant does not make objection no one else can do so. Lowenback v. Switzer, 1 Va. Dec. 141.

Alteration of Common Property.—One tenant in common has no right to change or alter the common property to the injury of the other without his consent. Woods v. Early, 95 Va. 307, 28 S. E. 374.

Cutting Timber. — In the case of McDodrill v. Pardee, etc., Lumber Co., 40 W. Va. 564, 21 S. E. 878, it is said: "If the life estate were ended, each and every cotenant would have the right to take possession peaceably, and have the reasonable enjoyment thereof in some of the ordinary methods of reaping profits from property of like character under like circumstances. Freem. Coten., § 251; Hawley v. Clowes, 2 Johns. Ch. 122. Thus, if timber standing on the land is of proper size and condition for advantageous sale, either of the cotenants, it is said, may lawfully proceed to cut and sell it; for in so doing he makes no unusual use of the real estate of which he is a tenant in fee. Freem. Coten., § 251. Baker v. Wheeler (1832) 8 Wend. 505, 24 Am. Dec. 66, and note, was an action of trover, where it is held, inter alia, that license by one tenant in common to a third person to cut timber on the common land is good, and gives such person title to the trees cut."

2. Use and Occupation.

a. In General.

By common law, one joint tenant, tenant in common, or parcener using the common land exclusively, but not ousting or excluding his co-owners, is not chargeable to them for use and occupation; but this rule has been changed by § 14, ch. 100, W. Va. Code, as to joint tenants and tenants in common, but not as to parceners. Ward v. Ward, 40 W. Va. 611, 21 S. E. 746, 52 Am. St. Rep. 911.

b. Rule as to Parceners.

By common law, one joint tenant, tenant in common, or parcener using the common land exclusively, but not ousting or excluding his co-owners, is not chargeable to them for use and occupation; but this rule has been changed by § 14, ch. 100, W. Va. Code, as to joint tenants and tenants in common, but not as to parceners. Ward v. Ward, 40 W. Va. 611, 21 S. E. 746, 52 Am. St. Rep. 911.

At common law and under § 14, ch. 100, of the West Virginia Code, one parcener using the common land exclusively, but not ousting or excluding his co-owners, is not chargeable to them for the use and occupation. Ward v. Ward, 40 W. Va. 611, 21 S. E. 746, 52 Am. St. Rep. 911, disapproving the language used in Fry v. Payne, 82 Va. 759, 1 S. E. 197.

c. Set-Off against Improvements.

Where it is proper to allow a coparcener for improvements, a charge for use and occupation may be set off against the improvements. Ward v. Ward, 40 W. Va. 611, 21 S. E. 746, 52 Am. St. Rep. 911.

3. Waste.

a. At Common Law.

By the common law one joint tenant or tenant in common could not recover against another for waste, because each was entitled to the possession of the undivided whole, and so might obtain redress as to waste on the part of his fellow by entering upon and occupying the premises. 2 Min. Inst. (4th Ed.) 475, 498. Williamson v. Jones, 43 W. Va. 562, 27 S. E. 411.

b. Under the Statutes.

But the statutes in Virginia and West Virginia now provide that if a tenant in common, joint tenant, or parcener commit waste, he shall be liable to his cotenants, jointly or severally, for damages. Va. Code, 1904, § 2776; W. Va. Code, 1899, ch. 92, § 3390; Williamson v. Jones, 43 W. Va. 562, 27 S. E. 411.

c. What Constitutes Waste.

In General.—It was said in Williamson v. Jones, 43 W. Va. 562, 27 S. E. 411, that those acts which would be waste in a tenant for life, would be such between tenants in common.

Taking Minerals.—Under the West Virginia Code providing that if a tenant in common, joint tenant or parcener commit waste, he shall be liable to his cotenants jointly and severally for damages, it has been held, that taking minerals from the land by a tenant in common is waste, for which he must account to his cotenant. Williamson v. Jones, 43 W. Va. 562, 27 S. E. 411; Cecil v. Clark, 47 W. Va. 402, 35 S. E. 11.

It is waste in a tenant in common to take petroleum oil from the land, for which he is liable to his cotenants to the extent of their right in the land. Williamson v. Jones, 43 W. Va. 562, 27 S. E. 411.

The extraction of coal by one tenant in common without consent of another is waste, for which he must account to that other. Cecil v. Clark, 47 W. Va. 402, 35 S. E. 11.

Working Mines, or Salt and Oil Wells.—It is not waste for a tenant in common to work open salt or oil wells or mines, but it is waste to open new ones. Williamson v. Jones, 43 W. Va. 562, 27 S. E. 411.

Cutting Timber.—Whether any particular act on the part of a joint tenant or tenant in common constitutes waste, depends on the circumstances of each particular case, and is often varied by the locality of the act complained of. Thus, the cutting of timber in some sections may be considered waste, while in others it is a positive benefit. Hence, in every case, the law on this subject must be applied with reasonable regard to circumstances. See McDodrill *v.* Pardee, etc., Lumber Co., 40 W. Va. 564, 21 S. E. 878; Findlay *v.* Smith, 6 Munf. 134; Macaulay *v.* Dismal Swamp Land Co., 2 Rob. 507.

In the case of McDodrill *v.* Pardee, etc., Lumber Co., 40 W. Va. 564, 21 S. E. 878, it is said: "If the life estate were ended, each and every cotenant would have the right to take possession peaceably, and have the reasonable enjoyment thereof in some of the ordinary methods of reaping profits from property of like character under like circumstances. Freem. Coten., § 251; Hawley *v.* Clowes, 2 Johns. Ch. 122. Thus, if timber standing on the land is of proper size and condition for advantageous sale, either of the cotenants, it is said, may lawfully proceed to cut and sell it; for in so doing he makes no unusual use of the real estate of which he is a tenant in fee. Freem. Coten., § 251. Baker *v.* Wheeler (1832), 8 Wend. 505, 24 Am. Dec. 66, and note, was an action of trover, where it is held, inter alia, that license by one tenant in common to a third person to cut timber on the common land is good, and gives such person title to the trees cut. * * * One tenant in common can not maintain an action on the case in the nature of waste against another tenant in common in possession of the whole, having a demise of the moiety from the first, for cutting down trees of a proper age and growth for being cut. Martyn *v.* Knowllys (1799), 8 Term R. 145; 1 Taunt. 241. The mere act of selling the standing timber was not waste. They were sales and grants by deed of some

interest in the realty, and, being duly recorded in the proper county, had the effect of notice to all subsequent purchasers; so that such purchaser took it subject to such rights, whatever they may be. The subsequent cutting of the timber constituted the waste, if any, which involves different questions; and, in any event, the plaintiffs would be entitled to recover only their proportionate part of the damages, measured by the quantity of their interest in the timber cut and carried away. See Freem. Coten., § 356; Carpentier *v.* Small, 35 Cal. 346; Cain *v.* Wright (1858), 5 Jones (N. C.) 282, 72 Am. Dec. 551. In fact, I think this is included in the meaning of our statute on the subject of waste between cotenants (§ 2 of chapter 92 of the Code.)"

d. Title to Proceeds of Waste.

A cotenant doing waste neither owns nor can sell what is not his. Williamson *v.* Jones, 43 W. Va. 562, 27 S. E. 411.

e. Measure of Recovery.

Cotenants, who commit waste, are liable to each other jointly or severally for the damages; but the amount of a recovery against a stranger or a grantee of a cotenant must be apportioned to correspond with his undivided interest in the land. "The propriety of limiting such recovery of the cotenant to an amount in damages proportionate to his interest in the land may receive some further indirect confirmation from § 14 of chapter 100 of the Code, which, among other things, provides that an action of account may be maintained by one joint tenant, or tenant in common, or his personal representative, against the other, for receiving more than comes to his just share or proportion, and against the personal representative of any such joint tenant or tenant in common. 'And if the property admits of use and occupation by several, and less than his just and proportionate share of the common property to the occupying cotenant, who in no way hinders or excludes the others, he is not accountable to his cotenants for the profits of that portion of the property owned by him within the meaning of this statute.' Dodson *v.* Hays, 29 W. Va. 577, 2 S. E. 415. But here the estate for life was not ended, and an undivided third interest in the immediate remainder in fee had, by our statute of descent, come to the father, the tenant for life. I take for granted that by operation of the law of merger an undivided third of the life tenant's freehold was thereby enlarged to a fee; but that such union of such part of his particular estate with such part of the immediate remainder in fee came to him by descent did not operate in any way to defeat, impair, or otherwise affect his own particular estate or the remainder. If it had the effect to merge the life tenant's whole legal estate, then it would be to be held for the use of the life tenant for life. See § 13, ch. 71, of the Code; Scott *v.* Scott (1868), 18 Gratt. 150, 160; Wiscot's Case (1599), 2 Coke 61. Crump *v.* Norwood, 7 Taunt. 362, goes to sustain the first view, and it would not affect the creditors of Lewis Couger, deceased, otherwise than as provided by § 5, of ch. 86 of the Code, making the heir liable to those entitled as creditors for the value thereof, with interest; and we see that he did by deed sell to defendant part of the standing timber trees here in controversy, which might have some bearing upon the case as to the remedy, and as to what would have been his liability, and what is the liability of his vendee growing out of his relation as life tenant to the owners of the remainder in fee, as governed by the doctrine of waste." McDodrill *v.* Pardee, etc., Lumber Co., 40 W. Va. 564, 21 S. E. 878.

If a tenant in common takes possession of the premises to the exclusion of his cotenant, and leases the same to third parties for the purpose of the mining and removal of the coal there-from, at a specified sum per ton, as royalty for the coal so removed, the cotenant so excluded may require an accounting to him for his just proportion of such royalty, as the proper measure of damages for such waste. Cecil *v.* Clark, 49 W. Va. 459, 39 S. E. 202.

When a tenant so taking possession and leasing the premises for operating the coal purchases front lands in his own right, and not as common property, which are absolutely essential for right of way for the removal of the coal, in accounting to his cotenant for his proportion of the royalty when the tort has been waived, legal interest on the amount of money invested in the purchase of such front lands is a just compensation for the use thereof. Cecil *v.* Clark, 49 W. Va. 459, 39 S. E. 202.

f. Jointly and Severally Liable.

Cotenants, who commit waste, are liable to each other jointly or severally for the damages. McDodrill *v.* Pardee, etc., Lumber Co., 40 W. Va. 564, 21 S. E. 878.

C. RENTS AND PROFITS.
1. At Common Law.

At common law neither a joint tenant, tenant in common, nor copaicener occupying the common property, and thus taking more than his share of the rents and profits, can be made to account to his fellows, unless he has been appointed bailiff or receiver by them. Each one has a right to enter and use the land, and this right can not be impaired by the fact that the others absent themselves or do not claim their right to a common enjoyment. Unless the one in possession denies the right of the others to enter and enjoy the estate, or agrees to pay rent, nothing can be claimed of him. It is presumed that the others consent to his use. He can not call on the others to help him farm or otherwise use the property, and, in case of loss from failure of crops or other cause, he can not call on the others to contribute to the loss. If the others do not wish to occupy the premises with their co-owners, the remedy of partition is at hand, or, if the property is indivisible, the court will sell it and divide the proceeds. Ward v. Ward, 40 W. Va. 611, 21 S. E. 746, 52 Am. St. Rep. 911; 2 Min. Inst. (4th Ed.) 475. See also, Graham v. Pierce, 19 Gratt. 28, 100 Am. Dec. 658.

2. Under the Statutes.

a. In General.

"By § 14, ch. 100, W. Va. Code, it is provided that an action of account may be maintained 'by one joint tenant or tenant in common, or his personal representative, against the other for receiving more than comes to his just share or proportion, and against the personal representative of any such joint tenant or tenant in common.' This statute originated in England, and there and in a majority of the American states it has received the construction, which I would think the proper one, that merely by exclusive occupation and use one tenant in common or joint tenant does not become liable to account to others, but only where he receives rent or proceeds of the estate from strangers. Freem. Coten., § 274; note to Early v. Friend, 16 Gratt. 21, 78 Am. Dec. 649; Chambers v. Chambers, 14 Am. Dec. 585, and note. But in Early v. Friend, 16 Gratt. 21, 78 Am. Dec. 649, which was decided at a date making it binding authority here, it is held, that one tenant in common may sue his cotenant, who has occupied the whole property, for an account of rents and profits. He is accountable whether he receives rents and profits from strangers, or receives them by occupying the premises himself, with interest from each year's close. Rust v. Rust, 17 W. Va. 901, holds just the same. In Dodson v. Hays, 29 W. Va. 577, 2 S. E. 415, syllabus 2, this doctrine was somewhat qualified in the holding that where the property is such as to admit of use by several, and less than his just share is used by one tenant in common in a manner not hindering or excluding the others from the use of their shares, he does not receive more than his share, within the meaning of § 14, ch. 100, Code, and is not accountable for the profits of that portion owned by him to his cotenants." Ward v. Ward, 40 W. Va. 611, 21 S. E. 746, 748, 52 Am. St. Rep. 911.

b. Illustrative Cases.

Tenant Not Liable for Rents and Profits unless He Has Received More than His Just Share.—Every tenant in common has a right to possess, use and enjoy the common property, without being accountable to his cotenants for rents and profits, except when he has received more than his just share thereof. Graham v. Pierce, 19 Gratt. 28, 100 Am. Dec. 658.

Where a tenant of land claims under a tenant in common adversely to other tenants in common, he will, in respect to rents and profits, be treated as a tenant in common with them. Ruffners v. Lewis, 7 Leigh 720, 30 Am. Dec 513.

Where a tenant in common uses the land for purposes allowable by law to a tenant in common, but uses no more than his share, and does not exclude his cotenants, he is not accountable to him for rents and profits. Cecil v. Clark, 47 W. Va. 402, 35 S. E. 11.

Necessity for Being Paid by Stranger.—By the words in the statute: "For receiving more than comes to his just share or proportion," it was held, that the legislature intended to make a tenant in common accountable to his cotenant for receiving more than his just share or proportion of the rents and profits, whether paid by a stranger or derived from his own occupation and enjoyment of the property. Early v. Friend, 16 Gratt. 21, 78 Am. Dec. 649.

No Liability Where Tenant Has Received No Rents and Profits.—Where one tenant in common holds the common property to the exclusion of his cotenant, he is not chargeable with rents or profits where none have been made, provided he has employed the property in good faith with a view to make it profitable, but has failed in doing so; nor is he chargeable with speculative profits where the real profits are susceptible of being ascertained. Ruffners v. Lewis, 7 Leigh 720, 30 Am. Dec. 513.

Where one cotenant solely occupies and uses the common property, and derives all the benefit which they could have derived from it had they been the sole owners; and so occupy and use it as plainly to indicate that they considered themselves as renters of the property, and not as tenants in common merely, this is sufficient to maintain an action of account under the statute. Early v. Friend, 16 Gratt. 21, 78 Am. Dec. 649, citing Ruffners v. Lewis, 7 Leigh 720, 30 Am. Dec. 513.

Liability Where Premises Are Occupied by One Cotenant.—Where one joint tenant or tenant in common has the possession and sole enjoyment of the common property, he is accountable to his cotenants for receiving more than his proportionate share of the rents and profits of the common property, whether he has rented the property out or has occupied and used the whole property himself. Early v. Friend, 16 Gratt. 21, 78 Am. Dec. 649; Graham v. Pierce, 19 Gratt. 28, 100 Am. Dec. 658; White v. Stuart, 76 Va. 546; Rust v. Rust, 17 W. Va. 901; Dodson v. Hays, 29 W. Va. 577, 2 S. E. 415.

Whenever the nature of the property is such as not to admit of its use and occupation by several, and it is used and occupied by one only of the tenants in common; or whenever the property, though capable of use and occupation by several, is yet so used and occupied by one as in effect to exclude the others, he receives more than comes to his just share and proportion of the rents and profits in the meaning of the statute. Early v. Friend, 16 Gratt. 21, 78 Am. Dec. 649; Rust v. Rust, 17 W. Va. 901; Dodson v. Hays, 29 W. Va. 577, 2 S. E. 415.

If one tenant in common uses the common land, and excludes his cotenant, he is accountable to such cotenant, though he does not take beyond his just share of rents and profits. Cecil v. Clark, 47 W. Va. 402, 35 S. E. 11.

A brother and sister were joint tenants of a furnace, forge, and a large quantity of land derived from their father, and the brother, who had conducted the business for some years in the lifetime of his father, continued to carry it on with the assent of his sister, without any contract with her. Held, that he must account to his sister for her share of the profits, and though they had attempted to come to an agreement upon a rent which should be paid for her half of the property, and the brother seemed to have thought that his proposition had been acquiesced in, and did not keep such accounts as he should have kept to enable him to render the account of profits to her yet she was entitled to have the account taken, and to have her share of the profits. Newman v. Newman, 27 Gratt. 714.

Where one of the cotenants entitled to partition had the possession and enjoyment of the whole land for many years, through want of knowledge of the title of the other cotenants, to whom he made their title known immediately after it was discovered by himself, it was considered equitable upon a bill filed by them for partition that he should account for their proportions of the rents received by him, deducting his disbursements for securing the title; that all the leases and agreements of lease he had made of the land should be acquiesced in by the plaintiffs; and that for the part which he had sold he should pay the price received with interest from the time of sale, the time when he received it not appearing to be different from that of the sale. Interest would also have been allowed the other cotenants on their proportions of the rents received by him from the time of filing their bill; but by their consent it was allowed from the beginning of the next year after the last receipt. Carter v. Carter, 5 Munf. 108.

c. Interest.

Interest is to be paid upon the annual rent found to be due at the end of each year from the tenant in possession to his cotenant; and the interest should be upon the amount due at the end of each year. Rust v. Rust, 17 W. Va. 901; Early v. Friend, 16 Gratt. 21, 78 Am. Dec. 649; Dodson v. Hays, 29 W. Va. 577, 2 S. E. 415.

It is proper to charge interest upon estimated rents and profits, where the land is occupied by the consent of the owner, or where one tenant in common holds and enjoys the whole land by the consent of his cotenant. Vance v. Evans, 11 W. Va. 342.

A part owner, being ignorant of the title of the other partners, remained in possession and enjoyment of the whole land for many years, but made their title known to the other partners immediately after it was discovered by himself. Upon a bill filed by them for partition, it was considered equitable, that he should account for their proportion of the rents received by him, deducting his disbursements for securing the title; that all leases he had made of the land should be acquiesced in by the plaintiffs; and that for the part he had sold he should pay the price received, with interest from the time of sale; the time when he received it not appearing to be different from that of sale. Carter v. Carter, 5 Munf. 108.

Interest also would have been allowed the other partners, on their proportions of the rents received by him, from the time of filing their bill; but, by their consent, it was allowed from

the beginning of the next year after the last receipt. Carter v. Carter, 5 Munf. 108.

d. Measure of Liability.

Statement of General Rule.—As a general rule, where a tenant in common uses the common property to the exclusion of his cotenants, or occupies and uses more than his just share or proportion, the best measure of his accountability to his cotenants is their shares of a fair rent of the property so used and occupied by him. Graham v. Pierce, 19 Gratt. 28, 100 Am. Dec. 658; Early v. Friend, 16 Gratt. 21, 78 Am. Dec. 649; Newman v. Newman, 27 Gratt. 714.

"Says Judge Moncure, in Early v. Friend, 16 Gratt. 21, 53, 78 Am. Dec. 649: 'He is not a fiduciary, nor a trespasser, but has the right to occupy and use the property. When he rents it out, and receives the rent, there is no difficulty in ascertaining the amount for which he is accountable. When, instead of renting it out, he occupies and uses the whole, to the exclusion of his cotenants, and thus, in effect, becomes himself the renter, there is more difficulty; but it seems that the just and true rule is to charge him with a reasonable rent for the use and occupation of the property, in the condition in which it was when he received it, and to hold him accountable to his cotenants for their just share of such rents.' Ruffners v. Lewis, 7 Leigh 720, 30 Am. Dec. 513; Thompson v. Bostick, 1 McMul. Eq. 75; Holt v. Robertson, Id. 475; Hancock v. Day, Id. 69; Sturton v. Richardson, 13 Mees. & W. 17; Graham v. Pierce, 19 Gratt. 28; Newman v. Newman, 27 Gratt. 714." Paxton v. Gamewell, 82 Va. 706, 1 S. E. 92.

Where the common property is rented out by one tenant in common, he is accountable to his cotenants for their share of the rents he has received. And where he occupies and uses the whole property himself, he is liable to his cotenants for a reasonable rent for it in the condition it was when he took possession. Early *v.* Friend, 16 Gratt. 21, 78 Am. Dec. 649; Rust *v.* Rust, 17 W. Va. 901; Dodson *v.* Hays, 29 W. Va. 577, 2 S. E. 415.

The defendants, who were joint owners with others of certain salt works, occupied the joint property from January 1, 1861, to January, 1869, without the consent of the other joint owners. During these years an extraordinary profit was realized, which could not at the beginning of such occupation have been anticipated. The property was, however, destroyed by armed forces in 1864. Held, that the defendants were liable for a reasonable rent, based on the condition of the property at the time of their taking possession, but were not accountable to the plaintiffs for the extraordinary profits realized by them during their occupancy, nor were they liable to the plaintiffs for rent after the destruction of the property. White *v.* Stuart, 76 Va. 546.

Accounting for Slaves.—Testator, in the commencement of his will, says: "Willing to make some arrangement of my affairs and equalize my estate among my children, I do, hereby, make this my last will and testament." He then, after making a provision for his widow, which includes two slaves, proceeds: "The residue of my real estate to be sold upon a credit, one-third in hand, and the other two-thirds in two equal annual payments, secured by a deed of trust upon the land; the balance of my slaves to be equally divided among my children, with those slaves which I have heretofore lent to my children, or their value; the remaining part of my personal estate to be sold and equally divided among my several children, charging my daughter, A. F., for advancements with 450 dollars, my daughter, K. C., with 600 dollars, and my son, S. W., with 600 dollars, as the balance for the land sold him, for which he has a deed." The testator in his lifetime had given slaves to some of his children, and loaned slaves to others. Held: 1. The children must account for the slaves delivered to them, and their increase, as of their value at the time of the division of the estate; or if any of the slaves have been sold, and the value at the time of the division can not be ascertained, then for their value at the time of the sale. 2. If any of the slaves delivered to the children have died, the loss is to be borne by the estate. Baldwin, J., dissenting. Kean *v.* Welch, 1 Gratt. 403.

In Moorman *v.* Smoot, 28 Gratt. 80, 85, it is said: "Without undertaking, therefore, now to decide whether in a case such as this the party settling is liable only for the value at the death of the life tenant, where that value appears, it is sufficient to say that in the absence of proof upon that point the court is bound to adopt the price for which the slaves were sold as the sum with which the appellant is to be charged in his account with his cotenants. Kean *v.* Welch, 1 Gratt. 403; Cross *v.* Cross, 4 Gratt. 257."

Where Rent Agreed on.—Where a guardian, duly qualified, has agreed with a coguardian of a brother of his ward's upon a rent to be paid for a store, the joint property of himself and the ward, and occupied by such guardian, and has regularly accounted for such to the other guardian, and, on his own ward's marriage, has settled in full with her husband on that basis; and, after the lunacy of such husband, has settled in full with the wife, and has continued to pay the rent agreed upon to the parties entitled, without complaint, during several years, he can not afterwards, in an action brought by his ward, be compelled to account for a higher rate than that agreed upon and paid by him. Paxton *v.* Gamewell, 82 Va. 706, 1 S. E. 92.

"The next question is as to the liability of W. C. Paxton for rent beyond his agreement, and beyond his settlement of the same with the parties, by payments in full. Our statute provides (Code, ch. 142, § 14), that an action of account may be maintained by one joint tenant, or tenant in common, or his personal representative, against the other as bailiff, for receiving more than comes to his just share or proportion; that is, that the joint tenant who has received more than his just share or proportion shall account for rents and profits actually received, more than his just share or proportion. He is a bailiff, not as a bailiff at common law, bound to manage the estate to the best advantage, and make all the profits he can for the owners; to keep and render them a full account of his transactions; to be held liable, not only for rents and profits actually received, but also for such as might have been received without his default. He is in as of his own right, not that of another, and he is made a bailiff by the statute, not by reason of his holding the property, but by reason of his receiving more than his just share; and, in an action of account against him, it is a necessary averment of the declaration that he has received more than his just share. Says Judge Moncure, in Early v. Friend, 16 Gratt. 21, 53. 'He is not a fiduciary, nor a trespasser, but has the right to occupy and use the property. When he rents it out, and receives the rent, there is no difficulty in ascertaining the amount for which he is accountable. When, instead of renting it out, he occupies and uses the whole, to the exclusion of his cotenants, and thus, in effect, becomes' himself the renter, there is more difficulty; but it seems that the just and true rule is to charge him with a reasonable rent for the use and occupation of the property, in the condition in which it was when he received it, and to hold him accountable to his cotenants for their just share of such rents.' Ruffners v. Lewis, 7 Leigh 720, 30 Am. Dec. 513; Thompson v. Bostick, 1 McMul. Eq. 75; Holt v. Robertson, 1 McMul. Eq. 475; Han-

cock v. Day, 1 McMul. Eq. 69; Sturton v. Richardson, 13 Mees. & W. 17; Graham v. Pierce, 19 Gratt. 28, 100 Am. Dec. 658; Newman v. Newman, 27 Gratt. 714." Paxton v. Gamewell, 82 Va. 706, 709, 1 S. E. 92.

Abatement of Rent Where Premises Destroyed.—In the absence of express covenant to pay rent, the occupying tenant is not liable for the same, where the premises are destroyed, whatever the rule may be in case of such express covenant. White v. Stuart, 76 Va. 546.

The defendants, who were joint tenants with others of certain salt works, occupied the joint property from 1861 to 1869, without the consent of the other joint owners. The property was destroyed by armed forces in 1864. Held, that the defendants were not liable to the plaintiffs for rent after such destruction. White v. Stuart, 76 Va. 546.

Annual Rental.—A tenant in common in sole possession claiming exclusive ownership, taking petroleum oil, and converting it to his exclusive use, is liable to account on the basis of rents and profits, not for annual rental. Williamson v. Jones, 43 W. Va. 562, 27 S. E. 411.

In an action by a cotenant to recover mesne profits, if the defendant at the time of the inception of the cause of action had knowledge of the plaintiff's title, although he honestly believed that he held the superior legal title, the measure of damages is not the actual receipts, but is the fair annual rental of the property, with legal interest, less the taxes paid by the defendant. Bodkin v. Arnold, 48 W. Va. 108, 35 S. E. 980.

Occupying Tenant Not Liable for Rents and Profits Arising from His Own Expenditures.—But the occupying tenant is liable only for a reasonable rent for the property in the condition in which it was at the time it went into his possession. The cotenants are not entitled to the benefit of the issues and profits made by the application of the skill, labor and capital of the occupying tenant upon the property. Early *v.* Friend, 16 Gratt. 21, 78 Am. Dec. 649; Graham *v.* Pierce, 19 Gratt. 28, 100 Am. Dec. 658; White *v.* Stuart, 76 Va. 546; Rust *v.* Rust, 17 W. Va. 901; Moore *v.* Ligon, 30 W. Va. 146, 3 S. E. 572.

In ascertaining what is a reasonable rent, where the report of the commissioner is concurred in by the court below, the appellate court will not reverse except in case of palpable error. White *v.* Stuart, 76 Va. 546.

Meaning of Rental Value. — The rental value of land is its condition at the time the tenant obtains possession thereof. Moore *v.* Ligon, 30 W. Va. 146, 3 S. E. 572, citing White *v.* Stuart, 76 Va. 546, 566.

The true annual rental value of land is not the value of all the farm products which can possibly be realized from its use, when the land is stocked, farmed, and managed with the greatest skill and industry, but it is the price which a prudent and industrious farmer can afford to pay for its use, after taking into consideration the probable amount and the market value of his crops, and the probable injuries thereto resulting from the ordinary changes of climate and season. Moore *v.* Ligon, 30 W. Va. 146, 3 S. E. 572.

Issues and Profits. — But there may be peculiar circumstances in a case making it proper to resort to an account of issues, profits, etc., as a mode of adjustment between the tenants in common. Graham *v.* Pierce, 19 Gratt. 28, 100 Am. Dec. 658; Early *v.* Friend, 16 Gratt. 21, 78 Am. Dec. 649; Newman *v.* Newman, 27 Gratt. 714.

Thus in the case of a tenancy in common in lead mines, and account of issues and profits is the proper mode of adjustment. And in settling the accounts of the operating tenants, they should not be charged a certain sum per ton for the ore raised from the mine, or credited with an estimated sum per ton for raising the ore and manufacturing the lead; but each so operating, is to be charged with all his receipts and credited with all his expenses, including those for necessary improvements, on account of the operation of the mine. Graham *v.* Pierce, 19 Gratt. 28, 100 Am. Dec. 658. See Williamson *v.* Jones, 43 W. Va. 562, 27 S. E. 411.

Where the occupying tenant was allowed all his expenses, in carrying on the business, including $1,500 a year for his services, and interest on his capital employed in it until it became self-sustaining, and was also allowed by the decree three-fifths of the net profits, it was held that he at least could not complain of the decree. Newman *v.* Newman, 27 Gratt. 714.

B. and C. are joint tenants of a furnace, forge, and a large quantity of land derived from their father, and B. who had conducted the business for some years in the lifetime of his father, continues to carry it on with the assent of his sister, C., without any contract with C. B. having been allowed all his expenses in carrying on the business, including $1,500 a year for his services, and interest on his capital employed in it until it became self-sustaining, and then being allowed by the decree three-fifths of the net profits, he at least can not complain of the decree. Newman *v.* Newman, 27 Gratt. 714.

Though there were efforts between B. and C. to agree upon a rent which should be paid by B. to C. for her half of the property, and B. seems to have thought that his proposition was acquiesced in, and did not keep such accounts as he should have kept to enable him to render the account of profits to her, yet C. is entitled to have the account taken, and to have her share of the profits. Newman *v.* Newman, 27 Gratt. 714, following Graham *v.* Pierce, 19 Gratt. 28, 100 Am. Dec. 658.

Speculative Profits.—In an action by a cotenant to recover mesne profits, the true measure of damages is compensation for the actual loss sustained by the plaintiff in being deprived of the use of his property, and speculative profits, founded on an exaggerated notion of the real value of the property, are not recoverable. Evidence tending to establish such speculative profits is inadmissible, as it may mislead the jury in arriving at the fair rental value of the property. Bodkin *v.* Arnold, 48 W. Va. 108, 35 S. E. 980.

Trespass for Mesne Profits.—The act of 1 Rev. Va. Code, ch. 118, § 1, p. 468, which authorizes the recovery of damages in writs of right, intends such damages as may be recovered in actions of trespass for mesne profits. And as from the form of the pleading, the statute of limitations applicable to the mesne profits, can not be pleaded, the tenant may give it in evidence upon the trial; and the demandant's recovery of mesne profits will be for five years next before the bringing the writ of right down to the recovery of possession. Purcell *v.* Wilson, 4 Gratt. 16, cited in Woodyard *v.* Polsley, 14 W. Va. 211, 220; McCann *v.* Righter, 34 W. Va. 186, 191, 192, 12 S. E. 499.

Punitive Damages.—In an action by a cotenant to recover mesne profits, where the action is not founded on the want of probable cause and maliciousness, punitive damages are not recoverable, and evidence tending to establish the same is not admissible. Bodkin *v.* Arnold, 48 W. Va. 108, 35 S. E. 980; Glen Jean, etc., R. Co. *v.* Kanawha, etc., R. Co., 47 W. Va. 725, 35 S. E. 978.

e. Ascertainment of Amount of Rent.

"How is the amount of such rent to be ascertained? In regard to the appellants, I think there can be no difficulty. Mrs. Early's interest of one-fourth of two-thirds of the property, was leased by her guardian to Thomas R. Friend, at an annual rent of three hundred dollars, for a term of ten years, subject to be determined, after her arrival at age or marriage, at the election of her or her husband. She arrived at age in 1843, and married in 1846, but, as it is averred in the answer of Joseph Friend and not disproved nor denied, neither she nor her husband has 'ever expressed any wish to change the terms of respondent, holding under the lease aforesaid, and hence he has always hitherto regarded himself as holding and occupying under the original rent reserved.' The lease commenced December 25, 1836, and of course expired, if not determined before by election as aforesaid, December 25, 1846. There was no such election to determine it before, and therefore, by its terms, it continued in force until the last-mentioned day. And Joseph Friend having after that day continued to hold and use the property as before, without any objection on the part of Early and wife or her trustee, he might be considered holding, on the terms of the previous lease; according to the authorities cited by his counsel, to wit: 2 Rob. Prac. 378, 379 (new ed.); Hyatt *v.* Griffiths, 79 Eng. C. L. R. 505; Humphreys *v.* Franks, 36 Eng. L. & E. 429. In McKay *v.* Mumford, 10 Wend. R. 351, it was held, that the presumption of law, that a tenant who holds over after the expiration of his lease continues to hold under the landlord and on the terms of the lease, does not apply to a tenant in common who leases the undivided interest of his cotenant. 'The fact of his not leaving possession,' said the court, 'does not authorize the inference that he still intends to hold under the lease; on the contrary the presumption is, that he holds under his own title, which gives him a right to the possession and enjoyment of the whole estate, liable, however, to account to his cotenants at law, 1 R. S. 90, or in equity, 8 Cow. R. 304. This presumption of possession by virtue of his own title may undoubtedly be rebutted, and then he would hold, as to the moiety of his cotenant, as any other tenant and subject to the same rules of law.' If there be any such presumption it is rebutted in this case by the express admission of Joseph Friend that after the expiration of the lease 'he always regarded himself as holding and occupying under the original rent reserved.' I therefore think that the rent for the interest of Mr. Early during the whole period of the use and occupation of the property by the Friends ought to be at the rate paid by the lease." Early v. Friend, 16 Gratt. 21, 55, 78 Am. Dec. 649.

f. Joint and Several Liability.

Where defendants holding lands by a joint title are decreed to surrender possession, and pay rents and profits, they are not jointly and severally, but only jointly liable. Hite v. Paul, 2 Munf. 154.

g. Pleading and Practice.

Equity Jurisdiction.—One tenant in common may maintain a suit in equity against his cotenant, who has occupied the whole of the common property, for an account of rents and profits. Early v. Friend, 16 Gratt. 21, 78 Am. Dec. 649; Rust v. Rust, 17 W. Va. 901; Ruffners v. Lewis, 7 Leigh 720, 30 Am. Dec. 513.

The statutory action for rents and profits where one cotenant has received more than his proper share, does not apply to a case of waste by a cotenant. Cecil v. Clark, 47 W. Va. 402, 35 S. E. 11; Williamson v. Jones, 43 W. Va. 562, 27 S. E. 411.

Prayer for Relief.—On a bill claiming a share of a tract of land and asking for partition and for general relief, under the prayer for general relief there may be a decree for an account of rents and profits though not specifically asked for in the bill. Rust v. Rust, 17 W. Va. 901, citing Humphrey v. Foster, 13 Gratt. 653; Hall v. Pierce, 4 W. Va. 107, 113; Bank v. Arthur, 3 Gratt. 173.

3. Rule as to Parceners.

Neither at common law nor under § 14, ch. 100, of the West Virginia Code is one parcener, merely from sole occupation chargeable in favor of coparceners for rents, unless he excludes them. Ward v. Ward, 40 W. Va. 611, 21 S. E. 746, 52 Am. St. Rep. 911.

D. IMPROVEMENTS AND REPAIRS.

In General.—Where one tenant in common lays out money in improvements on the estate, although the money so paid does not in strictness constitute a lien on the estate, yet a court of equity will not grant a partition without first directing an account, and a suitable compensation. To entitle the tenant in common to an allowance on a partition in equity, for the improvements made on the premises, it does not appear to be necessary for him to show the assent of his cotenants to such improvements, or a promise, on their part, to contribute their share of the expense, nor, is it necessary for him to show a previous request to join in the improvements, and their refusal. The allowance of compensation for improvements is, in all cases, made, not as a matter of legal right, but purely from the desire of the court to do justice, and therefore the compensation will be estimated so as to inflict no injury on the cotenant, against whom the improvements are charged. Ballou v. Ballou, 94 Va. 350, 26 S. E. 840.

Where improvements, such as clearing and fencing and building a house, are done by one tenant in common with the assent of the others, or when they know that such improvements are being made and do not object, such tenant in common is entitled to the full benefit of the increased value of the land either by having his improvements assessed at the rate the land would have been worth before the improvements were made, or, if the land is sold, to have an additional part of the price allowed him, which shall be equal to the increased price obtained as the result of his improvements. Dodson v. Hays, 29 W. Va. 577, 2 S. E. 415.

"Improvements made by one cotenant, independent of any agreement so to do, may sometimes be proper matter to be considered in taking an account; but under what circumstances, and to what extent, improvements may be considered in taking an account between cotenants, can not be stated with desirable precision. It is probable, however that they will not be made a subject of compensation, unless they are of an usual character and necessary for the ordinary and conceded use of the property." Freeman's Cotenancy & Partition, § 279. Quoted in Williamson v. Jones, 43 W. Va. 562, 27 S. E. 411.

In the case of a tenancy in common lead mines, the operating tenant in common should have a credit in his account for improvements made by him which were necessary to his operation of the mine. Graham v. Pierce, 19 Gratt. 28, 100 Am. Dec. 658.

Where a tenant in common improves the property at his own expense, without the assent of his cotenants, limitations do not begin to run against the equity for compensation till a partition is asked. Ballou v. Ballou, 94 Va. 350, 26 S. E. 840.

Right to Recover Directly from Cotenant Denied.—Where a tenant in common improves the property at his own expense, without the assent of his cotenants, he can not maintain an action of assumpsit to recover any part of the costs of improvement from his cotenants. Ballou v. Ballou, 94 Va. 350, 26 S. E. 840.

One cotenant can not compel another to make improvements on the common property, nor maintain an action against him personally to compel contribution to the expense of improvements made thereon without his consent, express or implied, nor fix it as a lien on his interest in the estate, except that at common law by the writ of de reparatione facienda all the tenants could be compelled to unite in the expenses of the necessary repairs of a house or mill owned by them. Ward v. Ward, 40 W. Va. 611, 21 S. E. 746, 52 Am. St. Rep. 911.

Permanent improvements made by one coparcener, without the request or agreement of the others, are not chargeable to the others personally or upon their shares in the land; but, if made by their request or agreement, they are a debt upon them, and a lien on their shares in the land. Ward v. Ward, 40 W. Va. 611, 21 S. E. 746, 52 Am. St. Rep. 911.

Where one joint tenant or tenant in common, without denying his cotenant's title, and without his cotenant's consent, makes improvements, he can not charge him, nor hold exclusive possession until reimbursed by rents and profits. Williamson v. Jones, 43 W. Va. 562, 27 S. E. 411.

One joint tenant, tenant in common, or coparcener can compel others to contribute to make necessary repairs to a mill or house, after request to assist and refusal. But this compulsion is as to future repairs, not those already made by one of the co-owners. This compulsion only applies to mills and houses, not to fences or other repairs to other properties. Ward v. Ward, 40 W. Va. 611, 21 S. E. 746, 52 Am. St. Rep. 911.

Where, however, the property is not susceptible of partition, and must be sold to provide the proceeds, the coparcener who made repairs and permanent improvements shall receive out of the proceeds that amount by which the property, at the date of sale, remains enhanced in value from the improvements, not their original cost. Ward v. Ward, 40 W. Va. 611, 21 S. E. 746, 52 Am. St. Rep. 911.

Lien. — Where improvements are made with the consent of the cotenants, they are personally bound, and the demand is a lien on their shares. Ward *v.* Ward, 40 W. Va. 611, 21 S. E. 746, 750, 52 Am. St. Rep. 911, citing Houston *v.* McCluney, 8 W. Va. 135; Freem. Coten., § 262.

When two joint tenants of real estate agree with each other that one shall, with his own money, erect improvements on the real estate jointly held, and have lien on the interest of the other for the money so expended, the agreement, with the actual erection of the improvements by the one and the acquiescence of the other, constitutes such a lien as will be recognized and enforced in a court of equity. Houston *v.* McCluney, 8 W. Va. 135.

Where improvements are made with the consent of the cotenants, they are personally bound, and the demand is a lien on their shares. Ward *v.* Ward, 40 W. Va. 611, 21 S. E. 746, 52 Am. St. Rep. 911.

But such lien is not valid, and will not be enforced in favor of the tenant who erects the improvements, against a creditor of the other, who has caused his interest in the property to be attached or a purchaser under such attachment, whether the creditor attaching, or the purchaser under the attachment, have notice of the previous equitable lien or not. Houston *v.* McCluney, 8 W. Va. 135.

Allowance for Improvements on Partition.—On partition the part improved, if it can be done without injury to others, should be assigned to the improver; but, where this can not be done, the cost of improvement can not be charged to him to whom it goes. Ward *v.* Ward, 40 W. Va. 611, 21 S. E. 746, 52 Am. St. Rep. 911.

Where a tenant in common has laid out money in erecting buildings, or making other substantial improvements, the court may, in entering a decree in partition, direct that the portion of the premises which has thus been enhanced in value shall be assigned to him, or if this can not be

done conveniently and it becomes requisite to proceed to a sale, that the purchase money shall be so apportioned as to reimburse him for his outlay. Dodson *v.* Hays, 29 W. Va. 577, 2 S. E. 415.

Where, however, the property is not susceptible of partition, and must be sold to divide the proceeds, to coparcener who made repairs and permanent improvements shall receive out of the proceeds that amount by which the property, at the date of sale, remains enhanced in value from the improvements, not their original cost. Ward *v.* Ward, 40 W. Va. 611, 21 S. E. 746, 52 Am. St. Rep. 911. See Dodson *v.* Hays, 29 W. Va. 577, 2 S. E. 415.

Amount Allowed.—Where property is not susceptible of partition, and must be sold to divide the proceeds, the coparcener, who made repairs and permanent improvements, should be allowed out of the proceeds of the sale that amount by which the property, at the date of the sale, remains enhanced in value from the improvements, not their original cost. Ward *v.* Ward, 40 W. Va. 611, 21 S. E. 746, 52 Am. St. Rep. 911.

Setting Off Improvements against Rents and Profits. — Improvements made by a tenant in possession may be set off against the rents and profits due from him to his cotenant. Ruffners *v.* Lewis, 7 Leigh 720, 743, 30 Am. Dec. 513; Graham *v.* Pierce, 19 Gratt. 28, 100 Am. Dec. 658; Moore *v.* Ligon, 30 W. Va. 146, 3 S. E. 572. See Newman *v.* Newman, 27 Gratt. 714.

"It is not the case of one making improvements in good faith believing the land to be his. The common law denied such an one relief, and it is only allowed by statute. Va. Code, ch. 91. It seems that, where a tenant in common or joint tenant is called on for rents and profits in equity, he may deduct ordinary repairs on the principle that he who asks help from a court of equity must do equity. Hannan *v.* Osborn, 4 Paige 343; Ruffners v. Lewis, 7 Leigh 720, 743, 30 Am. Dec. 513; 2 Minor Inst. 420; 1 Story, Eq. Jur., § 655; Graham v. Pierce, 19 Gratt. 28, 100 Am. Dec. 658, syllabus 6; Freem. Coten., § 279. Where partition is made, the part improved should, if not prejudical to others, be allotted to the one who made improvements, estimating its value without improvements. 2 Minor Inst. 420; Patrick v. Marshall, 4 Am. Dec. 670; Nelson v. Clay, 23 Am. Dec. 387. But, if this can not be done, he to whom the improvement falls does not have to pay for it. Nelson v. Clay, supra. Where improvements are made with the consent of the cotenants, they are personally bound, and the demand is a lien on their shares. Houston v. McCluney, 8 W. Va. 135; Freem. Coten., § 262." Ward v. Ward, 40 W. Va. 611, 21 S. E. 746, 749, 52 Am. St. Rep. 911.

Where an accounting is had between tenants in common, the expenditures of each year should be offset against the rents and profits of that year, and the claim for improvements in any one year should be liquidated in whole or in part by the rents and profits of that or any succeeding year. Ruffners v. Lewis, 7 Leigh 720, 30 Am. Dec. 513.

In Ruffners v. Lewis, 7 Leigh 720, parties holding adversely to the plaintiff, were treated as tenants in common with them, and as they had bored wells, and had discovered and produced salt water, were allowed improvements, including the costs of the wells, as set-offs against rents and profits, and even for abortive wells, the court saying: "The plaintiffs, if they will have advantage from their successes, must be content to share their disappointments and failures. He who takes the profit must share the burden." See Williamson v. Jones, 43 W. Va. 562, 27 S. E. 411.

In an action by a cotenant to recover mesne profits, the defendant is not entitled to offset his improvements against the rent, if at the time they were made he had knowledge of the plaintiff's title, although he in good faith believed his own title to be the better, in point of law. Bodkin v. Arnold, 48 W. Va. 108, 35 S. E. 980.

There is a difference between the case where the party making improvements seeks, as an actor or plaintiff, to set up a debt against the co-owner or his land for improvements, and one where the co-owner calls on the other to account for rents and profits; for in the former case, generally, the party will fail, and in the latter, if the party has acted in good faith, he will be allowed to set off improvements. Williamson v. Jones, 43 W. Va. 562, 27 S. E. 411. See opinion in Effinger v. Hall, 81 Va. 94; 3 Pom. Eq. Jur., § 1241.

In an action of trespass for mesne profits, the defendant is not entitled to offset his improvements against the rent, if at the time they were made he had knowledge of the plaintiff's title, although he in good faith believed his own title to be the better in point of law. Bodkin v. Arnold, 48 W. Va. 108, 35 S. E. 980.

Repairs.—"The rule applicable in the matter of repairs is different from that in the case of improvements. In the former case the weight of authority is that, when the repair of joint property is necessary to its use and preservation, one joint tenant, when his fellows refuse to unite, may have the property repaired and sue for compensation, but we have been referred to no authority which holds that this can be done in the case of improvements." Ballou v. Ballou, 94 Va. 350, 26 S. E. 840.

Where the plaintiff in an action of trespass for mesne profits seeks, in addition to the rent, to recover damages for waste occasioned by the failure of the defendant to make proper repairs, the improvements made by the defendant in the general nature of repairs should be taken into consideration in estimating the general depreciation of the value of the property through fault of the defendant. Bodkin *v.* Arnold, **48** W. Va. 108, 35 S. E. 980.

E. WEAR AND TEAR.

In an action by a cotenant to recover mesne profits, the defendant is not liable for natural wear and tear resulting from the lapse of time and the proper use of the property, but only for the damages occasioned by his negligence, misuse, or abuse. Bodkin *v.* Arnold, 48 W. Va. 108, 35 S. E. 980.

F. PURCHASE OF OUTSTANDING CLAIM OR TITLE.

In General.—It is well settled that a co-owner of property, finding a defect in the common title, can not purchase an outstanding title except for the common benefit. This rule is based on the community of interest in a common title creating such a relation of trust and confidence between the parties that it would be inequitable to permit one of them to do anything to the prejudice of the others in reference to the common property. The principle applies equally to joint tenants, tenants in common, coparceners, and all others having a common interest. Forrer *v.* Forrer, 29 Gratt. 134, 144; Battin *v.* Woods, 27 W. Va. 58; Bowers *v.* Dickinson, 30 W. Va. 709, 6 S. E. 335; Gilchrist *v.* Beswick, 33 W. Va. 168, 10 S. E. 371; Weaver *v.* Akin, 48 W. Va. 456, 37 S. E. 600.

"A cotenant can not take advantage of any defect in the common title by purchasing an outstanding title or incumbrance and asserting it against his companions in interest. The purchase is, notwithstanding his designs to the contrary, for the common benefit of all the cotenants. The legal title acquired by him is held in trust for the others, if they choose, within a reasonable time, to claim the benefit of the purchase, by contributing, or offering to contribute, their proportion of the purchase money." Freeman on Cotenancy, § 154, quoted with approval in Va. Coal, etc., Co. *v.* Kelly, 93 Va. 332, 24 S. E. 1020.

Two partners purchased a tract of land for partnership purposes. After the death of one of the partners, it was discovered that the title to one-third of the land was defective, and the surviving partner purchased this third interest and took the conveyance to himself. Held, that his purchase was for the joint benefit of himself and the heirs of the deceased partner, and that they were entitled to claim it upon paying their share of the purchase money. Forrer *v.* Forrer, 29 Gratt. 134.

One of several coparceners claiming under an ancestor who has a defective title can not purchase the outstanding title, falsely state the consideration in his deed, conceal the fact of purchase from his coparceners, and then rely upon lapse of time to defeat their right to get the benefit of such purchase. Pillow *v.* Southwest Va. Imp. Co., 92 Va. 144, 23 S. E. 32.

In Cecil *v.* Clark, 44 W. Va. 659, 30 S. E. 216, a quære is raised as to whether it is necessary, to enable one tenant in common to share in the benefit of an adverse title or incumbrance purchased by a cotenant, that the two tenants shall have acquired their right by separate instruments; and also as to whether a tenant in common, who has ousted his cotenant and claims adversely, can buy for his sole benefit an adverse incumbrance or title.

Purchase of Tax Title.—Where a cotenant permits the common property to be sold for taxes, and directly or indirectly secures the title in his own name, his deed will be avoided at the instance of his cotenants, or he will be held to be a trustee holding the legal title for their mutual benefit. A purchaser of the common property from such cotenant, with notice of the character of his title, will be limited in his holding to the actual interest of his grantor in such property. Parker *v.* Brast, 45 W. Va. 399, 32 S. E. 269, citing Hall *v.* Clark, 44 W. Va. 659, 30 S. E. 216; Battin *v.* Woods, 27 W. Va. 58;

Curtis *v.* Borland, 35 W. Va. 124, 12 S. E. 1113.

If one of several tenants in common purchases the land held in common at a tax sale or from a stranger, who bought it at such tax sale, such title so acquired will inure to the benefit of all the tenants in common. Battin *v.* Woods, 27 W. Va. 58.

A tax purchase by one tenant in common of the land owned in common is but a redemption, and inures to the benefit of the cotenants. The same is true in regard to a purchase under a sale of land under the common title forfeited for taxes, and sold by a commissioner of school lands. Cecil *v.* Clark, 44 W. Va. 659, 30 S. E. 216.

Notice.—In such case, before the cotenant can be held to have abandoned the benefit of the purchase, it must appear not only that he knew of the purchase, but of an adverse claim to its exclusive benefit, set up by his cotenant. He may reasonably presume the acquisition was made to support, not to defeat, the common title. Cecil *v.* Clark, 44 W. Va. 659, 30 S. E. 216; Buchanan *v.* King, 22 Gratt. 414; Rust *v.* Rust, 17 W. Va. 901, 905.

And in such case, the burden is upon the purchasing tenant to show that his cotenant had notice of the purchase and of the exclusive claim asserted by him. Buchanan *v.* King, 22 Gratt. 414.

When several parties, as tenants in common, own lands subject to a mortgage, and they enter into an arrangement by which one of such owners, with other parties, agrees to pay off the mortgage or buy in the land, and hold it subject to redemption by the other owners, and such arrangement is not fully complied with, but one of the owners, without explicit notice to the others that he is not acting under said arrangement, buys in the land for his own benefit for the balance due on the mortgage debt, which is less than one-tenth of the value of the lands, a court of equity will hold that the purchase was made for the benefit of all the owners. Gilchrist *v.* Beswick, 33 W. Va. 168, 10 S. E. 371.

If one of several joint owners of a lease, to cure a defect therein, takes an additional lease in his own name, he will be presumed to be acting for the common benefit of all the owners, and that such additional lease is a confirmation of the original lease. To oust his co-owners of such benefit, the second lessor must show that, after they had notice by his acts or words that he had intended to hold his lease adversely to them, they delayed for an unreasonable time in accepting the terms thereof. If for eleven months, by his conduct, letters and words, he leads his co-owners to believe that he has no intention of asserting the second lease in avoidance of the first, but during this period they continue mutually enjoying and developing the common property, he can not suddenly, and without reasonable notice to them, set up sole ownership under the second lease, and in this manner destroy the common ownership under the first. The dealings between co-owners must be fair and open, and free from deception and evil appearances. Weaver *v.* Akin, 48 W. Va. 456, 37 S. E. 600.

Different Owners of Soil and Minerals.—Although a cotenant can not take advantage of any defect in the common title by purchasing an outstanding title or incumbrance, and asserting it against his companions in interest, yet the owner of the surface of the land and the owner of the minerals under it, where each holds a separate and distinct title, are neither joint tenants, nor tenants in common. They are not the owners of undivided interests in the same subject, but are the owners of distinct subjects of entirely different natures. The title to the freehold of the one, either in the surface or the minerals, can not be acquired by adverse possession of the other, and the purchase of the outstanding title by the one does not enure to the benefit of the other. In the case at bar the evidence does not support the claim of a resulting trust or a constructive trust in favor of the appellant. Virginia Coal, etc., Co. *v.* Kelly, 93 Va. 332, 24 S. E. 1020.

G. SALE, CONVEYANCE OR LEASE OF COMMON PROPETY.

In General.—All purchases or sales made of or in respect to the common property of such joint owners by one of them, though made for his own benefit, will, at the option of his co-owners, be declared by a court of equity to be for the common benefit of all the owners. Gilchrist *v.* Beswick, 33 W. Va. 168, 10 S. E. 371.

Form and Sufficiency of Contract.— A release, and not a feofment, is the proper form of conveyance by one joint tenant to another. Patton *v.* Hoge, 22 Gratt. 443, 451.

"A feofment, and not a release, is the proper assurance between tenants in common." Patton *v.* Hoge, 22 Gratt. 443, 451.

A contract for the sale of joint property reduced to writing and signed by only one of two joint owners may be specifically enforced against both, according to the principle of law that the acts of one joint tenant in relation to the joint property, is the act of and for the benefit of all his cotenants unless specifically shown or stipulated to the contrary or repudiated. Elbon *v.* Adams, 44 W. Va. 237, 30 S. E. 150.

The enforcement of a contract for the sale of property belonging to joint tenants, reduced to writing but signed by only one of the joint owners, can not be defeated under the statute of frauds. Elbon v. Adams, 44 W. Va. 237, 30 S. E. 150.

Conveyance by Metes and Bounds.— A deed from a cotenant of a part of the land held in common, describing it by metes and bounds, can not in any way operate to the prejudice of the other tenants in common. They have the right to have the land partitioned, un-

affected by such deed. But in a partition in such a case a court of equity will allot the portion so conveyed to the purchaser thereof, if it can be done without prejudice to the rights of the other cotenants. Such a deed will become operative and pass the land to the grantee by metes and bounds, if the other tenants in common before partition confirm and ratify it, and after partition if that portion is allotted to the purchaser thereof; and in either case such deed will be binding on both the grantor and grantee. Worthington *v.* Staunton, 16 W. Va. 208; Boggess *v.* Meredith, 16 W. Va. 1; Robinett *v.* Preston, 2 Rob. 272, 273; Cox *v.* McMullin, 14 Gratt. 82; Buchanan *v.* King, 22 Gratt. 414, 422.

Although the party holding in common with others can do nothing to impair or vary in the slightest degree the rights of his cotenants, yet if he executes a deed for the specific portion of the common subject, or makes a contract in regard to it, and upon partition such portion falls in severalty to the parties so making the deed or contract, he will be bound by his act. Cox *v.* McMullin, 14 Gratt. 82. See also, McKee *v.* Barley, 11 Gratt. 340, 346; Robinett *v.* Preston, 2 Rob. 272, 273.

Title and Rights of Grantee.—A cotenant may convey at his pleasure his undivided interest in all the lands held in common without the knowledge or consent of his companions in interest. In this case the effect of the deed is to place the grantee in the deed in the same position that the grantor had previously occupied, and no possible injury could result to the other cotenants in the tract. Worthington *v.* Staunton, 16 W. Va. 208.

A deed from a tenant in common carries to the grantee only an undivided interest in the property, no matter by what description the property is conveyed. Woods *v.* Early, 95 Va. 307, 28 S. E. 374; Parker *v.* Brast, 45 W. Va. 399, 32 S. E. 269.

Sale to Partners.—"It is also well

settled that if real estate be purchased with partnership funds for partnership purposes, and used as partnership property, and the deed conveys the real estate to the individual partners, though such deed conveys the legal title of the land to them individually as tenants in common, or as joint tenants, yet upon the face of the deed it appears that they were partners, and the land was purchased for partnership uses, they will hold such land as trustee for the partnership, as against all creditors of one of the individual partners, whether claiming by judgment liens against him, by a deed of trust executed by him to secure his individual debts, or in any other manner." Cunningham *v.* Ward, 30 W. Va. 572, 5 S. E. 646, 649.

Conveyances between Parties.—A conveyance from one coparcener to another coparcener of his undivided interest in the common land does not pass his pre-existing demand against his coparceners or their interests in the land for improvements put upon the land, unless such demand is expressly released or transferred in the conveyance. Ward *v.* Ward, 50 W. Va. 517, 40 S. E. 472.

Sale of Entire Interest without Authority of All Tenants.—W. and his sisters, E., R. and M., were the joint owners of a tract of land. In 1863, E. and R., without authority from W. and M., but believing that they would concur, sold the whole tract to K. for $30,000 cash. On the 1st of April, 1863, a writing under seal was prepared, stating the contract, and drawn to be signed by the four owners. E. and R. and K. then signed it, and on that day and the next K. paid to G. and R. $25,509.33. Before the writing was signed, E. wrote to W., stating what they proposed to do, and W. replied, that he would sell his interest to K. for $7,500; K. to give his bond for one-half on demand, and the balance in one and two years, all secured by a lien on the land. This letter was shown to K., who proposed to pay $1,000 cash, and give his bonds

for the balance of the purchase money. E. objected, that this would not be satisfactory to W., but R. agreed to it, and K. paid her the $1,000, and executed his bonds to W., which he delivered to R., and R. handed to the wife of W. the $1,000, and K. was then put in possession of the land by E. and R., and continued to hold it. In June W. returned home on sick leave, and in a brief interview with K. he said, you have executed your bonds for the balance of the purchase money, and K. said he had, and would like him to go to Mr. C.'s and sign the contract; which W. did. At this time, W. says in his evidence, he had not seen the bonds, and did not know that K. had paid the $1,000. M. did not sign the paper, but refused to concur in the sale, though K. says he did not know until she filed her answer in his suit that she refused. In 1868 K. filed his bill against W., E., R. and M. to enforce the contract. Held, the arrangement between R. and K., as to the interest of W., not having been authorized by him, he was not bound by it. Kemper *v.* Ewing, 25 Gratt. 427.

Sale of Moiety.—J.'s devisees and W. are tenants in common of a hotel property, and J.'s executor and W. agree to sell the property at public auction; the deferred payments to be secured by separate bonds to each for his half of the purchase money, with a lien retained on the real property. The sale is made and W. becomes the purchaser, but refuses to execute the contract. J.'s executor sues W. for specific execution of the contract, and there is a decree in 1868 in his favor for specific execution, a personal decree against W. for the amount due, and for a sale of the whole property. Before the decree W. sells and conveys his moiety of the property to M. who pays the purchase money. Upon a bill by the judgment creditors of M. to subject his moiety of the property to the payment of their debts; held, W. bought at the sale but J.'s moiety of the property, and the lien of J.'s executor's decree only extends to that moiety, though the whole property was sold under the decree. Johnson *v*. National Exchange Bank, 33 Gratt. 473.

Abandonment of Purchase by Co-Owner.—"In the case of Cecil *v*. Clark, 44 W. Va. 659, 660, 30 S. E. 216, it was held, that 'before a cotenant can be held to have abandoned the benefit of the purchase, it must appear not only that he knew of the purchase, but of an adverse claim to its exclusive benefit set up by his cotenants. He may reasonably presume the acquisition was made to support, not to defeat, the common title.' Before abandonment can become conclusive so as to defeat a suit for partition, the co-owners must delay an unreasonable time after they have notice that the purchaser of the adverse title intends to hold it for his exclusive benefit; that is, an unreasonable time after they have been denied participation therein and there is a material change in the condition of the property or the circumstances of the parties." Weaver *v*. Akin, 48 W. Va. 456, 461, 37 S. E. 600.

Rescission and Cancellation.—If a tenant in common convey with covenant of general warranty a part of the common subject by metes and bounds, and upon partition afterwards made a material part of the land so conveyed is allotted to other tenants in common, so that the purchaser does not obtain the substantial inducement to his contract of purchase, upon the prayer of such purchaser a court of equity will cancel and annul such deed, and place the parties in statu quo. Worthington *v*. Staunton, 16 W. Va. 208.

M. on behalf of himself and P., joint owners of a tract of land, by contract under seal—but which contract was not authorized by P.—sold the same to A. receiving from A. on account of the cash payment $250, and $50, and A. also paid out for surveying the land for M. $255; afterwards at the suggestion and request of M. the contract was mutually, orally, rescinded, M. agreeing to repay to A. the said three sums so paid by A., with interest, M., acting upon such oral rescission resold the land to other parties. Held, that A. could recover in assumpsit from M. the money so paid by him. Arbogast *v*. Mylius, 55 W. Va. 101, 46 S. E. 809.

Lien for Payment of Purchase Money.—W., Z. and Y. are partners and joint tenants of real estate. W. and Z. sell their two-thirds interest in the real estate to Y., W. receiving $400 in cash for his interest, and Y. executing to Z. three notes, payable at different dates, amounting to $700, for his interest. The deed from W. and Z. to Y., which conveys the two undivided thirds of the property, reserves a lien as follows: "And the said Z. hereby retains a lien on the property hereby conveyed as security for the payment of the above recited notes received in payment of his interest; the said W. has been paid up in full for his interest." The lien is reserved on the two-thirds of the real estate conveyed in the deed. Patton *v*. Hoge, 22 Gratt. 443.

"Though the common-law right of survivorship in estates of joint tenancy has been abolished in Virginia by statute, yet many of the common-law incidents of the estate still remain, and especially the entirety of possession of each tenant, as well of every part as of the whole. When, therefore, two of these three joint tenants conveyed, or rather released, their interest in the joint subject to the other, they released an interest which pervaded the whole subject, and the lien which was expressly retained on the property conveyed by the deed naturally and properly, as well as literally, bound the whole property conveyed, embracing the interest of both of the grantors. Suppose the three joint tenants had joined in a conveyance of the whole property to a stranger, for a consideration payable to them all, and had expressly retained in the deed a lien on the property thereby conveyed for the security of the purchase money. Would not that lien have bound the whole property, and every part of it, for the payment of the whole consideration and every part of it? Certainly it would. Suppose one of the three grantors had received in cash his third of the purchase money; would not the same lien have existed in regard to the remaining two-thirds due to the other two grantors? Certainly it would. What difference can it make that two of the joint tenants release their interest to the third, and retain a lien on the property released for the payment of that part of the purchase money not paid in hand, though it be due and payable to one only of the releasors? What reason can there be for confining the lien to one-third only of the property, instead of extending it to the two-thirds conveyed? In this case, the whole consideration of the deed was $1,150, of which only $450 was paid to Williams, while the remainder, $700, was secured to Zimmerman. Why was this unequal division made of the purchase money, if they were equally interested in the subject conveyed? In law they were jointly and equally entitled; but in equity they may and must have been unequally entitled. The three had been partners, and we do not know what was the state of their accounts when the deed was made. It was such, however, between Williams and Zimmerman as that the latter was entitled to nearly two-thirds of the purchase money of their interests in the property. And if so, then in equity Zimmerman was entitled to nearly two-thirds of the property conveyed. We see in this a special reason for retaining a lien on the whole property conveyed for the payment of the purchase money due to Zimmerman. Then again, the subject conveyed embraced other property besides the tanyard, and the purchaser, Young, was to pay off the debts of the concern. Those debts, for aught we know, may consume the whole assets of the concern, besides the tanyard, and thus leave a subject for the operation of the lien in favor of Zimmerman not more than sufficient to discharge it. We see in this also a special reason for extending the said lien to the whole property conveyed." Patton v. Hoge, 22 Gratt. 443, 451.

Specific Performance.—"And a distinction is very properly recognized by the courts between the case of a vendor seeking to compel the vendee to perform, and that of the vendee asking a performance by the vendor. Though, therefore, the courts have refused, as in Dalby v. Pullen, 3 Sim. R. 29, and in other cases, to compel a vendee, who has contracted for the entirety of an estate, to take undivided aliquot parts of it, it by no means follows that it is improper to compel the vendor to convey such undivided parts, where the vendee is willing to accept them, with a proper abatement of the price, in lieu of the whole estate for which he contracted. On the contrary, in the case of the Attorney General v. Day, 1 Ves. sen. 218, Lord Hardwicke, whilst refusing to compel a vendee who had contracted for an entire estate, to take a moiety (a conveyance of the other by change of circumstances being impracticable), said: "On the other hand, if on the death of one of the tenants in common who contracted for a sale of the estate, the purchaser brings a bill against the survivor, desiring to take a moiety of the estate only, the interest in the money being divided by the interest in the estate, I should think (though I give no absolute opinion as to that) he might have a conveyance of the moiety from the survivor, although the contract can not be executed against the heirs of the other." The same principle is fairly to be deduced from the case of Roffey v. Shallcross, 4 Madd. R. 227, and also from a decision of Lord Eldon, in Ex parte Tilsley, reported in the note to that case; and is, I think, fully sustained in Sugden on

Vendors, vol. 1, 415-426, 7th Am. Ed. as well in the text as in the authorities cited in the notes. It is suggested that these views are in conflict with the decision of this court in Bailey v. James, 11 Gratt. 468. On an examination of that case it will be seen, that it is wholly different in character from the one before us. And I mentioned it only because of the suggestion just m ntioned, and for the purpose of saying that I do not mean to call in question the authority of that case by anything said in this." Clarke v. Reins, 12 Gratt. 98, 113.

"The wife being one of three equal joint owners of the land, and they and the husband having united in the sale, though the husband and wife will not be compelled to execute the contract on their part, the other two joint owners will be compelled to convey their undivided interests, upon the payment by the vendee of their shares of the purchase money." Clarke v. Reins, 12 Gratt. 98.

Lease.—One joint tenant, coparcener, or tenant in common, although he has a right to the possession of the whole against strangers, can not make a valid lease for more than his own part of the land; and, therefore, no more can be recovered in ejectment than the part to which the lessor, who is a joint tenant, tenant in common, or parcener, is entitled. Allen v. Gibson, 4 Rand. 468, 477.

If one of several joint owners of a lease, to cure a defect therein, takes an additional lease in his own name, he will be presumed to be acting for the common benefit of all the owners, and that such additional lease is a confirmation of the original lease. Weaver v. Akin, 48 W. Va. 456, 37 S. E. 600.

"It was his duty to have given them notice that unless within a certain reasonable time they accepted the terms of his lease he would deem the same abandoned by them, and would claim the exclusive benefit thereof, and until he did so they had the right to presume

he was acting for the common benefit. Cecil v. Clark, 44 W. Va. 660." Weaver v. Akin, 48 W. Va. 456, 37 S. E. 600.

Sale of Interest of Insane Persons. —In a proceeding by a committee of an insane person, under ch. 83, W. Va. Code, to sell the undivided interest of such insane person in the oil and gas underlying a tract of land, the cotenants of such person are not necessary or proper parties to such proceeding. South Penn Oil Co. v. McIntyre, 44 W. Va. 296, 28 S. E. 922.

H. PAYMENT OF TAXES.

The payment, by a tenant in common, of one undivided fourth of a tract of land, of one-fourth of the taxes and damages, when the whole tract has been returned delinquent for the non-payment of taxes, will not prevent the forfeiture of the entire tract of land or of any part thereof; for the statute authorized the land to be redeemed, only when all the taxes and damages were paid. The whole tract had been forfeited, and an undivided part of it could not under the statute be redeemed. Smith v. Tharp, 17 W. Va. 221, 237.

I. PAYMENT OF PURCHASE MONEY.

Where two persons purchase a tract of land jointly, and one of them pays more than his proportion of the purchase money, while the other takes a conveyance of the whole to himself, the person who has advanced more than his share has a lien on the land for the money so advanced. Hays v. Wood, 4 Rand. 272.

In such case, if the plaintiff does not pray to subject the land, but only for a personal decree for the balance due, equity will have jurisdiction. Hays v. Wood, 4 Rand. 272.

A. and B. are joint purchasers of real property. They give their notes for the payment of the purchase money, and receive a conveyance from the vendor. B. becomes insolvent, and A. pays more than a moiety of the purchase money. A. has a lien on the property to reimburse him all that he has paid above one moiety of the purchase money, in preference to the creditors of B., claiming under a deed of trust from B., unless they appear to be purchasers without notice. Tompkins *v.* Mitchell, 2 Rand. 428.

J. ADVERSE POSSESSION.

See the title ADVERSE POSSESSION, vol. 1, p. 212.

. **Actual Ouster or Disseisin Necessary.**—As possession of one joint tenant, tenant in common, or parcener, is prima facie the possession of his fellow, it follows that the possession of one is never adverse to the title of the other, unless there be proved an actual ouster or disseisin, or some other act amounting to the total denial of the plaintiff's right as cotenant. In short, there must be an exclusive enjoyment of the property accompanied with a denial of all right on the part of those claiming as coparceners, inconsistent with the asserted rights of others. Fry *v.* Payne, 82 Va. 759, 1 S. E. 197; Purcell *v.* Wilson, 4 Gratt. 16; Parker *v.* Brast, 45 W. Va. 399, 32 S. E. 269; Buchanan *v.* King, 22 Gratt. 414; Lagorio *v.* Dozier, 91 Va. 492, 22 S. E. 239; Cooey *v.* Porter, 22 W. Va. 120.

As the possession of one cotenant is the possession of all, laches, acquiescence, or lapse of time can not bar the right of entry of a cotenant until the actual disseisin has been effected by some notorious act of ouster brought home to his knowledge. Parker *v.* Brast, 45 W. Va. 399, 32 S. E. 269.

"The possession of one joint tenant or tenant in common or parcener is the possession of the other, and the possession of Starkey being under one cotenant, and not adverse to him, it was the friendly possession of the other." McNeeley *v.* South Penn Oil Co., 52 W. Va. 616, 630, 44 S. E. 508.

A tenant in common, out of possession, has a right to rely upon the possession of his cotenant, as one held according to the title, and for the benefit of all interested, until some action is taken by the other evidencing an intention to assert adverse and hostile claims. Justice *v.* Lawson, 46 W. Va. 163, 33 S. E. 102.

"It is undoubtedly true that the possession of one parcener is ordinarily regarded as the possession of all the others, and such possession, being subordinate and not adverse, can not, however long continued, operate as a bar to his coparceners. But it is equally true that such parcener in possession may disseise his coparceners and from the time of such disseisin his possession will be adverse. That one coparcener, joint tenant or tenant in common may disseise his cotenants there can be no legal doubt. The law on that question is fully settled. McClung *v.* Ross, 5 Wheat. 116; Purcell *v.* Wilson, 4 Gratt. 16; Clarke *v.* McClure, 10 Gratt. 305; Caperton *v.* Gregory, 11 Gratt. 505." Cooey *v.* Porter, 22 W. Va. 120, 124.

A parcener in possession may disseize his coparcener; and from the time of such disseisin his possession will be adverse. Cooey *v.* Porter, 22 W. Va. 120.

A special verdict in a writ of right, where the defense is the statute of limitations, must find either an actual disseisin or ouster of the demandants, or those under whom they claim, or facts which in law constitute such actual disseisin or ouster. Purcell *v.* Wilson, 4 Gratt. 16.

Proof of Disseisin or Ouster.— Though a great lapse of time, with other circumstances, may warrant the presumption of a disseisin or ouster by one coparcener or tenant in common, of another not laboring under disabilities, this presumption is a matter of evidence for the consideration of the jury, and not a question of law for the decision of the court upon a special verdict. Purcell *v.* Wilson, 4 Gratt. 16.

In Stonestreet *v.* Doyle, 4 Gratt. 356, 379, the court, citing Purcell *v.* Wilson, 4 Gratt. 16, as its authority, said that.

although a great lapse of time, with other circumstances, may warrant the presumption of a disseisin or ouster by one tenant or tenant in common, this presumption is a matter for the consideration of the jury, and not a question of law for the court.

The notice or knowledge required must be actual, as in the case of a disavowal or disclaimer of any right in his cotenants; or the acts relied on, as in the case of expulsion, making costly improvements and exercising exclusive ownership, must be of such an open, notorious character as to be notice of themselves. Cooey v. Porter, 22 W. Va. 120.

If a party obtains possession of land from another's tenant, he himself becomes that other's tenant, and can not be heard to set up title or possession in himself adverse to that under which he entered. If he would set up adverse possession he must restore that acquired through the tenant of another, and assert his adverse claim, or he must bring home to the landlord or a cotenant notice of his adverse claim and holding under it, or he must actually oust the tenant. Genin v. Ingersoll, 2 W. Va. 558.

Possession as Evidence of Notice.— Possession of cotenants, who own equal undivided moieties, by a common tenant resident on the land at the time of a sale of the whole tract by one of the cotenants, is notice sufficient, where the evidence shows such possession by the common tenant, of title in the other cotenant to the purchaser, although the deed to the cotenant whose interest is sought to be wrongfully sold, is not recorded. Genin v. Ingersoll, 2 W. Va. 558.

Intention Governs.—"The authorities it seems to me fully sustain the doctrine that it is the quo animo, the intention of the tenant or parcener in possession to hold the common property in severalty and exclusively as his own, with notice or knowledge to his cotenants of such intention, that con-

stitutes the ouster; therefore, any open, notorious act evincing such intention, or any explicit disclaimer or denial of the claims of his cotenants, or the assertion of a several and individual estate or title in himself to the entirety of the common property, will operate as a disseisin or ouster of his cotenants, and from the time they have notice or knowledge of such act, disclaimer or assertion of title his possession will be adverse and the statute of limitations will commence to run. Clymer v. Dawkins, 3 How. 674; Jackson v. Smith, 13 Johns. 406; Caperton v. Gregory, 11 Gratt. 505; Terrill v. Murray, 4 Yerg. 104; Peeler v. Guilkey, 27 Tex. 355; Lodge v. Patterson, 3 Watts 74." Cooey v. Porter, 22 W. Va. 120, 125.

It is the intention of the tenant or parcener in possession to hold the common property in severalty, and exclusively as his own, with notice or knowledge to his cotenants of such intention that constitutes the disseisin. Justice v. Lawson, 46 W. Va. 163, 33 S. E. 102.

"'A tenant in common, out of possession, has a right to rely upon the possession of his cotenant as one held according to the title, and for the benefit of all interested, until some action is taken by the other evidence an intention to assert adverse and hostile claim.' Hignite v. Hignite, 65 Miss. 447, 4 South. 345. McClung v. Ross, 5 Wheat. 116: 'One tenant in common may oust his cotenant, and hold in severalty; but a silent possession, unaccompanied with any act amounting to an ouster, or giving notice to the cotenant that his possession is adverse, can not be construed into an adverse possession.' Pillow v. Southwest Va. Imp. Co., 92 Va. 144, 23 S. E. 32 (syl., point 4). Cooey v. Porter, 22 W. Va. 120 (syl., point 4): 'It is the intention of the tenant or parcener in possession to hold the common property in severalty, and exclusively as his own, with notice or knowledge to his cotenants of such intention, that constitutes the disseisin.' It is insisted by appellants that the conveyances by deed of trust of the whole of the tract by W. A. Dingess to James A. Nighbert, and recording of the same, was an act of ouster and adverse possession. 'If one cotenant executes and delivers a deed of the entire estate, and the grantee causes the deed to be recorded, and enters into possession claiming title to the entirety, and openly exercises acts of ownership, this is a disseisin of the cotenants.' Busw. Lim., § 300; Parker *v.* Proprietors, 3 Metc. (Mass.) 91." Justice *v.* Lawson, 46 W. Va. 163, 33 S. E. 102, 107.

Acts Constituting Disseisin.

In General.—"What acts will amount to a disseisin is not always easily determined. While on the one hand a silent possession, accompanied with no act which can amount to an ouster or give notice to his coparceners that his possession is adversary, will not be construed into a disseisin or adverse possession, still on the other hand, where one coparcener occupies the common property notoriously as the sole owner, using it exclusively, improving it and taking to his own use the rents and profits therefrom and otherwise exercising over it such acts of ownership as manifest unequivocally an intention to ignore and repudiate any right or claim of his coparceners, such occupation will amount to a disseisin of his coparceners, and his possession will be regarded as adverse from the time they have knowledge of such acts or occupation. Tyler on Eject. & A. E. 927. It may be affirmed as a general rule, well established, that if one joint owner show by his acts or words that he means to hold out his cotenants and actually exclude them, it is an ouster and his possession becomes adverse. Humbert *v.* Trinity Church, 24 Wend. 587; Brackett *v.* Norcross, 1 Greenl. 89; Hargrave *v.* Powell, 2 Dev. & Batt. L. 97; Cloud *v.*

Webb, 10 Dev. 290." Cooey *v.* Porter, 22 W. Va. 120, 124.

Though the entry and possession by one coparcener enures to the benefit of all in the absence of proof to the contrary, yet when it appears that the coparcener, entering and taking possession, claimed the property as his own under color of title; that he took the profits to his own exclusive use, and denied the title of the other coparceners, of all which they had notice; the party so taking and holding is regarded as having disseised his cotenant. Caperton *v.* Gregory, 11 Gratt. 505, 508, citing Purcell *v.* Wilson, 4 Gratt. 16, which is also cited in Hannon *v.* Hannah, 9 Gratt. 146, 153.

"The notice or knowledge required must be either actual as in the case of a disavowal or disclaimer; or the acts relied on as an ouster, as in the case of expulsion, making costly improvements and exercising exclusive ownership, must be of such an open, notorious character as to be notice of themselves or reasonably sufficient to put the disseised cotenants on inquiry, which, if diligently pursued, will lead to notice or knowledge in fact. Lefavour *v.* Homan, 3 Allen 354; Lodge *v.* Paterson, 3 Watts 74." Cooey *v.* Porter, 22 W. Va. 120, 125.

Open, Notorious and Exclusive Possession.—"In Newell on Ejectment, § 72, p. 763, it is said: 'The possession of one cotenant is the possession of all the rest. * * * But when one tenant in common occupies the common property openly, notoriously and exclusively as the sole owner, improving it and receiving to himself the rents and profits, or exercising over the property such acts of ownership as evidence an intention to ignore the rights of his cotenants, such acts will amount to a disseizin and his possession will be regarded as adverse to his cotenants from the time they are shown to have knowledge of such acts and claims'; and authorities there cited. See also, Buswell on Limitations and Adverse Possession, § 298, to the same effect. Cooey v. Porter, 22 W. Va. 120; and in Justice v. Lawson, 46 W. Va. 163, 33 S. E. 102 (syl., pts. 3 and 4), it is held: 'One tenant in common may oust his cotenant, and hold in severalty, but, a silent possession, unaccompanied with any action amounting to an ouster, or giving notice to the cotenant that his possession is adverse, can not be construed into an adverse possession.' 'It is the intention of the tenant or parcener in possession to hold the common property in severalty and exclusively as his own, with notice or knowledge to his cotenants of such intention that constitutes the disseisin.' " Cochran v. Cochran, 55 W. Va. 178, 180, 46 S. E. 924.

When one tenant in common occupies the common property openly, notoriously and exclusively as the sole owner, keeping up the improvements, paying the taxes thereon and receiving to himself the rents and profits, and exercising over the property such acts of ownership as evidence an intention to ignore the rights of his cotenants, such acts amount to a disseizin and his possession will be regarded as adverse to his cotenants from the time they are shown to have knowledge of such acts and claims. Cochran v. Cochran, 55 W. Va. 178, 46 S. E. 924, approved and applied in Rodgers v. Miller, 55 W. Va. 576, 47 S. E. 354.

Where one parcener occupies the common property notoriously as the sole owner, using it exclusively, improving it and taking to his own use the rents and profits, or otherwise exercising over it such acts of ownership as manifest unequivocally an intention to ignore and repudiate any right in his coparceners, such occupation or acts and claim of sole ownership will amount to a disseisin of his coparceners, and his possession will be regarded as adverse from the time they have knowledge of such acts or occupation and claim of exclusive ownership. Cooey v. Porter, 22 W. Va. 120

Silent Possession Can Not Be Construed as Adverse.—One tenant in common may oust his cotenant, and hold in severalty, but a silent possession, unaccompanied with any action amounting to an ouster, or giving notice to the cotenant that his possession is adverse, can not be construed into an adverse possession. Justice v. Lawson, 46 W. Va. 163, 33 S. E. 102; Lagorio v. Dozier, 91 Va. 492, 22 S. E. 239; Emerich v. Tavener, 9 Gratt. 220, 238. See also, Purcell v. Wilson, 4 Gratt. 16.

Though the entry and possession by one coparcener enures to the benefit of all in the absence of proof to the contrary, yet when it appears that the coparcener, entering and taking possession, claimed the property as his own under color of title; that he took the profits to his own exclusive use, and denied the title of the other coparceners, of all which they had notice; the party so taking and holding is regarded as having disseised his cotenant. Caperton v. Gregory, 11 Gratt. 505, 508, citing Purcell v. Wilson, 4 Gratt. 16, which case is cited in Hannon v. Hannah, 9 Gratt. 146, 153; Cooey v. Porter, 22 W. Va. 120, 124, and footnote to Caperton v. Gregory, 11 Gratt. 505, to the point that a tenant in common may disseise his cotenants.

Purchase by Person Claiming under Inferior Title.—Where a person claiming an inferior paper title to land held by cotenants under a superior possessory title obtains possession of the land by any device from the cotenant in actual occupancy thereof, without the knowledge of the other cotenants, his entry will be held to have been under the cotenancy possession, and not under his adverse paper title, and to so continue until perfect disseisin of the other tenants, either presumed from lapse of time or some notorious act of adversary possession or disseisin brought home to the knowledge of the other cotenants. The burden of establishing such perfect disseisin is on the person alleging it. Davis *v.* Settle, 43 W. Va. 17, 26 S. E. 557.

Payment of Taxes Does Not Constitute an Ouster.—The payment of taxes on an undivided third, or a conveyance of a portion by metes and bounds, not followed by actual entry and possession, does not constitute an actual ouster by one tenant in common of his cotenant. Hannon *v.* Hannah, 9 Gratt. 146

"A person out of possession, holding an inferior paper title, can not buy out a cotenant in actual possession, to the detriment of the other cotenants, and then claim to enter under his inferior title adversely to them; but he will be held to have entered into and hold under the cotenancy possession, until actual perfect disseisin of them, by presumption from lapse of time, or as is said in the case of Pillow *v.* Southwest Va. Imp. Co., 92 Va. 144, 23 S. E. 32, by 'a clear, positive, and continued disclaimer of title and adverse right, brought home to the knowledge of the other coparceners. In that case it was held, that to make constructive possession under an adverse title amount to perfect disseisin in favor of those entering under the cotenancy possession, it must have continued the statutory period of ten years. It is different, however, if the possession is not under the cotenancy, but is entirely independent thereof. Every presumption is in favor of the cotenancy if it once existed, and it devolves on him alleging to prove perfect disseisin, or nonentry under such possession. It has not been done in this case, as no actual knowledge of even claim of disseisin was brought home to the plaintiff until after the institution of his suit. A coparcener can not be disseised without his knowing it until lapse of time raises a presumption against him which he is unable to explain or rebut; so that the tenant and landlord together must be regarded as the cotenants of the plaintiff, for they have failed to establish

perfect disseisin. Nor do they claim to be purchasers for value without notice, but, with full knowledge, they took the risk of plaintiff's claim, and entered on the land, and improved the same. They, therefore can not be protected as innocent purchasers for value, without notice, although they may have sincerely believed that they would be able to defeat the plaintiff of his right to recover in any suit instituted by him." Davis *v.* Settle, 43 W. Va. 17, 26 S. E. 557, 561.

Receipt of profits and the payment of taxes does not amount to a disseisin or ouster of the cotenant. Lagorio *v.* Dozier, 91 Va. 492, 22 S. E. 239, citing Rowe *v.* Bentley, 29 Gratt. 756, 760; Purcell *v.* Wilson, 4 Gratt. 16; Hannon *v.* Hounihan, 85 Va. 429, 12 S. E. 157; Creekmur *v.* Creekmur, 75 Va. 430, 436.

Sale or Conveyance by Cotenant.— The sale or conveyance to a stranger by one joint tenant, tenant in common, or coparcener, of the entire estate, and the grantee enters into possession under a deed claiming title to the entirety, and openly exercises acts of exclusive ownership, this works an ouster or disseisin of the other coparceners or tenants in common, and makes the possession of the other coparceners or tenants his vendor's cotenants. Parker *v.* Brast, 45 W. Va. 399, 32 S. E. 269; Bennett *v.* Pierce, 50 W. Va. 604, 40 S. E. 395.

Acts of exclusive ownership by one of two cotenants, such as the open sale, conveyance, and delivery of possession thereunder of the whole subject matter, amount to a complete ouster of the other cotenant, and unless he brings suit within ten years thereafter his right of recovery will be barred by the statute of limitations. Talbott *v.* Woodford, 48 W. Va. 449, 37 S. E. 580.

One of two joint tenants purchased a large tract including the land held jointly, and took the conveyance to himself. He then sold the large tract. It was held that the grantee in th, deed was tenant in common with the cotenant of his grantor; and that his possession was, in presumption of law, the possession of all, and was to be deemed in support, and not in derogation of the common title. The acts of the joint tenant in taking the conveyance to himself and conveying to his grantee were not such acts as were equivalent to an actual ouster under the Code of 1860, ch. 135, § 15. Buchanan v. King, 22 Gratt. 414.

Where one of several tenants in common, who is in possession of the premises, conveys the same to a third person, who enters under such conveyance, claiming title to the whole, there is an ouster of the other tenants, which will bar their right of entry, if continued for the length of time required to establish title by adverse possession. Johnston v. Virginia Coal, etc., Co., 96 Va. 158, 31 S. E. 85; Bennett v. Pierce, 50 W. Va. 604, 40 S. E. 395.

If, after the right of action has accrued and the statute of limitations has begun to run, such ousted cotenant dies, leaving infant heirs, the statute continues to run, and their rights are barred, notwithstanding their disability, in the same number of years as would bar their ancestor. They do not inherit the land, but a mere limited right of action, with days already numbered; and, unless they or their friends take the necessary legal steps to save the same within the period fixed by statute, their right of action is forever lost. Talbott v. Woodford, 48 W. Va. 449, 37 S. E. 580.

The act of one cotenant in purchasing a large tract of land which includes the land held jointly, and taking the conveyance to himself, and conveying to his grantee part of the large tract including the land held jointly, are not such acts as are equivalent to an actual ouster under the Virginia Code of 1860, ch. 135, § 15. Buchanan v. King, 22 Gratt. 414.

The making of a deed for the whole property by a cotenant to a stranger is not such act of ouster, unless actual adverse possession is taken thereunder. Parker v. Brast, 45 W. Va. 399, 32 S. E. 269.

Void Deed of Conveyance.—Where one coparcener or tenant in common conveys by deed his interest to another, though the deed be ineffectual to pass the legal title, though void, yet it is color of title, and ten years' possession under it would bar the coparcener or tenant making the deed. Swann v. Young, 36 W. Va. 57, 14 S. E. 426; Swann v. Thayer, 36 W. Va. 46, 14 S. E. 432; Bennett v. Pierce, 50 W. Va. 604, 608, 40 S. E. 395.

Burden of Proof.—A grantor claiming the common title of the cotenancy under a deed from one of the cotenants is under the burden of showing some notorious act of ouster or adversary possession, which has ripened into perfect title by its unbroken continuation during the statutory period of ten years, with the full knowledge and acquiescence of the disseised cotenants. Parker v. Brast, 45 W. Va. 399, 32 S. E. 269.

Joint Property of Husband and Wife.—Possession by a purchaser under an executory contract of sale made by the husband alone, of land owned in joint tenancy by husband and wife, is not adverse to the wife. McNeeley v. South Penn Oil Co., 52 W. Va. 616, 617, 44 S. E. 508.

Before Right of Entry and Action.—When a husband by executory contract during coverture sells land owned by him and his wife as joint tenants, and the purchaser takes possession, and then the wife dies, and then the husband conveys to the purchaser the whole tract by deed, the possession is not adverse to the heirs of the wife until the husband's death, as until then they have no right of entry or action, and the statute of limitations does not run against them until then. McNeeley v. South Penn Oil Co., 52 W. Va. 616, 617, 44 S. E. 508.

"To make a conveyance of the whole

tract by one joint tenant to a stranger so operate (as an ouster), there must be a possession taken under that deed, attributable to it alone. Freeman on Co. Ten., § 226; Hannon v. Hannah. 9 Gratt. 146. 'The making of a deed for the whole property by a cotenant to a stranger is not such act of ouster, unless actual adverse possession is taken thereunder.' Parker v. Brast, 45 W. Va. 399, 32 S. E. 269 (point 5)." McNeeley v. South Penn Oil Co., 52 W. Va. 616, 636, 44 S. E. 508.

Quære. Where man and wife are jointly seised of land, her interest being separate, and adverse possession under a distinct hostile title begins during the coverture; but before the period fixed as a bar by the statute of limitations has run out, the wife dies leaving children and husband surviving her; does the statute stop running as to the heirs until the close of the curtesy by the death of the husband? Does his failure to sue affect them? Is there a second or separate right of entry or action accruing to the heirs at the husband's death? How, when the husband during coverture has conveyed to the occupant, by deed purporting to pass in fee the whole tract? Does the statute run against the heirs before the husband's death? McNeeley v. South Penn Oil Co., 52 W. Va. 616, 617, 44 S. E. 508.

"If one tenant in common convey the whole by deed passing legal title, it is an ouster of his cotenant, but not if it is only a contract for title, for it is not adverse there to either owner." McNeeley v. South Penn Oil Co., 52 W. Va. 616, 630, 44 S. E. 508.

Claim under Void Title.—The character of the title, under which the disseisor asserts his ownership, is entirely immaterial. It is the fact, that he claims the property as his own, and not the goodness of his title, that makes his possession adverse. Cooey v. Porter, 22 W. Va. 120.

"His claim may be founded on a defective or even a void deed or paper as well as upon a valid instrument, or it may be simply in pais without any paper or color of title and resting wholly upon a naked assertion of title or claim in himself accompanied by exclusive possession. Caperton v. Gregory, 11 Gratt. 505; Jackson v. Brink, 5 Cow. 483; Jackson v. Ellis, 13 Johns. 118; Jackson v. Long, 7 Wend. 170; Leonard v. Leonard, 10 Mass. 231; Jackson v. Huntington, 5 Pet. 401; Towle v. Ayer, 8 N. H. 57; Walker v. Wilson, 8 N. H. 217; Comins v. Comins, 21 Conn. 413; Tyler on Eject. & Ad. E. 887, and cases cited." Cooey v. Porter, 22 W. Va. 120, 125.

A brother and his married sister being the owners of land in coparcenary, the latter, in 1837, by a paper purporting to be a deed signed and acknowledged by her but without privy examination or joined therein by her husband, conveyed to the former her interest in said land, he being at the time in possession thereof and so continuing thereafter until his death in 1859, when his devisees succeeded him and continued in possession up to 1881, at which time the heirs of the sister brought suit for partition of the land, the sister having remained under coverture until a short time before her death, which occurred in 1879; the brother and his devisees during the whole period from 1837 to 1881, having occupied the land notoriously as sole owners, using it exclusively, taking the entire rents and profits, making costly improvements thereon, and otherwise exercising over it such acts of ownership, as manifested an unequivocal intention to repudiate any right or claim of the sister in the land. Held, notwithstanding said deed was void as a conveyance or contract of sale, it was sufficient prima facie to give notice of an intention to hold adversely; and the subsequent possession of the brother and his devisees, under the circumstances operated as a bar to the right of the sister, although she continued under coverture the whole time; and the plaintiffs' bill was properly dismissed. Cooey v. Porter, 22 W. Va. 120.

Entry by Leave of Tenant.—In the case of Fry v. Payne, 82 Va. 759, 761, 1 S. E. 197, it is said: "As to adverse possession, there was no such possession. He entered, by leave of his mother, upon her dower land, and at her death he continued in possession; and as the possession of one joint tenant, tenant in common, or parcener, is prima facie the possession of his fellow, it follows that the possession of one is never adverse to the title of the other, unless there be proved an actual ouster or disseisin, or some other act amounting to total denial of the plaintiff's right as cotenant. In this case there was no exclusive enjoyment of the property, accompanied with a denial of all right on the part of those claiming as coparceners. William Thomas was in possession, and used the land; but there was nothing inconsistent with the asserted rights of others. His possession was the possession of all. There never was any ouster by him."

Questions of Law and Fact.—The question of ouster is a mixed question of law and fact to be determined by the jury under proper instructions from the court. Doe v. Hill, 10 Leigh 457.

In Stonestreet v. Doyle, 75 Va. 356, 379, the court, citing Purcell v. Wilson, 4 Gratt. 16, as its authority, said that, although a great lapse of time, with other circumstances, may warrant the presumption of a disseisin or ouster by one joint tenant or tenant in common, this presumption is a matter for the consideration of the jury, and not a question of law for the court.

During Coverture.—In the case of Buford v. North Roanoke Land Co., 90 Va. 418, 18 S. E. 914, it was held, that there could be no adverse possession as against a cotenant under coverture.

K. CONTRIBUTION AN EXONERATION.

See the title CONTRIBUTION AND EXONERATION, vol. 3, p. 477.

Purchase of Outstanding Title.—Although it is a general rule that a joint tenant or tenant in common can not purchase for his exclusive benefit an outstanding adverse incumbrance or title to the common property, yet his cotenant, to participate in its benefit, must, within a reasonable time, make his election to claim its benefit and contribute to the expense of its purchase. If he unreasonably delays until there is a change in the condition of the property, or in the circumstances of the parties, he will be held to have abandoned all benefit arising from the new acquisition. Morris v. Roseberry, 46 W. Va. 24, 32 S. E. 1019; Cecil v. Clark, 44 W. Va. 659, 30 S. E. 216; Buchanan v. King, 22 Gratt. 414; Pillow v. Southwest Va. Imp. Co., 92 Va. 144, 23 S. E. 32. See also, Bowers v. Dickinson, 30 W. Va. 709, 6 S. E. 335. See Cosby v. Lambert, 1 Rob. 225.

Where a joint tenant or tenant in common has obtained the assignment of the sheriff's certificate of sale and purchase from a party who purchased the land so held in common at the sheriff's sale of delinquent land, and as such assignee has obtained a deed therefor, and a party claiming to be a joint tenant or tenant in common with the party obtaining such deed seeks by a bill in equity to have said deed set aside as a cloud upon his title, he must tender with his bill a sufficient amount to reimburse the party who so obtained said deed, the amount paid for him in redemption of the land, and all subsequent taxes paid by him thereon, with interest. Morris v. Roseberry, 46 W. Va. 24, 32 S. E. 1019.

One tenant who discharges a lien on the common property, or pays more than his share of the purchase price is entitled to rateable contribution from his cotenants. "The right of a cotenant, who discharges an encumbrance upon the common property, or pays more than his share of the purchase price, to rateable contribution from his cotenants, is said to arise out of the trust relationship which exists among joint owners of property, rather than by way of subrogation. But whatever may have been its origin, the doctrine is firmly established by the authorities." Grove *v.* Grove, 100 Va. 556, 561, 42 S. E. 412.

The right of a tenant to enforce against the share of his cotenant the equitable lien arising from the payment, by the tenant, of more than his share of the purchase money, does not arise until suit for partition is brought, and the statute of limitations has no application to such suits. Grove *v.* Grove, 100 Va. 556, 42 S. E. 412.

V. Pleading and Practice.

A. SUITS AND ACTIONS BETWEEN COTENANTS.

1. Accounting.

See also, the title ACCOUNTS AND ACCOUNTING, vol. 1, p. 90.

a. At Common Law.

It seems that at common law joint tenants and tenants in common had no remedy against each other, where one alone received the whole profits of the estate, since he could not be charged as bailiff or receiver to his companion, unless he actually made him so. 1 Tho. Co. 788; Early *v.* Friend, 16 Gratt. 21, 43, 78 Am. Dec. 649; Rust *v.* Rust, 17 W. Va. 901.

"At common law, 'if one joint tenant, or tenant in common of land,' says Coke. 'maketh his companion his bailiff of his part, he shall have an action of account against him, as hath been said. But, although one tenant in common, or joint tenant, without being made bailiff take the whole profits, no action of account lieth against him: for in an action of account, he must charge him either as a guardian, bailiff, or receiver, as hath been said before; w: ch he can not do in this case, unless his companion constitute him his bailiff. And, therefore, all those books which affirm that an action of account lieth by one tenant in common or joint tenant

against another, must be intended, when the one maketh the other his bailiff, for otherwise, never his bailiff to render an account, is a good plea.' 1 Tho. Co. 787 marg. And in a note by the editor, it is said: 'At common law joint tenants and tenants in common had no remedy against each other, where one alone received the whole profits of the estate, since he could not be charged as bailiff or receiver to his companion, unless he actually made him so.' Id. 788, note (R)." Early *v.* Friend, 16 Gratt. 21, 42.

"At common law neither a joint tenant, tenant in common, nor coparcener occupying the common property, and thus taking more than his share of rents and profits, can be made to account to his fellows, unless he has been appointed bailiff or receiver by his fellows. Each one has right to enter and use the land, and this right can not be impaired by the fact that others absent themselves or do not claim their right to a common enjoyment. Unless the one in possession denies the right of the others to enter and enjoy the estate, or agrees to pay rent, nothing can be claimed of him. It is presumed that the others consent to his use. He can not call on the others to help him farm or otherwise use the property, and in case of loss from failure of crops or other cause, he can not call on the others to contribute to the loss. If the others do not wish to occupy the premises with their co-owners, the remedy of partition is at hand, or, if the property be indivisible, the court will sell it, and divide its proceeds. Lomax, Dig. 501, 481; 2 Minor Inst. 437, 429; Freem. Coten., § 269; note to Early *v.* Friend, 16 Gratt. 21, 78 Am. Dec. 649. This is the view stated in Freem. Coten., § 258; Gayle *v.* Johnston, 80 Ala. 395." Ward *v.* Ward. 40 W. Va. 611, 21 S. E. 746, 52 Am. St. Rep. 911.

b. Under the Statute.

In General.—"But the statute of 4 Anne, ch. 16, § 27, was passed in England to remedy this defect of the common law. And a similar statute was passed in Virginia at an early period, and has ever since continued in force. The Code of Virginia, p. 586, ch. 145, § 14, is in these words: 'An action of account may be maintained against the personal representative of any guardian, bailiff or receiver, and also by one joint tenant or tenant in common, or his personal representative, against the other as bailiff, for receiving more than comes to his just share or proportion, and against the personal representative of any such joint tenant or tenant in common.' This provision of statute law has been in force with us ever since this state came into existence and may be found in the Code of this state of 1868, § 14, ch. 100." Rust v. Rust, 17 W. Va. 901, 909.

The statutes in Virginia and West Virginia provide that an action of account may be maintained against the personal representative of any guardian or receiver, and also by one joint tenant or tenant in common, or his personal representative against the other for receiving more than comes to his just share or proposition, and against the personal representative of any such joint tenant or tenant in common. Va. Code, 1904, § 3294; W. Va. Code, 1899, ch. 100, § 3470; Williamson v. Jones, 43 W. Va. 562, 27 S. E. 411, 413, citing Rust v. Rust, 17 W. Va. 901; Fry v. Payne, 82 Va. 759, 1 S. E. 197.

Construction of the Statute.

In General.—This statute relates to rents and profits only in ordinary cultivation or other use authorized by law to one tenant in common, and does not touch such unauthorized use as waste. In the latter case he must account to his cotenant, but his liability is regulated by that section providing that if a tenant in common, joint tenant or parcener commit waste, he shall be liable to his cotenants jointly or severally for damages. Cecil v. Clark, 47 W. Va. 402, 35 S. E. 11.

Each tenant has a right to occupy and use the common property, but not to the exclusion of his cotenant. The occupation of one, does not necessarily exclude the occupation of the other, and the statute is not designed to take away or impair these rights of the occupying tenant, but to require them to be so used as not to interfere with those of his cotenants, and to hold him accountable only where he receives more than comes to his just share or proportion. But it is often difficult to determine when, by mere use and occupation of the property, the occupying tenant receives more than his just share. And it is still more difficult to lay down any general rule on the subject. Early v. Friend, 16 Gratt. 21, 78 Am. Dec. 649; Ruffners v. Lewis, 1 Leigh 720, 30 Am. Dec. 513; Ward v. Ward, 40 W. Va. 611, 21 S. E. 746, 52 Am. St. Rep. 911.

"Where one tenant in common takes wheat or apples, even in excess of his share, the law regards him as its sole owner; his cotenant having no title therein, though the producing tenant is accountable for taking more than his just share. But when one takes coal his cotenant has title to the very coal, after its severance from the land; and the taking tenant can be sued in trespass, or, if he sells, his cotenant can waive the tort, and sue for the money had and received, because the one has received money from the sale of property belonging to the other. When the one took the grain he did so with lawful authority, as he was entitled to occupy the land for the production of grain. But when he took the coal he did so without authority. His act was a wrong, a waste, in violation of the right of his cotenant; and this cotenant can follow up the property, and base his demand on its wrongful taking and conversion. The distinction is that one is waste, falling under a statute declaring, without qualification, that he who commits it shall answer, without any reference to whether he took more than his share or not, while the other is not waste, but authorized use, rendering him accountable, by the letter of the statute, only in case he takes more than his share. It does not seem that in cases in Virginia where tenants in common took salt water, lead, or iron ore, it was contended that they could keep all their proceeds, without account to their fellows, on the theory that what was taken was no more than their fair share, or that it came from the land assigned to them. Ruffners v. Lewis, 7 Leigh 720, 30 Am. Dec. 513; Early v. Friend, 16 Gratt. 21, 78 Am. Dec. 649; Graham v. Pierce, 19 Gratt. 28, 100 Am. Dec. 658; Newman v. Newman, 27 Gratt. 714." Cecil v. Clark, 47 W. Va. 402, 35 S. E. 11, 13.

"Where one cotenant occupies land for agricultural purposes in the production of yearly crops, fructus industriales, or other legitimate use for such a cotenant, it is plainly just that he be allowed to do so without accounting to his cotenant for such use, unless he occupies more than his share of the land; otherwise, he would not have the use of his share of the land. But, if he excludes his fellow from like enjoyment of his share, he must account to his cotenant for that cotenant's share, whether the occupation covers more or less than the share of the cotenant so occupying. Or, if he occupies more than his share, though he does not exclude his cotenant, thus not leaving open for his cotenant that cotenant's share for his enjoyment, he must account to him for taking more than his own just share of the profits. This liability to account did not exist at the common law. Use as much as he might, however profitable, one cotenant was not liable to account to another. But § 14, ch. 100, above quoted, changes this, by making him account for what is beyond his just share, to his fellow. Its only purpose is to

change the common-law rule of nonaccountability as to the ordinary use of the common property which a cotenant may legitimately make of it. Such legitimate use contemplated by that section does not waste the property by damaging the inheritance permanently, but leaves it, after such use, intact, uninjured, ready for partition, as before such use. That statute only says that if one cotenant, by such lawful use for ordinary purposes, get more than his fair share, he shall account for the excess to him entitled to the excess. Such construction of this statute was given in Williamson v. Jones, 43 W. Va. 562, 27 S. E. 411, and Ward v. Ward, 40 W. Va. 611, 21 S. E. 746, 52 Am. St. Rep. 911." Cecil v. Clark, 47 W. Va. 402, 35 S. E. 11, 12.

Whenever the nature of the property is such as not to admit of its use and occupation by several, and it is used and occupied by one only of the tenants in common; or whenever the property, though capable of use and occupation by several, is yet so used and occupied by one as in effect to exclude the others, he receives more than comes to his just share and proportion in the meaning of the statute. Early v. Friend, 16 Gratt. 21, 78 Am. Dec. 649; Rust v. Rust, 17 W. Va. 901; Dodson v. Hays, 29 W. Va. 577, 2 S. E. 415.

Where the nature of the property is such as not to admit of its use and occupation by several, and less than his just share and proportion of the common property is used and occupied by one tenant in common in a manner which tends in no way to hinder or exclude the other tenants in common from in like manner using and occupying the common property, such tenant does not receive more than comes to his just share and proportion in the meaning of the statute, and is not accountable to his cotenants for the profits of that portion of the property used by him. Dodson v. Hays, 29 W. Va. 577, 2 S. E. 415; Early v.

Friend, 16 Gratt. 21, 78 Am. Dec. 649; Rust v. Rust, 17 W. Va. 901.

Opening and Working Mines.—A tenant in common may work open salt or oil wells or mines and take all the profits, but he can not open new ones; though in the former cases he would have to account under the West Virginia Code because such acts are not waste. Williamson v. Jones, 43 W. Va. 562, 27 S. E. 411.

Exclusion of Owners.—"Another reason against allowing the trustees to keep all the money arising from the coal, without accounting to their cotenants, on the theory that the trustees took no more than their lawful share, is that the trustees denied all title in the Chapman and Hall heirs, took sole possession, and excluded them from the land. Those trustees can not say, or have the benefit of the theory, that they did not exclude the Chapmans and Halls, as they did not even concede their right when the Chapmans and Halls demanded a share in the land, but defended that suit through all the courts till the right of their adversaries was established. Therefore, if the taking of the coal is viewed, not as waste, but in the light of ordinary use for agriculture, and thus coming under § 14, ch. 100, of the Code, still the trustees must account, though they took less than their share, because of their exclusion of their co-owners. Early v. Friend, 16 Gratt. 21, 78 Am. Dec. 649 (Syl., point 2); Rust v. Rust, 17 W. Va. 901." Cecil v. Clark, 47 W. Va. 402, 35 S. E. 11, 13.

Parceners.—And applying the maxim "the mention of the one is the exclusion of the other," this statute has been held, not to apply to parceners. Ward v. Ward, 40 W. Va. 611, 21 S. E. 746, 52 Am. St. Rep. 911, disapproving 2 Min. Insts. 437.

One parcener receiving more of the rents and profits than his share, is liable to his coparceners in an action of account. Code, 1873, ch. 142, § 14. Fry v. Payne, 82 Va. 759, 1 S. E. 197, dis-

approved in Ward v. Ward, 40 W. Va. 611, 21 S. E. 746, 52 Am. St. Rep. 911.

Waste.—It has been held, in West Virginia, that this section does not apply to waste by a joint tenant in common. Cecil v. Clark, 47 W. Va. 402, 35 S. E. 11; Williamson v. Jones, 43 W. Va. 562, 27 S. E. 411.

The only purpose of this statute "is to change the common-law rule of non-accountability as to the ordinary use of the common property which a cotenant may legitimately make of it. Such legitimate use contemplated by that section does not waste the property by damaging the inheritance permanently, but leaves it, after such use, intact, uninjured, ready for partition, as before such use. That statute only says that if one cotenant, by such lawful use for ordinary purposes, get more than his fair share, he shall account for the excess to him entitled to the excess. Such construction of this statute was given in Williamson v. Jones, 43 W. Va. 562, 27 S. E. 411, and Ward v. Ward, 40 W. Va. 611, 21 S. E. 746, 52 Am. St. Rep. 911. Cecil v. Clark, 47 W. Va. 402, 35 S. E. 11.

If one tenant in common take coal from land without the consent of another, he must account to that other therefor, and can not keep the proceeds of the sale of the coal, without accounting, on the theory that the portion of land furnishing the coal is no more than his just share. The statute does not apply to this case. It relates to rents and profits only in ordinary cultivation or other use authorized by law to one tenant in common. Cecil v. Clark, 47 W. Va. 402, 35 S. E. 11.

Measure of Recovery.—"The propriety of limiting such recovery of the cotenant to an amount in damages proportionate to his interest in the land may receive some further indirect confirmation from § 14 of chapter 100 of the Code, which, among other things, provides that an action of account may be maintained by one joint tenant, or tenant in common, or his personal representative, against the other, for receiving more than comes to his just share or proportion, and against the personal representative of any such joint tenant or tenant in common. 'And if the property admits of use and occupation by several, and less than his just and proportionate share of the common property to the occupying co-tenant, who in no way hinders or excludes the others, he is not accountable to his cotenants for the profits of that portion of the property owned by him within the meaning of this statute.' Dodson v. Hays, 29 W. Va. 577, 2 S. E. 415. But here the estate for life was not ended, and an undivided third interest in the immediate remainder in fee had, by our statute of descent, come to the father, the tenant for life. I take for granted that by operation of the law of merger an undivided third of the life tenant's freehold was thereby enlarged to a fee; but that such union of such part of his particular estate with such part of the immediate remainder in fee came to him by descent did not operate in any way to defeat, impair, or otherwise affect his own particular estate or the remainder. If it had the effect to merge the life tenant's whole legal estate, then it would be to be held for the use of the life tenant for life. See § 13, chapter 71, of the Code; Scott v. Scott (1868), 18 Gratt. 150, 160; Wiscot's Case (1599), 2 Coke 61. Crump v. Norwood, 7 Taunt 362, goes to sustain the first view, and it would not affect the creditors of Lewis Couger, deceased, otherwise than as provided by § 5 of chapter 86 of the Code, making the heir liable to those entitled as creditors for the value thereof, with interest; and we see that he did by deed sell to defendant part of the standing timber trees here in controversy, which might have some bearing upon the case as to the remedy, and as to what would have been his liability, and what is the liability of his vendee growing out of his relation as life tenant to the owners of the re-mainder in fee, as governed by the doctrine of waste." McDodrill v. Pardee, etc., Lumber Co., 40 W. Va. 564, 21 S. E. 878, 884.

"Without undertaking therefore now to decide whether in a case such as this the party settling is liable only for the value at the death of the life tenant, where that value appears, it is sufficient to say that in the absence of proof upon that point the court is bound to adopt the price for which the slaves were sold as the sum with which the appellant is to be charged in his account with his cotenants. Kean v. Welch, 1 Gratt. 403; Cross v. Cross, 4 Gratt. 257." Moorman v. Smoot, 28 Gratt. 80, 85.

Necessary Allegations in Declaration. —In an action of account it is an essential averment of the declaration that the defendant has received more than his just share or proportion. Early v. Friend, 16 Gratt. 21, 78 Am. Dec. 649.

"The next question is as to the liability of W. C. Paxton for rent beyond his agreement, and beyond his settlement of the same with the parties, by payments in full. Our statute provides (Code, ch. 142, § 14), that an action of account may be maintained by one joint tenant, or tenant in common, or his personal representative, against the other as bailiff, for receiving more than comes to his just share or proportion; that is that the joint tenant who has received more than his just share or proportion shall account for rents and profits actually received, more than his just share or proportion. He is a bailiff, not as a bailiff at common law, bound to manage the estate to the best advantage, and make all the profits he can for the owners; to keep and render them a full account of his transactions; to be held liable, not only for rents and profits actually received, but also for such as might have been received without his default. He is in as of his own right, not that of another, and he is made a bailiff by the statute, not by reason of his holding the property, but by reason of his receiving more than his just share; and, in an action of account against him, it is a necessary averment of the declaration that he has received more than his just share." Paxton *v.* Gamewell, 82 Va. 706, 709, 1 S. E. 92.

Equity Jurisdiction.—And under this statute, it is held: One tenant in common may maintain a suit in equity against his cotenant, who has occupied the whole of the common property, for an account of rents and profits. Early *v.* Friend, 16 Gratt. 21, 78 Am. Dec. 649; Rust *v.* Rust, 17 W. Va. 901.

Where there are two administrators, their relations inter se are fiduciary and they may be held to account, each by the other, in a court of equity touching transactions between themselves connected with the administration of the trust. This equitable jurisdiction extends to cases of account between tenants in common, joint tenants, partners, and by analogy between executors and administrators, who have a joint and entire interest in the effects of the testator or intestate. Huff *v.* Thrash, 75 Va. 546.

In all cases in which an action of account would be the proper remedy at law, and in all cases where a trustee is a party, the jurisdiction of a court of equity is undoubted. Huff *v.* Thrash, 75 Va. 546.

2. Forcible Entry and Detainer.

One joint tenant or tenant in common might maintain a warrant of forcible entry and detainer against his companion. Allen *v.* Gibson, 4 Rand. 468, 477. See also, the title FORCIBLE ENTRY AND DETAINER, vol. 6, p. 168.

3. Improvements and Repairs.

See generally, the title IMPROVEMENTS, vol. 7, p. 317.

a. In General.

One joint tenant or tenant in common can not maintain an action against his cotenants personally to compel contribution to the expense of improvements made on the common property without his consent, express or implied, nor fix it as a lien on his interest in the estate, except that, at common law, by the writ of de reparatione facienda all the tenants could be compelled to unite in the expenses of the necessary repairs of a house or mill owned by them. Ward *v.* Ward, 40 W. Va. 611, 21 S. E. 746, 52 Am. St. Rep. 911.

b. Assumpsit.

The mere fact of improving the common property by a joint tenant does not raise an implied assumpsit on the part of cotenants to contribute to the expenses thereof, and no action will lie by the tenant making the improvements. Ballou *v.* Ballou, 94 Va. 350, 26 S. E. 840.

c. Partition.

In a suit in equity for partition, the court will grant compensation for repairs and improvements. Ballou *v.* Ballou, 94 Va. 350, 26 S. E. 840.

"The result of a decided preponderance of the authorities is that where one tenant in common lays out money in improvements on the estate, although the money so paid does not in strictness constitute a lien on the estate, yet a court of equity will not grant a partition without first directing an account, and a suitable compensation. To entitle the tenant in common to an allowance on a partition in equity, for the improvements made on the premises, it does not appear to be necessary for him to show the assent of his cotenants to such improvements, or a promise, on their part, to contribute their share of the expense, nor is it necessary for him to show a previous request to join in the improvements, and their refusal. The allowance of compensation for improvements is, in all cases, made, not as a matter of legal right, but purely from the desire of the court to do justice, and therefore the compensation will be estimated so as to inflict no injury on the cotenant against whom the improvements are charged. Freeman on Cotenancy and Partition, § 510; 3 Pomeroy's Eq. Jur., § 1389; 1 Story's Eq. Jur., § 655; Ruffners v. Lewis, 7 Leigh 720, 30 Am. Dec. 513." Ballou v. Ballou, 94 Va. 350, 352, 26 S. E. 840.

"A cotenant can not recover from his fellow tenants a share of the expense incurred by him in making improvements upon the common property, in the absence of an express assent on their part, or of such circumstances or dealings between the parties as will convince the court that an understanding existed to the effect that the expenses were to be repaid. Freeman on Cotenancy and Partition, § 262; 1 Wash. Real Prop., Marg. p. 421; notes to Robinson v. McDonald, 62 Amer. Dec., p. 483, and cases there cited. The right to claim compensation for improvements made under the circumstances disclosed by the record does not arise until the suit for partition is brought, and the right to partition arises whenever the parties may choose to assert it. Statutes of limitation have no application to suits for partition, nor to the equity for compensation which arises only when the partition is asked for." Ballou v. Ballou, 94 Va. 350, 353, 26 S. E. 840.

"The cases cited in support of the contention that Charles H. Ballou had a right of action against appellee for the improvements made are cases where the action was brought to recover compensation for repairs to the common property made by one cotenant. The rule applicable in the matter of repairs is different from that in the case of improvements. In the former case the weight of authority is that, when the repair of joint property is necessary to its use and preservation, one joint tenant, when his fellows refuse to unite, may have the property repaired and sue for compensation, but we have been referred to no authority which holds that this can

be done in the case of improvements." Ballou v. Ballou, 94 Va. 350, 353, 26 S. E. 840.

d. Writ De Reparatione.

The right of joint tenant or tenant in common at common law to compel others to unite in the expenses of the necessary reparation of a house or mill owned by them, was enforced by a writ of de reparatione facienda. But it did not apply to past repairs and could only be resorted to after request to unite in the repairs and refusal. Ward v. Ward, 40 W. Va. 611, 21 S. E. 746, 52 Am. St. Rep. 911; Ballou v. Ballou, 94 Va. 350, 26 S. E. 840.

"Next, as to improvements claimed by L. E. Ward. Can he be allowed for them? One joint tenant or tenant in common at common law could compel others to unite in the expenses of the necessary reparation of a house or mill owned by them, though the rule is limited to three parts of the common property, and does not apply to fences enclosing wood or arable land. The right was enforced by a writ de reparatione facienda. It did not apply to past repairs, and could only be resorted to after request to unite in the repairs and refusal 1 Lomax, Dig (504) 648; 2 Minor Inst. 430; 4 Kent, Comm. 370. It was confined to a mill or houses, because it is for the public good to maintain houses and mills, which are for the habitation and use of men—as Lord Coke said in Co. Litt 200b; Ind. 45b. 'If there be two joint tenants of wood or arable land, the one has no remedy against the other to make inclosure or reparation for safeguard of the wood or corn.' Bowles' Case, 11 Coke 82. I have no doubt this old common-law writ, though disused, might yet be resorted to. It applies to future, not past, repairs. Freem. Coten., § 261; Calvert v. Aldrich, 99 Mass. 76. I think it can be safely laid down, with the exception stated, no joint tenant, tenant in common, or parcener can compel his cotenant to make improvements, or

maintain an action against him personally to compel him to contribute to the expense of improvements made by him upon the estate, without his consent, express or implied, or fix it as a lien on his interest in the estate. One can not improve his fellow out of his estate. He has voluntarily put improvements on land of another, knowing his right, and he can not impose a debt on him or his estate without his consent. Freem. Coten., §§ 261, 262; Aldrich *v.* Husband, 131 Mass. 480; Id., 135 Mass. 317; Nelson *v.* Clay, 23 Am. Dec. 387; Hancock *v.* Day, 36 Am. Dec. 293; Scott *v.* Guernsey, 48 N. Y. 106; Calvert *v.* Aldrich, 99 Mass. 74; Mumford *v.* Brown, 16 Am. Dec. 440; Hancock *v.* Day, 36 Am. Dec. 293."
Ward *v.* Ward, 40 W. Va. 611, 21 S. E. 746, 749, 52 Am. St. Rep. 911.

And Judge Brannon in Ward *v.* Ward, 40 W. Va. 611, 21 S. E. 746, 749, 52 Am. St. Rep. 911, said: "I have no doubt this old common law writ, though disused, might yet be resorted to. It applies to future, not past, repairs. Freem. Coten., § 261."

4. Real Actions.

a. Ejectment.

See the title EJECTMENT, vol. 4, p. 887.

Cases Prior to Statute.—"In England, when an ejectment is brought by a joint tenant, parcener or tenant in common against his companion (to support which an actual ouster is necessary) the practice is for the defendant to apply to the court, upon affidavit, for leave to enter into a special rule, requiring him to confess lease and entry at the trial, but not ouster also, unless an actual ouster of the plaintiff's lessor by him, the defendant, should be proved. Adams on Ejectm. 236. But I regard this as a mere point of practice, conformable to rules invented from time to time by the courts to advance the remedy by ejectment, and to force the parties to go to trial on the merits, without be-ing entangled by formal objections to fictitious averments in the declaration. There are, however, essential differences between the rules of the several English courts themselves, and between those courts and our own. I do not believe we have ever adopted the special rule, the form of which is given in the appendix to Adams on Ejectm. No. 25, but in all cases our clerks make the entry of the consent rule in the form given by Robinson." Doe *v.* Hill, 10 Leigh 457, 464.

Ejectment may be maintained by one tenant in common against another; but in such case actual ouster must be shown by the plaintiff before he can maintain the action. The pro forma confession of ouster, which a defendant was required to make under the old "consent rule" before being allowed to plead, was not sufficient to satisfy this rule. Doe *v.* Hill, 10 Leigh 457.

In ejectment against a tenant in common by a cotenant, if the jury return a special verdict, actual ouster must be found therein, to entitle the plaintiff to judgment. The necessity of finding this fact is not dispensed with by the entry made, in Virginia, when the tenant in possession is admitted defendant, that he "confesses the lease, entry and ouster in the declaration supposed, and agrees to insist on the title only, at the trial." The confession that Richard Roe ousted John Doe, is not a confession that the real defendant ousted the real plaintiff; and when this latter ouster forms a part of the plaintiff's title to recover (as it does between tenants in common), the fact of such ouster must be proved. Roe *v.* Hill, 10 Leigh 457.

In Buchanan *v.* King, 22 Gratt. 414, 423, it is said: "It has been the established doctrine of the courts, that a tenant in common can not maintain ejectment against his companion without proof of an actual ouster. Difficulties often occur in determining whether certain acts constitute an ouster. Parties otherwise entitled to recover are defeated from an inability to prove it. It was, therefore, provided (Va. Code, 1860, ch. 135, § 15; Va. Code, 1887, § 2736), it should be sufficient for the plaintiff to prove some act amounting to a total denial of the plaintiff's right as cotenant. It was not intended to alter well-established principles of law governing the relations of joint tenants or tenants in common to each other, but simply to enlarge existing remedies. Doe v. Hill, 10 Leigh 457."

The statutes in Virginia and West Virginia provide that in an action of ejectment by one or more tenants in common, joint tenants, or coparceners, against their cotenants, the plaintiff shall be bound to prove actual ouster or some other act amounting to total denial of the plaintiff's right as cotenant. Va. Code, 1904, § 2736; W. Va. Code, 1899, ch. 90, § 3350.

A plaintiff in an action of ejectment can only recover that to which he hath the legal title. He can not recover the share of his cotenant or coparcener. If an ineffectual partition has been made, each joint tenant is still seized of his individual share of the whole, and can not recover more in an action of ejectment. Nye v. Lovitt, 92 Va. 710, 24 S. E. 345, 2 Va. Law. Reg. 29.

Evidence.—In ejectment between cotenants, where the defendants rely upon adversary possession, and acquiescence by the plaintiffs, letters by a party under whom the defendant's claim, and also a correspondence between one of the plaintiffs and the agent of the defendant, may be competent evidence to show for what purpose the tenants in possession had claimed the property, and the plaintiffs acquiesced in their claim. Stonestreet v. Doyle, 75 Va. 356.

Limitation of Actions.—As ejectment lies in Virginia for an undivided interest in realty, the infancy of one joint tenant will not prevent the running of the act of limitations as to the other joint tenants not under disability. Redford v. Clarke, 100 Va. 115, 40 S. E. 630.

b. Writ of Right.

In a writ of right by one joint tenant, tenant in common or coparcener, to recover an undivided part of the property, it was held, that the special verdict where the defense is the statute of limitations, must find either an actual disseisin or ouster of the demandants, or facts which in law constitute such actual disseisin or ouster. Purcell v. Wilson, 4 Gratt. 16.

c. Unlawful Detainer.

It was held, in Allen v. Gibson, 4 Rand. 468, 477, in an action of unlawful detainer, where the right to the possession of the property alone was involved, that one tenant in common might recover the possession of the whole land, against a person having no right whatever, without joining his cotenant. In delivering the opinion of the court, Judge Green said: "In a writ of right, and other real actions, the mere right is involved, and the proceeding and recovery must be according to the title; and, in ejectment, nothing can be recovered but that for which the lessor of the plaintiff can make a valid lease. One joint tenant, coparcener, or tenant in common, although he has a right to the possession of the whole against strangers, can not make a valid lease for more than his own part of the land, and therefore no more can be recovered in ejectment than the part to which the lessor, who is a joint tenant, tenant in common, or parcener, is entitled." Nye v. Lovitt, 92 Va. 710, 719, 24 S. E. 345, 2 Va. Law Reg. 29.

5. Trespass.

See generally, the title TRESPASS.

Where one cotenant brings against another an action of trespass to realty or an action on the case in lieu thereof under the statute, the place where the acts complained of were done is material and traversable, and the allegations thereof must in some way, either by the name of the land or close, by some or all of its abuttals, by naming a particular locality or in some other way, designate or describe such locus in quo with a reasonable degree of definiteness; otherwise the declaration will be bad on demurrer. McDodrill *v.* Pardee, etc., Lumber Co., 40 W. Va. 564, 21 S. E. 878.

Trespass for Mesne Profits.—In an action of trespass for mesne profits against his cotenant, if the defendant at the time of the inception of the cause of action had knowledge of the plaintiff's title, although he honestly believed that he held the superior legal title, the measure of damages is not the actual receipts, but is the fair annual rental of the property, with legal interest, less the taxes paid by the defendant. Bodkin *v.* Arnold, 48 W. Va. 108, 35 S. E. 980.

In such action the defendant is not entitled to offset his improvements against the rent, if at the time they were made he had knowledge of the plaintiff's title, although he in good faith believed his own title to be the better, in point of law. Bodkin *v.* Arnold, 48 W. Va. 108, 35 S. E. 980.

If, in addition to the rent, the plaintiff seeks to recover damages for waste occasioned by the failure of defendant to make proper, tenantable repairs, and his abuse and misuse of the property, the improvements made by the defendant in the nature of general repairs should be taken into consideration in estimating the general depreciation of the value of the property through fault of the defendant. Bodkin *v.* Arnold, 48 W. Va. 108, 35 S. E. 980.

6. Trover.

Trover lies by one tenant in common of a personal chattel against his cotenant for the appropriation of the chattel to his exclusive use, where the chattel is of such a nature as to be necessarily destroyed by the use thereof. Lowe *v.* Miller, 3 Gratt. 205,

46 Am. Dec. 188. See generally, the title TROVER AND CONVERSION.

7. Waste.

See generally, the title WASTE.

Accounting.—When a tenant in common has become liable for damages for waste, under W. Va. Code, 1899, ch. 92, § 2, p. 754, by the removal of coal from the premises, the cotenant injured may waive the tort, and require an accounting for money had and received, when the coal has been sold by such tenant. Cecil *v.* Clark, 49 W. Va. 459, 39 S. E. 202.

Tenants in common, committing waste against a cotenant, are wrong-doers, and may be sued on account thereof jointly or separately, and when sued jointly, it is not error to dismiss the cause as to one of them, on motion of the plaintiff, and over the objection of the other. Stewart *v.* Tennant, 52 W. Va. 559, 561, 44 S. E. 233.

Action for Rents and Profits.—The statutory action for rents and profits where one cotenant has received more than his proper share does not apply to a case of waste by cotenants. Cecil *v.* Clark, 47 W. Va. 402, 35 S. E. 11; Williamson *v.* Jones, 43 W. Va. 562, 27 S. E. 411.

8. Proceedings in Equity.

a. In General.

As one joint tenant or tenant in common was not allowed at common law to have an action ex contractu against his cotenant, except as bailiff, his only remedy was by bill in equity. The statute allowing an action of account between cotenants did not abridge the remedy in equity; and, where a case is presented involving a variety of adjustments, a bill in equity is still the usual mode of relief against a cotenant who has received more than his just share or proportion. 2 Min. Inst. (4th Ed.) 498; Early *v.* Friend, 16 Gratt. 21, 78 Am. Dec. 649; Rust *v.* Rust, 17 W. Va. 901; Dodson *v.* Hays, 29 W. Va. 577, 2 S. E. 415.

b. Partition.

See the title PARTITION.

Tenants in common of personal estate can not have partition at common law; and, therefore, a court of equity is the proper tribunal to decree a partition of it. Smith *v.* Smith, 4 Rand. 95.

Bill for Partition, and to Subject Interest to a Deed of Trust.—Under the provisions of § 2562 of the Virginia Code, as amended, a bill in equity may be filed by one tenant in common against another for the purpose of having partition of the property held in common, and to subject the interest of the defendant to a deed of trust thereon for the benefit of the complainant. Price *v.* Crozier, 101 Va. 644, 44 S. E. 890.

Misappropriation of Funds.—A complainant and a defendant jointly bought three lots which were conveyed to the defendant. Each paid one-half of the cash payment, and they gave their joint notes for the two deferred payments, which were secured by a deed of trust on the lots. Each paid his half of the first deferred payment, and when the last payment fell due the complainant paid one-half thereof, principal and interest, to the defendant, with the understanding that he would supply the remaining half, and pay it to their vendor. The defendant appropriated the amount to his own use, but gave the complainant a bond with condition to indemnify and save him harmless from any and all loss of every kind which he might sustain by reason of his failure to pay the amount so received, and also his own half of said installment to the vendor, which bond was secured by deed of trust on the interest of defendant's wife in a lot owned jointly by her and the complainant, and his brother. The defendant obtained title for one of the lots and conveyed it to the complainant. The other two lots were sold under the deed of trust given to secure the purchase price, and at the

sale brought only fifteen dollars each. Suit was brought by complainant for partition of the lot owned jointly by defendant's wife and the complainant and his brother, and to subject the wife's interest to the lien of the deed of trust. It was held, that the measure of complainant's recovery is the amount paid to the defendant, with interest thereon from the date of payment, and not merely half the price for which the two lots were sold, which amount is secured by the bond of indemnity, and the deed of trust given to secure the same. Price *v.* Crozier, 101 Va. 644, 44 S. E. 890.

c. Injunction.

See generally, the title INJUNCTIONS, vol. 7, p. 512.

A court of equity will grant an injunction in favor of a tenant in common to restrain the commission of a continuing and permanent injury, as where one tenant in common of a building erects a wall in the hallway thereof so as to interfere with the free enjoyment of the building. Woods *v.* Early, 95 Va. 307, 28 S. E. 374.

A court of equity has no jurisdiction to restrain one joint devisee of land from entering thereon, at the suit of a tenant claiming under the other devisees. Baldwin *v.* Darst, 3 Gratt. 132.

d. Cross Bill.

There were nine children tenants in common of slaves subject to the life estate of their mother. One of them, J., by his will gives to his brother, K., certain lands, plantation utensils, "and all the interest I may have in an undivided dower estate." J.'s widow marries T. and T. buys the shares of six of the children, one of them, K., and he buys of the husband of N., one of the children, her share; but her husband dies in the lifetime of N. and her mother. K. dies, and gives his interest under the will of J. to Y. T. sells two of the slaves to M., and M. afterwards sells them and the increase of one of them for $960. T. and his wife have removed from the state. After the death of the life tenant, S., who had not sold her interest in the slaves, files her bill against M, making N. and Y. defendants, setting out the facts, and claiming her interest in the slaves sold to M. It was not necessary that N. and Y. should file a cross bill in the cause in order to set up their claims against M. Moorman *v.* Smoot, 28 Gratt. 80. See the title CROSS BILLS, vol. 4, p. 100.

e. Equity Jurisdiction.

One tenant in common may maintain a suit in equity against his cotenant, who has occupied the whole of the common property. Early *v.* Friend, 16 Gratt. 21, 78 Am. Dec. 649; Rust *v.* Rust, 17 W. Va. 901.

f. Absent Defendants.

If A. and B. hold a tract of land in common, and A. sells it to C. and removes out of the state, B. may bring a suit in chancery against C. and A. as an absent defendant, to confirm the sale, and obtain a decree for his part of the purchase money. And, if in such case, C. had brought a suit against A. and B. to rescind the sale, and failed, but was permitted to retain part of the purchase money, until B.'s title should be tried by a jury; the latter will be entitled to avail herself of the proceedings in that cause. Pollard *v.* Coleman, 4 Call 245.

9. Joinder of Parties.

The Virginia Code provides that tenants in common may join and be joined as plaintiffs or defendants. Va. Code, 1904, § 3256.

One tenant in common may have the remedy of unlawful detainer for the whole land, against any party having no right whatever, without joining his cotenant. Allen *v.* Gibson, 4 Rand. 468.

Joinder in a Writ of Right.—In the case of Garrard *v.* Henry, 6 Rand. 110, 116, it is said: "But this finding shows, that whether she was seised in parcenary with the other demandants (as is implied by the finding) or jointly, or in common, her grantee must have been a tenant in common with the other demandants; all of whom are found to have better right than the tenants. And it is equally clear, that tenants in common can not properly join in a writ of right; and a joint writ, alleging a joint right in them, is false. So the other finding, that one of the demandants, who, if alive, would have had title, was dead before the emanation of the writ, leaving children who were his heirs, also falsified the writ. Either of these facts might have been pleaded in abatement of the writ, and if they can now be taken notice of, a judgment of abatement, or a final judgment upon the right, in favor of the tenants, must be the consequence."

Plea in Abatement.—Misjoinder of tenants in common should be pleaded in abatement. Garrard *v.* Henry, 6 Rand. 110.

10. Limitation of Actions.

See also, the title LIMITATION OF ACTIONS.

As ejectment lies in Virginia for an undivided interest in realty, the infancy of one joint tenant will not prevent the running of the act of limitations as to the other joint tenants not under disability. Redford *v.* Clarke, 100 Va. 115, 40 S. E. 630.

"Appellants maintain that the infancy of one joint tenant prevents the application of the act of limitations to other joint tenants not under disability, and authorities are cited to sustain that contention. These decisions, however, proceed upon the common-law doctrine that joint tenants must sue and be sued jointly. But that doctrine can have no application in this jurisdiction, where the common-law rule has been modified by statute, and where undivided interests may be sued for and recovered. V. C., ch. 125; Marshall *v.* Palmer, 91 Va.

344, 21 S. E. 672; Nye v. Lovitt, 92 Va. 710, 719, 24 S. E. 345, 2 Va. Law Reg. 29. The statute of limitations contains no exception in case of joint tenants where some are under disability, and there would seem to be no necessity for such an exception, under the statutory modification of the common-law rule, which no longer requires that all shall unite in suits affecting the joint property." Redford v. Clarke, 100 Va. 115, 120, 40 S. E. 630.

B. ACTIONS AGAINST THIRD PERSONS.

1. Caveat.

In Walton v. Hale, 9 Gratt. 194, a quære was raised as to whether a tenant in common of an undivided interest in land may maintain a caveat against the issuing of a grant of a third person, upon a survey of part of the land embraced within the limits of an amount in which he holds an undivided interest.

2. Ejectment.

A plaintiff in an action of ejectment can only recover that to which he has the legal title. He can not recover the share of his cotenant or coparcener. If an ineffectual partition has been made, each joint tenant is still seised of his individual share of the whole, and can not recover more in an action of ejectment. Nye v. Lovitt, 92 Va. 710, 24 S. E. 345, 2 Va. Law Reg. 29.

One joint tenant can not recover, in an action of ejectment in his own name, as sole plaintiff, the interests of himself, and his cotenants. He can only recover that to which he has the title, and if this be an undivided interest he must prove what his proportion is, else there must be judgment for the defendant. Marshall v. Palmer, 91 Va. 344, 21 S. E. 672.

3. Forcible Entry and Detainer.

One joint tenant or tenant in common may, in an action of unlawful detainer, recover the possession of the whole land, without joining his coten-

ant in the action. Voss v. King, 33 W. Va. 236, 10 S. E. 402; Allen v. Gibson, 4 Rand. 468. See the title FORCIBLE ENTRY AND DETAINER, vol. 6, p. 168.

4. Joinder of Parties.

The personal representative of one or more remaindermen dying during the lifetime of the life tenant, is tenant in common with the surviving remainderman, and must be joined with the remaindermen in an action to recover the property. Clarkson v. Booth, 17 Gratt. 490.

5. Survival of Actions.

Where two or more cotenants bring an action of trespass on the case to recover damages caused by the action of the defendant in constructing a dam and thereby overflownig their property, and one of the plaintiffs dies, the suit survives as to the other plaintiffs, and may be proceeded in by them. Rowe v. Shenandoah Pulp Co., 42 W. Va. 551, 26 S. E. 320.

In such a suit, if one of the parties plaintiff dies pending the suit the same should abate as to such deceased party; and it is error, upon the appointment of an administrator for the estate of such deceased party, to allow the suit to proceed in the name of such administrator and the survivors at the same time. Rowe v. Shenandoah Pulp Co., 42 W. Va. 551, 26 S. E. 320.

"Upon this question, Freeman on Cotenancy and Partition, in § 364, under the head of 'Death of Cotenant Pendente Lite,' says: 'In the two preceding sections we have considered the effect of the death of one cotenant after the accruing of a joint cause of action, and before the commencement of a suit thereon, and have found the rule to be universal that all joint causes of action survive to the last survivor, irrespective of the nature of the cotenancy, and further that, when the cause of action survives after the decease of all the cotenants, it vests in the personal representative of the last survivor. We shall now consider the effect of the death of one of the co-tenants pendente lite, for the purpose of ascertaining whether such death operates as an abatement of the suit. The general rule upon this subject is thus stated by Mr. Jickling: "If the whole interest of a party dying survive to the other party, so that no claim can be made by or against the representatives of the party so dying, the proceedings do not abate. Survivorship is a characteristic of joint tenancy, and hence, on the death of a joint tenant party to a suit, either as plaintiff or defendant, the suit does not abate." It is therefore certain that, if the plaintiffs are joint tenants, the death of one does not occasion an abatement of the action.' In § 362 the author says: 'When the cause of action is joint, it survives to the remaining cotenants on the death of either of them. This is true in every form of cotenancy. "It is to be observed that where damages are to be recovered for a wrong done to tenants in common, or parceners in a personal action, and one of them die, the survivor of them shall have the action; for, albeit the property or estate be several between, yet, as it appeareth here by Littleton, the personal action is joint."' Citing Co. Litt. 198a; 3 Rob. Prac. 164, where it is said: 'But if one, two or more mortgagees or other tenants in common shall die after there is possession adverse to them, and consequently after their cause of action accrues, then the right of action for this cause survives to the surviving mortgagees or tenants in common.' Citing Townsend v. Morris, 6 Cow. 123, where it is held that 'the damages for an eviction of two tenants in common to whom lands are granted with warranty are personal, and an action will lie for them by the survivor.' Also citing Nichols v. Campbell, 10 Gratt. 560, where it was held, 'Two trustees having brought an action of detinue to recover the trust property,

and one of them dying, the right of action survives to the other, and he may carry on the suit.' Robinson further says: 'This is according to Lord Coke; for he observes that where damages are to be recovered for a wrong done to tenants in common, or parceners in a personal action, and one of them dies, the survivor of them shall have the action.' Co. Litt. 198a. Again, in 9 Gray 177, in the case of Tyler v. Mather, it was held, that 'on the death of some of the complainants pending a complaint on Rev. St. ch. 116, for flowing land, the survivors alone may prosecute the suit, though some of the deceased complainants were tenants in common with some of the survivors.' Again, in the case of Watrous' Heirs v. McGrew, 16 Tex. 506, it was held, that: 'Where one of several tenants in common, who are coplaintiffs in an action of trespass to try title against a stranger, dies, it is not necessary to make the heirs or representatives of the deceased parties to the action. The right of action of the survivors is not affected by the death of their coplaintiff.' And in 35 Hun 622, in the case of Shale v. Schantz, it was held: 'An action brought by the members of a firm to recover damages for an alleged slander relating to the financial condition and credit of the firm does not abate by the death of one of the plaintiffs during its pendency. The entire cause of action vests in the surviving plaintiffs, and the action may be prosecuted by them.'" Rowe v. Shenandoah Pulp Co., 42 W. Va. 551, 26 S. E. 320.

C. PROCEEDING TO SELL. INTERESTS OF INSANE COTENANT.

In a proceeding by a committee of an insane person, under ch. 83, W. Va. Code, to sell the undivided interest of such insane person in the oil and gas underlying a tract of land, the cotenants of such person are not necessary or proper parties to such proceeding. South Penn Oil Co. *v.* McIntyre, 44 W. Va. 296, 28 S. E. 922.

VI. Severance.

A. JOINT TENANCY.

Joint tenancy is severed or dissolved by destroying any of its constituent unities; and if it be any other unity than that of possession, the holding then becomes a tenancy in common. For a discussion of the severance of the relation of joint tenancy, see 2 Min. Inst. (4th Ed.) 478, et seq.

B. TENANCY IN COMMON.

Since the unity of possession is the only unity in a tenancy in common, such tenancy is severed or dissolved by disuniting the possession and assigning to each tenant his share in severalty, or by uniting all the shares in the hands of some one of the tenants, or by agreeing to do one or the other of these things. See discussion of this subject in 2 Min. Inst. (4th Ed.) 501, et seq.

"The only way to destroy a cotenancy is either for part to buy out the others, or to exclude them from participation therein by such open and notorious acts of ouster as amount to a disseisin, and which has ripened by actual adverse possession into perfect title under the statute of limitations." Parker *v.* Brast, 45 W. Va. 399, 32 S. E. 269, 271.

Partition.—The usual mode by which a cotenancy is dissolved is by partition or the division of the common property between the several cotenants, so that they shall thereafter hold their respective shares in severalty. Partition may be affected either by act of the parties or by judicial proceedings. See the title PARTITION.

Joint Tort Feasors.

See the titles CONTRIBUTION AND EXONERATION, vol. 3, p. 483; FORMER ADJUDICATION OR RES ADJUDICATA, vol. 6, p. 337; RELEASE; TRESPASS.

Joint Trespass.

See the title TRESPASS.

Joint Trial.

See the title SEPARATE TRIALS.

Joint Trustees.

See the title TRUSTS AND TRUSTEES.

Jointure.

See the title DOWER, vol. 4, p. 809.

Joint Wills.

See the titles SPECIFIC PERFORMANCE; WILLS.

Journals of Legislature.

See the titles RECORDS; STATUTES.

JUDGES.

XI. De Facto Judges, 159.

XII. Special Judges, 159.

CROSS REFERENCES.

See the titles ABATEMENT, REVIVAL AND SURVIVAL, vol. 1, p. 3; ACKNOWLEDGMENTS, vol. 1, p. 104; AFFIDAVITS, vol. 1, p. 227; APPEAL AND ERROR, vol. 1, p. 418; ARBITRATION AND AWARD, vol. 1, p. 687; ARGUMENTS OF COUNSEL, vol. 1, p. 713; BAIL AND RECOGNIZANCE, vol. 2, p. 196; CHAMBERS AND VACATION, vol. 2, p. 767; CONSTITUTIONAL LAW, vol. 3, p. 140; CONTEMPT, vol. 3, p. 236; CONTINUANCES, vol. 3, p. 270; COURTS, vol. 3, p. 696; CRIMINAL LAW, vol. 4, p. 1; DE FACTO OFFICERS, vol. 4, p. 446; DEPOSITIONS, vol. 4, p. 549; ELECTIONS, vol. 5, p. 1; EVIDENCE, vol. 5, p. 295; EXECUTIONS, vol. 5, p. 416; HABEAS CORPUS, vol. 7, p. 1; INDICTMENTS, INFORMATIONS AND PRESENTMENTS, vol. 7, p. 371; JUDGMENTS AND DECREES; JURISDICTION; JURY; JUSTICES OF THE PEACE; MANDAMUS; NEW TRIALS; PROHIBITION; PUBLIC OFFICERS; VERDICT.

I. Eligibility and Qualification.

See post, "Special Judges," XII.

A. FIRST JUDGES OF COURT OF APPEALS.

Under the act of May, 1779, establishing the court of appeals, to consist of the judges of the high court of chancery, general court, and court of admiralty, the first judges of the court of appeals qualified without the intervention or presence of the executive, and without producing any commissions, as they had qualified under commissions in the courts to which they respectively belonged, and it was not thought necessary to produce them there, as that was a legislative court, and the judges, in construction of law, knew each other. First Case of Judges, 4 Call 1.

B. RESIDENCE WITHIN LOCAL JURISDICTION.

County Court Judge.—Section 13, art. 6, constitution of Virginia, 1776, provides that judges of the county court during their continuances in office shall reside in their respective counties or districts. Foster v. Jones, 79 Va. 642, 645.

II. Power of Legislature.

See generally, the title CONSTITUTIONAL LAW, vol. 3, p. 140. See post, "Special Judges," XII.

A. TO ELECT JUDGES.

See post, "Election to Office of Judge," III.

B. TO INCREASE DUTIES.

The legislature can not increase the duties of the judges of the court of chancery, general court, and court of admiralty, and therefore these judges could not be required to act as district judges. In re Judges' Case, 4 Call 135.

C. TO REMOVE JUDGES.

Judges may be removed from office for cause, by a concurrent vote of both houses of the general assembly; but a majority of all the members elected to each house must concur in such vote, and the cause of removal shall be entered on the journal of each house. Va. Const., 1902, Art. 6, § 104.

If an act of assembly speaking of an established court, says that the court of t..at name, shall consist of a certain number of judges, it ought not to be construed as meaning to remove the existing judges, but if it did, the legislature had no power to do it, as the judges were in under the constitution. In re Judges' Case, 4 Call 135.

D. TO REDUCE SALARIES.

Under the Virginia constitution, art. 5, § 8, there is a limitation upon the power of the legislature to reduce the salary of a judge during his term of office. Field v. Auditor, 83 Va. 882, 3 S. E. 707. See post, "Right to Compensation," VII, D.

The legislature can not reduce the salaries of the judges which are fixed, while the duties remain the same, and when public utility requires an increase of duty, there should be an analogous alteration of salary. In re Judges' Case, 4 Call 135.

E. TO CURTAIL JURISDICTION.

Where a county judge has been elected for a judicial district, composed of two counties, the legislature may curtail his jurisdiction, his territorial district having still at least eight thousand inhabitants, although it diminishes his salary. Foster v. Jones, 79 Va. 642. See Foster v. Supervisors, 79 Va. 633. See ante, "To Reduce Salaries," II, D; post, "Right to Compensation," VII, D. See the title JURISDICTION.

F. TO FILL VACANCIES.

See post, "Appointment to Fill Vacancies," IV; "Who May Elect," XII, B.

III. Election to Office of Judge.

See post, "Special Judges," XII. See generally, the title ELECTIONS, vol. 5, p. 1.

The constitution of the state of Virginia declares that "the two houses of assembly, shall by joint ballot, appoint judges of the supreme court of appeals, and general court, judges in chancery, judges of admiralty, etc.. to be commissioned by the governor, and continue in office during good behavior." Art. 14, Va. Const. In re Judges' Case, 4 Call 135. See also, Ex parte Fisher, 33 Gratt. 232, 234.

City Judge.—Section 14, art. 6, Va. constitution, provides "For each city or town in the state containing a population of five thousand, there shall be elected, on the joint vote of the two houses of the general assembly, one city judge who shall hold a corporation or hustings court of said city or town." Ex parte Fisher, 33 Gratt. 232, 234.

County Court Judge.—County court judges shall be chosen in the same manner as judges of the circuit courts. Foster v. Jones, 79 Va. 642, 645.

IV. Appointment to Fill Vacancies.

See generally, the title PUBLIC OFFICERS.

As to term of judge appointed to fill vacancy, see post, "Duration," V, B.

The constitution of Virginia (art. 5, § 22), authorizes the legislature to prescribe the manner of filling all vacancies in office, and to declare when an office is vacant, in cases not specially therein provided for, and makes no exception as to the office of judge. Burks v. Hinton, 77 Va. 1.

V. Term of Office.

See post, "Holding Over," XI, C; "When Office Terminates," XII, G.

A. BEGINNING OF TERM.

In General.—It is well settled by the

repeated decisions of this court, that the term of office of the different classes of judges in this case begin at a fixed and definite period. Watlington v. Edmonson, 1 Va. Dec. 587.

Corporation and Hustings Court Judges.—The constitution provides that the terms of office of judges of the hustings or corporation courts shall commence on the first day of January next following their appointment. Ex parte Fisher, 33 Gratt. 232, 234; In re Broadus, 32 Gratt. 779.

County Court Judge.—Under the constitution of Virginia it was provided that the terms of the judges of the county courts shall commence on the 1st of January, and they shall hold their office for six years, and until a successor is elected and qualified. The term of a judge having ended on the 31st of December, 1879, his successor was elected on the 12th of January, 1880. Held, his term commenced on the first of January, 1880; and he is the judge of the county from the time of his qualification, and authorized at once to exercise the authority and discharge the duties of the office. In re Broadus, 32 Gratt. 779.

B. DURATION.

Section 13, art. 6, Va. constitution, 1776, provided that the judges of county courts shall hold their office for the term of six years, except the first term under this constitution, which shall be three years. Foster v. Jones, 79 Va. 642, 645; Burks v. Hinton, 77 Va. 1.

Judge of County Court.—F. was duly commissioned and qualified, and acted as county judge for the two counties of K. W. and K. & Q. until the general assembly ascertained that K. & Q. county had eight thousand inhabitants and made it a judicial district, and J. was elected and commissioned, and qualified as county judge thereof, and assumed the office. Nevertheless F., claiming still to be judge of K. & Q. county, and to be entitled to the salary as such, applied to this court for a mandamus to compel the supervisors of K. & Q. to pay it. Held, F. is no longer judge of K. & Q. county court, and is of course not entitled to receive a salary as such. Foster v. Supervisors, 79 Va. 633.

Under § 14, art. 6, constitution, 1776, the judges of corporation and hustings courts hold their office for the term of six years. Ex parte Fisher, 33 Gratt. 232, 234.

The constitution provided that the judges of the corporation and husting courts should discharge the duties of their respective offices from their first appointment under the constitution until their terms began. Manchester was incorporated as a city in 1874, and having more than five thousand inhabitants was entitled to have a judge of its hustings court. In March, 1874, C. was elected and qualified as judge of said court. Held, this being the first judge of this court, under the constitution C.'s term of office commenced on the 1st of January, 1875, and would continue until the 31st of December, 1880; and he was, under the constitution, authorized to act as judge from the time of his qualification to the commencement of his term. Ex parte Fisher, 33 Gratt. 232. See also, In re Broadus, 32 Gratt. 779; Ex parte Meredith, 33 Gratt. 119; McCraw v. Williams, 33 Gratt. 510.

Judges Elected or Appointed to Fill Vacancies.—A judge of a county court who has been elected to fill a vacancy occasioned by the death of a former judge, is elected for a full term of six years, and not for the unexpired term of the former judge, and this is also true of judges of the court of appeals and the circuit courts. Ex parte Meredith, 33 Gratt. 119; The Bland and Giles County Judge Case, 33 Gratt. 443; McCraw v. Williams, 33 Gratt. 510; Montague v. Massey, 76 Va. 307; Neal v. Allen, 76 Va. 437.

Example.—B. was elected in January, 1874, judge of the county court of Halifax and commissioned by the governor, and proceeded to act as such. Held, his term of six years did not commence until the 1st of January, 1875, and continued until the 31st of December, 1880. McCraw v. Williams, 33 Gratt. 510.

But these cases have been overruled by the later cases and it is held, that a judge, elected to fill a vacancy, is elected not for a full term, but for that portion of the constitutional term that may not have expired. The words "term of office" refer to the tenure or duration of the office, and not to the incumbent. Jameson v. Hudson, 82 Va. 279; Howison v. Weeden, 77 Va. 704; Fitzpatrick v. Kirby, 81 Va. 467. See also, Burks v. Hinton, 77 Va. 1.

Example.—Pulaski having less than 8,000 inhabitants, and being, therefore, attached to Wythe, one judge was elected to hold the office of judge in both of those counties for a term of six years, which began January 1, 1880, and ended December 31, 1885. When Pulaski was separated from Wythe in 1882, only a portion of that term had expired. H. A. Jameson was elected to hold the office of county judge of Pulaski for the remainder of that term, and Isaac Hudson was elected to hold that office for the next ensuing term of six years. Upon petition of Jameson, filed after December 31st, 1885, for a peremptory mandamus to compel Hudson to surrender that office to the petitioner; held, the mandamus must be denied. Jameson v. Hudson, 82 Va. 279.

C. TERMINATION.

It is well settled that the terms of office of the different classes of judges in this state end at fixed and definite periods. Watlington v. Edmonson, 10 Va. Law J. 286, 1 Va. Dec. 587.

D. HOLDING OVER.

Article 6, § 25, Va. constitution, does not extend the term of office of judge, but simply enables the incumbent to hold over until his successor, whether elected or appointed, is chosen, in the way prescribed by law. Kilpatrick v. Smith, 77 Va. 347, 358. See Coleman v. Sands, 87 Va. 689, 702, 13 S. E. 148; Griffin v. Cunningham, 20 Gratt. 31. See the title PUBLIC OFFICERS. See post, "Holding Over," XI, C.

VI. Territorial Jurisdiction.

See post, "To Sit as Judge in Another County," VII, F. See the title JURISDICTION.

As to granting an injunction to compel a judge to refrain from acting outside his jurisdiction, see the title INJUNCTIONS, vol. 7, p. 512.

VII. Rights, Powers and Duties.

A. RIGHT TO OFFICE.

The judges composing the court of appeals may resign the office of judge of that court, and still be judges of the courts to which they respectively belonged. In re Judges' Case, 4 Call 135.

A claimant to the office of a judgeship does not forfeit or abandon his rights by failing to protest at once against the incompetency of the incumbent, or by becoming an attorney and practitioner in his court. The Bland and Giles County Judge Case, 33 Gratt. 443. See also, Montague v. Massey, 76 Va. 307, 313; McCraw v. Williams, 33 Gratt. 510; Watlington v. Edmonson, 10 Va. Law J. 286, 1 Va. Dec. 587.

Example.—In December, 1874, E. was elected by the legislature judge of the county courts of G. and B. counties, and on the 12th of the same month commissioned as such; the commission stating that he was elected to fill the unexpired term of his predecessor. In December, 1879, W. was elected judge of the same counties, and commissioned as such on the 20th of the same month. Without objection on the part of E., W. entered at once upon the duties of the office, and E.

qualified as an attorney and practiced in both of the courts over which W. presided, until the April term, 1880, when the court of appeals, having decided that the terms of all the county judges in Virginia, whether elected to fill vacancies or not, commenced on the first day of January next following their appointments, and were for the full term of six years, as fixed by the constitution, E. appeared and protested that he was the lawful judge. This claim W. refused to recognize, principally on the ground that E., by acquiescing in the assumption of the office of W. and becoming a practicing attorney in his court, held an office incompatible with the office of judge, and by this conduct had forfeited and abandoned his said office. On quo warranto by E. against W., held, E. was entitled to the office, and the fact that he only yielded to the legislative and executive construction of the constitution until the question was settled by the supreme court was no abandonment or forfeiture of his office. The Bland and Giles County Judge Case, 33 Gratt. 443.

Where defendant, claiming to be plaintiff's successor in the office as county judge, called on plaintiff to surrender the office on the ground that the supreme court had decided the question adversely to him in a case involving other parties, and plaintiff complied with the demand, he could not contend that he was ousted from office. Fitzpatrick v. Kirby, 81 Va. 467.

B. IN VACATION.

See the title CHAMBERS AND VACATION, vol. 2, p. 767.

C. TO SIGN BILLS OF EXCEPTION.

See the titles CERTIORARI, vol. 2, p. 734; EXCEPTIONS, BILL OF, vol. 5, p. 357.

A judge selected under W. Va. Code, ch. 112, to try a certain case, and who does try such case, may sign bills of exceptions therein within thirty days after the adjournment of the term at which the trial is had, as though he were the regular judge of such court. Carper v. Cook, 39 W. Va. 346, 19 S. E. 379.

D. RIGHT TO COMPENSATION.

In General.—Section 22, art. 6, of the Virginia constitution, provides that "all the judges shall receive such salaries and allowances as may be determined by law, the amount of which shall not be diminished during their term of office." Foster v. Jones, 79 Va. 642; Neal v. Allen, 76 Va. 437; Montague v. Massey, 76 Va. 307.

Judges of Special Court of Appeals. —The constitution provides that the judges of the supreme court of appeals and of the superior courts shall receive "fixed and adequate salaries." Therefore, a per diem compensation to the judges holding the special court of appeals, provided for by act of March, 1848, does not violate the constitution. Sharpe v. Robertson, 5 Gratt. 518.

Judge of General Court.—A judge of the general court, elected for and assigned to the seventh judicial circuit, has an additional salary allowed him in consequence of the great mass of judicial business in one of the courts of his circuit; that court is afterwards severed from the seventh circuit and formed into a new circuit, and a new judge appointed from the same; the former judge yet remaining judge of the seventh circuit. Held, that as the act establishing a new circuit, makes no mention of the additional salary allowed to the former judge, and does not in terms or by necessary implication take it away, it was not the intention of the legislature to take it away; and that, if the legislature had intended to take the additional salary away, and had so enacted, such enactment would have been unconstitutional. Com. v. Clopton, 9 Leigh 109.

Where Salary Payable.—Act, April 1, 1873, providing that the judges of the city corporation courts shall be paid out of the treasury of their respective corporations, has not been repealed, and applies to the judge of the chancery court of the city of Richmond. Holladay v. Auditor, 77 Va. 425.

The fact that the auditor has always included in his estimates and reports an amount sufficient to pay the city judge's salary, and that the legislature has always appropriated a sum in gross for the "officers of the government," out whereof the salary has always been paid, is evidence of the treasurer's disregard of the act of April 1, 1873, providing that judges of city courts shall be paid by their cities, but not of an intention on the part of the legislature to repeal that act. The auditor's estimates are no part of the appropriation acts of the legislature. Holladay v. Auditor, 77 Va. 425.

Waiver of Right.—Where a judge under second election accepts a diminished salary, under the acts of the assembly, without protest, he does not waive his rights. Neal v. Allen, 76 Va. 437; Montague v. Massey, 76 Va. 307.

E. POWER TO AWARD AND EN-FORCE INJUNCTIONS.

See the title INJUNCTIONS, vol. 7, p. 512.

F. TO SIT AS JUDGE IN AN-OTHER COUNTY.

A county court judge may sit as judge in a cause in another county when the lawfully qualified judge of that county is absent, or fails to attend, or is situated in a prescribed way; but it is necessary that these facts be entered of record. Gresham v. Ewell, 85 Va. 1, 3, 6 S. E. 700; Combs v. Com., 90 Va. 88, 17 S. E. 881.

Chapter 154, § 14, of the Virginia Code of 1873, which provides that, in certain cases, the judge of one county or district may hold a court in another county or district, is constitutional. Smith v. Com., 75 Va. 904.

G. POWER OF JUDGE TO SET ASIDE VERDICT.

See the title VERDICT.

H. CONTROL OF COURTHOUSE.

A judge of a circuit court has authority to control the courthouse in which he administers justice, to the extent at least, of preventing any interference with the discharge of the public business, and of having necessary jury rooms and other conveniences for that purpose. Where there is any such interference by the board of supervisors of a county, or any one else, the judge certainly has the right to inquire into it. If in doing so he violates the law or infringes upon the rights of others, his action may be corrected by a writ of error. But it is not a case in which prohibition will lie. Supervisors of Bedford v. Wingfield, 27 Gratt. 329.

I. AUTHORITY OVER JURY.

The authority of a judge who presides at a criminal trial, extends over the jury not only during the day whilst they are in court, but after the adjournment for the day; and it is not illegal or improper for the judge to take charge of a juror in the temporary absence of the sheriffs to whom the jury has been committed. Philips v. Com., 19 Gratt. 485. See the title JURY.

J. EXEMPTION FROM ARREST.

Judges are exempt from arrest in civil suits during their attendance at court. Com. v. Ronald, 4 Call 98. See generally, the title PRIVILEGE.

K. DUTY TO FILL VACATED OFFICE.

When the office of sheriff has become vacated, it is the duty of the county court judge to fill the vacancy in the mode prescribed by law. Shell v. Cousins, 77 Va. 328. See generally, the titles PUBLIC OFFICERS; SHERIFFS AND CONSTABLES.

L. NEGLECT OF DUTY.

In General.—Lack of time or lapse

of memory is no excuse for a judge's refusal to perform any duty imposed on him by law. Powell *v.* Tarry, 77 Va. 250.

M. POWERS OF SUCCESSOR AS TO PROCEEDINGS BEFORE FORMER JUDGE.

It is competent for a subsequent judge to hear and determine a motion to set aside a verdict of a jury and grant a new trial, where such motion was made before a preceding judge and left undetermined; but, in doing so, he must act on the evidence upon which the verdict was founded. What that evidence was may be ascertained by the note of the judge who presided at the trial, by his affidavit or that of the counsel in the case, by a re-examination of the witnesses, or by any other mode that may be lawful. Ott *v.* McHenry, 2 W. Va. 73.

VIII. Incapacities.

A. TO HOLD OTHER OFFICES.

The West Virginia constitution, § 16, art. 8, provides that "No judge, during his term of office, shall practice the profession of law, or hold any other office, appointment or public trust, under this or any other government, and the acceptance thereof shall vacate his judicial office. Nor shall he, during his continuance therein, be eligible to any political office." Building & Loan Ass'n *v.* Sohn, 54 W. Va. 101, 113, 46 S. E. 222. See also, Va. Const., 1902, art. 6, § 105.

Exception.—The judge of a corporation or hustings court in a city of the second class, may hold the office of commissioner in chancery of the circuit court for the county in which the city is located. Va. Const., 1902, § 105.

B. TO PRACTICE LAW.

The constitution of West Virginia, § 16, art. 8, provides that "no judge, during his term of office, shall practice the profession of law." Building & Loan Ass'n *v.* Sohn, 54 W. Va. 101,

113, 46 S. E. 222. See also, Va. Const., art. 6, § 105.

IX. Liabilities.

In Civil Actions.—When acting within their jurisdiction, judicial officers are exempt in civil actions from liability for their official acts, although such acts are alleged to have been done maliciously and corruptly. Johnson *v.* Moorman, 80 Va. 131. See also, Fansler *v.* Parsons, 6 W. Va. 486.

X. Disqualifications.

A. INTEREST.

General Rule.—It is a fundamental rule in the administration of justice that a person can not be a judge in a cause wherein he is interested, whether he be a party to the suit or not. Findley *v.* Smith, 42 W. Va. 299, 26 S. E. 370.

Character of Interest Which Disqualifies.—The interest of the judge must be in the subject matter, and not in the legal question involved, in order to disqualify. Forest Coal Co. *v.* Doolittle, 54 W. Va. 210, 46 S. E. 238.

In determining whether a judge is disqualified on account of interest, the superior court will ascertain what rights and interests are involved in the case and may be subjects of adjudication therein, and, if it be found that the judge has such interest as renders it impossible for him to adjudicate upon all the rights involved, without affecting his own, the writ will be awarded, without inquiry as to whether the parties will, or will not, call for adjudication upon the particular matter as to which the disqualification exists. Forest Coal Co. *v.* Doolittle, 54 W. Va. 210, 46 S. E. 238.

Example.—A judge who together with other persons, takes a lease on part of a tract of land against which a suit, instituted by the state for the sale thereof as school lands, is pending, is disqualified; and a dismissal as to the part on which the lease is will not remove his disqualification. Forest

Coal Co. *v.* Doolittle, 54 W. Va. 210, 46 S. E. 238.

Judge, Attorney in Fact.—A judge who, under a power of attorney, attaches a name of a surety to the bond of a county treasurer, is disqualified to approve a bond as required by Va. Code, 1887, § 812. Stuart *v.* Com., 91 Va. 152, 21 S. E. 246.

B. INTEREST WHICH REQUIRES REMOVAL OF CAUSE.

When the judge of a circuit court is so situated as to render it improper, in his judgment, for him to preside at the trial of a cause, the statute makes it lawful for him to remove the cause to another circuit. In such case, however, the propriety of removing or refusing to remove depends upon the self-consciousness of the judge, and an appellate court can not revise his decision. Boswell *v.* Flockheart, 8 Leigh 364.

Where Suit Brought.—When a judge of a circuit court is interested in a case, which but for such interest, would be proper for the jurisdiction of his court, the action or suit may be brought in any county in an adjoining circuit, the county seat of which county is nearest the county seat of the county wherein said Judge resides, and, in such case, the suit may be brought and prosecuted in such adjoining county, if none of the parties reside therein. McConaughey *v.* Bennett, 50 W. Va. 172, 40 S. E. 540.

C. JUDGE AS COUNSEL.

There is no statute which prohibits a judge from sitting in a case in which he is or has been counsel. Common law forbids his so doing, but if he acts, his acts are not void, but are binding until reversed or annulled in a proper proceeding. Louisville, etc., R. Co. *v.* Taylor, 93 Va. 226, 227, 24 S. E. 1013.

Prosecuting Attorney.—It is improper for a judge to try indictment signed by him as prosecuting attorney. State *v.* Cottrell, 45 W. Va. 837, 32 S. E. 162.

D. JUDGE AS A TAXPAYER.

Acts, 1881, ch. 62, § 1, providing that no judge shall be disqualified in any cause by reason of the fact that he is a taxpayer of the county, district or municipality interested in or a party to such cause, is constitutional. Wheeling *v.* Black, 25 W. Va. 266.

E. JUDGE ACTING AS CORONER.

A judge of an examining court is not legally disqualified, because, being a justice of the peace, he acted as coroner in taking the inquest upon the dead body of the man. Forde *v.* Com., 16 Gratt. 547. See the title JUSTICES OF THE PEACE.

F. JUDGE AS NOTARY PUBLIC.

The offices of judge of a criminal court and notary public are incompatible. Building & Loan Ass'n *v.* Sohn, 54 W. Va. 101, 103, 46 S. E. 222.

G. VALIDITY OF ACTS OF INTERESTED JUDGE.

A decree rendered by an interested judge is voidable only, and not void. Louisville, etc., R. Co. *v.* Taylor, 93 Va. 226, 24 S. E. 1013.

Mere formal orders may be entered by an interested judge. Findley *v.* Smith, 42 W. Va. 299, 26 S. E. 370.

H. HOW INTEREST OF JUDGE TAKEN ADVANTAGE OF.

Where a judge of an inferior court who is disqualified by reason of interest, is permitted to proceed to final judgment or decree, his interest is ground of error for which reversal may be had in the appellate court, and render the judgment or decree voidable; but he may be restrained, before judgment or final decree, at any stage of the case, by the writ of prohibition, and his disqualification may be made to appear upon the motion for the writ, without its having been first pleaded in the court below, passed upon adversely there and then established in the superior court on appeal or writ of error. Forest Coal Co. *v.* Doolittle, 54 W. Va. 210, 46 S. E. 238.

XI. De Facto Judges.

See the title DE FACTO OFFICERS, vol. 4, p. 446.

A. EXISTENCE.

There can be no judge de facto in any case where there is an incumbent in the office. Morriss v. Virginia Ins. Co., 85 Va. 588, 8 S. E. 383.

B. VALIDITY OF ACTS.

The acts of de facto judges are valid when they concern the public or the rights of third persons who have an interest in the act done. McCraw v. Williams, 33 Gratt. 510. See the title DE FACTO OFFICERS, vol. 4, p. 449.

Example.—A was elected in January, 1880, judge of the county court of Halifax, and commissioned by the governor; and believing that his term commenced immediately, he proceeded to hold the court and transact business. Held, he was a judge de facto; and his judgments are valid and binding, as if he had been a judge de jure. McCraw v. Williams, 33 Gratt. 510.

The judge of the court of appeals who were in office under military appointment when the state was restored to the union, holding over and continuing to exercise their office, their judgments and decrees are valid and binding. Griffin v. Cunningham, 20 Gratt. 31. See post, "Holding Over," XI, C.

C. HOLDING OVER.

Under act March 5, 1870, § 2, judges of the court of appeals in office under military appointment, were authorized to hold the office until their successors should be chosen and qualified. Griffin v. Cunningham, 20 Gratt. 31; Quinn v. Com., 20 Gratt. 138. See ante, "Holding Over," V, D.

XII. Special Judges.

A. WHO MAY BE ELECTED.

Any citizen of this state who is a "discreet and proper person, learned in the law," may be selected as judge to hold the term or try any particular cause in a circuit court. Winans v. Winans, 22 W. Va. 678.

B. WHO MAY ELECT.

Section 16, art. 8, of the constitution of 1872 of West Virginia authorizes the legislature to provide by law for the election of a special judge to hold a special as well as general term of the circuit court where, from any cause, the judge of such court shall fail to attend. Winans v. Winans, 22 W. Va. 678, 679. See ante, "Election to Office of Judge," III.

Acts, 1872-73, ch. 129, provides that where from any cause a judge shall fail to attend, or if in attendance, can not properly preside, the selection in the first instance shall be made by the attorneys at such court, and in the other by the parties or their attorneys in the particular cause. Winans v. Winans, 22 W. Va. 678.

Under acts, 1895, ch. 20, counsel for the prisoner in a murder case can not agree with the prosecuting attorney upon a member of the bar as special judge, to try the case. State v. Burnett, 47 W. Va. 731, 35 S. E. 983.

C. WHEN ELECTION JUSTIFIED.

When a regular judge is absent, and there is no person present authorized or willing to hold court, the election of a special judge is justified. State v. Carter, 49 W. Va. 709, 39 S. E. 611.

Where it is shown by the record that on the day fixed by law for the commencement of a regular term of the criminal court of a county the regular judge thereof being sick and failing to attend and hold said court, at the commencement of said term, the clerk of said court proceeded to hold an election for a special judge of said court as provided by chapter 112, § 11, Code of West Virginia, and several attorneys, named, being placed in nomination and the clerk of the said criminal court having held said election declares as the result thereof that J. W. V. received a majority of the votes cast by the attorney present and practicing in said court, and was duly elected judge of said criminal court, during the temporary absence of J., the regular judge, thereupon said J. W. V. appeared and took the several oaths prescribed by law; held, the law has been substantially complied with and the election is valid. Franklin v. Vandevort, 50 W. Va. 412, 40 S. E. 374.

The election of a special judge, where the regular judge is present holding the court, is prohibited by acts, 1897, ch. 49, unless the court by the regular judge enter of record an order for such election, which recites the facts specified in the act. State v. Cross, 44 W. Va. 315, 29 S. E. 527; State v. Newman, 49 W. Va. 724, 727, 39 S. E. 655.

Virginia Code, § 3049, provides that if a county judge is so situated as to render it improper for him to preside, and it be so entered of record, the judge of any other county court may hold said term, or any part thereof. The record showed that after the judge opened court the first and second days of the term, an order was entered, reciting his disability in the words of the statute and that K., judge of G. county, thereupon took his seat. The record stated that the orders of the second day including the adjourning order, were signed by K. Held, a compliance with the law. Combs v. Com., 90 Va. 88, 17 S. E. 881; Gresham v. Ewell, 85 Va. 1, 6 S. E. 700.

Constitutionality.—The act of the legislature, ch. 129, acts, 1872-73, which provides for electing a special judge by the member of the bar to hold the general term of a circuit court, where from any cause the judge fails to appear, or if present can not preside, is constitutional. State v. Williams, 14 W. Va. 851.

Whether the act of the legislature, ch. 129, acts, 1872-73, authorizes the election by the members of the bar, of a special judge to hold a special term of a circuit court where the judge who calls the special term fails to at-

tend, and if so, whether such act, as applied to a special term is constitutional or not, the court is equally divided. State v. Williams, 14 W. Va. 851.

Acts, 1881, ch. 3, § 2, providing for the election of a special judge of a circuit court, where the regular judge is disqualified to sit in any cause, is constitutional. Lynch v. Henry, 25 W. Va. 416.

Section 1 of chapter 129 of the acts of 1872-73 is constitutional; and under its provisions a special judge may be selected, as therein provided, to hold a special as well as a general or adjourned term of the circuit court, where the regular judge is not in attendance. Winans v. Winans, 22 W. Va. 678, 679.

D. NUMBER OF SPECIAL JUDGES.

The statute does not limit the number of elections of special judges. State v. Neuman, 49 W. Va. 724, 727, 39 S. E. 655; State v. Carter, 49 W. Va. 709, 39 S. E. 611.

There may be more than one special judge elected during the same term to hold a court in the absence of the regular judge, if, from the absence of the first elected judge, there be reason for the election of a second special judge. State v. Neuman, 49 W. Va. 724, 39 S. E. 655.

E. NECESSITY FOR OATH.

When a judge of a criminal court can not properly preside upon a felony case, and a special judge is selected as required by law, such judge must, before proceeding to exercise the authority or discharge the duties of the judgship, take the oath prescribed by § 5, art. 4, of the constitution, as well as that provided for in ch. 20, acts, 1895. State v. Burnett, 47 W. Va. 731, 35 S. E. 983. But see Tower v. Whip, 53 W. Va. 158, 44 S. E. 179, where it was held, that a judgment rendered by a special judge elected as provided by law, is neither void nor reversible merely because he did not take the oath in art. 4, § 5, of the constitution. He is at least a judge de facto.

F. OBJECTION TO AUTHORITY.

In General.—Where a litigant joins in the selection of a special judge to hear his case, without objection, he will not be permitted to raise technical objections to the selection and qualification of such judge after he has decided against such litigant. Whipkey v. Nicholas, 47 W. Va. 35, 34 S. E. 751.

In Appellate Court.—Where a special judge has tried a case and no objection was made on the trial to his authority, and the record is silent as to the mode of his appointment or election, no objection to his authority can be raised in the appellate court for the first time, provided that by law, he could have been elected, as the appellate court will presume that he was legally elected. State v. Lowe, 21 W. Va. 782; Jarrell v. French, 43 W. Va. 456, 27 S. E. 263; Winans v. Winans, 22 W. Va. 678; State v. Neuman, 49 W. Va. 724, 39 S. E. 655.

G. WHEN OFFICE TERMINATES.

Where a special judge is absent or refuses to hold his court when present, he vacates his continuance in office. State v. Carter, 49 W. Va. 709, 39 S. E. 611.

The appearance of the regular judge vacates the continuance in office of a special judge, without an order to this effect. State v. Carter, 49 W. Va. 709, 39 S. E. 611.

Judgment Notes.

See the title CONFESSION OF JUDGMENTS, vol. 3, p. 64.

JUDGMENTS AND DECREES.

CROSS REFERENCES.

See the titles APPEAL AND ERROR, vol. 1, p. 418; BANKRUPTCY AND INSOLVENCY, vol. 2, p. 232; BILL OF REVIEW, vol. 2, p. 384; CERTIORARI, vol. 2, p. 734; CONFESSION OF JUDGMENTS, vol. 3, p. 64; COURTS, vol. 3, p. 696; DEBT, THE ACTION OF, vol. 4 p. 269; DETINUE AND REPLEVIN, vol. 4, p. 634; DISMISSAL, DISCONTINUANCE AND NONSUIT, vol. 4, p. 683; DIVORCE, vol. 4, p. 734; ELEGIT, vol. 5, p. 58; EXECUTIONS, vol. 5, p. 416; EXECUTIONS AGAINST THE BODY AND ARREST IN CIVIL CASES, vol. 5, p. 474; EXECUTORS AND ADMINISTRATORS, vol. 5, p. 483; FOREIGN JUDGMENTS, vol. 6, p. 208; FORMER ADJUDICATION OR RES ADJUDICATA, vol. 6, p. 261; FORTHCOMING AND DELIVERY BONDS, vol. 6, p. 411; INJUNCTIONS, vol. 7, p. 512; JUDGES, ante, p. 150; JURISDICTION; JUSTICES OF THE PEACE; ORDERS OF COURT; RECORDS; SENTENCE AND PUNISHMENT; STARE DECISIS; VERDICT.

As to judgments on motion, see the title MOTIONS. As to judgments in evidence, see the title RECORDS. As to judgments in particular proceedings, see the appropriate titles.

I. Definition, Nature and General Consideration.

A. DEFINITIONS.

A judgment or decree is the sentence and adjudication made by the law, spoken through a court, upon facts admitted or proven. There can be no judgment or decree without matters of fact alleged. Freem. Judgm., § 2; Black, Judgm., § 1. Fowler v. Lewis, 36 W. Va. 112, 14 S. E. 447, 452.

"It is essential to a judgment that it be a judicial determination, an adjudication by the court." Bank v. McVeigh, 32 Gratt. 530.

A judgment, whether in a criminal or civil case, is the sentence of the law pronounced by the proper tribunal, as the result of the proceedings instituted for the redress of injury or the punishment of offenses. Pifer's Case, 14 Gratt. 710.

Whether the judgment be the act of the court, or be entered up by the clerk under the statute, the effect is the same. In either case it is the act of the law, and until reversed by the court which rendered it or by a superior tribunal, it imports absolute verity, and is as effectual and binding as if pronounced in a trial upon the merits. Neale v. Utz, 75 Va. 480.

"A judgment is the 'decision or sentence of the law, pronounced by a court or other competent tribunal, upon the matter contained in the record.' When, after the facts are found, the court pronounces the decision upon them, that is the judgment. That is the judicial act—the act of the court as a court speaking the sentence of the law, whereas the entering it in the roll, the docket, or the order or judgment book, * * * is an act of a different nature, a clerical or ministerial act, one to constitute merely a memorial to attest that the judicial act of pronouncing judgment was in fact done." Brannon, J., dissenting. McClain v. Davis, 37 W. Va. 330, 16 S. E. 629. See post, "Rendition and Entry," V.

A decree is the judicial decision of a litigated cause by courts of equity, admiralty and probate. In its accurate use the term is employed to distinguish decrees of equity courts from judgments of law courts, though the term judgment is often used to include both. Bouvier's Law Dictionary.

A decree is the conclusion of the law from the pleadings and the proofs. Keneweg Co. v. Schilansky, 47 W. Va. 287, 34 S. E. 773; Waldron v. Harvey, 54 W. Va. 608, 613, 46 S. E. 603; Vance Shoe Co. v. Haught, 41 W. Va. 275, 23 S. E. 553.

A judgment of his peers means a trial by jury. Jelly v. Dils, 27 W. Va. 267, 274.

For the definitions of the various classes of judgments, see post, "Classification of Judgments and Decrees," II.

B. DECREE FOR SPECIFIC PROPERTY OR FOR MONEY IN EFFECT A JUDGMENT.

Section 3557 of the West Virginia Code of 1899, provides that: "A decree for land or specific personal property, and a decree or order requiring the payment of money, shall have the effect of a judgment for such land, property, or money, and be embraced by the word 'judgment,' where used in any chapter under this title; but a party may proceed to carry into execution a decree or order in chancery other than for the payment of money, as he might have done if this and the following section had not been enacted." Section 1, ch. 139, of the West Virginia Code is to the same effect.

"The statute, Code, 1873, ch. 182, § 1, provides that 'a decree for land or specific personal property, and a decree or order requiring the payment of money, shall have the effect of a judgment for such land, property, or money, and be embraced in the word "judgment,"' etc. And by § 2 it is provided that 'the persons entitled to the benefit of any decree or order requiring the payment of money shall be deemed judgment creditors, although the money be required to be paid into a court, or a bank or other place of deposit. In such case, an execution on the decree or order shall make such recital thereof, and of the parties to it, as may be necessary to designate the case; and if a time be specified in the decree or order within which the payment is to be made, the execution shall not issue until the expiration of that time.'" Hutcheson v. Grubbs, 80 Va. 251, 253.

C. JUDGMENTS CONSIDERED AS CONTRACTS.

In General.—Freeman on Judgments, § 4, says: "Though it be conceded that a judgment is not a contract, yet perhaps courts are justified, in some cases, in treating it as though it were a contract, or rather, in determining that the word "contract," as used in some statute, was intended to include judgments. Thus it has been held, that a Code provision authorizing the union in one complaint of several causes of action, when they all arise out of contract, express or implied, warranted the joinder of two or more judgments as causes of action; that a statute investing justices with the jurisdiction over actions upon contracts for the recovery of money gave them authority to hear actions upon judgments; that where a statute classifies actions as being ex contractu or ex delicto, judgments must be treated as within the former class, their owners are entitled to the same remedies for their collection as if they were contracts, including the right to attachment." Therefore, there is the same right to file an affidavit under § 46 in an action on judgment as on a bond. Marstiller v. Ward, 52 W. Va. 74, 83, 43 S. E. 178, followed in Hutton v. Holt, 52 W. Va. 672, 44 S. E. 164. .

A judgment founded on a tort is in no sense a contract; therefore § 35, art. 8, of our constitution, as it only applies to judgments founded on tort, is not inhibited by § 10, art. 1, of the constitution of the United States, as it does not impair the obligation of a contract. White v. Crump, 19 W. Va. 583.

A judgment founded on a tort is in no sense a contract; therefore, § 35, art. 8, of the constitution of West Virginia, which provides, that: "No citizen of this state, who aided or participated in the late war between the government of the United States and a part of the people thereof on either side, shall be liable in any proceedings civil or criminal, nor shall his property be seized or sold under final process issued upon judgments or decrees heretofore rendered or otherwise because of any act done according to the usages of civilized warfare in the prosecution of said war by either of the parties thereto," is not inhibited by § 10, art. 1, of the constitution of the United States, as it does not impair the obligation of a contract. Peerce v. Kitzmiller, 19 W. Va. 564.

"It is clear, that a judgment founded upon a tort can in no case be regarded as a contract. There is no agreement of the parties; and there is no consideration. It is founded upon no agreement of the parties, and there

could have been no consideration moving the parties in such a case. Instead of harmony there was discord; instead of agreement there was disagreement; and it would be absurd to say, that under such circumstances there could be a contract between the parties." Peerce v. Kitzmiller, 19 W. Va. 564.

Judgments Considered as Debts of Record.—See post, "Actions on Judgments," XV. And see DEBT, vol. 4, p. 268. See also, the titles DEBT, THE ACTION OF, vol. 4, p. 283, et seq.; FOREIGN JUDGMENTS, vol. 6, p. 227.

D. JUDGMENTS TREATED AS PROPERTY UNDER WEST VIRGINIA CONSTITUTION.

Section 35, art. 8, of the constitution of West Virginia, treats judgments as property and provides for the carrying out of the provision by "due process of law;" and such judgments, as were contemplated by said section, were not to be declared void, until "by due process of law" it was ascertained, that they were recovered "because of acts done according to the usages of civilized warfare in the prosecution of the war," and when so ascertained, they were to be treated as nullities. White v. Crump, 19 W. Va. 583.

E. CONSTRUCTION.

Sufficient if Judgment or Decree May Be Made Certain.—As to the application to judgments and decrees of the maxim that is certain which may be made certain, see post, "Definiteness and Certainty," IV, B.

Reference to Bill and Other Proceedings.—Where a doubt arises as to the meaning and effect of a decree, it may be ascertained by reference to the bill and other proceedings, particularly where these are referred to in the decree itself. Walker v. Page, 21 Gratt. 636; Norvell v. Lessueur, 33 Gratt. 222, 227; Burging v. McDowell, 30 Gratt. 236, 242.

Effect of Reference in Decree to Record in Another Suit.—The decree referring to the record of another suit as an exhibit in the cause, makes it a part of the record, though it is not referred to in the bill or answer, nor made an exhibit by an entry on the order book. Craig *v.* Sebrell, 9 Gratt. 131; Tracey *v.* Shumate, 22 W. Va. 474, 511; Richardson *v.* Donehoo, 16 W. Va. 685. See the title EXHIBITS, vol. 5, p. 771.

Construction According to Plain Meaning and Import of Language.— H. files his bill to enforce his and the liens of other judgment creditors on the lands of S. An account of the liens and lands is taken. Report shows numerous liens and parcels of land. H.'s judgment was a lien on all the lands, and a vendor's lien on the parcel first aliened by S., viz.; to R. There were also three deeds of trust of different dates; the first and third securing each one debt on one parcel; and the second securing on all the lands numerous debts, as well judgments as debts not reduced to judgments. But this second trust deed was not enforceable until May 3d, 1882. Besides H.'s, there was no lien on R.'s parcel. Exceptions to report being overruled, the circuit court decreed that, unless within sixty days, S. paid the costs of the suit, the judgment of H. and the other judgments appearing from the report to be chargeable on the lands of S., then commissioners should sell so much of the lands of S., described in the report, as might be necessary to pay said costs and judgments, but should sell first so much of the land conveyed by S. to R. as might be necessary to pay said costs and the judgment of H.; and then sell so much of the other lands of S. as might be necessary to pay the balance (if any) of the judgment of H., and the other judgments chargeable thereon as set forth in the report. On appeal by defendants, held, by the plain mean-

ing and import of the language of the decree, R. could only prevent the sale of his land under it by the payment of all the judgments reported by the master and all the costs of the suit. Shultz *v.* Hansbrough, 76 Va. 817.

Decrees are not to be construed as adjudging by mere implication, and a decree will not be construed to so adjudge that a trust deed was fraudulent, or had been satisfied, when no decree expressly adjudges this, and if it did so, it would be in direct opposition to express evidence to the contrary. Fisher *v.* Dickenson, 84 Va. 318, 4 S. E. 737.

Construction of Decree Confirming a Report Containing Conflicting Statements.—Where an interlocutory decree merely confirms generally a report containing alternative conflicting statements, it must be understood that the court has reserved to itself the power of selecting, by its future decree, between such statements, and decreeing accordingly. M'Candlish *v.* Edloe, 3 Gratt. 330.

Where a decree for a deed does not direct specially whether a general or special warranty deed should be made, the defendants can only be required to make a deed with special warranty. Boggess *v.* Robinson, 5 W. Va. 402.

The word "curator" annexed to the name of a defendant against whom a decree is rendered is descriptive merely, and the decree is a personal decree, although there be superadded a direction to the defendant "as curator" to collect and apply certain funds to its payment. Fulkerson *v.* Taylor, 100 Va. 426, 41 S. E. 863.

Decision for Plaintiff Construed as Overruling Demurrers.—As to the rule that the judgment on a verdict virtually overrules all demurrers, to the declaration, and each count thereof, and that where the record on appeal does not show that a demurrer has been overruled, that must be presumed, if the court has decided on the merits

for the plaintiff, see the titles AP-
PEAL AND ERROR, vol. 1, p. 612;
DEMURRERS, vol. 4, p. 502.

As to presumptions on appeal in
favor of the judgment or decree below, see the title APPEAL AND ER-
ROR, vol. 1, p. 609, et seq.

Presumption That Judgment Is
against Defendants Mentioned in Writ
and Declaration.—When the writ and
declaration in the case are against two
defendants therein named, and the
record shows that the "defendants" appeared in court, by their attorney, and
pleaded in bar to the declaration, and
that the "defendants" made a motion,
at the same time, to the court, in the
cause, and afterwards, at another term
of court, the record recites "this day
came the parties," etc., judgment is
rendered in favor of the plaintiff
against the "defendants" it must be
taken that the judgment is against the
defendants mentioned in the writ and
declaration. Perry v. McHuffman, 7
W. Va. 306.

Where the principles of a decree of
the court of appeals seem to be opposed to its letter, the literal interpretation ought not to be relied on as
a binding precedent. Lewis v. Thornton, 6 Munf. 87.

As to the rule for determining what
was in issue and adjudicated by a
judgment or decree, see the title FOR-
MER ADJUDICATION OR RES
ADJUDICATA, vol. 6, p. 404, et seq.

II. Classification of Judgments and Decrees.

A. FINAL AND INTERLOCU-TORY.

1. In General.

Must Be Final or Interlocutory.—
In civil cases judgments are either in-
terlocutory or final. Pifer's Case, 14
Gratt. 710.

"All decrees are either interlocutory
or final; there is no middle class."
Harvey v. Branson, 1 Leigh 108.

A decree can not be in part final, and
in part interlocutory, in the same
cause, for and against the same parties who remain in court. Ryan v. Mc-
Leod, 32 Gratt. 367.

May Be Final as to One Party and
Not as to Another.—The supreme
court of Virginia has repeatedly decided that a decree may be final as to
one party and not as to another, depending upon the circumstances of the
case. Gardner v. Stratton, 89 Va. 900,
17 S. E. 553; Royall v. Johnson, 1 Rand.
421; Noel v. Noel, 86 Va. 109, 9 S. E.
584; Ryan v. McLeod, 32 Gratt. 367.

Where the rights or responsibilities
of several parties to a suit are perfectly distinct and several, and where
a final disposition of the cause as to
one, with a direction as to the payment of costs as between him and the
adverse party, does not in any degree
affect the rights or interests of any
other party, and where nothing which
can be brought into the cause by any
other party or which can be done by
the court as to the other party, can by
any possibility affect the rights or interests of the party as to whom such
decree has been made, such decree has
never been considered as interlocutory, but is final. Royall v. Johnson, 1
Rand. 421.

A suit was brought to construe a
will and to divide the land among the
parties entitled thereto. To this suit
the father and the two surviving children were made parties defendant, and
a decree was entered therein, adjudging
that the land be divided between the
two children and that the father had
no interest in it. It was subsequently
contended in a suit brought by a creditor to set aside a deed, made after the
decree, on the ground of fraud, and
subject the land to the payment of the
father's debts, that the doctrine of res
judicata had no application, because
the decree of partition was not a final
one. But as to the father the decree
was final, though it was not as to the

other parties. It settled the question that he had no interest in the land and that was the only question in which he was concerned. Gardner *v.* Stratton, 89 Va. 900, 17 S. E. 553. See the title FORMER ADJUDICATION OR RES ADJUDICATA, vol. 6, p. 281.

Decree Subsequent to Final Decree Erroneous.—After a final decree, which settles the right of all the parties and of the whole case made by the pleadings, any subsequent decree in the same cause is not made in a pending cause, and is therefore erroneous. Nelson *v.* Jennings, 2 Pat. & H. 369; Battaile *v.* Maryland Hospital, 76 Va. 63; Johnson *v.* Anderson, 76 Va. 766; Smith *v.* Powell, 98 Va. 431, 36 S. E. 522; Ruhl *v.* Ruhl, 24 W. Va. 279.

Where a final decree was entered in a suit, the cause was ended and the court could proceed no further. It had no further jurisdiction of the subject matter or of the parties in that proceeding, and any subsequent decree was a nullity, where it was rendered in the absence of the defendant upon the mere motion of the plaintiff by attorney, and without notice to any one. Johnson *v.* Anderson, 76 Va. 766. See Camden *v.* Haymond, 9 W. Va. 680.

After a final decree has been entered in a cause, upon proceedings regularly had, and to which no exceptions have been taken, it is error to allow an answer to be filed, and after reversing the former decree, to hear the case de novo. Crim *v.* Davisson, 6 W. Va. 465.

Where a bill has been dismissed with costs upon the hearing by a decree, this must of necessity be final, and if rendered in vacation, under the statute, it takes effect from the time it is entered of record by the clerk. The judge pronouncing it can not, by subsequent action impart to it a different character. Pace *v.* Ficklin, 76 Va. 292.

As to the finality of judgments or decrees in reference to appeals, see the title APPEAL AND ERROR, vol. 1, p. 437.

As to the finality of decrees in reference to bills of review, see the title BILL OF REVIEW, vol. 2, p. 388.

As to finality of judgments or decrees as affecting the doctrine of former adjudication or res adjudicata, see the title FORMER ADJUDICATION OR RES ADJUDICATA, vol. 6, p. 279.

2. Statement, Construction and Application of Principles Determining Finality.

a. General Principles Stated and Construed.

Criterion as to Finality of Judgment, Decrees or Orders.—According to the decisions both of the Virginia, and West Virginia courts the generally accepted definition of and distinction between final and interlocutory decrees would seem to be that when a decree makes an end of a case and decides the whole matter in controversy leaving nothing further for the court to do, it is a final decree, but when the further action of the court in the case is necessary to give completely the relief contemplated by the court, then the decree is to be regarded not as final but as interlocutory. Repass *v.* Moore, 96 Va. 147, 150, 30 S. E. 458; Yates *v.* Wilson, 86 Va. 625, 10 S. E. 976; Serles *v.* Cromer, 88 Va. 426, 428, 13 S. E. 859; Jameson *v.* Major, 86 Va. 51, 9 S. E. 480; Noel *v.* Noel, 86 Va. 109, 9 S. E. 584; Sims *v.* Sims, 94 Va. 580, 27 S. E. 436; Barker *v.* Jenkins, 84 Va. 895, 899, 6 S. E. 459; Parker *v.* Logan, 82 Va. 376, 4 S. E. 613; Miller *v.* Cook, 77 Va. 806; Johnson *v.* Anderson, 76 Va. 766; Battaile *v.* Maryland Hospital, 76 Va. 63; Rawlings *v.* Rawlings, 75 Va. 76, 87; Thomson *v.* Brooke, 76 Va. 160; Norfolk Trust Co. *v.* Foster, 78 Va. 413; Roanoke Nat. Bank *v.* Farmers' Nat. Bank, 84 Va. 603, 610, 5 S. E. 682; Sexton *v.* Patterson, 1 Va. Dec. 551;

Ryan *v.* McLeod, 32 Gratt. 367, 377; Smith *v.* Blackwell, 31 Gratt. 291, 300; Rogers *v.* Strother, 27 Gratt. 417; Ambrouse *v.* Keller, 22 Gratt. 769, 774; Burch *v.* Hardwicke, 23 Gratt. 51; Fleming *v.* Bolling, 8 Gratt. 292; Ruff *v.* Starke, 3 Gratt. 134; Vanmeter *v.* Vanmeter, 3 Gratt. 148; Cocke *v.* Gilpin, 1 Rob. 20, 21; Dunbar *v.* Woodcock, 10 Leigh 628; Hill *v.* Fox, 10 Leigh 587; Tennent *v.* Pattons, 6 Leigh 196, 208; Thorntons *v.* Fitzhugh, 4 Leigh 209, 213; Harvey *v.* Branson, 1 Leigh 108; Royall *v.* Johnson, 1 Rand. 421, 427; Alexander *v.* Coleman, 6 Munf. 328, 339; Chapman *v.* Armistead, 4 Munf. 382; Goodwin *v.* Miller, 2 Munf. 42; Sheppard *v.* Starke, 3 Munf. 29; Templeman *v.* Steptoe, 1 Munf. 339; Aldridge *v.* Giles, 3 Hen. & M. 136, 138; Mackey *v.* Bell, 2 Munf. 523; Fairfax *v.* Muse, 2 Hen. & M. 557, 558; Ellzey *v.* Lane, 2 Hen. & M. 590, 592; Allen *v.* Belches, 2 Hen. & M. 595; Bowyer *v.* Lewis, 1 Hen. & M. 554; Nelson *v.* Jennings, 2 Pat. & H. 369; Grymes *v.* Pendleton, 1 Call 54; McCall *v.* Peachy, 1 Call 55; Young *v.* Skipwith, 2 Wash. 300; Waldron *v.* Harvey, 54 W. Va. 608, 615, 46 S. E. 603; Fowler *v.* Lewis, 36 W. Va. 112, 14 S. E. 447; State *v.* Hays, 30 W. Va. 107, 120, 3 S. E. 177, 181; Ruhl *v.* Ruhl, 24 W. Va. 279, 283; Williamson *v.* Jones, 39 W. Va. 231, 19 S. E. 436; Morgan *v.* Ohio River R. Co., 39 W. Va. 17, 19 S. E. 588; Gillespie *v.* Bailey, 12 W. Va. 70; Manion *v.* Fahy, 11 W. Va. 482; Core *v.* Strickler, 24 W. Va. 689, 693; McKinney *v.* Kirk, 9 W. Va. 26, 28; Camden *v.* Haymond, 9 W. Va. 680; Butler *v.* Butler, 8 W. Va. 674; Warren *v.* Syme, 7 W. Va. 474.

In 4 Min. Inst., pt. 1 (3d Ed.), p. 1066, it is said: "The general doctrine is that any decree or order is final which disposes of whole subject, gives all the relief that was contemplated, provides with reasonable completeness for giving effect to the sentence, and leaves nothing to be done in the cause, save to superintend ministerially the execution of the decree."

The case of Cocke *v.* Gilpin, 1 Rob. 20, 21, is cited in Noel *v.* Noel, 86 Va. 109, 114, 9 S. E. 584, to the point that every decree that leaves anything to be done by the court is interlocutory as between the parties remaining in court, even though it disposes of the costs.

"According to the uniform decisions of this court, a decree which disposes of the whole subject, gives all the relief that is contemplated, and leaves nothing to be done by the court, is to be regarded as final; and, on the other hand, every decree which leaves anything to be done by the court in the cause is interlocutory as between the parties remaining in the court. Cocke *v.* Gilpin, 1 Rob. 21; Ryan *v.* McLeod, 32 Gratt. 367; Rawlings *v.* Rawlings, 75 Va. 76, and Wright *v.* Strother, 76 Va. 857." Sims *v.* Sims, 94 Va. 580, 581, 27 S. E. 436.

"In a law case a judgment, to be final, so as to warrant a writ of error, must end the issue presented by the whole case. Code, ch. 135, § 1, cl. 1; 2 Bart. Law Prac. 761." Riley *v.* Jarvis, 43 W. Va. 43, 26 S. E. 366.

"In the progress of a cause, it often becomes necessary to make orders of different kinds, in order to enable the court to come at the whole case, or to settle the details, after the principles of the cause are decided; all these are interlocutory orders or decrees." Harvey *v.* Branson, 1 Leigh 108.

"How, then, do we ascertain when a judgment or decree is final? That must always be ascertained, not by enquiring what ought to have been done by the court, but by inspecting the terms of the judgment or decree, and learning from its face what has been done. If it appears on the face of the judgment or decree, that 'further action in the cause is necessary to give completely the relief contemplated by the court, then the decree is to be regarded not as final, but interlocutory.' But 'when a decree makes an end of a case, and decides the whole matter in controversy, costs and all, leaving nothing further for the court to do, it is certainly a final decree. These principles have been repeatedly announced by this court, in chancery causes, and have been very recently reaffirmed in the latest case on the subject: Ambrouse v. Keller, 22 Gratt. 769. The same principle applies to judgment." Burch v. Hardwicke, 23 Gratt. 51.

"There is no case decided by this court, in which the decree has been held to be final where the judicial action of the court in the cause has not been exhausted. I do not mean that it is necessary the court by its decree should respond to all the questions in controversy, or to the whole relief prayed in the bill, its silence being often equally emphatic; but that this court has never held, where a given relief was contemplated, that the decree was final, if something remained to be done in the cause to render it effectual." Cocke v. Gilpin, 1 Rob. 20.

"A decree is final, when it either refuses or grants the redress sought by the party complaining. The plaintiff being the party who ordinarily seeks relief, the refusal of the court to allow it is usually accomplished by dismissing the bill. That of course terminates the cause, and sends the parties out of court. On the other hand, the case is also terminated by the granting of the whole relief contemplated by the court. In regard to that result, there can be no summary form by which it is to be accomplished; and we must look to the nature of the relief granted, in order to ascertain whether it is the final action of the court. Hence the difficulty which sometimes occurs in ascertaining whether a decree is final or interlocutory. An interlocutory decree may be merely preparatory to a decision upon the merits, by directing an inquiry necessary to the elucidation thereof, as for example the ordering of an issue; or it may go further, and deciding the principles as then presented by the record, institute proceedings for the purpose of enabling the court thereafter to apply those principles to the details of the subject, as for example directing an account; or it may approach still more nearly to the nature of a final decree, by granting relief in part, and suspending the action of the court as to the residue for further investigation, or by directing measures for entire relief to a certain extent, with a view to perfecting them thereafter, upon the supposition of contingencies or emergencies which can not be well provided for by anticipation; which last case may be illustrated by an order for the sale of property, without direction as to the application of the proceeds. And so, by various gradations, the interlocutory decree may be made to approximate the final determination, until the line of discrimination becomes too faint to be readily perceived. Thus it becomes necessary to resort to some criterion by which the distinction between the two kinds of decree may be preserved; and I regard it as comparatively of but little importance what that criterion is, provided it be uniform, and capable of a certain application; for so soon as it becomes established, the courts of original cognizance, and the parties to the controversy, by conforming to the rule, will avoid the greatest inconvenience which can occur—that of uncertainty whether further judicial action is to be had in the inferior or the appellate tribunal. For my own part, I am aware of no proper criterion but this: Where the further action of the court in the cause is necessary to give completely the relief contemplated by the court, there the decree upon which the question arises is to be regarded not as final, but interlocutory. I· say the further action of the court in the cause, to distinguish it from that action of the court which is common to both final and interlocutory decrees, to wit, those measures which are necessary for the execution of a decree that has been pronounced, and which are properly to be regarded as adopted, not in, but beyond the cause, and as founded on the decree itself or mandate of the court, without respect to the relief to which the party was previously entitled upon the merits of his case. Any other criterion than this seems to me liable to the objection of ambiguity or uncertainty." Cocke *v.* Gilpin, 1 Rob. 20.

In West Virginia and in Virginia an interlocutory decree is, after the adjournment of the term at which it was made, regarded not as an enrolled decree, but as an English decree would be regarded when entered in the registrar's book but not yet enrolled. Manion *v.* Fahy, 11 W. Va. 482, 494.

"The practice of enrollment being unknown in Virginia, it became necessary to substitute for the simple English rules, above explained, regulating the question, whether a decree should be modified or annulled, by motion, a petition for a rehearing or a supplemental bill in the nature of a bill of review, or an appeal or bill of review, or an original bill, some other rule which of necessity could be only based on the character of the decree, as there was no such distinction between decree, such as exists in England; that is, decrees which were entered on the registrar's book and decrees which had been enrolled on parchment. It was therefore determined that, what we call interlocutory decrees, should for the purpose of determining the manner in which they could be modified or annulled, be regarded as an English decree entered on the registrar's book, but not enrolled on parchment, and final decrees

should, for these purposes, be regarded as English decrees which had been enrolled on parchment. A necessity then arose with us of defining, what was an interlocutory decree and what a final decree; and though this has been a subject of discussion from our earliest judicial history, yet our courts have never yet laid down any really satisfactory definition of what is an interlocutory decree and what a final decree. The difficulty lay in the subject itself; for by various gradations the interlocutory decree may be made to approximate the final decree until the line of discrimination becomes too faint to be readily perceived." Manion *v.* Fahy, 11 W. Va. 482, 492.

By "further action of the court" is meant the further action of the court in the cause, not that action of the court which is common to both final and interlocutory decrees, and is necessary for the execution of the decree, and is regarded not in, but beyond the cause. Cocke *v.* Gilpin, 1 Rob. 20, 21; Yates *v.* Wilson, 86 Va. 625, 627, 10 S. E. 976; Serles *v.* Cromer, 88 Va. 426, 429, 13 S. E. 859; Fowler *v.* Lewis, 36 W. Va. 112, 14 S. E. 447; Camden *v.* Haymond, 9 W. Va. 680.

A decree made upon the hearing on the merits, which settles and adjudicates all the matters in controversy between the parties, is such a final decree that a bill of review will lie to it, although much may remain to be done before it can be completely carried into execution. Core *v.* Strickler, 24 W. Va. 689.

A decree in favor of receiver against executor and his sureties for a named sum, directed that receiver execute a bond in a specified sum before receiving any money under it. At a subsequent term the decree was amended as to the amount, and costs directed to be paid and execution to be issued, and the cause to be continued for a report. Held, this was a final decree, as all that remained to be done was outside the cause. Serles *v.* Cromer, 88 Va. 426, 13 S. E. 859.

Effect of Failure to Decree upon Unimportant Claim.—A decree which settles all matters in dispute in the cause, but omits to decree upon a claim set up in the bill, but which after circumstances had rendered unimportant and the plaintiff did not insist upon, is a final decree. Ruff *v.* Starke, 3 Gratt. 134.

Effect of Retention of Cause and Leave to Apply for Future Aid of Court.—It is a general rule that a decree entered upon hearing, which settles all the matters in controversy between the parties, is final though much remains to be done before it can be completely carried into execution, and even though to effectuate such execution the cause is retained and leave is given to the parties to apply for the future aid of the court. Thorntons *v.* Fitzhugh, 4 Leigh 209; Davenport *v.* Mason, 2 Wash. 200; Harvey *v.* Branson, 1 Leigh 108; Vanmeter *v.* Vanmeter, 3 Gratt. 148; Ruff *v.* Starke, 3 Gratt. 134; Tennent *v.* Pattons, 6 Leigh 196; Fleming *v.* Bolling, 8 Gratt. 292; Rogers *v.* Strother, 27 Gratt. 417; Core *v.* Strickler, 24 W. Va. 689; Rawlings *v.* Rawlings, 75 Va. 76.

Though a decree be `final, its finality will not prevent any proceedings by the court necessary and proper to carry it into complete execution. Baltimore, etc., R. Co. *v.* Vanderwerker, 33 W. Va. 191, 10 S. E. 289.

"In Harvey *v.* Branson, 1 Leigh 108, the court laid it down, that a decree which left no subject to be disposed of, no question to be decided by the court, was, in its nature, final; and Judge Brooke very correctly added, 'as to the reservations in this decree, those, and all similar reservations, are, in my view, simply provisions for the execution of the decree, as one final and conclusive, not reservations of any point for future consideration and

decision.' " Thorntons *v.* Fitzhugh, 4 Leigh 209.

A decree, final in its terms, is not rendered interlocutory by the retention of the cause on the docket, and the rendition of a subsequent decree in the same cause. Nelson *v.* Jennings, 2 Pat. & H. 369.

"In Tennent *v.* Pattons, 6 Leigh 196, Judge Carr said, that every decree which disposes of the whole cause and leaves nothing to be done, is a final decree. But there is a stronger case, a much stronger case, than this is, to show the finality of the decree under consideration. It is the case of Harvey *v.* Branson, 1 Leigh 108, which may be regarded as the leading case on this point. In that case, a decree had been rendered disposing of the whole subject, deciding all questions in controversy, ascertaining the rights of the parties and awarding costs, and a commissioner had been appointed to sell property, to account for and pay the proceeds to the parties, with liberty to them to apply to the court to add other commissioners, or substitute new commissioners, or have a decree for partition of the property directed to be sold. The court of appeals, by the unanimous opinion of all the judges who sat in the cause, held the decree to be final. The opinion delivered by Judge Carr, in that case, in which Judges Green and Brooke concurred, placed the question in a light too clear to admit of misapprehension or doubt. The principle of this case was affirmed in the cases of Paup *v.* Mingo, 4 Leigh 163, and Thornton *v.* Fitzhugh, 4 Leigh 209; in each of which, the causes were retained on the docket, for further proceedings to be had therein—showing clearly, that the mere fact of the cause being retained in court and on the docket, does not divest a decree of its finality." Nelson *v.* Jennings, 2 Pat. & H. 369, 381.

Testator by his will desires, that, when his affairs are settled and all his debts paid, his slaves be emancipated according to law, and those under age and over forty to be equally in the care of his wife, son and.daughter, and that the above may be done by his executors; upon bill in chancery by slaves (suing in forma pauperis) against the executor, charging that ample fund has been raised out of their profits to pay debts, and praying an account of administration, and of their profits, and decree for their manumission and for excess of profits above the debts, the chancellor, in 1809, finding that ample fund to pay the debts has been raised out of the profits, though debts not yet finally liquidated and paid, decrees, that the executor shall manumit them, reserving liberty to them to resort to the court, for a distribution of any surplus of profits which might remain after liquidation and payment of debts, or for other arrangement in respect to such surplus; the debts are not finally liquidated and paid till 1827, when there appears a surplus of profits; and now, the freedmen claim this surplus, the testator's next kin claim it, and the executor claims it. Held, the decree of 1809 is a final decree as to the manumission, but makes no disposition of the surplus of profits. Paup v. Mingo, 4 Leigh 163.

A legatee brought suit against the purchaser of real estate from an executor, and the sons of the deceased surety of the executor on his bond, holding the estate of the surety. The testator bequeathed an annuity to the legatee and the residue of his estate, which was ample to satisfy all legacies, after the payment of debts, to his son, who was the executor. The latter sold the real property, wasted the personal, and died insolvent. It was decreed in this case that the sons of the surety should each pay one-half of the annuities in arrear, and the costs of the suit, reserving liberty to the plaintiff, if the decree should prove unavailing against either, to resort to the court for a further decree against the other, and ordering the cause to be retained for the purpose of taking further accounts as to the annuities to accrue in the future. Notwithstanding the reservation this was a final decree, from which no appeal can be taken after the lapse of three years, and although the legacy was charged both on the real and personal property, yet the latter was primarily applicable to the legacy, and the decree was correct in subjecting the surety of the executor, before the purchaser of the real estate. Thorntons v. Fitzhugh, 4 Leigh 209.

Decree Not Interlocutory Merely Because Attachment Necessary to Its Enforcement.—In Rawlings v. Rawlings, 75 Va. 76, 87, it is said: "The inference which seems to have been drawn by Judge Tucker in Hill v. Fox, 10 Leigh 587, 591, that the decree in that case was interlocutory because an attachment was necessary to enforce it, would appear not to be consistent with the established doctrine as laid down in Cocke v. Gilpin, 1 Rob. 20; and Judge Brooke, who sat in both cases, took occasion to say in the latter case, that he 'concurred in the result of the opinion delivered by the president (in the former case), that the decree was interlocutory, but certainly not on the ground that it was to be enforced by attachment, as said by the president; because all decrees must be enforced by attachment when any party is in contempt of the court, and this necessity is most frequent in cases of final decrees.' "

Effect of Order Suspending Decree as to Part of Account Involved.—A decree which passes upon the whole subject in issue so as to be final in its nature, is not converted into an interlocutory decree by the addition thereto, of an order suspending the decree as to the amount of an item of the account involved in the cause, until the decision of another suit brought by another party against both the plaintiffs and defendants in the first suit, in which the amount of that item is claimed by the plaintiff. Fleming v. Bolling, 8 Gratt. 292; Nelson v. Jennings, 2 Pat. & H. 369, 381. See also, Davis v. Crews, 1 Gratt. 407.

The object of this order was not to reserve any question in the first case for future decision, but to prevent the enforcement of the decree until the second suit was decided. This does not convert the decree into an interlocutory one, but it still remains final. Fleming v. Bolling, 8 Gratt. 292.

Effect of Order Striking Cause from Docket.—Where land was sold by a commissioner as ordered, and the proceeds of the sale distributed and a final report was made, which showed a completion of his collections and a balance in his hands for final distribution, the cause was heard upon the papers formerly read and the report of the commissioners without exceptions. The court confirmed the report and decreed in conformity with it, and that "the cause should be stricken from the docket." This means that in the opinion of the court the cause is ended —that no further action of the court in the cause is necessary. That is the established definition of a final decree. It is, and in the nature of things must be an adjudication that everything has been done in the cause that the court intends to do, and there is no longer any necessity of retaining it on the docket. The unconditional order striking from the docket, appended to such a decree, absolutely and unequivocally imports judicial determination and a final disposition of the pending cause. The decree may be erroneous, but the error does not render it less final. The court by its order has put the cause beyond its control, and it can not upon discovery of the error recall it in a summary way and resume a jurisdiction which has been exhausted.

Battaile v. Maryland Hospital, 76 Va. 63.

Effect of Unauthorized Removal from Docket by Clerk.—Where a cause was removed from the docket, not by the order of the court, but by the clerk, and the decree was marked by him "final decree," because in his opinion there was nothing more to be done in it, this did not make it a final decree. The words marked on it do not determine its character and effect, the contents alone do this— and as there was nothing in the decree to show that the court intended to put an end to the cause, it was competent for the court to order it to be reinstated, and to take cognizance of the matters set forth in the petition filed in the suit. Ward v. Funsten, 86 Va. 359, 10 S. E. 415.

Effect of Order Allowing Execution to Issue under Virginia Code, § 3600. —At common law, no matter how long a term might last, a judgment did not become final until it ended, and the court had no power to direct an execution upon it. Until then, in the quaint language of Coke, "the record remains in the breast of the court and in their remembrance, and therefore the roll is alterable during that term as the judges shall direct; but when the term is past, then the record is in the roll, and admits of no alteration, averment or proof to the contrary." The inconvenience and injustice sometimes occasioned by this rule induced the legislature to provide a remedy, and § 3600 of the Code of Virginia was enacted, which provides that, "any court, after the fifteenth day of the term, may make a general order allowing executions to issue on judgments and decrees after ten days from their dates, although the term at which they are rendered be not ended." etc., but this section was not intended to, and does not, impart to such judgments, the quality of finality so as to deprive the court, during the term, of the power to correct, or if need be, annul an erroneous judgment. This statute manifestly enlarged the power of the court, and imparted to it an authority which at common law no court possessed. Baker v. Swineford, 97 Va. 112, 33 S. E. 542, holding the decision in Enders v. Burch, 15 Gratt. 64, to be obiter. See post, "Opening, Amending and Vacating," VII; "Judgments by Default and Decrees Pro Confesso," II, E.

Finality of Judgments, Orders and Decrees on Adjournment.—When a circuit court being about to end, without dispatching all its business, is adjourned, by the judge thereof, to a future day, by an order entered of record, as provided in § 4, ch. 112, of the West Virginia Code, all judgments, orders and decrees, rendered and made by such courts before or during the day on which such court adjourns to such future day, become final on such adjournment as if the adjournment itself were final, and can not be set aside at the adjourned term. Childers v. Loudin, 51 W. Va. 559, 42 S. E. 637.

Section 4, ch. 112, of the West Virginia Code, providing for the adjournment of the holding of a court to a future day when its term is about to end without dispatching all its business, as was done in this case, contains the following clause: "All judgments, orders and decrees, rendered and made by such court before, or during the day on which said court adjourned to such future day, as aforesaid, shall have the same force and effect in all respects as if said court had finally adjourned on that day." This statute has been construed in the case of Wickes v. Baltimore, etc., R. Co., 14 W. Va. 157, in which it is held, that by force of said statute the terms of the court as to a judgment rendered by it before or during the day on which such adjournment becomes final is ended, it is not competent for the court or

the judge thereof at the adjourned term or any other subsequent term to receive a bill of exceptions and sign it and make it a part of the record in the cause. This case was cited with approval in Amos v. Stockert, 47 W. Va. 119, 34 S. E. 821; Childers v. Loudin, 51 W. Va. 559, 42 S. E. 637.

An interlocutory decree being affirmed by the court of appeals, does not change its terms; but it remains to be executed here in the same manner as it did before the appeal; therefore, in this case, the appeal being affirmed without a deduction of war interest on a British debt, such deduction will be made in this court; especially as the plaintiff is asking the aid of the court to carry that decree into effect. Wilson v. Triplett, 4 Hen. & M. 433.

Where an appeal is taken from an interlocutory decree of a county court to the court of chancery, and that court affirms the decree, and an appeal is taken to the court of appeals; the decree of the court of chancery will be considered as interlocutory. Fretwell v. Wayt, 1 Rand. 415.

b. Application of Principles to Particular Judgments or Decrees.

(1) Instances of Final Judgments and Decrees.

A decree for the payment of money is a final decree, and is conclusive as to the questions thereby determined. W. Va. Code, 1891, ch. 135, § 1, cl. 7; Core v. Strickler, 24 W. Va. 689; Kearfott v. Dandridge, 45 W. Va. 673, 31 S. E. 947, 948.

A decree which provides for the distribution and payment of money is a final decree, and is subject to the statute of limitations relating to appeals, bills of review, and motions to correct nonappealable errors. Kearfott v. Dandridge, 45 W. Va. 673, 31 S. E. 947.

Award Entered as Decree of Court.—When the parties to a suit in equity agree to refer the matter in controversy to arbitrators, whose award is to be entered as the decree of the court, and the award is made and entered; this is a final decree, which can only be reversed or altered by bill of review. Davis v. Crews, 1 Gratt. 407.

Confirmation of Accounts.—A bill was filed by the legatees and devisees of an intestate asking for a settlement of accounts of his administrator. A full and complete settlement was duly made and filed without exception, being subsequently confirmed by the court. This decree of confirmation was final as to the administrator, and will not be reviewed on petition after three years. Bradley v. Bradley, 83 Va. 75, 1 S. E. 477.

Confirmation of Sale and Order for Disbursement and Conveyance.—A suit in chancery is brought to recover $758 in which an attachment is issued and levied upon a tract of land owned by the defendant; $718 of this sum is claimed to constitute a vendor's lien upon the land attached. The defendants answer the bill and contest their liability to pay the other $40. Depositions are taken by each party and when the cause is matured for hearing the court renders a decree for the purchase money and decrees the land to be sold. The land was sold and bought by the defendants, the sale confirmed, the price decreed to pay costs and sum decreed plaintiff, deed ordered to be executed and possession to be given by sheriff. At a subsequent term, the plaintiff moved the court, without notice, to set aside the last order and allow the commissioner's report to be amended as to the name of the security in the bond of the purchaser; it was so decreed, the report amended, and the same order of confirmation was re-entered, except that it provided if there was any surplus after paying debt, interest and costs, such surplus should be paid over to the receiver of the court. An appeal is allowed to this last order; giving its date. Held, that the first decree of confirmation was a final decree. McKinney v. Kirk, 9 W. Va. 26.

Order of Dismissal. — A decree which dismisses a suit was in these words: "The plaintiff failing to prosecute his suit, it is ordered that the same be dismissed." This decree is final, and after the end of the term at which it was rendered, it can only be set aside on appeal, or by bill of review. These remedies, however, must be pursued within the time limited by statute. Jones v. Turner, 81 Va. 709.

A decree, dismissing a bill as to a defendant, is as to such defendant a final decree. Dick v. Robinson, 19 W. Va. 159. A decree which dismisses a suit and directs the payment of costs, is a final decree, and the fact that two suits were heard together, the parties to which were not, and could not have been originally bound in one controversy, will not affect the finality of the decree. Home Bldg., etc., Co. v. London, 98 Va. 152, 35 S. E. 362.

(2) Judgments, Orders and Decrees Held to Be Merely Interlocutory.

"'A judgment merely for costs, without a final disposition of the cause, is not a final judgment.' 2 Cy. 593; 2 Ency. Pl. & Pr. 133." Hannah v. Bank, 53 W. Va. 82, 86, 44 S. E. 152.

An order declaring a summons void as an alias summons, but good as an original summons, is not appealable, under § 3454, Va. Code, 1887, as being a final judgment. Roger v. Bertha Zinc Co., 1 Va. Dec. 827.

The sustaining or overruling of a demurrer to a declaration is not a final judgment; to make it final there must be a judgment of dismissal. Gillespie v. Coleman, 98 Va. 276, 36 S. E. 377. See also, Hancock v. Richmond, etc., R. Co., 3 Gratt. 328; Trevilian v. Louisa R. Co., 3 Gratt. 326. Contra, Jeter v. Board, 27 Gratt. 910.

"It is also assigned as error, and

contended in argument, that the court had no right at a subsequent term to set aside its order sustaining a demurrer. This order, however, was not a demurrer to the entire declaration, which, if sustained, might determine the plaintiff's right to recover. It was a demurrer to a statement in aid of the declaration, and the ruling upon it could only be regarded as an interlocutory order, and Black on Judgments (volume 2, § 509) says: 'It is well settled that the doctrine of res judicata applies only to final judgments, not to interlocutory judgments or orders, which the court which rendered them has power to vacate or modify at any time.' Citing Webb v. Buckelew, 82 N. Y. 555." Rheims v. Standard Fire Ins. Co., 39 W. Va. 672, 20 S. E. 670, 676.

"I understand that it is everwhere admitted that an order merely sustaining a demurrer, without more, is a merely interlocutory order, not final. The case is in court till a final judgment ends it, and before that the order may be reviewed and recalled. It it contended that, after demurrer sustained, the same declaration can not be again filed. If there was final judgment, it could not; if not, there need be no further declaration, as the old one is yet alive. It is urged that a judgment sustaining a demurrer to a declaration has been held to be res judicata, and we are referred for authority to Poole v. Dilworth, 26 W. Va. 583, and Corrothers v. Sargent, 20 W. Va. 351, holding that a judgment upon a demurrer going to the merits is an effectual bar to further litigation as to every matter, whether specially stated in the pleading or not, provided it be clear it was necessarily decided in the suit. So it is when the adjudication is final, but everywhere we are told that to have such effect it must be final; technically final, not merely interlocutory. 5 Rob. Pr. 9; Burner v. Hevener, 34 W. Va. 775, 12 S. E. 861.

Sustaining a demurrer is not final, but revocable, unless carried into judgment, even where the demurrer goes to the whole case. 1 Black, Judgm., § 29." Clarke v. Ohio River R. Co., 39 W. Va. 732, 20 S. E. 696, 698.

An order is entered by the circuit court sustaining the defendant's demurrer to the plaintiff's declaration and each count thereof, which concludes as follows: "And thereupon this action is remanded to rules with leave to plaintiff to amend his declaration," and from this order the plaintiff obtains a writ of error to this court. Held, such order is not a final judgment from which a writ of error will lie to this court. White v. Chesapeake, etc., R. Co., 26 W. Va. 800.

An order sustaining a demurrer to a bill, and giving the plaintiff leave to amend in a specified time, can not be regarded as a final order, and as settling the principles of the cause, until after the time limited therein for the plaintiff to amend his bill has expired. London Virginia Mining Co. v. Moore, 98 Va. 256, 35 S. E. 722, citing Commercial Bank v. Rucker, 2 Va. Dec. 350.

A confession of judgment by one of several joint defendants, is only interlocutory, until the final decision of the cause as to the rest; and the confessing defendant must receive the same judgment as his codefendants. Taylor v. Beck, 3 Rand. 316. See the title CONFESSION OF JUDGMENTS, vol. 3, p. 68, et seq.

Decree Ordering Accounting and Report, Confirming Report, or Recommitting for Report.—A decree ordering an accounting, and report to the court at its next term, is an interlocutory decree. Sims v. Sims, 94 Va. 580, 27 S. E. 436, citing Templeman v. Steptoe, 1 Munf. 339; Barker v. Jenkins, 84 Va. 895, 899, 6 S. E. 459; Welsh v. Solenberger, 85 Va. 441, 8 S. E. 91.

Where by a decree certain inquiries

"in the cause" were directed to be made by a commissioner of the court, it was consequently not a final decree. Barker *v.* Jenkins, 84 Va. 895, 6 S. E. 459.

A decree, dismissing so much of a bill as claims one of two separate subjects in controversy, and as to the other, determining also the rights of the parties, but directing an account to be taken, is not final in any respect, between the parties retained in court, and their legal representatives, but is subject to revision in every part, at any time before a final decree, without the necessity of a bill of review. Templeman *v.* Steptoe, 1 Munf. 339.

Where the decree affirmed, on its face, orders that the cause be referred to a master to take further account and report, etc., such decree is interlocutory. Upon the cause being remanded to a court below for further proceedings, such interlocutory decree may be modified upon exceptions to the master's report on motion or otherwise. Miller *v.* Cook, 77 Va. 806, citing Smith *v.* Blackwell, 31 Gratt. 291.

A decree though deciding the right to the property in controversy, and awarding the costs of the suit, is still only interlocutory, if commissioners be appointed to carry it into effect, and the court has yet to act upon their report. Neither does it cease to be interlocutory in consequence of an order that the defendant be attached for failing to comply with it. Mackey *v.* Bell, 2 Munf. 523.

In a suit involving the right of access to a well, a decree was entered which directed that the plaintiff should have uninterrupted access to the water of the well, unless and until otherwise ordered by the court; that the injunction before awarded, which was only until the rights of the complainants could be considered and adjudicated, should be continued; that an account should be taken by a commissioner to ascertain the amount of expenses incurred by the father of the defendant, from whom the defendant claimed, and by the latter in keeping the well in repair, and the amount paid by the plaintiffs; and that the account when taken should be reported. The rights of the parties were not finally adjudicated; the injunction was not perpetuated; the decree directed an account to be taken and reported; but it did not determine the question of costs nor direct their payment. The decree was merely interlocutory. Warren *v.* Syme, 7 W. Va. 474.

In a suit for the administration of B.'s estate the commissioner classifies the debt of J. among the general creditors of B., and there is a decree confirming the report and distributing a fund in court pro rata among these creditors. There were several other decrees for accounts of further debts of B., and still a fund in court to be distributed, when J. made himself a defendant in the suit and filed his petition insisting that his was a fiduciary debt. Held, the decree confirming the report was an interlocutory decree, and J. was not concluded from setting up his claim as a fiduciary creditor of B. Smith *v.* Blackwell, 31 Gratt. 291.

A decree in a creditor's suit which ascertains the rights of one lien creditor, and remands the cause to a commissioner for a further report, is not a final decree. A decree to be final must decide the whole matter in contest, and leave nothing further for the court to do. Repass *v.* Moore, 96 Va. 147, 30 S. E. 458.

A decree recited that the case be recommitted to a commissioner to "report an account," and subsequently a decree was entered dismissing the complaint. Held, that the former decree was not a final judgment which would start the running of the statute of limitations. Penn *v.* Chesapeake, etc., R. Co., 2 Va. Dec. 224.

A decree confirming the report of

commissioner is not final. Fowler *v.* Lewis, 36 W. Va. 112, 14 S. E. 447.

In a suit, the object of which was to make a partition of the lands among the cotenants thereof, a decree was entered which approved and confirmed the report making the partition. It provided in express terms that, "leave is given the parties to whom the several parcels of lands are allotted by that report, and their alienees, to have such decree as the parties may agree upon finally settling their respective interests entered in the causes in vacation." It is evident that further action by the court to complete the relief contemplated was provided for, and it does not change the nature of the decree that no application for the further decree was ever made. It was nevertheless a pending cause and open to such orders and decrees as might be necessary. The applications for rehearing are always addressed to the sound discretion of the chancellor, and even if the decree was interlocutory, it can be reheard at any time before final decree, even after the lapse of a great length of time. Wright *v.* Strother, 76 Va. 857.

Decrees Ordering or Confirming Sale of Land.—A decree directing the sale of land to satisfy charges on it is not a final decree. Spoor *v.* Tilson, 97 Va. 279, 33 S. E. 609.

"A decree for a sale under a mortgage, or otherwise, is interlocutory because the sale is not consummated until approved by the court." Repass *v.* Moore, 96 Va. 147, 150, 30 S. E. 458.

A decree empowering an executor to sell the lands of his testator, for payment of debts, and report his proceedings, in execution thereof, to the court, is not final but interlocutory. Goodwin *v.* Miller, 2 Munf. 42.

A decree, which forecloses the equity of redemption in mortgaged property, and appoints commissioners to make the sale of it, is only interlocutory, and an appeal can not be allowed by the county court from such decree even in term time. Allen *v.* Belches, 2 Hen. & M. 595.

A decree, foreclosing a mortgage and directing a sale of the mortgaged premises, is an interlocutory decree. Fairfax *v.* Muse, 2 Hen. & M. 557.

Decree for Sale unless Sum Due Is Paid—Leave Given to Apply to Court. —In a suit brought to subject land to the payment of notes given for its purchase price, the court ascertained the indebtedness of the defendants to the plaintiffs to be a certain sum and a certain other sum to become due at a future time. The court decreed that unless the sum then due be paid in thirty days, certain commissioners should sell the land, which was subject to the vendor's lien of the two named sums, to pay the one then due. In this decree leave was given the plaintiff to apply for a decree to enforce the payment of the sum not yet due, under an attachment of other property of the defendant, the sale of which had not been prayed for in the bill. This was an interlocutory decree, and it may be reviewed on appeal after five years from its date. Camden *v.* Haymond, 9 W. Va. 680.

Decree for Conveyance with Condition.—In a suit by one partner against his copartner, for a settlement of the partnership accounts, and for a moiety of a tract of land purchased by the defendant in his own name, and paid for out of the partnership funds, a decree having been made declaring the land partnership property, and directing a settlement of the accounts, and the cause afterwards coming on to be further heard upon the report of the commissioner, the court decrees that the plaintiff pay to the defendant a sum of money appearing due by the report, and that the defendant thereupon convey to the plaintiff a moiety of the land; but if the plaintiff shall not, within six months from the date of the decree, pay the said money, that the marshal sell the moiety of the land, and out of the proceeds of sale, after defraying the expenses, pay to the defendant the money so decreed, and the residue, if any, to the plaintiff. And the court further decrees that the outstanding debts due to the firm be equally divided between the parties, and that the costs of the suit be equally borne by them. Held, this decree is interlocutory, and it may be reviewed upon an appeal, although there has been such lapse of time between the rendition of the decree and the appeal, as would preclude its being reviewed if the decree were final. Cocke v. Gilpin, 1 Rob. 20, approved by Miller v. Cook, 77 Va. 806.

Sale Decreed with Power Reserved to Confirm or Set Aside.—In a suit to subject land in the hands of the heirs to the payment of the debts of their ancestor, in the decree for sale the court reserved complete power over the sale, to confirm it or set it aside as the interest of the parties might require. No title could be made to the purchaser, without further action of the court, and what is most material to notice, no disposition is made of the purchase money; no directions given to the commissioner on the subject, so that the creditors could not receive a dollar of the proceeds, nor the heirs the surplus, without a further decree. If this be a final decree, the court has deprived itself of all control over the subject matter in controversy, and ended the cause, without giving the parties the slightest relief. The very fact that no direction is given as to the proceeds of sale, and that the commissioners are required to report their proceedings to the court, is conclusive that further action of the court was not only contemplated, but actually necessary. According to the uniform decisions of this court, a decree, which disposes of the whole subject, gives all the relief that is contemplated and leaves nothing to be done by the court,

is only to be regarded as final. On the other hand every decree which leaves anything in the cause to be done by the court, is interlocutory as between the parties remaining in the court. Ryan v. McLeod, 32 Gratt. 367.

In Summers v. Darne, 31 Gratt. 791, the decree of the county court, after declaring that the judgment liens have priority over the deed of trust, directs the sale of the land at public auction or at private sale, on credits stated, and that the commissioners should report their proceedings; and that a commissioner should ascertain and report the several liens on the land and their priorities.

Conveyance Set Aside and Report Ordered.—In an action to set aside certain conveyances and to subject the lands conveyed therein to the satisfaction of a judgment, a decree that sets aside the conveyances and refers the cause to a commissioner for inquiry and report, with a view to further action in the cause, is an interlocutory and not a final decree, as it is a step preliminary to subjecting the land to the judgment. Welsh v. Solenberger, 85 Va. 441, 8 S. E. 91.

Judgment or Orders in Condemnation Proceedings.—In Postal Tel. Cable Co. v. Norfolk, etc., R. Co., 87 Va. 349, 12 S. E. 613, it is held: "Judgment obtained by telegraph company appointing commissioners to fix a just compensation for land of railroad company proposed to be taken for the purpose of the former, in condemnation proceedings, is not final and appealable." And the same is held in Ludlow v. Norfolk, 87 Va. 319, 12 S. E. 612; Wheeling, etc., R. Co. v. Atkinson, 53 W. Va. 539, 44 S. E. 773.

"In the case of Pack v. Chesapeake, etc., R. Co., 5 W. Va. 118, it is held, that proceedings under the statute for taking lands for the use of internal improvement companies, is not a chancery but a law proceeding and no appeal can be taken from an interlocutory order therein, and in syllabus, point 2, it is held: 'Upon the coming in of a report of commissioners, which fact is entered of record, and the payment into court of the sum fixed as just compensation to landowners, the defendants, the landowners, move to set aside the original order appointing commissioners, which motion is overruled, and from this they appeal; and it is held, that the court not having acted upon the report, there is no final judgment, and therefore the appeal can not properly be taken.'" Wheeling, etc., R. Co. v. Atkinson, 53 W. Va. 539, 542, 44 S. E. 773.

An order directing a special commissioner to pay a certain sum of money to general creditors according to priorities, "if any there be;" not designating the creditors, the sum or pro rate sum they are entitled to, is an interlocutory order, and the court pronouncing the order has the right to retain the cause for a future direct action upon all matters that the interest and convenience of the parties, and the very justice of the case requires. Butler v. Butler, 8 W. Va. 674.

A decree can not be said to be final which directs a receiver to proceed "to get in all funds pertaining to the cause which have not heretofore been brought in and disposed of, and to make report thereof to the court," although it settles the rights of the parties to the funds in hand. It can not be said of such a decree that the relief contemplated has been completely given, or that no question is left undecided, and no further action "in the cause" is necessary. Unless this can be said of a decree it is not final. Gunnell v. Dixon, 101 Va. 174, 43 S. E. 340; Cocke v. Gilpin, 1 Rob. 20, 28; Rawlings v. Rawlings, 75 Va. 76, 78.

A decree directing the surveyor to make partition of a tract of land, and to make report, is not final, and can not be appealed from. Young v. Skipwith, 2 Wash. 300.

A decree approving and confirming the account of the representative of a trustee and ascertaining the balance due from the decedent's estate to the trust fund, without giving judgment for the same or making any other disposition of it, or without dismissing the case as to him, is not a final decree. Southern R. Co. v. Glenn, 98 Va. 309, 36 S. E. 395.

In a suit in chancery against several defendants, a decree that the complainant recover against one of them, the residue of the land claimed and owned by that defendant under the will of his father, after taking therefrom the portions sold out by him to the other defendants; that he yield possession, and execute a conveyance of the same in fee; "without which conveyance, however, the title is to be in the said complainant by force of this decree;" is not a final decree until the suit be disposed of as to all the defendants. Chapman v. Armistead, 4 Munf. 382.

A decree which declines to grant the relief prayed until the legislature enacts a further law on the subject is not a final decree, nor does it adjudicate the principles of the cause. From it no appeal lies. If a decision is desired the proper remedy is by mandamus to compel the trial court to hear and determine the cause. Board of Supervisors v. Alexandria, 95 Va. 469, 28 S. E. 882.

B. JUDGMENTS IN REM AND IN PERSONAM.

Judgments in Rem.—"Mr. Freeman, in his work on Judgments, says (§ 606): 'It seems to us that the true definition of a "judgment in rem" is that it is an adjudication against some person or thing, or upon the status of some subject matter, which, wherever and whenever binding upon any person, is equally binding upon all persons.' That is, it is a judgment which, being valid, binds all persons." Dulin v. McCaw, 39 W. Va. 721, 20 S. E. 681.

"A judgment in rem I conceive to be an adjudication pronounced upon the status of some particular subject matter by a tribunal having competent authority for the purpose. Such an adjudication, being a most solemn declaration, from the proper and accredited quarter, that the status of the thing adjudicated upon is as declared, excludes all persons from saying 'he thing adjudicated upon was not such as declared by the adjudication." Bruff v. Thompson, 31 W. Va. 16, 6 S. E. 352, 358. See the titles ATTACHMENT AND GARNISHMENT, vol. 2, p. 133; FOREIGN JUDGMENTS, vol. 6, p. 224; FORMER ADJUDICATION OR RES ADJUDICATA, vol. 6, p. 261.

A judgment in personam is "a judgment against a particular person, as distinguished from a judgment against a thing or a right or status." Black's Law Dict., tit. "Judgment in Personam."

C. JUDGMENTS BY CONSENT.

1. What Constitutes.

Definition and Nature.—A consent decree is a contract or agreement between the parties to the suit entered of record in the cause with the consent of the court. Such consent decree may or it may not be founded upon the pleadings and proofs in the cause. It is certainly not necessarily based upon the record or any report, paper, or exhibit filed in the suit. It may be wholly or in part independent of any matter or paper in the record, and may be even contradictory or the reverse of what these show ought to be the decree. In this respect it differs radically from a decree entered upon the decision of the court. Such decree must of necessity be founded upon the pleadings and proofs in the cause. Morris v. Peyton, 29 W. Va. 201, 11 S. E. 954, 961. See post, "Conformity to Pleadings and Proofs," III, E, 2.

A consent decree is not the judgment of the court upon the merits of the case, but the act of the parties to the suit. Myllius v. Smith, 53 W. Va. 173, 187, 44 S. E. 542; Morris v. Peyton, 29 W. Va. 201, 11 S. E. 954, 958.

Instances of Consent Judgments or Decrees.—Where the question is, whether it is proper to sell or rent real estate to pay the debts charged upon it, and the defendant "asks that it be rented instead of sold," and the complainants "assent thereto," and the court decrees thereupon, that it shall be rented instead of sold; this is a consent decree as to such question. Rose v. Brown, 17 W. Va. 649.

These are two actions of debt by the Bank of O. D. against J., the maker, and W. as the endorser, of the notes sued on, pending in the same court at the same time, in both of which the defense and the evidence is the same. There is a verdict and judgment for the plaintiff in one case; and the defendants propose to appeal. And then in the second case the following entry is made: "Bank of O. D. v. J. & al.—judgment by consent in favor of plaintiff for $10,760, the debt in the declaration mentioned, with interest thereon from the 1st day of January, 1866, till paid, and costs. Execution on the judgment to be stayed for ninety days; and in the event of an appeal being obtained and perfected in the Bank of O. D. v. J. & al., decided at this term, then this judgment to await the decision of the court of appeals, and abide the result thereof in the said case; provided the appeal bond in that case be sufficient to secure the amount of both judgments. C., p. q.: B. & W., p. d." The writ of error was obtained, but the appeal bond was only in the penalty of 200. The judgment was on the appeal reversed. Held, the entry in the second case, if a judgment at all, is a judgment by consent or confession, not absolute, but on the terms and conditions set out in the agreement annexed. Under the agreement, which is a continuing one, it is competent for the court which rendered it to deal with it in a summary way, and see that its terms are complied with. Bank v. McVeigh, 32 Gratt. 530.

Decrees Not Regarded as by Consent.—A decree was endorsed by the counsel in a cause, "submitted to us." All that this means is that it has been shown to counsel. It does not follow that they have not opposed or do not oppose it in every way they can, and it was not regarded at all as a consent decree. Gibson v. Burgess, 82 Va. 650.

When the parties to a suit in response to a decree of the court, appear before a commissioner and make a statement of their accounts, this does not amount to an acquiescence in the settlement, and does not justify the entering of a decree, based on such settlement, if it would not be authorized to do so, unless by consent of parties. Hall v. Taylor, 18 W. Va. 544.

2. By Whom Consent Given.

The parties to a suit can adjust matters and their rights between themselves and have a decree entered by consent of all parties without regard to the state of the pleadings or evidence in the cause. Seiler v. Union Mfg. Co., 50 W. Va. 208, 40 S. E. 547.

Necessity for Consent of All Parties Interested.—It was held, in Blair v. Thompson, 11 Gratt. 441, that there can not be a decree for a specific sum in lieu of dower without the consent of all the parties interested.

Infants Can Not Consent.—It is an error to give a joint decree in favor of all the plaintiffs, some of whom are infants, for the aggregate of all their debts against the defendants, notwithstanding it is stated to have been by consent of complainants, because infants are incapable of giving consent for want of discretion, and such con-

sent decree is invalid; nor can their next friend give consent for them. Armstrong v. Walkup, 9 Gratt. 372; Daingerfield v. Smith, 83 Va. 81, 1 S. E. 599.

By Counsel Adverse to Infants.—It is an error to allow counsel who represent interests adverse to infant parties to consent to a decree for them, and in such case a decree will be held invalid. Walker v. Grayson, 86 Va. 337, 338, 10 S. E. 51.

The consent of counsel to a decree is to be given upon their own conception of their instructions. Darraugh v. Blackford, 84 Va. 509, 514, 5 S. E. 542.

Presumption as to Consent by Real Parties in Interest.—In a suit brought in the name of one person for the benefit of another, a judgment stating that the parties appeared by their attorneys and by consent the suit was dismissed and judgment for defendant's cost against the person for whose benefit the suit was brought, it must be held, that the consent is the consent of the latter, and that the judgment is proper. Pates v. St. Clair, 11 Gratt. 22.

3. Rendition and Entry.

Time.—Parties can have a decree entered by consent without regard to the state of the pleadings or evidence in the case. Seiler v. Union Mfg. Co., 50 W. Va. 208, 40 S. E. 547.

Entry in Vacation.—See generally, the title CHAMBERS AND VACATION, vol. 2, p. 771. And see post, "Rendition and Entry," V.

In West Virginia, a decree adjudicating adverse claims or rights, entered by the judge of a circuit court in vacation, by consent of parties previously given in court and entered on record, is erroneous. Gilmer v. Baker, 24 W. Va. 72; Monroe v. Bartlett, 6 W. Va. 441; Johnson v. Young, 11 W. Va. 673; Rollins v. Fisher, 17 W. Va. 578.

In Virginia a decree which confirms a report of liens disposes of the cause on the merits, and can not be entered in vacation except by consent of the parties as provided in § 2437 of the Va. Code of 1887. Harris *v.* Jones, 96 Va. 658, 32 S. E. 455.

J. files his bill in the circuit court of Wood county, in the fourth judicial circuit, praying an injunction and for relief. The injunction was awarded, the cause removed to the circuit court of Ritchie county, in the second judicial circuit, and various proceedings there taken in the cause. The January term, 1872, of that court was held by the judge of the fourth judicial circuit instead of the judge of the second judicial circuit, but no decree or proceedings were had in the cause at that term, so far as the record shows. The judge of the fourth judicial circuit, after the adjournment of the circuit court of Ritchie county at its January term, in vacation, rendered a final decree in the cause dissolving the injunction and dismissing the bill at the complainant's costs. It concludes: "And by agreement of parties, it is ordered that this decree be entered among the proceedings of the next term of the circuit court of Wood county." At the April term, 1872, of the circuit court of Ritchie, held by its judge, the judge of the second judicial circuit, a decree was rendered in the cause, which first recited that at the January term, 1872, of said court, held by the judge of the fourth judicial circuit, the cause had been argued by counsel, and an agreement and consent was made in open court by the parties thereto, in person and by counsel, that the papers might be taken and the cause decided in vacation, and that any decree so made should be entered in the circuit court of Wood county at its then next term; and that it appeared that said cause was so decided in vacation by said judge of the fourth judicial circuit, and that his decree had been returned to the clerk of this court setting forth the final decree aforesaid rendered by the judge of the fourth judicial circuit, and then proceeded to order the papers of the cause to be transmitted to the clerk of the circuit court of Wood county, and that the said decree rendered by the judge of the fourth judicial circuit in vacation be entered on the chancery order book of the said court, at the next term thereof. At said next term of the circuit court of Wood county, a decree was entered in said cause, which first recited the transmission of the papers in the cause to the clerk of that court. It then proceeded to order the docketing of the cause in that court, and then ordered the said decree of the April term, 1872, of the circuit court of Ritchie county to be entered verbatim, which was done. Held, that no order having been made at the January term, 1872, of the circuit court of Ritchie county, that by consent of parties the cause might be decided in vacation, even if that term of the court had been held by the regular judge of that circuit, his decree in vacation would have been unauthorized and void; it not being decided whether, if such consent order had been made and entered on the record book, a decree rendered in vacation by the regular judge of that circuit would or would not be void. Johnson *v.* Young, 11 W. Va. 673.

On the adjournment of the January term, 1872, of the court the judicial power of the judge of the fourth judicial circuit to render a final decree in this cause ceased; and even if such consent decree that he might decide finally the cause in vacation had been entered, it would have conferred no such power upon him. Johnson *v.* Young, 11 W. Va. 673.

The recitals made in the decree, entered by the judge of the second judicial circuit at the April term of the circuit court of Ritchie county, of what occurred in open court at the January term, 1872, while the judge of the fourth judicial circuit was presiding, can not be regarded as the equivalent of a consent decree, of the January term, 1872, to submit the cause in vacation entered nunc pro tunc. Johnson v. Young, 11 W. Va. 673.

The judge of the circuit court of Ritchie county had no authority to order the decree, which had been made by the judge of the fourth judicial circuit in vacation, to be entered upon the chancery order book of the circuit court of Wood county. Johnson v. Young, 11 W. Va. 673.

The judge of the circuit court of Wood county ought not, pursuant to this order of the circuit court of Ritchie county, to have entered this decree made in vacation, and it did not do this when it entered the decree of the circuit court of Ritchie county, which merely recited this decree rendered in vacation. Johnson v. Young, 11 W. Va. 673.

"The entry of a consent decree is a statement on the record, not that theretofore the parties agreed to enter such a decree, but that they now (when the decree is entered) consent to its entry. And if they do not, when it is to be entered, consent to the court's entering it, it can not be so entered. Neither could the court enter such modified decree generally, as a decree made by the court without the consent of parties; for such a decree can only be entered on the merits of the case according to the judgment of the court; and this modified decree is not generally such a decree, but is one only which the parties formerly agreed to, and generally is not sustained by the facts in the record, and upon the propriety of which the court has never exercised its judgment." Manion v. Fahy, 11 W. Va. 482, 496.

4. Effect.

A judgment by consent must have the same force and effect as any other judgment, unless, upon principles of equity, some ground can be shown for relief. Richmond, etc., R. Co. v. Shippen, 2 Pat. & H. 327.

A decree by consent is binding unless procured by fraud or mistake, in which case relief is by original bill Darraugh v. Blackford, 84 Va. 509, 5 S. E. 542.

In a controversy in a county court about the confirmation of a report of commissioners appointed to assess damages for land taken for the use of a railroad company, no witnesses were examined, and a judgment was entered by consent against the company, confirming the report, and for the amount of damages assessed by the commissioners, for the purpose of removing the cause to the circuit superior court of the county by appeal, the counsel for both parties being of opinion, that an appeal lay of right to the circuit court. No such right of appeal existed, and the circuit court dismissed the appeal. Upon an appeal from an order of the circuit court dissolving an injunction to the judgment of the county court, held, that, although the damages were obviously excessive, and neither party intended that the judgment of the county court should be final and conclusive, that a court of equity could afford no relief against the judgment. Richmond, etc., R. Co. v. Shippen, 2 Pat. & H. 327.

Upon Whom Binding.—A consent decree can only bind the consenting parties. Myllius v. Smith, 53 W. Va. 173, 44 S. E. 542.

An order in a chancery cause entered "by consent of all parties represented by counsel, the pleadings and proofs are closed and this cause is submitted for a final adjudication," is binding upon all the parties who had, at the time of the entry of the order, appeared in the case. Myllius v. Smith, 53 W. Va. 173, 44 S. E. 542.

An Adjudication of Merits of Cause.—A consent decree dismissing a bill with costs, with no saving therein of the right to bring another suit, is an adjudication of the merits of the cause. Lockwood v. Holliday, 16 W. Va. 651. See the title FORMER ADJUDICATION OR RES ADJUDICATA, vol. 6, p. 276, et seq.

Where an order is made by consent in a justice's court, submitting the matter in controversy to arbitration, the submission is not revocable, except by order of the justice, under the statute, and that submission is a bar to a second suit for the same cause. Riley v. Jarvis, 43 W. Va. 43, 26 S. E. 366.

Effect as Curing and Supplying Irregularities and Insufficiencies.—Infirmities and insufficiencies of a bill are cured and supplied by decrees entered by consent. Scott v. Dameron, 2 Va. Dec. 635.

Consolidation—Decree for Sale—Irregularities Not Cured.—Where two cases were amalgamated by consent, and a decree for sale entered in the first case is made a decree for both cases by like consent, any error in decreeing a sale will not be cured thereby, as that consent merely cured any irregularities in the formalities of bringing the cases, consolidating the same and in making the decree. Buchanan v. Clark, 10 Gratt. 164.

5. Modification, Correction or Setting Aside.

a. Correction, Modification or Alteration.

A clerical error in entering a consent decree may be corrected by the original draft of the decree, furnished the clerk by the court, on motion at any time, under the provisions of § 5 of chapter 134 of the West Virginia Code. Manion v. Fahy, 11 W. Va. 482.

A consent decree, except where such clerical error has occurred, can never be modified or altered without the consent of parties, not even during the term at which it was entered. Manion v. Fahy, 11 W. Va. 482.

From the very nature of the consent decree it can not be altered or modified except by consent, unless there has been a clerical mistake, which mistake is corrected by a bill of review if the decree is final, or by a petition to rehear if it be interlocutory. Manion v. Fahy, 11 W. Va. 482; Morris v. Peyton, 29 W. Va. 201, 11 S. E. 954; Stewart v. Stewart, 40 W. Va. 65, 20 S. E. 862; Seiler v. Union Mfg. Co., 50 W. Va. 208, 40 S. E. 547. See the titles BILL OF REVIEW, vol. 2, p. 384; REHEARING.

"From the very nature of a consent decree, it can not be altered or modified, except by consent, unless there has been a clerical mistake, for though the court be satisfied that the parties had formerly agreed to have a decree, in substance, such as the modified one entered, which, by a mistake other than clerical, was not entered, but a different decree entered, how can the court enter this modified decree as a consent decree, when one of the parties is present and protests against its being entered as by his consent." Manion v. Fahy, 11 W. Va. 482.

"A case might arise when a party might be liable to a common-law action for refusing to carry out his agreement, and objecting to the entering of the consent decree as modified. But, except by consent of all parties, the court can not modify a consent decree, except in the case where the clerk, in entering the decree from the draft furnished him, has made a mistake. Such a mistake would formerly have been corrected by bill of review, or by bill in the nature of a bill of review, according to the English practice or here by a bill of review, if the decree was final, or a petition for a rehearing, if the decree was interlocutory. 8 Anon.; 1 Ves. 93; and Atkinson v. Marks, 1 Cow. 693. Now such clerical mistakes may be corrected on motion at a subsequent term. Code of W. Va., ch. 134, § 5, p. 638." Manion v. Fahy, 11 W. Va. 482, 497.

After the term at which a consent decree is entered it can not be set aside, modified, or altered without the consent of the parties, except only to correct a clerical error, which is a mistake made by the clerk in entering such consent decree, and it may be corrected by the original draft of the decree furnished the clerk by the court; or it may be a miscalculation or mistake in some arithmetical operation, whereby a sum entered in such consent decree, where all the parties are agreed on the basis of the calculation, and the mistake is simply an arithmetical mistake, or a simple blunder, in performing an arithmetical operation, all parties being agreed on the operation to be performed. Stewart *v.* Stewart, 40 W. Va. 65, 20 S. E. 862.

"There is, however, one species of mistake in a consent decree, if it can properly be called a mistake, which the court may correct at a subsequent term; that is, a clerical error. And when a clerical error is shown to exist it is corrected, because it is shown to the court that the decree as entered is not the decree intended to be entered by the parties or by any one of the parties. If it is the decree which any one of the parties intended to be entered, though it be not the decree which all the others intended to be entered, it is clearly not a clerical error, but an error or mistake of the parties themselves, they differing in opinion as to the decree which they had consented should be entered; or it may be a fraudulent preparation of a decree by one of the parties, when there was a perfect understanding as to what consent decree was to be entered. In neither of these cases, as we have seen, can the court correct such a decree by any order made in the cause. It can be corrected or set aside only by an original bill brought for the purpose. If, however, a correct decree is drawn up by the parties, who all understand it alike, and it is indorsed by the judge of the court to be entered, and the clerk in copying it onto the record book makes a mistake, whereby its meaning is changed materially, this is obviously a clerical error. It is no mistake of the parties, but a mistake of the clerk alone; and such a mistake, when made apparent to the court by producing the original decree given to the clerk to be entered, may be corrected by the court at a subsequent term, without the consent of all the parties. This is properly a clerical error; but the term is sometimes extended to include other errors. If, for instance, the parties have agreed upon the terms of a decree, and all the parties understand alike all the provisions to be inserted therein, and one of the parties, or a clerk, in making necessary arithmetical calculations, commits an error, so that a wrong amount is inserted in the decree, that would be regarded as a clerical error, which may be corrected at a subsequent term of the court, without the consent of all the parties, provided, of course, the existence of such error can be shown in the manner in which the law permits such error to be shown. Such clerical error can not be shown by depositions subsequently taken in the cause, but should clearly appear from the face of the decree itself, aided only by previous portions of the record or proceedings, as by a previous verdict, report of commissioner, bond or other writing filed in the cause, or by some part of the record previous to the entering of said consent decree." Morris *v.* Peyton, 29 W. Va. 201, 11 S. E. 954, 958.

When the error complained of is the insertion of a particular amount in a consent decree as the result of a calculation by one of the parties upon a basis which other parties regard as not in accord with the understanding of the parties, such error is not a clerical error, but a mistake of parties, and, if it be an error, it can be corrected only by original bill. Morris *v.* Peyton, 29 W. Va. 201, 11 S. E. 954.

b. Setting Aside or Annulling.

(1) During Term at Which Entered.

A consent decree may be set aside during the term at which it was entered, on motion, or by the court without any motion. Manion *v.* Fahy, 11 W. Va. 482.

(2) At Subsequent Term.

(a) In General.

After the termination of the term at which a consent decree was entered, it can never be set aside, except by consent, by any proceedings in the cause, though it had been entered by mistake, or by the fraud of one of the parties. Manion *v.* Fahy, 11 W. Va. 482; Rose *v.* Brown, 17 W. Va. 649; Armstrong *v.* Wilson, 19 W. Va. 108; Hoffman *v.* Ryan, 21 W. Va. 415; Stewart *v.* Stewart, 40 W. Va. 65, 20 S. E. 862.

The court at a subsequent term has no power to set aside, alter, or modify it without the consent of the parties except only to correct a clerical error. Seiler *v.* Union Mfg. Co., 50 W. Va. 208, 40 S. E. 547.

"This court has held, that after the close of the term, at which a consent decree was entered, it can never be set aside, except by consent, by any proceedings in the cause, though it had been entered by mistake or by the fraud of one of the parties. Manion *v.* Fahy, 11 W. Va. 482; Rose *v.* Brown, 17 W. Va. 649. A consent decree may be annulled on an original bill filed for the purpose, when it was procured by fraud or was entered by mistake of one or both of the parties differently from what it should have been entered. An original bill is necessary and proper to annul such consent decree whether the decree be final or interlocutory. Manion *v.* Fahy, 11 W. Va. 482. It is not pretended, that the cross bill filed

in this cause could be considered an original bill for the purpose of setting aside the consent decree theretofore entered in the cause. But before filing such original bill for the purpose of setting aside such consent decree it would be well for the party to inquire, whether the defense pleaded in the answer and cross bill, to wit, the usury and the fraud, could avail him, he having taken no steps whatever to defend himself at law. The question does not arise in this cause, but the following authorities are upon the subject: Brown *v.* Swann, 10 Pet. 497; Shields *v.* McClung, 6 W. Va. 79; Knapp *v.* Snyder, 15 W. Va. 434; Alford *v.* Moore, 15 W. Va. 597." Armstrong *v.* Wilson, 19 W. Va. 108, 114.

A decree or order made by consent can not be set aside either by rehearing or appeal or by bill of review, unless by clerical error anything has been inserted in the order as by consent, to which the party had not consented, in which case a bill of review might lie. Stewart *v.* Stewart, 40 W. Va. 65, 20 S. E. 862; Darraugh *v.* Blackford, 84 Va. 509, 514, 5 S. E. 542.

An appeal will not lie from a consent decree. Weekly *v.* Hardesty, 48 W. Va. 39, 35 S. E. 880; Manion *v.* Fahy, 11 W. Va. 482. See also, Hinton *v.* Bland, 81 Va. 588.

"It is well settled as to the effect of a consent decree or order, as said in Morris *v.* Peyton, 29 W. Va. 201, 212, 11 S. E. 954: 'As such a decree is not the judgment of the court upon the merits of the case but the act of the parties to the suit, it is obvious, that it can not be modified, set aside or annulled by any order in the cause made by the court below without the consent of all the parties to the cause, unless set aside during the same term of the court, which would leave matters in the same condition as if it had never been entered. Nor can it be appealed from, nor modified by this court, unless perhaps, it should be so entirely foreign to the matters in controversy in the cause, that for this or some other reason the court below had no jurisdiction or authority to enter any such decree by consent or otherwise.' Manion v. Fahy, 11 W. Va. 482; Rose v. Brown, 17 W. Va. 649; Seiler v. Union Mfg. Co., 50 W. Va. 208, 40 S. E. 547; 2 Beech Md. Eq. Pr., § 785." Myllius v. Smith, 53 W. Va. 173, 187, 44 S. E. 542.

If all the parties to the suit, who were or might be interested in the giving of the bond, were to enter a consent decree, that no bond should be executed, by a commissioner before sale of land by him, while it would be in violation of both the spirit, and the letter of the statute, yet on well-settled principles, it being a consent decree, it could not be reviewed. Neeley v. Ruleys, 26 W. Va. 686, 692.

In order that the rule that a decree by consent of parties even if erroneous can not be disturbed by the court, may apply such consent must be established by the clearest and most convincing proof. Gregg v. Sloan, 76 Va. 497.

In this case debtors in North Carolina granted all their property including choses in action due from their debtors in Virginia, and secured on land here. After recordation of deed in North Carolina, but before its recordation in Virginia a creditor of grantors, living in Virginia, attached the choses and the land securing them. The trustees petitioned to be made parties to the attachment suit, but no order making them such had been entered. A decree, purporting to be "by consent of parties through their counsel," was rendered, ascertaining plaintiff's debt and directing sale of land conveyed to secure the chose attached, and payment in full of plaintiff's debt. The counsel differed as to the extent of "the consent" given. The trustees enjoined the execution of the decree of the attaching creditor, who an-swered. Both causes being heard together, it was held, that the decree should have been set aside. "A decree so palpably unjust ought not to be permitted to stand on mere consent, unless such consent be established by the clearest and most convincing proof." Gregg v. Sloan, 76 Va. 497, 501.

"Dent, commissioner, under an order of the court in this cause, made a report of the liens on the land, in which he placed Corrothers' lien as the first lien and the judgments against Ryan in the order, in which they were obtained, as subsequent liens. A consent decree was rendered on the 30th of March, 1877, in accordance with this view, whereby a sale was ordered of this land to pay these liens; and a sale of it was made, but the court afterwards, on affidavits showing that this decree had never been consented to by some of the parties, set aside this consent decree, and being afterwards satisfied by the decision of this court in Manion v. Fahy, 11 W. Va. 482, that it had in this suit no authority to set aside this decree of March 3, 1877, except by consent, it, by consent annulled this order, and then by consent, set aside the decree of March 3, 1877, as well as the sale made under it." Hoffman v. Ryan, 21 W. Va. 415, 424.

Court Can Not Set Aside in Construing Decree.—The court in its decrees carrying into execution a consent decree may construe the same when necessary, but it can not set aside such consent decree, and enter one totally different therefrom, under the guise of construing it. Seiler v. Union Mfg. Co., 50 W. Va. 208, 40 S. E. 547.

The court in its decrees carrying into execution a consent decree must necessarily construe such consent decree, but it should not put a construction upon any clause therein until it is called upon to enter such a decree as renders it necessary to construe such clause. Morris *v.* Peyton, 29 W. Va. 201, 11 S. E. 954.

(b) Proceedings by Original Bill.

In General.—A consent decree may be annulled when it was procured by fraud or was entered, by mistake of one or both of the parties, differently from what it should have been on an original bill filed for the purpose. Manion *v.* Fahy, 11 W. Va. 482; Anderson *v.* Woodford, 8 Leigh 316; Armstrong *v.* Wilson, 19 W. Va. 108; Darraugh *v.* Blackford, 84 Va. 509, 5 S. E. 542; Estill *v.* McClintic, 11 W. Va. 399.

"A consent decree can not be affected by a bill of review but only by an original bill. Thompson *v.* Maxwell, 95 U. S. 391; Manion *v.* Fahy, 11 W. Va. 482; 3 Ency. Pl. & Pr. 608." Camden *v.* Ferrell, 50 W. Va. 119, 120, 40 S. E. 368.

An original bill is necessary and proper to annul such a consent decree, whether it be an interlocutory or final decree. Manion *v.* Fahy, 11 W. Va. 482; Armstrong *v.* Wilson, 19 W. Va. 108; Rose *v.* Brown, 17 W. Va. 649; Seiler *v.* Union Mfg. Co., 50 W. Va. 208, 40 S. E. 547.

A decree which has been entered in a cause by consent of parties is binding, and can only be set aside by a new suit, alleging improper procurement by surprise, fraud, or mistake of parties, and in a suit where a consent decree by some of the parties has been entered as by consent of all, leave should be given to any of the parties who did not consent thereto to bring a suit in a reasonable time to nullify it. Estill *v.* McClintic, 11 W. Va. 399.

In a suit to settle up a decedent's estate and to charge his personal and real estate with the payment of his debts, the plaintiff, a nonpreferred creditor, the administrator and a preferred creditor consent to the entry of a decree, whereby a particular creditor is declared to be a preferred creditor, and though none of the other nonpreferred creditors, parties to the suit, were consulted, this decree was entered as a decree rendered by the consent of all parties to the cause; such decree can not be modified or set aside by any subsequent proceedings in the cause, but the court should grant leave to any of the parties to the suit, who never consented to this decree to file in a reasonable time to be fixed by the court, an original bill to set it aside Estill *v.* McClintic, 11 W. Va. 399.

In such a suit if the court annuls the decree, it should proceed further, and in all respects restore the parties to the situation, they were in, when such consent decree was entered. Manion *v.* Fahy, 11 W. Va. 482.

After such consent decree has been thus annulled, the court should, in the suit in which it was entered, proceed to decide it upon its merits, as if no such consent decree had been entered. Manion *v.* Fahy, 11 W. Va. 482.

D. JUDGMENTS BY CONFESSION.

See the title CONFESSION OF JUDGMENTS, vol. 3, p. 64.

E. JUDGMENTS BY DEFAULT AND DECREES PRO CONFESSO.

1. Definitions and General Considerations.

a. Judgments by Default.

(1) Application of Term at Common Law.

"The term judgment by default strictly and technically applies to actions at common law only." Davis *v.* Com., 16 Gratt. 134; Watson *v.* Wigginton, 28 W. Va. 533, 544; Smith *v.* Knight, 14 W. Va. 749.

(2) Definition and Nature under the Statute.

(a) In General.

All judgments of every character, whether in common-law actions or on motions under some statute, when there has been no appearance by the defendant, are judgments by default within the meaning of § 3451, Va. Code, 1904, and § 5, ch. 134, W. Va. Code, 1899. Staunton Bldg., etc., Co. v. Haden, 92 Va. 201, 205, 23 S. E. 285; Brown v. Chapman, 90 Va. 174, 176, 17 S. E. 855; Goolsby v. St. John, 25 Gratt. 146, 159; Goolsby v. Strother, 21 Gratt. 107; Davis v. Com., 16 Gratt. 134; Cunningham v. Mitchell, 4 Rand. 189; National Exchange Bank v. McElfish, etc., Mfg. Co., 48 W. Va. 406, 409, 37 S. E. 541; Watson v. Wigginton, 28 W. Va. 533, 546; State v. Slack, 28 W. Va. 372, 375; Midkiff v. Lusher, 27 W. Va. 439; Forest v. Stephens, 21 W. Va. 316; Stringer v. Anderson, 23 W. Va. 482, 485; Adamson v. Peerce, 20 W. Va. 59, 61; Smith v. Knight, 14 W. Va. 749, 758; Holliday v. Myers, 11 W. Va. 276, 297; Carlon v. Ruffner, 12 W. Va. 297; Dickinson v. Lewis, 7 W. Va. 673; Baker v. Western Mining, etc., Co., 6 W. Va. 196; Meadows v. Justice, 6 W. Va. 198; Higginbotham v. Haselden, 3 W. Va. 266.

This is true even when under the law such judgments can not be entered, though the defendant had not appeared, unless the plaintiff proves his claim. "Such a judgment has much the appearance of a judgment on the merits of the case as shown by the proof introduced by the plaintiff, yet, as the defendant has wholly failed to appear for the reason assigned by Judge Allen in Davis v. Com., 16 Gratt. 136, * * * such a judgment is always regarded as a judgment by default within the meaning of the statute." Watson v. Wigginton, 23 W. Va. 533, 546. See post, "Proof of Case," II, E, 2, h.

Whether Defendant Legally Summoned or Not.—In Goolsby v. St. John, 25 Gratt. 146, which was a bill in equity to enjoin a judgment at law it was held, on the authority of Davis v. Com., 16 Gratt. 134, that all judgments, where there has been no appearance by the defendant, are judgments by default, within the meaning of this statute, whether the defendant was legally summoned or not. Brown v. Chapman, 90 Va. 174, 176, 17 S. E. 855. See post, "Sufficient Process Duly Served," II, E, 2, b.

A proceeding by notice, although not a technical judgment by default at common law, falls within the equity, and was intended to be embraced within the scope of these provisions of the West Virginia Code. Smith v. Knight, 14 W. Va. 749; Watson v. Wigginton, 28 W. Va. 533, 546. See also, Davis v. Com., 16 Gratt. 134.

Proceeding by Motion.—"The case of a motion comes within the reason of the statute, and I think the term judgment by default was intended to apply to all judgments where there was a default of appearance." Davis v. Com., 16 Gratt. 134. See also, Preston v. Auditor, 1 Call 471; Cunningham v. Mitchell, 4 Rand. 189. See also, Smith v. Knight, 14 W.' Va. 749; Watson v. Wigginton, 28 W. Va. 533, 546.

"In Cunningham v. Mitchell, 4 Rand, 189, there was a motion by a security to recover money from a person alleged to be a principal; there was no appearance for the defendant. In the report it is said judgment was rendered by default. And Judge Green, in delivering the opinion of the court, states that the defendant can not now, after submitting to a judgment by default, object in this court to the truth of the sheriff's return; thus giving to the judgment the effect of a judgment by default, and styling it a judgment by default. I think the legislature used the phrase in the same sense in the act under consideration, and that this must be considered as a judgment by default in the meaning of the law." Davis v. Com., 16 Gratt. 134; Watson v. Wigginton, 28 W. Va. 533, 545.

A judgment stating that the defendants were solemnly called not appear-

ing, on motion, etc., is a judgment by default; though it is stated at the foot of the judgment that on motion of the defendants the execution of this judgment is suspended for sixty days, upon the execution of a suspending bond, etc. Goolsby *v.* Strother, 21 Gratt. 107.

In National Exchange Bank *v.* McElfish, etc., Mfg. Co., 48 W. Va. 406, 409, 37 S. E. 541, it is said: "The defendants had all been served with process and no one of them appeared, although they were solemnly called. There can be no question about the judgment being taken by default."

Interlocutory or Final.—Judgment by default are either interlocutory or final. Pifer's Case, 14 Gratt. 710. See post, "When Defaults Become Final," II, E, 4.

(b) Effect of Appearance.

aa. General Rule.

"A judgment in a case in which there has been an appearance is not a judgment by default. Holliday *v.* Myers, 11 W. Va. 276; Carlon *v.* Ruffner, 12 W. Va. 297; Smith *v.* Knight, 14 W. Va. 749; Compton *v.* Cline, 5 Gratt. 137; Richardson *v.* Jones, 12 Gratt. 53; Goolsby *v.* Strother, 21 Gratt. 107; Stringer *v.* Anderson, 23 W. Va. 482." Bank *v.* Ralphsnyder, 54 W. Va. 231, 233, 46 S. E. 206; Watson *v.* Wigginton, 28 W. Va. 533; Steenrod *v.* Wheeling, etc., R. Co., 25 W. Va. 133, 137; McGraw *v.* Roller, 53 W. Va. 75, 44 S. E. 248.

If the record merely shows an appearance by the party complaining, the judgment will not be treated as being by default, although he may neither demur or plead, or it may appear that he withdrew all his pleas and defenses. Compton *v.* Cline, 5 Gratt. 137; Richardson *v.* Jones, 12 Gratt. 53; Stringer *v.* Anderson, 23 W. Va. 482; Goolsby *v.* Strother, 21 Gratt. 107. Steenrod *v.* Wheeling, etc., R. Co., 25 W. Va. 133, 137. See post, "Judgments after Withdrawal of Plea," II, E, 1, a, (2), (b), dd.

"If the defendant in a common-law action or a motion under some statute has appeared, though he subsequently withdrew his plea of defense, and the plaintiff either proves his cause and thereupon obtains his judgment, or he afterwards obtains his judgment by the confession of the defendant, such judgment in neither of these cases is a judgment by default within the meaning of this statute. (Holliday *v.* Myers, 11 W. Va. 297-298; Stringer *v.* Anderson, 23 W. Va. 482, 485.)" Watson *v.* Wigginton, 28 W. Va. 533, 546.

The judgment rendered in the case before us at the March term, 1881, was not a judgment by default within the meaning of the statute, nor in any other proper sense. The entry shows that the defendant had appeared and pleaded to the action and then at the term at which the judgment was entered he withdrew his plea and said that he could not gainsay the plaintiff's action. This was a judgment by confession. Stringer *v.* Anderson, 23 W. Va. 482, 485. See the title CONFESSION OF JUDGMENTS, vol. 3, p. 73.

Where parties appear by attorney, the judgment against them is not a judgment by default within the meaning of § 5, ch. 177, of the Code. Dillard *v.* Thornton, 29 Gratt. 392.

Answer or Other Pleading on File or Motion Pending.—"Black on Judgments (vol. 1, § 86) says: 'When an answer or other pleading of a defendant raising an issue of law or fact is properly on file in the case, no judgment by default can be entered against him. To authorize a default, the answer or other pleading must be disposed of by motion, demurrer, or in some other manner. * * * For the same reasons, a default can not be entered while a motion is pending.'" Johnston *v.* Bank, 41 W. Va. 550, 23 S. E. 517, 520. See post, "Judgment

Entered up or Order of Inquiry Executed," II, E, 3, d.

Appearance to Move to Set Aside, Reverse, etc.—Appellant contends that the judgment rendered against the defendants was not a judgment by default within the meaning of § 5, ch. 134, W. Va. Code, as to the appellee, because during the same term of which it was rendered he appeared and filed in the case a petition in the nature of a special plea, and might have interposed a demurrer or other pleadings and his appearance was before the judgment became final. If the judgment was rendered by default, it must maintain that character until it is opened in some way, set aside or reversed. An appearance for that purpose surely can not change the character of the judgment, and until the judgment was set aside, the defendants could not have interposed a demurrer on any other plea. National Exchange Bank v. McElfish, etc., Mfg. Co., 48 W. Va. 406, 37 S. E. 541.

bb. Appearance of Codefendant.

See post, "Codefendant's Appearing," II, E, 2, c, (2), (b).

cc. Judgment after Demurrer Overruled.

A judgment, rendered after a demurrer has been filed by the defendant and overruled, is not one by default. Bank v. Ralphsnyder, 54 W. Va. 231, 46 S. E. 206.

Judgment upon Proof of Case without Joinder of Issue.—In Bank v. Ralphsnyder, 54 W. Va. 231, 46 S. E. 206, the defendant appeared and demurred to the declaration which demurrer was overruled. No plea was ever filed at any time. The order giving judgment for the plaintiff recites that "the defendants being solemnly called came not to require a jury and the plaintiff requiring none, the plaintiff proved its case in open court." It was held, that under the West Virginia decision this judgment "would

hardly be regarded as a judgment by confession. A judgment by default it could not be because of the appearance. It is probably more than a judgment by nil dicit because it is a judgment upon proof as well as upon the failure of the defendants to say anything against the entry of the judgment. At any rate, it is a final judgment." See also, Holliday v. Myers, 11 W. Va. 276; Carlon v. Ruffner, 12 W. Va. 297.

"This view of the judgment in this case is strengthened by the recital in the order that the plaintiff proved its case in open court. If not strictly within the definition of a judgment of nil dicit, it very closely resembles such a judgment." Bank v. Ralphsnyder, 54 W. Va. 231, 234, 46 S. E. 206. See post, "Judgment of Nil Dicit," II, E, 1, a, (2), (b), ee.

dd. Judgment after Withdrawal of Plea.

A judgment rendered against the defendant after withdrawal of his plea is neither a judgment by default nor by confession. Holliday v. Myers, 11 W. Va. 276; Carlon v. Ruffner, 12 W. Va. 297; Bank v. Ralphsnyder, 54 W. Va. 231, 234, 46 S. E. 206.

It is a judgment rendered upon proof of the cause made to the court without issue joined between the parties then before the court. Carlon v. Ruffner, 12 W. Va. 297; Holliday v. Myers, 11 W. Va. 276; Bank v. Ralphsnyder, 54 W. Va. 231, 234, 46 S. E. 206.

In Holliday v. Myers, 11 W. Va. 276, the defendant appeared and plead to the action and then voluntarily withdrew their plea and suffered plaintiffs to prove their cause of action. Their mere appearance was held sufficient to make the judgment one rendered upon proof of the cause of action and not a judgment either by default or by confession within the meaning of the statute. Bank v. Ralphsnyder, 54 W. Va.

231, 234, 46 S. E. 206. See ante, General Rule," II, E, 1, a, (2), (b), aa.

ee. Judgment of Nil Dicit.

A judgment of nil dicit is "defined to be one rendered against a defendant who fails to put in a plea or answer to plaintiff's declaration by the day assigned. Bouv. L. Dic.; Black on Judg. § 79, 21 Am. & Eng. Ency. Law (23d) 541." Bank v. Ralphsnyder, 54 W. Va. 231, 234, 46 S. E. 206.

"In Story v. Nichols, 22 Tex. 87, the court said: 'A judgment by nil dicit is held by this court to possess a stronger implication in favor of the plaintiff's claim than an ordinary judgment by default; it is regarded as partaking of the nature of a judgment by confession as well as by default.' Under our decisions, it would hardly be regarded as a judgment by confession. A judgment by default it could not be because of the appearance." Bank v. Ralphsnyder, 54 W. Va. 231, 234, 46 S. E. 206. See ante, "Judgment after Demurrer Overruled," II, E, 1, a, (2), (b), cc.

ff. Judgment upon Proof of Cause without Issue Joined.

See ante, "Judgment after Demurrer Overruled," II, E, 1, a, (2), (b), cc; "Judgment after Withdrawal of Plea," II, E, 1, a, (2), (b), dd.

(3) In Criminal Cases.

See the title CRIMINAL LAW, vol. 4, p. 63.

At common law no judgment by default could be rendered in a misdemeanor case. State v. Slack, 28 W. Va. 372.

Effect of Statute.—But § 5, ch. 134, W. Va. Code, includes judgments for fines in misdemeanor cases, as well as judgments in civil cases, where such judgments are entered by default. State v. Slack, 28 W. Va. 372.

Under Code, W. Va., 1891, ch. 158, § 20, no judgment by default for imprisonment can be rendered for any misdemeanor either under chs. 32 or

151 or for other statutory misdemeanor, but there may be a judgment for a fine by default. A defendant may appear by counsel in any misdemeanor case, though it be punishable by imprisonment, but in no case can there be judgment of imprisonment without having the defendant present at its rendition. State v. Campbell, 42 W. Va. 246, 24 S. E. 875.

A tavern keeper who is presented for suffering faro and loo to be played at his house may be tried on the presentment alone, without any information; and if he refuses to answer to the presentment, judgment by default may be rendered against him. Com. v. Maddox, 2 Va. Cas. 19.

b. Judgment of Non Prosequitur.

Distinguished from Judgment by Default.—Speaking of default of the parties to prosecute or defend, 1 Bouv. Law Dict. 494, under the word "Default," says: "When the plaintiff makes default, he may be nonsuited; and, when the defendant makes default, judgment by default is rendered against him." This judgment as against defendant would be forever final; but the judgment of nonsuit against plaintiff would not be final, but would allow another suit. Com. Dig., "Pleader," E. 42, B. 11; Bouv. Law Dict., tit., "Judgment by Default." 7 Vin. Abr. 429; Dict. Plac. 208. Buena Vista, etc., Co. v. Parrish, 34 W. Va. 652, 12 S. E. 817, 818.

According to the practice in courts of record at common law, if the defendant appear and file his plea, and the plaintiff does not appear to reply to it, or do what is necessary to bring the cause to issue, there is judgment against him by non prosequitur. Where a defendant does not appear, there is judgment against him by default; or if he appears, and says nothing in defense, there is judgment against him by nil dicit; in both cases the judgment conceding to the plaintiff the relief called for by his action. Or, where he fails to answer any pleading of the plaintiff during the process of the pleading conducting to the issue, such judgment goes against him. In these cases he is taken to confess the allegation to which he makes no reply. It might seem that where the defendant files his defense, and the plaintiff fails to appear, the defendant ought to have the right to have his defense passed on by judgment, to give finality and rest to him, so that he may not be again harassed by a second suit; but the law contents itself with simply entering judgment of non prosequitur, commonly called in our practice "nonsuit," a term here covering judgment by non prosequitur, nolle prosequi, and technical nonsuits, as also judgments of nonsuit entered under the statute at rules. 4 Minor's Inst. 865. That there is this difference between defendant and plaintiff is settled. 3 Bl. Comm. 316, says: "Therefore, in the course of pleading, if either party neglects to put in his declaration, plea, replication, rejoinder, and the like, within the time allotted by the standing rules of the court, the plaintiff, if the omission be his, is said to be nonsuit, or not to follow and pursue his complaint, and shall lose the benefit of his writ; or, if the negligence be on the side of defendant, judgment may be had against him for such his default." 4 Minor's Inst. 864, et seq.; 2 Tuck. Bl. Comm. 270; 2 Bouv. Law Dict. 303, "Non Pros." Buena Vista, etc., Co. v. Parrish, 34 W. Va. 652, 12 S. E. 817, 818. See the title DISMISSAL, DISCONTINUANCE AND NONSUIT, vol. 4, p. 685.

In an action before a justice, where the plaintiff fails to appear and prosecute his action within one hour after the time for appearance mentioned in the summons or last order of continuance, and the defendant has filed no set-off or counterclaim, the proper judgment, if defendant ask it, is one dismissing the action, with costs to defendant, but without prejudice to a new action; and there can be no trial of the case on its merits by the justice or a jury, though defendant has filed a plea; and it is error for the justice to try the case, or to allow a jury trial, and render final judgment for defendant. Buena Vista, etc., Co. v. Parrish, 34 W. Va. 652, 12 S. E. 817. See the title JUSTICES OF THE PEACE.

c. Decrees Pro Confesso.

A decree by default is one on a bill taken pro confesso; and is on facts admitted on failure to deny them. Camden v. Ferrell, 50 W. Va. 119, 120, 40 S. E. 368.

Technically "a decree on a bill taken for confessed" is a decree rendered on a bill without plea or answer. Steenrod v. Wheeling, etc., R. Co., 25 W. Va. 133, 137; Watson v. Wigginton, 28 W. Va. 533, 549.

Appearance of Codefendant.—See post, "Codefendant's Appearing," II, E, 2, c, (2), (b).

2. Requisites and Validity.

a. Jurisdiction.

See post, "Jurisdiction," III, C.

(1) Judgments by Default.

A judgment by default, rendered without jurisdiction, under ch. 123, W. Va. Code, amended by ch. 46, acts, 1897, is void. Rorer v. People's Bldg, etc., Ass'n, 47 W. Va. 1, 34 S. E. 758.

Jurisdiction Questionable in Particular Instance.—When the judgment in the office by default is founded upon lawful process lawfully executed, and the court has general jurisdiction in cases of that character, but its jurisdiction in that particular instance was capable of being questioned, or the defendant is not subject to be sued, the judgment is liable to become final like any other, and if the defenses are not brought forward and insisted on in due time, they are not available.

The judgment is not capable of being successfully assailed in any collateral proceeding. (Terry v. Dickinson, 75 Va. 475, 477; Neale v. Utz, 75 Va. 480, 487.) 4 Minor's Institutes, pt. 1, p. 721. See post, "Sufficient Process Duly Served," II, E, 2, b; "Collateral Attack," II, E, 11.

Where process in an action of debt was served upon a defendant whilst he was in the military service of the confederate states, and there is an office judgment confirmed whilst he is in the service, the judgment is a valid judgment and can not be questioned in another suit. Terry v. Dickinson, 75 Va. 475.

There is a judgment in debt, by default, against four defendants in March, 1862. In August, 1872, one of the defendants moves the court to set it aside, on the ground that at the time of the judgment he was in the military service of the country. It appears, however, that at the time of the service of the process, and at the time the judgment became final, he was at home on furlough. The exemption of the defendant was a personal privilege of which the court could not ex officio take notice; and the objection should have been taken during the pendency of the proceedings. Turnbull v. Thompson, 27 Gratt. 306.

Where a suit has been brought against a member of the general assembly, and the process has been served upon him, and an office judgment has been entered up against him at the rules, whilst his privilege existed, and confirmed; he may, at the next term of the court, though his privilege has then ceased, upon motion, have all the proceedings subsequent to the issue of the process set aside, and the cause remanded to the rules. M'Pherson v. Nesmith, 3 Gratt. 237.

Judgment against Nonresident.—A personal judgment by default can not be rendered against a nonresident defendant, on publication merely; such a

judgment is void. "Even if there be attachment of effects of nonresidents, personal judgment on publication, without service of process or appearance, is a nullity, except as to effects attached. O'Brien v. Stephens, 11 Gratt. 610; Coleman v. Waters, 13 W. Va. 278; Gilchrist v. Oil, etc., Co., 21 W. Va. 115." Fowler v. Lewis, 36 W. Va. 112, 14 S. E. 447. See post, "Jurisdiction," III, C.

Obtained by Constructive Service.—See post, "Judgments by Default," II, E, 2, b, (1).

(2) Decrees Pro Confesso.

Jurisdiction of Nonresident Defendant.—There can be no personal decree, upon a bill taken as confessed, against a nonresident defendant who has not been served with process and who has not appeared in the case. McGavock v. Clark, 93 Va. 810, 22 S. E. 864. A decree against a nonresident defendant who has not appeared, based solely upon an attachment of his property, is void. McAllister v. Guggenheimer, 91 Va. 317, 21 S. E. 475; Hall v. Lowther, 22 W. Va. 570.

It is error to take a bill for confessed against a party proceeded against as a nonresident, and render a personal decree against him if he has not appeared in the cause. Barrett v. McAllister, 33 W. Va. 738, 11 S. E. 220; McCoy v. McCoy, 9 W. Va. 443. See also, Coleman v. Waters, 13 W. Va. 278, 311; O'Brien v. Stephens, 11 Gratt. 610.

No decree should be rendered affecting the interest of an absent defendant, unless it appear (if he be not otherwise brought before the court), "that he has been regularly proceeded against by order of publication duly published in a newspaper and posted at the front door of the courthouse. Craig v. Sebrell, 9 Gratt. 131, 133, citing Hadfield v. Jameson, 2 Munf. 53." McCoy v. McCoy, 9 W. Va. 443. See also, Coleman v. Waters, 13 W. Va.

278, 311; O'Brien v. Stephens, 11 Gratt. 610.

"The objection, for want of due publication against the absent defendant, may be taken by other defendants who may be affected by the decree against him; and if made in the appellate court, will prove fatal, though the absent defendant were not a party in the appeal." Craig v. Sebrell, 9 Gratt. 131, 133; McCoy v. McCoy, 9 W. Va. 443. See the titles JURISDICTION; SERVICE OF PROCESS; SUMMONS AND PROCESS.

Exercise According to Principles of Equity.—When a court of equity has properly taken jurisdiction of a cause against an absent defendant, it must proceed to give relief according to the principles of equity. Coleman v. Waters, 13 W. Va. 278.

b. Sufficient Process Duly Served.

See post, "Parties." II, E, 2, c.

(1) Judgments by Default.

"A judgment by default which does not appear to be founded upon sufficient process duly served is wholly void." Staunton Perpetual Bldg., etc., Co. v. Haden, 92 Va. 201, 206, 23 S. E. 285; Finney v. Clark, 86 Va. 354, 10 S. E. 569; Gray v. Stuart, 33 Gratt. 351, 356; Underwood v. McVeigh, 23 Gratt. 409; Lancaster v. Wilson, 27 Gratt. 624; Fairfax v. Alexandria, 28 Gratt. 16; Connolly v. Connolly, 32 Gratt. 657; Graham v. Graham, 4 Munf. 205; Stotz v. Collins, 83 Va. 423, 2 S. E. 737; Goolsby v. St. John, 25 Gratt. 146, 157; Gunn v. Turner, 21 Gratt. 382; Hill v. Bowyer, 18 Gratt. 364; Hatcher v. Lewis, 4 Rand. 152; Anderson v. Doolittle, 38 W. Va. 639, 18 S. E. 724; Ferguson v. Millender, 32 W. Va. 30, 9 S. E. 38; Midkiff v. Lusher, 27 W. Va. 439; Laidley v. Bright, 17 W. Va. 779; Ambler v. Leach, 15 W. Va. 677; Carlon v. Ruffner, 12 W. Va. 297; Vandiver v. Roberts, 12 W. Va. 493; Capehart v. Cunningham, 12 W. Va. 750; Houston v. McCluney, 8 W.

Va. 135. See ante, "Jurisdiction," II, E, 2, a; post, "Grounds for Relief," II, E, 8, b, (3), (c), cc.

Before Summons and Return.—A judgment by default against a defendant without any writ having been issued against or served upon him is void. Graham v. Graham, 4 Munf. 205.

A judgment by default can not be entered, when the writ has not been returned. Winchester v. Bank, 2 Munf. 339; Crews v. Garland, 2 Munf. 491.

Where the defendant appears not to have been included in the original process and the return thereon, the judgment entered in the suit is void, the presumption of jurisdiction being overcome by the record. Blanton v. Carroll, 86 Va. 539, 10 S. E. 329. See the title JURISDICTION.

If the writ be issued against, and served upon, one person only, who alone appears and pleads; yet, if the declaration be against him and another, and judgment be entered against "the defendants," such judgment is to be understood as against both, and therefore erroneous as to the one who never pleaded. And such erroneous judgment may be reversed (as to the person against whom it is improperly entered), upon appeal taken by the other defendant. Graham v. Graham, 4 Munf. 205.

A judgment entered in the clerk's office, before the execution and the return of the writ, is erroneous, and can not be supported by the writ's being returned executed to the term when the judgment is made final. The bail bond should be quashed, and all proceedings, back to the common order inclusive, should be set aside, and the cause remanded for further proceedings. Crews v. Garland, 2 Munf. 491; Winchester v. Bank, 2 Munf. 339.

When a defendant has not been served with process in the action, and has not appeared to the action, it is error for the clerk to enter office judgment against him for failing to appear and plead, and to award a writ of inquiry of damages; and it is also error under those circumstances for the court to have the damages assessed by the jury, and to enter judgment against the defendant for the damages found by the jury. Capehart v. Cunningham, 12 W. Va. 750; Carlon v. Ruffner, 12 W. Va. 297. See also, Bank v. Bank, 3 W. Va. 386, 391; Crews v. Garland, 2 Munf. 491; Winchester v. Bank, 2 Munf. 339.

Upon bill of S. against G. and P. to subject the land of G. to satisfy a judgment recovered against G., P. and others, it appears, and was so decided by the circuit court upon appeal from a judgment of the county court on a scire facias to revive the judgment, that no process had been served on P., and that he had not entered his appearance in the original action, and the scire facias was dismissed for a variance between the writ and the evidence. Held, the judgment against P. was void and a nullity, the court having no jurisdiction to render a judgment against him, he not having been served with process, or appearing in the cause. Gray v. Stuart, 33 Gratt. 351.

Due Execution.—A judgment by default with process badly executed would not be legal. The object of service of process is to bring the party into court. Mahany v. Kephart, etc., R. Co., 15 W. Va. 609, citing Bank v. Bank, 3 W. Va. 386. See the titles SERVICE OF PROCESS; SUMMONS AND PROCESS.

Return Must Show Lawful Execution.—Unless it appears from the record that the return was duly made, the judgment by default is void, and hence, if any prescribed interval of time is required to elapse between the date of service of the process and the return day, or before the judgment by default, it must appear by the record that such required interval did inter-

vene accordingly, or else the judgment by default is void, not voidable only. 4 Min. Inst. (3d Ed.) 647; Staunton Perpetual Bldg., etc., Co. v. Haden, 92 Va. 201, 23 S. E. 285. See also, Lewis v. Botkin, 4 W. Va. 533; Hoffman v. Shields, 4 W. Va. 490; Capehart v. Cunningham, 12 W. Va. 750.

In Staunton Perpetual Bldg., etc., Co. v. Haden, 92 Va. 201, 23 S. E. 285, it was held, that a judgment by default against a corporation, rendered on return of a summons which shows that it was executed on an officer of the company in a county other than that wherein the suit was brought, and was not served ten days before return day thereof, is a void judgment and may be assailed collaterally by third parties. See post, "Collateral Attack," II, E, 11.

Waiver of Void Service.—Where a judgment was obtained by default without legal service of process, the request of the attorney for the defendant that an item for attorney's fees, which was improperly included in the judgment, be omitted therefrom, is not a waiver of defective service, because the judgment, being void, could not be ratified. Staunton Perpetual Bldg., etc., Co. v. Haden, 92 Va. 201, 23 S. E. 285.

Notice Merely Defective or Irregular.—"The rule is, that if the notice is defective or irregular, but not to the extent of being substantially worthless, a judgment by default entered thereon will be regular and liable to be corrected or set aside on motion, or reversed above, but not absolutely void, and hence not open to collateral attack." Black on Judg., § 83. St. Lawrence Co. v. Holt, 51 W. Va. 370, 41 S. E. 351; Hill v. Bowyer, 18 Gratt. 364; Hatcher v. Lewis, 4 Rand. 152; Anderson v. Doolittle, 38 W. Va. 633, 18 S. E. 736; Ferguson v. Millender, 32 W. Va. 30, 9 S. E. 38; Laidley v. Bright, 17 W. Va. 779; Carlon v. Ruffner, 12 W. Va. 297, 299; Vandiver v. Roberts,

4 W. Va. 493; Midkiff *v.* Lusher, 27 W. Va. 439; Ambler *v.* Leach, 15 W. Va. 677, 701. See post, "Collateral Attack," II, E, 11.

Thus, where in debt against four obligors, one of whom is the high sheriff, the process goes into the hands of his deputy, who serves it upon him as well as the other three, to which he makes no objection; and there is a judgment by default against all of them, the process is properly served and the judgment is valid. Turnbull *v.* Thompson, 27 Gratt. 306.

In Williams *v.* Campbell, 1 Wash. 153, it was held, that if a writ be issued without an endorsement of the true nature of the action, the court may, upon inspection of the writ, dismiss the suit, if the motion be made during the term next after an office judgment has been entered, but not afterwards.

Where, contrary to law, the summons is directed to the sheriff of another county than the one in which the suit is brought, the judgment by default is erroneous, but not void. Brown *v.* Chapman, 90 Va. 174, 17 S. E. 855.

A judgment by default rendered upon a writ, a copy of which was not signed by the clerk, is erroneous, but not void. Laidley *v.* Bright, 17 W. Va. 779; Ambler *v.* Leach, 15 W. Va. 677.

Moreover, a judgment by default, rendered upon a writ, the date of which is blank, but otherwise regular, is valid and binding as a judgment, unless set aside by motion to the court or by writ of error. Ambler *v.* Leach, 15 W. Va. 677.

Where constructive service of process is allowed in lieu of personal service, the terms of the statute by which it is authorized and prescribed must be strictly followed, or the service will be invalid, and the judgment rendered thereon by default void. Staunton Perpetual Bldg., etc., Co. *v.* Haden, 92 Va. 201, 23 S. E. 285.

Default—Void Justice's Summons.— A justice can not issue a summons to a defendant to appear before him at a place, named, without his own district. A judgment by default rendered by such justice upon such summons is void. Stanton-Belment Co. *v.* Case, 47 W. Va. 779, 35 S. E. 851.

Partners.— In order for a joint judgment by default to be rendered against all the partners of a firm, process must be served on all, otherwise such joint judgment will be reversed in toto, under Code of West Virginia, ch. 134, § 5, on motion. Ferguson *v.* Millender, 32 W. Va. 30, 9 S. E. 38.

It was held, in Bowler *v.* Huston, 30 Gratt. 266, that a judgment in New York under the Code of Procedure of that state against the members of a dissolved partnership, one of whom was not served with process and did not appear in person or by attorney in the suit, is not such a judgment as is contemplated by the constitution and act of congress, as to such person.

(2) Decrees Pro Confesso.

In General.— A decree in chancery, upon default of defendants, who are not in contempt upon any proper process, is erroneous and will be reversed for such irregularity. Frazier *v.* Frazier, 2 Leigh 642.

Variance between Process and Bill. —Where neither the subpœna nor the decree nisi required the defendants to answer any such bill as was exhibited, and the parties named in the decree nisi are different from those between whom the decree was made and a decree by default was entered against those parties, they were not in contempt by any proper process, and such decree will be reversed on appeal. Frazier *v.* Frazier, 2 Leigh 642.

Cross Bill—Other Defendant than Plaintiff.— An answer, under § 35, ch. 125, W. Va. Code, containing new matter constituting a claim for affirmative relief, may be taken for confessed as against the plaintiff, but not against any other defendant, without service of process to reply to it. Goff *v.* Price, 42 W. Va. 384, 26 S. E. 287. See the title CROSS BILLS, vol. 4, p. 118.

Constructive Service. — See ante, "Jurisdiction," II, E, 2, a.

c. Parties.

See ante, "Sufficient Process Duly Served," II, E, 2, b.

(1) Parties Plaintiff.

Deceased Plaintiff.—A judgment rendered by default in a suit instituted in the name of a dead person is not void but merely erroneous or voidable, and can not be collaterally attacked, where the defendant is duly served but fails to appear and defend. Watt *v.* Brookover, 35 W. Va. 323, 13 S. E. 1007; McMillan *v.* Hickman, 35 W. Va. 705, 14 S. E. 227. See also, Evans *v.* Spurgin, 6 Gratt. 107.

(2) Parties Defendant.

(a) In General.

Parties Not Named in Writ, Declaration or Bill.—In a suit against a mercantile company, if the names of the parties be omitted in the writ and declaration, and the writ be served on a person not named in either, a judgment against the company for that person's failing to appear, can not be sustained. Scott *v.* Dunlop, 2 Munf. 349.

Upon a bill in chancery against several defendants, process issues against one not made a party defendant in the bill, and against whom there is no allegation therein, and no relief prayed, and a decree is made against him by default, and against the defendants, by some of whom an appeal is taken to the court of appeals, where the decree is reversed as to the appellants, and in all things else affirmed. Held, the decree is a mere nullity as to the party who was not named in the bill, and against whom the bill contained no allegation and prayed no relief. Mose-

ley *v.* Cocke, 7 Leigh 224; Ogden *v.* Davidson, 81 Va. 757.

Parties Named in the Writ but Not Served.—See ante, "Judgments by Default," II, E, 2, b, (1).

Infants.—It is error to take judgment against an infant by default, who is not stated on the record to have appeared by his guardian to defend the suit, or that the guardian appointed by the court ever acted, or had notice of such appointment. Fox *v.* Cosby, 2 Call 1. See the title INFANTS, vol. 7, p. 461.

And an office judgment against an infant, who in the writ, is named as defendant "by J. K., his guardian," can not be supported, but must be reversed in toto, if there be nothing in the record to show that J. K. was guardian by testament, or ex provisione legis, or guardian ad litem, appointed by the court. Brown *v.* M'Rea, 4 Munf. 439.

Deceased Defendant.—Where judgment by default is rendered against a defendant after his death, upon due service of process, such judgment is not void, but voidable, and can not be collaterally attacked. King *v.* Burdett, 28 W. Va. 601; Hooe *v.* Barber, 4 Hen. & M. 439, 440. See post, "Collateral Attack," II, E, 11.

Executor.—See post, "Against Executor," II, E, 7, c.

Partners.—See post, "Judgments by Default," II, E, 2, c, (2), aa.

Upon Failure of Sheriff to Return Bail Bond.—If the sheriff returns a writ executed, and the name of the appearance bail, but does not return the bail bond, or a copy thereof, to the clerk's office, together with the writ, judgment ought not to be entered against the defendant and bail, but against the defendant and the sheriff. Shelton *v.* Pollock, 1 Hen. & M. 423.

If judgment be entered against the defendant and sheriff, in a case in which the sheriff was not required to take appearance bail, the court ought to set it aside as to the sheriff, when this is disclosed before executing the writ of inquiry. Williams *v.* Campbell, 1 Wash. 153.

Disability Accruing Pending Suit. —The subsequent disability of the defendant does not render void a judgment by default where the court has once fairly acquired jurisdiction of the cause and parties. See Neale *v.* Utz, 75 Va. 480, holding that the judgment could not be collaterally assailed. See also, Turnbull *v.* Thompson, 27 Gratt. 306. See post, "Collateral Attack," II, E, 11.

(b) Codefendant's Appearing.

aa. Judgments by Default.

Order for an Inquiry of Damages Required.—When in a joint action upon a joint, or joint and several, demand, there has been service of process on all the defendants, in a case in which an order for an inquiry of damages is required, and the plaintiff has filed with his declaration the affidavit provided for in § 46, ch. 125, W. Va. Code, and one of the defendants has not appeared, but the others have appeared and filed pleas accompanied by counter affidavits as provided in said section, there can be no final judgment against the defendant in default until after the determination of the issues on the pleas. The judgment by default is dependent on the result of the trial of the issues joined, and the final judgment must be joint. State *v.* Corvin. 51 W. Va. 19, 41 S. E. 211.

That, in such case, when there is a judgment by default against one defendant, no final judgment as to him can be entered until the issues as to the other joint defendants are disposed of, and that such judgment by default is dependent upon the finding of those issues, is also well settled. Carlon *v.* Ruffner, 12 W. Va. 297; Enos *v.* Stansbury, 18 W. Va. 477; State *v.* Corvin, 51 W. Va. 19, 28, 41 S. E. 211.

Plea of Nil Debet by One Codefendant.—Where an action is brought against the makers and endorsers of a negotiable note, and one of the makers files a plea of nil debet, upon which the cause is discontinued as to him, and a judgment by default goes against the others for nonappearance, such judgment is valid against them. Va. Code, 1860, ch. 177, § 19.   Muse *v.* Farmers' Bank, 27 Gratt. 252.

Where one of several defendants appears and files a plea to an action of debt, which sets up no defense as to any one but himself, and no plea is entered for or by the codefendants, the office judgment is not set aside as to any of the parties but the one who moves so to do. Creigh *v.* Hedrick, 5 W. Va. 140, citing Enders *v.* Burch, 15 Gratt. 64; Alderson *v.* Gwinn, 3 W. Va. 229; Hinton *v.* Ballard, 3 W. Va. 582. See post, "Setting Aside Judgment Entered in the Office," II, E, 3.

Waiver of Plea by Appearance Bail. —If an office judgment be set aside and the suit defended by the appearance bail, and he afterwards waives his plea, judgment is to be entered against the defendant as well as the bail. Vanmeter *v.* Fulkimore, 1 Hen. & M. 329; Wallace *v.* Baker, 2 Munf. 334; Lee *v.* Carter, 3 Munf. 121.

Parties Served and Parties Withdrawing Plea.—In debt, on a note signed with a partnership name, the declaration charged, that the defendants, being partners, made the notes, and subscribed their partnership name thereto. Some of the defendants, upon whom process had been served, appeared and pleaded nil debet; and some filed with their plea affidavits denying such partnership. One of the defendants, upon whom process had been served, never appeared to plead to the action; and the office judgment was not set aside as to him. On two of defendants process was never served. After the filing of the said pleas and affidavits, the plaintiff, on his own motion, discontinued his action as to several of the defendants; and other defendants, who had pleaded, withdrew their pleas. The case was then submitted to the court, and proof heard; and the court rendered judgment on April 8, 1870, against all the defendants, who had withdrawn their pleas, except three, and except also the defendant, against whom the office judgment had been found and not set aside, but included in said judgment the two, whom process had not been served on. Five of the defendants appealed from the said judgment; but the two, upon whom the process had not been served, moved the court which rendered the judgment, during the pendency of said appeal, to reverse and correct the judgment. Upon that motion, said court corrected the judgment and remanded it to rules as to them, and also remanded it to rules as to the defendant, as to whom the office judgment had not been set aside. At the hearing of said motion, certain others, against whom the judgment had been rendered, appeared and asked leave to file certain pleas, and also affidavits denying the partnership; but the court refused to permit the same to be filed. Held, it was error under the circumstances not to have included in the judgment of April 8, 1870, the defendant, against whom the office judgment had been confirmed at rules, and who failed to appear and plead; and like error not to have included in said judgment the three defendants, who withdrew their pleas, and as to whom the case had not been discontinued. Carlon *v.* Ruffner, 12 W. Va. 297.

Joint Judgment—Default of Codefendant.—Where, in a joint action of debt against two, a judgment by default goes against one, and the other pleads to the action, and there is a trial, then there should be one and the same joint judgment against both.

Peasley *v.* Boatwright, 2 Leigh 195, 196.

bb. Decrees Pro Confesse.

General Rule.—Where a bill is filed against two or more defendants jointly interested, and is taken for confessed against one or more of them for want of appearance, and one or more of the other defendants appear, make defense, and disprove the complainant's case, the bill should be dismissed as to all the defendants. Aiken *v.* Connelley, 2 Va. Dec. 383, 384; Ashby *v.* Bell, 80 Va. 811; Terry *v.* Fontaine, 83 Va. 451, 458, 2 S. E. 743; Harrison *v.* Wallton, 95 Va. 721, 728, 30 S. E. 372; Echols *v.* Brennan, 99 Va. 150, 155, 37 S. E. 786; Payne *v.* Graves, 5 Leigh 561, 579; Cartigne *v.* Raymond, 4 Leigh 579; Findley *v.* Sheffey, 1 Rand. 73; Annonymous, 4 Hen. & M. 476.

"It would be unreasonable to hold that because one of the defendants had made default, the plaintiff should have a decree even against him, when the court is satisfied from the proofs offered by the other. that in fact the plaintiff is not entitled to a decree. See also, 2 Barton's Chy. Pr., § 240." Ashby *v.* Bell, 80 Va. 811.

For the answer of one codefendant to redound to the benefit of the other, their interests must not be separate and distinct. The answer of one defendant can only make an issue for another where the final relief sought, in its nature, affects all the parties alike, and does not apply where separate and distinct relief is sought against different defendants, and where the relief sought to be decreed in no wise affects other defendants. It is proper to take a bill for confessed as to all defendants thereto who have been personally served with process, or who have appeared in the cause and have failed to answer or make an issue therein. See Ashby *v.* Bell, 80 Va. 811.

The rule, does not apply where the defense set up by the defendant who answers is not common to all the defendants; as, for example, when the defense is infancy, bankruptcy, and the like. In such case, the decree against those who have made default is not affected, but will remain in full force as against them. Ashby v. Bell, 80 Va. 811.

Plea of Statute of Limitations.—In 1865, E. sued out distress warrant against estate of J., deceased, which has been committed to sheriff, administrator, who wasted it. Warrant was placed in hands of sheriff's deputy to levy. It was never levied, but was returned to, and remained effete in clerk's office until 1880, when E.'s administrator brought chancery suit against sheriff administrator and his two sureties, alleging the devastavit, and asking relief. Against principal and all his sureties, except A., the bill was taken for confessed. A. answered and plead statute of limitations. The suit being on the joint obligation of all the sureties, the defense by A., not being purely personal to him, enured to the benefit of all, and no decree can be entered against any. Ashby v. Bell, 80 Va. 811.

The appellee contended that the defense of the statute of limitations is a personal privilege, and to avail must be pleaded by the party who would take advantage of it. To a certain extent this proposition is undeniable. It is true, it is not for the court ex mero motu to interpose the defense in behalf of a defendant who does not choose to interpose it for himself. For, as was said by Judge Richardson in Smith v. Hutchinson, 78 Va. 683, "the court sits to determine all questions of law and practice under established rules, and not to interpose or plead * * * special defenses for defendants, who, by their conduct in failing to appear and make defense, in effect say that they can not gainsay the plaintiff's right." But here the interest of the defendants is joint, and

the defense set up by the appellant is, that the plaintiff's right of action is barred, not as against him alone, but all the sureties on his principal's bond. And it is difficult to see why the defense thus relied on should not enure to the benefit of all the sureties, and with the same effect, as if, instead of that defense, the appellant had pleaded and proved a release by the plaintiff, or payment in full of the asserted claim, or any other defense going to the foundation of the plaintiff's right to a decree at all. Ashby v. Bell, 80 Va. 811. See the title LIMITATION OF ACTIONS.

Payment.—See preceding paragraph.

Release.—"In Cartigne v. Raymond, 4 Leigh 579, a bill was filed by a distributee against an administrator and his surety, alleging that the administrator has not duly accounted, and prayed that an account be ordered, etc. The bill was taken for confessed as to the administrator, but the surety answered, and showed that on a final settlement, the plaintiff had released the administrator. The bill was dismissed as to both defendants, and on appeal to this court the decree was affirmed." Ashby v. Bell, 80 Va. 811.

Answer Denying Fraud Which Was Not Proved.—On debt contracted by F. in 1865, T. got judgment in 1873. In 1870, F. bought lands which were conveyed to his sister. In 1883, after death of F. and sister, the lands were sold in suit to settle sister's estate. Then T. brought his bill to apply proceeds to pay F.'s debts, on ground that the lands were conveyed to sister without consideration, to defraud F.'s creditors, and failed to explain delay to sue sooner. Answer to bill under oath denied fraud, and averred that the lands were conveyed to sister to satisfy judgment she had against F. No proof of fraudulency of judgment. Executions had been held up by order of sister. Plaintiff relied on loose declarations as to ownership of the lands. F. had acted for years as sister's agent, and she had income from other property. Administrator being called on to answer, answered the bill under oath, denying the fraud, which was not proved. The heirs did not answer. Held, complainant is not entitled to a decree pro confesso against the heirs; the defense made by administrator, not being purely personal to him, enuring to the benefit of all the defendants. Terry v. Fontaine, 83 Va. 451, 2. S. E. 743, citing Ashby v. Bell, 80 Va. 811.

In the case of Terry v. Fontaine, 83 Va. 451, 2 S. E. 743, Judge Lewis, in delivering the opinion of the court, held, that the answer of the administrator inured to the benefit of his co-defendants. The ground of the contention was that the administrator was not interested in the proceeds of the sales of the lands which were sought to be subjected, and that, therefore, he and his codefendants were not jointly interested in the subject matter of the suit. It said: "A sufficient answer, however, to this position, is that the bill prays that the administrator be made a defendant to the suit, and that he be required to answer the allegations of the bill on oath. He did answer, denying the charges of fraud contained in the bill; and it would be without reason, and doubtless without a precedent, to enter a decree for the plaintiff against those defendants who failed to answer, when the record shows he is not entitled to a decree." But this suit was brought by Terry against the heirs and administrators of Fontaine and his sister, Mrs. Thompson, charging that, after the contraction of the debt, Fontaine bought and paid for several tracts of land, and caused conveyances thereof to be made to his sister, without valuable consideration and with fraudulent intent, and that, pursuant to a decree in another suit, the lands had been sold by a special commissioner of the

court as the lands of his sister, to whom he had had them conveyed; and averring that the lands in reality belonged to Fontaine, and as such were liable to the satisfaction of plaintiff's judgment; that both Fontaine and his sister had died; and that, since the rendition of the decree, plaintiff had been informed that the said conveyances had been fraudulently caused to be made as aforesaid. And the prayer of the bill was that the personal representatives and heirs be made parties defendant and required to answer; that the conveyances be set aside; that the land be decreed to be the estate of Fontaine; that the special commissioner who sold the same, and who had collected a part of the purchase money and taken bonds for deferred payments, be enjoined, etc. All of the defendants made default, except the administrator of Mrs. Thompson, who demurred to the bill, and also answered. Testimony was taken, and at the hearing the bill was dismissed. Therefore, inasmuch as the special commissioner had sold these lands, which were charged to be the lands of Fontaine, as the property of Mrs. Thompson, and had collected part of the purchase money and taken bonds for the deferred payments, this money and these bonds, if not Fontaine's, were property to be administered by the administrator; and he, being the owner thereof in law, was required to defend the title thereto, and in defending the title as administrator the defense would necessarily also be for the benefit of the heirs.

d. Regular Proceedings at Rules and in the Office.

(1) Statutory Provision.

If a defendant, who appears, fail to plead, answer, or demur to the declaration or bill, a rule may be given him to plead. If he fail to appear at the rule day at which the process against him is returned executed, or, when it is returnable to a term, at the first day after it is so returned, the plaintiff, if he has filed his declaration or bill, may have a conditional judgment or decree nisi as to such defendant. No service of such decree nisi or conditional judgment shall be necessary. But at the next rule day after the same is entered, if the defendant continue in default, or at the expiration of any rule upon him with which he fails to comply, if the case be in equity, the bill shall be entered as taken for confessed as to him, and, if it be at law, judgment shall be entered against him, with an order for the damages to be inquired into, when such inquiry is proper. (Code, 1849, p. 651, ch. 171, § 42.) Va. Code, 1904, § 3284; W. Va. Code, ch. 125, § 44.

(2) Filing Declaration.

See post, "Declaration," II, E, 2, f, (1).

(3) Rule to Plead and Decree Nisi.

Rule to Plead.—If notice of the rule to plead be not served as the statute requires, the plaintiff can not proceed to judgment. Smithson v. Briggs, 33 Gratt. 180.

Such service is not now required. Va. Code, 1904, § 3284.

Upon a scire facias to revive a judgment a rule to plead is not necessary. Williamson v. Crawford, 7 Gratt. 202.

Service of Decree Nisi.—Where a defendant in chancery has not answered the bill, it is error to enter a final decree against him without the previous service of a decree nisi. And his appearing before commissioners appointed to take an account, or having notice of their proceeding to take it, does not preclude him from making this objection. Legrand v. Francisco, 3 Munf. 83. Such service is not now required, Va. Code, 1904, § 3284.

(4) Failure to Give Oyer When Craved.

If in an action of debt the bond or deed sued on is not filed with the declaration, and the defendant appears at rules and craves oyer of it, which the plaintiff does not give, and the defendant will not plead without oyer, the clerk may properly take the rules without regard to the craving of oyer, so that the case may be ready to be disposed of at the next term of the court. Smith v. Lloyd, 16 Gratt. 295.

(5) Form of Entry of Common Order and Common Order Confirmed.

See post, "Form of Entry before Execution Issues," II, E, 6, b.

(6) Correction of Irregular Confirmation of Common Order.

Where, in an action of debt, the common order is confirmed at rules irregularly, the defendant having pleaded to a part of the plaintiff's demand, this irregularity can not afterwards be corrected at rules. Southall v. Exchange Bank, 12 Gratt. 312.

(7) Placing Cause on Docket.

Effect of Irregularity.—If the proceedings in the office have been so irregular that the cause is not properly on the office judgment docket, the court should remand it to the rules for proper proceedings. Wall v. Atwell, 21 Gratt. 401.

Endorsement of Entry of Common Order and Common Order Confirmed.—If the common order and the common order confirmed have been regularly entered at rules, the cause is properly on the office judgment docket at the next term of the court; though no endorsement of the proceedings may have been made upon the papers in the cause. Wall v. Atwell, 21 Gratt. 401.

Docket Must Be Made Out before Term.—In Hale v. Chamberlain, 13 Gratt. 660, it is said: "The law then as now provided that the docket was to be made out before the term, and it followed that no cause could be put on the docket in which there was an office judgment, unless such office judgment had been obtained before the term; and where the office judgment was obtained on the same day the term commenced, the cause could not be put upon the docket at that term. White *v.* Archer, 2 Va. Cas. 201; Green *v.* Skipwith, 1 Rand. 460." See the title COURTS, vol. 3, p. 711.

A capias ad respondendum was issued, returnable to the rules, on the first Monday in April, and on that day common order was entered; the first Monday in May was the next rule day, on which day the common order was confirmed in the office. On the same day the court sat. Held, it was not regular to place that case on the office judgment docket of that term, because 1 Rev. Va. Code, 1819, ch. 128, § 76, pp. 506, 507, directs that the docket shall be made out before every term. White *v.* Archer, 2 Va. Cas. 201.

Plea to Action as Waiver.—A capias ad respondendum, in debt on bond, returnable to August rules, being returned executed, and that defendant not appearing, the clerk enters the common order; at September rules the defendant appears and puts in special bail, but does not plead; the plaintiff insists that the clerk shall enter a confirmation of the common order, so as to put the case on the office judgment lists of the next term, which the clerk refuses to do; at the next term, the court orders the case to be put on the office judgment, and then the defendant puts in a plea to the action; and at the ensuing term, there is a trial, verdict, and judgment for the defendant. The court held, without deciding whether it was regular or not to order the case to be put on the office judgment list, that the defendant's pleading to the action was a waiver of objection to the regularity of the order. Powell *v.* Watson, 3 Leigh 4.

e. Failure to Appear.

(1) Necessity.

See ante, "Definition and Nature under the Statute," II, E, 1, a, (2);

post, "Effect of Appearance," II, E, 10, a, (2), (b), bb.

(2) Excuses.

(a) In General.

See post, "Prevention of Enforcement," II, E, 9.

(b) Opportunity of Defense Denied by Rule of Court.

"It lies at the very foundation of justice, that every person who is to be affected by an adjudication should have an opportunity of being heard in defense, both in repelling the allegations of fact and upon the matters of law; and no sentence of any court is entitled to the least respect in any other court, or elsewhere, when it has been pronounced ex parte and without opportunity of defense. 'A tribunal which decides without hearing the defendant, or giving him an opportunity to be heard, can not claim for its decrees the weight of a judicial sentence. See Smith's Leading Cases, vol. 1, part 2, Ed. 1872, pp. 1118, 1119 and 1120.'" Fairfax *v.* Alexandria, 28 Gratt. 16.

Order of Judge Forbidding an Appearance.—Where in a proceeding to confiscate property of a person charged to be in rebellion, the counsel for such person does not enter an appearance for him, because in three cases against the same party, before the same judge, he was informed by the judge from the bench, that it was the rule of his court not to allow an appearance and defense by rebels and traitors, the counsel is not in default for failing to enter an appearance; and the decree of confiscation entered thereon is void and of no effect. Fairfax *v.* Alexandria, 28 Gratt. 16.

f. Proper Pleadings.

(1) Declaration.

(a) In General.

Necessity for Filing Declaration.—It is error sufficient to reverse an office judgment that the common order was entered before the plaintiff filed his declaration. Waugh v. Carter, 2 Munf. 333.

A judgment is not void, though no declaration was filed in the cause, and can only be avoided by the proper proceedings taken in due season in the court which rendered the judgment. Terry v. Dickinson, 75 Va. 475.

Upon a writ of scire facias to review a judgment, a declaration is not necessary. Williamson v. Crawford, 7 Gratt. 202.

Declaration Substantially Defective. —If the declaration be substantially defective, the judgment must be reversed in toto. The court observed that, "where the declaration was defective, it was the constant practice of this court to reverse the judgment altogether, and not to direct a repleader." Shelton v. Pollock, 1 Hen. & M. 423. See post, "Application of Statute of Jeofails," II, E, 8, c.

If a declaration in debt be blank as to the sums, the date of the obligation, the assignment thereof to the plaintiff, and as to the damages, a judgment by default rendered thereupon is erroneous; and ought to be reversed, and the suit dismissed with the costs of both courts. Blane v. Sansum, 2 Call 495.

Cause Sent Back to Be Proceeded in from the Writ.—It seems that where an office judgment is reversed on the ground that the declaration is radically defective, the appellate court, if the writ be correct, will not enter judgment for the defendant, but will send the cause back to be proceeded in from the writ. Hill v. Harvey, 2 Munf. 525; Shelton v. Welsh, 7 Leigh 175. See post, "Remand to Rules and Reinstating Cause," II, E, 8, b, (3), (d), ff.

Copy of Account in Action of Assumpsit.—In an action of assumpsit, if the plaintiff proceeds under the statute, Code of 1873, ch. 167, § 4, a copy of the account sued upon, served on

the defendant, must be intelligible to him and inform him of the precise nature of the claim of the plaintiff and its extent in order to warrant a judgment of default. Burwell v. Burgess, 32 Gratt. 472. See the title ASSUMPSIT, vol. 2, p. 1.

(b) Necessary Proceedings after Amendment.

When an order of court has been entered, granting the plaintiff leave to amend his declaration, and remanding the cause to rules, the case, after the amended declaration is filed, ought to be regularly proceeded in at the rules to an issue or office judgment, unless by consent an issue be made up in court; and if, without such proceedings at the rules, judgment be entered up in court against a defendant because he has not appeared and pleaded to the amended declaration, such judgment will be erroneous. Couch v. Fretwell, 10 Leigh 578.

(2) Want of or Defective Plea.

Want of Plea.—There can be no judgment by default for want of a plea except at the rules. Couch v. Fretwell, 10 Leigh 578. See ante, "Judgment after Withdrawal of Plea," II, E, 1, a, (2), (b), dd.

Plea to Part of Demand.—If the plea filed by the defendant at rules, does not go to the plaintiff's whole demand, he may sign judgment for so much as is not covered by the plea. Southall v. Exchange Bank, 12 Gratt. 312. See the title COURTS, vol. 3, p. 707.

g. Where Demurrer to Bill in Equity Overruled.

(1) Rule to Answer.

In General.—On overruling a demurrer to a bill in equity, the court should not at once decree against defendant as upon a bill taken for confessed, but should award a rule to answer the bill in a specified time. Hays v. Heatherley, 36 W. Va. 613, 15 S. E. 223; Moore v. Smith, 26 W. Va. 379; Pecks v.

Chambers, 8 W. Va. 210, 216; Sutton v. Gatewood, 6 Munf. 398.

If a defendant fails to answer the bill on the day specified in the order, the court may then and not till then enter a decree upon the merits of the case as stated in the bill. Moore v. Smith, 26 W. Va. 379. Pecks v. Chambers, 8 W. Va. 210, 216; Sutton v. Gatewood, 6 Munf. 398.

And though, when the demurrer is overruled, a rule be given to answer the bill but no day be specified in the order, the court can not enter a decree on the merits of the cause at a subsequent day of the term, if no answer be filed. Moore v. Smith, 26 W. Va. 379.

A decree of this kind can only be entered after the statute has been complied with, and the defendant has failed to answer on the day specified. Moore v. Smith, 26 W. Va. 379.

Where a demurrer was overruled, and the court in its discretion gave the defendant thirty days within which to answer, it was error for the court on the same day without an answer to decree against the defendant. Park v. Petroleum Co., 25 W. Va. 108.

This rule so required need not be served on the defendant, who is in court by having filed a demurrer, and therefore the rule is the equivalent of an order granting the defendant leave to file his answer before specified day, and this is the form, in which the order is usually and properly entered. Moore v. Smith, 26 W. Va. 379; Hays v. Heatherley, 36 W. Va. 613, 15 S. E. 223.

(2) Defendant Obstinately Insisting upon Demurrer.

That clause which was added to § 32, ch. 171, W. Va. Code, 1860, by the addition made in Code, 1868, to § 30, ch. 125, was not taken from § 59, ch. 71, Code, 1819 (see vol. 1, p. 257), but suggested by it: "If any defendant shall obstinately insist on a demurrer

and refuse to answer, where the court shall be of opinion that sufficient matter is alleged in the bill to oblige him to answer, and for the court to proceed upon, the bill shall be taken for confessed, and the matter thereof decreed accordingly." This was and is the regular chancery practice; for in default of answer, after day given by rule on overruling a general demurrer, the bill is taken against the defendant pro confesso, and the matter thereof proceeded in and decreed accordingly. Jennings v. Pearce, 1 Ves. Jr. 447. See Fost. Fed. Pr., § 122, and Append. rule 34, Eq. Pr., p. 671. Hays v. Heatherley, 36 W. Va. 613, 15 S. E. 223, 226.

h. Proof of Case.

(1) In General.

"The fair construction of a judgment by default at law, or bill in equity, taken as confessed, is, that the plaintiff, in either court, can recover no more than he can entitle himself to by proof, to be obtained according to the course of the court, which imposes no hardship upon him, as in either court, in case of an issue, he would have to prove his claim; and the judgment by default at law, or the bill, as confessed in equity, only fixed the period, beyond which the plaintiff shall not be delayed in obtaining his proof, and proceeding 'on to a hearing.'" Anonymous, 4 Hen. & M. 476.

(2) At Law.

On Writings for Payment of Money. —"At law, if a defendant makes default, in any action of debt, founded upon a bond, single bill, promissory note, or other writing, signed by himself, for the payment of money or tobacco, judgment may be entered thereupon for the same with interest; but if the bond, bill, note, or other writing be not filed, no judgment can be entered." Anonymous, 4 Hen. & M. 476. See the title BILLS, NOTES AND CHECKS, vol. 2, p. 497.

Action on the Case for Money Had and Received.—"Again, at law, an action on the case for money had and received is brought, and a judgment by default, and a writ of inquiry awarded, directing a jury to ascertain the damages, upon the execution thereof, the plaintiff can not recover more than what he can prove, and, if he is without proof, he shall not have a verdict for more than a cent." Annonymous, 4 Hen. & M. 476.

Relieving from Necessity of Proving Partnership.—In debt, on a note signed with a partnership name, the declaration charged, that the defendants being partners made the notes, and subscribed their partnership name thereto. Some of the defendants, upon whom process has been served, appeared and pleaded nil debet; and some filed with their plea affidavits denying such partnership. One of the defendants, upon whom process has been served, never appeared to plead to the action; and the office judgment was not set aside as to him. On two of defendants process was never served. After the filing of the said pleas and affidavits, the plaintiff, on his own motion, discontinued his action as to several of the defendants; and other defendants, who had pleaded, withdrew their pleas. The case was then submitted to the court, and proof heard; and the court rendered judgment against all the defendants, who had withdrawn their pleas, except three, and except also the defendant, against whom the office judgment had been found and not set aside, but included in said judgment the two, upon whom process had not been served. Five of the defendants appealed from the said judgment; but the two, upon whom the process had not been served, moved the court which rendered the judgment, during the pendency of said appeal, to reverse and correct the judgment. Upon that motion, said court corrected the judgment and remanded it to rules as to them, and also remanded it to rules as to the defendant, as to whom the office judgment had not been set aside. At the hearing of said motion, certain others, against whom the judgment had been rendered, appeared and asked leave to file certain pleas, and also affidavits denying the partnership; but the court refused to permit the same to be filed. Held, the defendant, against whom office judgment was confirmed at rules, not having appeared and filed his affidavit denying his partnership under said § 41, relieved the plaintiff from the necessity of proving the partnership as to him. Carlon *v.* Ruffner, 12 W. Va. 297.

Affidavit Required of Plaintiff.—See post, "When Default Becomes Final," II, E, 4.

(3) In Equity

General Rule.—"When the allegations of a bill are distinct and positive, and the bill is confessed, such allegations are taken as true without proof. But when its allegations are indefinite, or the demand of the plaintiff is in its nature uncertain, the certainty requisite to a proper decree must be afforded by proofs. 2 Rob. (old) Pr. 324; Thompson *v.* Wooster, 114 U. S. 104." Welsh *v.* Solenberger, 85 Va. 441, 8 S. E. 91; Price *v.* Thrash, 30 Gratt. 515. On a bill taken as confessed, the plaintiff can not obtain a final decree, without filing his documents, and proving his case. Annonymous, 4 Hen. & M. 476. See also, quære in Coleman *v.* Lyne, 4 Rand. 454.

Allegations Not Controverted.—Every material allegation of a bill not controverted by an answer shall, for the purposes of the suit, be taken as true and no proof thereof shall be required. Section 36, ch. 125, W. Va. Code; Gardner *v.* Landcraft, 6 W. Va. 36. Dickinson *v.* Railroad Co., 7 W. Va. 390.

Answer Not Responsive to Material Allegations.—Where an answer is not responsive to a material allegation of the bill, the plaintiff may except to it as insufficient, or may move to have that part of the bill taken for confessed. But if he do neither, he shall not on trial avail himself of any implied admission by the defendant, for where the defendant does not answer at all, the plaintiff can not take his bill for confessed without an order of the court to that effect, and having it served upon the defendant, and this is the only evidence of his admission. Dangerfield v. Claiborne, 2 Hen. & M. 17; Clinch River Mineral Co. v. Harrison, 91 Va. 122, 21 S. E. 660. See the title ANSWERS, vol. 1, p. 414.

It was formerly held, that when an answer controverts part of the plaintiff's claim, and does not deny the residue, a decree pro confesso may be entered for that part, and the rest set aside. Thompson v. Strode, 2 Hen. & M. 19.

Implied Admissions.—See two preceding paragraphs.

Specific Allegations of Fraud.—Where a bill to set aside conveyance contains positive and specific allegations of fraud, those allegations are taken as true on the bill being taken as confessed. Welsh v. Solenberger, 85 Va. 441, 8 S. E. 91; Price v. Thrash, 30 Gratt. 515.

In Price v. Thrash, 30 Gratt. 515, "a bill was filed against Price, a judgment debtor, and his alienees, to subject the lands in their possession to the satisfaction of the plaintiff's judgment, on the ground that the conveyances sought to be set aside were fraudulent. Price answered the bill, but the other defendants made default, and there was a decree for the plaintiff, setting aside the conveyances in question, and directing the land to be sold. Price alone appealed, and, among other things, contended that it was error, without proof, upon the bill taken for confessed as to the alienees, to decree a sale of the land which had been con-

veyed to them. But the court, speaking by Judge Burks, held otherwise, saying that in any view the decree in that respect was not to the prejudice of the appellant, and, moreover, that there was no error in the decree as against the alienees, because the allegations of the bill were positive and explicit, and were, therefore, properly treated as true on the bill taken for confessed as to them." Welsh v. Solenberger, 85 Va. 441, 8 S. E. 91.

Suit to Foreclose Mortgage.—In equity, if a suit be brought to foreclose a mortgage, and the bill be taken as confessed, a decree may be entered accordingly; but if the deed of mortgage, referred to by the bill, is not filled, no decree can be entered. Annonymous, 4 Hen. & M. 476.

Action for Settlement of Account.—"And so in equity, if a suit be brought for the settlement of accounts which could not be done at law, and the defendant makes default, yet the plaintiff shall not have a decree without proof; and for that purpose, the legislature hath provided, that 'the plaintiff may have a general commission to take depositions, or he may move the court to bring the defendant in to answer interrogatories, at his election, and proceed on to a hearing.'" Annonymous, 4 Hen. & M. 476.

Conveyance of Land—Mistake in Quantity.—A house and lot not conveyed to Mrs. M. and to her offsprings; Mrs. M. and her husband convey the same to a trustee and his heirs, to secure a debt; the trustee advertises the land to be sold in pursuance of the deed, but thinking that Mrs. M. had only a life estate, he proclaims that only an estate for her life will be sold, and that interest is sold to P. but the trustee conveys the whole fee simple; eight years after, M. and wife file a bill against P. to correct the mistake; and this bill is taken pro confesso. Held, as the bill was taken for confessed, the appellant has admitted the truth of these allegations. It is, therefore, immaterial to inquire whether parol evidence is admissible to prove the mistake of the trustee in selling only an estate for Mrs. M.'s life, and then conveying the whole fee. Pullen v. Mullen, 12 Leigh 434.

Effect of Failure of Codefendant to Controvert Material Allegations.—Although, "every material allegation of the bill not controverted by answer, shall for the purpose of the suit be taken as true, and no proof thereof shall be required" as provided by § 36 of chapter 125 of the Code of West Virginia, still, if one defendant does controvert the material allegations of the bill, by his answer, and his interest may be affected by the truth of such allegations, the failure of another defendant or defendants to do so, does not dispense with the necessity of proof, as to such allegations, as to the defendant who does controvert them, by his answer. Dickinson v. Railroad Co., 7 W. Va. 390. See the title ANSWERS, vol. 1, p. 411.

Decree against Absent Defendant—How Redress Obtained.—In a suit in equity against an absent defendant alleged to be indebted to the plaintiff, and a home defendant having effects in his hands, the plaintiff should prove himself in a legal manner to be a creditor of the absent defendant; but if a decree be rendered upon the bill taken for confessed without such proof, the absent defendant can not obtain redress by appealing from the decree; he must seek it in the mode prescribed by the statute, that is, he must appear in the court which pronounced the decree, and petition to have the cause reheard. Platt v. Howland, 10 Leigh 507. See post, "Limitation on Rights of Appellate Review," II, E, 10, a. See the title REHEARING.

Record as Evidence.—Notwithstanding the fact that the defendants, in a suit in chancery, are in default, yet the record or proceedings in another suit inter alios, is not competent evidence against them. Frazier v. Frazier, 2 Leigh 642.

i. Inquiry of Damages.
See the title INQUESTS AND INQUIRIES, vol. 7, p. 656.

3. Setting Aside Judgment Entered in the Office.

a. Statutory Provision Stated and Construed.
If a defendant against whom a judgment is entered in the office, whether an order for an inquiry of damages has been made therein or not, shall, before it becomes final, appear and plead to issue, and shall, in the case mentioned in section thirty-two hundred and eighty-six, in which an affidavit is required, file such affidavit with his plea, the judgment shall be set aside, unless an order for inquiry of damages has been executed; in which case, it shall not be set aside without good cause. (Code, 1849, p. 652, ch. 171, § 45.) Section 3288, Va. Code, 1904. The West Virginia Code, ch. 125, § 47, contains the same provision and in addition thereto provides that if the judgment has been entered up in court it shall not be set aside without good cause shown therefor. See Dillard v. Thornton, 29 Gratt. 392, in which the provision of the Code of 1849, p. 652, ch. 171, § 45, is quoted and discussed. Hunter v. Snyder, 11 W. Va. 198.

The words "final judgment" contained in, and as employed in, the fifty-third section of chapter one hundred and twenty-five of the Code of 1868, West Virginia, means the "final judgment" mentioned in the forty-sixth section of said chapter. In other words, they mean the "final judgment" mentioned in said forty-sixth section, which every judgment entered in the office in a case wherein there is no order for an inquiry of damages becomes final, by operation of that section, unless it be set aside by the defendant appearing and pleading to issue, as provided by the forty-seventh section of said chapter. Elliott *v.* Hutchinson, 8 W. Va. 452, 453. See W. Va. Code, 1899, ch. 125, § 47.

b. Time.

See post, "When Default Becomes Final," II, E, 4.

c. Plea and Affidavit.

(1) Necessity for Plea.

"Any appearance under our statute is an appearance to the action, but will not authorize the setting aside the office judgment unless by plea properly filed." James *v.* Gott, 55 W. Va. 223, 226, 47 S. E. 649. See post, "Waiver of Default," II, E, 5.

Requiring Suitor's Test Oath.— Where there has been a conditional judgment at rules, in an action of debt, and the case is on the docket for hearing, the judgment becomes final on the last day of the next term of court or on the fifteenth day thereof, which ever happens first, if there is no pleading to issue. And the filing of an affidavit, requiring the plaintiff to take the suitors' test oath, where there is no such pleading, is not sufficient to prevent a judgment by operation of law. Alderson *v.* Gwinn, 3 W. Va. 229. See post, "When Default Becomes Final," II, E, 4.

If after office judgment against the defendant and bail, the appearance bail, or any other person, becomes special bail, the judgment against the said appearance bail may be set aside, without the defendant's pleading to issue. In such case, the judgment stands confirmed against the defendant, although set aside as to the bail. The clerk ought to make an express entry in the order book, that the judgment is set aside as to the bail; but an omission to do so will not charge the bail, and the entry of special bail by the appearance bail, does virtually set aside the judgment against the said appearance bail. Keerle *v.* Norris, 2 Va. Cas. 117.

(2) Time of Filing.

(a) Action Wherein Order of Inquiry.

In an action wherein there is an order for an inquiry of damages, on contract or tort, a plea may be filed at the first term after office judgment, or at a later term. Marstiller *v.* Ward, 52 W. Va. 74, 43 S. E. 178, followed in Hutton *v.* Holt, 52 W. Va. 672, 44 S. E. 164.

(b) Action on Contract Wherein No Order of Inquiry.

In an action on contract wherein there is no order for an inquiry of damages, if a defendant does not plead to issue at the next term after office judgment, he can not thereafter do so, but the plaintiff may at any time demand judgment upon his affidavit before or afterwards filed, such as is required by § 46, ch. 125, W. Va. Code, 1899, or may prove his case for judgment. Marstiller *v.* Ward, 52 W. Va. 74, 43 S. E. 178, followed in Hutton *v.* Holt, 52 W. Va. 672, 44 S. E. 164.

Failure to Take Rule to Plead or Decree Nisi.—When the bill was filed, the plaintiffs were entitled to a rule to plead or reply as the case then stood (ch. 125, § 5, W. Va. Code); but the record does not disclose that the plaintiffs took any such rule, nor does it appear that any step was taken by the plaintiffs to mature their action for hearing beyond the mere filing of their bill at November rules. The statute of West Virginia provides that, after the suit has been brought, "that if the defendant fails to appear at the rule day at which the process against him is returned executed, * * * the plaintiff, if he has filed his declaration or bill, may have a conditional judgment or decree nisi as to such defendant." W. Va. Code, ch. 125, § 44. No decree nisi was taken, so far as the record discloses, the purpose of which is to notify the defendants that, unless they appear and plead at the next rules, "the bill shall be entered as

taken for confessed." Ib. The result
of this neglect kept the case open until the next rules, and left the plaintiffs in the same condition as if they
had failed to file their bill. Wilson v.
Winchester, etc., Co., 82 Fed. 15.

**Plea in Abatement—Plea Puis Dar-
rein Continuance.**—See post, "Character of Plea," II, E, 3, c, (3).

(3) Character of Plea.

"When a plea is offered to set aside
an office judgment, though the court
is to look only to the matter of the
plea, it should receive none (if objected to) that does not go to the
merits of the action. It should reject
all that contain no grounds of legal
defense. Wyche v. Macklin, 2 Rand.
426." Johnston v. Bank, 41 W. Va. 550,
23 S. E. 517, 519. See also, Downman
v. Downman, 1 Wash. 26; Baird v.
Mattox, 1 Call 257; Gray v. Campbell,
3 Munf. 251.

Barton, in his Law Practice (vol. 1,
p. 485), in speaking of the character of
the plea, says: "It must go to the
merits of the action, and must not be
of a nature merely calculated for delay; and although the plea, on its face,
contain a legal defense, yet if it conclude with a verification, and the defendant act in such a manner as to
show obviously that his design is only
to produce embarrassment and delay,
the court may for this cause reject or
strike out the plea. This authority
was not as definite in its nature as was
desirable, but it served to cause the
circuit courts to establish various rules
by which they test the bona fides of
the party offering the plea; and if there
was reason to suppose that a party is
not acting in good faith, but only intends to cause delay, the courts were
clearly justified in applying some test
by which this might be determined. A
common way has been to require an
affidavit from the party that he had a
good defense," etc. In Virginia the
statute on this point is substantially

the same as in this state. Johnston v.
Bank, 41 W. Va. 550, 23 S. E. 517, 519.

Looking to the early history of the
practice which prevailed in regard to
setting aside judgments by default, or
office judgments, Robinson, in his new
Practice (vol. 5, p. 200), says: "In
Virginia, as early as 1727, in certain
actions in the general court, there
might be a judgment by default in the
clerk's office, and it might be set aside
in term, on pleading to issue. There
was a like provision in the act of 1788,
establishing district courts, and it has
been extended to other courts." Under this provision, the practice has
been very liberal in allowing a defendant to plead that which did not make
an issue, but required subsequent
pleadings, provided the real justice of
the case, and not an intended delay,
was thereby promoted. In Downman
v. Downman, 1 Wash. 26, Pendleton,
P., said: "The intention of the law
was to leave a discretionary power
with the court to stop all dilatory and
frivolous pleas calculated for delay,
but to admit all fair ones." Hunt v.
Wilkinson, 2 Call 58. The mere want
of form in the plea is not a sufficient
cause for rejecting it. Downman v.
Downman, 1 Wash. 26. But it may
be rejected on other grounds. Gray
v. Campbell, 3 Munf. 251; Johnston v.
Bank, 41 W. Va. 550, 23 S. E. 517, 519.
See ante, "Time of Filing," II, E, 3,
c, (2).

Pleas Not Issuable.—In Downman
v. Downman, 1 Wash. 26; it was held,
that after office judgment, the court
has a discretionary power to admit any
plea which appears necessary for the
defendant's defense, though not issuable, and should refuse it only where
delay seems to be intended. Cited in
Johnston v. Bank, 41 W. Va. 550, 557,
23 S. E. 517, 519.

**Plea in Abatement—Plea Puis Dar-
rein Continuance.**—Our statute, however, provides (§ 17, ch. 125, W. Va.
Code) that, "where the declaration or

bill shows on its face proper matter for the jurisdiction of the court, no exception for want of such jurisdiction shall be allowed unless it be taken by plea in abatement, and the plea shall not be received after the defendant has pleaded in bar or answered to the declaration or bill after a rule to plead or a conditional judgment or decree nisi." See Simpson *v.* Edmiston, 23 W. Va. 675, where it is held, that "a plea in abatement to the jurisdiction can not be filed after a conditional judgment or decree nisi." McMillan *v.* Hickman, 35 W. Va. 705, 14 S. E. 227, 231; Hinton *v.* Ballard, 3 W. Va. 582. See also, Hunt *v.* Wilkinson, 2 Call 49, 50; Wall *v.* Atwell, 21 Gratt. 401; Bradley *v.* Welch, 1 Munf. 284; Wyche *v.* Macklin, 2 Rand. 426.

A plea in abatement, not being an issuable plea, can not be filed to set aside an office judgment, and must be filed at rules, before office judgment is entered, unless it be of matter which arose puris darrien continuance. Where cause, making the filing of a plea in abatement necessary, occurs after the office judgment is entered at rules, it may be filed at the first opportunity afterwards. Hinton *v.* Ballard, 3 W. Va. 582; Wyche *v.* Macklin, 2 Rand. 426; Hunt *v.* Wilkinson, 2 Call 49; Bradley *v.* Welch, 1 Munf. 284. See the title ABATEMENT, REVIVAL AND SURVIVAL, vol. 1, p. 2.

Plea puis darrien continuance may be pleaded after office judgment, and before the end of the next quarterly term. Hunt *v.* Wilkinson, 2 Call 49. See the title PLEADING.

An office judgment can not be set aside when it stands as an office judgment on the docket of the court, by a plea in abatement. Wall *v.* Atwell, 21 Gratt. 401.

Nil Debit—Set Forth in Affidavit.— The defendant filed his affidavit in support of his motion to set aside the judgment and permit him to plead; and on the face of his affidavit he stated that "there was not as he verily believed, any sum due from him to the plaintiff upon the demand or demands stated in the plaintiff's declaration," etc. It was held, that the statement is a complete plea of nil debit in itself, and is a plea to the merits with which an office judgment may be set aside. Johnston *v.* Bank, 41 W. Va. 550, 23 S. E. 517.

Statute of Limitation.—The plea of the statute of limitation is a plea to the merits with which an office judgment may be set aside. Tomlin *v.* How, 1 Gilmer 1, 9.

In Backhouse *v.* Jones, 5 Call 462, it was held, that the defendant can not plead the act of limitations upon setting aside the office judgment, after the next succeeding term, unless good cause is shown.

Non Est Factum.—The plea of non est factum to an action on a sealed instrument is a plea to the merits, with which an office judgment may be set aside. Franklin *v.* Cox, 4 Rand. 448.

General Demurrer.—But a general demurrer is an issuable plea, which ought to be received for the purpose of setting aside an office judgment. Syme *v.* Griffin, 4 Hen. & M. 277.

Defective Plea.—A defective plea, to an action upon an injunction bond, ought not to be received by the court, to set aside an office judgment. Gray *v.* Campbell, 3 Munf. 251.

(4) Affidavit as to Amount Due.

Section 46, ch. 125, W. Va. Code, says: "No plea shall be filed in the case either at rules or in court, unless the defendant shall file with the plea his affidavit that there is not as he verily believes any sum due from him to the plaintiff upon the demand or demands stated in the plaintiff's declaration * * *." "If such plea and affidavit be not filed, judgment shall be entered for the plaintiff by the court for the sum stated in his affidavit, with interest thereon from the date of the affidavit till paid." This language is imperative and gives the court no discretionary power in relation thereto. If the affidavit is not filed, the court must enter up judgment in favor of the plaintiff and if he refuses to do so and arbitrarily sets aside the office judgment, his action is coram non judice and he may be compelled to enter up judgment thereon by mandamus. Marstiller v. Ward, 52 W. Va. 74, 43 S. E. 178; Quesenberry v. People's Bldg., etc., Ass'n, 44 W. Va. 512, 30 S. E. 73, 75; Hurlburt v. Straub, 54 W. Va. 303, 306, 46 S. E. 163.

Where the plaintiff has filed with his declaration at rules the affidavit required by § 46, ch. 125, W. Va. Code, the circuit court has no authority to set aside the office judgment regularly entered, until the defendant has pleaded to issue and filed his counter affidavit with his plea, but it is the duty of such court in the absence of such affidavit to enter up judgment on the plaintiff's affidavit. Hurlburt v. Straub, 54 W. Va. 303, 46 S. E. 163.

When the defendant fails to file such affidavit at the first term of court at which such office judgment becomes final, he can not file it at any succeeding term of court. Hurlburt v. Straub, 54 W. Va. 303, 46 S. E. 163.

Affidavit by Attorney of Corporation—Personal Knowledge.—An affidavit in a case required of a defendant under § 46, ch. 125, W. Va. Code, 1891, made for a corporation by its attorney therein, not importing that he is conversant with the facts, but stating that he verily believes, from information given him by the corporation, that nothing is due the plaintiff, is not a sufficient affidavit with a plea to set aside an office judgment. Such affidavit calls for personal knowledge of the facts. Quesenberry v. People's Bldg., etc., Ass'n, 44 W. Va. 512, 30 S. E. 73.

Affidavit to Plea in Bar to Declaration in Assumpsit.—See the title ASSUMPSIT, vol. 2, pp. 57, 58.

d. Judgment Entered up or Order of Inquiry Executed.

See post, "Doctrine Abolished in West Virginia," II, E, 3, e, (3); "When Default Becomes Final," II, E, 4.

(1) General Rule.

In Post v. Carr, 42 W. Va. 72, 24 S. E. 583, it is held, that "after judgment by default has been entered up in court, or an order of inquiry of damages has been executed, under § 46, ch. 125, Code, it can not be set aside, and a defense to the action be allowed, under § 47, without good cause being shown therefor, and such good cause can only appear by showing fraud, accident, mistake, surprise or some other adventitious circumstance beyond the control of the party, and free from neglect on his part." Smith v. Parkersburg, etc., Ass'n, 48 W. Va. 232, 240, 37 S. E. 645. See post, "Grounds," II, E, 3, d, (2).

(2) Grounds.

Sickness of Defendant.—The first error assigned is that the court erred in setting aside a decree by default which was entered in the cause at the March term, 1891. This decree appears to have been made at the same term of the court at which said decree by default was entered, and this action was taken by the court upon an affidavit filed by the defendant, W. H. Smith, which showed that he was unable sooner to file his answer on account of sickness, and that he was the absolute owner of the 34-acre tract of land sought to be sold; and, the decree being still in the breast of the court, we can see no good reason why the answer should not have been allowed to be filed. The decree which was set aside, it is true, set aside the deed, and directed the sale of said tract of land; and while it might be regarded as an appealable decree, it can not be regarded as such a final decree as to preclude and prevent the court, for sufficient cause shown, to set it aside, and allow the defendant to file his answer. Bierne *v.* Ray, 37 W. Va. 571, 16 S. E. 864, 805.

Sickness of Defendant—Prevalance of Smallpox.—In an action of assumpsit upon a negotiable note, several parties are sued. Process is only served upon one, and the suit is allowed to abate as to the others. The plaintiff files with its declaration an affidavit, under § 46 of chapter 125 of the West Virginia Code, stating the amount he verily believes is due and unpaid from the defendant to him upon the demand, etc. At the next term of the court said defendant is dangerously sick, and unable to attend court. The attorney he relies on is deterred from going to the courthouse on account of the prevalence of smallpox in the town where the courthouse is situated. During the term, however, after judgment had been entered up against the defendant, an attorney appeared for him, and presented the affidavit of the defendant, in pursuance of the provisions of said § 46, and also presented the affidavit of said defendant's physician, showing his inability to attend court, on account of sickness, and also the affidavit of another party as to defendant's attorney's being deterred from attending court by smallpox, and moved the court to set aside the judgment and allow the defendant to plead. Said motion should have prevailed. Johnston *v.* Bank, 41 W. Va. 550, 23 S. E. 517.

Failure of Attorney to Defend.—The mere failure of an attorney to defend is not good cause for setting aside a judgment by default. Post *v.* Carr, 42 W. Va. 72, 24 S. E. 583; Hubbard *v.* Yocum, 30 W. Va. 740, 755, 5 S. E. 867; Hill *v.* Bowyer, 18 Gratt. 364. See ante, "General Rule," II, E, 3, d, (1).

(3) When Motion Acted on.

Where such a motion is made by a defendant during the term at which the judgment is entered, and good cause is shown why such judgment should be set aside and the defendant allowed to plead, the court should act on said motion during the term, and not continue the motion until the next term, and then hold that it can not then set it aside, on the ground that no plea was filed or offered with the affidavit of defendant at the former term, and that the court has no jurisdiction over said judgment, or authority to set it aside, after the end of the former term. Johnston *v.* Bank, 41 W. Va. 550, 23 S. E. 517.

Thus in Johnston *v.* Bank, 41 W. Va. 550, 23 S. E. 517, it was held, that where, under the circumstances of that cause, a motion was pending to permit the defendant to plead, and said motion is continued, and the consideration thereof deferred, until the next term, the motion having been docketed, such judgment will not become final at the last day of the first term. See post, "When Default Becomes Final," II, E, 4.

Continuance—Right of Cross-Examination.—"At the close of the forty-seventh section (Code, § 125), it is provided that: 'Any such issue may be tried at the same term unless the defendant show by affidavit filed with the papers good cause for a continuance. But the plaintiff shall have the right to cross-examine the defendant upon the matters contained in such affidavit;' that is, the affidavit for continuance." Johnston *v.* Bank, 41 W Va. 550, 23 S. E. 517.

e. After Judgment Becomes Final.

See post, "Motion in Lower Court to Reverse or Amend," II, E, 8, b, (3).

(1) Doctrine of Enders v. Burch, 15 Gratt. 64, Stated.

In the case of Enders *v.* Burch, 15 Gratt. 64, the supreme court of appeals of Virginia held: "'1st. If the term of the circuit court last more than fifteen days, all office judgments, in which no writ of inquiry is ordered, become final judgments on the fifteenth day, and can not afterwards be set aside by the court.' '2d. When a court authorizes executions to issue upon judgments, recovered during the term, the judgments become final from the time when executions may issue, and can not afterwards be set aside by the court.' '3d. A court having set aside an office judgment and the execution, which had issued upon it after the fifteenth day of the term, and permitted the defendant to plead, the plaintiff may have a supersedeas from this order; and though that part of the judgment, setting aside the judgment, is interlocutory, the appellate court will reverse the whole order.' " Hunter v. Snyder, 11 W. Va. 198, 203; Baker v. Swineford, 97 Va. 112, 33 S. E. 542, where it is said, that the first holding is by virtue of what is now § 3287, Va. Code, 1904. See also, Wickes v. Baltimore, etc., R. Co., 14 W. Va. 157, 165, in which it was held: If the judge of the court adjourns his court to a future day according to, and by authority of, the sixth section of chapter 15 of the acts of the legislature of 1872-73, (W. Va., vol. 17) the term of said court, quoad a judgment rendered by said court in a cause before or during the day, on which such adjournment becomes final, is ended. The court said: "According to my judgment in the construction of said sixth section, when the court adjourned on the said 15th day of June, that term of the court was ended quoad the judgment in this case, as much as though the court had adjourned until the first day of the next term, instead of adjourning to the 10th of July, 1876. See, as bearing upon this subject, Enders v. Burch, 15 Gratt. 64, and especially the opinion of the court delivered therein by Judge Moncure." See also, Alderson v. Gwinn, 3 W. Va. 229; Lazzele

v. Mapel, 1 W. Va. 43; Creigh v. Hedrick, 5 W. Va. 140, 142.

"Under these provisions of the Code, the fifteenth day of a term of a circuit court which consists of more than fifteen days, is, in effect, the last day of the term as to cases on the office judgment docket in which there is no order for an inquiry of damages, and in which the office judgment shall not have been set aside on or before that day. The office judgment in such cases becomes as final, to all intents and purposes, on that day, as if it were in fact the last day of the term. The court has no more power over it on a subsequent day of the term than at a subsequent term, and a motion to set it aside would be just as much coram non judice in the one case as the other. It has all the properties of a final judgment. An execution may forthwith be issued upon it, without any order of court, general or special, for that purpose. It can be corrected, set aside or reversed, only by proceedings in error in the same or a higher court. If the defendant has been taken by surprise, and has just ground for relief against the judgment, he can obtain it only in a court of equity." Enders v. Burch, 15 Gratt. 64. See post. "When Default Becomes Final," II, E, 4.

(2) Doctrine Questioned in Virginia.

The doctrine of Enders v. Burch, 15 Gratt. 64, as to the power of the lower court to set aside an office judgment and the execution which had been issued thereon after the 15th day of the term and allow the defendant to plead, was referred to in James River, etc., Co. v. Lee, 16 Gratt. 424, 433, by Moncure, J., the same judge who delivered the opinion in Enders v. Burch, 15 Gratt. 64, as possibly erroneous but the court in that case left the question undecided as it was not necessary in that case to decide the point. And the court was therefore of the opinion that a reargument of the question ought to be heard whenever it may come up for decision before a full court. Also, in Ballard v. Whitlock, 18 Gratt. 235, 243, the question was left undecided and the argument against the correctness of that decision was left unnoticed.

In Baker v. Swineford, 97 Va. 112, 115, 33 S. E. 542, it is said that what fell from the learned judge who delivered the opinion in the case of Enders v. Burch, 15 Gratt. 64, as to the power of the court, after the 15th day of the term, with respect to judgments upon which it permits executions to issue after ten days from that date, was an obiter dictum, entitled to great respect, but not binding as authority. "As a dictum its force is impaired by what was subsequently said by the same court in James River, etc., Co. v. Lee (16 Gratt. 424, 433), above quoted. We are at liberty, therefore, to consider the question as an open one. It is true that at common law executions issued only upon final judgments. It is also true at common law that 'during the term wherein any judicial act is done the record remains in the breast of the judges of the court and in their remembrance, and therefore the roll is alterable during that term as the judges shall direct; but when that term is past, then the record is in the roll, and admits of no alteration, averment or proof to the contrary.' 3 Tho. Co. Lit. 323, cited in Enders v. Burch, 15 Gratt. 64, 66." The court finally decides that under § 3600 of the Code the court has authority to direct execution to issue upon judgments under the conditions therein set forth, but such judgments do not thereby become final so as to deprive the court, during the term, of the power to correct, or if need be, annul them, if erroneous.

(3) Doctrine Abolished in West Virginia.

The legislature of West Virginia by the Code which took effect on the 1st day of April, 1869, made material changes in the 44th section of ch. 171, Va. Code, 1860 (which continued in force until the Code of West Virginia took effect), which changes abolished the doctrine of Enders v. Burch, 15 Gratt. 64, in reference to the power of a court to set aside an office judgment after the 15th day of the term. Hunter v. Snyder, 11 W. Va. 198.

H. brought an action of debt in the circuit court of Jefferson county, against N. T. S., executor of J. S., deceased, on the 31st day of August, 1874, to recover $1,000, due by note dated 31st day of August, 1869, and payable at the date thereof, made by N. T. S.'s testator, at the date aforesaid and during his life to H. On the 7th day of September, 1874, at rules in the clerk's office, H. filed his declaration; and a conditional judgment was taken against N. T. S. At the October rules thereafter the conditional judgment was confirmed in the clerk's office. Afterwards at a term of said court, and on the 12th day of November, 1874, the parties by their attorneys appeared in court. N. T. S., defendant, without objection from the plaintiff, filed a plea of non est factum; and the plaintiff joined issue thereon; and by consent of parties the cause was continued until the next term. The plea of non est factum filed is in the usual form, and is verified by the affidavit of the defendant. On the 3d day of April, 1875, the plea of non est factum theretofore pleaded by the defendant was, on his motion, withdrawn; and the defendant filed a plea of nil debit, without objection from the plaintiff; and the plaintiff replied generally thereto; and issue was thereon joined. The defendant filed with his last-named plea his affidavit to the effect, "that to the best of his knowledge and belief John Snyder never made and executed the note sued on in this cause, as charged in the declaration." On the 10th day of

November, 1875, on motion of the defendant, the cause was continued by the court until the next term thereof. And afterwards, on the 12th day of April, 1876, the parties appeared before the court, and without objection from the plaintiff or defendant, a jury was elected, tried and sworn the truth to speak upon the issue joined; and afterwards, on the 17th day of April, 1876, the jury found for the plaintiff $1,217.50; and on the 27th day of April, 1876, the court rendered judgment for the plaintiff upon the verdict of the jury for the amount thereof, with interest from the 17th day of April, 1876, and the costs of suit, to be paid out of the personal estate of the testator, etc. The term of the circuit court, at which the defendant filed the said plea of non est factum, commenced on the 20th day of October, 1874; and the 15th day of the term was the 5th of November thereafter; and that plea was therefore filed seven days after the 15th day of said term of court. The plea of nil debit was not filed until the next regular term. The plaintiff did not file the affidavit, required and prescribed by the 46th section, of ch. 125, of the Code. on the 15th day of the term, or at any time afterwards. It was assigned as error in the final judgment, rendered by the court upon the verdict of the jury before the appellate court, that all the proceedings in court in the cause, after said 15th day of said term, were coram non judice; that the action was debt upon a promissory note, and the defendant made no appearance in the cause, until several days after the said 15th day of the term, when the office judgment became final under the 46th section of said chapter 125 of the Code of West Virginia; neither of the orders, showing the filing of said pleas by the defendant, states that the common order was set aside. Held, that there is no error in the final judgment, rendered by the court in the cause by which the defendant is prejudiced, or of which he can be heard to complain in the appellate court. That the 46th section, of said chapter 125, of the Code of this state, is materially different from the 44th section, of chapter 171 of the Code of Virginia of 1860, and the decision of the supreme court of appeals, in the case of Enders v. Burch, 15 Gratt. 64, and of this court rendered in the case of Lazzele v. Mapel, 1 W. Va. 43; and also Alderson v. Gwinn, 3 W. Va. 229, 231, under and in construction of said 44th section, of chapter 171 of the Code of Virginia, do not apply to the said 46th section, of said chapter 125, of this state, by reason of the material difference in the provisions of said 46th section, of said chapter 125, and said 44th section, of said chapter 171 of said Code of 1860. Hunter v. Snyder, 11 W. Va. 198. See ante, "Judgment Entered up or Order of Inquiry Executed," II, E, 3, d.

4. When Default Becomes Final.

a. In Virginia.

See ante, "After Judgment Becomes Final," II, E, 3, e.

Where No Order for Inquiry of Damages.—"Every judgment entered in the office in a case wherein there is no order for an inquiry of damages * * * shall, if not previously set aside, become a final judgment * * * of the last day of the next term or the fifteenth day thereof (whichever shall happen first) * * *." Section 3287, Va. Code, 1904. Enders v. Burch, 15 Gratt. 64; McVeigh v. Bank of Old Dominion, 76 Va. 267; Dillard v. Thornton, 29 Gratt. 392; Baker v. Swineford, 97 Va. 112, 33 S. E. 542; James River, etc., Co. v. Lee, 16 Gratt. 424; Hunter v. Snyder, 11 W. Va. 198; Alderson v. Gwinn, 3 W. Va. 229; Lazzele v. Mapel, 1 W. Va. 43.

Judgment on Scire Facias or Summons.—Section 3287, Va. Code, 1904, provides that "no judgment by default on a scire facias or summons shall become final within two weeks after the service of such process." See Dillard v. Thornton, 29 Gratt. 392; Turnbull v. Thompson, 27 Gratt. 306.

In Mandeville v. Mandeville, 3 Call 225, it was held, that the defendant may be ruled to trial in the county court, at the first term after the office judgment.

Upon a scire facias to revive a judgment, if the writ is made returnable to the rules, and the defendant makes default, there should be an award of execution, which, if not set aside at the next term, becomes a final judgment as of the last day of the term. Williamson v. Crawford, 7 Gratt. 202.

Thirty Days Necessary to Ripen Cause for Hearing.—Va. Code, 1873, ch. 166, § 6, applies to judgments by default, and, perhaps to decrees or bills taken for confessed and not where the defendants appear and answer; and the thirty days necessary to elapse in order to ripen the cause for hearing on its merits, are thirty days from the service, not the return, of the process. Robinson v. Mays, 76 Va. 708.

Less than Month between Service and End of Term.—On September 30, 1867, a summons in debt on a single bill was sued out, returnable to the succeeding October rules, to which rules it was returned executed on the 3d of October; and the plaintiff filed his declaration, and the defendant not appearing, a conditional judgment was entered against him, which was confirmed at the succeeding rules held October 28, 1867, and final judgment was entered against the defendant on the last day of the succeeding term of the circuit court, which was October 31, 1867, which was less than one month after the service of process on the defendant. Held, the entry of final judgment against the defendant within one month after he was served with process was erroneous. Code, 1873, ch. 166, § 6. According to the true con-

struction of our statutes, where less than one month has elapsed between the service of process and the end of the succeeding term, the conditional judgment will become final at the term next succeeding the expiration of one month after the service of process. Dillard v. Thornton, 29 Gratt. 392.

Day after Conditional Judgment Confirmed.—It is error in a court of law to enter a judgment against a defendant, on the day after a conditional judgment has been confirmed at the rules. The defendant has until the next term after the conditional judgment is confirmed in the office, to set it aside, under the act of the assembly. Green v. Skipwith, 1 Rand. 460.

Day of Service of Process Counted.—In Turnbull v. Thompson, 27 Gratt. 306, it was held, that where a summons of debt was served on defendant on February 3, the judgment by default might become final on March 3, as under the statute, the day of service of the process may be counted. See also, Dick v. Robinson, 19 W. Va. 159, 165.

Until Quarterly Term Elapsed.—In Digges v. Dunn, 1 Munf. 56, 59, it was held, that an office judgment is not to be considered as a judgment till the ensuing quarterly term has elapsed.

Plea Entered by Codefendant Personal.—Where one of several defendants appears and files a plea to an action of debt, which sets up no defense as to any one but himself, and no plea is entered for or by the codefendants, the judgments become final against all others on the last day of the term at which the case is docketed. Creigh v. Hedrick, 5 W. Va. 140, citing Enders v. Burch, 15 Gratt. 64; Alderson v. Gwinn, 3 W. Va. 229; Hinton v. Ballard, 3 W. Va. 582.

In an Action of Ejectment.—See the title EJECTMENT, vol. 4, p. 916.

b. In West Virginia.

(1) In General.

Statutory Provision.—Section 46, ch. 125, W. Va. Code, provides as follows: "Every judgment entered in a clerk's office in a case wherein there is no order for an inquiry of damages, and every nonsuit or dismission entered therein, shall, if not previously set aside, become a final judgment on the last day of the next succeeding term of the court wherein the action is pending." Connolly *v.* Bruner, 48 W. Va. 71, 35 S. E. 927. See ante, "Judgment Entered Up or Order of Inquiry Executed," II, E, 3, d.

Action on Contract.—Under § 46, ch. 125, W. Va. Code of 1899, an office judgment in an action on contract, where there is no order for inquiry of damages, becomes final, so as to bar a defense, on the last day of the next succeeding term of the court after the entry of such office judgment. Marstiller *v.* Ward, 52 W. Va. 74, 43 S. E. 178, followed in Hutton *v.* Holt, 52 W. Va. 672, 44 S. E. 164; Connolly *v.* Bruner, 48 W. Va. 71, 35 S. E. 927.

Parties Proceeded against by Order of Publication.—Parties who are proceeded against by order of publication have one month after the order is completed to appear and plead; and it is error to confirm a conditional judgment at rules before the expiration of that time. Higginbotham *v.* Haselden, 3 W. Va. 266.

(2) Necessity for Affidavit as to Amount of Claim.

Under the 46th section of ch. 125 of the West Virginia Code, an office judgment can not become a final judgment on the 15th day of the term as was the case under the 44th section of ch. 171 of the Virginia Code of 1860, unless the affidavit required and prescribed by said 46th section is filed or offered to be filed in the case. If the affidavit is not filed, then no judgment can be entered by the court during the term, or after its adjournment by the clerk. The court said: "The affidavit fixes the amount of debt for which the judgment may be entered; and how is it possible for there to be a final judgment for a debt, without some amount or sum specified? The affidavit is clearly a prerequisite to the office judgment becoming a final judgment." Hunter *v.* Snyder, 11 W. Va. 198, reviewing Enders *v.* Burch, 15 Gratt. 64; Lazzele *v.* Mapel, 1 W. Va. 43; Alderson *v.* Gwinn, 3 W. Va. 229, 231; Creigh *v.* Hedrick, 5 W. Va. 140, 142. See also, Hurlburt *v.* Straub, 54 W. Va. 303, 46 S. E. 163; Marstiller *v.* Ward, 52 W. Va. 74, 75, 43 S. E. 178; followed in Hutton *v.* Holt, 52 W. Va. 672, 44 S. E. 164.

The proper construction of § 46, ch. 125, of the West Virginia Code, is that if the affidavit required by that section is filed during the first term of the court after the office judgment at rules, or at any time during the following vacation of the court, final judgment may be entered during that term in court on or before the fifteenth day thereof, or during that vacation by the clerk. But if the affidavit be not made during that term, or during the following vacation, then the clerk has no authority to enter up final judgment, but the plaintiff must prove his case before the court, before judgment is given him. Farmers' Bank *v.* Montgomery, 11 W. Va. 169; Hunter *v.* Snyder, 11 W. Va. 198.

Right to File in Action or Scire Facias on Judgment.—The words, "for the recovery of money arising out of contract," in § 46, ch. 125, W. Va. Code of 1899, include all actions in form ex contractu, but not those ex delicto, and thus includes an action or scire facias upon a judgment, and therefore the plaintiff may, in such action or scire facias upon a judgment, file the affidavit of the amount due him prescribed in that section. "Counsel for Ward presents the point that

§ 46 only allows the plaintiff to get judgment on affidavits in actions 'for the recovery of money arising out of contract,' and this action being one on a judgment is not one for recovery of money arising out of contract, as a judgment is not a 'contract,' and therefore the plaintiff had no right to file any affidavit, or ask judgment by force of it. Like the words 'final judgment' mentioned above, that depends upon the sense in which, or the purpose for which, the statute uses the word 'contract.' Sometimes the word 'contract' would include a judgment, sometimes not. Generally, it does not include a judgment." Marstiller v. Ward, 52 W. Va. 74, 75, 43 S. E. 178, followed in Hutton v. Holt, 52 W. Va. 672, 44 S. E. 164. See the title CONTRACTS, vol. 3, p. 307.

Time of Filing.—The affidavit of the amount which the plaintiff is entitled to recover specified in § 46, of ch. 125, W. Va. Code, 1899, need not necessarily be filed at rules or at the first term after entry of the office judgment. It may be filed later. Marstiller v. Ward, 52 W. Va. 74, 43 S. E. 178, followed in Hutton v. Holt, 52 W. Va. 672, 44 S. E. 164; Quesenberry v. People's Bldg., etc., Ass'n, 44 W. Va. 512, 30 S. E. 73.

Sufficiency of Affidavit.—An affidavit under § 46, ch. 125, W. Va. Code, 1899, made by a plaintiff as to the amount due him, which says that there is "due" him a certain sum, instead of saying that there is "due and unpaid," is not a sufficient affidavit to call for judgment under that section, by reason of the absence of the words "and unpaid." Marstiller v. Ward, 52 W. Va. 74, 75, 43 S. E. 178, followed in Hutton v. Holt, 52 W. Va. 672, 44 S. E. 164.

5. Waiver of Default.

In General.—A default may be waived. A party may waive a statutory right when such waiver is not contrary to public policy. The object of these provisions of the statute is to allow the plaintiff to have a judgment without unreasonable delay. The plaintiff may waive the benefit thereof, and agree that the office judgment shall not become final in accordance with the statute. James v. Gott, 55 W. Va. 223, 225, 47 S. E. 649; Williams v. Knight, 7 W. Va. 335; White v. Toncray, 9 Leigh 347, 352; Bowyer v. Hewitt, 2 Gratt. 193; Herrington v. Harkins, 1 Rob. 591.

What Constitutes—And Effect.—It will be considered that the default is waived if the plaintiff subsequently permits the defendant without objection to participate in the proceedings, as by filing an answer or demurrer. James v. Gott, 55 W. Va. 223, 226, 47 S. E. 649.

With the consent of the plaintiff, any appearance to the action, will prevent the office judgment becoming final by operation of law, so that judgment may not thereafterwards be taken by default but the office judgment may be entered up in court for want of a proper plea. James v. Gott, 55 W. Va. 223, 226, 47 S. E. 649.

At the term at which an office judgment would become final by operation of the statute, if the plaintiff agrees with the defendant to continue the case until the next term and such agreement and continuance is entered of record, they will prevent the office judgment becoming final by operation of the statute, and it can not thereafterwards become final until it is entered up as the judgment of the court. James v. Gott, 55 W. Va. 223, 47 S. E. 649.

The agreement of the plaintiff to a continuance is, in effect, such agreement, "for the case is carried over to the next term in the same condition that it was in when the agreement became a part of the record by consent of the parties. 9 Cyc. 150. The court could not have on its own motion entered a continuance to have such effect, nor could the defendants have had a continuance without filing their affidavit and pleading to issue. But the plaintiff had the right to grant to the defendants time until next term to file their affidavit and plead to issue, and thereby the operation of the law is interrupted and the finality of the office judgment prevented, and such office judgment can not thereafterwards become final until it is entered as the judgment of the court." James v. Gott, 55 W. Va. 223, 225, 47 S. E. 649.

"Such waiver prevents the office judgment from becoming final, and the defendant may afterwards, until it becomes final by order of court, file his affidavit and plead to issue. If a party agrees his legal rights away when he may, he must accept the consequence thereof." James v. Gott, 55 W. Va. 223, 225, 47 S. E. 649.

Before such office judgment becomes final by such entry, the defendant may have the same set aside by filing his counter affidavit and pleading to issue. James v. Gott, 55 W. Va. 223, 47 S. E. 649. See ante, "Setting Aside Judgment Entered in the Office," II, E, 3.

An office judgment set aside because no issue was joined or tried, with the presumed acquiescence of the plaintiff, has never become a final judgment by operation of the statute. Williams v. Knight, 7 W. Va. 335; James v. Gott, 55 W. Va. 223, 226, 47 S. E. 649.

Presumption That Order Was Entered by Consent.—When, on motion of the defendants, the judgment entered at rules in the clerk's office is set aside, and leave given the defendants to file a special plea in thirty days, an appellate court will presume, where no bill of exceptions has been filed, that such order was made by the consent or acquiescence of the plaintiffs. Williams v. Knight, 7 W. Va. 335,

following White v. Toncray, 9 Leigh 347, 352; Bowyer v. Hewitt, 2 Gratt. 193; Herrington v. Harkins, 1 Rob. 591.

If the defendants desired to repel such presumption, a bill of exceptions should have been filed to the action of the court. The propriety and necessity of this course is plainly pointed out in the case of White v. Toncray, 9 Leigh 347, 352; Williams v. Knight, 7 W. Va. 335. See also, Bowyer v. Hewitt, 2 Gratt. 193; Herrington v. Harkins, 1 Rob. 591.

6. Rendition and Entry—Record.

a. Duty of Court.

In General.—When the affidavit of the amount which the plaintiff is entitled to recover, prescribed in § 46, ch. 125, W. Va. Code of 1899, is filed in a case wherein there is an office judgment, but no order for an inquiry of damages, and the defendant fails to plead to issue at the next term after such office judgment, it is the duty of the court to render judgment for the plaintiff upon such affidavit. Marstiller v. Ward, 52 W. Va. 74, 75, 43 S. E. 178, followed in Hutton v. Holt, 52 W. Va. 672, 44 S. E. 164.

Mandamus to Enforce.—The duty of the court to render judgment for the plaintiff upon the affidavit prescribed in § 46, ch. 125, W. Va. Code, when the office judgment has become final, being ministerial, mandamus lies to enforce its performance. Marstiller v. Ward, 52 W. Va. 74, 75, 43 S. E. 178, followed in Hutton v. Holt, 52 W. Va. 672, 44 S. E. 164. See the title MANDAMUS.

b. Form of Entry before Execution Issues.

In the case of an office judgment, which becomes, by operation of law, a judgment of the succeeding term, the only entries usually made after the declaration is filed and before the execution issues, "are two short entries in the rule book, one in the words 'common order' and the other, 'common order confirmed.' These entries are identical, whether the suit be against the defendant in his own right, or en autre droit. The execution is issued upon the judgment as if it had been rightly entered in full. The clerk afterwards at his leisure enters a formal judgment in the case in a book kept for the purpose. The error, if any, in running out these short entries into form when the record is made up, is nothing but a clerical error, the correction of which belongs to the court whose officer committed it. The remedy is by motion to that court, and not by appeal to this. Eubank *v.* Ralls, 4 Leigh 308; Shelton *v.* Welsh, 7 Leigh 175; Digges *v.* Dunn, 1 Munf. 56." Snead *v.* Coleman, 7 Gratt. 305, 56 Am. Dec. 112. See post, "Grounds for Relief," II, E, 8, b, (3), (c), cc. See the title RECORDS.

c. Entry of Final Judgment or Decree.

(1) Time.

Writ of Inquiry Awarded.—Where the damages are not ascertained and a writ of inquiry of damages is awarded, on the return of this inquiry, the right to recover having been established, final judgment is entered up. Pifer's Case, 14 Gratt. 710.

Writ of Inquiry Unnecessary.—See ante, "When Default Becomes Final," II, E, 4; "Duty of Court," II, E, 6, a.

(2) Form.

In Digges *v.* Dunn, 1 Munf. 56, it is held, that a judgment at rules in the clerk's office of a county court ought to be entered as of the last day of the succeeding quarterly term.

Writing for Payment of Money Containing Indorsement of Credit.—See post, "Operation and Effect," II, E, 7.

(3) Effect.

"In 1 Black on Judgments, § 86, the law is stated to be: 'When a default has actually been entered against the defendant, he can not escape its consequence by filing a plea or answer, unless by consent of the plaintiff or leave of the court.'" James *v.* Gott, 55 W. Va. 223, 226, 47 S. E. 649. See ante, "When Default Becomes Final," II, E, 4; "Waiver of Default," II, E, 5.

Whenever final judgment by default is entered up, such final judgment finishes the proceedings, nothing more remains for the court to do, and execution may be done in pursuance of the judgment. Pifer's Case, 14 Gratt. 710.

Office Judgment against Defendant and Bail.—See post, "What Constitutes Record," II, E, 6, d.

(4) Presumption as to Truth of Recitals.

A decree entered on a bill taken for confessed as to all the defendants, which decree recites on its face that all the defendants had been duly served with process, and in the absence of anything in the record to the contrary, the presumption is conclusive that the recital is true. Moore *v.* Green, 90 Va. 181, 17 S. E. 872, citing Hill *v.* Woodard, 78 Va. 765; Ferguson *v.* Teel, 82 Va. 690. See the title APPEAL AND ERROR, vol. 1, p. 418.

d. What Constitutes Record.

Summons and Return Part of Record.—In all cases of a judgment by default, for want of appearance, the writ with the endorsement is a necessary part of the record, that it may be seen whether there was a proper foundation for the judgment. Nadenbush *v.* Lane, 4 Rand. 413; Wainwright *v.* Harper, 3 Leigh 270; Amiss *v.* McGinnis, 12 W. Va. 371, 374.

Receipt for Executions.—A judgment by default against a sheriff, for fines collected upon executions in behalf of the commonwealth, may be sustained, although his receipt for the execution is not inserted in the record. Segouine *v.* Auditor, 4 Munf. 398.

Facts Proven—Evidence.—It is not

necessary to make the facts proven, nor the evidence, a part of the record, in case of a judgment by default, and if any part of the evidence is referred to in the preamble to the judgment, this, of itself, is insufficient to preclude the fact that other evidence might have been heard by the court, unless it affirmatively appears from the record that this was all the evidence heard by the court. Anderson v. Doolittle, 38 W. Va. 629, 18 S. E. 724.

Copy of Bail Bond.—A clerk's entering and confirming an office judgment, at rules, against a defendant, and another person, as "security for his appearance," is not sufficient to make such person liable as appearance bail; but a copy of the bail bond should be inserted in the transcript of the record, for want of which, the judgment should be reversed. Quarles v. Buford, 3 Munf. 487. See also, Shelton v. Pollock, 1 Hen. & M. 423.

7. Operation and Effect.

a. Right of Recovery.

If there be an office judgment against the defendant, in an action on the case, and a writ of inquiry, and, afterwards, without any plea in the cause, the jury be sworn as if there were an issue, and a verdict be found for the defendant, the verdict will be set aside, and a new trial directed. M'Million v. Dobbins, 9 Leigh 422.

Right . to Cross Examine and Demurrer to Evidence—Only Question Being Quantum of Damages.—See post, "Application of Statute of Jeofails" II, E, 8, c.

b. Amount of Recovery.

A judgment by default, for want of appearance, founded on an instrument of writing for the payment of money, on which an endorsement of credit is made by the plaintiff himself, ought to be entered subject to such credit; or if the plaintiff refuses to take the judgment in that way, a writ of en-

quiry should be awarded. Rees v. Conococheague Bank, 5 Rand. 326.

c. Against Executor.

A judgment by default, against an executor, is prima facie admission of assets. Mason v. Peter, 1 Munf. 437.

d. Against Absent Defendants.

See the title REHEARING. See also, ante, "Jurisdiction" II, E, 2, "Sufficient Process Duly Served," II, E, 2, b.

Effect upon Right to Require Security of Plaintiff.—The time allowed by a decree against an absent defendant, within which he might show cause against it, having expired, the plaintiff is entitled to the benefit of the decree without giving the security originally required by it. Ross v. Austin, 4 Hen. & M. 502.

"It is too late now to open the decree, and therefore it is not necessary for the plaintiff to give the security thereby required." Ross v. Austin, 4 Hen. & M. 502.

8. Opening, Amending, Modification or Vacation.

a. During Term.

(1) Decrees Pro Confesso.

During the term at which a decree by default is entered, it is completely under the control of the court and may be modified or annulled on motion, or at the suggestion of the court without motion. Kelty v. High, 29 W. Va. 381, 1 S. E. 561. See also, post, "Motion in Lower Court to Reverse or Amend," II, E, 8, b, (3).

A decree by default for the plaintiff, in an action to cancel a conveyance as fraudulent, is not such a final decree as to prevent the court, for sufficient cause shown, from setting it aside during the term. Bierne v. Ray, 37 W. Va. 571, 16 S. E. 804.

In 1881, K. filed his bill against H. and wife, seeking to set aside, as fraudulent and void, a voluntary conveyance of certain lands from H. to his wife, and praying that the same may be sold to satisfy his judgment against H. On the ninth of December, 1881, the cause was heard upon the bill taken for confessed against H. and wife, and the court entered a decree annulling said conveyance, and directing a sale of the land conveyed to the wife to pay the judgment against H. On the twenty-third of December, 1881, and during the same term, the court on motion of H. and wife, set aside the decree of the ninth of December, 1881, and allowed them to answer the bill. It was held, that the court did not err in setting aside the decree of the ninth of December, 1881, and allowing the defendants to answer the bill. Kelty v. High, 29 W. Va. 381, 1 S. E. 561.

(2) Judgments by Default.

(a) While Interlocutory.

See ante, "Setting Aside Judgment Entered in the Office," II, E, 3; "When Default Becomes Final," II, E, 4.

(b) After Becoming Final.

After Final Judgment Entered or Writ of Inquiry Executed.—See ante, "Judgment Entered Up or Order of Inquiry Executed," II, E, 3, d; "After Judgment Becomes Final," II, E, 3, e.

Upon Motion to Reverse or Amend under Statute.—Amendment and reversal of defaults under § 3451, Va. Code, and § 5, ch. 134, W. Va. Code, whether motion made during term or at a subsequent term, is treated post, "Motion in Lower Court to Reverse or Amend," II, E, 8, b, (3).

b. At Subsequent Term.

(1) Upon Petition or Original Bill.

(a) In General.

A final decree by default may be set aside at a subsequent term, for good cause shown, in a case where relief can not be given by bill of review, or bill to impeach the decree for fraud in obtaining it. Erwin v. Vint, 6 Munf. 267, 268; Callaway v. Alexander,

8 Va—16

8 Leigh 114; Anderson v. Woodford, 8 Leigh 316; Hill v. Bowyer, 18 Gratt. 364, 375; Craufurd v. Smith, 93 Va. 623, 23 S. E. 235; Legrand v. Francisco, 3 Munf. 83.

A party against whom a final decree by default has been rendered may apply to the court to have the decree opened either by petition or original bill. Hill v. Bowyer, 18 Gratt. 364; Erwin v. Vint, 6 Munf. 267; Callaway v. Alexander, 8 Leigh 114. See also, Anderson v. Woodford, 8 Leigh 316; Craufurd v. Smith, 93 Va. 623, 23 S. E. 235; Legrand v. Francisco, 3 Munf. 83.

In either form it is an original proceeding, and may be commenced without previous leave of the court. Hill v. Bowyer, 18 Gratt. 364.

Not Abolished by Statute as to Correction on Motion.—In the case of Kendrick v. Whitney, 28 Gratt. 646, it is held, after speaking of the motion to correct error in a judgment by default, that "the statutory remedy is cumulative, and has not superseded or abolished petitions for rehearing, which may still be had according to the course of equity in the same manner as before the enactment of that statute." Gallatin Land, etc., Co. v. Davis, 44 W. Va. 109, 28 S. E. 747, 748. See also, Shenandoah, etc., Bank v. Shirley, 26 W. Va. 563.

Effect of Rejecting Petition.—If application is made to the court for leave to file a petition to open a decree, and the application is rejected, this is not a legal adjudication upon the case presented in the petition, as it would be in the case of the refusal to allow a bill of review to be filed, in which case the leave is necessary to entitle the plaintiff to file it; and the party may therefore file his original bill to have the decree opened. Hill v. Bowyer, 18 Gratt. 364.

Original Bill Can Not Be Treated as Bill of Review.—An original bill which seeks to correct errors in a decree by default apparent on its face, and also set it aside on the ground of mistake and surprise, having been filed without leave, can not be treated as a bill of review. But a copy of the original record being filed with the bill, the court may consider and correct any errors apparent on the face of the decree, which may be corrected by the court, under the Code, ch. 181, § 5. Hill v. Bowyer, 18 Gratt. 364. See post, "Motion in Lower Court to Reverse or Amend," II, E, 8, b, (3).

(b) Grounds.

Complainant Guilty of Laches—Failure of Attorney to Appear.—In suit by legatee against executor, for an account, and payment of the legacy, subpœna is served on the executor in June, 1828; order made for account in October, 1829; and decree by default against the executor, for the legacy, in May, 1831. Then, executor files bill against legatee, stating, that complaint is, and was at the institution of the former suit, a nonresident of the state; that shortly after the subpœna was served on him, he wrote to an attorney practicing in the court, requesting him to file his answer and attend to the suit for him; that the attorney never filed the answer or attended to the suit, and died during the progress of it, complainant being ignorant of his neglect or of his death, until after the decree, otherwise he would have employed other counsel; that though the commissioner's notice for taking the account was published in a newspaper, complainant, not taking that paper, never saw the notice or knew of the proceedings before the commissioner; and that, on a fair settlement, complainant would be found in advance to his testator's estate; and praying an injunction to restrain proceedings on the decree, and general relief. Held, upon the case stated in the bill, the complainant was guilty of laches, and is not entitled to relief.

Callaway v. Alexander, 8 Leigh 114. See the title LACHES.

Surprise—Effect of Laches.—A defendant upon whom process has been served, who wholly neglects his defense, or contents himself with merely writing to a lawyer who practices in the court to defend him, without giving him any information about his defense, or inquiring whether he is attending to the case, is not entitled to relief against a decree by default, on the ground of surprise, however grossly unjust the decree may be. Hill v. Bowyer, 18 Gratt. 364. See also, Post v. Carr, 42 W. Va. 72, 24 S. E. 583, 585; Hubbard v. Yocum, 30 W. Va. 740, 755, 5 S. E. 867, 875.

Mistake and Accident.—In Erwin v. Vint, 6 Munf. 267, 268, the circumstances shown were that the defendant against whom the decree was rendered was prevented by mistake and accident from filing his answer, and that, in fact, his title was good to the land in controversy. "The grounds alleged for setting aside the decree were, that the defendant, Erwin, had been prevented at one time by a mistake as to the day of session of the Court (which had frequently been changed by the legislature), and disabled by an accidental hurt to his knee at another time, from attending and filing his answer; and that the complainant, his executrix and devisee, was now prepared to show that, in fact, his title was good to the land, and paramount to any claim on the part of the other defendants, William, John and James Bells, or of the plaintiff, Vint, neither of whom had any title, in law or equity, to recover the said land, against him." See the title MISTAKE AND ACCIDENT.

Decree against Absent Debtor.—See the title REHEARING.

Want of Service of Process—Estoppel.—See the title ESTOPPEL, vol. 5, p. 287. See also, the title SERVICE OF PROCESS.

(2) Bill of Review.

Statutory Provisions as to Reversing Cumulative.—The provisions in chapter 134 of the West Virginia Code with reference to reversing a decree on a bill taken for confessed on motion do not preclude a party from resorting to a bill of review. Said provisions are merely cumulative, and have not abolished bills of review which may still be had according to the course of equity in the same manner as before the enacting of the statute. Gallatin Land, etc., Co. *v.* Davis, 44 W. Va. 109, 28 S. E. 747; Shenandoah, etc., Bank *v.* Shirley, 26 W. Va. 563. See also, Kendrick *v.* Whitney, 28 Gratt. 646. See generally, the title BILL OF REVIEW, vol. 2, p. 384.

A null decree by default may be assailed directly by bill of review where such bill of review suits the case. Morrison *v.* Leach, 55 W. Va. 126, 129, 47 S. E. 237; McCoy *v.* Allen, 16 W. Va. 724; Erwin *v.* Vint, 6 Munf. 267.

Error Apparent on Face of Decree. —In Law *v.* Law, 55 W. Va. 4, 9, 46 S. E. 697, the decrees complained of were based upon the bill, taken for confessed as against M. E. Law and her adult codefendant. It was said, if a bill of review, filed in the cause to set aside said decrees, "can be maintained for any reason, it must be on the ground that there is error of law apparent on the face of the said decrees, such as appear in the decrees themselves; the opinion of the court; or from the pleadings in the cause, and exhibits filed therewith; or from such error as arises from facts, either admitted by the pleadings, or stated as facts, settled, declared, or allowed by the decree. Neither the depositions nor the evidence in the cause can be looked to, to show error. Dunn *v.* Renick, 40 W. Va. 349, 22 S. E. 66; Hogg's Eq. Prac., supra, § 211." See also, Hill *v.* Bowyer, 18 Gratt. 364.

Based on Newly-Discovered Evidence.—"The bill of review is not for newly-discovered evidence. It would not lie for that cause to a decree taken pro confesso. Camden *v.* Ferrell, 50 W. Va. 119, 40 S. E. 368; Hogg's Eq. Prac., vol. 1, § 210." Law *v.* Law, 55 W. Va. 4, 9, 46 S. E. 697. But see, Hill *v.* Bowyer, 18 Gratt. 364; Erwin *v.* Vint, 6 Munf. 267.

A consent decree can not be affected by a bill of review, but only by an original bill. Thompson *v.* Maxwell, 95 U. S. 391; Manion *v.* Fahy, 11 W. Va. 482; 3 Ency Pl. & Pr. 608. True, a decree by default is not a consent decree fully; but is one on a bill taken pro confesso; and is on facts admitted on failure to deny them, and is enough analogous to a consent decree to justify the comparison. Camden *v.* Ferrell, 50 W. Va. 119, 120, 40 S. E. 368.

Limitations.—Three years is the limitation for a bill of review. Dunfee *v.* Childs, 45 W. Va. 155, 30 S. E. 102.

(3) Motion in Lower Court to Reverse or Amend.

(a) Statutory Provisions Stated and Construed Generally.

Section 5, ch. 134, of the West Virginia Code, is as follows: "The court in which there is a judgment by default, or a decree on a bill taken for confessed, or the judge of said court in the vacation thereof, may, on motion, reverse such judgment or decree, for any error for which an appellate court might reverse it, if the following section was not enacted, and give such judgment or decree as ought to be given. And the court in which is rendered a judgment or decree, in a cause wherein there is a declaration or pleading, or in the record of the judgment or decree, any mistake, miscalculation, or misrecital of any name, sum or quantity, or time, when the same is right in any part of the record or proceedings, or when there is any verdict, report of a commissioner, bond, or other writing, whereby such judgment or decree may be safely amended (or in which a judgment is rendered on a forthcoming bond for a sum larger than by the execution or warrant of distress appears to be proper, or on a verdict in an action for more damages than are mentioned in the declaration); or in the vacation of the court in which any such judgment or decree is rendered, the judge thereof may, on the motion of any party, amend such judgment or decree according to the truth and justice of the case." Stringer *v.* Anderson, 23 W. Va. 482; Ferrell *v.* Camden, 49 W. Va. 225, 230, 38 S. E. 581; Rader *v.* Adamson, 37 W. Va. 582, 16 S. E. 808. Section 3451, Va. Code, 1904, is similar. See Brown *v.* Chapman, 90 Va. 174, 17 S. E. 855; Goolsby *v.* St. John, 25 Gratt. 146; Goolsby *v.* Strother, 21 Gratt. 107; Hill *v.* Bowyer, 18 Gratt. 364; Davis *v.* Com., 16 Gratt. 134.

Constitutionality.—The statute which authorizes a court, or judge in vacation, to reverse a judgment by default, or a decree on a bill taken for confessed, for any error for which an appellate court might reverse it, is constitutional, being a statute passed in aid of judicial proceedings and which tends to their support by precluding parties from taking advantage of errors, apparent on the face of the proceedings, which do not affect their substantial rights. Such statutes are not regarded as an interference with judicial authority, but only in aid of judicial proceedings for the purpose of correcting errors, such as are mentioned in the statute. Ratcliffe *v.* Anderson, 31 Gratt. 105. See the title CONSTITUTIONAL LAW, vol. 3, p. 140.

Embraces Provisions of Former Statutes.—"These sections of the Code embrace the provisions contained in the Rev. Code of 1819, p. 512, §§ 108, 109, 110, authorizing clerical mistakes, etc., to be amended in certain cases by the court in which a judgment or de-

cree was rendered, or the judge thereof in vacation; and also the provision contained in the act of March 12, 1838, Sess. Acts, p. 74, extending the act of jeofails, to judgments rendered in the circuit courts for default of appearance, and providing for the reversal of such judgments by the court rendering them, or the judge thereof in vacation, for certain errors which would be ground for the reversal thereof in the court of appeals." Davis *v.* Com., 16 Gratt. 134. See post, "Application of Statute of Jeofails," II, E, 8 c.

Statute Cumulative.—See ante, "In General," II, E, 8, b, (1), (a); "Bill of Review," II, E, 8, b, (2).

Nature of Remedy and Purpose.—"This statute, it will be observed, contemplates a cheap, convenient and expeditious mode of proceeding, by motion and without pleadings." Hill *v.* Bowyer, 18 Gratt. 364.

"The object of the legislature was to save the parties the delay and costs of an appeal to correct such irregularities and formal errors; errors which seldom affect the merits of the controversy, and which would have been corrected at once by the court if pointed out." Davis *v.* Com., 16 Gratt. 134.

The spirit of the law is, to permit parties to ask the court below to correct errors, where there has been no appearance by the defendants, because the court is supposed in such a case, to be peculiarly liable to commit errors, there being only one party before the court. See Dickinson *v.* Lewis, 7 W. Va. 673; Davis *v.* Com., 16 Gratt. 134; Goolsby *v.* Strother, 21 Gratt. 107; Gates *v.* Cragg, 11 W. Va. 300, 306.

(b) Requisites of Valid Motion.

aa. Competent Parties.

Where a judgment is taken by default it is competent for the defendants or any of them to move under § 5, ch. 134, to reverse and set aside said judgment for any error for which an appellate court might reverse it, but for § 6 of same chapter. National Exchange Bank *v.* McElfish, etc., Mfg. Co., 48 W. Va. 406, 409, 37 S. E. 541.

bb. Reasonable Notice.

Every motion under this chapter shall be after reasonable notice to the opposite party, his agent or attorney in fact or at law. Ferrell *v.* Camden, 49 W. Va. 225, 230, 38 S. E. 581; Hill *v.* Bowyer, 18 Gratt. 364; Goolsby *v.* Strother, 21 Gratt. 107; Goolsby *v.* St. John, 25 Gratt. 146; Saunders *v.* Grigg, 81 Va. 506, 511.

The notice of the motion to reverse or cerrect is required to be only reasonable notice. The statute does not contemplate the more formal, expensive, and dilatory proceeding, by bill and regular process. Hill *v.* Bowyer, 18 Gratt. 364; Dillard *v.* Thornton, 29 Gratt. 392; Ballard *v.* Whitlock, 18 Gratt. 235.

In Dillard *v.* Thornton, 29 Gratt. 392, it was held, that a notice to reverse or correct a judgment by default, need not be in writing. See also, Ballard *v.* Whitlock, 18 Gratt. 235. This holding is overruled by § 3451, Va. Code, 1904.

"What is a reasonable notice depends on circumstances. In this case it appears by the record that the parties to the motion 'appeared by their attorneys,' and 'the said motion being maturely considered by the court,' it was ordered 'that the execution aforesaid. together with the judgment and all the proceedings thereunder, be quashed.' It does not appear that any objection was made or exception taken because the notice was not sufficient, or not reasonable." Ballard *v.* Whitlock. 18 Gratt. 235; Dillard *v.* Thornton. 29 Gratt. 392.

There is a decree by default against the defendant, and he gives notice to the counsel of the plaintiff that he will move the judge in vacation to reverse the same, and to make such order in the cause as might be deemed just and proper. This notice is not served on the plaintiffs, but on their counsel in the cause. The judge may properly refuse to entertain the motion, on the ground that the notice was too vague and indefinite to warrant the court to amend or reverse the decree, and also because it had not been served on the plaintiff. And for the same reasons the appellate court may dismiss the appeal as improvidently allowed. Coffman *v.* Sangston, 21 Gratt. 263; Board *v.* Parsons, 22 W. Va. 308, 311.

Parties Present by Counsel.—A judgment and award of execution upon a forfeited forthcoming bond, was entered by default, upon a day prior to that to which notice was given; the plaintiff gave a second notice to the obligors in the bond, for a judgment and award of execution thereon, who appeared and objected to the rendering of the judgment and award of execution asked. The court upon motion quashed the first judgment and execution, and rendered another judgment and award of execution on the bond. It was held, that the obligors being present by their counsel, they had reasonable notice of the motion to quash. Ballard *v.* Whitlock, 18 Gratt. 235.

Parties Entitled to Notice.—Section 5, ch. 134, W. Va. Code, 1899, in requiring "reasonable notice to the opposite party" of a motion to reverse a decree upon a bill taken for confessed, demands such notice to any party who has an interest in the maintenance of the decree whether plaintiff or defendant. Morrison *v.* Leach. 55 W. Va. 126, 47 S. E. 237. See also, Saunders *v.* Grigg, 81 Va. 506.

In Amiss *v.* McGinnis, 12 W. Va. 371. 373, it is said: "It seems that such notice was not only proper as to the defendants, who failed to answer, but it was the only remedy they had

to have the said decrees corrected."
See, in accord, Baker v. Western Mining, etc., Co., 6 W. Va. 196; Erwin v. Vint, 6 Munf. 267.

Waiver of Objections.—It is too late to make the objection in the appellate court that the notice was insufficient, when the parties appeared and made no such objection in the court below. Dillard v. Thornton, 29 Gratt. 392; Ballard v. Whitlock, 18 Gratt. 235.

Specification of Errors.—See post, "Specification of Error," II, E, 8, b, (3), (b), cc.

cc. Specification of Errors.

Doctrine in West Virginia.—On a motion to reverse a decree by default, the errors must be specified in the notice of the motion, or on the record in the motion, or in a written assignment of errors filed as a part of the record. Slingluff v. Gainer, 49 W. Va. 7, 8, 37 S. E. 771.

"A motion to reverse a decree by default under chapter 134 takes the place of an appeal, and by analogy to an appeal it should specify errors, either in the notice or on the record, or in a written assignment of errors filed. The invariable practice has been to specify the errors in the notice. There are some errors remediable by appeal, some by motion. The Code prohibits us from reversing a decree by default until the errors in it are presented to the court below. How can this court say on appeal that for given errors there was a motion to reverse, unless we can affirmatively see that those errors have undergone review in the court below?" Slingluff v. Gainer, 49 W. Va. 7, 37 S. E. 771. See, to the same effect, Gunn v. Turner, 21 Gratt. 382, which is apparently overruled by Saunders v. Grigg, 81 Va. 506.

In Laidley v. Bright, 17 W. Va. 801, it was urged that "unless a party, who asks a court to reverse a judgment by default on notice and motion under the statute, specifies in his notice a

particular ground of objection, he can not rely upon such grounds before the circuit judge or in the appellate court." It was said the case of Coffman v. Sangston, 21 Gratt. 263, strongly support these views. But Green, P., thought that the appellate court might look into the errors in the proceedings apparent on the face of the record although not specifically pointed out in the notice as the basis of the motion. This point, not being essential to the decision of the case, was expressly left undecided.

Former Doctrine in Virginia.—"In Gunn v. Turner, 21 Gratt. 382, it is held, that the notice must specify errors. This has, perhaps, been overruled in Saunders v. Grigg, 81 Va. 506, but, as 1 Barton's Law Prac. 574, asserts, the former decision is clearly the better one." Slingluff v. Gainer, 49 W. Va. 1, 13, 37 S. E. 771. See Coffman v. Sangston, 21 Gratt. 263; Laidley v. Bright, 17 W. Va. 779. In Gunn v. Turner, 21 Gratt. 382, it was held, that as there was no motion to reverse the judgment, on the ground that the process was not served on one of the defendants, that question could not be considered by the appellate court. "This ruling seems to be in accordance with the views generally held, the decided cases maintaining that a notice should describe a cause of action with as much certainty and particularity as in a declaration, and that where there are several grounds on which a motion may be granted, those upon which the moving party means to rely must be distinctly stated, either in the notice or in the affidavits which accompany it, and to the grounds thus stated the party will be confined upon the hearing." 1 Barton's Law Prac. 574.

Present Doctrine in Virginia.—The notice under § 3451, Va. Code, 1904, need not specify the errors for which the court is asked to correct or reverse its judgment by default, or decree on bill taken for confessed. Nowhere in Code, 1873, ch. 177, §§ 5, 6, now §§ 3451, 3452, Va. Code, 1904, is it required that the notice of a motion to reverse or correct a judgment or decree by default provided for in that chapter shall specify the errors on the face of the record, etc., for which the reversal is asked. Under Code, 1873, ch. 178, § 8, a petition for an appeal, etc., must assign error. Yet it is the well-known practice for appellate courts not to confine themselves to the errors specified in the petition, but to reverse the decree complained of for any substantial error disclosed by the record, whether mentioned in the petition or not. Saunders v. Grigg, 81 Va. 506, apparently overruling Gunn v. Turner, 21 Gratt. 382.

This court will in inspecting the whole record of the case examine and pass upon any errors which may be patent on the face of the record, which are substantive, which injuriously affect the appellant, and which may not have been by him manifestly waived, although they have neither been specified in the notice nor assigned in the petition for appeal. Saunders v. Grigg, 81 Va. 506, 507.

"It is true that objections on the mere ground of irregularity can not be made for the first time in the appellate court; but such is not the case as to objections based on grounds of substantial justice, as the necessity of there being jurisdiction over the subject matter and the parties to the suit, a good cause of action, a valid verdict, and a proper judgment." Saunders v. Grigg, 81 Va. 506, 507. See the title APPEAL AND ERROR, vol. 1, p. 548.

"In the case at bar the notice of the motion to reverse is very comprehensive, specifying six different errors, though not specifying the error assigned in the petition for appeal, to wit; that it was error in the court below to enter any decree for an account at the May term, 1880, when the appellant and several other defendants, obligors in the refunding bonds, had not been summoned, and were not before the court, although named as defendants in the bill and shown to be necessary parties and seriously interested in the subject matter of the accounts ordered. And neither the said notice nor the said petition mention it as error in the court below to have a report made under said decree of account, which was taken and reported before the appellant had been summoned or was before the court and whilst the cause was yet at rules as to him, any decree requiring him to pay money. And yet, if such errors were apparent on the face of the record when it was before the court below for inspection and reversal, upon motion under said fifth section for any error for which an appellate court would reverse the decree, upon an appeal to this court from the decree of the court below refusing to reverse it, for this court to shut its eyes to such errors, simply because they had not been designated, would be sheer denial of justice." Saunders v. Grigg, 81 Va. 506, 507.

(c) Scope of Remedy and Grounds of Relief.

aa. Motion to Reverse.

(aa) In General.

It will be observed that § 5, ch. 134, W. Va. Code, § 3451, Va. Code, 1904, is divided into "two clauses and embraces two distinct subjects, the first of which gives to the court (or judge in vacation) in which a judgment by default is entered, the right to reverse such a judgment for any error for which an appellate court might reverse it, and to give such judgment as ought to be given. Under this clause judgments by default only can be corrected. But errors in such judgment whether of law or fact may be corrected if they are of such character as could formerly have been reviewed and corrected by the appellate court. Barton's Law Pr. 171." Stringer *v.* Anderson, 23 W. Va. 482. See also, Shipman *v.* Fletcher, 91 Va. 473, 22 S. E. 458. See post, "Motion to Amend," II, E, 8, b, (3), (c), bb.

(bb) Judgment Not by Default.

A motion under § 5, ch. 134, W. Va. Code, or § 3451, Va. Code, 1704, to correct a judgment which is not a judgment by default will be dismissed. Stewart *v.* Stewart, 40 W. Va. 65, 20 S. E. 862; Stringer *v.* Anderson, 23 W. Va. 482; Bank *v.* Ralphsnyder, 54 W. Va. 231, 46 S. E. 206.

Judgment by Confession.—In an action of ejectment the land is described in the declaration by metes and bounds; the order giving judgment for the plaintiff for the land recites: "This day came the parties by their attorneys, and the defendant withdraws the plea of not guilty heretofore pleaded by him, and says that he can not gainsay the plaintiff's action;" judgment is then rendered describing the land by metes and bounds in the very terms of the declaration; and the order concludes as follows: "And it is further considered by the court, that the line on the plat (annexed to the plaintiff's declaration) and running S. 40 E. 119 poles between the points 'A.' and 'B.' be held firm, and stable as a division line betwen the plaintiff and defendant." This provision does not appear to be founded upon any matter or paper in the record and seems to be in conflict with the description of the land given in the former part of the order. Held, that, if said matter in the conclusion of said judgment is erroneous, it is not of that class of errors which can be corrected on motion under either the first or second clause, § 5, ch. 134, W. Va. Code. The first clause of said section is confined to judgments by default and this being a judgment by confes-

sion after appearance and not by default it can not be corrected under that clause. Stringer *v.* Anderson, 23 W. Va. 482.

Where Demurrer Overruled.—A motion to correct a judgment, rendered after a demurrer has been filed by the defendant and overruled for judicial error, made after the close of the term at which judgment was rendered, is properly overruled. Though such motion can not be entertained, a writ of error to the judgment may be allowed. Bank *v.* Ralphsnyder, 54 W. Va. 231, 46 S. E. 206.

(cc) Decree Not on Bill Taken for Confessed.

Where the decree sought to be reversed under § 5, ch. 134, W. Va. Code, or § 3451, Va. Code, 1904, is not a decree on a bill taken for confessed, the court will dismiss the motion. Bell *v.* List, 6 W. Va. 469.

Where a decree has been rendered in a cause upon a demurrer to the bill, an answer, a supplemental and amended answer, and replications thereto, upon depositions taken, and the report of a commissioner, which has been excepted to, the exceptions acted upon, and the principles of the cause have been adjudicated, such decree can not be reversed upon motion under ch 134, W. Va. Code. Rader *v.* Adamson, 37 W. Va. 582, 16 S. E. 808.

Answer to Bill—Reference by Court—A. filed his bill against B., the administrator of C., claiming a debt against the estate of C., claiming that he was entitled to have his debt paid out of the assets in the hands of the administrator. B. answered the bill and claims .that there was not sufficient assets to pay the debts against the estate. The court referred the cause, by consent of the parties to the bill, to a commissioner to ascertain, among other things, "What debts are due from said estate and respective priorities, if any, and any other matters deemed pertinent by any of the creditors of the said estate, or any of the parties in interest;" and directed the commissioner in the decree, before proceeding to state the account, to give notice to the creditors and all persons interested in the estate, by publication of the time and place of taking the same in some newspaper published in the city of Wheeling, at least four weeks before commencing to take the said account; and the court, in the decree, adjudged that such publication shall be equivalent to personal service. The commissioner proceeds to discharge his duties under the decree, and among other debts against the estate of A., he reports a debt as being due to B. of $4,000, in the aggregate exclusive of interest. The court hears the case upon the bill, answer of L., administrator, and report of the commissioner, to which no exceptions were filed, and directs what disposition shall be made of the assets, and orders that after paying the costs of suit and the funeral expenses, amounting to $169.68, out of the residue to pay the balance pro rata on the debts mentioned in schedule A to the extent of the funds in his hands. Schedule A is a list of the creditors of the estate, showing the amount due to each, filed with the commissioner's report and as part thereof, and B. is one of the creditors B. feeling aggrieved by this decree, moves the circuit court after due notice, to reverse and set aside said decree, and the circuit court, on motion, dismissed the motion to reverse Held, that it was not error in the circuit court to dismiss the motion, because the decree sought to be reversed was not a decree on a bill taken for confessed. Bell v. List. 6 W. Va. 469.

Error Not Apparent in Commissioner's Report.—In a litigated case where a final decree has been entered in a cause confirming the report of a commissioner, without exception or objection, errors alleged in said report and not appearing on the face of it can not be corrected by the trial court on motion under § 3451 of the Virginia Code. Shipman v. Fletcher, 91 Va. 473, 474, 22 S. E. 456.

bb. Motion to Amend.

The second clause, § 5, ch. 134, W. Va. Code, § 3451, Va. Code, 1904, is not confined to judgments by default, but is an enlargement of the old law on the subject of the correction of mistakes. But under this clause no error in the application of the law to the facts, or to what is known as judicial error, can be corrected; this can only be done, when the judgment is not by default, in an appellate court. The difference between the two clauses then is briefly this: A judgment by default may be corrected or reversed in the court which rendered it for either error of fact or an error of law including of course judicial errors; while a judgment under the second clause can only be corrected as to any mistake, miscalculation, misrecital, etc., where there is something in the record by which the correction may be certainly and safely made; hence such correction can never be of a judicial error. Richardson v. Jones, 12 Gratt. 53; Bart. Law Pr. 171. Stringer v. Anderson, 23 W. Va. 482, 484. See also, Shipman v. Fletcher, 91 Va. 473, 22 S. E. 456. See ante, "Motion to Reverse," II, E, 8, b, (3), (c), aa.

A clerical error is to be amended upon motion to the court; and is not a ground of appeal. Snead v. Coleman, 7 Gratt. 300, 56 Am. Dec. 112. See the title RECORDS.

cc. Grounds for Relief.

In General.—It is competent to submit a motion to the circuit court for a reversal and correction of the judgment or decree by default complained of, upon any ground on which it might have been reversed and corrected by an appellate court, if the statute had allowed an appeal without such previous application to the circuit court. Brown *v.* Chapman, 90 Va. 174, 17 S. E. 855; Hill *v.* Bowyer, 18 Gratt. 364; Davis *v.* Com., 16 Gratt. 134; Ratcliffe *v.* Anderson, 31 Gratt. 105; National Exchange Bank *v.* McElfish, etc., Mfg. Co., 48 W. Va. 406, 409, 37 S. E. 541.

Section 3451 (Va. Code, 1904) has no application to errors in the reasoning and conclusions of the court about contested matters. Shipman *v.* Fletcher, 91 Va. 473, 22 S. E. 458.

Want of Jurisdiction.—A judgment by default, rendered without jurisdiction, under ch. 123, W. Va. Code, amended by ch. 46, acts, 1897, is void and may be vacated on motion. Rorer *v.* People's Bldg., etc., Ass'n, 47 W. Va. 1, 34 S. E. 758.

Defective Summons or Service.—See ante, "Sufficient Process Duly Served," II, E, 2, b.

In Ambler *v.* Leach, 15 W. Va. 677, it was held: "A writ otherwise regular is not absolutely null and void if its date is blank and it is signed by the clerk. Such writ is voidable, and may be avoided by motion to quash if made by the defendant; but if not so avoided, or in some other manner, in the suit, and a judgment is rendered against the defendant by default on such writ, and such judgment is not set aside by motion to the court or by writ of error it is valid and binding." The inference to be drawn from this decision is clearly, that in the judgment of this court a judgment obtained by default on the service of such a writ, as was served on the three defendants residing in Cabell county, ought to be set aside on a motion made to the circuit court, such as was made in this case, and if refused by such court, then by this court on writ of error such judgment by default would be reversed. This is the inevitable conclusion to be drawn from that case; for when a judgment is obtained by default, the statute of jeofails has no effect on such judgment, and the

appellate court will look into the writ and all the other proceedings. Hatcher *v.* Lewis, 4 Rand. 152; Laidley *v.* Bright, 17 W. Va. 779, 790. See post, "Application of Statute of Jeofails," II, E, 8, c.

"Cases have been reversed for defects in the writ far less serious than the omission of the clerk to sign the writ at all, a defect so serious, that some courts, as we have seen, have held it to render the writ absolutely void. While such is not, we hold, the effect of such an omission, it is nevertheless a serious defect, much greater than defects, which have been held sufficient to reverse judgments by default. Thus an omission in the writ to claim the charges of protest was held in Hatcher *v.* Lewis [4 Rand. 152] sufficient to reverse a judgment by default." Laidley *v.* Bright, 17 W. Va. 779, 791.

On the trial of a motion to reverse a judgment by default under § 5, ch. 134, W. Va. Code, the court ought not to permit the clerk to correct the summons itself, though he has made a mistake by inadvertence in issuing it. Laidley *v.* Bright, 17 W. Va. 779, citing Ambler *v.* Leach, 15 W. Va. 677.

In such a case, if the judgment by default was a joint judgment against several deefndants, and it appears, that the writ, a copy of which was served on some of the defendants, was not signed by the clerk, such judgment should be reversed. Laidley *v.* Bright, 17 W. Va. 779, citing Ambler *v.* Leach, 15 W. Va. 677.

Absolute Want of Service.—When a defendant has not been served with process in the action, and has not appeared to the action, and the clerk has entered an office judgment against him for failing to appear and plead and awarded a writ of inquiry of damages; and under those circumstances the court has the damages assessed by the jury, enters judgment against the defendant for the damages found by the jury; such defendant has the right under the statute to move the court, after proper notice, to reverse the judgment and correct the proceedings, and upon the court's refusal to do so, then to bring the matter before the appellate court by writ of error. Capehart v. Cunningham, 12 W. Va. 750; Houston v. McCluney, 8 W. Va. 135. See ante, "Reasonable Notice," II, E, 8, b, (3), (b), bb.

Where judgment is given against persons, upon whom process has not been served, and who have not appeared to the action, the proper way to correct the error is upon motion before the court that rendered the judgment. Carlon v. Ruffner, 12 W. Va. 297, 299; Gunn v. Turner, 21 Gratt. 382.

Entry of Common Order Instead of Issuing New Summons.—Where the clerk enters the "common order," when he should have issued a new summons, this is a clerical misprision by the clerk, and the office judgment may be amended under Va. Code, 1873, ch. 177, §§ 5, 6, p. 1135. Goolsby v. St. John, 25 Gratt. 146, 157.

Codefendants Want of or Irregular Service of a Portion.—A joint judgment by default against several defendants, a portion of whom are not served with process, or if served, the service is irregular, is erroneous, and may be reversed on motion under W. Va. Code, ch. 134, § 5, though it has been satisfied by another defendant. Ferguson v. Millender, 32 W. Va. 30, 9 S. E. 38; Laidley v. Bright, 17 W. Va. 779; Carlon v. Ruffner, 12 W. Va. 297, 299; Vandiver v. Roberts, 4 W. Va. 493; Midkiff v. Lusher, 27 W. Va. 439.

A decree by default is entered against a guardian and his sureties although process had not been served upon one of the sureties. Upon a bill by the guardian and the other sureties to open the decree, no objection can be raised by them to the decree on this ground. Hill v. Bowyer, 18 Gratt. 364. See also, Ramsburg v. Kline, 96 Va. 465, 31 S. E. 608.

Return Fatally Defective.—On the other hand, where a return of a sheriff on process is fatally defective, and there has been on such return a judgment entered by default, the defendant, under W. Va. Code, § 5, ch. 134, may on motion have such judgment set aside for such error, and if the motion is overruled, the judgment will be reversed on writ of error. Midkiff v. Lusher, 27 W. Va. 439.

Return Showing Void Service on Corporation.—A judgment by default against a corporation, rendered on return of a summons which shows that the requirements of the statute have not been complied with, is a void judgment, and may be assailed collaterally by third parties. "It neither binds nor bars anyone. All acts performed under it, and all claims flowing out of it, are void." Staunton Perpetual Bldg., etc., Co. v. Haden, 92 Va. 201, 23 S. E. 285; Va. Code, 1887, §§ 3225, 3226.

Amendment of Return on Summons.—On a motion to reverse a judgment by default under § 5, ch. 134, W. Va. Code, for a defective return on the summon in the suit, the court ought to permit the sheriff to amend his return according to the facts, and if the amended return be good, the court may overrule the motion to reverse. Anderson v. Doolittle, 38 W. Va. 633, 18 S. E. 726; Laidley v. Bright, 17 W. Va. 779, citing Ambler v. Leach, 15 W. Va. 677.

Where under Va. Code, 1873, ch. 172, § 5, defendant moves the judge in vacation to reverse a judgment by default upon a defective return of substituted service of the summons, and to remand the case for trial; held, the court may then allow the sheriff to amend his return so as to show a proper service, and dismiss the defendant's motion. Stotz *v.* Collins, 83 Va. 423, 2 S. E. 737.

Waiver of Defective Service. — Where, upon a motion to reverse a judgment by default for defective service of process on a sheriff by his deputy, the defendant, who was sheriff, says he wishes to take no advantage of such return, if defective, this is a waiver or retraxit of the motion, and a release of error as to him, though he is a plaintiff in the motion to reverse; and, as he alone is prejudiced by the alleged defect, it is no ground for reversal as to any of the defendants. Anderson *v.* Doolittle, 38 W. Va. 628, 633, 18 S. E. 724.

Error in Calculation of Interest. — In the case of Bank *v.* Shirley, 26 W. Va. 563, it is held, that "An error in the calculation of interest can be corrected by motion on notice under § 5, ch. 134, of the Code. Gallatin Land, etc., Co. *v.* Davis, 44 W. Va. 109, 28 S. E. 747.

Where a judgment is rendered by default in the general court, upon motion, on a bond due the commonwealth; but the clerk, in entering the judgment, only allows interest from a date posterior to that, from which by the terms of the bond, interest was to run; this error may be amended, upon motion to the general court, at a succeeding term. 1 Rev. Va. Code 512, § 108; Com. *v.* Winstons, 5 Rand. 546.

Where the clerk erroneously enters judgment upon nil dicit in the county court, or an office judgment in the county or circuit courts, for interest from the date of the bond with a penalty, when it should have been with interest from the day of payment, as provided for in the bond, such error is a clerical mistake, amendable by the court, at a subsequent term. Eubank *v.* Ralls, 4 Leigh 308.

Motion Not Properly Docketed— Order Nunc Pro Tunc. — When, on an application to a trial court to correct a judgment by default, under the provision of § 3451 of the Virginia Code, it appears that no order was entered by the court on the day to which a notice of a motion for a judgment was returnable, but that judgment by default was entered at a subsequent term, it is within the power and discretion of the court to enter an order nunc pro tunc docketing the motion and continuing it to the next term, and validating the judgment, as between the original parties, and annexing a condition thereto that such judgment shall not affect the rights of innocent third persons whose rights have accrued since the original judgment, and before the nunc pro tunc order. Such order, when made, is an entirety, and is not valid as to the judgment and void as to the condition. The two provisions are dependent on each other. Powers *v.* Carter Coal, etc., Co., 100 Va. 450, 41 S. E. 867, citing Parker *v.* Pitts, 1 Hen. & M. 4; Amis *v.* Koger, 7 Leigh 221, 223.

Failure to Award Writ of Inquiry. — In debt on a decree for money, a conditional judgment is entered in the office, without awarding a writ of inquiry of damages, and the judgment not being set aside becomes final at the next term, and execution is sued out on the judgment; but at the ensuing term, the court set aside the judgment as irregularly entered, and gave defendants leave to plead to the action. Held, it was error to enter judgment in the office without awarding an inquiry or damages; and this was a clerical error, which the court properly corrected at a subsequent term. Shelton *v.* Welsh, 7 Leigh 175. The court in this case distinguished and explained Halley *v.* Baird, 1 Hen. & M. 25; Freeland *v.* Fields, 6 Call 12; Digges *v.* Dunn, 1 Munf. 56; Eubank *v.* Ralls, 4 Leigh 308. In the first case, i. e., Halley *v.* Baird, 1 Hen. & M. 25, the court decided, in conformity with the common law, and Freeland *v.* Fields, 6 Call 12, that a judgment entered in the order book and signed by the judge, in open court, could not be amended at a subsequent term; these facts were emphatically stated, and seemed to have been considered as vitally important. See the title INQUESTS AND INQUIRIES, vol. 7, p. 664.

Entry of Judgment as at Rules Only. —In Digges *v.* Dunn, 1 Munf. 56, it is held, that if judgment at rules in the clerk's office of a county court be entered as at the rules only, instead as of the last day of the succeeding quarterly term, it is merely a clerical misprision, and therefore amendable.

Erroneous Recital in Record of Judgment.—Where the defendant has not appeared and made defense to a motion, upon a notice, against him and his sureties, and judgment is rendered against him by the court at the instance of the plaintiff; and the record of the judgment erroneously states: "This day came the parties by their attorneys and neither party requiring a jury, all matters of law and fact are submitted to the court," it is not error for the court, upon the motion of the defendant at the same term, to set aside the judgment. And the court may do so ex mero motu. Smith *v.* Knight, 14 W. Va. 749.

Errors in Form of Judgment or Decree.—See ante, "Form of Entry before Execution Issues," II, E, 6, b.

Judgment—Failure of Clerk to Notice Memorandum.—Where the clerk enters up a judgment by nil dicit, in debt on bond for the payment of tobacco, without noticing a memorandum indorsed on the bond, such mistake is merely clerical and amendable upon motion, at a subsequent term. Gordon *v.* Frazier, 2 Wash. 130.

Executor—Judgment De Bonis Propriis.—Where a judgment by default de bonis propriis is erroneously entered against an executor, it is a clerical error to be amended upon motion

to the lower court, and is not a ground of appeal to the higher court. Snead *v.* Coleman, 7 Gratt. 300, 56 Am. Dec. 112.

Reformation of Judgment as to Admitted Credits.—Where certain plaintiffs give notice, that they will move the court to reform an office judgment, by allowing certain credits, and one of the credits claimed is endorsed on the bond, and the plaintiff endorses the other at the time of the motion, the court will refuse to reform the judgment. Gunn *v.* Turner, 21 Gratt. 382.

Premature Entry of Judgment.—A judgment and award of execution upon a forfeited forthcoming bond, having been entered by default, upon a day prior to that to which notice was given, the court in which the judgment and award of execution was rendered has jurisdiction on the motion of the plaintiff to set aside the judgment and quash the execution, upon reasonable notice to the defendants. Va. Code, ch. 181, § 5; ch. 187, § 23. Ballard *v.* Whitlock, 18 Gratt. 235.

Entry of final judgment by default against the defendant was made within one month after he had been served with process contrary to the provisions of the Va. Code, 1873, ch. 166, § 3. Under such judgment a fi. fa. was issued, and there was a proceeding by suggestion against persons indebted to the defendant. It was held, that such defendant may, upon proper notice, appear in such proceeding and have the judgment vacated, and all proceedings thereunder quashed. Dillard *v.* Thornton, 29 Gratt. 392. See ante, "In Virginia," II, E, 4, a; "Reasonable Notice," II, E, 8, b, (3), (b), bb.

"It is assigned as error that the judgment complained of was rendered in a collateral proceeding between the creditor and the garnishees. There is nothing in this objection. The judgment debtor had a direct interest in that proceeding, and had the right to appear and defend it, and if the judgment on which the proceeding was based was invalid, he had the further right, on his own motion, to have it vacated, and the summons of garnishment quashed." Dillard *v.* Thornton, 29 Gratt. 392, 398.

A judgment and award of execution upon a forfeited forthcoming bond was entered by default, upon a day prior to that to which notice was given. The plaintiff gave a second notice to the obligors in the forthcoming bond, for a judgment and award of execution thereon, who appeared and objected to the rendering of the judgment and award of execution asked. It was held, that the court may at the same time quash the first judgment and execution, and render another judgment and award of execution on the bond. Ballard *v.* Whitlock, 18 Gratt. 235.

dd. Imposing Conditions.

See ante, "Grounds for Relief," II, E, 8, b, (3), (c), cc.

(d) Procedure.

aa. Parties.

It is not necessary to make those defendants, upon whom process has been duly served, and against whom judgment has been rendered, parties to a motion made to correct a judgment by defendants, who have not been served with process, and who have not appeared to the action, but against whom the judgment had also been rendered. Carlon *v.* Ruffner, 12 W. Va. 297.

bb. Limitations.

The motion to reverse or correct errors in a judgment or decree by default, given by § 5, ch. 134, W. Va. Code, 1899, is barred after the lapse of five years from the date of the judgment or decree. Ferrell *v.* Camden, 49 W. Va. 225, 230, 38 S. E. 581; Dunfee *v.* Childs, 45 W. Va. 155, 30 S. E. 102; Dick *v.* Robinson, 19 W. Va. 159.

Section 3451, Va. Code, 1904, provides that such motions shall be barred after three years. Smith *v.* Powell, 98 Va. 431, 36 S. E. 522; Groseclose *v.* Harman, 1 Va. Dec. 564; Kendrick *v.* Whitney, 28 Gratt. 646; Goolsby *v.* Strother, 21 Gratt. 107. See also, Wrenn *v.* Thompson, 4 Munf. 377.

When the time allowed by § 3451, Va. Code, 1904, has expired, the decree becomes final and irreversible. Smith *v.* Powell, 98 Va. 431, 36 S. E. 522.

If, after lapse of the time allowed by § 3451, Va. Code, 1904, the case is reinstated by another party for other purposes, it is not competent for defendant to complain of such errors. Groseclose *v.* Harman, 1 Va. Dec. 564.

Two suits were instituted on the same day, in behalf of the same plaintiff. The writ in each case was against A. B. and C. D.; but endorsed to be served on A. B. only. In one case, bail was required; in the other not. The declarations included both A. B. and C. D. as defendants. The appearance bail, in the case in which bail was required, entered into a recognizance as special bail for them both; and (according to the transcript of the record) they appeared by their attorney, and pleaded payment. In the other case, no plea was filed, or appearance entered; except that A. B. on wnom the writ was served, came, in proper person, and acknowledged the plaintiff's action in both suits; whereupon, judgments were entered against him, and C. D. also. It was held, that C. D. was sufficiently a defendant to both suits; and that if there was error in the judgments, it could not be corrected, on motion, after five years had elapsed from the date of the judgments. Wrenn *v.* Thompson, 4 Munf. 377.

cc. Evidence.

On a trial in the circuit court to reverse a judgment for want of due notice of the original action, by order of publication, it is not error to receive proof of the posting of the order of publication at the front door of the courthouse. Higginbotham v. Haselden, 3 W. Va. 266. See ante, "Grounds," II, E, 8, b, (1), (b).

dd. Effect of Overruling Motion.

If the defendant makes a motion under § 5, ch. 134, W. Va. Code, and it is overruled, the decision of the circuit court overruling such motion, makes such judgment valid and binding, though before void, unless such decision be reversed; and he is entitled to reverse it though the judgment has been satisfied by another of the judgment debtors. Ferguson v. Millender, 32 W. Va. 30, 9 S. E. 38.

ee. Effect of Reversal.
(aa) As to Joint Judgments by Default.

Where a joint judgment is rendered against two or more defendants by default, it is error to reverse it on motion, under § 5, ch. 134, W. Va. Code, as to one defendant only, and not as to all. "In Jones v. Raine, 4 Rand. 386, syl., pt. 2, 'A joint judgment can not be reversed as to one defendant and affirmed as to the other.' Arrington v. Cheatham, 2 Rob. 492; Lenows v. Lenow, 8 Gratt. 349; Purcell v. Mc-Cleary, 10 Gratt. 246; Vandiver v. Roberts, 4 W. Va. 493; Lyman v. Thompson, 11 W. Va. 427; Carlon v. Ruffner, 12 W. Va. 297. And in Midkiff v. Lusher, 27 W. Va. 439, syl., pt. 3, 'When a joint judgment is rendered against two by default and for a defective return as to one, if it is reversed, it must be reversed as to both defendants.' Hoffman v. Bircher, 22 W. Va. 537." National Exchange Bank v. McElfish, etc., Mfg. Co., 48 W. Va. 406, 37 S. E. 541.

Where a joint judgment is rendered against two or more defendants by default, it is error to reverse it on mo-tion, under § 5, ch. 134, of the West Virginia Code, as to one defendant only, and not as to all. National Exchange Bank v. McElfish, etc., Mfg. Co., 48 W. Va. 406, 37 S. E. 541.

(bb) Motion by Joint Defendant Not Served.

In debt, on a note signed with a partnership name, the declaration charged, that the defendants being partners made the notes, and subscribed their partnership name thereto. Some of the defendants, upon whom process had been served, appeared and pleaded nil debet; and some filed with their plea affidavits denying such partnership. One of the defendants, upon whom process had been served, never appeared to plead to the action; and the office judgment was not set aside as to him. On two of defendants process was never served. After the filing of the said pleas and affidavits, the plaintiff, on his own motion, discontinued his action as to several of the defendants; and other defendants, who had pleaded, withdrew their pleas. The case was then submitted to the court, and proof heard; and the court rendered judgment against all the defendants, who had withdrawn their pleas, except three, and except also the defendant, against whom the office judgment had been found and not set aside, but included in said judgment the two, whom process had not been served on. Five of the defendants appealed from the said judgment; but the two, upon whom the process had not been served, moved the court which rendered the judgment, during the pendency of said appeal, to reverse and correct the judgment. Upon that motion, said court corrected the judgment and remanded it to rules as to them, and also remanded it to rules as to the defendant, as to whom the office judgment had not been set aside. At the hearing of said motion, certain others, against whom the judgment had been rendered, appeared and asked leave to file certain pleas, and also affidavits denying the partnership; but the court refused to permit the same to be filed. Held, upon the hearing of such a motion made by defendants, against whom the court had rendered judgment before process had been served on them, and who had not appeared, it is error for the said court to remand the cause to rules as to another defendant, upon whom process had been duly served, and office judgment was confirmed, but who had not appeared to the action, and against whom the court had failed to enter judgment. Carlon v. Ruffner, 12 W. Va. 297. See post, "Remand to Rules and Reinstating Cause," II, E, 8, b, (3), (d), ff.

(cc) Estoppel to Question Validity of Summons or Service.

Where a judgment by default is set aside to allow the defendant to appear and plead, the latter can not claim that he was not regularly brought into court. Morotock Ins. Co. v. Pankey, 91 Va. 259, 21 S. E. 487; Harvey v. Skipwith, 16 Gratt. 410, 414; Va. Code, § 3260.

ff. Remand to Rules and Reinstating Cause.

Remand to Rules.—Where a joint judgment by default is rendered against several defendants, and it is reversed on motion because the writ, a copy of which was served on some of the defendants, was not signed by the clerk, or where the notice is otherwise improperly executed as against one party, the cause should be remanded to rules to be properly proceeded with. Laidley v. Bright, 17 W. Va. 779. See also, Ambler v. Leach, 15 W. Va. 677; Vandiver v. Roberts, 4 W. Va. 493. See ante, "Declaration," II, E, 2, f, (1).

But upon the hearing of a motion made by defendants, against whom the court has rendered judgment before process has been served on them, and who had not appeared, it is error for the court to remand the cause to rules as to another defendant, upon whom process had been duly served, and office judgment was confirmed, but who had not appeared to the action, and against whom the court had failed to enter judgment. Carlon v. Ruffner, 12 W. Va. 297.

Reinstating Cause.—A final judgment by default having been set aside in the court below on the motion of the defendant, the court should have reinstated the cause upon the docket, with liberty to the defendant to plead, and to set aside the office judgment upon the usual terms, the said judgment to become final in case of his failure to set it aside. Dillard v. Thornton, 29 Gratt. 392; Green v. Skipwith, 1 Rand. 460.

gg. Correction of Order Vacating Judgment.

The court below having vacated the judgment of October 31, 1867, upon a motion of the defendant, where all parties appeared by their counsel, it had no jurisdiction to correct its action in that regard under § 5, ch. 177, Va. Code, 1873; but the proper remedy was by appeal. Dillard v. Thornton, 29 Gratt. 392. See post, "Appeal, Error and Supersedeas," II, E, 10.

(e) Release of Excess of Recovery.

The Virginia and West Virginia statutes, now § 3451, Va. Code, 1904, and ch. 134, § 5, W. Va. Code, 1899; § 4036, West's Code, contain a provision for the release by the plaintiff of any excess in the amount of the recovery beyond what it ought to be. Goolsby v. St. John. 25 Gratt. 146.

c. Application of Statute of Jeofails.

In cases of judgment by default for want of appearance, the statute of jeofails does not apply to cure errors and defects in the proceedings. Wainwright v. Harper, 3 Leigh 270; Hatcher v. Lewis, 4 Rand. 152; Payne v. Britton, 6 Rand. 101, 104; Bargamin *v.* Poitiaux, 4 Leigh 412; Laidley *v.* Bright, 17 W. Va. 779, 791.

But if the party has once appeared, though he makes default, afterwards, and then there is judgment against him by such default, the statute of jeofails is applicable. Bargamin *v.* Poitiaux, 4 Leigh 412.

Variance between Declaration and Writ.—In such cases, the writ is part of the record; and the writ in this case being in assumpsit and declaration in covenant, the variance is fatal. Wainwright *v.* Harper, 3 Leigh 270. See ante, "Declaration," II, E, 2, f, (1). See the title VARIANCE.

Where the judgment is by default, the error of claiming in the declaration costs of protest, when those costs are not demanded in the writ, may be taken advantage of. Hatcher *v.* Lewis, 4 Rand. 152. See also, Wainwright *v.* Harper, 3 Leigh 270.

Want of Issue.—Where in action of assumpsit, no plea has been filed, the only question is the quantum of damages, and that only after an order of inquiry of damages, it is error to allow defendant to cross-examine the witnesses and demur to the evidence, and such error is not cured by the statute of jeofails which does not cure a total want of issue. Petty *v.* Frick Co., 84 Va. 501, 10 S. E. 886.

9. Prevention of Enforcement.

a. By Prohibition.

Prohibition lies to prevent the enforcement of a judgment by default when the persons against whom the same was rendered had no notice of the time and place and were not present at the trial. Simmons *v.* Thomasson, 50 W. Va. 656, 41 S. E. 335.

b. In Equity.

(1) Effect of Adequate Remedy at Law.

See post, "Grounds of Relief," II, E, 9, b, (2).

A court of equity will not grant relief from the enforcement of a judgment by default or a decree on a bill taken for confessed, to a party who has a plain remedy at law. Brown *v.* Chapman, 90 Va. 174, 17 S. E. 855, in which it is said: In Goolsby *v.* St. John, 25 Gratt. 146, the court quoted with approval the remark in Hudson *v.* Kline, 9 Gratt. 379, that "it has been a favorite policy in this state, especially of late, not to afford relief in a court of equity to a party who has a plain remedy at law, except in cases of concurrent jurisdiction," and that "in all other cases he must avail himself of his legal remedy." See the title ADEQUATE REMEDY AT LAW, vol. 1, p. 161.

(2) Grounds of Relief.

In General.—A party can not get relief in equity, against a judgment by default, upon grounds which might have been successfully taken in a law court, unless some reason founded in fraud, accident, surprise, or some adventitious circumstances beyond the control of the party be shown, why the defense was not made in that court. Alford *v.* Moore, 15 W. Va. 597; Knapp *v.* Snyder, 15 W. Va. 434; Braden *v.* Reitzenberger, 18 W. Va. 286. See ante, "Effect of Adequate Remedy at Law," II, E, 9, b, (1).

Negligence of Defendant or Counsel.—"High on Injunctions at §§ 165, 166, says: 'In the absence of fraud or deception an injunction will only be allowed against a judgment which complainant has suffered to go against him by default. And where one has negligently permitted judgment to go against him by default, such negligence is sufficient to prevent him from obtaining the aid of an injunction against the judgment. Indeed in a case of default, a court of equity will refuse to consider the merits of the case any further than the question of complainant's negligence in asserting his rights at law, and no sufficient excuse appearing for his having neglected to defend at law, the injunction will be refused. Nor will the proceedings be enjoined merely because plaintiff obtained more relief than he was entitled to by his action, there being no misrepresentation or deception by which defendants were in any way misled.'" Harner v. Price, 17 W. Va. 523, 549.

W. is sued by R. in debt on the note of B. & Co. He employs counsel to defend the suit, and states to him that he never was a partner of B. & Co., or in any way liable for the debt. He lives in the county, but pays no further attention to the case. At the next term of the court the counsel examines the docket, and though he sees a case of R. against B. & Co., he does not suspect that that is the case against W., and therefore does not examine the papers; and no plea being entered, the office judgment is confirmed. Equity will not relieve W. Wallace v. Richmond, 26 Gratt. 67.

Irregularity in Summons.—An injunction will not be awarded to a judgment by default upon summons directed to sheriff of another county than the one where the action is brought, although the summons was issued contrary to law, as the judgment, though erroneous, is not void, and the defendant has a complete remedy at law by motion under Code, § 3451. Brown v. Chapman, 90 Va. 174, 17 S. E. 855.

Defective Return on Summons.—In 1866, S. sues G. & R., partners, in debt. The sheriff returns on the process, executed on G. by leaving copy at his house with sister, and on R. by leaving copy at his house with wife. On this return there is an office judgment confirmed. The stay law prevents an execution on this judgment, but there is a judgment upon notice for a year's interest upon this judgment in 1867, and also in 1868. In 1870, execution is issued on the judgment when G. & R.

enjoin it on the ground that a credit of $100 endorsed on the note should have been $600, and that the process was not properly served, and they had no notice of the suit. S. demurs to the bill for want of equity. Held, G. & R. having had notice of the judgment within the time limited for a motion to quash it, they had a remedy at law by motion to quash the sheriff's return, and therefore they are not entitled to relief in equity. Goolsby v. St. John, 25 Gratt. 146.

"Clearly they had a plain, cheap, summary, and complete remedy at law, which would formerly have been by a writ of error coram vobis (or coram nobis, for the writ has each of these names in the books) in the same court in which the error was committed, but is now by a mere motion to the court. 1 Rob. Prac., old edit., p. 644; Gordon v. Frazier, 2 Wash. 130. See also, 2 Saun. R., pp. 101 and 101a; Eubank v. Ralls, 4 Leigh 308; Shelton v. Welsh, 7 Leigh 175." Goolsby v. St. John, 25 Gratt. 146. See Va. Code, 1873, ch. 177, §§ 5, 6, p. 1135. See ante, "Grounds," II, E, 8, b, (1), (b).

Whether the error if any in this case was a mere clerical misprision, or an error in the judgment, or whether, being a mere clerical misprision, it comes within the meaning of §§ 5, 6, ch. 177, Va. Code, 1873, or not, there was a plain remedy at law for its correction by a mere motion to the court in which it was committed. Goolsby v. St. John, 25 Gratt. 146. See ante, "Motion in Lower Court to Reverse or Amend," II, E, 8, b, (3).

False Return of Service of Process. —A court of equity can not grant relief against a decree by default rendered against a defendant on the ground that no process was served on him, where the return of the officer and the recitals of the decree show that process was served on the defendant, unless the false return of service was procured or induced by the plaintiff, or he can in some way be connected with the deception. Preston v. Kindrick, 94 Va. 760, 27 S. E. 588; Ramsburg v. Kline, 96 Va. 465, 31 S. E. 608.

Although no process was served on a defendant he is not entitled to relief from a decree against him in the absence of proof that he did not have notice of the proceedings before the decree was rendered, and that he had a meritorious defense. Preston v. Kindrick, 94 Va. 760, 27 S. E. 588.

"Such a judgment is sustained, not because a judgment rendered without notice is good, but because the law will not permit any proof to weigh against that which the policy of the law treats as absolute verity, and remits the party injured to his remedy at law against the person by whom the record was falsified." Preston v. Kindrick, 94 Va. 760, 27 S. E. 588.

"In Goolsby v. St. John, 25 Gratt. 146, 156, where it did not appear affirmatively from the return that summons had been served in the manner prescribed by law, Judge Moncure said, in discussing that question, that 'if the summons had been executed in the manner prescribed by law, and that fact had appeared by the return made thereon by the sheriff, then the judgment would have been conclusive, even though the defendants may not have had actual knowledge of the existence of the action before the judgment was rendered.'" Preston v. Kindrick, 94 Va. 760, 27 S. E. 588.

Judgment Void for Want of Service. —Where for want of service of process judgment by default is void, collection of execution should be enjoined, the judgment vacated, and the cause remanded to be proceeded in at law by an alias summons properly served. Finney v. Clark, 86 Va. 354, 10 S. E. 569.

"Legal service" of summons against defendant was accepted by his son without his knowledge or authority;

and a judgment by defendant entered. Defendant applied to chancery court to enjoin the collection of said judgment, but raised no issue as to the merits. Plaintiff in his answer raised such issue. The court of its own motion, in vacation, made an order that a commissioner take an account of any set-offs of defendant against plaintiff in the action at law. Commissioner reported the judgment valid, and a decree was entered against defendant; held, the only question before the chancery court was the validity of the judgment, and it had no right to take jurisdiction of the merits of plaintiff's claim. Finney v. Clark, 86 Va. 354, 10 S. E. 569.

Failure to Take Advantage of Set-Off. —Where a party has been summoned to answer an action at law for the recovery of money, and allows judgment by default to go against him, although at the time of such recovery he had judgments against the plaintiff which he might have pleaded as a set-off, he can not, on the ground that he mistook the time at which the case was to be tried, combined with the fact of the insolvency of the plaintiff, come into equity to obtain the benefit of such set-off. Zinn v. Dawson, 47 W. Va. 45, 34 S. E. 784. See the title SET-OFF, RECOUPMENT AND COUNTERCLAIM.

On a Usurious Contract. —Notwithstanding the change in the statute declaring that usurious contracts shall be deemed to be for an illegal consideration, instead of void as formerly, a court of equity will relieve against a judgment by default on a usurious contract, and the measure of relief is that the lender can only recover the principal sum loaned or forborne, subject to the rule laid down in Munford v. McVeigh, 92 Va. 446, 23 S. E. 857, touching the application of payments. The measure of relief is the same in all cases involving the charge of usury, whether at law or in equity, no matter in what way the question is presented, if the usury be established. Greer *v.* Hale, 95 Va. 533, 28 S. E. 873. See the title USURY.

Failure to Plead Non Est Factum. —A party who might have pleaded non est factum in an action at law, and who merely wrote to counsel to defend him, is guilty of such neglect as will preclude him from relief in equity. Stanard *v.* Rogers, 4 Hen. & M. 438.

Mistake of Character of Suit.—In Mosby *v.* Haskins, 4 Hen. & M. 427, a judgment by default was opened where the party had made the mistake of supposing that the summons served upon him was process in a pending chancery suit instead of primal process in an action at law, the court further said: "Could there have been a more complete surprise, than in the first instance to have met with an execution instead of a capias. There certainly could not to my mind; and hence a good ground for relief in equity."

Relief of Bail.—Bail can not be relieved in equity against a judgment at law by default, without assigning some good cause why he did not defend himself at law. Brown *v.* Toell, 5 Rand. 543.

Scire Facias against Bail.—Upon a scire facias against special bail, he obtained a bail piece, arrested his principal, surrendered him to the jailer and took the jailer's receipt for his body, and gave notice thereof to the attorney of the plaintiffs, they not residing in the county. Notwithstanding all this, there was an office judgment upon scire facias against the bail, and he not appearing to defend the case at the next term, the office judgment was confirmed. It was held that equity will not relieve the bail. Allen *v.* Hamilton, 9 Gratt. 255.

(3) In Suit in Equity to Enforce Judgment.

In a suit in equity brought for the purpose of enforcing a judgment lien, which judgment was obtained against the defendant by default, the defendant will not be allowed in said chancery suit to make any defense against the judgment which might have been successfully made in a court of law, unless he shows some reason founded on fraud, accident, surprise, or some adventitious circumstance beyond his control, why the defense at law was not made. McNeel *v.* Auldridge, 34 W. Va. 748, 12 S. E. 851.

10. Appeal, Error and Supersedeas.

a. Limitation on Right of Appellate Review.

(1) Statutory Provisions Stated and Construed Generally.

Our statute provides, that "the court, in which there is a judgment by default, or a decree on a bill taken for confessed," may "on motion, reverse such judgment or decree, for any error for which an appellate court might reverse it, if the following section was not enacted, and give such judgment or decree as ought to be given." W. Va. Code, ch. 134, § 5. And the following section therein referred to—§ 6—declares that, "no appeal, writ of error, or supersedeas, shall be allowed or entertained by an appellate court or judge for any matter for which a judgment or decree is liable to be reversed or amended, on motion as aforesaid by the court which rendered it, * * * until such motion is made and overruled in whole or in part." Steenrod *v* Wheeling, etc., R. Co., 25 W. Va. 133, 136; Ferrell *v.* Camden, 49 W. Va. 225, 230, 38 S. E. 581; McGraw *v.* Roller, 53 W. Va. 75, 76, 44 S. E. 248; Watson *v.* Wigginton, 28 W. Va. 533, 543. The Virginia provision is similar and found in §§ 3451, 3452, Va. Code, 1904. Brown *v.* Chapman, 90 Va. 174, 17 S. E. 855; Goolsby *v.* St. John, 25 Gratt. 146; Hill *v.* Bowyer, 18 Gratt. 364; Davis *v.* Com., 16 Gratt. 134.

This statutory law is taken from

the Code of Virginia, ch. 181, §§ 5, 6; and they embrace the provisions contained in the Revised Code of 1819, §§ 108, 109, 110, p. 512, and also the provisions containd in the Virginia act of March 12, 1838 (sess. act, p. 74). Watson v. Wigginton, 28 W. Va. 533, 543. This statute is mandatory in its terms; and not only so, but it is remedial in its object and purpose. It was obviously intended to remedy the evil in the former practice of the courts which compelled parties prejudiced by errors in judgments or decrees of inferior courts, rendered in their absence and without contest or resistence— often mere inadvertencies—to incur the expense and delay of an appeal or writ of error to an appellate court for the correction of such errors. The statute must, therefore, under the well-settled rule, be construed liberally in order to advance the remedy intended to be given by it and to suppress the evil intended to be avoided by it. Steenrod v. Wheeling, etc., R. Co., 25 W. Va. 133, 136.

The language of the statute is too direct and positive to admit of construction. The plain import and object of its terms are to require all applications for the correction of errors in decrees rendered "on bills taken for confessed" to be made to the courts which rendered such decrees, and to prohibit the appellate court from allowing, or entertaining any appeal from such decrees until such application has been first made and overruled by such court. This statute has been often considered by the appellate courts in Virginia and of this state, but nearly all the cases relate to that part of it which refers to judgments by default. Steenrod v. Wheeling, etc., R. Co., 25 W. Va. 133, 137.

This statute was made for the protection of appellate courts by compelling litigants to first present their matters for adjudication to the lower courts without flooding the higher courts with unlitigated questions of fact and law. It applies strictly to judgments by default, and to all such questions and clerical errors as have not been matters of litigation and adjudication before the lower court. To any material question arising during the progress of litigation and adjudicated by the court, the statute does not apply, although a writ of error does not lie until after final judgment, but as to such adjudication does lie, although such final judgment is entered up by default. As when a final judgment is entered up by default after demurrer to a declaration or bill has been overruled. Watson v. Wigginton, 28 W. Va. 533, 549; McGraw v. Roller, 53 W. Va. 75, 44 S. E. 248.

"An inspection of the judgment, however, shows that it was not wholly by default, as the defendant appeared specially, and presented his motion to quash and plea in abatement, and obtained from the court an adjudication thereon, which was reviewed by this court whenever a final judgment was entered. As to this adjudication, the final judgment could never be treated as one by default, but must be regarded as one finally adjudicating the questions presented by the defendant by his special appearance. Such adjudication was inspected by this court at the instance of the defendant, nor was it necessary to make any further motion with regard thereto before obtaining his writ of error to this court. Hence, the writ of error was proper as to such adjudication." McGraw v. Roller, 53 W. Va. 75, 76, 44 S. E. 248.

Where the defendant does not appear in the inferior court, and a judgment is therefore rendered there against him, the law presumes that the court will correct its own errors so soon as they are brought to its notice by a party having a right to complain of them, and it therefore requires him to apply, in the first place, to that court or the judge thereof for relief, as being the cheapest and best remedy he could have. Whether the judgment be strictly or technically by default, or merely quasi by default, the effect and the reason of the law, are precisely the same. If authority be necessary to sustain this proposition, it is fully sustained by the case of Davis v. Com., 16 Gratt. 134; Goolsby v. St. John, 25 Gratt. 146, 156; Staunton Perpetual Bldg., etc., Co. v. Haden, 92 Va. 201, 23 S. E. 285.

(2) Prohibition of Appeal from Decree on Bill Taken for Confessed.

(a) In General.

There can be no appeal from a decree against a party on a bill taken for confessed as to him, until a motion to reverse shall first be made in the court that rendered the decree. Morrison v. Leach, 55 W. Va. 126, 47 S. E. 237; Ferrell v. Camden, 49 W. Va. 225, 230, 38 S. E. 581; Watson v. Wigginton, 28 W. Va. 533; McKinney v. Hammett, 26 W. Va. 628; Midkiff v. Lusher, 27 W. Va. 439; Steenrod v. Wheeling, etc., R. Co., 25 W. Va. 133, 137; Bock v. Bock, 24 W. Va. 586; Forest v. Stephens, 21 W. Va. 316; Adamson v. Peerce, 20 W. Va. 59; Hunter v. Kennedy, 20 W. Va. 343; Smith v. Knight, 14 W. Va. 749; Hartley v. Roffe, 12 W. Va. 401, 420; Dickinson v. Lewis, 7 W. Va. 673; Baker v. Western Mining, etc., Co., 6 W. Va. 196; Meadows v. Justice, 6 W. Va. 198; Gunn v. Turner, 21 Gratt. 382.

In Rowland v. Rowland, 11 W. Va. 262, 268, it is said: "The remedy of a party, against whom decrees had been rendered by default, is not by appeal, but by motion to the court that rendered the decree, to annul and set it aside." Citing Goolsby v. St. John, 25 Gratt. 146; Goolsby v. Strother, 21 Gratt. 107; Baker v. Western Mining, etc., Co., 6 W. Va. 196; Davis v. Com., 16 Gratt. 134; Hill v. Bowyer, 18 Gratt. 364. See also, Watson v. Wigginton, 28 W. Va. 533, 545.

This court has no jurisdiction of an appeal from a decree by default until relief has been sought under § 3451 of the Virginia Code, by motion to the court in which the decree was rendered. Smith v. Powell, 98 Va. 431, 36 S. E. 522. Gunn v. Turner, 21 Gratt. 382.

Any one has a right to appeal from an erroneous decree, as a general principle, whether on a bill taken for confessed or on appearance; but W. Va. Code, ch. 134, curtails this right of appeal in case of a decree on a bill taken for confessed to the extent that it requires first an unsuccessful motion in the circuit court; but this applies only to cases upon a bill taken for confessed; it is so limited; it does not apply to an erroneous decree upon a motion to reverse under ch. 134. From such decree appeal at once lies. That chapter gives it, as well as ch. 135. Midkiff v. Lusher, 27 W. Va. 439; Morrison v. Leach, 55 W. Va. 126, 129, 47 S. E. 237.

Appeal Dismissed as Improvidently Granted.—If an appeal from a decree against a party on a bill taken for confessed as to him, is taken without a motion to reverse having first been made in the court that rendered it, it will be dismissed as improvidently granted without considering the merits of such appeal. Morrison v. Leach, 55 W. Va. 126, 47 S. E. 237; Ferrell v. Camden, 49 W. Va. 225, 230, 38 S. E. 581, where it said: "In Dickinson v. Lewis, 7 W. Va. 673, it is held: 'When a party obtains an appeal and supersedeas to decrees of a circuit court, rendered upon bill taken for confessed as to him, before applying to the court in which the decree was rendered. or the judge thereof in vacation, to reverse or amend the errors of which he complains, his appeal and supersedeas will be dismissed as improvidently allowed.'" Ferrell v. Camden, 49 W. Va. 225, 230, 38 S. E. 581. See, to the same effect, Watson v. Wiggington, 28

W. Va. 533, 546; Midkiff *v.* Lusher, 27
W. Va. 439; Steenrod *v.* Wheeling,
etc., R. Co., 25 W. Va. 133; Bock *v.*
Bock, 24 W. Va. 586; Forest *v.*
Stephens, 21 W. Va. 316; Adamson
v. Peerce, 20 W. Va. 59, 61; Smith *v.*
Knight, 14 W. Va. 749; Hartley *v.*
Roffe, 12 W. Va. 401, 420; Dickinson
v. Lewis, 7 W. Va. 673; Baker *v.* Western Mining, etc., Co., 6 W. Va. 196;
Meadows *v.* Justice, 6 W. Va. 198;
Brown *v.* Chapman, 90 Va. 174, 17 S.
E. 855; Hill *v.* Bowyer, 18 Gratt. 364;
Davis *v.* Com., 16 Gratt. 134.

A null decree by default may be
annulled by appeal. Morrison *v.*
Leach, 55 W. Va. 126, 129, 47 S. E.
237; McCoy *v.* Allen, 16 W. Va. 724.

Appeal Taken as from Original Decree.—The provision of the Virginia
Code, ch. 181, § 5, now § 3451, Va.
Code, 1904, contemplates that if the
motion is overruled, wholly or in part,
the appeal shall afterwards be taken
from the original decree, as it stood
originally, if the motion is wholly
overruled, or as amended and corrected, if the motion is sustained in
part. Hill *v.* Bowyer, 18 Gratt. 364.

**(b) What Constitutes "A Decree on a
Bill Taken for Confessed."**

aa. In General.

There is no conflict in the Virginia
or West Virginia decisions as to what
is a judgment by default within the
meaning of the statute, which we are
construing; but our decisions have not
been harmonious as to what is "a decree on a bill taken for confessed"
within the meaning of the statute.
Watson *v.* Wigginton, 28 W. Va. 533,
546.

Where Defendant Fails to Appear.
—If in a chancery cause none of the
defendants have ever appeared in the
cause, demurred to the bill, filed answers or appeared before the commissioner, when the court had referred the
cause to a commissioner, or filed exceptions to his report or in any other

manner appeared in the cause, all the
decrees in such a cause would be on a
bill taken for confessed, within the
meaning of the statute. Where the defendant in a chancery suit has wholly
failed to appear, all our authorities
agree a decree though rendered on
proof is on a bill taken for confessed
within the meaning of this statute.
(Baker *v.* Western Mining, etc., Co.,
6 W. Va. 196; Dickinson *v.* Lewis, 7
W. Va. 673; Forest *v.* Stephens, 21 W.
Va. 316; McKinney *v.* Hammet, 26 W.
Va. 628.) Watson *v.* Wigginton, 28
W. Va. 533, 546. See post, "Upon
Failure of Defendant to Appear," II,
E, 10, a, (2), (c), aa.

Possibly there may be one exception to a proposition, which seems in
chancery causes generally to have
been universally adhered to, and that
is a chancery suit brought for a divorce, as in such a cause by statute,
the bill can not be taken for confessed. (Ch. 63, § 8, W. Va. Code, p.
441). Watson *v.* Wigginton, 28 W.
Va. 533, 547. See also, the title DIVORCE, vol. 4, p. 734.

In McKinney *v.* Hammett, 26 W. Va.
628, which was a suit against the heirs
of a deceased person to subject his
real estate to the payment of his debts,
none of the defendants answered or
appeared in any manner in the court
below. The cause was referred to a
commissioner. A report of the debts
and assets of the estate was made and
confirmed without objection or exception, and the real estate was ordered
to be sold, and then the sale was made
and confirmed without exception. It
was held, that, as all these decrees
were to be considered as entered upon
the bill taken for confessed, they could
not be reviewed by this court, till a
motion had been made in the court
below to have them reversed or corrected in the manner prescribed by §
5, ch. 134, W. Va. Code. This is all
that was decided in this case. Watson *v.* Wigginton, 28 W. Va. 533, 555.

bb. Effect of Appearance.

In General.—The language of the statute in regard to equity cases is essentially different from that in reference to actions at law. Any appearance by the defendant in the latter case prevents the judgment from being by default. The very word "default" means nonappearance—Bouv. Law Dict., "Default." But a bill may be taken for confessed after appearance. The mere appearance of the defendant, certainly does not prevent the bill from being taken for confessed. Technically a bill heard without plea or answer is a hearing on bill taken for confessed and a decree rendered in such case is "a decree on bill taken for confessed." Steenrod v. Wheeling, etc., R. Co., 25 W. Va. 133, 137. Watson v. Wigginton, 28 W. Va. 533, 549. See ante, "In General," II, E, 1, a, (2), (a).

In many cases the decree will be regarded as one on bill taken for confessed, though the defendant may have appeared in a variety of modes otherwise than by answer, on which the cause was heard, as, for instance, when he filed an answer but withdrew it, before the case was submitted to the court below on the hearing, or when he appeared simply to consent to a continuance or to a reference of the cause to a commissioner, and in a variety of other cases which might be suggested. But on the other hand cases may arise in which the defendant, the appellant, has filed no answer, and yet his appearance in other modes and certain actions taken by him in the court below may prevent decrees rendered against him being regarded as within the meaning of this statute decrees on bills taken for confessed. Watson v. Wigginton, 28 W. Va. 533, 562. See post, "Appeal Substantially from Decree Overruling Demurrer," II, E, 10, a, (2), (c), bb; "Decree Based on Facts Introduced after Filing Bill," II, E, 10, a, (2), (c), cc.

In Bock v. Bock, 24 W. Va. 586, and Hunter v. Kennedy, 20 W. Va. 343, "it is held, that in a chancery cause the simple fact, that a defendant has appeared in a cause, does not necessarily prevent a decree as to him being regarded as a decree on a bill taken for confessed as to him and therefore incapable of being reviewed at his instance by an appellate court, until he has moved the court below to correct the error." Watson v. Wigginton, 28 W. Va. 533, 555.

It, however, rarely happens that the claims set up by the plaintiff's bill are thus entirely ignored by all of the defendants, no one controverting them in any manner. They may controvert them in a variety of ways other than by filing their answers, which would of course take the case out of the operation of the statute, as of course, if all the defendants filed answers, there could not be rendered any "decree on the bill taken for confessed." The defendants might for instance file a demurrer to the bill, the demurrer might be overruled, and the defendants might thereafter fail to answer the bill or to further dispute in any manner the plaintiff's claim in his bill; would the decrees rendered in such a cause be regarded as "decrees on a bill taken for confessed?" Our decisions on this question have been conflicting. Watson v. Wigginton, 28 W. Va. 533, 547. See post, "Appeal Substantially from Decree Overruling Demurrer," II, E, 10, a, (2), (c). bb.

Instances.—In Bock v. Bock, 24 W. Va. 586, the defendants appeared and answered the bill, but subsequently and before hearing some of them withdrew their answers and brought the case before the supreme court. It was held, that the decree as to the defendants who had withdrawn their answers, was a decree on bill taken for confessed, and they were not in a position to appeal till the court below had been moved to correct the errors, of which they complained in such decree, though an appellant, who had answered and had an interest with them, might appeal. Watson *v.* Wigginton, 28 W. Va. 533, 555. See also, Hunter *v.* Kennedy, 20 W. Va. 343; Steenrod *v.* Wheeling, etc., R. Co., 25 W. Va. 133, 137.

In Hunter *v.* Kennedy, 20 W. Va. 343, "it was held, that when there was no appearance by the defendant in a cause except to make a qualified consent to a decree therein, and such a decree is entered on bill taken for confessed, and an appeal is taken from the decree, the appeal must be dismissed as improvidently awarded; for no appeal could be taken from the part consented to because of such consent, and no appeal would lie from the residue, because it was entered as a bill taken for confessed, no motion to correct having been made and overruled in the court below." Watson *v.* Wigginton, 28 W. Va. 533, 555.

(c) Rules for Construing Prohibition.
aa. Upon Failure of Defendant to Appear.

If a party defendant to a bill has failed to appear in the court below in any manner by filing plea, answer or demurrer or by filing exceptions to a report of a commissioner in chancery or commissioner of sale, which reports are the basis of the decree complained of, or if he has failed to appear in any other manner, such a defendant can not have his appeal entertained in this court, till he has made such a motion in the court below or to a judge in vacation, and it has been overruled in whole or in part. Watson *v.* Wigginton, 28 W. Va. 533.

Codefendant Who Answered Bill Uniting in Appeal.—But in such case, if any of the defendants having a joint interest with him in the matter complained of unite with him in the appeal and have answered the bill, this court will entertain jurisdiction of the appeal, and reverse or correct, if erroneous such decree, though no such motion had been made or overruled in whole or in part before the awarding of the appeal. Watson *v.* Wigginton, 28 W. Va. 533, 560.

F. brought his suit in equity for specific performance of the following contract: "Received of F. four thousand dollars, and he is to have all the lands owned by me in Webster County, West Virginia, and unsold at this date. As soon as I am well enough to do so, will make deeds, or have it done, and send to you. (Signed) G. D. C., per Mrs. C.,"—against the administrator with will annexed of G. D. C., Mrs. C. the widow and the heirs at law G. D. C., deceased, naming them, and D. and C., trustees, to whom the said widow and heirs at law had conveyed the legal title to all the real estate of which the said G. D. C. died seized; the prayer of the bill being that the said trustees and heirs at law be required to convey to plaintiff the said lands which were fully described in the bill, and, if the contract could not be specifically enforced, that plaintiff have a decree against the estate for the four thousand dollars and interest. The widow filed her answer and disclaimer, the administrator answered the bill, and the bill was taken for confessed as to said trustees and heirs at law. Upon the bill taken for confessed, a decree was entered requiring said trustees and heirs at law to convey to plaintiff the lands described in the bill. The administrator and heirs at law appealed from said decree. Held, that the rights of the administrator, as personal representative, were not affected by said decree; that the same having been rendered upon bill taken for confessed against all the parties whose interests were affected by said decree, and they having failed to move to have the same reversed or corrected in the court rendering the decree, as provided in § 5, ch. 134, W. Va. Code, said appeal can not be entertained in the appellate court (See § 6, ch. 134, W. Va. Code), and must be dismissed. Ferrell v. Camden, 49 W. Va. 225, 226, 38 S. E. 581; Baker v. Western Mining, etc., Co., 6 W. Va. 196; Davis v. Com., 16 Gratt. 134.

bb. Appeal Substantially from Decree Overruling Demurrer.

See ante, "Effect of Appearance," II, E, 10, a, (2), (b), bb.

If a defendant in a bill files no plea or answer but files a demurrer, simply on the ground that the plaintiff on the facts stated in the bill is entitled to no relief against him, and the court below overrules such demurrer and awards a rule against him, to answer the bill at a specified time, and he fails to do so, and a decree is rendered against him, and he makes no such motion to have it reversed or corrected in the court below, and he appeals from such decree, solely on the ground that the court rendered any sort of a decree against him, this court will, though he did not make such motion, entertain his appeal, because such appeal though in form an appeal from the last decree is in substance and in reality an appeal from the decree overruling his demurrer and deciding that the plaintiff was entitled to relief on the statements in the bill against him, and is therefore not to be regarded as a decree on a bill taken for confessed. But if the appellant in such case does not confine his appeal to the error committed by the court in overruling his demurrer simply carried out in the last decree but insists, that there are in addition thereto other and independent errors in the last decree against him, which should be reversed, even though the appellate court held, that the demurrer was properly overruled, this court will not entertain such appeal, because so far as these additional and independent errors are concerned, this last decree is to be regarded as a decree on a bill taken for confessed and can not be reversed by this court, till a motion to correct it has been made in the court below. The court said that the West Virginia decisions on the question have been conflicting and reviews them. Watson v. Wigginton, 28 W. Va. 533, 561.

In chancery cases the rule is that after the overruling of a demurrer and expiration of a rule to answer, a decree entered is appealable only as to matters settled by the demurrer, and is by confession as to errors committed in respect to matters subsequent to the demurrer. Watson v. Wigginton, 28 W. Va. 533. This rule does not apply to actions at law. The language of the statute in regard to equity cases is essentially different from that in reference to actions at law. Any appearance of the defendant in the latter case prevents the judgment from being by default. Steenrod v. Wheeling, etc., R. Co., 25 W. Va. 133, 137; McGraw v. Roller, 53 W. Va. 75, 44 S. E. 248; Bank v. Ralphsnyder, 54 W. Va. 231, 234, 46 S. E. 206. See ante, "In General," II, E, 1, a, (2), (a).

The words of our statute (W. Va. Code, ch. 125, § 30, p. 603) are: "If a demurrer be overruled there shall be a rule upon the defendant to answer the bill; and if he shall fail to appear and answer the bill on the day specified in the order, the plaintiff shall be entitled to a decree against him for the relief prayed for therein." This was not regarded by the court in Gates v. Cragg, 11 W. Va. 300, as the equivalent of a decree on a bill taken for confessed, when no appearance by demurrer, answer or otherwise had been made by the defendant. And it would seem that it ought not to be so regarded in all cases, but on the contrary it should not be held, that no such decree can in any case be regarded as a decree on a bill taken for confessed where the defendant has demurred, and the demurrer has been overruled, as was held in this case of Gates v. Cragg, 11 W. Va. 300; and this decision in going to this extent has been since overruled by this court in the case of Steenrod v. Wheeling, etc., R. Co., 25 W. Va. 133. Watson v. Wigginton, 28 W. Va. 533, 548. The general principles announced in Steenrod v. Railroad Co., are correct but to avoid mistakes they should be to some extent modified. In Gates v. Cragg, 11 W. Va. 300, 306, it was said: "If, however, the defendants have appeared and made defense, whether by demurrer, plea or answer, the final decree of the court can only be corrected, if erroneous, by the appellate court, for in such case the reason for allowing the correction of errors by motion in the court below does not exist. See Dickinson v. Lewis, 7 W. Va. 675; Davis v. Com., 16 Gratt. 134; Goolsby v. Strother, 21 Gratt. 107."

"The truth is, this court in Gates v. Cragg (11 W. Va. 300), failed to note the distinction, which is well pointed out by this court in the case of Steenrod v. Wheeling, etc., R. Co. (25 W. Va. 133), between the cases, where the errors complained of by the defendant in his appeal are errors necessarily resulting from the decree erroneously overruling the defendant's demurrer, and the cases, where the errors complained of by the appellant, the defendant, include also other errors independent of those resulting from such order overruling the defendant's demurrer. There is to my mind after duly considering the subject a clear distinction between the two cases. In the one the only error complained of in the final decree is an error necessarily resulting from the courts correctly carrying into effect a previous interlocutory order settling the principles of a cause and erroneously overruling the defendant's demurrer to the bill; such final decree, though no answer had been filed, not being a decree on a bill taken for confessed, but really simply a decree on the previous interlocutory order. From such a final decree an appeal lies, though no previous motion has been made in the court below to correct the errors in it. In the other case the appellant complains not only of the error committed in such interlocutory order but also of errors in the subsequent final decree, which errors are independent of those resulting merely from giving effect to an erroneous order overruling a demurrer to a bill. Such a final decree as this is, where no answer has been filed, a decree on a bill taken for confessed, and therefore a decree, which can not be appealed from, till after a motion has been made in the court below to correct such errors. These principles and these distinctions have been several times recognized by this court as proper. (Bock v. Bock, 24 W. Va. 586; Hunter v. Kennedy, 20 W. Va. 343.)" Watson v. Wigginton, 28 W. Va. 533, 554.

Failure to Answer after Rule Given. —Where a defendant in a chancery suit appears and demurs to the bill and his demurrer is overruled and a rule is given him to answer which he fails to do, and thereafter a decree is entered in the cause granting the relief prayed for in the bill, and such defendant obtains an appeal to this court from said decree without having moved in the court, which rendered it, to have the errors complained of corrected and assigns and complains of errors in said decree other than those resulting from the overruling of his demurrer; held, this is a decree on a bill taken for confessed and this court will not entertain the appeal but will dismiss the same as having been improvidently awarded. Steenrod v. Wheeling, etc., R. Co., 25 W. Va. 133.

Interlocutory Order Overruling Demurrer.—It will from these principles result, that an appeal may be taken from an interlocutory order overruling a demurrer, by which the principles of a cause are adjudicated, but not until after a decree has been entered carrying these principles into effect; but when this is done, if there be nothing done by the court below, which can be regarded as erroneous, except what merely results from giving effect to the erroneous order overruling the demurrer, an appeal will lie without first making a motion in the court below to correct such error, which arose merely from the order overruling the demurrer improperly; for these ought not to be regarded as errors in a decree on a bill taken for confessed; they are in point of fact errors substantially in the decree overruling the demurrer, which decree was of course not a decree on a bill taken for confessed. These principles are laid down by this court in Steenrod *v.* Wheeling, etc., R. Co., 25 W. Va. 133, and they accord with the principles laid down in Gates *v.* Cragg, 11 W. Va. 300. But while those cases accord in these respects, they differ in another point; the decree or decrees entered, after the time has expired given by the rule for the defendant to answer on the overruling of his demurrer to the bill, may contain not only errors arising necessarily from the error committed in the decree overruling the defendant's demurrer, but also errors in the subsequent decrees independent of those resulting merely from the erroneous decree overruling the defendant's demurrer and those resulting merely from giving effect to such erroneous decrees. If it does so, then the defendant can not without first moving to correct such error in the court below, appeal from such subsequent decree or decrees, if he has filed no answer; for so far as the independent and additional errors are concerned, these decrees are regarded as decrees on bill taken for confessed, as they were not committed when the demurrer was over-

ruled. Watson *v.* Wigginton, 28 W. Va. 533, 553.

(cc) Decree Based on Facts Introduced after Filing Bill.

See ante, "Effect of Appearance," II, E, 10, a, (2), (b), bb.

When the defendant, the appellant, has appeared in the court below otherwise than by filing a plea, answer or demurrer, and the decree, from which he appeals, was not based on any allegations of fact in the bill, which were treated by the court below as confessed or admitted, but was based on facts introduced into the case after the filing of the bill by the report of a commissioner or in some other manner, and in addition thereto the record shows, that these facts so introduced into the cause, on which the decree appealed from was based, were not treated by the court as facts taken for confessed and admitted, and also that the defendant appeared in the court below and controverted these facts and opposed the entry of the decree complained of based on these facts, such a decree will not be regarded as a decree on a bill taken for confessed, though the defendant has not pleaded or answered; and this court will entertain an appeal from it, though no such motion has been made in the court below to reverse or correct it. Watson *v.* Wigginton, 28 W. Va. 533.

The defendant has in fact done really the same thing in effect as making such motion, when he objected to the entering of such decree on such alleged facts. Watson *v.* Wigginton, 28 W. Va. 533, 563.

Upon Overruling Exceptions to Commissioner's Report.—Thus if the suit was to subject the real estate of a decedent to the payment of his debts, and the heirs filed no answer to the bill, but, after the case had been referred to a commissioner to ascertain the debts and assets of the estate, the heirs of the decedent were to appear and controvert certain debts sought to be proven before the commissioner not specified in the bill, but such debts were on the evidence allowed by the commissioner, and his action in the premises was excepted to by the heirs of the decedent, and their exceptions were overruled, and the commissioner's report confirmed, and a sale of the decedent's real estate ordered to be made to pay his debts as ascertained by such report, the heirs of the decedent could appeal from such decree, though they had made no motion in the court below to reverse or correct it, as such a decree ought not to be·regarded as a decree on a bill taken for confessed, though it would have been so regarded, had no exceptions been taken to the commissioner's report. And not only is such a decree not regarded as based on the facts stated in the bill taken as confessed, but the exceptions filed by the heirs to the commissioner's report overruled by the court answer precisely the same purpose, as a motion to correct the decree, because it allowed such debts against the estate; and it would be idle to require such motion for such purpose to be made, after the court had overruled such exceptions. Watson *v.* Wigginton, 28 W. Va. 533, 562.

So if in any chancery cause brought to have the defendant's land sold for any cause he filed no answer, and on the bill taken for confessed his land was decreed to be sold, and when it had been sold, the defendant appeared and by exception to the report of sale resisted the confirmation of the sale, because the land had not been properly advertised or for any other reason, and the defendant's exceptions were all overruled, and the sale confirmed by a decree of the court, such decree the defendant might appeal from because of errors in confirming such sale, though he made no motion

in the court, after such decree was entered, to reverse it for these errors. For though, if he had made no exceptions or appearance, such a decree might have been regarded as a decree on a bill taken for confessed, yet, if he filed such exceptions, and they were overruled, it ought not to be regarded as a decree on a bill taken for confessed, because it was not based on any facts stated in the bill treated as confessed or admitted to be true by the defendant but on facts occurring after the filing of the bill set out in the commissioner's report, which facts were not treated by the court as confessed or admitted by the defendant but as controverted by him by his formal exceptions to such report, which exceptions after consideration were overruled by the court. In such case it would be idle to require the defendant after the decree confirming the sale had been entered, to move the court to reverse such decree for the reasons, which he had already in writing urged as reasons, why such sale and report should not be confirmed. Watson *v.* Wigginton, 28 W. Va. 533, 562.

It may be fairly inferred from the opinion of the court pronounced by Judge Snyder in McKinney *v.* Hammett, 26 W. Va. 628, which was a suit against the heirs of a deceased person to subject his real estate to the payment of his debts, that, if the appellant, though he filed no answer, had, when the cause was referred to the commissioner, appeared before the commissioner and contested any debt whether claimed as a lien or not on the defendant's real estate in his lifetime and had excepted to the commissioner's report, because any particular debt had been audited against his estate in favor of the plaintiff or any one else, and the court had overruled his exception and confirmed the commissioner's report and ordered a sale of the defendant's real estate, and this sale had been made and reported to the court, and the defendant had excepted to this report of sale, but the court had overruled his exception and confirmed the report, and this defendant had appealed because only of the errors committed by the court below in overruling the appellant's exception to the commissioner's report and to the report of sale and for rendering decrees in accordance with said reports this court would have entertained the appeal, though the defendant had neither filed an answer nor made a motion to correct these errors in the court below. Watson v. Wigginton, 28 W. Va. 533, 555.

In Hartley v. Roffe, 12 W. Va. 401, it is held, that "when a creditor's bill is brought to sell lands of the debtor and defendant fails to answer or plead and decrees in the cause are made and entered on bill taken for confessed, but the defendant appears and files exceptions to the report of sales by the commissioner of the court, and the court overrules the exceptions to such report of sales, the appellate court will consider and determine the appeal and supersedeas of the debtor as to so much of the action of the court, as relates to said exceptions and the overruling thereof, but will generally dismiss the appeal and supersedeas as improperly allowed as to other decrees in the cause and parts thereof, which were made, and rendered on bill taken for confessed, the appellant not having applied to the circuit court, or the judge thereof in vacation, to reverse or correct the same according to the provisions of the fifth section of ch. 134 of the Code, before applying for and obtaining the appeal and supersedeas as to such decrees and parts thereof, as were made on bill taken for confessed." Beaty v. Veon, 18 W. Va. 291; Smith v. Knight, 14 W. Va. 749; Adamson v. Peerce, 20 W. Va. 59; Ferrell v. Camden, 49 W. Va. 225, 230, 38 S. E. 581.

Upon Overruling Motion for a New Trial.—In Watson v. Wigginton, 28 W. Va. 533, 534, an appeal was entered by the supreme court, where the defendant, the appellant, had filed no plea or answer and made no motion in the court below to correct or reverse the decree appealed from, but where the record showed, that an issue was tried by the order of the court, in which he was the interested party on one side, and the jury found a verdict against him, and he asked the court for a new trial, which the court overruled and against his objections entered up the decree appealed from, which was based solely on this verdict.

(3) Prohibition as to Entertaining Writ of Error or Supersedeas to Judgment by Default.

No writ of error can be entertained by an appellate court to any judgment by default, unless a motion has been made by the defendant and decided in the court below to correct the error complained of in such judgment. Watson v. Wigginton, 28 W. Va. 533; Adamson v. Peerce, 20 W. Va. 59; Smith v. Knight, 14 W. Va. 749; Holliday v. Myers, 11 W. Va. 276, 297; Brown v. Chapman, 90 Va. 174, 175, 17 S. E. 855; Goolsby v. St. John, 25 Gratt. 146; Goolsby v. Strother, 21 Gratt. 107; Cunningham v. Mitchell, 4 Rand. 189.

Supersedeas Dismissed as Improvidently Awarded.—If a party obtains a supersedeas to a judgment by default, before applying to the court in which the judgment was rendered, or the judge thereof, to correct the errors of which he complains, his supersedeas will be dismissed as improvidently awarded. Watson v. Wigginton, 28 W. Va. 533, 543; Adamson v. Peerce, 20 W. Va. 59, 61; Smith v. Knight, 14 W. Va. 749, 758; Higginbotham v. Haselden, 3 W. Va. 266, 269; Goolsby v. Strother, 21 Gratt. 107; Davis v. Com., 16 Gratt. 134; Cunningham v. Mitchell,

4 Rand. 189. See also, Saunders *v.* Grigg, 81 Va. 506, 511.

Appeal Dismissed as Improvidently Awarded.—If a party take an appeal from a judgment by default before applying to the court, which rendered it, or the judge thereof to correct the errors, of which he complains, his appeal will be dismissed as being improvidently taken. Davis *v.* Com., 16 Gratt. 134; Baker *v.* Western Mining, etc., Co., 6 W. Va. 196; Meadows *v.* Justice, 6 W. Va. 198; Smith *v.* Knight, 14 W. Va. 749; Adamson *v.* Peerce, 20 W. Va. 59, 61. See also, Brown *v.* Chapman, 90 Va. 174, 17 S. E. 855.

Error in Passing upon Pleadings and Matters Distinct from Trial.—The rule seems to be that if error be committed in passing upon the pleadings and other matters substantially distinct from the trial itself, a writ of error may be maintained notwithstanding no motion has been made in the trial court to set aside the judgment. Bank *v.* Ralphsnyder, 54 W. Va. 231, 236, 46 S. E. 206.

After Demurrer Overruled.—Ordinarily, where there is a judgment by default or after trial by jury, proceedings for error will not be entertained by this court until after a motion has been made in the court below to set the judgment aside, and there can be no good reason why the same rule should not apply in the case of a judgment rendered after a demurrer has been filed by the defendant and overruled. Bank *v.* Ralphsnyder, 54 W. Va. 231, 236, 46 S. E. 206.

b. Exceptions.

The evidence is not made a part of the record in case of a judgment by default, nor in any case, unless the party asks it. Anderson *v.* Doolittle, 38 W. Va. 629, 18 S. E. 724. Judgment is presumed to be right until the record discloses error. Ramsburg *v.* Erb, 16 W. Va. 777, 787; Harris *v.* Lewis, 5 W. Va. 575; Griffith *v.* Cor-

rothers, 42 W. Va. 59, 24 S. E. 569; Reed *v.* Nixon, 36 W. Va. 681, 15 S. E. 416. McClure-Mabie, etc., Co. *v.* Brooks, 46 W. Va. 732, 34 S. E. 921, 922. See post, "Burden of Proof and Presumption," II, E, 10, c. See the titles APPEAL AND ERROR, vol. 1, p. 418; EXCEPTIONS, BILL OF, vol. 5, p. 357.

c. Burden of Proof and Presumption.

In Reinhard *v.* Baker, 13 W. Va. 805, 811, it is said: "The appellant must show affirmatively, that there was error in the judgment of the court. They can not do so in the absence of all the evidence on which the court below acted. It must be presumed that the plaintiffs below proved the facts stated in their notice; and therefore that its judgment is right." See also, Gunn *v.* Turner, 21 Gratt. 382. See ante, "Exceptions," II, E, 10, b.

d. Scope of Review—Examination of Record.

In reviewing a judgment by default on a forthcoming bond, the appellate court will compare it with the execution on which it was taken. Glascock *v.* Dawson, 1 Munf. 605.

11. Collateral Attack.

A judgment by default or a decree pro confesso in order to be open to collateral attack must be void and not merely erroneous. See post, "Collateral Attack on Judgments and Decrees," IX. See also, ante, "Jurisdiction," II, E, 2, a; "Sufficient Process Duly Served," II, E, 2, b; "Parties," II, E, 2, c.

A judgment by default is conclusive in a collateral proceeding of all that is alleged in the complaint and nothing more. St. Lawrence Co. *v.* Holt, 51 W. Va. 370, 374, 41 S. E. 351.

A decree pro confesso is conclusive in a collateral proceeding of all that is alleged in the complaint and nothing more. St. Lawrence Co. *v.* Holt, 51 W. Va. 370, 374, 41 S. E. 351.

A null decree may be assailed collaterally. McCoy *v.* Allen, 16 W. Va. 724; Morrison *v.* Leach, 55 W. Va. 126, 129, 47 S. E. 237.

F. JUDGMENTS BY NIL DICIT.

A judgment of nil dicit is defined to be one rendered against a defendant who fails to put in a plea or answer to plaintiff's declaration by the day assigned, and closely resembles a judgment by default. Bank *v.* Ralphsnyder, 54 W. Va. 231, 234, 46 S. E. 206, citing Bouv. Law Dict.; Black on Judgm., § 79; 21 Am. & Eng. Ency. (2d Ed.) 541. See ante, "Judgments by Default and Decrees Pro Confesso," II, E.

G. JUDGMENTS ON AWARDS.

See generally, the title ARBITRATION AND AWARD, vol. 1, p. 687.

An award returned to court must be entered up as the judgment of the court, after rule or notice to the parties to show cause why it should not be entered as the judgment of the court, in order to constitute a lien, or have writ of execution. Turner *v.* Stewart, 51 W. Va. 493, 494, 41 S. E. 924.

Chapter 108 of the West Virginia Code allowing an award to be entered as the judgment of a court is only a cumulative remedy, and does not take from it its common-law force, though not entered as such judgment. Turner *v.* Stewart, 51 W. Va. 493, 495, 41 S. E. 924.

The circuit court has no power over an award made in pursuance of a submission under ch. 108, of the West Virginia Code, 1868, except to enter it as the judgment or decree of the court, or to reject or to refuse to so enter it, or perhaps to recommit it. Stevenson *v.* Walker, 5 W. Va. 427.

Enforcement.—Judgment or decree in an award, entered up as the judgment or decree of the court, may be enforced by an action at law or by a bill in equity; or if the award be for the payment of money an execution might issue for the same. Stevenson *v.* Walker, 5 W. Va. 427.

It was error for the court below to order the sale of real estate in a decree entering up an award as the decree of the court, when the same was not provided for or directed by the award. Stevenson *v.* Walker, 5 W. Va. 427.

H. CONDITIONAL JUDGMENTS.

As to conditional confessions of judgment, see the title CONFESSION OF JUDGMENTS, vol. 3, p. 79.

As to alternative judgments in detinue that the plaintiff recover the property sued for, or its value, see the title DETINUE AND REPLEVIN, vol. 4, p. 646.

I. JUDGMENTS NON OBSTANTE VEREDICTO.

See post, "Judgment Non Obstante Veredicto," III, F, 2.

J. DORMANT JUDGMENTS.

A dormant judgment is "one which has not been satisfied, nor extinguished by lapse of time, but which has remained so long unexecuted that execution can not now be issued upon it without first reviving the judgment." Black's Law Dict., tit., Dormant Judgment.

As to revival of dormant judgments, see post, "Revival of Judgments," XIV.

As to actions on dormant judgments, see post, "Actions of Judgments," XV.

K. JUDGMENTS ON APPEAL OR ERROR.

See the titles APPEAL AND ERROR, vol. 1, p. 418; CERTIORARI, vol. 2, p. 762.

L. JUDGMENTS IN CRIMINAL CASES.

See the title SENTENCE AND PUNISHMENT.

III. Requisites of Valid Judgments or Decrees.

A. BY WHAT LAWS GOVERNED.

Should Conform to Law of State Where Liability Is Fixed.—The decrees of courts of chancery in a state should conform to the law of the state where the liability of the parties is determined. De Ende v. Wilkinson, 2 Pat. & H. 663.

It is error for a court of chancery in Virginia to render a joint decree against heirs or legatees, whose liabilities are to be determined by the law of Louisiana, and are by that law several. De Ende v. Wilkinson, 2 Pat. & H. 663.

Validity Determined by Law in Force When Rendered.—The validity of a judgment is to be determined by the laws in force when it is rendered, and is not affected by subsequent changes therein. Anderson v. Hygeia Hotel Co., 92 Va. 687, 24 S. E. 269; Kennaird v. Jones, 9 Gratt. 183, 190.

For example, the legislature has no power to set aside a judgment, or to empower a court to set aside a judgment, rendered before the passage of the act, no matter how erroneous the judgment may be. Arnold v. Kelley, 5 W. Va. 446, citing Griffin v. Cunningham, 20 Gratt. 31.

The state of Virginia upon notices and motions by the name of "The Commonwealth" instituted and prosecuted by the auditor of public accounts on the 6th day of March, 1860, recovered two several judgments against Edmund S. Calwell "in the circuit court of Richmond" as one of the securities of John E. Lewis, late sheriff of Greenbrier county, the one being for $4,893.92, the balance of the land property, and capitation and September license taxes of 1854 due from said John E. Lewis, late sheriff of Greenbrier county, with interest thereon to be computed at the rate of six per centum per annum from the 17th day of January, 1855, until paid, and the costs of the motion, $13.44, and the other being for $1,073.86, the balance of June, 1855, license taxes, due from said John E. Lewis, late sheriff of Greenbrier county, with interest thereon to be computed at the rate of six per centum per annum from the 20th day of June, 1855, until paid, and $161.07 for damages thereon according to law, also the cost of the motion, $11.94. The law in force at the time said notices were given and motions made and judgments were rendered provided, that "the auditor of public accounts shall institute and prosecute all proceedings proper to enforce payment of money to the commonwealth —that the proceeding may be in the circuit court of the city of Richmond —that when it is at law, it may be by action or motion—that "every judgment on any such motion shall be in the name of the commonwealth." And the city of Richmond being the capital of the state of Virginia, as judicially known to the court, held, that each of said judgments is a valid judgment of the state of Virginia against said Edmund S. Calwell rendered in and by the circuit court of the city of Richmond, Virginia, though in the name of the commonwealth, "Commonwealth" under and by virtue of the law standing for and representing the state of Virginia for all purposes, of which all persons were bound to take notice. And the "circuit court of the city of Richmond" standing for and meaning the circuit court of the city of Richmond under and by virtue of the law, of which all persons were also bound to take notice. Chapter 42, Code of Virginia, 1860, §§ 1, 2, 4. Calwell v. Prindle, 19 W. Va. 604.

B. RENDITION BY LEGALLY CONSTITUTED COURTS PROCEEDING ACCORDING TO LAW.

1. Validity as Dependent on Character of Tribunal.

a. In General.

"The validity of a judgment as a bar depends primarily upon the organization and character of the tribunal from which it professes to emanate. And it is, first of all, requisite that the judgment should have been rendered by a legally constituted court—one known to and recognized by law." State v. Cross, 44 W. Va. 315, 29 S. E. 527, 529, quoting Black on Judgments, § 516. See the title FORMER ADJUDICATION OR RES AD-JUDICATA, vol. 6, p. 261.

"Judgment, if not by the proper judge, is of no effect." State v. Cross, 44 W. Va. 315, 29 S. E. 527, 529.

A decree rendered in November, 1861, by the pretended court of appeals of Virginia, at Richmond, acting under the authority of the citizens of Virginia in insurrection and open war with the United States and the restored government of Virginia, is not obligatory upon parties to a cause pending in said court on the 17th of April, 1861. Snider v. Snider, 3 W. Va. 200.

Judgment by Judge of Another County without Proper Entry on Record as to Reason for Presiding.— County judge of one county presided at trial of a cause in another county without entering upon record that the regular judge (personally present) was, in his opinion, so situated as to make it improper for him to preside. Held, the judgment is void, and its enforcement should be restrained by a writ of prohibition. Gresham v. Ewell, 85 Va. 1, 6 S. E. 700, Lewis, P., dissenting. See the title JUDGES, ante, p. 150.

As to the necessity for holding courts at time and place fixed by law, see generally, the titles COURTS, vol. 3, p. 701; JURISDICTION.

As to adjournment of terms of court, the validity of proceedings at adjourned terms, etc., see the title AD-JOURNMENT, vol. 1, p. 179.

b. Effect of Disqualification of Judge by Interest.

It is a fundamental rule in the administration of justice that a person can not be a judge in a cause wherein he is interested, whether he be a party to the suit or not. In West Virginia there is no statute bearing directly on the point, and a decree pronounced by a person thus interested in the cause is not void, but only voidable, as being a decree not according to law, and to be set aside only when brought under review, and upon objection taken. Findley v. Smith, 42 W. Va. 299, 26 S. E. 370.

Mere formal orders, such as are necessary to bring the cause before the proper tribunal, and where nothing is decided—mere orders entered to advance the cause towards a final hearing—may be entered by an interested judge, but that is the extent of his power. Findley v. Smith, 42 W. Va. 299, 26 S. E. 370.

For a full treatment of what constitutes disqualification of a judge, effect thereof, proper procedure in case of disqualification, etc., see the title JUDGES, ante, p. 150.

c. Proceedings by De Facto Judge.

A judgment given or an act done by any person by authority or color of any office is valid and binding, though it may afterwards be decided or adjudged that he was not lawfully elected or appointed or was disqualified to hold the office, or that the same had been forfeited or vacated. State v. Carter, 49 W. Va. 709, 39 S. E. 611. See generally, the titles DE FACTO OFFICERS, vol. 4, p. 449; JUDGES, ante, p. 150.

Judges by Military Appointment Holding Over.—The judgments and decrees of the judges of the court of appeals, who were in office under military appointment when the state was restored to the Union, holding over and continuing to exercise their office, are valid and binding. Griffin v. Cunningham, 20 Gratt. 31, and note.

Thus, where a judge by military appointment in Virginia, held a court and tried a criminal after the admission of the state to the union, his act was held to be valid. Quinn v. Com., 20 Gratt. 138, and note.

Rendition before Commencement of Judge's Term.—Where a judge was properly elected, and, believing that his term commenced immediately, proceeded to hold court, it was held that although the term of his predecessor had not then expired, he was a judge de facto, and his judgments were as valid and binding as if he had been a judge de jure. McGraw v. Williams, 33 Gratt. 510.

Effect of Failure of Special Judge to Take Prescribed Oath.—A judgment rendered by a special judge elected as provided by law, is neither void nor reversible merely because he did not take the oath in article 4, § 5, of the constitution. He is, at least, a judge de facto. Tower v. Whip, 53 W. Va. 158, 44 S. E. 179.

2. Power Must Be Exercised in Mode Established by Law.

In General.—Though the court may possess jurisdiction of a cause, of the subject matter and of the parties it is still limited in its modes of procedure and in the extent and character of its judgments. A departure from established modes of procedure will often render the judgment void. Anthony v. Kasey, 83 Va. 338, 341, 5 S. E. 176; Thurman v. Morgan, 79 Va. 367; Ogden v. Davidson, 81 Va. 757, 762; Nulton v. Isaacs, 30 Gratt. 726.

"The true doctrine of the law on this subject is, in our opinion, correctly laid down in the opinion of the supreme court of the United States, delivered by Mr. Justice Field in Windsor v. McVeigh, 3 Otto R. 274. 'The doctrine invoked by counsel,' said the court in that case, page 282, 'that where a court has once acquired jurisdiction, it has a right to decide every question which arises in the cause, and its judgment, however erroneous, can

not be collaterally assailed, is undoubtedly correct as a general proposition; but, like all general propositions, is subject to many qualifications in its application. All courts, even the highest, are more or less limited in their jurisdiction; they are limited to particular classes of actions, such as civil or criminal, or to particular modes of administering relief, such as legal or equitable,' etc. 'Though the court may possess jurisdiction of a cause, of the subject matter and of the parties, it is still limited in its mode of procedure, and in the extent and character of its judgments. It must act judicially in all things, and can not then transcend the power conferred by the law. If, for instance, the action be for a money demand, the court, notwithstanding its complete jurisdiction over the subject and parties, has no power to pass judgment of imprisonment in the penitentiary upon the defendant. If the action be for a libel or personal tort, the court can not order in that case a specific performance of a contract. If the action be for the possession of real property, the court is powerless to admit in the case the probate of a will. Instances of this kind show that the general doctrine stated by counsel is subject to many qualifications. The judgments mentioned, given in the cases supposed, would not be merely erroneous; they would be absolutely void, because the court in rendering them would transcend the limits of its authority in those cases.' 'So a departure from established modes of procedure will often render the judgment void; thus, the sentence of a person charged with felony, upon conviction by the court, without the intervention of a jury, would be invalid for any purpose. The decree of a court of equity upon oral allegations, without written pleadings, would be an idle act of no force beyond that of an advisory proceeding of the chancellor; and the reason is, that the courts are not authorized to exert their power in that way.' According to the principles thus laid down, the orders in question have not the force and effect of judgments. There is nothing in those principles at all in conflict with the opinion of this court, delivered by Judge Christian, in the case of Lancaster v. Wilson, 27 Gratt. 624. The distinction between the two is sufficiently obvious without any comment upon them here." Nulton v. Isaacs, 30 Gratt. 726.

Creditor, instead of proceeding at common law to recover his claim, obtains an order for its payment on summary rule to show cause. This is a departure from the established modes of procedure, and the order so obtained has not the force of a judgment, but is void on its face. Nulton v. Isaacs, 30 Gratt 726, 740; Thurman v. Morgan, 79 Va. 367.

As to effect of exceeding jurisdiction, see the title JURISDICTION.

After a final decree at one term giving the full relief warranted by the facts stated in the bill, the case is ended and out of court, and the court has no further jurisdiction of the subject matter or parties, and all orders and decrees at a later term are null and void. Waldron v. Harvey, 54 W. Va. 608, 46 S. E. 603.

C. JURISDICTION.

In General.—Before a court can render a valid judgment or decree it is essential that it should have jurisdiction of the person as well as of the subject matter. If either of these is wanting, all the proceedings are void. Haymond v. Camden, 22 W. Va. 181; Wilcher v. Robertson, 78 Va. 602; Seamster v. Blackstock, 83 Va. 232, 2 S. E. 36; Richardson v. Seevers, 84 Va. 259, 4 S. E. 712; Staunton Perpetual Bldg., etc., Co. v. Haden, 92 Va. 201, 23 S. E. 285.

It is no contempt of court to violate or disobey an order or decree which

the court had no authority to make. If the court had no jurisdiction to make said order it is without authority and void. Ruhl v. Ruhl, 24 W. Va. 279, citing Swinburn v. Smith, 15 W. Va. 483, 500.

"There must not only be jurisdiction as to the person affected by the decree by having him before the court by process or appearance, but there must be jurisdiction of the matter acted upon by having it also before the court in the pleadings. Multitudinous cases attest this elementary axiom of jurisdiction. If either is wanting, the decree or judgment is void, not merely voidable or erroneous. Hogg's Eq. Proced., § 573; Haymond v. Camden, 22 W. Va. 181 (point 5); McCoy v. Allen, 16 W. Va. 724; Shaffer v. Fetty, 30 W. Va. 248, 4 S. E. 278; Bland v. Stewart, 35 W. Va. 518, 14 S. E. 215." Waldron v. Harvey, 54 W. Va. 608, 613, 46 S. E. 603. See the title JURISDICTION. And see post, "Judgments for or against Persons Not Parties," III, D, 2.

Decree a Nullity if No Notice Is Given.—No doctrine is better settled than that every man is entitled to a day in court to defend his rights, and that a decree rendered against him, when he has had no opportunity for defense, is a nullity, and may be so pronounced by any court wherein it may be drawn into controversy. Ogden v. Davidson, 81 Va. 757; Myrick v. Adams, 4 Munf. 366; Robinson v. Dix, 18 W. Va. 528; Myers v. Nelson, 26 Gratt. 729; Beery v. Irick, 22 Gratt. 614; Purdie v. Jones, 32 Gratt. 827; Fultz v. Brightwell, 77 Va. 742; Hobson v. Yancey, 2 Gratt. 73; Shaffer v. Fetty, 30 W. Va. 248, 4 S. E. 278; Kyles v. Ford, 2 Rand. 1; Ferguson v. Teel, 82 Va. 690, 696; Lavell v. McCurdy, 77 Va. 763, 771; Bland v. Wyatt, 1 Hen. & M. 543; Carlon v. Ruffner, 12 W. Va. 297.

"As was said in Underwood v. McVeigh, 23 Gratt. 409: 'It lies at the very foundation of justice that every person who is to be affected by an adjudication should have an opportunity of being heard in defense both in repelling the allegations of fact and upon the matters of law; and no sentence of any court is entitled to the least respect in any other court or elsewhere, when it has been pronounced ex parte, and without opportunity of defense. A tribunal which decides without hearing the defendant or giving him an opportunity to be heard, can not claim for its decree or judgment the weight of a judicial sentence.' Such decree or judgment is a mere nullity, void in toto, and is no more effective than if it had never been pronounced. See also, Fairfax *v.* Alexandria, 28 Gratt. 16; Connolly *v.* Connolly, 32 Gratt. 657; Lancaster *v.* Wilson, 27 Gratt. 624." Gray *v.* Stuart, 33 Gratt. 351.

No decree should be rendered affecting the interest of an absent defendant, unless it appear (if it be not otherwise brought before the court), that he has been regularly proceeded against by order of publication duly published in a newspaper and posted at the front door of the courthouse. Craig *v.* Sebrell, 9 Gratt. 131, 133, citing Hadfield *v.* Jameson, 2 Munf. 53. McCoy *v.* McCoy, 9 W. Va. 443, 444.

It is error to decree on a petition filed by permission of the court, making numerous parties, both adults and infants, defendants thereto, on whom neither service of process is had, nor any appearance in any manner by them to such petition shown by the record. Morgan *v.* Morgan, 42 W. Va. 542, 26 S. E. 294.

Where defendants are not served with process, and do not in any way enter an appearance in a cause, a personal decree can not be entered against them, and the fact that they gave their depositions in a case does not authorize the court to give such a decree against them. Edichal, etc., Co.

v. Columbia, etc., Co., 87 Va. 641, 13 S. E. 100.

As to defendants, who are nonresidents, who have had no service of process upon them, have not appeared or authorized anyone to appear for them, no personal decree can be entered against them. McGavock *v.* Clark, 93 Va. 810, 22 S. E. 864; Coleman *v.* Waters, 13 W. Va. 278; Barrett *v.* McAllister, 33 W. Va. 738, 11 S. E. 220.

A decree in a suit instituted by a plaintiff within the union lines against defendants in the confederacy, who do not appear and are unnotified other than by order of publication, is void and may be so considered in that or any subsequent suit. Sturm *v.* Fleming, 22 W. Va. 404; Grinnan *v.* Edwards, 21 W. Va. 347; Haymond *v.* Camden, 22 W. Va. 181.

Generally, as to the necessity and sufficiency of proper process, and service thereof, see the titles SERVICE OF PROCESS; SUMMONS AND PROCESS.

Erroneous Exercise of Jurisdiction. —Where jurisdiction has been obtained over the person and subject matter no error in its exercise can make the judgment void. The authority to decide being shown, it can not be divested by being improperly or incorrectly employed. Lawson *v.* Moorman, 85 Va. 880, 9 S. E. 150.

"A judgment pronounced by a court having no jurisdiction is a mere nullity, not only voidable but entirely void. Such a judgment may be assailed anywhere and everywhere, in courts of the last resort, as well as in inferior courts. Wherever proceedings may be had to enforce such void judgment it may be opposed, and the jurisdiction of the court that pronounced it questioned and assailed. There is an obvious distinction between such a case where the court has no jurisdiction to enter the judgment complained of, and a case where the court, having a general jurisdiction over the subject matter, has erroneously exercised it. In the latter case the judgment can not be questioned in any collateral proceeding, and if not appealed from is final; but where the court is without jurisdiction its judgment must be treated as a mere nullity, and all proceedings under it, or depending on it are void." Withers v. Fuller, 30 Gratt. 547.

Generally, as to the distinction between want of jurisdiction, and an erroneous exercise of jurisdiction, as affecting the validity of a judgment or decree, see the title JURISDICTION.

As to presumptions as to jurisdiction in the case of courts of general and courts of limited jurisdiction, see the title JURISDICTION.

As to Collateral Attack on Judgments void for want of jurisdiction, see post, "Collateral Attack on Judgments or Decrees," IX. And see the title JURISDICTION.

D. PARTIES.
1. In General.

As Constituent Part of Court.—"In every court, there must be at least three constituent parts, the actor, the reus, and the judex; the actor or plaintiff who complains of any injury done, the reus, or defendant, who is called upon to make satisfaction for it; and the judex, or judicial power, which is to examine the truth of the fact, to determine the law arising upon that fact, and, if any injury appears to have been done, to ascertain and apply the remedy." 4 Min. Inst. (3d Ed.) p. 195.

As to who are proper and necessary parties, see generally, the title PARTIES.

Abatement of Suit for Want of Party.—Where there is no party in being in whose favor or against whom the court can render the judgment, as where the defendant is a corporation, but has become extinct, the proceeding will abate. Board v. Livesay, 6 W.

Va. 44, citing Rider v. Nelson, etc., Factory, 7 Leigh 154. See generally, the title ABATEMENT, REVIVAL AND SURVIVAL, vol. 1, p. 2.

As to reversal for want of proper parties, see generally, the title APPEAL AND ERROR, vol. 1, pp. 549, 632.

"Before a decree will be rendered in a cause, all parties materially interested therein must be before the court, either in person, or they must have been proceeded against by order of publication, if absent defendants, and if as to the absent defendants there has been no order of publication executed, and they were material parties, the decree will be reversed. But if there was no objection made in the court below as to the manner in which the order of publication was issued or executed, so as to bring the matter before the inferior court and have the question as to the sufficiency of the order of publication passed upon by that court, and the decree recites that the order of publication as to the absent defendants was 'duly executed,' the objection that it was not duly executed will not be entertained by the appellate court." Scott v. Ludington, 14 W. Va. 387.

Presumption That Parties Were Properly before the Court.—As to the presumption on appeal that parties were properly before the court, see the title APPEAL AND ERROR, vol. 1, p. 602, et seq.

2. Judgments for or against Persons Not Parties.

In General.—It is error to decree in favor of a person not a party in the cause. Bailey v. Robinsons, 1 Gratt. 4.

A decree or judgment affecting the rights of a person not before the court is a nullity as to such person. Bank v. Cook, 55 W. Va. 220, 222, 46 S. E. 1027.

"Upon plain principles, he whose rights are to be affected by any proceeding should be before the court, and have an opportunity to be heard. Otherwise he is not bound by the decree. Clark *v.* Long, 4 Rand. 452; Richardson *v.* Davis, 21 Gratt. 706, 709; Armentrout *v.* Gibbons, 25 Gratt. 371, 375; Barton's Ch. Pr. p. 219, vol. 1, § 74; Collins *v.* Lofftus, 10 Leigh 5; Com. *v.* Risks, 1 Gratt. 416; McDaniel *v.* Baskerville, 13 Gratt. 228; Story's Eq. Pl., §§ 207, 210; Fitzgibbon *v.* Barry, 78 Va. 755; Stovall *v.* Border Grange Bank, 78 Va. 188." Simon *v.* Ellison, 90 Va. 157, 158, 17 S. E. 436. See ante, "Jurisdiction," III, C.

Illustrations.—A court has no jurisdiction over a person who has not been made a party to a suit, and could render no decree against him, and if one was rendered it was a mere nullity. Hence, where in a creditors' suit to subject real estate, the debtor only is made defendant, although there is a prior deed of trust on the land, a decree in such suit is not binding on the trustee or the cestui que trust, nor does the service of a notice of the taking of accounts by the commissioner make them parties, or render such decree valid. McCoy *v.* Allen, 16 W. Va. 724.

In a suit in chancery erroneously brought by A. for the use of B. and B. not being a party to the suit, an order of the circuit court directing the costs to be taxed against the beneficiary, B., and not against A., is void as against B. and does not make him a party to the suit. Bank *v.* Cook, 55 W. Va. 220, 46 S. E. 1027.

It is premature and erroneous to decree an account to be taken of money received by a deceased party, when his personal representative is not before the court, upon proper process. Donahoe *v.* Fackler, 8 W. Va. 249.

No decree can be had against a party who is summoned as a garnishee in a suit in chancery, who is not made a party to the suit, and who does not appear and answer. Chilicothe Oil Co. *v.* Hall, 4 W. Va. 703.

A decree can not be made against a widow (restraining her from conveying her right of dower), in a suit to which she is not a party as widow, but only as administratrix of the decedent, and guardian of her children. Pennington *v.* Hanby, 4 Munf. 140.

Persons Not Named in Bill and against Whom No Allegations Made or Relief Sought.—A decree is a mere nullity as to persons not named as parties in the bill and against whom no allegations are made and no relief is asked. Moseley *v.* Cocke, 7 Leigh 224; Bland *v.* Wyatt, 1 Hen. & M. 543; Henderson *v.* Henderson, 9 Gratt. 394; James River, etc., Co. *v.* Littlejohn, 18 Gratt. 53, 81; Cronise *v.* Carper, 80 Va. 678, 681; Strother *v.* Mitchell, 8 Va. 149; Ogden *v.* Davidson, 81 Va. 757, 759; Strother *v.* Xaupi, 80 Va. 159; Newman *v.* Mollohan, 10 W. Va. 488, 503; Keystone Bridge Co. *v.* Summers, 13 W. Va. 476, 506; McCoy *v.* Allen, 16 W. Va. 724, 730; Renick *v.* Ludington, 20 W. Va. 511, 539; Rickard *v.* Schley, 27 W. Va. 617, 633; McNult *v.* Trogden, 29 W. Va. 469, 2 S. E. 328; Shaffer *v.* Fetty, 30 W. Va. 248, 4 S. E. 278; McKay *v.* McKay, 33 W. Va. 724, 11 S. E. 213, 217; Cook *v.* Dorsey, 38 W. Va. 196, 199, 18 S. E. 468, 469; Shinn *v.* Board of Education, 39 W. Va. 497, 506, 20 S. E. 604, 607; Bland *v.* Stewart, 35 W. Va. 518, 14 S. E. 215. See the title EQUITY, vol. 5, p. 130.

"A decree against one not named in the bill, and nowise comprehended in its general allegations, is a nullity. He is not bound by it, and has, therefore, no necessity to contest it, or answer to it. If he has been improperly named in the process, the plaintiff may indeed be subject to his action for vexing him by that service, when he was in fact not a party; but he can not file his answer where nothing is demanded of him." Moseley *v.* Cocke, 7 Leigh 224.

"If a person is not named in a bill,

and no allegation with reference to him appears therein, even if he is named in the summons, and he is served with process, he is not a party, and any decree against him would be void, and not res judicata; and though named in the prayer of the bill and in the summons, and served with it, but there is no allegation as to him, he is not a party, because there is nothing in the bill to which he could answer, and his rights are not adjudicated. Chapman v. Pittsburg, etc., R. Co., 18 W. Va. 184; Renick v. Ludington, 20 W. Va. 511, 536; McNult v. Trogden, 29 W. Va. 469, 471, 2 S. E. 328." Bland v. Stewart, 35 W. Va. 518, 14 S. E. 215.

Upon a bill in chancery against several defendants, process issues against one not made a party defendant in the bill, and against whom there is no allegation therein, and no relief prayed, and a decree is made against him by default, and against the defendants, by some of whom an appeal is taken to the court of appeals, where the decree is reversed as to the appellants, and in all things else affirmed. Held, the decree is a mere nullity as to the party who was not named in the bill, and against whom the bill contained no allegation and prayed no relief. Moseley v. Cocke, 7 Leigh 224.

Upon a bill in chancery against one defendant, she filed an answer which showed that a third party ought to have been made a defendant. Such third party thereupon tendered his answer to the bill, waiving service of any process; which answer was filed by leave of the court, on the motion of such third party; but the original bill was not amended, and there were no allegations against this person, and no relief prayed against him, and no allusion whatever made to him in the bill. Subsequently evidence was taken which proved the interest of such third person in the suit. Then the court had no jurisdiction over him, and he

was no party to the suit, and a decree either for or against him is a mere nullity, and should, if brought before an appellate court, be reversed and set aside. Shaffer v. Fetty, 30 W. Va. 248, 4 S. E. 278, 279.

3. Judgments for or against Parties by Representation.

Generally, as to parties by representation, see the title PARTIES.

As to the effect of judgments against parties by representation, see the title FORMER ADJUDICATION OR RES ADJUDICATA, vol. 6, p. 314.

4. Judgments for or against Deceased Persons.

In General. — Judgments for or against deceased persons are not generally regarded as void on that account. Such judgments are only voidable, and have been upheld in collateral proceedings. King v. Burdett, 28 W. Va. 601; Watt v. Brookover, 35 W. Va. 323, 13 S. E. 1007; Corrothers v. Sargent, 20 W. Va. 351; McMillan v. Hickman, 35 W. Va. 705, 14 S. E. 227; Robinett v. Mitchell, 101 Va. 762, 45 S. E. 287.

Where process has been regularly served on a defendant, and there is no appearance, and the defendant dies before judgment, and his death is not suggested on the record, and after his death judgment is rendered against him, such judgment is not void but voidable, and can not be collaterally attacked. King v. Burdett, 28 W. Va. 601; Evans v. Spurgin, 6 Gratt. 107.

"As regards a judgment against a party dead at its rendition, this court, in King v. Burdett, 28 W. Va. 601, held such judgment not void for the fact of death not appearing on the record, and that it was a lien enforceable in chancery, and such death could not be set up in defense of a bill to enforce it. In Evans v. Spurgin, 6 Gratt. 107, it was held, that the death of a defendant not having been suggested, a decree can not be impeached in a collateral action by evidence of his death. I think these decisions are binding authority on us, and in principle decide this point in the case." Watt *v.* Brookover, 35 W. Va. 323, 13 S. E. 1007.

In Freeman on Judgments (§ 153) the author says: "Judgments for or against deceased persons are not generally regarded as void on that account. Such judgments have sometimes been upheld in collateral proceedings on the ground that their rendition necessarily implied that the parties were then living, and that this implied finding in support of judgments ought not to be allowed to be impeached by evidence not contained in the record. A suit was prosecuted for the benefit of A. in the name of a nominal plaintiff, who was dead, without any objection being made by the defendant. Judgment was rendered by nil dicit. Defendant petitioned for a supersedeas. It was denied on the ground that the defendant was estopped from inquiry as to the death of plaintiff by his failure to plead it when he had an opportunity to do so, citing the case of Powell *v.* Washington, 15 Ala. 803." McMillan *v.* Hickman, 35 W. Va. 705, 14 S. E. 227, 231.

Black on Judgments (vol. 1, § 204) says, among other things, that, "in order to arrive at a just conclusion on this point it is necessary to take into account the time or stage of the cause at which the decease of the plaintiff occurs; and, first, if an action is commenced in the name of a person already dead (as where the decedent is the nominal plaintiff, and the one for whose benefit the suit is prosecuted is the real party in interest), or if one of several joint claimants is dead before action is brought, it is held, that the defendant must take advantage of the facts by plea in abatement at the peril of being estopped by his silence, and the judgment for plaintiff will not

be disturbed." McMillan *v.* Hickman, 35 W. Va. 705, 14 S. E. 227, 231.

"In Neale *v.* Utz, 75 Va. 480, a judgment against a convict was held unimpeachable in a collateral proceeding, though the party was civiliter mortuus. True, these cases were cases of judgment against persons, while here it is the case of one of the partners plaintiff dead at the institution of the action; but I concur in the opinion expressed in 1 Black, Judgm., § 204, that such a case 'can not be distinguished in principle from that of a defendant dying while the action is pending, where, as already shown (§ 200), the great preponderance of authority sustains the rule that the judgment is at least impervious to collateral attack, and must be vacated or reversed by proper proceedings. Both cases are equally governed by the principle that, when once the jurisdiction has attached, no subsequent error or irregularity in the exercise of that jurisdiction can make its judgment void.' Here the party was dead at the institution of the action in which judgment was rendered. Mr. Black, supra, states the law to be that, if an action is commenced in the name of a person already dead (as, where the decedent is the nominal plaintiff, and the one for whose benefit the suit is prosecuted is the real party in interest), or if one of several joint claimants is dead before action brought, it is held, that the defendant must take advantage of the fact by plea in abatement, at the peril of being estopped by his silence, and the judgment for plaintiff will not be disturbed. (The fact that defendant did not know of his death can make no difference as to this point.)" Watt *v.* Brookover, 35 W. Va. 323, 13 S. E. 1007, 1008.

"In Powell *v.* Washington, 15 Ala. 803, it was held, that where one, having the beneficial interest in a note, sued in the name of a dead payee, and there was judgment by default, the judgment was valid, and could not even be vacated by a proper proceeding to vacate it. In Milam Co. *v.* Robertson, 47 Tex. 222, and Case *v.* Rifelin, 1 J. J. Marsh 29, it was held, that a judgment for or against a party dead at the time, his death not appearing, is not void. Freeman on Judgments, § 153, states it as law that judgments for or against deceased parties are not void, and that, even where the fact of the death appears in the record they are not void, but only voidable, and are to be affected only by appeal. I am of opinion that, where the fact of death is apparent in the record of the judgment, its rendition would be error of law, to be corrected by appellate process; and, where it does not appear in the record, but is to be shown aliunde, it is called error in fact, to be corrected at common law by writ of error coram vobis, and now, under our Code (1889), ch. 135, § 1, by motion in lieu of that writ. 2 Tuck Com. Laws, 328; 4 Minor, Inst. 848. I do not intimate whether this judgment could have been affected in any way; whether the naming as a plaintiff a dead partner, when the cause of action survived to the other, who was also a party, would render the judgment erroneous. Some cases cited by authors as holding that judgments against dead persons are null do not do so. The word 'void' may be used in them, but in the sense of 'erroneous.' They were cases where, by proper proceedings, they were sought to be reversed, not attacked collaterally. Such are the cases of Colson *v.* Wade, 1 Murph. 43; Burke *v.* Stokely, 65 N. C. 569; Moore *v.* Easley, 18 Ala. 619." Watt *v.* Brookover, 35 W. Va. 323, 13 S. E. 1007, 1008.

Generally, as to death of party as ground for plea in abatement, see the title ABATEMENT, REVIVAL AND SURVIVAL, vol. 1, p. 2.

Party Civiliter Mortuus. — Where process is served upon a defendant on the day of his conviction for felony, but before the conviction has taken place, a judgment by default is obtained against the defendant while he is confined in the penitentiary, the judgment is not void, but voidable, and can not be assailed collaterally in a court of equity, or elsewhere. Neale *v.* Utz, 75 Va. 480.

Death of One of Several Plaintiffs. —The fact that a sole plaintiff, or one of several plaintiffs, is dead at the time of the institution of an action, such death not appearing on the record, does not render a judgment therein void, but only erroneous. Watt *v.* Brookover, 35 W. Va. 323, 13 S. E. 1007; King *v.* Burdett, 28 W. Va. 601.

Judgment Constitutes a Lien. — Where a suit is instituted in the name of a party who is dead at the time the suit is brought, and process is duly served upon the defendants, who suffer judgment to be rendered against them without pleading the death of the plaintiff in abatement in proper time during the pendency of the suit, the judgment so obtained is not absolutely void, but is erroneous, and until reversed in one of the modes prescribed by law, constitutes a lien upon the real estate of the defendant, and may be enforced as other judgment liens, and is not subject to collateral attack. McMillan *v.* Hickman, 35 W. Va. 705, 14 S. E. 227; Watt *v.* Brookover, 35 W. Va. 323, 13 S. E. 1007; King *v.* Burdett, 28 W. Va. 601. See post, "Judgment Liens," VI.

Error, How Corrected.—Where the fact of death is apparent in the record of the judgment, its rendition would be error of law, to be corrected by appellate process; and, where it does not appear in the record, but is to be shown aliunde, it is called error in fact, to be corrected at common law by writ of error coram nobis; but now, under Code of West Virginia 1889, ch. 135, § 1, it is corrected by motion in lieu of that writ. Watt *v.* Brookover, 35 W. Va. 323, 13 S. E. 1007; Williamson *v.* Appleberry, 1 Hen. & M. 206. See post, "Motion," VII, C, 4, b, (2).

A judgment against a defendant, who was dead at the time of its rendition, will be set aside on motion. Hooe *v.* Barber, 4 Hen. & M. 439.

Right of Court to Render Decree under West Virginia Code, § 9, ch. 127.—Section 9, ch. 127, of the West Virginia Code, provides that "when, in any suit in equity, the number of parties exceeds thirty, and any one of said parties, jointly interested with others in any question arising therein, shall die, the court may nevertheless proceed, if in its opinion all classes of interest in the case are represented, and the interest of no one will be prejudiced by the trial of the cause, to render a decree in such suit as if such person were alive, decreeing to the heirs at law, distributees, or representatives of such person, as the case may require, such interest as such person would have been entitled to had such person been alive at the date of the decree." The circuit court may, at its discretion, act upon this provision of the Code, and the supreme court will seldom interfere with the exercise of such discretion. Northwestern Bank *v.* Hays, 37 W. Va. 475, 16 S. E. 561.

5. Judgment against Insane Persons.

"A judgment against one insane at the time it is rendered is not void, and can not be collaterally attacked, and, not being void, is a lien on land. Freem. Judgm., § 152; 1 Black, Judgm., § 205; Vanfleet, Collat. Attack, § 616; Watt *v.* Brookover, 35 W. Va. 323, 13 S. E. 1007, and citations; 11 Amer. & Eng. Ency. Law, 127; 12 Amer. & Eng. Ency. Law, 90, note 4; Busw. Insan. § 124; authorities cited in opinion and syllabus in Sternbergh *v.* Schoolcraft, 2 Barb. 153; Allison *v.* Taylor, 32 Amer. Dec. 68; Wood *v.*

Bayard, 63 Pa. St. 320; Foster *v.* Jones, 23 Ga. 168." Withrow *v.* Smithson, 37 W. Va. 757, 17 S. E. 316. See post, "Judgment Liens," VI. And see the title INSANITY, vol. 7, p. 668.

6. Joinder of Parties.

a. Judgments against One or More Co-defendants.

In Actions on Joint and Joint and Several Obligations.—Generally, as to the common-law rule as to joint actions on contracts, the form and effect of such judgments, etc., and the changes effected in such rule by the statutes in Virginia and West Virginia, see the title FORMER ADJUDICATION OR RES ADJUDICATA, vol. 6, p. 325.

As to recovery against some defendants in actions on bonds, see the title BONDS, vol. 2, p. 568.

Judgment against Those Served.—Under Va. Code, ch. 167, § 50, where only one of several defendants is served with process, judgment is properly rendered against the defendant served. Norfolk, etc., R. Co. *v.* Shippers' Compress Co., 83 Va. 272, 2 S. E. 139; Gray *v.* Stuart, 33 Gratt. 351.

Writ Served on Part.—Where a writ is served on only a part of the defendants, the others being returned no inhabitants of the county, the court may render judgment against those upon whom the writ is served. Merchants, etc., Bank *v.* Evans, 9 W. Va. 373. For Va. Code, ch. 167, § 50, changes the common-law rule that all defendants in actions ex contractu must be summoned, before judgment can be had against any, by providing that judgment may be had against one defendant served with process, and a discontinuance as to others, or at the plaintiff's election, subsequent service of process and judgment, in the same suit against the other defendants. Beazley *v.* Sims, 81 Va. 644.

Under Va. Code, 1887, § 3396, providing that where, "in any action against two or more defendants, the process is served on part of them, the plaintiff may proceed to judgment as to any so served, and either discontinue it as to the others, or from time to time, as the process is served as to such others, proceed to judgment as to them until judgments be obtained against all," judgment may properly be entered against several defendants on whom process is served, though return is made that another defendant is dead. Dillard v. Turner, 87 Va. 669, 14 S. E. 123. See also, Newberry v. Sheffey, 89 Va. 286, 15 S. E. 548.

Where Part Only Appear and Plead. —It is not error to try a cause against a part of the defendants who have appeared and pleaded, and when there is an office judgment not set aside as to the other defendants. Hood v. Maxwell, 1 W. Va. 219.

In Actions against Joint Tort Feasors.—Generally, as to the rule in Virginia and West Virginia as to judgments in suits against joint tort feasors, see the title FORMER ADJUDICATION OR RES ADJUDICATA, vol. 6, p. 337.

If defendants have jointly participated in all of the fraudulent acts which entitle a complainant to a decree against them, the decree should be joint and several, with the right to the complainant to collect from either or all as he may be able, and should not undertake to segregate the sum which each defendant is to pay. Anderson v. Smith, 102 Va. 697, 48 S. E. 29.

G. institutes an action of trespass on the case, against J. and ten others, for arrest and false imprisonment. The defendants pleaded the statute of limitations and not guilty, and issues were thereon joined. Upon the issues the jury rendered a verdict for damages against eight of the defendants jointly, find two of the defendants not guilty, and omitted to find any verdict against F., the other defendant, and the circuit court entered joint judgment on the finding of the jury against the eight defendants for the damages assessed by the jury, and the costs. Held, that as the defendants against whom the verdict was rendered and the judgment thereon entered, were not prejudiced by the omission as to F., it was proper to enter the judgment on the verdict against the defendants who were found guilty. Jones v. Grimmet, 4 W. Va. 104.

In the case of Com. v. Bennet, 2 Va. Cas. 235, it was held, that on the trial of an indictment containing several counts, and the jury find the prisoner guilty on one of them, saying nothing about the others, the court should enter a judgment of conviction on the verdict, on the count on which the defendant was found guilty, and a judgment of acquittal on the others. Jones v. Grimmet, 4 W. Va. 104, 105.

In an action of trover and conversion against two, where the defendants appear and file a joint plea of not guilty and issue is thereon joined, it is competent for the jury to acquit one of the defendants and find the other guilty and assess damages against him. When in such action under such pleadings the jury find both defendants guilty, by a joint verdict, and a motion is made by the defendants to set aside such verdict and grant a new trial, it is competent and proper for the court to grant the motion, if the court is clearly of the opinion that there was no evidence against one of the defendants, before the jury tending to fix a legal liability upon him in the action. If the verdict in such case be set aside as to one of the defendants, no judgment can be rendered against the other. Tracy v. Cloyd, 10 W. Va. 19.

"It is declared, however, by Hillard, in his 2d volume on Torts, 3d edition, p. 314, that 'where several defendants in trespass plead one plea, and a joint verdict and damages are found against all, judgment must be rendered jointly against all. And if it be set aside as to part, no judgment can be rendered against the others. Though, where part are acquitted and part found guilty, setting aside the verdict as to the latter does not affect its validity as to the former.'" Tracy v. Cloyd, 10 W. Va. 19, 32.

b. Judgment as an Entirety.

At common law, a joint judgment erroneous as to some is erroneous and must be reversed as to all. Vance Shoe Co. v. Haught, 41 W. Va. 275; 23 S. E. 553; Jones v. Raine, 4 Rand. 386; Vandiver v. Roberts, 4 W. Va. 493; Lyman v. Thompson, 11 W. Va. 427; Lenows v. Lenow, 8 Gratt. 349; Purcell v. McCleary, 10 Gratt. 246; Gray v. Stuart, 33 Gratt. 351, 358; Arrington v. Cheatham, 2 Rob. 492; Lee v. Hassett, 41 W. Va. 368, 23 S. E. 559.

A joint judgment against two parties, where the service of notice is improperly executed as against one party, is erroneous, and must be reversed as to both. Vandiver v. Roberts, 4 W. Va. 493. See also, Gregory v. Marks, 1 Rand. 355, 386.

Under Statute.—"Section 26, ch. 135, W. Va. Code, authorizes this court to reverse in whole or in part, and, I think, changes the common-law rule as is intimated in Gray v. Stuart, 33 Gratt. 351." Per Brannon, J., in Vance Shoe Co. v. Haught, 41 W. Va. 275, 23 S. E. 553.

According to the ancient holding of the court, if there was a joint judgment against both of the defendants, when the record showed that only one of them was served with process, being void as to one, was void as to both. The judgment being entire, if it is a nullity with respect to one, it also is in the whole. "This ruling has since been seriously intrenched upon, departed from, and almost abrogated, by later decisions; the law now being

settled that when a suit is on a joint demand against several, and some are served with process, a joint judgment against all will be void as to those not served, but only erroneous as to those served, unless it comes within the provisions of § 19, ch. 131, Code, when, as between those against whom the plaintiff is bound and those against whom he is not bound, the judgment would stand on the same footing as though it were a separate demand as to the two classes." Lee v. Hassett, 41 W. Va. 368, 23 S. E. 559.

"While the courts of some states still hold to the doctrine of the entirety of a judgment, the courts of this state never have done so; and they are fully sustained by the voice of justice, reason, and authority. For why should a defendant against whom a judgment is proper and just have the right to vacate it, and escape its payment, because it is void as to some one else? When the person against whom it is void has reason to, and complains, it will be time enough for the court to interfere in his behalf. As to all others it is mere harmless error, and in no wise prejudicial. As was said in Poe v. Machine Works, 24 W. Va. 523, a judgment 'being void in toto as to the one, it was never a joint judgment, but only a judgment against the one as to whom the court had jurisdiction. Gray v. Stuart, 33 Gratt. 351.'" Lee v. Hassett, 41 W. Va. 368, 23 S. E. 559, 560.

When a suit is on a joint and several demand, a judgment against all would be void as to those not served with process, but valid as to those served, or appearing to answer the action. In either case a motion to quash an execution on such judgment should not be sustained in favor of the defendants served with process, or appearing to answer the action, as in one case the judgment would be binding, and in the other the proper proceeding would be in error, either by motion under the statute, or appeal. 1 Freem. Judgm., § 136; Hoffman v. Bircher, 22 W. Va. 537; Poe v. Machine Works, 24 W. Va. 517, 523. Lee *. Hassett, 41 W. Va. 368, 23 S. E. 559, 560.

Where a judgment is rendered against two partners of a partnership debt, and one of the partners has not been served with process, nor appeared to answer the action, such judgment is valid as to the partner served with process; and an execution issued thereon should not be quashed, on his motion, on the sole ground that the process was not served on his copartner. Lee v. Hassett, 41 W. Va. 368, 23 S. E. 559.

Reversal as to Parties Not Appealing.—At common law, a judgment erroneous as to one is erroneous and must be reversed as to all, but in equity under the West Virginia statute, if only one appeal from a joint decree, and the rights of the parties stand on different and separable grounds, there may be a reversal only in part. Vance Shoe Co. v. Haught, 41 W. Va. 275, 23 S. E. 553.

Generally, as to the adjudication of rights of parties not appealing, see the title APPEAL AND ERROR, vol. 1, p. 543, et seq.

Setting Aside Joint Decree against Lands of Five or More Defendants.— In Calvert v. Ash, 47 W. Va. 480, 35 S. E. 887, the decree was a joint one against the land of A. and B. It was held, that the decree directing the sale of this real estate must be regarded as an entirety although it was an erroneous decree, and that the circuit court committed no error in setting aside the entire decree.

7. Decree between Codefendants.
a. General Principles.
Case Must Be Made Out by Evidence Arising from Pleadings between Plaintiff and Defendant.—It is well settled that where a case is made out

between the codefendants by evidence arising from pleadings between the complainants and defendants, a court of equity may, and should render a decree between the codefendants; but when there are no such pleadings, a court of equity can not render a decree between the codefendants. Whitlock v. Gordon, 1 Va. Dec. 238; Strother v. Strother, 1 Va. Dec. 367; Mundy v. Vawter, 3 Gratt. 518; Law v. Sutherland, 5 Gratt. 357; Allen v. Morgan, 8 Gratt. 60; Braxton v. Harrison, 11 Gratt. 30; Blair v. Thompson, 11 Gratt. 441; Glenn v. Clark, 21 Gratt. 35; Steed v. Baker, 13 Gratt. 380; Alley v. Rogers, 19 Gratt. 366; Ould v. Myers, 23 Gratt. 383; Morriss v. Coleman, 1 Rob. 478; Yerby v. Grigsby, 9 Leigh 387; Toole v. Stephen, 4 Leigh 581; Dade v. Madison, 5 Leigh 401; Morris v. Terrell, 2 Rand. 6; Templeman v. Fauntleroy, 3 Rand. 434; Cocke v. Harrison, 3 Rand. 494; Fox v. Taliferro, 4 Munf. 243; McNeil v. Baird, 6 Munf. 316; Vance v. Evans, 11 W. Va. 342; Ruffner v. Hewitt, 14 W. Va. 737; Worthington v. Staunton, 16 W. Va. 208; Burlew v. Quarrier, 16 W. Va. 108; Kent v. Chapman, 18 W. Va. 485; Hoffman v. Ryan, 21 W. Va. 415; Tavenner v. Barrett, 21 W. Va. 656; Hansford v. Chesapeake Coal Co., 22 W. Va. 70; Titchenell v. Jackson, 26 W. Va. 460; Heard v. Chesapeake, etc., R. Co., 26 W. Va. 455, 460; Roots v. Mason City, etc., Co., 27 W. Va. 483; Vanscoy v. Stinchcomb, 29 W. Va. 263, 11 S. E. 927, 932; Radcliff v. Corrothers, 33 W. Va. 682, 11 S. E. 228; McKay v. McKay, 33 W. Va. 734, 11 S. E. 213, 217; Roberts v. Coleman, 37 W. Va. 143, 16 S. E. 482; Harrison v. Brewster, 38 W. Va. 294, 18 S. E. 568; Parsons v. Smith, 46 W. Va. 728, 34 S. E. 922; Yates v. Stuart, 39 W. Va. 124, 19 S. E. 423.

Where the equities between the defendants do not arise out of the pleadings and proofs between the plaintiffs and defendants, there can be no decree between codefendants. Blair *v.* Thompson, 11 Gratt. 441; Glenn *v.* Clark, 21 Gratt. 35. Ruffner *v.* Hewitt, 14 W. Va. 737, 741.

No decree can be made between codefendants, founded upon matters not stated in the bill, nor in litigation between the complainants and defendants, or some of them. Hoffman *v.* Ryan, 21 W. Va. 415.

"In relation to decrees between codefendants, I understand the rule in Virginia to be the same as that laid down by Lords Eldon and Redesdale in the House of Lords in the case of Chanity *v.* Lord Dunsany, 2 Sch. and Lef. 689, that 'whenever a case is made out between the defendants by evidence arising from the pleadings and proofs between the plaintiff and the defendants, a court of equity is entitled to make a decree between the defendants, and is bound to do so.' McNeil *v.* Baird, 6 Munf. 316; Allen *v.* Morgan, 8 Gratt. 60; Morris *v.* Terrell, 2 Rand. 6; Mundy *v.* Vawter, 3 Gratt. 518; Templeman *v.* Fauntleroy, 3 Rand. 434. There have been various cases decided in our court of appeals rejecting decrees between codefendants (and the case of Blair *v.* Thompson, 11 Gratt. 441, cited by the counsel of the appellants, is one of them), because the matter did not arise from the proceedings and proofs between the plaintiff and defendants. But none of them, I think, impugn the rule as above laid down that whenever a case does arise between the defendants upon such proceedings and proofs it is the right and duty of the court to decree between them, and make an end of the controversy, and save the necessity of other suits and further delay and expenses. And tested by that rule, it seems to me there can be no doubt of the right of the court to decree between the defendants in this case, because the questions of the making of the covenants in the several deeds by the defendants, and their ob-ligations arising out of them to the plaintiffs and towards each other, were put directly in issue by the proceedings, and were obliged to arise from the proceedings and proofs between the plaintiff and the defendants. I think, therefore, that there is nothing in the objection taken in the third assignment of error." Whitlock *v.* Gordon, 1 Va. Dec. 238, 251.

"The case of Taliaferro *v.* Minor, 2 Call 524, presents the first instance in which the practice was adverted to in this court. That was a suit by distributees against two administrators for an account and distribution. The report ascertained a balance to be due by one administrator to the estate of the other administrator; and a decree was rendered for such balance by the chancellor. But upon appeal it was reversed, because no contest appeared between the administrators, in the record, nor any account of their separate transactions, except in the statement of the accounts by the commissioner. The principle of the case is that the pleadings raised no issue between the codefendants as to the state of accounts between themselves." Blair *v.* Thompson, 11 Gratt. 441.

President Tucker in Hubbard *v.* Goodwin, 3 Leigh 522, thus refers to the subject of decrees between codefendants: "A defendant, who answers the plaintiff's bill, does not always go on to state his own case as it relates to the difference between him and his codefendant. There is no issue made up, nor any provision for taking their testimony in reference to the peculiar matters in controversy between them. And hence, in many cases, the contest between them can not come fairly before the court." Strother *v.* Strother, 1 Va. Dec. 367, 374.

In a case where the defendants had stated the case fully as it related to the difference between themselves, when that difference was the very subject of controversy in the case—when the issue was made up, and the testimony taken, so that the case did come fairly before the court, it would follow, by necessary implication, that the court should proceed to decree between the codefendants without requiring a cross bill. Strother v. Strother, 1 Va. Dec. 367.

As to the necessity for a cross bill to enable a defendant to have a decree against a codefendant, see the title CROSS BILLS, vol. 4, p. 111.

Reason for Rule.—"If the rule was not adhered to, the administration of justice would become extremely difficult, if not impossible in many cases. It could not be known when, where or how a chancery cause would terminate if all the parties, who had any interest in the subject matter of the bill, and who were therefore necessary defendants thereto, could, to save time and expense, by filing their answers in that cause, or cross bills, litigate all their differences which were in any way however remotely connected with the subject matter of the bill, and in which plaintiff had no special interest. The collateral issues in such a case might be interminable." Worthington v. Staunton, 16 W. Va. 208, 232.

Must Be Proper Case for Decree for Plaintiff.—There can be no decree in any case between codefendants when no decree can properly be rendered in favor of the plaintiff, whether this arises from the fact that the bill does not make out a case which entitles him to relief, or from the fact that the proof does not sustain the case as set out in the bill. Watson v. Wigginton, 28 W. Va. 533; Radcliff v. Corrothers, 33 W. Va. 682, 694, 11 S. E. 228, 232; Kinports v. Rawson, 36 W. Va. 237, 15 S. E. 66, 68; Glenn v. Clark, 21 Gratt. 35; Kennewig Co. v. Moore, 49 W. Va. 323, 38 S. E. 558; Roberts v. Coleman, 37 W. Va. 143, 16 S. E. 482.

Where the plaintiff in a suit is not entitled to any relief, there can be no decree between codefendants, nor any recovery by one defendant against another defendant. Western Lunatic Asylum v. Miller, 29 W. Va. 326, 1 S. E. 740; Hansford v. Coal Co., 22 W. Va. 70; Vance v. Evans, 11 W. Va. 342; Ould v. Myers, 23 Gratt. 383.

"I am clearly of opinion, that the court ought not in this cause to undertake to adjust the transactions between Hubbard and Kennedy. None of the cases in which the court has decreed between defendants have gone so far. I think it has been done in no case where the plaintiff was not entitled to a decree against both or either. The practice should not be extended further. The contest, if any, between defendants can never come fairly before the court. There is no issue made up, nor any provision for taking their testimony in reference to the peculiar matters in difference between them. Indeed, it does not follow, that in answer to a plaintiff's bill, the defendant should go on to state his own case in reference to his difference with his codefendant." Hubbard v. Goodwin, 3 Leigh 492.

"The case of Morris v. Terrell, 2 Rand. 6, and Mundy v. Vawter, 3 Gratt. 518, are the only cases in which the plaintiff was not entitled to a decree in any event against the defendant, as against whom a decree was made in favor of a codefendant. In Templeman v. Fauntleroy, and McNeil v. Baird, the plaintiff was entitled to a decree against the defendant charged in favor of the codefendant. In each case the liability of the party and the extent of it arose from the facts which entitled the plaintiff to any relief. They were, therefore, necessarily charged in the bill; the defendant had an opportunity of responding in his answer; and the evidence applied directly to the issue thus made up by the pleadings." Blair v. Thompson. 11 Gratt. 441.

It is no objection to a decree that it is nominally in favor of one defendant against another, if it be substantially in favor of the complainant. West v. Belches, 5 Munf. 187.

Issue Must Be Made.—The contest between codefendants can never come fairly before the court, where no issue is made up, nor any provision for taking their testimony as to the matters in difference between them. Hubbard v. Goodwin, 3 Leigh 492.

"The practice of decreeing between codefendants is not much favored by the courts. There is an increasing indisposition to extend that practice further than it has already been carried. In Taliaferro v. Minor, 1 Call 524, the court of appeals reversed the decree of the court below upon the ground that the pleadings raised no issue between the codefendants as to the state of the accounts between them. And in Blair v. Thompson, 11 Gratt. 441, Judge Allen laid down the rule to be, 'where the equities between the defendants do not arise out of the pleadings and proofs between plaintiffs and defendants, there can be no decree between codefendants.'" Glenn v. Clark, 21 Gratt. 35.

Necessity for Satisfactory Evidence.—Unless the matter has been put in issue by the pleadings, and there is satisfactory evidence of the facts, it is not deemed proper to decree in favor of one defendant against another. Yerby v. Grigsby, 9 Leigh 387.

Where the relief sought in a bill fails for want of proof, no relief can be administered between codefendants on answer filed praying it, but such answer must be dismissed with the bill, without prejudice to the rights of the defendants as between themselves. Kennewig Co. v. Moore, 49 W. Va. 323, 38 S. E. 558.

May First Subject Defendant Ultimately Liable.—A court of equity may enter a decree between codefendants, in a case where the same decree operates in favor of the complainant, by subjecting in the first instance that de-

fendant who ought ultimately to pay the debt. McNiel v. Baird, 6 Munf. 316.

Invited Error No Ground for Reversal.—A defendant, who by his answer asks the court to make inquiries through its commissioner, more extended than the statements in the bill might justify, and upon such inquiry to decree between him and a codefendant, is thereby precluded in the appellate court from assigning as error such enlarged extent of inquiry, or that a decree between codefendants was based thereon. Vance v. Evans, 11 W. Va. 342. See generally, the title APPEAL AND ERROR, vol. 1, p. 608.

Decree on Remand.—Where a decree for a sale of land which was bound for the payment of certain notes was interlocutory, although it was affirmed on appeal, there may be a decree between the codefendants when the cause goes back, if it is a proper case for such a decree. Alley v. Rogers, 19 Gratt. 366.

b. Application of Principles in Particular Instances.

Proper Cases for a Decree between Codefendants. — Judgment creditors seek to subject land of their debtor which has been conveyed in trust to secure a debt; and in their bill they charge that the deed was intended by the grantor to defraud his creditors, and the trustee and creditor in the deed were cognizant of the fraudulent intent at the time. The creditor answers and denies the fraud and proves his debt. Held, it is a proper case for a decree between defendants, and, the debt of the trust creditor having been established, for a decree in his favor for the debt. Barger v. Buckland, 28 Gratt. 850.

W., administrator of G., assigns the bond of T. to the executors of H., in discharge of a debt due from G. to H. The executors of H. sue T., and recover a judgment upon the bond; and he thereupon enjoins it on the ground that G. was indebted to him for a legacy left by R., of whom G. had been executor. And this injunction is afterwards perpetuated. Held, that the executors of H. are entitled to be substituted to the rights of T. against G.'s estate; and are not confined to their remedy upon the assignment of W. In this injunction suit the executors of H. and W. and the administrator de bonis non of G., are parties, and they consent to the decree perpetuating the injunction and also to a decree directing the executor of W., and the administrator de bonis non, to settle their accounts of admin'stration upon G.'s estate. Held, that it is a case in which there may be a decree between codefendants in favor of the executors of H. against G.'s estate. Braxton v. Harrison, 11 Gratt. 30.

"It is true that the right of Harrison's executions to have recourse against Grymes' estate accrued at the time of the perpetuation of the injunction; but it is not, I think, true that such right could not be enforced in the injunction suit. I think the case came within the reason and operation of the rule, that 'where a case is made out between defendants by evidence arising from pleadings and proofs between plaintiffs and defendants, a court of equity has a right and often is bound to make a decree between the defendants.' See 2 Rob. Pr. 397, and the cases cited; Fox v. Taliaferro, 4 Munf. 243; Dade v. Madison, 5 Leigh 401. Though a suit be disposed of as to the plaintiff, it may be retained until proper accounts can be taken, in order to render to one of the defendants the relief to which he may be entitled against the other. Morris v. Terrell, 2 Rand. 6. A defendant may in some cases object to a decree against him in favor of his codefendants, on the ground that there is no issue made up between them,

and their peculiar matters of difference have not been ascertained and settled. But the party entitled to make such objection may certainly waive it, and consent to a decree against him; and it may often be his interest to do so." Braxton v, Harrison, 11 Gratt. 30, 52.

D. draws an order on M., in favor of T., for $545, which M. accepts. T. recovers judgment against M. upon his acceptance; then M. files bill in equity against D. and T., praying injunction, on ground that the order was drawn for money won by D. of M. at unlawful gaming. D. in his answer acknowledges the gaming consideration, and avers that T. was informed of it, at the time he took the draft; but T. in his answer denies all knowledge of the gaming consideration; and there is no other evidence of the gaming but D.'s answer; chancellor dissolves the injunction, and allows T. to execute his judgment at law against M. but decrees, that, upon M.'s paying the amount of the debt to T., the other defendant, D., shall pay the same amount to M. Held, the decree is right, in all respects; the answer of D. was no evidence against T. but the gaming debt being paid under his order to T., he ought to pay it back to M. Dade v. Madison, 5 Leigh 401.

M. brought a bill to enforce a vendor's lien alleged to be due to himself. On the hearing of the cause the court decided that he had no lien or right in the premises and decreed costs against him; and being of opinion that it was a proper case for a decree between codefendants, for settling rights and equities, decreed a deed from one defendant to another. Held, that the decree for the deed between the defendants was not matter of which M. could complain. Mann v. Lewis, 3 W. Va. 215.

A decree can not be made between codefendants, unless it be based on pleadings and proofs between the plaintiffs and defendants. But in a bill asking that the lien on a debtor's land be audited, and their amounts and priorities settled, and the debtor's land sold to pay the same, though the bill admits that a particular debt is a lien and is unsatisfied, the debtor or any other lienor may dispute the validity of such lien, and such a controversy may be decided by the court without violating the above rule. Tavenner v. Barrett, 21 W. Va. 656, 658.

"It is by appellant's counsel insisted, that on the authority of numerous cases a decree can not be made between codefendants unless it be based on pleadings and proof between the plaintiff and defendant, and the following authorities are referred to to sustain this position: Vance v. Evans, 11 W. Va. 342; Worthington v. Staunton, 16 W. Va. 208, 244; Ould v. Myers, 23 Gratt. 383; and that it is a well settled principle, that a decree can not go outside of pleadings, see Burley v. Weller, 14 W. Va. 264, 273; Hunter v. Hunter, 10 W. Va. 321; Baugher v. Eichelberger, 11 W. Va. 217, 225; and also, Burlew v. Quarrier, 16 W. Va. 108. These propositions of law are unquestionably sound, but it does seem to me, that they have no sort of application to the case before us. The bill and amended bill both set out the various liens cla'med to be on the land, in the bill and amended bill named, including this deed of trust, and ask, that 'a commissioner be directed to ascertain and report any and all liens of any and every kind whatever existing against said property named, and the order of their priority, and that the court will decree a sale of said property or so much thereof as may be necessary to pay off and discharge the plaintiff's lien, and other liens existing against the said lands as aforesaid, and that a special commissioner be appointed for that purpose.' The amount and priority of the various liens including this deed of trust was

directly involved in this cause, as stated in the bill and amended bill, and as a matter of course any one of the defendants and more especially Sarah V. Barrett, had a right in her answer to insist, that any one of these liens was originally invalid or that the debt had been paid off; and surely she could not be deprived of this right by the plaintiff saying, that such lien was valid or such debt had not been paid off. There is in this case a direct issue made by the bill and the answer of Sarah V. Barrett, as to the validity of this deed of trust. The bill alleges it to be valid, and the answer of Sarah V. Barrett denies that it is valid. The decree therefore as to its validity or invalidity is based directly upon the pleadings and proofs between the plaintiff and the principal defendant, and according to the authorities cited by the appellant's counsel this is the very case, where the court may properly render a decree between codefendants. This question was thus fairly before the court for decision." Tavenner v. Barrett, 21 W. Va. 656, 685.

Where the representative of a sheriff is sued on account of an estate committed to his hands, and it appears that his deputy (who is also sued) had the entire management of the estate, the court may decree against the deputy, in the first instance, if assented to by the plaintiff, reserving liberty to him to resort to the court, for ulterior decree against the other parties; but if such consent be not given, it is the duty of the court to decree between defendants, in order to throw the burthen on the person ultimately liable. Cocke v. Harrison, 3 Rand. 494.

"Morris v. Terrell, 2 Rand. 6, was a case of a decree between codefendants. The principal in that case filed a bill against his agent and a purchaser of land from the agent, to set aside a sale for which the agent admitted he had received the purchase money, upon the ground that the agent had no authority to sell. The sale was set aside; the principal restored to his property; and the agent decreed to repay the purchase money received from the purchaser. In that case the authority of the agent to sell constituted the gravamen of the bill. His liability to refund to the purchaser resulted from the establishment of the fact that he had sold without authority; and the question was directly presented and arose from the allegations of the bill and the proofs to sustain them." Blair v. Thompson, 11 Gratt. 441.

"The case of Mundy v. Vawter, 3 Gratt. 518, agrees in principle with Morris v. Terrell, 2 Rand. 6. The bill of Vawter, the substituted trustee, made the purchasers of the land and the previous trustees and others who had united in a deed to Dillard, defendants, alleging that the sale was without authority. The court so held as to one-fourth of the subject, and gave the plaintiff a decree therefor; and then decreed over in favor of the purchaser against his grantors, in the order of their liability, upon the ground set forth in the decree, that the claim of the purchaser to relief upon the recovery from him, arose out of the decree against him upon the pleadings and proofs between the plaintiff and his grantors. There, as in the former case, the authority to sell constituted the stress of the case; and upon that depended the liability to refund. Upon that question the issue was fully made by the allegations of the bill to which the defendants ultimately made responsible to their vendee and codefendant, had an opportunity of responding by their answers. In another branch of the case of Mundy v. Vawter, the court refused a decree in favor of Norvell against his codefendants, because the pleadings did not make a proper case for such decree." Blair v. Thompson, 11 Gratt. 441.

Where one is compelled to pay a bond the second time, having wrongfully after notice paid it to a holder, who had no right to it, a decree in his favor against his codefendant, to whom he had so improperly paid it, should be for the sum he had so paid with interest, although it might be much less than the face of the bond and interest thereon. Pickens v. McCoy, 24 W. Va. 344.

When Such Decree Not Proper.— Bill by vendee of land to enjoin the payment of purchase money on the ground of defect of title to a part of the land. The bill states that the adverse claimant bought a part of the land under a sale for taxes, and another part from the attorney of his vendor, and charges generally that the deeds for the land sold for taxes were null and void, and the purchase from the attorney was fraudulent. And he makes his vendor and the adverse claimant defendants. The vendor in his answer charges, and sets out fraud in his attorney and the adverse claimant. The latter was in possession under his deeds, and this was known to plaintiff before his purchase. Held, the general allegation of fraud in the bill is not sufficient to raise that question; that there is no privity between plaintiff and the adverse claimant, and the equity between the latter and the vendor does not arise upon the pleadings and proofs between plaintiff and defendants, and is not therefore the proper subject of a decree between codefendants. Steed v. Baker, 13 Gratt. 380.

"In Allen v. Morgan, 8 Gratt. 60, the plaintiff, a judgment creditor of the intestate, filed a bill against the administrator of the debtor and his official sureties, charging a devastavit by the payment of debts of inferior dignity. Some of the sureties in their answers insisted that the devastavit had been committed by the fraudulent application of the assets by the administrator to the payment of a debt due to another of the sureties; and as the administrator was insolvent, they contended that this surety should be primarily liable, or that the other sureties should have a decree over against him. This court held, that although the plaintiff was entitled to a decree against all the defendants, there was nothing in the allegations of the bill and pleadings, which raised an issue between the codefendants, so as to let in evidence as to their liabilities as amongst themselves; and that it was not therefore a proper case for a decree between them." Blair v. Thompson, 11 Gratt. 441.

In a chancery suit brought by K. of Richmond against A. B. & Co. of Mercer county in West Virginia to enforce the lien of a judgment obtained before the war against A. B. & C. as partners on an accepted order known to the partners to include the amount due from the partnership to K. and also an individual debt due from C. to K.; held, the court ought not in such a suit to order a settlement of the partnership accounts with a view of ascertaining the amount, for which the lands of each partner should be primarily subject. and with a view to the rendering of a proper decree among the codefendants after such settlement; the case justifying such a decree between codefendants would not in such a cause be made out by evidence arising by pleadings and proofs between the complainant and defendants. Kent v. Chapman, 18 W. Va. 485.

H. procures the posting of advertisements for the sale of the lands of his wife's father, who is deceased, signed "The heirs." At said sale which is by public auction, H. bought one tract himself, and H. K. also bought one adjoining. Each takes possession of the tract purchased by him. Subsequently they agree on a division line and set a fence thereon,

and agree as to the portion of the fence to be kept up by the parties respectively. H. receives without objection, the full amount of the purchase money for his wife's share of the land purchased by H. K. H. afterwards declares his intention to be to convey to H. K., when the other heirs of his deceased father-in-law would convey to him, the property also purchased by him at the sale. Seven or eight years afterwards H. and wife bring their bill to set aside the sale of H. K., and to declare a deed made by the coheirs of the wife to H. K., to be void, and require the latter to restore possession and pay rents and profits for the use of the lands purchased by him. The coheirs of the wife are made defendants also with H. K. Held, not a proper case for decree between the codefendants, H. K. and the residue of the heirs. Hendrick v. Hern. 4 W. Va. 620, citing Heavener v. Godfrey, 3 W. Va. 426.

M., having filed a bill to enforce her claim to the land left to her by C., and made F. and the executor of C. defendants, and G., in his answer, having repudiated the sale of his land by his father, and insisted that the will of C. did not raise a case of election; but that he was entitled to hold both farms; though it may be that a part of the purchase money for his land is still due from C.'s estate, that question can not be considered in this case, and there can be no decree between these codefendants upon it. Glenn v. Clark, 21 Gratt. 35.

Instances of Decrees for Plaintiff against One Defendant Rather than Decree between Codefendants.—"Roberts v. Jordans, 3 Munf. 488, was an injunction to a judgment obtained by the assignee of a bond against the obligor, upon the allegation of payments to the obligee and assignor. This court directed the injunction to be made perpetual as to such sum only as had been paid to the assignor before notice of the assignment; but gave the plaintiff a decree over against the obligee and assignor for any sums received by the latter after notice of the assignment, as soon as the plaintiff should have paid the judgment. This was not a decree between codefendants, but in favor of the plaintiff against one of the defendants for money improperly received by him on a note he had assigned to a third person." Blair v. Thompson, 11 Gratt. 441.

"The case of Dade v. Madison, 5 Leigh 401, is similar in principle to the case last cited; a decree over in favor of the plaintiff against a defendant ultimately liable to pay back to the plaintiff money he had been compelled to pay under the order of such defendant in favor of a third person. Ruffners v. Barrett, 6 Munf. 207, is to the same effect; an injunction by the obligor to a judgment in favor of the assignee, upon the allegation of payment to the obligee before notice of the assignment. Upon proof of payment after notice of assignment the injunction was dissolved as to the assignee; but leave was given to proceed against the assignor. These cases, though referred to sometimes as instances of decree between codefendants, are in fact cases in which decrees were in fact rendered in favor of the plaintiff against one defendant upon a proper case made against him." Blair v. Thompson, 11 Gratt. 441.

E. PLEADING, ISSUES AND PROOFS.

1. Necessity.

a. Pleadings and Proofs.

Pleading Essential as Basis of Judgment.—A judgment or decree being the sentence and adjudication made by the law, spoken through a court, upon facts admitted or proven, there can be no judgment or decree without matters of fact alleged. Freem., Judg., § 2; Black, Judgm., § 1. Fowler v. Lewis, 36 W. Va. 112, 14 S. E. 447, 452.

A decree must have for its basis a proper pleading, else it is no decree. Martin v. Kester, 46 W. Va. 438, 33 S. E. 238; Turner v. Stewart, 51 W. Va. 493, 498, 41 S. E. 924.

"A decree, or any matter of a decree, which has no matter in the pleading to rest upon, is void, because pleadings are the very foundation of judgments and decrees." Waldron v. Harvey, 54 W. Va. 608, 613, 46 S. E. 603.

No Decree Where Failure of Pleading or Proof.—A decree is a conclusion of law from pleading and proofs and where there is a failure of either pleading or proofs there can be no decree. Kennewig Co. v. Schilansky, 47 W. Va. 287, 43 S. E. 773; Vance Shoe Co. v. Haught, 41 W. Va. 275, 23 S. E. 553; Waldron v. Harvey, 54 W. Va. 608, 613, 46 S. E. 603.

It is incumbent on the plaintiff to show, by his allegations and proofs, his right to a decree before he can require the defendant to sustain the affirmative allegations of his answer. Bryant v. Groves, 42 W. Va. 10, 24 S. E. 605, 606.

Waiver of Objection for Want of Proper Pleading.—Where defendant has taken depositions as if there had been a replication, the decree shall not be reversed for want of a replication. Va. Code, 1873, ch. 177, § 4. Jones v. Degge, 84 Va. 685, 5 S. E. 799.

Where there is an answer calling for a special reply, and there is a general replication to it, and the party filing it has gone on and taken depositions as if there were a special reply denying it, and there has been a full hearing of the merits, as if there had been such special reply, a decree will not be reversed for want of such special reply. Long v. Perine, 41 W. Va. 314, 23 S. E. 611. See the titles APPEAL AND ERROR, vol. 1, p. 500; PLEADING.

b. Issues.

General Rule as to Necessity.—It is well settled that, where a jury tries a case without an issue made up, the judgment will be reversed. Baltimore, etc., R. Co. *v.* Faulkner, 4 W. Va. 180; Ruffner *v.* Hill, 21 W. Va. 152; Curry *v.* Mannington, 23 W. Va. 14. Buena Vista, etc., Co. *v.* Parrish, 34 W. Va. 652, 12 S. E. 817, 818.

Where trials by jury have been had without issue joined they have invariably been set aside as wholly unauthorized by law. This has been repeatedly held in Virginia before, and in West Virginia since its formation, and must be regarded as settled law, correctly announcing the common-law rule on that subject. Stevens *v.* Taliaferro, 1 Wash. 155; Kerr *v.* Dixon, 2 Call 379; Taylors *v.* Huston, 2 Hen. & M. 161; Wilkinson *v.* Bennett, 3 Munf. 314, 316; Sydnor *v.* Burke, 4 Rand. 161; McMillion *v.* Dobbins, 9 Leigh 422; Rowans *v.* Givens, 10 Gratt. 250; Baltimore, etc., R. Co. *v.* Gettle, 3 W. Va. 376; Baltimore, etc., R. Co. *v.* Christie, 5 W. Va. 325; Gallatin *v.* Haywood, 4 W. Va. 1; Baltimore, etc., R. Co. *v.* Faulkner, 4 W. Va. 180; State *v.* Conkle, 16 W. Va. 736; State *v.* Douglass, 20 W. Va. 770; Ruffner *v.* Hill, 21 W. Va. 152, 159; Preston *v.* Salem Imp. Co., 91 Va. 583, 22 S. E. 486.

"In numerous cases, both in Virginia and in this state, it has been decided that a judgment entered upon the verdict of a jury sworn to try the issue joined, when no issue is in fact joined, or where there were more than one plea, and no issue had been joined on some one of such pleas, such judgment will, for that reason only, be set aside by the appellate court." Bennett *v.* Jackson, 34 W. Va. 62, 11 S. E. 734.

These decisions were rendered in a great variety of cases; in actions of debt, detinue, trespass on the case, assumpsit, writ of right, indictments and ejectments. In Ruffner *v.* Hill, 21 W. Va. 152, which was an action of eject-ment, the grounds of these decisions are stated thus: "By the common law the court had no right to make up the issue and impanel a jury to try it; but the parties by their pleading must first come to an issue, and then it is tried by a jury. When, therefore, the record shows that the parties by their pleadings have not come to any issue, but nevertheless the record shows that the issue was tried, this issue must either have been illegally made up by the court or by a blunder; it must have been assumed to have been made up by the parties, when in fact it was not."

In the case of Brown *v.* Cunningham, 23 W. Va. 109, it was held, that "a judgment based on a verdict in an action of ejectment or in any other action, civil or criminal, will be reversed by the appellate court if the record shows there was no issue made up between the plaintiff and defendant by the pleadings in the case." White *v.* Emblem, 43 W. Va. 819, 28 S. E. 761, 763.

In the case of State *v.* Douglass, 20 W. Va. 770, 771, it appears that the case was tried when no issue had been made up, and, although the case was presented to the jury precisely as though the issue had been made up, yet the attorney general conceded that, inasmuch as it appeared from the record that no plea was entered by the prisoner, the judgment of the court below should be reversed; and the court held that this was a fatal error, and that the court could not, on such a verdict, render any judgment, and proceeded to set aside the verdict, reverse the judgment, and remand the case. White *v.* Emblem, 43 W. Va. 819, 28 S. E. 761, 763.

The record not disclosing with certainty whether special pleas were filed, or if filed, showing that no replications were filed thereto, and no issues joined thereon, it was error to try the cause, and the judgment entered upon the verdict must be reversed. Williams v. Knight, 7 W. Va. 335.

Notwithstanding Verdict against Party Failing to Meet Affirmative Pleading of Opponent.—If a jury be impanelled to try the issue joined when, in reality, no issue is joined, the judgment must be reversed, and the verdict set aside, notwithstanding it was against the party who failed to meet, by a negative on his side, the affirmative matter pleaded on the other side. Wilkinson v. Bennett, 3 Munf. 314; Totty v. Donald, 4 Munf. 430; Taylors v. Huston, 2 Hen. & M. 161; Stevens v. Taliaferro, 1 Wash. 155; Kerr v. Dixon, 2 Call 379.

A judgment for the plaintiff in assumpsit, should be set aside, and a new trial granted, if there was no plea by the defendant. Johnson v. Fry, 88 Va. 695, 12 S. E. 973, 14 S. E. 183. See also, Petty v. Frick Co., 86 Va. 501, 10 S. E. 886.

If the intervention of a jury is waived and the evidence is heard by the court and judgment rendered, without issue having been joined, it is as equally erroneous as though the case had been tried by a jury. Baltimore, etc., R. Co. v. Faulkner, 4 W. Va. 180; Stevens v. Taliaferro, 1 Wash. 155.

The want of a similiter will not, after a trial, vitiate the verdict, and, as provided by Va. Code, 1860, ch. 181, § 3, it is not error after verdict. Brewer v. Tarpley, 1 Wash. 363; Baltimore, etc., R. Co. v. Faulkner, 4 W. Va. 180.

Determination of all Issues.—Where in an action of detinue for five slaves, the jury find for the plaintiff as to four of them, without also finding for the plaintiff or defendant, as to the fifth, the verdict will be set aside and a venire facias de novo awarded. Butler v. Parks, 1 Wash. 76.

Where issues are joined on the pleas of nul tiel record, and the act of limi-

tations, if the jury find for the plaintiff on the second plea, and the court, without taking any notice of the first plea, enters judgment, such judgment ought to be reversed, notwithstanding, on previous pleadings, which by consent were set aside, the court had pronounced · that, in fact, there was such a record. Gee v. Hamilton, 6 Munf. 32.

If a defendant pleads and demurs to the whole declaration, and the demurrer is overruled, judgment ought not to be entered, without first trying the issues joined on the other pleas. Waller v. Ellis, 2 Munf. 88.

In Morgantown Bank v. Foster, 35 W. Va. 357, 363, 13 S. E. 996, 997, issue was joined on a plea of nonassumpsit. The defendant then filed two special pleas, to which the plaintiff demurred. The lower court overruled the demurrer and gave final judgment for the defendant. The court of appeals held, that this was error, as there should have been no final judgment without the issue on the plea of nonassumpsit having been tried, withdrawn or otherwise disposed of. The court, citing Wilson v. Davisson, 5 Munf. 178, as authority, said: "It was error to give final judgment against the plaintiff with the issue on the plea of nonassumpsit left standing and undetermined. There could properly be no final judgment until the issue joined upon the plea of nonassumpsit was tried."

2. Conformity to Pleadings and Proofs.

a. In General.

Confined to Case Made by Pleadings.—It is a well-settled rule of pleading that judgment or decree can only be entered on the case as made by the pleadings; and evidence of matter not noticed in the pleadings will be of no avail, though it might show a right to a further judgment or decree. Welfley v. Shenandoah Iron, etc., Co., 83 Va.

768, 3 S. E. 376; Hubbard v. Blow, 4 Call 224; Gregory v. Peoples, 80 Va. 355; Edichal, etc., Co. v. Columbia, etc., Co., 87 Va. 641, 13 S. E. 100; Kent v. Kent, 82 Va. 205; Mundy v. Vawter, 3 Gratt. 518; Swope v. Chambers, 2 Gratt. 319; Blair v. Thompson, 11 Gratt. 449; Southall v. Farish, 85 Va. 403, 410, 7 S. E. 534; Adkins v. Edwards, 83 Va. 300, 305, 2 S. E. 435; Rorer Iron Co. v. Trout, 83 Va. 397, 2 S. E. 713; Potomac Mfg. Co. v. Evans, 84 Va. 717, 6 S. E. 2; Staples v. Staples, 85 Va. 76, 7 S. E. 199; Shenandoah Valley R. Co. v. Dunlop, 86 Va. 346, 350, 10 S. E. 239; Roanoke Gas Co. v. Roanoke, 88 Va. 810, 818, 14 S. E. 665; Tarter v. Wilson, 95 Va. 19, 25, 27 S. E. 618; Hunter v. Hunter, 10 W. Va. 321; Burley v. Weller, 14 W. Va. 264; Lamb v. Cecil, 25 W. Va. 288; Lamb v. Pannell, 25 W. Va. 298; Morris v. Peyton, 29 W. Va. 201, 11 S. E. 954; Smith v. Lowther, 35 W. Va. 300, 13 S. E. 999; Bland v. Stewart, 35 W. Va. 518, 14 S. E. 215; Roberts v. Coleman, 37 W. Va. 143, 16 S. E. 482; Vance Shoe Co. v. Haught, 41 W. Va. 275, 23 S. E. 553; Keneweg Co. v. Schilansky, 47 W. Va. 287, 34 S. E. 773. See the titles EQUITY, vol. 5, p. 125; PLEADING.

Variance between the declaration and the evidence, and between the judgment and the declaration, is error. Cook v. Berkley, 3 Call 378.

There can be no decree without allegations in the pleadings to support it. Coaldale Mining, etc., Co. v. Clark, 43 W. Va. 84, 27 S. E. 294.

Where there is no pleading to warrant a decree, or part of a decree, the decree, or such part of it, is not merely voidable, but void, as it is not on a matter in issue. Waldron v. Harvey, 54 W. Va. 608, 46 S. E. 603.

It is premature and erroneous to adjudicate and decide questions which are not properly presented in the pleadings, and to decree the payment of money by one party to another, when no such relief is sought or desired, and the proper parties are not all before the court. Donahoe v. Fackler, 8 W. Va. 249.

Although a plaintiff may present a good case by his proofs he is not entitled to a decree which is not justified by the allegations of his bill. Evans v. Kelley, 49 W. Va. 181, 38 S. E. 497.

When the evidence is defective as to a particular item, no decree should be made as to that. McConnico v. Curzen, 2 Call 358, 1 Am. Dec. 540.

A decree must be justified by the pleadings as well as by the proofs. Lang v. Smith, 37 W. Va. 725, 17 S. E. 213; Fadley v. Tomlinson, 41 W. Va. 606, 24 S. E. 645.

No rule is better settled than that a judgment or decree must be restricted to the case made by the pleadings, no matter what the evidence may show. Potomac Mfg. Co. v. Evans, 84 Va. 717, 6 S. E. 2; Mundy v. Vawter, 3 Gratt. 518; Campbell v. Bowles, 30 Gratt. 652.

A plaintiff must allege as well as prove the facts on which he claims relief. He can not obtain relief on any ground not alleged in his bill. Currey v. Lawler, 29 W. Va. 111, 11 S. E. 897.

For a plaintiff is no more entitled to recover without sufficient averments in his bill, than he is without proof of his averments when properly made. The one is as essential as the other, and both must concur or relief can not be granted. Pusey v. Gardner, 21 W. Va. 469.

In Gibson v. Green, 89 Va. 524, 526, 16 S. E. 661, the court said: "It is, moreover, a general rule, universally recognized, that a decree has to be founded on the allegata as well as the probata of the case; otherwise the pleadings, instead of being a shield to protect parties from surprise, would be a snare to entrap them. Putnam v. Day, 22 Wall. 60; Mundy v. Vawter, 3 Gratt. 518; 1 Bart. Ch. Pr. 260."

Equitable Relief Limited to Allegations and Prayer of Bill.—While a court of equity having jurisdiction for one purpose may go on and give full relief as to all matters comprehended under the allegations of fact in the pleadings, yet it is limited in its relief to the allegations of the bill or other pleading, and can not decree beyond their scope. Waldron v. Harvey, 54 W. Va. 608, 46 S. E. 603.

The allegations of the bill must correspond with the proof; and a decree based on a different case from that stated in the bill will be reversed. Bier v. Smith, 25 W. Va. 830, citing McFarland v. Dilly, 5 W. Va. 135; Baugher v. Eichelberger, 11 W. Va. 217; Floyd v. Jones, 19 W. Va. 359; Lamb v. Laughlin, 25 W. Va. 300.

When the pleadings contain no proper prayer therefor, it is error to decree affirmative relief. Harrison v. Brewster, 38 W. Va. 294, 18 S. E. 568; Middleton v. Selby, 19 W. Va. 167, 168.

A prayer for general relief will authorize a decree upon matter of the bill, though such decree is not asked by a prayer for specific relief; but not unless the matter of the bill warrants the decree in law. Waldron v. Harvey, 54 W. Va. 608, 46 S. E. 603.

It is well settled that when the bill contains allegations to support a decree and a prayer for general relief, a decree may be predicated thereon, although not specifically prayed for. Furbee v. Furbee, 49 W. Va. 191, 202, 38 S. E. 511; Vance Shoe Co. v. Haught, 41 W. Va. 275, 23 S. E. 553; Goff v. Price, 42 W. Va. 384, 26 S. E. 287; Bart. Chy. Pr., 281. Stewart v. Tennant, 52 W. Va. 559, 565, 44 S. E. 223, 231. See the title EQUITY, vol. 5, p. 125.

If matter appear in the answer of a defendant in equity, which is nowise alleged in the bill, it can not justify a decree against the defendant, though it might have been ground for such de-

cree if it had been alleged in the bill. Eib v. Martin, 5 Leigh 132.

When the answer of the defendant contains a claim which has no connection with the relief sought in the bill, and is not necessary to be considered in deciding the case as made by the bill, and the court in its decree expresses an opinion in favor of the defendant, this decree does not conclude the question when it is afterwards set up by the defendant in a cross bill in the cause. Niday v. Harvey, 9 Gratt. 454.

No decree can be found upon matters in a cross bill, which are not stated in the original bill, for as to them it is an original bill. Hansford v. Chesapeake Coal Co., 22 W. Va. 70.

Decree a nullity against persons not named in bill and against whom no allegations made or relief sought. See ante, "Judgments for or against Persons Not Parties," III, D, 2.

b. Applications of Rule.

If there be no count in the declaration based on the claim specified in a bill of particulars which by statute is declared to be no part of the declaration, the items it contains can not be proved, and no recovery can be had therefor. Riley v. Jarvis, 43 W. Va. 43, 26 S. E. 366.

Where a bill is filed for the sole purpose of having a certain paper, purporting to be a deed, declared a nullity, the court can not decree, upon such pleadings, that it be converted into a valid and proper deed, this not being prayed for in the bill. Miller v. Smoot, 86 Va. 1050, 11 S. E. 983.

Upon a bill for specific execution of an agreement, the agreement alleged in the bill must be proved by the evidence, and specific execution can only be decreed of the same agreement so alleged and proved, and specific execution must not be directed of a different contract. Pigg v. Corder, 12 Leigh 69.

Where a suit is brought in the county court, by a widow, for the sole purpose of having her dower assigned, and the court, after assigning dower, of its own accord decreed a sale of the residue of the land, the court transcended its jurisdiction, and its decree of sale is void. Seamster v. Blackstock, 83 Va. 232, 2 S. E. 36.

Damages beyond Those Claimed.— See generally, the title DAMAGES, vol. 4, p. 216.

As to damages in debt on bonds with collateral conditions, see the title BONDS, vol. 2, p. 573.

As to recovery of interest, see the title INTEREST, vol. 7, p. 819, and also above cross references.

Debts of Heirs Not Enforceable in Suit to Charge Ancestor's Estate.—A suit against a decedent's representative to charge his estate with a debt, the pleadings in which contain no allegation of debts against his heirs, and ask no relief as to their debts against land descended to them from such decedent, can not be made the vehicle of ascertaining and enforcing personal debts of such heirs against such land, and any decree entered therein as to that matter will be a nullity. Fowler v. Lewis, 36 W. Va. 112, 14 S. E. 447.

Single Creditor's Bill—Account of All Debts Erroneous.—In a single creditor's bill against all lienors on a tract of land designated in the bill, but which was not a general creditors' bill, it is an error to decree an account to be taken of all the debts due by the defendant, and which are valid liens on his land, their amounts and priorities. Such account not being asked by the bill, parties in interest may be taken by surprise. Baugher v. Eichelberger, 11 W. Va. 217.

Personal Decree against Trustee in Suit to Collect Debt of Cestui Que Trust.—Where there was no misconduct in the trustee of a married woman, it was error to enter a personal decree against him in a suit brought to enforce collection of a debt of his cestui que trust. Woodson v. Perkins, 5 Gratt. 345.

Judgment beyond Scope of Notice to Sheriff.—A notice to a sheriff and his sureties being of a motion for a balance of certain land, property and taxes, and the judgment being for a balance due upon these and also for a license, this is error for which the judgment will be reversed in the appellate court. Monteith v. Com., 15 Gratt. 172.

F. CONFORMITY TO VERDICT.
1. In General.

See generally, the titles SENTENCE AND PUNISHMENT; VERDICT.

In an action for defamation the trial court has no power to enter judgment for five dollars only, where the verdict was for that sum and costs; if the verdict is irregular, it should be set aside and a new trial awarded. The court had no power to change the verdict and then render judgment on it. Blackwell v. Landreth, 90 Va. 748, 19 S. E. 791.

In Lee v. Tapscott, 2 Wash. 276, a judgment in ejectment was reversed because it was for the land in the declaration mentioned when the verdict was for the plaintiff according to certain lines, upon the survey made in the cause.

Where, upon a trial for murder, the jury finds the prisoner guilty of involuntary manslaughter, and assesses upon him a fine of five hundred dollars, it is error for the court to enter a judgment discharging the prisoner. Such a judgment is not supported by the verdict. Price v. Com., 4 Va. Law J. 426, 33 Gratt. 819, 36 Am. Rep. 797.

In an action for damages the judgment should be for the amount assessed by the jury as damages and interest on this amount from the day the judgment is actually rendered, and not from the first day of the term at which the judgment is rendered. Hawker *v.* Baltimore, etc., R. Co., 15 W. Va. 628. See the title INTEREST, vol. 7, p. 819.

Where in an action of debt on a check, the declaration demands a sum certain with interest, and the verdict is simply for "the amount of the debt in the declaration mentioned," then, under § 2853 of the Virginia Code, judgment may be given "for the principal and charges of protest, with interest thereon from the date of such protest." Such a judgment is in conformity both with the verdict and the statute. Lake *v.* Tyree, 90 Va. 719, 19 S. E. 787.

As to what variance between a verdict and judgment in ejectment will be permitted, see Camden *v.* Haskill, 3 Rand. 462. And see the title EJECTMENT, vol. 4, p. 871.

2. Judgment Non Obstante Veredicto.

In General.—The court may refuse to receive a plea which presents an immaterial issue, or may strike it out if it has been filed, or may, either during the progress of the trial or after verdict, set aside the issue, or, in a proper case, render judgment notwithstanding the verdict. Duval *v.* Malone, 14 Gratt. 24.

"The court of its own motion, even after verdict, may disregard the finding of immaterial facts; and in a proper case judgment may be rendered non obstante veredicto; or if the case be not in a condition to warrant a judgment, a repleader may be awarded. 1 Rob. Prac. (old ed.) 222; Beale *v.* Botetourt Justices, 10 Gratt. 278; Boyles *v.* Overby, 11 Gratt. 202, and the cases there cited." Duval *v.* Malone, 14 Gratt. 24.

When Rendered for Plaintiff.— Where the only issue, in an action, is upon a plea in confession and avoidance, upon which a verdict has been found for the defendant, and it is afterwards decided that such plea is bad in substance, judgment should be entered for the plaintiff non obstante veredicto. Mason *v.* Harper's Ferry Bridge Co., 28 W. Va. 639, 640.

When Rendered for Defendant.— An action for deceit, practiced in a sale, not being maintainable against the personal representative of the deceased, therefore, though there is a verdict for the plaintiff, judgment non obstante veredicto should be rendered for the defendant. Boyles *v.* Overby, 11 Gratt. 202.

Verdict Unambiguous — Plaintiff's Case Defective.—If a verdict is imperfect by reason of any ambiguity or uncertainty, so that the court can not say for which party judgment ought to be given, a venire de novo ought to be awarded. Brown *v.* Ralston, 4 Rand. 504. But if the verdict be not ambiguous or uncertain in itself, but the case made by the plaintiff is a defective case, or defective title, then the judgment should be for the defendant, and a venire de novo should not be granted. Brown *v.* Ferguson, 4 Leigh 37, 24 Am. Dec. 707.

IV. Form of Judgment or Decree.

A. IN GENERAL.

By What Law Governed.—The law of the place where the suit is brought governs the remedy. This includes the mode of proceeding, the form of the judgment or decree, and the modes of carrying them into execution. Dulin *v.* McCaw, 39 W. Va. 721, 20 S. E. 681, 682.

Form Not Material if Fact of Judicial Determination Appears.—"It is essential to a judgment that it be a judicial determination, and adjudication by the court. If this appear, the form is not so material. Consideratum est per curiam, etc., is the old technical formula and the one generally followed; but a literal observance of it, although advisable, is not indispensable; language of like import will suffice." Bank *v.* McVeigh, 32 Gratt. 530.

Judgment on forthcoming bond, instead of awarding execution thereon, is, that plaintiff recover the debt against defendants. Held, irregular in form, yet well in substance. Harpers *v.* Patton, 1 Leigh 306.

Conclusion.—In trespass against an administrator for goods taken away by the intestate, judgment ought not to be reversed, for concluding, "and the defendant may be taken, etc.," instead of "and the defendant in mercy, etc." Vaughan *v.* Winckler, 4 Munf. 136. See the title TRESPASS.

"The usual form of a decree is: 'This cause came on this day to be heard, upon the papers heretofore read,' etc. Certainly it is not error to specify what papers were read, if the court prefers that style instead of the shorter form; and if the court deems proper to consider the whole record of its former proceedings in the cause before entering its decree, I can not see the impropriety in stating the fact in the decree, but it is right and proper." Linsey *v.* McGannon, 9 W. Va. 154.

As to the power of a court of equity to mould its decrees according to the circumstances of the particular case and to embrace and finally dispose of the rights of the parties, see the title JURISDICTION.

As to the form of particular judgments, see ante, "Classification of Judgments and Decrees," II. And see the specific titles.

B. DEFINITENESS AND CERTAINTY.

In General.—The general rule seems to be, that the judgment, being the voice of the law pronounced by the court on the matter in controversy, should be so certain as to leave nothing doubtful or unsettled. Thus, a judgment "that the plaintiff recover damages and expenses according to law, and the rules and regulations of the society" without specifying the amount or nature of damages and expenses, is erroneous for uncertainty. Stratton *v.* Mutual Assurance Soc., 6 Rand. 22.

If the judgment is ambiguous in its terms, the appellate court can not make it certain, upon the ground that the clerk of the county court might have moulded it into form, because it was only an entry on the minutes. Humphreys *v.* West, 3 Rand. 516.

An attachment ought not to be awarded against a party for refusing obedience to a decree, which as yet remains general and uncertain, and the extent of which, as it relates to him, he can not ascertain without applying to the court for a farther decree. Birchett *v.* Bolling, 5 Munf. 442. See the title CONTEMPT, vol. 3, p. 242.

A judgment subject to an uncertain credit is erroneous. The amount of the credit should be first ascertained by a writ of inquiry, and judgment should be rendered for the balance. Early *v.* Moore, 4 Munf. 262.

A judgment ought not to be entered on a bond for the sum of money, "subject to a credit for a hogshead of tobacco" without ascertaining its value; but the amount of such credit should in the first place, be ascertained by a writ of inquiry, and judgment should be rendered for the balance. Early *v.* Moore, 4 Munf. 262.

But it seems, that a verdict for a certain sum of money, with interest from a day specified, subject to a credit (without saying on what day such credit is to be applied) is not so uncertain as that the plaintiff can not take judgment upon it, and a judgment, in such case, for the damages aforesaid, in form aforesaid assessed, sufficiently follows the verdict. Lanier *v.* Harwell, 6 Munf. 79.

A verdict and judgment which awards the debt claimed in the declaration with interest, subject to a specified credit paid at a specified date, is certain enough. Barrett *v.* Wills, 4 Leigh 114, 26 Am. Dec. 315.

In Myers *v.* Williams, 85 Va. 621, 8 S. E. 483, a judgment allowing a conditional credit was sustained.

As to judgments conditional or alternative in form, see ante, "Conditional Judgments," II, H.

Sufficient if Judgment or Decree May Be Made Certain.—Where the bill and proceedings specifies the land, a decree for the sale of the land in the bill and proceedings mentioned, or so much as may satisfy the purposes of the decree, is sufficiently certain. That is certain which may be made certain, applied to the case. Barger *v.* Buckland, 28 Gratt. 850.

If the entry of the judgment, taken in connection with the record of the case in which it is made, has the requisite certainty of a judgment as to parties, amounts, dates, etc., the judgment is valid. Bank *v.* McVeigh, 32 Gratt. 530.

A decree ought not to be reversed for uncertainty, in matters, as to which it is only interlocutory, and may be perfected by application to the court. Birchett *v.* Bolling, 5 Munf. 442.

C. DATE.

The date of a decree or judgment, as shown by the record, marks the point of time from which the statute of limitation governing an appeal from, or writ of error thereto, commences to run. Cresap *v.* Cresap, 54 W. Va. 581, 46 S. E. 582.

It is believed to be the universal practice to state in the petition under § 3, ch. 135, of the Code of 1899, providing that: " 'No petition shall be presented for an appeal from, or writ of error or supersedeas to, any judgment, decree or order, whether the state be a party thereto or not, nor to any judgment of a circuit court or municipal court rendered in an appeal from

the judgment of a justice, which shall have been rendered or made more than two years before such petition is presented,' * * * the day on which the decree or judgment was made or entered, as the date of such decree or judgment. Such seems to be the construction placed upon the statute by the bar. No appeal from a decree, or writ of error to a judgment can be allowed; or correction thereof made under ch. 134 of the Code of 1899, until the same be entered on the record of the court. Certainly no execution can be issued thereon until the record thereof be made and signed by the judge. The execution must follow the judgment, and be supported by it. Freeman on Ex. 42; Herm. on Ev., vol. 1, § 42. It is a part, and continuation of the record." Cresap *v.* Cresap, 54 W. Va. 583, 46 S. E. 582. See the titles APPEAL AND ERROR, vol. 1, p. 499; EXECUTIONS, vol. 5, p. 416.

D. AMOUNT OF RECOVERY AND MEDIUM OF PAYMENT.

Statement of Amount, and Date from Which to Bear Interest.—A decree for money should state the amount which the defendant is to pay, and the date from which it is to bear interest. It is not sufficient to direct that the plaintiffs recover "the amounts of their respective notes and judgments, with interest thereon as separately and specifically set out in the bill." Spoor *v.* Tilson, 97 Va. 279, 33 S. E. 609.

As to judgments for costs, see the title COSTS, vol. 3, p. 604.

Judgment for One Amount to Be Discharged by Payment of Less Amount.—In Ross *v.* Gill, 1 Wash. 87, the judgment was for one amount (£490) to be discharged by the payment of a lesser amount. This last clause was held surplusage, and unwarranted by law, but, as the plaintiff did not complain, it was regarded as a release of so much of the judgment. At all events it was a defect of which the defendant could not complain.

Correction of Decree Erroneous as to Amount.—When the record of a cause clearly shows that a party has obtained a decree for an amount greater than he is entitled to by reason of some inadvertency or clerical error, such party may in the same court, at any future term, by an entry of record, release a part of the amount of such decree without notice to the adverse party. Shipman v. Bailey, 20 W. Va. 140.

"The decree complained of is for a greater amount that it should be, which is evidently occasioned by a miscalculation of interest. The decree is for three thousand and twenty-eight dollars and sixty cents, with interest, when it should be two thousand, eight hundred and ninety-two dollars and eighty cents, with interest. This error can be corrected in the court below under § 5, ch. 134, of the Code, page 637, and may be corrected in this court under § 6, same chapter. Connor v. Fleshman, 4 W. Va. 693." Pumphry v. Brown, 5 W. Va. 107, 110. See post, "Statutory Provisions," VII, B, 1, b, (2); "Motion," VII, B, 2, c.

Judgment for Sterling Money Value. —In an action of debt upon a protested bill of exchange drawn for sterling money, if the declaration is for the current money value of the sum for which the bill was drawn, the judgment being for the sum so demanded, will be reversed on a writ of error. The suit should have been for the sterling money. Scott v. Call. 1 Wash. 115; Skipwith v. Baird, 2 Wash. 135. In the latter case, Scott v. Call was distinguished on the ground that the damages were considered as being laid in current money, whereas they ought to have been laid in sterling money.

A sterling judgment may be reduced into currency at the time of entering judgment on the forthcoming bond. Scott v. Hornsby, 1 Call 41.

Fixing Rate of Exchange.—It is necessary on judgments for sterling money, that the court should fix the rate of exchange. Taylor v. M'Clean, 3 Call 557.

After the verdict for the plaintiff, in debt on a bond, the penalty of which was in current money, with condition to pay so much sterling money, the judgment should be for the current money mentioned in the penal part of the bond, to be discharged by the sterling money in the declaration, and the court ought to settle the rate of exchange, which on an appeal should appear on the record. Terrell v. Ladd, 2 Wash. 150.

Judgment for Certificate.—In a suit at common law, judgment can not be entered for certificates. Graves v. Webb, 1 Call 443.

Judgment for Confederate Notes.— It seems that a judgment on a contract for the payment of confederate notes, should be entered for confederate notes; the scale of depreciation must be applied at the day when the money was payable. Dearing v. Rucker, 18 Gratt. 426.

Judgment on a penal bond should be for the penalty, to be discharged by the payment of the sum actually due. Moore v. Fenwick, Gilmer 214.

In an action of debt on a bond, the judgment is always entered for the penalty to be discharged by the principal and interest; and if that exceed the penalty, the defendant has his election, and may satisfy it by paying the penalty. Atwell v. Towles, 1 Munf. 175.

In an action upon a sheriff's bond in the name of the commonwealth, for the benefit of a person aggrieved by the misconduct of the sheriff, the judgment should be entered for the penalty, to be discharged by the payment of the damages assessed and costs, "and such other damages as may be hereafter assessed upon suing out a scire facias, and assigning new breaches, by the plaintiff or any other person or persons injured." Bibb v. Cauthorne, 1 Wash. 91.

Judgment on Caveat.—A judgment, on a caveat, that no grant shall issue to the caveatee on his inclusive survey, where it appears that he has any other claim or survey, by which he may possibly hold a part of the land, ought to be so worded as not to affect his right under such claim or survey. Preston v. Harvey, 2 Hen. & M. 55.

E. STATEMENT IN DECREE AS TO COMPLIANCE WITH PRELIMINARIES TO HEARING.

It is not necessary to state, in a decree in chancery, that all the preliminary steps towards maturing the cause for hearing were taken; it being intended, where the cause is set for hearin, that it was regularly done, unless the party attempting to impugn the decree show the contrary. Quarrier v. Carter, 4 Hen. & M. 242.

"In 1 Harrison's Ch. Prac. 108 (old ed.), it is said, that, in drawing the decree, it is not held to be sufficient to recite therein the bill and answer, and then add that, upon reading the proofs, and hearing what was alleged on either side, it was decreed so and so; but that the facts which were proved and allowed by the court to be proved, must be particularly mentioned in the decree. It is nowhere said, however, that it is necessary, or proper, to insert in a decree, that all the previous and preliminary measures necessary to prepare a cause for hearing had been complied with, and therefore the omission of these in the decree would be no objection thereto. In the same book, p. 110, the form of a decree is given us, in which the substance of the proofs is stated in the decree, together with that of the bill and answer; but no other matters of the character last mentioned are stated therein. If, then, circumstances of this last description form, properly, no part

of the decree of the court, even in England, where the decrees are drawn very particularly and minutely by the register; and a bill of review of the kind we are now considering is confined to matters of error apparent on the face of the decree itself; an omission similar to that now alleged is no ground for a bill of review; for such circumstances neither do appear in practice, nor ought they properly to appear on the face of the decree itself." Quarrier v. Carter, 4 Hen. & M. 242.

It is the better practice for a decree to show on its face, that the cause was regularly matured for hearing, but it is not error to enter a decree in a cause which does not show this, if the cause was in fact matured for hearing. Riggs v. Lockwood, 12 W. Va. 133. See the title HEARING, vol. 7, p. 41.

F. ASSIGNMENT OF REASONS FOR JUDGMENT.

In General.—Every court ought to state, on record, legal grounds for their judgment; especially subordinate courts, liable to have their judgments reversed in a superior court. Preston v. Auditor, 1 Call 471.

If the decree of the trial court is right, the supreme court will affirm it, though it does not approve the reasons assigned by the trial court. Boyd v. Cleghorn, 94 Va. 780, 27 S. E. 574.

It is not necessary to assign in a decree any reason for the decision, and, if a decree is substantially right, it should be affirmed, although the court below may have given an erroneous or insufficient reason for its judgment. Ballard v. Chewning, 49 W. Va. 508, 39 S. E. 170; Newell v. Wood, 1 Munf. 555; Easley v. Craddock, 4 Rand. 423. See the title APPEAL AND ERROR, vol. 1, p. 624.

Duty of Supreme Court to State Reasons for Decision and to Prepare Syllabus.—See the title COURTS, vol. 3, p. 709.

The clause in the constitution of West Virginia, requiring the supreme court of that state to "decide every point, fairly arising upon the record, and give its reasons therefor in writing" is directory, and does not affect the common-law doctrine of res judicata. Henry v. Davis, 13 W. Va. 230; Hall v. Bank, 15 W. Va. 323.

V. Rendition and Entry.

See the titles CONFESSION OF JUDGMENTS, vol. 3, p. 73; JUSTICES OF THE PEACE.

A. DISTINCTION BETWEEN RENDITION AND ENTRY.

1. In General.

"Five or six sections of the Code, immediately succeeding § 114, show that the object of the legislature was to draw a marked distinction between the rendition of a judgment and its entry. When, therefore, in § 114, the legislature provides, 'In other cases judgment shall be entered within 24 hours (Sundays excepted), after the trial,' it is taking unwarranted liberty with their language to say that when they used the word 'entered' they meant 'rendered;' or to hold that the judgment, if rendered, might be entered after the lapse of not only twenty-four hours, but of 2 years after its rendition, as was attempted in this case." McClain v. Davis, 37 W. Va. 330, 16 S. E. 629, 630.

The distinction between rendition and entry that runs through all the cases seems to be that failure to comply with the statute as to entry, or errors or irregularities in the entry, do not vitiate the judgment, whereas this will make the rendition absolutely void. See Long v. Pence, 93 Va. 584, 25 S. E. 533; Roach v. Blakey, 89 Va. 767, 17 S. E. 228; Snead v. Coleman, 7 Gratt. 300, 305; McClain v. Davis, 37 W. Va. 330, 16 S. E. 629, dissenting opinion of Brannon, J.

2. As to Time of Rendition and Entry.

There is a marked distinction between the rendition and entry of a judgment, when its validity is attacked because not entered or rendered in time. Thus a failure to enter within the time prescribed by statute does not render the judgment void, whereas a judgment not rendered within such time is absolutely void. McClain v. Davis, 37 W. Va. 330, 16 S. E. 629, dissenting opinion of Brannon, J.; Packet Co. v. Bellville, 55 W. Va. 560, 47 S. E. 301.

Although the statute requires that a judgment of a justice shall be entered within twenty-four hours after trial (Sundays excepted) a judgment rendered within such time, but entered after the time thus directed, is not void. Packet Co. v. Bellville, 55 W. Va. 560, 47 S. E. 301.

Where a judgment in an action tried before a justice is rendered and publicly announced by the justice on the day and at the close of the trial, although the clerical work of entering the judgment upon his docket is not performed until a few days thereafter, the statute is substantially complied with. Packet Co. v. Bellville, 55 W. Va. 560, 47 S. E. 301.

In Hutchinson's Treatise, § 131, it is said: "Although the statute requires that a judgment of a justice shall be entered as we have seen without delay, or within twenty-four hours after trial (Sundays excepted) a judgment entered after the time or the day thus directed by the statute is not absolutely void. It is irregular but will be effectual as a judgment until reversed or properly set aside." Packet Co. v. Bellville, 55 W. Va. 560, 47 S. E. 301, citing McClain v. Davis, 37 W. Va. 300, 16 S. E. 629.

Judgment of Justice.—It has been held, where two justices presided at a trial at which a verdict was rendered, but no judgment thereon was entered, and subsequently, nearly two years afterwards, the same justices, without notice, met and undertook to enter a judgment upon the verdict nunc pro tunc, that such entry nunc pro tunc was unauthorized and illegal, and wa's properly treated by the circuit court as a nullity. McClain *v.* Davis, 37 W. Va. 330, 16 S. E. 629, Brannon, J., dissenting.

"The language of this court, as above quoted from the opinion, precluded the idea that the entry of a judgment within the time prescribed by the statute is not essential to its validity. But, secondly, were it otherwise, the language of the Code (see § 114, ch. 50), taken in connection with other provisions in pari materia, is too unequivocal to admit of misconstruction. Where the language is unambiguous, no ambiguity can be authorized by interpretation." McClain *v.* Davis, 37 W. Va. 330, 16 S. E. 629, 630.

Judgment Neither Rendered Nor Entered in Time.—"We do not have to decide whether, where it appears that both the rendering and the entry in the docket of a judgment by a justice took place after the time fixed therefor by statute, the judgment would be void, or merely irregular and reversible on appeal. In some states, especially Wisconsin, it is held void in several decisions; but the judge delivering the opinion in Wearne *v.* Smith, 32 Wis. 414, expressed himself dissatisfied with those decisions. In Watson *v.* Davis, 19 Wend. 371, which is urged upon us as authority to hold this judgment void, it is held, that it is 'erroneous,' and subject to reversal. In Martin *v.* Pifer, 96 Ind. 245, and Stillman *v.* McConnell, 36 Kan. 398, 13 Pac. Rep. 571, such judgments were held not void, but erroneous; and in Robinson *v.* Kious, 4 O. St. 593, Judge Thurman said the failure to render judgments within time might not make them void, but only irregular and reversible. Nothing is presumed in favor of the jurisdiction of inferior courts, but when once jurisdiction of the

cause and parties is established, as is clearly the case here, courts should be averse to holding mere missteps in the proceedings, mere irregularities, simple nullities, because to do so destroys rights of parties, and the maxim is that it is better that serious proceedings shall have force than fail. If, then, a judgment rendered and entered after the time fixed by law be not void, but simply erroneous, as I think it would be at worst, it could be reversed only by appeal; and as the motion to revive the judgment in this case stands as a scire facias in courts of record under the common law, mere irregularity could not avail as a defense to a writ of scire facias. Fost. Sci. Fa. 27; 12 Amer. & Eng. Enc. Law, 150; 1 Black, Judgm., 496." McClain *v.* Davis, 37 W. Va. 330, 16 S. E. 629, 633, dissenting opinion of Brannon, J.

Effect of Failure to Comply with Statutes.—"Though statute require judgment to be forthwith rendered and entered upon the return of a verdict, a judgment rendered·in due time will not be reversed because not entered in the docket until two or three days thereafter." Packet Co. *v.* Bellville, 55 W. Va. 560, 47 S. E. 301.

B. RENDITION.

1. Time of Rendition.

a. Judgments in Criminal Cases.

Upon an indictment in the county court against C. the jury render a verdict of guilty, and that he be imprisoned in the county jail for ten months, and pay a fine of ten dollars. No judgment on the verdict is entered at that term, nor is the case continued; but at the next term of the court the judgment is rendered. Before the ten months has expired, C. escapes from jail, and is afterwards retaken. Held, the cause was pending in court, and it was proper to render the judgment on the verdict at the next term of the court. Cleek *v.* Com., 21 Gratt. 777.

"The verdict did not finally dispose of the case, but was merely an interlocutory proceeding in it. Notwithstanding the verdict, the case was still pending, and stood over for judgment, which might have been rendered on the same day, or on a subsequent day of the same term, or might be rendered at a subsequent term. There could have been no doubt of this, if the case had been continued on the record for judgment, either to another day of the same term, or to a subsequent term. But no such continuance was entered on the record; and the only question is, whether the omission of such an entry on the record worked a discontinuance of the case. Now, that very question is expressly answered by the statute, and no other answer is needed. The Code, p. 686, ch. 161, § 16, declares that 'all causes upon the docket of any court, and all other matters ready for its decision, which shall not have been determined before the end of a term, whether regular or special, shall, without any order of continuance, stand continued to the next term.' And again, at p. 834, ch. 207, § 26, in special reference to criminal cases, the Code declares that 'there shall be no discontinuance of any criminal prosecution by reason of the failure of the court to award process or to enter a continuance on the record.' It follows that the first question must be determined in the affirmative, and that the county court of Bath had power, at the August term of the court, to render judgment on the verdict found at the preceding July term of the court." Cleek *v.* Com., 21 Gratt. 777.

b. **In Vacation.**

J. files his bill in the circuit court of Wood county, in the fourth judicial circuit, praying an injunction and for relief. The injunction was awarded, the cause removed to the circuit court of Ritchie county, in the second judicial circuit, and various proceedings there taken in the cause. The January term, 1872, of that court was held by the judge of the fourth judicial circuit instead of the judge of the second judicial circuit, but no decree or proceedings were had in the cause at that term, so far as the record shows. The judge of the fourth judicial circuit, after the adjournment of the circuit court of Ritchie county at its January term, in vacation, rendered a final decree in the cause dissolving the injunction and dismissing the bill at the complainant's costs. It concludes, "And by agreement of parties, it is ordered that this decree be entered among the proceedings of the next term of the circuit court of Wood county." At the April term, 1872, of the circuit court of Ritchie, held by its judge, the judge of the second judicial circuit, a decree was rendered in the cause, which first recited that at the January term, 1872, of said court, held by the judge of the fourth judicial circuit, the cause had been argued by counsel, and an agreement and consent was made in open court by the parties thereto, in person and by counsel, that the papers might be taken and the cause decided in vacation, and that any decree so made should be entered in the circuit court of Wood county at its then next term; and that it appeared that said cause was so decided in vacation by said judge of the fourth judicial circuit, and that his decree had been returned to the clerk of this court setting forth the final decree aforesaid rendered by the judge of the fourth judicial circuit, and then proceeded to order the papers of the cause to be transmitted to the clerk of the circuit court of Wood county, and that the said decree rendered by the judge of the fourth judicial circuit in vacation be entered on the chancery order book of the said court, at the next term thereof. At said next term of the circuit court of Wood county, a decree was entered in said cause, which first recited the transmission of the papers in the cause to the clerk of that court. It then proceeded to order the docketing of the cause in that court, and then ordered the said decree of the April term, 1872, of the circuit court of Ritchie county to be entered verbatim, which was done. Held, the judge of the circuit court of Wood county ought not, pursuant to this order of the circuit court of Ritchie county, to have entered this decree made in vacation, and it did not do this when it entered the decree of the circuit court of Ritchie county, which merely recited this decree rendered in vacation. That no order having been made at the January term, 1872, of the circuit court of Ritchie county, that by consent of parties the cause might be decided in vacation, even if that term of the court had been held by the regular judge of that circuit, his decree in vacation would have been unauthorized and void; it not being decided whether, if such consent order had been made and entered on the record book, a decree rendered in vacation by the regular judge of that circuit would or would not be void. The judge of the circuit court of Ritchie county had no authority to order the decree, which had been made by the judge of the fourth judicial circuit in vacation, to be entered upon the chancery order book of the circuit court of Wood county. The appellate court will not dismiss the appeal in this cause, because, the decrees aforesaid were rendered without sufficient authority, but will take jurisdiction of the cause and decrees so far, and so far only as to reverse these decrees, and remand the cause to the circuit court of Wood county, there to be proceeded with and heard and determined according to the rules and usages governing courts of equity in this state. It is not proper for the appellate court to determine and decree upon the merits of the cause, as the cause has never been heard or acted upon either by the circuit court of Ritchie county, or the circuit court of Wood county, but only by the judge of the fourth judicial circuit in vacation, who had no authority to render such decree, or decide the cause. Johnson v. Young, 11 W. Va. 673.

c. Adjourned Term.

Upon the above facts it was further held, that on the adjournment of the January term, 1872, of the court the judicial power of the judge of the fourth judicial circuit to render a final decree in this cause ceased; and even if such consent decree that he might decide finally the cause in vacation had been entered, it would have conferred no such power upon him. Johnson v. Young, 11 W. Va. 673.

d. Doctrine of Relation.

See post, "Judgment Liens," VI.

2. Several Defendants.

Where only one of several defendants has been served with process, judgment may be rendered against him. Code, 1873, ch. 167, § 50; Norfolk, etc., R. Co. v. Shippers Compress Co., 83 Va. 272, 2 S. E. 139.

3. Mandamus to Compel Rendition.

When an affidavit is filed of the amount which the plaintiff is entitled to recover, prescribed in § 46, ch. 125, W. Va. Code, 1899, in a case wherein there is an office judgment, but no order for an inquiry of damages, and the defendant fails to plead to issue at the next term after such office judgment, it is the duty of the court to render judgment for the plaintiff upon such affidavit, and such duty being ministerial, mandamus lies to enforce its performance. Marstiller v. Ward, 52 W. Va. 74, 75, 43 S. E. 178, followed in Hutton v. Holt, 52 W. Va. 672, 44 S. E. 164.

4. Judgment as Evidence of Rendition.

See the title FORMER ADJUDICATION OR RES ADJUDICATA, vol. 6, p. 338.

C. ENTRY.

1. Terms Defined.

"Our statute says the judgment must be 'entered' within the time. What does the word 'entered' here mean? It means that judgment must be rendered —pronounced—within the time, but not necessarily entered in the docket within that time. In Conwell v. Kuykendall, 29 Kan. 707, though the section of the statute required judgment within four days, the court said, to obviate difficulty, the word 'entered' should be interpreted as 'rendered;' that when the justice formed his mind, and announced it, that was judgment, while recording it afterwards would do; that it was the almost universal practice in all courts to announce judgments, and afterwards record them. That the word 'entered,' in § 114, means 'rendered,' is shown from the fact that the justice is to ascertain balance after credits, and enter judgment, thus showing that it means the formation and decision of the mind as to the legal result of the case; and it is shown by the further important fact that it is other sections (178 and 179) which command him to enter certain things in the docket, among them the judgment. The judgment of the justice shall be stated; that is, the one already entered or announced." McClain v. Davis, 37 W. Va. 330, 16 S. E. 629, 631, dissenting opinion of Brannon, J.

"**What is a judgment?** Upon such a question as that involved in this case, we must have a correct conception of what it is. The docket entry is not the judgment, but only evidence that a judgment was rendered. Judgment is what is ordered and considered; not the mere entry of what is ordered and considered. We sometimes speak of the record entry as the judgment, but it is no more the judgment, accurately speaking, than a note for money is the money or debt itself. Hickey v. Hinsdale, 8 Mich. 267. A judgment is the 'decision or sentence of the law, pronounced by a court or other competent tribunal, upon the matter contained in the record.' 3 Black, Comm. 395; Jac. Law Dict.; Freem. Judgm., § 2. When, after the facts are found, the court pronounces the decision of them, that is the judgment." McClain v. Davis, 37 W. Va. 330, 16 S. E. 629, 631, dissenting opinion of Brannon, J.

2. What Constitutes the Entry.

"The question as to what constitutes the entry is an entirely different one. All that can be said upon that subject is that the very least required to give validity to the judgment is some written evidence contained in the papers or on the docket that it has been rendered, and this writing must be made within the twenty-four hours (Sundays excepted), as prescribed by the statute." McClain v. Davis, 37 W. Va. 330, 16 S. E. 629, 630.

3. Entry a Judicial or Ministerial Act.

The entry of judgment is in no respect the exercise of judicial power but the performance of a mere ministerial act. "An omission, therefore, to make such an entry will not render the entire proceedings a nullity. It may be made by the justice at any time, and will, for the purpose of sustaining the proceedings, be regarded as made." Packet Co. v. Bellville, 55 W. Va. 560, 564, 47 S. E. 301; Marstiller v. Ward, 52 W. Va. 74, 84, 43 S. E. 178, followed in Hutton v. Holt, 52 W. Va. 672, 44 S. E. 164.

After a justice has rendered and publicly announced his judgment in an action at the close of the trial, the entry thereof upon the justice's docket is purely ministerial, and not judicial. Packet Co. v. Bellville, 55 W. Va. 560, 47 S. E. 301.

4. Form of Entry.
a. In General.

A failure to comply with the statute as to the form of entry makes the judgment voidable and not void. Chalfants *v.* Martin, 25 W. Va. 394, 398.

b. Expressions in Entry.

In a proceeding by an assignee of a note against a remote assignor to recover on the contract implied by the assignment, the note is a necessary piece of evidence for the plaintiff in order to prove the assignment, and also to show the measure of the plaintiff's recovery; for, in the absence of proof to the contrary, the law presumes that the assignor received for the note a sum equal to that specified in it. The fact that the note was seen and inspected by the court need not be expressed in the entry of the judgment, but the expression of it does not vitiate the judgment, nor show that the judgment was rendered on the note, and not on the contract implied from the assignment. Long *v.* Pence, 93 Va. 584, 25 S. E. 593.

c. Entry "Subject to Control of Court."

In an action to subject the land of a debtor to the payment of a judgment, the land was rented by order of court to the debtor himself, and he executed to the commissioner five notes for the rent. Two of the notes were paid, and on default in the payment of the third proceedings were taken against the debtor and his sureties, which resulted in an order for the rerenting of the land for the term of one year, for enough to pay the amount due on the rent note. This judgment was suspended, but, instead of taking an appeal, the debtor obtained an injunction against the enforcement of the decree, and from the order dissolving the injunction, and from the order for rerenting, the debtor appealed. This appeal and supersedeas the debtor set up in a plea in abatement in an action against him on another of the rent notes. Held, that it was proper to overrule the plea, and enter judgment "subject to the control of the court," in the action on the first note. As the judgment was entered "subject to the control of the court" in the former action, there was no occasion for a writ of error. Moore *v.* Peirce, 1 Va. Dec. 698.

d. Conformity to Verdict.

See ante, "Requisites of Valid Judgments or Decrees," III.

In an action for defamation the trial court has no power to enter judgment for five dollars only, where the verdict was for that sum and costs, but if the verdict was irregular, it should have been set aside and a new trial awarded. Blackwell *v.* Landreth, 90 Va. 748, 19 S. E. 791.

e. Judgments of Appellate Court.

See the title MANDATE AND PROCEEDINGS THEREON.

The provision of § 4060 of the Code requiring the judgment of the appellate court to be certified to the trial court and entered by the latter as its judgment is substantially complied with by simply transcribing the judgment of the appellate court on the order book of the trial court. Reed *v.* Com., 98 Va. 817, 36 S. E. 399.

5. Time of Entry.

a. In General.

See ante, "Distinction between Rendition and Entry," V, A.

b. In Vacation.

In General.—A court has no power to enter an order or judgment in vacation, unless so authorized by statute. Kinports *v.* Rawson, 29 W. Va. 487, 2 S. E. 85; Johnson *v.* Young, 11 W. Va. 673; Monroe *v.* Bartlett, 6 W. Va. 441.

A decree confirming a report of liens disposes of the cause on its merits, and can not be entered in vacation except by consent of parties, as provided in § 3427 of the Virginia Code. Harris *v.* Jones, 96 Va. 658, 32 S. E. 455.

Entry by Consent of Parties—The Statute.—Any motion, action at law, or chancery cause, pending in a circuit, or corporation court, or any matter of law or fact, arising in such motion, action at law, or chancery cause, may, by consent of parties, either in person or by counsel, next friend or guardian ad litem, in term time entered of record, or by like consent in vacation, be submitted to the judge of said court for such decision and decree, judgment, or order, therein in vacation as might be made in term (and such court may, either in term or vacation, without such consent, when it desires time to consider of its judgment as to any motion, action at law, chancery cause, or matter of law, or fact arising therein, which has been fully argued and submitted, direct such motion, action at law, chancery cause, or matter of law, or fact, to be submitted for decision, and decree, judgment, or order in vacation); provided, that no such consent shall be necessary as to any defendant against whom the cause, action, or motion has been matured by order of publication, and who has not appeared by motion, demurrer, plea, or answer. When such consent is in vacation, the judge shall certify the fact to the clerk of the court in which the motion, action at law, or chancery cause is pending, to be entered in the law, or chancery order book, as the case may be. The judge acting in vacation under this section, in addition to the other powers herein given to him, shall have authority to do any and all things, and to enter all judgments, decrees, or orders, in behalf of, or at the request of, a party desiring to make an appeal, or to apply for a writ of error, that the court might do, or enter, in term time. The judge shall certify the judgments, orders and decrees made by him in vacation to the clerk aforesaid, to be entered in like manner as the vacation consent. All judgments, orders, and decrees so made and entered, shall have the same force and effect as if made and entered in term, except that in the case of a judgment, order, or decree for money, the same shall be effective only from the time of day at which it is received in the clerk's office to be entered of record. (1872-73, p. 18; 1884, p. 57; 1895-96, p. 177; 1897-98, p. 754; 1901-02, p. 729; 1902-03-04, p. 77; 1904, p. 312.) Va. Code, 1904, § 3427.

Illustrative Cases.—A decree adjudicating adverse claims or rights, entered by the judge of a circuit court in vacation, by consent of the parties previously given in court and entered on the record, is erroneous and, perhaps, void; sed quære, will so much of such decree, as constitutes simply an order or direction ex parte and administrative in its character, be held erroneous, if proper in itself, merely because it was thus entered in vacation? It is held, not to be void. Gilmer v. Baker, 24 W. Va. 72.

Virginia Code, 1773, ch. 167, § 53, provides that any chancery cause may, by consent, be submitted to the judge of the court, wherein pending for determination in vacation. Act of July 11th, 1870 (acts, 1869-70, p. 427), athorizes, in certain events, the judge of the hustings court of the city of Richmond to perform any duty required by law of the judge of the chancery court. Where such cause pending in the chancery court of said city was, by consent (the infant defendants being represented by guardian ad litem), submitted July 8th, 1873, to the judge thereof for decrees in vacation, and a decree beneficial to said infants was entered in vacation by the judge of the said hustings court, acting as judge of said chancery court; held, the judge of the hustings court, sitting as judge of said chancery court, was the judge of the latter court, and the decree valid. Morriss v. Virginia Ins. Co., 85 Va. 588, 8 S. E. 383.

A vacation decree only becomes effective from the time it is entered in the chancery order book of the clerk of the court in which the case is pending. Lee v. Willis, 99 Va. 16, 37 S. E. 826.

c. On Sundays or Holidays.

See the title SUNDAYS AND HOLIDAYS.

Sundays.—Entry of vacation decree made on Sunday is a void entry, and the decree, signed by the judge, remains as if it had not been copied into the order book. Lee v. Willis, 99 Va. 16, 37 S. E. 826, citing Michie v. Michie, 17 Gratt. 109; Read v. Com., 22 Gratt. 924, 934.

Holidays.—Judgments, orders and decrees may be validly entered on public holidays. Va. Code, 1904, § 2844a.

d. Decree on Commissioner's Report.

See the title REFERENCE.

Under § 7, ch. 8, W. Va. acts, 1895, if a decree is entered on a commissioner's report before the term next after the term at which the same was filed, such decree is so entered at the risk of a party excepting and showing error within the time given by statute. Kanawha Coal Co. v. Ballard Coal Co., 43 W. Va. 721, 29 S. E. 514.

e. After Final Decree.

After a final decree has been entered in a cause, no further decree can be regularly entered therein. Smith v. Powell, 98 Va. 431, 36 S. E. 522.

6. Entry of Judgments Nunc Pro Tunc.
a. Power of Courts.

The power of courts to make entries of judgment and orders nunc pro tunc, in proper case and in furtherance of the ends of justice, has been recognized and exercised from the earliest times; and the period in which the power may be exercised is not limited. Weatherman v. Com., 91 Va. 796, 26 S. E. 349.

All cases on the court docket, not determined before the end of the term, stand as continued without an order of continuance (see Va. Code, 1887, § 3124). Held, it is in the power of a court, at its July term, to enter up the judgment nunc pro tunc which it had omitted on the verdict at its April term. Van Gunden v. Kane (1892), 88 Va. 591, 14 S. E. 334.

b. Discretion of Court.

It is nowhere questioned that every application to the court to enter up a judgment nunc pro tunc, or what is the same thing in effect, to cure by such an order a defect in the proceedings upon which the judgment was originally entered, is an application addressed to the discretion of the court. Powers v. Carter Coal, etc., Co., 100 Va. 450, 457, 41 S. E. 867.

c. Civil and Criminal Cases.

In proper cases, to further the ends of justice, courts may make entries of judgments and orders nunc pro tunc in either civil or criminal cases, and the time within which this may be done is not limited. If the entry is one which the judge may be compelled, by mandamus, to make, he may make it of his own motion. Weatherman v. Com., 91 Va. 796, 22 S. E. 349.

Upon an indictment in the county court against C., the jury render a verdict of guilty, and that he be imprisoned in the county jail for ten months, and pay a fine of ten dollars. No judgment on the verdict is entered at that term, nor is the case continued; but at the next term of the court, the judgment is rendered nunc pro tunc. Before the ten months has expired, C. escapes from jail, and is afterwards retaken. Held, the cause was pending in court, and it was proper to render the judgment on the verdict at the next term of the court. C. is not entitled to be discharged at the end of the ten months; but is to be kept in prison beyond that period for the length of time he was out when he escaped; and this, though C. has been indicted for his escape. Cleek *v.* Com. (1871), 21 Gratt. 777.

d. Interlocutory Orders.

"That an interlocutory order may be entered nunc pro tunc has been decided by the supreme court of the United States. In re Wight, 134 U. S. 136." Vance *v.* Ravenswood, etc., R. Co., 53 W. Va. 338, 341, 44 S. E. 461.

e. Judgments of Justices.

See the title JUSTICES OF THE PEACE.

On the 8th day of April, 1886, two justices presided at a trial at which a verdict was rendered, but no judgment thereon was entered. Subsequently, nearly two years afterwards, the same justices, without notice, met and undertook to enter a judgment upon the verdict nunc pro tunc. Held, such entry nunc pro tunc was unauthorized and illegal, and was properly treated by the circuit court as a nullity. "It is well known that the justice's court has no regular term, and if his proceedings are to be carried in his own breast for years, and then entered in a case no longer pending, his docket and proceedings would soon be in a chaotic condition, and absolutely useless for any practical purpose." McClain *v.* Davis, 37 W. Va. 330, 16 S. E. 629, 630, Brannon, J., dissenting.

f. On Whose Motion.

In proper cases, to further the ends of justice, courts may make entries of judgments and orders nunc pro tunc in either civil or criminal cases, and the time within which this may be done is not limited. If the entry is one which the judge may be compelled, by mandamus, to make, he may make it of his own motion. Weatherman *v.* Com., 91 Va. 796, 22 S. E. 349.

g. When Proper.

In General.—"There are two classes of cases in which it has been held proper to enter judgments and decrees nunc pro tunc. The first class embraces those cases in which the suitors have done all in their power to place the cause in a condition to be decided by the court, but in which, owing to the delay of the court, no final judgment has been entered. The second class embraces those cases in which judgments, though pronounced by the court, have, from accident or mistake of the officers of the court, never been entered on the records of the court." The cases falling within the first class mentioned nearly always arise from the death of one of the parties, after submission of the cause and before judgment is actually rendered, and it becomes necessary to enter judgment nunc pro tunc, in order to prevent the other party from being prejudiced by the delay of the court, and without fault on his part. * * * The second class of cases includes those in which formal judgment has been pronounced by the court, but not entered in the record by reason of some accident or mistake, or through the neglect, omission, or misprison of the clerk. The court which has ordered a judgment, which the clerk has failed or neglected to enter in the record, has power, even after the term at which it was rendered has passed, to order the judgment so rendered to be entered nunc pro tunc, provided there be satisfactory evidence that the judgment was rendered as alleged, and of the nature and extent of the relief granted by it." Vance *v.* Ravenswood, etc., R. Co., 53 W. Va. 338, 342, 44 S. E. 461.

Negligence, Mistake or Misprison.—Where the omission of the entry of the judgment already rendered, is the result of negligence, mistake or misprison of the clerk, an entry nunc pro tunc is proper. Vance *v.* Ravenswood, etc., R. Co., 53 W. Va. 338, 44 S. E. 461.

An interlocutory order, omitted to be entered by neglect or inadvertence on the part of the clerk of a court, may be ordered, by the court, to be entered nunc pro tunc, by way of amendment, so as to make the record show what has actually transpired in the cause, upon clear and satisfactory evidence, consisting of uncontradicted affidavits, and papers filed, and orders entered, in the cause. Vance *v.* Ravenswood, etc., R. Co., 53 W. Va. 338, 44 S. E. 461.

Nonresidence of Counsel.—"After said order was entered, the defendant moved the court to enter final judgment for it nunc pro tunc, as of the August term, 1898, and the action of the court in overruling that motion and declining to make the entry is assigned as error. In support of this motion, the defendant presented the affidavit of the retired judge who had presided at the trial, setting forth, in substance, the proceedings, and stating that, at said August term, he had 'rendered his opinion upon said demurrer to the evidence, and sustained said demurrer to the evidence,' but 'judgment was not entered in accordance with the opinion of the court, so rendered, because counsel for the defendant were nonresidents of Roane county, and none of them were present to see that a proper order was prepared and to ask that the same be entered.' * * * The affidavit offered in support of the motion, clearly shows on its face that the omission of the entry of the judgment which the judge says he rendered, was not the result of negligence, mistake or misprision of the clerk. He says that judgment was not entered in accordance with opinion because counsel for the defendant were nonresidents and none of them were present to see that a proper order was prepared and to ask that the same be entered. The clerk was not ordered to enter any judgment. Hence, it can not be said that any judgment was rendered, even if the court had announced his opinion that the demurrer should be sustained and his intention

to render judgment. Whether, under conditions bringing a case within the rules above referred to, under which a great many of the courts enter judgment nunc pro tunc, this court would do so and whether, if it did so, it would adopt these rules to the extent to which such judgments have been entered by other courts, can not be decided here, but even if those rules were adopted to their fullest extent, they did not warrant the entry of such judgment under the conditions existing at the time the court overruled defendant's motion therefor." Vance *v.* Ravenswood, etc., R. Co., 53 W. Va. 338, 342, 44 S. E. 461.

h. Time of Entry.

In General.—In proper cases, to further the ends of justice, courts may make entries of judgments and orders nunc pro tunc in either civil or criminal cases, and the time within which this may be done is not limited. If the entry is one which the judge may be compelled, by mandamus, to make, he may make it of his own motion. Weatherman *v.* Com., 91 Va. 796, 22 S. E. 349.

After Stay of Issuance of Execution. —Where, in an action of unlawful detainer, the jury finds for the plaintiff, and a stay of the issuance of a writ of possession for sixty days is entered to allow the defendants to apply to the circuit court for a writ of error and supersedeas, and they fail to present their petition therefor during the two following terms, it is proper at the third term to enter judgment nunc pro tunc as of the time the stay was granted, under the provisions of Va. Code, 1887, § 3124, which provides that "all causes upon the docket of any court, and all other matters ready for its decision, which shall not have been determined before the end of a term, whether regular or special, shall, without any order of continuance, stand continued to the next term." Van

Gunden v. Kane, 88 Va. 591, 14 S. E. 334.

Entry in Vacation.—J. files his bill in the circuit court of Wood county, in the fourth judicial circuit, praying an injunction and for relief. The injunction was awarded, the cause removed to the circuit court of Ritchie county, in the second judicial circuit, and various proceedings there taken in the cause. The January term, 1872, of that court was held by the judge of the fourth judicial circuit instead of the judge of the second judicial circuit, but no decree or proceedings were had in the cause at that term, so far as the record shows. The judge of the fourth judicial circuit, after the adjournment of the circuit court of Ritchie county at its January term, in vacation, rendered a final decree in the cause dissolving the injunction and dismissing the bill at the complainant's costs. It concludes, "And by agreement of parties, it is ordered that this decree be entered among the proceedings of the next term of the circuit court of Wood county." At the April term, 1872, of the circuit court of Ritchie, held by its judge, the judge of the second judicial circuit, a decree was rendered in the cause, which first recited that at the January term, 1872, of said court, held by the judge of the fourth judicial circuit, the cause had been argued by counsel, and an agreement and consent was made in open court by the parties thereto, in person and by counsel, that the papers might be taken and the cause decided in vacation, and that any decree so made should be entered in the circuit court of Wood county at its then next term; and that it appeared that said cause was so decided in vacation by said judge of the fourth judicial circuit, and that his decree had been returned to the clerk of this court setting forth the final decree aforesaid rendered by the judge of the fourth judicial circuit; and then proceeded to order the pa-

pers of the cause to be transmitted to the clerk of the circuit court of Wood county, and that the said decree rendered by the judge of the fourth judicial circuit in vacation be entered on the chancery order book of the said court, at the next term thereof. At said term of the circuit court of Wood county, a decree was entered in said cause, which first recited the transmission of the papers in the cause to the clerk of that court. It then proceeded to order the docketing of the cause in that court, and then ordered the said decree of the April term, 1872, of the circuit court of Ritchie county to be entered verbatim, which was done. Held, the recitals made in the decree, entered by the judge of the second judicial circuit at the April term of the circuit court of Ritchie county, of what occurred in open court at the January term, 1872, while the judge of the fourth judicial circuit was presiding, can not be regarded as the equivalent of a consent decree, of the January term, 1872, to submit the cause in vacation entered nunc pro tunc. Johnson v. Young, 11 W. Va. 673.

i. Sufficiency and Proof of Rendition to Warrant Entry.

A mere announcement by a judge in court of his opinion to sustain a demurrer to evidence, without an order or direction to the clerk to enter judgment accordingly, is not a sufficient rendition of judgment to warrant the entry of it as final judgment nunc pro tunc, when it further appears that absence of counsel was the reason for not ordering it to be entered at the time of the announcement. Vance v. Ravenswood, etc., R. Co., 53 W. Va. 338, 44 S. E. 461.

"Upon the other hand, in Shelton v. Welsh, 7 Leigh 175, it was held, that a clerical error might be corrected at a subsequent term. In the present case, if it were conceded that a justice of the peace could at any time enter a judgment nunc pro tunc, after the termination of his session at which it was rendered, he certainly could not do so except upon reasonable notice to the parties interested, nor could he at any time do so from his own recollection of what had occurred, but would have to rely exclusively upon some sufficient evidence appearing in the record or papers in the case, showing that such a judgment had been rendered." McClain v. Davis, 37 W. Va. 330, 16 S. E. 629, 631, Brannon, J., dissenting.

j. Right of Court to Annex Conditions.

When, on an application to a trial court to correct a judgment by default, under the provision of § 3451 of the Code, it appears that no order was entered by the court on the day to which a notice of a motion for a judgment was returnable, but that judgment by default was entered at a subsequent term, it is within the power and discretion of the court to enter an order nunc pro tunc docketing the motion and continuing it to the next term, and validating the judgment, as between the original parties, and annexing a condition thereto that such judgment shall not affect the rights of innocent third persons whose rights have accrued since the original judgment, and before the nunc pro tunc order. Such order, when made, is an entirety and is not valid as to the judgment and void as to the condition. The two provisions are dependent on each other. Powers v. Carter Coal, etc., Co., 100 Va. 450, 41 S. E. 867, citing Parker v. Pitts, 1 Hen. & M. 4; Amis v. Koger, 7 Leigh 221, 223.

k. Rights of Third Persons.

It is said by Freeman, in his work on Judgments, § 66: "The entry of judgments or decrees nunc pro tunc is intended to be in the furtherance of justice. It will not be ordered so as to affect third persons who have acquired rights without notice of the

rendition of any judgment. Generally, such conditions will be imposed as may be necessary to save the interest of third parties, who have acted bona fide, and without notice; but if such conditions are not expressed in the order of the court, they are, nevertheless, to be considered as made part of it by force of the law. The public are not expected or required to search in unusual places for evidence of judgments. They are bound to take notice of the regular records, but not of the existence or signification of memoranda made by the judge, and upon which the record may happen to be afterwards perfected." Powers v. Carter Coal, etc., Co., 100 Va. 450, 456, 41 S. E. 867.

l. Correction of Clerical Errors Nunc Pro Tunc.

Mr. Black thus lays down the rule: "That a court has a right at a term, subsequent to one at which a judgment is rendered, to correct, by an order nunc pro tunc, a clerical error or omission in the original entry, is indisputable. The error, whether of omission or commission, must appear from the record of the proceedings in which the entry of judgment is made." 1 Black, Judgm., § 131. McClain v. Davis, 37 W. Va. 330, 16 S. E. 629, 631, Brannon, J., dissenting.

It is intended to commit the estate of David Clarkson to the sergeant of Lynchburg, but by a clerical mistake the name is written "Daniel" Clarkson; over four years afterwards, and after action brought by the sergeant under this committal, the court, on his motion, corrects the mistake by an order nunc pro tunc. Held, the mistake was a mere clerical error, which the court at a subsequent term had a right to correct by an order nunc pro tunc, and the order relating back to the former order, the estate was well committed. Clarkson v. Booth (1868), 17 Gratt. 490.

m. Signing Nunc Pro Tunc.

If a court would have the right to enter a judgment and authenticate the record thereof now for then, it follows as clearly as the greater includes the less, the whole a part, that the judge may sign in like manner the record of a judgment rendered or a proceeding had at a previous term and duly entered by the clerk upon the order book. Weatherman v. Com., 91 Va. 796, 800, 22 S. E. 349.

n. Effect of Judgment.

"When a judgment is entered nunc pro tunc, its effect, so far as it operates by relation of the earlier date, must be confined to the rights and interests of the original parties; at least it will not be allowed to work detriment to the rights of innocent third persons acquiring interests without notice of the rendition of any judgment." Powers v. Carter Coal, etc., Co., 100 Va. 450, 456, 41 S. E. 867.

o. Estoppel.

Where a plea and statement of grounds of defense are offered by one of several defendants and received by the court at one term, but the order of the court at that term states that there was no appearance for the defendants, and gives judgment against all of them, and, at a subsequent term, by agreement of parties shown by the record, a nunc pro tunc order is entered showing the filing of said statement of defenses and special plea, and made up thereon and tried, treating the judgment at the former term as set aside, the plaintiff is thereafter estopped to deny that such order was the effect of the nunc pro tunc order. Rocky Mount Loan, etc., Co. v. Price, 103 Va. 298, 49 S. E. 73.

7. Clerical Errors and Mistakes.

In General.—"In whatever respect the clerk may have erred in entering judgment, the court may on proper evidence, nullify the error by making the judgment entry fully and correctly express the judgment rendered." 1 Freem, Judgm., § 72; Davis v. Trump, 43 W. Va. 191, 27 S. E. 397.

Mistake in Entry.—In an action on a nonnegotiable note in which the homestead exemption is waived, the statement in the entry of the judgment that the homestead is waived does not vitiate the judgment. The judgment in this respect will be amended and affirmed. Long v. Pence, 93 Va. 584, 25 S. E. 593.

Judgment Erroneously Entered in Singular Number.—The validity of a judgment against two defendants is not affected because of a merely clerical error in entering the same against them in the singular number, "defendant," instead of the plural number, "defendants." Roach v. Blakey, 89 Va. 767, 17 S. E. 228.

Office Judgments.—"Suppose the judgment ought to have been de bonis testatoris, would it be proper to reverse the judgment on that account? I think not. The judgment in the case was an office judgment, which not having been set aside, became by operation of law, a judgment of the succeeding term. In such a case the only entries usually made after the declaration is filed and before the execution issues, are two short entries in the rule book, one in the words 'common order' and the other, 'common order confirmed.' These entries are identical, whether the suit be against the defendant in his own right, or en autre droit. The execution is issued upon the judgment as if it had been rightly entered in full. The clerk afterwards at his leisure enters a formal judgment in the case in a book kept for the purpose. The error, if any, in running out these short entries into form when the record is made up, is nothing but a clerical error, the correction of which belongs to the court whose officer committed it. The remedy is by motion to that court, and not by appeal to this. Eubank v. Ralls, 4 Leigh 308; Shelton *v.* Welsh, 4 Leigh 175; Digges *v.* Dunn, 1 Munf. 56. I am for affirming the judgment." Snead *v.* Coleman, 7 Gratt. 300, 305, 56 Am. Dec. 112.

Notice.—"In the third place, this entry of the judgment made by these justices seems to have been done upon their own mere motion, and without any notice whatever to the defendant in the court below. It is a well-established rule that, if they regarded the omission of the entry as a mere clerical error, they could only correct such error upon reasonable notice to the other party. This is the well-established practice in the circuit courts, and in this court. See Code, ch. 134, §§ 1, 5." McClain *v.* Davis, 37 W. Va. 330, 16 S. E. 629, 630.

Remittitur.—An error in stating a credit on a judgment below, in entering up the judgment, can be cured by filing a release in the clerk's office, by the plaintiff, for the sum improperly allowed him. Werninger *v.* Wilson, 2 W. Va. 1, 2.

8. Effect of Failure to Enter.

The clerk of a county court having by mistake failed to enter a judgment on a verdict, and an appeal being taken, such appeal ought to be dismissed, notwithstanding the county court afterwards, during the pendency of the appeal, corrects the error, by having a judgment entered and certified to the district court. Tatum *v.* Snidow, 2 Hen. & M. 542.

In Turberville *v.* Self, 4 Call 580, although the county court gave no judgment on the verdict, the district court affirmed it with damages, and the court of appeals (probably from oversight), did the same.

9. Proceedings against Several Parties.

Where in a proceeding at law against several parties, judgments against one or more are entered at one time, and against others at another time, one ex-ecution may be issued against all. Walker *v.* Com., 18 Gratt. 13.

10. Signature.

Statutes Directory.—"The authorities generally hold that the statutes relating to the recordation of deeds and the docketing of judgments are merely directory, and the failure of the clerk or other officer to comply with their provisions can not affect the rights of parties, claiming under such deeds or judgments. In Beverley *v.* Ellis, 1 Rand. 102, it is decided that where a deed is duly proved, or acknowledged and left with the clerk for recordation, it is considered as recorded from that time, although it was never recorded, but lost by the negligence of the clerk. In Rollins *v.* Henry, 78 N. Car. 342, it was held, that the requirement of the statute that a judge shall sign all judgments rendered in court is merely directory, and his omission to do so will not vitiate it as to strangers." Shadrack *v.* Woolfolk, 32 Gratt. 707, 713.

Signing Nunc Pro Tunc.—If a court would have the right to enter a judgment and authenticate the record thereof now for then, it follows as clearly as the greater includes the less, the whole a part, that the judge may sign in like manner the record of a judgment rendered or a proceeding had at a previous term and duly entered by the clerk upon the order book. Weatherman *v.* Com., 91 Va. 796, 800, 22 S. E. 349.

A judge may sign a day's proceedings in the order book at the next term nunc pro tunc. Weatherman *v.* Com., 91 Va. 796, 798, 22 S. E. 349. See Va. Code, § 3114.

Criminal Cases.—Signing the orders is no step in the prosecution of a criminal, and no part of the trial, but is simply the authentication of what has been done, and where the record shows that the accused was present when the proceedings were had, he need not be present when the orders are signed. Weatherman v. Com., 91 Va. 796, 22 S. E. 349.

11. Mandamus to Compel Entry.

See the title MANDAMUS.

The entry of judgment is a mere ministerial act and may be enforced by mandamus. Marstiller v. Ward, 52 W. Va. 74, 84, 43 S. E. 178, followed in Hutton v. Holt, 52 W. Va. 672, 44 S. E. 164, citing McClain v. Davis, 37 W. Va. 330, 16 S. E. 629; Weatherman v. Com., 91 Va. 796, 22 S. E. 349.

"The cases above, Enders v. Burch, 15 Gratt. 64, and Alderson v. Gwinn, 3 W. Va. 229, showing that all further proceedings after the end of the term are without authority, coram non judice, seems to show that the duty to enter judgment is simply ministerial or clerical, and thus justify mandamus. The entry of judgment is a mere ministerial act, and does not constitute the judgment itself, being only record evidence of what the law has adjudged, and that entry may be enforced by mandamus. What other remedy? 17 Am. &. Ency. L. (2d Ed.) 768; 19 Id. 839; 20 Id. 793. See McClain v. Davis, 37 W. Va. 330, 16 S. E. 629." Marstiller v. Ward, 52 W. Va. 74, 84, 43 S. E. 178, followed in Hutton v. Holt, 52 W. Va. 672, 44 S. E. 164.

12. Error.

The statutes provide that no judgment or decree shall be stayed or reversed for any informality in the entry of the judgment or decree by the clerk. W. Va. Code, 1899, ch. 134, § 4034; Va. Code, 1904, § 3449.

The informal entry of a judgment is not a ground for reversing it. Code of Virginia, § 3449. Long v. Pence, 93 Va. 584, 589, 25 S. E. 593.

Any informality in the entry of a judgment by the clerk must be corrected by the court below, and is no ground for reversal in this court. Roach v. Blakey, 89 Va. 767, 17 S. E. 228.

"Another error is assigned in the brief by counsel for the appellants, which will here be noticed. He insists, that there was no judgment, because it was not entered as the statute requires, the judgment being for the penalty, to be discharged by a smaller sum, when the statute now requires that the damage shall be ascertained and judgment shall be given for such damages. If this were an error, as no prejudice results to the defendant therefrom, the decree would not be reversed. (Bank v. Fleshman, 22 W. Va. 317.) But if there is anything in the assignment of error to the prejudice of the defendant, it can not be inquired into here. The question whether or no the judgment was erroneously entered, should have been raised in that case and not in this. There certainly is a judgment, and it is just as certain that it is not void, although in the proper court might have been reversed, because voidable." Chalfants v. Martin, 25 W. Va. 394, 398.

D. JUDGMENT BOOK AND INDEX.

As to docketing and indexing judgments to acquire a lien, etc., see post, "Judgment Liens," VI.

Loss of Judgment Book.—Where any book containing judgments, decrees, orders or proceedings of a court, or proceedings at rules, is lost, and there can be again entered correctly, by means of any writing, any matters which were in such book, the court may cause its clerk to have such matters re-entered, and such entries shall have the same effect as the original entries. W. Va. Code, 1899, ch. 130, § 3934. See Va. Code, 1904, § 3338.

Where any such book, or any book containing the record of wills, deeds or other papers, or where any paper filed in a clerk's office is lost, the clerk in whose office such book or paper was, upon the production to him of any original paper which was recorded in the said book, or any attested copy of the record thereof, or of an attested copy of anything else in such book, or of any paper so filed, shall, on application, record or file the same anew. The record shall show whether it is made from an original or a copy, and how the paper from which it is made was authenticated or attested. Such record shall have prima facie the same effect that the record or papers for which it is substituted would have had. W. Va. Code, 1899, ch. 130, § 3935. See Va. Code, 1904, § 339.

Index.—The clerk of every court shall have an index to each book he is required to keep, making convenient reference to every order, record, or entry therein. Every execution, and every judgment or decree for money, shall be indexed as well in the name or the person against whom, as in the name of the person in whose favor the. same is. A clerk failing to perform any duty required of him by this section, shall forfeit not less than twenty nor more than one hundred dollars. W. Va. Code, 1899, ch. 117, § 3742. See Va. Code, 1904, § 3183.

Order Assigning Dower.—The clerk of the court wherein there is any partition of, or assignment of dower in, land under any order, or any recovery of land under judgment or decree, shall transmit to the clerk of the county court of each county wherein such land is, a copy of such order, judgment or decree, and of such partition or assignment, and of the order confirming the same, and along therewith, such description of the land as may appear in the papers of the cause, and the report of such partition or assignment. Such clerk shall record the same in his deed book, and index it in the name of the person who had the land before, and also in the name of the person who became entitled under such partition, assignment or recovery. And every such record shall be as effectual, in cases of partition, to convey the legal title of such lands to the person to whom the same is assigned by the report of the commissioners, and decree of the courts as deeds of partition would be if duly made by the parties. A clerk failing to perform any duty required of him by this section, shall forfeit not less than twenty dollars nor more than one hundred dollars. W. Va. Code, 1899, ch. 117, § 3740. See Va. Code, 1904, § 2510.

VI. Judgment Liens.

A. ORIGIN, NATURE AND EXTENT OF LIEN.

See the title ELEGIT, vol. 5, p. 58.

1. Origin and History.

a. At Common Law and under the Writ of Elegit.

Let us inquire for a moment into the origin, nature, and extent of the judgment lien. At common law, lands of the debtor could not be taken to satisfy his debts, except judgments due to the king, and judgments therefore did not operate as liens on land. But by the statute of Westm. 2, 13 Edw. I, ch. 18, substantially adopted in this state (1 Rev. Code, ch. 134, § 1, pp. 524, 525, 526, 527), a new execution was provided, the writ of elegit, by which a moiety of the lands of the debtor could be subjected to the satisfaction of the judgment. The statute, however, did not in express terms give a lien on the land. It provided for the writ, and prescribed the form of it. By its terms, the officer was required to deliver to the creditor all the goods and chattels of the debtor, saving the oxen and beasts of his plough, and also a moiety of all his lands and tenements whereof the debtor at the day of obtaining his judgment was seized, or at any time afterwards, by reasonable price and extent, to have and to hold the said goods and chattels to the creditor as his own proper goods and chattels, and the said moiety as his freehold, to him and his assigns, until thereof the judgment be satisfied ("until he shall have levied thereof the debt and damages aforesaid)." It was by the judicial construction given to this writ, that the judgment was said to be a lien on the land. The lien resulted from the mandate of the writ to deliver to the creditor, by reasonable price and extent, a moiety of all the lands and tenements of the debtor, whereof he was seized at the date of the judgment or at any time afterwards. The lien was an incident of the writ and depended for its existence and continuance upon the capacity to sue out the writ. As long as this capacity lasted, even although revived after being temporarily suspended, the lien continued, and whenever it finally ceased, the lien which was dependent upon it was extinguished. As the mandate of the writ extended to all the lands and tenements of which the debtor was seized at the date of the judgment, or at any time afterwards, it was by force of this mandate also that the lien of the judgment overreached all subsequent conveyances, although made to purchasers for valuable consideration without notice of the judgment, and extended to all the lands of the debtor within the jurisdiction of the state. Price v. Planters' Nat. Bank, 92 Va. 468, 481; Hutcheson v. Grubbs, 80 Va. 251, 254; Borst v. Nalle, 28 Gratt. 423; Renick v. Ludington, 14 W. Va. 367; Calwell v. Prindle, 19 W. Va. 604, 655.

Elegit Abolished.—The lien resulting from the writ of elegit was not abolished in Virginia until the revisal of 1849, and a lien given by statute upon the debtor's entire real estate. Gordon v. Rixey, 76 Va. 694; Hutcheson v. Grubbs, 80 Va. 251.

It was abolished in West Virginia by the Code of 1868, ch. 140, § 2. Calwell v. Prindle, 19 W. Va. 604.

b. Statutory Provisions.

Act of 1843.—"In the interest and for the protection of such purchasers, the act of March 3, 1843, was passed, which provided for the docketing of judgments; and further, that 'no judgment, decree, bond or recognizance thereafter rendered, should bind the land of any party to the same against a bona fide purchaser for valuable consideration without notice, unless the same be docketed in the county or corporation in which the land lay, within twelve months after the rendition or forfeiture of such judgment, decree, bond, or recognizance, or ninety days before such land shall have been conveyed to such purchaser.'" Borst v. Nalle, 28 Gratt. 423.

Except as thus modified in respect to purchasers by the act of 1843 the lien of the judgment continued the same in all respects as to its nature, extent, and mode of enforcing it, until the general revision of 1849. Up to that time, as we have seen, it was a mere incident of the writ of elegit, resulting by construction from the mandate of the writ, and dependent for its existence and continuance on the capacity to sue out the writ. It was now made for the first time, as to judgments thereafter to be rendered, an express, direct, positive, absolute lien on all the real estate of, or to which the judgment debtor should be possessed or entitled, at or after the date of the judgment, or if it was rendered in court, at or after the commencement of the term at which it was so rendered, with the same qualifications as to purchasers for valuable consideration without notice, as was made by the act of 1843. Code of 1860, ch. 186, §§ 6, 8; Code of West Virginia, ch. 139, §§ 5, 7, 9. The writ of elegit was preserved and made to conform to the statutory lien of the judgment; and an additional remedy in equity was given for the enforcement of the lien. Code of 1849, ch. 186, § 9; Code of 1860, ch. 186, § 9; Code of West Virginia, ch. 139, § 8. The lien of the judgment being now express, positive and in no way dependent upon the elegit, and the remedy in equity being preferred in practice, the elegit soon fell into disuse, and was finally abolished by the legislature, Code of West Virginia, ch. 140, § 2, and was abolished by the legislature of Virginia in 1873. Code of 1873, ch. 1873, § 26. Renick v. Ludington, 14 W. Va. 367, 374; Borst v. Nalle, 28 Gratt. 423.

Revisal of 1849.—It was, however, not until the revisal of 1849 that the lien resulting from the elegit was abolished, and a lien given by statute upon the debtor's entire real estate. This lien, conferred by the 6th section of ch. 182, Va. Code, 1873, is absolute and unconditional. It is thus provided that every judgment for money thereafter rendered in .this state against any person, shall be a lien upon all the real estate of or to which such person shall be possessed or entitled, at or after the date of such judgment. Gordon v. Rixey, 76 Va. 694, 702.

By the revisal of 1849 the writ of ca. sa. was abolished, and the lien of the judgment was expressly given on all the real estate of or to which the defendant is possessed or entitled. The lien of the fi. fa. was enlarged and the operation of the elegit (which, however, is now abolished) was extended so as to embrace; not a moiety only, but all the debtor's real estate. And it was further provided that the lien of a judgment may always be enforced in a court of equity. Va. Code, 1849, ch. 186, § 9; Va. Code, 1873, ch. 182, § 9; Hutcheson v. Grubbs, 80 Va. 251, 255.

Present Statutory Provisions.—Every judgment for money rendered in this state heretofore or hereafter, against any person, shall be a lien on all real estate of or to which such person shall be possessed or entitled at or after the date of such judgment, or, if it was rendered in court, at or after the commencement of the term at which it was so rendered. W. Va. Code, 1899, ch. 139, § 4145.

Every judgment for money rendered in this state heretofore or hereafter against any person shall be a lien on all the real estate of or to which such person is or becomes possessed or entitled at or after the date of such judgment. Va. Code, 1904, § 3567.

Docketing.—See post, "Docketing and Indexing Judgments," VI, D.

The only exception to, or limitation upon, this sweeping enactment, is found in the eighth section of the same chapter, which declares that no judgment shall be a lien on real estate as against a purchaser thereof without notice, unless it be docketed as directed. Gordon v. Rixey, 76 Va. 694, 702.

2. Nature of the Lien.

Legal or Equitable Right.—The lien of a judgment given by the statute is a legal lien. Hutcheson v. Grubbs, 80 Va. 251, 257.

A judgment creditor has a legal lien on the lands of his debtor, and has a right to rest on that lien without pursuing his debtor's personal property. Blakemore v. Wise, 95 Va. 269, 28 S. E. 332.

A judgment creditor who comes into a court of equity to enforce his lien upon land is not asserting an equitable right or seeking equitable relief. His judgment is a legal lien. Flanary v. Kane, 102 Va. 547, 559, 46 S. E. 312.

Liens of judgments and their priorities and the right to enforce the same, are plain legal rights, expressly created by statute, and can not be judicially modified to soften the supposed hardship of secret incumbrances. Gurnee v. Johnson, 77 Va. 712.

In Borst v. Nalle, 28 Gratt. 423, 430, and in Price v. Thrash, 30 Gratt. 515, it was held, that the lien of a judgment is an express, absolute statutory lien on the debtor's real estate, and the right to resort to the courts to enforce it is a legal right without terms or conditions to be imposed. Gordon v. Rixey, 76 Va. 694, 704.

To the point that the lien of a judgment constitutes a legal lien, Leake v. Ferguson, 2 Gratt. 419, is cited in Hill v. Manser, 11 Gratt. 522, 525; Gordon v. Rixey, 76 Va. 694, 702; Hutcheson v. Grubbs, 80 Va. 251, 254; Werdenbaugh v. Reid, 20 W. Va. 588.

"Such a lien is a right of high order, and is under the law and by force of law, a plain, direct, positive charge upon real estate. Having once attached, it continues, unless it is in some way discharged, as long as the real estate on which it rests remains the property of the judgment debtor. It accompanies the land in its descent to heirs, follows it into the possession of volunteers, and even into the hands of purchasers for value, if they have notice, or even if they do not have notice, provided the judgment is docketed in the manner and within the time prescribed by law." Renick v. Ludington, 14 W. Va. 367, 375.

Analogous to Claim of Donee. — Pomeroy, in his valuable work on Equity Jurisprudence (2d Ed., vol. 2, § 685), in speaking of the lien of a judgment, says: "The lien of a judgment is analogous to the claim of a donee. It is general, not specific. The beneficiary under a trust, the vendee under an agreement, the holder of a lien created by a contract in rem, deals concerning a specific thing. He parts with the consideration upon the security of that specific thing. The judgment creditor has not dealt with that specific thing. He has not parted with value in contemplation of it. His lien is general, and not confined to it. It is just, therefore, that, so far as their intrinsic natures are concerned, his claim should be considered as inferior to the interest arising from a trust, or from a contract in rem. His lien only extends to what his debtor really has; that is, to the thing, subject to all the equities in it existing at the date of the judgment." Wise v. Taylor, 44 W. Va. 492, 29 S. E. 1003, 1005.

Judgment an "Accrued Right."—The state of Virginia upon notices and motions by the name of "The Commonwealth" instituted and prosecuted by the auditor of public accounts on the 6th day of March, 1860, recovered two several judgments against Edmund S. Calwell "in the circuit court of Richmond" as one of the securities of John E. Lewis, late sheriff of Greenbrier county, the one being for $4,895.92, the balance of the land property, and capitation and September license taxes of 1854 due from said John E. Lewis, late sheriff of Greenbrier county, with interest thereon to be computed at the rate of six per centum per annum from the 17th day of January, 1855, until paid, and the costs of the motion, $13.44, and the other being for $1,073.86, the balance of June, 1855, license taxes, due from said John E. Lewis, late sheriff of Greenbrier county, with interest thereon to be computed at the rate of six per centum per annum from the 29th day of June, 1855, until paid, and $161.07 for damages thereon according to law, also the cost of the motion, $11.94. The law in force at the time said notices were given and motions made and judgments were rendered provided, that "the auditor of public accounts shall institute and prosecute all proceedings proper to enforce payment of money to the commonwealth—that the proceeding may be in the circuit court of the city of Richmond—that when it is at law, it may be by action or motion—that "every judgment on any such motion shall be in the name of the commonwealth." And the city of Richmond being the capital of the state of Virginia, as judicially known to the court, the said two judgments were docketed in the clerk's office of the county court of Greenbrier county by the clerk thereof, in the name of "the

Commonwealth against Edmund S. Calwell," on the 29th day of September, 1860, in the judgment lien docket kept in the clerk's office of said county court for the purpose of docketing judgments under the fourth section of said ch. 186 of said Code of 1860. Said judgments as docketed plainly show the date and the amount of each judgment and the date of the docketing of each judgment and the amount and date of each credit. But the judgment was not indexed in the name of the defendant, Edmund v. Calwell. Held, the liens of said two judgments upon said lands were in no wise impaired or discharged by any of the provisions of the Code of this state of 1868, such judgment liens upon such lands being accrued rights, were not intended to be affected by said Code. (Sections 1 and 2 of ch. 176 of the Code of 1868.) Calwell v. Prindle, 19 W. Va. 604, citing Borst v. Nalle, 28 Gratt. 423, 430, holding that such a lien is a civil right.

B. INSTRUMENTS EMBRACED BY STATUTE.

Bonds and Recognizances.—Those sections of the Virginia Code relating to the docketing of judgments, entering and satisfaction thereof, liens of judgments and enforcement of such liens, shall be construed as embracing recognizances, and bonds having the force of a judgment. Va. Code, 1904, § 3580. See W. Va. Code, 1899, ch. 139, § 4143.

The Virginia Code of 1860, ch. 186, provided that the word "judgment" in the section relating to liens shall include any bond or recognizance which has the force of a judgment. Calwell v. Prindle, 19 W. Va. 604, 654; Dickinson v. Railroad Co., 7 W. Va. 390.

C. NATURE AND REQUISITES OF JUDGMENTS.

1. Requisites and Validity.

See ante, "Requisites of Valid Judgments or Decrees," III.

a. In General.

There is a wide difference between a judgment null and void and one erroneous and voidable; the one is no lien, the other is until reversed. If the judgment is not a nullity, it is a valid lien on the land sought to be subjected. Watt v. Brookover, 35 W. Va. 323, 13 S. E. 1007, 1008.

"There was no jurisdiction in the court to confirm the office judgment, and it is utterly void, for there was no process served, or appearance, and not even attachment of property. Such a judgment is no lien, and may be attacked in a collateral proceeding. Houston v. McCluney, 8 W. Va. 135; Capehart v. Cunningham, 12 W. Va. 750, opinion in Wilson v. Bank, 6 Leigh 570, 574; Wynn v. Wyatt, 11 Leigh 584; Pennoyer v. Neff, 95 U. S. 715; Gray v. Stuart, 33 Gratt. 351; Underwood v. McVeigh, 23 Gratt. 409; Freem., Judgm., § 495; 1 Black, Judgm., §§ 220, 22; Lemar v. Hale, 79 Va. 147; Wade v. Hancock, 76 Va. 620; Windor v. McVeigh, 93 U. S. 274; Hahn v. Kelly, 94 Amer. Dec. 742; Cooper v. Reynolds, 10 Wall. 318; Harris v. Hardeman, 14 How. 334. Even if there be attachment of effects of nonresidents, a personal judgment on publication, without service of process or appearance, is a nullity, except as to effects attached. O'Brien v. Stephens, 11 Gratt. 610; Black, Judgm., § 231; Cooper v. Reynolds, 10 Wall. 318; Coleman v. Waters, 13 W. Va. 278; Gilchrist v. West Virginia Oil, etc., Co., 21 W. Va. 115." Fowler v. Lewis, 36 W. Va. 112, 14 S. E. 447, 451.

b. Must Be for Sum Certain.

To create a lien the judgment must be for a specific sum of money. Thus, a decree providing that if the defendant does not, in a given time, pay the plaintiff a certain sum, that certain real and personal property of the defendant, on which the plaintiff has a specific lien, shall be sold, is not a judgment which creates a lien on other real estate of the defendant. Linn *v.* Patton, 10 W. Va. 187.

c. Jurisdiction to Determine Validity.

In a chancery suit brought to enforce the lien of a judgment upon real estate, a circuit court has jurisdiction to determine whether or not such judgment is valid, although it may be void upon its face, and the writ of prohibition does not lie to restrain the judge of such court from proceeding in such case. Sperry *v.* Sanders, 50 W. Va. 70, 40 S. E. 327.

2. Particular Judgments as Constituting Liens Considered.

a. Decrees.

(1) Early Doctrine.

Originally no decree of a court of chancery of any kind was a lien upon the lands of the defendant debtor nor could it be made so by issuing an elegit to enforce the payment of the sum decreed; for no execution of any sort could be issued on a decree of a chancery court. Decrees were enforced by the chancery court awarding against the defendants, against whom the decrees were, an attachment, his failure to pay the debt decreed to be paid, being regarded as a contempt of the court. If, when the attachment issued, the debtor-defendant could not be found, the chancery court issued an attachment with proclamations, and if this was also returned, not found, a commission of rebellion was issued by the chancery court, or a writ of sequestration, first nisi and then absolute, might be issued after an attachment in the proclamation, or a commission of rebellion had issued. Hook *v.* Ross, 1 Hen. & M. 310.

(2) Later Doctrine.

But at a very early day it seemed to the legislature of Virginia to be right, not only that courts of equity should have the power of carrying their decrees into execution, but that such execution ought to be had by the most direct, simple and efficacious means. As early as 1787 an act was passed, that after a final decree of a court of chancery for lands, slaves, money or things of a specific nature the parties obtaining such decree might issue any appropriate writ of execution thereon, a fi. fa., ca. sa., elegit, or any other writ, which could be issued on a like judgment in a common-law court. And by an act passed January 23, 1798, like writs of execution in like cases might be issued on interlocutory decrees. This law was greatly changed in the Code, 1849, by the provisions to be found in title 53, chs. 186 to 189 inclusive. Chapter 189, §§ 1, 2, were as follows (page 708 of Code of 1849): "1. A decree for land or specific personal property and a decree or order requiring the payment of money, shall have the effect of a judgment for such land, property or money and be embraced by the word 'judgment' when used in any chapter under this title. But a party may proceed to carry into execution a decree or order in chancery other than for the payment of money, as he might have done if this and the following sections had not been enacted. 2. The persons entitled to the benefit of any decree or order requiring the payment of money shall be deemed judgment creditors, though the money be required to be paid into court, or a bank, or other place of deposit. In such case, an execution on the decree or order shall make such recital thereof, and of the parties to it, as may be necessary to designate the case; and if a time be specified in the decree or order, within which the payment is to be made, the execution shall not issue until the expiration of that time." The sixth section of said ch. 186 of Code of 1849, p. 709, provided that "every judgment for money rendered in this state heretofore or hereafter shall be a lien on all the real estate of or to which such person shall be possessed or entitled at or after the date of such judgment or if it was rendered in court at or after the commencement of the term at which it was rendered" with an exception in reference to judgments rendered prior to July 1, 1850, when this Code went into effect. These provisions of the Code of Virginia of 1849 have ever since been in force both in Virginia and West Virginia (Code of W. Va., ch. 139, §§ 1, 2, 5, Warth's Code, pp. 772, 773). Of course since this statute law went into effect a decree of a chancery court against a party personally has been a lien on his lands, just as the judgments of a common-law court against him personally are a lien on his land. Rickard *v.* Schley, 27 W. Va. 617, 625.

A decree in chancery, equally with a judgment at law, creates a lien on lands. Scriba *v.* Deane, 1 Brock. (U. S.) 166; Lee *v.* Swepson, 75 Va. 173; Parker *v.* Clarkson, 4 W. Va. 407; Haleys *v.* Williams, 1 Leigh 140, 19 Am. Dec. 743; Buchanan *v.* Clark, 10 Gratt. 164; Withers *v.* Carter, 4 Gratt. 407; Parrill *v.* McKinley, 6 W. Va. 67; Burbridge *v.* Higgins, 6 Gratt. 119.

(3) Present Rule.

The statutes provide that a decree for land or specific personal property, and a decree or order requiring the payment of money, shall be embraced by the word "judgments," wherever used in any section relating to the lien of judgments. Va. Code, 1904, § 3557; W. Va. Code, 1899, ch. 139, § 4141; Rickard *v.* Schley, 27 W. Va. 617, 625.

Our statute (Code, W. Va., p. 880, ch. 139, § 1) provides that "a decree for land or specific personal property, and a decree or order requiring the payment of money, shall have the effect of a judgment for such land, property, or money, and shall be embraced by the word 'judgment,' where used in any of the succeeding chapters;" and § 5 of said chapter provides that every

judgment for money rendered in this state heretofore or hereafter against any person shall be a lien on all real estate of or to which such person shall be possessed or entitled at or after the date of such judgment, or, if it was rendered in court, at or after the commencement of the term at which it was so rendered, except as follows, etc. Snyder *v.* Botkin, 37 W. Va. 355, 16 S. E. 591, 594.

Judgments for money, whether docketed or not, bind the unaliened lands of the debtor; certainly those owned by him at the date of the judgments, and, it may be, those subsequently acquired, in the order in which the judgments are recovered, and the same is true of decrees for money; and so, though not docketed, they bind the debtor's lands subsequently aliened to a purchaser with notice, even though he be a purchaser for value; but unless docketed they are not liens on lands subsequently aliened to bona fide purchasers for value without notice—and a trustee in a deed of trust given to secure a debt, and the creditor secured, are purchasers for value within the meaning of the registration laws. Code of 1860, ch. 186, §§ 6, 8, 11; Code of 1873, ch. 182, §§ 1, 6, 8, 11. Rhea *v.* Preston, 75 Va. 757, citing Hill *v.* Rixey, 26 Gratt. 72; Borst *v.* Nalle, 28 Gratt. 423, 428; Williams *v.* Lord, 5 Va. Law J., 243, 250; Williams *v.* Lord, 75 Va. 390.

Orders of Court of Chancery.—R. obtains a decree against his guardian and his sureties for a certain sum of money; and sues out an execution, which is levied, and a forthcoming bond taken, and forfeited. The court on its chancery side, on notice to the obligors in the forthcoming bond, renders a judgment in favor of R. against them; and this judgment is docketed. Held, "The orders of the circuit court of Henry entered on the chancery side thereof on the 5th day of September, 1859, were in form and legal effect judgments, and can not be held to be mere awards of executions. * * * It is plain, under these statutes, that the order referred to above is in terms and legal effect a judgment, and being recorded, is a lien on all the lands of the defendants and those in the hands of purchasers conveyed after the docketing of said judgment." Reed *v.* Rainey, 31 Gratt. 265.

In a suit to subject land to the payment of debts, the commissioner of sale was directed, after his report of sale had been confirmed, to pay out of the funds in his hands the debts of the creditors named in the decree. He failed to do this, became insolvent and then transferred his land to secure one of his creditors. The first and second sections of ch. 18 of the Virginia Code, 1873, provided that a decree requiring the payment of money shall have the effect of a judgment for so much money. The sixth section makes such judgment a lien on the real estate of the person who is directed to make the payment of said money. Under the operation of these provisions the above decree constitutes a valid lien upon the lands of the commissioner of sale. Lee *y.* Swepson, 76 Va. 173.

Where a personal decree is entered against a defendant in a suit in the nature of a foreign attachment, this decree is a lien on the debtor's land, and the creditor may come into equity to subject the land, although the decree has not been revived against the administrator of the debtor and no execution has ever been issued upon it. Burbridge *v.* Higgins, 6 Gratt. 119.

Decrees against Receivers.—Under §§ 1, 2, ch. 139, of the Code of West Virginia, a decree against a general receiver of the court requiring him to pay out of funds then in the hands of the general receiver to a party to the cause, in which the decree is rendered, a certain sum on a named future day has the effect of a judgment for such sum of money with interest from the day, on which it is to be paid, with a stay of execution till that day, and is a lien on the lands of such general receiver and the person entitled to the benefit of such decree or order is to be deemed a judgment creditor and may enforce his lien as other judgment creditors by a suit in equity. "Whether a decree or order requiring the payment of money by a commissioner of sale or by a receiver general or special out of funds in his hands, whether such payment is required to be made immediately or at a certain fixed period in the future, is to have the effect of a judgment and be a lien on the lands of such commissioner of sale or general or special receiver has never been decided in this state, though it has been decided in Virginia under the same statute law, that a decree entered directing a commissioner of sale out of funds reported in his hands to pay certain creditors named has under said §§ 1, 2, the effect of a judgment and is a lien on the lands of such commissioner of sale (Lee *v.* Swepson, 76 Va. 173). The reasoning by which this conclusion was reached, would necessarily give to a decree or order directing a receiver to pay money reported to be in his hands to certain creditors the effect of a judgment and make it a lien on all the lands of such general receiver." Rickard *v.* Schley, 27 W. Va. 617.

Cases Distinguished. — Rickard *v.* Schley, 27 W. Va. 617, and Lee *v.* Swepson, 76 Va. 173, are distinguished in Gay *v.* Skeen, 36 W. Va. 582, 15 S. E. 64.

b. Judgments by Confession.

See the title CONFESSION OF JUDGMENTS, vol. 3, p. 76.

Under § 5, ch. 139, W. Va. Code of 1899, a judgment for money confessed before a justice against any person is a lien from the date of said judgment, on the real estate of or to which such person shall be possessed or entitled at or after such date. But as against a purchaser for valuable consideration without notice, it is not a lien until the same is docketed in the judgment lien docket in the office of the clerk of the county court as provided in § 4, ch. 139, W. Va. Code, 1899. Nuzum v. Herron, 52 W. Va. 499, 44 S. E. 257; Shadrack v. Woolfolk, 32 Gratt. 707.

A judgment confessed by an administrator de bonis non, is no lien upon the lands of the intestate. And a decree showing upon its face, that it was enforcing such a judgment as a lien against such land, may be reviewed and reversed upon a proper bill of review brought for that purpose by the heirs. Custer v. Custer, 17 W. Va. 113.

A defendant bought a tract of 166 acres of land for $1,400, giving a deed of trust to secure the purchase money. He afterwards paid $800 in cash, in consideration of the vendor's releasing 66 acres of the land, and agreeing to look to the other 100 acres for payment of the balance of $600, for which the defendant executed new notes. These were assigned to the plaintiff, in whose favor the defendant afterwards confessed judgment thereon. Held, that the lien of this judgment extended to the defendant's interest in the whole tract of 166 acres, notwithstanding the release of part of it from the vendor's lien, of which the plaintiff had no notice. McFarland v. Fish, 34 W. Va. 548, 12 S. E. 548.

c. Judgments in Favor of Commonwealth.

"Since 1788, a judgment in favor of the commonwealth binds all the lands of a public collector. And by the act of February 23d, 1822, supplement to Rev. Code 339, the law is made general, and applies to all public debtors. The question upon the act of 1788, arose in the case of Nimmo v. Com., 4 Hen. & M. 57. A judgment had been obtained against the sheriff in 1786. In 1799, a scire facias was sued out to revive

the judgment against his executor, who pleaded fully administered. In his account adduced in support of his plea, he had charged himself with the proceeds of a tract of land which his testator had devised to be sold. The general court held he was bound to take notice of judgments against his testator, and disallowing his credits, charged him with the proceeds of the land sold as legal assets. In the petition for a supersedeas, it was assigned for error, that the proceeds of the land were equitable assets, and as such distributable pari passu among all the creditors of the testator; and that if even legal assets, the bond debts were entitled to share, since the judgment was prior to the act of assembly subjecting lands to the judgment of the commonwealth." Leake v. Ferguson, 2 Gratt. 419.

The state of Virginia upon notices and motions by the name of "The Commonwealth" instituted and prosecuted by the auditor of public accounts on the 6th day of March, 1860, recovered two several judgments against Edmund S. Calwell "in the circuit court of Richmond" as one of the securities of John E. Lewis, late sheriff of Greenbrier county, the one being for $4,893.92, the balance of the land property, and capitation and September license taxes of 1854 due from said John E. Lewis, late sheriff of Greenbrier county, with interest thereon to be computed at the rate of six per centum from the 17th day of January, 1855, until paid, and the costs of the motion, $13.44, and the other being for $1,073.86, the balance of June, 1855, license taxes, due from said John E. Lewis, late sheriff of Greenbrier county, with interest thereon to be computed at the rate of six per cent. per annum from the 20th day of June, 1855, until paid, and $161.07 for damages thereon according to law, also the cost of the motion, $11.94. The law in force at the time said notices were given and motions made and judgments were rendered provided, that "the auditor of public accounts shall institute and prosecute all proceedings proper to enforce payment of money to the commonwealth—that the proceeding may be in the circuit court of the city of Richmond—that when it is at law, it may be by action or motion—that "every judgment on any such motion shall be in the name of the commonwealth." And the city of Richmond being the capital of the state of Virginia, as judicially known to the court, held, that by virtue of the said Virginia act of February 3d, 1863, the said judgments with their said liens upon the said lands of said Edmund S. Calwell in the said 20th day of June, 1863, passed to and belonged to the state of West Virginia, and said judgments on the date last aforesaid became and from thence continued to be positive liens in favor of the state of West Virginia upon the lands of said Edmund S. Calwell within the limits of the state of West Virginia, including his lands in the said county of Greenbrier. Held, that each of said judgments with their liens passed to and became vested in the state of West Virginia under and by virtue of the said act of the General Assembly of Virginia, passed February 3d, 1863, on the 20th day of June, 1863. That each of said judgments belonged to the state of Virginia with their liens until the said 20th day of June, 1863. Calwell v. Prindle, 19 W. Va. 604.

d. Judgments against Deceased Persons.

"The fact that a sole plaintiff, or one of several plaintiffs, is dead at the time of the institution of an action, such death not appearing on the record, does not render a judgment therein void, but only erroneous, and such judgment is a lien on real estate. "As regards a judgment against a party dead at its rendition, this court,

in King v. Burdett, 28 W. Va. 601, held such judgment not void for the fact of death not appearing on the record, and that it was a lien enforceable in chancery, and such death could not be set up in defense of a bill to enforce it. In Evans v. Spurgin, 6 Gratt. 107, it was held that, the death of a defendant not having been suggested, a decree can not be impeached in a collateral action by evidence of his death. I think these decisions are binding authority on us, and in principle decide this point in the case." Watt v. Brookover, 35 W. Va. 323, 13 S. E. 1007.

Where suit is instituted in the name of a party who is dead at the time the suit is brought, and process is duly served upon the defendants, who suffer judgment to be rendered against them without pleading the death of the plaintiff in abatement in proper time during the pendency of the suit, the judgment so obtained is not absolutely void, but is erroneous. Such judgment, until reversed in one of the modes prescribed by law, constitutes a lien upon the real estate of the defendant, and may be enforced as other judgment liens, and is not subject to collateral attack. McMillan v. Hickman, 35 W. Va. 705, 14 S. E. 227.

e. Judgments against Insane Persons.

A judgment against a person insane at its rendition is not for that cause void, and is a lien on land. Withrow v. Smithson, 37 W. Va. 757, 17 S. E. 316.

f. Judgments and Decrees against Personal Representatives.

See the title EXECUTORS AND ADMINISTRATORS, vol. 5, p. 729.

A judgment recovered by a creditor against an administrator is not a lien on the realty of the intestate. Laidley v. Kline, 8 W. Va. 218; Woodyard v. Polsley, 14 W. Va. 211, 218; Custer v. Custer, 17 W. Va. 113; Merchants' Nat. Bank v. Good, 21 W. Va. 455;

Saddler *v.* Kennedy, 36 W. Va. 636; Broderick *v.* Broderick, 28 W. Va. 378; Board *v.* Callihan, 33 W. Va. 209, 10 S. E. 382; McKay *v.* McKay, 33 W. Va. 724, 11 S. E. 213; Laidley *v.* Kline, 23 W. Va. 565, 578.

Laidley *v.* Kline, 8 W. Va. 218, is cited in Custer *v.* Custer, 17 W. Va. 113, 124, to support the proposition that a judgment obtained by a creditor against the administrator is not a judgment lien on the realty of the intestate.

Although, under the legislation of this state, as contained in the Code, real as well as personal estate is made subject to the payment of the just debts of the intestate, still the realty which descended to the heir should not be decreed to be sold for the payment of judgment liens until resort is first had to the personal estate, so far as practicable, and without producing unreasonable delay. Laidley *v.* Kline, 8 W. Va. 218.

An administrator de bonis non of D. C. confessed judgment in favor of the administrator of M. C., pursuant to a written agreement made between them. The administrator of M. C. then filed a bill in chancery against the administrator de bonis non of D. C. and the widow and heirs of D. C. to enforce the said judgment as a lien against the lands of D. C. Held, such a judgment is not a lien upon the lands of which D. C. died seized. The decree showing upon its face, that it was enforcing such a judgment as a lien against such land, may be reviewed and reversed upon a proper bill of review filed for that purpose by the heirs. "Such a judgment is not a lien upon the land, and should not be enforced against the land. The agreement is made a part of the decree itself, and it shows upon its face, that it is not such an agreement, as administrators could enter into, so as to bind the heirs; and to enforce a confessed judgment rendered upon it against the

lands, that have descended to heirs and in which the widow is entitled to dower, would open the door to fraud; and besides the widow and children of the intestate are in no wise privy to the agreement, and can not be prejudiced by any judgment thereon, however it might affect the administrator himself." Custer *v.* Custer, 17 W. Va. 113, 126.

A conditional decree, directing an executor to pay certain debts due from him in his fiduciary capacity, when he shall have collected certain other specified claims or debts coming to his testator's estate, constitutes no lien upon the real estate of such executor. Neither could execution be issued thereon and enforced against him without further proceedings in the cause wherein such decree has been rendered; nor will a bill in chancery be maintained to enforce the lien of such decree against the real estate of such executor. Gay *v.* Skeen, 36 W. Va. 582, 15 S. E. 64, citing Rickard *v.* Schley, 27 W. Va. 617; Lee *v.* Swepson, 76 Va. 173.

Cases Distinguished.—"It is not necessary to decide in this case whether a decree against an executor, directing him to pay a balance found due on the settlement of his accounts, and for which he is liable de bonis propriis, becomes a lien upon his real estate, which may be enforced like the lien of any other personal judgment. Whatever might be the law in such a case as that, it is quite certain that a conditional decree directing an executor to pay certain debts due by his testator, or due from him in his fiduciary capacity, when he shall have collected certain other claims or debts coming to his testator's estate, is no lien upon the real estate of such executor; neither could execution be issued thereon, and enforced against him without further proceedings in the case, and in the court where such decree has been rendered. In the case of

Rickard *v.* Schley, 27 W. Va. 617, it was held, that 'a decree against a general receiver, requiring him to pay out of funds then in the hands of the general receiver, to a party to the cause in which the decree is rendered, a certain sum on a named future day, has the effect of a judgment for such sum of money with interest from the day on which it is to be paid, with a stay of execution till that day, and is a lien on the lands of such general receiver, and a person entitled to the benefit of such decree or order is to be deemed a judgment creditor, and may enforce his lien as other judgment creditors, by a suit in equity.' It might well be argued that a similar decree against any other fiduciary, such as an executor or an administrator, would be embraced in the reasoning and principle decided in Rickard *v.* Schley. But it is necessary to observe that the decree or order must be based upon a fund 'then in the hands of the' receiver or other fiduciary at the time the decree is entered. This is quite obvious upon a consideration of the facts of the case, and the language of the opinion of Judge Green on page 630, in which he says: 'Such an order on an officer of the court to pay money to certain persons at a fixed future time out of funds in his hands when the order is made, is, under our statute, in its effect equivalent to a judgment, with a stay of execution till such fixed future day.' Precisely the same point was ruled in the case which Judge Green was following, and approving Lee *v.* Swepson, 76 Va. 173. In the latter case the order was for the commissioner to pay money 'out of the funds reported in his hands,' and this was regarded as a personal decree against the commissioner, and a judgment for money fixing a lien upon his real estate. In the latter case the words which we have quoted above from the opinion of Judge Staples are italicized in the syllabus, thus showing

their importance in construing the principle intended to be settled, namely, that when an officer of the court is directed to pay out of a fund then in his hands certain debts, this order becomes a lien as a judgment against the real estate of such officer in favor of such creditors as he has been directed to pay. This is as far as the cases have ever gone under §§ 1, 2, 5, ch. 139, of the Code, or the Code of Virginia, which is similar. All that we are required to decide in the present case, and all that we do decide, is that a decree against an executor, directing him to collect certain debts coming to the estate of his testator, and apply them, when collected, to discharge certain specified debt or debts due from the estate, does not fix a lien as a judgment against the real estate of such executor." Gay *v.* Skeen, 36 W. Va. 582, 15 S. E. 64, 65.

g. Judgments of Foreign Courts.

The judgments of foreign courts do not constitute liens upon lands within this state. A judgment rendered by a court in the state of Ohio is not a lien upon lands in this state. Dickinson *v.* Railroad Co., 7 W. Va. 390, 417.

h. Judgments of United States Courts.

"The fifth section of chapter one hundred and thirty-nine of the Code of West Virginia provides that 'every judgment for money, rendered in this state, heretofore or hereafter, against any person, shall be a lien on all the real estate of, or to, which such person shall be possessed or entitled, at, or after, the date of such judgment, or if it was rendered in court, at, or after, the commencement of the term at which it was so rendered, etc.' And the eighth section of the same chapter provides that 'the lien of a judgment may always be enforced in a court of equity.' Do not these sections apply as well to judgments of the United States courts held within this state, as to judgments of our state courts? I apprehend they do, and I think there is no difference of opinion upon this subject among members of the legal profession. And so of the fourth section of the same chapter, in relation to the docketing of judgments and the preservation of judgment liens. If these sections apply to judgments of the circuit and district courts of the United States, why may not the fifth section of chapter one hundred and thirty apply to the records and judicial proceedings of these courts? The language is equally broad: It is 'a copy of any record or paper in the clerk's office of any court, may be admitted as evidence in lieu of the original, etc.' My present conviction is that said fifth section does embrace the records and judicial proceedings of these courts. And that to entitle them to be received as evidence in our state courts it is only necessary that they should be authenticated in the same manner as said section requires the records and judicial proceedings of our own courts to be certified to entitle them to be received as evidence. Such, according to my understanding, has, heretofore, been the universal practice of our state courts, and that practice so far as I have learned has been sanctioned by the legal profession of the state." Dickinson v. Railroad Co., 7 W. Va. 390, 418.

i. Judgment on Scire Facias.

A judgment on a scire facias for award of execution does not constitute a lien on real estate. Lavell v. McCurdy, 77 Va. 763.

j. Awards.

See the title ARBITRATION AND AWARD, vol. 1, p. 706.

An award is not of itself a lien on land. To make it a lien, or to give execution, it must be made the judgment or a decree of a court. Turner v. Stewart, 51 W. Va. 493, 494, 41 S. E. 924.

D. DOCKETING AND INDEXING JUDGMENTS.

1. Docketing Judgments.

a. Instruments Embraced by Statute.

The sections in Virginia and West Virginia relating to the docketing of judgments embrace recognizances and bonds having the force of a judgment. Va. Code, 1904, § 3580; W. Va. Code, 1899, ch. 139, § 4143; Dickinson v. Railroad Co., 7 W. Va. 390; Calwell v. Prindle, 19 W. Va. 604.

b. As to Whom Docketing Necessary.

(1) As between Purchasers and Judgment Creditors.

Former Rule.—Prior to the statute, it was held, that the lien of a judgment is a legal lien, and a purchaser of the title from the debtor, takes it subject to the lien, though he had no notice of it. Leake v. Ferguson, 2 Gratt. 419.

"The history of these statutes (i. e., the statute requiring the docketing of judgments) will show that they were framed for the protection of bona fide purchasers of real estate claiming, under alienation by or through the judgment debtor, real estate which, under former laws, would have been subject to the lien of the judgment, even in the hands of alienees, for value without notice. For, under these laws, the lien of the judgment, deriving its efficacy from the elegit, extended to a moiety of the debtor's lands, whether owned at the date of the judgment, or subsequently acquired; whether in the possession of the debtor himself or of bona fide purchasers from him. The case of Leake v. Ferguson, 2 Gratt. 419, 420, is a striking illustration of the harsh operation of this rule. In that case the purchaser had been in possession of the land for nearly fifteen years. He had paid full value for it, and he had no notice of any defect in the title. And yet the lien of the judgment was enforced against him in favor of a party who might have been justly charged with having slept upon his rights. Judge Allen said: 'The lien of a judgment is a legal lien, and the question of notice has no influence upon it. The purchaser takes the legal title, subject to the legal lien, whether a purchaser with or without notice.' See also, Taylor v. Spindle, 2 Gratt. 44; Rodgers v. M'Cluer, 4 Gratt. 81. The great hardship of these and like cases led, no doubt, to the act of 1843, the first law ever passed in Virginia requiring the docketing of judgments. See acts of 1842-43, p. —, revisal of 1849." Gordon v. Rixey, 76 Va. 694, 707.

Act of March 3d, 1843.—In the interest and for the protection of purchasers the act of March 3, 1843, was passed, which provided for the docketing of judgments, and further, that "no judgment, decree, bond or recognizance thereafter rendered should bind the land of any party to the same against a bona fide purchaser for valuable consideration without notice, unless the same should be docketed in the county or corporation, in which the land lay, within twelve months after the rendition, or forfeiture, of such judgment, decree, bond or recognizance, or ninety days before such land shall·have been conveyed to such purchaser." Renick v. Ludington, 14 W. Va. 367, 374.

"Except as thus modified in respect to purchasers by the act of 1843 the lien of the judgment continued the same in all respects as to its nature, extent, and the mode of enforcing it until the general revision of the laws of 1849, when the law was enacted substantially, as I have quoted it from the Code of 1860. Up to that time as we have seen, it was a mere incident of the writ of elegit, resulting by construction from the mandate of the writ, and dependent for its existence and continuance on the capacity to sue out the writ. It was now made for the first time as to judgments thereafter to be rendered an express, direct, positive, absolute lien on all the real estate, of or to which the judgment debtor should be possessed or entitled at or after the date of the judgment, or if it was rendered in court, at or after the commencement of the term, at which it was so rendered, with the same qualification as to purchasers for valuable consideration without notice, as was made by the act of 1843. The lien of the judgment being now express, positive and in no way dependent upon the elegit, and the remedy in equity being preferred in practice, the elegit soon fell into disuse and was finally abolished by the legislature of Virginia. Va. Code, 1873, ch. 183, § 26, p. 1175. It was also abolished in this state by the Code of 1868. W. Va. Code, ch. 140, § 2." Calwell v. Prindle, 19 W. Va. 604, 656.

Virginia Code, 1860.—Chapter 186 of the Code of Virginia of 1860 provided: No judgment shall be a lien on real estate as against a purchaser thereof for valuable consideration without notice, unless it be docketed according to the third and fourth sections of this chapter in the county or corporation, wherein such real estate is, either within a year next after the date of such judgment, or ninety days before the conveyance of such estate to such purchaser. Calwell v. Prindle, 19 W. Va. 604, 655.

Present Code Provisions.—No judgment shall be a lien on real estate as against a purchaser thereof for valuable consideration without notice until and except from the time that it is duly docketed in the clerk's office of the county or corporation wherein such real estate may be. (1872-73, p. 242; 1901-2, p. 427.) Va. Code, 1904, § 3570.

"No judgment shall be a lien on real estate as against a purchaser thereof for valuable consideration without notice. unless it be docketed according to the provisions of this chapter in the county or corporation wherein such real estate is, either within twenty days after the date of such judgment, or fifteen days before the conveyance of such real estate to such purchaser." Va. Code, 1904, § 3570; Wicks v. Scull, 102 Va. 290, 293, 46 S. E. 297.

No judgment shall be a lien on real estate as against a purchaser thereof for valuable consideration without notice, unless it be docketed according to the third and fourth sections of this chapter in the county wherein such real estate is, either within sixty days next after the date of the judgment or before a deed therefor to said purchaser, is delivered for record to the clerk of the county court. Provided, that the judgment of a justice of the peace shall not be a lien on real estate as against such purchaser, until the same is docketed as aforesaid. W. Va. Code, 1899, ch. 139, § 4146.

A judgment is not a lien on real estate as against subsequent purchasers for value and without notice, unless it is docketed in the mode and within the time prescribed by statute. Va. Code, 1873, ch. 182, § 8; W. Va. Code, ch. 139, § 7; Gurnee v. Johnson, 77 Va. 712; Duncan v. Custard, 24 W. Va. 730, 737; Renick v. Ludington, 14 W. Va. 367; Hill v. Rixey, 26 Gratt. 72; Gordon v. Rixey, 76 Va. 694; Bankers' Loan, etc., Co. v. Blair, 99 Va. 606, 39 S. E. 231; Maxwell v. Leeson, 50 W. Va. 361, 365, 40 S. E. 420; Rhea v. Preston, 75 Va. 757; Reed v. Ramey, 31 Gratt. 265; Northwestern Bank v. Hays, 37 W. Va. 475, 16 S. E. 561.

In Rhea v. Preston, 75 Va. 757, the court, citing Hill v. Rixey, 26 Gratt. 72, states the law as follows: "Judgments for money, whether docketed or not, bind the unaliened lands of the debtors, certainly those owned by him at the date of the judgments, and, it may be those subsequently acquired, in the order in which the judgments are recovered, and the same is true of decrees for money; and so though not docketed, they bind the debtor's land subsequently aliened to a purchaser with notice, even though he be a purchaser for value, but unless docketed, they are not liens on lands subsequently aliened to bona fide purchasers for value without notice—and a trustee in a deed of trust given to secure a debt and the creditors secured are purchasers for value within the meaning of our registry laws."

It will be seen that the only person protected by this section is a purchaser of real estate, for value without notice, which would otherwise be subject to the lien of the judgment. With respect to every other person, it is a matter of no sort of consequence whether the judgment be or be not docketed. Gordon v. Rixey, 76 Va. 694, 702.

The docketing of a judgment as of a day past, may be corrected, and will not affect rights acquired by third persons before the correction was made. Johnson v. National Exchange Bank, 33 Gratt. 473.

Duty to Docket.—To docket his judgment is a creditor's privilege, not his duty. If he fails to docket it, he may lose his lien on the real estate aliened to a purchaser for value without notice. Gurnee v. Johnson, 77 Va. 712.

Purpose of Statute.—"The history of these statutes (i. e., the statute requiring the docketing of judgments) will show that they were framed for the protection of bona fide purchasers of real estate claiming, under alienation by or through the judgment debtor, real estate which, under former laws, would have been subject to the lien of the judgment, even in the hands of alienees, for value without notice. For, under these laws the lien of the judgment, deriving its efficacy from the elegit, extended to a moiety of the debtor's lands, whether owned at the date of the judgment, or subsequently acquired; whether in the possession of the debtor himself or of bona fide purchasers from him. The case of Leake v. Ferguson, 2 Gratt. 419, 420, is a striking illustration of the harsh operation of this rule. In that case the purchaser had been in possession of the land for nearly fifteen years. He had paid full value for it, and he had no notice of any defect in the title. And yet the lien of the judgment was enforced against him in favor of a party who might have been justly charged with having slept upon his rights. Judge Allen said: 'The lien of a judgment is a legal lien, and the question of notice has no influence upon it. The purchaser takes the legal title, subject to the legal lien, whether a purchaser with or without notice.' See also, Taylor v. Spindle, 2 Gratt. 44; Rodgers v. McCluer, 4 Gratt. 81. The great hardship of these and like cases led, no doubt, to the act of 1843, the first law ever passed in Virginia requiring the docketing of judgments. See acts of 1842-43, p. —, revival of 1849." Gordon v. Rixey, 76 Va. 694, 701.

Statute Does Not Create the Lien.— "It is a mistake to suppose, that the 9th section of ch. 186 of the Code of 1860, amended by § 7 of ch. 136, Code of West Virginia, was intended to create a lien against the purchaser by docketing the judgment. The lien is created by § 5 of ch. 139 of the Code of West Virginia, and attaches to all the real estate of the debtor, and continues, except so far as is qualified by § 7. The qualification is, that it shall not extend to real estate aliened after judgment to purchasers for value, who had no notice of the judgment, unless the judgment be docketed in the manner and within the time prescribed. The implication is irresistible, that if so docketed it shall be a lien; that is, that the lien, which was created by § 5, shall continue as to such purchasers. Renick v. Ludington, 14 W. Va. 367, 375.

(2) As between Judgment Debtor and Creditor.

Moreover, it has been held, that as between the judgment creditor and debtor the statute requiring the judgment to be docketed has no application or force. Renick v. Ludington, 14 W. Va. 367; Grantham v. Lucas, 24 W. Va. 231; McClaskey v. O'Brien, 16 W. Va. 791; Gatewood v. Goode, 23 Gratt. 880; Renick v. Ludington, 20 W. Va. 511.

"Numerous cases have been cited upon the statutes of the different states requiring all judgments to be docketed. Upon the question the decisions are very conflicting. In many of them it has been held that it is the duty of the creditor to see to it that his judgment is properly docketed. If he fails to do so, he loses the benefit of the judgment lien. But in all these cases the controversy was between the judgment creditor on the one hand and the bona fide purchaser on the other for valuable consideration without notice. If, in the present case, the right of such a purchaser was' involved, very different considerations might govern. This, however, is a controversy between creditors, who, it is well settled, stand upon no higher ground than the common debtor. If the judgment is valid as to the debtor, it is equally so as to the creditor, unless it can be impeached on some ground of fraud or collusion. The authorities generally hold, that the statutes relating to the recordation of deeds and docketing of judgments are merely directory, and the failure of the clerk or other officer to comply with their provisions can not affect the rights of parties claiming under such deeds or judgments." Shadrack v. Woolfolk, 32 Gratt. 707.

At the March term, 1861, of the county court of Monroe, a judgment was rendered at the suit of the bank of V., plaintiff, against W., S. and G., the latter living in the county of Bath. Execution of fi. fa. was issued on this judgment and levied on the property of W., and the sheriff returned, after June, 1861, a levy upon the personal property of W., that the property was appraised and offered for sale, and not bringing valuation it was returned. G. died during the war, leaving real estate in Bath county, and also in West Virginia; and after his death some of his creditors filed their bill in the circuit court of Bath, to subject his real estate to the payment of his debts. The commissioner reported the above judgment as a debt by judgment having priority. A copy of the judgment was certified by the clerk of Monroe circuit court, "and as such, keeper of the records of Monroe county court, and which by law are a part of the records of my office." The circuit court confirmed the report. Held, the judgment constituted, as between the parties thereto, a lien on the real estate in Virginia belonging to the judgment debtors or any of them, whether the said judgment was docketed in the counties in which the real estate might be or not. Gatewood v. Goode, 23 Gratt. 880.

(3) As against the State.

President Johnson, in a dictum, in Hoge v. Brookover, 28 W. Va. 304, was of opinion that the act requiring judgment liens to be docketed in order to preserve them as against purchasers of the property, to which they are attached, does not affect a judgment in favor of the state. See Va. Code 1904, § 3565.

In the case of Calwell v. Prindle, 19 W. Va. 604, 605, the judgments considered were recorded in Virginia prior to the separation. The "docketing act" was held not to deprive the state of West Virginia of the judgment; but it was not held, that it was necessary that the state should docket its judgments in order to preserve the liens. The quære was propounded, whether the statute of limitations would apply.

There is nothing in the case contrary to the position taken here, and the reasoning is in perfect harmony with our position.

(4) As against Assignees.

If as against the assignee of purchase money bonds, the creditor is not required to docket his judgment, a failure to docket can raise no equity in behalf of such assignee. So far as he is concerned, the rights of the judgment creditor are precisely the same as they would be if the statute had neer been passed requiring judgments to be docketed. Gordon v. Rixey, 76 Va. 694, 704.

(5) As against Subsequent Creditors.

Judgment, though undocketed, is good against subsequent creditors, with or without notice. Gordon v. Rixey, 76 Va. 694.

"It has been said, however, that if the creditor may neglect for years to docket his judgment, no one can ever be safe in taking an assignment of bonds, however well secured by lien on real estate, and however apparently free from every defect affecting their value, for the assignee may, at any remote period, be surprised by a secret encumbrance, or some latent equity, of the existence of which he can have no notice. This argument might be addressed to the legislature with more propriety than to the courts. The statutes of registration do not profess, and were not designed, to guard against all the mischiefs which arise from conflicting titles or successive alienations of property. An undocketed judgment is good against subsequent creditors, with or without notice, and yet the subsequent creditor may have trusted the debtor upon the faith of his ownership of an apparently unencumbered estate." Gordon v. Rixey, 76 Va. 694, 703.

An undocketed judgment is good against subsequent creditors with or without notice, and yet the subsequent creditor may have trusted the debtor upon the faith of his ownership of an apparently unencumbered estàte. It has been repeatedly held, by this court, that the lien of a judgment is an express, absolute, statutory lien on the debtor's real estate, and the right to resort to the courts to enforce it is a legal right without terms or conditions to be imposed, except the one which we have noticed as the sole exception,' which protects the purchaser without notice against an unrecorded lien upon the land which he buys. As to all other persons and all other real estate the rights of the judgment creditor are precisely the same as they would be if the statute had never been passed, requiring judgments to be docketed. Gurnee *v.* Johnson, 77 Va. 712, 727.

c. Computation of Time—Stay Law.

The act of March 2, 1866, sess. acts, 1865-66, p. 191, ch. 77, § 1, "to preserve and extend the time for the exercise of certain civil rights and remedies," is retrospective in its operation, and applies in favor of a judgment creditor as to the docketing of his judgment. Hill *v.* Rixey, 26 Gratt. 72, citing Hart *v.* Haynes, 1 Va. Dec. 201.

The docketing of a judgment is an act to be done to preserve or prevent the loss of a civil right or remedy, w'thin the meaning of the acts of March 4, 1862, acts of 1861-62, ch. 81, and of March 2, 1866, Code of 1873, ch. 146, §§ 6, 7, p. 998, 999. And therefore in computing the time within which a judgment is required by § 8, ch. 186, of the Code of 1860, to be docketed, in order to preserve the lien of such judgment against purchasers, the period between the 17th of April, 1861, and the 2d of March, 1866, is not to be computed as a part of such time. Borst *v.* Nalle, 28 Gratt. 423.

Under the act of March 2, 1866, entitled "An act to preserve and extend

the time for the exercise of certain civil rights and remedies" (which act .confirms those of February 23, 1862, and March 14, 1862), in computing the time within which A. was required, by ch. 186, §§ 6, 8, of the Code of 1860, to docket his judgment in order to preserve the lien thereof, the period from April 17, 1861, to March 2, 1866, must be excluded. Hart *v.* Haynes, 1 Va. Dec. 201, 202.

d. Effect of Actual or Constructive Notice.

(1) Of Undocketed Judgments.

(a) Prior to the Statute.

"The lien of a judgment is a legal lien. The question of notice has no influence upon it, or had not until the passage of the recent statute requiring judgments to be recorded to preserve the lien. What influence that statute may have upon a purchaser with notice of an unrecorded, judgment, it is unnecessary now to consider, as this case must be decided according to the laws previously in force. By those laws, the debtor was left in the enjoyment of the legal title, subject to the right of the judgment creditor to charge the lands; and the purchaser from the debtor took the legal title subject to the legal lien, whether a purchaser with or without notice of the judgment." Leake *v.* Ferguson, 2 Gratt. 419.

"The definition given by the counsel, of the nature and source of the judgment lien, is inaccurate and erroneous in all its parts. Notice, actual or constructive, is in no respect an element in the constitution of the legal lien of the judgment creditor, on the legal estate of the debtor. That lien, where it exists, deriving its existence from the mandate of the elegit to deliver a moiety of the lands. etc., of which the debtor was seized at the date of the judgment, at a reasonable extent, overreaches all intermediate conveyances, 'without regard to the point of notice or not notice. A judgment creditor whose lien is against the legal estate, may pursue his remedy notwithstanding a sale, though the sale be bona fide, and without notice; and he can not be deprived of his remedy, or have his priority disturbed.' 3 Pres. on Abs. 327. That lien does not arise from the presumption of the court, that the purchaser has notice of the judgment; but results from the express grant of the law, imported by the terms of the execution which the law authorizes him to use. In such case the inquiry into notice or no notice, actual or constructive, is supererogatory. The question of notice (and that is always one in respect to actual notice), only arises when equitable interests of the debtor are pursued by the creditor, against a purchaser for value, having the legal estate, or a right to call for it; or where the neglect of the creditor to have his judgment registered, or docketed, has impaired the legal force of the lien. 3 Preston on Abs. 328. Davis v. Strathmore, 16 Ves. 419. The reference to Gilbert on Ex'ons 12, was, I apprehend, not apposite. The effect of the common-law scire facias in a real action, is not the measure of the force and effect of the statutory lien of the elegit." Taylor v. Spindle, 2 Gratt. 44.

The history of these statutes requiring the docketing of judgments will show that they were framed for the protection of bona fide purchasers of real estate claiming, under alienation by or through the judgment debtor, real estate which, under former laws, would have been subject to the lien of the judgment, even in the hands of alienees, for value without notice. For, under these laws, the lien of the judgment, deriving its efficacy from the elegit, extended to a moiety of the debtor's lands, whether owned at the date of the judgment, or subsequently acquired; whether in the possession of the debtor himself or of bona fide purchasers from him. The case of Leake v. Ferguson, 2 Gratt. 420, is a striking illustration of the harsh operations of this rule. In that case the purchaser had been in possession of the land for nearly fifteen years. He had paid full value for it, and he had had no notice of any defect in the title. And yet the lien of the judgment was enforced against him in favor of a party who might have been justly charged with having slept upon his rights. Judge Allen said: "The lien of a judgment is a legal lien, and the question of notice has no influence upon it. The purchaser takes the legal title, subject to the legal lien, whether a purchaser with or without notice." See also, Taylor v. Spindle, 2 Gratt. 44; Rodgers v. McCluer, 4 Gratt. 81. The great hardship of these and like cases led, no doubt, to the act of 1843, the first law ever passed in Virginia requiring the docketing of judgments. See acts of 1842-43, p. —, revisal of 1849. Gordon v. Rixey, 76 Va. 694, 701.

(b) Under the Statute.

Whatever the rule may be elsewhere, in Virginia and West Virginia, subsequent purchasers are bound by actual notice of a judgment never entered on the judgment lien docket as required by the statute. Johnson v. National Exchange Bank, 33 Gratt. 473; Cold River, etc., Co. v. Webb, 3 W. Va. 438; Craig v. Sebrell, 9 Gratt. 131; Rhea v. Preston, 75 Va. 757; Heermans v. Montague, 2 Va. Dec. 6; McClaskey v. O'Brien, 16 W. Va. 791; Wicks v. Scull, 102 Va. 290, 46 S. E. 297.

In West Virginia the judgment is a lien on the land as against the debtor, and on land conveyed by him after the judgment in the hands of his vendee purchasing after the docketing of the judgment or without docketing if he have notice of it. He takes the land encumbered by the judgment. He stands in the shoes of the judgment debtor, having acquired the land with notice of the judgment creditor's rights, and thus he can be in no better plight than the judgment debtor. Maxwell *v.* Leeson, 50 W. Va. 361, 365, 40 S. E. 420.

Judgments for money, whether docketed or not, bind the unaliened lands of the debtor; certainly those owned by him at the date of the judgments, and, it may be, those subsequently acquired, in the order in which the judgments are recovered, and the same is true of decrees for money; and so, though not docketed, they bind the debtor's lands subsequently aliened to a purchaser with notice, even though he be a purchaser for value; but unless docketed they are not liens on lands subsequently aliened to bona fide purchasers for value without notice—and a trustee in a deed of trust given to secure a debt, and the creditor secured, are purchasers for value within the meaning of the registration laws. Code of 1860, ch. 186, §§ 6, 8, 11; Code of 1873, ch. 182, §§ 1, 6, 8, 11. Rhea *v.* Preston, 75 Va. 757, citing Hill *v.* Rixey, 26 Gratt. 72; Borst *v.* Nalle, 28 Gratt. 423, 428; Williams *v.* Lord, 5 Va. Law J. 243, 250; Williams *v.* Lord, 75 Va. 390.

Judgment is a lien upon land in the hands of a purchaser, though at the time of the conveyance execution upon the judgment was suspended by an injunction. And the lien exists though the judgment was not docketed, the purchaser having had notice thereof. Craig *v.* Sebrell, 9 Gratt. 131.

In the case of Renick *v.* Ludington, 14 W. Va. 367, it was held, by this court, that "Section seven of chapter one hundred and thirty-nine was enacted for the protection of purchasers for valuable consideration without notice of judgments; but that protection only extends to the land so conveyed to such purchaser, it being liable to the satisfaction of judgments docketed

only." Of course this last section of the syllabus means, or was intended to mean, liable for the satisfaction of judgments of which the purchaser had notice or which were docketed according to law, and to such judgments only. Reaffirmed in Renick *v.* Ludington, 20 W. Va. 511.

Section seven of chapter one hundred and thirty-nine of said Code of 1868 was enacted mainly for the protection of purchasers for valuable consideration without notice of judgments; but that protection only extends to the land so conveyed to such purchaser, it being liable for the satisfaction of judgments of which the purchaser had notice, or which were docketed according to law, and to such judgments only; and so of section eight of chapter one hundred and eighty-six of the Code of Virginia of 1860. McClaskey *v.* O'Brien, 16 W. Va. 791.

A deed of trust creditor may be bound by actual notice of an undocketed judgment. Cold River, etc., Co. *v.* Webb, 3 W. Va. 438.

Place of Docketing.—Purchaser of land under decree in county wherein it lies, is not affected by constructive notice of judgment in another county which is not docketed in former county until after sale is confirmed and purchase money paid, though title is retained. Logan *v.* Pannill, 90 Va. 11, 17 S. E. 744.

Docketing a judgment in the clerk's office of the county court of a county out of which a city is subsequently carved is not constructive notice of such judgment to a purchaser for value of land acquired by the judgment debtor several years after the incorporation of the city. Wicks *v.* Scull, 102 Va. 290, 46 S. E. 297.

Lands in Another County.—A purchaser of land at a judicial sale in the county where the land lies, under a decree of the circuit court of that county, can not be affected by constructive notice of a judgment obtained in another county, which is not recorded in the county where the land is situated, before the confirmation of the sale; actual notice or knowledge of the judgment must be brought home to the purchaser before the payment of the purchase money. Logan v. Pannill, 90 Va. 11, 17 S. E. 744.

Notice to Agent or Trustee.—Previous actual notice or knowledge by a subsequent purchaser's agent or trustee of a prior unrecorded lien on his real estate, will affect the creditor, provided the notice or knowledge was imparted or given to the agent in the same transaction, unless one transaction is closely followed by and connected with the other. Morrison v. Bausemer, 32 Gratt. 225; Johnson v. National Exchange Bank, 33 Gratt. 473.

The trustee in a deed to secure creditors is a purchaser for value, and notice to him is notice to the beneficiaries. Merchants' Bank v. Ballou, 98 Va. 112, 32 S. E. 481; Wicks v. Scull, 102 Va. 290, 46 S. E. 297.

The beneficiaries in a deed of trust are affected with notice to the trustee, although he did not know of the existence of the deed or of an intention to make it until it was recorded, and then immediately declined the trust. Merchants' Bank v. Ballou, 98 Va. 112, 32 S. E. 481.

Sufficiency of Proof.—Though T., the trustee, had been the judge who made the decree against W., yet, he stating in his answer, and also in his deposition, that he had no recollection of the decree when the deed was made and recorded; held, in order to affect the creditor by the previous notice or knowledge of his agent or trustee, of the existence of a prior unrecorded lien on the real estate which is conveyed for his security, it is necessary that the notice or knowledge should have been given or imparted to the agent in the same transaction, unless one transaction is closely followed by and connected with the other. In this

case the evidence does not establish notice. Johnson v. National Exchange Bank, 33 Gratt. 473.

"It may be conceded that notice to the trustee was in effect notice to the creditor secured by the deed of trust. But, as was held by this court in Morrison v. Bausemer, Moncure, P., delivering the opinion of the court, 32 Gratt. 225, 229, 'if a trustee in a deed of trust to secure a debt had notice or knowledge of the existence of a judgment against the grantor in the deed of trust at a time anterior to the execution of the deed of trust, but have no remembrance of such existence at the time of such execution, the trust creditor will not be at all affected by such anterior notice or knowledge on the part of such trustee.' In that case it appeared that the trustee, Newman, about a year before the execution of the deed of trust to him and Trout, had notice or knowledge of the existence of said judgment. He was then writing in the clerk's office of the court which rendered the judgment, and as deputy or assistant of the clerk, made a copy of it, and signed the clerk's name to it for the creditor. There was no evidence that he remembered the fact at the time the deed of trust was executed, except what might be presumed from the fact of his having made a copy of it. Upon his examination as a witness, he could not say that he had any recollection about it one way or the other at the time the deed of trust was executed. In that case it was held, that the proof of notice was insufficient." Johnson v. National Exchange Bank, 33 Gratt. 473.

M. claimed to subject the proceeds of land under a deed of trust duly recorded. B. claimed priority of M.'s deed under an unrecorded judgment rendered before the deed of trust was executed, on the ground that N., a trustee in M.'s deed, had notice of the judgment at the time of the execution of the deed. Held, if an agent, before the commencement of his agency, receive notice of an unrecorded lien on real estate of which his principal afterwards becomes a purchaser, such notice of the agent will not be imputable to the principal unless there be very strong evidence that at the time of the purchase, the agent remembered the fact that he had received such notice. Though N., then a deputy clerk in the clerk's office where the judgment was recovered, made a copy of said judgment about twelve months before the execution of M.'s deed, this is, not of itself sufficient evidence of his recollecting the fact when the deed was executed; and there being no other evidence of the fact, the deed of M. has priority over the judgment of P. Morrison v. Bausemer, 32 Gratt. 225.

Proof of Notice.—Plain and unambiguous recitals in a deed of trust may constitute sufficient notice to the trust creditors of a prior undocketed judgment against their debtor. Cold River, etc., Co. v. Webb, 3 W. Va. 438, citing Wiley v. Givens, 6 Gratt. 277; Hannon v. Hannah, 9 Gratt. 146.

Where the recitals of a deed under which a purchaser claims show that a third person was formerly the equitable owner of the land, such purchaser is charged with notice of that fact, and the land is bound in his hands for prior judgments against such equitable owner which have been duly docketed. Flanary v. Kane, 102 Va. 547, 46 S. E. 312.

W. obtained a judgment against the C. R. N. Co. His judgment was never placed on the lien docket. More than two years afterwards the company gave a trust to secure its creditors, including the debt due to W., which was therein described as the balance due on a judgment to W., "rendered in the United States District Court, held at Charleston, Kanawha county, in the spring of 1856. The balance being now about two thousand dollars." W. filed a bill to enforce his judgment, and the defendants alleged a want of notice by reason of its not being docketed, and also that they had no actual notice of it. Held, that the trustee and trust creditors claiming the benefit of the trust are estopped by the recital of the deed from averring a want of notice of the judgment, at the time of the execution of the deed. There being nothing in the record to show that W. had any notice or knowledge of a judgment on a suggestion issued on an execution against him, whereby a part of the proceeds of the sale of the works of the company, by the trustee, were applied to the payment of the judgment on the suggestion, it is held, that he can not be presumed to have accepted the provisions of the trust in consequence of this judgment on the suggestion; especially as his suit had been pending for many years, to enforce his lien. Cold River, etc., Co. v. Webb, 3 W. Va. 438.

Presumption.—In Farley v. Bateman, 40 W. Va. 540, 22 S. E. 72, it was held, that the fact that a subsequent purchaser had notice of a prior undocketed judgment may be inferred from circumstances as well as proved by direct evidence. Judge Dent, in delivering the opinion of the court, said: "The question presented in this case is whether the defendant Mann was a purchaser for valuable consideration without notice of plaintiffs' undocketed judgment. The fact of notice may be inferred from circumstances as well as proved by direct evidence; and where the facts and circumstances are such as to raise a presumption of notice, the burden of proof is shifted, and it devolves upon the defendant purchaser to prove want of notice. Newman v. Chapman, 2 Rand. 93; French v. Loyal Co., 5 Leigh 627, 635."

(2) Of Unrecorded Deeds.

(a) In General.

But under the recording acts, a contract in writing for the sale of real estate, not recorded before a creditor has docketed his judgment against the vendor, is subordinate to such judgment, whether the judgment creditor had notice of such contract or not. Dobyns v. Waring, 82 Va. 159; March v. Chambers, 30 Gratt. 299; Eidson v. Huff, 29 Gratt. 338.

As against the creditors of a judgment debtor an unrecorded deed of the latter is a mere nullity. It has no existence as to them, and their rights are to be determined as if it had never been executed. Such creditors have the right to subject the land so conveyed to the payment of their judgments, and also to subject the improvements put on the land by the grantee, although they knew of the existence of the deed. Such creditors are not affected by knowledge of the conveyance and the fact that the alienee is making improvements. Flanary v. Kane, 102 Va. 547, 46 S. E. 312.

The words "without notice" in the statute declaring unrecorded deeds void as to creditors and subsequent purchasers, refer to purchasers alone, and not to creditors as well. Price v. Wall, 97 Va. 334, 33 S. E. 599, citing Eidson v. Huff, 29 Gratt. 338; March v. Chambers, 30 Gratt. 299; Dobyns v. Waring, 82 Va. 159.

Illustrative Cases.—At the February term, 1857, of the court, a judgment was recovered against S., and H. as his surety, on a forthcoming bond, and it was docketed on the 1st of April, 1857. An execution was issued on this judgment, and it was paid by H. On the 8th of October, 1856, S., by written agreement under seal, sold to E. a house and lot, and delivered possession, and on the 18th of the same month S. conveyed the same to E. This deed was acknowledged on the same day, H. being one of the justices who took the acknowledgment; but it was not presented in the clerk's office for record until March 9th, 1857. Upon a bill by H., against E. and S., to be substituted to the lien of the judgment against S., it was held: Notice of a deed or written agreement for the sale of land does not affect a creditor of the grantor. "It has been argued, however, that Mrs. Hanger's possession of the house and lot was sufficient notice to all the world of her title, and was equivalent in law to the recordation of the deed and title bond. To sustain this position the learned counsel for the appellant has cited certain cases of other states in which it has been held that possession is notice of the purchaser's equity. Whatever may be the rule elsewhere, it is perfectly clear that in Virginia the possession of the grantee or vendee does not dispense with the necessity of recordation so far as creditors are concerned. Whether such possession is sufficient to put a purchaser upon inquiry, and thus affect him with notice, is a question we are not called on to decide. We are now dealing with the rights of creditors only. As to them both the deed and title bond are void unless recorded, whether they (the creditors) have or have not notice. This distinction between creditors and purchasers was made at an early day in the registration laws, and has been recognized for more than forty years, through all the amendments and revisals of our statutes, and by the decisions of our courts. The unrecorded deed or contract is only void as to purchasers for a valuable consideration without notice, and it is void as to creditors also, even though they may have notice. It is not our province to consider whether this distinction rests upon any just or solid ground. It is sufficient for us that it exists and is the well-settled law. It does not matter, therefore, that Mrs. Hanger had actual possession of the premises; and it is equally immaterial that the appellee had actual notice of the deed to Mrs. Hanger." Eidson v. Huff, 29 Gratt. 338, 341.

Subrogation.—At the February term, 1857, of the court, a judgment was recovered against S., and H. as his surety, on a forthcoming bond, and it was docketed on the 1st of April, 1857. An execution was issued on this judgment, and it was paid by H. On the 8th of October, 1856, S., by written agreement under seal, sold to E. a house and lot, and delivered possession, and on the 18th of the same month S. conveyed the same to E. This deed was acknowledged on the same day, H. being one of the justices who took the acknowledgment; but it was not presented in the clerk's office for record until March 9th, 1857. Upon a bill by H., against E. and S., to be substituted to the lien of the judgment against S., it was held: H. is entitled to be substituted to the lien of the judgment. The judgment having been docketed within twelve months from the date of its being rendered, and the deed not having been recorded within sixty days from its acknowledgment, the judgment is a lien upon the house and lot as against the deed. The agreement not having been recorded, it is void as to the creditor, and as to H. claiming under him, though H. had notice of the deed and E. had possession of the house and lot. Notice of a deed or written agreement for the sale of land does not affect a creditor of the grantor. Eidson *v.* Huff, 29 Gratt. 338.

(b) Possession as Notice.

The Virginia Code provides that the possession of any such estate or term, without notice or evidence of title, shall not be notice to subsequent purchasers for valuable consideration. Va. Code, 1904, § 2465.

e. Conclusiveness of Notice.

The regular docketing of judgments under the statute gives constructive, but nevertheless conclusive, notice thereof to all the world. Citizens' Nat. Bank *v.* Manoni, 76 Va. 802.

Purchasers of land are conclusively affected with notice of judgments duly obtained and docketed against the owner, and no lis pendens or other notice of a suit to subject the land to such judgment is needed to affect them. Sharitz *v.* Moyers, 99 Va. 519, 39 S. E. 166.

Section 14, ch. 139, of the Virginia Code does not affect the common-law doctrine of lis pendens, where a judgment lien had, under the provisions of the Code, been previously acquired on the land, and duly docketed. "The common-law doctrine of lis pendens, as applied to this case, is in no way affected by § 14 of ch. 139 of the Code, which provides that: 'The pending of an action, suit or proceeding to subject real estate to the payment of any debt or liability, upon which a previous lien shall not have been acquired in some one or more of the methods prescribed by law, shall not bind or affect a purchaser of such real estate, unless, and until a memorandum, setting forth the title of the cause, the court in which it is pending, the several objects of the suit, the location and quantity of the land, as near as may be, and the name of the person whose estate therein is intended to be affected by the action or suit, shall be filed with the recorder of the county in which the land is situated;' because in this case a lien by judgment had been previously acquired, and duly docketed." Harmon *v.* Bryam, 11 W. Va. 511, 521.

f. Place of Docketing.

A judgment is not a lien on real estate unless docketed in the county or corporation in which the land is situated. W. Va. Code, 1899, ch. 139, § 4146; Va. Code, 1904, § 3570.

Docketing a judgment in the clerk's office of the county court of a county out of which a city is subsequently carved, is not constructive notice of such judgment to a purchaser for value of land acquired by the judgment debtor several years after the incorporation of the city. Wicks v. Scull, 102 Va. 290, 46 S. E. 297.

Lands in Another County.—Where a creditor has judgments in one county against persons who have an interest in lands in another county, and knows of the pendency of a suit to partition such lands, and he does not intervene in such suit or record his judgments in the latter county till after a sale of the land is confirmed, and does not give the purchaser actual notice of his judgments before the purchase money is paid, he can not subject the land to the payment of such judgments. Logan v. Pannill, 90 Va. 11, 17 S. E. 744.

Purchase Money Bonds.—It was held, in Logan v. Pannill, 90 Va. 11, 17 S. E. 744, that a judgment not docketed in the county wherein the land of the debtor, lies, and is sold under a decree in partition, does not, upon being docketed in such county, become a lien upon bonds for the purchase money in the hands of the assignee who has no notice of the judgment, though title to the land was retained by the prior owners as security for the payment of the bonds, because the bonds are personalty, and not subject to the lien of any judgment when no execution is sued out upon them.

Cloud on Title.—A judgment, though not docketed in the county or corporation in which land lies, constitutes a cloud on the title of a purchaser for value and without notice of such land from the judgment debtor which he may file a bill, to remove, as the fact of the existence of the judgment may still be established by extrinsic evidence, and as long as such an issue can be made, the judgment constitutes a cloud upon the title of the purchaser, and depreciates its value. Wicks v. Scull, 102 Va. 290, 46 S. E. 297.

g. Effect of Separation of Virginia and West Virginia.

The state of Virginia upon notices and motions by the name of "The Commonwealth" instituted and prosecuted by the auditor of public accounts on the 6th day of March, 1860, recovered two several judgments against Edmund S. Calwell "in the circuit court of Richmond" as one of the securities of John E. Lewis, late sheriff of Greenbrier county, the one being for $4,893.92, the balance of the land property, and capitation and September license taxes of 1854 due from said John E. Lewis, late sheriff of Greenbrier county, with interest thereon to be computed at the rate of six per centum per annum from the 17th day of January, 1855, until paid, and the costs of the motion, $13.44, and the other being for $1,073.86, the balance of June, 1855, license taxes, due from said John E. Lewis, late sheriff of Greenbrier county, with interest thereon to be computed at the rate of six per centum per annum from the 20th day of June, 1855, until paid, and $161.07 for damages thereon according to law, also the cost of the motion, $11.94. The law in force at the time said notices were given and motions made and judgments were rendered provided, that "the auditor of public accounts shall institute and prosecute all proceedings proper to enforce payment of money to the commonwealth —that the proceeding may be in the circuit court of the city of Richmond —that when it is at law, it may be by action or motion—that "every judgment on any such motion shall be in the name of the commonwealth." And the city of Richmond being the capital of the state of Virginia, as judicially known to the court, held: The said two judgments were docketed in the clerk's office of the county court of Greenbrier county by the clerk thereof, in the name of "the commonwealth against Edmund S. Calwell," on the 29th day of September, 1860, in the judgment lien docket kept in the clerk's office of said county court for the purpose of docketing judgments under the fourth section of said ch. 186 of said Code of 1860. Said judgments as docketed plainly show the date and the amount of each judgment and the date of the docketing of each judgment and the amount and date of each credit. But the judgment was not indexed in the name of the defendant, Edmund S. Calwell. Held also, that under ch. 186, §§ 4, 8, of the said Code of 1860, indexing was not a necessary part of the docketing of the judgment; the docketing is complete without the indexing for the purpose of preserving the liens of the judgments upon the real estate of the said judgment debtor in Greenbrier county, as against a purchaser therefor for valuable consideration without notice. That said docketing of each of said judgments as aforesaid preserved the lien of each of said judgments upon the real estate of said Edmund S. Calwell, in the county of Greenbrier, in favor of the state of Virginia, as against a purchaser thereof for valuable consideration without notice until the 20th day of June, 1863 and preserved the lien of each of said judgments upon the real estate of the said Edmund S. Calwell, in the said county of Greenbrier, in favor of the state of West Virginia, as against a purchaser thereof for valuable consideration without notice, on the said 20th of June, 1863, and from thence forward. Calwell v. Prindle, 19 W. Va. 604.

Where a judgment was recovered in the county court of Monroe county, W. Va., in March, 1861, against three debtors, W., S. and G., and the latter lived in Bath county, but during the war, died, leaving real estate in Bath county, it was held that the judgment constituted as between the parties thereto, a lien on the real estate in Bath county, whether the judgment was docketed or not, and the lien of the judgment on the lands of G. in Bath county, was neither lost nor im-

paired by reason of the division of the state of Virginia into two states, and the falling of the county of Monroe into the state of West Virginia, moreover, the certificate of the clerk of the circuit court of Monroe county, West Virginia, of the records of which court the records of the former county court of Monroe form a part, is proper evidence of the judgment. Gatewood v. Goode, 23 Gratt. 880.

h. Particular Judgments Considered.

(1) Judgments by Confession.

Where a judgment by confession amounts to a preference under § 2, ch. 74, W. Va. Code, and has not been docketed in the office of the clerk of the county court in the judgment lien docket as provided in § 4, ch. 139, Code, a creditor is not limited to four months in which to attack it by suit as a preference. Quære, whether, when so docketed the creditor must sue within four months thereafter. Nuzum v. Herron, 52 W. Va. 499, 44 S. E. 257.

(2) Judgments of United States Courts.

Judgments and decrees rendered in a circuit or district court of the United States within this state may be docketed in the clerks' offices of courts of this state in the same manner and under the same rules and requirements of law as judgments and decrees of courts of this state. (1889-90, p. 22.) Va. Code, 1904, § 3559a. See Dickinson v. Railroad Co., 7 W. Va. 390.

(3) Judgments of Justices.

Under § 5, ch. 139, W. Va. Code, a judgment for money rendered by a justice against any person is a lien from the date of said judgment, on the real estate of or to which such person shall be possessed or entitled, at or after such date. But such judgment is not a lien on real estate as against a purchaser thereof for valuable consideration, without notice, until the same is docketed in the judgment lien docket in the office of the clerk of the county court as provided in § 4, ch. 139, Code. Nuzum *v.* Herron, 52 W. Va. 499, 44 S. E. 257, 259.

(4) Judgments in Favor of Commonwealth.

Whenever a judgment is recovered in favor of the commonwealth, it shall be the duty of the attorney-general or other attorney representing the commonwealth, to cause the said judgment to be docketed in all counties and corporations wherein there is any real estate owned by any person against whom the judgment is recovered. (1884, p. 82.) Va. Code, 1904, § 3565. But see Hoge *v.* Brookover, 28 W. Va. 304

i. Construction of Statute.

(1) In General.

The authorities generally hold that the statutes relating to the docketing of judgments are merely directory, and the failure of the clerk or other officer to comply with their provisions can not affect the rights of parties claiming under such deeds or judgments. Shadrack *v.* Woolfolk, 32 Gratt. 707, 712.

"Numerous cases have been cited upon the statutes of the different states requiring all judgments to be docketed. Upon this question the decisions are very conflicting. In many of them it has been held, that it is the duty, of the creditor to see to it that his judgment is properly docketed. If he fails to do so, he loses the benefit of the judgment lien. But in all these cases the controversy was between the judgment creditor on the one hand and the bona fide purchaser on the other for valuable consideration without notice. If, in the present case, the right of such a purchaser was involved, very different considerations might govern. This, however, is a controversy between creditors, who, it is well settled, stand upon no higher ground than the common debtor. If the judgment is valid as to the debtor, it is equally so as to the creditor, unless it can be impeached on some ground of fraud or collusion. The authorities generally hold that the statutes relating to the recordation of deeds and docketing of judgments are merely directory, and the failure of the clerk or other officer to comply with their provisions can not affect the rights of parties claiming under such deeds or judgments." Shadrack *v.* Woolfolk, 32 Gratt. 707.

"The law requiring judgments to be docketed is an enactment of great public utility, founded upon the same considerations of public policy as the laws requiring the recordation of deeds, title bonds and marriage contracts. By discountenancing secret trusts and liens they encourage the sale of property, and protect the rights of innocent purchasers. The very fact that the judgment could not be enforced was an additional reason for requiring it to be docketed. The creditor might justly claim that the indulgence granted the debtor should not impair his legal rights and remedies; but he could not justly claim that this indulgence should also release him (the creditor) from a compliance with the laws intended for the protection of third persons. The object of the seventh section was to prevent the bar of the statute in favor of the debtor, but not to relieve the creditor of the duty he owed to innocent purchasers. In this view I am sustained by the opinion of Judge Bouldin in Sexton *v.* Crockett, 23 Gratt. 857." Hill *v.* Rixey, 26 Gratt. 72, 79.

(2) Retrospective Operation.

The act of March 3, 1843, sess. acts, 1842-43, p. 51, does not apply to purchasers before the passage of the act. As to such the lien of a prior judgment is valid though not recorded. McCance *v.* Taylor, 10 Gratt. 580, followed in Hoge *v.* Brookover, 28 W. Va. 304, 313.

"It is alleged that Taylor's lien was lost by his omission to docket his judgment, according to the provisions of the statute, March 3d, 1843, sess, acts, p. 52, § 3. Before considering this objection, it must be observed that the estate held by McCance, before that statute took effect, was subject to the lien of Taylor's judgment in case it should be affirmed. It was insisted, nevertheless, that Taylor, to preserve his priority, should have docketed his judgment; that the statute operates retrospectively and gives a new rule of priority between lienors by judgment and purchasers before March 3d, 1843. This construction I hold to be in contravention of a well-settled rule; to be at war with the obvious purpose of the statute. The rule referred to is, that statutes should be construed prospectively." McCance *v.* Taylor, 10 Gratt. 580.

On this subject, see, citing McCance *v.* Taylor, 10 Gratt. 580, Duval *v.* Malone, 14 Gratt. 24, 29, footnote to Price *v.* Harrison, 31 Gratt. 114; Hoge *v.* Brookover, 28 W. Va. 304, 313; Murdock *v.* Franklin Ins. Co., 33 W. Va. 407, 417, 10 S. E. 777, 780; State *v.* Mines, 38 W. Va. 125, 134, 18 S. E. 470, 473.

Sess. acts, 1842-43, p. 52, § 3. "That hereafter, no judgment or decree of any court within this commonwealth, heretofore rendered, for the payment of money or tobacco, and no forthcoming bond or recognizance, or other bond having the force of a judgment, heretofore executed or acknowledged, shall bind the lands of any party to the same, against a bona fide purchaser for valuable consideration, without notice, unless the same shall be docketed in the manner provided in the first section of this act, in the county or corporation in which such land may lie, within twelve months after the passage of this act, or ninety days before such land shall have been conveyed to such purchaser. Section 4. "That no judg-ment or decree, bond or recognizance, hereafter rendered, executed or acknowledged, shall bind the land of any party to the same against a bona fide purchaser, for valuable consideration, without notice, unless the same shall be in like manner docketed in the county or corporation in which the land may lie, within twelve months after the rendition or forfeiture of such judgment, decree, bond or recognizance, or ninety days before such land shall have been conveyed to such purchaser." Recognizances in favor of the commonwealth are excepted out of the operation of the act. See Va. Code, 1904, § 3569

j. The Judgment Docket.

The Judgment Docket and Its Contents.

"Docket and Index Distinguished.—The act of 1843 provided, that 'if any clerk shall fail to docket without delay, in the manner herein prescribed, any judgment, etc., which he shall be required to docket, or shall fail to make and preserve the index hereby required of him, he shall be liable to the action of the party aggrieved for such damages as he may sustain thereby.' It will thus be seen that the docket is one thing, and the index another, and quite a different thing. Nothing can more strongly enforce this distinction than the language of the second section just quoted. The clerk is required to docket only when requested, but it is his duty to index, whether requested or not. While the statute imposes upon the creditor the duty of requiring the clerk to docket the judgment, it imposes no duty upon him with respect to the indexing. With that the creditor need not concern himself. Certainly he is not compelled to make any demand upon the clerk by the express terms of the provision. The sole object of the indexing, as disclosed in the statute, is 'for the purpose of a more convenient reference, to facilitate the search, to enable parties more readily to find that which is contained in the docket.' The index is a guide to the docket; it saves labor and trouble in examining the docket, but it is not the docket itself, nor a part of it." Old Dominion, etc., Co. *v*. Clarke, 28 Gratt. 617.

"**The first act passed upon this subject was in April, 1843.** A recurrence to that act will very materially aid us in reaching a correct conclusion. The first section provides, it shall be the duty of the clerk of the county court to keep in well-bound books a judgment docket, in which shall be regularly docketed all such unsatisfied final judgments, decrees, etc., as any person interested therein shall require him to docket. In such docket there shall be plainly set down in separate colums the date of such judgment or decree, the name, description and residence of the parties, the amount of the debts, costs, etc., appearing in each case, and the amount and date of the credits, if any. We have here plainly pointed out what constitutes a docket, the manner and form in which it shall be made out, and the facts it is required to set forth for the information of parties concerned. Having thus provided for a docket, the act makes provision for an index as follows: 'And, for the purpose of more convenient reference, there shall be made and preserved in the same books a plain and accurate index of all judgments, decrees, etc., docketed, and every judgment, etc., in the said index shall be set down in alphabetical order, the names of the debtors, and each of them.'" Old Dominion, etc., Co. *v*. Clarke, 28 Gratt. 617.

The Va. Code of 1860 provided as follows: "3· In the following section the word 'judgment' shall include any undertaking, bond, or recognizance which has the force of a judgment. 4. The recorder of every county shall keep in his office, in a well-bound book, a judgment docketed, in which he shall docket without delay any judgment in this state, when he shall be required to do so by any person interested, on such person's delivering him an authenticated abstract of it. In such docket there shall be stated, in separate columns: 1. The names of the parties. 2. The amount of the judgment; 3. The value of specific property (if any) recovered by it; 4. The date of the judgment; 5. The court in which it was rendered; 6. The date of docketing it. And it shall be the duty of the clerk of the court in which, or of the justice before whom, any judgment is rendered to include in the abstract thereof the foregoing particulars." Dickinson *v*. Railroad Co., 7 W. Va. 390, 394.

Chapter 186 of the Code of Virginia of 1860 provided: The clerk of each county and corporation court shall keep in his office, in a well-bound book, a judgment docket, in which he shall docket without delay any judgment in this state, when he shall be required to do so by any person interested, on such persons delivering him, if the judgment be not in his court or office, an authenticated abstract of it. In such docket there shall be stated in separate columns the date and amount of the judgment, the date of docketing it, the alternative value of any specific property secured by it, and the amount and date of any credits on the judgment with the names, description and residence of the parties, so far as they appear in his office or in such abstract. Calwell *v*. Prindle, 19 W. Va. 604, 654.

The present Va. Code provides that the clerk of the chancery court of the city of Richmond, and of every circuit and corporation or hustings court except the hustings court of the city of Richmond, and except circuit courts of cities, shall keep in his office, in a well-bound book, a judgment docket, in which he shall docket, without delay, any judgment for money rendered in this state by any state or federal court, when he shall be required so to do by any person interested, on such person delivering to him an authenticated abstract of it; and shall docket every judgment for money rendered in his court or office, and every such judgment, the abstract of which is delivered to him by the clerk of the circuit or other court of his corporation, and also upon the request of any person interested therein, any such judgment rendered by a justice whose book has been filed in his office under the provisions of section twenty-nine hundred and forty-four, or of which an abstract is delivered to him certified by the justice who rendered it. The clerk of the circuit or other court of each corporation, except the clerk of the circuit or of a city court of the city of Richmond, shall, without delay, deliver to the clerk of the corporation or hustings court of his corporation, and the clerk of the circuit or of a city court of the city of Richmond to the clerk of the chancery court of said city, an authenticated abstract of every judgment for money rendered in his court or office, except that judgments, decrees, or orders against fiduciaries for which they are not personally liable, and against commissioners and receivers of any court, and against any bank or incorporated company doing a banking business for money deposited under or subject to the order of any court, or by a commissioner or receiver thereof, shall not be docketed, nor abstracts thereof delivered by the clerks of the circuit courts to the clerks of the corporation or hustings court, or by the clerks of the circuit or city courts of Richmond to the clerk of the chancery court of the said city, unless required by the plaintiff in such judgment, decree, or order, or some person interested therein, to be so certified and docketed, and then only at the cost of such plaintiff or person so interested. (1884, p. 82; 1902-3-4, p. 777.) Va. Code, 1904, § 3559.

In such docket there shall be stated, in separate columns, the date and amount of the judgment; the names of all the parties thereto; the alternative value of any specific property recovered by it; the date of docketing it; the amount and date of any credits thereon; the court in which, or the justice by whom it was rendered; and when paid off or discharged, in whole or in part, the time thereof, and by whom such payment or discharge was made, where there is more than one defendant. And in case of a judgment or decree by confession or in vacation the clerk shall also enter in such docket the time of day at which the same was confessed, or at which the same was received in his office to be entered of record. And it shall be the duty of the clerk of any circuit or city court for a corporation in which a judgment is confessed or entered in vacation, to certify to the clerk of the hustings or corporation court thereof the time of day of such confession or the time at which the vacation decree was received in his office to be entered, except that in the city of Richmond he shall certify the same to the clerk of the chancery court of said city. (1884, p. 82; 1897-8, p. 507; 1902-3-4, p. 777.) Va. Code, 1904, § 3560.

The present W. Va. Code provides: The clerk of every circuit and municipal court shall, without delay, make out and deliver a duly certified abstract of every judgment rendered by such court, and every justice of the peace shall, without delay, make out and deliver a duly certified abstract of every judgment rendered by him, or by any other justice, the docket of which is in his possession and under his control, to any person interested therein who may demand the same, and pay or tender the fee therefor, in which abstract shall be stated the names in full of the plaintiff or plaintiffs, and the defendant or defendants, as they appear in the papers and proceedings in the cause, and if the defendants are sued as partners, the partnership name shall be stated; the amount of the judgment and the amount of the costs, stating each separately; the value of specific property (if any) recovered by it, and the damages (if any) for its detention; the date of the judgment and the court in which, or the justice by whom, the judgment was rendered. Any clerk or justice who shall fail to deliver such abstract as herein required, shall be guilty of a misdemeanor and fined fifty dollars. And the clerk of every county court shall keep in his office in a well bound book a judgment docket, in which he shall docket without delay any judgment rendered by any justice of the peace or court of this state or by any circuit or district court of the United States within this state, upon the delivery to him of such authenticated abstract thereof for that purpose, and the payment or tender of his fee therefor. In such docket there shall be stated, in separate columns: I. The names in full of the plaintiff or plaintiffs, and the defendant or defendants, as they are stated in such abstract, and if it appear by such abstract that the defendants were sued as partners, their partnership name shall also be stated. II. The amount of the judgment and of the costs, stating each separately. III. The value of any specific property recovered by the judgment, and the damages (if any) for its detention. IV. The date of the judgment. V. The court in which or the justice by whom it was rendered. VI. The date of docketing the judgment. W. Va. Code, 1899, ch. 139, § 4144.

Certifying the Judgment.—"It is objected, that neither of the judgments is properly certified (as required by the statute). Each judgment is headed: 'In the circuit court of the city of Richmond, March 6, 1860,' then the title of each case is given and then the judgment of the court, and at the bottom of the judgments are the words: 'A copy teste;' and then the signature 'James Ellet, clerk.' These copies are attested in the usual way attestations of such copies are made and are required to be made by clerks in order to be evidence. See § 5, ch. 176, of the Code of 1860. It is true, it would perhaps have been more satisfactory, if the clerk had appended to his name 'clerk of the circuit court of the city of Richmond,' but considering the heading to the copy: 'In the circuit court of the city of Richmond,' etc., and the attestation as it appears, I think it is substantially sufficient to meet the requirements of the statute." Calwell v. Prindle, 19 W. Va.· 604, 665.

The Abstract.—The "authenticated abstract" of a judgment mentioned and referred to in § 4 of ch. 186 of the Code of Virginia of 1860, in relation to docketing judgments, is answered and fulfilled by presenting to the clerk of the county court an attested copy of the judgment in lieu of an "authenticated abstract" of the judgment; such copy of a judgment answers substantially for all purposes the requirements of said fourth section, and includes all that an abstract could show and more. "While there is a difference between an authenticated abstract of a judgment and an authenticated copy of a judgment, still it must be admitted, that an authenticated copy of a judgment contains all the information and more than an authenticated abstract of the judgment, and is in fact more reliable for the clerk to act upon. An authenticated copy of a judgment for the purpose of said fourth section includes an authenticated abstract, because it contains all such abstract could and more; and in my opinion the requirement of said section is complied with, when an official copy of the judgment is delivered to the clerk instead of an official abstract of the judgment." Calwell *v.* Prindle, 19 Va. 604, 664.

"It is objected, 'that they are not abstracts (as required by § 4), but purport on their face to be copies of judgments.' It will be seen by reference to the fourth section of ch. 186 of the Code of 1860, that if the judgment is in the county court of the county, of which the clerk required to docket it is clerk, an abstract of the judgment is not required to be delivered to such clerk, that he may docket the judgment; but in that case it is evidently contemplated, that he shall docket it from the record of the judgment in his office on being required to docket the judgment by any person interested. In that case the law supposes, that the clerk has in his custody the recorded judgment of the court, which is all, that is necessary to enable him to docket the judgment in the judgment docket book, which he is required to keep in his office. But where the judgment was not rendered in his court, then an authenticated abstract of the judgment or an authenticated copy of the judgment is necessary for the information of the clerk, 1st, as to there being such a judgment, and 2d, to enable him to docket it." Calwell *v.* Prindle, 19 W. Va. 604, 664.

Proof of Docketing Abstract.—An authenticated copy from the recorder's docket of an official abstract of a judgment docketed under the provisions of the third and fourth sections of chapter 139 of the Code of 1868 of West Virginia, is evidence that such abstract was docketed, and when, and of notice to purchasers of lands upon which the alleged judgment is claimed to be a lien, when the existence of such judgment is properly proved; but where the judgment is put in issue, ordinarily, an authenticated copy of such abstract, as docketed by the recorder, will not be received as proof of the judgment and dispense with the necessity of producing a properly authen-ticated copy of the judgment. Dickinson *v.* Railroad Co., 7 W. Va. 390; Anderson *v.* Nagle, 12 W. Va. 98.

"Well-Bound Book."—The fourth section of ch. 186 of the Virginia Code of 1860, in so far as it relates to the quality of a judgment docket book, is directory. Calwell *v.* Prindle, 19 W. Va. 604.

"It is objected, that the book from which the copies were taken is not such a 'well-bound book' as § 4 requires. The attestation of the clerk of the county court to one of the copies is as follows: 'A true copy from the judgment lien docket, as it now remains 'in the clerk's office of Greenbrier county court,' and to the other: 'A true copy from the judgment lien docket as it now remains in the clerk's office of Greenbrier county court.' I see no substantial difference in the attestations of the clerk; the only difference is, in the one the words 'the judgment lien docket' are italicized, and in the other they are not. The clerk also after his attestive certificate certifies, that the book though old is substantially bound and well preserved for so old a book; that said book was used for docketing judgments from August 16, 1843, to May 15, 1861, and that he finds one judgment docketed therein the 1st day of May, 1866; that there is in the office no other book kept during that time or period for such purpose; that no judgments were docketed in his office from May 15, 1861, until February, 1866, from which time another book was commenced and used for that purpose; that the said first book was always treated and used in the office as a judgment lien docket, and was always exhibited as such to any persons wishing to see such a docket for the time, which it covers, and copies from said book were always furnished to persons desiring them certified as from the judgment lien docket. I have doubts whether portions of these certificates as to facts stated can be proved by a certificate of the clerk, and whether, if such facts are relied on, if deemed material, they should not be proved by deposition. But I do not deem it necessary now to decide that question, as in my opinion the direction of the statute as to "a well-bound book," is simply directory as to the quality of the book, and so far as my knowledge extends, it has always been so considered by the legal profession." Calwell v. Prindle, 19 W. Va. 604, 666.

"Stating the Different Items."—"It is objected, that § 4 requires, that the different items 'shall be stated in separate columns.' This raises the question whether the statute in this respect is mandatory or simply directory. I am of the opinion, that the statute in this respect must be held as simply directory and not mandatory, if for no other reason, because the thing directed to be done in this particular is not the essence of the thing required. Lord Mansfield in Rex v. Loxdale, 1 Burr. 447; Pott. Dwarr. on Statutes, etc., of 1871, 222, 223, 224, 226, notes; Marchant v. Langworthy, 6 Hill. 646; Striker v. Kelly, 7 Hill. 9; People v. Cook, 8 N. Y. 67; People v. Cook, 14 Barb. 290; People v. Schermerhorn, 19 Barb. 558. In the last case it was held, that a state is directory, where the thing directed to be done is an immaterial matter, where a compliance is matter of convenience rather than substance. In Dwar. on Statutes at page 226 in a note it is said: 'And in general it may be laid down as a rule, that when a statute directs certain proceedings to be done in a certain way or at a certain time, and the form or period does not appear essential to the judicial mind, the law will be regarded as directory, and the proceedings under it will be held valid, though the command of the statute as to form and time has not been strictly obeyed; the time and manner not being the essence of the thing required to be done.'

This it seems to me states a good general rule upon the subject." Calwell v. Prindle, 19 W. Va. 604, 666.

Names of Parties.—"It is objected that the names of the parties to said judgments are not given (as required by § 4). The plaintiff is stated in the first judgment to be 'the Commonwealth;' and the defendant is stated to be 'Edmund S. Calwell, one of the sureties of John E. Lewis, late sheriff of Greenbrier county. First case upon a motion instituted and prosecuted by the auditor of public accounts.' The plaintiff in the second judgment is stated to be 'the Commonwealth' and the defendant is stated to be 'Edmund S. Calwell, one of the sureties of John E. Lewis, late sheriff of Greenbrier county, second case upon a motion instituted and prosecuted by the auditor of public accounts.' The 4th section of ch. 42 of said Code of 1860, expressly provides, that 'every judgment on any such motion shall be in the name of the Commonwealth.' So that the name of the plaintiff is given as designated and required by the law, and no one could be misled or deceived as to who was the plaintiff in the judgments." Calwell v. Prindle, 19 W. Va. 604, 665.

Date of Judgment.—"It is objected, that 'the dates of the judgments are not given' (as required by § 4). I am of opinion, that 'March 6, 1860,' in the connection and place in which the words and figures are used, do plainly import the date of each of the judgments, and that they import such date so clearly, that no one could be mistaken or misled thereby." Calwell v. Prindle, 19 W. Va. 604, 664.

The Court in Which Rendered.—"It is objected, that the court, in which the judgments were rendered, is not given (as required by § 4). The words 'Greenbrier county clerk's office, to wit,' at the head of one of the copies, and the words, 'The state of West Virginia, Greenbrier county, to wit,' at the head of the other, were manifestly prefixed by the clerk of the county court of Greenbrier county, as will be at once seen by the words immediately following: 'In the circuit court of the city of Richmond, March 6, 1860,' and what follows in each of said copies. The 'circuit court of the city of Richmond' is the court designated by the law. See §§ 1 and 2 of ch. 42 of the Code of 1866, supra. The law seems to suppose, that that was a sufficient designation of the court without designating, that the city of Richmond was in the state of Virginia." Calwell *v.* Prindle, 19 W. Va. 604, 665.

"**Date of the Docketing.**"—"It is objected, that 'the date of the docketing is not given' (as required by statute). The docketing and the date thereof is distinctly stated as to each judgment in these words: 'Docketed September 29, 1860.'" Calwell *v.* Prindle, 19 W. Va. 604, 666.

"It does not appear that the judgment was docketed in pursuance of the statute, which provides, among other things, that the record shall show the date of docketing said judgment. There was simply an abstract of such judgment from the record, but nothing to show that it was ever docketed in the judgment lien docket; and if it was actually entered in the judgment lien docket, of which there is no evidence, the date of docketing does not appear, which is one of the essentials to the docketing; however, as the judgment was permitted to die for want of issuing execution thereon, the docketing the same was immaterial, as that could have nothing to do with keeping it alive." Woods *v.* Douglass, 52 W. Va. 517, 522, 44 S. E. 234.

2. Indexing Judgments.

a. Former Rule in Virginia and West Virginia.

The Virginia Code of 1860 provided that every judgment shall, as soon as it is docketed, be indexed in the name of each defendant. If a clerk shall fail to do this, he shall pay a fine of not less than thirty nor more than three hundred dollars, to any person who will prosecute therefor. Dickinson *v.* Railroad Co., 7 W. Va. 390.

Under these statutes it was decided that indexing is not a necessary part of the docketing of a judgment, but the land is subject to the lien of the judgment without it. Old Dominion, etc., Co. *v.* Clarke, 28 Gratt. 617; Calwell *v.* Prindle, 19 W. Va. 604.

"We come then to the fourth section, which provides that 'no judgment or decree shall bind the land against a bona fide purchaser for valuable consideration without notice, unless the same shall be docketed in the manner prescribed in the first section.' Now if this section had provided that the judgment shall not constitute a lien unless docketed and indexed according to the first section, the question would be free from difficulty. But it does not say so. The forfeiture results only from a failure to docket; and as we have seen, the docketing is complete without the indexing. If the clerk fails to make the index as prescribed by the statute and the purchaser is misled, the latter doubtless may have his action for damages. But this is no concern of the creditor. Having docketed his judgment, he may safely leave the rest to the clerk, whose duty as to the index does not depend upon any act or request of the creditor. The provisions found in the revisal of 1849 are substantially the same as the act of 1843. The only difference is, that in the former the revisors omitted the phrase 'for the purpose of a more convenient reference.' It is certain that no material change was thereby intended. It was probably thought those words were unnecessary, and consequently they were left out in conformity with the plan of condensing all the statutes." Old Dominion, etc., Co. *v.* Clarke, 28 Gratt. 617.

"The second section provides, that 'if any clerk shall fail to docket without delay, in the manner herein prescribed, any judgment, etc., which he shall be required to docket, or shall fail to make and preserve the index hereby required of him, he shall be liable to the action of the party aggrieved for such damages as he may sustain thereby.' It will thus be seen that the docket is one thing, and the index another, and quite a different thing. Nothing can more strongly enforce this distinction than the language of the second section just quoted. The clerk is required to docket only when requested, but it is his duty to index, whether requested or, not. While the statute imposes upon the creditor the duty of requiring the clerk to docket the judgment, it imposes no duty upon him with respect to the indexing. With that the creditor need not concern himself. Certainly he is not compelled to make any demand upon the clerk by the express terms of the provision. The sole object of the indexing, as disclosed in the statute, is 'for the purpose of a more convenient reference, to facilitate the search, to enable parties more readily to find that which is contained in the docket.' The index is a guide to the docket; it saves labor and trouble in examining the docket, but it is not the docket itself, nor a part of it." Old Dominion, etc., Co. *v.* Clarke, 28 Gratt. 617.

C. obtained a judgment against B. and P., as partners trading under the firm of B. & Co. He delivered an abstract of his judgment to the clerk of the county court of the county, wherein there was a tract of land belonging to P.; and the same was properly entered by the clerk in the body of the judgment docket, but was not indexed in the name of P., but merely in the name of "B. & Co." Subse-

quently P. sold and conveyed his land to O., who had no knowledge of C.'s judgment. Upon a bill filed by C. to subject the land in the hands of O. to the lien of his judgment, held, that under ch. 186, §§ 4, 8, Code of 1860, indexing was not a necessary part of the docketing, and that the land was therefore subject to the lien of C.'s judgment. Old Dominion, etc., Co. *v.* Clarke, 28 Gratt. 617.

b. Present Rule in Virginia.

But § 3561 of the Virginia Code of 1904 directed that "every judgment shall, as soon as it is docketed, be indexed by the clerk in the name of each defendant, and shall not be regarded as docketed as to any defendant in whose name it is not so indexed." Fulkerson *v.* Taylor, 100 Va. 426, 436, 41 S. E. 863.

This, of course, abrogates the rule in Old Dominion, etc., Co. *v.* Clarke, 28 Gratt. 617.

Mistake as to Name of Party to Judgment.—Where the plaintiff obtains judgment against Mrs. T. Frank S., which is indexed in the name of Mrs. T. Frank S., on July 31, 1891, but in 1897 is indexed in the judgment lien docket as against May M. S. such docketing and indexing of the judgment are not constructive notice to a purchaser that the judgment constituted a lien on the property of May M. S. in the absence of evidence that the purchaser had actual knowledge of the judgment or knew that Mrs. T. Frank S. and May M. S. were the same persons. Bankers' Loan, etc., Co. *v.* Blair, 99 Va. 606, 39 S. E. 231.

Docketing and indexing a judgment in the name of "Mrs. John Smith" is no notice of a judgment against Mary Smith, who is in fact the wife of John Smith. Bankers' Loan, etc., Co. *v.* Blair, 99 Va. 606, 39 S. E. 231.

Use of Word "Same."—Where the name of a judgment debtor is entered in the index of the judgment lien docket, giving reference to page of the docket, and immediately under his name the word "same" is written; also giving reference to page of docket, this is a sufficient compliance as to second-named judgment with the provisions of § 3561 of the Code requiring judgments to be indexed, although it is safer for clerks to comply with the letter of the statute. The object of the statute requiring judgments to be docketed and indexed is to apprise third persons who exercise ordinary care and prudence of the existence and character of the judgment. Fulkerson *v.* Taylor, 102 Va. 314, 46 S. E. 378.

The object of the provisions of the Code for docketing and indexing abstracts of judgment is to apprise third persons—as, for instance, intending purchasers—of the existence and character of the judgment if they exercise ordinary care and intelligence. Cooke *v.* Avery, 147 U. S. 377, 13 Sup. Ct. 346, 37 L. Ed. 209. In the case cited, which involved the construction of a statute similar to the one under consideration, the supreme court of the United States said: "The only ground upon which this abstract and index could be held insufficient was that the names of the plaintiffs were not given in full in either abstract or index. Was this omission fatal to the lien? The circuit court did not think so, and we concur in that view. Willis *v.* Smith, 66 Tex. 31 (17 S. W. 247). 'The object of the statute is not to incumber the register with full information, but to excite inquiry and indicate the source of full information.' It appears to us that the source of full information was so indicated in this instance that no reasonably prudent or cautious inquirer could go astray." Fulkerson *v.* Taylor, 102 Va. 314, 317, 46 S. E. 378.

An allegation in a bill that a judgment sought to be enforced was duly docketed is a sufficient allegation of the indexing of the judgment as re-

quired by § 3561 of the Code, but if the fact of indexing be put in issue it must be proved, and it would seem that this is not sufficiently done by the mere production of an abstract of the judgment which does not certify that it was duly docketed, and makes no reference to the indexing. Fulkerson *v.* Taylor, 100 Va. 426, 41 S. E. 863.

c. Present Rule in West Virginia.

Every judgment docketed by the clerk of the county court as aforesaid shall at the same time be indexed by him in an index to be kept in or annexed to said judgment docket, in full, the name of the defendant, and if more than one defendant, in the full name of each, as they appear in the said abstract. If the defendants are sued as partners, it shall also be indexed in the partnership name appearing by such abstract. Any clerk of a county court failing to perform any duty required of him by this section shall be guilty of a misdemeanor, and be fined fifty dollars; and he and his securities in his official bond shall moreover be liable to any person injured by such failure for all such damages as he may sustain by reason thereof. W. Va. Code, 1899, ch. 139, § 4144.

It would seem that the doctrine of Calwell *v.* Prindle, stated above, still holds in West Virginia.

Under ch. 186, §§ 4, 8, of the Code of 1860, indexing was not a necessary part of the docketing of the judgment; the docketing was complete without the indexing for the purpose of preserving the liens of the judgments upon the real estate of the said judgment debtor in Greenbrier county, as against a purchaser thereof for valuable consideration without notice. Calwell *v.* Prindle, 19 W. Va. 604, following Old Dominion, etc., Co. *v.* Clarke, 28 Gratt. 617.

"It is further objected that neither of said two judgments were indexed (as required by the statute). The clerk certifies, that the said two judgments are indexed as follows: 'The space in the index under the letter "C" is filled up and runs out just where the column for "E" begins, and there where the "C" space ends and before any indexing under "E" is this note, "See after J;" and upon the page after the letter "J" in the said index the indexing under "C" is resumed, and after thirty-nine entries in letter "C" the following are found: Commonwealth v. Calwell, E. S. '81; Same v. Same, '81.' The clerk also certifies, that said judgments are not otherwise docketed than as above. This precise question was presented to and decided by the court of appeals in Virginia in cases, in which the facts appearing were much stronger than in the case at bar. The case to which I refer, is Old Dominion, etc., Co. v. Clarke, 28 Gratt. 617. The syllabus of the case is: 'C. obtained a judgment against B. and P. as partners trading under the firm of B. & Co. He delivered an abstract of his judgment to the clerk of the county court of the county, wherein there was a tract of land belonging to P., and the same was properly entered by the clerk in the body of the judgment docket, but was not indexed in the name of P., but merely in the name of "B. & Co." Subsequently P. sold and conveyed his land to O., who had no knowledge of C.'s judgments. Upon a bill filed by C. to subject the lands in the hands of O. to his judgments, held, that under ch. 186, §§ 4, 8, Code of 1860 indexing was not a necessary part of the docketing.' This case was decided in 1877. Judge Staples delivered the unanimous opinion of the court." Calwell v. Prindle, 19 W. Va. 604, 667.

d. Judgments and Decrees of United States Courts.

Judgments and decrees rendered in a circuit or district court of the United States within this state may be indexed in the clerks' offices of courts of this state in the same manner and under the same rules and requirements of law as judgments and decrees of courts of this state. (1899-90, p. 22.) Va. Code, 1904, § 3559a. See Dickinson v. Railroad Co., 7 W. Va. 390.

e. Fines and Penalties.

The Code of West Virginia provides: "3. In the following section the word 'judgment' shall include any undertaking, bond, or recognizance which has the force of a judgment. 4. The recorder of every county shall keep in his office, in a well-bound book, a judgment docket, in which he shall docket without delay any judgment in this state, when he shall be required to do so by any person interested, on such person's delivering him an authenticated abstract of it. In such docket there shall be stated, in separate columns: 1. The names of the parties; 2. The amount of the judgment; 3. The value of specific property (if any) recovered by it; 4. The date of the judgment; 5. The court in which it was rendered; 6. The date of docketing it. And it shall be the duty of the clerk of the court in which, or of the justice before whom, any judgment is rendered to include in the abstract thereof the foregoing particulars. Every judgment shall, as soon as it is docketed, be indexed in the name of each defendant therein. If a recorder fail to do anything required of him by this section, he shall pay a fine of not less than thirty nor more than three hundred dollars to any person who will prosecute therefor." Dickinson v. Railroad Co., 7 W. Va. 390, 394.

In West Virginia, any clerk or justice who shall fail to deliver a duly certified abstract as the statute provides, shall be guilty of a misdemeanor and fined fifty dollars. W. Va. Code, 1899, ch. 139, § 4144.

E. NECESSITY FOR ISSUANCE OF EXECUTION OR SCIRE FACIAS.

See post, "Limitations and Laches," VI, K, 6, a, (8).

Issuance of Elegit.—In Taylor *v.* Spindle, 2 Gratt. 44, 57, Stuart *v.* Hamilton, 8 Leigh 503, was cited as sustaining the lien of a judgment from its date, though there was no elegit or election of one at any time, and though the suit in equity was commenced about nine years after the judgment was rendered.

The lien on land created by a judgment, depended upon the right of the plaintiff to sue out an elegit, and it was not essential to the existence of the lien, that the elegit should have actually issued before the judgment creditor can come into equity for relief. Scriba *v.* Deane, 1 Brock. (U. S.) 166; Taylor *v.* Spindle, 2 Gratt. 44.

Eppes v. Randolph.—It was held, in an early case that judgments did not bind lands after twelve months from the date, unless execution be taken out within that time, or an entry of elegit be made on the record. Eppes *v.* Randolph. 2 Call 125.

Eppes v. Randolph Criticised.—"Notwithstanding that the dictum in that case, that it is necessary to the preservation of the lien of the judgment against subsequent purchasers from the debtor, that the creditor should either sue out, or enter of record his election of the writ of elegit, has been occasionally referred to as an adjudication, it has, as far as my researches have informed me, never been acted on by this court, or governed the practice of the country. On the contrary, very recently after the decision of that case. the court in the case of Tinsley *v.* Anderson, 3 Call 329. sustained the lien of the judgment from its date, where execution had issued within the year and a day, irrespective of the nature of the execution, and without inquiry whether the creditor had entered on the record his election of the elegit. So in the case of Stuart *v.* Hamilton, 8 Leigh 503, though there was no elegit or election of one at any time, and the suit in equity was commenced about nine years after the judgment was rendered. So in the case of United States *v.* Morrison, 4 Peters 124, though there was no elegit or election of one, and though there had been a voluntary suspension of execution for years, the lien of the judgment was sustained against parties claiming under a conveyance for valuable consideration made during the period of the suspension. I do not refer to the cases of Coleman *v.* Cocke, 6 Rand. 618, and M'Cullough *v.* Sommerville, 8 Leigh 415, because in them, the relief was granted against volunteers or fraudulent grantees, and on that ground distinguishable from, and not ruling the case where the relief is sought against a purchaser for valuable consideration. But it is useless to refer to particular cases. The efficacy of the judgment, on which the right to issue execution has not been suffered to expire, has never been questioned even, in any case that has fallen under my notice except the dictum before cited in Eppes *v.* Randolph, 2 Call 125. Tracing that dictum to its source, we shall ascertain its accuracy; and when ascertained, the dictum will furnish a curious example of the application of the function ascribed to the suing out, or election on the record of the elegit, in the case to which it is applied, in such manner as wholly to change that function." Taylor *v.* Spindle. 2 Gratt. 44.

In Taylor *v.* Spindle, 2 Gratt. 44, 57, the court, in expressing its disapproval of the dictum in Eppes *v.* Randolph, 2 Call 125, that it is necessary to the preservation of the lien of the judgment against subsequent purchasers from the debtor, that the creditor should either sue out, or enter of record his election of the writ of elegit, said that, on the contrary, the principal case sustained the lien of the judgment from its date, where execution had issued within the year and a day, irrespective of the nature of the execution, and without inquiry whether the creditor had entered on the record his election of the elegit. So also, in the case of United States v. Morrison, 4 Peters 124, though there was no elegit or election of one, and though there had been a voluntary suspension of execution for years, the lien of the judgment was sustained against parties claiming under a conveyance for valuable consideration made during the period of the suspension.

The late act of March, 1843, respecting the docketing of judgments, clearly evinces that in the opinion of the legislature, the lien of the judgment creditor operated from the date of the judgment and contained thenceforward without qualification or impediment, while the creditor had or could get the capacity to issue the elegit on it, irrespective of intervening abatements, suspension or delays; and that the judgments docketed according to the act, would in like manner, preserve the past, and continue the existing lien indefinitely; that is, until from some supervening cause, it should be lost by the loss of the rightful capacity to sue execution on the judgment. These words used by Judge Stanard in Taylor v. Spindle, 2 Gratt. 44, were quoted in Borst v. Nalle, 28 Gratt. 423, 431; Renick v. Ludington, 14 W. Va. 367, 376. To the same effect, see Taylor v. Spindle cited in Michaux v. Brown, 10 Gratt. 612, 620; Hutcheson v. Grubbs, 80 Va. 251, 255; Werdenbaugh v. Reid, 20 W. Va. 588, 591 (citing also, Watts v. Kinney, 3 Leigh 272, 293; Burbridge v. Higgins, 6 Gratt. 119).

Issuance of Execution.—As in this state an execution can not be levied on lands, and the lien of a judgment on lands in this state is created directly by our statute, it is in no manner dependent on the issuing of an execution. Renick v. Ludington, 20 W. Va. 511, 551.

The lien of a judgment upon land arises from the judgment per se irrespective of execution upon it so long as the judgment is not barred by limitations. Maxwell v. Leeson, 50 W. Va. 361, 362, 40 S. E. 420.

This lien is a legal lien, born alone of the judgment, not of an execution, a lien independent of any execution, the only efficacy of an execution being to keep it alive. If it is capable of execution, or may be revived by sci. fa., the lien may be enforced on land in equity, not because of an execution, but without execution, the lien of the judgment on the land being one thing, the lien of an execution on personalty being another thing—just as distinct from each other as is the personal debt of a note secured by deed of trust on land and the lien of that deed on the land. 2 Minor Ins. 314. Maxwell v. Leeson, 50 W. Va. 361, 365, 40 S. E. 420.

Scire Facias.—The lien of a judgment upon land exists, though execution may be suspended by the death of the defendant, and may be enforced in equity without revival by scire facias so long as the scire facias may lie on the judgment. Maxwell v. Leeson, 50 W. Va. 361, 40 S. E. 420.

"In the case of The Bank of the Old Dominion v. Allen, 76 Va. 200, 206, this court appears to have treated the question as settled. That was a case in which a creditor's bill was filed to subject the lands of the debtors to the payment of the liens and encumbrances thereon, and no execution had issued on the judgment then under consideration, but the right to revive it upon scire facias still existed. Burks, J., says: 'There was no necessity of reviving the judgment.'" James v. Life, 92 Va. 702, 705, 24 S. E. 275.

F. COMMENCEMENT AND DURATION OF LIEN.

1. In General.

The statutes give a direct, positive, express, and absolute lien of a judgment against all the lands of or to which the debtor shall be possessed or entitled at or after the date of such judgment, or if it was rendered in court, at or after the commencement of the terms, at which it was so rendered; and such lien continues until it is in some legal manner discharged. Code, W. Va., ch. 139, § 5; Code, Va. 1860; 1904, § 3567; McClaskey v. O'Brien, 16 W. Va. 791, 792; Duncan v. Custard, 24 W. Va. 730; Anderson v. Nagle, 12 W. Va. 98; Borst v. Nalle, 28 Gratt. 423; Gurnee v. Johnson, 77 Va. 712; Renick v. Ludington, 20 W. Va. 511; Snyder v. Botkin, 37 W. Va. 355, 16 S. E. 591; Foley v. Ruley, 50 W. Va. 158, 40 S. E. 382.

Prior to the statute a judgment was a lien upon the lands owned by the debtor at the date of the judgment. Rodgers v. M'Cluer, 4 Gratt. 81.

Section 5, ch. 139, of the West Virginia Code, gives a positive express lien of a judgment against all the lands, of or to which the debtor shall be possessed or entitled at or after the date of such judgment, or if it was rendered in court, at or after the commencement of the term, at which it was so rendered; and such lien continues until it is in some legal manner discharged. Renick v. Ludington, 14 W. Va. 367.

Chapter 186 of the Code of Virginia of 1860 provided: Every judgment for money rendered in this state heretofore or hereafter against any person, shall be a lien on all the real estate, of or to which such persons shall be possessed or entitled, at or after the date of such judgment, or if it was rendered in court, at or after the commencement of the term at which it was so rendered. Calwell v. Prindle, 19 W. Va. 604, 655.

The difference in the provisions of the Va. and W. Va. Code in respect to the commencement of the lien, is that the W. Va. Code gives a judgment the effect of a lien after its date, or, if it was rendered in court at or after the commencement of the term at which it was so rendered; but the Virginia Code drops these latter words, and makes it a lien at or after its date, and as will be seen further on the Virginia Code expressly provides that the lien of a judgment shall in no case relate back to the day or other time prior to that on or at which a judgment was rendered. W. Va. Code, 1899, ch. 139, § 4145; Va. Code, 1904, § 3567.

2. Particular Judgments Considered.

a. Judgment in Favor of Commonwealth.

The state of Virginia upon notices and motions by the name of "The Commonwealth" instituted and prosecuted by the auditor of public accounts on the 6th day of March, 1860, recovered two several judgments against Edmund S. Calwell "in the circuit court of Richmond" as one of the securities of John E. Lewis, late sheriff of Greenbrier county, the one being for $4,893.92, the balance of the land property, and capitation and September license taxes of 1854 due from said John E. Lewis, late sheriff of Greenbrier county, with interest thereon to be computed at the rate of six per centum per annum from the 17th day of January, 1855, until paid, and the costs of the motion, 13.44, and the other being for $1,073.86, the balance of June, 1855, license taxes, due from said John E. Lewis, late sheriff of Greenbrier county, with interest thereon to be computed at the rate of six per centum per annum from the 20th day of June, 1855, until paid, and $161.07 for damages thereon according to law, also the cost of the motion, $11.94. The law, in force at the time said notices were given and motions made and judgments were rendered, provided, that "the auditor of public accounts shall institute and prosecute all proceedings proper to enforce payment of money to the commonwealth —that the proceeding may be in the circuit court of the city of Richmond —that when it is at law, it may be by action or motion—that "every judgment on any such motion shall be in the name of the commonwealth." And the city of Richmond being the capital of the state of Virginia, as judicially known to the court; held, the said judgments and each of them were and continued to be positive liens in favor of the state of Virginia upon all the lands of the said Edmund S. Calwell in the state of Virginia, including those in the county of Greenbrier, now of the state of West Virginia, from the time of their rendition until the said 20th day of June, 1863. Calwell v. Prindle, 19 W. Va. 604.

b. Judgment Revived by Scire Facias.

The dictum of the judge, delivering the opinion of the court in the case of Eppes v. Randolph, 2 Call 103, "that a judgment revived by scire facias only operates prospectively, so as to give a lien from the time of its revival, and has no retrospective effect so as to avoid mesne alienations," was examined and disapproved in Taylor v. Spindle, 2 Gratt. 44.

c. Judgment against Sheriff.

A judgment against a sheriff is, under ch. 195, W. Va. Code, 1872, a lien from the time he is served with notice or summons pursuant to which the judgment is afterwards rendered, and is superior to a deed of trust executed by the sheriff after such service of summons. Hoge v. Brookover, 28 W. Va. 304.

d. Forfeited Forthcoming Bond.

See the title FORTHCOMING AND DELIVERY BONDS, vol. 6, p. 427.

A forfeited forthcoming bond has the force of a judgment, so as to create a lien upon the lands of the obligors, only from the time the bond is returned to the clerk's office. Cabell v. Given, 30 W. Va. 760, 5 S. E. 442; Central Land Co. v. Calhoun, 16 W. Va. 361; Jones v. Myrick, 8 Gratt. 179, 210; Lipscomb v. Davis, 4 Leigh 303, 305.

Though a forthcoming bond is forfeited, and not quashed, yet in equity the lien of the original judgment still exists; and if the obligors in the bond prove insolvent, so that the debt is not paid, a court of law will quash the bond so as to revive the lien of the original judgment. Jones v. Myrick, 8 Gratt. 179.

Where the only evidence of the time a forthcoming bond was returned to the clerk's office was an indorsement as follows: "Notice proved and docketed in court, 10 October, 1868, and mo. to quash,"—such bond would have the force of a judgment from the date in the endorsements, and the requirement by the statute (Code, W. Va., 1860, ch. 189, § 2) that the clerk of a court shall indorse on a forfeited forthcoming bond, "the date of its return," is directory. Cabell v. Given, 30 W Va. 760, 5 S. E. 442.

e. Judgment with Stay of Execution.

A judgment, with a stay of execution, creates no lien on land, until the plaintiff has a right to issue execution thereon. Scriba v. Deane, 1 Brock. (U. S.) 166; Enders v. Board, 1 Gratt. 364, 378.

3. Doctrine of Relation.

See the title RELATION.

a. At Common Law.

"At common law, all judgments were, by legal fiction, it is said, supposed to be entered on the first day of the term of the court at which they were recovered. This rule has always prevailed in this state whenever the action, in which the judgment was rendered, was in such condition that it might have been then tried, if it had happened to occupy the first place on the docket. And the law, not regarding fractions of a day, the lien of a judgment began by relation at the first moment of the first day of the term. Mutual Assurance Society *v.* Stanard, 4 Munf. 539; Coutts *v.* Walker, 2 Leigh 268; Skipwith *v.* Cunningham, 8 Leigh 272; Horsley *v.* Garth, 2 Gratt. 471, 474; Withers *v.* Carter, 4 Gratt. 407, 50 Am. Dec. 78; Jones *v.* Myrick, 8 Gratt. 179; Brockenbrough *v.* Brockenbrough, 31 Gratt. 580; Yates *v.* Robinson, 80 Va. 475; and Janney *v.* Stephen, 2 Pat. & H. 11." Hockman *v.* Hockman, 93 Va. 455, 25 S. E. 534.

The lien of a judgment upon the lands of the party relates back to the commencement of the term at which it is obtained. Mutual Assurance Society *v.* Stanard, 4 Munf. 539; Jones *v.* Myrick, 8 Gratt. 179.

Reasons for Rule.—This general principle of the common law, like many others, is of such remote antiquity, and so long recognized without dispute, that the reasons and policy on which it was founded are in a great degree left to conjecture. Coutts *v.* Walker, 2 Leigh 268; First Nat. Bank *v.* Huntington, etc., Co., 41 W. Va. 530, 23 S. E. 792; Smith *v.* Parkersburg Co-Op. Ass'n, 48 W. Va. 232, 37 S. E. 645.

b. Under the Statutes.

In West Virginia.—"This doctrine or rule had been always recognized in Virginia before we had a statute, but it is now embodied in a statute, as regards the effect of the judgment as a lien. Code, ch. 139, § 5; Mutual Assurance Society *v.* Stanard, 4 Munf. 539; Coutts *v.* Walker, 2 Leigh 268; Skipwith *v.* Cunningham, 8 Leigh 272; Withers *v.* Carter, 4 Gratt. 407, 418." Smith *v.* Parkersburg Co-Op. Ass'n, 48 W. Va. 232, 37 S. E. 645, 653.

In Dunn *v.* Renick, 40 W. Va. 343, 22 S. E. 66, it is said: "By reason of this rule that the whole term is one day, the common-law rule was that a judgment rendered on any day, has relation to, and is a judgment of, its first day." Tidd. Prac. 547; 1 Lomax Dig. 287; 1 Black., Judg., § 441; 2 Freem., Judg., § 369; Farley *v.* Lea, 32 Am. Dec. 680. This doctrine or rule had always been recognized in Virginia before we had a statute, but is now embodied in a statute, as regards the effect of the judgment as a lien. Code, ch. 139, § 5; Mutual Assurance Society *v.* Stanard, 4 Munf. 539; Coutts *v.* Walker, 2 Leigh 268; Skipwith *v.* Cunningham, 8 Leigh 272; Withers *v.* Carter, 4 Gratt. 407, 418. The court, in Dunn *v.* Renick, supra, holds: "Though a decree or judgment relate to the first day of a term, yet if the case was not ready for hearing or trial, and therefore no judgment or decree could have been given on such first day, it does not relate to the first day, but has the date of its actual entry on the record." This rule of law seems to be necessary, in order to give effect to the proceedings of the courts. Without it, the administration of justice might be thwarted in many cases by successive alienations of property, pending the suit, wherein the property is the object of the litigation. All men are presumed to take notice of the proceedings in courts of justice. Cresap *v.* Cresap, 54 W. Va. 581, 582, 46 S. E. 582.

In Virginia.—But this rule has been changed by statute in Virginia providing that the lien of a judgment shall in no case relate back to a day or other time prior to that on or at which the judgment was rendered. Va. Code, 1904, § 3567.

c. Rule in Equity.

The rule that "a judgment has relation to the first day of the term at which it is rendered, is allowed in equity as well as at law." First Nat. Bank *v.* Huntington, etc., Co., 41 W.

Va. 530, 533, 23 S. E. 792; Yates *v.* Robertson, 80 Va. 475; Hockman *v.* Hockman. 93 Va. 455, 25 S. E. 534; New South Bldg., etc., Ass'n *v.* Reed, 96 Va. 345, 31 S. E. 514; Smith *v.* Parkersburg Co-Op. Ass'n, 48 W. Va. 232, 37 S. E. 645, ·653.

d. Cause Must Be Matured.

But though a decree or judgment relates to the first day of the term, yet if the case was not ready for hearing or trial, and therefore no judgment or decree could have been given on such first day had it occupied the first place on the docket, it does not relate to the first day, but has the date of its actual entry of record. Dunn *v.* Renick, 40 W. Va. 349, 22 S. E. 66; Yates *v.* Robertson, 80 Va. 475; First Nat. Bank *v.* Huntington, etc., Co., 41 W. Va. 530, 23 S. E. 792; Withers *v.* Carter, 4 Gratt. 407; Hockman *v.* Hockman, 93 Va. 455, 25 S. E. 534; Cresap *v.* Cresap, 54 W. Va. 581, 582, 46 S. E. 582.

The fiction of law which gives a judgment relation to the first day of the term, applies to all cases in which the judgment might have been rendered on that day; but not to a case in which it could not have been then rendered. Withers *v.* Carter, 4 Gratt. 407, cited in Smith *v.* Parkersburg Co-Op. Ass'n, 48 W. Va. 232, 37 S. E. 645; Yates *v.* Robertson, 80 Va. 475; Hockman *v.* Hockman, 93 Va. 455, 456, 25 S. E. 534; Brockenbrough *v.* Brockenbrough, 31 Gratt. 580, 600; Womer *v.* Ravenswood, etc., R. Co., 37 W. Va. 287, 290, 16 S. E. 488, 489; Dunn *v.* Renick, 40 W. Va. 349, 22 S. E. 66; First Nat. Bank *v.* Huntington, etc., Co., 41 W. Va. 530, 533, 23 S. E. 792.

e. Commencement of Term.

The commencement of the term to which the lien of a judgment has relation is the last day of the term upon which the court sits. Skipwith *v.* Cunningham, 8 Leigh 272. See Brown *v.* Hume, 16 Gratt. 456, 462.

But the term is not considered as commencing on the day appointed by law for its commencement, when in point of fact the court is not held until afterwards. Skipwith *v.* Cunningham, 8 Leigh 272.

Section 5, ch. 139, of the W. Va. Code provides that "every judgment for money rendered in this state heretofore or hereafter against any person shall be a lien ·on all real estate of or to which such person shall be possessed or entitled at or after the date of such judgment, or, if it was rendered in court, at or after the commencement of the term at which it was so rendered," etc. "This was a judgment rendered in court, at a term, the commencement of which had been fixed, as required by law, at a former regular term, and it can not be said, because there may be some case or cases on the docket that one of the judges is interested in, that the term can not commence as to that case or those cases until the other three judges were present. With as much propriety could it be said that, because the judge of the circuit court is so situated that he can not try some particular case, the term does not commence until a special judge is elected to try the case, or a judge from some other circuit takes the bench. I therefore think the decree which is sought to be enforced in this case related back to the first day of the term, to wit, to the 12th day of October, 1886." Snyder *v.* Botkin, 37 W. Va. 355, 16 S. E. 591, 595.

In Dunn *v.* Renick, 40 W. Va. 349, 22 S. E. 66, after quoting Judge Tucker in Dew *v.* District Judges, 3 Hen. & M. 27: "The term 'session,' when applied to courts means the whole term and in legal construction the whole term is construed as but one day, and that day is always referred to the first day or commencement of the term," Judge Brannon says: "I hardly think that, because our statute contemplates adjournment from day to day, and provides that each day's proceedings shall be separately recorded and signed by the judge, it cuts up the term into separate days, and individuates each day from another, and changes the common-law rule. By reason of this rule that the whole term is one day, the common rule was that a judgment rendered on any day has relation to, and is a judgment of, its first day. Tidd, Prac. 547; 1 Lomax Dig. 287; Black, Judgm., § 441; 2 Freem., Judgm., § 369; Farley v. Lea, 32 Am. Dec. 680." Smith v. Parkersburg Co-Op. Ass'n, 48 W. Va. 232, 37 S. E. 645, 653.

f. Particular Judgments Considered.

(1) Enjoined Judgments.

Where an injunction to a judgment is only perpetuated as to part of it, or a reversal is only as to part of a judgment, the lien of the part not affected continues from the date of the judgment. Grafton, etc., R. Co. v. Davisson, 45 W. Va. 12, 29 S. E. 1028.

Relation after Dissolution of Injunction.—Though a judgment is enjoined by a purchaser of land at the time of the purchase, yet, upon the dissolution of the injunction, the lien relates back to the date of the judgment, and so has priority over the equity of the purchaser. Michaux v. Brown, 10 Gratt. 612.

(2) Judgment on Attachment.

The rule that a judgment lien relates to the first day of a term, applies to a judgment on an attachment, and is not confined to realty, and such judgment will thereby override an assignment to an assignee for the benefit of creditors. Smith v. Parkersburg Co-Op. Ass'n, 48 W. Va. 232, 37 S. E. 645.

(3) Judgments by Confession.

A judgment confessed in court in a pending suit and the oath of insolvency taken thereon by the debtor upon his surrender by his bail, has relation to the first moment of the first day of the term; but a forfeited forthcoming bond which is not returned to the clerk's office until some day in the term after the first, when there is an award of execution thereon, had no relation; and therefore the assignment by operation of law under the first has preference over the lien of the forthcoming bond. Jones v. Myrick, 8 Gratt. 179.

Judgment by Confession in Vacation.—The lien of a judgment or decree begins with the first moment of the day on which it attaches. If it is a judgment by confession entered in vacation, the lien commences with the first moment of the day of such entry, irrespective of the hour at which the entry was in fact made. Hockman v. Hockman, 93 Va. 455, 25 S. E. 534.

(4) Office Judgments.

An office judgment confirmed on the last day of a term, and a judgment confessed on the first day of the same term, must be treated as judgments rendered on the same day, at the same time, and both judgments stand as of the same date; because of the well-settled rule which has already been set forth, that the office judgment would relate to the first day of the term, the law taking no notice of the fraction of a day. Brockenbrough v. Brockenbrough, 31 Gratt. 580.

g. Priorities.

Priority over Deeds, Deeds of Trust and Mortgages.—"It was the rule of common law (and this rule still obtains in some of the states) that the judgments of courts of record all relate back to the first day of the term, and are considered as rendered on that day, and therefore their lien will attach to the debtor's realty from the beginning of the term, and it will override a conveyance or mortgage made on the second or any succeeding day although prior to the rendition of the judgment." Black, Judgm. 441; Smith v. Parkersburg Co-Op. Ass'n, 48 W.

Va. 232, 37 S. E. 645. See also, Mutual Assurance Society *v.* Stanard, 4 Munf. 539; Coutts *v.* Walker, 2 Leigh 268.

Overreaches a Deed of Trust.—It is well settled, as a general rule, that the lien of a judgment upon the land of the debtor relates back to the commencement of the term at which the judgment was obtained, and over-reaches a deed of trust on the land executed by the debtor on or after the first day of the term. Skipwith *v.* Cunningham, 8 Leigh 272; Brown *v.* Hume, 16 Gratt. 456, 462; Brockenbrough *v.* Brockenbrough, 31 Gratt. 580.

Under Va. Code, § 3567, providing that a judgment is a lien as of the first day of the term at which it was rendered, a judgment rendered after the recordation of a deed of trust, but at a term which commenced prior to such recordation, is prior to the deed. New South Bldg., etc., Ass'n *v.* Reed, 96 Va. 345, 31 S. E. 514.

Priority over Deed Recorded Same Day.—Prior to the statute, the lien of a judgment, moreover, has priority over a conveyance recorded on the same day on which the judgment was entered, though the endorsement of the clerk shows that the judgment was, in fact, entered, after the deed was filed for record. Hockman *v.* Hockman, 93 Va. 455, 25 S. E. 534.

Priority over Assignment for Benefit of Creditors.—"It is insisted that the assignment to the assignee for the benefit of the creditors being prior to the judgment on the attachment, the lien of the attachment ceased the moment the transfer was made, and that the judgment lien does not by statute relate to the first day of the term except upon realty. The statute is only declaratory of the common law, so far as the judgment lien on real estate is concerned, but it does not change the rule of the common law, as laid down in § 441, Bl. on Judgts. 'It was the rule of the common law (and this rule still obtains in some of the states) that the judgments of a court of record all relate back to the first day of the term, and are considered as rendered on that day, and therefore their lien will attach to the debtor's realty from the beginning of the term, and will override a conveyance or mortgage made on the second or any succeeding day, although actually prior to the rendition of the judgment. This general principle of the common law, like many others, is of such remote antiquity, and so long recognized without dispute, that the reasons and policy on which it was founded are in a great degree left to conjecture.' This rule has always been recognized in Virginia, in cases matured for a term and ready for judgment on the first day of the term, and is so recognized in this state. In Dunn *v.* Renick, 40 W. Va. 349, 22 S. E. 66, after quoting Judge Tucker in Dew *v.* Judges, 3 Hen. & M. 2, 27, 'The term session, when applied to courts, means the whole term; and in legal construction the whole term is construed as but one day, and that day is always referred to the first day or commencement of the term.' Judge Brannon says: 'I hardly think that because our statute contemplates adjournment from day to day, and provides that each day's proceedings shall be separately recorded and signed by the judge, it cuts up the term into separate days, and individuates each day from another and changes the common-law rule. By reason of this rule that the whole term is one day, the common rule was that a judgment rendered on any day has relation to, and is a judgment of, its first day. Tidd Prac. 547; 1 Lomax Dig. 287; Black, Judgts., § 441; 2 Freem., Judgm., § 369; Farley *v.* Lea, 32 Am. Dec. 680. This doctrine or rule had been always recognized in Virginia before we had a statute, but is now embodied in a statute, as regards the effect of the judgment as a lien. Code, ch. 139, § 5; Mutual Assurance Society *v.* Stanard, 4 Munf. 539; Coutts *v.* Walker, 2 Leigh 268; Skipwith *v.* Cunningham, 8 Leigh 272; Withers *v.* Carter, 4 Gratt. 407, 418." Smith *v.* Parkersburg Co-Op. Ass'n, 48 W. Va. 232, 37 S. E. 645.

G. PROPERTY AND INTERESTS SUBJECT TO LIEN.

1. Real Estate.

a. In General.

The statutes provide in substance that every judgment for money rendered heretofore or hereafter, against any person, shall be a lien on all real estate of or to which such person shall be possessed or entitled. W. Va. Code, 1899, § 4145; Va. Code, 1904, § 3567.

b. Title or Interest of Judgment Debtor.

(1) In General.

It is well settled that where statute enactments do not interfere, a judgment creditor can acquire no better right to the estate of a debtor than the debtor himself has when the judgment is recovered. He takes it subject to every liability under which the debtor held it, and subject to all the equities which exist in favor of third parties; and a court of equity will limit the lien of the judgment to the actual interest which the debtor has in the estate. Snyder *v.* Martin, 17 W. Va. 276; Pack *v.* Hansbarger, 17 W. Va. 313; Snyder *v.* Botkin, 37 W. Va. 355, 16 S. E. 591; Cleavenger *v.* Felton, 46 W. Va. 249, 33 S. E. 117; Shipe *v.* Repass, 28 Gratt. 716; Floyd *v.* Harding, 28 Gratt. 401; Borst *v.* Nalle, 28 Gratt. 423; Sharitz *v.* Moyers, 99 Va. 519, 39 S. E. 166; Powell *v.* Bell, 81 Va. 222; Wise *v.* Taylor, 44 W. Va. 492, 29 S. E. 1003; Bowman *v.* Hicks, 80 Va. 806; Coldiron *v.* Asheville Shoe Co., 93 Va. 364, 25 S. E. 238; Burkholder *v.* Ludlam, 30 Gratt. 255; First Nat. Bank *v.* Turnbull, 32 Gratt. 695; Hughes *v.* Harvey, 75 Va. 200, 210;

Cowardin *v.* Anderson, 78 Va. 88, 90; Nutt *v.* Summers, 78 Va. 164, 173; Braxton *v.* Bell, 92 Va. 229, 237, 23 S. E. 289; Young *v.* Devries, 31 Gratt. 304, 309; Summers *v.* Darne, 31 Gratt. 791, 800; Smith *v.* Gott, 51 W. Va. 141, 41 S. E. 175; Dingus *v.* Minneapolis Imp. Co., 98 Va. 737, 37 S. E. 353; Sinclair *v.* Sinclair, 79 Va. 40.

"It is well settled that ordinarily no greater interest in real estate than the judgment debtor himself has is available for the satisfaction of a judgment against him. In other words, that the right of the judgment creditor is limited to the debtor's interest in the land sought to be subjected. The creditor is in no sense treated as a purchaser, and has no equity beyond what belongs to the debtor. These propositions have often been affirmed by this court. Floyd *v.* Harding, 28 Gratt. 401; Borst *v.* Nalle, 28 Gratt. 423; Summers *v.* Darne, 31 Gratt. 791." Cowardin *v.* Anderson, 78 Va. 88, 89.

"It is well-settled law in this state that a judgment creditor can acquire no better right to the estate of the debtor than the debtor himself has when the judgment is recovered. He takes it subject to every liability under which the debtor held it and subject to all the equities which existed in favor of third parties and a court of equity will limit the lien of the judgment to the actual interest which the debtor has in the estate. The leading case on this subject is Snyder *v.* Martin, 17 W. Va. 276, in which Judges Johnson and Green give it exhaustive consideration, reviewing many authorities, both English and American, Judge Johnson, however, dissenting. Pack *v.* Hansbarger, 17 W. Va. 313, 324, in which the opinion of the court was delivered by Judge Haymond, announces the same principle and the subject is there reviewed and discussed at great length. It is reiterated again in Snyder *v.* Botkin, 37 W. Va. 355, 16 S. E. 591, in which

Judge English delivered the opinion of the court. See also, Farmers' Transportation Co. *v.* Swaney, 48 W. Va. 272, 37 S. E. 592; Standard Mercantile Co. *v.* Ellis, 48 W. Va. 309, 37 S. E. 593; Shipe *v.* Repass, 28 Gratt. 716; Floyd *v.* Harding, 28 Gratt. 401; Freeman on Judgments, § 357; .Brown *v.* Pierce, 7 Wall. (U. S.) 205; Withers *v.* Carter, 4 Gratt. 407; Bierne *v.* Ray, 49 W. Va. 129, 38 S. E. 530." Smith *v.* Gott, 51 W. Va. 141, 145, 41 S. E. 175.

A judgment creditor can not subject to the lien of his judgment real estate or some interest therein not owned by the debtor at or after the recovery of the judgment. Powell *v.* Bell, 81 Va. 222, 235.

"It has been over and over again decided that the judgment creditor can acquire no better right to the estate than the debtor himself has when the judgment is recovered." Floyd *v.* Harding, 28 Gratt. 401; Withers *v.* Carter, 4 Gratt. 407, approved.

"The lien of the judgment creditor operates only on the estate which belongs to the debtor." Shipe *v.* Repass, 28 Gratt. 716.

"A judgment can confer upon the creditor no greater or better estate than the debtor had. Whatever the debtor owns (except that which is exempted by statute), is subject to the lien of the judgment creditor; but the lien can not cover that which the debtor does not own. As was said by Judge Staples, in Floyd *v.* Harding, 28 Gratt. 401, 'It has been over and over decided, that the judgment creditor can acquire no better right to the estate than the debtor himself has when the judgment is recovered. He takes it subject to every liability under which the debtor held it, and subject to all the equities which exist at the time, in favor of third parties, and a court of chancery will limit the lien of the judgment to the actual interest which the debtor has in the estate. The creditor is in no sense a purchaser—he

has no equity whatever beyond what justly belongs to his debtor—his claim is to subject to his lien, such estate as the former owns, and no more. These principles have been time and again announced by the court of England—by this court, and by the supreme court of the United States, and by the courts of many other states of the union.' See cases cited by Judge Baldwin, in Withers *v.* Carter, 4 Gratt. 407, and cases cited by Judge Staples, in Floyd *v.* Harding, 28 Gratt. 401. In a still more recent case, Borst *v.* Nalle, 28 Gratt. 423, decided at the late Richmond term, Judge Burks, delivering the unanimous opinion of this court, says: 'Authorities might be multiplied without number to show that where statute enactments do not interfere, one creditor can never get by his judgment more than his debtor actually owns, and to this he will be, as he should be, confined by courts of equity.' See the numerous cases cited by Judge Burks in that case." Shipe *v.* Repass, 28 Gratt. 716.

The lien of a judgment can not be enforced against a tract of land in which the judgment debtor has neither right nor title, according to the well-settled rule that where statutory enactments do not interfere, only the actual interest of the judgment debtor can be subjected to sale to satisfy judgments against him. Sharitz *v.* Moyers, 99 Va. 519, 39 S. E. 166, citing Dingus *v.* Minneapolis Imp. Co., 98 Va. 737, 37 S. E. 353.

Illustrative Cases.—In 1855, H. bought of K. a lot of land for $433.33, and paid one-third cash, but took neither deed nor other writing nor possession. Some time prior to July 14th, 1856, T., as trustee of B., verbally purchased the lot of H. for same price, and paid him what he had paid, and assumed the remaining two-thirds due to K. And by writing, under seal of that date, B. directed her trustee to obtain a conveyance of said lot from

K., reserving vendor's lien for the two-thirds still due on the purchase money, and to employ her trust fund in building a house upon it. This T. did, after having first got a written order from H., directing K. to convey the lot as aforesaid. The deed is dated August 1st, 1856, but it was not recorded until 1859. Afterwards, in May, 1857, S. got a judgment against H., and sued to subject the lot to the judgment. Held, T. having paid H. for his entire interest in the lot, and got possession of it before S.'s judgment was obtained, had a valid, equitable title to the lot, and the lot is not subject to the lien of the judgment of S. against H. Powell v. Bell, 81 Va. 222.

Held, H. had bought the lot verbally, and had sold it verbally, and been paid back his money, and his vendor had acquired possession of the lot before the rendition of the judgment against H., so H. had, when the judgment was obtained, no interest in the lot whereof the judgment lien creditor could avail. Powell v. Bell, 81 Va. 222.

"The statute (Code, 1873, ch. 182, § 6), makes every judgment for money rendered in this state, theretofore or thereafter, against any person, a lien on all the real estate of or to which such person shall be possessed or entitled, at or after the date of such judgment, etc. It certainly can not be said that Heflin was either possessed or entitled to the real estate in question, or that he was entitled to any interest therein, either at or after the recovery of the judgment in this case. Hence, the settled doctrine of this court is, 'that the creditor can never get by his judgment more than his debtor really owns.' See Borst v. Nalle, 28 Gratt. 423, 433, and subsequent decisions which need not be cited." Powell v. Bell, 81 Va. 222, 233.

Lands forfeited by nonentry on the assessor's land books under Code, W. Va., 1868, ch. 31, § 24, vests in the state upon the forfeiture by the mere force of the statute, and therefore a judgment against the former owner rendered after such forfeiture is no lien on the land. Wiant v. Hays, 38 W. Va. 681, 18 S. E. 807.

In 1856, N. sold and conveyed, for gold, land to R. H. D. and J. W. D., who reconveyed same to secure purchase money. In 1866, R. H. D. was released, and the land was conveyed to J. W. D., who reconveyed it to secure the purchase money, which was expressly made payable in gold, or its equivalent. By decision of this court, in Summers v. Darne, 31 Gratt. 791, it became res judicata that this arrangement was no novation of the debt, and that N.'s lien was superior to the lien of judgments obtained against J. W. D. between the trust deed of 1856 and the trust deed of 1866. At the sale of the land under the second deed of trust, N. purchased it at a sum equal to the amount of his debt, including principal, interest and gold premiums. Held, as judgment creditor can acquire no more nor better rights to a debtor's land than the debtor himself has, N. has priority over such creditors for the gold premiums also. Nutt v. Summers, 78 Va. 164.

If B., a judgment debtor, purchases land and procures it to be conveyed to J. as the purchaser, and J. conveys it in trust to secure a bona fide debt, the creditor not being informed that it had been so purchased by B. and conveyed to J. the judgment creditor has no lien upon the land for his debt as against the creditor under the deed of trust. Moore v. Sexton, 30 Gratt. 505.

"The docketing of the judgment is required to give notice to subsequent purchasers. But the docketing of a judgment against Benjamin Beville could give no notice of a lien of the judgment upon the land of James A. Beville, the holder of the legal title, by virtue of a secret equitable title which Benjamin Beville once had to the land, of which the bona fide purchaser for value from James A. Beville of the legal title, had no notice." Moore *v.* Sexton, 30 Gratt. 505.

Vendor's Lien and Judgment.— Where the vendor's lien is retained in a contract for the sale of land, though the contract is not recorded, the vendor's lien has priority to that of the judgment creditors of the vendee. "The question we have to determine is, whether the judgment creditors of Hurt have acquired by their judgment, a superior lien to that of Repass, retained as a vendor's lien in the contract of sale referred to. It is true this contract of sale was never recorded. But the question is not to be determined by the provisions of the registry acts. It must depend upon principles outside of and independent of those acts. Whether the contract of sale was recorded or not, can make no difference. The lien of the judgment creditor operates only on the estate which belongs to the debtor." Shipe *v.* Repass, 28 Gratt. 716.

Equity of Redemption.—"The judgments being subsequent to the date of the deed of trust, they would be postponed until the deed of trust was satisfied. Their lien attached only to such interest as the grantor, their debtor, retained in the lands after executing the deed of trust; that is, to his equity of redemption." Hale *v.* Horne, 21 Gratt. 112.

Property Transferred before Recovery of Judgment.—Aside from any question of recordation, judgments acquired after lands have been aliened to a purchaser in good faith and for value, do not attach as liens to such land. Bowman *v.* Hicks, 80 Va. 806.

Partition.—The children of A., who is living, and seized of a tract of land in fee simple, agree to partition the land among themselves, and executed deeds for the parcels severally allotted to each; in pursuance of what was supposed to be a contract between B., and C., two of said children, the portion coming to B., is conveyed by a deed signed by the other children to C., but this deed is never deliverd to C., but was handed by B., to his brother Albert; subsequently, and while the parent is still living, B., admits in suit, by his creditor to enforce a judgment lien, that he is the owner of the land, which was thus to have been allotted to him, but for which no deed was made to him, but to C. Under this admission the court decreed the land to be sold, A., the parent, being no party to the suit. Held, that A. had no such equity in the land as was bound by a judgment lien, and that a decree and sale of said land passed no title to the purchaser. Parrill *v.* McKinley, 6 W. Va. 67.

(2) Apparent Interest of Judgment Debtor.

Mr. Freeman in his work on Judgments at § 356, p. 309, says: "Whenever a lien attaches to any personal property, it becomes a charge upon the precise interest which the judgment debtor has, and no other. The apparent interest of the debtor can neither extend nor restrict the operation of the lien, so that it shall encumber any greater or less interest than the debtor in fact possesses." Quoted in Pack *v.* Hansbarger, 17 W. Va. 313, 325.

"The judgment lien 'is a lien only on the interest of the judgment debtor whatever it may be. Therefore, though he seems to have an interest, yet if he have none in fact, no lien can attach.'" Pack *v.* Hansbarger, 17 W. Va. 313, 325.

Independent of any statute law the lien of a judgment is a charge upon the precise interest, which the judgment debtor has, and upon no other. The apparent interest of the debtor can neither extend nor restrict the operation of the lien, so that it shall encumber any greater or less interest than the debtor in fact possesses. The judgment creditor has a charge on the interests of the defendant in the land, just as they stood at the moment the lien attached, therefore though he seems to have an interest, yet if he have none in fact, no lien can attach. The rights of the judgment lien owner can not exceed those, which he might acquire by a purchase from the defendant with full notice of all existing legal or equitable rights belonging to third persons. The attaching of a judgment lien upon the legal title forms no impediment to the assertion of all equities previously existing over the property. The judgment lien is in equity but a charge on the equity held by the defendant, where the lien attaches. It can only hold the legal estate subject to the equity. It is well settled, that a judgment lien on the land of the debtor is subject to every equity, which existed against the debtor at the rendition of the judgment; and courts of equity will always limit the lien to the actual interest of the judgment debtor. The lien of the judgment creates a preference over subsequently acquired rights, but a court of equity will always protect the equitable rights of third persons existing at the time the judgment lien attaches. Snyder v. Martin, 17 W. Va. 276, 298.

(3) Transitory or Instantaneous Seisin.

Transitory seisin is not such an interest as becomes subject to a lien of a judgment. Straus v. Bodeker, 86 Va. 543, 10 S. E. 570.

Where land is conveyed to judgment debtor, and eo instanti reconveyed by him to trustee to secure the purchase money, he has no interest subject to the judgment lien as against the trust deed. Straus v. Bodeker, 86 Va. 543, 10 S. E. 570.

This is a doctrine well established and frequently applied. It is stated almost in the words employed by Judge Staples in Summers v. Darne, 31 Gratt. 791, and by Chancellor Kent in his Commentaries, vol. 4, pp. 173, 174, where he says: "In one instance, a mortgage will have preference over a prior docketed judgment, and that is the case of a sale and conveyance of land, and a mortgage taken at the same time in return to secure the payment of the purchase money. The deed and the mortgage are considered as parts of the same contract, and constituting one act; and justice and policy equally require that no prior judgment against the mortgagor should intervene and attach upon the land during the transitory seizen to the prejudice of the mortgage." Cowardin v. Anderson, 78 Va. 88, 90; Straus v. Bodeker, 86 Va. 543, 548, 10 S. E. 570.

Priority of Mortgage Executed Back to Secure Purchase Money.—Where a purchaser, contemporaneously with the delivery of a conveyance of the purchased land, executes a mortgage, trust deed, or other incumbrance to secure the purchase money, he acquires a temporary seisin, and not such an interest in the land as becomes subject to the lien of a judgment against him in preference to the deed of trust. And it applies equally in favor of a third person who advances the purchase money, and at the time of conveyance takes a mortgage on the land for his indemnity. Cowardin v. Anderson, 78 Va. 88; Summers v. Darne, 31 Gratt. 791, 801; Straus v. Bodeker, 86 Va. 543, 10 S. E. 570.

Where a purchaser contemporaneously with delivery of conveyance of the purchased land executes a trust deed to secure the purchase money, he acquires a temporary seizin, and not such an interest in the land as becomes subject to the lien of a judgment against him in preference to the deed of trust. The judgment creditor acquires no preference over the trust deed, whether the latter be directly for the vendor's benefit or for the benefit of a lender of the money to pay the purchase money, or whether the trust deed be recorded or not, the latter and the conveyance being parts of one transaction. Cowardin v. Anderson, 78 Va. 88.

"The testimony shows that the deed from Courtney to Coulling and the trust deed from Coulling and wife to Courtney and Walford were delivered at the same time, and were intended by the parties to operate simultaneously. The two deeds must, therefore, be treated, not as separate and distinct contracts, but as constituting one and the same transaction. And, hence, it results that Coulling acquired a transitory seizin only, and not such an interest in the land as became subject to the lien of a judgment against him in preference to the deed of trust." Cowardin v. Anderson, 78 Va. 88, 90.

Under Va. Code, 1873, ch. 182, § 6, giving judgment creditors a lien on all realty of or to which the judgment debtor is possessed or entitled, where land is conveyed to a judgment debtor, and eo instanti reconveyed by him to a trustee to secure the purchase money, he has no interest subject to the lien of the judgment as against the trust deed. Straus v. Bodeker, 86 Va. 543, 10 S. E. 570.

(4) Effect of Rescission or Cancellation.

Where a contract for the sale of real estate has been rescinded by a competent court having jurisdiction of the parties and of the subject, and the vendor and vendee have been restored to their former rights, judgments against the vendee do not attach as liens to said real estate, because the vendee has no interest to which the judgments could attach as liens. It is immaterial whether the contract was rescinded because of fraud in its procurement, or the failure of the vendee to comply with his contract. Nelson v. Turner, 97 Va. 54, 33 S. E. 390.

Cancellation of Deed.—In the case of Graysons v. Richards, and Grayson v. Beaty, 10 Leigh 57, the syllabus is as follows: "A father by deed of gift conveys land to a son, and shortly after the son voluntarily surrenders the deed to the father to be cancelled, with design to divest the title out of himself and restore it to the father, and the deed is cancelled. Held, the son's title is not divested by the cancellation of the deed, and the land shall be charged in equity with the debts of the son. In such a case, a creditor having obtained a judgment against the son subsequent to the cancellation of the deed, under which the son has taken the oath of insolvency, is not only entitled to satisfaction of his judgment out of the land as still the property of the son, but he may also claim satisfaction out of it of a simple contract debt which the son owes; and other creditors of the son who have not recovered judgments against him, coming in at the same time, shall be entered to claim satisfaction of the debts due them out of the same land." "It would seem from the principles decided in this case, that the legal title passed by the deed from Wilkinson to W. P. Golden, and that the said W. P. Golden has never in fact divested himself of the legal title, and that it is yet in him but of course subject to the judgment debts in the bill mentioned, as that deed was never recorded. And according to said decision in 10 Leigh the said deed from Wilkinson to George W. Golden did not pass the legal title to said George W., for the reason that it had already passed out of said Wilkinson to said W. P. Golden; and perhaps, as the deed as made acknowledged and delivered to W. P. Golden was changed by the erasure of the name of W. P. Golden and the insertion of the name of George W. Golden in lieu of the name of W. P. Golden, the deed as thus changed as to the grantee therein could not have been lawfully admitted to record without reacknowledgment of the deed after the said material change was made. But the deed was not admitted to record until after the judgments in the bill mentioned against said Wilkinson were rendered and docketed according to law, and it is therefore unnecessary to decide whether the said deed from Wilkinson to said George W. Golden was improperly admitted to record or not." Delaplain *v.* Wilkinson, 17 W. Va. 242, 271.

(5) Trust Property.

Where the judgment debtor's interest in the lands sought to be subjected to which the lien of a judgment is alleged to attach, is a mere equitable title held in trust for others, it is not such an interest as can be subjected to the lien of a judgment. Coldiron *v.* Asheville Shoe Co., 93 Va. 364, 25 S. E. 238.

Although the judgment debtor holds the legal title to land, yet if it is charged with a trust, it is paramount to the rights of judgment creditors. Dingus *v.* Minneapolis Imp. Co., 98 Va. 737, 37 S. E. 353.

"Judgments constitute liens only on such real estate of the debtor, of or to which he is possessed or entitled, at or after the date of the judgment. Code of Virginia, § 3567. Kelly was neither possessed of, nor entitled to the lands in Lee county, when the judgments sought to be enforced against them were recovered. He had neither the possession nor any beneficial interest in them. At no time did he hold anything beyond the mere equitable title, and this he held as the agent of the parties who were rightfully entitled to the lands, or in trust for them; and no statute required, in such case, the recordation of the title bonds to prevent judgments against him from attaching as liens on the lands." Coldiron *v.* Asheville Shoe Co., 93 Va. 364, 372, 25 S. E. 238.

C.'s real estate is encumbered with liens, and a suit is pending to enforce them. Pending the suit C. dies, leaving four heirs. H., a daughter, married S. H. E.; and there is a marriage settlement investing in J. A. E., a trustee, the real estate inherited by the daughter, H., for her sole and separate use. In the pending suit a decree is rendered by the circuit court of Lynchburg, in 1854, against her trustee, for the one-fourth of the liens against the real estate of which her father, C., died seized. S. H. E., her husband, and J. A. E., her trustee, with the consent and approbation of the husband, joined in a deed to J. N. C. for two tracts of land in Kanawha county, included in the marriage settlement, and against which the decree was rendered; and a lien is retained in the deed for 11,000 dollars, the whole of the purchase money, and a deed of trust was executed by J. N. C. at the date of the deed, to secure 9,600 dollars, parcel of said purchase money. J. N. C. never paid all the purchase money, and became involved, and executed sundry deeds of trust on his lands, and judgment liens were also obtained against him. Held: I. That the lien of the decree against E., the trustee, resting on the estate conveyed in the deed of settlement, was paramount to the rights and title of the grantors and cestui que trust therein, and the provisions of the deed of settlement could not be carried into effect, as to any part of the property, so long as the lien remained unsatisfied, and they could neither sell it for the purposes of reinvestment, nor could the cestui que trust enjoy the rents and profits, or any part thereof, for at least five years, and under the circumstances, it was clearly competent to sell a part of the estate and discharge the lien, in order that the residue might be enjoyed by the cestui que trust, and in doing so, there was no violation of the spirit of the deed of settlement, at least none that the cestui que trust could be heard to complain of. II. That J. N. C. having paid into the Saving Bank at Lynchburg, and to the receiver of the circuit court of Lynchburg, the amount of the sum secured by the trust deed executed by him to the trustee, J. A. E., a part of which payment was made with the consent of the trustee, to discharge the lien decreed by that court against the lands conveyed him by the trustee and the cestui que trust and her husband, the lien of the trust thereby became discharged, and the lands were subject to the claims of the creditors of J. N. C. III. That J. N. C. should be charged with the amount of the purchase money, 11,000 dollars, and credited with the amount he paid at sundry times into the bank, to the credit of the decree of the Lynchburg court, 11;847 dollars and 16 cents; and the residue of the purchase money should be paid to the trustee of the cestui que trust, to be held for her use according to the provisions of the marriage settlement. Parker *v.* Clarkson, 4 W. Va. 407.

Title of Trustee under Resulting Trust.—Where one with another's money buys an estate, and takes the conveyance in his own name, by presumption of law, a trust results in favor of him whose money is thus used. Such trust may be established by parol proof, but the proof must be clear. Kane *v.* O'Conners, 78 Va. 76. If part only of the purchase money has been paid of another's funds, the land will be charged proportionately, and judgment creditors of the grantee can subject only his portion or interest therein. Briscoe *v.* Ashby, 24 Gratt. 454; Sinclair *v.* Sinclair, 79 Va. 40.

(6) Creditor Secured by Deed of Trust.

A creditor whose debt is secured by deed of trust on real estate has no such interest in the land conveyed as amounts to a right of property therein, or as would be bound by judgment against the creditor. Augusta Nat. Bank *v.* Beard, 100 Va. 687, 42 S. E. 694.

(7) Title of Former Owner of Forfeited Lands.

The title to land forfeited for non-entry on the assessor's land books, by § 7, p. 90, acts, 1869 (Code, 1868, ch. 31, § 34), vested in the state upon the forfeiture, by the mere force of the statute, and without judicial or other proceeding declaring the forfeiture, and therefore a judgment against the former owner, rendered after such forfeiture, is no lien on such land. Wiant *v.* Hays, 38 W. Va. 681, 18 S. E. 807.

(8) Title of Husband to Wife's Property.

Subsequent lien creditors can not compel the sale of the wife's property to pay the husband's debt, for which she is surety, so as to give them the benefit of the husband's property. If her property is taken to pay a prior lien against her husband, for which she is surety, she is entitled to be subrogated thereto as against subsequent lien creditors. Hall *v.* Hyer, 48 W. Va. 353, 37 S. E. 594. See Rau *v.* Shaver, 102 Va. 68, 45 S. E. 873.

Where a deed of trust to secure a husband's individual indebtedness binds the property of both wife and husband, a court of equity will protect the interest of the wife as surety for her husband, and will compel a sale and application of the husband's interest or property first, if the same can be done without substantially prejudicing the rights of the trust creditor. Hall *v.* Hyer, 48 W. Va. 353, 37 S. E. 594.

In 1878, in suit under Va. Code, 1873, ch. 148, § 1, against S., a nonresident, R. got judgment and an order to sell the attached land. S. and wife got sale enjoined, their bill stating that in

1872, S., then not in debt, bought at judicial sale the land for $4,300, paid $1,500, and becoming unable in 1875 to pay balance, his wife paid it with her own funds on agreement the purchase should enure pro tanto for her separate benefit; but that commissioner had conveyed it to him and her and the survivor. She asked that her part be laid off to her. R. answered, denying that she paid anything, and prayed that his answer be treated as a cross bill, the deed be set aside as null, and the land sold to pay his judgment. The circuit court excluded the depositions of S. and wife, and being of opinion that they had failed to prove their averments, and that the land was liable to the judgment, decreed sale. At same term the court permitted S. and wife to file demurrer and answer to R.'s answer, taken as a cross bill, the same failing to allege any grounds why the deed should be annulled. In 1879, commissioners reported sale. S. and wife excepted to its confirmation, and filed bill of review of the former decree. The circuit court overruled the demurrer and the exception, confirmed the sale, and ordered commissioners to pay the net proceeds to R. On appeal here, held; S.'s moiety of the land should be subjected to R.'s judgment. The injunction should be perpetuated as to the moiety of his wife. Scott v. Rowland, 82 Va. 484, 4 S. E. 595.

Share of Joint Tenants.—Where, upon partition of real estate among joint tenants, the share of one of them who is a married woman, is released to her and her Husband by the other joint tenants, such release does not vest in the husband any such right or title in the portion set apart to his wife, as may be subject to judgment liens against the husband. Sharitz v. Moyers, 99 Va. 519, 39 S. E. 166, citing Bolling v. Teel, 76 Va. 487, 492; Dooley v. Baynes, 86 Va. 644, 649, 10 S. E. 974.

Two sisters, being the joint owners of a tract of two hundred acres of land, married and afterwards partitioned the land by mutual conveyances, their husbands joining in the deeds, but, by inadvertance, the conveyance of the share of one of the sisters was made to her and her husband. The husband having died, his judgment creditors, claiming that he was the owner of an undivided half of the one hundred acres of the land so conveyed, sought to enforce the alleged liens of their judgments thereon and to subject the one-half of said land to the satisfaction thereof. Held, that the equitable title to the whole of said one hundred acres is owned by the widow of said decedent and that the creditors have no liens upon any part of the same. Smith v. Gott, 51 W. Va. 141, 41 S. E. 175.

Lien of Husband's Judgment on Curtesy during Wife's Life.—Where property which constitutes a wife's separate estate is conveyed by a deed in which the husband unites, a judgment against him does not constitute a lien on the husband's estate by curtesy in such property, since during the wife's life the husband had no interest in the property to which the judgment could attach. Bankers' Loan, etc., Co. v. Blair, 99 Va. 606, 39 S. E. 231.

The husband has no interest, during the coverture, in the wife's statutory separate estate upon which judgments can attach as liens, and an alienation by husband and wife, during the coverture, defeats his curtesy. "The cross bill claims that the judgments are at least liens upon the husband, T. Frank Simmons', estate by curtesy in the property. The property was the wife's statutory separate estate. During her life he had no interest in it upon which the lien of the judgments could attach, and she having aliened the property by a conveyance in which he united, his right by the curtesy was defeated. Breeding v. Davis, 77 Va. 639; Campbell v. McBee,

92 Va. 68, 22 S. E. 807." Bankers' Loan, etc., Co. *v.* Blair, 99 Va. 606, 611, 39 S. E. 231.

(9) Adverse Possession against Debtor.

When the conveyance is by an unrecorded deed, and the vendee has held the property adversely for the period of ten years, before a judgment is recovered against the grantor, the land can not thereafter be subjected to the lien of such judgment. As soon as such deed is made and delivered, though unrecorded, the holder thereunder will be adverse to the world. Parkersburg Nat. Bank *v.* Neal, 28 W. Va. 744. See Bowman *v.* Hicks, 80 Va. 806.

(10) Equities Held by Third Parties against Debtor.

(a) In General.

There are cases in Virginia and West Virginia holding that notwithstanding the recording acts, judgment liens yield to prior equitable mortgages, and other trusts and equitable estates. Withers *v.* Carter, 4 Gratt. 407; Snyder *v.* Martin, 17 W. Va. 276, 299, Johnson, P., dissenting; Floyd *v.* Harding, 28 Gratt. 401; Pack *v.* Hansbarger, 17 W. Va. 313; Powell *v.* Bell, 81 Va. 222.

"It may therefore be laid down as a universal rule established by many cases, that a judgment lien is always subject to every possible description of equity held by a third party against the debtor at the time the judgment lien attached; and that it is immaterial, whether the rights of such third party consist of an equitable estate or interest in the judgment debtor's land, an equitable lien on his land, or a mere equity against the debtor which attaches to or affects his land. Nor is it at all material, whether the judgment debtor has or has not, when he contracted his debt or obtained his judgment or docketed the same, notice of such equitable estate, equitable lien, or mere equity. If they be prior in time to the judgment, they will al-

ways be preferred to the judgment lien." Snyder *v.* Martin, 17 W. Va. 276, 301.

It is a long-established rule of courts of equity that (apart from any positive provision of a statute to the contrary) where one has an equitable interest in land, with a good right to call for the conveyance of the legal title, and a subsequent encumbrancer (e. g., a judgment creditor), whose debt did not originally affect the land, acquires the legal title, he shall notwithstanding be postponed to the equitable claimant. For since the subsequent encumbrancer did not originally take the land for his security, nor had in his view an intention to affect it, when afterwards the land is affected by his lien, and he comes in claiming under the very person that is obliged in conscience to make the assurance good, he stands in that person's place and is postponed, despite his legal title, to the superior equity of the adverse claimant. 2 Lomax Dig. 487; Burgh *v.* Francis, 1 P. Wms. 276: Finch *v.* Earl of Winchelsea, 1 P. Wms. 282; Coleman *v.* Cocke, 6 Rand. 618; Withers *v.* Carter, 4 Gratt. 407, 411; Pack *v.* Hansbarger, 17 W. Va. 313, 324; Delaplain *v.* Wilkinson, 17 W. Va. 242, 267.

A good equitable title acquired by a purchaser is paramount in equity to subsequent judgment of the vendor's creditors recovered before the vendee has obtained a conveyance of the legal title, or though he has obtained one that is void in law. Withers *v.* Carter, 4 Gratt. 407, 412.

One who purchases and pays for a tract of land becomes the equitable owner thereof, though he cause his vendor to convey to a third person to whom he sells it. Flanary *v.* Kane, 102 Va. 547, 46 S. E. 312, 681.

Arguments for and against Doctrine. —"The argument that 'the equitable estate of the purchaser is good against creditors of the vendor,' has no application under our recording statutes; and the cases cited in Floyd *v.* Harding, 28 Gratt. 401, in support of the position have no reference to the rights of creditors under such statutes. It never could have been intended by the legislature to put a party claiming under a parol contract in a better condition than one who had a deed or written contract for the land. No premium should be placed upon a plain violation of the statute of frauds. And it certainly is a high premium put on such violation to place a man, who has a mere parol contract partly executed, in a safer position as to creditors than one who has taken the trouble to obey the statute and have a deed or contract executed to him for the land, and which may have been lost or destroyed." Snyder *v.* Martin, 17 W. Va. 276, 297, dissenting opinion of Johnson, J.

The dissenting opinion of Johnson, J., in Snyder *v.* Martin, 17 W. Va. 276, was approved by Holt, J., in his dissenting opinion in Snyder *v.* Botkin, 37 W. Va. 355, 16 S. E. 591.

But another judge said: "Our recording acts above copied furnish to a purchaser perfect protection by simply requiring all deeds to be recorded, and if unrecorded, rendering them void as to purchasers for valuable consideration without notice. Such purchasers needed no protection against equitable titles and liens. The creditor by these acts is obviously protected to the extent of requiring all contracts for the sale of lands, when in writing, and all deeds conveying lands to be recorded and by declaring them void against creditors, if not recorded. This is all the protection these acts afford the creditor, and is in truth all the protection which can be afforded him by any recording act. These acts do not, and no recording act could, afford a creditor any protection against any equitable title or lien, which was not evidenced by writing, such, for instance, as an equitable title to land arising from a parol contract having been made and so far executed as to entitle the purchaser to a specific execution of the parol contract, or any other constructive trust, or any resulting trust. Nor has the legislature thought proper to protect the judgment creditor by any other form of legislation against these sorts of equitable titles and liens; for we have seen that the statute of frauds furnishes him no such protection." Snyder *v.* Martin, 17 W. Va. 276, 309.

"I have not been able to find in our recording acts the least evidence, that the legislature intended to avoid for the benefit of a creditor an equitable title, which was preceded by a verbal contract, and which was based on a fraud attempted by the seller in refusing to make a deed for the land, after it had been improved by the purchaser. I could not expect to find such intention in any recording act. It would be entirely out of place in such an act." Snyder *v.* Martin, 17 W. Va. 276, 310.

"I now proceed to inquire, whether the statute in question, to wit, the 4th and 5th sections of ch. 74 of the Code of this state (which are the same as §§ 4, 5, ch. 118, Code of Virginia of 1849, as we have already stated) make void an equitable interest in land acquired by verbal contract of purchase executed by possession, etc., as to subsequent judgment creditors. And first it must be observed, that verbal contracts are not mentioned in either of the sections, and neither are equitable interests in land acquired by purchase by verbal contract mentioned in either of the said sections. No contracts are named in either sections except contracts in writings and deeds of conveyance. It can not be said that the words "contract in writings" as used necessarily include or were intended to include verbal contracts of purchase of lands with as much plausibility as it might have been said before the said decision of Withers *v.* Carter, that the 4th section of said ch. 99, 1 Revised Code of 1819, p. 362, included contracts in writing for the conveyance or sale of lands as well as deed conveying lands. But, as we have seen, it was properly held that it did not." Snyder *v.* Martin, 17 W. Va. 276, 339.

(b) Illustrative Cases.

In the opinion in White *v.* Denman, 1 O. St. 112, it is said: "It is a principle of familiar application in equity jurisprudence that a specific equitable interest in real estate, whether it be created by an executory agreement for the sale and conveyance of land, or by a deed so defectively executed as not to pass the legal estate, but treated in equity as a contract to convey, or even a vendor's lien, is upheld by courts of equity, and uniformly takes priority, not only over judgment liens and assignments in bankruptcy but also assignments for the benefit of creditors generally." Atkinson *v.* Miller, 34 W. Va. 115, 11 S. E. 1007, 1009.

Judge Green, in Snyder *v.* Martin, 17 W. Va. 276, 299, shows, by many cases, that judgment liens yield to prior equitable mortgages, and other trusts and equitable estates created by written contract, and on page 301, says: "It may therefore be laid down as a universal rule, established by many cases, that a judgment lien is always subject to every possible description of equity held by a third party against the debtor at the time the judgment lien attached, and that it is immaterial whether the rights of such third party consist of an equitable estate or interest in the judgment debtor's land, an equitable lien on his land, or a mere equity which attaches to or affects his land. Nor is it at all material whether the judgment debtor has or has not, when he contracted his debt, or obtained his judgment, or docketed the same, notice of

such equitable estate, equitable lien, or mere equity. If they be prior in time to the judgment, they will always be preferred to the judgment lien. The authorities we have cited abundantly sustain this conclusion, and there is no exception to this universal rule, except where such exception has been made by some statute law." It follows, therefore, that this defective deed of trust as an equitable mortgage, being prior in time to the judgments of the appellants, takes precedence over them though it might, in this latter view, be subordinate to deeds of trust. And so, whether we view this deed of trust as a contract for a conveyance recordable under the statute, which we hold it to be, or as an equitable mortgage recordable under the statute, or as an equitable mortgage not recordable under the statute, it is to be preferred to the judgments of the appellants, and on both grounds their appeal is not well taken. Atkinson *v.* Miller, 34 W. Va. 115, 11 S. E. 1007.

A judgment lien is subject to any express trust existing, when the judgment lien attaches. Snyder *v.* Martin, 17 W. Va. 276, 299.

A judgment creditor must yield to a prior equitable estate created by a written contract. Snyder *v.* Martin, 17 W. Va. 276, 300.

A judgment lien must yield to a prior resulting trust in a third party. Snyder *v.* Martin, 17 W. Va. 276, 300.

Constructive Trust.—A judgment lien will be postponed to a prior constructive trust. Snyder *v.* Martin, 17 W. Va. 276, 300.

Although if a son obtain a conveyance for land purchased by his father, that conveyance may be set aside for fraud by a creditor of the father, whilst the land is in the hands of the son; yet, if the son sell and convey the land to a third person for valuable consideration, who has no notice of the fraud between father and son, such third person being a bona fide purchaser, will be protected in his purchase against the creditors of the father, from the operation of the statute of frauds, by its proviso. And if the deed to such bona fide purchaser be not duly recorded, yet he will be protected in his purchase against a creditor of the father, who obtains a decree against the father, after the bona fide purchase so made, because such a purchaser has a prior equity to such creditor. For, if the original vendor had never made a deed to the son, yet the purchaser, holding the equitable title transferred from the father to the son, and from the son to him, would have had a better right to call on the original vendor for a conveyance of the legal title, than any creditor of the father obtaining a judgment against him, after his transfer of the equitable right to the son. Coleman v. Cocke, 6 Rand. 618.

Contest between Judgment Creditor and a Purchaser.—If a judgment debtor purchases land and procures it to be conveyed to another as the purchaser, and he conveys it in trust to secure a bona fide debt, and the creditor is not informed that it has been purchased by the judgment debtor and conveyed to another as the purchaser, the judgment creditor has no lien upon the land for his debt as against the creditor under the deed of trust. Moore v. Sexton, 30 Gratt. 505.

Vendor's Liens.—The judgment lien must yield to prior vendors' liens or specific liens of any kind or prior equities of any description. Snyder v. Martin, 17 W. Va. 276, 300.

"But as now by statute law in this state the secret vendor's lien has been abolished, and it can have no existence, only when reserved on the face of the deed, which must be recorded, there can be no question, that in this state a vendor's lien, when it has any existence, will have priority over a subsequent judgment." Snyder v. Martin, 17 W. Va. 276, 301.

Equitable Mortgages.—On the well-established principles of courts of equity an equitable mortgage ought to have priority over a subsequent judgment lien. Snyder v. Martin, 17 W Va. 276, 300.

Defective Conveyance. — A paper made for a deed of trust conveying land to secure a debt signed by the grantor but without a seal, though not effectual as a deed of trust at law, is an equitable mortgage, enforceable in equity, and may be recorded under § 4, ch. 74, W. Va. Code, 1868, and when recorded is a lien valid against subsequent judgment creditors. The syllabus in Pratt v. Clemens, 4 W. Va. 443, and point 2 of the syllabus in Shattuck v. Knight, 25 W. Va. 590, disapproved. Atkinson v. Miller, 34 W. Va. 115, 11 S. E. 1007.

When a paper purporting to be a deed of trust does not appear to have been executed under the seals of the grantors, it does not create a lien so as to defeat subsequent judgment creditors. And such paper does not come within the provisions of the fourth section of ch. 118, Code of Virginia, 1860, for while it might be technically a contract for a conveyance of the land, it is in substance nothing more than a contract for a lien upon the land to be created by a deed of trust. Pratt v. Clemens, 4 W. Va. 443, disapproved in Atkinson v. Miller, 34 W. Va. 115, 11 S. E. 1007.

Equity of Purchaser under Unrecorded Parol Contract.—See post, "Doctrine of Floyd v. Harding," VI, G, 1, b, (10), (e), for a full discussion.

"Whenever, therefore, after a parol contract has been entered into for the sale of land, and it has been so far performed by the parties as to place the purchaser in a position, that if the contract was treated as void, it would operate as a fraud on the purchaser, he will therefore be regarded by a court of equity as the equitable owner of the land, and on his performing his contract in a full court of equity will decree that a deed shall be made to him by the seller. In other words, such oral contract, when followed up by such part performance, originates a constructive trust, just as other frauds give rise to constructive trusts. This constructive trust having been raised, I can conceive of no reason why it should not like all other constructive trusts, equitable estates and equities be preferred to a subsequent judgment lien. We have seen, that every imaginable equity attached to the land is preferred to a subsequent judgment lien. Why should this equity be excepted from this universal rule? Not because it originated in a fraud, which bound only the conscience of the seller, and therefore not binding the conscience of the judgment creditor of the seller, it ought not to be enforced against him; for if this were so, the same reasoning would apply to every constructive trust originating in the fraud of the judgment debtor. Yet we have seen, that all such constructive trusts have ever been held to be enforceable against the subsequent judgment creditor of the party committing the fraud. This preference, which a court of chancery always gives to the equity of a third person over a subsequent judgment lien, ought not to be set aside by reason of its acknowledgment being in contravention to the policy of the statute of frauds." Snyder v. Martin, 17 W. Va. 276, 304.

"Unquestionably therefore a purchaser of land by parol contract, to the full extent that a court of equity would recognize his equity against the party, who by parol contract had agreed to sell him the land, should be held in a court of equity to have rights superior to any subsequent judgment creditor, whether the judgment creditor had or had not notice of his contract to purchase the land, unless some statute law has rendered the judgment creditor's lien superior to his equity. It is claimed that the statute of frauds produced this effect, and that after its passage the judgment creditor's lien must be held as superior to any equitable estate or right, which a third party had before the rendition of the judgment acquired from the debtor to any land, which was based in whole or in part on the fact, that he had made a parol contract for the purchase of the land. We will now consider whether this be the real effect of the statute of frauds." Snyder v. Martin, 17 W. Va. 276, 302.

A purchaser of land by parol contract which has been so far executed as to vest in him the right to compel his vendor to execute the parol contract in a court of equity has an equitable right in said land so purchased, which a court of equity will fully protect against the lien of a subsequent judgment creditor of his vendor. Snyder v. Botkin, 37 W. Va. 355, 16 S. E. 591.

(c) Doctrine of McClure v. Thistle.

Under the first recording act it was held, that a deed executed before judgments have been obtained against the grantor, under which the purchaser has been put in possession and paid the purchase money, but which was not recorded until after the judgments were obtained, is void as against such creditors, and the land conveyed thereby is subject to satisfy the judgments. M'Clure v. Thistle, 2 Gratt. 182; Delaplain v. Wilkinson, 17 W. Va. 242, 262; Snyder v. Martin, 17 W. Va. 276, 289; Pack v. Hansbarger, 17 W. Va. 313, 323; Anderson v. Nagle, 12 W. Va. 98, 104; Murdock v. Welles, 9 W. Va. 552, 557; Hart v. Haynes, 1 Va. Dec. 201, 206; Campbell v. Nonpareil Co., 75 Va. 291, 295; Powell v. Bell, 81 Va. 222, 225; Withers v. Carter, 4 Gratt. 407, 409; Eidson v. Huff, 29 Gratt. 338, 345. See also, Trout v. Warwick, 77 Va. 731; Davis v. Landcraft, 10 W. Va. 718.

"It has been decided by the supreme court of the United States, in the case of Bayley *v.* Greenlief, 7 Wheat. 46, and by this court in Moore *v.* Holcombe, 3 Leigh 597, that the judgment lien has priority over the equitable lien of the vendor for the purchase money. The principle of these decisions is decisive of this question. The legal title of the grantee being void as to creditors, his equitable title must be void as against the legal lien of the judgment." M'Clure *v.* Thistle, 2 Gratt. 182.

The rule that where one has an equitable interest in land with a good right to call for the conveyance of the legal title, and a judgment creditor whose debt did not originally affect the land, acquires the legal title, he shall notwithstanding be postponed to the equitable claimant, as was announced in Withers *v.* Carter, 4 Gratt. 407, 411, can not stand against the positive provisions of the statute declaring that unrecorded and unregistered contracts in writing for the conveyance or sale of real estate for a greater term than five years, are void as to creditors and purchasers for valuable consideration. Delaplain *v.* Wilkinson, 17 W. Va. 242.

It is certain that the statute providing that contracts in writing for the sale or conveyance of real estate for a term greater than five years, shall be void as to creditors and subsequent purchasers for value without notice, until recorded, overturns as to written conveyances, the rule in Withers *v.* Carter, 4 Gratt. 407, and would seem to put at rest all attempts to reconcile this case with McClure *v.* Thistle, 2 Gratt. 182. This question is dealt with at length in Delaplain *v.* Wilkinson, 17 W. Va. 242, 267.

A contract in writing for the sale of land, in which the vendee is put in possession, and makes valuable improvements, but which is not recorded as required by statute, is void as to a judgment recovered against the vendor and docketed as required by statute. Delaplain *v.* Wilkinson, 17 W. Va. 242. The court said that the statute requiring the recordation of contracts in writing for the conveyance and sale of real estate placed such written contracts unrecorded upon the same footing with purchasers for valuable consideration without notice, as unrecorded deeds. This being so then every unrecorded or unregistered contract in writing for the conveyance or sale of real estate for a greater term than five years, is void as to judgment creditors who have properly docketed their judgments. Following McClure *v.* Thistle, 2 Gratt. 182, and disapproving Withers *v.* Carter, 4 Gratt. 407.

Issuance of Ca. Sa.—The land is equally subject, in such case, to satisfy a creditor, who has issued a ca. sa. upon his judgment, upon the service of which the grantor in the deed has been discharged as an insolvent debtor. McClure *v.* Thistle, 2 Gratt. 182.

(d) Doctrine of Withers v. Carter.

Further as to this, see post, "Doctrine of Floyd *v.* Harding," VI, G, 1, b, (10), (e).

Present Status of Doctrine in Virginia.—The recording acts providing that every contract in writing in respect to real estate shall be void as to creditors and subsequent purchasers for valuable consideration without notice, until and except from the time that it is duly admitted to record in the county or corporation wherein the real estate embraced in the contract or deed may be, abrogate the doctrine of Withers *v.* Carter, 4 Gratt. 407, so far as executory contracts in writing for the sale of land are concerned, and place them on the same footing as conveyances of the legal title. But as will be shown further on, in discussing the doctrine of Floyd *v.* Harding, 28 Gratt. 401, it was held, that the statute applied only to contracts in writing and in no way affected the case of a parol contract for the sale of land, and that a purchaser taking possession under such a contract is vested with a valid equitable title not subject to the lien of a judgment subsequently obtained against the vendor. See Eidson *v.* Huff, 29 Gratt. 338; Hart *v.* Haynes, 1 Va. Dec. 201, 206; Anderson *v.* Nagle, 12 W. Va. 98, 111; Delaplain *v.* Wilkinson, 17 W. Va. 242, 268; Pack *v.* Hansbarger, 17 W. Va. 313, 335; Snyder *v.* Martin, 17 W. Va. 276, 290.

The only cases which can now fall under the influence of Withers *v.* Carter, 4 Gratt. 407, are those where there has been a verbal contract attended with circumstances of part performance. We will premise, that it is now well settled that, except perhaps in a few exceptional cases, nothing short of a delivery of possession will confer the equitable title, and entitle the vendee to specific execution. Lester *v.* Foxcroft, Lead. Cas. in Eq., vol. 1, pt. 2 (4 Amer. Ed.). In such cases the vendee acquires an equitable title (as much now as before the recording acts), which the court of equity will recognize, protect and enforce. The necessity of recordation arises from the statute. The recording act does not embrace such oral contracts nor require their recordation, whereof they are insusceptible from their very nature. To uphold the validity of such titles, prior to the conveyance of the legal title, is certainly not contrary to the letter of the recording acts; nor, as it seems to us, to their spirit. In order to acquire the equitable title under such oral contract, it is necessary that the vendee should be put in possession. This circumstance gives notice to the world, or at least suffices to put all persons on inquiry. It is an open and notorious fact, not secret like a deed or a written contract, which may be pocketed, and the world never know of the change of title. This necessity of putting the vendee in possession will also prevent the danger of collusive and pretended sales, which is deprecated by Judge Wingfield. The recording act makes a distinction which is founded upon this very principle in the case of chattels; for a mortgage thereof must be recorded; but a bill of sale (where generally there must be a transfer of possession) need not be. Of course there is an obvious difference between chattels and lands—possession being, in a much greater degree, the badge of ownership, with the former; but still the illustration has some application. But, however that may be, where there is no deed or contract which can be recorded, such a case can not be embraced, in any sense, within the recording act; and if the circumstances are such as to confer an equitable title, it results as a necessary consequence that that title will be protected in equity, inasmuch as it can not be affected by a failure to comply with a statute with whose requisitions compliance is not only not required, but is impossible. And, to the question, whether it could have been intended that such a verbal contract, accompanied by circumstances of part performance, should stand upon a better footing than the deed conveying the full legal title, or the written contract, we answer, no, if the deed, or contract, is recorded pursuant to the statute, full opportunity for which is given; but yes, if they are not so recorded; such intention could not only have been entertained, but, in our judgment, has in effect been declared.

"The principal question before us is, whether the appellee's judgment is a lien upon the house and lot in the possession of Mrs. Hanger or her alienees. The position of the appellant is, that although the deed to Mrs. Hanger may be invalid as to creditors of Shelby for want of recordation in due time, the executory contract of October 8th, 1856, although never recorded, vested in Mrs. Hanger an equitable title paramount to the lien of the judgment. This pretension is based upon the decision of this court in Withers *v.* Carter, 4 Gratt. 407, in which it was held, that although the statute avoids an unrecorded deed as against creditors of the grantor, it does not affect a pre-existing equitable estate acquired by purchase from him. Since that decision was made, an important change, as is well known, has been made in the laws relating to the registration of deeds. This change was effected at the revisal of 1849. The statute then adopted, and which is still in force, declares that every contract in writing in respect to real estate shall be void as to creditors and subsequent purchasers for valuable consideration, without notice, until and except from the time that it is duly admitted to record in the county or corporation wherein the real estate embraced in said contract or deed may be. By a subsequent section it is provided that if the writing is admitted to record within sixty days from the time of its being acknowledged before and certified to by a justice, notary public or other person authorized to certify the same for record, it shall, unless it be a mortgage or deed of trust. be as valid as if it had been recorded on the day of its acknowledgment. Code of 1860, ch. 119, §§ 4, 5, 7. These provisions effectually abrogated the rule laid down in Withers *v.* Carter, so far at least as executory contracts in writing for the sale of land are concerned, and placed them upon precisely the same footing as conveyances of the legaI' title. See the case of Hart *v.* Haynes. decided by the special court of appeals, and reported in the number of the Law Journal for February, 1877, p. 109." Eidson *v.* Huff. 29 Gratt. 338, 340.

Status of Withers v. Carter in West Virginia.—"It is manifest, I think, that the principles settled in the case of Withers *v.* Carter, 4 Gratt. 407. as to equitable interests in land applies to and covers an equitable interest in land

acquired by a purchaser by verbal contract executed by possession, etc., as well as to written contracts. The syllabus of the case and the language employed by the very able judge, who delivered the opinion of the court, in discussing and declaring the great principles of equity governing as to the holders of such equitable interests as against subsequent judgment creditors, clearly shows such to be the fact. And the principles declared by the court in its opinion in that case as to equitable interests in land and the protection, to which such equitable interests were entitled and would receive in a court of equity as against subsequent judgment creditors, I regard as a rule governing property which should not be departed from by this court at this late day, unless very peculiar circumstances, if at all. When a rule, by which the title to real property is to be determined, has become established by positive law or by deliberate judicial decision, its inherent correctness or incorrectness, its justice or injustice, in the abstract, are of far less importance than that it should itself be constant and invariable." Pack *v.* Hansbarger. 17 W. Va. 313, 338.

The Argument in Hart v. Haynes.—"But in the case of Withers *v.* Carter, 4 Gratt. 407, decided by a court of three judges, which seems to me to be exactly similar in principle, and only differs in its details from the former in that the contract for the sale and purchase was in writing, and the purchaser (Carter) had only paid two-thirds of the price of the land bought by him from Triplett, and had, according to the terms of the contract, gotten a deed of conveyance, properly acknowledged and certified, which, however, was never recorded in consequence of its having been lost by the messenger by whom it was sent to the clerk's office to be recorded, a different rule seems to have been laid down. It is true that Judge Baldwin, in his opinion in the latter case, undertakes to distinguish it from McClure *v.* Thistle, 2 Gratt. 182, upon the ground that there was a pre-existing executory contract for the sale of the land by Triplett to Carter at the time the deed was made, and that the statute only made the deed void and did not affect the previous existing contract (which he assumes was not the case in McClure *v.* Thistle); and that as Carter had fully paid so much of the purchase money as entitled him, under the contract, to a deed of conveyance, and had been put into possession, he had a complete equitable title to the same, which a court of chancery would have executed; and which, therefore, protected it against the creditors who obtained judgments after the sale. The distinction attempted to be made between the two cases is based upon the argument that there was a preceding executory contract by which Triplett was bound to convey the land to Carter, which was a still existing contract (notwithstanding the execution of the deed of conveyance); and as the statute then in force did not require such a contract to be recorded, but merely permitted it, and when it was done, gave it the effect of a deed and notice as to creditors and purchasers, and did not avoid it if not recorded; and although the deed of conveyance to Carter was rendered void by the statute as to the creditors of Triplett, yet it did not affect Carter's previous equitable estate, and he was entitled to have his equitable title and estate protected and enforced against them in a court of equity. While in McClure *v.* Thistle, it did not appear there was any preceding executory contract, but that the payment, delivery of possession and deed of conveyance were all at the same time, for anything that appeared in the case. It seems to me that there is, of necessity, obliged to be a verbal agreement preceding every written contract. How is there ever to be a written contract unless the parties before hand agree upon its terms? It is true, that such a contract in relation to the sale of land would be void under the statute of frauds, unless it had been so far performed by one of the parties as to entitle him to have a specific performance in equity; but when it has been so far performed by the purchaser as to entitle him, in a court of equity, to compel the vendor to convey the legal title, he has as good and complete an equitable title as if he stood upon a written executory contract." Hart *v.* Haynes, 1 Va. Dec. 201, 206.

"It always seemed to me that the decision in Withers *v.* Carter, 4 Gratt. 407, could not stand with that in McClure *v.* Thistle, 2 Gratt. 182, or with the letter and spirit of the statute. I think it can not be fairly inferred that the legislature, when it declared that an unrecorded deed should be void as to creditors and purchasers without notice, meant that the party might go behind that and set up an unrecorded executory contract on which the deed was founded, and in that way defeat the very object of the statute. For what good purpose should the deed (the highest evidence of title) be held void, if behind that, there may be an equitable title resting upon an unrecorded executory contract on which the deed is founded, to the whole beneficial interest which may be protected against the creditors as to whom the deed is void.'" Hart *v.* Haynes, 1 Va. Dec. 201, 209.

"To hold that an equitable title resting upon a parol contract partly performed could be set up against creditors would tend not only to defeat the letter and spirit of the statute, but would have a very pernicious and evil tendency in itself, and open a wide door to frauds and perjuries. The remedy allowed the creditor against the lands of the debtor, by the law, is of much more importance and much more frequently resorted to now, than it formerly was—and if the doctrine should be established that such an equitable title can be set up against a creditor, when one under an unrecorded written contract can not, what is to prevent a fraudulent combination between the debtor and a pretended purchaser from defeating the creditor in every instance? They will have nothing to do but for the one to pretend to have sold and the other to have purchased and paid for the land before the judgment was recovered— no one may know anything of the supposed purchase but themselves. They, under the law as it now stands, will be competent witnesses; and they may, and in most instances will be the sole witnesses to prove the supposed sale and purchase, and there can be none to contradict them, and thus every creditor may be defeated and defrauded. This, I think, shows the wisdom of the statute, and the propriety of adhering to its letter and spirit." Hart v. Haynes, 1 Va. Dec. 201, 211.

"There is no need to quarrel with Withers v. Carter, 4 Gratt. 407, now, and whether it can be distinguished from McClure v. Thistle, 2 Gratt. 182, is not now a question of any great interest or importance, because by the 4th and 5th sections of ch. 118 of the Code of 1849, all written contracts in relation to land, are put upon the same footing of deeds, and are declared void as to creditors and purchasers without notice, unless recorded." Hart v. Haynes, 1 Va. Dec. 201, 209, opinion of Wingfield, J.

The decision in Hart v. Haynes, 1 Va. Dec. 201, reaffirms the principles settled by McClure v. Thistle, 2 Gratt. 182, but does not necessarily trench upon the doctrine of Withers v. Carter, 4 Gratt. 407.

(e) **Doctrine of Floyd v. Harding.**

aa. Interest of Vendee under Unrecorded Parol Contract.

In General.—And the rule announced in Withers v. Carter, 4 Gratt. 407, that the statute requiring the recordation of deeds does not apply to a written executory contract for the sale of land, and thus does not affect a pre-existing equitable estate acquired by such contract, so that one, who under such a contract has paid the purchase money due and been put in possession of the land, has a valid equitable title not subject to the lien of a subsequent judgment creditor of the vendor, though abrogated so far as executory contracts in writing for the sale of land are concerned, has been held to apply with equal force to a pre-existing equitable estate acquired under a parol contract. Under this statute it has been held, repeatedly, that land sold and purchased under a parol contract, the purchaser having paid the purchase money, and having been put into possession, and holding the same under such contract, before a judgment is recovered against the vendor, is not subject to satisfy the judgment. In the language of Judge Staples in Floyd v. Harding, 28 Gratt. 401, to require the vendee to record such a paper would be to require him to "perform an impossibility." Floyd v. Harding, 28 Gratt. 401; Eidson v. Huff, 29 Gratt. 338, 340; Long v. Hagerstown, etc., Co., 30 Gratt. 665, 669; Young v. Devries, 31 Gratt. 304, 309; Campbell v. Nonpareil Co., 75 Va. 291, 296; Hurt v. Prillaman, 79 Va. 257, 263; Bowman v. Hicks, 80 Va. 806; Brown v. Butler, 87 Va. 621, 13 S. E. 71; Pack v. Hansbarger, 17 W. Va. 313, 338, Snyder v. Botkin, 37 W. Va. 355, 16 S. E. 591; Hicks v. Riddick, 28 Gratt. 418; Shipe v. Repass, 28 Gratt. 716; Dobyns v. Waring, 82 Va. 159, 166; Trout v. Warwick, 77 Va. 731; Burkholder v. Ludlam, 30 Gratt. 255; Withers v. Carter, 4 Gratt. 407; Marling v. Marling, 9 W. Va. 79; Powell v. Bell, 81 Va. 222; Delaplain v. Wilkinson, 17 W. Va. 242; Snyder v. Martin, 17 W. Va. 276; Farmers' Transportation Co.

v. Swaney, 48 W. Va. 272, 37 S. E. 592; Renick *v.* Ludington, 20 W. Va. 511, 569; Anderson *v.* Nagle, 12 W. Va. 98.

In an opinion delivered by Judge Haymond in Pack *v.* Hansbarger, 17 W. Va. 313, 336, the court reviewed the statutes from the earliest times bearing on this subject, and the cases of McClure *v.* Thistle, 2 Gratt. 182; Withers *v.* Carter, 4 Gratt. 407, and arrived at the following conclusion: "I might refer to other decisions of this court bearing upon the same subject; but the principle is so well established and sanctioned with us, and is so familiar to the legal profession, that to cite them would be a work of supererogation. These decisions, however, establish the principle as ∙recognized and established with us, that a purchaser by verbal contract executed by possession, payment, etc., has a good equitable title or interest in the land so purchased under and by virtue of such contract against his vendor, which a court of equity will upon proof thereof enforce by compelling a conveyance of the legal title, and that such equitable title∙ or interest in the land so acquired will in equity generally be enforced against the vendor, when properly established, as readily as if the contract of sale had been in writing. This being established, it must follow that in the case of a purchaser of lands by verbal contract, where the purchaser has acquired an equitable title or interest in the land under such contract, that the vendor of such purchaser is considered in equity the trustee of the purchaser as to the legal title to the land, as much as though the contract of sale had been in writing. These principles being established, if a good equitable interest has been acquired in lands by a purchaser under a verbal contract, which a court of equity will recognize, respect and enforce against the vendor, it must follow, that a court of equity

will protect such equitable title or interest against a subsequent judgment creditor of the vendor, where no deed has been made, and generally where a deed has been made but is void because not recorded prior to the judgment, unless such verbal contract, under which such equitable interest is acquired, is embraced and included by the statute, the same as written contracts, for the conveyance or sale, or deeds conveying land, where they have not been recorded, so far as relates to creditors and purchasers for valuable consideration without notice."

The decision of Floyd v. Harding, 28 Gratt. 401, that the registry acts do not apply to a parol contract for land so that one who under a parol contract has paid the purchase money and been put in possession of land has a valid equitable title not subject to the lien of a subsequent judgment creditor of the vendor, is followed in Burkholder *v.* Ludlam, 30 Gratt. 255; March *v.* Chambers, 30 Gratt. 299; Long *v.* Hagerstown, etc., Co., 30 Gratt. 665; Trout *v.* Warwick, 77 Va. 731; Halsey *v.* Peters, 79 Va. 60; Bowman *v.* Hicks, 80 Va. 806; Powell *v.* Bell, 81 Va. 222; Brown *v.* Butler, 87 Va. 621, 13 S. E. 71; Reynolds *v.* Necessary, 88 Va. 125; 13 S. E. 348; Frame *v.* Frame, 32 W. Va. 463, 9 S. E. 901. See 2 Minor's (4th Ed.), 851, et seq. The principal case is distinguished in Campbell *v.* Nonpareil Co., 75 Va. 291, 297 and Eidson *v.* Huff, 29 Gratt. 338. See also, Hicks *v.* Riddick, 28 Gratt. 418. Subsequent to these decisions it was provided by statute, Code, § 2463, that "every contract, not in writing, made in respect to real estate or goods and chattels, in consideration of marriage, or made for the conveyance or sale of real estate on a term therein of more than five years, shall be void, both at law and in equity, as to purchasers for valuable consideration without notice and creditors." See also, Barton's Ch. Pr. 396,

522, 636, 932, 950, 990, 1030, 1032, 1063.

Doctrine Criticised.—In Snyder v. Martin, 17 W. Va. 276, 291, Judge Johnson in a clear and cogent opinion, makes the following just criticism of this harsh and unreasonable construction of the statute which started with the decision of Floyd v. Harding, 28 Gratt. 401: "These decisions were made by the court of appeals of our mother state, construing our own statute laws enacted long before the separation, and they are entitled to our earnest consideration, and should not be departed from except for most cogent reasons. But we are compelled to say, if they correctly propound the law, a very strange condition of our recording acts is exhibited, a good illustration of which is found in Young et al. v. Devries, the last case of the series, in which case it appeared, that all the claimants of the lands sought to be subjected had paid their purchase money, and had been in possession of the lands from the time of their respective purchases, some under written contracts of purchase, and others under parol contracts. Those who had taken the precaution to have their contracts reduced to writing, and who did not have them recorded, and were turned off from the lands they had occupied, and were compelled to give them up to be sold to satisfy the judgment liens; but those who had been more negligent, and did not take the trouble to procure written contracts or deeds, were protected and their homes saved to them. It was called gross negligence in the former not to record their contracts; but the others were protected, because these contracts were such as the statute did not require to be recorded, and which it would be impossible to admit to record. Thus in the one case the direct calamity is visited upon one for his gross negligence, and a premium given to the other for what was certainly a

8 Va—25

grosser negligence. It is settled law in Virginia and in this state, that creditors stand on higher ground than purchasers, and are not chargeable with actual notice of unrecorded deeds and contracts. The manifest policy of our recording acts is, that persons shall not be permitted to obtain credit on the fact, that the records disclose that they are the legal or equitable owners of property, and then be allowed to escape the payment of their debts by secret transfers of such property. But if such transfers either legal or equitable are placed upon record, the creditor is bound thereby. If the late Virginia decisions are correct, two rules bind the creditor now instead of one. He must not be content, when trusting his neighbor, with an examination of the records of his county to ascertain what real estate he owns, but if he would be safe, he must not only do this, he must also enquire who is in possession of the property, and whether he claims it, and how. It may be that the party, who claims to have a right to the land, is in possession by his tenant, and it would be still more difficult to ascertain who in fact claimed to be the owner of the land. The whole question turns upon what construction is given to our recording acts taken in connection with the statute of frauds."

Part Payment of Purchase Money Not Sufficient.—A purchaser of land under a parol contract who has been let into possession and paid a part of the purchase price is not entitled to priority for the payments made over a subsequent judgment against his vendor. In order for a purchaser under a contract which is not required to be recorded, to be protected against subsequent judgments against his vendor, he must, before the date of such judgment, have become invested with a perfect equitable title. Fulkerson v. Taylor, 102 Va. 314, 46 S. E. 378; Bowman v. Hicks, 80 Va. 806.

The provisions of § 2472 of the Code, which protects a subsequent purchaser under an unrecorded title to the extent of payments made when he receives notice of a prior unrecorded deed or writing and gives him a lien on the property purchased for so much of the purchase money as he had paid before notice, has no application to judgment creditors. "Prior to the Code of 1887, a subsequent purchaser under a contract not required to be recorded was not protected against a prior unrecorded conveyance unless he had paid the whole purchase price before he received notice of the unrecorded conveyance. 4 Minor's Inst. 968, and cases there cited. Now, under § 2472 of that Code, such a purchaser is protected to the extent of the payments made when he receives notice of the prior unrecorded deed or writing, and has a lien on the property purchased for so much of the purchase money as he had paid before notice. But this highly equitable provision has no application to judgment creditors. The word 'writing,' in that section, refers to contracts in writing by which a party acquires some interest in, not to judgments by which a party acquires a mere lien upon, land." Fulkerson v. Taylor, 102 Va. 314, 319, 46 S. E. 378.

Parol Contract Must Be Certain and Definite.—But in order that an equitable right held by a bona fide purchaser, under a parol contract, who has paid the purchase money and received possession, may be preferred in equity to the liens of judgment creditors subsequently acquired against the vendor, the parol contract relied on must be certain and definite in its terms, and sustained by satisfactory proof. Hurt v. Prillaman, 79 Va. 257; Floyd v. Harding, 28 Gratt. 401; Wright v. Pucket, 22 Gratt. 370.

Unpaid Purchase Money. — But though the land in the hands of a vendee under a parol contract is not subject to a judgment against the vendor, it is liable to the extent of the unpaid purchase money. Withers v. Carter, 4 Gratt. 407; Floyd v. Harding, 28 Gratt. 401; Bowman v. Hicks, 80 Va. 806.

A creditor by judgment or decree may in equity subject the debtor's equitable interest in land sold by him, for the purchase money unpaid. And such creditor will be preferred to an assignee of the purchase money claiming under an assignment made subsequent to the judgment or decree. Withers v. Carter, 4 Gratt. 407.

There is a creditor by judgment prior to a sale of land by his debtor, and there is a purchase money unpaid sufficient to satisfy the judgment, when another creditor recovers a judgment against the same debtor. This last can not insist that the first shall go against the land, and leave the purchase money unpaid for him; but the purchaser of the land is entitled to have the purchase money applied to relieve his land. Withers v. Carter, 4 Gratt. 407.

Illustrative Cases.—Where A. sells land to B. by parol contract, and B. takes possession and control of said land, he thereby acquires an equitable title to the same, which will be protected from a judgment subsequently obtained against his grantor; and the fact that shortly before said judgment was recorded in the judgment lien docket such vendee obtained a deed for said land from his vendor, which he failed to record, will not render said land liable to be subjected to the payment of said judgment. Snyder v. Botkin, 37 W. Va. 355, 16 S. E. 591, Holt. J., dissenting, citing Renick v. Ludington, 20 W. Va. 511, 559; Pack v. Hansbarger, 17 W. Va. 313; Snyder v. Martin, 17 W. Va. 276.

Where a party sells land, by a verbal contract, to another, without receiving the purchase price, and subsequently becomes surety for his vendee, whereby the vendee agrees to allow his vendor to retain the legal and equitable title to the land until he pays the purchase money and until his liability as surety is discharged, which agreement is not recorded, and later the vendee becomes a bankrupt, it was held that as against the other judgment creditors of the vendee (bankrupt) the agreement between the vendor and vendee is valid though not recorded, and that they only have the equities of the vendee against the vendor. Coffman *v.* Niswander, 26 Gratt. 737.

In 1856, L. sells land to T. by parol contract, receives all the purchase money and puts T. into possession. In January, 1867, L. executes a deed to T., by which he releases all his claims to the land to T. and warrants the title. T. then sells the land to W. and W. conveys to F. In March, 1866, B. recovers a judgment against L., which is docketed within the year. In a suit against F. to subject the land to satisfy the judgment against L., held, that the registry acts do not apply to a parol contract for land, and T. having paid all the purchase money, and having been put into possession, so that he had a valid equitable title to the land, it is not subject to the lien of the judgment against L. The valid equitable title of T. is not so merged in the legal title acquired by the deed of L. to him, as to subject the land to the lien of the judgment against L. Floyd *v.* Harding, 28 Gratt. 401.

H., by a parol contract, sells to McN. a tract of land, and McN. upon faith of such contract pays H. the full amount of the purchase money and is put into possession of said land; and McN. and those claiming under him, after so taking possession of the land, continue in possession of the same, etc., upon faith of said contract. Some time after all this occurred, but while said McN. was still in possession, P. obtained a judgment against H., his debtor, and caused it to be duly docketed. H. some time after said parol contract had been so executed made a deed to McN. for said land, which was not admitted to record, until after the said judgment was rendered. Held, that while said deed is void as to P.'s said judgment, McN. and those claiming said land under him by parol contract, executed by payment of part of the purchase money to McN. and by the delivery of possession by said McN. to his said parol vendees of the land and the making of improvements thereon by the last-named vendees, have an equitable interest in said land by virtue of said parol contract between H. and McN., executed as aforesaid, prior and superior to the judgment lien of said P., and that in a suit in equity brought by said P. to enforce the lien of such judgment against said land said equitable interest of McN. and his parol vendees so acquired in said land will be protected against said judgment, and the land will not be sold to pay said judgment of P. Pack *v.* Hansbarger, 17 W. Va. 313.

L. owned a tract of land which he cultivated, and a younger brother and two sisters lived with him, but not as tenants. There were liens on the land, and L. owed his brother and sisters money. By parol contract L. sold the land to his brother and sisters, they assuming to pay the liens, and paying the balance in his bonds, which they delivered to him, and they took and held possession of the land. L. afterwards conveyed the land to them, but before the deed was recorded H. docketed a judgment which he had recovered against L. after the parol agreement had been made and carried into effect. Held, the judgment is not a lien upon the land. Long *v.* Hagerstown, etc., Co., 30 Gratt. 665.

In 1855, H. bought of K. a lot of land for $433.33, and paid one-third cash, but took neither deed nor other writing nor possession. Some time prior to July 14th, 1856, T., as trustee of B., verbally purchased the lot of H. for same price, and paid him what he had paid, and assumed the remaining two-thirds due to K. And by writing, under seal of that date, B. directed her trustee to obtain a conveyance of said lot from K., reserving vendor's lien for the two-thirds still due on the purchase money, and to employ her trust fund in building a house upon it. This T. did, after having first got a written order from H., directing K. to convey the lot as aforesaid. The deed is dated August 1st, 1856, but it was not recorded until 1859. Afterwards, in May, 1857, S. got a judgment against H., and sued to subject the lot to the judgment. Held, the valid, equitable title of T. in the lot was not so merged in the legal title acquired by the subsequent deed of K. to him as to subject the lot to the lien of said judgment. Powell *v.* Bell, 81 Va. 222.

Circuit court of N. directs W., trustee for his wife, to buy, subject to its approval at price not exceeding $6,000, payable out of her funds in its hands, a home for her. In 1873, trustee contracts by writing with H. for 240 acres in A. at $12,000, subject to court's approval. In March, 1874, trustee reports contract with H.; but court is told that only 100 acres thereof at $6,000—cash, $2,500, balance in three annual payments—is to be paid for out of her funds. H.'s conveyance of the 100 acres to trustee is filed as escrow until cash payment made. Court confirms report quoad the 100 acres, and "the deed as escrow, until cash payment made and recorded," and provides for paying not only the cash but the other payments. On November 6th, 1874, all the purchase money, except $419.59, is paid, and during that year that balance is paid. Deed is recorded April 13, 1876. Written contract never was. T.'s ad-

ministrator and others got judgments against H. March 15th, 1876, which were docketed two days later. In suit to subject the 100 acres to those judgments, held, but as that balance was paid, and trustee held possession of the 100 acres under a parol contract and equitable title, before T.'s administrator and others got their judgments against H., that land is wholly exempt from the lien thereof. Floyd *v.* Harding, 27 Gratt. 401, approved in Trout *v.* Warwick, 77 Va. 731.

B. held adverse, open and notorious possession of land from 1849 to 1862, when D. asserted claim to it, and B. buys up his claim under verbal contract, paying his price in full, and remains in such possession until 1881, when creditors of D., by judgments obtained since 1862, sue to subject the land to their judgments. Held, apart from B.'s title by such possession, he was a complete purchaser from D. before their judgments were obtained, and their liens never attached to the land. "The hustings court erred in holding the lands in the hands of the appellants, Bowman and Branches, liable to the judgment liens of the appellees against Davis; and the said lands, under the decisions in Withers *v.* Carter, 4 Gratt. 407, and Floyd *v.* Harding, 28 Gratt. 401, are free and exempt from such liability, except to the extent of the unpaid purchase money, admitted by the deposition and answer filed by the appellants, Branch, for the 200-acre tract purchased by Olive Branch." Bowman *v.* Hicks, 80 Va. 806, 810.

Effect of Recording Acts.—The statutes in Virginia and West Virginia provide that every contract made in respect to real estate, for goods and chattels in consideration of marriage, or made for the conveyance or sale of real estate, for a term therein for more than five years, and every deed conveying such estate or term, and every deed of gift or deed of trust or mortgage conveying real estate or goods and chattels, shall be void as to creditors and subsequent purchasers for valuable consideration without notice, until and except from the time it is duly admitted to record in the county wherein the property embraced in such contract or deed may be. Snyder v. Martin, 17 W. Va. 276; Land v. Jeffries, 2 Rand. 211; Prior v. Kinney, 6 Munf. 510.

Barton, in his Chancery Practice (vol. 2, p. 981), says: "The registry law, however, is only applicable to written contracts, and when one has purchased land by parol contract, and has been put in possession, so that he has a valid, equitable title to the land, it is not subject to judgments recovered against the vendor after the sale; whereas, if he had a written contract, and failed to record it, the contract would be invalid as against subsequent purchasers for value without notice." In the case of Floyd v. Harding, 28 Gratt. 401, the court of appeals of Virginia held, that "the registry acts do not apply to a parol contract for land, and T. having paid all the purchase money, and having been put into possession, so that he had a valid, equitable title to the land, it is not subject to the lien of L. (the vendor). The valid, equitable title of T. is not so merged in the legal title acquired by the deed of L. to him as to subject the land to the lien of the judgment against L." Quoted in Snyder v. Botkin, 37 W. Va. 355, 16 S. E. 591, 596.

Soon after the decision of Withers v. Carter, 4 Gratt. 407, and possibly induced by it, an important change was made in the laws relating to registration of deeds. The statute, which is still in force (Code, 1849, ch. 118, § 5; Code, 1860, ch. 118, § 5; Code, 1887, § 2465), declares that every contract in writing in respect to real estate shall be void as to creditors and subsequent purchasers for valuable consideration, without notice, until and except from the time it is duly admitted to record in the county or corporation wherein the real estate embraced in said contract or deed may be. This statute effectually abrogated the rule laid down in Withers v. Carter, 4 Gratt. 407, so far as executory contracts in writing for the sale of land are concerned, and placed them on the same footing as conveyances of the legal title. Eidson v. Huff, 29 Gratt. 338, 344; Hart v. Haynes, 1 Va. Dec. 201, 206, 209, 213 (see discussion of Withers v. Carter, 4 Gratt. 407, in opinion of Wingfield, J.); Anderson v. Nagle, 12 W. Va. 98, 111; Delaplain v. Wilkinson, 17 W. Va. 242, 268; Pack v. Hansbarger, 17 W. Va. 313, 335; Snyder v. Martin, 17 W. Va. 276, 290. But in Floyd v. Harding, 28 Gratt. 401, the court said that the statute last above mentioned applied only to contracts in writing and in no way affected the case of a parol contract for the sale of land, and that a purchaser taking possession under such a contract is vested with a valid equitable title not subject to the lien of a judgment subsequently obtained against the vendor.

bb. Interest of Vendee under Unrecorded Written Contract.

But the rule is otherwise in the case of a written contract. Because of the decision in Withers v. Carter, 4 Gratt. 407, holding that the registry acts did not avoid the executory contract, which is the equitable title, the change was made so as to embrace all "contracts in writing." It has been repeatedly held, since that time, that such contracts unrecorded are void as to judgment creditors. Eidson v. Huff, 29 Gratt. 338; March v. Chambers, 30 Gratt. 299; Young v. Devries, 31 Gratt. 304; Hart v. Haynes, 1 Va. Dec. 201; Anderson v. Nagle, 12 W. Va. 98; Delaplain v. Wilkinson, 17 W. Va. 242, distinguishing Floyd v. Harding, 28 Gratt. 401; Dobyns v. Waring, 82 Va. 159, 166, distinguishing Floyd v. Harding, 28 Gratt. 401.

"Under Code, 1873, ch. 114, § 5, unrecorded contracts for the sale of real estate are void as to creditors with or without notice. Guerrant *v.* Anderson, 4 Rand. 208. In the case here the evidence proves that there was a written contract for the sale of real estate that was not recorded before a creditor had got and docketed his judgment against the vendor; and the case does not come within the principle of Floyd *v.* Harding, 28 Gratt. 401." Dobyns *v.* Waring, 82 Va. 159.

Sufficiency of Bill and Answer.—"All that the bill alleges on this point is, that Waring sold and conveyed to Jones, subsequent to the docketing of the appellant's judgment, and calls on Jones to answer the bill 'in all material matters.' The bill contains no intimation as to whether there was prior to the deed of conveyance from Waring to Jones any executory contract, either written or verbal. In the light of the case made by the bill, it was wholly immaterial whether there was such prior contract, or, if so, whether it was written or verbal, until it was properly averred and proved. It was competent for Jones to set up in his answer, as he did, that there was no written contract, which is tantamount to averring that there was a verbal contract prior and superior to the appellant's claim. But the averment thus made was of affirmative matter, and must be proved. It is not proved, and is not evidence for the appellees. 2 Rob. Pr. (old Ed.) 330; Shurtz *v.* Johnson, 28 Gratt. 657. But for this, authorities need not be cited." Dobyn *v.* Waring, 82 Va. 159, 167.

(f) **Interest of Vendee under Instrument Not Required to Be Recorded.**

An auctioneer's memorandum, though sufficient to satisfy the statute of frauds, is not such a contract in writing as the recording acts require to be recorded, and may be treated as a parol contract; thus exempting the land in the hands of alienees from the lien of judgments against their vendor. Brown *v.* Butler, 87 Va. 621, 13 S. E. 71.

Deed in Escrow.—Circuit court of N. directs W., trustee for his wife, to buy, subject to its approval at price not exceeding $6,000, payable out of her funds in its hands, a home for her. In 1873, trustee contracts by writing with H. for 240 acres in A. at $12,000, subject to court's approval. In March, 1874, trustee reports contract with H.; but court is told that only 100 acres thereof at $6,000—cash, $2,500, balance in three annual payments—is to be paid for out of her funds. H.'s conveyance of the 100 acres to trustee is filed as escrow until cash payment made. Court confirms report quoad the 100 acres, and "the deed as escrow, until cash payment made and recorded," and provides for paying not only the cash but the other payments. On November 6th, 1874, all the purchase money, except $419.59, is paid, and during that year that balance is paid. Deed is recorded April 13, 1876. Written contract never was. T.'s administrator and others got judgments against H. March 15th, 1876, which were docketed two days later. In suit to subject the 100 acres to those judgments, held, this is not a case coming within the operation of the statute requiring the registry of titles. The purchase being directed by the court of N., and conditional upon its approval, was not the purchase of the trustee, but of the court itself, and there was no purchase until that approval was given. If it did not come within the operation of that statute, there was no contract in writing between W. and H. for the purchase of the 100 acres, which could have been placed on record, the failure to register which rendered said land liable to said judgments. Trout *v.* Warwick, 77 Va. 731.

Perfection of Equitable Title.—In order for a purchaser, under a contract which is not required to be recorded, to be protected as to subsequent judgments against his vendor, he must, before the date of such judgment, have become invested with a perfect equitable title. Withers v. Carter, 4 Gratt. 407, 412, 50 Am. Dec. 78; Floyd v. Harding, 28 Gratt. 401, 416; March v. Chambers, 30 Gratt. 299, 303; Long v. Hagerstown, etc., Co., 30 Gratt. 665; Brown v. Butler, 87 Va. 621, 13 S. E. 71; Powell v. Bell, 81 Va. 222; Fulkerson v. Taylor, 102 Va. 314, 319, 46 S. E. 378.

Protection to Purchaser.—"Prior to the Code of 1887 a subsequent purchaser under a contract not required to be recorded was not protected against a prior unrecorded conveyance unless he had paid the whole purchase price before he received notice of the unrecorded conveyance. 4 Minor's Inst. 968, and cases there cited. Now, under § 2472 of that Code, such a purchaser is protected to the extent of the payments made when he receives notice of the prior unrecorded deed or writing, and has a lien on the property purchased for so much of the purchase money as he had paid before notice. But this highly equitable provision has no application to judgment creditors. The word 'writing,' in that section, refers to contracts in writing by which a party acquires some interest in, not to judgments by which a party acquires a mere lien upon, land." Fulkerson v. Taylor, 102 Va. 314, 319, 46 S. E. 378.

(11) Title of Assignor under Unrecorded Assignment.

A person has equitable title to land under an executory written contract, and by written assignment transfers it to another, which assignment is not recorded, and a judgment goes against the assignor. The assignment is void as to such judgment, and the equitable right to the land under the contract and assignment subject to the judg-

ment, because of failure to record the assignment. Damron v. Smith, 37 W. Va. 580, 16 S. E. 807.

(12) Interest of Delinquent Purchaser.

Where a party purchases land, and pays a part of the purchase money, but fails to pay the balance, whereby the land is resold, he has an equitable interest in the land, which is liable to a judgment subsequently obtained against him by another party, on a debt existing against the delinquent purchaser at the time he made them partial payment on the land. Davis v. Vass, 47 W. Va. 811, 35 S. E. 826.

(13) Property Aliened before Judgment Rendered.

Aside from any question of recordation, after-acquired judgments do not attach to lands in the hands of a bona fide purchaser for value; in short, a complete purchaser from the debtor before the liens attach. Bowman v. Hicks, 80 Va. 806.

(14) Antecedent Trust Lien.

A party acquiring a judgment lien on real estate can not in any manner interfere with the rights acquired by a party holding an antecedent, bona fide unsatisfied trust lien on the same property. Wise v. Taylor, 44 W Va. 492, 29 S. E. 1003, 1006.

Where the owner of real estate has executed a valid deed of trust upon the same to secure the payment of a loan (which is evidenced by note or bond) contracted to be paid in installments, which have not yet matured, when a creditor obtains a judgment against the grantor in said trust deed, and proceeds to enforce his judgment lien in a court of equity, he can only subject the equity of redemption; and the court has no power to change the terms and conditions of the deed of trust as to the maturity of the loan thereby secured. Wise v. Taylor, 44 W. Va. 492, 29 S. E. 1003.

(15) Strangers Paying Purchase Money.

If a third person furnishes the money to pay for land which is conveyed to a married woman under a written contract with her husband, as her agent, by which it is agreed that such third person shall have a lien on the land until the purchase money is refunded, and the land is conveyed to the wife, the judgment creditors of the husband can not subject said land to their judgments until said purchase money has been refunded. Rau v. Shaver, 102 Va. 68, 45 S. E. 873.

c. Separate Estate of Married Women.

See the title SEPARATE ESTATE OF MARRIED WOMEN.

In West Virginia, the statute provides that an action may be maintained against the husband and wife jointly for any debt of the wife contracted before marriage; but the execution of any judgment in such action shall issue against, and such judgment shall bind the separate estate and property of the wife only, and not that of the husband. W. Va. Code, 1899, ch. 66, § 2959.

If a married woman at the time of contracting a debt, in 1886, had a statutory separate estate, and intended to charge it with the payment of the debt, she may be sued on it in a court of law, and a personal judgment may be rendered against her under the provisions of §§ 2289, 2298, of the Code. And although the plaintiff may now obtain a personal judgment against her, he can only subject to its payment such separate estate as she owned when the contract was made, or so much thereof as is owned by her when the lien of the judgment and execution thereon attaches. Duval. v. Chelf. 92 Va. 489, 23 S. E. 893, citing Crockett v. Doriot, 85 Va. 240, 3 S. E. 128.

A married woman's separate property is not subject to the control of her husband, nor liable for the payment of his debts, and a court of equity will protect her rights. Hall v. Hyer, 48 W. Va. 353, 37 S. E. 594.

W. purchased a lot of land in September, 1866, for $1,150, from D. M., who executed and delivered to her a deed therefor, and afterwards she sent said deed to the clerk's office by S., for the purpose of having it recorded, and said S., upon consulting an attorney, without the knowledge or consent of W. (who was then a married woman, but living apart from her husband), had said deed altered by inserting therein his name as grantee, in the room and stead of hers, and subsequently informed W. that said change was made to protect said property from her husband, should he return. She sold said property for $2,500; and, after paying a balance owed by W. on the purchase money, for which a vendor's lien was retained, and an amount borrowed by her from S. to make part of the cash payment thereon, a balance of $1,950 was left of the proceeds of said sale, which amount was received and retained by S., who declared to W. he would hold the same in trust for her, and purchase for her a better home, when she could hold it. Said W. and S. intermarried in the fall of 1869, and in 1875 and in 1877 said W. purchased, at commissioner's and tax sale, two tracts of land—one containing 110 acres, and the other 31 acres—situated in Preston county, W. Va., where she resided; and part of the purchase money therefor was paid by S. out of money in his hands belonging to his then wife. Said purchase was reported as made by her, and the report of sale was confirmed. At the time of said commissioner's and tax sales, and confirmation thereof, no judgment lien existed against said S.; and, so far as the pleadings show, no debts existed against him. Held, that said land, purchased by the wife of S. at said commissioner's and tax sale, could not be subjected to sale by the creditors of S. to satisfy judgments acquired and docketed after said sale and confirmation. Cale *v.* Shaw, 33 W. Va. 299, 10 S. E. 637.

d. Remainders.

Vested Remainders.—Under the provision of § 3567 of the Code which declares that "every judgment for money rendered in this state, heretofore or hereafter, against any person, shall be a lien on all the real estate of or to which such person is or becomes possessed or entitled, at or after the date of such judgment," a judgment is a lien on an after-acquired vested remainder in possession. Wilson *v.* Langhorne, 102 Va. 631, 47 S. E. 871.

e. Equitable Interests.

(1) In General.

A judgment creditor has a lien in equity on the equitable estate of the debtor, in like manner as he has a lien at law on his legal estate. Coutts *v.* Walker, 2 Leigh 268; Michaux *v.* Brown, 10 Gratt. 612.

"In Michaux *v.* Brown, 10 Gratt. 612, 619, J. Allen says: 'Although this equity of redemption could not be taken in execution at law, it was upon the general principle of a court of equity, bound in equity, as it would have been bound at law if it had been a legal estate. And in equity the judgment is a lien upon the whole of the debtor's equitable estate.'" Hale *v.* Horne, 21 Gratt. 112.

In equity, judgments are liens on the whole of the debtor's equitable estate; and the whole is first to be applied to the elder judgment, then the whole of the residue to the junior judgment; and in neither case is only a moiety to be applied to their satisfaction. Haleys *v.* Williams, 1 Leigh 140, 19 Am. Dec. 743. See Buchanan *v.* Clark, 10 Gratt. 164; Withers *v.* Carter, 4 Gratt. 407; Parrill *v.* McKinley, 6 W. Va. 67.

Judgment against Cestui Que Trust. —A judgment creditor, who has recovered judgment against the cestui que trust, under a deed of marriage settlement to a trustee, can not, while the annuitant is still living, subject such equitable interest, at law, to the satisfaction of his debt, but such equitable interest is bound by the judgment in equity, which will apply it to the satisfaction of the debt. Coutts *v.* Walker, 2 Leigh 268.

Title of Assignor in Unrecorded Assignment.—Where a person has an equitable title to land under an executory written contract, and by written assignment transfers it to another, which assignment is not recorded, and a judgment goes against the assignor, the assignment is void as to such judgment, and the equitable right to the land under the contract and assignment is subject to the judgment, because of failure to record the assignment. Damron *v.* Smith, 37 W. Va. 580, 16 S. E. 807.

(2) Equity of Redemption.

See the title MORTGAGES AND DEEDS OF TRUST.

A judgment is a lien upon an equity of redemption in land, and will be preferred to a subsequent purchaser of the equity of redemption not having the legal title. And the lien of the judgment extends to the whole equity of redemption. Michaux *v.* Brown, 10 Gratt. 612; Hale *v.* Horne, 21 Gratt. 112.

The equity of redemption in land conveyed in trust to secure debts is subject to the lien of judgments subsequently obtained. Hale *v.* Horne, 21 Gratt. 112, citing Michaux *v.* Brown, 10 Gratt. 612.

A decree creates a lien on the debtor's equity of redemption under his deed of trust; for though the equity of redemption could not be sold under a fi. fa. and was not extendible, yet the decree constituted an equitable lien thereon, entitled to priority over subsequent liens by judgment or otherwise. Findlay *v.* Toncray, 2 Rob. 374, 377, citing Haleys *v.* Williams, 1 Leigh 140; Coutts *v.* Walker, 2 Leigh 268. Haleys *v.* Williams is also cited in Nickell *v.* Handly, 10 Gratt. 336, 339; and in McClung *v.* Beirne, 10 Leigh 394, 405, citing the case, it is said, the equity of redemption in land conveyed in trust should have been first sold out and out—not a moiety only, but the whole.

"In Michaux *v.* Brown, 10 Gratt. 612, 619, J. Allen says: 'Although this equity of redemption could not be taken in execution at law, it was upon the general principle of a court of equity, bound in equity as it would have been bound at law if it had been a legal estate. And in equity the judgment is a lien upon the whole of the debtor's equitable estate." Hale *v.* Horne, 21 Gratt. 112.

"It is perfectly clear, that whatever interest Wm. M. Mitchell had in these lands, after he had conveyed them in trust, was subject to the lien of his subsequent judgment creditors; and that his vendors, who purchased with notice of those judgments, purchased subject to the judgment liens, and that whatever portion of the purchase money remained, after satisfying the incumbrance of the deed of trust, was liable to satisfy the judgments; and the land in the hands of the vendees, is bound for the payment thereof to the judgment creditor. Hence, it follows, that their bond for the purchase money, in the hands of Mitchell, or of the trustee, remaining after the trust creditors were satisfied out of the trust fund, was liable to the judgments; and no one could release the vendees, or the land they had purchased, from the judgment lien, except the judgment creditors themselves." Hale *v.* Horne, 21 Gratt. 112.

A judgment creditor has a right to come into a court of equity to enforce his judgment lien against the lands conveyed in a deed of trust prior to the obtaining of the judgment, subject to the debts secured by the trust; and after the debts secured by the trust fall due and no sale is made thereunder, the court will interfere for the benefit of judgment liens younger than the trust and will direct a sale of the land, and not the redemption alone, to satisfy the debts of both classes of creditors. Laidley *v.* Hinchman, 3 W. Va. 423.

Judgment Subsequent to Deed of Trust.—A creditor, whose judgment is subsequent to a deed of trust on the debtor's land, has only a lien on his equity of redemption, and can not have the deed of trust enforced, and the land sold to pay the debts thereby secured, until default. Wytheville Crystal Ice, etc., Co. *v.* Frick Co., 96 Va. 141, 30 S. E. 491; Shurtz *v.* Johnson, 28 Gratt. 657; Wise *v.* Taylor, 44 W. Va. 492, 29 S. E. 1003.

Satisfaction and Discharge.—The equity of redemption in land conveyed in trust to secure debts is subject to the lien of judgments subsequently obtained, in the order of their priority in date. Hale *v.* Horne, 21 Gratt. 112.

The equity of redemption in land conveyed in trust by a judgment debtor must first be sold to satisfy a judgment before recourse can be had to aliened lands. McClung *v.* Beirne, 10 Leigh 394; Michaux *v.* Brown, 10 Gratt. 612. See Buchanan *v.* Clark, 10 Gratt. 164.

Amount of Lien.—The damages on the dissolution of an injunction to a judgment become, as to the party obtaining it, a part of the judgment, and are embraced in the lien of the judgment upon the equity of redemption. Michaux *v.* Brown, 10 Gratt. 612.

f. Purchase Money.

A judgment creditor has no lien upon purchase money due to a judgment debtor for lands sold by him and which are subject to the judgment lien. Blakemore *v.* Wise, 95 Va. 269, 28 S. E. 332, 64 Am. St. Rep. 781. See Rau *v.* Shaver, 102 Va. 68, 45 S. E. 873; Davis *v.* Vass, 47 W. Va. 811, 35 S. E. 826. See ante, "Doctrine of Floyd *v.* Harding," VI, G, 1, b, (10), (e).

g. Homestead Exemption.

A judgment creditor who has the first lien on real estate of his debtor, has the right to subject the same to the payment of his judgment, though his debt contains no waiver of the homestead exemption, and the subsequent liens which are paramount to the homestead are in excess of the whole value of the land. If the debtor claims the homestead it may be set apart to him, and the judgment paid out of the residue, but, if necessary to pay subsequent liens which are paramount to the homestead, the land so set apart should be subjected. Strayer *v.* Long, 93 Va. 695, 26 S. E. 409.

Lien of judgment attached before homestead claimed in land, can not be enforced during the homestead's existence; but after homestead abandoned, it has priority over a trust deed executed during the occupancy of the land as a homestead. Blose *v.* Bear, 87 Va. 177, 12 S. E. 294.

h. Subsequently Acquired Realty.

The lien of a judgment extends to all the land owned by the judgment debtor at the date thereof, or which may have been afterwards acquired. McClung *v.* Beirne, 10 Leigh 394; Brockenbrough *v.* Brockenbrough, 31 Gratt. 580; Hill *v.* Manser, 11 Gratt. 522.

So long as a judgment might be revived, it was a lien upon a moiety of all the lands owned by the debtor at the date of the judgment, or which are afterwards acquired, in whoseoever hands they may have come. Taylor *v.* Spindle, 2 Gratt. 44.

The lien of a judgment will attach to after-acquired lands of a debtor.. And such lands acquired and aliened by the debtor subsequent to the rendition of a judgment, are within the terms and reason of § 10, ch. 186, W. Va. Code, 1860. Handly *v.* Sydenstricker, 4 W. Va. 605.

Judgments for money, whether docketed or not, bind the unaliened lands to the debtor; certainly those owned by him at the date of the judgments, it may be, those subsequently acquired in the order in which the judgments are recovered, and the same is true of decrees for money; and so, though not docketed, they bind the debtor's lands subsequently aliened to a purchaser with notice, even though he be a purchaser for value; but unless docketed, they are not liens on lands subsequently aliened to bona fide purchasers for value without notice, and a trustee in a deed of trust given to secure a debt and the creditor secured are purchasers for value within the meaning of the registration law. Rhea *v.* Preston, 75 Va. 757; Hill *v.* Rixey, 26 Gratt. 72.

Judgment against Bankrupt.—Judgments matured against bankrupt after his adjudication on pre-existing provable debts, are not liens on his after-acquired lands; but a bankrupt is released by his discharge from them, as well as from the debts whereon they are founded. Blair *v.* Carter, 78 Va. 621.

In 1868, H. L. M. was adjudged a bankrupt. His land was sold by decree of bankrupt court, free of liens, and purchased by himself, and conveyed to him by his assignees. Later, he sold it to J. H. M., who conveyed it in trust to secure debt to B. Under this trust, it was sold and purchased by B. In 1879, C. brought creditor's bill to subject the land in B.'s hands to liens of judgments recovered against H. L. M., after his adjudication as bankrupt on pre-existing provable debts. Held, the judgments were released by H. L. M.'s discharge, and are not liens on the land in B.'s hands. Blair *v.* Carter, 78 Va. 621.

i. Lands Exchanged.

If upon an exchange, the parties executed mutual conveyances, but the grantee of one tract fails to record his deed, judgment against the grantor binds the land so given in exchange as well as that received in exchange, the rights of the parties are not affected by the character of the consideration for the unrecorded deed. Price *v.* Wall, 97 Va. 334, 33 S. E. 599.

j. Lands Held Jointly.

Property Held by Tenants in Common.—J.'s devisees and W. are tenants in common of a hotel property, and J.'s executor and W. agree to sell the property at public auction; the deferred payments to be secured by separate bonds to each for his half of the purchase money, with a lien retained on the real property. The sale is made and W. becomes the purchaser, but refuses to execute the contract. J.'s executor sues W. for specific execution of the contract, and there is a decree in 1868 in his favor for specific execution, a personal decree against W. for the amount due, and for a sale of the whole property. Before the decree W. sells and conveys his moiety of the property to M. who pays the purchase money. Upon a bill by the judgment creditors of M. to subject his moiety of the property to the payment of their debts; held, W. bought at the sale but J.'s moiety of the property, and the lien of J.'s executor's decree only extends to that moiety, though the whole property was sold under the decree. Johnson *v.* National Exchange Bank, 33 Gratt. 473.

Right of Joint Owner.—A joint owner of property, who, being a party to a suit, allows his undivided interest in such property to be sold to satisfy judgment liens thereon, can not file a bill of review to set aside the decrees in such suit, for the sole purpose of having the property, not being susceptible of partition, sold as a whole, for by his negligence he has waived whatever rights he may have had in this

respect. Chancellor *v.* Spencer, 40 W. Va. 337, 21 S. E. 1011.

k. Partnership Property.

In a chancery suit brought by K. of Richmond against A. B. & C. of Mercer county in this state to enforce the lien of a judgment obtained before the war against A. B. & C. as partners on an accepted order known to the partners to include the amount due from the partnership to K. and also an individual debt due from C. to K.; held: The lands of each partner ought to be held primarily responsible for the portion of K.'s judgment, which corresponds with his interest in the profits and losses of the partnership under the articles of copartnership. Kent *v.* Chapman, 18 W. Va. 485.

In joint action against partners, judgment is confessed by one, and later, during the same term, is rendered against the other. Held, cause of action was not merged by the confession, and the judgment rendered is valid, though the rule is, that a judgment against one of a firm on a joint liability, merges the original cause of action, and bars another suit against remaining partners. Judgment of firm creditor against each partner is paramount as to their individual assets to any unsecured claim against either of them. Such firm creditor must exhaust the partnership assets before resorting to the individual assets. Pitts *v.* Spotts, 86 Va. 71, 9 S. E. 501.

A judgment against a partnership on a partnership contract is a valid lien on the separate estate of one of the partners, and entitled to priority over more unsecured open-account creditors. Pitts *v.* Spotts, 86 Va. 71, 9 S. E. 501.

l. Trees on Land.

Trees growing on the land are a part of the land and subject to a judgment lien. Goff *v.* McLain, 48 W. Va. 445, 37 S. E. 566.

m. Lands Bought with Pension Money.

See the titles EXEMPTIONS FROM EXECUTION AND ATTACHMENT, vol. 5, p. 766; PENSIONS.

Where a pensioner receives pension drafts under the act of congress and transfers said drafts or the proceeds thereof to a third person, who in consideration thereof conveys or agrees to convey to the wife of the pensioner a tract of land; and thereafter a suit is brought by judgment creditors of the pensioner, whose judgments existed at the time said pension drafts were received; held: Under § 4747, U. S. Rev. Sts., said land is not liable for the payment of said judgments. "The said statute is as follows: 'No sum of money due, or to become, to any pensioner, shall be liable to attachment, levy or seizure by or under any legal or equitable process whatever, whether the same remains with the pension office, or any officer, or agent thereof, or in course of transmission to the pensioner entitled thereto, but shall enure wholly to the benefit of such pensioner.'" Hissem v. Johnson, 27 W. Va. 644, 646.

F. becomes the purchaser of a tract of land containing 166½ acres from S. and executes a deed of trust thereon to secure the purchase money. When the purchase money and its accrued interest amounted to $1,400, F., having received pension money to the amount of $800, agreed with S. that, if he would release 66½ acres, part of said tract, from said trust lien, and look to the remaining 100 acres for the residue of said purchase money, he would pay him $800 in cash, and execute his three notes, for $200 each, payable in one, two, and three years, with interest, for the residue of said purchase money. S., for a valuable consideration, assigned said three notes, for $200 each, to McFarland, who held them, until maturity, when F. voluntarily confessed judgment on said three $200 notes in favor of McFarland, the plaintiff, agreeing to give him six months' time. At the end of the time McFarland brought a suit to subject the entire 166½ acres to the satisfaction of the judgment lien. F. resisted the enforcement of said judgment lien on two grounds: First, by reason of the agreement between S. and himself that S. would look alone to the remaining 100 acres of said land for the payment of said $600 and interest, of which agreement he claimed McFarland had notice; second, because said 66½ acres of land was paid for with money received from the United States government as pension money. Held, that under the circumstances shown in this case, the entire 166½ acres of land was liable to be subjected to the lien of the judgment confessed by said F. as aforesaid. McFarland v. Fish, 34 W. Va. 548, 12 S. E. 548.

"In our own state, in the case of Hissem v. Johnson, 27 W. Va. 644, which seems to be relied on by the appellee in this case, Snyder, J., in delivering the opinion of the court, says: 'I do not think this statute was intended to exempt pension money, after it has been received by the pensioner, entirely from liability for his debts. In other words, I do not think it was intended to add to the exemption laws of the state by exempting the proceeds of pensions from liability for the debts of the pensioner, even if congress had the right to create such an exemption, which I very much doubt.' The case under consideration is clearly distinguishable from the case of Hissem v. Johnson, 27 W. Va. 644. In this case the defendant Fish says he paid the $800 in cash. It was not paid in government checks, as the evidence showed the payments were made in Hissem v. Johnson. In this case it does not appear how long the defendant Fish had been in possession of said money, where it had been kept, or

and by distinct conveyances. Winston v. Johnson, 2 Munf. 305.

Subrogation.—B. sold a tract of land to V. for $550, of which V. paid $250, and went into possession of the land, occupying it with his family. V. paid no more on the land, and left his family to maintain themselves, but returned home and remained at his pleasure. B., claiming that V. had relinquished his purchase, sold the land to I., the wife of V., for $306, she paying in cash $70 from her own means, and giving her notes for the residue of the purchase money. D., having a judgment against V., rendered on a debt existing at the time V. paid the $250 on the land, filed his bill to enforce his judgment against V.'s equitable interest in the land. Held, I., having purchased the land in good faith, without knowledge of D.'s debt against V., and having paid the $70 from her own means, is entitled to be substituted to the rights of B. as vendor to that amount prior to the claim of D. The balance of the purchase money unpaid and due to B. from I. is the first lien on the said land. Davis v. Vass, 47 W. Va. 811, 35 S. E. 826.

If one of two or more tracts of land, which are subject to a judgment lien, be sold and conveyed by the judgment debtor, and the deed has been duly recorded and the purchase money paid, a subsequent judgment creditor is not entitled to subrogation to the prior lien, because such a decree would conflict with the equity of the purchaser. And in such case, where the land sold is subject to an encumbrance which is also a charge on other land belonging to the vendor, and the land is sold with an express or implied agreement that the title shall be clear, the vendee is not liable to contribution. It is the duty of the vendor, who has been paid in full, to discharge an encumbrance on the land, and if the lien extends to other land, that and not the land conveyed is the primary fund for the payment of the debt. McClaskey v. O'Brien, 16 W. Va. 791.

Parties—Intervention.—When a suit in equity is brought by a judgment creditor to enforce his lien against the land of his debtor, and persons claiming to be purchasers of the debtor's land complain that they were not made parties to that suit, their remedy, if they have notice of that suit, is by motion or petition to be made parties defendant thereto, and not by an independent suit to set aside the decree in the cause, upon the principal ground that the judgment therein sought to be enforced was itself void. Neale v. Utz, 75 Va. 480.

Chancery Practice—Relief Granted Judgment Creditor.—It is the settled practice in Virginia, to entertain the suit of the judgment creditor for relief in equity, when the debtor has, subsequent to the judgment, conveyed his land in trust for the payment of debts, or on other trusts authorizing the sale of the land. And in such case, the court will decree a sale to satisfy the judgment. Taylor v. Spindle, 2 Gratt. 44.

Equity Jurisdiction.—Purchasers of land from a judgment debtor file a bill, making the judgment creditor and other purchasers of land from the debtor, parties, assailing the judgment, setting out the different purchases, and insisting that if the judgment is valid the plaintiffs are entitled to have it paid rateably by the purchasers; and they ask for this and for general relief. The creditor answers, maintaining the validity of his judgment and claiming to have his debt paid out of the lands held by his debtor at the date of the judgment. The purchasers who are defendants, make no objection to the jurisdiction, but claim exemption from liability to the judgment; and one of them insists that a fund in court arising from the sale of lands conveyed in trust for his benefit shall be paid to him. Held, it is a proper case for the jurisdiction of a court of equity, which should settle the rights and liabilities of the parties and decree between them. Though the plaintiffs ask for a rateable contribution by the parties, yet as they set out all the facts and ask for general relief, and it appears that the fund in court is primarily liable to satisfy the judgment, that fund will be so applied to the relief of the plaintiffs. Michaux *v.* Brown, 10 Gratt. 612.

H. PRIORITIES.

1. Between Judgments.

In General.—The Virginia Code provides that the liens of judgments against the same person shall attach to all his real estate liable thereto under section thirty-five hundred and sixty-seven in the order of the dates respectively of said judgments, and the judgments shall be made payable thereout in the same order; and where there are rendered at the same term of court two or more judgments against the same person in suits or in proceedings by motion, both or all of which were matured, at the rules or otherwise, and were upon the docket at the commencement of the term, there shall be no priority between or among them, but said judgments shall be paid rateably out of the real estate upon which they are liens. Such judgments shall take priority over judgments by confession entered at the same term, and over judgments rendered at the same term in any proceeding by motion instituted during the term. An extract of any judgment shall, upon motion, be granted to any party interested immediately upon its rendition, subject to the future action of the court rendering the same. This act shall be in force from its passage (March 29, 1902), but shall not affect in any manner liens existing at the date of its passage. (Code, 1849, p. 710, ch. 186, § 11; 1901-1902, p. 427.) Va. Code, 1904, § 3576.

The West Virginia Code provides that where two or more judgments are rendered against the same person, and the lien thereof on his real estate commences on the same day, the creditors having such judgments shall be entitled to satisfaction out of said real estate rateably. W. Va. Code, 1899, ch. 139, § 4149.

Code, 1873, ch. 182, § 6, makes every judgment rendered in this state, a lien on all the debtor's real estate, and the prior judgment hath priority as between the judgments, whether docketed or undocketed. Gurnee *v.* Johnson, 77 Va. 712; Max Meadows Land, etc., Co. *v.* McGavock, 98 Va. 411, 36 S. E. 490. See Blakemore *v.* Wise, 95 Va. 269, 28 S. E. 332.

In case the proceeds of lands, on which several judgments obtained at the same time are liens, are insufficient to pay them all, they must be paid pro rata. Janney *v.* Stephen, 2 Pat. & H. 11.

When a person has paid off several executions against another, for some of which he was bound as surety, and for others not bound at all, and when he has received personal property of the debtor, sufficient to satisfy them in part, the oldest judgments will be presumed to have been satisfied out of the proceeds of the judgment debtor's property, as they constitute a prior lien on the same. Janney *v.* Stephen, 2 Pat. & H. 11.

If several creditors by judgments of different dates, resort to a court of equity, for satisfaction out of an equitable interest of their debtor in real estate, they are to have satisfaction out of the fund, according to the order of their judgments in point of time, the elder being entitled to priority over the younger. Haleys *v.* Williams, 1 Leigh 140; Fox *v.* Rootes, 4 Leigh 429.

"It is objected to this view, that it in effect gives to subsequent judgments precedence of those prior in date; whereas as between creditors the judgments take effect in the order of time, whether docketed or not. This is true, but it is because the registration laws so provided. A judgment creditor may lose his lien as against a purchaser by a failure to docket, and a subsequent creditor to him may preserve his judgment lien against the same purchaser by a prompt compliance with the statute. In such case the purchaser takes precedence of the prior though not of the subsequent judgment. This is the necessary result of the preference given to him who is most vigilant in the exercise of his rights. The books are full of familiar illustrations of the rule." Hill *v.* Rixey, 26 Gratt. 72, 81.

"Though it has been decided, that a judgment creditor, who has suffered the year to elapse without taking out execution, can not afterwards overreach in equity, a bona fide purchaser of the debtor's land (such purchase being made after the year), yet this applies, neither in terms nor in principle, to a subsequent judgment creditor, who has not laid out his money on the land, nor trusted the debtor on that fund, but on his general credit; and the same majority considers it a settled rule, that when, in equity the question is as to the priority of judgment creditors, they are ranked according to the date of their judgments, without inquiring, as between them, whether such judgments have been kept alive by process; the capacity to renew by scire facias being, in such case, considered in that forum as sufficient proof of the lien; provided it appears, that these judgments are still due." Fox *v.* Rootes, 4 Leigh 429.

As between the judgment creditor and debtor the statute with regard to docketing judgments has no application or force. The judgment liens in their priorities should be fixed according to the dates of the judgments. Grantham *v.* Lucas, 24 W. Va. 231.

Exception Prescribed by Statute.— In a controversy between different judgment creditors, priority of time has been held to be priority of right, except in the exception provided by the eighth section. Gurnee *v.* Johnson, 77 Va. 712, 728.

Decree of Sale and Judgments.— Where land is sold, under a decree of court having jurisdiction of the subject, to pay a deed of trust debt, and a judgment debt, which are liens on the land in full force, the deed of trust and judgment as liens, also, the decree of sale made in the cause, being prior in date to a judgment, which was obtained after such decree of sale, and also docketed on the proper judgment lien docket before a sale was made by the special commissioner appointed to make said sale in the decree of sale, a sale made after the recovery and docketing of such judgment by said special commissioner, and the deed made to the purchaser at such sale, for the land purchased, by such special commissioner appointed in and by the decree of the court confirming such sale, is valid, and passes the title to the purchaser as against the judgment and any lien thereof, although such sale, the decree of the court confirming the same, and such deed of such special commissioner to the purchaser for the land, were made subsequent to the recovery and docketing of said judgment, unless something is alleged and shown in proper form and manner against said sale, decree and deed, other than the mere fact that the sale, decree of confirmation thereof, and such deed were made subsequent to the recovery and docketing of the judgment. Davis *v.* Landcraft, 10 W. Va. 718.

Land having been sold to pay a junior judgment, and the sale confirmed and a decree entered directing the purchase money to be paid to the plaintiff as it is collected, the land is liable in the hands of the purchaser for a prior judgment, and it was error to direct the payment of those judgments out of the purchase money in preference to the plaintiff's judgment, upon petitions filed in the cause by the prior judgment creditors. Sexton *v.* Patterson, 1 Va. Dec. 551, 552.

Illustrative Cases.—Where two judgments were recovered, one in 1868, and the other in 1869, and the one last recovered is docketed in 1870, while the one first obtained is docketed in 1871; but both are docketed before a contract in writing or deed to a purchaser for valuable consideration without notice is recorded, the judgment first recovered though last docketed had priority. Anderson *v.* Nagle, 12 W. Va. 98.

By a written contract between W. and G. executed on January 30th, 1866, W. sold to G. a tract of land, at which time G. paid part of the purchase money, and W. bound himself by the contract to make to G., upon payment of the balance of the purchase money, a deed for said land. The contract was duly executed and acknowledged, but never recorded. On May 21st, 1866, W. and wife conveyed said land to G. by deed with general warranty, which was acknowledged on that day, and duly recorded on the next. At the time of the execution of the deed G. owed a balance of $311.83 of the purchase money, with interest from January 1, 1866, for which he was requested by W. to execute his bond to S. instead of himself, which, with the assent of S., who was present, was accordingly done. On May 16th, 1866, during the term of the county court of Caroline, which began on the 14th of that month, H. and J. each recovered judgments against W., which were duly docketed on June 6, 1866. On February 11, 1861, A. recovered a judgment against W., which was docketed May 16, 1866. On May 29, 1866, at a term of the circuit court of Caroline, which began on that day, P. recovered a judgment against W., which was docketed July 2, 1866. Upon these facts it was held: As between the judgment of A. and the judgments of H. and J., the former being prior in point of time, is entitled to preference of satisfaction. Hart *v.* Haynes, 1 Va. Dec. 201.

W. owned two tracts of land, viz.: "Hart's bottom" and "Connery." J. obtained in April, 1868, a judgment against W., which was not docketed until July, 1870. After the date of J.'s judgment, but before April 22d, 1870, B. and others obtained judgments against W., which were duly docketed. W., on April 22d, 1870, executed a trust deed on "Hart's bottom," to secure a loan of $15,000 from G., which deed was recorded May 2d, 1870. In contest for priority between G. and the judgment creditors, held: The judgment of J. from its date was a lien on all the real estate of W., and though undocketed, being prior in date, hath priority of lien over the judgments of B. and others, as to both tracts. Gurnee *v.* Johnson, 77 Va. 712.

Between Confessed Judgments.— When more than one judgment or decree is confessed or entered in vacation on the same day, they shall have priority as among themselves in the order with respect to the time when they are respectively confessed or received for record in the clerk's office of the court entering the same; provided, that when several judgments are confessed together they shall all be deemed to have been confessed as of the time the first was confessed, and the clerk shall enter such time on the margin of his order book. Va. Code, 1904, § 3567.

When all the creditors, assailing a fraudulent or voluntary conveyance, are judgment creditors, the lien of each dates from the time he obtained his judgment, and not from the date of the filing of his bill, answer or petition, attacking the fraudulent or voluntary conveyance, and the priorities among them must be settled according to the dates of their judgments. Foley v. Ruley, 50 W. Va. 158, 40 S. E. 382.

Determination of Priority.—Where there are several judgment creditors whose judgments are of equal dignity with that of the plaintiff, it is proper they should be convened in a suit by a creditor seeking to enforce his judgment; but if it appears from the pleadings and proof, that such judgment creditors are enforcing their liens or debts in another court, against the parties liable for such other debts, and that there is a large fund under the control of the latter court, applicable to such judgments or debts, it is error to decree the sale of land, on the failure of the debtor to pay the entire amount of such judgment, without taking any steps to ascertain what would remain unpaid, after the application of such fund to the liquidation of such judgments. The court should, before decreeing the land to be sold, cause an inquiry into that matter, so as to be enabled to prescribe the liens and their priorities, that the rights of all the parties in interest may be protected. Murdock v. Welles, 9 W. Va. 552.

2. Between Undocketed Judgments and Purchasers for Valuable Consideration.

See ante, "Docketing and Indexing Judgments," VI, D.

a. Prior to the Statute.

In Renick v. Ludington, 14 W. Va. 367, 381; it is said: "The lands of a purchaser were before the act of 1843 liable to satisfy the lien of the judgment, not upon any presumption, that he had notice of the judgment, for in many cases he could not have notice, but because the lien of the judgment was the grant of the law, imported by the terms of the elegit. Taylor v. Spindle, 2 Gratt. 44; Leake v. Ferguson, 2 Gratt. 419."

The lien of a judgment is a legal lien, and a purchaser of the legal title from the debtor takes it subject to the lien, though he had no notice of it. Leake v. Ferguson, 2 Gratt. 419.

A judgment is a lien on the lands of the debtor after they pass into the hands of bona fide purchasers, if at the date of the judgment they were owned by the debtor. Rodgers v. McCluer, 4 Gratt. 81.

The case of Fox v. Rootes, 4 Leigh 429, was an appeal from a decree of the superior court of chancery of Fredericksburg, which was decided in December, 1828. There were only three judges present at the hearing—Cabell, Coalter and Carr. The following is a copy of the decree: "A majority of the court is of opinion, that the plaintiffs claiming under the deed from Rootes senior to Fox, dated the 1st of March 1821, are purchasers for valuable consideration, and as such, within the protection of that part of our statute of frauds, which is substantially taken from 27 Eliz. ch. 4. They have, therefore, an undoubted right to apply to a court of equity for the purpose of removing out of their way, any obstruction to the fair and just enforcement of their incumbrance. With respect to the deed executed by Thomas Rootes senior to his son Thomas Rootes, bearing date the 18th of February 1813, purporting to convey to his son the Gouldhill tract of land in the proceedings mentioned, and which deed it is the object of the bill to set aside, it appears to a majority of the court, 1. that this was a voluntary deed; 2. that it was not recorded until eight years after its date; 3. that during all the intervening time, the existence of the deed was carefully concealed from the world; the grantor remained in full possession of the land from the year 1817, and exercised over it every act of ownership, with the knowledge and assent of the grantee. A majority of the court is, therefore, of opinion, that as to the purchasers under the deed to Fox, and the decree creditors, also parties to this suit, the said deed of 1813, is fraudulent and void. With respect to the priorities between the purchasers under Fox's deed, and the decree creditors, the court is of opinion, that all these creditors take precedence of the purchasers: Baylor's creditors, 1. on the ground of actual notice; and 2. because at the date of the deed to Fox, the lien of their decrees was in full force: Dunlop, because though it does not appear, that he had taken out execution within the year, yet as his decree is stated in Fox's deed as an existing debt, and provision therein made for its payment, those claiming under that deed are purchasers with full notice of the decree, and can not be received, especially in equity, to contest its priority of lien. As to the decree creditors before the court, it appears that they are, 1st, Dunlop, who obtained a decree in 1818; and 2ndly, Baylor's creditors, namely Martin's ex'ors, Graves, Hoomes, Guy, Jones's ex'ors, Taliaferro, Chiles's adm'r, Pemberton and Tenant (these nine being represented by Battaile), also Catlett, Davis, Grinnan, Green and Patton, all of whom obtained decrees in the same suit in 1820. A majority of the court is of opinion, that as between these two classes of creditors, Dunlop has priority; though it has been decided, that a judgment creditor, who has suffered the year to elapse without taking out execution, can not afterwards overreach in equity, a bona fide purchaser of the debtor's land (such purchase being made after the year), yet this applies, neither in terms nor in principle, to a subsequent judgment creditor, who has not laid out his money on the land, nor trusted the debtor on that fund, but on his general credit; and :he same majority considers it a settled rule."

b. **Under the Statute.**

In General.—The statutes provide in substance that no judgment shall be a lien on real estate as against a purchaser thereof for valuable consideration without notice, unless it is docketed in the mode and within the time prescribed by the statute. Va. Code, 1904, § 3570; W. Va. Code, 1899, ch. 139, § 4146; Duncan *v.* Custard, 24 W. Va. 730, 737; Hill *v.* Rixey, 26 Gratt. 72.

By Va. Code, 1873, ch. 182, §˙8, no judgment is a lien on real estate as against purchasers thereof for a valuable consideration without notice, unless it be docketed in the mode and within the time prescribed. If docketed, the judgment, if prior in time, hath priority over such purchaser. Gurnee *v.* Johnson, 77 Va. 712.

"A judgment creditor may lose his lien as against a purchaser by a failure to docket, and a subsequent creditor to him may preserve his judgment lien against the same purchaser by a prompt compliance with the statute. In such case the purchaser takes precedence of the prior though not of the subsequent judgment. This is the necessary result of the preference given to him who is most vigilant in the exercise of his rights. The books are full of familiar illustrations of the rule." Hill *v.* Rixey, 26 Gratt. 72.

Where a valid judgment has been docketed, it is notice which will affect all subsequent purchasers of land from any of the defendants in the judgment. Redd *v.* Ramey, 31 Gratt. 265; Sharitz *v.* Moyers, 99 Va. 519, 39 S. E. 166.

Judgments for money, whether docketed or not, bind the unaliened lands of the debtor; certainly those owned by him at the date of the judgments, and, it may be, those subsequently acquired, in the order in which the judgments are recovered, and the same is true of decrees for money; and so, though not docketed, they bind the debtor's lands subsequently aliened to a purchaser with notice, even though he be a purchaser for value; but unless docketed they are not liens on lands subsequently aliened to bona fide purchasers for value without notice—and a trustee in a deed of trust given to secure a debt, and the creditor secured, are purchasers for value within the meaning of the registration laws. Code of 1860, ch. 186, §§ 6, 8, 11; Code of 1873, ch. 182, §§ 1, 6, 8, 11. Rhea v. Preston, 75 Va. 757, citing Hill v. Rixey, 26 Gratt. 72; Borst v. Nalle, 28 Gratt. 423, 428; Williams v. Lord, Va. Law J. 243, 250; S. C., 75 Va. 390.

And undocketed judgments are subject to subsequent recorded mortgages. Duncan v. Custard, 24 W. Va. 730.

"We have said enough, we think, to show that by a proper construction of the several statutes, the lien of a judgment attaches to and follows the lands of the debtor into the hands of a purchaser for value, and continues, provided the judgment is docketed; and, if so docketed, that it is a lien from the date of the judgment as against such purchaser, in like manner and with like effect, as against the debtor; and while the docketing a judgment does not per se create a lien as against a purchaser for value, without notice, yet it is an act necessary, under our statutes, to be done, in order to preserve, or prevent the loss of the lien as against such purchaser." Gurnee v. Johnson, 77 Va. 712, 729.

Illustrative Cases.

Judgments.—W. owned two tracts of land, viz.: "Hart's bottom" and "Connery." J. obtained in April, 1868, a judgment against W., which was not docketed until July, 1870. After the date of J.'s judgment, but before April 22d, 1870, B. and others obtained judgments against W., which were duly docketed. W., on April 22d, 1870, executed a trust deed on "Hart's bottom," to secure a loan of $15,000 from G., which deed was recorded May 2d, 1870. In contest for priority between G. and the judgment creditors, held: J.'s judgment being undocketed at the time of G.'s deed, and G. being a purchaser for value without notice of J.'s judgment, the lien of that judgment on "Hart's Bottom," was lost as against G., whose deed, as to that tract, hath priority over that judgment. Gurnee v. Johnson, 77 Va. 712.

The judgments of B. and others being docketed at the time of G.'s deed, have priority over the deed as to "Hart's Bottom," but G. hath the right to hold that tract of land as against these judgments, until the real estate of W. (if any) unaliened at the date of G.'s purchase has been exhausted. Code, 1873, ch. 182, § 10. Gurnee v. Johnson, 77 Va. 712.

On the 5th day of May, 1874, C. conveyed his property to B., who on the same day conveyed it to E., the wife of C. On March 20, 1875, a deed of trust on a part of the land so conveyed, executed by C. and wife to secure a debt to M., is recorded; on the 30th day of March another deed of trust on the same land to secure a debt to B. is recorded; and on July 8, 1876, another deed of trust on the same land to secure a debt to Bowles is recorded. Judgments were recovered against C. as follows: One on the 29th day of October, 1875; another on the 19th day of November, 1875, and a third on the 28th day of November, 1876. It does not appear whether the judgments were docketed. Held, if the two judgments recovered before the trust deeds were executed were docketed within ninety days from their rendition, respectively, or before said trust deeds were recorded, they would take precedence over such trust liens, provided there was not sufficient other property to discharge them. Duncan v. Custard, 24 W. Va. 730, citing Renick v. Ludington, 14 W. Va. 367.

In 1856, W. conveyed to P. a tract of land in York county, in trust to secure a debt of $8,000 with interest. In May, 1866, W. conveyed his equity of redemption in this land to N., in trust to secure a debt of $2,000 then lent to him. All the parties to this deed then living in Baltimore, the deed provided that in default of payment the trustee should sell, "at such place as he may think proper," the said property at public auction, etc. In July, 1869, the trustee advertised and sold the said equity of redemption at public auction in Baltimore, when the creditor became the purchaser; and she afterwards sold it at a small advance, but not sufficient to pay the whole of her debt. At the time of the sale by the trustee the amount of the prior lien was ascertained. In November, 1859, M. recovered two judgments against W. in Accomac county; and J. and S., who claimed to have paid these judgments, had them docketed in York county in May, 1867. On a bill of J. and S. to set aside the said sales and conveyances, held, the deed of trust having been taken without any notice to the trustee or creditor of the existence of the judgments in Accomac, and before these judgments were docketed in York county, the liens of the judgments were subsequent to that of the deed of trust and presented no objection to the sale. Shurtz v. Johnson, 28 Gratt. 657.

"The judgments sought to be enforced by the bill in this case were recovered November 5th, 1859. They were never docketed in the county of York where 'Temple Farm' lies, until May 21st, 1867. At the time the deed was made to Williams (trustee), May 31st, 1866, neither the trustee nor the creditors secured by the deed had any notice of them. If they had been docketed in said county within twelve months from the date of their recovery, they would have constituted liens on White's equity of redemption of the deed to Peachy (trustee), as of the date of their recovery (Code of 1860, ch. 186, §§ 6, 8); which, being prior, would have been superior to the lien created by the deed to Williams (trus-

tee). The trustee in the last-named deed and the creditors secured therein are 'purchasers for valuable consideration' within the meaning of § 8, ch. 186, Code of 1860, and having had no notice of the judgment at the time the deed was executed and recorded, the lien created by the deed takes precedence of the lien of the judgments. Evans v. Greenhow, 15 Gratt. 153; Exchange Bank v. Knox, 19 Gratt. 739." Shurtz v. Johnson, 28 Gratt. 657.

In a contest between a judgment lien creditor whose judgment was never placed on the docket, and a lien created by a deed of trust on the property of a navigation company, as to which is superior and has priority, a claim of the deed of trust creditor that his debt due from the company should have preference inasmuch as it was created and accrued to him for the repairs made and done by him on its works, which repairs were indispensable to their restoration and profit, is unfounded. Cold River, etc., Co. v. Webb, 3 W. Va. 438.

By a written contract between W. and G. executed on January 30th, 1866, W. sold to G. a tract of land, at which G. paid part of the purchase money, and W. bound himself by the contract to make to G., upon payment of the balance of the purchase money, a deed for said land. The contract was duly executed and acknowledged, but never recorded. On May 21st, 1866, W. and wife conveyed said land to G. by deed with general warranty, which was acknowledged on that day, and duly recorded on the next. At the time of the execution of the deed G. owed a balance of $311.83 of the purchase money, with interest from January 1, 1866, for which he was requested by W. to execute his bond to S. instead of himself, which, with the assent of S., who was present, was accordingly done. On May 16th, 1866, during the term of the county court of Carolina, which began on the 14th of that month,

H. and J. each recovered judgments against W., which were duly docketed on June 6, 1866. On February 11, 1861, A. recovered a judgment against W., which was docketed May 16, 1866. On May 29, 1866, at a term of the circuit court of Carolina, which began on that day, P. recovered a judgment against W., which was docketed July 2, 1866. Upon these facts it was held: The said period being excluded, A.'s judgment was duly docketed within less than a year next after its date. The said judgment and the judgments in favor of H. and J. having been recovered before the conveyance of May 21, 1866, and duly docketed as required by ch. 186, § 8, of the Code of 1860, constitute liens on the land in the hands of G., the purchaser. Hart v. Haynes, 1 Va. Dec. 201.

Inasmuch as the said judgments constituting liens on the land exceed the value thereof, there is a total failure of consideration for the bond for $311.83; and inasmuch as S., under the circumstances of this case, stands in the shoes of W., G. is entitled to have the collection of said bond perpetually enjoined. Hart v. Haynes, 1 Va. Dec. 201.

R. recovers a judgment against G. in 1860, but it is not docketed until December, 1868. W. and others recover judgments against G. in 1861 and 1865, which were docketed in November and December, 1865, and in 1866. In November, 1865, G. conveys land in trust to secure other creditors, and in the same month it is left with the clerk to be recorded, but not being stamped, and the tax on the deed and fee for recording not being paid until November, 1867, it is not admitted to record until that time. Held: The deed having been recorded before the judgment of R. was docketed, the lien of the deed has priority over the judgment of R. The deed was not of record until November, 1867, though left with the clerk in No-

vember, 1865; and the judgments of W. and others having been docketed before the deed was recorded, they have priority over the deed. Hill v. Rixey, 26 Gratt. 72.

Father conveyed property in trust to secure two debts to son and to trustee of his wife, by deed in statutory form, giving no priority. One of the debts secured to son arose out of a judgment against father, prior to deed, in favor of a third person, which son had paid, but no assignment thereof had been made. It was only referred to in the deed as an execution against father, which son had paid. Upon question whether this was entitled to priority, held, it is not. All three of the debts must be paid pari passu. But even if this judgment had been the property of son, by bona fide purchase for value, and a lien on the land when it was conveyed, son lost his property by unequivocally accepting the deed, recognized no priority, as attested by his execution thereof. Clark v. Moore, 76 Va. 262.

Decrees.—J.'s devisees and W. are tenants in common of a hotel property, and J.'s executor and W. agree to sell the property at public auction; the deferred payments to be secured by separate bonds to each for his half of the purchase money, with a lien retained on the real property. The sale is made and W. becomes the purchaser, but refuses to execute the contract. J.'s executor sues W. for specific execution of the contract, and there is a decree in 1868 in his favor for specific execution, a personal decree against W. for the amount due, and for a sale of the whole property. Before the decree W. sells and conveys his moiety of the property to M. who pays the purchase money. Upon a bill by the judgment creditor of M. to subject his moiety of the property to the payment of their debts, the decree of J.'s executor was left with the clerk of the county court to be docketed on the 4th of February, 1870, but was not then put upon the docket. In July, 1870, the decree was found in the office and was then docketed, but was dated February the 4th. In May of the same year W. conveyed a tract of land to T. and C. in trust to secure a debt to G., which was recorded. Held, the decree was not duly recorded until July, and the deed to T. and C. had preference of satisfaction out of the land. Johnson v. National Exchange Bank, 33 Gratt. 473.

The decree of J.'s executor was left with the clerk of the county court to be docketed on the 4th of February, 1870, but was not then put upon the docket. In July, 1870, the decree was found in the office and was then docketed, but was dated February the 4th. In May of the same year W. conveyed a tract of land to T. and C. in trust to secure a debt to G., which was recorded. Held, the decree was not duly recorded until July, and the deed to T. and C. had preference of satisfaction out of the land. Johnson v. National Exchange Bank, 33 Gratt. 473.

. R. obtains a decree against his guardian and his sureties for a certain sum of money; and sues out an execution, which is levied, and a forthcoming bond taken, and forfeited. The court on its chancery side, on notice to the obligors in the forthcoming bond, renders a judgment in favor of R. against them; and this judgment is docketed. Held, the judgment is a valid judgment, and having been docketed, it is notice which will affect all subsequent purchasers of land from any of the defendants in the judgment. Reed v. Ramey, 31 Gratt. 265.

Judgment of Sheriff.—Whether in a creditor's bill judgments paid by the sheriff, who has the execution in his hands, will have priority over the liens of subsequent creditors, is not decided, as in this cause such creditors do not object to it, and the debtor is not prej-

udiced by such preference being given. Beard v. Arbuckle, 19 W. Va. 135.

Judgment against Sheriff.—Chapter 195 of the acts of 1872 (which applies to this case) gave effect to the lien of a judgment against a sheriff from the time he was served with notice or summons, pursuant to which the judgment was afterwards rendered, and declared void as to such judgment any transfer or assignment of his property made after the service of such notice or summons; therefore, a deed of trust executed by the defaulting sheriff after such service of summons or notice is under the operation of such statute void as to such judgment. Quære: Does the act requiring judgment liens to be docketed in order to preserve them as against purchasers of the property, to which they are attached, affect a judgment in favor of the state? Section 39 of ch. 18 of the acts of 1882 operates prospectively and does not affect a case arising under ch. 195 of the acts of 1872. Hoge v. Brookover, 28 W. Va. 304.

Judgment of Justice.—Under § 5, ch. 139, W. Va. Code, 1899, a judgment for money rendered by a justice against any person is a lien from the date of said judgment, on the real estate of or to which such person shall be possessed or entitled at or after such date. But such judgment is not a lien on real estate, as against a purchaser thereof for valuable consideration, without notice, until the same is docketed in the judgment lien docket in the office of the clerk of the county court as provided in § 4, ch. 139, Code, 1899. Nuzum v. Herron, 52 W. Va. 499, 44 S. E. 257.

Construction of Statute.—But the protection to purchasers for valuable consideration without notice of a judgment given them under § 7, ch. 139 of the West Virginia Code, only extends to the land so conveyed to such purchaser, it being liable to the satisfaction of judgments docketed according to law and to such judgments only. Renick *v.* Ludington, 14 W. Va. 367; McClaskey *v.* O'Brien, 16 W. Va. 791.

Who Are Purchasers for Valuable Consideration.

In General.—It is well settled that the creditors and the trustees secured in a deed of trust are purchasers for value; but it can not be said that they are in all cases purchasers for value without notice, for whether or not they are affected with notice will depend upon the circumstances of the case. Evans *v.* Greenhow, 15 Gratt. 153; Exchange Bank *v.* Knox, 19 Gratt. 739, 747; Antoni *v.* Wright, 22 Gratt. 833, 873; Shurtz *v.* Johnson, 28 Gratt. 657; Cammack *v.* Soran, 30 Gratt. 292, 296; Williams *v.* Lord, 75 Va. 390, 404; Witz *v.* Osburn, 83 Va. 227, 230, 2 S. E. 33; Throckmorton *v.* Throckmorton, 91 Va. 42, 47, 22 S. E. 162; Chapman *v.* Chapman, 91 Va. 397, 400, 21 S. E. 813; Cox *v.* Wayt, 26 W. Va. 807, 817; Harden *v.* Wagner, 22 W. Va. 356, 365; Duncan *v.* Custard, 24 W. Va. 730, 737; Western Mining, etc., Co. *v.* Peytona Cannel Coal Co., 8 W. Va. 406, 441; Kimmins *v.* Wilson, 8 W. Va. 584, 591; Farmers' Bank *v.* Willis, 7 W. Va. 31, 47; Ruffner *v.* Mairs, 33 W. Va. 655, 661, 11 S. E. 5, 7; Peters *v.* Bain, 133 U. S. 670, 10 Sup. Ct. 361, 363; Wickham *v.* Lewis, 13 Gratt. 427; Richeson *v.* Richeson, 2 Gratt. 497; Weinberg *v.* Rempe, 15 W. Va. 829; Merchants' Bank *v.* Ballou, 98 Va. 112, 32 S. E. 481; Fischer *v.* Lee, 98 Va. 159, 160, 35 S. E. 441; Davis *v.* Beazley, 75 Va. 491; Zell Guano Co. *v.* Heatherly, 38 W. Va. 409, 18 S. E. 611; Harrison *v.* Farmers' Bank, 9 W. Va. 424.

The contention of the appellant is, that under the registry acts, purchasers are understood to be all persons who, by contract, have acquired a direct interest in the subject, whether by way of lien, as by mortgage or deed of trust, or by absolute conveyance, in contradistinction to creditors whose liens arise by act of law; that in this case the assignment of the bonds to the appellant carried with it the vendor's lien, and as this lien is secured by the deed from Moseley to Bondurant, the appellant is to be treated as a purchaser under that deed to the same extent as though the bonds had been secured by deed of trust or mortgage, and as such purchaser the appellant has priority over the judgment which was not duly docketed. The proposition of the learned counsel with respect to the persons who are to be regarded as purchasers under the registry acts, is taken from 2d Minor's Inst., page 876, and is no doubt entirely correct. The learned author does not, of course, mean to say that every person holding a lien by contract on real estate is to be considered a purchaser. His statement is, that "he is a purchaser who has acquired a direct interest in the subject by way of lien, or by mortgage, or by deed of trust, or by absolute conveyance." It has been repeatedly held, by this court, that creditors secured by deeds of trust are regarded in the light of purchasers, and it is well settled that a mortgagee is also a purchaser to the extent of his interest in the premises. Wickham *v.* Lewis, 13 Gratt. 427, 436; Conrad *v.* Atlantic Ins. Co., 1 Peters 442. And the reason is that both the trust and the mortgage operate as conveyances of the estate, in the one case to the trustee, and in the other to the mortgagee. Gordon *v.* Rixey, 75 Va. 694, 698.

Assignee of purchase money bonds, secured by vendor's lien, is assignee of a chose in action only and not such purchaser of the land for value as will be protected by Virginia Code, 1873, ch. 182, § 8. He is entitled to the rights of his assignor, and no more. "It is very true that in some of the states it has been held that the assignee of a mortgage debt is a purchaser within the meaning and policy of the recording acts. These decisions are, however, based upon special statutes, authorizing the registration of such assignments. These statutes do not treat the assignee as a purchaser of real estate, but as the assignee of a chose in action. The object in recording the assignment is to protect the assignee against a subsequent sale of the mortgage by the apparent holder, as also to prevent a wrongful discharge of the mortgage by the mortgagee. In Virginia there are no laws requiring or authorizing the assignment of debts to be recorded, and such recordation, if made, would not constitute constructive notice to third persons. In any and every view that may be taken, it is clear that the appellant is not a purchaser of real estate or of any interest therein in any proper sense of the word." Gordon *v.* Rixey, 76 Va. 694, 701.

A deed of trust creditor is entitled to be held a purchaser for value within the meaning of the statute in relation to docketing judgments. McClaskey *v.* O'Brien, 16 W. Va. 791; First Nat. Bank *v.* Simms, 49 W. Va. 442, 44, 38 S. E. 525; Wicks *v.* Scull, 102 Va. 290, 46 S. E. 297; Freeman *v.* Eacho, 79 Va. 43; Tabb *v.* Tabb, 82 Va. 48; Carr *v.* Branch, 85 Va. 597, 605, 8 S. E. 476; Williams *v.* Lord, 75 Va. 390, 404; Wickham *v.* Martin, 13 Gratt 427, 437; Evans *v.* Greenhow, 15 Gratt 153, 157; Exchange Bank *v.* Knox, 19 Gratt. 739; Shurtz *v.* Johnson, 28 Gratt. 657; Hill *v.* Rixey, 26 Gratt. 72.

Within the meaning of this statute, the trustee and creditors secured by a deed of trust, are "purchasers for valuable consideration." Shurtz *v.* Johnson, 28 Gratt. 657, citing Evans *v.* Greenhow, 15 Gratt. 153; Exchange Bank *v.* Knox, 19 Gratt. 739, 747.

A trustee in a deed of trust given to secure a debt and the creditor secured, are purchasers for value within the meaning of the statute. Rhea *v.* Preston, 75 Va. 757; Hill *v.* Rixey, 26 Gratt. 72.

Judgments for money, whether docketed or not, bind the unaliened lands of the debtor; certainly those owned by him at the date of the judgments, and, it may be, those subsequently acquired, in the order in which the judgments are recovered, and the same is true of decrees for money; and so, though not docketed, they bind the debtor's lands subsequently aliened to a purchaser with notice, even though he be a purchaser for value; but unless docketed they are not liens on lands subsequently aliened to bona fide purchasers for value without notice—and a trustee in a deed of trust given to secure a debt, and the creditor secured, are purchasers for value within the meaning of the registration laws. Code of 1860, ch. 186, §§ 6, 8, 11; Code of 1873, ch. 182, §§ 1, 6, 8, 11. Rhea *v.* Preston, 75 Va. 757, citing Hill *v.* Rixey, 26 Gratt. 72; Borst *v.* Nalle, 28 Gratt. 423, 428; Williams *v.* Lord, 5 Va. Law J., 243, 250; Williams *v.* Lord, 75 Va. 390.

E. J. O'B. executed a deed of trust upon two hundred acres of land in Barbour county, part of a larger tract, to a trustee to secure a debt to R.; afterwards H., who held a deed of trust upon the larger tract including the said two hundred acres, purchased of said E. J. O'B. the entire tract including said two hundred acres, and E. J. O'B. made to H. a general warranty deed for the land by him so purchased, and H. properly applied a part of the purchase money to the payment of the deed of trust debt of said R. and paid the residue. About seven years after the commencement of these suits, and over a year after a decree had been rendered therein by the court declaring the said debt of R. a paramount lien on said two hundred acres,

8 Va—27

R. executed a release of his said deed of trust, which was admitted to record in said county. If H. released and extinguished the said debt of R. with the lien thereof by such payment for all purposes and in any event, and it clearly appeared that such was the intention of the parties at the time, and a release was executed by R., then perhaps H. might not be entitled to the benefit of the lien of R.'s deed of trust debt for his protection in a court of equity against intervening judgment debts; but unless it does so clearly appear, then in a court of equity, under the circumstances appearing, H. is entitled to be regarded as a purchaser of said R.'s trust deed and the lien thereof, or to the benefit of it for his protection to the amount thereof with its interest against such intervening judgment creditors, it not appearing that injustice would thereby be done. McCleskey *v.* O'Brien, 16 W. Va. 791, 793.

The law is well settled that the purchaser of an equitable title can never claim the rights of a bona fide purchaser. The simple fact that his vendor has no legal title is of itself sufficient to give him notice that he is purchasing an imperfect title and to deprive him of the character of a bona fide purchaser and the protection which the law accords to such purchaser. Poe *v.* Paxton, 26 W. Va. 607; Richards *v.* Fisher, 8 W. Va. 55; Coles *v.* Withers, 33 Gratt. 186; Morehead *v.* Horner, 30 W. Va. 548, 4 S. E. 448, 450.

It is well settled, that the grantee in a trust deed is a purchaser for valuable consideration. (Wickham *v.* Lewis, 13 Gratt. 427; Evans *v.* Greenhow, 15 Gratt. 153; Weinberg *v.* Rempe, 15 W. Va. 829, 831.) Duncan *v.* Custard, 24 W. Va. 730, 737.

3. Between Judgments and Unrecorded Conveyances.

See ante, "Docketing and Indexing Judgments," VI, D. See the title RECORDING ACTS.

a. Between Judgments and Unrecorded Deeds.

Under the statute of 1819, which provided "that all bargains and sales and other conveyances whatsoever of any lands, whether made for passing any estate of inheritance," etc., should be void as to all creditors and subsequent purchasers for valuable consideration without notice, unless they should be proved and lodged with the clerk to be recorded according to the directions of the act—see 1 Revised Code, page 362—it was decided in the case of McClure *v.* Thistle, 2 Gratt. 182, by a full court: That a house and lot in the city of Wheeling, sold and conveyed by David Agnew to McClure in 1835, and which he had fully paid for and been in possession of from the date of his deed and purchase (but which deed, although duly acknowledged and certified at the time of its date, was not recorded until May, 1842), was void as to the creditors of Agnew, who had obtained judgments subsequent to the purchase of the lot by McClure and before the recording of the deed. This decision would seem to be plainly in accordance with the letter and policy of the statute last cited, which was the existing law on the subject at the time it was made.

The present statutes now provide that every contract in writing, made in respect to real estate or goods and chattels in consideration of marriage, or made for the conveyance or sale of real estate, or a term therein for more than five years, and every deed conveying any such estate or term and every deed of gift or deed of trust or mortgage conveying real estate or goods and chattels, shall be void as to creditors and subsequent purchasers for valuable consideration without notice, until and except from the time it is duly admitted to record in the county or corporation wherein the property embraced in such contract, deed or bill of sale may be. Va. Code, 1904, § 2465; W. Va. Code, 1899, ch. 74, § 5.

Beginning with this decision in McClure v. Thistle, 2 Gratt. 182, it has been held repeatedly in both Virginia and West Virginia that a judgment docketed before the recordation of a conveyance takes priority, and the land conveyed thereby is subject to satisfy the judgment. Hart v. Haynes, 1 Va. Dec. 201, 206; Powell v. Bell, 81 Va. 222, 225; Campbell v. Nonpareil Co., 75 Va. 291, 295; Heermans v. Montague, 2 Va. Dec. 6; Price v. Wall, 97 Va. 334, 33 S. E. 599; March v. Chambers, 30 Gratt. 299; Fulkerson v. Taylor, 102 Va. 314, 46 S. E. 378; Delaplain v. Wilkinson, 17 W. Va. 242, 262; Snyder v. Martin, 17 W. Va. 276, 289; Pack v. Hausbarger, 17 W. Va. 313, 323; Anderson v. Nagle, 12 W. Va. 98, 104; Murdock v. Welles, 9 W. Va. 552, 557; Duncan v. Custard, 24 W. Va. 730, 735.

A judgment lien must yield to unrecorded deeds where the recording statutes only declare them void against purchasers without notice. Snyder v. Martin, 17 W. Va. 276, 299.

As against the creditors of a judgment debtor an unrecorded deed of the latter is a mere nullity. It has no existence as to them, and their rights are to be determined as if it had never been executed. Such creditors have the right to subject the land so conveyed to the payment of their judgments, and also to subject the improvements put on the land by the grantee, although they knew of the existence of the deed. Such creditors are not affected by knowledge of the conveyance and the fact that the alienee is making improvements. Flanary v. Kane, 102 Va. 547, 46 S. E. 312, 681.

Words and Phrases in Statute.— Under the statute declaring deeds void

as to creditors and subsequent purchasers for value, whether with or without notice, until and except from the time they are duly admitted to record, an unrecorded deed is void as to judgment creditors, whether the debt upon which the judgment was obtained was contracted before or after the date of the unrecorded deed. The word "subsequent" in that statute applies to purchasers only. The change in the position of the word "creditors" in that section, was not to affect the modification of the law, but it was made that in order that the words "without notice" might more clearly refer to purchasers alone, and not to creditors as well; and in order that there might be no apparent conflict between the language of the statute, and the decisions of the court previously made in Eidson v. Huff, 29 Gratt. 338; March v. Chambers, 30 Gratt. 299; Dobyns v. Waring, 82 Va. 159; Price v. Wall, 97 Va. 334, 33 S. E. 599; Robinson v. Commercial, etc., Bank, 1 Va. Dec. 769; Blakemore v. Wise, 95 Va. 269, 28 S. E. 332; Jones v. Byrne, 94 Va. 751, 27 S. E. 591.

A deed executed on September 3, 1889, but not recorded by the grantee until January 3, 1896, is void as to a judgment docketed December 14, 1894, and the land conveyed under such deed may be subjected to the satisfaction of the judgment, whether the debts on which the judgment is based, were contracted before or after such deed. The word "subsequent" in § 2465 of the Virginia Code, 1904, applies to purchasers only. Price v. Wall, 97 Va. 334, 33 S. E. 599, citing Eidson v. Huff, 29 Gratt. 338; March v. Chambers, 30 Gratt. 299; Dobyns v. Waring, 82 Va. 159.

The word "creditors" in this statute means, all creditors who but for the deed or writing will have a right to subject the land embraced therein to the payment of their debts. Snyder v.

Martin, 17 W. Va. 276, 41 Am. Rep. 670.

The principle of Withers v. Carter, 4 Gratt. 407, 416, and Floyd v. Harding, 28 Gratt. 401, is, that the purchaser having a good equitable title prior to and independent of the writing, will not forfeit it merely because he may afterwards attempt to consummate his right by a deed or title bond. In other words, when there is a parol agreement under which the purchaser is in possession, and which is valid without a writing, the subsequent execution of a writing can not invalidate the title previously acquired without it. This principle is adverted to and relied upon in Withers v. Carter, 4 Gratt. 407, 416, as distinguishing that case from McClure v. Thistle, 2 Gratt. 182. McClure v. Thistle, 2 Gratt. 182, is cited in this connection in Eidson v. Huff, 29 Gratt. 338, 345; Delaplain v. Wilkinson, 17 W. Va. 242, 268; Pack v. Hansbarger, 17 W. Va. 313, 334; Anderson v. Nagle, 12 W. Va. 98, 108; Snyder v. Martin, 17 W. Va. 276, 289. See also, Snyder v. Botkin, 37 W. Va. 355, 16 S. E. 591; Campbell v. Nonpareil Co., 75 Va. 291, 296. In Pack v. Hansbarger, 17 W. Va. 313, 338, it was said: "It is true, that the equitable ground of priority, protection and relief is not admitted and administered against the positive provisions of a statute to sustain the prior against the subsequent encumbrancer, as in the case of McClure v. Thistle, 2 Gratt. 182." McClure v. Thistle, 2 Gratt. 182 is cited on this point in Delaplain v. Wilkinson, 17 W. Va. 242, 268.

· Statute Prospective.—This statute is wholly prospective in its operation, and does not validate a recordation invalid under previous laws, where rights have accrued under those laws. Campbell v. Nonpareil Co., 75 Va. 291.

Retrospective Operation of Statute. —The act of March 2, 1866, sess. acts, 1865-66, p. 191, ch. 77, § 1, "to preserve and extend the time for the exercise of certain civil rights and remedies," is retrospective in its operation, and applies in favor of a judgment creditor as to the docketing of his judgment. The act of March 2, 1866, sess. acts, 1865-66, ch. 69, p. 180, called the stay law, does not apply to a judgment creditor to relieve him from the necessity of docketing his judgment. R. recovers a judgment against G. in 1860, but it is not docketed until December, 1868. W. and others recover judgments against G. in 1861 and 1865, which were docketed in November and December, 1865, and in 1866. In November, 1865, G. conveys land in trust to secure other creditors, and in the same month it is left with the clerk to be recorded, but not being stamped, and the tax on the deed and fee for recording not being paid until November, 1867, it is not admitted to record until that time. Held: The deed having been recorded before the judgment of R. was docketed, the lien of the deed has priority over the judgment of R. The deed was not of record until November, 1868, though left with the clerk in November, 1865; and the judgments of W. and others having been docketed before the deed was recorded, they have priority over the deed. Hill v. Rixey, 26 Gratt, 72.

Purchasers of Different Parcels.—If the first alienee of a portion of the lands liable to judgment liens fails to put his deed of record, and a subsequent alienee, who bought another portion of said lands liable to judgment liens, puts his deed of record, still the lands of such last alienee must be liable for such judgment liens before the land of the first alienee. The reason for the last of the above rules is, that the 5th section of ch. 74 of the Code of West Virginia, p. 474, declaring "that every deed, etc., shall be void as to creditors and purchasers for valuable consideration without notice, until and except from the time it is duly admitted to record," does not apply to purchasers of different parcels of land from the same vendor, but only refers to "subsequent purchasers" of the same subject as that embraced in the instrument declared void. Renick v. Ludington, 20 W. Va. 511, 567.

The provision of § 5, ch. 114 of the Va. Code of 1873, that every deed, etc., "shall be void as to creditors, and subsequent purchasers for valuable consideration without notice, until and except from the time it is duly admitted to record," etc., does not apply to purchasers of different tracts of land from the same vendor, but refers only to "subsequent purchasers" of the same subject, as that embraced in the instrument declared to be void. Harman v. Oberdorfer, 33 Gratt. 497.

Illustrative Cases. — A judgment creditor, whose judgment has been duly docketed, and who has brought suit to enforce the lien on the judgment debtor's land, is entitled to priority over a grantee of the judgment debtor claiming under a deed not recorded until after the commencement of the suit, after the expiration of twenty months from its execution and acknowledgment; since such a deed is void, under Code, § 2465, as to creditors whose rights have attached before it was recorded. Robinson v. Commercial, etc., Bank, 1 Va. Dec. 769, citing Strayer v. Long, 86 Va. 557, 562, 10 S. E. 574.

A deed, executed before judgment had been obtained against the grantor, under which the purchaser had paid the purchase money and had been put in possession, but which was not recorded until after the judgment was obtained, is void as against such creditor, and the land thereby conveyed is subject to satisfy the judgment. Parkersburg Nat. Bank v. Neal, 28 W. Va. 744.

A deed executed on the ninth of August, 1869, but not recorded until seventh of October, is void as to a judgment obtained and entered upon the fifth of October, and duly docketed, according to the provisions of the seventh section of chapter one hundred and thirty-nine of the Code. Such deed, being made bona fide and upon valuable consideration, is not void as to judgments obtained after its recordation. Murdock v. Welles, 9 W. Va. 552, citing McClure v. Thistle, 2 Gratt. 182, 183.

A contract in writing was executed for the sale of land, before judgments were obtained against the vendor, and the deed executed in pursuance of said contract was not recorded until after the said judgments were duly docketed and the contract was never recorded. Such contract and deed are void as to such creditors; and the land so contracted to be sold, and so conveyed is subject to the satisfaction of the judgments. Anderson v. Nagle, 12 W. Va. 98.

By a written contract between W. and G. executed on January 30th, 1866, W. sold to G. a tract of land, at which G. paid part of the purchase money, and W. bound himself by the contract to make to G., upon payment of the balance of the purchase money, a deed for said land. The contract was duly executed and acknowledged, but never recorded. On May 21st, 1866, W. and wife conveyed said land to G. by deed with general warranty, which was acknowledged on that day, and duly recorded on the next. At the time of the execution of the deed G. owed a balance of $311.83 of the purchase money, with interest from January 1, 1866, for which he was requested by W. to execute his bond to S. instead of himself, which, with the assent of S., who was present, was accordingly done. On May 16th, 1866, during the term of the county court of Caroline, which began on the 14th of that month, H. and J. each recovered judgments against W., which were duly docketed on June 6, 1866. On February 11,

1861, A recovered a judgment against W., which was docketed May 16, 1866. On May 29, 1866, at a term of the circuit court of Caroline, which began on that day, P. recovered a judgment against W., which was docketed July 2, 1866. Upon these facts it was held: The contract of January 30, 1866, never having been recorded, as required by ch. 118, §§ 4, 5, 7, of the Code of 1860, was void as to the judgment creditors of W., whose judgments were duly docketed. Hart v. Haynes, 1 Va. Dec. 201, criticising and disapproving Withers v. Carter, 4 Gratt. 407.

In March v. Chambers, 30 Gratt. 299, it appeared that in January, 1866, Chambers, by an agreement in writing, sold to Ramey a lot in Danville, Va., and in the same month conveyed it to him. The agreement was never recorded, and the deed was not recorded until September 18, 1873. Ramey paid all his purchase money, and on the 15th of August, 1866, conveyed the lot to John G. Ramey, to secure a debt of $4,000. On the 1st of July, 1872, March, Price & Co. obtained a judgment against Chambers, which was duly docketed March 11, 1873. Ramey was declared a bankrupt in April, 1868; and in the following month the register in bankruptcy conveyed the lot to his assignee. In September, 1868, on the joint application of the assignee and of John G. Ramey, as a lien creditor of the bankrupt, the court in bankruptcy ordered a sale of the lot; and John G. Ramey bought it, and received the deed in due form from the assignee; and, upon a proceeding by March, Price & Co. to subject the lot to the lien of their judgment, it was held, that it was so liable, notwithstanding all the conveyances and proceedings in relation to it. Followed in Heermans v. Montague, 2 Va. Dec. 6, 20.

By a written contract between W. and G. executed on January 30th, 1866, W. sold to G. a tract of land, at which G. paid part of the purchase money, and W. bound himself by the contract to make to G., upon payment of the balance of the purchase money, a deed for said land. The contract was duly executed and acknowledged, but never recorded. On May 21st, 1866, W. and wife conveyed said land to G. by deed with general warranty, which was acknowledged on that day, and duly recorded on the next. At the time of the execution of the deed G. owed a balance of $311.83 of the purchase money, with interest from January 1, 1866, for which he was requested by W. to execute his bond to S. instead of himself, which, with the assent of S., who was present, was accordingly done. On May 16th, 1866, during the term of the county court of Caroline, which began on the 14th of that month, H. and J. each recovered judgments against W., which were duly docketed on June 6, 1866. On February 11, 1861, A. recovered a judgment against W., which was docketed May 16, 1866. On May 29, 1866, at a term of the circuit court of Caroline, which began on that day, P. recovered a judgment against W., which was docketed July 2, 1866. Upon these facts, it was held: P.'s judgment having been recovered after the deed from W. and wife was made and recorded, constitutes no lien on the land. Hart v. Haynes, 1 Va. Dec. 201.

"If the land encumbered by Morgan's deed were the only land owned by Thomas at the time the deed went to record, it might be a question presenting difficulty, whether the deed or the judgments were entitled to priority —the deed being declared by the statute void as to creditors (whether with or without notice) 'until and except from the time that it is duly admitted to record,' etc., and the undocketed judgments not a lien on real estate as against purchasers thereof for valuable consideration without notice. The question, in its general bearing, is of great importance and was but little argued. I give no opinion upon it, as it is not necessary to do so in the present case; for, if it be conceded that the lien of the judgments is superior, still they were properly postponed to the deed, under the circumstances." Rhea v. Preston, 75 Va. 757, 768.

If a grantee of land who has failed to record his deed, induce the grantor to make a new deed to the grantee's wife, who records the same, and, together with her husband, executes a deed of trust on the property for a loan with which to pay the purchase price, the deed and deed of trust, when recorded, operate to invest the trustee with the title to the property, as against the creditors of the grantor, and they can not subject it to judgments obtained against the grantor subsequent to such recordation. As against creditors of the grantor, the unrecorded deed is a mere nullity, and must be treated as if it had never been executed. Such creditors can not treat the deed as a nullity for some purposes, and as valid for others. The fact that it may be valid between the parties, and as to subsequent purchasers with notice, does not affect them. Bankers' Loan, etc., Co. v. Blair, 99 Va. 606, 39 S. E. 231.

This is a controversy as to priority of right between a judgment creditor, asserting the lien of a judgment on a certain real estate on the one hand, and subsequent purchasers of said real estate on the other hand, who claim by deed under one who took the same as purchaser from one of the judgment debtors, who conveyed by deed made and recorded subsequent to the rendition and docketing of the judgment, there being of record no prior executory contract. Held, the judgment creditor has priority. Dobyns v. Waring, 82 Va. 159.

If upon an exchange of lands the parties execute mutual conveyances, but the grantee of one tract fails to record his deed, a judgment against his grantor binds the land so given in exchange as well as that received in exchange. The rights of the parties are not affected by the character of the consideration for the unrecorded deed. Having failed to record his deed as provided by law, the land conveyed thereby is bound by the lien as effectually as if the judgment debtor had never parted with it. Price v. Wall, 97 Va. 334, 33 S. E. 599.

Unrecorded Title Bond.—At the February term, 1857, of the court, a judgment was recovered against S. and H. as his surety, on a forthcoming bond, and it was docketed on the 1st of April, 1857. An execution was issued on this judgment, and it was paid by H. On the 8th of October, 1856, S., by written agreement under seal, sold to E. a house and lot, and delivered possession, and on the 18th of the same month S. conveyed the same to E. This deed was acknowledged on the same day, H. being one of the justices who took the acknowledgment; but it was not presented in the clerk's office for record until March 9th, 1857. Upon a bill by H. against E. and S., to be substituted to the lien of the judgment against S., held: The judgment having been docketed within twelve months from the date of its being rendered, and the deed not having been recorded within sixty days from its acknowledgment, the judgment is a lien upon the house and lot as against the deed. The agreement not having been recorded, it is void as to the creditor, and as to H. claiming under him, though H. had notice of the deed and E. had possession of the house and lot. "It was held, that the deed had priority over the judgment of Rixey and Starke, because that judgment, although rendered in November, 1860, was not docketed until December 11th, 1868, more than twelve months after the recordation of the deed. But it was also held, that the other judgments had priority over the deed, although not docketed until after the execution of the deed, but before it was recorded; and the reason was they (the judgments) were docketed within twelve months from the time they were rendered. The doctrine laid down in Hill *v.* Rixey is therefore in direct conformity with the views here expressed, and lead inevitably to the same conclusion." Eidson *v.* Huff, 29 Gratt. 338, 342.

"In the present case the only question is as to the necessity of recording a title bond and deed as against a creditor whose judgment has been duly docketed. By the provisions of the 8th section, chapter 186, Code of 1860, the judgment lien is preserved if it is docketed within a year from its date, or ninety days before the conveyance of the estate to a purchaser. Here the judgment was rendered at the February term, 1857, and was docketed on the 1st of April thereafter. On the other hand the title bond was never recorded. The deed to Mrs. Hanger bears date October 18th, 1856. It was acknowledged before and certified to by two justices of the peace on the same day, but was not recorded until March 9th, 1857, nearly five months after such acknowledgment; so that the judgment was recovered before the deed was recorded. If the deed had been recorded within sixty days from its acknowledgment it would be held valid as a recorded deed from the time of such acknowledgment. But not being so recorded, it is only valid as to creditors and purchasers, without notice, from the day of its actual admittance to record." Eidson *v.* Huff, 29 Gratt. 338.

Deed in Escrow.—Circuit court of N. directs W., trustee for his wife, to buy, subject to its approval at price not exceeding $6,000, payable out of her funds in its hands, a home for her. In 1873, trustee contracts by writing with H. for 240 acres in A. at $12,000, subject to court's approval. In March, 1874, trustee reports contract with H.; but court is told that only 100 acres thereof at $6,000—cash, $2,500 balance in three annual payments—is to be paid for out of her funds. H.'s conveyance of the 100 acres to trustee is filed as escrow until cash payment made. Court confirms report quoad the 100 acres, and "the deed as escrow, until cash payment made and recorded," and provides for paying not only the cash but the other payments. On November 6th, 1874, all the purchase money, except $419.59, is paid, and during that year that balance is paid. Deed is recorded April 13, 1876. Written contract never was. T.'s administrator and others got judgments against H. March 15th, 1876, which were docketed two days later. In suit to subject the 100 acres to those judgments; held, the deed delivered as an escrow in the proceedings of a court of equity, administering trust funds, is not within the intendment of that statute. Briscoe *v.* Ashby, 24 Gratt. 454, 469, approved in Trout *v.* Warwick, 77 Va. 731.

Held, that deed, so delivered as an escrow, could not have been placed on record until W. had become entitled to it by paying the cash payment on November 6th, 1874, when all the purchase money, except $419.59, was paid. Trout *v.* Warwick, 77 Va. 731.

Estoppel.—Where the owner of a tract of land conveys the same to his brother by a deed absolute on its face, and allows the said deed to remain for years on the record of the county in which the land lies, thus giving notice to the world of the title thereto in said brother, and third parties extend credit to that brother, and allow him to become indebted to them, and said third parties obtain judgments against said brother for the debts thus created, and docket the same in the county where the land is situated, such creditors thereby acquire a valid lien upon said land, and the party who conveyed said land to his brother, and allowed the deed to so remain recorded, is estopped from claiming title to said land, as against said creditors. Per Holt, P., and English, J. Greer v. Mitchell, 42 W. Va. 494, 26 S. E. 302.

As between Parties.—It is well settled in Virginia that an unrecorded conveyance is good as between the parties to the instrument and their representatives. In re Wynne, Fed. Cas. No. 18,117, citing Glazebrook v. Ragland, 8 Gratt. 332; McClure v. Thistle, 2 Gratt. 182; Wiley v. Givens, 6 Gratt. 277; Johnston v. Slater, 11 Gratt. 321.

A deed executed on the ninth of August, 1869, but not recorded until seventh of October, is void as to a judgment obtained and entered up on the fifth of October, and duly docketed, according to the provisions of the seventh section of chapter one hundred and thirty-nine of the Code. Such deed, being made bona fide and upon valuable consideration, is not void as to judgments obtained after its recordation. It is error to decree such deed "null and void" in a decree in favor of the judgment creditor; it should be so held as to the creditor, it being good between the parties. Murdock v. Welles, 9 W. Va. 552.

Form and Sufficiency of Recordation. —See the title RECORDING ACTS.

Acknowledgment.—See the title ACKNOWLEDGMENTS, vol. 1, p. 104.

A clerk of the county court endorses on a deed that it was on that day exhibited in his office, acknowledged by the parties thereto and admitted to record. In fact the deed was acknowledged and the certificate endorsed thereon, out of the office, and was then taken by the clerk to the office and deposited there. Held, the deed was valid as a recorded deed from the date of the certificate. Carper v. M'Dowell, 5 Gratt. 212.

Fraud of Clerk.—"It is this principle of fraud, upon which the decision of this court in Horsely v. Garth, 2 Gratt. 471, so much relied on by the counsel for the appellee. is founded. In that case, the deed, acknowledged before justices, was not delivered to the clerk for recordation, by the agent of the grantees, until after the lien of the judgment creditor had attached, by relation to the first day of the term; and yet the clerk, knowingly and willfully, for the purpose of giving the registration the same effect as if made in due time; contrary to law and the truth of the case, did certify that the deed was delivered to him and admitted to record at an earlier day, and so surreptitiously divested the priority of the judgment creditor. A principal must be taken to know what was known to his agent; 1 Hov. on Frauds 184; and therefore the attitude of the grantees in relation to the proceeding, was the same as if they had delivered the deed to the clerk with their own hands. Under such circumstances, a court of equity will not stop to inquire into the motives with which the act was done, when the effect of it was to make the registration operate fraudulently in regard to the subsisting rights of the creditor entitled to priority. The grantees could not conscientiously avail themselves of an undue advantage so obtained, and redress could only be had by the interposition of a court of equity." Carper v. M'Dowell, 5 Gratt. 212.

Voluntary Release.—Where a grantee of land fails to record his deed until after a judgment is obtained against the grantor, the lien of the judgment plaintiff will not be postponed, as to other land of the grantor, to the liens of judgments rendered after such deed was recorded, because such judgment plaintiff voluntarily released his lien on the land conveyed. Blakemore v. Wise, 95 Va. 269, 28 S. E. 332.

A variance between the date as it appears in the deed certified by the justices, and in their certificate, does not avoid the registry of the deed, if the identity of the deed certified and the deed recorded is satisfactorily ascertained by other parts of the certificate, and the annexation thereof to the deed. Horsley *v.* Garth, 2 Gratt. 471.

The endorsement of the clerk on the deed of the day when it was left with him to be recorded, and his return to the court, of deeds left with him to be recorded, is not conclusive as to the day when the deed was so left; but the true day may be shown by parol testimony. Horsley *v.* Garth, 2 Gratt. 471.

The carrying a deed to the clerk's office to be recorded is not enough to make it good, as a recorded deed, from that day. It must be left with the clerk to be recorded. Horsley *v.* Garth, 2 Gratt. 471.

A deed which was lost after it was executed, and before it was recorded, is void as against the creditors of the grantors, and can not be set up against them in a suit by the grantee brought more than eight months after its execution. Withers *v.* Carter, 4 Gratt. 407.

Place of Recordation.—The court is of opinion, that where a deed conveys several tracts of land lying separately, in different counties, the recordation thereof in only one of the counties is not effectual, in regard to the tract or tracts lying in the other county or counties, within the true intent and meaning of the statute regulating conveyances, 1 Rev. Code, ch. 99; and therefore, that the deed of trust in the proceedings mentioned, made by John Horsley and wife in March, 1836, to Frederick M. Cabell and Alexander Munday as trustees, though recorded in the counties of Nelson, Amherst and Buckingham, is null and void in regard to the lands conveyed by said deed lying in the county of Greenbrier, and the lots lying in the city of Richmond, as against the creditors of said Horsley, by judgments against him recovered in the courts of this commonwealth before the due recordation of said deed in the county of Greenbrier and city of Richmond respectively. Horsley *v.* Garth, 2 Gratt. 471, 490.

Where a navigable stream is the dividing line between two counties, and so separates lands conveyed by deed, as to throw part thereof into the county on one side of said stream, and part thereof into the county on the opposite side of the same, the parts so separated must be regarded as distinct tracts lying in different counties, within the true intent and meaning of said statute; and the recordation of such deed in one of the counties is not effectual in regard to the part lying in the opposite county; and therefore, that the recordation of the deed of trust aforesaid in the counties of Nelson and Amherst, is null and void in regard to all the lands which it conveys, lying in the county of Buckingham, as against the creditors of said Horsley, by judgments against him recovered in the courts of this commonwealth before the due recordation of said deed in the county of Buckingham. Horsley *v.* Garth, 2 Gratt. 471, 490.

Payment of Tax and Registration Fees.—"The other judgments were rendered and docketed before the deed of trust was admitted to record on the 6th of November, 1867. It is said, however, that the deed must be considered as recorded from the day of its delivery to the clerk. This was the 8th of December, 1865. But as the proper revenue stamps were not then affixed, nor the tax and registration fees then paid, the clerk was under no obligation to record the deed. All the cases which hold that the instrument is to be regarded as actually recorded from the time of delivery to the clerk, proceed upon the idea, that the party has done all that is incumbent upon him to do, and nothing remains to be done as a prerequisite to the recordation. This, of course, can not be predicated of a conveyance which is deposited in the office without prepayment of the necessary fees and charges imposed by authority of the government." Hill v. Rixey, 26 Gratt. 72, 80.

b. Between Judgments and Unrecorded Deeds of Trust and Mortgages.

In General.—Under the recording acts all deeds of trust and mortgages are utterly void as to creditors and purchasers without notice, unless properly recorded. As to such creditors and purchasers the title is regarded as remaining in the grantor. No distinction is made between deeds of trust executed and deeds of trust merely executory. Both the letter and the policy of the recording acts are opposed to any such distinction. Campbell v. Nonpareil Co., 75 Va. 291.

Between Judgments and Unrecorded Deeds of Trust.—A prior deed of trust unrecorded is null and void as to a subsequent judgment; and the judgment is a lien upon the land embraced in the deed. McCance v. Taylor, 10 Gratt. 580.

If the owner of a tract of land executes a deed of trust, conveying his land to a trustee to secure certain debts, and afterwards a judgment is rendered against him, which is duly docketed, and he then makes a contract with a third party to advance for him the amount secured by the deed of trust, and to secure such advance, mortgages this land to the person advancing the money for him, and such mortgagee pays off the debts secured by the deed of trust, it would be a complete satisfaction of these debts both in law and in equity; the deed of trust becomes wholly inoperative, and the mortgagee can not be

subrogated to the rights of the cestui que trust and have the deed of trust kept alive for his benefit, thus securing priority over the judgment debtor. Hoffman v. Ryan, 21 W. Va. 415.

Where a party conveys land in trust to secure the payment of a debt, and subsequently sells lands he holds as trustee for his wife and children to pay the debts, the wife and children have an implied trust in their favor on the tract of land deeded to secure the payment of the debt, which refers back to the date of the trust deed, and has priority over judgment creditors who recovered judgments between the recording of the deed and the payment out of the proceeds of the land held by him as trustee for his wife and children, even though the judgments were recovered before the payment by the husband. Warwick v. Warwick, 31 Gratt. 70.

A judgment creditor, whose debtor, after being taken in execution, has been discharged from custody by the jailor, for nonpayment of the jail fees, is remitted to the lien of his judgment, and will be entitled to satisfaction out of the debtor's land, in preference to creditors claiming under a deed of trust executed by the debtor, conveying the land, but not recorded in the county where it lies. McCullough v. Somerville, 8 Leigh 415.

On the 29th of July, 1869, the Nonpareil F. B. & K. Co. executed a deed of trust for the benefit of its creditors, conveying real estate located in Henrico county, within a mile of the corporate limits of the city of Richmond. The deed was admitted to record in the clerk's office of the county court of Henrico, on the 7th of August, 1869, and in the clerk's office of the chancery court of Richmond on the 30th of November, 1876. On the 3d of April, 1876, C. & Co. recovered judgment against the grantor, which was duly docketed. On the 30th of

June, 1875, the trustees sold and conveyed a portion of the trust property to a purchaser, whose deed was recorded in Henrico court on the 6th of November, 1875, and in the chancery court of Richmond on the 30th of November, 1876. In a suit brought to enforce the judgment lien, held, the deed of trust not having been legally recorded prior to the rendition of the judgment, is absolutely void as to the judgment creditors, notwithstanding the trust had been executed by a sale and conveyance of the property; for in this respect the statutes of registration make no distinction between executed and unexecuted trusts, but are designed to give notice of the state of the title as affected by successive alienations, as well as by encumbrances. Quære: Whether, if the sale had been made under a decree in a suit brought for the purpose, instead of being made for the sole act of the trustee, the consequences would have been the same? The dicta of Baldwin and Daniel, JJ., in Glazebrook v. Ragland, 8 Gratt. 332, 344, criticised in Campbell v. Nonpareil Co., 75 Va. 291.

Consideration for Deed.—In April, 1868, R. conveyed land with general warranty to C., and C. conveyed it in trust to secure four bonds for the purchase money. The trust deed was recorded, but the deed to C. was not, until March, 1869. One of the bonds was paid by C. R. assigned the other three to W., and B. and J., J. being the last assignee. In July, 1868, D. recovered a judgment against R., and afterwards filed his bill to subject a small tract of land of R. to satisfy it. In May, 1873, C. was declared a bankrupt, and upon petition by J. the bankrupt court had C.'s land sold, and fixed the priorities of the creditors, making D. the first and J. the last, the proceeds of the land not being sufficient to pay all; but directing the fund should be retained until it was ascer-

tained how much D. would get from the proceeds of the other tract. In March, 1871, R. executed a declaration of homestead, which embraced all his personal property; and on the 10th of August, 1871, he conveyed this property to P. in trust for his wife and children. In January, 1874, J. having purchased D.'s judgment, he filed a bill against R. and his wife and children and P., in a state court, to subject this personal property to satisfy this judgment; and in April, 1874, there was a decree in the bankrupt court, by which the proceeds of C.'s land was distributed among the assignees of his bonds, it not being enough to satisfy J. And it being suggested to the court, that beside the small tract of land aforesaid, there was personal property of R., which might be subjected to pay the said judgment, which was sufficient for that purpose, it was decreed that no part of the proceeds of C.'s land should be applied to pay the judgment of D. Held, the deed of R. to P. being not upon consideration deemed valuable in law, having been made after the judgment, was also null and void as to D.'s debt. Russell v. Randolph, 26 Gratt. 705.

Docketing Conclusive to All.—The regular docketing of a judgment is constructive but in law conclusive notice to all the world of the lien of such judgment, and will give such judgment priority over a deed of trust executed after the docketing thereof. Citizens' Nat. Bank v. Manoni, 76 Va. 802.

Place of Recordation.—By the charter of the city of Lynchburg jurisdiction is given to the court of hustings for said city, not only within the limits of the corporation, but also for the space of one mile without and around said city. A deed of trust conveying real estate lying outside the corporation limits, but within one mile without and around said city, is to be recorded in the clerk's office of the corporation court of the city. And being so recorded it is valid, and has priority over subsequent judgments against the grantor in the deed docketed in the clerk's office of the county court. Blackford *v.* Hurst, 26 Gratt. 203, reaffirmed in Burgess *v.* Belvin, 32 Gratt. 663; Campbell *v.* Nonpareil Co., 75 Va. 291; Boston *v.* Chesapeake, etc., R. Co., 76 Va. 185.

Judicial Sales.—"When a suit is brought in a court of equity for the execution of a trust deed, a decree is rendered for the sale of the property, and a sale and conveyance made to the purchaser under the sanction of the court, the title of the purchaser is good against the judgment creditor of the grantor, although the deed of trust has never been recorded. If this doctrine can be sustained at all, it is upon the ground that all the parties interested in the property are before the court, and the purchaser holds not under the deed of trust, but under the decree, which is his muniment of title. In tracing that title, he need not go back to the deed of trust, but only to the proceedings and decree in equity under which he claims. I do not see with what propriety this doctrine can be invoked to show that an unrecorded deed of trust is valid against a judgment lien, where the sale and conveyance are made by the trustee himself, and not under the decree of a court. In such case the purchaser must trace his title through the unrecorded deed of trust. He must stand or fall by that title; and if the deed be invalid, he is without support." Campbell *v.* Nonpareil Co., 75 Va. 291, 294, citing Glazebrook *v.* Ragland, 8 Gratt. 332.

Between Judgments and Unrecorded Mortgages.—M. and J. are bound as sureties for E. who conveyed slaves to a trustee to indemnify them, and to secure divers other debts; and judgment against E., the principal, and M.

and J., the sureties, and judgments against E. for all other debts so secured, are recovered at the same time; after which the trustee appoints J., one of the cestuis que trust, his agent to carry the trust slaves to a southwestern market, and E., the mortgagor, accompanies him, carrying out three other slaves; J. and E. co-operate in selling the trust slaves, and E. sells the other three slaves, for a gross sum of 12,325 dollars for both parcels of slaves, and bring back a bill of exchange for 2,000 dollars, and 10,325 dollars in money. The trustee receives the bill of exchange from E. and makes efforts to get it cashed, but, the acceptors having failed, without success, and sends it to an attorney for collection; of the 10,325 dollars, he, with the acquiescence of M. and J. permits E. to retain 1,000 dollars, and receives 9,325 dollars, out of which, with the acquiescence of M. and J. he pays no dividend to them or to the creditor to whom they are sureties, but applies the whole to the other debts secured by the mortgage; and after all these transactions, E. by deed of trust conveys his land to indemnify K., another surety for him, and the trustee sells the land under this deed, and K. becomes the purchaser. Held, that the judgment against E. and M. and J., his sureties, gave the judgment creditor a lien on E.'s land, prior to the lien which K. acquired by his subsequent mortgage, and M. and J. are entitled to the benefit of that prior lien; that the other judgments of the same date against E. gave those judgment creditors prior liens on E.'s land, and their judgments being satisfied out of a fund in which M. and J. had a right to participate, they are entitled, by subrogation to the benefit of these liens also; and as these liens together bound the whole of E.'s land, therefore, not a moiety only, but the whole of the proceeds of the land sold under the subsequent deed of trust to K. is liable to be applied to the satisfaction of M. and J.'s claim. Kent *v.* Matthews, 12 Leigh 573.

Place of Recordation — Boats.—A canal boat, which plied between Richmond and a point in Fluvanna county, was owned by one Tutwiler, who resided in said county. He sold the boat to Cox, who lived in Richmond, and took a mortgage thereon to secure the purchase money, which mortgage he forthwith recorded in Fluvanna county, and within twelve months thereafter in the city of Richmond. Between the dates of the recordation of the mortgage in the two places, judgment creditors of Cox issued fieri facias, under which the boat was seized at Richmond. Upon a bill filed by Tutwiler's administratrix to assert her (alleged) prior lien, held, that the mortgage in favor of her intestate was properly recorded, and she therefore had priority. Lucado *v.* Tutwiler, 28 Gratt. 39.

Defective Deeds of Trusts and Mortgages.

Equitable Mortgage.—A paper made for a deed of trust conveying land to secure a debt signed by the grantor, but without a seal, though not effectual as a deed of trust at law, is an equitable mortgage, enforceable in equity, and if recorded under § 4 of ch. 74 of the West Virginia Code of 1868, will take priority over a judgment lien. Atkinson *v.* Miller, 34 W. Va. 115, 11 S. E. 1007, disapproving Pratt *v.* Clemens, 4 W. Va. 443; Shattuck *v.* Knight, 25 W. Va. 590; White *v.* Deman, 16 O. 59, and following Alexander *v.* Newton, 2 Gratt. 266; Snyder *v.* Martin, 17 W. Va. 276, 299; Knott *v.* Shepherdstown Mfg., Co., 39 W. Va. 790, 5 S. E. 266; Fidelity Ins., etc., Co. *v.* Shenandoah Val. R. Co., 33 W. Va. 761, 11 S. E. 58; White *v.* Denman, 1 O. St. 112.

A deed conveys land to a trustee to hold for the separate use of a married woman, "expressly reserving, however, to the said E. A. C. (the woman) the right to sell and unite with her husband and her said trustee in conveying all or any part of said lands, whenever she may elect to do so." She and her husband make a deed of trust on the land, acknowledged by them properly, to which the trustee is not a party; but, by an underwriting under his hand and seal of same date with the trust, he agrees "that the above trust deed may be executed, and, in the event that a sale of the above named lands shall have to be made, I will unite in the deed conveying, provided the said sale is made according to the terms of this trust deed." The instrument is recorded. Held, that though informal for the want of the trustee as a formal party, and not passing legal title, yet it creates a lien on the land as an equitable mortgage. Bensimer *v.* Fell, 35 W. Va. 15, 12 S. E. 1078, 29 Am. St. Rep. 774.

4. Between Judgments and Unacknowledged Deeds.

The act approved March 1, 1894 (acts, 1893-94, page 580), to the extent that it attempts to validate deeds theretofore made for the benefit of corporations which had been acknowledged before a notary public or other officer who was a stockholder in such corporation, is unconstitutional and void so far as it affects the lien of judgments recovered and docketed against the grantors in such deeds prior to the approval of said act. Such acknowledgment is invalid. Merchants Bank *v.* Ballou, 98 Va. 112, 32 S. E. 481.

5. Between Judgments and Homestead.

While the lien of a judgment which attaches before a homestead in the land is claimed, can not be enforced during the existence of the homestead, yet it will have priority on the land after the homestead is abandoned over a deed of trust executed during the occupancy of the land as a homestead. Blose *v.* Bear, 87 Va. 177, 12 S. E. 294.

In March, 1871, R. executed a declaration of homestead, which embraced all his personal property; and on the 10th of August, 1871, he conveyed this property to P. in trust for his wife and children. In January, 1874, J. having purchased D.'s judgment, he filed a bill against R. and his wife and children and P., in a state court, to subject this personal property to satisfy this judgment; and in April, 1874, there was a decree in the bankrupt court, by which the proceeds of C.'s land was distributed among the assignees of his bonds, it not being enough to satisfy J. And it being suggested to the court, that beside the small tract of land aforesaid, there was personal property of R., which might be subjected to pay the said judgment, which was sufficient for that purpose, it was decreed that no part of the proceeds of C.'s land should be applied to pay the judgment of D. It was held, that that declaration on homestead by R. having been after D. had recovered his judgment, was null and void as to D.'s debt. The deed of R. to P. being not upon consideration deemed valuable in law, having been made after the judgment, was also null and void as to D.'s debt. Russell *v.* Randolph, 26 Gratt. 705. See also, Va. Code, §§ 3642; Rose *v.* Sharpless, 33 Gratt. 153; Holt *v.* Williams, 13 W. Va. 704; 2 Minor's Inst. (4th Ed.) 912.

Where some of the judgments against a defendant are paramount to a claim of homestead asserted by his heirs, and others not, it is not error to decree a sale of the land, without prejudice to the rights of the heirs as inheritors of the land encumbered by judgments against their ancestor. The creditors whose judgments were paramount to the homestead were entitled to a sale of the land for the satisfaction of their judgments. The right of the heirs to a homestead, if entitled thereto, is in the surplus of the fund arising from a sale of the lands which remain after the satisfaction of the liens paramount to the homestead. Hawpe *v.* Bumgardner, 103 Va. 91, 48 S. E. 554.

One who becomes a householder or head of a family after a judgment lien has fastened on his land, is not entitled to a homestead exemption in the land paramount to that lien until its discharge. Code, 1873, ch. 183, § 5. Kennerly *v.* Swartz, 83 Va. 704, 3 S. E. 348.

. "Section 17 of the same act declares that 'no exemption under this act shall affect or impair any prior lien on any real or personal estate, or any claim for the purchase money thereof, or for work or labor performed as a domestic; nor shall anything in this act contained exempt any property from taxation, or from sale of taxes.' Of course, by the very terms of the statute the writing designating the homestead was to have no effect until it was recorded in the proper county. Taking the different sections I have quoted, it means it is to have no effect until recorded, and when recorded, it shall not affect prior liens, etc. We have seen that the forfeited forthcoming bond had the force of a judgment lien on the real estate of B. V. Given from the 10th day of October, 1868. His declaration of homestead was not recorded until the 27th day of March, 1869. So the judgment lien is not defeated by the homestead, but the homestead is liable to be subjected to the payment thereof." Cabell *v.* Gives, 30 W. Va. 760, 5 S. E. 442, 449.

A judgment creditor who has the first lien on real estate of his debtor worth nearly $30,000, has the right to subject the same to the payment of his judgment, though his debt contains no waiver of the homestead exemption, and the subsequent liens which are paramount to the homestead are in excess of the whole value of the land. If the debtor claims the homestead it may be set apart to him, and the judgment paid out of the residue, but, if necessary to pay subsequent liens which are paramount to the homestead, the land so set apart should be subjected. Strayer *v.* Long, 93 Va. 695, 26 S. E. 409.

Between Judgment and Deed of Trust Executed during Homestead.—After a homestead has been abandoned, a judgment lien attaching before the homestead was claimed in the land has priority over a trust deed executed during occupancy of the land as a homestead. Blose *v.* Bear, 87 Va. 177, 12 S. E. 294.

6. Between Judgments and Purchase Money Mortgages.

In General.—Judgments recovered against the vendor of land and docketed before his deed of conveyance to the purchaser is admitted to record, have priority over the notes given by such purchaser for deferred payments on the land, though such notes are secured by a deed of trust made contemporaneously with the deed of conveyance to him, and duly recorded before the recovery of such judgments. Jones *v.* Byrne, 94 Va. 751, 27 S. E. 591.

Illustrative Cases.—K. conveyed F., by deed, a house and lot, which deed was duly recorded on the 16th day of March, 1863, subsequent to the docketing of two judgments by a judgment creditor of K. F. afterwards sold the house and lot to H. At the request of F., H. executed two bonds in favor of M. for $1,000 of the money, and delivered them to M. who, in consideration thereof, surrendered to F. a bond held on F. by him (M.) and released the security thereon. M. obtained judgment on the bonds against H. H.

then filed a bill in equity against K. F. and M. enjoining the collection of the judgment, on the ground of judgment liens existing on the property. Held, that as to M. the bonds were good, and enforceable against H. Henning *v.* Fisher, 6 W. Va. 238.

A. became the purchaser of a tract of land, and executed his bonds for the deferred payments of the purchase money, with B. as surety, and to secure any sums which, as surety, he might be compelled to pay upon the said purchase money bonds, executed a deed of trust upon the land, which was duly recorded in the clerk's office. Subsequently to the execution and the recording of the deed of trust, A. became indebted to a number of persons, who obtained judgments against him, and then brought suit to subject his land to a lien of a judgment. A. then appears and alleges that B. had paid a part of the purchase money on the bonds, and that by virtue of the deed of trust securing him against loss as security on the purchase money bonds, B. had a lien prior and superior to the judgments of his creditors. It was held, that B. did not pay the money as surety for A. but as an advancement to his daughter, the wife of A., and the lien of the creditors is prior to the alleged payment. Bowman *v.* Reinhart, 89 Va. 435, 16 S. E. 279.

B. sold a tract of land to V. for $550, of which V. paid $250, and went into possession of the land, occupying it with his family. V. paid no more on the land, and left his family to maintain themselves, but returned home and remained at his pleasure. B., claiming that V. had relinquished his purchase, sold the land to I., the wife of V., for $306, she paying in cash $70 from her own means, and giving her notes for the residue of the purchase money. D., having a judgment against V., rendered on a debt existing at the time V. paid the $250 on the land, filed his bill to enforce his judgment against V.'s equitable interest in the land. Held, the balance of the purchase money unpaid and due to B. from L. is the first lien on the said land. Davis *v.* Vass, 47 W. Va. 811, 35 S. E. 826.

When the vendor by his deed "covenants with the vendee for general warranty of title, and that he is seized of the land conveyed in fee simple, and has good right and title to convey the same, and that the same shall not be subject to any liability from incumbrances now thereon," and there are recorded judgment liens on the land at the time of the conveyance, a court of equity will not enjoin or stay the collection of a judgment against the vendee for the purchase money of the land, unless the bill shows that the vendor has no other lands sufficient to satisfy such judgment liens, and that he is unable to pay them because of his pecuniary condition. Wamsley *v.* Stalnaker, 24 W. Va. 214.

If the owner of a tract of land executes a deed of trust, conveying his land to a trustee to secure certain debts, and afterwards a judgment is rendered against him, which is duly docketed, and he then makes a contract with a third party to advance for him the amount secured by the deed of trust, and, to secure such advance, mortgages this land to the person advancing the money for him, and such mortgagee pays off the debts secured by the deed of trust, it would be a complete satisfaction of these debts both in law and equity; the deed of trust becomes wholly inoperative, and the mortgagee can not be subrogated to the rights of the cestui que trust and have the deed of trust kept alive for his benefit, thus securing priority over the judgment debtor. Hoffman *v.* Ryan, 21 W. Va. 415.

Instantaneous Seisin. — See ante, "Property and Interests Subject to Lien," VI, G.

8 Va—28

The judgment creditor acquires no preference over the deed of trust, whether the latter be directly for the vendor's benefit or for the benefit of a lender of the money to pay the purchase money, or whether the trust be recorded or not, the latter and the conveyance being parts of one transaction. Cowardin *v.* Anderson, 78 Va. 88. See Summers *v.* Darne, 31 Gratt. 791.

In 1856, N. sold and conveyed for gold land to R. H. D. and J. W. D., who reconveyed same to secure purchase money. In 1866, R. H. D. was released, and the land was conveyed to J. W. D., who reconveyed it to secure the purchase money, which was expressly made payable in gold, or its equivalent. By decision of this court, in Summers *v.* Darne, 31 Gratt. 791, it became res judicata that this arrangement was no novation of the debt, and that N.'s lien was superior to the lien of judgments obtained against J. W. D., between the trust deed of 1856 and the trust deed of 1866. At the sale of the land under the second deed of trust, N. purchased it at a sum equal to the amount of his debt, including principal, interest and gold premiums. Held, N. is entitled to his lien for the gold premiums as well as for the principal and interest. Nutt *v.* Summers, 78 Va. 164.

7. Between Judgments and Vendor's Lien.

See the title VENDOR'S LIEN.

Where the vendor's lien is retained in a contract for the sale of land, though the contract is not recorded, the vendor's lien has priority to that of the judgment creditors of the vendee. Shipe *v.* Repass, 28 Gratt. 716.

An insolvent purchaser of property, who had paid a part of the price, and taken a deed to himself as trustee for his wife, in which a vendor's lien was reserved, not having recorded such deed, surrendered it, and caused another to be made by his vendor to a third person, who paid the remainder of the purchase money, as security for its repayment and for other indebtedness. Held, that, as against a judgment creditor of the purchaser, the grantee became subrogated to the vendor's lien to the extent of the payment advanced, but that, as to the remaining indebtedness secured, his lien was subject to that of the judgment. Kline v. Triplett, 2 Va. Dec. 429.

A vendor sells a tract of land, puts the vendee in possession, but retains the title to the whole tract to secure a part of the purchase money. This vendee then sells a portion of said tract to another on credit, puts him in possession, takes his bond for the purchase money, but having no title, attempts to make none. The first vendee then dies, and his vendor and another, qualify as his executors; the bond of the second vendee for the land purchased by him is assigned, with his knowledge, to one of the distributees of the estate of the first vendee (his vendor) by the executors, who, having paid the whole purchase money to the first vendor for the whole tract, then (November 11th, 1863), unite in a deed directly to the second vendee, for that portion of the land purchased by him, with knowledge of the outstanding unpaid bond. A judgment was obtained on this bond April 11th, 1866, and duly docketed April 20th, 1866, and in January, 1868, a bill was filed to subject the land, for which this judgment was, a portion of the purchase money, to its payment, asserting a vendor's lien thereon. On the 12th of June, 1866, the said second vendee conveyed his whole property to a trustee for the benefit of creditors named in the deed. At June rules, 1869, another bill was filed against the said second vendee, his trustee and others, by another judgment creditor of the second vendee to

enforce his judgment lien. On the 15th of September, 1869, a decree was rendered in the two suits which had been consolidated for an account of the liens and their priorities; and three days thereafter, another decree was rendered for the sale of the second vendee's real estate (no objection was made to the decree for sale before the report of liens and priorities was made). There were a large number of judgments of the same class with that of the 11th of April, 1866, for which a vendor's lien was claimed, amounting to more than the value of the whole real estate to be sold. The circuit court held, that the holder of the said judgment of the 11th of April, 1866, had no claim in equity to a vendor's lien for the amount of his judgment and dismissed his bill as to this claim. Held, this was erroneous. The conveyance by the first vendor, and as executor of the first vendee, to the second vendee of the land purchased by him, and the acceptance of the same by said second vendee, without the knowledge or assent of the holder of the bond given for part of the purchase money, and with the knowledge that this land was held as security for said bond, was a fraud on the rights of the holder of the judgment rendered on that bond, and neither the said second vendee nor his judgment creditors, who occupy no better position with reference to the same, than he, can claim any benefit from said conveyance; and the funds derived from the sale of the land for the price of which said judgment was obtained, must be first applied to the payment of that judgment, and this is not in conflict with the provisions of § 1, ch. 119, Va. Code, 1860, with reference to vendor's liens. Stovall v. Hardy, 1 Va. Dec. 342.

Is not the equitable vendor's lien paramount also to the liens of the judgment creditors of the vendor?

"The necessary conclusion from the views thus stated is, that this implied equitable lien for unpaid purchase money can not prevail against purchasers for value without notice, nor against liens of mortgages, trust or judgment creditors, but that it will be enforced only against the vendee, his heirs, purchasers with notice and the general or unsecured creditors of the vendor. This is all that is claimed by counsel for the appellant in this cause, and I think it is all that he is entitled to. Moore v. Holcomb, 3 Leigh 597. But as some members of this court are unwilling to decide definitely (as such decision is not asked and does not appear to be material in this cause, so far as the record before us disclosed), that this equitable lien is not paramount also to the liens or rights of judgment creditors of the vendor, that question is left undecided." Poe v. Paxton, 26 W. Va. 607, 608.

Vendor's Lien Reserved on Face of Conveyance.—A vendor's lien reserved on the face of the conveyance will have priority over a judgment against the grantee. Kline v. Triplett, 2 Va. Dec. 429.

Assignee of Vendor's Lien.—In 1867, on bond of M. and B. to P., assigned by P. to R., the latter obtained judgment, which was docketed in 1869. In 1866, M. granted his land to B., reserving lien for purchase money, and in 1870 assigned the purchase money bonds to G. for value without notice of the judgment. In contest for priority between R., as judgment creditor, and G., as assignee of the vendor's lien and of the bonds thereby secured, it was held, the lien of the judgment hath priority. Gordon v. Rixey, 76 Va. 694.

8. Between Judgments and Assignments for Creditors.

A deed of trust conveying land for the benefit of creditors, which is executed by the maker of the deed and the trustees and duly recorded, before a judgment is obtained against the maker, will intercept the lien of the judgment, although the creditors may not have given their assent to the deed until after the judgment. In such case even in a court of equity the equity of the judgment creditor will generally be considered inferior to the equity of the creditors claiming under the deed. Calwell v. Prindle, 19 W. Va. 604, 651.

A deed of trust by a bank for the benefit of creditors, conveying to the trustees all its property of every kind, wheresoever situated, will take priority over an execution lien, the judgment being obtained after the title of the trustees was perfected. The lien can only operate on what belongs to the bank, and after this conveyance the assets were no longer the property of the bank, but belonged to the trustee, who took as a purchaser for value. Harrison v. Farmers' Bank, 9 W. Va. 424.

9. Between Judgments and Dower.

Wife's right of dower, whether inchoate or consummate, is an existing lien, and a covenant against incumbrances is broken by its existence. This lien is inferior to all which attached prior to the marriage, but superior to those acquired after marriage without her consent. Ficklin v. Rixey, 89 Va. 832, 17 S. E. 325.

Judgments against a man before marriage are paramount to the claim of his widow to dower. Offield v. Davis, 100 Va. 250, 40 S. E. 910.

Where the owner of a tract of land has allowed the same to be incumbered by deeds of trust and judgment liens, and while it is in that condition he intermarries, and then he and his wife make a conveyance of the land to a third party, in which she did not effectively join, being then an infant, who, out of the purchase money, pays off and discharges said liens in order to relieve the property therefrom, he is entitled to be subrogated to the rights of the parties holding said liens, and such liens are paramount to said wife's right of dower on the decease of her husband. Blair *v.* Mounts, 41 W. Va. 706, 24 S. E. 620.

10. Between Judgments and Tax Lien. See the title TAXATION.

"It is well established that the tax lien has priority, and that a tax sale is made clear of prior encumbrances. Simmons *v.* Lyles, 32 Gratt. 752; Com. *v.* Ashlin, 95 Va. 145, 28 S. E. 177; Thomas *v.* Jones, 94 Va. 756, 27 S. E. 813. These cases hold that the tax is superior in dignity to judgment liens, and to the vendor's lien. There is no distinction in principle between the cases, for the same reason that the tax is held to be superior in dignity to a judgment lien and a vendor's lien; it must be paramount to a deed of trust lien. Indeed, it is said in Thomas *v.* Jones, 94 Va. 756, that taxes are prior in dignity to all other liens; must be so from the very necessity of the case, otherwise the state would be powerless to collect her revenue." Stevenson *v.* Henkle, 100 Va. 591, 598, 42 S. E. 672.

Taxes on real estate, though assessed against a vendee subsequent to his purchase, have priority over the vendor's lien for purchase money. The provision of § 661 of the Code that "the right or title to such estate shall stand vested in the grantee in such deed as it was vested in the party assessed with the taxes or levies on account whereof the sale was made" refers to the character of the title which shall be vested in the grantee, whether it be a fee simple, or otherwise. The purchaser does not take it subject to the liens resting thereon at the time the taxes were assessed. Thomas *v.* Jones, 94 Va. 756, 27 S. E. 813.

"The second inquiry involves the order of priority between the tax lien and the vendor's lien. This court has held, in Simmons *v.* Lyle, 32 Gratt. 752, that taxes are a prior lien to judgments obtained and duly docketed long prior to the date at which the taxes were assessed. There is no distinction, in principle, between the two cases; for the same reason that the tax is held to be prior in dignity to the judgment lien, it must be preferred to the vendor's lien. That taxes are prior in dignity to all other liens must be so from the very necessity of the case, otherwise the state would be powerless to collect her revenue. The liens upon the land would, as in the case at bar, often be greater than the value of the land, and the tax lien being inferior, the land would escape all taxation. The provision in § 661 of the Code, that 'the right or title to such estate shall stand vested in the grantee in such deed as it was vested in the party assessed with the taxes or levies on account whereof the sale was made,' refers to the character of the title that shall be vested in the grantee in such deed, whether it be a fee simple or otherwise. It has no reference to liens, and does not mean, as contended, that the purchaser takes the land subject to the liens resting thereon at the time the taxes are assessed." Thomas *v.* Jones. 94 Va. 756, 758, 27 S. E. 813. This was approved in Com. *v.* Ashlin, 95 Va. 145, 149, 28 S. E. 177.

The lien of the commonwealth on land for taxes assessed thereon after the death of the owner is superior and paramount to the right of creditors of the decedent to subject the land to the payment of their debts. Where this lien has been perfected by a sale of the land for delinquent taxes and a purchase thereof by the commonwealth, she stands as a purchaser for value. If she offers to relinquish her title only upon payment of the taxes justly due, creditors of the decedent can not complain. While the real estate of a decedent is assets for the payment of his debts, that fact alone does not give a lien on his real estate for the payment of such debts, nor does a judgment against the personal representative of the decedent constitute such lien. Com. *v.* Ashlin, 95 Va. 145, 28 S. E. 177, following Simmons *v.* Lyles, 32 Gratt. 752; Thomas *v.* Jones, 94 Va. 756, 27 S. E. 813.

11. Between Judgments and Mechanic's Lien.

See the title MECHANICS' LIENS.

The effect of § 2483 of the Code is to modify the registry law as contained in § 2465 so far as to give priority to a mechanic's lien on the lands of the grantee, who has failed to record his deed, over judgenmts subsequently obtained against his grantor. Pace *v.* Moorman, 99 Va. 246, 37 S. E. 911.

If the owner of the full equitable estate in land causes buildings to be erected thereon, for the cost of which a mechanic records a lien, such lien, by the terms of § 2483 of the Virginia Code, takes priority, as to both land and buildings, over all liens thereafter acquired on the lands of such owner, and also over all judgments thereafter recovered against the grantor of such owner holding the mere legal title to the land. If the mechanic's lien has been enforced by sale of the property, the purchaser has the right to stand in the shoes of the mechanic before the sale. Pace *v.* Moorman, 99 Va. 246, 37 S. E. 911.

12. Debts of Decedents.

See the title EXECUTORS AND ADMINISTRATORS, vol. 5, p. 572.

The judgment obtained during the life of an intestate is a lien upon the lands in the hands of his heirs for the payment thereof, and is entitled to priority of payment out of the pro-ceeds of the sale thereof over a simple contract creditor, who acquired no equal or superior lien for his debt upon the realty during the life of the debtor. Laidley *v.* Kline, 8 W. Va. 218.

There is no priority given by statute, Code, 1860, ch. 130, § 25, p. 598, to a debt due as administrator, over a lien created by judgment in the lifetime of the judgment debtor, who is also the administrator. Alderson *v.* Henderson, 5 W. Va. 182.

13. Claims of United States.

See the title UNITED STATES.

Quære, whether the United States have any priority over an individual creditor for satisfaction out of the lands of a deceased debtor; and if not, whether the United States, having got the first decree in the federal court, or the individual creditor who brought suit first in the state court, shall have preference; or whether the real assets should be rateably distributed? King *v.* Ashley, 5 Leigh 408.

14. Doctrine of Relation.

See ante, "Commencement and Duration of Lien," VI, F.

The statute is only declaratory of the common law, so far as the judgment lien on real estate is concerned, but it does not change the rule of the common law as laid down in § 441, Black, Judgm.: "It was the rule of the common law (and this rule still obtains in some of the states) that the judgments of a court of record all relate back to the first day of the term, and are considered as rendered on that day; and therefore their lien will attach to the debtor's realty from the beginning of the term, and will override a conveyance or mortgage made on the second or any succeeding day, although actually prior to the rendition of the judgment. This general principle of the common law, like many others, is of such remote antiquity, and so long recognized without dispute that the reasons and policy on which it was founded are in a great decree left to conjecture." This rule has always been recognized in Virginia in cases matured for a term and ready for judgment on the first day of the term and is so recognized in this state. Smith *v.* Parkersburg Co-Op. Ass'n, 48 W. Va. 232, 37 S. E. 645, 652.

The rule that a judgment lien relates to the first day of a term, applies to a judgment on an attachment, and is not confined to realty, and such judgment will thereby override an assignment to an assignee for the benefit of creditors. Smith *v.* Parkersburg Co-Op. Ass'n, 48 W. Va. 232, 37 S. E. 645.

As between Judgments and Deeds of Trust.—A decree rendered or judgment confessed in vacation operated as a lien upon the first moment of the day on which the decree was rendered or judgment confessed regardless of the time of the day at which it is actually rendered or confessed, and took precedence over the deed of trust admitted to record during the same day, though in point of fact the deed of trust may have been recorded before the decree was rendered, or the judgment confessed. The law takes no notice of the fraction of the day as to the decree, while the deed, as against subsequent purchasers for value and without notice, and creditors, is only operative from the time it is admitted to record. Hockman *v.* Hockman, 93 Va. 455, 25 S. E. 534.

But this has been changed by statute in Virginia. Va. Code, 1904, § 3567.

It seems that even prior to the statute in Virginia, a judgment would not be considered as relating to the first day of a term for the purpose of giving it priority over a conveyance to a purchaser for valuable consideration without notice. Skipwith *v.* Cunningham, 8 Leigh 272; Withers *v.* Carter,

4 Gratt. 407; Brockenbrough *v.* Brockenbrough, 31 Gratt. 580.

I. AMOUNT OF LIEN.

In General.—One who purchases land subject to a judgment lien is not affected by a subsequent judgment against the same land for an amount in excess of such lien to which he was not a formal party and in which the true amount of the first judgment lien was not litigated, and he may satisfy such lien by the payment of the amount called for by the judgment under which he purchased. Bensimer *v.* Fell, 35 W. Va. 15, 12 S. E. 1078.

A purchaser of land which is subject to the lien of a judgment takes it subject only to the amount called for by the judgment, and it is not liable to the judgment increased by usury under a subsequent agreement between the creditor and judgment debtor. Bensimer *v.* Fell, 35 W. Va. 15, 12 S. E. 1078, 29 Am. St. Rep. 774.

Penalty of Bond.—A judgment being rendered for the penalty of a bond, to be discharged by the payment of the principal sum due and interest; and the payment of the money having been delayed by an injunction until the principal sum due and the interest exceed the penalty, the lien of the judgment only extends to the penalty, the damages upon the dissolution of the injunction, and the costs at law, without continuing interest. Michaux *v.* Brown, 10 Gratt. 612.

Interest on Judgment.—If the judgment does not carry interest on its face, it can only be recovered by action or suit upon the judgment; it is not a part of the judgment and of course can not be recovered by execution thereon, nor does the lien of this judgment extend to it. Tazewell *v.* Saunders, 13 Gratt. 353, 368, citing Mercer *v.* Beale, 4 Leigh 189; Michaux *v.* Brown, 10 Gratt. 612; Mower *v.* Kip, 6 Paige's R. 88.

Costs and Damages in Appellate Court.—The lien is not only for the damages, interest and costs recovered by the original judgment, but also for the damages and costs to which the creditor became entitled by the judgment of affirmance. McClung v. Beirne, 10 Leigh 394, cited with approval in McCance v. Taylor, 10 Gratt. 580, 588; Michaux v. Brown, 10 Gratt. 612, 621, and distinguished and explained in Bailey v. McCormick, 22 W. Va. 95, 102.

Damages on Dissolution of Injunction to Judgment.—The damages on the dissolution of an injunction become, as to the party obtaining it, a part of the judgment; and are embraced in the lien of the judgment upon the equity of redemption. Michaux v. Brown, 10 Gratt. 612.

Lien of Creditors Suing to Set Aside Fraudulent Conveyance.—A creditor at large, successfully suing to set aside a deed conveying property in fraud of creditors, has a lien on the property from time of suit brought; and a creditor, who comes into the suit, shall have a like lien from the filing of his petition. Such lien is a lien only upon the property conveyed, and not, like the lien of a judgment, on all of debtor's estate. Davis v. Bonney, 89 Va. 755, 17 S. E. 229.

Accordingly, it was held in Frayser v. Richmond, etc., R. Co., 81 Va. 388, that the lien of the execution there in question extended to certain moneys of the judgment debtor, under the control of the court, after receivers had been appointed. It is true the receivers had not qualified when the execution went into the officer's hands to be executed; but that was an immaterial circumstance, so far as the extent of the lien was concerned, as the qualification of a receiver does not affect the control of the court over the property which goes into his possession, he being merely the hand of the court. In other words, the receiver's possession is the possession of the court appointing him. Beverley v. Brooke, 4 Gratt. 187; Harman v. McMullin, 85 Va. 187; Davis v. Bonney, 89 Va. 755, 760, 17 S. E. 229.

Former Rule.

Lien on Moiety.

In General.—The writ of elegit enabled the creditor to subject to the satisfaction of the judgment only a moiety of his debtor's lands. Price v. Planters' Nat. Bank, 92 Va. 468, 23 S. E. 887; Hutcheson v. Grubbs, 80 Va. 251, 254; Borst v. Nalle, 28 Gratt. 423; Calwell v. Prindle, 19 W. Va. 604; Renick v. Ludington, 14 W. Va. 367; Leake v. Ferguson, 2 Gratt. 419.

"It was decided in Haleys v. Williams, 1 Leigh 140, that a judgment is a lien on the whole of the debtor's equitable estate; and the whole fund and not a moiety is to be applied to the judgment. In that case the legal title was in a trustee for the security of a debt having priority to the judgments. Green, Judge (whose opinion in this respect was concurred in by the other judges, as a decree was entered conforming to it), stated that a court of equity, upon the principle that equity follows the law, would, if it were practicable, subject only a moiety; but that was impracticable; as equity could only enable the creditor to reach the equity of redemption by allowing him to redeem; which can not be done with a proper regard to the rights of the mortgagee, without requiring him to redeem in toto, and not for a moiety only; and when redeemed, the judgment creditor has a right to stand in the shoes of the mortgagee, and to tack his judgment. The debtor would not ask to redeem without paying the judgment, as well as the mortgage debt, upon the principle that he who asks must do equity. But where the legal estate is in the debtor at the date of the judgment, the creditor can only subject a moiety; and a subsequent all'enation by the debtor can not enlarge his rights. Even where the alienation is fraudulent, equity merely removes the fraudulent conveyance out of his way. Stilman v. Ashdown, 2 Atk. R. 477; Ibid. 607; McNew v. Smith, 5 Gratt. 84." Buchanan v. Clark, 10 Gratt. 164.

If there be two decrees on the same day against a defendant's land, the whole, and not a moiety only of the land, ought to be directed to be sold; for, at law, each of two judgments would have taken a moiety of the land, and both of course the whole, if it had been extendible at law. Coleman v. Cocke, 6 Rand. 618.

Legal Estates.—"Where the legal estate is in the debtor at the date of the judgment, the creditor can only subject a moiety; and a subsequent alienation by the debtor can not enlarge his rights." Buchanan v. Clark, 10 Gratt. 164; Mutual Assurance Society v. Stanard, 4 Munf. 539; Blow v. Maynard, 2 Leigh 29, 37; Haleys v. Williams, 1 Leigh 140, distinguished and explained.

Where a fieri facias has been issued upon a judgment within a year and a day, the judgment is a lien upon a moiety of all the land owned by the debtor at the date of the judgment, or which were afterwards acquired, in the hands of a bona fide purchaser for value, and without notice. Taylor v. Spindle, 2 Gratt. 44. See Kent v. Matthews, 12 Leigh 573.

If a debtor conveys land fraudulently and retains other lands, on setting aside the conveyance at the suit of a judgment creditor, there will be a decree for the sale of only one moiety of the whole, embracing in the moiety the land retained by the debtor. McNew v. Smith, 5 Gratt. 84.

But upon setting aside a conveyance of real estate as fraudulent, at the suit of a judgment creditor the court can not decree a sale of only one moiety of the lands to satisfy the judgment. McNew v. Smith, 5 Gratt. 84.

Judgment in Favor of Commonwealth.—It was held, in Leake v. Ferguson, 2 Gratt. 419, that prior to the act of 1822, Sup. Rev. Code, ch. 282, § 1, p. 339, the judgment in favor of the commonwealth against his generals debtors, only bound one-half the land of the debtor.

Equitable Estates.—In equity, judgments are liens on the whole of the debtor's equitable estate in lands; so that not a moiety only but the whole fund is first to be applied to satisfy the elder judgment, and not a moiety only but the whole of the residue is then to be applied to satisfy the younger judgment. Haleys v. Williams, 1 Leigh 140.

Present Rule.—But the statutes now expressly provide that the judgment shall be a lien on all the debtor's real estate. Va. Code, 1904, § 3567; W. Va. Code, 1899, ch. 139, § 4145.

As against Creditor or Purchaser.—Chapter 186 of the Code of Virginia of 1860 provides: A judgment rendered before the commencement of this act shall as against a purchaser or creditor, claiming under a deed made or judgment obtained before the day of such commencement, or as against the heirs or devisees of a person dying before that day, affect no more of such real estate, than would have been liable thereto under the laws in force on the day before this chapter takes effect. Calwell v. Prindle, 19 W. Va. 604, 655.

And the present Va. Code provides that a judgment rendered before the first day of July, eighteen hundred and fifty, shall, as against a purchaser or creditor, claiming under a deed made or judgment obtained, or as against the heirs or devisees of a person dying, before that day, affect no more of such real estate than would have been liable thereto under the laws in force on the day before the first day of July, eighteen hundred and fifty. (Code, 1849, p. 709, ch. 186, § 7.) Va. Code, 1904, § 3569. McCance *v.* Taylor, 10 Gratt. 580.

Amount as Affecting Right to Enforce.—The Virginia Code provides: If the amount of the judgment does not exceed twenty dollars, exclusive of interest and costs, no bill to enforce the lien thereof shall be entertained, unless it appear that sixty days before the institution of the suit, the judgment debtor or his personal representative, and the owner of the real estate on which the judgment is a lien, or, in case of a nonresident, his agent or attorney (if he have one in this state), had notice that the suit would be instituted, if the judgment was not paid within that time. (1877-78, p. 68.) Va. Code, 1904, § 3572.

J. SUSPENSION OR DISCHARGE OF LIEN.

1. By Act of Legislature.

A judgment is such a vested right of property that the legislature can not, by a retroactive law, either destroy or diminish its value. It can not alter its amount or destroy the effect theretofore given to it as a lien on real estate. The right to the lien upon the debtor's real estate is, in many cases, the sole inducement to the credit, which constitutes the basis of the judgment. Without the benefit of that lien, guaranteed by the law at the time the judgment is taken, the credit would not have been given. Merchants' Bank *v.* Ballou, 98 Va. 112, 32 S. E. 481.

2. By Act of Debtor.

a. In General.

When a judgment creditor has obtained his judgment and caused it to be docketed, his lien is perfect and complete, and can not be defeated or impaired by any act of his debtor in which he did not participate. Strayer *v.* Long, 93 Va. 695, 26 S. E. 409.

b. Sale of Property Subject to Lien.

Where a party has a judgment lien upon land, and is proceeding by suit in equity to subject such land to the satisfaction of said judgment, the judgment debtor can not, by severing the timber trees growing on said land, and selling same to a codefendant, who has full notice of the pendency of said suit and its object, defeat or displace the lien of said judgment creditor. Goff *v.* McLain, 48 W. Va. 445, 37 S. E. 566.

3. Cancellation of the Security.

A judgment becomes a lien on property conveyed to the judgment debtor as a trustee for his wife, where the husband, who was insolvent, paid the consideration, and such is not divested by a return and cancellation of the deed unrecorded. Kline *v.* Triplett, 2 Va. Dec. 429.

4. Recovery of Another Judgment.

The lien of a judgment shall not be impaired by the recovery of another judgment thereon. Va. Code, 1904, § 3574.

5. By Execution.

See the title EXECUTIONS, vol. 5, p. 465.

a. In General.

The return or destruction of the execution does not destroy the lien of the judgment, unless there has been really a satisfaction of the execution or judgment, or unless it is shown that a purchaser was deceived or mislead by such return of the execution. Renick *v.* Ludington, 20 W. Va. 511, 551.

A mere levy of an execution is not a satisfaction of a judgment. Rhea *v.* Preston, 75 Va. 757, 772.

At the March term 1861, of the county court of Monroe, a judgment was rendered at the suit of the bank of V., plaintiff, against W., S. and C., the latter living in the county of Bath. Execution of fi. fa. was issued on this judgment and levied on the property of W., and the sheriff returned, after June, 1861, a levy upon the personal property of W., that the property was appraised and offered for sale, and not bringing valuation it was returned. G. died during the war, leaving real estate in Bath county, and also in West Virginia; and after his death some of his creditors filed their bill in the circuit court of Bath, to subject his real estate to the payment of his debts. The commissioner reported the above judgment as a debt by judgment having priority. A copy of the judgment was certified by the clerk of Monroe circuit court, "and as such, keeper of the records of Monroe county court, and which by law are a part of the records of my office." The circuit court confirmed the report. Held, that the lien was not discharged by the levy of the execution upon the property of W., one of the debtors, by the sheriff of Monroe county; nor was the execution satisfied by the act of the sheriff, returning the property so levied on to W., in obedience to the ordinance of the Virginia convention of 1861, whether such ordinance was valid or not; said act of the sheriff being entirely his own act, neither prompted nor assisted by the plaintiff in the judgment. Gatewood v. Goode, 23 Gratt. 880.

Indorsement on an Execution.—It was held, in Saunders v. Prunty, 89 Va. 921, 17 S. E. 231, where an execution issued on a judgment was indorsed levied, April 14, 1861, on a negro named Wyatt, and was returnable on the first Monday in May following, that there was no prima facie presumption that the judgment was satisfied by such levy as the stay law was passed on the 30th of April, 1861, which fully accounts for no sale having been made, and a succession of stay laws prevented the sale of the slave, until the property was destroyed by emancipation. See also, Shannon v. McMul-lin, 25 Gratt. 211; Hamilton v. McConkey, 83 Va. 533, 5 S. E. 724.

Presumption of Satisfaction.—With the report of a commissioner was returned an execution endorsed to the effect that on April 14th, 1861, a fi. fa. had been levied on one slave, the property of defendant, and held up by order of plaintiff. On April 30th, 1861, the stay law was enacted, and continued in force until emancipation. Held, it is not to be presumed from the levy that the judgment was satisfied. Saunders v. Prunty, 89 Va. 921, 17 S. E. 231.

b. Forthcoming Bond.

See the title FORTHCOMING AND DELIVERY BONDS, vol. 6, p. 411.

The lien of a judgment shall not be impaired by a forthcoming bond taken on an execution thereon, such bond having the force of a judgment. Va. Code, 1904, § 3474; Cooper v. Daugherty, 85 Va. 343, 7 S. E. 387.

"Until a delivery bond shall have been forfeited, I presume it would not be considered as a discharge of the original judgment, or even as changing its character." Cooke v. Piles, 2 Munf. 151; Rhea v. Preston, 75 Va. 757.

In Lusk v. Ramsay, 3 Munf. 417, 454, Judge Roane said he entirely concurred in the opinion of Judge Cabell in Cook v. Piles, 2 Munf. 151, that a forthcoming bond is no satisfaction of a judgment until the forfeiture; and Judge Roane further expressed the opinion that, until such satisfaction has taken place, the lien created under the judgment is not extinguished.

The taking of a forthcoming bond on a judgment and execution against the obligor of an assignment bond, is not such a satisfaction of the judgment, as will preclude the assignees from having recourse against the assignors. Smith v. Triplett, 4 Leigh 590, cited in Garland v. Lynch, 1 Rob. 545, 565.

Faulty Forthcoming Bond.—A faulty forthcoming bond, whilst in force, is a satisfaction of the judgment, and a second execution can not issue until it is quashed. Downman *v.* Chinn, 2 Wash. 189; Rhea *v.* Preston, 75 Va. 757.

Where judgment is obtained against a principal and surety to a bond, and the latter gives a forthcoming bond, which is forfeited, the original judgment is not thereby satisfied, although any further proceedings on it will be barred, until the forthcoming bond shall be quashed. Randolph *v.* Randolph, 3 Rand. 490; Rhea *v.* Preston, 75 Va. 757.

Fi. Fa. Returned "No Property."—Where a fi. fa. issued on a judgment based on a forthcoming bond has been returned "no property," equity will regard the bond as a nullity, and the original judgment as in full force. Cooper *v.* Daugherty, 85 Va. 343, 7 S. E. 387. The court in this case said: "And in Rhea *v.* Preston, 75 Va. 757, it is said by this court: 'When the obligors in a forthcoming bond, which has been forfeited and returned, though solvent when the bond was taken, become insolvent afterwards, the plaintiff may have the bond quashed, and be restored to his original judgment. And though the bond be not quashed, a court of equity will regard it as a nullity, and the original judgment in full force.' Jones *v.* Myrick, 8 Gratt. 179, 211; Leake *v.* Ferguson, 2 Gratt. 419, 432; Robinson *v.* Sherman, 2 Gratt. 178; Garland *v.* Lynch, 1 Rob. 545; Powell *v.* White, 11 Leigh 309."

6. Failure to Docket.

"Section 5, therefore, gives to the judgment creditor a positive express lien, on all the real estate, of which the debtor at the time was possessed, or to which he was entitled; which lien by the terms of the statute must continue, until it is in some way actually discharged. Can it be, that it is discharged or lost, by the failure of the creditor to docket it? The docketing of the judgment does not preserve the lien nor does the failure to docket discharge the lien, as to any lands, the title to which remained in the judgment debtor, because under 5th section the lien is created and must continue, unless in some way lost. The docketing of the judgment as we have seen, does not create the lien, nor can the failure to docket, as between the judgment creditor and debtor, discharge the lien. It is only where the right of a purchaser for valuable consideration without notice of the judgment intervenes, that the docketing of the judgment can have any effect upon the lien. What effect does it have? As to so much of the land, and so much only, as has been conveyed to such purchaser, the liens of judgment creditors are affected." Renick *v.* Ludington, 14 W. Va. 367, 376.

7. Death of Judgment Debtor.

A judgment obtained during the life of an intestate is a lien upon his lands in the hands of his heirs for the payment thereof, and is entitled to priority of payment out of the proceeds of the sale thereof over a simple contract creditor, who acquired no equal or superior lien for his debt upon the realty during the life of the debtor. Laidley *v.* Kline, 8 W. Va. 218, followed in Maxwell *v.* Leeson, 50 W. Va. 361, 366, 40 S. E. 420.

"The law also provided the more comprehensive writ of ca. sa., which extended to all the lands of the defendant, and by the levy of which the creditor acquired an inchoate lien, which became consummate upon the defendant's taking the oath of insolvency. If the latter died in execution, the lien was lost. Stuart *v.* Hamilton, 8 Leigh 503." Hutcheson *v.* Grubbs, 80 Va. 251, 255.

8. Agreement between Parties.

A judgment is recovered and an execution issued thereon, and while it is in the hands of the sheriff, an agreement is made between the creditor and debtor, by which certain claims are transferred to the creditor in satisfaction of the judgment, and thereupon the sheriff, at the instance of the creditor, returns the execution "satisfied," but it appears, that the agreement on the part of the debtor was fraudulent and the execution was not in fact satisfied; the lien of the judgment is not destroyed, and the position and priority is not disturbed, although its payment may affect purchasers of part of the land of the debtor, but it does not appear in the pleadings and proofs, that such return was brought home to the purchaser, and by it he was misled to his injury. Renick v. Ludington, 14 W. Va. 367.

Breach of Agreement—Remedy.—In a case where, by virtue of an agreement between a judgment debtor and a judgment creditor, the judgment ought to be entered as satisfied, but in lieu thereof the creditor has an execution issued and levied upon the goods of the debtor, the latter can not obtain relief by injunction in a court of equity, for the reason that he has a complete and adequate remedy at law. Should the court, in such a case, after having granted an injunction, dissolve the same at a final hearing, it ought not to enter a personal decree against the plaintiff for the amount of the original judgment enjoined, but should simply dissolve the injunction, and dismiss the bill, with costs, and without prejudice to the plaintiff as to his defense at law against the enforcement of the execution. Howell v. Thomason, 34 W. Va. 794, 12 S. E. 1088.

9. Waiver or Release.

By an executory contract between A. and B., the former bound himself to convey to the latter, upon the payment of the purchase money, certain real estate. Subsequently B. conveyed said real estate to C., reserving in the deed a lien to indemnify A. against certain judgments, which B. was then primarily bound to pay; afterwards A. conveyed the legal title to said real estate to B., reserving a lien in the deed for his indemnity against said judgments; the legal title is never conveyed to C. In a suit by A. to subject the said real estate to the payment of the amount he was compelled to pay to satisfy said judgments, held, A. was entitled to subject said real estate in the hands of C. to such payment. A.'s right to do so was not lost or impaired by the fact that after B. had conveyed to C. he released B. from all liability for said judgments, nor because at the time he instituted his suit said judgments had become barred by the statute of limitations, the lien of A. depending upon the instrument reserving it, and not upon said judgments. Morehead v. Horner, 30 W. Va. 548, 4 S. E. 448.

Release of Surety.—A recovered judgment against B and C, his surety, and issued execution, which was levied on the property of B. A, on receiving a part payment of the judgment, gave B further time for the payment of the balance, and ordered the property to be released to B. It was held that in consequence the judgment was discharged at law, and the surety, not having assented to, or acquiesced in the agreement, was discharged in equity, and could have an injunction against a second execution. Baird v. Rice, 1 Call 18, 1 Am. Dec. 497.

Effect of Release or Waiver of Lien on One Parcel.—A judgment creditor having, by his contract, waived or lost his right to subject the land first liable to satisfy his judgments, is not entitled to subject the lands next liable for the whole amount of his judgment but only for the balance after crediting thereon the value of the land first liable. Jones *v.* Myrick, 8 Gratt. 179.

Release of Lands Aliened by Debtor.—The lands aliened by the debtor constitute a secondary fund for the payment of the judgment, and neither a release of these lands, nor the failure to subject certain notes for unpaid purchase money on land is prejudicial to subsequent judgment creditors who obtained their judgments after the alienation, but before the release by the first judgment creditor. Blakemore *v.* Wise, 95 Va. 269, 28 S. E. 332.

Effect of Release, by Prior Party of Property Subject to Second Deed.—If a prior judgment lienor releases the property subject to a second deed of trust, the proceeds of which are amply sufficient to satisfy his judgment lien, he can not enforce payment of such judgment lien out of the property subject to a first deed of trust until such latter trust is fully satisfied. First Nat. Bank *v.* Simms, 49 W. Va. 442, 38 S. E. 525.

10. Reversal of Judgment.

It is familiar doctrine, that where a decree is reversed in part and affirmed as to the residue, the reversal in part does not destroy the lien of so much of the decree as is unreversed or affirmed; and one prominent reason for this is, that equity looks to the substance of things, and not to the mere form. 2 Barton's Chy., § 295; Knifong *v.* Hendricks, 2 Gratt. 212; Moss *v.* Moorman, 24 Gratt. 97. Shepherd *v.* Chapman, 83 Va. 215, 224, 2 S. E. 273.

But the rule does not apply to a reversal of judgment and award of a new trial. Shepherd *v.* Chapman, 83 Va. 215, 2 S. E. 273.

"In Chapman *v.* Shepherd, 24 Gratt. 377, this court reversed the decree of the circuit court so far only as it allowed compound interest on the amount due from Chapman's estate, from October 7, 1851, instead of from August 4, 1853, and affirmed it in all other respects. Held, such reversal did not affect the lien of the decree so far as it was affirmed." Shepherd *v.* Chapman, 83 Va. 215, 2 S. E. 273.

11. Arrest on Capias Ad Satisfaciendum.

See the title EXECUTIONS AGAINST THE BODY AND ARREST IN CIVIL CASES, vol. 5, p. 474.

It has undoubtedly been established, by a series of decisions, that where a defendant in execution under a ca. sa. has been discharged from his imprisonment by the direction or with the consent of the plaintiff, no action will ever again lie on the judgment on which the execution is founded, the judgment being considered as satisfied. Nor can any new execution ever issue on that judgment, even though the defendant was discharged on an express understanding on his part, that he should be liable again to be taken in execution, on his failure to comply with the terms on which the discharge took place. Noyes *v.* Cooper, 5 Leigh 186, citing Windrum *v.* Parker, 2 Leigh 361.

If a debtor be arrested on a ca. sa. and discharged by order of the creditor or his agent, no other execution can be had on the same judgment or decree. Windrum *v.* Parker, 2 Leigh 361.

Joint Judgment—Effect of Service of Ca. Sa. on One.—It was held, in Leake *v.* Ferguson, 2 Gratt. 419, that on a joint judgment against several, the service of ca. sa. on one, and the execution and forfeiture of a forthcoming bond by him, did not extinguish the lien of the judgment upon the land of the others.

In Leake *v.* Ferguson, 2 Gratt. 419, 432, it is said, the creditor here resorted to the ca. sa., and after taking out the ca. sa. and having it executed he can no longer stand on the lien of the judgment. Citing Rogers *v.* Marshall, 4 Leigh 425. This is certainly true, under the decisions of this court so far as respects the creditor, and with respect to debtor on whom the ca. sa. is executed. Yet the services of the ca. sa. is not an actual discharge of the judgment. Also, in Werdenbaugh v. Reid, 20 W. Va. 588, 592, it is said, the writ of ca. sa. was by statute expressly made a lien on all the real and personal estate of the debtor from the time it was levied. But this lien, while express, conferred upon the creditor an inchoate right until the debtor took the oath of insolvency; if he died in jail, the security of the creditor was lost. Citing Stuart v. Hamilton, 8 Leigh 503, 507; Rogers v. Marshall, 4 Leigh 425.

In such a case, the party upon whom the ca. sa. was served, and who executed the forthcoming bond, having been a surety of the principal debtor in the judgment, his surety in the forthcoming bond having paid the debt, is entitled to be substituted to the creditor's remedies against the land of the principal debtor; and this, though the land was sold by the principal debtor, and had come into the hands of a bona fide purchaser for value without notice, before the service of the ca. sa. Leake v. Ferguson, 2 Gratt. 419.

Land, conveyed by deed of trust, which is void as to subsequent judgment creditors, because unrecorded, is subject to satisfy the judgments of a creditor, although he has issued a ca. sa. upon his judgment, whereupon the grantor in the deed is discharged as an insolvent. McClure v. Thistle, 2 Gratt. 182.

Effect on Lien of Discharge of Debtor Taken under Ca. Sa.—A judgment creditor, whose debtor, after being taken in execution, has been discharged from custody by the jailer, for nonpayment of the jail fees, is remitted to the lien of his judgment, and will be entitled to satisfaction out of the debtor's land, in preference to creditors claiming under a deed of trust executed by the debtor, conveying the land, but not recorded in the county where it lies. McCullough v. Sommerville, 8 Leigh 415.

Priority.—A debtor is taken in execution under a ca. sa. while in custody, the commonwealth obtains a judgment against him, and sues out a fi. fa., under which his lands are sold; and then the debtor takes the oath of insolvency, and is discharged from custody under H.'s ca. sa. The lien of H.'s ca. sa. executed, given by the statute (1 Rev. Code, 1819, page 528, § 10), does not take priority over the lien of the commonwealth's judgment. Foreman v. Loyd (1830), 2 Leigh 284. This case expressly overrules a contrary doctrine in Jackson v. Heiskell (1829), 1 Leigh 257, which, however, was decided by a court of three judges, one of whom, Judge Cabell, thought the point ought to be argued before a full court, and reserved the right to reconsider the question whenever the question arose again.

A. recovers a judgment against B. at August term, and sues out a ca. sa. thereon in October, under which B. is taken in execution, and in November takes the oath of insolvency, and is discharged, under the statute for the relief of insolvent debtors; in the interval between the date of A.'s judgment and the service of his ca. sa. on B. sundry mortgages are executed by B. and duly recorded, to secure sundry debts to other creditors. Held, that by the actual service of A.'s ca. sa. on B. the lien of A.'s judgment was destroyed, and A. could then stand only on the lien given to the ca. sa. executed by the statute of executions, 1 Rev. Code, ch. 134, § 10, and that, therefore, the mortgagees are entitled to the benefit of their mortgages. Rogers v. Marshall, 4 Leigh 425. See also, the unreported case of Fox v.

Rootes, 4 Leigh 429, referred to by the court in Rogers v. Marshall, and reported in a note to that case.

12. Discharge of Debtor in Bankruptcy.

As to the effect of bankruptcy proceedings, on judgment liens, see the title BANKRUPTCY AND INSOLVENCY, vol. 1, pp. 232, 234, 247.

The lien of a judgment is not defeated by the discharge of the debtor as a bankrupt; it may be enforced in the state courts. McCance v. Taylor, 10 Gratt. 580.

In such case the elegit sued out upon the judgment may be in the usual form; and in executing it the sheriff must take notice of the bankruptcy of the debtor, and disregarding all property of the debtor not subject to the lien, levy it upon that which is so subject. McCance v. Taylor, 10 Gratt. 580. See, citing McCance v. Taylor, 10 Gratt. 580; Beall v. Walker, 26 W. Va. 741, 745.

"The first link in the chain of Taylor's title is his judgment against Green; this gave Taylor a lien on the real estate whereof Green was seized at the date of the judgment. It is objected that this judgment and of consequence the lien, its incident, ceased to exist by operation of Green's discharge as a bankrupt under the act of congress approved 19th of August, 1841, entitled an act to establish a uniform system of bankruptcy throughout the United States. In reply to this objection it may be said, that the lien in question is preserved by the express terms of the last proviso in § 2. That proviso, so far as applicable to our case, is in these words, 'that nothing in this act contained shall be construed to annul, destroy or impair any liens, mortgages or other securities on property, real or personal, which may be valid by the laws of the states respectively, and which are not incon-sistent with the provisions of the second and fifth sections of this act.' (Taylor's lien is not affected by the exception.) The supreme court of the United States, in Ex parte Christy, 3 How. S. C. R. 292, 318, 319, and in Norton's assignee v. Boyd, 3 How. S. C. R. 426, 436, 437, declare that the liens mentioned in the proviso remain in full force, and may be made available by the state courts; that the United States district courts in bankruptcy should not interfere with their execution except under peculiar circumstances in those cases mentioned. In this case the court in bankruptcy did not take cognizance of the subject, but left it to the state courts. It may be safely said that these decisions of the supreme court have not placed limits too narrow upon the power of the federal judiciary. It must therefore be held that the judgment and the lien incident thereto, were not discharged by Green's bankruptcy. They are left to the cognizance of the state courts to be enforced by appropriate remedies." McCance v. Taylor, 10 Gratt. 580.

13. Injunction to Judgment.

An injunction to a judgment merely suspends execution upon the judgment, and does not destroy the lien. Craig v. Sebrell, 9 Gratt. 131.

"The judgment being a lien and charging the whole of the equitable estate, has any thing occurred to displace it? It constituted a lien at the time of its rendition. The creditor then had the capacity to take out an elegit, and that right was never lost or even suspended through any act or omission of his own. Even if, as was argued, there has been any necessity for a scire facias to revive the judgment the lien would have continued so long as the capacity to revive existed, and would have related to the date of the judgment. Taylor v. Spindle, 2 Gratt. 44. But there was no necessity to revive. The judgment was rendered on the 18th of June, 1819, and on the 24th of June, 1819, there was an execution and return. The injunction was dissolved on the 20th of July, 1826, and on the 28th of September, 1826, another execution issued. Upon such dissolution the party was remitted to the lien of his original judgment. Whilst the creditor could get, or as in this case had, the capacity to issue an elegit, the lien of the judgment having once attached, continued to operate, notwithstanding any supervening suspension interposed by the injunction. Taylor v. Spindle, ubi supra." Michaux v. Brown, 10 Gratt. 612.

Where an injunction to a judgment is only perpetuated as to a part of it, or a reversal is only as to a part of a judgment, the lien of the part not affected continues from the date of the judgment. Grafton, etc., R. Co. v. Davisson, 45 W. Va. 12, 29 S. E. 1028, 77 Am. St. Rep. 790; Moss v. Moorman, 24 Gratt. 97; Graham v. Citizens' Nat. Bank, 45 W. Va. 701, 32 S. E. 245.

Upon a bill in chancery to enjoin a judgment at law, and for a retrial, there must not be a decree before such retrial annulling the judgment and granting a new trial in the law court; but the judgment is allowed to stand as security for what may be found to be justly due, and the injunction allowed to stand until after the retrial, and the decree should direct an issue or issues to be tried in the circuit court to find what the nature of the case requires, and upon the verdict the court should perpetuate or dissolve, wholly or partially, the judgment. "The court must not at once set aside the judgment, and grant a new trial, when it determines that a retrial should be had, but must await its result, as the judgment ought to stand as security until it is finally determined whether

it shall be perpetually enjoined or not. Knifong v. Hendricks, 2 Gratt. 212; Bank v. Hupp, 10 Gratt. 23, 33; Wynne v. Newman, 75 Va. 811; Bart. Ch. Prac. 58; 2 Story, Eq. Jur., § 1574. The judgment ought to be allowed to stand as security until the final decree, as its lien is good for what may be found to be really due, though obtained by fraud, accident, or surprise, and though what may be due be the whole or only part of the debt recovered (Farmers' Bank v. Vanmeter, 4 Rand. 553, Judge Green's opinion; Judge Lee's opinion, Bank v. Hupp, 10 Gratt. 33); just as a judgment reversed in part is all the while a lien (2 Bart. Ch. Prac. § 295; Moss v. Moorman, 24 Gratt. 97)." Grafton, etc., R. Co. v. Davisson, 45 W. Va. 12, 29 S. E. 1028, 1030.

14. Effect of Division of Virginia and West Virginia.

The lien of a judgment which had attached to land in either Virginia or West Virginia prior to the separation, was not lost upon the division of these two states, whereby the county in which the judgment lien originally attached fell either within the one state or the other. Calwell v. Prindle, 19 W. Va. 604; Gatewood v. Goode, 23 Gratt. 880.

The state of Virginia upon notices and motions by the name of "The Commonwealth" instituted and prosecuted by the auditor of public accounts on the 6th day of March, 1860, recovered two several judgments against Edmund S. Calwell "in the circuit court of Richmond" as one of the securities of John E. Lewis, late sheriff of Greenbrier county, the one being for $4,893.92, the balance of the land property, and capitation and September license taxes of 1854 due from said John E. Lewis, late sheriff of Greenbrier county, with interest thereon to be computed at the rate of six per centum from the 17th day of January,

1855, until paid, and the costs of the motion, $13.44, and the other being for $1,073.86, the balance of June, 1855, license taxes, due from said John E. Lewis, late sheriff of Greenbrier county, with interest thereon to be computed at the rate of six per centum per annum from the 20th day of June, 1855, until paid, and $161.07 for damages thereon according to law, also the cost of the motion, $11.94. The law in force at the time said notices were given and motions made and judgments were rendered provided, that "the auditor of public accounts shall institute and prosecute all proceedings proper to enforce payment of money to the commonwealth"— that the proceeding may be in the circuit court of the city of Richmond— that when it is at law, it may be by action or motion—that "every judgment on any such motion shall be in the name of the commonwealth." And the city of Richmond being the capital of the state of Virginia, as judicially known to the court, held, that said judgments did not cease to be liens upon the lands of said Calwell within the state of West Virginia, upon the last-named state becoming one of the states of the union, to wit, on the 20th day of June, 1863, nor did the liens of said judgment upon the lands of said Calwell within the state of West Virginia in any wise become discharged or released by the state of West Virginia becoming one of the United States. Calwell v. Prindle, 19 W Va. 604.

At the March term, 1861, of the county court of Monroe, a judgment was rendered at the suit of the bank of V., plaintiff, against W., S. and G., the latter living in the county of Bath. Execution of fi. fa. was issued on this judgment and levied on the property of W., and the sheriff returned, after June 1861, a levy upon the personal property of W., that the property was

appraised and offered for sale, and not bringing valuation it was returned. G. died during the war, leaving real estate in Bath county, and also in West Virginia; and after his death some of his creditors filed their bill in the circuit court of Bath, to subject his real estate to the payment of his debts. The commissioner reported the above judgment as a debt by judgment having priority. A copy of the judgment was certified by the clerk of Monroe circuit court, "and as such, keeper of the records of Monroe county court, and which by law are a part of the records of my office." The circuit court confirmed the report. Held, that the lien of said judgment on the lands of G., in Bath county, was neither lost nor impaired by reason of the division of the state of Virginia into two states, and the falling of the county of Monroe into the state of West Virginia. Gatewood v. Goode, 23 Gratt. 880.

15. Entry of Satisfaction.

See post, "Satisfaction and Discharge," XIII.

A judgment is recovered, and an execution issued thereon, and while it is in the hands of the sheriff, an agreement is made between the creditor and debtor, by which certain claims are transferred to the creditor in satisfaction of the judgment, and thereupon the sheriff, at the instance of the creditor, returns the execution "satisfied," but it appears, that said agreement on the part of the debtor was fraudulent and the execution was not in fact satisfied, the lien of the judgment is not destroyed, and its position and priority is not disturbed, although its payment may effect purchasers of part of the land of the debtor, where it does not appear in the pleadings and proofs, that such return was brought home to the purchaser, and by it he was misled to his injury. Renick v Ludington, 14 W. Va. 367.

The object of § 2498 of the Code is to afford a summary remedy for having marked satisfied the liens therein mentioned upon proof that the debt has been actually paid or discharged, and was not intended to enable persons to have such liens marked satisfied because liable to be defeated by presumption of payment, or because barred by the statute of limitations. Does this statute include judgments? In the annotation to this section it is said that in practice judgments have been marked satisfied under this section. Turnbull v. Mann, 94 Va. 182, 26 S. E. 510.

16. Dismissal of Writ of Error.

In a writ of error in the supreme court from a judgment, an order is made reciting that it appeared from a writing filed that the "matters in difference herein" have been settled, and dismissing the writ of error "agreed" on motion of the plaintiff in error; such order is not a bar against the judgment, and does not discharge it. Fletcher v. Parker, 53 W. Va. 422, 44 S. E. 422.

17. Judgment against Partners.

In a chancery suit brought by K. of Richmond against A. B. & C. of Mercer county in this state to enforce the lien of a judgment obtained before the war against A. B. & C. as partners on an accepted order known to the partners to include the amount due from the partnership to K. and also an individual debt due from C. to K.; held, the court in such a case ought not to decree the lands of C. primarily liable for so much of the judgment, as was barred on his individual account with K., as a settlement of the partnership accounts might show the other partners indebted to him in a still greater amount, and the equities between the codefendants ought not in such a suit to be inquired into by the court. The lands of each partner ought to be held primarily responsible for the portion of K.'s judgment, which corresponds with his interest in the profits and losses of the partnership under the articles of copartnership. Kent v. Chapman, 18 W. Va. 485. See Pitts v. Spotts, 86 Va. 71, 9 S. E. 501.

18. Judgment upon Equitable Estates.

See ante, "Priorities," VI, H.

" 'It is a settled rule,' says J. Green, in Haleys v. Williams, 1 Leigh 140, 'in respect to the satisfaction of judgments, and other liens upon an equitable fund, that all are to be paid according to their priority in point of time; 'qui prior est in tempore, potior est in jure.' In that case the fund was equitable so far as the judgment creditors were concerned; the legal title being in trustees, for the security of other creditors, who had thereby a priority over the judgment creditors; which is precisely this case." Hale v. Horne, 21 Gratt. 112.

Amongst incumbrances, where all having nothing but equities, and none the legal title, their equities being equal, they are entitled to satisfaction according to the priority of their incumbrances in point of time, upon the maxim qui prior est in tempore, potior est in jure. Coutts v. Walker, 2 Leigh 268, 280, citing Haleys v. Williams, 1 Leigh 140. To the same effect Haleys v. Williams, 1 Leigh 140, cited in Michaux v. Brown, 10 Gratt. 612, 619; Hale v. Horne, 21 Gratt. 112, 122; Findlay v. Toncray, 2 Rob. 374, 377.

Judgment creditors may, in equity, have satisfaction out of the equitable estate of their debtor, in real estate, according to the order of their judgments in point of time, the oldest having priority over the youngest. Haleys v. Williams, 1 Leigh 140, 19 Am. Dec. 743.

Order of Liability of Equity of Redemption.—The equity of redemption in land conveyed in trust to secure debts, is subject to the lien of judgments subsequently obtained in the order of their priority in date. Hale v. Horne, 21 Gratt. 112; Michaux v. Brown, 10 Gratt. 612.

19. Marshaling the Assets.

See the title MARSHALING ASSETS AND SECURITIES.

a. In General.

The West Virginia Code provides that where the real estate liable to the lien of a judgment is more than sufficient to satisfy the same, and it, or any part of it, has been aliened, as between the alienees for value, that which was aliened last shall, in equity, be first liable, and so on with other successive alienations until the whole judgment is satisfied. And as between alienees who are volunteers under such judgment debtor, the same rule as to the order of liability shall prevail. But any part of such real estate retained by the debtor himself shall be first liable to the satisfaction of the judgment. W. Va. Code, 1899, ch. 139, § 4148.

The statute (Va. Code, 1873, ch. 182, § 10) provided, that "where the real estate liable to the lien of a judgment is more than sufficient to satisfy the same, and it or any part of it has been aliened, as between the alienees for value, that which was aliened last shall, in equity, be first liable, and so on with successive alienations until the whole judgment is satisfied. And as between alienees who are volunteers under such judgment debtor, the same rule as to the order of liability shall prevail; but any part of such real estate retained by the debtor shall be first liable to the satisfaction of the judgment." Harman v. Oberdorfer, 33 Gratt. 497, 501.

And the present Virginia Code provides that where the real estate liable to the lien of a judgment is more than sufficient to satisfy the same, and it, or any part of it, has been aliened, as among the alienees for value, that which was aliened last, shall, in equity, be first liable, and so on with other successive alienations, until the whole judgment is satisfied. And as among alienees who are volunteers under such judgment debtor, the same rule as to the order of liability shall prevail; but as among the alienees for value and volunteers, the lands aliened to the latter shall be subjected before the lands aliened to the former are resorted to; and, in either case, any part of such real estate retained by the debtor shall be first liable to the satisfaction of the judgment. (Code, 1849, p. 709, ch. 186, § 10.) Va. Code, 1904, § 3575.

Doubly Charged Fund.—If in a suit brought by a judgment creditor against the judgment debtor to sell his lands to satisfy the liens thereon, one of his creditors has a lien on two parcels of land, to only one of which the other lien creditors can resort for the payment of their debt, a court of equity will require such creditor having two securities to exhaust the one to which he only can resort for the payment of his debt, before he is entitled to charge the other land of the debtor, to which alone the other lien creditors can resort. Kanawha Valley Bank v. Wilson, 25 W. Va. 242, 243; Ball v. Setzer, 33 W. Va. 444, 10 S. E. 798; McClaskey v. O'Brien, 16 W. Va. 791; Pitts v. Spotts, 86 Va. 71, 9 S. E. 501.

In April, 1868, R. conveyed land with general warranty to C., and C. conveyed it in trust to secure four bonds for the purchase money. The trust deed was recorded, but the deed to C. was not, until March, 1869. One of the bonds was paid by C. R. assigned the other three to W., and B. and J., J. being the last assignee. In July, 1868, D. recovered a judgment against R., and afterwards filed his bill to subject a small tract of land of R. to satisfy it. In May, 1873, C. was

declared a bankrupt, and upon petition by J. the bankrupt court had C.'s
land sold, and fixed the priorities of
the creditors, making D. the first and
J. the last, the proceeds of the land
not being sufficient to pay all; but directing the fund should be retained
until it was ascertained how much D.
would get from the proceeds of the
other tract. In March, 1871, R. executed a declaration of homestead,
which embraced all his personal prop·
erty; and on the 10th of August, 1871,
he conveyed this property to P. in
trust for his wife and children. In
January, 1874, J. having purchased D.'s
judgment, he filed a bill against R.
and his wife and children and P., in a
state court, to subject this personal
property to satisfy this judgment; and
in April, 1874, there was a decree in
the bankrupt court, by which the proceeds of C.'s land was distributed
among the assignees of his bonds, it
not being enough to satisfy J. And it
being suggested to the court, that beside the small tract of land aforesaid,
there was personal property of R.
which might be subjected to pay the
said judgment, which was sufficient for
that purpose, it was decreed that no
part of the proceeds of C.'s land
should be applied to pay the judgment
of D. Held, as holder of the bond J.
had but one fund upon which he can
rely for payment, whilst D. has two
funds for the satisfaction of his judgment, the land and the personal property embraced in the deed of homestead and deed of trust. And a court
of equity will marshal the assets, and
compel D. to exhaust the fund upon
which J. had no claim, that J. may appropriate the only fund within his
reach. Russell v. Randolph, 26 Gratt.
705.

Error.—It is error for the circuit
court not to determine, by marshaling
the same, out of which of the proceeds
of several properties various judgments

and trust liens should be paid accord-
ing to their priorities. First Nat.
Bank v. Simms, 49 W. Va. 442, 38 S.
E. 525.

b. As between Trust Creditors of Same Debtor.

As between two trust creditors of
the same debtor, secured on separate
properties, a prior judgment lien must
be first paid out of the proceeds of the
property subject to the second trust,
to the relief of the property subject to
the first, both by reason of the statute and the doctrine of subrogation.
First Nat. Bank v. Simms, 49 W. Va.
442, 38 S. E. 525. See Woods v. Douglas, 46 W. Va. 657, 33 S. E. 771; Ball
v. Setzer, 33 W. Va. 444, 10 S. E. 798.

"There can be no question that a
deed of trust creditor is an alienee for
value, and entitled to have prior judgment lienors enforce their judgment
against lands unaliened at the date of
such trust, even against subsequent
trust creditor under § 8, ch. 139, Code.
This is also the settled law of subrogation, that a trust creditor may require a judgment lienor to resort to
lands of the debtor not subject to such
trust even though such lands are subject to subsequent trust liens. Ball v.
Setzer, 33 W. Va. 444, 10 S. E. 798;
Woods v. Douglas, 46 W. Va. 657, 33
S. E. 771." First Nat. Bank v. Simms,
49 S. Va. 442, 444, 38 S. E. 525.

c. As between the Judgment Debtor and His Alienee.

In General.—Any part of the real
estate liable to the lien of a judgment,
retained by the debtor shall be first
liable to the satisfaction of the judgment. Va. Code, 1904, § 3575; W. Va.
Code, 1899, ch. 139, § 4148.

If the judgment debtor retains sufficient lands to pay the judgment they
should be first subjected. Blakemore
v. Wise. 95 Va. 269, 28 S. E. 332.

Equity requires, where a judgment
lien is sought to be enforced, that the

lands owned by the debtor at the time of the attempted enforcement, should be applied to the discharge of the judgment before resorting to lands upon which the judgment was also a lien, then in the hands of his alienee. Handly v. Sydenstricker, 4 W. Va. 605.

If a judgment is obtained which is a lien on the lands of the judgment debtor, and the judgment debtor sells and conveys part of it, generally the judgment creditor should be required in the first instance to exhaust the unsold portion. McClaskey v. O'Brien, 16 W. Va. 791.

Where there have been successive judgments against a common debtor, who has aliened a part of his lands after the first judgment, but before the other judgments were recovered, the first judgment creditor is entitled to priority of satisfaction out of the land still held by the judgment debtor, although he released his lien on the land so aliened after the recovery of the other judgments. Blakemore v. Wise, 95 Va. 269, 28 S. E. 332.

Illustrative Cases.—The judgment is not a lien on notes given by a purchaser for unpaid purchase money for the land on which the judgment is a lien, nor do such notes, together with unaliened lands on the judgment debtor, constitute a common fund for the payment of the judgment. If the judgment debtor retains sufficient lands to pay the judgment they should be first subjected. The lands aliened by the debtor constitute a secondary fund for the payment of the judgment, and neither a release of these lands, nor the failure to subject said notes is prejudicial to subsequent judgment creditors who obtained their judgments after the alienation, but before the release by the first judgment creditor. Blakemore v. Wise, 95 Va. 269, 28 S. E. 332.

Where some of the land conveyed by a judgment lien is included in a deed of trust, subsequent to the judgment and the residue of it is not, such residue, not included, should first be sold to satisfy the prior judgment, and if insufficient to discharge the judgment, then the lands included in the deed of trust should be sold, and so much of the proceeds thereof, as, with the proceeds of the land not included in the deed, amount to a moiety of the whole, should be applied to the satisfaction of the judgment. If there is another judgment having priority over the deed of trust, the proceeds of the other moiety of the land sold, included in the deed of trust, should be applied to satisfy it. Buchanan v. Clark, 10 Gratt. 164.

There is a creditor by judgment prior to a sale of land by his debtor, and there is purchase money unpaid sufficient to satisfy the judgment, when another creditor recovers a judgment against the same debtor. This last can not insist that the first shall go against the land, and leave the purchase money unpaid for him; but the purchaser of the land is entitled to have the purchase money applied to relieve his land. Withers v. Carter, 4 Gratt. 407.

When various judgments are rendered against a debtor, and the junior judgments are docketed, and the senior undocketed, and in this state of things the debtor conveys a part of the land to a purchaser for valuable consideration without notice of the undocketed judgments, and the docketed judgment liens are not discharged, the liens of the undocketed judgments must be discharged out of the proceeds of the unsold lands, although the effect might be to require the holders of the docketed judgments to resort in whole or in part to the land so conveyed for the satisfaction of their judgment liens. Renick v. Ludington, 14 W. Va. 367; McClaskey v. O'Brien, 16 W. Va. 791, 792;

Renick *v.* Ludington, 20 W. Va. 511, approved in Gurnee *v.* Johnson, 77 Va. 712, 730. See also, Duncan *v.* Custard, 24 W. Va. 730.

Sufficiency of Answer.—If a defendant in chancery, whose land is sought to be subjected to the lien of a judgment against his vendor, answers that other lands of his vendor, or lands of a subsequent alienee of his vendor, are liable to the complainant's demand, the answer is not liable to exception for insufficiency, and the defendant should be allowed to show those facts. "From that answer it appears that Logan & Brewer and Kirkpatrick had liens upon two tracts of land owned by J. J. Kelly, Jr., the title to which remained in J. J. Kelly, Sr., until 1897, which were worth more than the sum of the judgments sought to be enforced in this suit, and that Logan & Brewer, assignors of Hamblen, and Kirkpatrick, entered into a compromise with J. J. Kelly, Jr., who agreed to pay, and did pay, them one-third of their demands; whereupon a consent decree was entered reciting the compromise and dismissing the bill. This, we think, was error. If the facts stated in the answer be true, the land of J. J. Kelly, Jr., title to which remained in J. J. Kelly, Sr., until 1897, should have been subjected to the lien of the judgments to the exoneration of the lands of William J. Kelly, title to which J. J. Kelly, Sr., parted with as far back as 1894. See Jones *v.* Myrick, 8 Gratt. 179; Building, etc., Ass'n *v.* Fellers, 96 Va. 337, 31 S. E. 505." Kelly *v.* Hamblen, 98 Va. 383, 390, 36 S. E. 491.

d. As between Principal and Surety.

In a suit to enforce judgment liens on the lands of the principal debtor and his sureties, the principal's lands should be exhausted before subjecting that of the sureties. Wytheville Crystal Ice, etc., Co. *v.* Frick Co., 96 Va.

141, 30 S. E. 491; Womack *v.* Paxton, 84 Va. 9, 5 S. E. 550; Stovall *v.* Border Grange Bank, 78 Va. 188; Horton *v.* Bond, 28 Gratt. 815; Gentry *v.* Allen, 32 Gratt. 254; Ross *v.* M'Lauchlan, 7 Gratt. 86.

"In suit to enforce judgment lien on lands of principal debtor and his sureties, principal's lands should be exhausted before subjecting that of sureties. Horton *v.* Bond, 28 Gratt. 815. In such suit a receiver should not be appointed of the lands of one surety before subjecting the lands of principal and before taking any steps against the lands of the cosurety." Stovall *v.* Border Grange Bank, 78 Va. 188.

Where judgment is rendered against a principal and his sureties, which is paid by the sureties, the judgment is a lien in favor of the sureties prior to a subsequent trust deed, although the sureties have permitted the proceeds of other property conveyed by their principal in trust for them to be applied in satisfaction of another judgment against their principal. Kent *v.* Matthews, 12 Leigh 573.

Parties to Negotiable Paper.—Upon a bill by a judgment creditor to subject the lands of his debtors to satisfy a judgment obtained against them as the maker and endorsers of a note, whose liabilities inter sese are successive, it is error to decree a sale of the lands of the last endorser before resorting to the lands of the maker and prior endorsers of such note, unless to require the plaintiff to exhaust the estates of those debtors, whose liability is prior to the last endorser, will in the opinion of the court unduly delay the plaintiff in the collection of his debt. Shenandoah Valley Nat. Bank *v.* Bates, 20 W. Va. 210, citing Horton *v.* Bond, 28 Gratt. 815.

e. Docketed and Undocketed Judgments.

Where various judgments are rendered against a debtor, and the junior judgments are docketed, and the senior undocketed, and in this state of things the debtor conveys a part of the land to a purchaser for valuable consideration without notice of the undocketed judgments, and the docketed judgment liens are not discharged, the liens of the undocketed judgments must be discharged out of the proceeds of the unsold lands, although the effect might be to require the holders of the docketed judgments to resort in whole or in part to the land so conveyed for satisfaction of their judgment liens. Renick v. Ludington, 14 W. Va. 367; Renick v. Ludington, 20 W. Va. 511; Duncan v. Custard, 24 W. Va. 730; Gurnee v. Johnson, 77 Va. 712, 730.

On the 5th day of May, 1874, C. conveys his property to B., who on the same day conveyed it to E., the wife of C. On March 20, 1875, a deed of trust on a part of the land so conveyed, executed by C. and wife to secure a debt to M., is recorded; on the 30th day of March another deed of trust on the same land to secure a debt to B. is recorded; and on July 8, 1876, another deed of trust on the same land to secure a debt to Bowles is recorded. Judgments were recovered against C. as follows: One on the 29th day of October, 1875; another on the 19th day of November, 1875, and a third on the 28th day of November, 1876. It does not appear whether the judgments were docketed. Held, the proceeds of the tract of land, on which are the three trust liens, if the two prior judgments were not docketed, and those interested in the trusts had no notice of such judgments, must be applied to pay said liens in the order in which the trust deeds were recorded, and any surplus must go to the payment of the judgments in the order above indicated. Duncan v. Custard, 24 W. Va. 730.

f. Proceeds of Land Sold by Commissioner.

The proceeds of lands of a judgment debtor sold by a commissioner must be applied to the satisfaction of specific liens against such lands according to their respective priorities, and a judgment subsequently rendered can not be made a general lien on such lands until the specific liens are paid. Hutton v. Lockridge, 22 W. Va. 159

g. Release of Doubly Charged Fund.

See generally, the title MARSHALING ASSETS AND SECURITIES.

If a prior judgment lienor releases the property subject to a second deed of trust, the proceeds of which are amply sufficient to satisfy his judgment lien, he can not enforce payment of such judgment lien out of the property subject to a first deed of trust until such latter trust is fully satisfied. First Nat. Bank v. Simms, 49 W. Va. 442, 38 S. E. 525.

If a judgment creditor has as such a lien covering the debtor's lands and also certain lands which the debtor has sold, such creditor may release the land so sold without impairing his right to assert his judgment lien against all the other lands of the debtor, though at the date of such release junior judgment liens existed against the judgment debtor. The junior judgment creditors have no right to complain of such release, though when it was made the lands released had not been fully paid for and the judgment creditor did not insist that the balance of the purchase price be paid towards the satisfaction of his judgment or of the judgment in favor of the junior judgment creditors. Blakemore v. Wise, 95 Va. 269, 28 S. E. 332, 64 Am. St. Rep. 781.

h. Superior Rights of Third Parties.

The equity of a judgment creditor to marshal the assets, as a means of obtaining payment out of a fund that is not subject to the lien of a judgment, will not be enforced against a bona fide purchaser, unless the equity springs out of some contract between the purchaser and vendor. McClaskey v. O'Brien, 16 W. Va. 791; Withers v. Carter, 4 Gratt. 407; Schultz v. Hansbrough, 33 Gratt. 567, 582; Hall v. Hyer, 48 W. Va. 353, 37 S. E. 594; Ball v. Setzer, 33 W. Va. 444, 10 S. E. 798.

i. Contribution and Exoneration.

If a defendant in chancery, whose land is sought to be subjected to the lien of a judgment against his vendor, answers that other lands of his vendor, or lands of a subsequent alienee of his vendor, are liable to the complainant's demand, the answer is not liable to exception for insufficiency, and the defendant should be allowed to show those facts. "From that answer it appears that Logan & Brewer and Kirkpatrick had liens upon two tracts of land owned by J. J. Kelly, Jr., the title to which remained in J. J. Kelly, Sr., until 1897, which were worth more than the sum of the judgments sought to be enforced in this suit, and that Logan & Brewer, assignors of Hamblen, and Kirkpatrick, entered into a compromise with J. J. Kelly, Jr., who agreed to pay, and did pay, them one-third of their demands; whereupon a consent decree was entered reciting the compromise and dismissing the bill. This, we think, was error. If the facts stated in the answer be true, the land of J. J. Kelly, Jr., title to which remained in J. J. Kelly, Sr., until 1897, should have been subjected to the lien of the judgments to the exoneration of the lands of William J. Kelly, title to which J. J. Kelly, Sr., parted with as far back as 1894. See Jones v. Myrick, 8 Gratt. 179; Building, etc., Ass'n v. Fellers, 96 Va. 337, 33 S. E. 505." Kelly v. Hamblen, 98 Va. 383, 390. 36 S. E. 491.

Real Estate by Personalty.—A judgment creditor has a legal lien on the lands of his debtor, and has a right to rest on that lien without pursuing his debtor's personalty. Blakemore v. Wise, 95 Va. 269, 28 S. E. 332.

The act of 5 George 2, ch. 7, § 4, subjecting lands, slaves, etc., in the colonies to payment of debts, was the law of Alexandria county in the District of Columbia from June 24th, 1812. In favor of a judgment creditor of a deceased debtor, his real estate was not merely a secondary fund for the payment of the debt, but the real and personal estate were equally liable. The judgment creditor might file a bill in equity against the executor and devisees to subject the real and personal estate to the payment of his debt. Suckley v. Rotchford, 12 Gratt. 60.

On the 5th day of May, 1874, C. conveys his property to B., who on the same day conveyed it to E., the wife of C. On March 20, 1875, a deed of trust on a part of the land so conveyed, executed by C. and wife to secure a debt to M., is recorded; on the 30th day of March another deed of trust on the same land to secure a debt to B. is recorded; and on July 8, 1876, another deed of trust on the same land to secure a debt to Bowles is recorded. Judgments were recovered against C. as follows: One on the 29th day of October, 1875; another on the 19th day of November, 1875, and a third on the 28th day of November, 1876. It does not appear whether the judgments were docketed. Held, whether docketed or not, all the personal property, if any, not included in the deeds of trust and all the real estate not included in such trust should first be sold to pay said judgments in the order they were rendered. Duncan v. Custard, 24 W. Va. 730, citing Renick v. Ludington, 14 W. Va. 367.

j. Inverse Order of Alienation.

Prior to Statute.—The first case dealing with this question held, that where a judgment is obtained against a debtor, and then the debtor aliens to divers alienees by divers conveyances, all the debtor's lands in the hands of his several alienees, are alike liable to the judgment creditor, and the lands in the hands of the several alienees must contribute pro rata to satisfy the judgment. Beverley v. Brooke, 2 Leigh 425.

But later cases review the decision in Beverley v. Brooke, 2 Leigh 425, on this point and expressly overrule it, or refer to it as overruled. And the rule established in both Virginia and West Virginia now is, that where land which is subject to a lien of a judgment, or other incumbrances, is aliened to different purchasers by successive alienations, it is chargeable in the hands of the purchasers in the inverse order of alienation. Indeed Beverley v. Brooke, 2 Leigh 425, seems to be the only Virginia case that ever held otherwise. McClung v. Beirne, 10 Leigh 394, overruling Beverley v. Brooke, 2 Leigh 425; Harman v. Oberdorfer, 33 Gratt. 497; Nelson v. Turner, 97 Va. 54, 33 S. E. 390; Hutton v. Lockridge, 22 W. Va. 159; Rodgers v. McCluer, 4 Gratt. 81; Alley v. Rogers, 19 Gratt. 366, 389; Jones v. Phelan, 20 Gratt. 229; Jones v. Myrick, 8 Gratt. 179; Brengle v. Richardson, 78 Va. 406; Londons v. Echols, 17 Gratt. 15, 20.

In Conrad v. Harrison, 3 Leigh 532, a debtor mortgaged certain lands to three different creditors successively to secure debts due them. It was held, that the third mortgagee could not call on the second mortgagee to contribute pro rata to the satisfaction of the debt due the first mortgagee. The proposition affirmed in Beverley v. Brooke, 2 Leigh 425, that where "a judgment is recovered against a debtor, and the debtor aliens his lands to divers alienees and by divers conveyances, all the debtor's lands, in the hands of his several alienees, are alike liable to the judgment creditor, and the lands in the hands of several alienees must contribute pro rata to satisfy the judgment," was doubted, but held not applicable to the case at bar. Judges

Cabell and Tucker (pp. 541, 546) distinguished Beverley v. Brooke, 2 Leigh 425, from the case at bar on the ground that Beverley v. Brooke, 2 Leigh 425, was not a case of subsequent incumbrances after a prior mortgage, but after a prior judgment. Judge Carr, while he concurred in the opinion of the court in each case, said that he could not reconcile them, but that in each he decided as he thought right.

The land last sold by the debtor is to be first applied to the satisfaction of the judgment. And this, though the last purchaser obtained a conveyance before the first; the first having previously had a good equitable title. Rodgers v. McCluer, 4 Gratt. 81.

Lands subject to a judgment lien which have been sold or encumbered by the debtor, are to be subjected to the satisfaction of the judgment in the inverse order in point of time of the alienations and encumbrances; the land last sold or encumbered being first subjected. Jones v. Myrick, 8 Gratt. 179, approved in Kelly v. Hamblen, 98 Va. 383, 36 S. E. 491.

Without evidence of any preceding executory agreements between the parties, or any evidence of the time of the delivery of the deeds, except what may be inferred from their dates, P., a judgment debtor, by one deed (dated January 1, 1860, acknowledged February 1, 1860, and recorded April 13, 1860), conveyed one tract of land to H. and by another deed (dated February 1, 1860, acknowledged February 1, 1860, and recorded February 24, 1860), conveyed another tract to B. In proceedings to subject both tracts to the payments of judgments obtained against P., prior to either deed, held: The tract to B. was the last aliened, and, therefore, under § 10, ch. 182 of the Code of 1873, first liable to satisfy the judgments. Harman v. Oberdorfer, 33 Gratt. 497.

In the absence of any averment in the pleading, or of proof, that several tracts of land which have been aliened to the same person by a judgment debtor, after the recovery of the judgments, are more than sufficient to pay such judgments, it is not error to decree that the lands shall be offered in parcels and also as a whole, and the best price offered accepted. "Without considering whether § 3575 applies to a case like this, where the several alienations are to the same person, it is sufficient to say that the section referred to provides that, when the real estate liable to the lien of a judgment is more than sufficient to satisfy the same, and it, or any part of it, has been aliened, as among the alienees for value, that which was aliened last shall in equity be first liable, etc." Preston v. National Exchange Bank, 97 Va. 222, 226, 33 S. E. 546.

Lands Primarily Liable.—Lands being liable for judgments in the inverse order of alienation, those primarily liable should be first subjected before proceeding against the purchaser whose land is only secondarily liable. Nelson v. Turner, 97 Va. 54, 33 S. E. 390.

Oldest Unpaid General Lien.—The holder of the oldest unpaid judgment lien is entitled to be first paid out of the property of the debtor, where his lien is a general one. Max Meadows Land, etc., Co. v. McGavock, 98 Va. 411, 36 S. E. 490.

Parties to Suit Subsequent to Order for Account of Liens.—Where a judgment creditor brings suit to enforce his lien, and after an account of liens is ordered to be taken by the commissioner and other liens are proved, several other judgment creditors become parties to the suit and prove their liens, they are entitled to have the lands sold for their relief in the order of their respective merits and rights, and each is entitled to relief in the cause according to the merits of his cause, and the lands of the debtor are liable in the inverse order of alienation under Va. Code, 1873, ch. 182, § 10. Brengle v. Richardson, 78 Va. 406.

Statutory Provisions.—And this rule is now embodied in the statutes which provide that where the real estate liable to the lien of a judgment is more than sufficient to satisfy the same, and it, or any part of it, has been aliened, as among the alienees for value, that which was aliened last, shall, in equity, be first liable, and so on with other successive alienations, until the whole judgment is satisfied. And as among alienees who are volunteers under such judgment debtor, the same rule as to the order of liability shall prevail. Va. Code, 1904, § 3575; W. Va. Code, 1899, ch. 139, § 4148.

"The law is now well settled that where land which is subject to the lien of a judgment or other incumbrance, is sold in parcels to different persons by successive alienations, it is chargeable in the hands of the purchaser in the inverse order of such alienations. This rule is not only established by the decisions of courts of equity, but in Virginia it is prescribed by statute. Harman v. Oberdorfer, 33 Gratt. 497." Per Staples, J. Whitten v. Saunders, 75 Va. 563, 567; Renick v. Ludington, 20 W. Va. 511, 567. See also, Schultz v. Hansbrough, 33 Gratt. 567; Miller v. Holland, 84 Va. 652, 5 S. E. 701.

The statute in West Virginia provides that: "Where the real estate liable to the lien of a judgment is more than sufficient to satisfy the same, and it, or any part of it, has been aliened, as between the alienees for value, that which was aliened last shall, in equity, be first liable, and so on with other successive alienations until the whole judgment is satisfied." Section 9, ch. 139, W. Va. Code, p. 666; Renick v. Ludington, 20 W. Va. 511; Jackson v. Hull, 21 W. Va. 601, 616.

Construction of Statute.—The 9th section of ch. 139 of Code of West Virginia, p. 666, provides: "When real estate liable to the lien of a judgment is more than sufficient to satisfy the same and it, or any part of it, has been aliened as between the alienees for value, that which was aliened last shall in equity be prior liable and so on in the other successive alienations until the whole judgment is satisfied. And as between alienees who are volunteers under such judgment debtor, the same rule as to order of liability shall prevail. But any part of such real estate retained by the debtor himself shall be first liable to the satisfaction of the judgment." A person becomes the alienee of land, under the true construction of the 9th section of ch. 139 of the Code of West Virginia, p. 666, as soon as he makes a valid contract of purchase, a contract which a court of equity would enforce, that is, either a written contract or a verbal contract accompanied by the delivery of possession, and if the contract be verbal, the date of the alienation will not be the time the contract was made, but the time possession was taken under the contract. Renick v. Ludington, 20 W. Va. 511, 566, following Harman v. Oberdorfer, 33 Gratt. 497.

If the lands owned by the debtor are not sufficient to satisfy the judgment lien, then the real estate last owned and aliened is liable until it is fully satisfied. And in a suit for the purpose of enforcing the lien, unless it should appear with reasonable certainty that the land first liable would be sufficient to discharge it, it would not be error to decree and advertise together the sale of all the land upon which the lien existed, and then proceed to sell it in the order in which it was liable until a sufficient sum is realized to pay off the judgment and costs of suit. Handly v. Sydenstricker, 4 W. Va. 605, citing McClung v. Beirne, 10 Leigh 394.

If the first alienee of a portion of the land liable to judgment liens fails to put his deed of record, and a subsequent alienee, who bought another portion of the lands, liable to the judgment liens, puts his deed of record, still the lands of such last alienee must be held liable for such judgment liens

before the lands of the first alienee. Renick v. Ludington, 20 W. Va. 511.

Where land subject to an encumbrance is sold successively in parcels, each of them will be liable in the inverse order of alienation. "If a judgment or mortgage is a lien on three tracts of land belonging to the same person, who sells one of them to A., another afterwards to B. and finally the third to C., A. is entitled to exoneration at the expense of B. and C. while B. has a similar right against C., and if an execution is issued on the judgment, the court may direct that C.'s land shall be first exposed to sale, next B.'s and that A.'s shall not be held, unless the other tracts do not produce enough to satisfy the debt. McClaskey v. O'Brien, 16 W. Va. 761, 838.

k. Lands Sold Contemporaneously.

But where the different parcels of land are sold contemporaneously they must contribute pro rata to the satisfaction of the judgment. Harman v. Oberdorfer, 33 Gratt. 497, followed in Renick v. Ludington, 20 W. Va. 511, 567.

When the proceeds of lands, on which several judgments, obtained at the same time, are liens, are insufficient to pay them all, they must be paid pro rata. Janney v. Stephen, 2 Pat. & H. 11.

Where several lots of land are sold on the same day, on the same terms, to several parties, all of whom are immediately put in possession under the same agreement, as to the deeds conveying the lots, and the trust deeds to secure the purchase money—although the deeds conveying them are really delivered and recorded at different times—they will all be regarded as "alienations," within the meaning of the statute (ch. 182, § 10, Code, 1873), as of the same day (day of sale); and in subjecting them to the payment of a judgment docketed against a vendor at the time of the sale, each lot must bear its proportion, according to their relative values on the day of sale, and subjected in accordance with the principles of Horton v. Bond, 28 Gratt. 815. Harman v. Oberdorfer, 33 Gratt. 497.

l. As between Successive Alienees for Value and Volunteers.

And the Virginia Code contains a provision that where the real estate liable to the lien of a judgment is more than sufficient to satisfy the same, and it, or any part of it, has been aliened, as among the alienees for value and volunteers, the lands aliened to the latter, shall be subjected before the lands aliened to the former are resorted to. The West Virginia Code does not contain this qualification of the "Inverse Order of Alienation" rule stated above. See Va. Code, 1904, § 3575.

K. PROCEEDINGS TO ENFORCE THE LIEN.

1. Right to Enforce.

The maxim that he who asks equity must do equity only applies to an actor who is seeking some equitable relief. It has no application to a judgment creditor seeking to enforce his lien on debtor's land. He is not asserting an equitable right, or seeking equitable relief. His judgment is a legal lien which he has the right to enforce without terms or conditions. Flanary v. Kane. 102 Va. 547, 46 S. E. 312.

In Gordon v. Rixey, 76 Va. 694, 704, Judge Staples, speaking for the court, said: "In Borst v. Nalle, 28 Gratt. 423, 430, and in Price v. Thrash, 30 Gratt. 515, it was held, that the lien of a judgment is an express absolute statutory lien on the debtor's real estate, and the right to resort to the courts to enforce it is a legal right, without terms and conditions imposed." Leake v. Ferguson, 2 Gratt. 419; 2 Minor's Inst. 314, 315. Flanary v. Kane, 102 Va. 547, 559, 46 S. E. 312.

Liens of judgments and their priorities and the right to enforce the same, are plain legal rights, expressly created by statute, and can not be judicially modified to soften the supposed hardship of secret encumbrances. Gurnee v. Johnson, 77 Va. 712.

2. Nature of Suit.

A chancery suit to enforce a judgment is a collateral suit. Fulkerson v. Taylor, 102 Va. 314, 46 S. E. 378.

3. Jurisdiction.

a. Equity Jurisdiction.

(1) In General.

Jurisdiction to enforce the lien of a judgment shall be in equity. Va. Code, 1904, § 3571.

Chapter 186 of the Code of Virginia of 1860 provided: The lien of a judgment may always be enforced in a court of equity, etc. Calwell v. Prindle, 19 W. Va. 604, 655.

(2) Necessity of Exhausting Personalty.

Section 8. ch. 139, W. Va. Code, 1868, confers upon courts of equity, jurisdiction and authority to enforce judgment liens against the lands of the judgment debtor, whether he has personal property or estate, out of which the judgment might be made by process of execution, or not. Marling v. Robrecht, 13 W. Va. 440; Pecks v. Chambers, 8 W. Va. 210.

"I do not understand that, before a court of equity can decree the sale of real estate to satisfy a judgment lien, the personal estate of the debtor must first be exhausted, as in the case of a proceeding against the estate of a decedent. Courts of equity are always open for the enforcement of a judgment lien." Gardner v. Landcraft, 6 W. Va. 36, 42.

By the ninth section of ch. ,182 of the Code of 1873, which is the act of 1849, it is provided that "the lien of a judgment may always be enforced in a court of equity. If it appear to such court, that the rents and profits of the real estate, subject to the lien. will not satisfy the judgment in five years, the court may decree the said estate, or any part thereof, to be sold, and the proceeds thereof applied to the judgment." This court, in a late case, quoting the above statute, declared that, looking to the policy of the legislature and to the broad and comprehensive language of the enactment, that a judgment creditor, if he should so elect, might resort to a court of equity to enforce the lien of his judgment against the real estate of his debtor, without first proceeding by execution at law to subject the personal estate, or assigning any reason for not doing so. The remedy against the real estate in equity is declared, not dependent upon the inadequacy of the legal remedy to satisfy the judgment out of the personal estate, or the insufficiency of such estate for that purpose, but that it may always be resorted to, whether there be or be not personal estate of the debtor sufficient to satisfy the judgment. The remedy is given in general terms, and if it had been intended to limit its application to cases in which there was no personal estate of the debtor, or when such estate was not sufficient to satisfy the judgment, it would doubtless have been so provided in express terms. Stovall v. Border Grange Bank, 78 Va. 188, 190.

"The eighth section of chapter one hundred and thirty-nine of the Code of West Virginia provides that 'the lien of a judgment may always be enforced in a court of equity.' The word 'always' as employed in this section, may properly be construed to mean 'at any time.' I have quoted the whole of said eighth section, and it is materially different from the ninth section of chapter one hundred and eighty-six of the Code of Virginia of 1860 which was in force in this state when the Code of this state took effect. The said ninth section provides that 'the lien of a judgment may always be enforced in a court of equity. If it appear to such court that the rents and profits of the real estate, subject to

the lien, will not satisfy the judgment in five years, the court may decree the said estate, or any part thereof, to be sold, and the proceeds applied to the discharge of the judgment.' The said eighth section of chapter one hundred and thirty-nine of the Code confers upon courts of equity jurisdiction and authority to enforce judgment liens at any time without qualification. Whatever may have been the law and practice in relation to the right' to resort to the writ of elegit for the collection of judgment debts or the practice of courts of equity in former times in relation to the enforcement of judgment liens by the sale of lands, it seems to me that the said eighth section of chapter one hundred and thirty-nine of the Code of this state confers upon courts of equity jurisdiction and authority to enforce the judgment liens against the land of the judgment debtor at any time without reference to whether the judgment debtor has personal property or estate out of which the judgment might be made by process of execution or not." Pecks v. Chambers, 8 W. Va. 210, 213.

(3) Adequate Remedy at Law.

(a) Rule in Virginia.

aa. Former Rule.

"Previous to the general revision of the laws in 1849, there were two legal remedies by which the judgment creditor was enabled to reach the lands of his debtor. One was through the execution of ca. sa. under which the debtor was taken and imprisoned, and might be discharged from imprisonment on surrendering his property, and the other was by elegit, whereby all the goods and chattels of the debtor (except his oxen and beasts of the plow), and a moiety of all his lands and tenements whereof he was seized at the date of the judgment or at any time afterwards, were delivered to the creditor by reasonable price and extent, to have and to hold the goods and chattels as his own, and the moiety of the land as his freehold until thereof the judgment was satisfied. The creditor having these legal remedies, equity had no jurisdiction to decree a sale of the lands to satisfy the judgment unless it was made to appear that the remedy at law to enforce the judgment was inadequate. It was always regarded that the legal remedy by elegit was inadequate where it was shown that the rents and profits of the land would not satisfy the judgment within a reasonable time, and in such case a court of equity would take jurisdiction and decree a sale. Such was the state of the law in 1849, when the ca. sa. was abolished, and to supply its place other existing remedies were enlarged and some new ones were provided. The liens of judgments and decrees for money, which theretofore had been mere incidents of the elegit and attached to a moiety only of the debtor's land, were made express, direct, positive, absolute charges on all the real estate of the debtor, and the elegit was made to conform to the statutory lien. Borst v. Nalle, 28 Gratt. 423, 430. Code of 1873, ch. 182, §§ 6, 1. The lien of the fi. fa. was enlarged so as to extend to all the personal estate of or to which the judgment debtor is possessed or entitled, although not levied on or capable of being levied on under the law, as it then existed, and this additional lien was made continuous; that is, it was provided that it should 'cease whenever the right of the judgment creditor to levy the fieri facias under which the lien arises, or to levy a new execution on his judgment, ceases or is suspended by a forthcoming bond being given and forfeited, or by a supersedeas or other legal process,' and means were provided for enforcing this lien. Code of 1873, ch. 184. And it was at the same time enacted as follows: 'The lien of a judgment may always be enforced in a court of equity. If it appear to such court, that the rents and profits of the real estate subject to the lien will not

satisfy the judgment in five years, the court may decree the said estate, or any part thereof, to be sold, and the proceeds applied to the discharge of the judgment.' Code of 1873, ch. 182, § 9." Price v. Thrash, 30 Gratt. 515.

"Looking to the policy of the legislature at the revision, and to the broad and comprehensive language of the enactment, I do not doubt that a judgment creditor, if he so elect, may resort to a court of equity to enforce the lien of his judgment against the real estate of his debtor, without first proceeding by execution at law to subject the personal estate, or assigning any reason for not doing so. The remedy in equity against the real estate (now the only remedy since the elegit was abolished, acts, 1871-72, ch. 373, p. 469), is not dependent upon the inadequacy of the legal remedy to satisfy the judgment out of the personal estate, or the insufficiency of such estate for that purpose, but it may 'always' be resorted to, whether there be or not personal estate of the debtor sufficient to satisfy the judgment." Price v. Thrash, 30 Gratt. 515.

bb. Present Rule.

Equity now has jurisdiction to enforce a judgment lien against the land of the debtor, notwithstanding the judgment creditor has not exhausted his remedy at law. Price v. Thrash, 30 Gratt. 515; Va. Code, 1873, ch. 122, §§ 6, 9; Va. Code, 1887, § 3571; Hutcheson v. Grubbs, 80 Va. 251, 257; Gordon v. Rixey, 76 Va. 694; Stovall v. Border Grange Bank, 78 Va. 188, 191; Moore v. Bruce, 85 Va. 139, 7 S. E. 195; Morrison v. Wilkinson, 1 Va. Dec. 772.

It is not necessary since the revision of the law in 1849, that a judgment creditor shall exhaust his remedies at law before going into equity to subject the land of his debtor or his fraudulent alienees to his judgment. The remedy in equity against the real estate is not dependent upon the inadequacy of the legal remedy to satisfy the judgment out of the personal estate, or the insufficiency of such estate for that purpose, but it may always be resorted to whether there is or is not personal estate of the debtor, sufficient to satisfy the debtor. Price v. Thrash, 30 Gratt. 515; Stovall v. Border Grange Bank, 78 Va. 188.

Judgment creditor need not exhaust his remedies at law, before going into chancery, to subject his debtor's land. Code, 1873, ch. 182, § 9; Price v. Thrash, 30 Gratt. 515; Stovall v. Border Grange Bank, 78 Va. 188.

It has been held, that the language of the statute, Va. Code, 1873, ch. 182, § 9, "The lien of a judgment may always be enforced in a court of equity," implies only a purpose to confer jurisdiction on courts of equity to enforce the lien, whether the remedies at law are adequate or not. Hutcheson v. Grubbs, 80 Va. 251.

Judgments in Favor of State.—And this privilege is extended to judgments in favor of the commonwealth. Com. v. Ford, 29 Gratt. 683.

Elegit.—It is not necessary that a judgment creditor should have issued an elegit on his judgment, before coming into equity for relief. Taylor v. Spindle, 2 Gratt. 44.

Fi. Fa.—The lien of a judgment may always be enforced in equity without fi. fa. thereon. Code, 1873, ch. 182, § 9. Price v. Thrash, 30 Gratt. 515; Moore v. Bruce, 85 Va. 139, 7 S. E. 195.

Under Va. Code, 1873, ch. 182, § 9, a judgment lien may be enforced in equity without a fi. fa. thereon, it being unnecessary for the judgment creditor, under that act, to exhaust his remedies at law before going into equity to subject the land of his debtor, or his fraudulent alienees to satisfy his judgment. Moore v. Bruce, 85 Va. 139, 7 S. E. 195; Price v. Thrash, 30 Gratt. 515.

Fi. Fa. Need Not Be Returned "Nulla Bona."—Under the statute, Code, 1873,

ch. 182, § 9, it is not necessary that an execution of fieri facias should have been returned nulla bona, before the plaintiff in the judgment may sue in equity to subject the lands of his debtor to satisfy the judgment. Barr v. White, 30 Gratt. 531.

Bill by T., a judgment creditor of P., against P. and his alienees, to subject to the satisfaction of his judgment the land still held by P., and the lands in the hands of the alienees, charges that the deeds to these alienees were fraudulent and without consideration. The bill is taken for confessed as to all the parties but P., who answers denying the fraud, and saying they were on valuable consideration. The court below holds the deeds to have been fraudulent, and decrees a sale of the land, and P. alone appeals. Held, it is not necessary, since the revision of the law in 1849, that a judgment creditor shall exhaust his remedies at law before going into equity to subject the land of his debtor or his fraudulent alienees to satisfy his judgment, Code of 1873, ch. 182, §§ 6, 9. The remedy in equity against the real estate is not dependent upon inadequacy of the legal remedy to satisfy the judgment out of the personal estate, or the insufficiency of such estate for that purpose, but it may always be resorted to whether there be or not personal estate of the debtor, sufficient to satisfy the judgment. Price v. Thrash, 30 Gratt. 515.

(b) Rule in West Virginia.

Former Rule.—Until the late statute in West Virginia requiring the issue of an execution preliminary to a chancery suit upon a judgment, such chancery suit could have been maintained without any execution. Marling v. Robrecht, 13 W. Va. 440; Maxwell v. Leeson, 50 W. Va. 361, 367, 40 S. E. 420.

Present Rule.—But the West Virginia Code provides that the lien of a judgment may be enforced in a court of equity after an execution of fieri facias thereon has been duly returned, to the office of the court or to the justice from which it issued, showing by the return thereon that no property could be found from which such execution could be made; provided, that such lien may be enforced in equity without such return, when an execution or fieri facias has not issued within two years from the date of the judgment. W. Va. Code, 1899, ch. 139, § 4147.

A bill to enforce a judgment lien must state that a writ of fieri facias has been returned "No property found," or that no execution issued within two years from the date of the judgment. This is not required as to judgments of date before the act of March 13th, 1891. Dunfee v. Childs, 45 W. Va. 155, 30 S. E. 102.

Retrospective Operation of Statute. —Chapter 95, acts, 1891, requiring the issue and return of a fieri facias unsatisfied before a chancery suit to enforce the lien of a judgment, does not apply to suits pending when it went into force. Burns v. Hays, 44 W. Va. 503, 30 S. E. 101.

(4) Determination of Validity of Judgment.

In a chancery suit brought to enforce the lien of a judgment upon real estate, a circuit court has jurisdiction to determine whether or not such judgment is valid, although it may be void upon its face, and the writ of prohibition does not lie to restrain the judge of such court from proceeding in such cause. Sperry v. Sanders, 50 W. Va. 70, 40 S. E. 327.

"The proceeding sought to be restrained is a suit in chancery, brought to enforce the alleged lien of a judgment, alleged to be void, against the real estate of the petitioner, and to have the same sold for the purpose of paying off and satisfying said judgment. Such cause of action clearly belongs to the chancery jurisdiction of the circuit court. The court has power and jurisdiction to hear and determine all cases of that class. It may consider whether the judgment is valid and determine that question in this case as well as in any other. Having the right to consider that question and to hear and determine it, its jurisdiction of the cause is complete and prohibition does not lie to prevent it from so proceeding even if it should err in the determination of the question to the extent of holding a judgment good and valid which is clearly void upon its face. Such error would not amount to an act in excess of the court's legitimate powers nor to an abuse of its jurisdiction. Should the court decide the question wrong, the defendant's remedy, if any, would be by appeal, as in any other chancery cause in which the court has jurisdiction and an erroneous decree is entered. Prohibition does not lie for the correction of errors and it can not take the place of any of the ordinary proceedings for the correction of errors." Sperry v. Sanders, 50 W. Va. 70, 73, 40 S. E. 327.

b. Jurisdiction of Federal Courts.

See the title UNITED STATES.

"It has been repeatedly held, by this court, and by the supreme court of the United States, that it was competent for judgment lien creditors to seek the enforcement of their liens in a state court. Spilman v. Johnson, 27 Gratt. 33, 38; Ray v. Norseworthy, 23 Wall. 134." McAllister v. Bodkin, 76 Va. 809, 814.

A judgment of state court, regularly docketed, before the debtor was adjudicated a bankrupt, was assigned to third person, who had no notice of the proceedings in the bankrupt court, made no claim and received nothing from the bankrupt's funds there administered. Judgment debtor afterwards sold to purchaser, for value, land owned by him at time of his bankruptcy. On bill filed in state court for benefit of assignee of the judgment against judgment debtor, his assignee in bankruptcy, and the purchaser, to subject the land to pay the judgment; held, the judgment having been obtained before the bankruptcy, state court has jurisdiction to enforce its lien on the land in possession of the alienee of the bankrupt; and conceding that the bill should have been filed in the name of the assignee in bankruptcy, yet he, being a defendant, made no objection to the jurisdiction. Had the point been made at proper time, the difficulty would have been removed. It is too late to raise the objection for the first time here in argument. Ferrell v. Madigan, 76 Va. 195.

Quære: Have the decisions of the supreme court of the United States application to judgments of state courts prior to the adjudication in bankruptcy, the liens whereof have not been affected by the proceedings in the bankrupt court? Ferrell v. Madigan, 76 Va. 195.

All interest on property held by a bankrupt, and all property which he has fraudulently conveyed, come within the jurisdiction of the bankrupt court. But that court has no jurisdiction over property bona fide conveyed to a purchaser by the bankrupt before he is declared a bankrupt. And a creditor by judgment docketed against the bankrupt recovered before a bona fide conveyance of land, may proceed in a state court to enforce his judgment lien against said land. Parker v. Dillard, 75 Va. 418.

Judgments obtained and docketed, and liens acquired before the debtor is adjudicated a bankrupt, may, after he is discharged as such, be enforced in the state courts at the instance of persons who were not parties to the bankrupt proceedings, on lands owned by him before his adjudication and allotted him for his homestead. McAllister v. Bodkin, 76 Va. 809.

4. Creditors' Suits.

See the title CREDITORS' SUITS, vol. 3, p. 780.

In General.—A creditor's bill is one of the favorite means employed to enforce a judgment. Hansucker v. Walker, 76 Va. 753.

"The authorities cited seem to fully sustain the proposition that a creditors' bill may be maintained by one or more lien creditor in behalf of themselves and others similarly situated against a living man." Preston v. Aston. 85 Va. 104, 114, 7 S. E. 344.

A creditor who brings his suit against a debtor to enforce the lien of his judgment against his debtor's land should sue on behalf of himself and all other judgment creditors, excepting those made defendants, and he should make formal defendants in his suit all other creditors who have obtained judgments in the courts of record in the county in which the debtor owns lands which are sought to be subjected to the payment of the judgments, and also all creditors who have obtained judgments in any part of the state, which have been recorded in the judgment lien docket of said county; and that if all the judgment creditors are not made parties to such a suit either formally, or informally by being called by publication before a commissioner under a decree of the court to present their judgments, and this is disclosed in any manner by the record, the appellate court will reverse any decree ordering the sale of the lands, or the distribution of the proceeds of such sale. Neely v. Jones, 16 W. Va. 625; Norris v. Bean. 17 W. Va. 655; Pappenheimer v. Roberts. 24 W. Va. 702, 708; Jackson v. Hull. 21 W. Va. 601.

Though a suit be brought by one judgment creditor only, to enforce the lien of his judgment. and though it does not make other judgment creditors parties. and though it be not in terms a suit for the benefit of the plaintiff and other judgment creditors, yet the court may make it a suit for all lienors by ordering an account of all liens to be taken. or on a reference to convene lienors, any may prove their liens. Upon such order to convene liens it is a suit for the benefit of all presenting liens, though no mention of such liens be made in the bill. Dunfee v. Childs, 45 W. Va. 155, 30 S. E. 102.

Illustrative Cases.—Where a suit is brought by one judgment creditor for the purpose of enforcing his lien upon the real estate of the defendant, such becomes a lien creditor's bill from the date of the entry of the decree, referring the cause to a commissioner for an account of the real estate of the defendant, the liens thereon and the order of priority. Repass v. Moore, 96 Va. 147, 30 S. E. 458.

Five suits pending by creditors to enforce liens on judgment debtor's lands. No account taken, but on proof of sufficiency of rents to pay the liens in five years, decree in each suit to rent entered, but not executed. Creditor, with lien older than those asserted in those suits, brings his bill reciting these facts, charging sale of lands to be necessary, and praying for convening all the lien holders, for account of liens and lands, for hearing the suits together, for annulling the decrees to rent, and for sale of the land. Decree accordingly. Held, no error. Preston v. Aston, 85 Va. 104, 7 S. E. 344.

B., as cestui que trust, in two deeds of trust made to L., as trustee, filed his bill in equity in the name of himself and said trustee, to enforce his trust liens upon a particular tract of land of E., alleging priority over all other liens by one of his trust liens, but admitting the priority of certain other trust liens and judgment liens, designated by his bill and exhibits, over his second trust lien, and made those particular lienors parties to the suit, and praying to convene those creditors before a commissioner, to ascertain and audit their respective debts in the order of their priorities; and that the land, or so much thereof as may be necessary to pay B.'s debts, be sold. E. was owner of other tracts of land, upon which the said judgment creditors and others had liens, but the bill took no notice thereof. Held, the bill was a single creditors' bill against all lienors on the particular tract of land designated in the bill, but was not a general creditors' bill, such as would have called for marshaling all the lien debts existing upon all the lands of E. Baugher v. Eichelberger, 11 W. Va. 217.

Appellate Practice.—If in a bill brought by a judgment creditor against a debtor to enforce the lien of his judgment against his lands, the creditor should fail to sue on behalf of himself and all other judgment creditors, but the court should afford to all judgment creditors an opportunity to have their judgments audited before a commissioner by directing a publication to be made, calling on them to present their judgments for auditing, the appellate court will regard this as a creditors' bill, the same as if the plaintiff in his bill had sued on behalf of himself and all other judgment creditors except those made defendants. Neely v. Jones, 16 W. Va. 625.

Another Suit Pending.—When a suit under § 7, ch. 139, W. Va. Code, 1891, has been begun by one judgment creditor for himself and all other lienors to enforce the lien of a judgment on land, no other lien holder can sue for the same purpose. If he does, the pendency of the first suit may be pleaded in bar and dismissal of the second suit. "In the case of liens against the realty of a living judgment debtor, our statute, in § 7, ch. 139, Code, 1891, has gone far beyond the rule of chancery practice before it, if it be as I have stated above. That statute plainly intends one suit, and one only, to enforce all liens resting upon the land, and to prohibit multiplicity of suits, devouring the land to the injury of both debtor and creditors. I think that, after a suit is brought by one lien holder for the benefit of himself and others, no other can sue, and though the suit be not so brought, yet another can not sue after an account of liens is ordered for the benefit of all. The statute allows a defense of this kind to a second suit, because it says that the court may enjoin it and compel him who brings it to come in and assert his lien in the first suit, or may make such order in relation to it as the court or judge may deem right to protect the interests of all parties, and I have no doubt that the pendency of the first suit may be set up by plea in bar of the second suit, and that the court may dismiss the second suit upon it with costs, because that suit is brought in violation of law." Foley v. Ruley, 43 W. Va. 513, 27 S. E. 268, 269.

One judgment creditor can bring his own suit on his own judgment to enforce his lien, unless he has been made a formal party in another suit. As against the estate of a dead man, it is also so. It is true that, after an order of account in a suit to administer a dead man's estate, if another creditor, with knowledge of it, bring a suit for the same purpose, he will pay the costs of his suit. Laidley v. Kline, 23 W. Va. 565. This seems to have been the established chancery practice to prevent numerous suits against a dead man's estate, all his assets being a fund for the payment of his creditors, and to avoid their exhaustion by numerous suits; but I do not understand that to be the practice in suits to enforce liens against land of a living man. As to the estate of a dead man there was no prohibition against separate suits by separate creditors until the court had made an order of reference for the convention of all the creditors, thus making the suit one for the benefit of all creditors; but our statute has very properly gone beyond this, and fully provided for a chancery suit to administer his real estate for the benefit of his creditors, and has provided that if, after the commencement of that suit, any creditor commence another suit, either in law or in equity, no costs shall be recovered in such last-mentioned suit. Whether in such case a plea setting up the pendency of the former suit would be in bar, calling for the dismissal of the second suit, is not before us. That would rest on the construction of that statute—ch. 86, Code, 1891. Foley v. Ruley, 43 W. Va. 513, 27 S. E. 268, 269.

A., a judgment creditor, suing on behalf of himself and all other judgment creditors of C. D. E. and the estate of B. against the said C. D. E. and the administrator of B., defendants, files his bill, in which he avers, that his judgment is founded on a note drawn by B. and endorsed successively by C. D. and E.; that a creditors' bill is pending in the same court against the administrator, widow and heirs of B. and also separate suits against C. and D. to subject the lands of said B. C. and D. to the payment of their respective debts; that said B. C. D. and E. each own lands in the county, against which it is believed there are judgment liens; and prays, that said liens and their respective priorities be ascertained and said lands sold to pay said liens. The defendants demurred to said bill as follows: It shows, that creditors' bills are now pending against the defendants C. and D. and the heirs of B. having the same object that this suit has. Held, the defendant, E., against whom and whose lands the plaintiff has a right to proceed for the payment of his judgment against him, not being a party to any of the three creditors' suits then pending, the pendency of said suits does not prevent the plaintiff from bringing this suit. Shenandoah Valley Nat. Bank v. Bates, 20 W. Va. 210.

Suspension of Suit by Payment.— Payment of some of the debts included in a decree made on a commissioner's report convening liens, under § 7, ch. 139, Code, 1891, in a suit by a judgment creditor for himself and other lienors, will not suspend its execution, or call for a rehearing or restatement of liens. A suit to enforce liens, under § 7, ch. 139, Code, 1891, by one judgment creditor, suing for himself and other lienors, will not be suspended by payment of the debt of the plaintiff after an order of reference. It may and will proceed in the name of the plaintiff, unless an order be made substituting another person as plaintiff. Shumate *v.* Crockett, 43 W. Va. 491, 27 S. E. 240.

Sale Pending Suit.—When a suit by a judgment creditor is brought to enforce his lien on land, and that of other lienors, under § 7, ch. 139, W. Va. Code, and the creditor and trustee under a deed of trust are formal parties, pending this suit a sale can not be made under the deed of trust. Parsons *v.* Snider, 42 W. Va. 517, 26 S. E. 285, 286.

5. Suit by Administrator.

Where an administrator is proceeding in a court of equity to enforce the lien of a judgment recovered by him against persons who are distributees of the estate, the cause can not be delayed, until there is a settlement of the administrator's accounts. Wyatt *v.* Thompson, 10 W. Va. 645.

"Wyatt, as administrator of Nancy Smith, deceased, had recovered judgment against the defendants, Harriman, Forqueran and Nancy Thompson, and according to the 8th section of ch. 139 of the Code, the plaintiff had the right to enforce his judgment liens at any time against the lands of the judgment debtors. Pecks *v.* Chambers, 8 W. Va. 210. And if there was any reason why in that particular case it ought not to have been done, it was for the defendants to show it, which as we have seen, they failed to do." Wyatt *v.* Thompson, 10 W. Va. 645, 652.

6. Pleading and Proof.

a. Pleading and Practice.

(1) Remedies to Enforce Lien.

(a) Execution.

See the title EXECUTIONS, vol. 5, p. 416.

Previous to the general revision of the laws in 1849, there were two legal remedies by which the judgment creditor was enabled to reach the lands of his debtor. One was through the execution of ca. sa. under which the debtor was taken and imprisoned, and might be discharged from imprisonment on surrendering his property, and the other was by elegit, whereby all the goods and chattels of the debtor (except his oxen and beasts of the plow), and a moiety of all his lands and tenements whereof he was seized at the date of the judgment or at any time afterwards, were delivered to the creditor by reasonable price and extent, to have and to hold the goods and chattels as his own, and the moiety of the land as his freehold until thereof the judgment was satisfied. Price *v.* Thrash, 30 Gratt. 515, 524.

When the mode of enforcing money judgments against land was by elegit, which was a writ of execution operative of its own force upon the land, a scire facias went against the heir and terre tenant; but even then the sci. fa. might go against the heir alone. 2 Minor Ins. 206; 1 Lomax Dix. 383. Since the abolition of elegit, and the substitution for it by express statute of a lien by the judgment on land, the enforcement of that judgment by a suit in equity, to which the terre tenant must be a party, and in which he can have full defense, there is in practice no such thing as a revival of a judgment by sci fa. against heirs or terre tenants. They are brought into chancery to answer the legal lien of the judgment, not an execution. Maxwell *v.* Leeson, 50 W. Va. 361, 368, 40 S. E. 420.

(b) Bill in Equity.
aa. Original Bill.
(aa) In General.

The lien of a judgment can not be otherwise enforced against land than by suit in equity. Schilb v. Moon, 50 W. Va. 47, 40 S. E. 329.

Judgment liens are generally enforced by a bill in equity. Virginia Iron, etc., Co. v. Roberts, 103 Va. 661, 49 S. E. 984; Citizens' Nat. Bank v. Manoni, 76 Va. 802.

(bb) Definiteness and Certainty.

G., judgment debtor, is tenant by curtesy in 250 acres of land, subject to widow's dower; in suit by junior judgment creditor, 91½ acres are set aside for dower and interest of G. in residue sold and purchased by H.; pending subsequent suit by senior judgment creditor to sell same land, widow dies and G.'s interest in the 91½ acres vests; and, without amendment of pleadings, is first sold in exoneration of H.'s land. Held, not error for which decree will be reversed. The court could not look to proceedings in first suit, referred to in second suit, to ascertain what land had been sold therein. Groseclose v. Harman, 1 Va. Dec. 564.

(cc) Multifariousness.

See the title MULTIFARIOUSNESS.

"In Norris v. Bean, 17 W. Va. 655, this court decided that, in a suit to enforce a judgment lien, all the several plaintiffs as well as all the several defendants in all the judgments in courts of record in counties in which the lands sought to be subjected lie, which have been rendered against the judgment debtor alone or the judgment debtor and other defendants jointly, should be made parties. It is apparent, therefore, that all the defendants in the suit at bar are necessary parties, and the bill is not multifarious." Shenandoah Valley Nat. Bank v. Bates, 20 W. Va. 210, 217.

A bill in equity is brought to subject to the lien of the plaintiff's judgment, his debtor's estate alleged to have been fraudulently conveyed to various persons, who are charged with having combined and colluded with the debtor to defraud the plaintiff, and who are all made parties. Held, the bill is not multifarious. Almond v. Wilson, 75 Va. 613; Com. v. Drake, 81 Va. 305.

A bill in equity is brought to subject to the lien of the plaintiff's judgment his debtor's estate, alleged to have been fraudulently conveyed to various persons, all of whom are made defendants; but there is no charge of combination and confederacy among the alienees. Held, the bill is not multifarious. Although a plaintiff can not demand several matters of different natures against several defendants, a demurrer will not lie, even though the defendant be unconnected with each other, where there is one common interest centering on the point in issue in the cause. Almond v. Wilson, 75 Va. 613.

A bill in a suit in equity brought for the purpose of subjecting property to the lien of an attachment and also to have a confessed judgment lien on the attached property declared fraudulent as to the plaintiff's lien, is not multifarious. Stewart v. Stewart, 27 W. Va. 167.

A bill which seeks to enforce payment of a small judgment for costs against an administrator d. b. n. out of funds in his hands; to sell the real estate of the decedent to pay such judgment; to establish a devastavit against the administrator, and surcharge and falsify his accounts; to convene the heirs and creditors of said administrator, now deceased; to settle the accounts of his administrator, and sell his real estate; to convene the heirs, settle the accounts of the administrator, and distribute the estate of the third decedent; to convene the devisees, settle the accounts of the executor, and distribute the estate of a fourth decedent is multifarious and un-equitable. Crickard *v.* Crouch, 41 W. Va. 503, 23 S. E. 727.

A., a judgment creditor, suing on be-half of himself and all other judgment creditors of C. D. E. and the estate of B. against the said C. D. E. and the administrator of B., defendants, files his bill, in which he avers, that his judgment is founded on a note drawn by B. and endorsed successively by C. D. and E.; that a creditors' bill is pending in the same court against the administrator, widow and heirs of B. and also separate suits against C. and D. to subject the lands of said B. C. and D. to the payment of their respec-tive debts; that said B. C. D. and E. each own lands in the county, against which it is believed there are judgment liens; and prays, that said liens and their respective priorities be ascer-tained and said lands sold to pay said liens. The defendants demurred to said bill as follows: It is multifarious, because the plaintiff's judgment is joint against all the defendants, and he im-properly unites all the creditors hav-ing several judgments against any of said defendants severally. The bill is not multifarious. Shenandoah Valley Nat. Bank *v.* Bates, 20 W. Va. 210.

It is not multifarious for a bill to seek to subject judgment debtor's alleged interest in lands, chattels, etc., to the payment of plaintiff's debt. Thomas *v.* Sellman, 87 Va. 683, 13 S. E. 146.

(dd) Allegations.

Existence of Other Lienors.—A plaintiff is not required to allege in his bill and prove that there are no other lienors. Howard *v.* Stephenson, 33 W. Va. 116, 10 S. E. 66, 72.

In the case of McCoy *v.* Allen, 16 W. Va. 724, 725, it was held, that "if a creditor files a bill to subject the real estate of a debtor to a judgment lien, and in his bill fails to state that there is any other lien on this real es-tate, or to ask the auditing of other

liens, and makes only the debtor a party defendant, though the court in such cases by its decree directs a com-missioner to ascertain all liens and their priorities, still the court can not, upon the report of the commissioner that a prior deed of trust had been satisfied, decree that the debt secured by it has been paid, and order its re-lease. Such a decree of the court is a mere nullity, and not binding on the trustee or cestui que trust, because they were not parties to the suit; nor does such order of reference, or an actual service of notice by the commissioner on the cestui que trust, make him a party, or render such decree valid as against him." McMillan *v.* Hickman, 35 W. Va. 705, 14 S. E. 227, 229.

Suit by Receiver.—It is unnecessary to allege, in a chancery suit, brought by a special receiver, to enforce a judgment lien against the lands of a judgment debtor, that the suit in which the judgment on the common-law side of the court was had, or that the chan-cery suit brought to enforce the judg-ment, was brought by the receiver, by the direction of the court which ap-pointed the receiver. Howard *v.* Stephenson, 33 W. Va. 116, 10 S. E. 66.

H., special receiver, obtained a judg-ment in the circuit court of Mason county against R. & S. He then brought a chancery suit in said cir-cuit court to enforce the lien of this judgment against the lands of S. in said county. Held, such suit might be brought by H. for his own benefit, and that of all other judgment creditors of S., or he might make other judgment creditors of S. defendants, in which case the court would have had to audit all the judgment liens against S. be-fore he decreed a sale of his land; and, if H. made only S. a defendant, and did not bring his suit as a creditors' bill, yet, where S. alleges that he had other judgment creditors, the court would have converted this suit into a creditors' bill by directing a commis-sioner to audit all judgment liens against S., and it would have done the same had any other judgment creditors, by petition or otherwise, asked the court so to do. Howard v. Stephenson, 33 W. Va. 116, 10 S. E. 66.

Rents and Profits.—See the title JUDICIAL SALES.

Under the Code of West Virginia, 1868, it would seem unnecessary to aver, in a bill to enforce a judgment lien, that the rents and profits will not pay the debt in five years. Handly v. Sydenstricker, 4 W. Va. 605.

Subrogation.—Failure to ask specifically for subrogation is not ground for a demurrer to a bill filed by a surety against his principal to subject the lands of the principal to the lien of a judgment which he has paid as surety, where the bill alleges a state of facts which shows that the complainant is entitled to subrogation, and contains a prayer for general relief. Hawpe v. Bumgardner, 103 Va. 91, 48 S. E. 554.

Prayer for Relief.—Where a bill is filed to subject land to the payment of a judgment, if the bill contains a prayer for general relief, the decree of the court may extend beyond the land described in the bill, without any subsequent amendment of the pleadings. Groseclose v. Harman, 1 Va. Dec. 564.

(ee) Variance.

See the title VARIANCE.

Where the bill sets out a judgment correctly, as stated in the record of the judgment, there is no variance because a scire facias issued against garnishees, recites it as of a different amount, or that the endorsement on the papers by the clerk, of the proceedings in the cause, of the date of the judgment, is different from that stated in the bill. Fisher v. March, 26 Gratt. 765.

bb. Amended Bill.

See the title AMENDMENTS, vol. 1, p. 321.

In an action by a judgment creditor to subject property to his judgment, on the ground that an unrecorded deed of the property to the debtor had been fraudulently surrendered and cancelled, where the evidence showed that the deed was to the debtor as trustee for his wife, and the heirs of the wife, who was dead, were then made parties, and evidence taken as to such provision in the deed, a decree holding the provision fraudulent and void as against the complainant will not be reversed because the bill was not amended to charge the fraudulent character of the deed. Kline v. Triplett, 2 Va. Dec. 429.

Where a suit in equity is pending to enforce judgment liens against a debtor's lands, the fact, that persons after the commencement of a suit have acquired judgments against the debtor, generally does not make it necessary for the plaintiff to file an amended bill, making the answer of such subsequent or pendente lite judgment creditors parties to the suit; nor is it necessary for them generally to file their petitions asking to be made parties, if their judgments are obtained before the order of reference is made in the cause, or in time after the order of reference for them to prove their judgment before the commissioner. For such subsequent judgment creditor may be allowed to prove his judgment before his commissioner under the general order of reference, and thus make himself at least a quasi party to the cause, and be bound thereby as to his debt. Marling v. Robrecht, 13 W. Va. 440.

If in a suit to enforce a judgment lien, against the lands of a judgment debtor, the judgment creditor fails to mention a piece of land subject thereto, an amended bill may be filed in the cause, praying that such land be sold to satisfy their judgment lien thereon. Delaplain v. Wilkinson, 17 W. Va. 242.

Where a bill is filed to subject land to the payment of a judgment, if the bill contains a prayer for general relief, the decree of the court may extend beyond the land described in the bill, without any subsequent amendment of the pleadings. Groseclose v. Harman, 1 Va. Dec. 564.

cc. Cross Bill.

See the title CROSS BILLS, vol. 4, p. 100.

A suit to enforce the lien of a judgment, if found subsisting in a suit to cancel satisfaction thereof, may, during pendency of latter suit, be maintained by the owners of the judgment, in the nature of a cross bill. Higginbotham v. May, 90 Va. 233, 17 S. E. 941.

dd. Supplemental Bill.

See the title SUPPLEMENTAL PLEADINGS.

Where a suit is brought to enforce a judgment lien, and is revived in the name of an administrator d. b. n., who subsequently assigns the judgment to another, and the suit proceeds in the name of the administrator d. b. n., and it is charged in the answer of a defendant that a party other than the assignee of such administrator had become the owner of the judgment, and that it had been paid off and ratified therein, it becomes necessary for the assignee to file a supplemental bill, and it is error in the court to refuse to permit him to do so. List v. Pumphrey, 3 W. Va. 672.

B., as cestui que trust, in two deeds of trust made to L., as trustee, filed his bill in equity in the name of himself and said trustee, to enforce his trust liens upon a particular tract of land of E., alleging priority over all other liens by one of his trust liens, but admitting the priority of certain other trust liens and judgment liens, designated by his bill and exhibits, over his second trust lien, and made those particular lienors parties to the suit, and praying to convene those creditors before a commissioner, to ascertain and audit their respective debts in the order of their priorities; and that the land, or so much thereof as may be necessary to pay B.'s debts, be sold. E. was owner of other tracts of land, upon which the said judgment creditors and others had liens, but the bill took no notice thereof. Held, upon such a bill, it is error to decree an account to be taken by a commissioner "of all debts due by E.," "and which are valid and subsisting liens on his lands, the amounts of said debts, the persons to whom due, and their priority;" and to show "the quantity and annual and fee simple value of all the lands of E." The bill not having contemplated, nor asked for such an account, parties interested, relying on the essential inquiry as made by the bill, may thus be taken by surprise, and not collect testimony to meet the commissioner's inquiry. If after-discovered facts and testimony render it necessary for an account of such scope, the complainant should be permitted to file a supplemental bill, and thus present a proper cause for such an account. Baugher v. Eichelberger, 11 W. Va. 217.

(c) Answer and Replication.

Answer.—Where an answer in a suit for the enforcement of a judgment lien is filed and not replied to, the allegations therein, whether responsive to the bill or not, must be taken as true. If such answer raises a substantial defense to the case made by the bill, it will bar the plaintiff's equity. Snyder v. Martin, 17 W. Va. 276.

If a defendant in chancery, whose land is sought to be subjected to the lien of a judgment against his vendor, answers that other lands of his vendor, or land of a subsequent alienee of his vendor, are liable to the complainant's demand, the answer is not liable to exception for insufficiency, and the defendant should be allowed to show those facts. Kelly v. Hamblen, 98 Va. 383, 36 S. E. 491.

Where a suit is brought to enforce

a judgment lien, and is revived in the name of an administrator de bonis non, who subsequently assigns the judgment to another, and the suit proceeds in the name of the administrator de bonis non, and it is charged in the answer of a defendant that a party other than the assignee of such administrator, had become the owner of the judgment, and that it had been paid off and satisfied to him, it becomes necessary for the assignee to file a supplemental bill, and it is error in the court to refuse to permit him to do so. List *v.* Pumphrey, 3 W. Va. 672.

Replication.—Where a bill is filed to enforce a judgment lien, and the answer avers payment and a receipt of plaintiff's attorney for the amount· of the judgment, a general replication to the answer puts in issue the execution of the receipt, the authority of the attorney to receive the money, and whether or not it was procured by a fraudulent combination between the judgment debtor and the attorney of the judgment creditor with the purpose to defraud such creditor. Chalfants *v.* Martin, 25 W. Va. 394.

When a suit for the enforcement of a judgment lien, is set for hearing by the plaintiff, and heard on bill, answer and exhibits, and the court directs a dismissal of the bill, the plaintiff can not as a matter of right reply to the answer. Snyder *v.* Martin, 17 W. Va. 276.

(d) Mandamus.

See the title MANDAMUS.

Mandamus is in this state a proper remedy to enforce the payment of judgments against municipal corporations, when executions on such judgments have been issued and returned "no property found." Under such circumstances a judgment against a town in this state will be enforced by mandamus, though the judgment had been rendered for medical attendance on a pauper in a town, in which it was not the duty of the common council to support the poor residing in the town. Wells *v.* Mason, 23 W. Va. 456, citing Fisher *v.* Charleston, 17 W. Va. 595, 615.

A mandamus lies in behalf of a judgment creditor against a municipal corporation, where an execution has been issued on the judgment, and it has been returned "no property found." In such a case no demand on the proper municipal authorities to levy a special tax to pay such judgment is necessary as preliminary to the right of the creditor to apply to the court for a mandamus. In such a case it is not necessary in the petition, that the plaintiff should expressly allege, that this judgment, on which such execution has been so returned, has not been paid; but such nonpayment must be alleged in the alternative writ, as it is regarded as a declaration, and in this state such nonpayment must be alleged in every declaration. Fisher *v.* Charleston, 17 W. Va. 595.

(2) Election of Remedies.

"For a time there were two remedies to enforce a judgment against land, elegit and a suit in equity. Code, 1849 and 1860, ch. 186, §§ 6, 9; ch. 187, § 2. While those two remedies were existent the creditor could resort to either. Borst *v.* Nalle, 28 Gratt. 430. In case of death the creditor had to revive if he desired to proceed by. elegit; whereas, if he desired to proceed by a chancery suit to enforce the lien of his judgment, he could do so without revival. This shows the execution and the judgment are separate and distinct." Maxwell *v.* Leeson, 50 W. Va. 361, 368, 40 S. E. 420.

(3) Necessity of Revival.

A bill in equity may be maintained against the personal representative of a decedent and his devisees or heirs at law to subject the real estate of the decedent to the payment of a judgment recovered against him in his lifetime, without first reviving such judgment at law. James v. Life, 92 Va. 702, 24 S. E. 275; Taylor v. Spindle, 2 Gratt. 44; Burbridge v. Higgins, 6 Gratt. 119, 127; Suckley v. Rotchford, 12 Gratt. 60, 68.

The right of a judgment creditor to bring his suit in equity against the personal representative and heirs or devisees of his deceased debtor before reviving his judgment at law has been generally recognized in the courts of this state. James v. Life, 92 Va. 702, 24 S. E. 275.

A decree is a lien on the debtor's land and the creditor may come into equity to subject the land, though the decree has not been revived against the administrator of the debtor, and no execution has ever issued upon it. For this proposition Burbridge v. Higgins, 6 Gratt. 119, is cited and followed in James v. Life, 92 Va. 702, 705, 24 S. E. 275; Werdenbaugh v. Reid, 20 W. Va. 588, 591.

"As statute law makes the judgment a direct legal lien on the land until it is barred—I say makes the judgment a lien—an equity suit may be brought to enforce that lien notwithstanding the death of a party, either party, may have suspended right of execution upon the judgment until revival. Burbridge v. Higgins, 6 Gratt. 119, 120." Maxwell v. Leeson, 50 W. Va. 361, 365, 40 S. E. 420.

(4) Parties.

(a) In General.

All interested in the relief sought by a bill to enforce a judgment lien on lands should be made parties—either plaintiffs or defendants. "The second ground of demurrer was that one of the defendants in the suit at law, in which the judgment was obtained, and who was one of the judgment debtors, was not made a party defendant in this suit. All persons who are interested in the relief sought by a bill should be made parties defendants to the bill, unless they are already joined as plaintiffs, and the prayer for process must be so framed as to bring all persons interested in that relief before the court, either as plaintiffs or defendants. This is elementary." Stovall v. Border Grange Bank, 78 Va. 188, 191.

The West Virginia Code provides that in every suit to enforce the lien of a judgment in equity all persons having liens on the real estate sought to be subjected by judgment or otherwise, shall be made parties, plaintiff or defendant, or if the number of such persons exceed ten the suit may be brought by any one or more of them, for the benefit of himself and such other lien holders as will come in and contribute to the expenses of the suit. And whether the suit be so brought or not, every such lien holder, whether he be named as a party to the suit or not, or whether he be served with process therein or not, may present, prove and have allowed any claim he may have against the judgment debtor, which is a lien on such real estate, or any part thereof, and from and after the time he presents any such claim he shall be deemed a party plaintiff in such suit. W. Va. Code, 1899, ch. 139, § 4147; Jackson v. Hill, 21 W. Va. 601, 616; McMillan v. Hickman, 35 W. Va. 705, 14 S. E. 227, 229.

(b) Parties Plaintiff.

aa. In General.

In a suit to subject land to the lien of a judgment, it is not necessary to make any of the other lien creditors besides the plaintiffs formal parties, as they are in effect made parties, by the opportunity given them of proving their claims before the commissioner, whose account was taken upon due notice given in the usual way; especially when such other lien creditors seem to have availed themselves fully of the opportunity. Brumback v. Keyser, 1 Va. Dec. 96.

Lienors and persons owning the remainder are not necessary parties to bill to enforce a judgment, as creditors can subject only their debtors' interest in the land. The omission of a necessary party, who voluntarily appears, is harmless error. Moore *v.* Bruce, 85 Va. 139, 7 S. E. 195.

bb. Real Parties in Interest.

"A suit in equity can not be brought in the name of one party for the use of another." "Where a judgment at law was recovered in the name of A. for the use of B. and afterwards A. brought a chancery suit in his own name for the use of B., the judgment creditor, and B. was not a party to the suit, and a decree was rendered, enforcing said judgment lien, it was reversed for want of proper parties and remanded for proper parties to be made. See also, Grove *v.* Judy, 24 W. Va. 294; Neely *v.* Jones, 16 W. Va. 625." Bank *v.* Cook, 55 W. Va. 222, 46 S. E. 1027, citing Kellam *v.* Sayer, 30 W. Va. 198, 3 S. E. 589.

H. brings his suit in equity to enforce a judgment lien and files his bill therein in his own name for the use and benefit of L., and L. is not made a party to the suit. Held, that while this mode of bringing suits at law for well-known reasons is allowed and recognized in a class at least, still it is not allowed in equity, as the general rule in equity is, that all persons materially interested in the subject matter of the suit should be made parties thereto. This case is not an exception to the general rule; and the bill was demurrable. McClaskey *v.* O'Brien, 16 W. Va. 791.

cc. Judgment Creditors.

A suit to enforce the lien of a judgment, may be maintained by the judgment creditor, during the pendency of an action by attorneys to cancel satisfaction of such judgment, if it should be found to be subsisting in such latter suit; this second action should be treated as a cross bill in the first action. Higginbotham *v.* May, 90 Va. 233, 17 S. E. 941.

A judgment creditor has a right to come into a court of equity to enforce his judgment lien against the lands conveyed in a deed of trust prior to the obtaining of the judgment, subject to the debts secured by the trust; and after the debt secured by the trust falls due and no sale is made thereunder, the court will interfere for the benefit of judgment liens younger than the trust, and will direct a sale of the land, and not the redemption alone to satisfy the debts of both classes of creditors. Laidley *v.* Hinchman, 3 W. Va. 423.

Pendente Lite Judgment Creditors. —Where a suit in equity is pending to enforce judgment liens against a debtor's land, the fact, that persons after the commencement of the suit have acquired judgments against the debtor, generally does not make it necessary for the plaintiff to file an amended bill, making the answer of such subsequent or pendente lite judgment creditors parties to the suit; nor is it necessary for them generally to file their petitions asking to be made parties, if their judgments are obtained before the order of reference made in the cause, or in time after the order of reference for them to prove their judgments before the commissioner. For such subsequent judgment creditor may be allowed to prove his judgment before the commissioner under the general order of reference, and thus make himself at least a quasi party to the cause, and be bound thereby as to his debt. Marling *v.* Robrecht, 13 W. Va. 440.

While with the view of saving a multitude of suits and of costs, pendente lite judgment creditors may be permitted to prove their judgments before the commissioner under the general order of reference, and file petitions in the cause asking to be made parties defendant thereto, still the filing of such petitions by such pendente lite judgment creditors should not be allowed from time to time without limit, so as to unnecessarily delay the plaintiff's cause. Marling v. Robrecht, 13 W. Va. 440.

dd. Receivers.

See the title RECEIVERS.

A receiver has authority to bring a suit to enforce a judgment lien, and in the absence of any denial of his authority, he is not required to allege or prove it. If it does not appear from the record that he did not have leave of court, and such leave is not denied or disputed, it will be presumed to exist. Howard v. Stephenson, 33 W. Va. 116, 10 S. E. 66.

A special receiver may bring a chancery suit to enforce the lien of a judgment against the judgment debtor's lands, for his own benefit, and that of all the other judgment creditors of the judgment debtor, or he might make other judgment creditors of the debtor defendants, in which case the court would have to audit all the judgment liens against the debtor, before it decreed a sale of the land; and if the special receiver made only the judgment debtor a defendant, and did not bring his suit as a creditors' bill, yet, where the judgment debtor alleges that he has other judgment creditors, the court will convert this suit into a creditors' bill by directing a commissioner to audit all judgment liens against the judgment debtor; but it would do the same had any other judgment creditors, by petition or otherwise, asked the court to do so. Howard v. Stephenson, 33 W. Va. 116, 10 S. E. 66.

Commissioner sold land and received the money without giving bond or accounting. Purchaser was required to pay it again. Receiver got judgment against him and surety. Execution was returned "no effects." Before the return, commissioner executed trust deed to secure purchaser. Receiver filed in pending creditor's suit against commissioner, his petition to enforce his execution lien against fund secured to purchaser. Latter resisted on the ground (1), that he claimed the fund as his homestead, and (2), that he had assigned it. Receiver then brought suit to enforce his judgment lien against lands of purchaser and surety. Held, receiver was entitled to maintain his suit to enforce said judgment on said lands. Va. Code, 1873, ch. 182, § 9, p. 1167; Eggleton v. Whittle, 84 Va. 163, 4 S. E. 222.

H., special receiver, obtained a judgment in the circuit court of Mason county against R. & S. He then brought a chancery suit in said circuit court to enforce the lien of this judgment against the lands of S. in said county. Held, it was unnecessary in this chancery suit to allege in the bill that the suit in which the judgment on the common-law side of the court was had, or this chancery suit, was brought by the receiver, by the direction of the court which appointed the receiver. Howard v. Stephenson, 33 W. Va. 116, 10 S. E. 66.

ee. Assignor and Assignee.

The assignor and assignee of a judgment may be properly made coplaintiffs in a chancery suit to enforce the lien of the judgment on the debtor's lands. Neely v. Jones, 16 W. Va. 625, 626.

ff. Purchasers of Debtor's Lands.

Where there are several purchasers of land subject to a judgment lien, some may file a bill to question the lien, and if it is valid, asking that the different purchasers may be subjected to pay it. And though they ask for a rateable contribution, this will not prevent the court's subjecting the land last sold to satisfy the creditor. Michaux v. Brown, 10 Gratt. 612.

(c) Intervenors.

See the title INTERVENTION.

It is the constant practice in this state, where a suit is pending to enforce judgment liens against a debtor's lands, to permit other lien creditors of such debtor to file petitions in such suit making themselves parties thereto. Marling *v.* Robrecht, 13 W. Va. 440. Such petition can only be filed by leave of the court, and an opportunity must be given to any party in interest to answer it. But where no new parties are brought into the suit by the petition, and especially where the cause is subsequently referred to a commissioner, so that all the parties interested can be heard and make their objections, it is not the practice to serve process to answer the petition. Kendrick *v.* Whitney, 28 Gratt. 646; Marling *v.* Robrecht, 13 W. Va. 440; Jackson *v.* Hull, 21 W. Va. 601, 613.

Where a vendor of land, who has retained the title, files a bill against the widow and infant children of the vendee, for a sale of land to satisfy his debt, the judgment creditors of the vendee may make themselves parties to the cause, and have the land, subject to the vendor's lien, and the widow's dower, applied to the payment of their debts. Simmons *v.* Lyles, 27 Gratt. 922.

In a suit to subject land to the lien of a judgment, if any of the lien creditors have been omitted in the original suit, when the cause is remanded they may still have an opportunity of coming in by petition and present their claims and have a report made upon them. Brumback *v.* Keyser, 1 Va. Dec. 96.

If in a suit by a judgment creditor to sell the lands of his debtor for the payment of his judgment, any judgment creditor, who has not been made a party, formally or informally, having an unsatisfied judgment against such debtor, which was recovered before such suit was brought, may at any time before final decree file his petition in said cause setting up his judgment and praying to be made a party to such suit, and to have his rights under such judgment adjudicated, and if this right be denied him, it will be error for which the decree of the cir-

cuit court, denying such right, will be reversed. Pappenheimer *v.* Roberts, 24 W. Va. 702.

Upon a bill filed by a judgment creditor, suing on behalf of himself and all other lien creditors of the defendant, a creditor holding a vendor's reserved lien on a part of the lands of the defendant may come in by petition, and assert his lien, and it is immaterial whether the rents and profits of that and other lands of the vendee will, within five years, pay and satisfy the amount of such lien. He is entitled to a decree for the sale of the land on which he has a vendor's lien, although he may also have a judgment for the amount. Kane *v.* Mann, 93 Va. 239, 24 S. E. 938.

(d) Parties Defendant.

aa. In General.

The necessary parties defendant in a bill to enforce a judgment lien are: I. The judgment debtor himself. II. The trustees in all deeds of trust on the judgment debtor's lands sought to be subjected to the payment of judgment liens. III. If the deeds of trust are deeds to secure the payment of a limited number of debts, then the cestuis que trust in these deeds including not only the parties, to whom the debts secured are due, but also all the obligors in these debts, if there be any other obligor than the grantor or judgment debtor, and if the trusts are of different character, then all the cestuis que trust in them, unless from their indefinite description or some other good reason they would not all be made defendants in any suit in equity brought by an adverse claimant against the trustee respecting the trust property. IV. All the several plaintiffs as well as all the several defendants in all judgments in the courts of record in the counties, in which the lands sought to be subjected lie, which have been rendered against the judgment debtor alone or the judgment debtor and other defendants jointly, and also all the plaintiffs and all the defendants in any such judgments, whether rendered by courts of record or by justices in any part of the state, which have been docketed on the judgment lien docket of said county or counties. See Neely v. Jones, 16 W. Va. 625. V. Any other party, who according to the general rules of equity in the particular case has such a direct interest in the subject matter or object of the suit, as would render it necessary, that he should be made a defendant to the suit, as for instance the transferee or other owner of any debt secured by a deed of trust on any part of the real estate sought to be subjected to the payment of the judgment debts. Norris v. Bean, 17 W. Va. 655; Shenandoah Valley Nat. Bank v. Bates, 20 W. Va. 210; Jackson v. Hull, 21 W. Va. 601, 615.

In a proceeding in chancery by a judgment creditor to subject the real estate of his debtor to the payment of his judgment lien, it is the duty of the plaintiff to make all the lien creditors of the debtor known to him, and which are disclosed by records of the courts of the counties in which the lands sought to be sold are situated, parties to the suit. McMillan v. Hickman, 35 W. Va. 705, 14 S. E. 227; McCoy v. Allen, 16 W. Va. 724, 725; Bilmyer v. Sherman, 23 W. Va. 656.

"If the record shows that there were any others who claim liens on this land, it would have been necessary to have made them parties before the land was decreed to be sold. See Neely v. Jones, 16 W. Va. 625; Code, W. Va., ch. 139, § 7. But in this case it does not appear from the record in any way, either by evidence, pleading, or by suggestion to the court below in any manner, that there were others who claimed liens on this land, and that these lienors and their priorities and the amount of their liens would have to be ascertained before there could be a decree to sell the land."

Howard v. Stephenson, 33 W. Va. 116, 10 S. E. 66, 72.

bb. Judgment Creditors.

In General.—In a proceeding in chancery by a judgment creditor to subject the real estate of his debtor to the lien of his judgment, it is the duty of the plaintiff to make all the lien creditors of the debtor known to him, and which are disclosed by the judgment lien docket, or the records of the court of the counties in which the lands sought to be sold are situated, parties to the suit. McMillan v. Hickman, 35 W. Va. 705, 14 S. E. 227; Bilmyer v. Sherman, 23 W. Va. 656; McCoy v. Allen, 16 W. Va. 724, 725; Jackson v. Hull, 21 W. Va. 601; Shenandoah Valley Nat. Bank v. Bates, 20 W. Va. 210; Grove v. Judy, 24 W. Va. 294.

A creditor, who brings suit against a debtor to enforce against his lands a judgment lien, should sue on behalf of himself and all other creditors excepting those made defendants, and he should make formally defendants in the suit all creditors who have obtained judgments in the courts of record in the county or counties in which the debtor owns lands sought to be subjected to the payment of the judgments, also all creditors who have obtained judgments in courts of record or before justices in any part of the state, and have had them docketed on the judgment lien docket of such county or counties. Neely v. Jones, 16 W. Va. 625, 626; Livesay v. Feamster, 21 W. Va. 83; Norris v. Bean, 17 W. Va. 655; Pappenheimer v. Roberts, 24 W. Va. 702.

In a suit brought by a judgment creditor to enforce his judgment lien he should make formal defendants to the suit all creditors, who have obtained judgments against the debtor in the courts of record in the county wherein the lands lie, which he seeks to subject, and if he fails to do so, he should in the order of reference in the cause provide for calling in all judgment creditors of the debtor by publication; and if this be not done, this court in such a case will reverse on order of the court confirming the commissioner's report and ordering a sale of the debtor's lands. Livesay v. Feamster, 21 W. Va. 83, citing Neely v. Jones, 16 W. Va. 625; Caldwell v. Bean, 17 W. Va. 655.

Judgment creditors are necessary parties in proceedings to subject lands, upon which they are liens, to the payment of other judgment liens. Hoffman v. Shields, 4 W. Va. 490; Livesay v. Feamster, 21 W. Va. 83.

If a suit be brought by a judgment creditor to sell the lands of his debtor for the payment of his judgment, and it appears on the face of the bill that other creditors have unsatisfied judgments against said debtor duly recorded on the judgment lien docket in the county wherein the said lands are situated, such other creditors are necessary parties to such a suit. Pappenheimer v. Roberts, 24 W. Va. 702.

"This court has heretofore held, that judgment creditors are necessary parties in proceedings to subject the lands upon which they have liens, to the payment of other judgment liens; so that this is a settled question so far as this court is concerned. Snyder v. Brown, 3 W. Va. 143." Hoffman v. Shields, 4 W. Va. 490, 492.

Illustrative Cases.—S. conveyed to W. a tract of land on condition that he should pay certain parties, who subsequently became the heirs and legatees of S., certain sums of money to become due and payable annually after his death. One of the legatees and her assignee of a part of the sum bequeathed to her, brought a bill after the death of S. to subject the land, there being but little personal estate or the sum due thereon from W. to payment of their claims. The administrators with the will annexed and W. only were made parties defendant. The court decreed that the complain-

ant's claims and the debts due sundry creditors be paid by W., and in default thereof, that the land be sold. Held, it appearing by the answer of W. that there was a judgment creditor, he ought to have been made a party. Snyder v. Brown, 3 W. Va. 143.

M. was adjudged a bankrupt and discharged in 1873. He claimed as his homestead certain land, which the bankrupt court allotted him, but without notice to his creditors, who were lienors by judgments recovered in 1857. Those creditors in 1878 filed their bill in the state court to enforce their liens on said land, but did not make T., who was the assignee in bankruptcy of M., a party. M. demurred, answered, and pleaded that the enforcement of the judgments was barred by the lapse of twenty years between their date and the filing of the bill. The demurrer was overruled and decree of sale entered, but the commissioner of sale was not directed to give the usual bond. On appeal by M., held, the decree of the state court for sale of the land does not impinge the decree of the bankrupt court allotting the land to M. for his homestead, because the judgment lienors were not parties to the proceedings wherein the latter decree was rendered. McAllister v. Bodkin, 76 Va. 809.

A., a judgment creditor, suing on behalf of himself and all other judgment creditors of C. D. E. and the estate of B. against the said C. D. E. and the administrator of B., defendants, files his bill, in which he avers, that his judgment is founded on a note drawn by B. and endorsed successively by C. D. and E.; that a creditors' bill is pending in the same court against the administrator, widow and heirs of B. and also separate suits against C. and D. to subject the lands of said B. C. and D. to the payment of their respective debts; that said B. C. D. and E. each own lands in the county, against which it is believed there are judgment liens; and prays, that said liens and their respective priorities be ascertained and said lands sold to pay said liens. The defendants demurred to said bill as follows: It improperly seeks to charge the lands of said B. C. D. and E. with the payment of all the judgment liens against all or any of said parties, and yet none of the parties having such liens are made parties to the bill. Under the rule announced by this court in Neely v. Jones, 16 W. Va. 625, it appearing that judgments against the defendants were of record in the county, where the defendant's lands lie, the first ground of demurrer should have been sustained by the court. Shenandoah Valley Nat. Bank v. Bates, 20 W. Va. 210.

Error.—C. brought his bill to enforce judgment liens against the real estate of M. E. P., wife of L. P., and made other lien holders thereon parties defendant. R. & Sons afterwards filed their bill against M. E. P. and L. P., alleging that the deed from the father of L. P. for the real estate sought to be subjected was made to M. E. P. in fraud of the creditors of L. P. and asking to have it set aside, and the real estate subjected to the payment of their judgment against L. P., which existed at the date of the deed, but failed to make the judgment creditors of M. E. P. parties to their bill. The cases were heard together, the deed set aside, and R. & Sons' judgment declared to be the first lien on the property. Held error to hear the cases together, or to decree upon the bill of R. & Sons until the proper parties were brought in. Crim v. Price, 46 W. Va. 374, 33 S. E. 251.

In a suit by a vendor to enforce a vendor's lien, other lienors having judgment liens on the vendee's lands ought not to be made parties to such suit, nor should a notice to all persons holding liens on the real estate of the debtor be published under § 7, ch. 126, of acts of 1882, said section having no application to a suit brought to enforce a vendor's lien. "This section applies to a creditors' bill brought by one or more judgment creditors to enforce their liens against the debtor's real estate. It has no application to a suit brought by a vendor against his vendee to enforce his vendor's lien, which is still to be conducted as it always was, it being unnecessary to make other lien creditors parties to the suit either formally or informally, and of course unnecessary to have them convened before a commissioner, and their liens and priorities ascertained." Moreland v. Metz, 24 W. Va. 119, 130.

Nonresident judgment creditors are necessary parties to a bill in equity to enforce a judgment lien, and the order of publication must be properly executed against him before a decree can be rendered. Hoffman v. Shields, 4 W. Va. 490.

"It has been questioned, whether it was necessary to make persons, occupying the position these persons did, formally parties to such a suit, and whether it was not sufficient for a party, who files a bill to subject the land of a living debtor to the satisfaction of a judgment, to make all other judgment creditors parties to the suit by the plaintiff suing on behalf of himself and all other judgment creditors. In this court it would seem to have been held, in the case of Hoffman v. Shields, 4 W. Va. 490, that it was necessary to make all such judgment creditors formally parties. In this case there was another error fatal to the appellees and the court does not appear to have maturely considered this question. We can not follow to its full extent the apparent decision in this case, because the judgments of all the courts in the state, as well as the judgments of all justices of the peace, are liens on the lands of the debtor, and it would be impracticable, if not impossible, for the plaintiff, who desired to enforce his judgment lien to make all the judgment creditors in the state formal parties defendant in his bill, as he could not ascertain who they were. They being an undefined class having a like interest with the plaintiff, he ought on general principles to be allowed to sue on behalf of himself and all other judgment creditors without making them formal parties." Neely v. Jones, 16 W. Va. 625, 647.

Suit by Surety.—It is necessary, in a bill to enforce a judgment lien by a surety, where such surety has paid the judgment, that the original judgment creditors, whose judgment he had paid, be made parties. Conaway v. Odbert, 2 W. Va. 25; Hoffman v. Shields, 4 W. Va. 490.

The judgment creditor in a judgment upon a negotiable note, must be a party to a suit in equity by a subsequent endorser to enforce substitution to the lien of the judgment against the land of the prior endorser. Schilb v. Moon, 50 W. Va. 47, 40 S. E. 329.

Decree of Sale.—Where there are several judgment creditors whose judgments are of equal dignity with that of the plaintiff, it is proper that they should be convened in a suit by a creditor seeking to enforce his judgment; but if it appears from the pleadings and proof, that such judgment creditors are enforcing their liens or debts in another court, against the parties liable for such other debts, and that there is a large fund under control of the latter court, applicable to such judgments or debts, it is error to decree a sale of the land, on the failure of the debtor to pay the entire amount of such judgment, without taking any steps to ascertain what would remain unpaid, after the application of such fund to the liquidation of such judgments. Murdock v. Welles, 9 W. Va. 552.

Appellate Practice.—If all the judgment creditors are not made parties to a suit by a creditor against a debtor to enforce against his lands a judgment lien, either formally or informally, and this is disclosed in any manner by the record, the appellate court will reverse any decree ordering the sale of the land or the distribution of the proceeds of such sale. Neely v. Jones, 16 W. Va. 625, 626.

In Neely v. Jones, 16 W. Va. 625, it was held, that a creditor, who brings suit against a debtor to enforce against his lands a judgment lien, should sue on behalf of himself and all other judgment creditors except those made defendants, and should make formally defendants in the suit all creditors, who have obtained judgments in the courts of record in the county or counties in which the debtor owns lands which are sought to be subjected to the payment of their judgments, also all creditors who have obtained judgments in courts of record in the county or counties in which the debtor owns lands, which are sought to be subjected to the payment of the judgment, also all creditors who have obtained judgments in courts of record or before justices in any part of the state and have had them docketed on the judgment lien docket of said county or counties. If all the judgment creditors are not made parties to such suit either formally or informally, and this is disclosed in any manner by the record, the appellate court will reverse any decree ordering the sale of the lands or the distribution of the proceeds of such sale. But if all the judgment creditors are made parties to such suit informally, by being called by publication before a commissioner under a decree of the court to present their judgments, then this court would not reverse a decree ordering sale of the lands of the debtor or distribution of the proceeds of such sale, merely because the record disclosed, that some of the judgment creditors had not been made formal defendants, who ought to have been so made, unless it appears that objection was made to the rendering of such decree on this ground in the court below, and before such decree was rendered. If in such a bill the creditor should fail to sue on behalf of himself and all other judgment creditors, the court should afford to all judgment creditors an opportunity to have their judgments audited before a commissioner by directing a publication to be made calling upon them to present their judgments for auditing; and in such case the appellate court would regard such bill as a creditors' bill, the same as if the plaintiff had sued on behalf of himself and all other judgment creditors except those made defendants. Jackson v. Hull, 21 W. Va. 601, followed in Grove v. Judy, 24 W. Va. 294, 297.

It is settled 'by the decisions of this court, that a creditor, who brings a suit against his debtor to enforce a judgment lien, whether he brings such suit on behalf of himself and other lien creditors or alone, should formally make defendants to his bill all creditors of such debtor, who have obtained judgments in the courts of record in the county or counties, in which the lands sought to be subjected are situated, and also the creditors who have obtained judgments in any part of the state and have had them entered on the judgment lien docket in such county or counties; and unless such judgment creditors are formally made defendants, or informally made such (by being called by publication before a court, under an order of reference, to file their judgment in such suit), and this is disclosed in any manner by the record, the appellate court will reverse any decree ordering the sale of lands or the distribution of the proceeds of such sale. But if all such creditors are made parties informally, then this court will not reverse such decree merely because the record shows that some of them are not made formal parties, unless it appears that objection was made to the rendering of such decree in the court below before it was entered. Neely v. Jones, 16 W. Va. 625; Norris v. Bean, 17 W. Va. 655; Shen-

andoah Valley Nat. Bank v. Bates, 20 W. Va. 210, 215.

cc. Judgment Debtors.

It is obvious that the judgment debtor must be a formal defendant to the bill. Norris v. Bean, 17 W. Va. 655, 666. .

Where a special receiver obtained judgment against two debtors in the circuit court of a county, and then brought a chancery suit in that court to enforce the lien of this judgment against the lands of one of the debtors in the county where the judgment was obtained, it was held unnecessary to make the other judgment debtor a party defendant in this chancery suit, as in it the plaintiff sought no redress against him or his property. Howard v. Stephenson, 33 W. Va. 116, 10 S. E. 66.

dd. Assignor and Assignee.

After a cause has been revived in the name of an administrator de bonis non, he assigns a judgment, which is the subject matter of the suit, to another, and the suit proceeds in the name of the administrator de bonis non, without making the assignee a party. Held, that the cause might so proceed until final decree. List v. Pumphrey, 3 W. Va. 672.

In creditors' suit, assignor with recourse of obligation, whereon is founded a judgment sought to be enforced, and subsequent alienees of land sought to be subjected, are proper parties. James River, etc., Co. v. Littlejohn, 18 Gratt. 53, 83; Preston v. Aston, 85 Va. 104, 7 S. E. 344.

Assignee in Bankruptcy.—M. was adjudged a bankrupt and discharged in 1873. He claimed as his homestead certain land, which the bankrupt court allotted him, but without notice to his creditors, who were lienors by judgments recovered in 1857. Those creditors in 1878 filed their bill in the state court to enforce their liens on said land, but did not make T., who was the assignee in bankruptcy of M., a party. M. demurred, answered, and pleaded that the enforcement of the judgments was barred by the lapse of twenty years between their date and the filing of the bill. The demurrer was overruled and decree of sale entered, but the commissioner of sale was not directed to give the usual bond. On appeal by M., held, under the bankrupt laws of the United States the legal title to the bankrupt's homestead, does not vest in his assignee; and if it does vest, eo instante the homestead is allotted him, and legal title thereto reverts to him. Therefore the assignee had no interest in the subject of this suit and was not a necessary party. The assignee had not even a reversionary interest in the subject of this suit, as by Code, 1873, p. 1171, ch. 183, § 8, if the homestead be not aliened in the householder's lifetime, after his death it continues for benefit of his widow and children, until her death or marriage, and after her death or marriage until the youngest child becomes twenty-one years of age; after which it passes to his heirs or to his devisees, not subject to dower, but subject to all his debts. In no event does it pass to his assignee in bankruptcy. McAllister v. Bodkin, 76 Va. 809.

ee. Joint Defendants.

H., special receiver, obtained a judgment in the circuit court of Mason county against R. & S. He then brought a chancery suit in said circuit court to enforce the lien of this judgment against the lands of S. in said county. Held, it was unnecessary to make R. a defendant in this chancery suit, as in it the plaintiff sought no redress against him or his property. Howard v. Stephenson, 33 W. Va. 116, 10 S. E. 66. See Preston v. National Exchange Bank, 97 Va. 222, 33 S. E. 546.

In a suit of this sort it is the duty of the plaintiff to make not only all judgment creditors, whose judgments appear in the clerks' office in the counties, in which lie the lands he seeks to subject, formal parties defendant, but if any of these judgments are joint judgments against the judgment debtor of the plaintiff and third persons, such third persons should be made formal defendants in the bill and served with process, as they evidently have a direct interest, that such joint judgments should be audited in their proper place as to priority and paid, as they are personally bound to pay them, if not so paid. Norris v. Bean, 17 W. Va. 655, 670.

ff. Lienors for Unpaid Purchase Money.

In a suit in equity, to sell land to satisfy a judgment lien, or to enforce the payment of the purchase money, if it appears that there is a prior lien for unpaid purchase money on the land, those entitled to the benefit of such prior purchase money lien, should be made parties to the suit. Dickinson v. Railroad Co., 7 W. Va. 390.

gg. Purchasers of Debtors' Lands.

In General.—Subsequent alienees of the land sought to be subjected are proper parties to the suit. James River, etc., Co. v. Littlejohn, 18 Gratt. 53, 83; Preston v. Aston, 85 Va. 104, 7 S. E. 344.

No subsequent decree or judgment for an amount beyond the legal call of the first judgment, in a suit to which such purchaser is not a formal party, or wherein the true amount due by reason of the judgment was not in fact litigated, can estop such purchaser from satisfying the demand by payment of a sum lawfully called for by the judgment as it was when he purchased. Bensimer v. Fell, 35 W. Va. 15, 12 S. E. 1078, 1079, 29 Am. St. Rep. 774.

In suit to settle estate of R., deceased, C. set up a judgment against G., insolvent principal, and R. and P., sureties. G. and P. were not named in the bill. Leave was given to amend the bill, and make parties G. and P., and J. C., the alienee of P.'s land, which was bound by the judgment lien. Amended bill was filed, and C. and J. C., but not P., were summoned to answer it, but by order of plaintiff's attorney, it was dismissed at same rules at which it was filed. Account of liens was ordered and taken, showing that $616 was P.'s portion, and a lien on P.'s lands aliened to J. C., who had been summoned to appear, and who did appear before the commissioner. Circuit court confirmed report, and decree that J. C. pay to its receiver said sum of money. On appeal, held, J. C. was not, in any fair sense of the term, a party to the suit. J. C. not being a party, the decree is a nullity as to him. Without the presence of P. before the court, his lands could not be subjected to the judgment. In no aspect of the case was there any foundation for the personal decree against J. C. Cronise *v.* Carper, **80** Va. 678.

Pendente lite purchasers need not be made parties. Where judgments are docketed or deeds of trust recorded, or liens otherwise acquired, and a chancery suit to enforce same is pending, there need be no notice of the pendency of such chancery suit, under § 13, ch. 139, Code, 891, to bind purchasers purchasing after the docketing of such judgment or recordation of such deeds of trust or lien. They are pendente lite purchasers, under the common-law rule. Shumate *v.* Crockett, 43 W. Va. 491, 27 S. E. 240, citing Harmon *v.* Bryam, 11 W. Va. 511; Lynch *v.* Andrews, 25 W. Va. 751, 754; Stout *v.* Philippi Mfg., etc., Co., 41 W. Va. 339, 23 S. E. 571; O'Connor *v.* Dills, 43 W. Va. 54, 26 S. E. 354.

In 1881, H., and in March, 1882, J. against W. & Q., and in July, 1882, S. against W. alone, brought their respective bills to enforce judgments on lands alleged therein to belong to W., who answered admitting the ownership, whilst Q. failed to answer. In each suit there was a decree to rent. Commissioner reported his inability to rent for enough to pay the judgments, and in October, 1882, there was a decree in these three suits heard together to sell. In February, 1883, J. filed a supplemental bill alleging that he had just learned that these lands had, before the institution of these suits, been sold under proceedings in bankruptcy and bought by W., who still owed part of the purchase money. In these suits there was an account of liens and lands, the latter being reported as the lands of W., who was present and did not object. In April, 1883, account was confirmed and sale decreed and made in June, 1883, to J., Q. being present and T. having notice thereof, and neither objecting. Sale was confirmed, and J. had paid half the purchase money on 18th June, 1884. Twelve months after such payment Q., T. and W. filed their cross bills, making all W.'s creditors parties, and charged that just after the sale in bankruptcy in 1878, W. had sold by parol, and by deed recorded in October, 1882, conveyed to Q. ninety-three acres, and to T. thirty acres of said land by deed recorded in November, 1882, and that both had paid him the price thereof, which he had paid to his assignee in bankruptcy on the purchase money due him, and had each made improvements on said parcels of land and prayed that the decree of sale be set aside. Defendants answered the cross bill, denying the parol sales and the alleged payments thereon, which sales and payments were not established by evidence. Held: Q. and T., being pendente lite purchasers, were not necessary parties to the suits to enforce the judgments against W. Price *v.* Thrash. 30 Gratt. 515; McGee *v.* Johnson. 85 Va. 161, 7 S. E. 374.

Sureties.—Where there is a judgment at law against a principal debtor and his two sureties, and a bill is filed in equity for the purpose, inter alia, of enforcing the lien of the judgment against the real estate of the principal and the real estate of one of the sureties, his cosurety is a proper party, and, being made a party, is not in any way served with process, and does not appear, and a joint personal decree is pronounced against them; held, the cosurety decreed against, who was before the court, has right of complaint that the court entered a void decree against his cosurety. Findley v. Smith, 42 W. Va. 299, 26 S. E. 370.

B. & S. for use of McC., obtained a judgment at law, in November, 1859, against G. and O'B., et. al., his sureties. A suit in equity was instituted by his lien creditors for the purpose of subjecting the real estate of said O'B. to the payment of their liens against it. G. was the owner of a tract of twenty-four and one-half acres of land and was a party defendant to the suit, but no proceedings were taken therein against said twenty-four and one-half acres. G. died pending the suit which was revived in the name of C., his only heir, who conveyed the twenty-four and one-half acres to D. Held, that said suit being for the purpose of enforcing the liens against the real estate of O'B. and not in any way involving or affecting the twenty-four and one-half acres, D. was not a pendente lite purchaser thereof, therefore not a necessary party. Woods v. Douglass, 52 W. Va. 517, 44 S. E. 234.

Fraudulent Alienees.—If in a suit brought by a judgment creditor to sell the lands of his debtor for the payment of his judgment, the plaintiff seeks to set aside as fraudulent and void certain deeds alleged to have been made by the judgment debtor with intent to hinder, delay and defraud the plaintiff in the collection of his debt, in order to charge the lands thereby conveyed with the payment of his judgment, such alleged fraudulent alienees are necessary parties to such suit, although they may have conveyed the said lands granted them, respectively, to other persons who are defendants in the suit.

Pappenheimer v. Roberts, 24 W. Va. 702.

Administrator and Heirs of Purchaser.—In a creditor's suit afterwards brought by another creditor to convene and enforce liens against lands of such judgment debtor, but not against the land so sold, there is a personal decree against the debtor based on such judgment for an amount beyond the legal call of the judgment by reason of such usury, and the lands of such debtor are decreed to sale to pay that, and other liens ascertained by a commissioner's report of liens under an order to convene them, and after publication of notice to creditors, and such purchaser's administrators and heirs are not formal parties, but prove a debt before the commissioner; and afterwards an amended bill is filed to subject the land which had been sold to such purchaser to said debt. Held, that the administrators and heirs of such purchaser are not precluded by such convention of creditors and such decree from disputing the amount of the debt as fixed by such decree, and the land so sold is to be held liable only for the amount legally called for by the judgment. Bensimer v. Fell, 35 W. Va. 15, 12 S. E. 1078, 29 Am. St. Rep. 774.

Remedies.—When a suit in equity is brought by a judgment creditor to enforce his lien against the land of his debtor, the persons claiming to be purchasers of the debtor's land complain that they were not made parties to that suit, their remedy, if they have notice of the suit, is by motion or petition to be made parties defendant thereto, and not by an independent suit to set aside the decree in the other cause, upon the principal ground that the judgment therein sought to be enforced was itself void. Neale v. Utz, 75 Va. 480.

hh. Trustee and Cestui Que Trust.

In General.—It is well settled that in a suit to enforce a judgment lien against lands covered by a deed of trust, both the trustee and cestui que trust are necessary parties defendant. Bansimer v. Fell, 39 W. Va. 448, 19 S. E. 545; McMillan v. Hickman, 35 W. Va. 705, 14 S. E. 227; Bilmyer v. Sherman, 23 W. Va. 656; McCoy v. Allen, 16 W. Va. 724, 725.

"And at this term it was held, in Farmers' Bank v. Watson, 39 W. Va. 342, 19 S. E. 413—a case where there was a convention of lien holders—that the trustees and beneficiaries must be formal parties. The position that any judicial action can have effect to prejudice persons or rights in no way present, when their presence is necessary, is untenable." Bansiber v. Fell, 39 W. Va. 448, 19 S. E. 545, 546.

The trustee and cestui que trust in a deed of trust which constitutes a lien on real estate which a judgment creditor is seeking by bill in equity to subject to the payment of his lien, are necessary and indispensable parties to such a bill; and it is reasonable that the trustee, being the custodian of the legal title, should be before the court when the object of the bill is a sale of the legal title to satisfy the liens existing against the land. It has been held, that it is necessary in such a suit to ascertain the liens existing against the land thus sought to be subjected, and it is conceded at once that such an ascertainment would not be binding unless the trustee holding the legal title was before the court. McMillan v. Hickman, 35 W. Va. 705, 14 S. E. 227, 229.

"If we treat the said deed of trust as valid, the trustee and cestui que trust's administrators were necessary parties, under McCoy v. Allen, 16 W. Va. 724, 732, and Bilmyer v. Sherman, 23 W. Va. 656, in the former case the opinion saying: 'Only the undefiled class of judgment creditors holding liens similar to the plaintiff can be made in such case quasi parties. If the trustee holding the legal title to the land and his cestui que trust are

not made formally defendants, they can not, by any such decree, be made quasi parties, and can not be bound by any decree of the court.' Those cases were before the act of 1882 as to suits to enforce judgment liens, and as the language of § 7, under that act is liens 'by judgment or otherwise,' and in the form of notice, 'all claims held * * * which are liens on his real estate,' any lien in any manner arising is contemplated; but, in cases where the legal title is outstanding in a trustee, it is still necessary to make the trustee, and, I should say, also the beneficiary, under the deed, formal parties. Again, the statute bars those not presenting their claims only from participation in the proceeds of the sale of the land, not from the personal debt, unless that be expressly involved in the case, in the pleadings, or made so by contestation before the commissioner." Bensimer v. Fell, 35 W. Va. 15, 12 S. E. 1078, 1084, 29 Am. St. Rep. 774.

Trustees in Deed of Trust.—In a proceeding in chancery by a judgment creditor to subject the real estate of his debtor to the payment of his judgment lien, where there are liens by trust deeds, the trustees in such deeds must be made formal parties before any sale of the debtor's lands can be ordered, and such trustees can not be made informal parties by publication. McMillan v. Hickman, 35 W. Va. 705, 14 S. E. 227; Norris v. Bean, 17 W. Va. 655; Jackson v. Hull, 21 W. Va. 601, 615.

In a suit to enforce the lien of a judgment, creditors of the debtor under a deed of trust are necessary parties. Kennedy v. Davisson, 46 W. Va. 433, 33 S. E. 291.

The trust creditors in interest should be made parties to a bill by a judgment creditor to enforce his lien against the subject of the trust. Laidley v. Hinchman, 3 W. Va. 423.

"It is almost equally obvious, that the trustees in all deeds of trust executed by the debtor, conveying any portion of his lands, sought to be subjected in trust to secure the payment of his debts, must be made formally defendants in such a bill and be brought before the court. The trustees have the legal title to the land sought to be sold by the court, and any conveyance made by a special commissioner could only convey the title of the parties to the suit, if the trustees were not parties, the purchasers by a decree of the court would not get a legal title to the land. This is a special reason, why in a suit of this character the trustee in any deed of trust, conveying any portion of the land sought to be sold, should be made a formal defendant. But even without this special reason the uniform practice is in all cases to make the trustees parties to every suit touching the subject of the trust. In the language of Story the trustees have the legal interest, and therefore they are necessary parties.' Story Eq. Pl., § 207." Norris v. Bean, 17 W. Va. 655, 667.

Cestui Que Trust.—To the general rule, that in all such cases the cestuis que trust should be made formal defendants and served with process, there are some exceptions, as for instance, when the cestuis que trust are very numerous, or the description of them is so general, as to make it difficult or impracticable to ascertain in the first instance, who are all the persons included therein, or many of them are unknown. In some of these excepted cases the trustees are supposed to represent the interest of the cestuis que trust. See Story's Eq. Plead., §§ 150, 207. But we need not consider these exceptional cases, for it is clear, when the trustee is the mere holder of the legal title of the land, which has been conveyed to him to secure a limited number of specified debts, that the cestuis que trust must be made parties defendant and served with process, such a case coming within the general rule, and none of the excep-

tional cases have any analogy to such a case. Norris v. Bean, 17 W. Va. 655, 669.

"The cestuis que trust are necessary parties as formal defendants in a suit, when, as in this case, the deeds of trust simply convey portions of the real estate sought to be subjected to sale in trust to secure a small number of specified debts. The general rule, where a chancery suit is brought to sell or in any manner to affect or in any way respecting trust property, that is, property conveyed to trustees upon trusts, is, that not only must the trustees be parties formally, but also all the cestuis que trust must be formal parties to such a suit." Norris v. Bean, 17 W. Va. 655, 668.

Notice to Lienholders.—In a suit under § 7, ch. 139, Code, 1891, to subject land to a judgment lien, if there be liens thereon by deeds of trust the trustee and creditors therein must be made formal parties; and they do not become quasi parties, so as to affect their rights, by notice to lienholders. Bansimer v. Fell, 39 W. Va. 448, 19 S. E. 545.

Publication.—"In McMillan v. Hickman, 35 W. Va. 705, 14 S. E. 227, it was held that in a suit to subject a debtor's land to a judgment, lien creditors known to the plaintiff, and disclosed by the judgment lien docket or records of the court of the county in which the land lies, must be made parties, and that where there are liens by trust deeds the trustees must be made formal parties, and can not be made informal parties by publication. See also, Turk v. Skiles, 38 W. Va. 404, 18 S. E. 561." Bansimer v. Fell, 39 W. Va. 448, 19 S. E. 545, 546.

In the case of Bilmyer v. Sherman, 23 W. Va. 656, this court held (fifth point of syllabus) that, "where there are liens by trust deeds, the trustees in such deeds must be made formal parties before any sale of the debtor's lands can be ordered. Such trustees can not be made informal parties by publication; and where a decree of sale is made in the absence of a trustee, this court will reverse the decree, although the cestui que trust had his debt audited in the suit." McMillan *v.* Hickman, 35 W. Va. 705, 14 S. E. 227, 229.

ii. Life Tenant and Remainderman.

On the other hand, the remaindermen are not necessary parties to a bill to subject a life estate to the lien of a judgment. Moore *v.* Bruce, 85 Va. 139, 7 S. E. 195.

In a suit by creditors to subject the real estate of a decedent to the payment of his debts, where it appears that the decedent devised his real estate to his wife in life, with remainder in fee in equal parts to his two children, but, if either died without issue, remainder over to his sister, with power to the wife to sell and reinvest proceeds, if deemed advisable, the sister is not a necessary party. New *v.* Bass, 92 Va. 383, 23 S. E. 747.

jj. Tenant by Dower.

"Besides these four classes of parties who must generally be made formal defendants in all suits of this character, there may be of course in particular cases a necessity to make other parties, as for instance, a widow, who claimed a right of dower in a tract of land owned by the judgment debtor to be sold, which dower had not been assigned her, and in this case T. J. Grove, for he should be made a defendant in the amended bill, which must be filed, because it appears from the petition of George Bean, that in some way, not in any manner explained, Grove has or claims to have a right to the two debts payable to George Bean and secured by a deed of trust on a portion of the land sought to be subjected in this case." Norris *v.* Bean, 17 W. Va. 655, 671.

kk. Personal Representatives and Devisees and Legatees.

In a chancery suit to enforce the lien of a judgment against a principal and sureties, where it appears that judgment has also been obtained against the personal representative of another surety for the same debt, such personal representative and sole devisee and legatees of the deceased surety are necessary parties in order that the deceased surety's part of the judgment remaining unpaid, after exhausting the realty of the principal, may be ascertained, and his estate subjected to its payment. Wytheville Crystal Ice, etc., Co. *v.* Frick Co., 96 Va. 141, 30 S. E. 491.

In a suit in chancery to enforce a lien in judgment against the principal and sureties, if other judgments are proved upon which others than those before the court are also bound, it is not necessary to make such others parties. Wytheville Crystal Ice, etc., Co. *v.* Frick Co., 96 Va. 141, 30 S. E. 491.

Joint Obligors.—Moreover, a judgment at law being obtained against one of two obligors, in a joint and several bond, and no proceedings to enforce it appearing, a court of equity ought not to charge the lands of the other obligor, in the possession of his devisees, without having made the obligor, against whom the judgment was rendered, or his representatives, parties to the suit. Foster *v.* Crenshaw, 3 Munf. 514.

ll. Heirs.

Where, in a suit by a judgment creditor to subject lands in the hands of a bona fide purchaser for the vendee, the purchaser dies pending the suit, his heirs are necessary parties. Taylor *v.* Spindle, 2 Gratt. 44; Bensimer *v.* Fell, 35 W. Va. 15, 12 S. E. 1078. 29 Am. St. Rep. 774.

A., a judgment creditor, suing on behalf of himself and all other judgment creditors of C. D. E. and the estate of B. against the said C. D. E. and the administrator of B., defendants, files his bill, in which he avers, that his judgment is founded on a note drawn by B. and endorsed successively by C. D. and E.; that a creditors' bill is pending in the same court against the administrator, widow and heirs of B. and also separate suits against C. and D. to subject the lands of said B. C. and D. to the payment of their respective debts; that said B. C. D. and E. each own lands in the county, against which it is believed there are judgment liens; and prays, that said liens and their respective priorities be ascertained and said lands sold to pay said liens. The defendants demurred to said bill as follows: The heirs of said B. deceased are not made parties. The creditors' bill pending in the same court against the heirs of B. can be heard with this cause, and thus the necessity of making said heirs parties to this suit may be obviated. Shenandoah Valley Nat. Bank v. Bates, 20 W. Va. 210.

mm. Fraudulent Alienees.

A bill is filed to subject lands to the satisfaction of a judgment after the death of the debtor, and charging fraud in certain conveyances by the debtor to his son. The son having conveyed some of the lands to third persons, all such persons must be made parties to the cause. Henderson v. Henderson, 9 Gratt. 394.

(e) Effect of Omission to Make Necessary Parties.

Harmless Error.—The omission of a necessary party, who voluntarily appears, is harmless error. Moore v. Bruce, 85 Va. 139, 7 S. E. 195.

Reversible Error.—It is error to proceed to render a decree in a suit to enforce a judgment lien, without having all necessary parties before the court. Hoffman v. Shields, 4 W. Va. 490; Findlay v. Smith, 42 W. Va. 299, 26 S. E. 370.

If in a suit brought by a judgment creditor to subject the lands of his debtor to the payment of his judgment, and the land has been sold under a decree in the cause, and the sale has been confirmed, and it appears that the nec-

essary parties were not formally or informally before the court, the decree ordering the sale to be made, as well as the decree confirming the sale made in pursuance thereof, will be reversed and the sale set aside. Pappenheimer v. Roberts, 24 W. Va. 702.

If in a suit brought by a judgment creditor to sell the lands of his debtor for the payment of his judgment, all the judgment creditors are not made parties, either formally or informally, and this fact is disclosed by the record, the appellate court will reverse any decree directing the sale of the lands or the distribution of the proceeds thereof. Neely v. Jones, 16 W. Va. 625; Pappenheimer v. Roberts, 24 W. Va. 702; Grove v. Judy, 24 W. Va. 294; Donahue v. Thackler, 21 W. Va. 124; Turk v. Skiles, 38 W. Va. 404, 18 S. E. 561; Hitchcox v. Hitchcox, 39 W. Va. 607, 20 S. E. 595.

In Farmers' Bank v. Watson, 39 W. Va. 342, 19 S. E. 413, it is held: "If a lien creditor, in filing a bill to enforce his lien against real estate, neglects to make necessary parties thereto in accordance with the former decisions of this court, all decrees entered will be reversed, and the proceedings thereunder annulled, and the bill will be remanded to be properly amended." Bilmyer v. Sherman, 23 W. Va. 656; McMillan v. Hickman, 35 W. Va. 705, 14 S. E. 227; Neely v. Jones, 16 W. Va. 625; Norris v. Bean, 17 W. Va. 655; Crim v. Price, 46 W. Va. 374, 33 S. E. 251, 252.

"As then this record discloses, that there were parties, who ought to have been made formal defendants in this cause, who were never so made, or on whom no process was served, and who never appeared in the cause, and who have direct interest in both the subject matter and object of this suit, and who were not even informally parties, as were the judgment debtors, and all the decrees rendered in this cause were rendered in their absence and without notice to them, it must follow that all of these decrees must be set aside, reversed and annulled excepting only a part of the decree rendered on September 5, 1872." Norris *v.* Bean, 17 W. Va. 655, 671.

Demurrer.—If in a suit brought by a judgment creditor to sell the lands of his debtor for the payment of his judgment, the want of such proper parties appears on the face of the bill, it will for that cause be demurrable, and the defect may be taken advantage of by demurrer or at the hearing of the cause. But where the demurrer for such cause is sustained, the plaintiff should have leave to amend his bill. Pappenheimer *v.* Roberts, 24 W. Va. 702.

Exceptions and Objections.—"If the plaintiff, however, should omit to make any or all of the parties named in the fourth class above named defendants but whom the court has afforded an opportunity to have their debts audited by directing them to be called before a commissioner to audit their debts, and such call has been duly published and no objection has been made to their being thus informally made parties in the court below, till after a decree is rendered, such decree would not be reversed in the appellate court for the failure of the plaintiff to make all or any of the fourth class above named formal defendants in the bill. See Neely *v.* Jones, 16 W. Va. 625." Norris *v.* Bean, 17 W. Va. 655.

(5) Consolidation of Suits.

See the title CONSOLIDATION OF ACTIONS, vol. 3, p. 125.

Where the suits are by different plaintiffs, proceeding against different funds of the defendant, to satisfy separate and distinct liens; and where, as in the present case, the judgment lien of the plaintiffs in one of the suits against the defendants, was created long subsequent to the institution of the other creditor's suit, and subsequent to the report of the master ascertaining the liens and their priorities, and a decree confirming the same adjudicating the merits of the cause and enforcing the liens of such other creditors against the property of defendant elected by them for that purpose, it was not improper to refuse consolidation. Beach *v.* Woodyard, 5 W. Va. 231.

Suits in equity for the enforcement of liens are properly heard together when it is necessary to protect the interests of all concerned, and to prevent inconsistent and conflicting decrees from being entered in the several causes. Preston *v.* National Exchange Bank, 97 Va. 222, 33 S. E. 546.

C. brought his bill to enforce judgment liens against the real estate of M. E. P., wife of L. P., and made other lien holders thereon defendant. R. & Sons afterwards filed their bill against M. E. P. and L. P., alleging that the deed from the father of L. P. for the real estate sought to be subjected was made to M. E. P. in fraud of the creditors of L. P., and asking to have it set aside, and the real estate subjected to the payment of their judgment against L. P., which existed at the date of the deed, but failed to make the judgment creditors of M. E. P. parties to their bill. The cases were heard together, the deed set aside, and R. & Sons' judgment declared to be the first lien on the property. Held, error to hear the cases together, or to decree upon the bill of R. & Sons until the proper parties were brought in. Crim *v.* Price, 46 W. Va. 374, 33 S. E. 251.

(6) Joinder of Suits.

A chancery suit may be brought to enforce a judgment against A., and at the same time to avoid a fraudulent or voluntary conveyance of land by A. Damron *v.* Smith, 37 W. Va. 580, 16 S. E. 807.

(7) Abatement of Suit.

See the title ABATEMENT, REVIVAL AND SURVIVAL, vol. 1 p. 16.

(8) Limitations and Laches.

(a) Limitations.

aa. In General.

The principle is now settled by statute, that the lien of a judgment ceases with the life of a judgment. Hutcheson v. Grubbs, 80 Va. 251; Code, § 3573; Ayre v. Burke, 82 Va. 338, 4 S. E. 618; Brown v. Butler, 87 Va. 621, 626, 13 S. E. 71.

Coextensive with Execution and Scire Facias.—See the title EXECUTIONS, vol. 5, p. 464. See post, "Revival of Judgments," XIV; "Actions on Judgments," XV.

In General.—Formerly judgments did not bind lands after twelve months from the date unless execution be taken out within that time or entry of elegit be made on the record. For this proposition, Eppes v. Randolph, 2 Call 125 is cited in Tinsley v. Anderson, 3 Call 329, 333; Nimmo v. Com., 4 Hen. & M. 57, 68; Claiborne v. Gross, 7 Leigh 331, 345; note to Lane v. Ludlow, 14 Fed. Cas. 1082. In Taylor v. Spindle, 2 Gratt. 44, it is said, the dictum of the judge, delivering the opinion of the court in Eppes v. Randolph, 2 Call 125: "That a judgment revived by scire facias only operates prospectively, so as to give a lien from the time of its revival, and has no retrospective effect so as to avoid mesne alienations," examined and disapproved. See also, Coleman v. Coke, 6 Rand. 618, 628; Werdenbaugh v. Reid, 20 W. Va. 588, 596; Bank of United States v. Winston, 2 Fed. Cas. 743. In Smith v. Charlton, 7 Gratt. 425; Daniel, J., says: "Yet I presume it has not been doubted since the decisions in Eppes v. Randolph, 2 Call 125, 186, and Nowland v. Cromwell, 6 Munf. 185, that this one year's limitation could not avail a defendant where there had been a stay of execution by his own agreement, or by force of an injunction obtained at his own instance." See also, citing Eppes v. Randolph, 2 Call 125; Hutsonpiller v. Stover, 12

Gratt. 579, 581; note to Alston v. Munford, 1 Fed. Cas. 581.

Where a fieri facias has been issued upon a judgment within the year and a day, the judgment is a lien upon a moiety of all the lands owned by the debtor at the date of the judgment, or which were afterwards acquired, in the hands of bona fide purchasers for value, without notice. Taylor v. Spindle, 2 Gratt. 44.

So long as a judgment may be revived, it was formerly a lien upon a moiety of all the lands owned by the debtor at the date of the judgment, or which were afterwards acquired, into whosoever hands they might have come. Taylor v. Spindle, 2 Gratt. 44.

In Werdenbaugh v. Reid, 20 W. Va. 588, 593, it is said: "In determining the time within which the lien of a judgment might be enforced in a court of equity, it was uniformly held, that whenever the capacity of having execution upon the judgment was barred, the lien of the judgment was destroyed and no suit could be brought to enforce it. 2 Minor's Inst. 272; 1 Lomax Dig., § 10, p. 288, and cases cited. Taylor v. Spindle, 2 Gratt. 44."

Present Rule.—And it is settled law now that the lien of a judgment ceases, when the right to sue out execution on the judgment, or to revive it by scire facias, is barred by the statute of limitations. Reilly v. Clark, 31 W. Va. 571, 8 S. E. 509; Laidley v. Kline, 23 W. Va. 565; Werdenbaugh v. Reid, 20 W. Va. 588; Shipley v. Pew, 23 W. Va. 487; Serles v. Cromer, 88 Va. 426, 13 S. E. 859; Kennerly v. Swartz, 83 Va. 704, 3 S. E. 348; McCarty v. Ball, 82 Va. 875, 1 S. E. 189; Eppes v. Randolph, 2 Call 125.

No suit shall be brought to enforce the lien of a judgment upon which the right to issue an execution, or bring a scire facias, or an action, is barred by sections thirty-five hundred and seventy-seven and thirty-five hundred and seventy-eight. Va. Code, 1904, § 3573.

Where no scire facias is sued out to revive a judgment within ten years after its recovery, all remedy on the judgment is barred. Bank *v.* Allen, 76 Va. 200, 205, citing Va. Code, 1873, ch. 182, § 12.

The right to enforce the lien of a judgment, although the statute declares that it may always be enforced in a court of equity, is confined to the time that an action may be brought or scire facias sued out thereon, and after that time the lien ceases to exist. Werdenbaugh *v.* Ried, 20 W. Va. 588, 596, citing Bart. Ch. Pr. 109; Eppes *v.* Randolph, 2 Call 125; Stuart *v.* Hamilton, 8 Leigh 503; Taylor *v.* Spindle, 2 Gratt. 44; Brown *v.* Campbell, 33 Gratt. 402; Michaux *v.* Brown, 10 Gratt. 612, 619.

The right to file a bill in equity to enforce a judgment lien is coextensive as to time with the right to sue out an execution on such judgment. James *v.* Life, 92 Va. 702, 24 S. E. 275, citing Hutcheson *v.* Grubbs, 80 Va. 251.

The lien of a judgment upon land exists, though execution may be suspended by the death of the defendant, and may be enforced in equity without revival by scire facias so long as the scire facias may lie on the judgment. Maxwell *v.* Leeson, 50 W. Va. 361, 40 S. E. 420.

If either party to a judgment die, while no execution can go without revival against the personal representative by sci. fa., yet the lien on the land still exists as long as a sci. fa. may be sued out, and that is within * the period limiting the judgment. Laidley *v.* Kline, 23 W. Va. 565; Maxwell *v.* Leeson, 50 W. Va. 361, 366, 40 S. E. 420.

In Werdenbaugh *v.* Reid, 20 W. Va. 588, it is held: "The lien of judgment upon which no execution was ever issued will not be enforced in a court of equity in a suit brought after the lapse of ten years from the date of the judgment." Woods *v.* Douglass, 52 W. Va. 521, 44 S. E. 234.

In no event can a judgment be re- vived, under our statute (§ 11, ch. 139, Code), after ten years have elapsed from the return day of the last execution issued thereon, and, if more than five years of that period elapse during the life of the execution debtor, then the creditor has only the remainder of the ten years within which to revive the judgment against the personal representative of such debtor. Handy *v.* Smith, 30 W. Va. 195, 3 S. E. 604.

Lands in Hands of Bona Fide Purchaser.—The Virginia Code provides that no suit shall be brought to enforce the lien of a judgment, upon which the right to issue an execution or bring a scire facias or action is barred by §§ 3577, 3578. This implies, as has been frequently decided, that as long as the right to issue an execution, or bring a scire facias or action thereon exists, the lien may be enforced in equity, and this is so not only when the lands subject to the lien of the judgment are in the hands of the judgment debtor, but also in the hands of subsequent purchasers, whether they had actual notice or not, if the judgment was duly docketed. Taylor *v.* Spindle, 2 Gratt. 44; Leake *v.* Ferguson, 2 Gratt. 419; Borst *v.* Nalle, 28 Gratt. 423; Hutcheson *v.* Grubbs, 80 Va. 251; Flanary *v.* Kane, 102 Va. 547, 557, 46 S. E. 312.

Illustrative Cases.—On May 5, 1855, the plaintiff recovered a judgment against the defendants, and sued out execution thereon within the year. The last execution was returnable to the first Monday in January, 1859, upon which no return of any officer was ever made. On September 16, 1874, the plaintiff filed his bill against the defendants to enforce the lien of his judgment against the real estate of the defendants, which was resisted on the ground that the lien of the judgment was barred by the statute of limitations. Held, that on September 16, 1874, when the plaintiff's suit was instituted, the lien of his judgment had ceased to exist, and that his suit to enforce same could not be sustained. Shipley *v.* Pew, 23 W. Va. 487, citing Werdenbaugh *v.* Reid, 20 W. Va. 588.

On May 5, 1855, the plaintiff recovered a judgment against the defendants, and sued out execution thereon within the year. The last execution was returnable to the first Monday in January, 1859, upon which no return of any officer was ever made. On September 16, 1874, the plaintiff filed his bill against the defendants to enforce the lien of his judgment against the real estate of the defendants, which was resisted on the ground that the lien of the judgment was barred by the statute of limitations. Held, that the lien of the plaintiff's judgment ceased to exist when his right to sue out other executions, or to bring a scire facias or action thereon, was barred by the statute of limitations. Shipley *v.* Pew, 23 W. Va. 487, cited in Northwestern Bank *v.* Hays, 37 W. Va. 475, 16 S. E. 561, 563.

On May 5, 1855, the plaintiff recovered a judgment against the defendants, and sued out execution thereon within the year. The last execution was returnable to the first Monday in January, 1859, upon which no return of any officer was ever made. On September 16, 1874, the plaintiff filed his bill against the defendants to enforce the lien of his judgment against the real estate of the defendants, which was resisted on the ground that the lien of the judgment was barred by the statute of limitations. Held, that the plaintiff's right to sue out other executions, or to bring a scire facias or action upon his judgment, expired at the end of thirteen years, ten months and fourteen days, from the return day of said last execution. Shipley *v.* Pew, 23 W. Va. 487.

In April, 1887, suit was brought to enforce the liens of two judgments, one dated February 23, 1866, the other dated November 2, 1866, both duly docketed, but execution had been issued on neither. Held, right to enforce had ceased by limitation. (Code, §§ 3573, 3577, 3578.) "The provision of the statute (Code, § 3573) is express that no suit shall be brought to enforce the lien of a judgment upon which the right to issue an execution, or bring a scire facias, or an action, is barred by §§ 3577, 3578; and by § 3577 it is provided that 'on a judgment, execution may be issued within a year, and a scire facias, or an action, may be brought within ten years after the date of the judgment; and where execution issues within the year, other executions may be issued, or a scire facias, or an action, may be brought within ten years from the return day of an execution on which there is no return by an officer, or within twenty years from the return day of an execution on which there is no such return.'" Brown *v.* Butler, 87 Va. 621, 623, 13 S. E. 71.

Subrogation.—See the title SUBROGATION.

Section 3573 of the Virginia Code shall not be construed to impair the right to subrogation to which any person may become entitled while the lien is in force, provided he instituted proceedings to enforce such right within five years after the same accrued. Va. Code, 1904, § 3574.

"Last of notes given to satisfy the Illinois judgment was paid January, 1880. Yet the Illinois judgment was marked satisfied December, 1869. General creditors' bill filed July, 1873, to enforce judgment against maker, and order of account of debts, etc., entered October, 1873. Held, the statute of limitations does not bar the claim of endorser or his assignee to be subrogated to plaintiff's rights in judgment against maker. Order of account entered, all lien creditors became parties, and at liberty to assert their demands in that suit." Bank *v.* Allen, 76 Va. 200.

bb. Limitation on Actions of Ejectment.

The statute of limitations fixing the

time within which an action of ejectment may be brought to recover land has no application to a suit to enforce the lien of a judgment on land. The lien of a judgment is a fixed, definite, statutory lien, running for the time prescribed by § 3573 of the Code, and enforceable not only against lands while in the hands of the judgment debtor, but also in the hands of subsequent purchasers, whether they had actual notice or not, if the judgment was duly docketed. Flanary *v.* Kane, 102 Va. 547, 46 S. E. 312.

"The statute of limitations invoked has no application to this case. This is clear from the language of that statute, § 2915 of the Code, and of the statute, § 3573, which limits the time within which judgment liens may be enforced in equity. Section 2915 applies only to the right to make an entry or to bring an action to recover land. The suit of a judgment creditor to enforce his lien against land is not a suit to recover it. He has no right to the possession of the land." Flanary *v.* Kane, 102 Va. 547, 557, 46 S. E. 312.

cc. Judgments against State.

The state of Virginia upon notices and motions by the name of "The Commonwealth" instituted and prosecuted by the auditor of public accounts on the 6th day of March, 1860, recovered two several judgments against Edmund S. Calwell "in the circuit court of Richmond" as one of the securities of John E. Lewis, late sheriff of Greenbrier county, the one being for $4,893.92, the balance of the land property, and capitation and September license taxes of 1854 due from said John E. Lewis, late sheriff of Greenbrier county, with interest thereon to be computed at the rate of six per centum from the 17th day of January, 1855, until paid, and the costs of the motion, $13.44, and the other being for $1,073.86, the balance of June, 1855, license taxes. due from said John E. Lewis, late sheriff of Greenbrier county, with interest

thereon to be computed at the rate of six per centum per annum from the 20th day of June, 1855, until paid, and $161.07 for damages thereon according to law, also the cost of the motion, $11.94. The law in force at the time said notice were given and motions made and judgments were rendered provided, that "the auditor of public accounts shall institute and prosecute all proceedings proper to enforce payment of money to the commonwealth —that the proceeding may be in the circuit court of the city of Richmond —that when it is at law, it may be by action or motion—that "every judgment on any such motion shall be in the name of the commonwealth." And the city of Richmond being the capital of the state of Virginia, as judicially known to the court, held, the statute of limitations did not commence to run against the state of Virginia as to said judgment for any purpose prior to the 20th day of June, 1863, when they with their liens passed to the state of West Virginia. The statute of limitations did not commence to run against the state of West Virginia for any purpose by virtue of her laws as to said judgments until the 1st day of April, 1869. (Code of 1868, ch. 35, § 20.) Calwell *v.* Prindle, 19 W. Va. 604.

dd. Rule Where Lien Not Dependent on Judgment.

By an executory contract between A. and B., the former bound himself to convey to the latter, upon the payment of the purchase money, certain real estate. Subsequently B. conveyed said real estate to C., reserving in the deed a lien to indemnify A. against certain judgments, which B. was then primarily bound to pay; afterwards A. conveyed the legal title to said real estate to B., reserving a lien in the deed for his indemnity against said judgments; the legal title is never conveyed to C. In a suit by A. to subject the said real estate to the payment of the amount he was compelled to pay to satisfy said judgments, held, that A.'s right to it was not lost or impaired, because at the time he instituted his suit said judgment had become barred by the statute of limitations, the lien of A. depending upon the instrument reserving it, and not upon the judgment. Morehead *v.* Horner, 30 W. Va. 548, 4 S. E. 448, citing Wayt *v.* Carwithen, 21 W. Va. 516.

ee. Rule Where Judgment Is Secured by Mortgage.*

It was said, by the court, in Paxton *v.* Rich, 85 Va. 378, 7 S. E. 531: "The case of Hutcheson *v.* Grubbs, 80 Va. 251, referred to by counsel, has no application. In that case it was held that the lien of a judgment ceases with the life of the judgment, and obviously so, because the lien is a legal lien, conferred by statute, and is not collateral to, but grows out of the judgment itself. Hence the lien and the judgment are inseparable, and the extinguishment of the latter is the extinguishment of the former. But not so where there is a judgment for a debt secured by a mortgage, deed of trust, or a vendor's lien. There the lien is collateral to the judgment and may be enforced in equity although the judgment be barred or annihilated."

ff. Statutory Limitations on Execution and Scire Facias.

The West Virginia Code provides that on a judgment, execution may be issued within two years after the date thereof, or if none be so issued, the court in which the judgment was rendered may thereafter, and within ten years from the date of the judgment, upon ten days' notice to the party against whom the same is, order an execution to issue thereon for such sum as remains unpaid. Where execution issues within two years as aforesaid, other executions may be issued on such judgment without notice, within ten years from the return day of the last execution issued thereon, on which there is no return by an officer, or which has been returned unsatisfied. And an action, suit or scire facias may be brought upon a judgment on which no execution issued within the said two years, or where there has been a change of parties by death or otherwise, at any time within ten years next after the date of the judgment. But if such action, suit or scire facias be against a personal representative of a decedent, it shall be brought within five years from the qualification of such representative. W. Va. Code, 1899, ch. 139, § 4150.

The Virginia Code provides that on a judgment, execution may be issued within a year, and a scire facias or an action may be brought within ten years after the date of the judgment; and where execution issues within the year, other executions may be issued, or a scire facias or an action may be brought within ten years from the return day of an execution on which there is no return by an officer, or within twenty years from the return day of an execution on which there is such return; except that where the scire facias or action is against the personal representative of a decedent, it shall be brought within five years from the qualification of such representative; and in computing time under this section, there shall, as to writs of fieri facias, be omitted from such computation the time elapsed between the first day of January, eighteen hundred and sixty-nine, and the twenty-ninth day of March, eighteen hundred and seventy-one. Any return by an officer on an execution showing that the same has not been satisfied, shall be a sufficient return within the meaning of this section. (1870-71, p. 341.) Va. Code, 1904, § 3577.

On a judgment, execution may be issued within two years after the date thereof under the Code of West Virginia. Gardner *v.* Landcraft, 6 W. Va. 36, 37.

Retrospective Operation of Statute.
—Section 3 of ch. 141 of the West Vir-

ginia Code and §§ 11, 12, ch. 139, prescribing limitations to the time, in which executions may issue on a judgment, apply alike to judgments obtained before and to those obtained since this Code went into operation. Spang v. Robinson, 24 W. Va. 327.

The ten years' statute of limitations, which in §§ 11, 12, ch. 139, of the West Virginia Code, is made applicable to judgments, applies to judgments rendered before the 1st day of April, 1869, at which date the Code took effect. Northwestern Bank v. Hays, 37 W. Va. 475, 16 S. E. 561.

gg. Computation of Time.

The West Virginia Code provides that no execution shall issue, nor any action, suit or scire facias be brought on any judgment in this state after the time prescribed in the preceding section, except that in computing the time, the period mentioned in the fourth section of chapter one hundred and thirty-six of this Code, and any time during which the right to sue out execution on the judgment is suspended by the terms thereof, or by legal process, shall be omitted from the computation; and the sixteenth, seventeenth, eighteenth and nineteenth sections of chapter one hundred and four of this Code shall apply to the right to bring such action, suit or scire facias, in like manner as to any right, action, suit or scire facias, mentioned in those sections; and except that when the judgment is for the penalty of a bond, but to be discharged by the payment of what is then ascertained, and such sums as may be afterwards assessed or found due upon a scire facias on the judgment, assigning a further breach of the bond, such scire facias may be brought within ten years after such breach. W. Va. Code, 1899, ch. 139, § 4151.

The Virginia Code provides that no execution shall issue, nor any scire facias or action be brought, on a judgment in this state, other than for the commonwealth, after the time prescribed by the preceding section, except that, in computing the time, any time during which the right to sue out execution on the judgment is suspended by the terms thereof, or by legal process, shall be omitted; and sections twenty-nine hundred and thirty-one, twenty-nine hundred and thirty-two, twenty-nine hundred and thirty-three, twenty-nine hundred and thirty-four, and twenty-nine hundred and thirty-eight shall apply to the right to bring such action or scire facias in like manner as to any right, action or scire facias mentioned in those sections; and except that when the judgment is for the penalty of a bond, but to be discharged by the payment of what is then ascertained, and such sums as may be afterwards assessed or found due upon a scire facias on the judgment, assigning a further breach of the bond, such scire facias may be brought within ten years after such breach. This section is qualified by the following section. (Code, 1849, p. 710, ch. 186, § 13.) Va. Code, 1904, § 3578.

Suspension of Right to Sue Out Execution.—In order that a proceeding instituted may have the effect of suspending the right to sue out execution on a judgment under ch. 182, § 13, of the Code, 1873, it must be brought for that purpose, and when such is not the object of the suit, the rights of the judgment creditor under his judgment will be unaffected. Dabney v. Shelton, 82 Va. 349, 4 S. E. 605; Straus v. Bodeker, 86 Va. 543, 10 S. E. 570.

Legal Process.—Where nonresident judgment creditors are summoned by order of publication and no order is made to suspend the issuing of executions, a suit to enforce a contract for the sale of the judgment debtor's land, is no such "legal process" as, under Code, 1873, ch. 182, § 13, suspends judgment creditors' right to sue out executions and stops the running of the statute of limitations against such judgments. Straus v. Bodeker, 86 Va. 543, 10 S. E. 570.

Petitions filed during that period by judgment creditor in a chancery suit brought to subject the lands of judgment debtor to the payment of judgment liens, and dismissed without any order on it except an order of dismissal seven years after it was filed, did not suspend the right to sue out execution upon the judgment, and does not bring the case under the saving clause contained in § 13 of said chapter. Dabney v. Shelton, 82 Va. 349, 4 S. E. 605.

January 1, 1869, and March 29, 1871. —The right to file a bill in equity to enforce a judgment lien is coextensive as to time with the right to sue out an execution on such judgment. And, in computing the time within which an execution is to be sued out, the time between January 1, 1869, and March 29, 1871, is excluded by express statutory provision. Section 3577, Va. Code. James v. Life, 92 Va. 702, 24 S. E. 275; Hutcheson v. Grubbs, 80 Va. 251; Dabney v. Shelton, 82 Va. 349, 4 S. E. 605.

M. was adjudged a bankrupt and discharged in 1873. He claimed as his homestead certain land, which ' the bankrupt court allotted him, but without notice to his creditors, who were lienors by judgments recovered in 1857. Those creditors in 1878 filed their bill in the state court to enforce their liens on said land, but did not make T., who was the assignee in bankruptcy of, M., a party. M. demurred, answered, and pleaded that the enforcement of the judgments was barred by the lapse of twenty years between their date and the filing of the bill. The demurrer was overruled and decree of sale entered, but the commissioner of sale was not directed to give the usual bond. On appeal by M., held: The right to enforce the judgment liens was not barred, as, after deducting the time between the 17th

of April, 1861, and the 1st of January, 1869, there can not be computed twenty years between the date of the judgments and the filing of the bill in this cause. McAllister v. Bodkin, 76 Va. 809.

hh. Postponement, Suspension and Interruption of Statute.

Parol Evidence to Avoid Bar.—To avoid the bar of the statute of limitations in respect to the right to enforce the lien of a judgment, the creditor must bring his case within one of the exceptions declared in the statute, and he can not, by parol evidence or otherwise, avoid such bar upon any ground not embraced in the statute. Reilly v. Clark, 31 W. Va. 571, 8 S. E. 509.

Removal from Commonwealth.—"In Ficklin v. Carrington, 31 Gratt. 219, it was laid down that debtor's removal from the state operates, propria vigore, to obstruct prosecution of plaintiff's right to enforce a judgment lien. In Wilson v. Koontz, 7 Cranch 202, construing the same statute, it was held, that removal of defendant must have actually obstructed plaintiff. In the case here, plaintiff was not actually or constructively obstructed." Brown v. Butler, 87 Va. 621, 13 S. E. 71.

Sale of real estate whereon the judgment is previously a lien is not, of itself, an obstruction of plaintiff to enforce a judgment lien. Brown v. Butler, 87 Va. 621, 13 S. E. 71.

Execution and Return.—See the title EXECUTIONS, vol. 5, p. 462.

Where ten years or more have elapsed since rendition of judgment, and no execution was issued upon it, and no writ of scire facias was sued out to revive it, within the period of ten years, the said judgment is barred by the statute of limitations, both at law and in equity. Code, 1873, ch. 182, §§ 12, 13; Hutcheson v. Grubbs, 80 Va. 251. Dabney v. Shelton, 82 Va. 349, 4 S. E. 605.

Return No Property.—Where an action is brought to subject real estate to the payment of a judgment, ten years after its rendition, it is not barred by the statute of limitations when the record shows that within a year thereafter an execution had been issued and returned, "no property." Hutcheson v. Grubbs, 80 Va. 251, distinguished in Kennerly v. Swartz, 83 Va. 704, 3 S. E. 348.

Returned Not Levied.—An execution, while in the hands of the sheriff, is endorsed by the attorneys for the plaintiff as follows: "The sheriff is hereby directed to return this execution without levying it." It was held, that this was a sufficient return to make the twenty years' period applicable. Rowe v. Hardy, 97 Va. 674, 34 S. E. 625.

Voidable Execution.—An execution issued on an unconditional decree for money, in contravention of the agreement of the parties entered of record, is voidable only, and is sufficient to stop the running of the act of limitations on the decree. Fulkerson v. Taylor, 100 Va. 426, 41 S. E. 863.

"The administratrix of L. D. Fulkerson, in an answer filed on the 8th day of June, 1901, set up the plea of the statute of limitations to the judgment of Baylor, upon the ground that more than ten years had elapsed between the date of its rendition and the institution of this suit, and that no valid execution had ever issued thereon. She filed with her answer a notice served upon the personal representative of the judgment creditor, that she would on the 7th day of that month move the circuit court to quash the execution in question upon the ground that it was prematurely issued. Upon the same day upon which the answer was filed, a decree was entered in this cause overruling a motion made by the administrator of L. D. Fulkerson. What that motion was is not disclosed by the record. If it was the motion to quash the execution, it does not appear to have been made on the day named in the notice, and besides, could not

have been legally made in this case. Conceding that the execution was improperly issued, it was not void, but only voidable. Until it is avoided it must be regarded as a valid execution, and could not be avoided by plea or proof in this, a collateral suit. Fulkerson v. Taylor, supra. In Beale v. Botetourt Justices, 10 Gratt. 278, the execution issued more than a year and a day from the date of the decree, without and proceeding by way of scire facias or otherwise to authorize the same. In that case it was held—though the conclusion may not have been necessary to a decision of the case—that the validity of the execution could not be attacked in that, a collateral proceeding. The reasoning, however, of Judge Moncure in that case, and the authorities cited by him, sustain the doctrine that an execution issued improperly, which is voidable, but not void, upon a judgment or decree rendered in one case, can not be attacked in another case in which such judgment is sought to be enforced, but that if such execution is to be avoided, it must be done in some independent proceeding instituted for that purpose." Fulkerson v. Taylor, 102 Va. 314, 313, 46 S. E. 378.

Where an execution has been issued upon a judgment more than ten years after the return day of the last preceding execution issued thereon, and a suit is brought by the creditor to enforce the lien of such judgment against the real estate of his debtor, the issuance of such execution will not avoid the bar of the right to enforce such lien, notwithstanding the execution is merely voidable, and not liable to be assailed in a collateral suit. Reilly v. Clark, 31 W. Va. 571, 8 S. E. 509.

Pendency of Suit.—As a general rule, the pendency of a suit operates to suspend the statute of limitations as to the parties thereto so far as the subject matter of that suit is concerned. But the suspension only exists as to that particular suit, and not as to the

the cause of action involved therein. Quære: In view of the provisions of § 3573 of the Code, does the pendency of a general creditor's suit suspend the act of limitations as to a judgment sought to be enforced in another suit? "Even if it were a general creditor's suit, it may well be doubted whether under the provisions of § 3573 of the Code, the doctrine invoked, which is not founded upon legislative enactment, but is a mere rule of courts of equity for the more convenient administration of the debtor's estate, and to avoid a multiplicity of suits (Callaway *v.* Saunders, 99 Va. 350, 352, 38 S. E. 182), could suspend the running of the statute of limitations or prevent its being relied on as a defense when it is sought to enforce the judgments in any proceeding other than the general creditor's suit in which the judgments has been asserted, the general rule being that the pendency of a suit operates to suspend the statute as to parties thereto so far as the subject matter of that suit is concerned. But the suspension only exists as to that particular suit, and not as to the cause of action involved therein. Dabney *v.* Shelton, 82 Va. 349, 351, 4 S. E. 605; Straus *v.* Bodeker, 86 Va. 543, 547, 10 S. E. 570." Gunnell *v.* Dixon, 101 Va. 174, 179, 43 S. E. 340.

Suit Dismissed.—A suit brought by the judgment creditor to enforce satisfaction of his judgment, suspends the operation of the statute of limitations during its pendency. But if it is dismissed without satisfaction of the judgment, it will not prevent the bar of the statute to another suit brought after its dismissal. Braxton *v.* Wood, 4 Gratt. 25, cited in Shipley *v.* Pew, 23 W. Va. 487, 497; Horner *v.* Speed, 2 Pat. & H. 616.

Bill in Equity in Aid of Execution.—Under the law of West Virginia, a plaintiff, after obtaining a judgment for his debt can issue a writ of fieri facias against the personalty of the defendant; if the execution be returned un-satisfied in whole or in part, and he wishes to reach the land of the defendant, he must file a bill in equity in aid of the execution. Such chancery suit will have the effect of holding the statute of limitations in abeyance until the date of the final decree. Ryan *v.* Kanawha Val. Bank (W. Va.), 71 Fed. Rep. 812.

Creditor's Suit.—Although a suit is brought by only one creditor to subject the lands of a debtor to the payment of the complainant's judgment only, the suit becomes a lien creditor's suit as soon as a decree is entered therein referring the cause to a commissioner to take an account of the defendant's lands and of the liens thereon; and the effect of such a decree is to suspend the act of limitations as to all the lien creditors of the defendant. Repass *v.* Moore, 96 Va. 147, 30 S. E. 458.

A bill filed by the grantor against the grantee's personal representative and heirs to have a deed absolute on its face declared to be a mortgage, and which results in a decree for an account of the liens which the grantee had undertaken to pay as a consideration for the conveyance, and of the liens against the land at the time of the conveyance, is not a creditor's bill which will stop the running of the statute of limitations on judgments against the grantor. Gunnell *v.* Dixon, 101 Va. 174, 43 S. E. 340.

Where a bill is filed by one creditor as plaintiff, on behalf of himself and others, the statute of limitations will cease running against any of the creditors, who come in under the decree, from the time such suit was commenced. Ang. on Lim., § 331. But if the suit be commenced by one creditor, who does not sue in behalf of himself and other creditors, and an order of reference is made in such suit convening by publication all the lien creditors of the same judgment debtor; in such case the statute will cease running against creditors, who may come into such suit, only from the date of the order of reference. Ewing v. Ferguson, 33 Gratt. 548; Jackson v. Hull, 21 W. Va. 601, 612.

Where a suit is brought by a lien creditor against his debtor to subject the lands of the latter to the payment of his debt, and during the pendency of such suit another lien creditor of such debtor, by leave of the court, files his petition in said suit and is made a party thereto, and process is ordered against the defendant to answer such petition, which is not issued at once but is subsequently issued and duly served on the defendant; held, that in such case the statute of limitations ceases to run against the debt of such petitioner at the time he files his petition and not at the time, when the process to answer it is served on the defendant. Jackson v. Hull, 21 W. Va. 601.

Entry of Order of Reference.—In a creditors' suit, where the object and purpose are to ascertain all the liens upon the debtor's real estate, and their priorities, and to provide for their payment, the statute of limitations will in general cease to run against such liens after the entry of an order of reference. Northwestern Bank v. Hays, 37 W. Va. 475, 16 S. E. 561.

An order of reference for an account of liens suspends the running of the statute of limitations as to all creditors who come in under the order, and prove their liens in the suit. It also suspends the statute as to such lien creditors as for good cause have not proved their debts, but thereafter come in by petition and assert their liens, without unreasonable delay, and while the fund sought to be subjected is still under the control of the court. The evidence in the case in judgment shows good cause for delay in asserting the lien. Gunnell v. Dixon, 101 Va. 174, 43 S. E. 340.

Death.—B. & S. for use of McC., obtained a judgment at law, in Novem-

ber, 1859, against G. and O'B., et al., his sureties. A suit in equity was instituted by his lien creditors for the purpose of subjecting the real estate of said O'B. to the payment of their liens against it. G. was the owner of a tract of twenty-four and one-half acres of land and was a party defendant to the suit, but no proceedings were taken therein against said twenty-four and one-half acres. G. died pending the suit which was revived in the name of C., his only heir, who conveyed the twenty-four and one-half acres to D. Held: The fact that G. was a party defendant to a suit for the enforcement of liens against the realty of O'B. would not prevent the running of the statute of limitations as to a judgment against G. Woods v. Douglass, 52 W. Va. 517, 44 S. E. 234.

"In Werdenbaugh v. Reid, 20 W. Va. 588, this court decided that the right to enforce the lien of a judgment in a court of equity ceased when the right to sue out execution on the judgment, or to revive it by scire facias, became barred by the statute of limitations. Shipley v. Pew, 23 W. Va. 487. The plaintiff's right to relief, therefore, depends wholly upon the question whether or not, at the time they instituted this suit, their right to sue out execution upon, or to revive, their judgment, had become barred by the statute of limitations. By our statute, where execution issues within two years, other executions, may be issued on the judgment within ten years from the return day of the last execution. But, when the execution debtor dies, the right to revive the judgment by scire facias is limited to five years from the qualification of the personal representative of the debtor. Section 11, ch. 139, Code. It is therefore clear that, if Smith had lived ten years after the return day of the last execution, the plaintiff's right to relief would have been completely barred." Handy v. Smith, 30 W. Va. 195, 3 S. E. 604, 605.

Limitation Not Suspended by Agreement.—In a suit to enforce the lien of a judgment against real estate brought more than ten years after return day of the last execution issued thereon, the creditor can not avoid the bar of the statute by a parol agreement binding him not to sue out execution or enforce the judgment until within ten years before the bringing of such suit. Reilly v. Clark, 31 W. Va. 571, 8 S. E. 509.

Injunction to Judgment.—Upon the dissolution of an injunction to a judgment, execution may issue thereon within a year and a day from the dissolution of the injunction, without a scire facias, though the injunction was in force for more than ten years. Hutsonpiller v. Stover, 12 Gratt. 579.

New Promise.—A charge that a confession of judgment was obtained by fraudulently representing that the lien on the defendant's land, for which lien the judgment was confessed, was still in force, when in fact, it was at the time barred by the statute of limitations, of which the defendant was ignorant, is not sustained when it appears that, while the lien was in force, the defendant, for a valuable consideration, gave the plaintiff a promise in writing to pay the lien, for this he might have been compelled to do. Bradshaw v. Bratton, 96 Va. 577, 32 S. E. 56.

ii. Who May Plead.

Where a suit in equity is brought by a judgment creditor to subject the lands of the debtor to the satisfaction of his judgment, and the plaintiff in the bill sets forth the fact that there is another judgment against the same defendant, older in point of time, but which has not been kept alive by issuing executions as required by statute, but the defendant is in life, and does not plead the statute of limitations as to said older judgment, the plaintiff in said suit in equity has no right to file or rely on such plea.

Welton v. Boggs, 45 W. Va. 620, 32 S. E. 232.

Question: Can one judgment creditor of a living debtor plead the statute of limitations against another? "I do not now say whether one judgment lienor can plead the statute against other lienors of a common living debtor. It is not necessary to say here how this is. He is a general lienor, while a mortgagee is a lienor on that particular property. It was left open in the opinion in Woodyard v. Polsley, 14 W. Va. 211, and in Lee v. Feamster, 21 W. Va. 108, 111, and Conrad v. Buck, 21 W. Va. 396, 411." McClaugherty v. Croft, 43 W. Va. 270, 27 S. E. 246, 248.

jj. How Defense Made.

The defenses of the statute of limitations and laches and stale demands may be made by demurrer in a suit to enforce the lien of a judgment. Woods v. Douglass, 52 W. Va. 517, 44 S. E. 234, citing Thompson v. Whittaker Iron Co., 41 W. Va. 574, 23 S. E. 795.

kk. Enforcement in Equity.

In General.—And it seems to be equally well settled that the lien of a judgment is not enforceable in equity after it ceases to be enforceable at law, such a lien being a creature of statute. Sutton v. McKenney, 82 Va. 46; Hutcheson v. Grubbs, 80 Va. 251; McCarty v. Ball, 82 Va. 872, 1 S. E. 189; Shipley v. Pew, 23 W. Va. 487, 498; Werdenbaugh v. Reid, 20 W. Va. 588.

"The judgment sought to be enforced in equity in this suit was dead in law, and directly and expressly barred by the statute; and, being so barred by the law, it is equally barred in equity. Coles v. Ballard, 78 Va. 139, 149, citing Rowe v. Bentley, 29 Gratt. 756, 759; Hutcheson v. Grubbs, 80 Va. 251." McCarty v. Ball, 82 Va. 872, 874, 1 S. E. 189.

Courts of equity follow the law as respects Code, Va. 1873, ch. 182, §§ 12, 13, which declares that no execution shall issue, nor any scire facias or action be brought, on a judgment after the lapse of ten years from the return day of an execution on which there is no return by an officer, or after twenty years from the return day of an execution on which there is such return. Hence if a legal claim, barred at law, is asserted in equity, it is equally barred there. McCarty v. Ball, 82 Va. 872, 1 S. E. 189.

In the case of Hutcheson v. Grubbs, 80 Va. 251, Lewis, P., said: "It is needless to multiply words and authorities upon a proposition which we deem too plain to admit of doubt. Our conclusion, therefore, is, that the lien of a judgment is a legal lien, conferred by the express terms of the statute, though enforceable in equity, and ceases with the life of the judgment upon which it is founded." See opinion of Burke, Judge, in Rowe v. Bentley, 29 Gratt. 756, and authorities cited. Ayre v. Burke, 82 Va. 338, 341, 4 S. E. 618.

Lien of judgment ceases with the judgment's life. This lien, created by statute, is not collateral to, but grows out of, judgment. So long as judgment is enforceable at law by levy of fi. fa. it may be enforced in equity, and no longer, unless judgment be on debt secured by mortgage, trust deed or vendor's lien. Hutcheson v. Grubbs, 80 Va. 251; Paxton v. Rich, 85 Va. 378, 7 S. E. 531.

This court in the case of Werdenbaugh v. Reid, 20 W. Va. 588, decided that "the lien of a judgment on which no execution has ever issued, will not be enforced in a court of equity in a suit brought after the lapse of ten years from the date of such judgment." Jackson v. Hull, 21 W. Va. 601, 612.

"Comfort is sought from this quotation by putting over much stress upon the word 'always.' This fallacy is easily exploded. We have long had a statute (§ 9, ch. 182, Code, 1873), which declares: 'The lien of a judgment may always be enforced in a court of equity,' and, strange to say, much controversy arose as to its interpretation, but it was finally construed to mean that the lien can not be enforced in equity after it ceases to be enforceable at law." Corey v. Moore, 86 Va. 721, 736, 11 S. E. 114.

Death of Judgment Debtor.—The lien of a judgment, on which no execution has ever issued, will not be enforced in a court of equity in a suit brought after the lapse of ten years from the date of the judgment, and where the debtor dies, the time in which it can be enforced may be less, as in no case can it exceed five years after the qualification of his personal representative, unless perhaps, it may be kept alive by suing out successive executions after the death of the debtor, or, by having sued out a scire facias, continued his right to do so. Werdenbaugh v. Reid, 20 W. Va. 588.

(b) Laches.

See the title LACHES.

"As to the contention that the judgment creditors were guilty of laches in asserting their claims, it is only necessary to say that a judgment creditor's right to enforce his lien under the registry acts is not affected by his knowledge of the fact that the property has been aliened and that the alienee is making improvements thereon. When he dockets his judgment as provided by statute, he has done all he is bound to do, and parties dealing with the property do so at their peril and in complete subjection to the lien. Graeme v. Cullen, 23 Gratt. 266, 307; Wood v. Krebbs, 33 Gratt. 685, 692." Flanary v. Kane, 102 Va. 547, 560, 46 S. E. 312.

On debt contracted by F. in 1865, T. got judgment in 1873. In 1870, F. bought lands which were conveyed to his sister. In 1883, after death of F. and sister, the lands were sold in suit to settle sister's estate. Then T. brought his bill to apply proceeds to pay F.'s debts, on ground that the lands were conveyed to sister without consideration, to defraud creditors, and failed to explain delay to sue sooner. Held, the bill should be dismissed for laches. Terry *v.* Fontaine, 83 Va. 451, 2 S. E. 743.

(9) Costs.

In a suit to subject land to the payment of a judgment lien and to set aside deeds for fraud against the creditor, it is the practice to decree that the costs of the suit shall be first paid out of the proceeds of the sale of the land. Hinton *v.* Ellis, 27 W. Va. 422.

b. Proof.

See the title RECORDS.

Necessity of Proof.—Although, "every material allegation of the bill not controverted by answer, shall for the purposes of the suit be taken as true, and no proof thereof shall be required" as provided by § 36 of ch. 125 of the Code of West Virginia, still, if one defendant does controvert the material allegations of the bill to enforce the judgment lien, by his answer, and his interest may be affected by the truth of such allegations, the failure of another defendant or defendants to do so, does not dispense with the necessity of proof, as to such allegations, as to the defendant who does controvert them, by his answer. Dickinson *v.* Railroad Co., 7 W. Va. 390.

Such parts of the bill, for the enforcement of a judgment lien, as are not controverted by the answer, must also be taken as true. Snyder *v.* Martin, 17 W. Va. 276.

Authenticated Copy.—Where a judgment or decree is obtained for a debt, in a proceeding in chancery to enforce the lien of such judgment or decree against lands, ordinarily it is not necessary that a complete copy of the whole record of the case in the court in which the judgment or decree was had, should be produced or filed, but only a properly authenticated copy of such judgment or decree. In such case a copy of the judgment is an extract from the record of the cause, and not a complete copy of the whole record, and being an extract from the record, and a copy of the judgment, as entered, it may be read as evidence in the cause. Dickinson *v.* Railroad Co., 7 W. Va. 390; Sayre *v.* Edwards, 19 W. Va. 352, 353; White *v.* Clay, 7 Leigh 68; Wynn *v.* Harman, 5 Gratt. 157.

An authenticated copy from the recorder's docket of an official abstract of a judgment docketed under the provisions of the 3d and 4th sections of ch. 139 of the Code of 1868, of West Virginia, is evidence that such abstract was docketed, and when, and of notice to purchasers of lands upon which the alleged judgment is claimed to be a lien, when the existence of such judgment is properly proved; but where the judgment is put in issue, ordinarily, an authenticated copy of such abstract, as docketed by the recorder, will not be received as proof of the judgment and dispense with the necessity of producing a properly authenticated copy of the judgment. Dickinson *v.* Railroad Co., 7 W. Va. 390, 391.

"The third and fourth sections of ch. 139 of the Code provides for docketing judgments upon delivery to the recorder, of authenticated abstracts thereof. The docketing of judgments, as provided for, is intended for a special purpose, and that is to enable persons who may desire to purchase lands, etc., in any county, to know at what place, and in what description of record book they can learn the fact as to whether there are judgment liens; or, in other words, it is intended as notice to purchasers, that they may be put upon intelligent inquiry. An authenticated copy, from the recorder's docket, would be evidence as to where the abstract was docketed, and of notice to third persons of the existence of the judgment, when such judgment was properly proved; but would not, I apprehend, in a suit where the existence of the judgment was put in issue by the pleadings, be received, ordinarily, as proof of the judgment, and dispense with the necessity of producing an authenticated copy of the judgment itself. When the judgment, or an authenticated copy thereof, is produced, then an authenticated copy from the recorder's docket is simply proof that an abstract of the judgment was docketed as, and at, the place, prescribed by law, to have its legal effect touching the preservation of the judgment lien as against subsequent purchasers, etc." Dickinson v. Railroad Co., 7 W. Va. 390, 414.

"The remaining and important question is, did the plaintiff have a valid judgment? A duly certified copy of the record of the judgment, attested by the clerk of the circuit court of Cabell county was produced and read in evidence as a part of the plaintiff's bill, and the law makes such attested copy evidence in lieu of the original. See Code, 1891, p. 821, ch. 130, § 5; 2 Freem., Judgm. § 407. And such original imports absolute verity, and when read proves itself, and, the judgment being valid on its face, the court determines by inspection the existence of the record and the validity of the judgment." First Nat. Bank v. Huntington, etc., Co., 41 W. Va. 530, 23 S. E. 792, 793, 56 Am. St. Rep. 878.

Complete Copy of Whole Record Unnecessary.—In bringing suit to enforce the lien of the justice's judgment, it was not necessary to produce the whole record, but only a transcript of the justice's docket; and it was not required of the plaintiff to allege and show due service of the process. The transcript of the docket to the extent that it attempts to give the return of the officer who served the summons is mere surplusage so far as plaintiff's suit was concerned, and is wholly insufficient to sustain the demurrer, and justify the dismissal of the bill. Moran v. American Fire, etc., Co., 44 W. Va. 42, 28 S. E. 728, 729.

Where a judgment or decree is obtained for a debt, in a proceeding in chancery to enforce the lien of such judgment or decree against lands, ordinarily, it is not necessary that a complete copy of the whole record of the case in the court in which the judgment or decree was had, should be produced or filed, but only a properly authenticated copy of such judgment or decree. Dickinson v. Railroad Co., 7 W. Va. 390.

In such case a copy of the judgment is an extract from the record of the cause, and not a complete copy of the whole record, and being an extract from the record, and a copy of the judgment, as entered, it may be read as evidence in the cause. Dickinson v. Railroad Co., 7 W. Va. 390.

Certificate of Clerk.—At the March term, 1861, of the county court of Monroe, a judgment was rendered at the suit of the bank of V., plaintiff, against W., S. and G., the latter living in the county of Bath. Execution of fi. fa. was issued on this judgment and levied on the property of W., and the sheriff returned, after June, 1861, a levy upon the personal property of W., that the property was appraised and offered for sale, and not bringing valuation it was returned. G. died during the war, leaving real estate in Bath county, and also in West Virginia; and after his death some of his creditors filed their bill in the circuit court of Bath, to subject his real estate to the payment of his debts. The commissioner reported the above judgment as a debt by judgment having priority. A copy of the judgment was certified by the clerk of Monroe circuit court, "and as such, keeper of the records of Monroe county court, and which by law are a part of the records of my office." The circuit court confirmed the report. Held, that the certificate of the clerk of the circuit court of Monroe county, in West Virginia, of the records of which court the records of the former county court of Monroe form a part, was proper evidence of such judgment; and there appearing no other judgment binding said lands, or any debt of G. of superior dignity, there was no error in the decree. Gatewood *v.* Goode, 23 Gratt. 880.

"**An abstract**, ordinarily, means a mere brief and not a copy of that from which it is taken. This paper, then, being only an abstract of an alleged judgment, and attested only as an abstract, and not as a copy, and the existence of the judgment being denied, and the abstract, excepted to as not being legal evidence of the judgment, it can not be read as proof of the judgment against the railroad company. It would be extremely dangerous to accept mere abstracts of judgments as proof of the original. I don't think it necessary that a complete copy of the whole record of the case in the district court should be produced, but only a properly authenticated copy of the judgment. White *v.* Clay, 7 Leigh 68, 78, 82; Wynn *v.* Harman, 5 Gratt. 175." Dickinson *v.* Railroad Co., 7 W. Va. 390, 413.

An abstract as applied to records ordinarily means a mere brief, and not a copy of that from which it is taken, and a paper writing being only an abstract of an alleged judgment, and attested as an abstract, although attested by the clerk of the court in which the judgment was rendered, can not ordinarily be read as proof of the alleged judgment, where the existence of the judgment is denied. Dickinson *v.* Railroad Co., 7 W. Va. 390.

A mere abstract, not being a copy of a judgment, does not prove the existence of the judgment, if controverted. Thomson *v.* Mann, 53 W. Va. 432, 44 S. E. 246.

"Upon the question as to whether such an abstract as was filed in this case, taken from the judgment lien docket, was sufficient when the existence of such judgment is denied, and proof thereof is called for in the answer, this court held, in the case of Dickinson *v.* Railroad Co., 7 W. Va. 390 (§ 7 of syllabus), that 'an authenticated copy from the recorder's docket under the provisions of the third and fourth sections of ch. 139 of the Code of 1868 of West Virginia is evidence such abstract was docketed, and when, and of notice to purchasers of lands upon which the alleged judgment is claimed to be a lien when the existence of such judgment is properly proved; but when the judgment is put in issue, ordinarily, an authenticated copy of such abstract as docketed by the recorder will not be received as proof of the judgment, and dispense with the necessity of producing a properly authenticated copy of the judgment;' and the same thing is held precisely in the case of Anderson *v.* Nagle, 12 W. Va. 98. (§ 2 of syllabus.)" Snyder *v.* Botkin, 37 W. Va. 355, 16 S. E. 591, 595.

Proof of Rendition.—Where the fact to be shown is merely that a decree or judgment has been rendered, proof of the other proceedings ordinarily (though perhaps not universally), will not be necessary, but the adversary party will be at liberty to show any other matter in the record which may avoid the effect of that which is introduced. Dickinson *v.* Railroad Co., 7 W. Va. 390.

Judgments of United States Courts. —Section 5 of ch. 130 of the Code of 1868 of West Virginia applies as well to the records of the district court of the United States, held within this state, as to the records of the courts of this state; and a copy of a judgment rendered in the district court of the United States, in this state, attested by the clerk of such court, according to the provisions of said last-named section and chapter, will ordinarily be received as evidence of the existence of such judgment. Dickinson *v.* Railroad Co., 7 W. Va. 390, 391.

Objections in Appellate Court.— Where the confession of a judgment before a justice is alleged in the bill, giving date and amount, and admitted by defendant in his answer, and proved in the cause by oral testimony, without objection or exception, the question of the sufficiency of the proof of the existence of such judgment, because the record of it was not produced, can not be raised the first time in the appellate court. Nuzum *v.* Herron, 52 W. Va. 499, 44 S. E. 257.

Burden of Proof.—The burden is upon the judgment creditor seeking to subject land in the hands of his debtor's alienee for value to show that the land is liable. If the bill alleges a sale and no conveyance, but does not allege an unrecorded written contract, and the answer denies a written contract, and avers a verbal contract and such performance thereunder prior to May 1, 1888, as would have entitled the purchaser to specific performance as against his vendor, there can be no recovery unless the averments of the answer are overcome. Fulkerson *v.* Taylor, 100 Va. 426, 41 S. E. 863.

7. The Judgment or Decree.

See the title JUDICIAL SALES.

a. In General.

A decree in a suit brought by a judgment creditor should upon its face show the amount and priority of every debt against the land of the judgment debtor, the person to whom the same is payable, and the fund out of which it is entitled to be paid; and therefore a decree in such a cause, that the judgment debtor (naming him) "do pay to the complainant and other judgment and trust creditors of the said debtor the several sums ascertained to be due to them respectively by the report of the commissioner contained on pages 33 and 34 of his report," is erroneous. Kanawha Valley Bank *v.* Wilson, 25 W. Va. 242, 243.

b. Conformity to Pleadings.

Where a suit in equity is brought by a party to enforce his judgment lien against real estate which his debtor holds jointly with another, and both of the owners of the real estate are made parties to the suit, and served with process, although no allegation is made or lien asserted against the party holding the real estate jointly with such judgment debtor, and the cause being referred to a commissioner to ascertain the liens existing against the real estate, and their priorities, who reports a judgment lien existing against the real estate belonging to the party who is not the judgment debtor mentioned in the bill, it is error to decree a sale of the entire property, and such a decree may be set aside by a bill of review filed in proper time. Calvert *v.* Ash, 47 W. Va. 480, 35 S. E. 887.

B., as cestui que trust, in two deeds of trust made to L., as trustee, filed his bill in equity in the name of himself and said trustee, to enforce his trust liens upon a particular tract of land of B., alleging priority over all other liens by one of his trust liens, but admitting the priority of certain other trust liens and judgment liens, designated by his bill and exhibits, over his second trust lien, and made those particular lienors parties to the suit, and praying to convene those creditors before a commissioner, to ascertain and audit their respective debts in the order of their priorities; and that the land, or so much thereof as may be necessary to pay B.'s debts, be sold. E. was owner of other tracts of land, upon which the said judgment creditors and others had liens, but the bill took no notice thereof. Held: The bill having for its object the enforcement of B.'s specific claims on a certain tract of E.'s land, B. could have a decree touching only the object of the bill. Baugher *v.* Eichelberger, 11 W. Va. 217.

So also, where a bill to enforce a judgment lien, filed against the judgment debtor, alleges that after the judgment was rendered, the debtor obtained an injunction against the judgment, giving Cl. and T. as sureties in the injunction bond, that the injunction was dissolved and the bill dismissed, but the bill only seeks the sale of the judgment debtor's real estate, a personal decree against Cl. for a balance of the judgment, after exhausting the judgment debtor's estate would be proper, but under this bill, a decree for the sale of the real estate of Cl. would be erroneous. Sinnett *v.* Cralle, 4 W. Va. 600.

Where a bill is filed to subject land to the payment of a judgment, if the bill contains a prayer for general relief, the decree of the court may extend beyond the land described in the bill, without any subsequent amendment of the pleadings. Groseclose *v.* Harman, 1 Va. Dec. 564.

c. Time to Redeem.

It is not per se error to decree a sale of land to enforce judgment liens without giving the debtor time to redeem, as in the foreclosure of mortgages, though such practice ought not in general to be pursued, but where the debtor does not show that he has sustained any damage by the failure to do so, it is not ground for setting aside the sale. Crawford *v.* Weller, 23 Gratt. 835.

d. Suit to Set Aside Fraudulent Conveyance.

Where a suit has been brought to subject lands to the payment of a lien and to set aside fraudulent conveyances, where the report of sale has been made, and it is found there will not be sufficient money produced by the sale to pay the liens, expenses of sale and costs, for whatever costs remaining after providing for the payment of the liens and expenses of sale, there should be rendered a personal decree against all the fraudulent grantors and grantees. Hinton *v.* Ellis, 27 W. Va. 422.

e. Joint and Several Judgments.

One of several joint judgment debtors may be proceeded against to enforce the payment of his part of the judgment, where the complainant has released him on the record from all liability for the shares of the other judgment debtors. Moreover, this objection, raised for the first time in an appellate court, comes too late. Preston *v.* National Exchange Bank, 97 Va. 222, 23 S. E. 546.

Where a suit in equity is brought by a party to enforce his judgment lien against real estate which his debtor holds jointly with another, and both of the owners of said real estate are made parties to the suit, and served with process, although no allegation is made or lien asserted against the party holding said real estate jointly with such judgment debtor, and the cause being referred to a commissioner to ascertain the liens existing against said real estate, and their priorities, who reports a judgment lien existing against the real estate belonging to said party who is not the judgment debtors mentioned in the bill, it is error to decree a sale of the entire property, and such decree may be set aside by bill of review filed in proper time. Calvert *v.* Ash, 47 W. Va. 480, 35 S. E. 887.

f. Notice to Lien Holders.

See the title JUDICIAL SALES.

No decree for the distribution of the proceeds of real estate shall be made in a suit in equity to enforce the lien of a judgment, until a notice to all persons holding liens on the real estate of the judgment debtor be posted and published under a decree of the court. And the Code provides the form of notice. W. Va. Code, 1899, ch. 139, § 4147; Bensimer *v.* Fell, 35 W. Va. 15, 12 S. E. 1078, 29 Am. St. Rep. 774.

A decree under § 7, ch. 139, W. Va. Code, 1887, upon a report of a commissioner after notice to lien holders, adjudging liens on the lands of a debtor, is conclusive as between the various lienors proving liens, though not formal parties, as to the existence and amounts of their debts for the purposes of that cause as to the lands of the debtor; and if there be a personal decree against the debtor for such liens, not merely because of the statute, but on general principles of law, the decree would be conclusive generally as between, not only the creditor and debtor, but also conclusive as between the various lienors, as to the existence and amounts of their respective debts. Bensimer *v.* Fell, 35 W. Va. 15, 12 S. E. 1078, 29 Am. St. Rep. 774.

Any lienor holding the debt against the judgment debtor constituting a lien on his land, not proving his lien in such proceeding, would be thereby barred from sharing in the proceeds of the sale of land under the decree, except in the surplus remaining after payment of the liens decreed, though not a formal party. But a debt secured by deed of trust would not be so barred, unless the trustee and cestui que trust be formal parties. They must still in such suit be made formal parties, under § 7, ch. 139, as found in the edition of the Code issued in 1887, under ch. 126, acts, 1882. Bensimer *v.* Fell, 35 W. Va. 15, 12 S. E. 1078, 29 Am. St. Rep. 774.

g. Settlement of Accounts.

The court ought not, in a chancery suit brought to enforce the lien of a judgment between partners, order a settlement of partnership accounts with a view of ascertaining the amount for which the lands of each partner should be primarily subject, and with a view to the rendering of a proper decree among the codefendants after such settlement. Kent *v.* Chapman, 18 W. Va. 485.

h. Decree Annulling Unrecorded Deed.

In a suit to enforce a judgment lien, it is error to decree an unrecorded deed null and void in a decree in favor of the judgment creditor; it should be so held as to the creditor, it being good between the parties. Murdock *v.* Welles, 9 W. Va. 552.

Where a deed is fraudulent as to creditors, but good between the parties, in a suit to subject the land to the liens of creditors it is error to decree the conveyance void in toto. Duncan *v.* Custard, 24 W. Va. 730, citing Murdock *v.* Welles, 9 W. Va. 552.

i. Construction of Decree.

Bill to enforce judgment lien, alleged prior trust deed to be fraudulent or satisfied. Debtor denied the allegation, and charged the judgment to be usurious. Account of liens was taken. Report did not sustain charge of usury, nor allude to trust deed, which was not filed with the bill, and was at no time before the master or the court. No evidence was presented tending to prove the alleged fraud or satisfaction. Report was excepted to, but it was confirmed, and the land decreed to be sold. Upon appeal here, the decree, which was silent as to the trust deed, was reversed, and the judgment reduced by reason of the manifest usury to the principal loaned, and the cause remanded. Held, these decrees are not to be constructed as adjudging by implication, the trust deed to be fraudulent or satsfied, when no decree expressly so adjudges, and when, if any did so adjudge, it would be in opposition to evidence to the contrary. Fisher *v.* Dickenson, 84 Va. 318, 4 S. E. 737.

j. Equitable Relief.

See post, "Equitable Relief," VIII, A.

In a suit in equity, brought for the purpose of enforcing a judgment lien, which judgment was obtained against the defendant by default, the defendant will not be allowed in said chancery suit to make any defense against said judgment which might have been successfully made in a court of law, unless he shows some reason founded on fraud, accident, surprise, or some adventitious circumstance beyond his control, why the defense at law was not made. McNeel *v.* Auldridge, 34 W. Va. 748, 12 S. E. 851.

After a judgment has been recovered in an action at law, and a suit in equity has been pending for more than ten years to enforce the lien of the judgment, the defendant can not prevent the enforcement of this judgment, on the ground that they did not employ counsel to defend them in the action at law, and that their appearance by counsel was false, when it appears in the record of the action at law, in which the judgment was recovered, the defendant did appear by counsel and file pleas. Cabell *v.* Given, 30 W. Va. 760, 5 S. E. 442.

k. Satisfaction and Discharge.

Where a suit in chancery is instituted to enforce a judgment lien and the bill alleges that there is but one other judgment lien on real estate sought to be held liable to the satisfaction of the judgment, and sets it up also as a lien on the land, the decree should provide for the payment of both judgments, if the land is subject thereto. Anderson *v.* Nagle, 12 W. Va. 98.

l. Former Adjudication or Res Adjudicata.

See the title FORMER ADJUDICATION OR RES ADJUDICATA, vol. 6, p. 261.

Divisible and Indivisible Causes of Action.—While a judgment may not be divided into different causes of action, yet a suit brought to enforce the lien thereof, prosecuted in good faith, though ineffectually, is not a bar to a subsequent suit by the same complainant against the same defendant to enforce satisfaction of the same judgment. Kelly *v.* Hamblen, 98 Va. 383, 36 S. E. 491.

A judgment is an indivisible cause of action, and when once an action is instituted upon it and prosecuted to a final judgment or decree, no other suit or action can be brought upon it. It is true, that a judgment is an indivisible cause of action in the sense that it may not be divided or split up into several causes of action. Subject to the discretion of courts in the imposition of costs, as many successive actions may be brought upon a judgment as may be needful in the opinion of the

plaintiff, but there can, of course, be but one satisfaction. Kelly *v.* Hamblenn, 98 Va. 383, 389, 36 S. E. 491.

Parties and Persons Concluded.

In General.—No decree in a suit to enforce a judgment lien will be binding, unless all necessary parties are before the court. McMillan *v.* Hickman, 35 W. Va. 705, 14 S. E. 227.

In a suit for partition, where no sale is necessary and none is made for the purpose of partition, the court is without jurisdiction to sell the land assigned to one of the parties to satisfy his share of the costs of partition. The judgment for such costs would probably be a preferred lien on the land, but would have to be enforced like other judgment liens by a bill in equity. If such a decree could be held to bind the parties to the suit, it certainly would not bind a third party, claiming an interest in the land, who was not a party to the suit, and had no notice of the proceedings. After the purposes of the suit have been accomplished and costs decreed, the suit is ended. Virginia Iron, etc., Co. *v.* Roberts, 103 Va. 661, 49 S. E. 984.

A creditor holding a debt against a judgment debtor constituting a lien on his land, who is not made a formal party to a judgment adjudging creditors' liens on the land of the debtor, and who does not prove his lien in such proceeding, is thereby barred from sharing in the proceeds of the sale under the decree, except in the surplus remaining after the satisfaction of the liens decreed. The debt, as a personal debt against the debtor, is not barred by such proceeding. Bensimer *v.* Fell, 35 W. Va. 15, 12 S. E. 1078.

A judgment adjudging creditors' liens on the land of a debtor will not bar a lien thereon created by a former owner of the land because of a failure to prove the lien, unless its owner is made a formal party to the proceeding. Bensimer *v.* Fell, 35 W. Va. 15, 12 S. E. 1078.

Purchaser of Debtor's Land.—In a suit to settle estate of R., deceased, C. set up a judgment against G., insolvent principal, and R. and P., sureties. G. and P. were not named in the bill. Leave was given to amend the bill, and make parties G. and P., and J. C., the alienee of P.'s land, which was bound by the judgment lien. Amended bill was filed, and C. and J. C., but not P., were summoned to answer it, but by order of plaintiff's attorney, it was dismissed at same rules at which it was filed. Account of liens was ordered and taken, showing that $616 was P.'s portion, and a lien on P.'s lands aliened to J. C., who had been summoned to appear, and who did appear before the commissioner. Circuit court confirmed report, and decreed that J. C. pay to its receiver said sum of money. On appeal, held, J. C. was not in any fair sense of the term, a party to the suit. J. C. not being a party, the decree is a nullity as to him. Without the presence of P. before the court, his lands could not be subjected to the judgment. In no aspect of the case, was there any foundation for the personal decree against J. C. Cronise v. Carper, 80 Va. 678, citing Moseley v. Cocke, 7 Leigh 224, 226; Henderson v. Henderson, 9 Gratt. 394; Taylor v. Spindle, 2 Gratt. 44.

No subsequent decree or judgment for an amount beyond the legal call of the first judgment, in a suit to which such purchaser is not a formal party, or wherein the true amount due by reason of the judgment was not in fact litigated, can estop such purchaser from satisfying the demand by payment of a sum lawfully called for by the judgment as it was when he purchased. Bensimer v. Fell, 35 W. Va. 15, 12 S. E. 1078, 29 Am. St. Rep. 774.

Trustee and Cestui Que Trust.—A judgment adjudging creditors' liens on land of a debtor will not bar a holder of a debt by deed of trust, who does not prove his debt, from sharing in the proceeds of the sale under the de-cree, unless the trustee and cestui que trust are made formal parties thereto. Bensimer v. Fell, 35 W. Va. 15, 12 S. E. 1078.

8. Appeal and Error.

See the title APPEAL AND ER-ROR, vol. 1, p. 418.

a. Amount in Controversy.

Where several judgment creditors with judgments each below $300, unite in one suit to enforce their liens on the judgment debtor's land, and their bill is dismissed by the court below, this court has no jurisdiction to entertain their appeal. Umbarger v. Watts, 25 Gratt. 167; Thompson v. Adams, 82 Va. 672; Pitts v. Spotts, 86 Va. 71, 9 S. E. 501.

The lien of a judgment which does not amount to more than $100, exclusive of costs, is sought by suit in equity to be enforced against what is claimed to be the life estate of B. in a certain tract of land, and there is a decree for the sale of such life estate, but the controversy, so far as it concerns B., is simply pecuniary Held, this court has no jurisdiction to entertain an appeal on behalf of B. alone. Berry v. Cunningham, 37 W. Va. 302, 16 S. E. 463. See Faulconer v. Stinson, 44 W. Va. 546, 29 S. E. 1011; McClaugherty v. Morgan, 36 W. Va. 191, 14 S. E. 992; Davis v. Vass, 47 W. Va. 811, 35 S. E. 826.

b. Exceptions and Objections.

See the title APPEAL AND ER-ROR, vol. 1, p. 547.

On a bill to enforce the lien of a judgment, a contention that the commissioner's report fails to show which one of the debtors is entitled to certain credits will not be considered on appeal, when all parties had ample opportunity to be heard before the commissioner, and failed to make any objections. National Exchange Bank v. Preston, 2 Va. Dec. 652.

Where the confession of a judgment before a justice is alleged in the bill giving date and amount and admitted by defendant in his answer and proved in the cause by oral testimony without objection or exception, the question of the sufficiency of the proof of the existence of such judgment because the record of it was not produced can not be raised the first time in the appellate court. Nuzum *v.* Herron, 52 W. Va. 499, 44 S. E. 257.

A judgment debtor can not object in the appellate court for the first time that he has not been allowed credits to which he was entitled, or that others were jointly bound with him for the judgment. Preston *v.* National Exchange Bank, 97 Va. 222, 33 S. E. 546.

9. Remedies to Prevent Enforcement.

a. Injunction.

"There can be no doubt that courts of equity have sometimes restrained by injunction the collection of judgments which had been previously satisfied. See Bowen *v.* Clark, 46 Ind. 405; Scogin *v.* Beall, 50 Ga. 88; Craft *v.* Thompson, 51 N. H. 536. But the more recent and better authorities hold that, when the remedy at law is as complete and adequate as the remedy in equity, the chancery court will not interfere by injunction. Thus, in this very recent work on the Law of Judgments (1891), Mr. Black says: 'Whether a bill in equity for an injunction is the proper remedy to prevent a judgment creditor from proceeding to collect anew a judgment which has been in fact satisfied, has been disputed. Some of the cases hold that such an application is meritorious and should be allowed. But others, and we think with better reason, consider that equity ought not to interfere in such a case, inasmuch as the party has a prompt and adequate remedy at law.' Black, Judgm., § 390. So Mr. High, in his last edition on Injunctions (1890, § 123), says: 'There is also noticeable want of harmony in the authorities upon the question of the right to enjoin the enforcement of a judgment which has been already paid,

either in whole or in part. The better-considered doctrine upon this subject, and that most in harmony with the general principles underlying the preventive jurisdiction of equity, is that an injunction should not be granted for the purpose of staying or preventing a sale under execution on the ground of payment, in whole or in part, and that in all such cases the person aggrieved should be left to pursue his remedy at law.' In support of this position Mr. High cites Hall *v.* Taylor, 18 W. Va. 544. Upon turning to that case, we find that it fully sustains the position that a defendant can not, in a court of equity, enjoin the collection of an execution issued to enforce a judgment already satisfied, because he has an adequate and summary remedy at law, viz., the motion to quash the execution because the judgment has been paid." Howell *v.* Thomason, 34 W. Va. 794, 12 S. E. 1088, 1089.

In a case where, by virtue of an agreement between a judgment debtor and a judgment creditor, the judgment ought to be entered as satisfied, but in lieu thereof the creditor has an execution issued and levied upon the goods of the debtor, the latter can not obtain relief by injunction in a court of equity, for the reason that he has a complete and adequate remedy at law. Should the court, in such a case, after having granted an injunction, dissolve the same at a final hearing, it ought not to enter a personal decree against the plaintiff for the amount of the original judgment enjoined, but should simply dissolve the injunction, and dismiss the bill, with costs, and without prejudice to the plaintiff as to his defense at law against the enforcement of the execution. Howell *v.* Thomason, 34 W. Va. 794, 12 S. E. 1088.

b. Prohibition.

See the title PROHIBITION.

Prohibition lies to prevent the enforcement of a judgment by default when the persons against whom the same was rendered had no notice of the time and place and were not present at the trial. Simmons *v.* Thomason, 50 W. Va. 656, 41 S. E. 335.

County judge of one county presided at trial of a cause in another county without entering upon record that the regular judge (personally present) was, in his opinion, so situated as to make it improper for him to preside, held, the judgment is void, and its enforcement should be restrained by a writ of prohibition. Gresham *v.* Ewell, 85 Va. 1, 6 S. E. 700. Lewis, P., dissenting.

c. Motion to Quash Execution.

The provision of the West Virginia Code on this subject is as follows: "A motion to quash an execution may, after reasonable notice to the adverse party, be heard and decided by the court whose clerk issued the execution, or, if a circuit court, by the judge thereof in vacation; and such judge or court may, without such notice, make an order staying proceedings on the execution until such motion can be heard and determined. A copy of the order so made must be served upon the officer in whose hands the execution is." Page 870, § 17. It will thus be seen that this provision is ample to protect an execution debtor from the levy of an execution upon a satisfied judgment, and is fully as complete and far less expensive and cumbersome than the resort to a court of chancery. See Cockerell *v.* Nichols, 8 W. Va. 159; Farmers' Bank *v.* Montgomery, 11 W. Va. 169; McCoy *v.* Allen, 16 W. Va. 724, 733. Howell *v.* Thomason, 34 W. Va. 794, 12 S. E. 1088, 1089.

VII. Opening, Amending, Modifying or Vacating Judgments or Decrees.

A. CONTROL OF COURT OVER JUDGMENTS OR DECREES.

1. General Rules as to Power during and after Term.

a. During Term.

A court has full control over its or-

ders, judgments or decrees during the term, and may, in its discretion, revise, amend, supplement or·vacate such orders judgments or decrees. Spilman *v.* Gilpin, 93 Va. 698, 25 S. E. 1004; Barnes' Case, 92 Va. 794, 23 S. E. 784, 796; Clendenning *v.* Conrad, 91 Va. 410, 21 S. E. 818; Shipman *v.* Fletcher, 91 Va. 473, 22 S. E. 458; Price *v.* Com., 33 Gratt. 819; Lingle *v.* Cook, 32 Gratt. 262; Winston *v.* Giles, 27 Gratt. 530; Bunting *v.* Willis, 27 Gratt. 144, 158; Enders *v.* Burch, 15 Gratt. 64; Snead *v.* Coleman, 7 Gratt. 300; Garland *v.* Marx, 4 Leigh 321; Eubank *v.* Ralls, 4 Leigh 308; Com. *v.* Winstons, 5 Rand. 546; Bent *v.* Patten, 1 Rand. 25; Vaughan *v.* Freeland, 2 Hen. & M. 477; Cogvill *v.* Cogvill, 2 Hen. & M. 467; Marr *v.* Miller, 1 Hen. & M. 204; Halley *v.* Baird, 1 Hen. & M. 25; Cawoods Case, 2 Va. Cas. 527; Freeland *v.* Fields, 6 Call 12, 15; Gordon *v.* Frazier, 2 Wash. 130, 135; Vance *v.* Railway Co., 53 W. Va. 338, 340, 44 S. E. 461; Barbour County Court *v.* O'Neal, 42 W. Va. 295, 26 S. E. 182; Post *v.* Carr, 42 W. Va. 72, 24 S. E. 583; Morgan *v.* Ohio River R. Co., 39 W. Va. 17, 19 S. E. 588; Bierne *v.* Ray, 37 W. Va. 571, 16 S. E. 804; Kelty *v.* High, 29 W. Va. 381, 1 S. E. 561; Stringer *v.* Anderson, 23 W. Va. 482; National Bank *v.* Jarvis, 26 W. Va. 785; Smith *v.* Knight, 14 W. Va. 749, 759; Green *v.* Pittsburgh, etc., R. Co., 11 W. Va. 685; Manion *v.* Fahy, 11 W. Va. 482. And see post, "Final Judgments or Decrees," VII, A, 1, b, (2).

"During the term of the court at which a decree is entered it is completely under the control of the court, and may be modified or annulled on motion, or at the suggestion of the court without motion." Kelty *v.* High, 29 W. Va. 381, 1 S. E. 561.

"Speaking of a final decree, Prof. Minor, in part 2, vol. 4, p. 1506, of his Institutes, says: 'It must be understood that it is not properly a decree at all until the end of the term at which it is pronounced, being then in fieri, and in the breast of the court.'" Kelty *v.* High, 29 W. Va. 381, 1 S. E. 561.

During the term, the proceedings of the court are said to be in its breast, and it may strike out, modify or set them aside. Cawood's Case, 2 Va. Cas. 527; Clendenning *v.* Conrad, 91 Va. 410, 21 S. E. 818; Kelty *v.* High, 29 W. Va. 381, 1 S. E. 561; Morgan *v.* Ohio River R. Co., 39 W. Va. 17, 19 S. E. 588, 589; Green *v.* Pittsburg, etc., R. Co., 11 W. Va. 685.

"During the term, the record remains in the breast of the judges of the court, and in their remembrance, and therefore the roll is alterable during that term as they shall direct. 1 Rob. Pr., old edition." Smith *v.* Knight, 14 W. Va. 749, 759.

"When we say that the record is in the breast of the court to be changed during the term, we only mean that proceedings attested by it have not yet obtained that irrevocable character which places them beyond the power of the court after the term. We only mean that the court can, for good reasons, and under proper circumstances, modify, set them aside, or otherwise affect them during the term. By no means do we mean that a party who has, by due process of law, obtained the final judgment of the law upon his cause, can have his property in that judgment arbitrarily taken from him at the unwarranted behest of his adversary." Post *v.* Carr, 42 W. Va. 72, 24 S. E. 583.

After a decree in a chancery cause has been passed upon and entered by the circuit court, it may be modified or set aside during the same term for good cause shown. What is sufficient cause is a matter in the sound discretion of the circuit court. Mathews *v.* Tyree, 53 W. Va. 298, 44 S. E. 526.

"Every court, whether appellate or original, has during the term complete control of its decrees and proceedings, and may review or modify them at its pleasure." Summers *v.* Darne, 31 Gratt. 791.

Correction during Term Notwithstanding Issuance of Execution.—At common law no judgment became final until the end of the term at which it was rendered, regardless of the duration of the term, and until final no court could direct an execution to issue on it. Section 3600 of the Virginia Code, however, confers on courts authority to direct executions to issue on judgments under the conditions therein set forth, but such judgments do not thereby become final so as to deprive the court during the term, of the power to correct, or if need be annul them if erroneous. Baker *v.* Swineford, 97 Va. 112, 33 S. E. 542, discussing and criticising Enders *v.* Burch, 15 Gratt. 64.

"At common law, no matter how long a term might last, a judgment did not become final until it ended, and the court had no power to direct an execution upon it. The inconvenience and injustice sometimes occasioned by this rule induced the legislature to provide a remedy. It enlarged the power of the court, and imparted to it an authority which at common law no court possessed. A statute, the manifest purpose of which was to enlarge the power of the court, will not be construed to limit that power unless such a result be unavoidable. There seems no incongruity in so modifying the common law as to permit an execution to issue upon a judgment and at the same time preserving to the court jurisdiction to correct any error in the judgment during the continuance of the term at which it was rendered. The common law is in force with us except in so far as it has been changed by statute." Baker *v.* Swineford, 97 Va. 112, 116, 33 S. E. 542.

May Set Aside or Modify in Whole or in Part.—"It has been held by this court that 'until the term ends, every judgment or decree entered may for good reason be modified or set aside in whole or in part. The court has a discretion to do this in the exercise of which this court will not interfere except for the most cogent reasons.' Parkersburg Nat. Bank v. Neal, 28 W. Va. 744. What is good reason for setting aside a judgment at law has been settled in the case of Post v. Carr, 42 W. Va. 72, 24 S. E. 583, where it is said in first point in syllabus, 'Such good cause can only appear by showing fraud, accident, mistake, surprise or some other adventitious circumstances beyond the control of the party and free from neglect on his part.'" Mathews v. Tyree, 53 W. Va. 298, 304, 44 S. E. 526.

Discretion of Court.—Until the term ends every judgment or decree may for good reason be modified or set aside in whole or in part. The court has a discretion to do this, in the exercise of which the supreme court will not interfere except for the most cogent reasons. Parkersburg Nat. Bank v. Neal, 28 W. Va. 744.

When a judgment is set aside by the court during the term at which it was rendered, the appellate court will presume that it was rightfully set aside unless the contrary affirmatively appears by the record. Green v. Pittsburg, etc., R. Co., 11 W. Va. 685, 686.

Power to Set Aside Judgment in Criminal Cases.—Upon the trial of P. for murder, the jury found him not guilty of the murder, but guilty of involuntary manslaughter, and assessed upon him a fine of $500. And the court thereupon entered a judgment discharging him. At the same term of the court, in the absence of P., the court set aside the judgment, and entered a judgment against him, for the fine of $500, and six months' imprisonment, and directed him to be arrested and committed to prison. Held: 1. The first judgment was erroneous. 2. During the same term of the court the matter was under the control of the court; and it was competent for the court to set aside the first and render the second judgment. 3. It was not necessary that P. should be present in court when the second judgment was entered. Price v. Com., 33 Gratt. 819.

b. After Expiration of Term.

(1) Interlocutory Judgments or Decrees.

In General.—After the close of the term, the court may modify or set aside any judgment or decree made at a former term, if it be interlocutory and not final in character. 1 Black, Judg., § 308; Spilman v. Gilpin, 93 Va. 698, 25 S. E. 1004; Miller v. Cook, 77 Va. 806, 819; Wayland v. Crank, 79 Va. 602; Ryan v. McLeod, 32 Gratt. 367; Roberts v. Cocke, 1 Rand. 121; Repass v. Moore, 96 Va. 147, 30 S. E. 458; Com. v. Beaumarchais, 3 Call 122; Barbour County Court v. O'Neal, 42 W. Va. 295, 26 S. E. 182; Rheims v. Standard Fire Ins. Co., 39 W. Va. 672, 20 S. E. 670, 676; Clarke v. Ohio River R. Co., 39 W. Va. 732, 20 S. E. 696; Morgan v. Ohio River R. Co., 39 W. Va. 17, 19 S. E. 588; Bierne v. Ray, 37 W. Va. 571, 16 S. E. 804; Chesapeake, etc., R. Co. v. Pack, 6 W. Va. 397.

"During the term of the court all its proceedings are in its breast, and its judgments and decrees may be set aside upon motion. When the term is ended, final judgments have passed beyond the power of the court except to a very limited extent, regulated by statute, and final decrees, except in so far as the power to control them is regulated by statute, or by the law governing bills of review, but in courts of law where proceedings are far less plastic than in courts of equity interlocutory orders may be controlled, and the record amended and made to speak the truth until a final judgment has been entered and the term ended at which it was entered." Spilman v. Gilpin, 93 Va. 698, 704, 25 S. E. 1004.

"Black on Judgments (vol. 2, § 509) says: 'It is well settled that the doctrine of res judicata applies only to final judgments, not to interlocutory judgments or orders, which the court which rendered them has power to vacate or modify at any time.' Citing Webb *v*. Buckelew, 82 N. Y. 555." Rheims *v*. Standard Fire Ins. Co., 39 W. Va. 672, 20 S. E. 670, 676.

It is not a sufficient ground for reversing an interlocutory decree, that no day was given to an infant defendant to show cause against it, after he should come of age; because such omission may be corrected in the final decree. Pickett *v*. Chilton, 5 Munf. 467. See the title INFANTS, vol. 7, p. 497.

See, however, Davis *v*. Demming, 12 W. Va. 246, in which it is held, that after the close of the term of the court, in which a decree is rendered settling any of the principles of a cause, though such decree be interlocutory, the court can not set aside or disregard such decree, unless it is done upon a petition for a rehearing.

Generally, as to the distinction between final and interlocutory judgments and decrees, illustrations, etc., see ante, "Final and Interlocutory," II, A.

An order which merely sustains a demurrer to a declaration, or strikes out a count or item of claim, but followed by no judgment as to it, is interlocutory in nature, and the count or item of claim may be reinstated in the declaration at a subsequent term. Clarke *v*. Ohio River R. Co., 39 W. Va. 732, 20 S. E. 696.

It is well settled that whether an interlocutory decree confirming a commissioner's report shall be modified or wholly set aside, or not, is generally a matter resting in the sound discretion of the chancellor, to be exercised according to the particular circumstances of each case. Kendrick *v*. Whitney, 28 Gratt. 646; Fultz *v*. Brightwell, 77 Va. 742; 1 Bart. Ch. Pr., 339. Newberry *v*. Stuart, 86 Va. 965, 967, 11 S. E. 880.

An interlocutory decree directed a sale of land to satisfy a debt, in a case where it might have been proper to decree satisfaction out of the rents and profits. This was not in controversy in the court below nor was it brought to the notice of the court although the party had ample opportunity to apply for an alteration of the decree. On appeal the decree will not be reversed for such cause, but affirmed with directions that the cause be remanded, the decree corrected and that the debt be satisfied out of the rents and profits, if it can be done so within a reasonable time. Manns *v*. Flinn, 10 Leigh 93.

(2) Final Judgments or Decrees.

General Rule.—When the term of court is ended final judgments have passed beyond the power of the court except to a very limited extent, regulated by statute, and final decrees also, except in so far as the power to control them is regulated by statute, or by the law governing bills of review. Spilman *v*. Gilpin, 93 Va. 698, 25 S. E. 1004; Wright *v*. Strother, 76 Va. 857; Nelson *v*. Kownslar, 79 Va. 468; Battaile *v*. Maryland Hospital, 76 Va. 63; Reid *v*. Strider, 7 Gratt. 76, 83; Bank *v*. Craig, 6 Leigh 399; Glass *v*. Baker, 6 Munf. 212; Davis *v*. Crews, 1 Gratt. 407; Bank *v*. Ralphsnyder, 54 W. Va. 231, 235, 46 S. E. 206; Snyder *v*. Middle States Loan, etc., Co., 52 W. Va. 655, 44 S. E. 250; Barbour County Court *v*. O'Neal, 42 W. Va. 295, 26 S. E. 182; Clarke *v*. Ohio River R. Co., 39 W. Va. 732, 20 S. E. 696; Morgan *v*. Ohio River R. Co., 39 W. Va. 17, 19 S. E. 588; Crawford *v*. Fickey, 41 W. Va. 544, 23 S. E. 662; Ruhl *v*. Ruhl, 24 W. Va. 279; Hall *v*. Bank, 15 W. Va. 323; Green *v*. Pittsburg, etc., R. Co., 11 W. Va. 685, 686; Crim *v*. Davisson, 6 W. Va. 465; Childers *v*. Loudin, 57 W. Va. 559, 42 S. E. 637. See ante, "During Term," VII, A, 1, a.

"It is a rule of the common law, that during the term wherein any judicial act is done the record remains in the breast of the judges of the court and in their remembrance and therefore the roll is alterable during that term as the judges shall direct; but when that term is past, then the record is in the roll and admits of no alteration, averment or proof to the contrary. 3 Tho. Co. Lit. 323, 1 Rob. Pr. 638 (old.)" Enders *v.* Burch, 15 Gratt. 64; Baker *v.* Swineford, 97 Va. 112, 116, 33 S. E. 542.

A court can not examine the propriety of a decree made at a former term inter partes, or set aside such decree of a former term, on the ground that it decided matters coram non judice at the time. Bank of Virginia *v.* Craig, 6 Leigh 399.

"In the case of Ruhl *v.* Ruhl, 24 W. Va. 279, this court held (fifth point of syllabus) that: 'After the close of the term, the parties to a cause in which a final decree has been pronounced are no longer in court; and no further order or decree as to them can be made therein, unless they are again brought into court by bill of review, or by some other recognized legal method. After a final decree, the court has no further jurisdiction, either of the subject matter or of the parties, and all subsequent orders or decrees entered without notice to the parties are void.' And the same ruling applies to a judgment at law." Barbour County Court *v.* O'Neal, 42 W. Va. 295, 26 S. E. 182, 183.

In Vaughan *v.* Freeland reported in note to Cogbill *v.* Cogbill, 2 Hen. & M. 467, 478, the court of appeals reversed the judgment of the district court, being of opinion "that the order made for amending the record, and altering the judgment entered on the said verdict at another and subsequent term after the verdict given, and judgment entered thereon, fully drawn up, read and signed by the judges in open court was erroneous, the said amendment after the term not being authorized by law."

Motion Made during Term Continued until Next Term.—Generally, the judgment of a court is under and subject to its control during the term at which it is rendered, and it may set the judgment aside, at any time before the end of the term without notice; but when that term ends, such judgment becomes final and passes beyond the control of the court, unless perhaps a motion be made during such term to set it aside, and such motion is continued until the next term. Green *v.* Pittsburg, etc., R. Co., 11 W. Va. 685. See also, Reid *v.* Strider, 7 Gratt. 76; Wynn *v.* Wyatt, 11 Leigh 584.

Control of Court over Proceedings during Preceding Vacation.—See generally, the titles CHAMBERS AND VACATION, vol. 2, p. 771; CONFESSION OF JUDGMENTS, vol. 3, p. 77; COURTS, vol. 3, p. 707.

B. AMENDMENT AND CORRECTION.

1. Power of Court to Amend or Correct.

a. During Term.

As has been seen, during the term, at which rendered judgments or decrees are in the breast of the court, and it may amend the same in its discretion. See ante, "During Term," VII, A, 1, a.

Notice to Parties Unnecessary.—During the term the proceedings being in the breast of the court and under its control, are liable to be stricken out, altered or amended without notice to the parties. Clendenning *v.* Conrad, 91 Va. 410, 21 S. E. 818; Green *v.* Pittsburg, etc., R. Co., 11 W. Va. 685.

b. After Term.

(1) In General.

Early Common-Law Rule and Modification Thereof.—"At common law, the courts might amend their records so as to make them truthfully set forth what had occurred, while the proceeding was in fieri, but not after the term at which final judgment was rendered. This rule resulted in such great hardship that relief was given by early English statutes. Stat. 1, ch. 6, 14, Edw.

111; Stat. 1, ch. 4, 9 Edw. V; ch. 12, 8 Henry VI. See 17 Ency. Pl. & Pr. 919." Vance *v.* Railway Co., 53 W. Va. 338, 340, 44 S. E. 461.

"In 17 Ency. Pl. & Pr. 920, it is said that the rule now very generally obtains that a court may amend its record as to clerical errors and misprisions as well after the term as during it, and, for this, decisions of a great many of the states are cited, including two in Virginia. Com. *v.* Winstons, 5 Rand. 546, and Marr *v.* Miller, 1 Hen. & M. 204." Vance *v.* Railway Co., 53 W. Va. 338, 341, 44 S. E. 461.

"From the English statute of 14 Ed. 3, Stat. 1, ch. 6, which is said to have been the first statute of amendment, down to our statute of 1819, 1 Rev. Code, ch. 128, § 108, p. 512, the legislative will has leaned to the amendment of mere misprisions, without the necessity of encountering the expense and trouble of a writ of error." Eubank *v.* Ralls, 4 Leigh 308, 315.

"The principles of the common law inhibited the allowance of a writ of error in the same court in which the judgment was rendered, for any error in the judgment of the court itself; for, if that were allowed, it would be infinite. But where the error was in the process, or a misprision of the clerk it might be corrected by the same court, without involving inconsistency, or leading to endless contests about what the record ought to be." Eubank *v.* Ralls, 4 Leigh 308.

"At the common law, an error committed by the court, not in a point of judgment, but such as might be called a misprision of the court, could be amended; but no misprision of the clerk was amendable after the term." Com. *v.* Winstons, 5 Rand. 546.

In Halley *v.* Baird, 1 Hen. & M. 25, it was held, that the "district court has no power or jurisdiction to reverse, alter, or amend a judgment given at a former term of the said court which had been entered on the order book, and signed by a judge in open court." McClain *v.* Davis, 37 W. Va. 330, 16 S. E. 629, 631.

As it is error in a court to amend a record, after the term at which the judgment was rendered, therefore, if the record omits to state that a plea was entered, and issue joined, the court can not, after the term at which judgment was rendered, direct a plea to be entered, nunc pro tunc, upon the evidence of the clerk that a plea was filed, and issue joined. Sydnor *v.* Burke, 4 Rand. 161.

The rule at common law as modified is that during the term wherein any judicial act is done, the records are in the breast of the court and in their remembrance and may be amended; but after the term no amendment can be made, except of a mere clerical misprision. Cawood's Case, 2 Va. Cas. 527; Manion *v.* Fahy, 11 W. Va. 482, 496; Smith *v.* Knight, 14 W. Va. 749; National Bank *v.* Jarvis, 26 W. Va. 785; Bunting *v.* Willis, 27 Gratt. 144, 158; Lingle *v.* Cook, 32 Gratt. 262; Kelty *v.* High, 29 W. Va. 381, 1 S. E. 561; Morgan *v.* Ohio River R. Co., 39 W. Va. 17, 19 S. E. 588; Barnes *v.* Com., 92 Va. 794, 23 S. E. 784. See also, Emory *v.* Erskine, 7 Leigh 267; Shelton *v.* Welsh, 7 Leigh 175.

As to amendments of judgments by confession, see the title CONFESSION OF JUDGMENTS, vol. 3, p. 64.

As to amendments of consent judgments or decrees, see ante, "Judgments by Consent," II, C.

As to amendments of default judgments or decrees pro confesso, see ante, "Judgments by Default and Decrees Pro Confesso," II, E.

(2) Statutory Provisions.

(a) Provisions Stated.

Section 3447 of the Virginia Code (Code, 1849, p. 680, ch. 181, § 1), provides that for any clerical error or error in fact for which a judgment or decree may be reversed or corrected on writ of error coram vobis the same may be reversed or corrected on motion after reasonable notice by the court, or if the judgment or decree be in a circuit court, by the judge thereof in vacation.

Section 1, ch. 134, of the West Virginia Code, 1899, is to the same effect, except that correction may be "by the court or by the judge thereof in vacation." Shipman v. Fletcher, 91 Va. 473, 22 S. E. 458; Bank v. Ralphsnyder, 54 W. Va. 231, 235, 46 S. E. 206; Stewart v. Stewart, 40 W. Va. 65, 20 S. E. 862. And see cases cited to following paragraph.

The Code of West Virginia, 1899, ch. 134, § 5, further provides that the court in which is rendered a judgment or decree, in a cause wherein there is in a declaration or pleading, or in the record of the judgment or decree, any mistake, miscalculation, or misrecital of any name, sum, quantity or time, when the same is right in any part of the record or proceedings, or when there is any verdict, report of a commissioner, bond, or other writing, whereby such judgment or decree may be safely amended; or in which a judgment is rendered on a forthcoming bond for a sum larger than by the execution or warrant of distress appears to be proper, or on a verdict in an action for more damages than are mentioned in the declaration; or in the vacation of the court in which any such judgment or decree is rendered, the judge thereof may, on the motion of any party, amend such judgment or decree according to the truth and justice of the case; or in any such case the party obtaining such judgment or decree may, in the same court, at any future term, by an entry of record, or in the vacation, by a writing signed by him, attested by the clerk, and filed among the papers of the cause, release a part of the amount of his judgment or decree; and such release shall have the effect of an amendment, and make the judgment or decree operate only for what is not released. Every

motion under this chapter shall be after reasonable notice to the opposite party, his agent or attorney in fact or at law, and shall be within five years from the date of the judgment or decree. The Code of Virginia is to the same effect, save that it requires written notice, and that the time of motion is limited to three years from the date of the judgment or decree. Va. Code, 1887, 1904, § 3451; Va. Code, 1873, ch. 177, § 5; Va. Code, 1849, ch. 181, §§ 5, 6; Va. Rev. Code, 512. Preston v. Kindrick, 94 Va. 760, 27 S. E. 588; Shipman v. Fletcher, 91 Va. 473, 22 S. E. 458; Roach v. Blakey, 89 Va. 767, 17 S. E. 228; Marshall v. Cheatam, 88 Va. 31, 13 S. E. 308; Thompson v. Carpenter, 88 Va. 702, 14 S. E. 181; Dickerson v. Clement, 87 Va. 41, 12 S. E. 105; Alvey v. Cahoon, 86 Va. 173, 9 S. E. 994; Dillard v. Dillard, 77 Va. 820; Massey v. King, 1 Va. Dec. 63; Goolsby v. St. John, 25 Gratt. 146; Strother v. Hull, 23 Gratt. 652; Hill v. Bowyer, 18 Gratt. 364; Davis v. Com., 16 Gratt. 134; Armstrong v. Pitts, 13 Gratt. 235; Richardson v. Jones, 12 Gratt. 53; Powell v. Com., 11 Gratt. 822; Tyree v. Donnally, 9 Gratt. 64; Snead v. Coleman, 7 Gratt. 300; Shelton v. Welsh, 7 Leigh 175; Eubank v. Ralls, 4 Leigh 308; Garland v. Marx, in note to above case, p. 321; Com. v. Winstons, 5 Rand. 546; Bent v. Patten, 1 Rand. 25; Banks v. Anderson, 2 Hen. & M. 20; Marr v. Miller, 1 Hen. & M. 204; Gordon v. Frazier, 2 Wash. 130; Bank v. Ralphsnyder, 54 W. Va. 231, 235, 46 S. E. 206; Triplett v. Lake, 43 W. Va. 428, 27 S. E. 363; Shumate v. Crockett, 43 W. Va. 491, 27 S. E. 240; Crawford v. Fickey, 41 W. Va. 544, 23 S. E. 662; Barbour County Court v. O'Neal, 42 W. Va. 295, 26 S. E. 182; Morgan v. Ohio River R. Co., 39 W. Va. 17, 19 S. E. 588; Withrow v. Smithson, 37 W. Va. 757, 17 S. E. 316; Watt v. Brookover, 35 W. Va. 323, 13 S. E. 1007; Howard v. Stephenson, 33 W. Va. 116, 10 S. E. 66; Crumlish v. Shenandoah Valley R. Co., 28 W. Va.

623, 627; King v. Burdett, 28 W. Va. 601; Martin v. Smith, 25 W. Va. 579, 583; Ohio River R. Co. v. Harness, 24 W. Va. 511; Stringer v. Anderson, 23 W. Va. 482; Alleman v. Knight, 19 W. Va. 201; Smith v. Knight, 14 W. Va. 749; Manion v. Fahy, 11 W. Va. 482; Gates v. Cragg, 11 W. Va. 300; Pumphry v. Brown, 5 W. Va. 107; Boggess v. Robinson, 5 W. Va. 402; Connor v. Fleshman, 4 W. Va. 693.

The Virginia Statute of 1819, ch. 128, § 108, provides that: "Where in the record of any judgment or decree of any superior court of law or equity, there shall be any mistake, miscalculation, or misrecital of any sum or sums of money, tobacco, wheat, or any other such thing, or of any name or names, and there shall be among the record or proceedings in the suit in which such judgment or decree shall be rendered, any verdict, bond, bill, note, or other writing of the like nature or kind, whereby such judgment or decree may be safely amended, it shall be the duty of the court in which such judgment shall be rendered, and of the judge thereof in vacation, to amend such judgment or decree thereby, according to the very truth and justice of the case; provided the opposite party have notice." Com. v. Winstons, 5 Rand. 546; Eubank v. Ralls, 4 Leigh 308.

(b) Provisions Construed and Applied.
aa. Provisions Construed.

The second clause of § 5, ch. 134 of the West Virginia Code, authorizes amendments and corrections only in cases of mistakes and misrecitals when the same may be safely amended from some other part of the record. The clause is confined to mere clerical and not judicial errors. Judicial errors, where the judgment is not by default, can be corrected only by an appellate court. Stringer v. Anderson, 23 W. Va. 482. See also, Connor v. Fleshman, 4 W. Va. 693; Ohio River R. Co. v. Harness, 24 W. Va. 511.

Section 3451 of the Virginia Code, provides for the correction of such errors as misprisions of the clerk and what may be termed clerical misprisions of the court. This has been the construction heretofore placed upon the statute. It has no application to errors in the reasoning and conclusions of the court about contested matters. Shipman v. Fletcher, 91 Va. 473, 22 S. E. 458. See also, Rees v. Conococheague Bank, 5 Rand. 326.

The purpose of the statute was to provide a prompt and inexpensive remedy for the correction of errors by the court that made them. Shipman v. Fletcher, 91 Va. 473, 22 S. E. 458.

Virginia Code, § 3451, applies only to judgments by default and to decrees on bills taken for confessed, and to cases of mistake or miscalculation, for which no appeal lies to the supreme court. Thompson v. Carpenter, 88 Va. 702, 14 S. E. 181; Stringer v. Anderson, 23 W. Va. 482.

"Those only are clerical errors which are made by the clerk which depend only upon a comparison and calculation to be made by him, and may be safely reformed by reference to other statements contained in the proceedings." Gordon v. Frazier, 2 Wash. 130; Bent v. Patten, 1 Rand. 25.

"Upon this question, Minor, in his Institutes (volume 4, pt. 1, at page 854), says: 'It is clear that the provision was intended to apply exclusively to those inadvertencies of the clerk which depend upon a comparison and calculation to be made by him, and which may be safely reformed by reference to other statements in writing obtained in the proceedings, and not at all to judicial errors growing out of a mistaken application of the law to the facts, notwithstanding such mistaken application be made by the clerk alone, and the court be not directly privy to it.'" Stewart v. Stewart, 40 W. Va. 65, 20 S. E. 862.

The Virginia statute of 1819, ch. 128, § 108, does not (as did the former laws) confine the power to amend, to mistakes, etc., made by the clerk only; but, extends to those also made by the court, if they be not errors in the judgment of the court, but only in the sum, name or quantity, which indeed would be properly clerical mistakes, in the court reducing its judgments to writing. Com. v. Winstons, 5 Rand. 546.

"The statute of 1819, * * * not confining itself to clerical errors, or errors in the process, or to the mere ministerial acts of the officer of the court, extends to the very judgment of the court itself; it provides, that 'where, in the record of the judgment, there shall be any mistake, etc., and among the records of the proceedings, there shall be any verdict, bond, bill, note or other writing of the like nature or kind, whereby such judgment may be safely amended, the court in which such judgment shall be rendered, shall amend it according to the very right of the case.' Here, it is clearly manifested, that though the error be in the judgment itself, if there appears to have been a mistake in it, it shall be amended. Thus, if a verdict be rendered for £100, and the judgment on it entered for 100 dollars, there is an obvious mistake, which may be corrected under the statute of 1819, by the verdict, to which it may be fairly presumed the court designed to conform. This statute, I think, relieves us from much of the former difficulty in relation to the distinction between clerical errors and errors in the judgment of the court. For, if it appears, that there is a mere mistake, miscalculation or misrecital, the statute is imperative, that the correction shall be made. But if, upon the inspection of the proceeding, the matter complained of appears to have proceeded from error in the opinion of the court, and not from mere mistake, the case is not within the statutes; for the mistake, whether of the clerk or of the judge, to which the statute refers, is not an error of judgment, but an error in which the judgment has no participation." Eubank v. Ralls, 4 Leigh 308.

"Since this statute, then, I conceive, there are two classes of errors amendable by the same court in which the judgment is rendered: 1. All such errors as were deemed clerical, or were amendable before the act; and 2, all such mistakes even in the judgment of the court, as can be amended by any verdict, bond, note, or bill, etc., in the record." Eubanks v. Ralls, 4 Leigh 308.

The amendments authorized by Va. Code, ch. 181, § 5, p. 681, providing for the reversal and amendment of judgments in certain cases in the same court, are amendments to support the judgment, not amendments to give ground for reversing it. Powell's Case, 11 Gratt. 822.

The power of amendment, allowed by 1 Rev. Code 512, § 108, applies to a motion as well as to an action, and extends to the general court. Com. v. Winstons, 5 Rand. 546.

bb. Application of Provisions.

(aa) Proper Grounds for Motion.

An erroneous entry of a decree may be rectified upon motion, at a succeeding term; and any mistake committed by the officers of the court or gentlemen of the bar may be corrected in like manner. Marr v. Miller, 1 Hen. & M. 204.

Any informality in the entry of the judgment by the clerk must be corrected in the court below, and is no ground for reversal in the appellate court. Roach v. Blakey, 89 Va. 767, 17 S. E. 228.

Where a clerk commits a merely clerical error in entering up a judgment, the injured party may if he please, proceed by writ of error coram nobis, which is a plain, cheap, summary, and complete remedy at law, but the proceeding now, is merely by motion to the court. Gordon *v.* Frazier, 2 Wash. 130; Goolsby *v.* St. John, 25 Gratt. 146.

An error in entering a judgment against two defendants in the singular, and not the plural number, is a mere clerical error, which may be corrected by the trial court upon motion. Roach *v.* Blakey, 89 Va. 767, 17 S. E. 228.

Omission of Entry of Order. — Quære, whether, in case of an order made by this court, but the entry omitted by inadvertence of the court or misprision of the clerk, such omission may be corrected at a subsequent term? And per Tucker, P., it seems that it may. Emory *v.* Erskine, 7 Leigh 267.

Where a decree is entered in a cause, the pleadings and proofs in which did not authorize such, it is a mere error of the court where it has jurisdiction of the parties and of the subject matter, and it does not exceed its jurisdiction in rendering a personal decree, it only commits an error for which relief could have been had under § 3451, of the Virginia Code. Preston *v.* Kindrick, 94 Va. 760, 27 S. E. 588.

A mistake or misrecital of a sum in a decree will be corrected on motion after notice, under § 5, ch. 134, W. Va. Code, 1891. Shumate *v.* Crockett, 43 W. Va. 491, 27 S. E. 240.

"There was in the decree what I shall call a clerical mistake. The commissioner reported a debt of B. Prince & Co. as $96.58, and the decree, by mispunctuation, makes out of the same figures a debt of $9,658,—a signal instance of the power of punctuation, especially if, as claimed, it be good ground on this appeal, if it were in time, for the reversal of the whole decree. The petition of Willie C. Crockett, as I interpret it, assigned this as a ground of rehearing. This is, under § 5. ch. 134, Code, 1891, a mistake or misrecital of a sum, and the decree is amendable by the commissioners' report within five years. This petition is good to correct that error. Crumlish

v. Shenandoah Valley R. Co., 28 W. Va. 623, 627; Martin *v.* Smith, 25 W. Va. 579, 583; Triplett *v.* Lake, 43 W. Va. 428, 27 S. E. 363." Shumate *v.* Crockett, 43 W. Va. 491, 27 S. E. 240, 241.

Mistake in Date from Which Damages Given.—In entering the judgment, damages are given from a date anterior to the date of the return of the venditioni exponas. As this writ is properly described in the notice, and damages from the return day thereof claimed, and it is made a part of the record, the error was merely clerical, and might have been corrected by the court in term, or by the judge in vacation, upon motion, by reference to the writ. It is not, therefore, a ground for reversing the judgment, but the same will be amended and affirmed, if there is no other error. Tyree *v.* Donnally, 9 Gratt. 64.

If the court, in enforcing a vendor's lien, aggregates the amount and interest to the date of the decree, and then decrees that the defendants. pay interest in such aggregate amount for several months prior to the date of the decree, this is such a mistake as may be safely amended on motion, under § 5 of ch. 134 of the West Virginia Code, and which should be amended on motion in the circuit court. Triplett *v.* Lake, 43 W. Va. 428, 27 S. E. 363.

Where in entering the decree the name T. K. Menefee is used instead of T. K. Menefee & Co., it is held. that it is clerical error which might be corrected. Henley *v.* Menefee, 10 W. Va. 771.

(bb) Errors Not Grounds for Motion.

An error in the order of the court, or an omission to make an entry in the order book, is not a clerical. but a judicial error. Cawood's Case, 3 Va. Cas. 527.

An error in the judgment itself of a court can never be corrected by the same court. Gordon *v.* Frazier, 2 Wash. 130.

Allowance of Too Much Interest.—
Where an action is brought on a note,
which was executed at the time when
five per centum was the legal rate of
interest, upon which the defendant acknowledged the action for the principal with interest from the date of the
note; on which acknowledgment a
judgment was rendered for the principal, with interest at the rate of six
per centum per annum; this is not a
mere clerical error, but one which can
only be rectified by an appellate court.
1 Rev. Va. Code, 512; Bent *v.* Patten,
1 Rand. 25.

**Bond for $188, Declared on as Bond
for $108.—**Where an action of debt is
brought upon a bond for $188, but is
declared on as a bond for $108, the
bond being in fact for $188, this not
such a clerical error as may be
an ended under the 108th section of the
statute of jeofails, 1 Rev. Va. Code,
ch. 128, p. 512. Compton *v.* Cline, 5
Gratt. 137.

If the jury finds a right verdict, and
the district court records it wrongly,
entering judgment upon it as recorded,
they can not correct error by the true
verdict, at a subsequent term. Freeland *v.* Fields, 6 Call 12.

Insanity.—A writ of error coram nobis, or a motion in lieu of it, is not a
proper process to reverse a judgment,
because the defendant was insane at
the time of its rendition, as the judgment can be attacked for such cause
only in equity. Withrow *v.* Smithson,
37 W. Va. 757, 17 S. E. 316.

"Death, infancy, and coverture are
conceded grounds of error in fact, as
a basis for writ of error coram nobis;
and I would consider insanity of like
nature, and ground for that writ, and
not for equity jurisdiction, were it a
cause at law for reversal of a judgment.
But I do not think that insanity of the
defendant at the date of the judgment
is a reason for the reversal of the
judgment by proceedings at law.
Some authorities look that way. It is
stated in 1 Freem., Judgm., § 94, that

insanity is a matter to affect judgment
by writ of error coram nobis. But no
case cited supports this, and § 152 is
pointedly to the contrary. Likewise,
Allison *v.* Taylor, 32 Amer. Dec. 68."
Withrow *v.* Smithson, 37 W. Va. 757,
17 S. E. 316.

2. Procedure.

a. In General.

No Correction by Original Suit.—
The superior court of chancery can
not correct errors in a decree of an
inferior court by an original suit, although in that way it may impeach
such a decree for fraud, and under peculiar circumstances lend its aid to
carry a decree of an inferior court into
effect. Banks *v.* Anderson, 2 Hen. &
M. 20; Graves *v.* Graves, 2 Hen. & M.
22, 23.

**Amendable on Motion in Summary
Way, or by Bill of Review.—**A decree
which is final in all respects, except
that "liberty is reserved to the parties,
or either of them, to resort to the
court for its further interposition, if
it should be found necessary," may be
amended, on motion, in a summary
way, or by bill of review. Sheppard
v. Starke, 3 Munf. 29.

b. Error Coram Nobis.

In General.—The remedy for a mere
clerical error was formerly by a writ
of error coram nobis (or coram vobis)
in the same court in which the error
was committed. Goolsby *v.* St. John,
25 Gratt. 146; Gordon *v.* Frazier, 2
Wash. 130; Bent *v.* Patten, 1 Rand. 25;
Richardson *v.* Jones, 12 Gratt. 53. See
the title APPEAL AND ERROR, vol.
1, p. 434.

The clerk having entered up a judgment by nil dicit, in the district court,
in debt on a bond for the payment of
tobacco, without noticing a memorandum endorsed on the bond, this court
considered the mistake to be merely
clerical and amendable upon motion at
a subsequent term. But the injured
party may if he please, proceed by
writ of error coram nobis; although

in this latter case, he is not entitled to costs. Gordon *v.* Frazier, 2 Wash. 130.

When Writ Lies.—A writ of error coram nobis lies where some defect is alleged in the process or execution thereof, or some misprision of the clerk, or some error in the proceedings arising from a fact not appearing upon their face, as where the judgment is rendered against a party after his death, or who is an infant or feme covert. Gordon *v.* Frazier, 2 Wash. 130; Bent *v.* Patten, 1 Rand. 25; Richardson *v.* Jones, 12 Gratt. 53.

An injunction ought not to be granted on the ground that the plaintiff was dead before the judgment was obtained in his name. This error should be rectified by a writ of error coram nobis. Williamson *v.* Appleberry, 1 Hen. & M. 206.

When Writ Does Not Lie.—A writ of error coram nobis does not lie to correct any error in the judgment of the court, nor to contradict or put in issue a fact directly passed upon and affirmed in the judgment itself. If this could be done there would be no end to litigation and little security for the titles to property. Richardson *v.* Jones, 12 Gratt. 53.

The death of the lessor of the plaintiff, previous to the judgment in ejectment, is no ground for a writ of error coram nobis, notwithstanding that circumstance was not stated in the record, and no security for costs was given; because an ejectment does not abate by the death of the lessor of the plaintiff. Purvis *v.* Hill, 2 Hen. & M. 614. See ante, "Provisions Construed and Applied," VII, B, 1, b, (2), (b).

Limitation to Proceedings. — The statute of limitations of writs of error, if it applies to writs of error coram nobis at all, can not be relied on without being pleaded. Eubank *v.* Ralls, 4 Leigh 208.

If the defendant in a writ of error coram nobis, plead in nullo est erratum, and conclude to the court, the trial must be by the court. Gordon *v.* Frazier, 2 Wash. 130.

c. Motion.

(1) In General.

By both the Virginia and West Virginia Codes it is now provided that on motion after reasonable notice, the court, or the judge in vacation, may reverse or correct a judgment or decree for any clerical error, or error in fact, for which the judgment or decree may be reversed or corrected on writ of error coram nobis. Va. Code, 1904, § 3447; W. Va. Code, 1899, ch. 134, § 1. Goolsby *v.* St. John, 25 Gratt. 146; Bank *v.* Ralphsnyder, 54 W. Va. 231, 235, 46 S. E. 206; Manion *v.* Fahy, 11 W. Va. 482; Dillard *v.* Dillard, 77 Va. 820. And see cases cited ante, "Provisions Stated," VII, B, 1, b, (2), (a).

"For many years, as well in England as with us, relief has been generally obtainable on simple motion wherever a writ of error coram nobis is applicable, and consequently the proceeding has fallen gradually into disuse. (Gordon *v.* Frazier, 2 Wash. 130; 1 Rob. Pr. [1st Ed.] 644, 645.) And now it is expressly provided by statute, that for any clerical error, or error in fact for which a judgment may be reversed or corrected on writ of error vobis, the same may be reversed or corrected on motion, after reasonable notice, by the court, or if the judgment be in a circuit court, by the judge thereof in vacation. (V. C., 1873, ch. 177, § 1; V. C., 1887, ch. 169, § 3447.)" Minor's Institutes, pt. 1, p. 1055.

When Proper.—See ante, "Provisions Construed and Applied," VII, B, 1, b, (2), (b).

As to the correction or reversal of default judgments or decrees pro confesso on motion, see ante, "Judgments by Default or Decrees Pro Confesso," II, E.

(2) Jurisdiction.

In General.—Under the Codes, the power to reverse or correct on motion is given to the court wherein the judgment or decree is rendered, or to the judge in vacation. Bank *v.* Ralphsnyder, 54 W. Va. 231, 235, 46 S. E. 206; Dillard *v.* Dillard, 77 Va. 820; Powell *v.* Com., 11 Gratt. 822. And see cases cited, ante, "Provisions Stated," VII, B, 1, b, (2), (a).

Jurisdiction of Circuit Superior Courts of Law over Judgments of Former Circuit Courts of Law.—The present circuit superior courts of law and chancery have jurisdiction to correct on motion mistakes in judgments of the former circuit courts of law. Garland *v.* Marx, reported in note to Eubank *v.* Ralls, 4 Leigh 308, 321.

(3) By Whom Made.

The amendments provided for by the Code may be made on the motion of any party. See ante, "Provisions Stated," VII, B, 1, b, (2), (a), and cases cited.

(4) Time of Motion.

The motion to amend under the West Virginia Code, 1889, ch. 134, § 5, shall be within five years after the date of the judgment or decree. This was also the time prescribed by the Virginia Code, 1873, ch. 177, § 5. Marshall *v.* Cheatham, 88 Va. 31, 13 S. E. 308. See also, Kendrick *v.* Whitney, 28 Gratt. 646. Under the Virginia Code, 1904, § 3451, however, the motion must be within three years from the date of the judgment or decree. See ante, "Provisions Stated," VII, B, 1, b, (2), (a), and cases cited.

(5) Notice of Motion.

The motion to amend a judgment or decree must be after reasonable notice to the opposite party, his agent or attorney in fact or at law. W. Va. Code, 1899, ch. 134, § 5; Va. Code, 1904, § 3451; Hill *v.* Bowyer, 18 Gratt. 364; Beery *v.* Irick, 22 Gratt. 614; Shumate *v.* Crockett, 43 W. Va. 491, 27 S. E. 240; Dillard *v.* Dillard, 77 Va. 820. See ante, "Provisions Stated," VII, B, 1, b, (2), (a), and cases cited.

The Virginia Code, 1904, § 3451, re-quires written notice. Under the Virginia Code, 1873, ch. 177, § 5, however, it seems that written notice was not necessary. See Dillard *v.* Thornton, 29 Gratt. 392.

As to the right to amend without notice during the term, see ante, "During Term," VII, A, 1, a.

(6) Source of Amendment—Necessity for Error to Appear of Record.

In General.—The Codes of Virginia and West Virginia authorize the amendments by the court or judge on motion, of a judgment or decree "according to the truth and justice of the case," in a cause "wherein there is in a declaration or pleading, or in the record of the judgment or decree, any mistake, misrecital of any name, sum, quantity or time, when the same is right in any part of the proceedings, or when there is any verdict, report of a commissioner, bond, or other writing, whereby such judgment or decree may be safely amended; or in which a judgment is rendered on a forthcoming bond for a sum larger than by the execution or warrant of distress appears to be proper, or on a verdict in an action for more damages than are mentioned in the declaration." Va. Code, 1904, § 3451; W. Va. Code, 1899, ch. 134, § 5. Stringer *v.* Anderson, 23 W. Va. 482; Richardson *v.* Jones. 21 Gratt. 53. See ante. "Provisions Stated." VII, B, 1, b, (2). (a), and cases cited.

There is no doubt but the court may amend upon motion where a mistake is committed by their clerk, if there be something to amend by. Gordon *v.* Frazier, 2 Wash. 130.

"The second clause of § 5 of ch. 134 of the West Virginia Code authorizes amendments and corrections only in cases of mistakes and miscalculations or misrecitals when the same may be safely amended from some other part of the record." Stringer *v.* Anderson, 23 W. Va. 482.

The act of 1819 applies only as to

such corrections as can be safely made by the judge by referring to other statements in the record. It was never intended to make him an appellate court over himself. It was never intended that his decisions made in open court, and upon argument should be reversed by himself, at his own chamber in vacation." Bent v. Patten, 1 Rand. 25.

The amendments authorized by Virginia Code, ch. 181, § 5, p. 181, providing for the reversal and amendment of judgments in certain cases in the same court, at a subsequent term, or by the judge in vacation, are to be based upon something in the record, and not upon the recollection of the judges who presided at the trial, or by evidence aliunde. Powell's Case, 11 Gratt. 822; Richardson v. Jones, 12 Gratt. 53; Mc-Clain v. Davis, 37 W. Va. 330, 16 S. E. 629; Barnes v. Com., 92 Va. 794, 23 S. E. 784.

"Waiving the question whether the provisions in the Code, ch. 181, § 5, p. 681, authorizing amendments in judgments or decrees of a court in certain cases by the judge in vacation after the adjournment of the term, can apply to a case of felony, in which all the proceedings should regularly be had in presence of the accused, or to any criminal case, I am yet of opinion, that no such amendment of the record as that attempted to be made in this case, by the action of the judge, in vacation, on the 11th of May, 1854, is within the scope of that provision. It was intended to authorize amendments in support of a judgment, in cases in which there was something in the record by which they could safely be made. It could not have been intended to authorize an amendment to be made upon the individual recollection of the judge, or upon proof aliunde. Nor was the application in this case to amend the judgment, nor was it designed to aid the judgment when made. It was an application to introduce something into the record as part

thereof, not before found therein, depending on the recollection of the judge, or upon proofs to be submitted to him; and its object was to provide a means of reversing the judgment, not of sustaining it." Powell v. Com., 11 Gratt. 822.

Illustrations.—Where, by an error of the clerk, a judgment by confession is entered instead of a nil dicit, this is not such a clerical misprision as can be corrected by the court at the next term, under either the first or the fifth sections of ch. 181, of the Virginia Code, p. 680, which only applies where the error appears in some part of the record. Richardson v. Jones, 12 Gratt. 53.

Where the error is a mere mistake of the court, and is plainly in conflict with the report of the commissioner which was confirmed by the decree, such decree can be safely amended by the report, in pursuance of the Virginia Code of 1849, ch. 181, §§ 5, 6. Massey v. King, 1 Va. Dec. 63.

A clerk, failing to pay the taxes received by him, on law process, into the treasury, is liable to the penalty of $600, even though he should have accounted for the same with the auditor The auditor has a remedy for this delinquency by motion. On such a motion, where the judgment is informal, it may be amended by referring to the notice. Steptoe v. Auditor, 3 Rand. 221.

It was held in Cox v. Thomas, 9 Gratt. 312, that though the copy of the judgment against the high sheriff in the record, does not show in what court or when it was rendered, it is a mere clerical omission in copying the judgments into the record, and if these facts appear from any other part of the record, it will be held sufficient in the appellate court, when the objection was not made in the court below.

(7) Effect of Failure to Move to Amend.

No appeal, writ of error, or supersedeas shall be allowed or entertained by an appellate court or judge, for any matter for which a judgment or decree is liable to be reversed or amended on motion by the court which rendered it, or the judge thereof until such motion be made and overruled in whole or in part. Va. Code, 1873, ch. 177, § 6; Va. Code, 1904, § 3452; W. Va. Code, 1899, ch. 134, § 6; Hill v. Bowyer, 18 Gratt. 364; Goolsby v. St. John, 25 Gratt. 146; Bent v. Patten, 1 Rand. 25; McGraw v. Roller, 53 W. Va. 75, 44 S. E. 248; Smith v. Powell, 98 Va. 431, 36 S. E. 522; Armstrong v. Pitts, 13 Gratt. 235; Smith v. Knight, 14 W. Va. 749; Howard v. Stephenson, 33 W. Va. 116, 10 S. E. 66. See the title APPEAL AND ERROR, vol. 1, pp. 464, 574. And see ante, "Judgments by Default and Decrees Pro Confesso," II, E.

A clerical error is to be amended upon motion to the court; and is not a ground for an appeal. Snead v. Coleman, 7 Gratt. 300.

A cause is heard upon the report of a commissioner which had not been returned for the legal period. The decree being merely interlocutory, the error should have been corrected by application to the court below; and it is not ground for an appeal unless, upon application, the court below refuses to correct it. Armstrong v. Pitts, 13 Gratt. 235.

"The statute relied on was made for the protection of appellate courts by compelling litigants to first present their matters for adjudication to the lower courts without flooding the higher courts with unlitigated questions of fact and law. It applies strictly to judgments by default, and to all such questions and clerical errors as have not been matters of litigation and adjudication before the lower court. To any material questions arising during the progress of litigation and adjudicated by the court, the statute does not apply, although a writ of error does not lie until after final judgment, but as to such adjudication does

lie, although such final judgment is entered up by default. As when a final judgment is entered up by default after demurrer to a declaration or bill has been overruled." McGraw v. Roller, 53 W. Va. 75, 44 S. E. 248.

(3) Effect of Amendment after Appeal Allowed.

Both in Virginia and West Virginia it is provided by statute, that when an appellate court hears a case wherein an appeal, writ of error, or supersedeas has been allowed, if it appear that, either before or since the same was allowed the judgment or decree has been so amended (by the court rendering it) the appellate court shall affirm the judgment or decree unless there be other error. Va. Code, 1873, ch. 177, § 6; Va. Code, 1904, § 3452; W. Va. Code, 1899, ch. 134, § 6. Triplett v. Lake, 43 W. Va. 428, 27 S. E. 363; Goolsby v. St. John, 25 Gratt. 146. See the title APPEAL AND ERROR, vol. 1, p. 574.

d. Order Nunc Pro Tunc.

See ante, "Rendition and Entry," V.

3. Amendment and Affirmance on Appeal.

Under the sections of the Virginia and West Virginia Codes authorizing the amendment and correction of judgments and decrees for certain errors and providing that no appeal, etc., shall be allowed unless a motion for such amendment shall have been made and overruled below either in whole or in part, it is further provided that on appeal if it appear that the amendment ought to and has not been made, the appellate court may make such amendment, and affirm the judgment or decree, unless there be other error. Va. Code, 1873, ch. 177, § 6; Va. Code, 1904, § 3452; W. Va. Code, 1899, ch. 134, § 6. Pumphry v. Brown, 4 W. Va. 107; Shumate v. Crockett, 43 W. Va. 491, 27 S. E. 240.

When a decree has been entered against a person, who is not a party to the suit, it may be corrected by motion in the lower court, and can be corrected in the appellate court. Boggess v. Robinson, 5 W. Va. 402. Generally, as to amendment and affirmance on appeal, see the title APPEAL AND ERROR, vol. 1, p. 624.

C. OPENING, MODIFICATION OR VACATION.

1. Power of Court to Open, Modify or Vacate.

Generally, as to the power of the court during and after the term at which a judgment or decree was rendered to open, modify or vacate such judgment or decree, see ante, "General Rules as to Power during and after Term," VII, A, 1.

2. What Judgments or Decrees May Be Opened or Vacated.

Judgments by Confession.—See the title CONFESSION OF JUDGMENTS, vol. 3, p. 77.

Judgments by Consent.—See ante, "Judgments by Consent," II, C.

Judgments by Default and Decrees Pro Confesso.—See ante, "Judgments by Default and Decrees Pro Confesso," II, E.

Divorce Decrees.—See the title DIVORCE, vol. 4, p. 748.

Void Judgments or Decrees.—A void judgment or decree may be vacated, notwithstanding the fact that such judgments are open to collateral attack. Finney v. Clark, 86 Va. 354, 10 S. E. 569; Rorer v. People's Bldg., etc., Ass'n, 47 W. Va. 1, 34 S. E. 758, 759; Snyder v. Middle States Loan, etc., Co., 52 W. Va. 655, 657, 44 S. E. 250.

See, however, Monroe v. Bartlett, 6 W. Va. 441, 443, in which the court said: "When considering the question whether proceedings in error might or ought to be brought, it should be remembered that there are some errors so obvious and gross that they render the judgment void. But even in such case, error for the reversal of such judgment might be sustained, and that would be the better way as being more direct and posi-

tive." Quoted in Conrad v. County of Lewis, 10 W. Va. 784. See also, Snyder v. Middle States Loan, etc., Co., 52 W. Va. 655, 657, 44 S. E. 250.

As to what judgments or decrees are void and open to collateral attack, see ante, "Requisites of Valid Judgments or Decree," III; post, "Collateral Attack on Judgments or Decrees," IX.

3. Grounds.

Fraud, Accident, Mistake or Surprise.—When judgments and decrees have been pronounced or suffered by fraud, accident or mistake, upon a proper proceeding, they may be annulled. Chesapeake, etc., R. Co. v. Pack, 6 W. Va. 397, 398.

When a decree has been obtained by fraud, the court will restore the parties to their former situation, whatever their rights may be. Keran v. Trice, 75 Va. 690.

A court of equity will review and reverse a decree founded on a mistake in the record evidence, not occasioned by the culpable negligence or misconduct of the party complaining. Clark v. Sayers, 48 W. Va. 33, 35 S. E. 882.

Fraud, to set aside a decree, must be fraud in the procurement thereof, and not in alleged mistakes and additions in a store account settled by note more than five years previous to such decree, and on which it is founded. Alleged fraud must be proven, and it is not sustained by evidence of mistaken additions on the face of a store account always open to inspection, and long settled by note. Bodkin v. Rollyson, 48 W. Va. 453, 37 S. E. 617.

Surprise or accident are grounds for an original bill or petition to open a decree. Anderson v. Woodford, 8 Leigh 316; Hill v. Bowyer, 18 Gratt. 364. See post, "Original Bill," VII, C, 4, b, (3), (d).

"That equity will for accident or mistake impeach and set aside decrees is settled. Byrne v. Edmonds, 23 Gratt. 200; 1 Story, Eq. Jur., § 78; Pom., Eq. Jur., §§ 836, 871, 1377." Baxter *v.* Tanner, 35· W. Va. 60, 12 S. E. 1094, 1096.

A decree sustaining a demurrer to a bill upon the ground of laches, whereby the plaintiff is completely taken by surprise, should be set aside on his motion, when, during the same term of the court, he asks leave to file an amended bill, which fully explains any charge of laches. Cottrell *v.* Watkins. 89 Va. 801, 17 S. E. 328, 19 L. R. A. 754.

During the term of court, the counsel representing the parties plaintiff and defendant in a case, in the presence of the regular judge, are talking over the business remaining unfinished, the defendant in said case being present, who understands from the conversation that his case should not be taken up before the next Tuesday for trial, which conversation was on Friday; and under this impression the defendant, with his witnesses, left the court. On Saturday a special judge was elected, who went upon the bench on Monday morning, and tried the case, in the absence of said defendant and his witnesses. and in ignorance of said misunderstanding, although an attorney for the defendant was in town, and had notice that a jury was being called in the case, on account of some feeling existing between himself and the special judge, and on account of his being too unwell to attend to business, and sent another attorney to state the matters to the court in reference to said understanding. The trial is proceeded with, and a judgment is rendered against the defendant, although he claims to have had a good defense. The trial of the cause, under the circumstances, works such a surprise upon the defendant that a motion to vacate the judgment. set aside the verdict, and award a new trial, should have prevailed. Simpkins *v.* White, 43 W. Va. 200, 27 S. E. 241.

An action was brought in 1875 in the county court. Two years there-after it was transferred to the circuit court. No order except continuances was made in it after such transfer. The judge of said circuit court could not preside at the trial, and in 1887 the plaintiff, in the absence of the defendant and his counsel, caused a special judge to be elected; and, without the knowledge of the defendant, the case was tried, and a verdict and judgment rendered for the plaintiff. The defendant, being notified of such judgment, moved the court to set the same aside because of the facts above stated; and upon his affidavit, alleging surprise, and the full payment of the debt sued on, the circuit court set aside the judgment and awarded the defendant a new trial. Held, no error. "In numerous cases, both in Virginia and this state, it has been decided that a judgment entered upon the verdict of a jury sworn to try the issue joined, when no issue is in fact joined, or where there were more than one plea, and no issue had been joined on some one of such pleas, such judgment will for that reason only be set aside by the appellate court. Many of these cases are cited in Ruffner *v.* Hill, 21 W. Va. on page 159." Bennett *v.* Jackson, 34 W. Va. 62, 11 S. E. 734.

Mistakes of judgment, or want of attention or capacity of counsel, afford no just or proper grounds for granting a motion to reopen a case. Smith *v.* Parkersburg Co-Op. Ass'n., 48 W. Va. 232, 37 S. E. 645.

Judgment Void for Want of Jurisdiction.—"The court being without jurisdiction, its judgment is void, and may be vacated on motion. Freem., Judgm., § 98." Rorer *v.* People's Bldg., etc., Ass'n., 47 W. Va. 1, 34 S. E. 758, 759.

Where for want of service of process judgment is void, collection of execution should be enjoined. the judgment vacated. and the cause remanded to be proceeded in at law by an alias summons properly served. Finney *v.* Clark, 86 Va. 354, 10 S. E. 569.

Irregularities which do not render a judgment void, while not ground for assailing such judgment in collateral proceedings, may furnish grounds for reversal by proper proceedings taken in due season in the court which rendered the judgment. Terry *v.* Dickinson, 75 Va. 475; Neale *v.* Utz, 75 Va. 480.

As to the rule that erroneous or irregular judgments or decrees can not be attacked collaterally, see post, "Erroneous or Irregular Judgments," IX, C.

Opening Interlocutory Decree on Ground of Newly-Discovered Evidence.—It is error in the chancellor to refuse an application to open an interlocutory decree, founded upon affidavits of a discovery of important matter since such decree was rendered. Roberts *v.* Cocke, 1 Rand. 121.

Infancy.—As to opening judgments or decrees rendered against infants, see the title INFANTS, vol. 7, p. 497, et seq.

Insignificant Errors in Amount.—A judgment regularly obtained should not be set aside for an error of a few cents in the amount for which the judgment should have been rendered. The rule de minimis lex non curat should be applied. Ramsburg *v.* Kline, 96 Va. 465, 31 S. E. 608.

Action and Judgment against Two on Joint and Several Note of Three Persons.—A judgment can not be set aside on the ground that the note upon which the judgment was rendered was the joint and several note of three persons, while the action was brought and judgment obtained against only two of them. No evidence could be introduced on that subject until after the judgment had been set aside. Such evidence might be used after the judgment was set aside in order to prevent a new judgment, but not to set aside a judgment already in force. Ramsburg *v.* Kline, 96 Va. 465, 31 S. E. 608.

As to grounds for opening or vacating judgments by default and decrees

pro confesso, see ante, " Judgments by Default and Decrees Pro Confesso," II, E.

4. Procedure.

a. During Term.

On Motion or at Suggestion of Court.—During the term of the court at which a decree is entered it is completely under the control of the court and may be modified or annulled on motion, or at the suggestion of the court without motion. Kelty *v.* High, 29 W. Va. 381, 1 S. E. 561; Manion *v.* Fahy, 11 W. Va. 482; Smith *v.* Knight, 14 W. Va. 749.

During the term of the court, its judgments and decrees may be set aside on motion. Spilman *v.* Gilpin, 93 Va. 698, 25 S. E. 1004.

A decree procured by fraud may be so set aside during the term at which it was made, but not afterwards. Manion *v.* Fahy, 11 W. Va. 482.

Notice Unnecessary.—During the term the court rendering the judgment may set the same aside, without notice. Green *v.* Pittsburg, etc., R. Co., 11 W. Va. 685.

During the term all the proceedings are in the breast of the court and under its control, and liable to be stricken out, altered or amended during the term, without notice to the parties, who are conclusively presumed to know that a decree entered at an early day of the term of the court has been modified by the decree, entered at a later day. Clendenning *v.* Conrad, 91 Va. 410, 21 S. E. 818.

Disposition of Motion in Discretion of Court.—The action of the court below in overruling a motion to set aside a judgment before the expiration of the term at which the judgment was rendered, on the ground that there was an unauthorized appearance by attorney as to the judgment debtor, when several orders entered in the case at former terms show a general appearance for him by attorney, will not be disturbed by the appellate court unless the motion was supported by a clear preponderance of evidence. Chilhowie Lumber Co. *v.* Lance, 50 W. Va. 636, 41 S. E. 128.

Review of Decision on Motion.—If a defendant does not on the record object or except to the judgment of the court in overruling a motion to set aside the judgment entered at the same term of the court, the appellate court will not review such action of the circuit court. Perry *v.* Horn, 22 W. Va. 381. See generally. the title EXCEPTIONS, BILL OF, vol. 5, p. 357.

b. After Term.

(1) In General.

A judgment can be set aside or altered only in the mode prescribed, and by the court or officer invested with jurisdiction to do so by law. Marshall *v.* Cheatam, 88 Va. 31, 13 S. E. 308.

A final decree upon the merits after answer filed can not be reheard, reviewed or otherwise disturbed in the court below, after the end of the term at which it was pronounced, except for such matter as constitutes ground for a bill of review for error apparent in the decree, bill of review for newly-discovered evidence, or an original bill to impeach it for sufficient cause, such as fraud in its procurement. Snyder *v.* Middle States Loan, etc., Co., 52 W. Va. 655, 44 S. E. 250.

A decree once passed, and the term ended, can only be disturbed by petition, bill of review, bill to impeach, or by appeal. Nelson *v.* Kownslar, 79 Va. 468.

"For the review of a final decree upon the hearing, after the end of the term, the methods are appeal, bill of review for error apparent, bill of review for newly-discovered matter, original bill to set it aside for fraud in its procurement or other supervenient cause, or, if it be utterly void for want of jurisdiction, motion to vacate it, some of the authorities say, but in this last case, it is said in Conrad *v.*

County of Lewis, 10 W Va. 784, that appeal is the better remedy." Snyder *v.* Middle States Loan, etc., Co., 52 W. Va. 655, 657, 44 S. E. 250.

As to the manner of opening or vacating judgments or decrees other than those rendered on hearing, see the title CONFESSION OF JUDGMENTS, vol. 3, p. 64. And see ante, "Judgments by Consent," II, C; "Judgments by Default and Decrees Pro Confesso," II, E.

(2) Motion.

(a) In General.

Statutory Provisions.—Under § 3447 of the Virginia Code, 1904, and § 1, ch. 134, of the West Virginia Code, 1899, a judgment or decree may be reversed or corrected on motion for any clerical error or error in fact for which a judgment or decree may be reversed or corrected on writ of error coram nobis (or coram vobis). For a full treatment of these statutory provisions, and of § 3451 of the Virginia Code, and § 5, ch. 134 of the West Virginia Code, including errors to which they are applicable, to whom the motion must be made, time of making, necessity for notice, etc., see ante, "Statutory Provisions," VII, B, 1, b, (2); "Procedure," VII, B, 2.

"Under chancery practice, unaffected by statute, an interlocutory decree may be set aside in some cases on mere motion; in others, by petition for rehearing, the distinction between cases where it can be done by motion and where it must be by petition not being clearly defined. Bart. Ch. Pr. 126; Chancellor Taylor's opinion in Banks *v.* Anderson, 2 Hen. & M. 20; Sand. Eq. 690." Fowler *v.* Lewis, 36 W. Va. 112, 130, 14 S. E. 447, 453.

As to opening or vacating default judgments, or decrees pro confesso, on motion or petition, see ante, "Judgments by Default and Decrees Pro Confesso," II, E.

(b) Form of Motion.

Under no circumstances will a court

entertain a mere oral motion to review and set aside its former decree solemnly pronounced and duly recorded. The petition must be in writing, presented in due form, and must contain the requisite averments. Scott v. Rowland, 82 Va. 484, 4 S. E. 595.

(c) Evidence in Support of Motion.

"This court laid down the rule in Smith v. Johnson, 44 W. Va. 278, as follows: 'When a defendant, by bill in equity, seeks to nullify a judgment at law obtained against him without service of process, upon unauthorized appearance by attorney, to succeed he must have a clear preponderance of evidence sustaining the allegation of his bill.' Proceedings by motion and by bill in equity in such case are both direct and not collateral and the rule must be the same. Wandling v. Straw, 25 W. Va. 692, 703." Chilhowie Lumber Co. v. Lance, 50 W. Va. 636, 642, 41 S. E. 128.

(d) Discretion of Court as to Imposition of Terms.

"The rule of law as stated in 15 Ency. of Pl. and Pr. 288, is: 'A court, upon an application to open or vacate a judgment may, in the exercise of its discretion, impose such terms upon the applicant as a condition of granting such application, as under the circumstances it may see fit, or it may grant the application and open or vacate the judgment unconditionally without the imposition of terms; it being entirely in the discretion of the court to impose them or not, according to its view of what the justice of the case requires.'" Powers v. Carter Coal, etc., Co., 100 Va. 450, 456, 41 S. E. 867. See ante, "Judgments by Default and Decrees Pro Confesso," II, E.

(3) Petition for Rehearing or Bill in Equity.

(a) In General.

"The mode of modifying or annulling the decrees of a chancery court, other than consent decrees differs in this state considerably from the modes adopted in England and in some of the states of the union. This difference is caused principally by our having never adopted the English practice of enrolling decrees. By this English practice the decree, whatever its character, is first entered in the registrar's book; but this entry does not, strictly speaking, make it a record. It is subsequently enrolled upon parchment, when it is regarded as a complete and perfect record. The time, which intervenes between this entry of the decree on the registrar's books and the enrollment of it on parchment, is generally considerable. During this intervening time, the record not being regarded as complete and perfect, the decree may be modified or annulled for errors appearing on the face of the record, upon a petition for a rehearing, whether these errors be errors in the judgment of the court, or errors arising from inadvertence; though, if the error be a clear mistake made by the court, or by the counsel in drawing the decree, or if some ordinary direction has been omitted, or a clerical mistake made, the correction may be made, after the decree is entered and before it is enrolled, upon motion simply. But if the error be in matter of substance, the proper mode of correcting it is by a petition for a rehearing." Manion v. Fahy, 11 W. Va. 482, 490.

"If, however, after the decree has been entered, and before it is enrolled, new matter is discovered, which ought to cause a modification or annulling of the decree, it must, by the English practice, be brought forward by a supplemental bill, in the nature of a bill of review; and it can not be done by a petition for a rehearing; but it is accompanied by a petition to rehear the cause at the same time, it is heard on this supplemental bill. Such a bill can not be filed without the leave of the court, nor without an affidavit similar to that required on a bill of review proper being filed. And to sustain such a bill the same proof is required, as would be required, if it had been a bill of review, filed after the enrollment of a decree." Manion *v.* Fahy, 11 W. Va. 482, 491.

"If a decree has been procured by fraud, discovered after the decree is entered but before it is enrolled, the proper mode of correcting it by the English practice is neither by a petition for a rehearing nor by a supplemental bill, in the nature of a bill of review, but the correction must be asked by an original bill in the nature of a bill of review. See Mussell *v.* Morgan, 3 Bro. Ch. R. 74, 79. Such a bill is not a continuance of a former suit, as a supplemental bill in the nature of a bill of review is; but it is a new suit, and like any other original bill, it may be filed without the leave of the court. After the decree has been enrolled, no matter what may be the character of the decree, whether it be an interlocutory decree in the sense in which we use the term, or a final decree, it can, according to the English practice, be modified or annulled by the court, who pronounced the decree only by bill of review, which may be filed for error of law, apparent on the face of the record, or because of newly-discovered matter. If, however, this enrolled decree was procured by fraud, it can only be set aside by an original bill, in a new suit, and can not be annulled by a bill of review." Manion *v.* Fahy, 11 W. Va. 482, 491.

(b) Rehearing.

As to when a rehearing is proper, procedure, etc., see the title REHEARING.

(c) Bill of Review.

As to when a bill of review will lie, manner and scope of proceedings, etc, see the title BILL OF REVIEW, vol. 2, p. 383.

(d) Original Bill.

aa. When Proper.

Where a final decree has been procured by fraud, it should be annulled or modified, not by a bill of review proper, but by an original bill, or by an original bill in the nature of a bill of review. Keran *v.* Trice, 75 Va. 690; Hill *v.* Bowyer, 18 Gratt. 364; Evans *v.* Spurgin, 11 Gratt. 615; Anderson *v.* Woodford, 8 Leigh 316; Banks *v.* Anderson, 2 Hen. & M. 20; Law *v.* Law, 55 W. Va. 4, 11, 46 S. E. 697; Snyder *v.* Middle States Loan, etc., Co., 52 W. Va. 655, 44 S. E. 250; Slinguff *v.* Gainer, 49 W. Va. 7, 12, 37 S. E. 771; Springston *v.* Morris, 47 W. Va. 50, 34 S. E. 766, 767; Manion *v.* Fahy, 11 W. Va. 482, 491; Davis *v.* Landcraft, 10 W. Va. 718. And see Carter *v.* Allen, 21 Gratt. 241.

If a decree in a cause has been procured by fraud, discovered after the decree is entered on the record, and after the adjournment of the term at which it is entered, it can be set aside, only by an original bill, in a new suit, and can not be annulled by a bill of review. Law *v.* Law, 55 W. Va. 4, 46 S. E. 697.

"The reason why a final decree procured by fraud can not be reversed on a bill of review which constitutes a continuance of the old cause, but the decree must be set aside by a new suit, would seem to be this: A bill of review which opens the final decree is allowed on a newly-discovered fact which affects the merits of the case set out in the bill and proceedings, and which ought therefore to be heard in finally disposing of the case. But facts, which establish fraud in procuring the final decree, have no effect whatever on the cause of action set forth in the bill and proceedings, and if the decree was opened, then facts establishing fraud would not be considered in entering up the new decree, but the new decree would be entered up on the pleading and evidence which were in the cause, when the decree assailed was made. The setting aside of a final decree, thus procured by fraud, would seem to be the proper subject for a new suit, having no connection with the real merits of the original suit. If this be the reason why a new suit must be brought, it would follow that though the decree procured by fraud was an interlocutory decree, it could still only be annulled by a new suit, setting up the fraud. Under the English rule, if the decree had been entered by fraud, but had not been enrolled, the new facts constituting the fraud, it would seem, could not be brought before the court in that suit by a bill in the nature of a bill of review; for only such new facts can be brought forward in that way as are newly discovered and material to the decision of the case, as made by the bill and pleadings. And for the same reason, here or in Virginia, the facts constituting the fraud, by which the court was induced to enter an interlocutory decree, it would seem, ought not to be brought forward by a petition for a rehearing, for as we have seen, such petition is a mere substitute for a bill in the nature of a bill of review under the English practice." Manion v. Fahy, 11 W. Va. 482, 494.

"In State v. Vest, 21 W. Va. 796, it is held, that 'A record imports such absolute verity, that no person against whom it is pronounced will be permitted to aver or prove anything against it.' Judge Green, who delivered the opinion of the court in that case, says, upon that point: 'It is certainly a rule invariably recognized by the courts, that a record imports such absolute verity, that no person against whom it is pronounced will be permitted to aver or prove anything against it. This rule is well established, and we now here refer to but a few of the many cases in which this doctrine has been held. See Rex v. Carlisle, 2 Barns. Ad. 971; 23 Eng. Ch. R. 226; Braden v. Reitzenberger, 18 W. Va. 286; Carper v. McDowell, 5 Gratt. 212, 226; Harkins v. Forsyth, 11 Leigh 294; Taliaferro v. Pryor, 12 Gratt. 277; Vaughn v. Com., 17 Gratt. 386; Quinn v. Com., 20 Gratt. 138. Whatever,

therefore, on the face of a book of record has been duly authenticated by the signature of the judge, must be held to be an absolute verity, and it can not be contradicted; and so also any paper actually referred to on the record book as filed or as constituting a part of the record is to be regarded as a part of the record, and is as much a verity as if it had been spread out at length as a part of the record.' But in Springston v. Morris, 47 W. Va. 50, it is also held, that the recitals of a decree, which is directly attacked for fraud, are not presumed to be absolute verities, but are subject to impeachment. Judge Dent, speaking for the court, says: 'Defendants insist that the plaintiffs have no right to question the recitals of the decree confirming the sale. State v. Vest, 21 W. Va. 796. This is not the rule where a decree is directly impeached for fraud or surprise in its procurement. It may be an absolute verity as to what occurred in court and was there recorded, but not as to the recitals therein contained as to what occurred other than in the presence of the court at the time of the entry of the decree. Black, Judgm., § 238. If such rule were to be held good in all cases, no decree could be impeached for fraud or surprise; and yet such is ordinary equity jurisdiction. Bart. Ch. Prac. (2d Ed.) p. 841. The doctrine of the absolute verity of the record must always yield to that higher equitable doctrine that fraud vitiates all things. "It is the just and proper pride of our mature system of equity jurisprudence that fraud vitiates every transaction; and however men may surround it with forms, solemn instruments, proceedings conforming to all the details required in the laws, or even by the formal judgment of courts, a court of equity will disregard them all, if necessary, that justice and equity may prevail." Warner v. Blakeman, 43 W. N. Y. 507; Freem., Judgm., § 489. The proper way in which to attack such decree, when the object is merely to set aside the d cree, and then permit the original suit to continue to final hearing is by an original bill in the nature of a bill of review. Manion *v.* Fahy, 11 W. Va. 482.'" Law *v.* Law, 55 W. Va. 4, 10, 46 S. E. 697.

Surprise, Accident or Mistake.—An original bill is the proper remedy where a decree has been obtained by surprise or mistake. Anderson *v.* Woodford, 8 Leigh 316.

The party against whom a decree has been rendered, without his appearance, may apply to the court to have the decree opened either by petition or by original bill on the grounds of alleged accident and surprise. In either form it is an original proceeding, and may be commenced without previous leave of the court. Hill *v.* Bowyer, 18 Gratt. 364.

"A decree, other than a consent decree, which has been entered by surprise or by mistake of the parties, would seem to stand upon the same footing and whether interlocutory or final, should be set aside by a new suit for the purpose. The case in 8 Leigh was one of surprise rather than fraud. The authorities, however, on the question whether an interlocutory decree, not entered by consent, but procured by fraud, surprise or mistake of the parties, can be set aside by a bill in the nature of a bill of review, or by a petition for a rehearing, are not clear or distinct, though the probable inference to be drawn from them is, that such interlocutory decrees can not be so set aside, but only by an original bill." Manion *v.* Fahy, 11 W. Va. 482, 495.

"The petition can not be treated as a bill of review, because it suggested no error on the face of the record, and brought in no newly discovered matter touching the matter in litigation in the pleadings in the case. True, it brought in a new matter, but not a new matter entering into the matters in litigation, but an outside matter, an accident affecting the decree. Probably, the pleader intended it for a petition for a rehearing; but a petition for rehearing is applicable only to interlocutory decrees. I am impelled to the conclusion that as the relief sought, the setting aside of the decree, depends on this accident, wholly outside of the pleadings of the cause, or the matters involved in them, relief must be had by an original, independent suit to set aside and annul the decree because of accident. Manion *v.* Fahy, 11 W. Va. 482, 496; Knapp *v.* Snyder, 15 W. Va. 434; Morris *v.* Peyton, 29 W. Va. 201, 213; Armstrong *v.* Wilson, 19 W. Va. 108. Callaway *v.* Alexander, 8 Leigh 114, and Anderson *v.* Woodford, 8 Leigh 316, will show that relief against a decree for fraud, surprise or the like must be by original bill. It is a new matter not involved in the pleadings in the case, outside the case, and relief can not be given by an order in the case." Slingluff *v.* Gainer, 49 W. Va. 7, 12, 37 S. E. 771.

An infant under the statute allowing him to show cause against a decree, may do so by original bill, although the cause alleged is error of law apparent on the face of the decree. When such bill seeks relief, by way of cancellation of a deed and an accounting for waste, rents, issues and profits, consequent upon the reversal of the decree, and fully sets forth the defects in the decree, and incorporates the pleadings, decrees and orders as exhibits, the suit is not collateral, but directly attacks the erroneous decree, and the record of the cause in which it was pronounced may be introduced upon the hearing as evidence. Stewart *v.* Tennant, 52 W. Va. 559, 44 S. E. 223.

As to original bills to impeach decrees pro confesso, see ante, "Judgments by Default and Decrees Pro Confesso," II, E.

As to original bills to impeach consent decrees, see ante, "Judgments by Consent," II, C.

bb. Leave of Court Unnecessary.

A bill to impeach a decree for fraud may be filed without leave of court previously obtained. Keran *v.* Trice, 75 Va. 690; Banks *v.* Anderson, 2 Hen. & M. 20.

" 'There is no doubt,' says Mr. Justice Story, 'of the jurisdiction of courts of equity to grant relief against a former decree, where the same has been obtained by fraud and imposition; for these will infect judgments at law and decrees of all kinds; but they annul the whole in the consideration of the courts of equity. * * * Where a decree has been so obtained, the courts will restore the parties to their former situation, whatever their rights may be. This kind of bill may be filed without leave of the court being first obtained for the purpose, the fraud used in obtaining the decree being the principal point in issue, and being necessary to be established by proof, before the propriety of the decree can be investigated.' Story's Eq. Plead., § 426." Keran *v.* Trice, 75 Va. 690, 698.

cc. Necessity for Procedure within Reasonable Time.

One who would set aside a decree by reason of mistake must proceed within a reasonable time after knowledge of it, else he will be barred of relief by laches. Seymour *v.* Alkire, 47 W. Va. 302, 34 S. E. 953. See generally, the title LACHES.

dd. Parties.

Generally, as to who are proper and necessary parties in equity proceedings, see the title PARTIES.

A decree of confirmation founded on a false report of sale made may be impeached by an interested party guiltless of culpable fraud or neglect. Springston *v.* Morris, 47 W. Va. 50, 34 S. E. 766.

The persons whose right would or might be affected by setting aside the decrees complained of were necessary parties to any suit brought for that purpose, or in which such relief could be granted. Story, Eq. Pl., § 420; Harwood *v.* Railroad Co., 17 Wall. 78; 3 Am. & Eng. Ency. Pl. & Prac. 620, etc. Harrison *v.* Wallton, 95 Va. 721, 30 S. E. 372, 374.

A decree of a court of equity set aside on the ground of fraud, upon a bill against the heirs at law of the party procuring the decree. Evans *v.* Spurgin, 11 Gratt. 615.

ee. Allegations of Bill.

In General.—Generally, as to the essential allegations of a bill in equity, see the title EQUITY, vol. 5, p. 127, et seq.

A bill to set aside a decree must state the decree and the proceedings which led to it, with the circumstances of fraud, or whatever the ground may be on which it is impeached. Davis *v.* Landcraft, 10 W. Va. 718.

"Judge Story, in his work on Eq. Plead., § 28, says: 'It may be proper, however, to remark, that every material fact, to which the plaintiff means to offer evidence, ought to be distinctly stated in the premises; for otherwise he will not be permitted to offer or require any evidence of such fact. A general charge or statement, however, of the matter of fact is sufficient; and it is not necessary to charge minutely all the circumstances, which may conduce to prove the general charge; for these circumstances are properly matters of evidence, which need not be charged in order to let them in as proofs.' Again, at paragraph 241, he says: 'In the next place it may be affirmed, as an elementary rule of the most extensive influence, that the bill should state the right, title or claim of the plaintiff, with accuracy and clearness; and that it should, in like manner, state, the injury or grievance of which he complains, and the relief which he asks of the court. In other words, there must be such certainty in the averment of the title upon which the bill is founded, that the defendant may be distinctly informed of the nature of the case which he is called on to meet. The other material facts ought, also, to be plainly, yet succinctly, alleged, and with all necessary and convenient certainty, as to the essential circumstances of time, place, manner and other incidents.'" Davis *v.* Lancraft, 10 W. Va. 718, 745.

Allegations as to Fraud.—In Harrison *v.* Walton, 95 Va. 721, 30 S. E. 372, it was held, that "whether it is essential, in order that a judgment or decree may be set aside and annulled for fraud, that the suit shall be brought expressly for that purpose, and that the bill shall state a case of actual fraud, it is unnecessary to decide or express any opinion upon in this case, as the bill is fatally defective as a bill for that purpose in another respect."

A bill to impeach a decree for fraud is an original bill in the nature of a bill of review, and should state the decree and the proceedings which led to it, with the circumstances of fraud on which it is impeached. Keran *v.* Trice, 75 Va. 690.

"In all suits instituted for the purpose of impeaching transactions on the ground of fraud, it is essential that the nature of the case should be distinctly and accurately stated. It must be shown in what the fraud consists, and in what manner it has been effected. Where it is sought to set aside or annul a regular judgment or decree upon the ground that it was obtained by fraud practiced upon a party or upon the court during the trial, or in prosecuting the suit, or in obtaining the judgment or decree, it is necessary, it is said, that the bill should state a case which shows actual fraud (Kerr, Fraud & M. 353; Patch *v.* Ward, 3 Ch. App. 203. See also, Milford & T. Pl. & Prac. 190, 191; U. S. *v.* Throckmorton, 98 U. S. 61); and that the suit should be brought for the express purpose of impeaching the de-

cree, otherwise it will be regarded as a collateral attack (2 Freem. Judgm., 4th Ed., 336; 12 Am. & Eng. Ency. Law, 147j; Milford & T. Pl. & Prac. 190, 191)." Harrison *v.* Wallton, 95 Va. 721, 30 S. E. 372, 374.

"In Mitford's Pleading, by Jeremy, at page 94, it is said that 'a bill to set aside a decree for fraud must state the decree, and the proceedings which led to it, with the circumstances of fraud on which it is impeached. The prayer must necessarily be varied according to the nature of the fraud used, and the extent of its operation in obtaining an improper decision of the court.' Story, in his work on Eq. Plead., § 257, says, 'that every fact essential to the plaintiff's title to maintain the bill, and obtain the relief, must be stated in the bill, otherwise the defect will be fatal. For no facts are properly in issue, unless charged in the bill; and of course no proofs can be generally offered of facts not in the bill; nor can relief be granted for matters not charged, although they may be apparent from other parts of the pleadings and evidence; for the court pronounces its decree secundum allegata et probata.' Cooper's Eq. Plead., pp. 5, 7; § 28, Story's Eq. Plead." Davis *v.* Landcraft, 10 W. Va. 718, 739.

A bill to impeach a decree for fraud need not charge fraud in terms, but it is sufficient if it states facts and circumstances which, if true, make a case of fraud and imposition. **Keran** *v.* **Trice,** 75 Va. 690, 698.

A charge in general terms in a bill to set aside a decree for fraud where it is the point on which the merits of the case turns, and does not come in collaterally and incidentally, will warrant the production of evidence to particular facts. Cooper's Eq. Plead., p. 7. Davis *v.* Landcraft, 10 W. Va. 718, 743.

Charging Notice of Fraud.—In Carter *v.* Allan, 21 Gratt. 241, the bill was held fatally defective as a bill to impeach for fraud, as against B. for failing to charge him with notice of the fraud.

ff. Amendment Changing Bill of Review to Original Bill.

Where a bill of review is filed in a cause to set aside certain decrees therein alleged to have been procured by fraud, and a demurrer is sustained to said bill as a bill of review; and the plaintiff therein asks leave to amend the same, and have it taken and treated as an original bill, for the purpose of setting aside said decrees, for fraud; and said bill can be so amended as to make it a bill, sufficient in substance for the purpose sought, it is error in the court to refuse to allow such amendment to be made therein, and to treat the same when so amended as an original bill. Law *v.* Law, 55 W. Va. 4, 46 S. E. 697.

5. Effect of Vacating or Setting Aside.

Upon Execution Issued on Judgment.—When a judgment is set aside, the execution which has issued upon it falls with it, without any express order to quash the execution. Ballard *v.* Whitlock, 18 Gratt. 235.

A reversed or vacated decree does not constitute an estoppel; on it no plea of res adjudicata can rest. 2 Blach, Judgm., § 511; Freem., Judgm., § 333. Fowler *v.* Lewis, 36 W. Va. 112, 14 S. E. 447, 453. See the title FORMER ADJUDICATION OR RES ADJUDICATA, vol. 6, p. 261.

VIII. Relief against Enforcement of Judgments.

A. EQUITABLE RELIEF.

1. When Proper.

General Principles Determining Propriety of Equitable Relief.—The grounds upon which a court of equity will grant relief against a judgment at law are well defined and firmly established. It will not relieve a party against a judgment rendered in consequence of his default upon grounds which might have been successfully taken at law, unless some reason founded in fraud, accident, mistake, surprise or some adventitious circumstances beyond his control be shown why the defense was not made. This proposition has been so repeatedly affirmed that it has become a principle and maxim of equity as well settled as any other. It has been acted upon and recognized in numerous cases in the Virginia courts. The principle is founded in wisdom and sound policy and springs from the positive necessity of prescribing some period at which litigation must cease. Injustice alone does not entitle a party to relief, but he must show himself free from laches, and that he has done everything that could reasonably be required of him. If the court of equity should relieve persons from the consequences of their own neglect, it would directly encourage such conduct. Diligence and vigilance would cease to be the rule, and all certainty in judicial proceedings would be destroyed. But they have always granted relief when it is shown that some good reason prevented a defense from being made at law. Hoge *v.* Fidelity Loan, etc., Co., 103 Va. 1, 48 S. E. 494; Thomas *v.* Jones, 98 Va. 323, 36 S. E. 382; Preston *v.* Kindrick, 94 Va. 760, 27 S. E. 588; Brown *v.* Chapman, 90 Va. 174, 17 S. E. 855; Corey *v.* Moore, 86 Va. 721, 11 S. E. 114; Canada *v.* Barksdale, 84 Va. 742, 6 S. E. 10; Barnett *v.* Barnett, 83 Va. 504, 2 S. E. 733; Moore *v.* Lipscombe, 82 Va. 546, 549; Dey *v.* Martin, 78 Va. 1; Pendleton *v.* Taylor, 77 Va. 580; Yuille *v.* Wimbish, 77 Va. 308; Wallace *v.* Richmond, 26 Gratt. 67; Richmond Enquirer Co. *v.* Robinson, 24 Gratt. 548; Penn *v.* Reynolds, 23 Gratt. 518, 523; Holland *v.* Trotter, 22 Gratt. 136, 139; Sanders *v.* Branson, 22 Gratt. 364; Haseltine *v.* Brickey, 16 Gratt. 116, 120; Meem *v.* Rucker, 10 Gratt. 506; Slack *v.* Wood, 9 Gratt. 40; Hudson *v.* Kline, 9 Gratt. 379; Allen *v.* Hamilton, 9 Gratt. 255; Knifong *v.* Hendricks, 2 Gratt. 212; Hendricks *v.*

Compton, 2 Rob. 192; Mason *v.* Nelson, 11 Leigh 227; Tapp *v.* Rankin, 9 Leigh 478; Turner *v.* Davis, 7 Leigh 227; Morgan *v.* Carson, 7 Leigh 238; Donally *v.* Ginatt, 5 Leigh 359; Bierne *v.* Mann, 5 Leigh 364; 'Arthur *v.* Chavis, 6 Rand. 142; Brown *v.* Street, 6 Rand. 1; Green *v.* Judith, 5 Rand. 1, 29; Chapman *v.* Harrison, 4 Rand. 336, 343; Oswald *v.* Tyler, 4 Rand. 19; Faulkner *v.* Harwood, 6 Rand. 125; Poindexter *v.* Waddy, 6 Munf. 418; Fenwick *v.* McMurdo, 2 Munf. 244; Auditor *v.* Nicholas, 2 Munf. 31; DeLima *v.* Glassell, 4 Hen. & M. 369; Mosby *v.* Haskins, 4 Hen. & M. 427; Degraffenreid *v.* Donald, 2 Hen. & M. 10; Turpin *v.* Thomas, 2 Hen. & M. 139; Richmond, etc., R. Co. *v.* Shippen, 2 Pat. & H. 327; Hord *v.* Dishman, 5 Call 279; Foushee *v.* Lea, 4 Call 279; Mosby *v.* Leeds, 3 Call 439; Maupin *v.* Whiting, 1 Call 224; Ashby *v.* Kiger, Gilmer 153; Tarpley *v.* Dobyns, 1 Wash. 185; Farmers', etc., Warehouse Co. *v.* Pridemore, 55 W. Va. 451, 465, 47 S. E. 258; Bank *v.* Ralphsnyder, 54 W. Va. 231, 46 S. E. 206; Hickok *v.* Caton, 53 W. Va. 46, 44 S. E. 178; Sibley *v.* Stacey, 53 W. Va. 292, 293, 44 S. E. 420; Iron Co. *v.* Quesenberry, 50 W. Va. 451, 457, 40 S. E. 487; Bodkin *v.* Rollyson, 48 W. Va. 453, 455, 37 S. E. 617, 618; Grafton, etc., R. Co. *v.* Davisson, 45 W. Va. 12, 29 S. E. 1028; Parsons *v.* Snider, 42 W. Va. 517, 26 S. E. 285; Rollins *v.* National Casket Co., 40 W. Va. 590, 21 S. E. 722, 723; Newlon *v.* Wade, 43 W. Va. 283, 27 S. E. 244; Powell *v.* Miller, 41 W. Va. 371, 23 S. E. 557; Zinn *v.* Dawson, 47 W. Va. 45, 34 S. E. 784, 785; Graham *v.* Citizens' Nat. Bank, 45 W. Va. 701, 32 S. E. 245; Shay *v.* Nolan, 46 W. Va. 299, 33 S. E. 225; Howell *v.* Thomason, 34 W. Va. 794, 12 S. E. 1088; Kanawha, etc., R. Co. *v.* Ryan, 31 W. Va. 364, 6 S. E. 924; Hubbard *v.* Yocum, 30 W. Va. 740, 5 S. E. 867; Bias *v.* Vickers, 27 W. Va. 456; Sayre *v.* Harpold, 33 W. Va. 553, 11 S. E. 16; Knott *v.* Seamands, 25 W. Va. 99; Ensign Mfg. Co. *v.* Mc-

Ginnis, 30 W. Va. 532, 4 S. E. 782, 787; Ludington *v.* Tiffany, 6 W. Va. 11; Shields *v.* McClung, 6 W. Va. 79; Chesapeake, etc., R. Co. *v.* Pack, 6 W. Va. 397; Ferrell *v.* Allen, 5 W. Va. 43; Black *v.* Smith, 13 W. Va. 780; Smith *v.* McLain, 11 W. Va. 654, 655; Harner *v.* Price, 17 W. Va. 523; Hevener *v.* McClung, 22 W. Va. 81; Alford *v.* Moore, 15 W. Va. 597; Braden *v.* Reitzerberger, 18 W. Va. 286. See the titles ACTIONS, vol. 1, p. 157; ADEQUATE REMEDY AT LAW, vol. 1, p. 161; INJUNCTIONS, vol. 7, p. 512.

Excuses for Failure to Defend at Law.—Relief will always be granted in equity when it is shown that the failure to successfully defend at law was because of the acts or representations of the opposite party, or agents, or the result of fraud, accident, surprise or some other adventitious circumstance beyond the control of the complainant. Louisville, etc., R. Co. *v.* Taylor, 93 Va. 226, 24 S. E. 1013; Rosenberger *v.* Bowen, 84 Va. 660, 5 S. E. 697; Moore *v.* Lipscombe, 82 Va. 546; Dey *v.* Martin, 78 Va. 1; Slack *v.* Wood, 9 Gratt. 40; Mason *v.* Nelson, 11 Leigh 227; Faulkner *v.* Harwood, 6 Rand. 125; Poindexter *v.* Waddy, 6 Munf. 418; Kincaid *v.* Cunningham, 2 Munf. 1; Mosby *v.* Haskins, 4 Hen. & M. 427; Degraffenreid *v.* Donald, 2 Hen. & M. 10; Hord *v.* Dishman, 5 Call 279; Smith *v.* McLain, 11 W. Va. 654; Shields *v.* McClung, 6 W. Va. 79.

When a defendant at law is precluded by a certain course of proceedings at law from defending the action, which by just set-offs would have extinguished the debt, he may be relieved in equity from the judgment, as that court has jurisdiction of the case. Mann *v.* Drewry, 5 Leigh 296.

Notwithstanding a judgment against administrators in an action of debt, and a subsequent judgment against them personally, relief in equity was granted them where the peculiar state of the assets made it difficult to plead at law in relation thereto, and because at the trial of the second action their counsel was absent, in consequence whereof they were wholly undefended, and a verdict was obtained against them contrary to justice without any negligence or default on their part. Pendleton *v.* Stuart, 6 Munf. 377.

" 'The ground upon which relief in equity against a judgment is commonly justified is, that the complainant had a cause of action or defense, of the benefit of which he was deprived in the original action, under circumstances which make it inequitable for the prevailing party to enforce the judgment; and if this is the only ground upon which the claim for relief can rest, it must be denied, unless the complainant shows he had some cause of action or of defense, or at least, had there been a fair trial, that the judgment would probably have been more favorable to him.' 2 Freem. on Judgments, § 498. He must show the judgment unjust. 1 Black on Judgments, § 393; 3 Pom. Eq., § 1364." Iron Co. *v.* Quesenberry, 50 W. Va. 451, 453, 40 S. E. 487. See the title INJUNCTIONS, vol. 7, p. 512.

" 'It may be laid down, says High on Injunctions, § 125, 'as a general rule, that ignorance of important facts material to the establishing of a defense to the action at law, will in the absence of laches on the part of the defendant warrant a court of equity in extending a relief by injunction against the judgment.' But, in Mum *v.* Rucker, 10 Gratt. 506, it was held, as follows: '1· An injunction to a judgment at law will not be sustained where defendant at law has failed to make his defense at law from ignorance of the nature of the proceeding against him, and a misapprehension of the steps it was necessary to take in order to subject him. 2. The mere averment by a plaintiff in his bill asking for an injunction to a judgment at law, of the facts constituting his excuse for not defending himself at law, is not suffi-

cient; he must prove them.' " Harner *v.* Price, 17 W. Va. 523, 548.

When the grounds given for relief in equity were available as defenses at law, then no jurisdiction will be taken in equity. Harnsbarger *v.* Kinney, 13 Gratt. 511; Mackey *v.* Mackey, 29 Gratt. 158; Allen *v.* Hamilton, 9 Gratt. 255; Harvey *v.* Fox, 5 Leigh 444; Haden *v.* Garden, 7 Leigh 157; Hendricks *v.* Compton, 2 Rob. 192.

It is immaterial that the act preventing the defense was done in good faith and without fraudulent intention. Thomas *v.* Jones, 98 Va. 323, 36 S. E. 382. See the title ACTIONS, vol. 1, p. 157.

The mere fact that a party has mistaken his rights, and so has failed to make his defense at law, does not entitle him to relief in equity. Hoge *v.* Fidelity Loan, etc., Co., 103 Va. 1, 48 S. E. 494.

A court of equity can not relieve against a judgment at law merely on the ground that it was erroneous, even though the plaintiff at law was not entitled to recover, or not entitled to recover in that form of action, and the judgment was obtained by default. To give jurisdiction in equity in such a case, there must be some suggestion of fraud or surprise, or some good reason assigned as an excuse for the failure to make a defense at law. Turpin *v.* Thomas, 2 Hen. & M. 139; Auditor *v.* Nicholas, 2 Munf. 31; Chapman *v.* Harrison, 4 Rand. 336; Branch *v.* Burnley, 1 Call 147; Kincaid *v.* Cunningham, 2 Munf. 1; Turner *v.* Davis, 7 Leigh 227; Allen *v.* Hamilton, 9 Gratt. 255.

Chancery will not enjoin a judgment at law and grant a new trial merely for error in the law court, but only because of fraud, accident, surprise, or some adventitious circumstance unknown to the party before judgment, and beyond his control. Graham *v.* Citizens' Nat. Bank, 45 W. Va. 701, 32 S. E. 245.

A court of equity will not interfere

by injunction to correct simple errors of judgment in a court of law, or to give relief against a judgment of a court of law, because of mere error of judgment in such courts. The remedy in such case to the party aggrieved is by appeal, writ of error or supersedeas, in courts of appellate jurisdiction, and not by injunction. Black *v.* Smith, 13 W. Va. 780, 802.

Failure of proof upon the trial at law will not, in the absence of fraud, accident, mistake or other adventitious circumstances, warrant a court of equity in granting relief against a judgment. "Thus, where complainant asks an injunction against a judgment, alleging in his bill that he is now able to prove the matter of his plea in defense of the action at law, which he was unable to prove at the trial, but does not suggest fraud, accident, mistake, or other circumstances as the cause of such failure of proof, the injunction will not be allowed. High on Inj., ch. 3, § 168; Shields *v.* McClung, 6 W. Va. 79; Hogg's Eq. Pr. 472, 473." Farmers', etc., Warehouse Co. *v.* Pridemore, 55 W. Va. 451, 465, 47 S. E. 258.

Negligence of Party or Agent as Precluding Relief.—It is generally held that where a party, through his own or his agent's or attorney's negligence, fails to avail himself of a defense which he might have made at law, he will not be relieved in equity. Wallace *v.* Richmond, 26 Gratt. 67; Haseltine *v.* Brickey, 16 Gratt. 116, 120; Callaway *v.* Alexander, 8 Leigh 114, 31 Am. Dec. 640; Slack *v.* Wood, 9 Gratt. 40; Dey *v.* Martin, 78 Va. 1; Wray *v.* Davenport, 79 Va. 26; Holland *v.* Trotter, 22 Gratt. 136, 141; Canada *v.* Barksdale, 84 Va. 742, 746, 6 S. E. 10; Shields *v.* McClung, 6 W. Va. 79; Meem *v.* Rucker, 10 Gratt. 506; Donally *v.* Ginatt, 5 Leigh 359; Richmond Enquirer Co. *v.* Robinson, 24 Gratt. 548; Gentry *v.* Allen, 32 Gratt. 254, 257; Ayres *v.* Morehead, 77 Va. 586, 589; Black *v.* Smith, 13 W. Va. 780, 800; Braden *v.* Reitzenberger, 18 W. Va.

286, 290; Crumlish *v.* Shenandoah Valley R. Co., 40 W. Va. 627, 22 S. E. 90; Green *v.* Massie, 21 Gratt. 356; Stanard *v.* Rogers, 4 Hen. & M. 438; Ross *v.* Reid, 8 Gratt. 229.

Relief in equity against a judgment will not be granted where the complainant is not shown to have exercised proper diligence in making his defense at law, but the judgment is due to his inattention and laches. Collins *v.* Jones, 6 Leigh 530; Slack *v.* Wood, 9 Gratt. 40.

The negligence of an officer of a corporation, in allowing a judgment to be rendered against his corporation as garnishee when the debt had been previously assigned to another party, and notice thereof had been given to another officer, will exclude the corporation from relief in equity against the judgment. Richmond Enquirer Co. *v.* Robinson, 24 Gratt. 548.

Newly-Discovered Evidence.—Chancery will not relieve against a judgment at law on the ground of newly-discovered evidence, where there is no suggestion of fraud, accident, mistake or any other circumstance preventing the party from having made the defense at law. Norris *v.* Hume, 2 Leigh 334, 21 Am. Dec. 631.

Equity will not relieve a party against a judgment at law, on the ground of after-discovered evidence, or of a defense, of which he was ignorant, until judgment was rendered, unless he shows, that by the exercise of ordinary diligence he could not discover such evidence or defense, or that he was prevented from employing the same by fraud, accident or the act of the opposite party, unmixed with laches or negligence on his part. Shields *v.* McClung, 6 W. Va. 79; Knapp *v.* Snyder, 15 W. Va. 434; Slack *v.* Wood, 9 Gratt. 40; Richmond Enquirer Co. *v.* Robinson, 24 W. Va. 548; Hevener *v.* McClung, 22 W. Va. 81; Farmers', etc., Warehouse Co. *v.* Pridemore, 55 W. Va. 451, 464, 47 S. E. 258.

Paupers, who have brought a suit at law for freedom and failed, may afterwards go in equity and obtain relief, when some were infants held in slavery, and the evidence now exhibited was not then in their power; some of the witnesses having determined to tell the truth since the trial at law. Talbert *v.* Jenny, 6 Rand. 159.

A judgment at law will be enjoined on ground of mistake by the jury, ascertained by after-discovered evidence; and the subject of the action being an account, it will not direct a new trial but will itself give proper relief. Rust *v.* Ware, 6 Gratt. 50.

The defendant in an action on an indemnifying bond for the benefit of a trustee in a deed of trust, after judgment against him, comes into equity on the ground of after-discovered evidence establishing fraud to some of the debts secured. The ground of equity jurisdiction being made out, the court will not direct a new trial, because it would not probably afford relief, but will retain the cause and allow the plaintiff to impeach the deed, notwithstanding his unsuccessful effort to do so at law. Billups *v.* Sears, 5 Gratt. 31, 50 Am. Dec. 105.

Defense Cognizable Only in Equity. —It is well settled that courts of equity will interfere by injunction, either pending an action or after judgment, where there is a distinct defense to the claim asserted by law, which is solely cognizable in equity. And it is equally well settled that where a court of equity has awarded jurisdiction for one purpose, it will ordinarily proceed to a final disposition of the cause. Penn *v.* Ingles, 82 Va. 65; Walters *v.* Farmers' Bank, 76 Va. 12; Rust *v.* Ware, 6 Gratt. 50.

Where a party is entitled to avail himself of an equitable defense under the statute—§ 5, ch. 126, W. Va. Code, 1899, but does not do so, and a judgment is given against him at law, he will still be entitled to relief in a court of equity under § 6 of said statute; and

to entitle him to relief in equity against the judgment it is not necessary that he should aver in his bill any reason or excuse for not availing himself of such equitable defense at law. Bias *v.* Vickers, 27 W. Va. 456; Ludington *v.* Tiffany, 6 W. Va. 11.

Judgments for Gaming Debt.—A court of equity has jurisdiction to relieve against a judgment founded on a gaming debt, although the party failed to defend himself at law, and gives no good reason for such failure. Skipwith *v.* Strother, 3 Rand. 214.

In an action at law on a promise founded on a gaming consideration, the defendant may come into equity for relief if he was surprised at the trial and the judgment was given against him, although he made no effort to obtain a new trial in the law court. White *v.* Washington, 5 Gratt. 645. See the title GAMBLING CONTRACTS, vol. 6, p. 689.

To Restrain Sale under Execution on Fraudulent Judgment.—A court of equity has jurisdiction to enjoin the sale of property under an execution upon a judgment; which the plaintiffs charge was obtained by fraud, and they are without adequate remedy at law. McFarland *v.* Dilly, 5 W. Va. 135; Walker *v.* Hunt, 2 W. Va. 491, 492; Morrison *v.* Wilkinson, 1 Va. Dec. 772.

To Restrain Collection of Satisfied Judgment.—See post, "Satisfaction and Discharge," XIII.

Usury as Ground for Relief.—See generally, the title USURY.

It is well settled in Virginia that a court of equity will interfere with a judgment at law, to relieve against usury. This was held in Young *v.* Scott, 4 Rand. 415, and the doctrine has since been recognized in a number of cases; the latest being Exchange, etc., Bank *v.* Fugate, 93 Va. 821, 23 S. E. 884. It would serve no good purpose to advert to the reasons which led to the exercise of this jurisdiction; for, whether those reasons commended themselves to our judgment or not, it would be our duty to enforce the law as established. The change in the statute declaring that usurious contracts shall be deemed to be for an illegal consideration, instead of void, as formerly, furnishes no warrant for departing from the long-established doctrine that a court of equity will go behind a judgment, to relieve against usury. Nor do the recent decisions of Lynchburg Nat. Bank v. Scott, 91 Va. 652, 22 S. E. 487, and Munford v. McVeigh, 92 Va. 446, 23 S. E. 857, construing that change in the statute, furnish any ground for that contention. Greer v. Hale, 95 Va. 533, 28 S. E. 873, 874.

No Relief Where Parties in Pari Delicto.—Where one person executes his bond to another to enable him to use it as a means of inducing innocent strangers to buy certain patent rights, the obligor can obtain against the bond no relief in equity, he being in pari delicto with the defendant. Barnett v. Barnett, 83 Va. 504, 2 S. E. 733. See the title MAXIMS.

2. Procedure to Obtain.

As to the manner of application for equitable relief by injunction against judgments, the time, manner, requisites and procedure, see the title INJUNCTIONS, vol. 7, p. 512.

3. Extent of Relief.

Chancery Acts on Parties Not Directly on Judgment.—Chancery can not reverse or set aside a judgment of a law court for error or other cause, and order the law court to grant a new trial; but it can act on the person of the owner of the judgment by injunction against the enforcement of the judgment, and direct a trial by jury, and, upon verdict, either perpetuate or dissolve, in whole or in part, the injunction. Graham v. Citizens' Nat. Bank, 45 W. Va. 701, 32 S. E. 245. See also, Farmers', etc., Warehouse Co. v. Pridemore, 55 W. Va. 451, 463, 47 S. E. 258.

In Wynne v. Newman, 75 Va. 811, a bill was brought to obtain a new trial of an issue in an action at law, in which there was a verdict and judgment for the defendant. At the hearing the court annulled the judgment, set aside the verdict, and ordered a new trial in the action at law. The appellate court, in holding that even if the complainant was entitled to relief, the mode of granting it was improper, said: "A court of chancery, under our system of jurisprudence, is invested with no such power as this. It may act on the parties, but not directly on the judgment, nor on the court which rendered it. Such judgment by a court having jurisdiction to render it, can be vacated only by some direct proceeding at law, either in the court in which the judgment was recovered or some other court having appellate jurisdiction. See 2 Story's Eq. Jurisprudence, § 1571; Graham & Waterman on New Trials, ch. 17, pp. 1482, 1483 and cases cited." See the titles INJUNCTIONS, vol. 7, p. 512; NEW TRIALS.

In strictness, there is no such thing as an injunction to a judgment, because the court of chancery does not act upon the law court, and neither reverses, rescinds nor amends the judgment. It acts upon the party only, restrains him from enforcement by execution, and punishes him as for contempt for any violation of its mandate. Beckley v. Palmer, 11 Gratt. 625.

"The court of chancery acts in personam, and not upon the court of law, which must decide all cases coming before it according to the legal rights of the parties." Nichols v. Campbell, 10 Gratt. 560.

"The tribunal of the court of equity, does not act immediately upon that of the court of law, nor in any manner disrespectful to it; it only acts upon the party, and for good reasons existing in relation to him, restrains him from proceeding further." Ashby v. Kiger, Gilmer 153.

"That the injunction operates upon

the party only, and not upon the court, would seem to be a truism requiring **no** argument to support it." Epes *v.* Dudley, 4 Leigh 145.

"The ordinary jurisdiction of the chancellor is confined to fraud, force and accident; but it is sometimes concurrent with the law, and occasionally affords relief, where the law gives no remedy; or judgment has been obtained from inadvertence or surprise. Heard *v.* Stomford, Cas. T. Talb. 174; Kent *v.* Bridgman, Prec. Ch. 233. Not that it creates a new right in the former case, or exercises appellate jurisdiction in the latter. But, in the first, it merely gives effect to existing rights which the law would enforce, if its forms permitted; and in the second, it prevents the party, who has improperly acquired an unconscionable advantage at law, from making use of it." Foushee *v.* Lea, 4 Call 279.

One County Court May Relieve against Judgment of Another County Court.—The court of one county may on its equity side relieve against a judgment at law, rendered in another county court, by way of original jurisdiction. Although it can not award a new trial in that court, yet it may direct the issue to be tried at its own bar. Ambler *v.* Wyld, 2 Wash. 36.

B. PROHIBITION.

Generally, as to when a writ of prohibition will lie, the nature and effect thereof, procedure, etc., see the title PROHIBITION, WRIT OF.

Lies in Case of Void Judgments.— All judgments in excess, want or abuse of legitimate powers are void and subject to prohibition. Hein *v.* Smith, 13 W. Va. 358; Ensign Mfg. Co. *v.* McGinnis, 30 W. Va. 532, 4 S. E. 782; Brodley *v.* Archibald, 33 W. Va. 229, 10 S. E. 392; Wilkinson *v.* Hoke, 39 W. Va. 403, 19 S. E. 520; Charleston *v.* Beller, 45 W. Va. 44, 30 S. E. 152; Yates *v.* Taylor County Court, 47 W. Va. 376, 35 S. E. 24. Simmons *v.* Thomasson, 50 W. Va.

656, 660, 41 S. E. 335. See the title JUSTICES OF THE PEACE.

The judgment of the court ordering or confirming a donation made out of the county treasury without lawful au thority is void, and will be prohibited. Yates *v.* Taylor County Court, 47 W. Va. 376, 35 S. E. 24, 25.

Prohibition lies to prevent the enforcement of a judgment by default when the persons against whom the same was rendered had no notice of the time and place and were not present at the trial. Simmons *v.* Thomasson, 50 W. Va. 656, 41 S. E. 335.

To proceed to judgment against persons not served with process or in default of any notice is an excess of legitimate powers authorizing the writ of prohibition. But not so if the notice is merely defective. Simmons *v.* Thomasson, 50 W. Va. 656, 659, 41 S. E. 335.

While there is some apparent conflict of authority as to the stage of the cause in the court below at which the application for the writ may be made, as to whether it should be made before or after the decision of the court, the distinction is as to whether the want of jurisdiction in the subordinate court which is relied on as the foundation of the writ, is apparent upon the proceedings sought to be prohibited; and, where this want of jurisdiction is thus apparent upon the record, the superior tribunal may interpose the aid of a prohibition at any stage of the proceedings below, even after verdict, sentence or judgment. Ensign Mfg. Co. *v.* McGinnis, 30 W. Va. 532, 4 S. E. 782, 789.

"In French *v.* Noel, 22 Gratt. 454, it was held, by the court of appeals of Virginia, 'that after the judgment of the circuit court has been rendered, as well as before, the person injured by the judgment may apply to the court of appeals for a writ of prohibition to restrain the appellant and the judge from proceeding to enforce the judgment.' And this court, in Hein *v.* Smith, 13 W. Va. 358, announced the same doctrine." Ensign Mfg. Co. *v.* McGinnis, 30 W. Va. 532, 4 S. E. 782, 790.

M. recovered against C. a judgment for $41 with interest and costs, which for value received he assigned to E. who afterwards became indebted to C., $48.90, who, to recover the same, sued E. before a justice. E. pleaded to C.'s demand said judgment as a set-off. To this plea C. replied that E. had procured said assignment with the fraudulent intent of depriving him of his legal right to exempt $200 of personalty, which right he said he had claimed against M. Upon the trial of the issue on this replication, C. demanded a jury, who found in his favor a verdict for the whole of his demand. On motion of E., this verdict was set aside, and a new trial granted. Upon this new trial, C. again demanded a jury, who found a verdict in favor of E. for $5.79, for which he had judgment, with costs. C. afterwards presented his bill. of complaint to the judge of the circuit court setting up the foregoing facts, but alleging no other grounds for equitable relief; praying that E. might be perpetually enjoined from collecting said judgment of $5.79, and from using said assigned judgment as a set-off against his demand of $48.90, and that he may be compelled to pay to C. his demand of $48.90, and for general relief. E. answered the bill, and pleaded the trial and judgment as res adjudicata; but, upon final hearing, said judge perpetually enjoined E. from collecting said judgment of $5.79, and decreed that E. pay C. the whole amount of his demand, with the costs of his injunction, and also all costs incurred by him in prosecuting his unsuccessful civil suit before the justice. Upon a petition filed by E. alleging the foregoing facts, and praying that a writ of prohibition might issue against C. and the said judge, prohibiting them from proceeding in said

chancery cause, it was held, that the judgment for $5.79, rendered in favor of E. by the justice upon the verdict of the jury, on said new trial, was final and irreversible, and was conclusive between the parties thereto as to all matters involved in that controversy. Held, further, that it is proper, in such case, that a prohibition should be awarded against C. and the said judge, prohibiting them from all further proceedings to enforce the said decree. Held, further, that inasmuch as it is apparent upon the face of the record that under the cicumstances of this case, said judge had no jurisdiction to grant the relief prayed for in said bill of injunction, the prohibition may be awarded as well after as before the rendition of said decree. Ensign Mfg. Co. *v.* McGinnis, 30 W. Va. 532, 4 S. E. 782.

"In Hutson *v.* Lowry, 2 Va. Cas., 42, H. owed L. $80, for which he executed to him four single bills of $20 each, dated the same day, and payable, respectively, in one day, one, two, and three months thereafter. After the last note became payable, L. on the same day brought four several suits against H. upon said single bills for $20 each, and recovered against him four several judgments, and on the same day sued out an execution on each of said judgments, and placed the same in the hands of the constable to be levied, who collected the amounts thereof, and returned the executions satisfied "and money ready to render." The defendant notified the constable not to pay over the money to the plaintiff in the executions, and upon these facts applied to the superior court for a writ of prohibition to prevent the justice from all further proceedings in the cases because he had no jurisdiction, as all the notes constituted but one debt. The questions arising in the case were adjourned to the general court, which decided that although the judgments had been actually rendered, the execution levied, and the money collected and in the hands of the constable, the prohibition will still go, the defendant having given notice to the constable not to pay the money to the plaintiff. 8 Bac. Abr. 224." Ensign Mfg. Co. *v.* McGinnis, 30 W. Va. 532, 4 S. E. 782, 789.

"In Jackson *v.* Maxwell, 5 Rand. 636, J. sued M. before a justice, who rendered judgment against M. for $10, from which he appealed to the county court, where the appeal was dismissed, as improvidently granted. Thereupon he filed his petition in the county court, and upon the facts therein stated obtained from that court a writ of prohibition prohibitiing the justice from enforcing said judgments. J. then filed his petition in the superior court, praying a writ of prohibition to the proceedings of the county court, and the superior court adjourned to the general court the questions arising in the case, which court decided that the county court had not jurisdiction by prohibition in any case; that, when a county court shall exceed its jurisdiction by issuing such writ, the superior court of law may and ought, upon proper application, to award a writ of prohibition to such county court, prohibiting it from further exercise of such jurisdiction or the enforcing any order or judgment made under color thereof." Ensign Mfg. Co. *v.* McGinnis, 30 W. Va. 532, 4 S. E. 782, 789.

Will Not Lie Where Judgment Merely Erroneous.—"The office of the writ of prohibition, we need hardly say, is not the correction of mere errors. The writ lies only to restrain an inferior court from acting in a matter of which it has no jurisdiction, or from exceeding the bounds of its jurisdiction. Hence, if the inferior court has jurisdiction of the subject matter of the controversy, and the parties are before it, or have had notice and an opportunity to be heard, a mistaken exercise of that jurisdiction does not render its judgment void, or justify a resort to the extraordinary remedy by prohibition. Or, as it has been tersely expressed, the writ of prohibition does not lie to prevent a subordinate court from deciding erroneously, or from enforcing an erroneous judgment, in a case in which it has a right to adjudicate. High, Extr. Rem., § 772; Hogan *v.* Guigon, 29 Gratt. 705; Nelms *v.* Vaughan, 84 Va. 696, 5 S. E. 704." Grigg *v.* Dalsheimer, 88 Va. 508, 13 S. E. 993.

As to the distinction between void and erroneous judgments, see post, "Collateral Attack on Judgments or Decrees," IX. And see the title JURISDICTION.

IX. Collateral Attack on Judgments or Decrees.

A. GENERAL RULES AS TO COLLATERAL ATTACK.

Not Open to Such Attack unless Want of Jurisdiction Appears from Face of Record.—Where a court of general jurisdiction acts within the scope of its general powers, its judgments will be presumed to be in accordance with its jurisdiction and can not be collaterally impeached unless the record discloses a want of jurisdiction. Neale *v.* Utz, 75 Va. 480; Pennybacker *v.* Switzer, 75 Va. 671; Wade *v.* Hancock, 76 Va. 620; Johnson *v.* Wagner, 76 Va. 587; Bank *v.* Allen, 76 Va. 200, 202; Woodhouse *v.* Fillbates, 77 Va. 317; Wimbish *v.* Breeden, 77 Va. 324; Panrill *v.* Calloway, 78 Va. 387; Brengle *v.* Richardson, 78 Va. 406; Wilcher *v.* Robertson, 78 Va. 602; Hill *v.* Woodard, 78 Va. 765; Wright *v.* Smith, 81 Va. 777; Perkins *v.* Lane, 82 Va. 59; Ferguson *v.* Teel, 82 Va. 690; Richardson *v.* Seevers, 84 Va. 259, 4 S. E. 712; Blanton *v.* Carroll, 86 Va. 539, 10 S. E. 329; Lawson *v.* Moorman, 85 Va. 880, 9 S. E. 150; Spotts *v.* Com., 85 Va. 531, 8 S. E. 375; Ex parte Marx, 86 Va. 40, 9 S. E. 475; Pugh *v.* McCue, 86 Va. 475, 10 S. E. 715; Shipman *v.* Fletcher, 91 Va. 473, 22 S. E. 458; Harrison *v.* Wallton, 95 Va. 721,

30 S. E. 372; Turnbull *v*. Mann, 99 Va. 41, 37 S. E. 288; Fulkerson *v*. Taylor, 102 Va. 314, 46 S. E. 378; Sargeant *v*. Irving, 2 Va. Dec. 338; Cardoza *v*. Epps, 2 Va. Dec. 133, 137; Rootes *v*. Tompkins, 3 Gratt. 98; Cook *v*. Hays, 9 Gratt. 142; Burbridge *v*. Higgins, 6 Gratt. 119; Beale *v*. Botetourt, 10 Gratt. 278; Robisons *v*. Allen, 11 Gratt. 785; Pates *v*. St. Clair, 11 Gratt. 22; Hutcheson *v*. Priddy, 12 Gratt. 85; Baylor *v*. Dejarnette, 13 Gratt. 152; Andrews *v*. Avory, 14 Gratt 229; Gibson *v*. Beckham, 16 Gratt. 321, 327; Com. *v*. Byrne, 20 Gratt. 165; Howery *v*. Helms, 20 Gratt. 1; Wilson *v*. Smith, 22 Gratt. 493; Cline *v*. Catron, 22 Gratt. 378; Myers *v*. Nelson, 26 Gratt. 729; Shelton *v*. Jones, 26 Gratt. 891; Adams *v*. Logan, 27 Gratt. 201; Lancaster *v*. Wilson, 27 Gratt. 624; Spilman *v*. Johnson, 27 Gratt. 33, 41; Fairfax *v*. Alexandria, 28 Gratt. 16; Pulaski County *v*. Stuart, 28 Gratt. 872, 879; Quesenberry *v*. Barbour, 31 Gratt. 491, 500; Nulton *v*. Isaacs, 30 Gratt. 726, 742; Burnley *v*. Duke, 2 Rob. 102; Fisher *v*. Bassett, 9 Leigh 119; Lemon *v*. Reynolds, 5 Munf. 552; Ford *v*. Gardner, 1 Hen. & M. 72; Edmunds *v*. Venable, 1 Pat. & H. 121; Smith *v*. Henning, 10 W. Va. 596; Davis *v*. Landcraft, 10 W. Va. 718; Ambler *v*. Leach, 15 W. Va. 677; Patton *v*. Merchants' Bank, 12 W. Va. 587; Hall *v*. Hall, 12 W. Va. 1, 13; Ramsberg *v*. Erb, 16 W. Va. 777; Smith *v*. Johnson, 44 W. Va. 278, 29 S. E. 509; Moran *v*. American Fire, etc., Co., 44 W. Va. 42, 28 S. E. 728; Cecil *v*. Clark, 44 W. Va. 659, 30 S. E. 216; Miller *v*. White, 46 W. Va. 67, 33 S. E. 332; St. Lawrence Co. *v*. Holt, 51 W. Va. 370, 41 S. E. 351; Starr *v*. Sampelle, 55 W. Va. 442, 450, 47 S. E. 255; Lee *v*. Smith, 54 W. Va. 98, 46 S. E. 352; McMillan *v*. Hickman, 35 W. Va. 705, 14 S. E. 227; Anderson *v*. Doolittle, 38 W. Va. 629, 18 S. E. 724.

" 'Where the court has jurisdiction of the parties and the subject matter in the particular case, its judgment, unless reversed or annulled in some proper proceeding, is not open to attack or impeachment, by parties or privies, in any collateral action or proceeding whatever.' Black on Judg., § 245." Lee *v*. Smith, 54 W. Va. 98, 46 S. E. 352.

Where the record of a judgment or decree of a court of general jurisdiction is offered in evidence collaterally in another suit, it can not be impeached except for the want of jurisdiction in the court that rendered it. And such inquiry is confined to the question whether such court had jurisdiction of the subject matter of the suit, and can not extend to the question, whether it had jurisdiction in the particular case. Fisher *v*. Bassett, 9 Leigh 119; Cox *v*. Thomas, 9 Gratt. 323, 328. Hall *v*. Hall, 12 W. Va. 1, 3.

In Wandling *v*. Straw, 25 W. Va. 692, syl., pt. 1, it is held, that "the validity of a judgment of a court of record can not be collaterally attacked, on the ground that the court had no jurisdiction, unless the want of jurisdiction appears upon the face of the record." Smith *v*. Johnson, 44 W. Va. 278, 29 S. E. 509, 511.

"The judgment of a court having general jurisdiction, acting within the scope of its authority, is presumed to be right and unimpeachable in a collateral suit or proceeding, unless the want of jurisdiction clearly appears on the face thereof. If such be the case, it is void. Railroad Co. *v*. Ashby's Trustees, 86 Va. 232, 9 S. E. 1003; 1 Freem., Judgm., § 120a. To render such a judgment void for want of service, the record, as a whole, must positively show that the summons was not served on the defendant; in other words, that the return of the officer is so defective as to be invalid. This must affirmatively appear, and not be a question of doubt." Moran *v*. American Fire, etc., Co., 44 W. Va. 42, 28 S. E. 728, 729.

To impeach a judgment where there is nothing in the record to show affirmatively that process was not served, but on the contrary it appears that the cause was matured at rules as to all the defendants, "it being a judgment of a court of general jurisdiction, and the party being within its jurisdictional limits, it is not enough to raise a doubt merely; nor will it suffice that the record fails to show that notice was given, the onus lies upon the party assailing the judgment to show that it is wrong, and it is only when he satisfies the conscience of the court that the judgment is wrong that it should be disturbed, the recognized rule being that every thing must be presumed in favor of the proceedings of a court of general jurisdiction, unless there is a plain excess or want of authority." Ferguson v. Teel, 82 Va. 690, 697, citing Wade v. Hancock, 76 Va. 620; Harman v. Lynchburg, 33 Gratt. 37, 43.

Where a defendant is proceeded against as a person in being and as a nonresident of this state, and an order of publication was accordingly made and regularly executed, its effect is equivalent to an averment on the record that he had in fact been summoned, which averment can not be contradicted in a collateral proceeding. Wilcher v. Robertson, 78 Va. 602.

"If it appears by the record that an attorney appeared for the defendant in a court of general jurisdiction, such appearance gives the court jurisdiction of the person of the defendant; and, if the attorney so appeared without his authority, that fact can not be shown in a defense at law in any action or proceeding upon the judgment, where the same may properly be used as evidence of the right thereby established." Smith v. Johnson, 44 W. Va. 278, 29 S. E. 509, quoting Wandling v. Straw, 25 W. Va. 692.

"When a person seeks to show that an attorney at law was not authorized to appear for him, he is confronted by a legal presumption. It is at the present time the settled rule, that although an attorney can not, without special authority, admit service of jurisdictional process upon his client, yet it will be presumed in all collateral proceedings, and perhaps on appeal or in error, that a regular attorney at law who appeared for a defendant, though not served, had authority to do so. 2 Ency. Pl. & Prac. 682." Smith v. Johnson, 44 W. Va. 278, 29 S. E. 509. See the titles APPEARANCES, vol. 1, p. 667; ATTORNEY AND CLIENT, vol. 2, p. 145.

Whether a judgment be the act of the court, or be entered up by the clerk under the statute, the effect is the same; in either case it is the act of the law, and until reversed by the court which rendered it, or by a superior tribunal, it imports absolute verity, and is as effectual and binding as if pronounced upon a trial on its merits. Neale v. Utz, 75 Va. 480.

Application to Judgments of Courts of Special or Limited Jurisdiction.— When the jurisdiction of a court of special or limited jurisdiction affirmatively appears, the judgment of such a court is as secure from collateral attack as is the judgment of a court of general jurisdiction. Shank v. Ravenswood, 43 W. Va. 242, 27 S. E. 223; Cecil v. Clark, 44 W. Va. 659, 30 S. E. 216; Ex parte Marx, 86 Va. 40, 9 S. E. 475. See the title JURISDICTION.

"It seems settled that, where the facts essential to give jurisdiction to an inferior or special tribunal of limited authority are shown by its record, the same presumption prevails in favor of its jurisdiction as prevails in favor of the jurisdiction of superior courts of general jurisdiction, and the statement of jurisdictional facts can not be denied upon a collateral attack, nor will its plain errors affect it. 12 Am. & Eng. Ency. Law, p. 274; Bigelow Estop. 66; 1 Herm. Estop., Res Jud., 405; Van Fleet, Coll. Attack, 538; Morrow v. Weed, 6 Am. Dec. 122; 1 Black, Judgm., § 287." Shank v. Ravenswood, 43 W. Va. 242, 27 S. E. 223, 224.

Where the jurisdiction of even an inferior court is dependent on a fact which the court is required to ascertain and settle by its decision, such decision is held conclusive; and, furthermore, it has been claimed that this principle is not confined to determinations of a judicial character. Cecil *v.* Clark, 44 W. Va. 659, 30 S. E. 216, 223.

Court of General Jurisdiction Exercising Special Statutory Powers.— Where a court of general jurisdiction acts within the scope of its general powers, its judgments will be presumed to be in accordance with its jurisdiction, and can not be collaterally impeached. So also, when a court of general jurisdiction has conferred upon it special powers by special statute, and such special powers are exercised judicially, that is, according to the course of the common law and proceedings in chancery, such judgment can not be impeached collaterally. Pulaski County *v.* Stuart, 28 Gratt. 872.

Application to Strangers to Judgment.—"While it is true that the plea of res adjudicata can be filed only by the parties to the suit in which the judgment was entered, or their privies, it is equally true that judgments of courts, where they do not undertake to adjudicate the existing rights of persons who are not parties to the suit, can not be questioned in collateral proceedings, but are binding on the courts and on all persons so far as they affect the rights of those who were parties." Turnbull *v.* Mann, 99 Va. 41, 45, 37 S. E. 288.

"In the absence of fraud or collusion, a judgment for money conclusively establishes the relation of debtor and creditor, not only as respects the parties themselves, but all other persons. * * * Unless there is good reason to impute fraud or collusion, a judgment is conclusive of the existence and amount of the debt, and can not be impeached collaterally either by

parties or strangers." Gentry *v.* Allen, 32 Gratt. 254.

"Mr. Freeman, in his work on Judgments, § 335 (3d Ed.), after referring to the right of strangers to impeach a judgment, and the grounds upon which the right is placed, says: 'It must not, however, be understood that all strangers are entitled to impeach a judgment. It is only those strangers who, if the judgment were given full credit and effect, would be prejudiced in regard to some pre-existing right, that are permitted to impeach the judgment.'" Wilcher *v.* Robertson, 78 Va. 602.

As to the right of third persons to impeach collaterally for fraud, see post, "Fraud or Collusion as Ground for Collateral Attack," IX, D.

As to who may impeach a judgment or decree in proceedings for that purpose, see ante, "Opening, Amending, Modifying or Vacating Judgments or Decrees," VII; "Equitable Relief," VIII, A.

Generally, as to the doctrine of res adjudicata, see the title FORMER ADJUDICATION OR RES ADJUDICATA, vol. 6, p. 261.

Presumptions as to Jurisdiction.— For a full treatment of the question of presumptions as to jurisdiction, see the title JURISDICTION.

Effect of Affirmative Findings as to Jurisdictional Facts.—See the title JURISDICTION.

Methods of Direct Attack.—As to proceedings on appeal or in error, see the title APPEAL AND ERROR, vol. 1, p. 418. As to proceedings by bill of review, see the title BILL OF RE-VIEW, vol. 2, p. 383. As to proceedings to open or vacate, see ante, "Opening, Amending, Modifying or Vacating Judgments or Decrees," VII. As to bills for injunction and other equitable relief, see ante, "Equitable Relief," VIII, A.

Proceedings by motion to vacate a judgment, and by bill in equity are both direct and not collateral. Chilhowie Lumber Co. *v.* Lance, 50 W. Va. 636, 41 S. E. 128.

Impeachment in Actions on Foreign Judgments.—As to the right to impeach the jurisdiction of the court in actions on foreign judgments, see the title FOREIGN JUDGMENTS, vol. 6, p. 212.

B. VOID JUDGMENTS.

General Rule.—A void judgment is no judgment at all, but a mere nullity and may be assailed in any court, anywhere, whenever any claim is made or rights asserted under it. Neale *v.* Utz, 75 Va. 480, 484; Wade *v.* Hancock, 76 Va. 620; Fultz *v.* Brightwell, 77 Va. 742; Lavell *v.* McCurdy, 77 Va. 763; Ogden *v.* Davidson, 81 Va. 757; Dillard *v.* Central Virginia, etc., Co., 82 Va. 734, 1 S. E. 124; Seamster *v.* Blackstock, 83 Va. 232, 2 S. E. 36; Blanton *v.* Carroll, 86 Va. 539, 10 S. E. 329; Staunton Perpetual Bldg., etc., Co. *v.* Haden, 92 Va. 201, 23 S. E. 285; Louisville, etc., R. Co. *v.* Taylor, 93 Va. 226, 24 S. E. 1013; Turner *v.* Barraud, 102 Va. 324, 46 S. E. 318; Gray *v.* Stuart, 33 Gratt. 351; Dillard *v.* Thornton, 29 Gratt. 392; Hollins *v.* Patterson, 6 Leigh 457; Ambler *v.* Leach, 15 W. Va. 677; Sturm *v.* Flemming, 22 W. Va. 404; Grinnan *v.* Edwards, 21 W. Va. 347; Haymond *v.* Camden, 22 W. Va. 181; White *v* Foote Lumber Co., 29 W. Va. 385, 1 S. E. 572; Hall *v.* Hall, 30 W. Va. 779, 5 S. E. 260; Fowler *v.* Lewis, 36 W. Va. 112, 14 S. E. 447; Morgan *v.* Ohio River R. Co., 39 W. Va. 17, 19 S. E. 588.

It neither binds nor bars any one, and all proceedings under it are ineffectual to confer title, or afford protection to any one. Neale *v.* Utz, 75 Va. 480, 484.

A decree which is void, not merely erroneous, may be attacked directly by appeal or bill of review, or by collateral attack. Waldron *v.* Harvey, 54 W. Va. 608, 609, 46 S. E. 603.

A void judgment does not bind any one, and no act of ratification can impart vitality to it. Its payment may be resisted by other creditors interested in the fund sought to be subjected, and who would be prejudiced thereby. Staunton Perpetual Bldg., etc., Co. *v.* Haden, 92 Va. 201, 23 S. E. 285.

"In Freeman on Judgments, § 117, it is said: 'A void judgment is in legal effect no judgment. By it no rights are divested. From it no rights are obtained. Being worthless in itself, all proceedings founded upon it are equally worthless. It neither binds nor bars any one. All acts performed under it, and all claims flowing out of it, are void. A purchaser at a sale by virtue of its authority finds himself without title and without redress. If it be null, no action upon the part of the plaintiff, no inaction upon the part of the defendant, no resulting equity in the hands of third persons, can invest it with any of the elements of power or of vitality.'" Staunton Perpetual Bldg., etc., Co. *v.* Haden, 92 Va. 201, 207, 23 S. E. 285.

"The difference between holding that a judgment may be reversed on error or set aside by the court which rendered it, and disregarding it as a nullity while still untouched, is the whole difference between what is absolutely void and what is merely voidable, and involves consequences of too much moment to be lightly disregarded." Hill *v.* Woodard, 78 Va. 765, 769.

If a court does not have jurisdiction, it is a matter of no importance, however correct its proceedings and decisions may be. Its judgments are nullities, and may not only be set aside in the same court, but may be declared void by every court in which they are called in question. To render a judgment or decree binding, the court rendering the same must have jurisdiction both of the parties and the subject matter. Staunton Perpetual Bldg., etc., Co. *v.* Haden, 92 Va. 201, 23 S. E.

285; Blanton v. Carroll, 86 Va. 539, 10 S. E. 329; Greshan v. Ewell, 85 Va. 1, 6 S. E. 700; Richardson v. Seevers, 84 Va. 259, 4 S. E. 712; Anthony v. Kasey, 83 Va. 338, 5 S. E. 176; Dorr v. Rohr, 82 Va. 359; Lemar v. Hale, 79 Va. 147; Wilcher v. Robertson, 78 Va. 602; Johnson v. Anderson, 76 Va. 766; Withers v. Fuller, 30 Gratt. 547; Underwood v. McVeigh, 23 Gratt. 409, 418; Cox v. Thomas, 9 Gratt. 322, 326; Hickam v. Larkey, 6 Gratt. 211, 212; Hopkirk v. Bridges, 4 Hen. & M. 413; Kyles v. Ford, 2 Rand. 1; Wynn v. Wyatt, 11 Leigh 584; Wilson v. Bank, 6 Leigh 570, 574; Ex parte Barker, 2 Leigh 719; St. Lawrence Co. v. Holt, 51 W. Va. 370, 41 S. E. 351, 357; Hoback v. Miller, 44 W. Va. 635, 29 W. Va. 1014; Hartigan v. Board, 49 W. Va. 14, 38 S. E. 698; Mayer v. Adams, 27 W. Va. 244; Chapman v. Maitland, 22 W. Va. 329; Capehart v. Cunningham, 12 W. Va. 750; Camden v. Haymond, 9 W. Va. 680; Houston v. McCluney, 8 W. Va. 135; and cases cited ante, under, "General Rule," IX, B. See ante, "Jurisdiction," III, C. And see also, the title JURISDICTION.

"All proceedings of a court which has no jurisdiction of the subject matter on which it undertakes to act are void * * *. Such proceedings are absolutely void. The want of legal authority can not be supplied. No assent of parties in such a case can confer any jurisdiction. They are in the words of our definition wholly void, without force or effect, as to all persons and for all purposes, and are incapable of being, or being made, otherwise." Ambler v. Leach, 15 W. Va. 677, 683.

Though the court has jurisdiction of the subject matter and the parties, yet it is limited in its mode of procedure and the extent and the character of its judgment; and if it transcend such limits, its judgments are void and may be so treated collaterally. Anthony v. Kasey, 83 Va. 338, 5 S. E. 176.

A judgment on a writ of scire facias

for money, and not merely for award of execution, is in excess of the jurisdiction of the court, and is absolutely void, and may be so declared either in a direct or a collateral proceeding. Lavell v. McCurdy, 77 Va. 763.

A judgment rendered without service of process is void, and may be collaterally attacked. Lavell v. McCurdy, 77 Va. 763, 771, citing Kyles v. Ford, 2 Rand. 1; Hickam v. Larkey, 6 Gratt. 211, 212; Underwood v. McVeigh, 23 Gratt. 409, 418; Gray v. Stuart, 33 Gratt. 351, 358; Wade v. Hancock, 76 Va. 620. See the title SERVICE OF PROCESS.

In 1859, suit in A. county, in names of widow and heirs of P. B., all of whom, during the war, were outside confederate lines, and nonresidents, to sell house and lot descended upon them. Sale in 1860 to R. B. confirmed. F., administrator of P. B., as commissioner, collected nearly the entire purchase money in gold, or its equivalent. Under decree of 10th of June, 1863, in that suit, to which he was no party, and which involved no settlement of his accounts and indebtedness, without notice to widow and heirs, F. deposited the amount of the purchase money in confederate currency with the general receiver of the court. In 1873, widow and heirs filed bill, treated as ancillary to original suit, and as petition to rehear decrees therein, to hold F. and the property liable for the purchase money, which bill the circuit court sustained. On appeal by F., held, that decree, entered without notice to those interested in the fund, and in a cause wherein the administrator was no party, was a void decree, and may be so treated collaterally. Fultz v. Brightwell, 77 Va. 742, Lacy, J., dissenting.

A judgment or decree, pronounced in an action at law or suit in equity instituted during the late civil war by a plaintiff residing within the union lines, in a court within said lines, against parties residing within the confederate lines and in the confederate military service, without any appearance by, or notice to such parties other than an order of publication published within the union lines, is absolutely void and may be so treated in the same or any subsequent collateral suit or proceeding. The doctrine of the cases of Grinnan v. Edwards, 21 W. Va. 347, and Haymond v. Camden, 22 W. Va. 181, 208, approved. Sturm v. Fleming, 22 W. Va. 404.

A personal judgment for money against a nonresident, on publication, without service of process or appearance, is void, is no lien on land, and may be attacked collaterally. Fowler v. Lewis, 36 W. Va. 112, 14 S. E. 447.

"Even if there be attachment of effects of nonresidents, a personal judgment on publication, without service of process or appearance, is a nullity, except as to effects attached. O'Brien v. Stephens, 11 Gratt. 610; Black, Judgm., § 231; Cooper v. Reynolds, 10 Wall. 318; Coleman v. Waters, 13 W. Va. 278; Gilchrist v. West Virginia Oil, etc., Co., 21 W. Va. 115." Fowler v. Lewis, 36 W. Va. 112, 14 S. E. 447, 451.

When the record shows in any court, whether superior or inferior, that the court has proceeded without notice, and without any sufficient excuse or reason for the want of notice, any presumption in its favor is at an end, and it may not only be reversed as erroneous, but be impeached and set aside collaterally as void. Richardson v. Seevers, 84 Va. 259, 267, 4 S. E. 712.

No presumption exists in favor of the validity of judgments even of courts of general jurisdiction, where want of jurisdiction affirmatively appears on the face of the proceedings. Want of jurisdiction makes such judgments null; and they may be so treated by any court in any proceeding, direct or collateral. Wade v. Hancock, 76 Va. 620; Dillard v. Central Virginia Iron Co., 82 Va. 734, 1 S. E. 124. See the title JURISDICTION.

C. ERRONEOUS OR IRREGULAR JUDGMENTS.

1. General Rule.

Judgment Merely Erroneous Not Subject to Collateral Attack.—In order that a judgment or decree may be subject to collateral attack, it must be void and not merely erroneous. Pates v. St. Clair, 11 Gratt. 22.

Objections to a decree which merely show that it is erroneous, but fall short of showing that it is void, can not be made in a collateral proceeding. Lemmon v. Herbert, 92 Va. 653, 24 S. E. 249.

The judgment of a court possessing competent jurisdiction in the proceeding before it and over the person against whom it is rendered, is binding and conclusive; and however irregular or erroneous it may be, yet so long as it remains unreversed, it can not be drawn in question in a collateral proceeding; nor can any allegation be made against its validity. Rhea v. Shields, 103 Va. 305, 49 S. E. 70; Fulkerson v. Taylor, 102 Va. 314, 46. S E. 378; Robinett v. Mitchell, 101 Va. 762, 45 S. E. 287; Chesapeake, etc., R. Co. v. Washington, etc., R. Co., 99 Va. 715, 40 S. E. 20; Lemmon v. Herbert, 92 Va. 653, 24 S. E. 249; Dorr v. Rohr, 82 Va. 359, 365; Fox v. Cottage, etc., Ass'n, 81 Va. 677; Neale v. Utz, 75 Va. 480; Terry v. Dickinson, 75 Va. 475; Withers v. Fuller, 30 Gratt. 547; Shelton v. Jones, 26 Gratt. 891; Durrett v. Davis, 24 Gratt. 302; Cline v. Catron, 22 Gratt. 378, 321; Gibson v. Beckham, 16 Gratt. 321, 334; Andrews v. Avory, 14 Gratt. 229; Hitchcox v. Rawson, 14 Gratt. 526; Baylor v. Dejarnette, 13 Gratt. 152; Franklin v. Depriest, 13 Gratt. 257; Pates v. St. Clair, 11 Gratt. 22; Cook v. Hays, 9 Gratt. 142; Rootes v. Tompkins, 3 Gratt. 98; First Nat. Bank v. Hyer, 46 W. Va. 13, 32 S. E. 1000; Findley v. Findley, 42 W. Va. 372, 26 S. E. 433; St. Lawrence, etc., Co. v. Holt, 51 W. Va. 370, 41 S. E. 351; Northwestern Bank v. Hays, 37 W. Va. 475, 16 S. E. 561; McMillan v. Hickman, 35 W. Va. 705, 14 S. E. 227; Gilmer v. Baker, 24 W. Va. 72, 89; Poe v. Machine Works, 24 W. Va. 517; Smith v. Henning, 10 W. Va. 596. See the title JURISDICTION.

Irregularities which do not render a judgment void, do not furnish ground for assailing such judgment in any collateral proceeding, although they may furnish ground for reversal by proper proceedings taken in due season in the court which rendered the judgment. Terry v. Dickinson, 75 Va. 475; Neale v. Utz, 75 Va. 480.

A voidable judgment, until set aside in a proper proceeding for that purpose, possesses all the attributes of a valid judgment. Robinett v. Mitchell, 101 Va. 762, 766, 45 S. E. 287.

"As was said in Lancaster v. Wilson, 27 Gratt. 624, 629, with respect to collateral attack on judgments: 'It is not merely an arbitrary rule of law, established by the courts, but it is a doctrine founded upon reason and the soundest principles of public policy. It is one which has been adopted in the interest of the peace of society, and the permanent security of titles.' Hooe v. Barber, 4 Hen. & M. 439; Evans v. Spurgin, 6 Gratt. 107, 52 Am. Dec. 105; Neale v. Utz, 75 Va. 480; Wilcher v. Robertson, 78 Va. 602." Robinett v. Mitchell, 101 Va. 762, 765, 45 S. E. 287.

"The decree being the adjudication of the tribunal having jurisdiction of the subject matter and of the parties can never be collaterally impeached for any defect, irregularity or error in the proceedings, however manifest or palpable it may be. In such case the question of jurisdiction enters into and becomes an essential part of the judgment of the court. This principle has again and again been affirmed by this court. The cases of Fisher v. Bassett, 9 Leigh 119; Cook v. Hays, 9 Gratt. 142; Andrews v. Avory, 14 Gratt. 229; and Gibson v. Beckham, 16 Gratt. 321; are familiar illustrations. It is unnecessary to consume time in quoting

from these decisions, as they are well understood by the profession. In Gibson v. Beckham, Judge Allen entered into an exhaustive discussion of this whole doctrine, and a critical examination of all the authorities. The rule as laid down in that case is, that where a court has cognizance of the subject matter, its judgment, though it may be erroneous, is not void; it is binding until set aside or reversed, and can not be questioned incidentally; acts done and bonds taken under it bind the obligors and sureties as well as principals." Shelton v. Jones, 26 Gratt. 891.

"If the court has cognizance of the cause, advantage can not be taken of an erroneous judgment collaterally; for although the error be apparent, the judgment remains in force until reversed. Drury's Case, 8 Coke 141b; Tarlton v. Fisher, Doug. R. 671. The only question, then would seem to be whether the subject matter was within the jurisdiction of the court; if it was if the jurisdiction of the court extended over that class of cases, it was the province of the court to determine for itself whether the particular case was one within its jurisdiction." Cox v. Thomas, 9 Gratt. 323.

"There is a manifest distinction * * * between an erroneous judgment and a void judgment. The first is a valid judgment though erroneous, until reversed, provided it is the judgment of a court of competent jurisdiction. The latter is no judgment at all. It is a mere nullity.. The first can not be assailed in any other court but an appellate court. The latter may be assailed in any court, anywhere, whenever any claim is made, or rights asserted under it." Gray v. Stuart, 33 Gratt. 351.

The mere fact that the court erred in deciding that a case is within the jurisdiction of a court of equity renders a decree merely erroneous and not void; therefore, it is not open to collateral attack. Lemmon v. Herbert, 92 Va. 653, 24 S. E. 249, citing Fisher v.

Bassett, 9 Leigh 119; Cox *v.* Thomas, 9 Gratt. 323; Gibson *v.* Beckham, 16 Gratt. 321.

Vanfleet on Col. Attack, § 1, says: "And as no one would think of holding a judgment of the court of last resort void if its jurisdiction were debatable or even colorable, the same rule must be applied to the judgments of all judicial tribunals. This is the true theory of judicial action when viewed collaterally. If any jurisdictional question is debatable or colorable, the tribunal must decide it; and an erroneous conclusion can only be corrected by some proceeding provided by law for so doing, commonly called a direct attack." These considerations, and authorities lead to the conclusion that in a case in which it is questionable or debatable whether a court has jurisdiction, and it erroneously decides that it does have its judgment or degree, is erroneous and voidable only, and subject to correction only by proper proceedings in the court which rendered it or by an appellate court, and is not void or open to collateral attack. St. Lawrence Co. *v.* Holt, 51 W. Va. 370, 371, 41 S. E. 351.

When jurisdiction is acquired in a particular case by statute, if the court fails to comply with the details of the statute in hearing the cause, the error may be reviewed upon appeal, but is no ground for collateral attack. Wimbish *v.* Breeden, 77 Va. 324.

Bonds taken in judicial proceedings bind obligors if the court have jurisdiction, though its action be erroneous, but not void. The action of the court can not be incidentally questioned by impeaching the bonds. Findley *v.* Findley, 42 W. Va. 372, 26 S. E. 433.

An execution issued in contravention of the agreement of the parties is not void, but voidable. Until avoided it is a valid execution, and can not be assailed by plea or proof in a chancery suit to enforce the judgment on which it issued. The chancery suit is a col-

lateral suit. Fulkerson *v.* Taylor, 102 Va. 314, 46 S. E. 378.

The seizure of the property of the defendant under the proper process of the court, is generally the foundation of the court's jurisdiction in proceedings in rem, and defective or irregular affidavits, though they might reverse a judgment or decree in such case for error, in departing from the directions of the statute, do not render such a judgment or decree, or the subsequent proceedings void. Hall *v.* Hall, 12 W. Va. 1.

Where there is no service of process or appearance, and the seizure of property of defendant is the foundation of jurisdiction, defective or irregular affidavits for attachment, though they might reverse a judgment in the case for error in departing from the statute, do not make the suit one without jurisdiction, if the court have jurisdiction in cases of that class. A total want of affidavit for attachment in such case would show there was no jurisdiction, but a mere insufficient averment in the affidavit would not. Cooper *v.* Reynolds, 10 Wall. 309. Miller *v.* White, 46 W. Va. 67, 33 S. E. 332.

2. Application of Rule to Judgment of Various Tribunals.

Generally, as to the nature and extent of the jurisdiction of the various courts, presumptions in favor of their jurisdiction, etc., see the title JURISDICTION.

The circuit court is a court of general jurisdiction, taking cognizance of all actions at law between individuals, with authority to pronounce judgments and to issue executions for their enforcement. Where its jurisdiction is questioned it must decide the question itself. And whenever the subject matter is a controversy at law between individuals, the jurisdiction is presumed from the fact that it has pronounced the judgment; and the correctness of such judgment can be inquired into only by some appellate tribunal. Cox *v.* Thomas, 9 Gratt. 323; Ballard *v.* Thomas, 19 Gratt. 14.

A judgment of a circuit court upon a notice and motion, in favor of creditor against a high sheriff or his administratrix, for the default of his deputy in not paying over money collected on an execution which issued from the county court, is conclusive of the jurisdiction of the court, unless reversed on appeal; and its validity can not be called in question by the deputy or his sureties, on a motion by the high sheriff or his administratrix against them, founded on said judgment. Cox *v.* Thomas, 9 Gratt. 323.

In such a case if it does not certainly appear that the proceeding by the creditor against the high sheriff commenced in the circuit court, the court in favor of the judgment, will presume that such proceeding was commenced in the county court and removed to circuit court, or had been retained in the circuit court after a reversal of the judgment of the county court; and it is for the deputy and his sureties to produce the whole record to repel the presumption. Cox *v.* Thomas, 9 Gratt. 323.

A circuit court acting in proceeding by a commissioner of school lands to sell forfeited land under chapter 134, acts, 1872-73, though the proceeding be in nature administrative, not judicial, is yet, so far as its jurisdiction is concerned, to be regarded as a court of general jurisdiction, and in a collateral proceeding no proof of the existence of facts essential to jurisdiction is required, nor can the same be received to disprove their existence. It is presumed that the court ascertained those facts giving it jurisdiction to exist. Cecil *v.* Clark, 44 W. Va. 659, 30 S. E. 216.

"It is none the less a court of general jurisdiction as to its procedure because the general nature of its function in the case was administrative because of the matter on which it acted. Notwithstanding the character of the sub-

ject matter before it, the court had to ascertain whether the fact giving jurisdiction existed; and, being a court of general jurisdiction, if it is not stated on its record that such facts exists, it would be presumed that it had been established to its satisfaction. But I find the order does state it, and the principle then comes in that, 'when the record of an inferior court (even if it were such) does show affirmatively the jurisdictional fact, it is conclusive.' 1 Black., Judgm., 287; 12 Am. & Eng. Law, 274; Bigelow, Estop. 66." Cecil *v.* Clark, 44 W. Va. 659, 30 S. E. 216, 223.

County courts, with respect to purely judicial powers, are courts of general jurisdiction, and their judgments are presumed to be right; therefore they can not be collaterally attacked, however erroneous they may be. Chesapeake, etc., R. Co. *v.* Washington, etc., R. Co., 99 Va. 715, 40 S. E. 20; Shelton *v.* Jones, 26 Gratt. 891.

In a collateral attack upon a condemnation proceeding before a county court it is not necessary to the validity of its judgment that it should appear on the face of the proceedings how the defendant was notified. It is sufficient that it appears that the defendant was duly notified. Chesapeake, etc., R. Co. *v.* Washington, etc., R. Co., 99 Va. 715, 40 S. E. 20.

The county court which lays the county levy is not a special tribunal erected for that special purpose. It is the ordinary county court; and that court is a court of general jurisdiction. Therefore, though the record does not show that the justices had been summoned for the purpose, or a majority were present, the act of the court in laying the levy can not be questioned in any collateral proceeding. Ballard *v.* Thomas, 19 Gratt. 14.

A county court having laid the county levy, and directed the sheriff to pay certain claims upon the county out of it, and the sheriff having received the commissioner's book and proceeded to collect the levy as far as it could be collected, and returned a list of insolvents; upon a motion by one of the creditors of the county, whose claim was directed to be paid out of the levy, against the sheriff and his sureties to recover the amount, it is not competent for the defendants to object that the county court was not legally constituted to be authorized to lay the levy when it was done; nor can they object that the commissioner's book was irregularly made out and not properly authenticated. Cook v. Hays, 9 Gratt. 142.

It is well settled, that the county court is a court of general jurisdiction in regard to probates and the grant of administrations; that it has jurisdiction in regard to the whole subject matter; and that though it may err in taking jurisdiction of a particular case, yet the order is generally not void, but only voidable on citation or appeal, and cannot be questioned in any collateral proceeding. Fisher v. Bassett, 9 Leigh 119; Burnley v. Duke, 2 Rob. 102; Schultz v. Schultz, 10 Gratt. 358; Cox v. Thomas, 9 Gratt. 323; Hutcheson v. Priddy, 12 Gratt. 85; Andrews v. Avory, 14 Gratt. 229.

In Ballow v. Hudson, 13 Gratt. 672, 681, the court said: "The cases in this court in regard to grants of administration, although not bearing directly upon the question here, yet seem to illustrate the general principle that the judgment of a court of general jurisdiction over the subject is conclusive until it is avoided, or expires by its own limitation; and this although the facts of the particular case were not such as to give the court jurisdiction over that case. Fisher v. Bassett, 9 Leigh 119; Burnley v. Duke, 2 Rob. 102."

If the county court commits an estate to the sheriff for administration, before the expiration of three months from the death of the testator or intestate, the act is not void but voidable. In such a case the county court, hav-ing general jurisdiction to grant administration, the act of the court in committing the estate to the sheriff can not be questioned in any collateral proceeding. Hutcheson v. Priddy, 12 Gratt. 85.

"The jurisdiction of a county court upon this subject is a general jurisdiction conferred by the statute to grant probate of wills, and to hear and determine suits and controversies testamentary and concerning administrations. Code, ch. 122, § 23, p. 519; ch. 130, § 4, p. 541. It is a court of record, and its judgments or sentences can not be questioned collaterally, if it have jurisdiction of cases ejusdem generis. Where it has jurisdiction over that class of cases, whether the court erred or not in determining that the facts were proved upon which the power to grant administration in the particular case depended, is not to be inquired into collaterally. It must be supposed to have been inquired into and decided upon those facts at the time of making its order, and its decision if erroneous would be voidable only and not void. Accordingly under the influence of these considerations, it has been held in this court that a grant of administration by the court of a county not authorized by the facts of the case to make such grant (the decedent having had no residence, and having left no estate of any kind in the county by the court of which the grant was made), was not void but voidable only; overruling previous decisions of the general court to the contrary in Barker's Case, 2 Leigh 719; and Case of Robinson's Estate, November term, 1828, cited in Barker's Case. Fisher v. Bassett, 9 Leigh 119; Burnley v. Duke, 2 Rob. 102. See also, Schultz v. Schultz, 10 Gratt. 358, 377; Cox v. Thomas, 9 Gratt. 323." Hutcheson v. Priddy, 12 Gratt. 85.

Court of Probate.—"It is well settled by the decisions of this court, that the sentence of a court of probate, of competent jurisdiction, admitting a will or writing in nature of a will, to probate, is conclusive evidence of the due making thereof, and that it can not be denied in any collateral proceeding touching the will; that its validity can be tested only by resorting to the means provided by law for that specific purpose. See West *v.* West, 3 Rand. 373; Vaughn *v.* Doe, 1 Leigh 287; Wills *v.* Spraggins, 3 Gratt. 555; Parker *v.* Brown, 6 Gratt. 554." Robisons *v.* Allen, 11 Gratt. 785.

The judgment of a justice of the peace, whose jurisdiction of the case appears, is as secure from collateral attack as is the judgment of a court of general jurisdiction. The only difference is that in respect to the former, the jurisdiction must affirmatively appear, whereas in the latter case jurisdiction is presumed. Ex parte Marx, 86 Va. 40, 9 S. E. 475.

"The law is well settled that a conviction by a magistrate, who has jurisdiction over the subject matter, is conclusive evidence of the facts stated in it when collaterally assailed." Ex parte Marx, 86 Va. 40, 45, 9 S. E. 475.

The judgment of a justice can not be attacked collaterally for mere amendable clerical omissions not in any wise invalidating the judgment, or rendering it uncertain as to time, parties, or the amount thereof. Fishburne *v.* Baldwin, 46 W. Va. 19, 32 S. E. 1007; Newlon *v.* Wade, 43 W. Va. 283, 286, 27 S. E. 244.

A judgment of a justice founded on a sufficient summons can not be collaterally attacked in equity on the ground alone that the cause of action arose in another county, the place of the defendant's residence. Such question is purely legal, and does not give equity jurisdiction to review such judgment. Newlon *v.* Wade, 43 W. Va. 283, 27 S. E. 244.

While a writ of prohibition will be awarded to prevent a justice of the peace from taking jurisdiction of a debt in excess of one hundred dollars which has been split up into notes, each less than one hundred dollars, all of which are due, and for which separate warrants are being prosecuted before him, yet where such warrants have proceeded to judgment before the justice, with the consent or acquiescence of the defendant, such judgments can not be thereafter collaterally assailed by third persons. This result does not in any degree impinge upon the maxim that consent can not give jurisdiction, as the justice had jurisdiction over the amount represented in each judgment. Adams *v.* Jennings, 103 Va. 579, 49 S. E. 982.

Authority of Commissioners to Appoint an Assistant.—A commissioner of the revenue under § 7 of the act of 1867, in relation to the assessment of taxes on licenses, appoints an assistant commissioner, and the appointment is approved by the proper court. The question whether the facts existed which authorized the commissioner to appoint an assistant, can not be made in a collateral proceeding. Com. *v.* Byrne, 20 Gratt. 165.

"Whether the facts necessary to authorize the appointment of an assistant commissioner existed in this case, was a question for the county court of Henrico to determine. That court accordingly determined that they did exist, by appointing John A. Eacho assistant commissioner, who qualified as such according to law; which appointment was made on the motion of Sidney W. Blankinship, the commissioner. And that determination is conclusive of the question, being a judgment of a court of competent jurisdiction, upon a subject matter within such jurisdiction." Com. *v.* Byrne, 20 Gratt. 165.

Proceedings of town council to annex territory can not be collaterally attacked. Shank *v.* Ravenswood, 43 W. Va. 242, 27 S. E. 223.

3. Application of Rule to Particular Judgments.

Default Judgments.—The principles which uphold the jurisdiction of the courts in all this class of cases is not at all affected by the fact that the judgment is by default. For whether the judgment be the act of the court, or be entered up by the clerk under the statute, the effect is the same. In either case it is the act of the law, and until reversed by the court which rendered it or by a superior tribunal, it imports absolute verity, and is as effectual and binding as if pronounced upon a trial upon the merits. Freeman, §§ 330-1, 487-541. Neale *v.* Utz, 75 Va. 480, 487.

Judgments for or against Deceased Party.—While the decisions are irreconc...bly in conflict as to the effect of a judgment rendered for or against a party after his death, the decided weight of authority seems to be that where a court of general jurisdiction renders such judgment, it is not for that reason void. The judgment, though erroneous and voidable, if assailed in a direct proceeding for that purpose, is effective unless and until set aside, and may not be collaterally attacked. That is the settled doctrine of this court, and a different rule would lead to great inconvenience and mischief. Robinett *v.* Mitchell, 101 Va. 762, 765, 45 S. E. 287. See ante, "Judgments for or against Deceased Persons," III, D, 4.

A judgment against one insane at the time it is rendered is not void, and can not be collaterally attacked, and, not being void, is a lien on land. Freem., Judgm., § 152; 1 Black, Judgm., § 205; Vanfleet, Collat. Attack, § 616; Watt *v.* Brookover, 35 W. Va. 323, 13 S. E. 1007, and citations; 11 Amer. & Eng. Ency. Law, 127; 12 Amer. & Eng. Ency. Law, 90, note 4; Busw. Insan., § 124; authorities cited in opinion and syllabus in Sternbergh *v.* Schoolcraft, 2 Barb. 153; Allison *v.* Taylor, 32 Amer. Dec. 68; Wood *v.* Bayard, 63 Pa. St. 320; Foster *v.* Jones, 23 Ga. 168. Withrow *v.* Smithson, 37 W. Va. 757, 17 S. E. 316.

Where there has been an appointment of a committee of a lunatic by a court having jurisdiction of the subject, the regularity of the appointment can not be inquired into by any other court (except by appeal). Edmunds *v.* Venable, 1 Pat. & H. 121.

A decree in a suit in equity by a committee of a lunatic against the sureties of a former committee, is evidence in a suit by the sureties who have satisfied the decree, against a purchaser from the first committee of bonds belonging to the estate of the lunatic, to show that they have been required to answer for the default of the first committee, and in such collateral proceeding the propriety of the decree can not be inquired into. Edmunds *v.* Venable, 1 Pat. & H. 121.

Purchase by Committee of Idiots' Lands—Decree Valid until Reversed. —A bill is filed by a committee of two idiots, for the sale of the land, and there is a decree for the sale, and a sale; and the report of the marshal of the court shows that the land was purchased by the committee. This report is confirmed, and the marshal is directed to convey the land to such committee; which is done. The committee afterwards sells and conveys this land to a third person, who sues to recover the land. Though the decree confirming the sale to the committee was erroneous, and such committee is forbid by the statute to purchase or own the land during the incompetency of the idiots, yet the decree is not void but voidable, and can not be impeached collaterally, and until it is reversed, must be held to be valid, and as passing a good title to the committee. Cline *v.* Catron, 22 Gratt. 378, 379.

Appointment of Guardian by Chancery Court.—"If the chancery courts have no power to appoint guardians in the first instance, but only to remove and appoint, it would seem to be clear where they have appointed, the validity of that appointment can not be questioned in a collateral proceeding. No other court, unless it be an appellate tribunal, is authorized to examine the records to ascertain whether the occasion was one for the proper exercise of the power in question. They are courts of general jurisdiction and their decrees and orders are conclusive until reversed by a proper proceeding. This principle has received the sanction of the courts in innumerable instances." Durrett v. Davis, 24 Gratt. 302.

A decree approving the action of a receiver of the court in a case where the court had jurisdiction of the subject matter and of the parties can not be attacked in a collateral proceeding, but must remain in force until reversed on appeal, or by proper proceedings in that case. Turnbull v. Mann, 99 Va. 41, 37 S. E. 288, citing Pennybacker v. Switzer, 75 Va. 671; Harrison v. Wallton, 95 Va. 721, 30 S. E. 372.

A commissioner's deed of real estate, and the decrees of courts of competent jurisdiction under which the deed was made, are always admissible in an action of ejectment against a stranger to the suit, and can not be attacked because of irregularities or error in the cause in which they are made. Turnbull v. Mann, 99 Va. 41, 37 S. E. 288.

Where there is a valid attachment and levy of the same, a decree of a court of competent jurisdiction, an order or decree of sale, and a sale by a commissioner appointed by the court, and confirmation thereof, with directions to the commissioner to make a deed to the purchaser, and commissioner's deed made to the purchaser, or his assignee by deed, the proceeding can not be held void when introduced collaterally in another suit; nor can such deed of the commissioner be held void in such other suit, because not made to the purchaser, but, to his assignee by deed, in which the said commissioner was directed by the purchaser to make the deed for the realty to such assignee, if the execution and delivery of such deed of assignment of the purchaser be properly proved,

when such deed of the commissioner to such assignee is offered in evidence at the trial, in connection with a copy of the proceedings had in the chancery cause, in which said realty was decreed to be sold, sale made and confirmed, etc. In such case, said deed of the commissioner to such assignee should be admitted as evidence tending to show title in such assignee. Hall v. Hall, 12 W. Va. 1.

A decree in favor of legatees against an executor and his sureties, in a proper suit for that purpose, is conclusive as to the amount decreed, and also that the claim of the legatees is not barred by the statute of limitations. Such a decree so long as it remains unreversed, is binding on all of the parties to the suit in which it was rendered, and can not be collaterally assailed. Smith v. Moore, 102 Va. 260, 46 S. E. 326, citing Franklin v. Depriest, 13 Gratt. 257; Crawford v. Turk, 24 Gratt. 176; Supervisors v. Dunn, 27 Gratt. 608; Carr v. Meade, 77 Va. 142.

If a decree in chancery erroneously authorizes execution to issue on the foot of the decree, this is error, which may be corrected by an appeal or other direct proceeding, but the decree can not be attacked in a collateral proceeding. Northwestern Bank v. Hays, 37 W. Va. 475, 16 S. E. 561.

A decree in a cause for the sale of land, where there is no error apparent on its face and no exception taken to it, can not be attacked collaterally. Myers v. Nelson, 26 Gratt. 729.

F. conveys land to Q. in trust for J., the daughter of F. and wife of Q., for her life, and then to her children. Afterwards J. and her children, who are infants under fourteen years of age, by their next friend, filed their bill against Q., the trustee, for the sale of the land, and there is a decree for the sale, and a sale made more than six months after the decree, and this sale is confirmed, and a conveyance to the purchaser. In an action of ejectment by the children of J., after her death, to recover the land from a vendee of the purchaser; held, the court having had jurisdiction of the case under the statute, the validity and propriety of the decree for the sale of the land can not be questioned in a collateral proceeding. Quesenberry v. Barbour, 31 Gratt. 491.

"The subject was undoubtedly within the jurisdiction of the court which rendered the decree. It was the sale of a trust estate; and one, too, in which infants were interested; in each of which cases the statute law existing at the time of the rendition of the decree authorized the court to make the same. The judgment or decree of a court of competent jurisdiction over the subject matter thereof is conclusive against the parties thereto until it is set aside or reversed by some proceeding in the case in the same or an appellate court. It can not be set aside or annulled in any collateral proceeding. The authorities on this subject are very numerous, and many of them are cited in the pointed argument of the learned counsel for the defendant in error in this case. The following are cited from the decisions of this court: Fisher v. Bassett, 9 Leigh 119; Ballard v. Thomas, 19 Gratt. 14; Devaughn v. Devaughn, 19 Gratt. 556; and Durrett v. Davis, 24 Gratt. 302." Quesenberry v. Barbour, 31 Gratt. 491.

Decree Confirming Sale.—A sale made pending the suit by agreement of the parties, in person or by counsel, which sale is afterwards approved and confirmed by the court, is as valid as if made under a previous decree of the court in the suit, and can no more be impeached collaterally than if so made. Wilson v. Smith, 22 Gratt. 493.

Reservation in Decree.—In a suit to sell land for the purchase money, on which there is a sawmill that is part of the freehold, and the decree to sell provides that the sale shall not include the mill, a sale of the land does not pass the mill to the purchaser. Though there is nothing in the record

to warrant the reservation, it is not void, but voidable only by appeal, and can not be collaterally assailed. First Nat. Bank v. Hyer, 46 W. Va. 13, 32 S. E. 1000.

Where the right of eminent domain has been exercised in behalf of a rail-road company, and the land has been condemned, damages assessed and paid, and the company placed in possession of such land, the title thereby acquired, in so far as it is without reservation, becomes adverse to all other claimants of the property so condemned. Nor can such proceedings be collaterally attacked, except for fraud. Kanawha, etc., R. Co. v. Glen Jean, etc., R. Co., 45 W. Va. 119, 30 S. E. 86.

As one railroad company may under some circumstances condemn the land of another for its purpose, the right to so condemn is determined by the adjudication in the condemnation proceedings, and such determination can not be collaterally attacked. The judgment in the condemnation proceedings concludes all questions that could have been therein raised or determined. Chesapeake, etc., R. Co. v. Washington, etc., R. Co., 99 Va. 715, 716, 40 S. E. 20.

An award of execution on a forfeited forthcoming bond can not successfully be objected to on account of the invalidity of the original judgment, unless such judgment is null and void. Pates v. St. Clair, 11 Gratt. 22.

A decree in personam against an absent debtor, is entitled to all the respect to which any other decree is entitled, in all collateral controversies. So that if property is sold under an execution issued thereon, the title to said property can not be impeached by objections to the form or merits of the decree. Rootes v. Tompkins, 3 Gratt. 98.

In a suit in the nature of a foreign attachment, the subpoena is served upon the absent defendant, and there is a personal decree against him in favor of the plaintiff, for the amount of the debt. In another suit brought by the plaintiff to obtain satisfaction of this decree, the validity of the decree in the first suit can not be questioned. Burbridge v. Higgins, 6 Gratt. 119.

D. FRAUD OR COLLUSION AS GROUND FOR COLLATERAL ATTACK.

There is apparently an irreconcilable conflict both in the Virginia and West Virginia decisions as to collateral attack upon judgments on the ground of fraud or collusion, and no attempt has been made in this section to do more than set out the cases upon this point.

A judgment of a court of record can not be impeached in another action, except for want of jurisdiction in the court, or fraud in the parties or actors in it. Lancaster v. Wilson, 27 Gratt. 624; McMillan v. Hickman, 35 W. Va. 705, 14 S. E. 227, 231.

Want of jurisdiction or fraud in procurement of a judgment may be shown in any collateral proceeding. Gray v. Stuart, 33 Gratt. 351, 358; Underwood v. McVeigh, 23 Gratt. 409, 417; Wilcher v. Robertson, 78 Va. 602.

. "Want of jurisdiction or fraud in the procurement of a judgment may be shown in any case, and when established will in any court invalidate the judgment; but nothing else will, when relied upon in another suit, which brings into question collaterally the judgment of a court of competent jurisdiction. Lancaster v. Wilson, 27 Gratt. 624, and cases there cited." Gray v. Stuart, 33 Gratt. 351.

Where a judgment creditor files a bill against a debtor to subject his lands to the lien of his judgment, and makes a trust creditor of the same debtor who holds a deed of trust on the land a party, such trust creditor can not question the validity of the judgment against the debtor, except upon grounds that would avoid it, between the judgment creditor and the debtor, or on the ground that there was fraud and collusion between them

in procuring the judgment. Gentry v. Allen, 32 Gratt. 254.

A judgment for a debt in favor of A against B is conclusive, not only between the parties, but even as to strangers, to establish the existence and amount of the liability, and strangers can only impeach it for fraud or collusion. Bensimer v. Fell, 35 W. Va. 15, 12 S. E. 1078.

"Bump., Fraud. Conv. 576, states the rule to be that the 'judgment may be impeached collaterally by proof that the court had no jurisdiction, or that it was obtained by fraud or collusion, or that it was entered illegally, but not beyond this.'" Bensimer v. Fell, 35 W. Va. 15, 12 S. E. 1078.

"Wait, Fraud. Conv., § 270, says that when a judgment is conclusive between the parties, it is 'competent evidence tending to prove the debt, even as to third parties, until something is shown to the contrary by way of impeachment. A third party may, as a general rule, show that the judgment was collusive, and not founded on actual indebtedness or liability. Were this rule otherwise, the greatest injustice would result, since a stranger to the record can not ordinarily move to vacate the judgment or prosecute a writ of error or appeal.'" Bensimer v. Fell, 35 W. Va. 15, 12 S. E. 1078.

"In Garland v. Rives, 4 Rand. 282, a case to set aside a fraudulent conveyance, it is held, that the judgment against the grantor is prima facie evidence against the debtor or mere strangers, unless they can impeach it on the ground of fraud," etc. Bensimer v. Fell, 35 W. Va. 15, 12 S. E. 1078.

"In the opinion in Chamberlayne v. Temple, 2 Rand. 396, it is said that a judgment against donor establishes a debt against donee, unless impeached on the ground of fraud or for any other just ground." Bensimer v. Fell, 35 W. Va. 15, 12 S. E. 1078.

A decree, or decrees, of a court can

not be impeached in a court of equity for fraud in a collateral proceeding. If done at all, it must be done in a cause wherein the decree is sought to be impeached by the pleadings directly. In other words, it must be done in a cause where the fraud is put in issue properly by the pleadings. Davis v. Landcraft, 10 W. Va. 718, 741.

A judgment or decree for a debt in favor of A. against B. is conclusive, both between the parties and as to strangers, of the existence, justness and amount of the debt, and can be impeached by a party or a stranger only for fraud or collusion. It can be impeached therefor, not collaterally, but only by a direct proceeding to set it aside by original bill or cross bill or answer. Turner v. Stewart, 51 W. Va. 493, 41 S. E. 924, citing Bensimer v. Fell, 35 W. Va. 15, 12 S. E. 1078; First Nat. Bank v. Huntington, etc., Co., 41 W. Va. 530, 23 S. E. 792.

In a suit for partition of land, whether partition can be conveniently made in kind or not, and whether the interest of those who are entitled to the subject or its proceeds will be promoted by a sale of the entire subject or not, are questions for the court in which the suit is pending to decide, and its decision can not be questioned in any collateral suit, except on the ground of fraud or surprise. In such a case, a sale made pending the suit by agreement of the parties, in person or by counsel, which sale is afterwards approved and confirmed by the court, is as valid as if made under a previous decree of the court in the suit, and can no more be impeached collaterally than if so made. Wilson v. Smith, 22 Gratt. 493.

A decree erroneous in itself, or collusive between the parties to it, can not be examined into in a collateral proceeding; but it is conclusive upon the matters thereby adjudicated until set aside in some proceeding for the purpose. Where a sale of land has been made under such decree, the title

8 Va—36

passes. Baylor v. Dejarnette, 13 Gratt. 152.

"With regard to these and the other supposed errors in the proceedings it is sufficient to say that they can not be examined into when the decree is offered in evidence in a court of law. And so with regard to the charge of collusion. If there was any improper arrangement between those parties to subject the property to a debt with which it was not chargeable in whole or in part, or if any wrong were done in throwing the whole burden upon that part of the land held by George D. Baylor, the remedy is not to be sought in the exclusion of the decree which was the basis of the defendant's title. All these are matters purely of equitable cognizance with which the court of law has no concern. To undertake to reverse the proceedings would be to usurp the province of the court of chancery, and to do what even that court would not do in this collateral way." Baylor v. Dejarnette, 13 Gratt. 152.

In the case of First Nat. Bank v. Huntington, etc., Co., 41 W. Va. 530, 23 S. E. 792, the syllabus is as follows: "In a suit in equity to enforce a judgment lien against the real estate of the judgment debtor, the judgment, as between the judgment creditor and other judgment creditors, is conclusive of the justness and amount of the debt. Such judgment, valid on its face, can not be impeached by such other creditor except for fraud; and that can not be done otherwise than in a direct proceeding brought to set it aside on that ground." The opinion of the court is, however, in part as follows: "The remaining and important question is, did not plaintiff have a valid judgment? A duly-certified copy of the record of the judgment, attested by the clerk of the circuit court of Cabell county, was produced and read in evidence as a part of the plaintiff's bill, and the law makes such attested copy evidence in lieu of the original. See Code, 1891,

p. 821, ch. 130, § 5; 2 Freem., Judgm., § 407. And such original imports absolute verity, and when read proves itself, and, the judgment being valid on its face, the court determines by inspection the existence of the record and the validity of the judgment. And, as against other creditors, it is conclusive of the justness and amount of the debt, and can not, on a bill to enforce the lien against real estate, be impeached, except for fraud and collusion." Citing Bensimer *v.* Fell, 35 W. Va. 15, 25, 13 S. E. 1078, and referring to McNeel *v.* Auldridge, 34 W. Va. 748, 12 S. E. 851; Garland *v.* Rives, 4 Rand. 282.

X. Interest.

See the titles INTEREST, vol. 7, p. 819; USURY.

A. IN GENERAL.

Interest is recovered on a judgment either as a debt or damages. If the judgment does not carry interest on its face, it can be recovered like any debt by action or suit upon the judgment, but it is not given as a matter of course; if the decree provides for the payment of interest it is recovered in the shape of damages. Mercer *v.* Beale, 4 Leigh 189; Jones *v.* Williams, 2 Call 102; Tazewell *v.* Saunders, 13 Gratt. 353, 368; Stuart *v.* Hurt, 88 Va. 343, 13 S. E. 438.

B. RIGHT TO RECOVER.

In General.—In Tazewell *v.* Saunders, 13 Gratt. 353, 368, Judge Moncure says: "In this state interest is generally recoverable on a judgment, both at law and in equity." He then adds: "But if the judgment does not carry interest on its face, it can only be recovered by action or suit upon the judgment."

Rule in Equity.—Prior to Va. Stat. 1804, chancery courts could not grant interest, subsequent to the date of the decree, on debts not bearing interest in terms. Dillard *v.* Tomlinson, 1 Munf. 183; Deanes *v.* Scriba, 2 Call

415. Nor, prior to said statute, could the court of appeals, in affirming a decree appealed from, allow interest on the amount of the decree pending the appeal. Scott *v.* Trents, 4 Hen. & M. 356. Since the 1st of May, 1804, when interest is allowed in equity, it should not stop when the balance of account is struck, nor at the date of the decree, but should run to the payment of such balance. Snickers *v.* Dorsey, 2 Munf. 505. See Va. Code, 1887, § 3391.

In Action for Tort.—Prior to statutory enactment (Va. Code, 1887, § 3390), interest could not be allowed upon a verdict in an action of tort. Brugh *v.* Shanks, 5 Leigh 598. See also, Hepburn *v.* Dundas, 13 Gratt. 219.

That a court of equity will under circumstances give interest on a judgment sounding only in damages and not carrying interest in terms, can not be denied. Mercer *v.* Beale, 4 Leigh 189, 196, citing Beall *v.* Silver, 2 Rand. 401. To the same effect, the principal case is cited in Laidley *v.* Merrifield, 7 Leigh 346, 360.

But judgments in actions for tort now bear interest by express statutory enactment. Va. Code, 1904, § 3390; Fry *v.* Leslie, 87 Va. 269, 12 S. E. 671.

Judgment on Nil Dicit or Non Sum Informatus.—In a debt on a bill penal, a judgment entered upon nil dicit or non sum informatus, ought not to be reversed on the ground that the declaration, though describing the bill penal correctly as to the principal sum, penalty and date, omits to mention that the debt is payable, "with interest from a day prior to the date," and that the judgment, in conformity with the bill penal, is entered for the penalty, to be discharged by the principal, with such interest, and costs. Harper *v.* Smith, 6 Munf. 389. See Mosby *v.* Taylor, Gilmer 172.

Judgment or Decree for Costs.—A judgment or decree for costs, as a general rule, does not bear interest. Costs are considered in some sense as damages. "Said Judge Roane in Mc-

Rea *v.* Brown, 2 Munf. 46: 'The general principle is that costs are considered as an appendage to the judgment, rather than a part of the judgment itself; that they are considered, in some sense, as damages, and are always entered, in effect, as an increase of damages by the court. This doctrine is to be found in 3 Blackstone's Com. 399. I presume it was on the ground of this general principle that this court reversed the judgment in the case of Hudson *v.* Johnson, which gave damages on the costs; for as costs are in the nature of damages, and damages and interest are considered, in some sense, as the same, it might seem that the judgment gave, in effect, interest upon interest, or compound interest, which has been always highly discountenanced by the courts and the legislature.'" Ashworth *v.* Tramwell, 102 Va. 852, 47 S. E. 1011; Douglass *v.* McCoy, 24 W. Va. 722.

It was held, in McRea *v.* Brown, 2 Munf. 46, that the 5th section of the act passed January 20, 1804, entitled, "An act concerning the proceedings in courts of chancery, and for other purposes," did not authorize a judgment for interest upon the costs of suit.

C. COMPUTATION OF INTEREST.

1. Period at Which Interest Begins.

a. In West Virginia.

(1) From Date of Judgment or Decree.

Judgment or Decree for Payment of Money.

In General.—The West Virginia Code provides that: "Every judgment or decree for the payment of money, except where it is otherwise provided by law, shall bear interest from the date thereof, whether it be so stated in the judgment or decree or not." W. Va. Code, 1899, ch. 131, § 3988.

Where a decree is made for the payment of money, whether it is a personal decree against the debtor or merely against property liable for the payment of the money so decreed to be paid, the decree should be entered for the aggregate of principal and interest at the date of the decree with interest thereon from that date. Cranmer *v.* McSwords, 26 W. Va. 412, 413; Shipman *v.* Bailey, 20 W. Va. 140; Merchants' Nat. Bank *v.* Good, 21 W. Va. 455; Douglass *v.* McCoy, 24 W. Va. 722, 728.

It is provided by our statute (§ 16 of ch. 131 of the Code) that: "In all cases where a judgment or decree is rendered or made for the payment of money, it shall be for the aggregate of principal and interest due at the date of the verdict if there be one, otherwise at the date of the judgment or decree, with interest thereon from such date except in cases where it is otherwise provided." So in the case of Hawker *v.* Railroad Co., 15 W. Va. 628, 644, Green, P., delivering the opinion of the court, said: "The court erred in giving judgment for interest on damages found by the jury prior to the day the judgment was actually entered; that is, the 7th day of May, 1878. The judgment entered by the circuit court erroneously gave interest from the first day of the term at which the judgment was entered; that is, from April 18, 1878." Triplett *v.* Lake, 43 W. Va. 428, 27 S. E. 363, 366.

Again, in the case of Lamb *v.* Cecil, 25 W. Va. 288, Johnston, P., in the opinion of the court, says: "It was error to decree interest on the aggregate of principal and interest from a time anterior to the rendition of the decree,"—citing Fowler *v.* Baltimore, etc., R. Co., 18 W. Va. 579. He adds that, while this error would require the decree to be corrected, yet, as the difference is not sufficient to give this court jurisdiction, it would, if there were no other error, be reversed, with costs to the appellee, and a decree entered for the correct amount; citing Bee *v.* Burdett, 23 W. Va. 744. Triplett *v.* Lake, 43 W. Va. 428, 27 S. E. 363, 366.

In enforcing a vendor's lien for purchase money, the court, in rendering its decree, will ascertain the aggregate amount of principal and interest due on the notes executed for such purchase money, for which the vendor's lien is retained, to the date of the decree, and decree that interest be paid on such aggregate from the date of the decree. Triplett *v.* Lake, 43 W. Va. 428, 27 S. E. 363.

Harmless Error.—The court erred in giving interest from the date of verdict instead of from date of judgment; but, as it only amounts to a few dollars, the judgment will not be reversed for that reason, but, in that respect will be here corrected and affirmed with costs and thirty dollars damages according to law. Quarrier *v.* Baltimore, etc., R. Co., 20 W. Va. 424, 428.

While it is error to give interest upon the aggregate of principal and interest from a time anterior to the decree, yet if the difference in amount is less than $100, and that is the only error appearing by the record, the decree will be reversed with costs to the appellee, and a decree will be entered for the proper amount. Lamb *v.* Cecil, 25 W. Va. 288, citing Fowler *v.* Baltimore, etc., R. Co., 18 W. Va. 579; Bee *v.* Burdett, 23 W. Va. 744.

In Absence of Verdict.—Where a judgment or decree is made for the payment of money it shall be for the aggregate of principal and interest due at the date of the verdict, if there be one, otherwise at the date of the judgment or decree, with interest thereon from such date, except in cases where it is otherwise provided. Baer's Sons, Grocer Co. *v.* Cutting, etc., Co., 42 W. Va. 359, 26 S. E. 191, citing Hawker *v.* Baltimore, etc., R. Co., 15 W. Va. 628, 629.

Amendment.—If the court, in enforcing a vendor's lien, aggregates the amount of principal and interest to the date of the decree, and then decrees that the defendants pay interest in such aggregate amount for several months prior to the date of the decree, this is such a mistake as may be safely amended on motion, under § 5 of ch. 134 of the Code, and which should be amended on motion in the circuit court. Triplett *v.* Lake, 43 W. Va. 428, 27 S. E. 363.

Constitutionality of Statutes.—The 16th section of ch. 131, W. Va. Code, providing, that a judgment or decree for the payment of money, shall be for the aggregate of the principal and interest due at the date of the judgment or decree, with interest thereon from that date, does not violate the provision of the constitution of the United States, prohibiting any state to pass a law impairing the obligation of contracts. Fleming *v.* Holt, 12 W. Va. 144; Douglass *v.* McCoy, 24 W. Va. 722, 728.

Recovery on Bond Conditioned for Payment of Money.—When there is a recovery on a bond conditioned for the payment of money, as well as in all cases where a judgment or decree is rendered or made for the payment of money, it shall be for the aggregate of principal and interest due at the date of the verdict if there be one, otherwise at the date of the judgment or decree, with interest thereon from such date, except in cases where it is otherwise provided. W. Va. Code, 1899, ch. 131, § 3986.

This section is constitutional. Fleming *v.* Holt, 12 W. Va. 144; Douglass *v.* McCoy, 24 W. Va. 722.

Judgments on Tort.—And in other cases, as on verdict in a case of tort, the judgment must bear interest from the date thereof. Talbott *v.* West Virginia, etc., R. Co., 42 W. Va. 560. 26 S. E. 311, citing Hawker *v.* Baltimore, etc., R. Co., 15 W. Va. 628; Murdock *v.* Franklin Ins. Co., 33 W. Va. 407, 10 S. E. 777.

In an action for damages the judgment should be for the interest on the amount assessed by the jury as damages from the day the judgment is actually rendered, and not from the first day of the term at which the judgment . is rendered. Hawker *v.* Baltimore, etc., R. Co., 15 W. Va. 628. See Mercer *v.* Beale, 4 Leigh 189.

In an action for damages the judgment should be for the amount assessed by the jury and interest on this amount from the day the judgment is actually rendered, and not from the date of the verdict. Hawker *v.* Baltimore, etc., R. Co., 15 W. Va. 628; Fowler *v.* Baltimore, etc., R. Co., 18 W. Va. 579, 586.

(2) From Date of Verdict.

Judgments on Contract.—The jury in an action founded on contract, may allow interest on the principal due, or any part thereof, and in all cases they shall find the aggregate of principal and interest due at the time of the trial, after allowing all credits, payments and set-offs, and judgment shall be entered for such aggregate with interest from the date of the verdict. W. Va. Code, 1899, ch. 131, § 3984.

Under W. Va. Code, judgments on contracts, as provided by § 14 of the same chapter of the Code, bear interest from the date of the verdict. Talbott *v.* West Virginia, etc., R. Co., 42 W. Va. 560, 26 S. E. 311; Fowler *v.* Baltimore, etc., R. Co., 18 W. Va. 579; Hawker *v.* Baltimore, etc., R. Co., 15 W. Va. 628; Murdock *v.* Franklin Ins Co., 33 W. Va. 407, 10 S. E. 777.

What Law Governs.—In an action on a contract, a verdict is rendered for the plaintiff for a sum of money while § 14, ch. 131, Code, 1868, as originally enacted, was in force, providing that judgment should be entered for the amount found, with interest from the date of the judgment, and judgment is not entered on such verdict until 1887, when said § 14, as amended by ch. 120, acts, 1882, is in force, providing that on verdicts judgments shall be rendered, with interest from date of verdict. Such judgment should have called for interest from its date, according to the law in force when the verdict was rendered, and not from the date of the verdict. Murdock *v.* Franklin Ins. Co., 33 W. Va. 407, 10 S. E. 777.

Correction and Amendment.—A judgment rendered .in June, 1870, provides for the recovery of interest from 1866, which is held to be erroneous under §§ 14, 16, ch. 131, page, 627, Code of West Virginia. But such error can be corrected in the court below by § 5, ch. 134, and in this court by § 6 of same chapter, and it is accordingly corrected. Connor *v.* Fleshman, 4 W. Va. 693.

b. In Virginia.

In General.—By Virginia Code, 1904, § 3390, it is provided that "the jury, in any action founded on contract, may allow interest on the principal due, or any part thereof, and fix the period at which such interest shall commence. And in any action whether on contract or for tort, the jury may allow interest on the sum found by the verdict, or any part thereof, and fix the period at which the interest shall commence. If a verdict be rendered which does not allow interest the sum thereby found shall bear interest from its date, and judgment shall be entered accordingly." Stuart *v.* Hurt, 88 Va. 343, 13 S. E. 438.

Tort Actions.—Upon a payment in an action for a tort depending when the act, Va. Code, ch. 177, § 14, p. 673, went into operation, it is proper to charge interest from the date of the verdict. Lewis *v.* Arnold, 13 Gratt. 454.

It was held in a West Virginia case, that under the Code of Virginia, 1860, p. 732, § 14, providing that the jury may allow interest on the sum found by the verdict, and fix the period at which the interest shall commence, that the jury may allow interest on the sum found by the verdict in an action of trespass and fix the period at which it shall commence; therefore, it is not error for the circuit court to instruct the jury that the defendant is liable, if at all, for the value of the property taken, with interest on that value from the time it was taken. Shepherd *v.* McQuilkin, 2 W. Va. 90.

Where Verdict Does Not Allow Interest.—Under Virginia Code 1887, § 3390, which provides that if a verdict does not allow interest, the sum thereby found shall bear interest from the date of the verdict, the judgment on a verdict for damages in an action of tort must allow interest from the date of the verdict, when interest is not given by the verdict. Fry *v.* Leslie, 87 Va. 269, 12 S. E. 671.

Injunction to Judgment.—If a defendant in a judgment for costs enjoins the collection of the judgment upon the grounds which do not affect its validity, or furnish any foundation for restraining the plaintiff from prosecuting to judgment his claim, although it may be proper to stay its payment, he is liable for interest on the judgment from the time the injunction was granted. Shipman *v.* Fletcher, 95 Va. 585, 29 S. E. 325.

Judgment Secured by Mortgage.—Where judgment was recovered for the principal debt, with damages in lieu of interest, and costs, and the debtor executed a mortgage to secure the payment, interest was allowed on the aggregate of princ'pal, damages and costs, from the date of the mortgage till payment. Laidley *v.* Merrifield, 7 Leigh 346.

Judgment on Scire Facias.—Upon a scire facias against bail, it is error to give a judgment for the aggregate amount of principal, interest, and costs of the first judgment, with interest thereon. Bowyer *v.* Hewitt, 2 Gratt. 193.

Judgment on Replevy Bond.—Judgment ought not to be entered on a three months' replevy bond, for interest from a day anterior to the date of the bond, but it may be for interest from that date, on the rent and costs of the distress added together. And if the bond be taken, including interest from a day anterior to its date, such erroneous interest may be deducted, and judgment entered for the right sum. Williams *v.* Howard, 3 Munf. 277.

Interest upon estimated hires and profits of slaves, should be allowed only from the date of the decree, and it is error to allow interest from the date of the report ascertaining the amount of such hires and profits. Shields *v.* Anderson, 3 Leigh 729.

2. Decree in Suit to Subject Real Estate Fraudulently Conveyed.

In a suit to subject real estate, conveyed by a debtor in his lifetime without valuable consideration, to the payment of a simple contract debt, it is error for the court to take the amount of a judgment for such debt recovered against the administrator of such debtor as the foundation for its decree and to give interest on the amount of such judgment—said amount being for the principal and interest on the original debt at the date of said judgment. The decree in such case should be for the original debt with the interest aggregated thereon to the date of the decree, and then interest on such aggregate until paid. Merchants' Nat. Bank *v.* Good, 21 W. Va. 455.

3. Part Payments.

It is error in a commissioner to allow interest on part payments of a judgment; the proper rule is to bring the interest on the principal sum up to the date of each payment, and deduct it from the amount of that payment—thus making the partial payments first applicable to the interest. See De Ende *v.* Wilkinson, 2 Pat. & H. 663, cited with approval in Hurst *v.* Hite, 20 W. Va. 193.

4. Judgment against Deputy.

On a motion by a sheriff against his deputy, where judgment has been obtained by the commonwealth against him for taxes, judgment must be entered for the principal sum, and the interest, and not for the penalty to be discharged by that sum and interest. Asberry *v.* Calloway, 1 Wash. 72.

5. Where No Jury Impanelled.

In any suit in equity, or in an action founded on contract, where no jury is impanelled, judgment or decree may be rendered for interest on the principal sum recovered, until such judgment be paid; and where there is a jury, which allows interest, the judgment shall, in like manner, be for such interest until payment. (Code, 1849, p. 673, ch. 177, § 18.) Va Code, 1904, § 3391; Stuart *v.* Hurt, 88 Va. 343, 13 S. E. 438.

6. Rate of Interest.

A judgment upon the default of the sheriff, or other officer responsible for fines collected, ought not to be rendered for interest at the rate of fifteen per cent. per annum; but for five per cent. damages, and five per cent. per annum interest, on the whole amount, as in the case of public taxes. Segouine *v.* Auditor, 4 Munf. 398.

Where a bond by its terms bears interest at three per cent., per annum from date, a decree for the payment thereof should be for the aggregate sum due, the interest being computed at the rate of three per cent. to the date of the decree, and then the decree should provide for the payment of interest thereon at the rate of three per cent. until paid. A decree providing for interest at six per cent. on such aggregate sum is erroneous. Pickens *v.* McCoy, 24 W. Va. 344.

A contract for the payment of interest at the rate of eight per cent. from date until paid, if such rate is authorized by the laws of the place where the contract is made, may be computed at such rate to the date of the decree under the provisions of § 16, ch. 131, of the Code of West Virginia, and the decree for the aggregate sum thus computed will continue to bear interest at such rate. Shipman *v.* Bailey, 20 W. Va. 140.

D. INTEREST ON INTEREST OR COMPOUND INTEREST.

See the title INTEREST, vol. 7, p. 840.

West Virginia.—The West Virginia statute provides that, "when a decree or judgment is rendered or made for the payment of money, it shall be for the aggregate of principal and interest due at the time of the judgment or decree, with interest thereon from that date." Code, ch. 131, § 16. Before the enactment of this statute, the rule of the common law was that the decree should be rendered for the principal of the debt with interst on that only. Neither the accrued interest nor the costs could be made an interest-bearing fund, for the reason that that would have been compounding interest which was not lawful. Our statute has so far modified the common law as to require the court to include in the decree the interest accrued on the debt at the date of the decree, so as to make it as well as the principal of the debt bear interest from that date. Tiernan *v.* Minghini, 28 W. Va. 314, 323.

Under W. Va. Code, ch. 131, § 16, providing that where a judgment is rendered for the payment of money, "it shall be for the aggregate of principal and interest due at the date of the verdict if there be one, otherwise at the date of the judgment or decree, with interest thereon," it was held that, where this had been done, it was error in a subsequent decree to reaggregate the debt by calculating interest to the date of the subsequent decree, and then to add this interest to the sum of the first decree and give interest on the second aggregate from the date of the last decree. Tiernan *v.* Minghini, 28 W. Va. 314.

"When such aggregation has been once made and a decree entered for the same with interest thereon from that date, it does not authorize a second aggregation of the same debt in the same cause in subsequent decrees providing for the payment of the said first decree, much less would it permit the aggregation of the costs of the suit then accrued to be made in such second decree. The costs do not bear interest either by virtue of the statute or the common law. However, when a suit is brought to enforce a judgment or decree rendered in another and distinct suit, it seems that in such suit there may be an aggregation of the principal, interest and costs recovered in the first action or suit, because these constitute the debt sought to be enforced in the second suit thus brought. Douglass v. Mc-Coy, 24 W. Va. 722, 727; Fleming v. Holt, 12 W. Va. 144; Merchants' Nat. Bank v. Good, 21 W. Va. 455." Tiernan v. Minghini, 28 W. Va. 314, 323.

It is not error to aggregate principal and interest to date of judgment, or decree, and allow interest on said aggregate from date of judgment, or decree, until paid. Fleming v. Holt, 12 W. Va. 144; Ruffner v. Hewitt, 14 W. Va. 737.

Virginia.—In a late case the court pointed out that the rule which declares that interest shall not bear interest does not hold in the case of judgments and decrees, because the decree changes the character of the interest, and converts it into a debt. Stuart v. Hurt, 88 Va. 343, 13 S. E. 438. Compare Bowyer v. Hewitt, 2 Gratt. 193; Ashworth v. Tramwell, 102 Va. 852, 47 S. E. 1011.

E. ABATEMENT OF INTEREST.

"Judgments and decrees for money being contracts of the highest character, of course, and for reasons before stated, to abate any portion of the interest included in them, would necessarily impair their obligation. Moreover by such judgments and decrees, the rights of the parties, in whose behalf they were rendered, to the money ordered to be paid, whether principal or interest, have become vested, and can not be divested, as provided by the act of the assembly. Griffin v. Cunningham, 20 Gratt. 31." Roberts v. Cocke, 28 Gratt. 207; Merchants' Bank v. Ballou, 98 Va. 112, 32 S. E. 481. See, in accord, Linkous v. Shafer, 28 Gratt. 775; Kent v. Kent, 28 Gratt. 840; Pretlow v. Bailey, 29 Gratt. 212; also, Crawford v. Fickey, 41 W. Va. 544, 23 S. E. 662.

After judgment is obtained for a debt, both principal and interest, the court has no more power to abate any part of the interest, on the ground that the creditor was within the enemy's lines, than to abate the principal. The matter has passed into judgment, and it is too late, then, to raise the question of such abatement. Rowe v. Hardy, 97 Va. 674, 34 S. E. 625.

It was held in Roberts v. Cocke, 28 Gratt. 207, that so much of the act of April 2, 1872, as empowers the courts to review judgments and decrees, upon motion, and to abate interest as provided therein is repugnant to the United States constitution and the constitution of Virginia, and therefore void.

In a chancery suit brought by K. of Richmond against A. B. & C. of Mercer county in this state to enforce the lien of a judgment obtained before the war against A. B. & C. as partners on an accepted order known to the partners to include the amount due from the partnership to K. and also an individual debt due from C. to K.; held: There should be no abatement of the interest on the judgment during the war, Richmond and Mercer county being judicially known to the court not to be in territories which were hostile to one another during the war. Kent v. Chapman, 18 W. Va. 485, citing Simmons v. Trumbo, 9 W. Va. 358.

F. CONSTRUCTION OF VERDICT.

Where a declaration calls for a sum certain with interest, and the verdict is simply for the amount of the debt mentioned in the declaration, then under sec. 2853, of the Virginia Code, the legal effect of the verdict is a finding of interest also. Lake *v.* Tyree, 90 Va. 719, 19 S. E. 787.

G. PLEADING.

Necessity for Demand.—Judgment can not be given for interest, if the declaration does not demand interest. Hubbard *v.* Blow, 4 Call 224.

XI. Arrest of Judgment.

A. IN GENERAL.

"The motion in arrest of judgment is quite common in our practice; resorted to out°of abundant caution, as there may be some serious defect appearing on the fact of the record not cured by our statute of jeofails. Sections 9, 15, 29, ch. 125; § 8, ch. 131; ch. 135; 4 Minor, Inst., pt. 1, p. 848, et seq., where the subject is discussed and the cases are considered." Gerling *v.* Agricultural Ins. Co., 39 W. Va. 689, 20 S. E. 691, 692.

B. GROUNDS OF ARREST.

1. Errors Apparent on Face of Record.

It is a well-established rule of law that a motion in arrest of judgment lies only to correct an error that is apparent on the face of the record. Gray's Case, 92 Va. 772, 22 S. E. 858; Hall's Case, 80 Va. 555; Watts' Case, 4 Leigh 672; Stephen's Case, 4 Leigh 679; Hughes *v.* Frum, 41 W. Va. 445, 23 S. E. 604; Gerling *v.* Agricultural Ins. Co., 39 W. Va. 689, 20 S. E. 691; State *v.* Martin, 38 W. Va. 568, 18 S. E. 748; Com. *v.* Linton, 2 Va. Cas. 476.

A motion in arrest of judgment, only lies for some error appearing on the face of the record which vitiates the proceedings. Gerling *v.* Agricultural Ins. Co., 39 W. Va. 689, 20 S. E. 691.

A motion in arrest of judgment lies only to correct an error apparent on the face of the record. It does not lie to correct an error in improperly receiving a juror, when the impropriety, if any, is only shown by a bill of exception. Gray *v.* Com., 92 Va. 772, 22 S. E. 858, citing Com. *v.* Stephen, 4 Leigh 679; Watt's Case, 4 Leigh. 672.

Illustrative Cases.—A motion in arrest of judgment, based on the theory that the basis of recovery being upon the verbal assignment of a promissory note, and there being no special count in the declaration alleging the assignment and the insolvency in the maker of the note, those facts being stated only in the bill of particulars, there could be no recovery, is properly overruled, because the bill of particulars containing the only hint of this assignment, and being no part of the declaration, and the ground of recovery appearing only from the evidence, "we can not say that the defect or fact precluding judgment appears by the record." Hughes *v.* Frum, 41 W. Va. 445, 23 S. E. 604.

2. Grounds for Reversal.

See the title APPEAL AND ERROR, vol. 1, p. 418.

Anything which is good cause for arresting a judgment, is good cause for reversing it, though no motion in arrest is made. Matthews *v.* Com., 18 Gratt. 989, cited in Randall *v.* Com., 24 Gratt. 644, 646; Lemons *v.* State, 4 W. Va. 757; State *v.* Miller, 6 W. Va. 609; State *v.* McClung, 35 W. Va. 280, 286, 13 S. E. 654, 656.

3. Defects in Indictment.

See the title INDICTMENTS, INFORMATIONS AND PRESENTMENTS, vol. 7, p. 456.

In General.—Where an indictment is so defective that any judgment thereon rendered against the defendant would be erroneous, he may take advantage of such defect by motion to quash the indictment, or by demurrer thereto, or by motion in arrest of judgment. State *v.* Ball, 30 W. Va. 382, 4 S. E. 646.

Witnesses before Grand Jury.—Judgment can not be arrested, after verdict against a defendant, because the presentment does not state whether the witnesses on whose evidence it was found, were called by the grand jury, or sent to them by the court, or because the name of the prosecutor was not written at the foot of the information. Com. v. Chalmers, 2 Va. Cas. 76.

No Offense Charged.—On the other hand where an information is filed on a defective presentment, but the defendant pleads to the information and there is a verdict against him, he can arrest the judgment because the presentment charged no offense. Com. v. Chalmers, 2 Va. Cas. 76.

Upon an indictment for forging a check upon the bank of Virginia, and obtaining therefor money current in the commonwealth of Virginia, and verdict of guilty; held, motion in arrest of judgment must be overruled. Second Case v. Swinney, 1 Va. Cas. 150.

Upon an indictment for forging a check upon the bank of Virginia, and obtaining a note of the said bank therefor (under the act of November 18th, 1789, passed before the existence of the said bank), and a verdict of guilty; held, judgment must be arrested. Com. v. Swinney, 1 Va. Cas. 146.

Feloniously.—If an indictment for felony found by a grand jury has omitted to charge, that the criminal act done was done feloniously, and after the grand jury is discharged the word "feloniously" is inserted in the indictment so as to render it in form a good indictment, when before it was fatally defective, and the defendant pleads not guilty, and the jury find a verdict against him, he may then move the court to have the indictment restored to its original and true form, and when so restored judgment may be arrested for the fatal defect in the indictment. If in such an alleged case the court below refuses to hear the evidence offered to prove such unauthorized interlineation of the word "feloniously," the appellate court will reverse the judgment entered upon such verdict, and will remand the case with instructions to the court below, on such motion, to hear the parol evidence and restore the indictment, if it has been changed, to its original and true form, and then to determine the motion in arrest of judgment, treating, in deciding such motion, the indictment, on which the defendant had been tried as if at the trial it had been in its true and original form. State v. Vest, 21 W. Va. 796.

Finding Indictment.—If a person is put upon trial for a felony before an indictment is found against him by a grand jury in court of competent jurisdiction, this is a ground for motion in arrest of judgment. Matthews v. Com., 18 Gratt. 989.

Present West Virginia Practice.—"In what manner may the defendant avail himself of such defect in the indictment? The law affords him three modes whereby he may take advantage of such defect, he may move to quash the indictment, or demur thereto, or, after verdict found against him, he may move in arrest of judgment. At common law a demurrer to the indictment was seldom resorted to, for the reason that any objection which would have been fatal on demurrer (with few exceptions) was equally fatal on motion in arrest of judgment. Whart. Crim. Pl., § 759; Archb. Crim. Pl. 115. But the remedy by motion in arrest of judgment is now rendered much less effectual by statutes in many of the states which now require certain objections formerly available on motion in arrest of judgment, to be made before verdict found. By § 11, ch. 158, Code, it is declared that, 'judgment in any criminal case, after a verdict, shall not be arrested or reversed upon any exception to the indictment or other accusation, if the offense be charged therein with sufficient certainty for judgment to be given thereon according to the very right of the case.' While the motion in arrest of judgment has by this statutory provision been rendered less effectual than it was at common law, the remedy by demurrer to the indictment remains unimpaired, and may be resorted to in all cases where the defendant would be entitled to move in arrest of judgment. In all cases where an indictment is so defective that any judgment to be given upon it against the defendant would be erroneous, the court in its discretion may quash it; thus an indictment found in a court having no jurisdiction of the offense will be quashed in a superior court, and so where the finding is on its face bad, or where the indictment charges an offense excluded by a statute of limitations, and for many other reasons which it is unnecessary to recite here. 1 Archb. Crim. Pr. 102; Whart. Crim. Pl., § 385; 1 Bush. Crim. Proc., §§ 168, 771." State v. Ball, 30 W. Va. 382, 4 S. E. 646, 648.

"But the court will not quash an indictment except in a very clear case, but in doubtful cases will leave the party to his demurrer or motion in arrest of judgment. But a party indicted may also demur to the indictment against him wherever it is defective in substance or form, and upon such demurrer he may take advantage of any error to the same extent as he might by motion in arrest of judgment, and because of the efficiency of the latter remedy the demurrer at common law was seldom resorted to; but since many of the errors which were formerly sufficient to arrest the judgment are no longer available for that purpose, the demurrer in this state is a more efficient remedy than a motion to quash the indictment, or a motion in arrest of judgment. The demurrer admits the facts demurred to, and refers their legal sufficiency to the court. It puts in issue the legality of the whole proceedings and compels the court to examine the validity of the whole record. But as already intimated, there are many errors which can not now be taken advantage of by motion in arrest of judgment. Among these are duplicity, which is fatal on motion to quash, or on demurrer or where there has been a misjoinder of counts and the defendant has gone to trial without motion to quash, or to put the prosecutor to election; and so with all essential averments the truth of which would be implied by the verdict, or for any other defect in charging the offense. Where, according to our statute, it is charged in the indictment with sufficient certainty for judgment to be given thereon according to the very right of the case. Whart. Crim. Pl. §§ 759, 760; 1 Bish. Crim. Proc. §§ 1282, 1286; 1 Archb. Crim. Pr. 178, 180." State v. Ball, 30 W. Va. 382, 4 S. E. 646, 649.

While the motion in arrest of judgment has, by § 11 of ch. 158 of the Code, been rendered less effectual than it was at common law, yet the remedy by demurrer to the indictment remains unimpaired, and may be resorted to in all cases where the defendant is entitled to move in arrest of judgment. State v. Ball, 30 W. Va. 382, 4 S. E. 646.

Where a party is indicted in this state, he may demur to the indictment, and upon such demurrer take advantage of all defects therein to the same extent he may do by motion in arrest of judgment. State v. Ball, 30 W. Va. 382, 4 S. E. 646.

4. Defects in Pleadings.

In General.—Where the declaration sufficiently sets forth a good cause of action, a motion in arrest of judgment will be overruled. Travis v. Peabody Ins. Co., 28 W. Va. 583, 584.

Joinder of Counts.—Counts ex delicto can not be joined in the same declaration with counts ex contractu. Such misjoinder makes the declaration bad on demurrer. But unless a demurrer has been filed and overruled, such misjoinder will not be grounds for motion in arrest of judgment or writ of error. Code, 1873, ch. 177, § 3. Norfolk, etc., R. Co. v. Wysor, 82 Va. 250.

It is a good ground for arresting judgment and awarding a repleader after a general verdict for the pln-tiff, that there were two counts in the declaration; the one, beginning in covenant, and concluding in case; and, the other, entirely in case. To which, the defendant pleaded only, "that he had not broken the covenants." Terrell *v.* Page, 3 Hen. & M. 118.

Negligence.—Although a declaration be less specific in its allegations of negligence than it should have been, and the evidence was permitted to go beyond the averments of the declaration, still where there was no demurrer to the declaration, no objection to the evidence when offered, and no motion to strike it out after it was received, and the case has proceeded to a verdict against the defendant, and it is manifest that the defendant has presented his whole case to the jury, and has suffered no prejudice, and that the verdict is in accordance with the very right of the case, a motion in arrest of judgment for failure of the declaration to state a case of actionable negligence should be overruled. Virginia, etc., R. Co. *v.* Bailey, 103 Va. 205, 49 S. E. 33.

Pleading Consideration.—In the action of assumpsit, if no consideration for promise be laid in the declaration, judgment ought to be arrested, notwithstanding it be founded on a written agreement. Hall *v.* Smith, 3 Munf. 550; Mosely *v.* Jones, 5 Munf. 23.

Omission to Lay Damages.—After verdict, the damages having been left blank in the declaration, the court will inspect the writ and supply them from it. Digges *v.* Norris, 3 Hen. & M. 268.

"This was an action of assault and battery, in which the time and the damages were left blank in the declaration; and the pleas were 'not guilty,' and 'son assault demesne.' After a general verdict for the plaintiff for 300 dollars damages, the defendant moved in arrest of judgment, assigning the blanks in the declaration as grounds of arrest. The district court overruled the motion, and gave judgment for the plaintiff; whereupon the de-

fendant appealed to this court. A copy of the writ (in which the damages were laid at 1,000 dollars), was inserted in the record by the clerk of the district court, though no entry was made of oyer of the writ, nor any order of the court for its insertion." Digges *v.* Norris, 3 Hen. & M. 268.

Failure to Set Forth Award.—A judgment in favor of a plaintiff, ought to be arrested after verdict, where he neglects to set forth the award in his declaration, and reply generally, in debt on bond with condition to perform an award, to be made by certain arbitrators, and aver a breach of the condition by special replication, the conditions being made a part of the record by oyer, and the defendant having pleaded "conditions performed." Green *v.* Bailey, 5 Munf. 246.

Action in Requiring Bill of Particulars.—On the other hand, motion in arrest of judgment is not the proper method of raising the question as to the propriety of the court's action in requiring the defendants in ejectment to file the particulars of their defense; the question should be raised by a bill of exceptions. Virginia Coal, etc., Co. *v.* Fields, 94 Va. 102, 26 S. E. 426.

Profert.—Nor will judgment be arrested for omission to make profert of a bill. Terrell *v.* Atkinson, 2 Wash. 143.

5. Objections to Jury.
See the title JURY.

Improperly Receiving Juror.—A motion in arrest of judgment does not lie to correct an error in improperly receiving a juror, where the impropriety, if any, is only shown by a bill of exceptions. Gray's Case, 92 Va. 772, 22 S. E. 858.

Qualification of Jurors—Petty Juror Not a Freeholder.—Nor is it a good reason for arresting a judgment on a motion in arrest, that several of the petty jury were not freeholders, when this is a matter of fact not appearing on the record. Stephen's Case, 4 Leigh 679.

Conviction of Crime.—So, a motion for arrest of judgment does not lie because a juror, convicted of a felony, had been pardoned in 1868. Puryear *v.* Com., 83 Va. 51, 1 S. E. 512; Edward's Case, 78 Va. 39, 43.

6. Venire Facias.

Irregularites in any writ of venire facias whereby the defendant is not injured, are not grounds for arresting the judgment, where no objection was made before jury sworn. But ordering persons to be summoned without a writ of venire facias is good ground for motion in arrest of judgment, though the objection was not made before jury sworn. Vawter *v.* Com., 87 Va. 245, 12 S. E. 339.

But omission to direct a new venire facias or omission of any statutory essential apparent on the record, is such an error as may be taken advantage of after verdict by motion in arrest of judgment. Hall *v.* Com., 80 Va. 555.

7. Jurisdiction and Venue.

See the titles JURISDICTION; VENUE.

In General.—Questions of jurisdiction may be raised by demurrer; by motion for instructions; by motion in arrest of judgment, on general issue; and by writ of error. Ryan *v.* Com., 80 Va. 385.

Nonresidence.—Nonresidence is not a ground for arresting a judgment; if it is good ground for objection to the jurisdiction of the court, it must be taken by plea in abatement before the defendant pleads in bar. Washington, etc., Tel. Co. *v.* Hobson, 15 Gratt. 122. See Va. Code, ch. 171, § 19, p. 648.

Jurisdiction over Felonies.—But if upon an indictment for a felony the prisoner is tried and found guilty in the county or corporation court having no jurisdiction to try the prisoner, the verdict should be arrested, and all proceedings subsequent to the indictment should be quashed. Rider *v.* Com., 16 Gratt. 499.

Examining Court.—After a verdict convicting a prisoner of a felony, a plea in arrest of judgment, that he has not been examined for the offense by a court of competent jurisdiction (alleging that the corporation court, by which he was examined, has no criminal jurisdiction), ought to be overruled; because the said plea suggests matter making no part of the record, but matter which, if true, is proper for a plea in abatement, or for a motion to quash the indictment. Com. *v.* Cohen, 2 Va. Cas. 158.

Nonresidence of Plaintiff in Federal Court.—A plaintiff in a federal court must state himself to be the citizen or subject of a foreign state, in order to entitle the court to jurisdiction. And if he omits it, the defendant may take advantage of the omission by motion in arrest of judgment. Shedden *v.* Custis, 6 Call 241.

Laying the Venue.—It is not error sufficient in arrest of judgment, in an action of assumpsit in a superior court of a county, that the declaration lays the venue in a different county and omits to state that the cause of action arose within the jurisdiction of the court. Buster *v.* Ruffner, 5 Munf. 27.

8. Defects in Verdict.

See the title VERDICT.

Where there is no objection to the form or sufficiency of the verdict, a motion in arrest of judgment will be overruled. Travis *v.* Peabody Ins. Co., 28 W. Va. 583, 584.

Verdict Uncertain and Defective.—But, judgment against a prisoner tried for a felony will be arrested, where the verdict against him is too uncertain and defective to authorize a judgment thereon. Com. *v.* Hatton, 3 Gratt. 623.

Where the amount of damages assessed by the jury is within the amounts laid in both the writ and the declaration, a motion in arrest of judgment is properly overruled. Swindell *v.* Harper, 51 W. Va. 381, 41 S. E. 117.

9. Parties.

See the title PARTIES.

Joinder of Parties.—When a person, who ought to join as plaintiff, is omitted, and the objection appears upon the pleadings, the defendant may demur, move in arrest of judgment, or bring a writ of error. Prunty *v.* Mitchell, 76 Va. 169.

10. Variance.

See the title VARIANCE.

After issue joined in ejectment on the title only, and a verdict for the plaintiff, for the land in one of the counts in the declaration mentioned, it is no ground for arrest of judgment, that the two counts laid demises of the same land from different persons. See Rev. Code, vol. 1, ch. 76, § 35, p. 112. Throckmorton *v.* Cooper, 3 Munf. 93.

11. Defects in Form of Recognizance.

See the title BAIL AND RECOGNIZANCE, vol. 2, p. 213.

No action or judgment on a recognizance shall be defeated or arrested by reason of any defect in the form of the recognizance, if it appear to have been taken by a court or officer authorized to take it, and be substantially sufficient. W. Va. Code, 1899, ch. 162, § 4631.

12. Former Conviction or Acquittal.

See the title AUTREFOIS, ACQUIT AND CONVICT, vol. 2, p. 181.

Where a former conviction or acquittal was on the same indictment still being further prosecuted, no plea of former conviction or acquittal is necessary. Objection to being further tried, or a motion in arrest of judgment, gives the accused the benefit of the former acquittal or conviction. Otherwise where former trial was upon another indictment in the same or other court. State *v.* Cross, 44 W. Va. 315, 29 S. E. 527.

Indictment against S. S. for second offense of petit larceny alleges former conviction and punishment of S. S. for a like offense, but does not in terms allege that the court in which the first offense was tried had competent authority to try the same; nor that the former conviction remains in force; nor that such conviction appears by the record; nor that S. S. formerly convicted is the same person who is charged with the subsequent offense. Verdict, guilty. Held, none of the omissions aforesaid in the indictments is a ground for arresting the judgment. Stroup *v.* Com., 1 Rob. 754.

13. Statute of Limitations.

See the title LIMITATION OF ACTIONS.

After verdict for the plaintiff, on the plea of nil debet, it is no ground for arresting the judgment, that the claim, as shown by the declaration, was barred by act of limitations. Murdock *v.* Herndon, 4 Hen. & M. 200.

If an indictment for an offense, the prosecution of which is by statute limited to a certain time after the offense was committed, shows upon its face that at the time the indictment was found the prosecution of the offense was barred by such statute, it is fatally defective, and the defendant may take advantage of such defect on motion to quash the indictment, or by demurrer thereto, or by motion in arrest of judgment. State *v.* Ball, 30 W. Va. 382, 4 S. E. 646.

14. Arraignment.

See the title CRIMINAL LAW, vol. 4, p. 37.

Where the clerk, in arraigning the prisoner, erroneously states to the jury the maximum punishment for the offense, but the jury fix the maximum punishment, showing that they were not misled by the error of the clerk, such error is not sufficient to set aside or arrest the judgment. Mitchell *v.* Com., 75 Va. 856. See also, Burgess *v.* Com., 2 Va. Cas. 483.

15. Summons and Process.

If by direction of the plaintiff, the writ be served on one only of two partners in trade, when the declaration shows that the plaintiff knew the names of both, and he gets a verdict upon the plea of nonassumpsit, pleaded by the partner, on whom the writ was served, judgment ought to be arrested. Shields *v.* Oney, 5 Munf. 550.

C. TIME OF MOTION.
1. After Verdict.

Where the objection to sending to the jury an indictment endorsed with verdict of guilty found at a first trial is delayed until after verdict, such error, if any, can not be remedied by motion in arrest of judgment. Forbes *v.* Com., 90 Va. 550, 19 S. E. 164; Angel *v.* Com., 2 Va. Cas. 231.

Where the administrator of a defendant in detinue, who dies pending the action, consents that the cause shall stand revived against him, and instead of pleading de novo, goes to trial upon the plea put in by his intestate, he can not, after verdict against him, arrest the judgment because of his own failure to plead anew. Greenlee *v.* Bailey, 9 Leigh 526.

Errors of Committing Magistrate.— Judgment will not be arrested because of errors in the examination before the committing magistrate, or because he was not examined for the felony of which he is indicted, for such objection comes too late after verdict. Morris *v.* Com., 9 Leigh 636; Angel *v.* Com., 2 Va. Cas. 231.

2. At Subsequent Term.

It seems, that the party, to whom a new trial is granted, may, at the next term, without claiming such trial, file errors in arrest of judgment. Hall *v.* Smith, 3 Munf. 550.

D. MOTION FOR NEW TRIAL AFTER MOTION IN ARREST.

A motion in arrest of judgment is a waiver of a motion for a new trial. Hall *v.* Smith, 3 Munf. 550.

E. HEARING AND DETERMINATION OF MOTION.
1. Motion in Arrest and Motion for New Trial.

Where a motion in arrest of judg-ment and a motion for a new trial are made at the same time, and are acted upon by the court at the same time, the order in which they may be considered by the court is not material; as under such circumstances the motion in arrest of judgment can not be regarded as a waiver of objection to its verdict, or as an admission that the verdict is objectionable. "The court, having first overruled the motion in arrest of judgment, could not then go back to the motion for a new trial, but should have proceeded to judgment on the verdict. For this Sims *v.* Alderson (1836), 8 Leigh 479, is cited, where it is said: 'It is well settled that a party can not move for a new trial after a motion in arrest (4 Barn. & C. 160); but the inference is that if the motions are simultaneous, and disposed of at the same time, in one judgment, no matter in what order, then the rule does not apply; as under such circumstances the motion in arrest of judgment can not be regarded as an admission that the verdict is unobjectionable, and, the motions being made together, they are disposed of in one judgment. If the motion in arrest had been made and overruled, and then the motion made for a new trial, it might be said that the motion came too late; for the only action the court could then take would be to render judgment on the verdict.' It will be noticed that in the case of Sweeney *v.* Baker, 13 W. Va. 158, 216, the two motions were made together, in the same order as in this case, and both were acted on at the same time, and both overruled, which was there held not to be improper." Gerling *v.* Agricultural Ins. Co., 39 W. Va. 689, 20 S. E. 691, 692.

If a motion in arrest of judgment and a motion for a new trial are made simultaneously, they may properly be both acted upon by the court; as under such circumstances the motion in arrest of judgment can not be regarded as an admission that the verdict was unobjectionable. Sweeney *v.* Baker, 13 W. Va. 158.

2. Discharge of Accused.

Where the court, at a trial for murder, ⁻overrules a motion in arrest of judgment, but sets aside the verdict the next day ex mero motu, the defendant is not entitled to discharge on the ground that his motion in arrest of judgment has been allowed. Curtis *v.* Com., 87 Va. 589, 13 S. E. 73.

F. APPELLATE PRACTICE.

Objection for First Time on Appeal. —Anything which is good cause for arresting a judgment is good cause for reversing it, though no motion in arrest be made. They are not bound to make the objection by motion in arrest of judgment but may make it for the first time in the appellate court. Matthews *v.* Com., 18 Gratt. 989, cited in Randall *v.* Com., 24 Gratt. 644, 646; Lemons *v.* State, 4 W. Va. 757; State *v.* Miller, 6 W. Va. 609; State *v.* Mc-Clung, 35 W. Va. 280, 286, 13 S. E. 654, 656.

Where the indictment and the verdict are fatally defective, a judgment may be reversed by the appellate court, though no motion in arrest of judgment was made in the court below. Randall *v.* Com., 24 Gratt. 644; Old *v.* Com., 18 Gratt. 915.

Remand.—The appellate court, upon overruling a motion in arrest of judgment, will not send the case back for a decision upon the motion for a new trial, but will proceed to give final judgment for the plaintiff. Sims *v.* Alderson, 8 Leigh 479.

XII. Assignment of Judgments.

See the title ASSIGNMENTS, vol. 1, p. 745.

A. WHAT CONSTITUTES.

1. Form and Sufficiency.

In General.—There is no actual necessity of a formal written assignment of a judgment. Bank *v.* Allen, 76 Va. 200, 206.

Words which show an intention of transferring or appropriating a decree of foreclosure to or for the use of another, if based upon a valuable consideration, will, in contemplation of a court of equity, operate as assignment. If the written assignment of a bond, which is not in the custody nor under the control of the assignor, is delivered to the assignee, this is a sufficient delivery to pass the equitable title to the bond, and the bond itself need not be delivered. Tatum *v.* Ballard, 94 Va. 370, 26 S. E. 871.

A writing given by a client to his attorney in a suit authorizing the attorney to retain out of the judgment, when recovered, a part for his compensation, is an assignment of such part. Bent *v.* Lipscomb, 45 W. Va. 183, 31 S. E. 907.

Mere Authority to Collect.—A., claiming the benefit of a judgment of R. against T. as being transferred to him by R. for payment of a debt due by R. to him, brings assumpsit against R.'s attorney for the money collected by him on the judgment; and produces in proof of his claim, a written paper signed by R. authorizing A. to prosecute and recover the amount of R.'s claim against T. Held, this imports a mere authority to A. to collect the debt for R. not an assignment or transfer thereof to A. Green *v.* Ashby, 6 Leigh 135.

Written Acknowledgment of Indebtedness.—R. and D., by a writing signed with their names, acknowledge themselves to be due S. $969.87, which they promised to pay as soon as the money can be made on a judgment in the hands of the sheriff of Greenbrier county, in favor of D. against F., et al., with interest from date. Held, that the said writing does not, by any of its provisions, have the effect to transfer, or assign, the said judgment debt to S., either at law or in equity. Feamster *v.* Withrow, 9 W. Va. 296, citing Eib *v.* Martin, 5 Leigh 132.

Parol Agreement.—If a sheriff with

his own money pays off an execution, which has been or is in his hands, without the request of the defendant, but at the time he pays such execution or judgment, there is an understanding or agreement between him and the plaintiff, that he shall have the benefit of the judgment and issue another execution in the name of the plaintiff for the use of the defendant, this amounts to a purchase by the sheriff of the judgment, and he has a right as against the defendant to issue another execution on the judgment for the use of himself. Hall *v.* Taylor, 18 W. Va. 544.

2. Equitable Assignments.

An agreement to transfer certain judgments, if the assignee would pay the amount due on them, operates as an equitable assignment of the judgments, when this amount is paid. Neely *v.* Jones, 16 W. Va. 625, 645.

B. EFFECT OF ASSIGNMENT.

1. Assignee Takes Subject to Equities.

Effect on Rights of Parties to Negotiable Paper.—No assignment of a judgment will deprive a prior endorser of any rights and equities he may have or be entitled to, against a subsequent endorser, because the assignment would not place the assignee in a better position than he would be in without it. Conaway *v.* Odbert, 2 W. Va. 25.

Judgment against Surety.—The assignee of a judgment obtained by the principal against the surety will in such case stand in no better position than the principal. Brandt on Suretyship and Guaranty 278. Mattingly *v.* Sutton, 19 W. Va. 19, 31.

The purchaser of a tract of land on which there is the lien of a judgment against two persons, one of whom is surety, where the lien of the judgment continues on the land in the hands of the purchasers, by purchasing and taking an assignment of the judgment discharges the surety pro tanto. Johnson *v.* Young, 20 W. Va. 614.

2. Warranties.

By an assignment of a judgment, although without recourse, the assignor warrants that the judgment is what it purports to be, that he has done nothing to prevent the assignee from collecting it, and that it has not been paid; but, being without recourse, he is not answerable for the insolvency of the judgment debtor. Findley *v.* Smith, 42 W. Va. 299, 26 S. E. 370; Arnold *v.* Hickman, 6 Munf. 15.

3. Rights of Assignor after Assignment.

The assignor of a judgment, or the claim on which it is founded, upon which judgment was recovered, has no control over it, nor of an execution issued thereon, taken out by the assignee. Clarke *v.* Hogeman, 13 W. Va. 718.

When a valid assignment is once made, the assignor has no further interest in the claim; and of course no subsequent assignment of the judgment, recovered on such claim, can give any right to such subsequent assignee. Clarke *v.* Hogeman, 13 W. Va. 718.

4. Good Faith in Assignment.

Where appellant is the owner of two judgments sought to be enforced, if one of the judgments was acquired after suit brought, by assignment, which purports on its face to be for value, it must be presumed to have been made in good faith until the contrary is made to appear. Filler *v.* Tyler, 91 Va. 458, 22 S. E. 235.

5. Set-Offs against Assignee.

See the title SET-OFF, RECOUPMENT AND COUNTERCLAIM.

Judgment debtor of bank deposited money with its branch subject to his own check, and the money was lost by the bank's failure; held, the deposit did not discharge the judgment, and is no set-off against the assignee thereof. Spilman *v.* Payne, 84 Va. 435, 4 S. E. 749.

C. PRIORITIES.

As between the assignees of a judgment, the maxim, qui prior est tempore potior est jure, applies. Clarke *v.* Hogeman, 13 W. Va. 718.

It matters not, that the subsequent assignee had no notice of the prior assignment; for neither can have anything more by virtue of the assignment than an equitable title to the claim; and the maxim, qui prior est tempore potior est jure, applies. Clarke *v.* Hogeman, 13 W. Va. 718.

As between Lien of Attorney and Judgment.—See the title ATTORNEY AND CLIENT, vol. 2, p. 168.

An attorney at law has a lien upon a judgment recovered by him for his client for his compensation, which lien is good against an assignee of the judgment, though he had no notice of the lien. Bent *v.* Lipscomb, 45 W. Va. 183, 31 S. E. 907.

Notice of an attorney's lien upon a judgment recovered by him for his compensation is necessary as to a debtor,. but not as to the assignee of the judgment. Bent *v.* Lipscomb, 45 W. Va. 183, 31 S. E. 907, citing Renick *v.* Ludington, 16 W. Va. 378; 3 Am. & Eng. Ency. Law, 2d Ed., 473.

D. RIGHTS OF ASSIGNEE ON RE-VERSAL OF ASSIGNED JUDG-MENT.

To the point that where a judgment is assigned and afterwards reversed, the assignee may thereupon sue the assignor without appealing the case to a higher court, Arnold *v.* Hickman, 6 Munf. 15, was cited in Taylor *v.* Cox, 32 W. Va. 148, 9 S. E. 70.

If a judgment of a county court be assigned, and afterwards reversed by the superior court of law, the assignee may thereupon sue the assignor, without carrying the case to the court of appeals. Arnold *v.* Hickman, 6 Munf. 15.

Assumpsit may be brought against the assignor of a judgment, afterwards reversed, notwithstanding the assignment was by a sealed instrument; for, in such case, the sealed instrument is not the ground of the action, but only inducement thereto. Baird *v.* Blaigrove, 1 Wash. 170; Arnold *v.* Hickman, 6 Munf. 15.

E. ASSIGNMENT OF JUDGMENTS IN TRUST.

E. held judgments amounting to about $20,000 against her son, B., and assigned them in trust for stated objects, the balance on such trusts as B. might appoint, and if he failed to appoint, then in trust to pay the interest to B., free from liens of any of his present creditors. E. reserved power to revoke the trust, and afterwards assigned the judgments to B. Held, under the premises, the judgments having become B.'s absolutely, the trust ceased and could not be interposed as against his creditors and mortgagees. Carter *v.* Hough, 86 Va. 668, 10 S. E. 1063.

Acceptance of Assignment.—Where a judgment is assigned to a party for the benefit of infant children, and the same judgment was assigned to another party for the benefit of said children, and in a chancery suit pending both of said assignees file petitions respectively, claiming to be entitled to the control of said judgment, the successful party in said contest must be regarded as having accepted said assignment, and subsequently as holding said judgment as trustee for said infant children. Feamster *v.* Feamster, 35 W. Va. 1, 13 S. E. 53.

F. RESCISSION OF ASSIGNMENT.

See the title RESCISSION, CANCELLATION AND REFORMA-TION.

Circumstances of misrepresentation may furnish grounds for rescinding an assignment of judgments, as where judgments worth $1,350 were assigned in consideration of $200. Lowe *v.* Trundle, 78 Va. 65.

G. PLEADING AND PRACTICE.

1. In Whose Name Suit to Be Brought.

"Under our law, an assignment of a note, a judgment, or other chose in action does not pass legal, but only equitable, title. The common law forbade their assignment, and then our statute legalized it, and gave a right of action in the assignee's name; and with Judge Carr, in Garland v. Richeson, 4 Rand. 266, if it were an original question, I would hold that the assignee takes legal title, but it is firmly settled otherwise in that case and Clarke v. Hogeman, 13 W. Va. 718; Tingle v. Fisher, 20 W. Va. 497, 498, and other cases. Therefore, unless we can see a statute to otherwise allow, a scire facias or action on a judgment must be in the name of the plaintiff in the judgment, or his personal representative, because there is the legal title." Wells v. Graham, 39 W. Va. 605, 20 S. E. 576.

Scire Facias to Revive Judgment.— An assignee of a judgment can not, in his own name, maintain a writ of scire facias to revive it. "There is no inconvenience to result from this holding, as execution can be awarded in the name of the plaintiff in the judgment, or his representative, which name the assignee has always a right to use, even beyond the control of that party, or, if preferable, the order of award of execution can recite that it is for the use of the assignee." Wells v. Graham, 39 W. Va. 605, 20 S. E. 576.

The pendente lite purchaser of a judgment rendered by a justice may continue to prosecute the claim in the circuit court in the name of his assignor, the plaintiff, when appealed to that court by the defendant. Garber v. Blatchley, 51 W. Va. 147, 41 S. E. 222.

2. The Bill.

When the bill alleges assignment of judgment sued on to plaintiff, and it is not controverted in pleadings or otherwise, it must be taken as admitted. Groseclose v. Harman, 1 Va. Dec. 564.

3. Supplemental Bill.

Where a suit is brought to enforce a judgment lien, and is revived in the name of an administrator de bonis non, who subsequently assigns the judgment to another, and the suit proceeds in the name of the administrator de bonis non, and it is charged in the answer of a defendant that a party other than the assignee of such administrator, had become the owner of the judgment, and that it had been paid off and satisfied to him, it becomes necessary for the assignee to file a supplemental bill, and it is error in the court to refuse to permit him to do so. List v. Pumphrey, 3 W. Va. 672.

4. Parties.

Where the assignment of a decree of foreclosure is absolute and unconditional, the assignor is not a necessary party to a suit by the assignee to enforce collection of the chose. Tatum v. Ballard, 94 Va. 370, 26 S. E. 871.

After a cause has been revived in the name of an administrator de bonis non, he assigns a judgment, which is the subject matter of the suit, to another, and the suit proceeds in the name of the administrator de bonis non, without making the assignee a party. Held, that the cause might so proceed until final decree. List v. Pumphrey, 3 W. Va. 672.

The assignor and assignee of a judgment may be properly made coplaintiffs in a chancery suit to enforce the lien of it on the debtor's lands. Neely v. Jones, 16 W. Va. 625.

5. Statute of Limitations.

One of two assignees claiming the same judgment can not plead the statute of limitations as against the other. Clarke v. Hogeman, 13 W. Va. 718.

XIV. Satisfaction and Discharge.

See the titles PAYMENT; SUBROGATION.

See ante, "Judgment Liens," VI.

A. WHAT CONSTITUTES.
1. In General.

H. recovers a judgment against W. and P. Afterwards W. and H. die, and K. qualifies as the executor of W. and the administrator of H. As administrator of H., K. sues out a scire facias to revive the judgment against P., the surviving obligor, and he appears and files a general plea of payment, without stating the nature of the payment. He proves that H. in his lifetime assigned the judgment to D., who was a debtor of T., who was a debtor of W.; and that under an agreement between T. and D. that T. would take in payment of his debt, any debt on W. which K. would take in payment of T.'s debt to W., D. obtained this judgment from H., and assigned it to K., who credited the amount on T.'s debt to W. There was a verdict for the defendant, and on motion for a new trial; held: The evidence should have been excluded from the jury, the defendant's plea not describing the payment so as to give plaintiff notice of its nature, as required by the statute, Code of 1860, ch. 172, § 4. K. having taken the assignment to himself, and credited the amount upon the debt due from T. to W., he made himself liable to his testator's estate for that amount; but having taken the assignment to himself, he was the owner of the judgment, and might as administrator of H. maintain the scire facias to revive the judgment at law. The arrangement does not constitute a payment of the judgment at law, though it may constitute grounds of equities between W. and P. Peory *v.* Peery, 26 Gratt. 320.

2. Deposits.

Insolvent bank holds judgment against principal and surety, and deposits of surety, on which it pays sixty per cent., but which third party had contracted to take at par. Surety pays judgments with his deposits, under agreement with principal to repay the face value of the deposits so used.

Where surety pays part of such judgment with his deposits, principal, compromising balance, may have the judgment assigned to surety for fifty cents on the dollar of the amount paid by him, though the bank pays less dividend. Southall *v.* Farish, 85 Va. 403, 7 S. E. 534.

Deposit in Branch Bank.—Where the judgment debtor of a bank deposited money with the branch subject to his own check, and the money was lost by the bank's failure, it was held that the deposit did not discharge the judgment. Spilman *v.* Payne, 84 Va. 435, 4 S. E. 749.

3. Collateral Security for Payment of Judgment.

Where the security furnished by a deed of trust, given as additional or collateral security for the payment of a judgment, is entirely lost to the judgment creditor, he may enforce the judgment for its full amount against other property of the judgment debtor. In the case in judgment, the evidence shows that the deed of trust was not intended as a novation of the debt, and that the sale made by the trustee, at which the judgment creditor purchased, was not made subject to the vendor's lien on the property conveyed in trust. Deaton Grocery Co. *v.* Pepper, 98 Va. 587, 36 S. E. 988.

4. Necessity of Acceptance.

Where a judgment debtor, who is absent in the army, sends confederate money to his son to pay the judgment, and. the payment is made to the clerk, who deposits the money in the bank, with an "ear-mark," and subsequently the judgment debtor and his son see the judgment creditor and tell him of this payment, but the latter does not accept in so many terms, such payment to the clerk does not discharge the judgment. Moore *v.* Tate, 22 Gratt. 351.

B. PAYMENT BY WHOM.
1. By Officers and Strangers.

A sheriff or other officer, who has

or has had an execution process in his hands, if he pays the judgment or claim without the request or authority of the defendant, where it is not afterwards approved or ratified by the defendant, is regarded precisely as any other stranger would be regarded and he can not bring an action of assumpsit to recover of the defendant the amount so paid by him. Neely *v*. Jones, 16 W. Va. 625, 635.

"It has been said that public policy forbids that a sheriff or other officer, who pays a judgment, on which the execution is or has been in his hands, should be placed on the footing of a stranger who pays the judgment, and that such sheriff or other officer, whether he takes an assignment of the judgment or not, is not entitled to the benefit of the lien created by the judgment on the debtor's lands, at least as against other creditors having liens by judgment or otherwise, or as against purchasers of the land for valuable consideration without notice that the sheriff had such claim. See The People *v*. Omondaga, 19 Wend. 79; Clevinger *v*. Miller, 27 Gratt. 740; Feamster *v*. Withrow, 12 W. Va. 611, 659. I can not see that public policy forbids the sheriff, who pays a judgment under these circumstances, to occupy the same position so far as the debtor himself is concerned, and to have against him the same rights, as a stranger would have who paid the judgment, whether there was an equitable assignment made at the time or not, his rights varying according to the facts as do those of the stranger; and there is nothing in either of these cases, which would lead to the conclusion, that as against the debtor himself the sheriff would not occupy the same position and have the same rights as a stranger under the same circumstances." Neely *v*. Jones, 16 W. Va. 625, 642.

In the case of Clevinger *v*. Miller, 27 Gratt. 740, it was held, that: 'A sheriff or other officer, who pays an execution in his hands for collection, without an assignment at the time, of the judgment on which it is founded, or the debt, is not entitled to be subrogated to the lien of the creditor whose debt he has paid, as against other creditors having liens by judgment or otherwise." Cited in Feamster *v*. Withrow, 12 W. Va. 611, 658.

Rights and Remedies.—If a sheriff, who has had or who has an execution in his hands, pays the amount of the debt to the creditor without intending to extinguish the debt, whether he takes an assignment of the judgment or not, may have a right under circumstances to enforce the payment of the debt against the debtor. Beard *v*. Arbuckle, 19 W. Va. 135; Rhea *v*. Preston, 75 Va. 757.

If a sheriff, who has had or who has an execution in his hands, pays the debt to the creditor, whether he takes an assignment of the judgment or not, will have the same rights and remedies against the debtor that a mere stranger would have. But quære: Does not public policy forbid that such sheriff should have the same rights and remedies as against subsequent judgment creditors, who have acquired liens on the debtor's lands, or against a purchaser of such lands for valuable consideration without notice that the sheriff set up such a claim. Neely *v*. Jones, 16 W. Va. 625; Hall *v*. Taylor, 18 W. Va. 544.

2. By Purchaser of Land Subject to Lien.

No subsequent decree or judgment for an amount beyond the legal call of the first judgment, in a suit to which such purchaser is not a formal party, or wherein the true amount due by reason of the judgment was not in fact litigated, can estop such purchaser from satisfying the demand by payment of a sum lawfully called for by the judgment as it was when he purchased. Bensimer *v*. Fell, 35 W. Va. 15, 12 S. E. 1078, 1079, 29 Am. St. Rep. 774.

A creditor's forbearance to enforce a judgment against land on which it was a lien is a sufficient consideration for a promise by a subsequent purchaser of the land to pay it, although the landowner was not previously liable for the judgment. Bradshaw v. Bratton, 96 Va. 577, 32 S. E. 56.

C. PAYMENT TO WHOM.

1. To Attorneys.

An attorney at law may receive the money recovered from the defendant, and his receipt will discharge the judgment. Branch v. Burnley, 1 Call 147; Smock v. Dade, 5 Rand. 639.

Branch v. Burnley, 1 Call 147, and Hudson v. Johnson, 1 Wash. 10, are cited in Wilkinson v. Holloway, 7 Leigh 285, as authority for the proposition, that an attorney at law who has possession of the evidence of debt, or had obtained a judgment for his client, may receive from the debtor payment of the debt, and the creditor having confided in him not only to sue if necessary, but also to collect and receive the money, is bound by the payment. They place the attorney at law on the footing of an agent delegated to receive money.

"There is no doubt of the authority of an attorney in good faith to receive payment of a judgment due his client. (Smock v. Dade, 5 Rand. 639; Wilkinson v. Holloway, 7 Leigh 285; Smith v. Lamberts, 7 Gratt. 138, 143; Wiley v. Mahood, 10 W. Va. 206, 228.) It is not denied that at the time, when A. J. Conway is said to have received the payment, he was the attorney of the plaintiff, and if the money was in good faith paid to him, it was a good payment on the judgment. Of course he could not take in full discharge of the judgment anything less than the full amount due; for an attorney without authority from his client has no power to compromise a claim and take for it less than the sum due." Chalfants v. Martin, 25 W. Va. 394, 398.

Before Authority Revoked.—The payment of a judgment or decree to an attorney of record, who obtained it, before his authority is revoked and due notice of such revocation given to the defendant, is valid and binding on the plaintiff so far as the defendant is concerned, and his receipt will discharge the judgment. Harper v. Harvey, 4 W. Va. 539; Yoakum v. Tilden, 3 W. Va. 167; Branch v. Burnley, 1 Call 147.

Medium of Payment.—An attorney at law employed to collect a debt may receive payment in money but has no right to accept bonds, notes or anything else in satisfaction or as collateral security for the debt without express authority from his client; and if he does, it will be no payment, and will not bind his client, unless he expressly or impliedly ratifies the act of his attorney. Kent v. Chapman, 18 W. Va. 485.

Pleading.—Where a bill is filed to enforce a judgment lien, and the answer avers payment and a receipt of plaintiff's attorney for the amount of the judgment, a general replication to the answer puts in issue the execution of the receipt, the authority of the attorney to receive the money, and whether or not it was procured by a fraudulent combination between the judgment debtor and the attorney of the judgment creditor with the purpose to defraud such creditor. Chalfants v. Martin, 25 W. Va. 394.

2. To Next Friend.

"The next friend is one to prosecute and look after the suit. His duties and powers end with judgment recovered. He can not receive pay of it; but payment must be made to the regular guardian or to the court. Lawson v. Kirchner, 50 W. Va. 344, 40 S. E. 344, 14 Ency. Pl. & Pr. 998, 1037; Miles v. Kaigler, 30 Am. Dec. 425; Smith v. Redus, 44 Am. Dec. 429." Fletcher v. Parker, 53 W. Va. 422, 424, 44 S. E. 422.

D. MEDIUM OF PAYMENT.

1. In Payments to Attorneys of Record.

The payment of the judgment or decree to an attorney of record must be a payment of money, or if not a payment of money, it must be accepted by the plaintiff in lieu of money, or the attorney must have special authority to receive it. Harper v. Harvey, 4 W. Va. 539; Wilkinson v. Holloway, 7 Leigh 285.

Confederate Money.—The payment of confederate states treasury notes made to an attorney, without the authority of the plaintiff to receive them, was held not a payment in money that would satisfy a judgment or decree against the defendant. Harper v. Harvey, 4 W. Va. 539.

Bond.—An attorney at law has no power to receive in satisfaction of his client's judgments a bond from the judgment debtor. Smock v. Dade, 5 Rand. 639.

2. Notes and Drafts.

See generally, the title PAYMENT. The note of a debtor does not operate as a payment of an antecedent debt unless so intended by the parties. In the absence of such intention, express or implied, the note is treated as a conditional payment merely. If such antecedent debt has passed into a judgment, the same rule applies; the new note is considered simply as a conditional satisfaction of the judgment, and upon the dishonor of the former, the latter revives and may be enforced at law or in equity. When the parties provide for the extinguishment of the judgment, it may be fairly presumed that they contemplated the extinguishment of the debt upon which it is founded. If the substituted note is accepted in satisfaction of the judgment, the presumption is, in the absence of proof to the contrary, that it was accepted in satisfaction of the debt represented by the judgment. Morriss v. Harvey, 75 Va. 726.

"In the case of Witherby v. Mann, 11 Johns. 516, it was held, that 'when a negotiable note has been received, expressly in satisfaction of a judgment, it is an extinguishment of the judgment debt.' But in this case it was proved by the judgment creditor, that 'he had received from the plaintiff, his promissory note for $52.17, being the amount of that judgment, which note remained unpaid, and was received by him in full satisfaction of the judgment, and for which he gave a receipt as for so much money, being the amount of the. judgment.' See Cox v. Boone, 8 W. Va. 500; Miller v. Miller, 8 W. Va. 542; Hoffman v. Walker, 26 Gratt. 314; Parker v. Cousins, 2 Gratt. 372; McGuire v. Gadsby, 3 Call 234; Farmers' Bank v. Mutual Assurance Society, 4 Leigh 69, 88; Taylor v. Bank, 5 Leigh 471." Feamster v. Withrow, 12 W. Va. 611, 651.

When T. L. F. made his negotiable note with security or endorsers to a bank and the note became due and payable and was not paid at maturity, and suit was brought and judgment recovered by the bank, and S. W. N. F., one of the securities, after the recovery of such judgment, made and delivered his negotiable note to said bank, with security or endorsers for the balance due on said judgment, including costs payable at one hundred and sixteen days after date, said last-named note will not be considered as a satisfaction and extinguishment of said judgment debt, unless it is clearly proven that said last-named note was by agreement of the bank accepted and received by it in absolute satisfaction and extinguishment of said judgment, and the onus of proving that the last-named note was by express agreement accepted and received by the bank in absolute satisfaction and extinguishment of said judgment debt, rests upon the party so claiming it to have been so accepted and received. And especially is this so in a court of equity where in a cause said surety is seeking indemnity and reimbursement from his principal for alleged loss sustained by reason of his suretyship, it appears that said surety paid said last-named negotiable note on its renewal in depreciated bank notes or confederate treasury notes at their nominal value. Feamster *v.* Withrow, 12 W. Va. 611.

When it appears that the payment claimed to have been of a judgment debt made by the surety was in a negotiable note and not money, or its equivalent, the surety, if his action is brought before the debt has been actually paid in money or its equivalent, such as personal or real property, can not recover against his principal in an action at law for money paid by him as his security, unless he clearly proves that his said negotiable note was accepted and received by the creditor by express agreement in absolute and complete satisfaction and discharge of the pre-existing debt, and of the principal debtor therefrom. Feamster *v.* Withrow, 12 W. Va. 611, 654.

Debt and Judgment.—"It seems to me that if the judgment is to be regarded as satisfied, the debt must be considered as also satisfied. As will be hereafter seen, the general rule applying in all this class of cases, is that the debtor's own note does not operate as a payment of an antecedent debt, unless intended by the parties. In the absence of such intention, expressed or implied, the note is treated as a conditional payment merely, that is, when actually paid. If the debt has passed into a judgment, the same rule applies; the new note is considered simply as a conditional satisfaction of the judgment, and upon the dishonor of the former, the latter revives and may be enforced at law or in equity. On the other hand, when the parties provide for the extinguishment of the judgment, it may be fairly presumed they contemplate the extinguishment of the debt upon which it is founded. If the substituted note is accepted in satisfaction of the judgment, the presump-

tion is, in the absence of proof to the contrary, it was accepted in satisfaction of the debt represented by the judgment. By the judgment, the nature of the cause of action is changed, and the debt loses all its validity and ceases to bind the parties. Its force and effect are then expended, and all remaining legal liability is transferred to the judgment." Morriss *v.* Harvey, 75 Va. 726, 730.

When the parties provided for the extinguishment of the judgment it may be fairly presumed they contemplate the extinguishment of the debt upon which it is founded. If the substituted note is accepted in satisfaction of the judgment the presumption is, in the absence of proof to the contrary, that it was accepted in satisfaction of the debt represented by the judgment. Morriss *v.* Harvey, 75 Va. 726.

Draft.—C. being indebted to M. by judgment, gave (with the privity of M., but without his express authority), to S., who, by virtue of an order from M., had an interest in the same judgment, a draft on L., which was partly paid, and never returned. M. received of a person who undertook the collection a part of the draft, amounting to more than his share of the judgment, and paid the surplus to the assignee of S. It was adjudged that C. was entitled to a credit against the judgment, for the full amount of the draft. See Kyd on Bills of Exchange, 125, 126. Campbell *v.* Mosby, 4 Munf. 487.

E. TENDER.

See the title TENDER.

A tender of money in payment of a judgment, will not authorize a court of equity to stop the execution, where there is neither allegation nor proof that the defendant in the execution kept the money on hand for the discharge of the judgment. Shumaker *v.* Nichols, 6 Gratt. 592.

F. COMPROMISE.

See the title COMPROMISE, vol. 3, p. 37.

1. By Next Friend.

A next friend of an infant can not compromise a judgment recovered in action in the name of the infant by such next friend, and on part payment release the judgment. Fletcher v. Parker, 53 W. Va. 422, 44 S. E. 422.

2. By Attorneys.

An attorney at law, employed to collect a debt merely as such, has no power to compromise after judgment, and accept a sum of money less than the full amount of the judgment as satisfaction. Watt v. Brookover, 35 W. Va. 323, 13 S. E. 1007.

G. PROMISE TO PAY JUDGMENT BARRED BY STATUTE.

Refraining from instituting proceedings to subject land to the payment of a judgment which is a lien thereon, on a written promise by the owner of the land to pay the judgment, constitutes a valuable consideration for the promise to pay the judgment, although the landowner was not previously liable for the judgment. Bradshaw v. Bratton, 96 Va. 577, 32 S. E. 56.

H. PAYMENTS ON JUDGMENTS SUBSEQUENTLY REVERSED.

If payments have been made on a judgment which has been reversed, they should be credited on the debt on which the judgment was rendered. Effinger v. Kenney, 92 Va. 245, 23 S. E. 742.

Where a decree which fixes the amount of a debt, and directs the sale of real estate unless the debt is paid, is reversed on appeal because the amount of the debt is not properly ascertained, this of necessity sets aside the sale, if one has been made, and reverses the decree directing the sale. The trial court should then proceed to ascertain the amount of the debt in accordance with the mandate of the appellate court, if any; and, if none, should proceed de novo, allowing all proper credits. If payments have been made on a judgment which has been reversed, they should be credited on the debt on which the judgment was rendered. Effinger v. Kenney, 92 Va. 245, 23 S. E. 742.

It is error to render judgment against several defendants, one of them not served with process and not appearing, for which he may reverse the judgment, under § 5, ch. 134, of the Code, by motion. If he make such motion, and it is overruled, the decision of the circuit court overruling such motion makes such judgment valid and binding, though before void, unless such decision be reversed; and he is entitled to reverse it though the judgment has been satisfied by another of the judgment debtors. Ferguson v. Millender, 32 W. Va. 30, 9 S. E. 38.

Right of Recovery.—Money paid upon a judgment afterwards reversed may be recovered; but where a defendant after suit brought and after a decree of reference to a commissioner not settling his liability, with full knowledge of all the facts, voluntarily pays a part of the demand against him, and a decree is afterwards rendered against him for the residue of the demand, which upon appeal is reversed, and the plaintiff's bill dismissed, he can not recover the part so paid, because it was paid under his own mistake of law voluntarily with full knowledge of all the facts. Beard v. Beard, 25 W. Va. 486.

Remedy of defendant paying the decree is by motion, rule, or petition in the suit wherein the decree was rendered, to compel the creditor to refund. Fleming v. Riddick, 5 Gratt. 272; Green v. Brengle, 84 Va. 913, 6 S. E. 603.

Assumpsit.—Where a decree is collected, and the money paid to plaintiff's attorneys and disposed of as he directs, after reversal, action will not lie against the attorneys to recover the money paid by a defendant that did not appeal, because of want of privity between him and them. Bank of United

States *v.* Bank of W., 6 Peters 8; Green *v.* Brengle, 84 Va. 913, 6 S. E. 603.

I. APPLICATION OF PAYMENTS.

See generally, the title PAYMENT.

In covenant by M. against B. judgment is recovered by M. in 1792, for £2,500 damages; fi. fa. is sued out by M. and returned nulla bona; then both parties die; and, afterwards, the executor of B. makes sundry payments, at sundry times, to M.'s administrator. Held, all such payments shall be applied to the principal of the debt due on the judgment; and M. is only entitled to the balance of principal with interest from the date of the judgment, and shall not be allowed to compute interest on the whole debt from date of the judgment, and apply the partial payments, first to the satisfaction of interest so computed, and then to the principal. Mercer *v.* Beale, 4 Leigh 189.

Usurious Interest.—Under Code, § 2824, plaintiff, who was a judgment creditor of R. & Co., filed his bill against the defendant, making his allegations in accordance with the provisions of said section, and praying that, if more than legal interest had been received by the defendant from R. & Co. in their dealings during the five years next theretofore, the excess should be applied, as far as necessary, to the satisfaction of his judgment against R. & Co. Held, such excess should be applied to satisfy plaintiff's judgment. Ryan *v.* Krise, 89 Va. 728, 17 S. E. 128, followed in Clark *v.* Krise, 89 Va. 739, 17 S. E. 132.

J. COMPELLING PAYMENT.

1. Powers of Commissioners.

Under the fifth section of ch. 141 of the Code a commissioner may in the manner prescribed by that section compel the debtor to convey his real estate lying out of this state to satisfy the creditor's judgment; but he is not authorized to compel the debtor to execute an assignment of his chose in action for such purpose. If he does compel in the manner prescribed by that section such an assignment of his chose in action by the debtor, the courts will hold that such assignment was made under duress, and it will be held either absolutely void or at least voidable. Spang *v.* Robinson, 24 W. Va. 327.

2. By Mandamus.

See the title MANDAMUS.

Mandamus does not lie to enforce the payment of an order issued by the board of education and for the satisfaction of a judgment recovered against it. Poling *v.* Board of Education, 50 W. Va. 374, 40 S. E. 357.

3. Bill Quia Timet.

See the title QUIETING TITLE.

If a bank has obtained a judgment on a negotiable note, which it had discounted, against both the maker and each of the two endorsers and has had such judgment properly docketed on the judgment lien docket of the only county, where either the maker or the first or second endorser of such note has any real estate, and has issued a fieri facias on such judgment and placed it in the hands of the sheriff, the second and last endorser has not a right as a matter of course to file a bill quia timet asking a court of equity to compel the payment of this judgment out of the sale of the real estate of the maker and first indorser of such note, simply because he alleges that he is afraid, that his own real estate may be subjected to the payment of this judgment, while the real estate of the maker and first endorser remains unsubjected. Before the court in the exercise of a sound discretion, which in such a case it must exercise, can entertain such a bill, it must be satisfied from facts stated in the bill, that the plaintiff has reasonable ground to apprehend injury, from the fact that he is the last indorser on such note, and if no facts are stated justifying the inference, that the plaintiff may be injured by the failure of the bank to make the judgment out of the maker and first indorser or their lands, such a bill should not be entertained but should be dismissed on a general demurrer. Watson *v.* Wigginton, 28 W. Va. 533, 534.

K. PROOF OF PAYMENT.

1. Presumptions and Burden of Proof.

Presumptions.—See the title PAYMENT.

The rule as to presumption of payment from lapse of time applies in the case of a debt evidenced by judgment. Criss *v.* Criss, 28 W. Va. 388.

Presumption of payment of a judgment can not arise from lapse of time less than the period of limitation. James *v.* Life, 92 Va. 702, 24 S. E. 275.

Legal and Natural Presumption.—Upon a scire facias to revive a judgment which had been suspended by an injunction for forty-six years, issue was made up on the plea of payment and upon the trial the court instructed the jury, that the pendency of the injunction cause repelled the legal presumption of payment which would have arisen from lapse of time if the injunction had not been pending, and it was held, that such instruction was proper, and it was not necessary to distinguish to the jury between legal presumption and natural presumption arising from lapse of time. Hutsonpiller *v.* Stover, 12 Gratt. 579.

Lapse of Twenty-Three Years.—It was held in Brown *v.* Campbell, 33 Gratt. 402, 412, that under the circumstances of the case, the proof is sufficient to establish the payment of a debt on which judgment had been rendered and execution issued twenty-three years before the filing of a bill to enforce the payment of the judgment. See also, Cox *v.* Carr, 79 Va. 28.

Rebuttal of Presumption. — The debtor died in May, 1885, and only a few months before his death made two payments on account of the judgment, to wit: The sum of $265

on January 9, 1885, and $100 on March 7, 1885, which was an admission on his part that up to that time the judgment had not been discharged. Updike *v.* Lane, 78 Va. 132; Coles *v.* Ballard, 78 Va. 139; Rowe *v.* Hardy, 97 Va. 674, 681, 34 S. E. 625.

Burden of Proof.—"The debt, as stated above, is due by judgment, and is a matter of record. The burden of establishing payments and proving that there was no longer any balance due upon it devolved upon the administrators of the debtor. Credit was allowed for all payments of which they produced any evidence. At their instance, the commissioner required the administrator of the creditor and his attorney to produce before him all books and papers in their possession or under their control showing the amounts that had been paid on account of the debt, or a certified statement thereof from the books. They did so, and furnished, among other credits, some for which no receipts were produced. All payments that were acknowledged, or of which there was any evidence, were allowed. There is no evidence that any payment was made for which credit was not allowed by the commissioner. His statement of the debt and report of the balance found to be due on the judgment, with the exception of an abatement of interest for the three years that the creditor was within the lines of the federal army, was approved by the court and a decree entered for its payment. The decree accords with the evidence and is proper and right." Rowe *v.* Hardy, 97 Va. 674, 680, 34 S. E. 625.

2. Declarations and Admissions.

Where there is a judgment, and the parties, by unmistakable acts and declarations, show that they consider the judgment satisfied and extinguished, there is less difficulty in treating the debt represented by the judgment as also satisfied. Morriss *v.* Harvey, 75 Va. 726, 733.

Hearsay Evidence.—"We do not think, however, that a mere oral statement of the sheriff that a debt has not been paid could be introduced as hearsay testimony, to the prejudice of the debtor. Nor should his statement that the debt has been paid be permitted to be proved as hearsay, to the prejudice of the creditor." Northwestern Bank *v.* Hays, 37 W. Va. 475, 16 S. E. 561, 563.

3. Weight and Sufficiency of Evidence.

To justify the court in determining that the judgment had been paid, the evidence should have established the fact with reasonable certainty, and it seems to me that the evidence adduced, bearing on that subject, but considering the whole evidence, the most reasonable conclusion to be deduced therefrom, is, that the said judgment debt was never paid. Feamster *v.* Withrow, 9 W. Va. 296, 312.

Defendant testified that he had satisfied a judgment filed in creditors' suit, with a debt due from plaintiff, who swore the contrary, and showed by receipts how he paid the debt, and that at time of alleged satisfaction judgment had been assigned as collateral to a third party, by whom it was subsequently reassigned. Held, confirmation of report of commissioner, showing judgment unpaid, was proper. Barrett *v.* Wilkinson, 87 Va. 442, 12 S. E. 885.

In a creditor's suit appellee filed a claim, evidenced by a judgment, which was resisted on the ground that it had been paid. The debtor testified that he had paid it by a debt due to him from appellee, but was not corroborated. Appellee testified that it had not been paid, and produced receipts to show how he had otherwise paid his debt. It also appeared that at the time it was alleged to have been so satisfied appellee had assigned it as collateral for a debt to a third person, afterwards taking a reassignment. Held, that a finding that the judgment was

unpaid was proper. Barrett *v.* Wilkinson, 87 Va. 442, 12 S. E. 885.

L. SET-OFF.

This question will be fully treated under the title SET-OFF, RECOUPMENT AND COUNTERCLAIM.

The practice in this matter of setting off judgments is indicated in 2 Freem. Judgm., § 467, where it is said: "The satisfaction of a judgment may be wholly or partly produced by compelling the judgment creditor to accept in payment a judgment against him in favor of the judgment debtor, or, in other words, by setting off one judgment against another. This is usually brought about by a motion in behalf of the party who desires to have his judgment credited upon. or set off against a judgment against him. The court, in a proper case, will grant the motion. Its power to do this can not be traced to any particular statute, and exists only in virtue of its general equitable authority over its officers and suitors." Zinn *v.* Dawson, 47 W. Va. 45, 34 S. E. 784, 786.

M. MERGER.

See the title MERGER.

N. EXECUTION AGAINST PROPERTY OR BODY OF DEBTOR.

See ante, "Judgment Liens," VI. See also, the title EXECUTIONS, vol. 5, p. 464.

O. CONTRIBUTION BETWEEN TORT FEASORS.

See the title CONTRIBUTION AND EXONERATION, vol. 3, p. 483.

Where judgments have been rendered since the twenty-fourth day of March, one thousand, eight hundred and seventy-three, or may hereafter be rendered in actions ex delicto against several persons jointly, and satisfaction of said judgments has been, or may be. made by any one or more of the said parties. the others shall be liable to contribution to the same extent as if the judgments were upon actions ex contractu. W. Va. Code, 1904, ch. 136, § 4086.

P. PREVENTING COLLECTION OF JUDGMENTS ALREADY SATISFIED.

1. Bill in Equity for Injunction—Adequate Remedy at Law.

There can be no doubt that courts of equity have sometimes restrained by injunction the collection of judgments which had been previously satisfied. See Bowen v. Clark, 46 Ind. 405; Scogin v. Beall, 50 Ga. 88; Craft v. Thompson, 51 N. H. 536. But the more recent and better authorities hold that, when the remedy at law is as complete and adequate as the remedy in equity, the chancery court will not interfere by injunction. Thus, in this very recent work on the Law of Judgments (1891), Mr. Black says: "Whether a bill in equity for an injunction is the proper remedy to prevent a judgment creditor from proceeding to collect anew a judgment which has been in fact satisfied, has been disputed. Some of the cases hold that such an application is meritorious and should be allowed. But others, and we think with better reason, consider that equity ought not to interfere in such a case, inasmuch as the party has a prompt and adequate remedy at law." Black, Judgm., § 390. So Mr. High, in his last edition on Injunctions (1890, § 123), says: "There is also noticeable want of harmony in the authorities upon the question of the right to enjoin the enforcement of a judgment which has been already paid, either in whole or in part. The better-considered doctrine upon this subject, and that most in harmony with the general principles underlying the preventive jurisdiction of equity, is that an injunction should not be granted for the purpose of staying or preventing a sale under execution on the ground of payment, in whole or in part, and that in all such cases the person aggrieved should be left to pursue

his remedy at law." In support of this position Mr. High cites Hall v. Taylor, 18 W. Va. 544. Upon turning to that case, we find that it fully sustains the position that a defendant can not, in a court of equity, enjoin the collection of an execution issued to enforce a judgment already satisfied, because he has an adequate and summary remedy at law, viz., the motion to quash the execution because the judgment has been paid. Howell v. Thomason, 34 W. Va. 794, 12 S. E. 1088, 1089.

Where the debtor in an execution objects that a previous execution has been levied by the sheriff upon sufficient property to satisfy the judgment, and that he has improperly misapplied the proceeds of the sale of the property, or if he insists that payment has been made to the sheriff which has not been credited on the execution, if he has an opportunity to apply to the court of law from which the execution issued, for redress, he has no right to come into equity for relief. Beckley v. Palmer, 11 Gratt. 625.

A party claiming that he has not been credited for all the money paid by him to the sheriff, on a judgment, may have any injustice done to him in that respect corrected by the court from whence the execution issued; and it is not a case for an injunction and relief in equity. Morrison v. Speer, 10 Gratt. 228, distinguishing Crawford v. Thurmond, 3 Leigh 85.

Difficult and Complicated Questions. —A. recovers a judgment against B., and C., who had prosecuted the suit to judgment, as A.'s agent, sues out a fi. fa. upon it, and indorses on the execution, that it is partly for his, C.'s, own benefit; before this execution is delivered to the sheriff, B. the debtor, makes satisfaction to A. of the full amount of the debt, and A. gives him a receipt in full and discharge. Held, though B. the debtor, might have made a motion to quash the execution, and thus had remedy at law, yet a court of·

equity has jurisdiction to give him relief by way of injunction to inhibit further proceedings on the execution. Crawford v. Thurmond, 3 Leigh 85.

Insolvency.—Equity will enjoin the collection of a judgment in favor of an insolvent plaintiff, who is a judgment debtor to the defendant, to the extent of such indebtedness. Beard v. Beard, 25 W. Va. 486.

Jurisdiction and Venue.—A bill praying an injunction to a judgment upon the ground of payment or satisfaction by levy on sufficient property of another defendant in execution, sufficient to discharge it, must be filed in the county where the judgment was recovered; and the circuit court of another county has no jurisdiction of the case. In such case it is not necessary that the objection to the jurisdiction should be made by demurrer or plea; but it may be taken at the hearing of the cause. Beckley v. Palmer, 11 Gratt. 625.

2. Motion to Quash Execution.

See the title EXECUTIONS, vol. 5, p. 444.

The provision of the West Virginia Code on this subject is as follows: "A motion to quash an execution may, after reasonable notice to the adverse party, be heard and decided by the court whose clerk issued the execution, or, if a circuit court, by the judge thereof in vacation; and such judge, or court may, without such notice, make an order staying proceedings on the execution until such motion can be heard and determined. A copy of the order ·so made must be served upon the officer in whose hands the execution is." Page 870, § 17. It will thus be seen that this provision is ample to protect an execution debtor from the levy of an execution upon a satisfied judgment, and is fully as complete and far less expensive and cumbersome than the resort to a court of chancery. See Cockerell v. Nichols, 8 W. Va. 159; Farmers' Bank v. Montgomery, 11 W.

Va. 169; McCoy v. Allen, 16 W. Va. 724, 733. Howell v. Thomason, 34 W. Va. 794, 12 S. E. 1088, 1089.

Quære: If a party against whom a judgment has been rendered in a court of law, may come into equity to set up payments he has made to the attorney of the plaintiff in the action at law, where it is insisted by the plaintiff at law that the debtor was forbid to pay to the attorney, and the attorney was so informed by the plaintiff. "The court is of opinion that the plaintiff below had, and still has, upon the case made by his bill, a plain and adequate remedy at law, by motion, on reasonable notice, to quash the execution in the circuit court which rendered the judgment, or before the judge thereof in vacation. (Code of 1873, p. 1178, § 40.) And nothing appearing on the face of his bill, or in the pleadings or evidence, from which it could be inferred that his remedy at law would be unavailing or inadequate, and that there was a necessity for invoking the aid of a court of equity, upon the authority of Morrison v. Speer, 10 Gratt. 228, and Beckley v. Palmer, 11 Gratt. 625, the court of chancery had no jurisdiction to hear and determine his case. In the former case Judge Daniel, who delivered the opinion concurred in by the other judges, says: 'I can see nothing in this case on which to ground the jurisdiction of a court of chancery. The original bill sets out a single execution, and payments made to the sheriff in satisfaction of it, which had not been fully credited. No reason is alleged why the appellee had not applied, or might not still apply to a court of law from which the execution issued to remedy the injustice of which he complained; and there is an entire absence from the case of those peculiar features which induced this court, in the case of Crawford v. Thurmond, 3 Leigh 85, to sanction the interference of the chancellor.' Every word of the foregoing remarks might be spoken with equal appropriateness to this case as to that, except that the payments are alleged in this case to have been made to the judgment plaintiff's attorney instead of to the sheriff, as in that—an immaterial difference." Coleman v. Anderson, 29 Gratt. 425, 427.

In a case where, by virtue of an agreement between a judgment debtor and a judgment creditor, the judgment ought to be entered as satisfied, but in lieu thereof the creditor has an execution issued and levied upon the goods of the debtor, the latter can not obtain relief by injunction in a court of equity, for the reason that he has a complete and adequate remedy at law. Should the court, in such a case, after having granted an injunction, dissolve the same at a final hearing, it ought not to enter a personal decree against the plaintiff for the amount of the original judgment enjoined, but should simply dissolve the injunction, and dismiss the bill, with costs, and without prejudice to the plaintiff as to his defense at law against the enforcement of the execution. Howell v. Thomason, 34 W. Va. 794, 12 S. E. 1088.

Q. ENTRY OF SATISFACTION.
1. Statutory Provisions.

The fact of the payment or discharge, either in whole or in part, of any judgment so docketed, and if there be more than one defendant, by which defendant it was paid or discharged, shall be entered, as aforesaid, by the clerk upon the return of any execution showing such satisfaction or upon the certificate of the clerk from whose office such execution was issued, that the same has been satisfied in whole or in part, or upon the direction of the judgment creditor or his attorney, and the clerk of the circuit or other court of each corporation, except the clerks of the circuit or city courts of the city of Richmond, whenever it appears from the return of an execution issued thereon that any judgment rendered in his court or office has been

satisfied, in whole or in part, shall, without delay, certify the fact of such satisfaction, and if there be more than one defendant, by which defendant it was satisfied, to the clerk of the corporation or hustings court of his corporation, and the clerks of the circuit or city courts of the city of Richmond to the clerk of the chancery court of the said city. (1884, p. 82; 1902-3-4, p. 778.) Va. Code, 1904, § 3562.

In all cases where payment or satisfaction of any judgment so docketed is made which does not appear by the return of an execution to the office of the clerk where the judgment is docketed or which is not required to be certified to him under the preceding section, it shall be the duty of the judgment creditor, himself, or by his agent or attorney, to cause such payment, or satisfaction, whether in whole or in part, and if there be more than one defendant, by which defendant it was paid or discharged, to be entered within ninety days after the same is made, on said judgment docket; or, if the judgment has not been docketed, then on the execution book in the office of the clerk from which the execution issued. And for any failure to do so, after the same is made, such judgment creditor shall be liable to a fine of twenty dollars. Such entry of payment or satisfaction shall be signed by the creditor, his duly authorized agent or attorney, and be attested by the clerk in whose office the judgment is docketed, or, when not docketed, by the clerk from whose office the execution issued. (1884, p. 82; 1902-3-4, p. 778.) Va. Code, 1904, § 3563.

Holder of note sending it to attorneys with instructions to renew, if possible, but otherwise to sue, and after judgment is obtained receiving from them new note and money, with intimation that if a small balance is soon paid they will receive it in satisfaction of the judgment, which holder accepts and announces the balance due, but doing nothing further for five years, thereby ratifies the act of the attorneys in endorsing the judgment as "satisfied." Higginbotham *v.* May, 90 Va. 233, 17 S. E. 941.

2. Compelling Entry of Satisfaction.

Statutory Provisions.—A defendant in any judgment, his heirs or personal representatives, may, on motion, after ten days' notice thereof to the plaintiff in said judgment, or his assignee, or if he be a nonresident such notice to his attorney, if he have one, or, if he be dead, to his personal representative, apply to the court in which the judgment was rendered, to have the same marked satisfied, and upon proof that the judgment has been paid off or discharged, such court shall order such satisfaction to be entered on the margin of the page in the book wherein the said judgment was entered, and a certificate of such order to be made to the clerk of the court in which such judgment is required by section thirty-five hundred and fifty-nine to be docketed, and the clerk of such court shall immediately, upon the receipt of such certificate, enter the same in the proper column of the judgment docket opposite the place where the said judgment is docketed. (1884, p. 82.) Va. Code, 1904, § 3564.

The object of § 2498 of the Virginia Code is to afford a summary remedy for having marked satisfied the liens therein mentioned upon proof that the debt has been actually paid or discharged, and was not intended to enable persons to have such liens marked satisfied because liable to be defeated by presumption of payment, or because barred by the statute of limitations. Turnbull *v.* Mann, 94 Va. 182, 26 S. E. 510.

Audita Querela or Motion.—The audita querela to compel the entry of a judgment satisfied, is an obsolete remedy, and has been substituted in modern practice by motion. Smock *v.* Dade, 5 Rand. 639.

A tender of money in payment of a judgment, will not authorize the quashing an execution issued thereon, unless the tender is followed by the payment of the money into court, and a motion to enter satisfaction on the record. Shumaker *v.* Nichols, 6 Gratt. 592.

Trial of the Issue.—If on a motion (to quash an execution, or enter a judgment satisfied), the relief of the party depends on matters of fact, the court has a discretion to direct a jury to try the facts. Smock *v.* Dade, 5 Rand. 639.

R. CANCELLING OR SETTING ASIDE SATISFACTION.

1. Form of Application.

A suit in equity is the proper remedy to vacate an entry of satisfaction. Bradshaw *v.* Bratton, 96 Va. 577, 32 S. E. 56; Higginbotham *v.* May, 90 Va. 233, 17 S. E. 941.

2. Grounds for Vacating.

Entry of satisfaction of a judgment may be stricken off for fraud or mistake by motion to the court. Higginbotham *v.* May, 90 Va. 233, 17 S. E. 941, citing 2 Black on Judgments, § 1016; Bradshaw *v.* Bratton, 96 Va. 577, 32 S. E. 56.

A charge that a satisfaction of judgment was obtained by fraudulently representing that the lien on the defendant's land for which lien the judgment was confessed, was still in force, when in fact it was at the time barred by the statute of limitations, of which the defendant was ignorant, is not sustained where it appears that, while the lien was in force, the defendant, for a valuable consideration, gave to the plaintiff a promise in writing to pay the lien. The defendant only did voluntarily what he might have been compelled to do, and has suffered no injury. Bradshaw *v.* Bratton, 96 Va. 577, 32 S. E. 56.

A judgment is recovered, and an execution issued thereon, and while it is in the hands of the sheriff, an agreement is made between the creditor and debtor, by which certain claims are transferred to the creditor in satisfaction of the judgment, and thereupon the sheriff, at the instance of the creditor, returns the execution "satisfied," but it appears, that said agreement on the part of the debtor was fraudulent and the execution was not in fact satisfied, the lien of the judgment is not destroyed, and its position and priority is not disturbed, although its payment may affect purchasers of part of the land of the debtor, where it does not appear in the pleadings and proof, that such return was brought home to the purchaser, and by it he was misled to his injury. Renick v. Ludington, 14 W. Va. 367.

3. Parties to Suit.

A suit to cancel satisfaction of judgment, on the ground that it was procured by fraud or mistake, may be maintained by the attorneys who obtained the judgment. Higginbotham v. May, 90 Va. 233, 17 S. E. 941.

S. THE DECREE OF SALE.

See the title JUDICIAL SALES.

Where a suit in chancery is instituted to enforce a judgment lien, and the bill alleges that there is but one other judgment lien on the real estate sought to be held liable to the satisfaction of the judgment, and sets it up also as a lien on the land, the decree should provide for the payment of both judgments, if the land is subject thereto. Anderson v. Nagle, 12 W. Va. 98.

It is a settled practice in Virginia, to entertain the suit of the judgment creditor for relief in equity, when the debtor has, subsequent to the judgments, conveyed his land in trust for the payment of debts, or on other trusts authorizing the sale of land. And in such case, the court will decree a sale to satisfy the judgment. Taylor v. Spindle, 2 Gratt. 44.

XIV. Revival of Judgments.

A. BY SCIRE FACIAS.

See the title SCIRE FACIAS.

1. Origin and History of Writ.

Prior to Statute.—It is not definitely known whether this right to a scire facias was a right at common law or by virtue of the statute of Westminster 2. Judge Carr in Allen v. Cunningham, 3 Leigh 395, seems to have thought it was by virtue of that statute, and this is the prevailing opinion. See Holt v. Lynch, 18 W. Va. 567.

But Judge Green in the case of Dykes v. Woodhouse, 3 Rand. 291, claims that the scire facias existed at common law.

The practice of the English courts, in relation to writs of scire facias for the renewal of judgments, as well as other matters of practice, came to us on the settlement of the country, and has prevailed here, so far as adapted to the organization of our courts, and compatible with our own legislation. Williamson v. Crawford, 7 Gratt. 202.

Under the Statute.—It has been decided in West Virginia that § 10, ch. 139, of the West Virginia Code, set out below, gives the remedy for revival of judgments and it will be seen that the provision in the Virginia Code is substantially the same. Wells v. Graham, 39 W. Va. 605, 20 S. E. 576.

2. Office and Nature of Writ.

Office and Purpose.—The purpose of the writ of scire facias is to give notice to the defendant of an application for award of execution, which can not be had without an order to that effect, where execution had not been sued out upon the judgment within a year and a day. Williamson v. Crawford, 7 Gratt. 202; Bolanz v. Com., 24 Gratt. 31.

So "in all cases where the writ of scire facias is required either to revive a previous judgment, above a year old, or where a person has become interested in the suit, who was not a party to the judgment, it is a judicial writ to warn the defendant to plead any matter in bar of the execution; and in these cases it is only a quasi continuation of the former suit brought merely to revive the former judgment, and is then properly called a writ of execution." See Foster on Scire Facias, Law Library, 45. The whole office of the writ is to obtain, upon due notification to the defendant, in such cases, execution of the judgment. Lavell *v.* McCurdy, 77 Va. 763.

Nature.—A scire facias is not an original action, but a mere continuation of the same suit. Wells *v.* Graham, 39 W. Va. 605, 20 S. E. 576; Lavell *v.* McCurdy, 77 Va. 763.

A scire facias is a continuation of the same suit, a process in cases of suspension of execution from dormancy of the judgment by death or other cause, to have an award of execution in the name of a new party, and not to try the matter over again, and if the court go beyond this and render an original judgment, as in an original action, it exceeds its jurisdiction proper upon such a writ, and its judgment is void. Hogg's Plead. & Forms (2d Ed.) 508; 2 Barton L. Prac. 1024; 1 Black, Judgm., 498; Lavell *v.* McCurdy, 77 Va. 763; Wade *v.* Hancock, 76 Va. 620. Maxwell *v.* Leeson, 50 W. Va. 361, 368, 40 S. E. 420.

3. When Writ May Issue.
a. Nature, Requisites and Validity of Judgment.
(1) Final Judgments and Decrees.

Under the Virginia Code of 1873, the decree must have become final before it might be revived. Serles *v.* Cromer, 88 Va. 426, 13 S. E. 859.

(2) Judgments Quando Acciderint.

Scire facias may be brought upon a judgment "when assets" or "if assets" to ascertain whether there is not a surplus of assets after paying the debts which have priority to his judgment. Braxton *v.* Wood, 4 Gratt. 25.

An action of debt or scire facias may be brought upon judgment "when assets," or "if assets;" and if upon the plea of plene administravit, the issue is found for the executor or administrator, the plaintiff may take another

judgment when assets.   Braxton *v.* Wood, 4 Gratt. 25.

(3) Validity of Judgment.
(a) In General.

A judgment absolutely void can not be revived. Gray *v.* Stuart, 33 Gratt. 351.

Upon bill by S. against G. and P. to subject the land of G. to satisfy a judgment recovered against G., P. and others, it appears and was so decided by the circuit court upon appeal from a judgment of the county court on a scire facias to revive the judgment, that no process had been served on P., and that he had not entered his appearance in the original action, and the scire facias was dismissed for a variance between the writ and the evidence. Held, the judgment against P. was void and a nullity, the court having no jurisdiction to render a judgment against him, he not having been served with process, or appearing in the cause. Gray *v.* Stuart, 33 Gratt. 351.

There is a manifest distinction between an erroneous judgment and a void judgment. The first is a valid judgment though erroneous, until reversed, provided it is the judgment of a court of competent jurisdiction. The latter is no judgment at all. It is a mere nullity. The first can not be assailed in any other court but an appellate court. The latter may be assailed in any court, anywhere, whenever any claim is made, or right asserted under it. Gray *v.* Stuart, 33 Gratt. 351; Staunton Perpetual Bldg., etc., Co. *v.* Haden, 92 Va. 201, 23 S. E. 285; Poe *v.* Machine Works, 24 W. Va. 517, 524.

(b) Pendency of Injunction to Judgment.

See post, "Limitations," XIV, A, 11. The dependency of an injunction to a judgment at law, will not prevent the revival of the judgment upon the death of either the plaintiff or defendant; the injunction operates upon the judgment on the scire facias, to restrain and prohibit the issue of execution thereon. Richardson *v.* Prince George Justices, 11 Gratt. 190; Hutsonpiller *v.* Stover, 12 Gratt. 579.

"The plea that the judgment had not been suspended by an injunction, offered no bar to the scire facias. It but served to point to another matter which might be made the subject of a plea in bar, and which, if not successfully answered, would defeat the action. It is true the scire facias does allege that execution of the judgment had been suspended by an injunction; but this allegation was unnecessary, and may be treated as surplusage; and a naked traverse of such a matter offers no sufficient defense to the action. If the defendant desired to set up the statute of limitations in his defense, it was his duty to plead it distinctly and directly. He could not be entitled to the benefit of it upon a collateral issue. If the plea were strictly true and there never had been an injunction, it does not follow that the judgment could not be revived. And if the defendant had pleaded the statute of limitations, the plaintiffs might have replied some matter (other than the pendency of the injunction) which might serve to take the case out of its operation, but of the benefit of which, upon the issue tendered, they might be deprived. I think, therefore, this plea also was properly rejected by the court." Richardson *v.* Prince George Justices, 11 Gratt. 190, 196.

"I can perceive no good reason why a party plaintiff, whose judgment has been enjoined, may not be permitted, upon the death of the defendant pending the injunction, to revive it against his personal representative. Such a proceeding can be no breach of the injunction, the object of which is to restrain the party from enforcing the judgment by execution, and reaping its fruits, until the matters of equity alleged can be heard and considered.

All that the court of chancery intends to restrain is execution. The plaintiff may proceed so far as to be able to take out execution the instant the injunction is dissolved. 1 Eden on Injunct. 97. Now, where the defendant dies after the injunction, unless the plaintiff can go on and revive against his representative, he will not be in a situation, upon the dissolution of the injunction, to issue his execution, but must then be delayed till he can sue out his scire facias and obtain the order of revival; and thus, by the supervening death of the defendant, he is placed in a worse condition than when the injunction was allowed; while, if he is allowed to go on and revive his judgment, notwithstanding the injunction, he is merely reinstating himself to the right which he then had or issuing his execution as soon as the injunction is dissolved. In fact, the right to sue out execution upon his dissolution is the very condition of an injunction to a judgment; and if the judgment creditor die pending the injunction, the court of chancery will in a summary way impose it as a condition on the complainant to consent to revive at law, under the penalty of having his injunction dissolved if he refuse. Medley *v.* Pannill, 1 Rob. 63. And there can be no conceivable difference in this respect whether the necessity for the revival is occasioned by the death of the judgment creditor or the judgment debtor. The inconvenience to be remedied is precisely the same in both cases; and what the court of chancery would itself enforce in a summary way by a rule, it surely would not regard as a breach of the injunction when sought to be accomplished by the ordinary process of law. The judgment creditor must take care to stop with the order reviving his judgment. Thus far may he go but no farther; and the judgment of the court upon the scire facias is to be regarded as in strict subordination to the injunction to the original judgment of which it is the mere continuation." Richardson v. Prince George Justices, 11 Gratt. 190, 198.

Averments.—The scire facias stated the judgment had been suspended by injunction. This was an unnecessary allegation, and may be treated as surplusage; and a plea that the judgment had not been suspended by injunction, offered no bar to the scire facias. Richardson v. Prince George Justices, 11 Gratt. 190.

The scire facias further stated that the injunction had been dissolved. A plea that the injunction had not been dissolved is bad, and an issue made upon it is immaterial. Therefore, though the court admits improper evidence upon it, offered by the plaintiff, it is not cause for reversing the judgment. Richardson v. Prince George Just.ces, 11 Gratt. 190.

Upon a judgment in ejectment, if execution of the writ of habere facias possessionem be prevented for several years by injunction, the plaintiff is entitled to the writ on motion upon a rule to show cause, without a scire facias, provided not more than a year has elapsed since the affirmance, by the court of appeals, of the decree dissolving the injunction and dismissing the bill in chancery. In such case, if the term laid in the declaration has expired pending the proceedings on the injunction, the court to which the motion is made for the writ of habere facias possessionem, may cause the term to be enlarged and award the writ, upon a rule to show cause, served upon the defendant. Noland v. Seekright, 6 Munf. 185.

Smith v. Charlton Criticised.—In Richardson v. Prince George Justices, 11 Gratt. 190, 199, it is said: "Judge Baldwin, in delivering his opinion in the case of Smith v. Charlton, 7 Gratt. 425, 466, intimates that pending a writ of error or injunction or cessat, an action of debt or scire facias can not be brought upon the judgment. He cites no authority for the proposition, and so far as it respects the injunction, it is an intimation thrown out arguendo and by way of illustration. He probably did not advert to the distinction between the nature and effect of an injunction and that of a writ of error or cessat. At all events it was a point not at all material to the decision in that case, and the remark of the judge as it respects the injunction, must be regarded as obiter merely." Smith v. Charlton, 7 Gratt. 425, also cited in Hutsonpiller v. Stover, 12 Gratt. 579, 582; Werdenbaugh v. Reid, 20 W. Va. 588.

b. Grounds for Issuance of Writ.

(1) In General.

"It is needless here to attempt to classify the numerous cases and their distinctions, in which the proceeding by scire facias is appropriate. In our practice this remedy is most frequently resorted to, to continue a former suit to execution; and this may be, either when this writ is required to revive a judgment by or against the same party, or when it is required to revive a judgment where there is, as in this case, a new party to the suit." Lavell v. McCurdy, 77 Va. 763, 769.

(2) To Revive Dormant Judgments.

At Common Law.—By the common law, the failure of the plaintiff to sue out execution within the year, so far created the presumption of a payment, satisfaction or release of the judgment, as to compel the plaintiff to bring his action on the judgment; and thus give the defendant an opportunity, by pleading, to put in issue such supposed payment, satisfaction or release. By the statute of Westminster 2, 13 Edward 1, ch. 45, a scire facias is given to the plaintiff to revive his judgment where he has omitted to sue out execution within the year; and is now the remedy most usually resorted to for such purpose. Notwithstanding the year's neglect drives the plaintiff, generally, to his action or scire facias, the English cases furnish many exceptions to the rule. Smith v. Charlton, 7 Gratt. 425,

447; Beale *v.* Botetourt Justices, 10 Gratt. 278.

In Beale *v.* Botetourt Justices, 10 Gratt. 278, 281, the court held that, "a judgment on which no execution is issued within a year and a day from its date, is, generally, so far presumed to be satisfied as to render a scire facias to revive it if necessary. See dicta to the same effect, in Nimmo *v.* Com., 4 Hen. & M. 57, 67, in Spotts *v.* Com., 85 Va. 531, 8 S. E. 375, and again in Smith *v.* Charlton, 7 Gratt. 425, 447.

Present Statutory Provisions.—In Virginia, on a judgment, execution may be issued within a year, and a scire facias or an action may be brought within ten years after the date of the judgment; and where execution issues within the year, other executions may be issued, or a scire facias or an action may be brought within ten years from the return day of an execution on which there is no return by an officer, or within twenty years from the return day of an execution on which there is such return; except that where the scire facias or action is against the personal representative of a decedent, it shall be brought within five years from the qualification of such representative; and in computing time under this section, there shall, as to writs of fieri facias, be omitted from such computation the time elapsed between the first day of January, eighteen hundred and sixty-nine, and the twenty-ninth day of March, eighteen hundred and seventy-one. Any return by an officer on an execution showing that the same has not been satisfied, shall be a sufficient return within the meaning of this section. (1870-71, p. 341.) Va. Code, 1904, § 3577.

In West Virginia on a judgment, execution may be issued within two years after the date thereof, or if none be so issued, the court in which the judgment was rendered may thereafter, and within ten years from the date of the judgment, upon ten days, notice to the party against whom the same is, order an execution to issue thereon for such sum as remains unpaid. Where execution issues within two years as aforesaid, other execution may be issued on such judgment without notice, within ten years from the return day of the last execution issued thereon, on which there is no return by an officer, or which has been returned unsatisfied. And an action, suit or scire facias may be brought upon a judgment on which no execution issued within the said two years, or where there has been a change of parties by death or otherwise, at any time within ten years next after the date of the judgment. But if such action, suit or scire facias be against a personal representative of a decedent, it shall be brought within five years from the qualification of such representative. W. Va. Code, 1899, ch. 139, § 4150.

For the treatment of cases arising under this statute, see ante, "Judgment Liens," VI. And see post, "Limitations," XIV, A, 11.

(3) To Revive Judgment by or against Same Party.

This remedy is most frequently resorted to to continue a former suit to execution; and this may be, either when this writ is required to revive a judgment by or against the same party, or when it is required to revive a judgment where there is a new party to the suit. Lavell *v.* McCurdy, 77 Va. 763.

(4) To Charge New Parties.

Foster on Scire Facias 99, says: "It is a general rule that in all cases where a new person who was not a party to a judgment or recognizance derives a benefit by, or becomes chargeable to the execution, there must be a scire facias to make him a party to the judgment. But where the execution is not beneficial or chargeable to a person not a party to the judgment, then it seems this rule does apply, and a scire facias is not necessary.

* * * The reason for the rule is that the execution must be warranted by the judgment, and a new party being a stranger to the judgment, he not being named on the record, the judgment would not warrant an execution for or against him until he should be made a party." In the place cited in Foster, and also on page 189, Foster says, that "where a sole plaintiff or defendant dies after judgment, a scire facias must be sued out by or against his personal representative, in order that execution may be had of the goods and chattels of the party against whom the judgment is given." See Bart. L. Prac. 1022. Maxwell v. Leeson, 50 W. Va. 361, 365, 40 S. E. 420.

Where a new person, who was not a party to the judgment, derives a benefit by, or becomes chargeable to the execution upon it, there must be a scire facias to make him a party to the judgment. Allen v. Cunningham, 3 Leigh 395, 401; Holt v. Lynch, 18 W. Va. 567, 572.

It is a rule whenever it is sought to fix a party on a judgment given against another, it must be done by scire facias; the rule being that where a new person, who was not a party to a judgment, derives a benefit by, or becomes chargeable to the execution, there must be a scire facias to make him a party to the judgment. Lavell v. McCurdy, 77 Va. 763, 769.

The object of a scire facias to revive a judgment is to make the record consistent, by suggesting a change of parties to get an execution in new names, and then show by the record why there is a departure in the execution from the judgment and justify such variance. Maxwell v. Leeson, 50 W. Va. 361, 40 S. E. 420.

"What is the reason for a scire facias to revive a judgment? It is to make the record consistent. It would not do, where the judgment was between living parties, to issue an execution in favor of or against their administrators, as this would not har-monize with the record of the judgment; and hence we resort to a scire facias suggesting a change of parties in order to get an execution in new names, and thus show by the record why there is a departure in the execution from the judgment, and justify such variance." Maxwell v. Leeson, 50 W. Va. 361, 364, 40 S. E. 420.

"From a consideration of these authorities I understand the law to be, that at common law before the statute of 2 Westm. the judgment creditor was entitled to sue out a scire facias at common law and proceed to his execution in those cases, where he desired to charge in execution a person, who was not a party to the judgment, that is, where the original party to the judgment is dead, and it is desired to charge his representative. But if there was any party to the judgment still surviving, although one or more in the same interest was dead, he was not put to his scire facias to revive, but could proceed in execution against the surviving party." Holt v. Lynch, 18 W. Va. 567, 574.

(5) Where Execution Debtor Escapes or Is Discharged.

If a debtor charged in execution escapes, the creditor may obtain a new execution, either by scire facias, or upon motion after reasonable notice. Fawkes v. Davison, 8 Leigh 554; Stuart v. Hamilton, 8 Leigh 503.

Or he may have new execution in the same manner after the discharge of the debtor for nonpayment of jail fees. Stuart v. Hamilton, 8 Leigh 503.

(6) Real and Personal Actions.

"At common law no scire facias would issue on a judgment except in real actions. In all personal actions, where the lapse of time or the change of parties had been such as to prevent the taking out execution, the party entitled to the judgment was obliged to bring an action of debt on it, 2 Inst. 269. To remedy this inconvenience the statute of Westminster 2, 1 Edw

I., ch. 45, gave a scire facias in personal actions." Green, Judge, in the case of Dykes *v.* Woodhouse, 3 Rand. 291, disagrees with this view of Judge Carr, that the scire facias sprang from the statute of Westminster 2, but claims, that it existed at common law, and that the statute only covered, so far as it regards this question, those cases where the execution was not sued out within the year. He says: "It is said, that the scire facias in personal actions was given by the statute of Westminster 2, ch. 45, and did not exist at common law, Bac. Abr. scire facias c. 1. Lord Holt, in Withers *v.* Harris, 2 Salk. 600, doubted whether this was true as a general proposition, but submitted to the weight of authority. I think any one, who will examine the statute at large, will agree with Lord Holt." Holt *v.* Lynch, 18 W. Va. 567, 572.

4. From Whence Issued.

A scire facias to revive a suit, or action, decree, or judgment can only be issued in the suit or action to be revived; and if the suit was in equity, the scire facias must also be in equity, and governed by the rules of that court; and if the action was at law, the proceeding must conform to the rules of that court. Garrison *v.* Myers, 12 W. Va. 330.

In this state the statute as to reviving suits is as follows: By § 4 of ch. 127 of the Code it is provided, that "In any stage of any case, a scire facias may be sued out, for or against the committee of any party, who is insane or a convict; or for or against a party before insane, the powers of whose committee have ceased; or for or against the personal representative of the decedent, who, or whose personal representatives, was a party; or for or against the heirs, or devisees of a decedent, who was a party; or for the assignee or beneficiary party, to show cause why the suit should not proceed in the name of him or them;

or where the party dying, or whose powers cease, or such insane person or convict, is plaintiff or appellant, the person or persons, for whom such scire facias might be sued out, may without notice or scire facias move, that the suit proceed in his or their name. In the former case after the service of the scire facias, or in the latter case on such motion, if no sufficient cause be shown against it, an order shall be entered, that the suit proceed according to such scire facias or motion. Any such new party (except in an appellate court) may have a continuance of the case at the term, at which such order is entered; and the court may allow him to plead anew, or amend the pleadings, as far as it deems reasonable, but in other respects the case shall proceed to final judgment or decree, for or against him, in like manner as if the case had been pending for or against him, before such scire facias or motion." It is clear that a scire facias, to revive a suit or action, decree or judgment, can only be issued in the suit to be revived; and if the suit was in equity, the scire facias must be in equity, and be governed by the rules of that court; and if the action was at law, the proceedings must conform to the rules of that court. Therefore we do not think the court erred, in treating the scire facias in this cause, as being a proceeding in equity. Garrison *v.* Myers, 12 W. Va. 330, 334.

5. Summons and Service of Process.

See titles SERVICE OF PROCESS; SUMMONS AND PROCESS.

A summons, issued by a justice of the peace, requiring the defendant to appear before him at his office, at a proper time therein specified, to answer the complaint of the plaintiff, "In a civil action for the recovery of money due on a judgment on the docket of J. A. Connelly, late a justice, to show cause why said judgment should not revive and be re-entered and execution issue thereon, in which the plaintiff will demand judgment for one hundred and sixty-two dollars and —— cents, exclusive of interest and cost." is sufficient. Meighen v. Williams, 50 W. Va. 65, 40 S. E. 332.

A writ of scire facias summoning the defendants "before the—of our said circuit court," is properly quashed. Raub v. Otterback, 89 Va. 645, 16 S. E. 933.

Where defendants are nonresidents, and the scire facias is not executed on them in the county where suit is brought, and the writ was not executed at least ten days before the return day, the service was illegal. Code, §§ 3215, 3220. Raub v. Otterback, 89 Va. 645, 16 S. E. 933.

Where service on one of the defendants, outside of the state, by private individual, is not made fifteen days before the return day, such service is not only not equivalent to order of publication, but is illegal. Raub v. Otterback, 89 Va. 645, 16 S. E. 933.

Where the affidavit of service outside of the state by private individual fails to show that the affiant was not interested in the suit, such service was also illegal. Raub v. Otterback, 89 Va. 645, 16 S. E. 933.

Where a writ of scire facias to revive a decree describes a judgment, and there is no demand for an attachment against property, and no indication that the defendants have property in the state, and the writ has only been served outside the state by private individual (such service being equivalent only to an order of publication); held, such will not warrant a personal judgment. Raub v. Otterback, 89 Va. 645, 16 S. E. 933, citing Smith v. Chilton, 77 Va. 535.

6. Return of Writ.

Time of Return.—A writ of scire facias to award execution on a judgment is included under the statute providing that process from any court, whether original, mesne, or final, ex-

cept a summons for a witness, shall be returnable within ninety days after its date (Code, 1873, ch. 166, § 2), hence if such a writ is not on its face returnable within that period, it is void and any judgment rendered thereon is void. Objection in such case may be taken by demurrer. Lavell v. McCurdy, 77 Va. 763, citing Warren v. Saunders, 27 Gratt. 259.

A writ of scire facias returnable at rules "on the first day of the next term—June term, 1889," that day being the second Monday in June, whereas there was no rules until the third Monday, was invalid. Code, § 3226. Raub v. Otterback, 89 Va. 645, 16 S. E. 933.

Place of Return.—The writ may be returnable at rules in the office, or in court. And the order awarding execution is made upon due return of the process unless good cause be shown against it. If the writ is returnable to rules, it is made at rules, and if not set aside at the next succeeding term, becomes a final judgment of the last day of the term. If the writ is returnable to the court, the order is made in court. It is not necessary to send the case to rules, because it is not a proceeding which requires a declaration or a rule to plead; the purpose for which rule days are required in the office. Va. Code, 1860, ch. 171, § 4. Bolanz v. Com., 24 Gratt. 31; McVeigh v. Bank, 76 Va. 267; Williamson v. Crawford, 7 Gratt. 202; Smith v. Hutchinson, 78 Va. 683.

Hence there is no error in a judgment overruling a motion to send the case to rules, nor in a judgment that the plaintiffs have execution against the defendant, etc. Though such judgment is unnecessary, as the judgment at rules, awarding execution, not having been set aside, would by operation of law, become a final judgment as of the last day of the term, still it would not to the prejudice of the plaintiff in error. McVeigh v. Bank, 76 Va. 267.

Return of Two Nihils.

Provisions of Statute.—Act of 1819. "On writs of scire facias for the renewal of judgments, no judgment shall be rendered on the return of two nihils, unless the defendant resides in the county, or unless he be absent from the commonwealth, and have no known attorney therein. But such scire facias may be directed to the sheriff of any county of the commonwealth wherein the defendant or his attorney shall reside or be found, which being returned served, the court may proceed to judgment thereupon, as if the defendant had resided in the county." Act of 1831. "That all writs of scire facias which shall issue to revive either a pending suit, or a judgment or decree in any of the courts of this commonwealth, where it shall appear by affidavit of the plaintiff or other person, filed with the clerk, that the defendant is out of the commonwealth, may be served on the defendant's agent or attorney in fact, if any he have within the commonwealth, or if he have no such agent or attorney known, by publication for four weeks successively previous to the return day of such court, in some newspaper published in this commonwealth." Williamson v. Crawford, 7 Gratt. 202.

Construction of Statute.—The act, 1 Rev. Va. Code, ch. 128, § 65, p. 505, in relation to a scire facias to revive a judgment, is not repealed by the act of March 29th, Supp. Rev. Code, ch. 197, § 2, on the same subject. Williamson v. Crawford, 7 Gratt. 202.

This last act is not repealed by the act of 1831, Supp. Rev. Code, p. 258, providing that upon the affidavit therein prescribed, service of the scire facias was authorized, where the defendant was out of the commonwealth, upon his agent or attorney in fact or by publication, since this last act is merely permissive. Williamson v. Crawford, 7 Gratt. 202.

Award of Execution.—The practice in Virginia, like that in England, is to award execution upon the return of two nihils except that it is restricted by the act of 1792, 1 Rev. Va. Code, ch. 128, § 65, to cases where the defendant resides in the county or where he is absent from the commonwealth and has no known attorney therein. Lyons v. Gregory, 3 Hen. & M. 237.

"The practice of the English courts, in relation to writs of scire facias for the renewal of judgments, as well as other matters of practice, came to us on the settlement of the country, and has prevailed here, so far as adapted to the organization of our courts, and compatible with our own legislation. By that practice, execution was awarded on the return of two nihils, and it was recognized by our acts of 1792 (1 Rev. Code, ch. 128, § 65, p. 505), but was restricted by that act to cases where the defendant resided in the county, or where he was absent from the commonwealth, and had no known attorney therein. By the act of 1831 (Supp. Rev. Code, p. 258), upon the affidavit therein prescribed being made and filed, service of the scire facias was authorized, where the defendant was out of the commonwealth, upon his agent or attorney in fact, or by publication in some newspaper as therein provided for. But this last-mentioned act is permissive only, and in no wise abolishes the previously-existing practice. The purpose of the writ of scire facias is to give notice to the defendant of an application for award of execution, which can not be had without an order to that effect, where execution had not been sued out upon the judgment within a year and a day; and the order is made in court, or at the rules, upon due return of the process, unless good cause can be shown to the contrary; and it is not a proceeding which requires a declaration or a rule to plead. The default of the defendant in not appearing to show cause, is a sufficient foundation for award of execution, which if made at the rules, and not set aside at the next succeeding term, becomes a final judgment of the last day of the term. The provisions of the 6th section of ch. 170 of the New Code, are not applicable to the present case, which occurred before the same took effect." Williamson v. Crawford, 7 Gratt. 202, 204.

Evidence of Insolvency.—Where a writ of scire facias is sued out on a judgment on a forthcoming bond, and returned "no property," this return is conclusive evidence of the insolvency of the execution debtor. Cooper v. Daugherty, 85 Va. 343, 7 S. E. 387, 393, citing Goodall v. Stewart, 2 Hen. & M. 105, 111.

7. Parties.

a. Parties Plaintiff.

(1) In General.

A scire facias must be brought in the name of the plaintiff in the judgment or his personal representative, because there is the legal title. Wells v. Graham, 39 W. Va. 605, 20 S. E. 576.

It is a general rule, that no person can bring a writ of error, who is not a party or privy to the record; but the right to bring the writ of error in case of the death of the party, against whom the judgment was rendered, will be in the personal representative without a revival of the judgment, because the personal representative stands in the shoes of the deceased, and has the same rights, as his intestate had, with reference to the judgment. Phares v. Saunders, 18 W. Va. 336.

(2) Assignee of Judgment.

An assignee of a judgment can not, in his own name, maintain a writ of scire facias to revive it. "There is no inconvenience to result from this holding, as execution can be awarded in the name of the plaintiff in the judgment, or his representative, which name the assignee has always a right to use, even beyond the control of that party, or, if preferable, the order of award of execution can recite that

it is for the use of the assignee." Wells v. Graham, 39 W. Va. 605, 20 S. E. 576.

Section 4, ch. 127, W. Va. Code, 1891, provides that "in any stage of any case, a scire facias may be sued out for or against * * * the assignee or beneficiary party to show cause why the suit should not proceed in the name of him or them," but a suit is no longer pending after judgment. Wells v. Graham, 39 W. Va. 605, 20 S. E. 576.

"Seeing the remedies given for revival of judgments, we then appeal to the common law, or some statute, if to be found, to tell us who shall move in those remedies. The common law tells us it must be the plaintiff in the judgment, or his personal representative. 1 Black, Judgm., § 488; 21 Am. & Eng. Ency. Law, 858. There is no statute allowing an assignee of a judgment to sue in his own name by action or scire facias. Section 14, ch. 99, Code, enables 'the assignee of any bond, note, account or writing not negotiable' to sue in his own name, but does not include judgment. This is a circumstance strong against the contention of the appellants. They urge that the scire facias is an original action. This seems not to be so. 1 Black, Judgm., § 482; 21 Am. & Eng. Ency. Law, 855. If it were, they could not use it, as § 14, ch. 99, does not give an assignee right to sue on a judgment in his own name. That equity allows a suit by assignee argues nothing, as it allows suit on equitable title." Wells v. Graham, 39 W. Va. 605, 20 S. E. 576.

"Except for § 10, ch. 139, Code, we might with more readiness apply § 4, ch. 127, to the case; but as § 10, ch. 139, relates in terms to the revival of judgments, we must go by it, and not the other provision. It provides that an action, suit, or scire facias may be brought on a judgment. It does not give right to an assignee to revive. It is true, it does not give right to any particular person to use those remedies for revival, only giving such remedies; but I mean it is this section which gives the remedy for revival of a judgment, not § 4, ch. 127." Wells *v.* Graham, 39 W. Va. 605, 20 S. E. 576.

H. recovers a judgment against W. and P. Afterwards W. and H. die, and K. qualifies as the executor of W. and the administrator of H. As administrator of H., K. sues out a scire facias to revive the judgment against P. the surviving obligor, and he appears and files a general plea of payment, without stating the nature of the payment. He proves that H. in his lifetime assigned the judgment to D., who was a debtor of T., who was a debtor of W.; and that under an agreement between T. and D. that T. would take in payment of his debt, any debt on W. which K. would take in payment of T.'s debt to W. D. obtained this judgment from H., and assigned it to K., who credited the amount on T.'s debt to W. There was a verdict for the defendant, and on motion for a new trial, held: K. having taken the assignment to himself, and credited the amount upon the debt due from T. to W., he made himself liable to his testator's estate for that amount; but having taken the assignment to himself, he was the owner of the judgment, and might as administrator of H. maintain the scire facias to revive the judgment at law. Peery *v.* Peery, 26 Gratt. 320.

(3) Heirs.

Heirs named in a decree as being entitled to any balance of the price of lands sold to pay debts, after paying the costs and debts, without proof that said price sufficed to pay the costs and debts and leave a balance; held, not to have such an interest in such decree as entitled them to revive the suit. Riely *v.* Kinzel, 85 Va. 480, 7 S. E. 907.

b. Parties Defendant.
(1) In General.

"Where the execution goes only against personalty, only the personal representative is a necessary party. It goes to show that only he need be a party to a scire facias whose property is to be taken by execution under it. It goes to show that only a party to be benefited or prejudiced directly by force of the execution itself need be a party to the scire facias." Maxwell *v.* Leeson, 50 W. Va. 361, 365, 40 S. E. 420.

(2) Bail.

See the title SCIRE FACIAS.

If the defendant in an action of covenant die, after judgment by default against him and the bail for his appearance, and before a writ of inquiry executed, the plaintiff can not have a scire facias against the bail, but only against the executors or administrators of the defendant. Saunders *v.* Gaines, 3 Munf. 225.

(3) Terre Tenants.

Where the plaintiff in a judgment or decree for money dies, it is not necessary that a writ of scire facias to revive and have execution in the name of his personal representative against the defendant still living should make terre tenants parties, and an award of execution upon a scire facias which keeps alive the lien of the judgment or decree on land as to the defendant, will also keep the lien alive as to the terre tenants, though not parties to the scire facias. Maxwell *v.* Leeson, 50 W. Va. 361, 40 S. E. 420, disapproving the rule in 21 Am. & Eng. Ency. L. (1st Ed.) 8; Black on Judgm.

The court saying in this case: "We never have in the Virginias made heirs parties to writs of scire facias to revive money judgments, though on judgments or decrees for the recovery of land, where a writ of habere facias possessionem must issue, as in ejectment, there should be a revival against the heirs, because that writ operates directly on the land. When the mode of enforcing money judgments against land was by elegit, which was a writ of execution operative of its own force upon the land, a scire facias went against the heir and terre tenant; but even then the scire facias might go against the heir alone." Maxwell *v.* Leeson, 50 W. Va. 361, 40 S. E. 420.

(4) Personal Representative, Heirs and Devisees.

In an action of trespass q. c. f. if the defendant dies after verdict and judgment, the plaintiff has a right to a scire facias against the personal representative of the defendant, though not against his heir or devisee; and the personal representative has a right to reverse the judgment, on appeal, if he can. Harris *v.* Crenshaw, 3 Rand. 14.

"We never have in the Virginias made heirs parties to writs of scire facias to revive money judgments, though on judgments or decrees for the recovery of land, where a writ of habere facias possessionem must issue, as in ejectment, there should be a revival against the heirs, because that writ operates directly on the land." Maxwell *v.* Leeson, 50 W. Va. 361, 368, 40 S. E. 420.

(5) Alienees of Judgment Debtor.

"We never make alienees of the judgment debtor parties to a scire facias to revive judgments." Maxwell *v.* Leeson, 50 W. Va. 361, 364, 40 S. E. 420.

(6) Curator.

When a court of probate, under the 24th section of the statute concerning wills, appoints a person to collect and preserve the estate of a decedent until administration be granted, such appointee can not properly be sued on a bond of the decedent. If he be sued and judgment rendered against him, a scire facias upon the judgment will not lie, after administration is granted, against the administrator, nor will the judgment be any bar to a new action against the administrator, upon his decedent's bond. Wynn *v.* Wynn, 8 Leigh 264.

c. Demurrer.

A demurrer will lie to a petition to revive a decree if it fails to make all the parties to the original suit parties to the petition, or if it make parties of persons whose only connection with the transaction is that they are the last in the list of purchasers of the land sold under the decree. Riely *v.* Kinzel, 85 Va. 480, 7 S. E. 907.

8. Form and Sufficiency of the Proceeding.

a. Necessity for Declaration or Rule to Plead.

Upon a scire facias to revive a judgment, neither a declaration nor a rule to plead is necessary. And if the writ is made returnable to the rules, and the defendant makes default, there should be an award of execution, which, if not set aside at the next term, becomes a final judgment as of the last day of the term. Williamson *v.* Crawford, 7 Gratt. 202; Smith *v.* Hutchinson, 78 Va. 683.

"Upon the authority of Williamson *v.* Crawford, 7 Gratt. 202, which is recognized in a later case—Bolanz *v.* Com., 24 Gratt. 31, 38—as accurately expounding the law of this state, the court is of opinion that there is no error in the judgment of the court below. Upon a scire facias to revive a judgment, neither a declaration nor rule to plead is necessary. And if the writ is made returnable to rules, as it was in this case, and the defendant makes default, it is unnecessary to give him a rule to plead, but there should be an award of execution, which, if not set aside at the next term, becomes a final judgment as of the last day of the term." McVeigh *v.* Bank, 76 Va. 267, 268.

b. Necessity for Order of Court.

In Williamson *v.* Crawford, 7 Gratt. 202, Baldwin, J., delivering the opinion of the court, said: "The purpose of the writ of scire facias is to give notice to the defendant of an application for award of execution, which can not be had without an order to that effect, where execution had not been sued out upon the judgment within a year and a day; and the order is made in court or at rules, upon due return of process, unless good cause be shown to the contrary; and it is not a proceeding which requires a declaration or a rule to plead. The default of the defendant in not appearing to show cause is a sufficient foundation for award of execution, which, if made at the rules, and not set aside at the succeeding term, becomes a final judgment of the last day of the term." Quoted in Smith *v.* Hutchinson, 78 Va. 683, 688.

But in another case it was said: "Neither declaration nor rule is necessary upon a scire facias to revive a judgment. If scire facias is returnable to rules, and defendant makes default, there should then be an award of execution, which, if not set aside at the next term, becomes a final judgment as of the last day of the term. No order of the court is necessary in such case, but could prejudice no one." McVeigh *v.* Bank, 76 Va. 267.

c. Averments.

(1) Suggestion of Death.

A scire facias should suggest the death of the party or other cause of revival. Wells *v.* Graham, 39 W. Va. 605, 20 S. E. 576.

"This scire facias suggests no death or cause of revival. It should have done so, if the plaintiff is dead, as the judgment says he is." Wells *v.* Graham, 39 W. Va. 605, 20 S. E. 576.

P. obtained a rule against T. and others to show cause why a writ of possession should not be awarded against them, requiring them to deliver certain lands into his possession which had been decreed him in a suit, to which they were not parties. They answered that they were in possession as tenants under S., who had been a party to the suit of P., and that the decree in favor of the latter was erroneous, and that S. had deceased since the rendition of the decree, and that the bill should have been dismissed as to S. Held, the decree being final as to S., it was unnecessary to suggest his death and waive the suit against his heirs in order to proceed with the rule. Trimble *v.* Patton, 5 W. Va. 432.

(2) Acquisition of Property Since Judgment.

A writ of scire facias need not set forth what goods, lands, etc., have been acquired by the defendant, since the date of the judgment. Lang *v.* Lewis, 1 Rand. 277.

(3) Scire Facias against Heir.

A scire facias against the heir upon a judgment recovered against the ancestor, need not aver proceedings against the personal representative, without effect. But if no such proceedings have been had against the personal representative, the heir must set up such defense by plea, in the nature of a plea in abatement, not by demurrer. Rogers *v.* Denham, 2 Gratt. 200.

(4) Scire Facias on Office Judgment.

A scire facias upon an office judgment in a suit at law, which does not aver that the office judgment was confirmed by the court or by rise of the next court, will be fatally defective. The case of Evans *v.* Freeland, 3 Munf. 119, is a sufficient authority to prove this proposition; Lee, J., delivering the opinion of the court in Roach *v.* Gardner, 9 Gratt. 89, 92.

A scire facias, purporting to be founded upon a judgment entered at rules, in the clerk's office of a county court, but not mentioning that judgment was confirmed, by not being set aside at the ensuing quarterly term, nor even that such quarterly term occurred prior to the suing out of the said scire facias, ought to be quashed, as not setting forth any legal cause of action. Evans *v.* Freeland, 3 Munf. 119.

(5) Surplusage.

At Whose Instance Awarded.— Where a judgment is in the name of four persons, as justices of a certain county suing for the benefit of the marshal of the district court of chancery, the fact that the scire facias recites that it was awarded at the instance of the administrator of such marshal instead of the four parties on the record, is not a fatal defect, for though it might be more regular for the scire facias to recite that it was awarded at the instance and on behalf of the plaintiffs on the record, as it would have been good if the averment at whose instance it had issued had been wholly omitted, such an averment is mere surplusage, and does not vitiate the scire facias. Richardson *v.* Prince George Justices, 11 Gratt. 190.

"The objection that the scire facias recites it was awarded at the instance of P. P. Mayo, administrator of Charles L. Wingfield, instead of Benjamin Harrison, and the other three parties who are the plaintiffs on the record, is one rather of form than of substance. It might have been more regular for the scire facias to recite that it was awarded at the instance and on behalf of the plaintiffs on the record, but as it would have been good if the averment at whose instance it had issued had been wholly omitted, I regard it as mere surplusage, and not serving to vitiate; and the rather because the requirement of the process is that the defendant shall show, if anything he can, why execution should not be awarded against him 'according the judgment aforesaid,' thus contemplating conformity to the judgment in the manner of the process sought, while it recognizes the right of the party for whose benefit it was designed to be taken. I think the demurrer and motion to quash were properly overruled." Richardson *v.* Prince George Justices, 11 Gratt. 190, 194.

"In this case the marshal being dead, the scire facias recites that it was awarded at the instance of M., his administrator. Though it might have been more regular for the scire facias

to recite that it was awarded at the instance and on behalf of the plaintiffs on the record, yet as it would have been good if the averment at whose instance it had issued had been wholly omitted, the recital was mere surplusage, and does not vitiate the scire facias." Richardson *v.* Prince George Justices, 11 Gratt. 190.

(6) Quashal.

Where the scire facias fails to set forth any legal cause of action it ought to be quashed. Evans *v.* Freeland, 3 Munf. 119.

d. Pleas and Defenses.

(1) In General.

To a scire facias to revive a judgment payment, release, set-off or other matter arising after judgment, may be pleaded, but not any matter existing prior to the judgment. Maxwell *v.* Leeson, 50 W. Va. 361, 362, 40 S. E. 420, 88 Am. St. Rep. 875, citing 1 Black, Judgm., § 491; May *v.* Bank, 2 Rob. 56, 40 Am. Dec. 726.

(2) Payment.

See the title PAYMENT.

That payment can be pleaded to a scire facias is well settled. May *v.* Bank, 2 Rob. 56, 40 Am. Dec. 726; Lauer *v.* Ketner, 42 Am. St. Rep. 833; 2 Barton Law Prac. 1036; 1 Black, Judgm., § 494. Maxwell *v.* Leeson, 50 W. Va. 361, 369, 40 S. E. 420, 88 Am. St. Rep. 875.

Payment may be pleaded to a scire facias, hence the order on a scire facias may be for the unpaid balance of a decree. Execution in such case should recite the original judgment and also that on the scire facias, and then account for the variance. Maxwell *v.* Leeson, 50 W. Va. 361, 40 S. E. 420, 88 Am. St. Rep. 726.

Sufficiency of Plea.—A plea of payment does not require the defendant to produce the record. Hutsonpiller *v.* Stover, 12 Gratt. 579.

H. recovers a judgment against W. and P. Afterwards W. and H. die, and K. qualifies as the executor of W. and the administrator of H. As administrator of H., K. sues out a scire facias to revive the judgment against P., the surviving obligor, and he appears and files a general plea of payment, without stating the nature of the payment. He proves that H. in his lifetime assigned the judgment to D., who was a debtor of T., who was a debtor of W.; and that under an agreement between T. and D. that T. would take in payment of his debt, any debt on W. which K. would take in payment of T.'s debt to W., D. obtained this judgment from H., and assigned it to K., who credited the amount on T.'s debt to W. There was a verdict for the defendant, and on motion for a new trial, held: The evidence should have been excluded from the jury, the defendant's plea not describing the payment so as to give plaintiff notice of its nature, as required by the statute, Code of 1860, ch. 172, § 4. K. having taken the assignment to himself, and credited the amount upon the debt due from T. to W., he made himself liable to his testator's estate for that amount; but having taken the assignment to himself, he was the owner of the judgment, and might as administrator of H. maintain the scire facias to revive the judgment at law. The arrangement does not constitute a payment of the judgment at law, though it may constitute grounds of equities between W. and P. Peery v. Peery, 26 Gratt. 320.

Presumption of Payment.—See the title PAYMENT.

Upon a scire facias to revive a judgment which had been suspended by an injunction for forty-six years, issue was made up on the plea of payment; and upon the trial the court instructed the jury, that the pendency of said injunction cause repelled the legal presumption of payment which would have arisen from lapse of time if said injunction had not been pending. Held, the instruction was proper; and it was not necessary to distinguish to the jury between the legal presumption, and the natural presumption arising from the lapse of time. Hutsonpiller v. Stover, 12 Gratt. 579.

(3) Usury.

See the title USURY.

A defendant may plead to a scire facias brought to revive a decree, which was obtained against him by default, that the original contract was usurious. Lane v. Elizey, 4 Hen. & M. 504.

(4) Set-Off.

See the title SET-OFF, RECOUPMENT AND COUNTERCLAIM.

To a scire facias to revive a judgment, matters of set-off, arising after the judgment, may be pleaded. Maxwell v. Leeson, 50 W. Va. 361, 362, 40 S. E. 420.

(5) Release.

See the title RELEASE.

To a scire facias to revive a judgment matter of release arising after the judgment may be pleaded. Maxwell v. Leeson, 50 W. Va. 361, 362, 40 S. E. 420.

(6) Transfer of Sufficient Assets to Sheriff under Insolvency Act.

It is not a good plea to a scire facias, that the defendant had transferred, conveyed, etc., to the sheriff, goods and chattels, lands, etc., according to the act of assembly, to a greater value, etc., and that no proceedings had been had under the act of assembly, against the said lands, etc. Lang v. Lewis, 1 Rand. 277.

Nor is it a good plea that the defendant had transferred, in like manner, various debts, etc., and that the proceedings prescribed by the act of assembly, etc., to recover such debts, had not been had. Lang v. Lewis, 1 Rand. 277.

(7) Nul Tiel Record.

Upon a plea of nul tiel record to a scire facias, as the court below has the whole record before it, in the absence of the record in the appellate court, it will be presumed, that the part of the record recited in the scire facias was before the court below, and that the order reviving the decree is correct. Garrison v. Myers, 12 W. Va. 330.

(8) Character of Obligation on Which Judgment Rendered.

Neither the scire facias nor any other part of the record, showing what was the character of the obligation or other liability upon which the judgment was rendered, and the defendant's plea not averring that it was such a statutory bond as required that there should · be a relator in any action brought upon it, and that the relator should be the party, having the legal right to sue, it must be regarded as a common-law bond or liability subject to be sued on in the names of the payees without a relator, or for the benefit of the holder or any party entitled to the benefit of it; and whether W. was marshal or M. ·was his administrator, is a question in which defendant has no interest; and it can not be raised by him by plea in bar to the plaintiff's claim. Richardson v. Prince George Justices, 11 Gratt. 190.

(9) Scire Facias by Husband and Wife.

Sci. fa. by husband and wife, upon a judgment recovered by wife dum sola, suggesting that since rendition of the judgment, the wife had intermarried with the husband. Plea, actio non, because at the date of the emanation of the sci. fa. the wife was not married to the husband as suggested in the writ; concluding to the contrary. And plea held naught, upon general demurrer: 1. Because the matter of it is properly pleadable in abatement only, not in bar; 2. Because it neither distinctly negatives the fact suggested in the writ, nor affirms any matter to avoid the action; and 3. Because, instead of concluding with a verification, it concludes to the country. Buck v. Fouchee, 1 Leigh 64.

(10) Contemnor's Disabilities.

See the title CONTEMPT, vol. 3, p. 263.

A defendant's being in contempt to the first process of the court, is not a contempt to the decree, and forms no objection to his pleading to a scire facias brought to revive that decree. Lane v. Elizey, 4 Hen. & M. 504.

9. Waiver.

As the object of the scire facias is merely to give the defendant a day in court to show cause why the judgment should not be revived, the defendant may waive this benefit; and if he has no such cause to show, it will be to his interest to waive it, for he will thereby save the costs of the scire facias. Beale v. Botetourt Justices, 10 Gratt. 278.

10. Variance.

See the title VARIANCE.

In Richardson v. Prince George Justices, 11 Gratt. 190, the court held, admitting that if a scire facias to revive a judgment varied in a material matter from the judgment in the description thereof, such a variance would be fatal, that the fact that the judgment was in the name of four persons described as justices of Prince George county suing for the benefit of the marshal of the district court of chancery, without giving his name, while the scire facias averred that his name was Charles T. Wingfield, constituted no variance, being intended merely to furnish additional names of identification.

That the scire facias reciting a judgment says it was "for debt" while such words do not appear in the minute of the judgment produced of record and in stating the costs the scire facias does not add, to "146 lbs." the word "nett" before "tobacco" as does the minute produced, and in the scire facias, the 15s. recovered in part of costs is not followed by the words and figures "or 150 lbs. tobacco" though this follows in·the judgment rendered upon the scire facias, do not institute fatal variance, since they only reduce the minute to the form which the clerk might legally have given it in an execution or order book. Lyons *v.* Gregory, 3 Hen. & M. 237.

An order reviving a judgment and awarding execution for money in the name of a personal representative of a deceased party for a less sum than the original recovery by reason of partial payments since the judgment, is not void as a new judgment or because of variance in amount from the original judgment. Maxwell *v.* Leeson, 50 W. Va. 361, 40 S. E. 420.

A judgment is recovered in the name of B. H. and three others, justices of P. G. county, for the benefit of the marshal of the superior court of chancery for the Williamsburg district. The defendant being dead, a scire facias issued to revive the judgment, which, after setting out the plaintiffs, and the recovery of the judgment for the benefit of the marshal, adds, which marshal was W. Held, this is not a variance. Richardson *v.* Prince George Justices, 11 Gratt. 190.

Where the bill sets out a judgment correctly, as stated in the record of the judgment, there is no variance because a scire facias issued against garnishees, recites it as of a different amount, or that the endorsement on the papers by the clerk, of the proceedings in the cause, of the date of the judgment, is different from that stated in the bill. Fisher *v.* March, 26 Gratt. 765.

How Taken Advantage of.—In order to take advantage of a variance between the judgment and a writ of scire facias, the defendant must plead nul tiel record or crave oyer of the record and demur. Hutsonpiller *v.* Stover, 12 Gratt. 579; Wood *v.* Com., 4 Rand. 329.

"A party may plead nul tiel record, and if upon inspection by the court, the record is not such as is described in the pleadings, he will. have judgment; or he may crave oyer of the record, which makes the record a part of the pleadings in that case; 18 Vin. Abr. 184, pl. 20, 21; and when it is

spread upon the record by oyer, if the party admits that the record of which oyer is given him is the true record, and relies that it does not support the pleadings or scire facias, it seems to me that he should not deny that there is such a record; by plea; but, that he ought to demur, upon the ground that it varies from the pleadings or scire facias. If he denies the verity of the record of which oyer is given, he should plead nul tiel record after oyer." Wood *v.* Com., 4 Rand. 329.

"It is no doubt true that if a scire facias for the purpose of reviving a judgment, be found to vary in a material matter from the judgment in the description which it undertakes to give of it, advantage may be taken of it in the proper mode, and the variance will prove fatal. But waiving the question whether a proper mode of making such an objection could be by a general demurrer or motion to quash, I am of opinion that no such variance appears in the present case. It is true the judgment was in the names of four persons described as justices of Prince George county, suing for the benefit of the marshal of the district court of chancery held at Williamsburg, without giving his name, while the scire facias avers that his name was Charles L. Wingfield. But this is no variance. It is intended to furnish an additional means of identification of the person for whose benefit the judgment had been rendered, and to show the right of the party at whose instance the present proceeding was taken. It is an averment in nowise repugnant to, but strictly consistent with, all the terms of the judgment, while the names, sums, dates and other elements of description, which the judgment affords, are found accurately given in the scire facias." Richardson *v.* Prince George Justices, 11 Gratt. 190, 194.

Dismissal.—Upon bill by S. against G. and P. to subject the land of G. to satisfy a judgment recovered against

G., P. and others, it appears and was so decided by the circuit court upon appeal from a judgment of the county court on a scire facias to revive the judgment, that no process had been served on P., and that he had not entered his appearance in the original action, and the scire facias was dismissed for a variance. between the writ and the evidence. Held, the judgment against G. is a valid judgment; and is not affected by the judgment of the circuit court dismissing the scire facias for a variance between the writ and the evidence. Gray *v*. Stuart, 33 Gratt. 351.

11. Limitations.

a. In General.

At Common Law.—"There is no limitation, by statute, to an action of debt or scire facias upon a judgment, except only in the case of a judgment on which no execution has been taken out; and in cases of executors and administrators, upon a judgment against their testator or intestate. In all other cases, these remedies are left us at the common law; and at common law, there was nothing like a limitation upon them, except the presumption of satisfaction, arising from a delay to proceed upon the judgment for twenty years which might be repelled by circumstances." Randolph *v*. Randolph, 3 Rand. 490.

Under Early Statutes.—There was formerly no limitation by statute, to an action of debt, or scire facias on a judgment, except only in the case of a judgment on which no execution had been taken out; and except in cases of executors and administrators, on a judgment against their testator or intestate. Randolph *v*. Randolph, 3 Rand. 490. Herrington *v*. Harkins, 1 Rob. 591, is cited in Smith *v*. Charlton, 7 Gratt. 425, 450. See Fleming *v*. Dunlop, 4 Leigh 338.

"In Randolph *v*. Randolph, 3 Rand. 490, Judge Green remarked, that there is no limitation by statute to an action of debt or scire facias upon a judgment, except only in the case of judgment on which no execution has been taken out, and in case of executors, etc. The correctness of this observation, as to a scire facias where an execution has been taken out and not returned, came under the consideration of this court in Fleming *v*. Dunlop, 4 Leigh 338. There an execution had been sued out within the year, and another at a subsequent period, but neither returned; and to a scire facias sued out more than ten years after the judgment, the statute was held to be a bar. But Judge Tucker concurred with Judge Green in the opinion that debt would not be barred. At common law there was no limitation to the action of debt; nothing but the presumption of payment or satisfaction, arising from a delay to proceed upon the judgment for 20 years. This being the law, the statute provided that judgments, where execution hath not issued, may be revived by scire facias of an action of debt brought thereon within ten years next after the date of such judgment, and not after. No other reference is made to the action of debt. At common law, if no execution was issued within the year, a presumption of satisfaction or release was raised, and the plaintiff was driven to his action of the judgment. To this the statute of Westminister the 2d superadded a scire facias, to give the plaintiff the benefit of the original judgment. And the first provision in the 5th section of our statute limits the remedy to ten years. Where an execution had issued but was not returned, the execution could not be kept alive for want of continuances on the roll, and the party was driven to his scire facias or action. 4 Leigh 343. The second clause of the 5th section was designed to relieve the plaintiff from this inconvenience, and does so by authorizing him to obtain other executions within ten years without a scire facias. But unless he procures a return on the execution within the ten years, the act is a bar to obtaining any other execution on the judgment. But nothing is said as to the action of debt." Herrington *v.* Harkins, 1 Rob. 591.

Difference between Early and Present Statutes.—The only practical difference between the law as it stood in the first revised Code of 1819 and the statute now in force is, that in addition to the limitation imposed by the former, which went only to judgments when execution had not issued, the present statute also imposes a limitation as to the writ of scire facias or action, although execution did issue within the year, and although other executions may have issued; the limitation in such case being ten years from the return day of an execution on which there is no return, or twenty years from the return day of an execution on which there is such return. But this difference in the two statutes in no manner changes the principle or practice requiring the statute to be pleaded if relied on. Nor can it be said that the writ in the case under consideration was demurrable; for although prima facie barred by the recitals therein, yet had the statute been pleaded, some one or more of the exceptions in the statute or other matter might have been replied so as to avoid the bar. Hence the propriety and manifest justice of the rule requiring the statute to be pleaded. And in a case like this, if the statute be not pleaded, and no other adequate defense be made, it is the plain duty of the court to give judgment for the plaintiff according to the writ. Smith *v.* Hutchinson, 78 Va. 683, 688.

Our statute, § 12, ch. 182, Code, 1873, provides that: "On a judgment execution may be issued within a year, and a scire facias or action may be brought within ten years after the date of the judgment; and where execution issues within the year, other executions may be issued, or a scire facias or action may be brought within ten years from the return day of an execution on which there is no return by an officer, or within twenty years from the return day of an execution on which there is such return." Then follow the exceptions. By the succeeding 13th section, of the same chapter, it is declared: "No execution shall issue, nor any scire facias or action be brought, on a judgment in this state, other than for the commonwealth, after the time prescribed by the preceding section." Then follow the enumerated exceptions to that section. The law, as it formerly stood, imposed no limitation to a scire facias upon a judgment, except only in the case of a judgment on which no execution had issued; and in cases of executors and administrators, upon judgments against their testators or intestates. In all other cases, the remedy was left as at the common law; and at common law there was nothing like a limitation in such case, except the presumption of satisfaction arising from a delay to proceed upon the judgment for twenty years, which might be repelled by circumstances. 1 R. C. 1819, p. 489, and Green, J., in Randolph *v.* Randolph, 3 Rand. 490, 493. The effect of these provisions, limiting writs of scire facias upon judgments, was considered in Day *v.* Pickett, 4 Munf. 104; Gee *v.* Hamilton, 6 Munf. 32; and Peyton *v.* Carr, 1 Rand. 435, 436. In each of these cases the statute was pleaded; and they may be said to illustrate in practice the principle, which we take to be undeniable, that where in a case in which no execution issued within the year, and which prima facie is barred, the practice is for the clerk to issue the scire facias, and leave the defendant to plead the statute, and the plaintiff to reply the exceptions, so far as they may be applicable to his case. Smith *v.* Hutchinson, 78 Va. 683, 687.

Present Statutory Provisions.—The Virginia Code provides, that on a judgment, execution may be issued within a year, and a scire facias or an action may be brought within ten years after the date of the judgment; and where execution issues within the year, other execut ons may be issued, or a scire facias or an action may be brought within ten years from the return day of an execution on which there is no return by an officer, or within twenty years from the return day of an execution on which there is such return; except that where the scire facias or action is against the personal representative of a decedent, it shall be brought within five years from the qualification of such representative; and in computing time under this section, there shall, as to writs of fieri facias, be omitted from such computation the time elapsed between the first day of January, eighteen hundred and sixty-nine, and the twenty-ninth day of March, eighteen hundred and seventy-one. Any return by an officer on an execution showing that the same has not been satisfied, shall be a sufficient return within the meaning of this section. (1870-71, p. 341.) Va. Code, 1904, § 3577.

The West Virginia Code provides that on a judgment, execution may be issued within two years after the date thereof, or if none be so issued, the court in which the judgment was rendered may thereafter, and within ten years from the date of the judgment, upon ten days' notice to the party against whom the same is, order an execution to issue thereon for such sum as remains unpaid. Where execution issues within two years as aforesaid, other executions may be issued on such judgment without notice, within ten years from the return day of the last execution issued thereon, on which there is no return by an officer, or which has been returned unsatisfied. And an action, suit or scire facias may be brought upon a judgment on which no execution issued within the said two years, or where there has been a change of par-

ties by death or otherwise, at any time within ten years next after the date of the judgment. But if such action, suit or scire facias be against a personal representative of a decedent, it shall be brought within five years from the qualification of such representative. W. Va. Code, 1899, ch. 139, § 4150.

Distinction between Virginia and West Virginia Statute.—Under the provisions of the 11th and 12th sections of ch. 139 of the Code a judgment may be revived by scire facias against the personal representative of the judgment debtor within ten years from the return day of the last execution issued thereon, although that time may be more than ten years after the date of the judgment; provided such revival be made within five years from the date of the qualification of such representative. "In support of this construction it will be noticed that there is a very material difference between our statute and that of Virginia in the context of this last mentioned provision. In the Virginia statute it commences with the word 'except' and forms a part of the preceding sentence; while in ours, and new matter forming an independent or parenthetical sentence, separates it from the former sentence corresponding with the one in the Virginia statute, and thus making a separate and distinct sentence. In ours it commences with the word 'But' and forms a sentence separate from the new parenthetical provision which precedes it. This separation of the two provisions and alteration of the text indicates very distinctly to my mind that it was not intended to be a qualification merely of the new provision; that is, judgments on which no execution has issued within two years, but to all judgments mentioned in the preceding part of the section and including those which had been kept in force by issuing executions on them up to the death of the judgment debtor." Laidley v. Kline, 23 W. Va. 565, 576.

b. When Statute Begins to Run.

When the debtor dies, the scire facias must be brought within five years from the qualification of the representative of such deceased debtor, and after five years from such qualification the lien of the judgment on the land of decedent must cease; unless, perhaps, it might be kept alive longer by the suing out of successive executions after the death of the debtor, or, by having sued out a scire facias against his personal representative, continued his right to do so. Braxton v. Wood, 4 Gratt. 25; Smith v. Charlton, 7 Gratt. 425; Werdenbaugh v. Reid, 20 W. Va. 588, 601.

In no event can the judgment be revived, or suit brought to enforce it, after ten years have elapsed from the return day of the last execution; and if more than five years of that period elapse during the lifetime of the execution debtor, then the creditor has only the remainder of the ten years within which to revive his judgment, or bring his suit, although such remainder may be less than five years, and there may be no personal representative of his estate. Laidley v. Kline, 23 W. Va. 565, 576; Handy v. Smith, 30 W. Va. 195, 3 S. E. 604.

Under §§ 11, 12, ch. 139, of the Code a judgment can be revived by scire facias against the personal representative of the debtor within ten years from the return day of the last execution, though that time may be more than ten years from the date of the judgment; provided such revival be made within five years from the qualification of such representative. Sherrards v. Keiter, 32 W. Va. 144, 9 S. E. 25; Werdenbaugh v. Reid, 20 W. Va. 588.

"The circuit court evidently proceeded under the view that under § 11, ch. 139, Code, 1868, where there has been a change of parties by death, 10 computable years after its date would bar the judgment, notwithstanding less than 10 years had elapsed from the return day of the last execution; but that construction of that section has been overruled by the case of Laidley v. Kline, 23 W. Va. 565, holding, in point 5 of the syllabus, that under §§ 11, 12, ch. 139, Code, 1868, a judgment may be revived by scire facias against a personal representative of the judgment debtor within 10 years of the return day of the last execution issued thereon, although that time may be more than 10 years after the date of the judgment; provided such revival be made within five years from the date of the qualification of such representative. Therefore the plea averring that more than ten years had elapsed from the date of the judgment was not good, because the scire facias alleged that two executions had issued, the last returnable in May, 1860, and the plea therefore did not answer its averment, and the demurrer to it should have been sustained." Sherrards v. Keiter, 32 W. Va. 144, 9 S. E. 25, 26.

On May 5, 1855, the plaintiff recovered a judgment against the defendants, and sued out execution thereon within the year. The last execution was returnable to the first Monday in January, 1859, upon which no return of any officer was ever made. On September 16, 1874, the plaintiff filed his bill against the defendants to enforce the lien of his judgment against the real estate of the defendants, which was resisted on the ground that the lien of the judgment was barred by the statute of limitations. Held, that the plaintiff's right to sue out other executions, or to bring a scire facias or action upon his judgment, expired at the end of thirteen years, ten months and fourteen days, from the return day of said last execution. Shipley v. Pew, 23 W. Va. 487.

A judgment obtained against a testator in his lifetime, and not revived against his personal representative after his death, within five years from the time of his qualification, is barred

by the statute of limitations. Peyton
v. Carr, 1 Rand. 435.

c. **Postponement, Suspension or Interruption of Statute.**

In General.—"By the common law, the failure of the plaintiff to sue out execution within the year, so far created the presumption of a payment, satisfaction or release of the judgment, as to compel the plaintiff to bring his action on the judgment; and thus give the defendant an opportunity, by pleading, to put in issue such supposed payment, satisfaction or release. By the statute Westminster 2, 13 Edward 1, ch. 45, a scire facias is given to the plaintiff to revive his judgment where he has omitted to sue out execution within the year; and it is now the remedy most usually resorted to for such purpose. Notwithstanding the year's neglect drives the plaintiff, generally, to his action or scire facias, the English cases furnish many exceptions to the rule. As when a writ of error is brought on a judgment, the delay in executing the judgment being imputable to the defendant, execution may issue after the judgment is affirmed, although more than a year and a day have elapsed since the judgment was signed. 1 Salk. 322. So if a plaintiff had a judgment with a 'cessat executio' for a given time, he may within a year and a day after the expiration of the time allowed by the 'cessat executio' take out execution without a scire facias. 1 Salk. 322. So when the plaintiff is prevented from suing out his execution within the year by the defendant's obtaining an injunction out of chancery, he may upon the dissolution of the injunction, have execution without resorting to the scire facias. This was for a time disputed, but is now well-settled law. 2 Burr. R. 660. And even where a year after judgment had expired before the writ of error was sued out, and the judgment is affirmed, or plaintiff in error is nonsuited, or the writ of error discontinued, the plaintiff may sue out execution, the writ of error being held to have revived the judgment. 1 Show. 402. In most of the states of this union the same rule prevails either by force of the common law or by virtue of legislative enactment; and the same or like exceptions will be found to obtain." Smith v. Charlton, 7 Gratt. 425, 447.

"Whilst the second clause of the fifth section prescribes a limitation to the remedies of plaintiffs in the cases where they have so far availed themselves of the means of enforcing judgment as to sue out execution, but have obtained no return thereon, the first clause of the section was, in my opinion, designed to prescribe the limitation to their remedies, where having a right to sue out executions, they have wholly failed to exercise the right. By the term 'judgments' in the first clause, are intended judgments clothed as judgments ordinarily are, with the capacity of being enforced; judgments upon which the plaintiffs have the right to sue out execution. Where the exercise of this right is stayed or suspended by the agreement of the parties, or by the restraints of legal proceedings set on foot at the instances of the defendant, the limitation will not begin to run in favor of the defendant till the time of such stay or suspension has expired. Judgments which show upon their faces that there is now no right to enforce them by execution, and that such right is to depend on other proceedings yet to be instituted, do not, in my opinion, come within the meaning and operation of the statute at all." Smith v. Charlton, 7 Gratt. 425, 451.

Stay of Execution.—"The language of the first section of our execution law, 1 Rev. Code, p. 524, ch. 134, is 'that all persons who have or shall hereafter recover any debt, etc., by the judgment of any court of record within this commonwealth, may at their election prosecute writs of fieri facias, etc., within the year, for taking the goods, etc., etc.' The language of the statute is explicit in confining the peremptory right to sue out execution 'within the year.' Yet I presume it has not been doubted since the decision in Eppes *v.* Randolph, 2 Call 125, 186, and Noland *v.* Seekright, 6 Munf. 185, that this one year's limitation could not avail a defendant where there has been a stay of execution by his own agreement, or by force of an injunction obtained at his instance. In any of the instances above cited of stay of execution, whether by 'cessat executio' or the parol agreement of the parties, or by injunction or supersedeas, I presume it will not be doubted that the plaintiff might at the end and expiration of the time bring his action of debt upon the judgment, instead of suing execution thereon; and that if the judgment had been thus suspended for more than ten years, he might meet the statute of limitations by showing that though his judgment was more than ten years old, and one upon which no execution was issued, and thus falling within the very words of the statute, yet that it was so situated that no execution could be sued out on it, and therefore that it did not fall within the true meaning and design of the statute." Smith *v.* Charlton, 7 Gratt. 425, 448.

Execution without Scire Facias.—"If an execution be issued without a scire facias, and the defendant move to quash it, the plaintiff may show that another execution was issued within a year and a day from the date of the judgment; or that he was prevented from issuing one by writ of error, injunction, cessat executio, or agreement of the parties, until within a year and a day next before the date of that which is moved to be quashed; and the motion will thereupon be overruled." Beale *v.* Botetourt Justices, 10 Gratt. 278.

New Promise.—A plea of the act of limitations, in bar to a scire facias to revive a judgment, can not be repelled by a replication that the defendant within five years next before the suing out of the scire facias, promised to pay the amount of the judgment. Day *v.* Pickett, 4 Munf. 104.

Indulgence or Agreement.—An execution on a judgment stayed by indulgence or agreement is no replication to the bar of the statute of limitations, for it neither suspends the capacity to maintain debt or scire facias on the judgment, nor falls within any of the savings of the proviso. Indeed a replication of an express promise to pay the debt is bad. Smith *v.* Charlton, 7 Gratt. 425, 474, citing Day *v.* Pickett, 4 Munf. 104 as its authority. In Mercer *v.* Beale, 4 Leigh 189, 203, it is said: "Since this act (Statute of Limitations), no judgment can be revived, or be the foundation of an action of debt, against the executor, after the expiration of five years, unless the persons entitled were non compos, etc. No promise of payment, no assumpsit, or acknowledgment, could have the effect of removing the bar. Such assumpsits may serve as the foundation of a new action, or may take a debt out of other clauses of the statute, but not out of those which limit the right of reviving judgments by debt or $s_{ci}r_e$ facias. Day *v.* Pickett, 4 Munf. 104, before cited."

Twenty-eight years after final decree, confirming sale of land for payment of claims, and after nearly all the parties and witnesses are dead, the record lost, and the property passed through many hands on faith of the title acquired under the decree, a clause in said decree, which provides that "any of the parties to this suit have leave to ask any such further order as may be necessary to enforce the same;" held, insufficient to authorize the revival of the suit. Riely *v.* Kinzel, 85 Va. 480, 7 S. E. 907.

Death of Either Party.—When an action has accrued to a party capable of suing against a party who may be sued, the statute of limitations begins to run; unless this be prevented by the case coming within some exception to the statute; and after it has begun to run its running is not suspended because of the subsequent death of either of the parties, or because of the lapse of time before either has a personal representative. "But it is insisted by the appellants that, as Smith died thirty-three days before the ten years expired, they had, under the second clause of the statute, five years from the date of the qualification of his personal representative to revive their judgment or bring this suit. It is claimed that this provision is a limitation within itself, independent of the ten-years' limitation in the first part of the statute; and that 'it matters not whether the five years fall wholly within the ten years, or wholly without the ten years, in cases not barred, or partly within and partly without the same.' This position is plainly untenable. The law is well settled that, when to a party capable of suing an action has accrued against a party who may be sued, the statute begins to run, unless this be prevented by the case coming within some exception to the statute. After it has begun to run, its running will not be suspended because of the subsequent death of either party, or because of the lapse of time before either has a personal representative. 1 Rob. Pr. (New Ed.) 591, 609; Jones v. Lemon, 26 W. Va. 629; Harshberger v. Alger, 31 Gratt. 52, 67; Wilsons v. Harper, 25 W. Va. 179." Handy v. Smith, 30 W. Va. 195, 3 S. E. 604, 605.

Issuance of Execution and Return.— The right to issue a scire facias upon a judgment is not barred by the act of limitations, in a case where execution was issued in due time, and returned "no effects," though more than ten years elapsed between the return of the execution, and date of the scire facias. Gee v. Hamilton, 6 Munf. 32.

Where execution has issued within the year, the plaintiff has no right to a scire facias, hence where such fact appears by the evidence on issues of payment and nul tiel record on a writ of scire facias, a judgment dismissing the writ with costs to the defendant is proper. Miller v. Cox, 9 W. Va. 8.

In Hutcheson v. Grubbs, 80 Va. 251, 255, it is said, the time, however, within which executions and writs of scire facias could be issued on judgments was prescribed by statute; and in Fleming v. Dunlop, 4 Leigh 338, it was said by Judge Carr, that where no execution issued within the prescribed time the judgment was annihilated. To the same effect, Fleming v. Dunlop, 4 Leigh 338, is cited in Ayre v. Burke, 82 Va. 338, 340, 4 S. E. 618; Dabney v. Shelton, 82 Va. 349, 351, 4 S. E. 605; White v. Offield, 90 Va. 336, 339, 18 S. E. 436; Werdenbaugh v. Reid, 20 W. Va. 588, 592.

Judgment recovered by D. P. & Co. against F. in September, 1810, and execution sued out in the same month, and another in October, 1815, but neither returned; to a scire facias to revive the judgment against F.'s executor, sued out in July, 1826, defendant pleads in bar, the statute of limitations. 1 Rev. Code, ch. 128, § 5. Plaintiffs reply the two executions sued out in September, 1810, and October, 1815; on demurrer to this replication. Held, the statute is a bar of the scire facias. Fleming v. Dunlop, 4 Leigh 338.

Sufficiency of Return.— Under the Virginia statute providing that a judgment is barred after the lapse of ten years from the return date of an execution on which there is no return by an officer, but a scire facias or action may be brought within twenty years from the date of an execution on which there is such return, it was held, that an order of the attorneys for the plaintiff to return the execution without levying it. indorsed by them on the writ shortly after it came into the sheriff's hands, was a sufficient return to make the twenty years' period apply. Rowe v. Hardy, 97 Va. 674, 34 S. E.

625, citing Hamilton *v.* McConkey, 83 Va. 533.

Amended Return.—A judgment obtained on twenty-first of August, 1847, on which execution issues on twenty-sixth of August, 1847, which is placed in hands of sheriff same day, who returns money made, but who, afterwards, by leave of the court, makes an amended return, from which it appears that he had received no money, but had taken property and choses in action and credit upon his own indebtedness to the execution debtors. After this amended return was made the plaintiffs sued out a scire facias alleging that no execution had issued within a year. On the trial of this scire facias, the above facts appearing in evidence, the court, to whom the matter was submitted for trial, on the issues of payment and nul tiel record, entered judgment dismissing the scire facias with costs to defendant. Held, no error, and the judgment is affirmed. Miller *v.* Cox, 9 W. Va. 8.

Pendency of Injunction.—See ante, "When Writ May Issue," XIV, A, 3.

The statute of limitations to judgments does not run whilst an injunction to the judgment is pending. Hutsonpiller *v.* Stover, 12 Gratt. 579.

Where execution has been stayed by injunction, the plaintiff may sue out execution within one year after it shall have been dissolved, without scire facias. Hutsonpiller *v.* Stover, 12 Gratt. 579, 582, citing Noland *v.* Seekright, 6 Munf. 185, as authority. To the same effect, Noland *v.* Seekright, 6 Munf. 185, is cited in Smith *v.* Charlton, 7 Gratt. 425, 449.

If the defendant in a judgment dies whilst an injunction to the judgment is pending, though the injunction may not be dissolved for more than five years after his death, the statute requiring judgments to be revived within five years does not run during the pendency of the injunction; and the judgment may be revived after the five

years from the death of the defendant. And this though the judgment might have been revived whilst the injunction was in force. Hutsonpiller *v.* Stover, 12 Gratt. 579.

Upon the dissolution of an injunction to a judgment, execution may issue thereon within a year and a day from the dissolution of the injunction without a scire facias, though the injunction was in force for more than ten years. Hutsonpiller *v.* Stover, 12 Gratt. 579.

Injunction was awarded, before expiration of the ten years, against sale of the executor's home place, but said decree was not assailed nor the issuance of said execution affected. Held, there was no such suspension as would permit revival after lapse of ten years, under Code, 1873, ch. 1882, § 13. Serles *v.* Cromer, 88 Va. 426, 13 S. E. 859, citing Straus *v.* Bodeker, 86 Va. 543, 10 S. E. 570; Dabney *v.* Shelton, 82 Va. 349, 4 S. E. 605.

Suspension by Legal Process.—Petitions filed during the period of ten years after the rendition of judgment by judgment creditor in a chancery suit brought to subject the lands of judgment debtor to the payment of judgment liens, and dismissed without an order on it except that of dismissal seven years after it was filed, did not suspend the right to sue out execution upon the judgment, and does not bring the case under the saving clause contained in § 13 of said chapter, which provides "except that in computing the time, any time during which the right to sue out execution on the judgment is suspended by the terms thereof, or by legal process, shall be omitted." Dabney *v.* Shelton, 82 Va. 349, 4 S. E. 605. See Werdenbaugh *v.* Reid, 20 W. Va. 588.

The act, Code, ch. 186, § 13, p. 710, which directs that the time for which the right to sue out execution on a judgment is suspended by the terms thereof or by legal process shall be omitted in computing the limitation, applies to judgments recovered previous to the act, which are suspended by injunction at the time when the act went into operation. Hutsonpiller *v.* Stover, 12 Gratt. 579.

Nonsuit. — A judgment obtained against a testator in his lifetime, and not revived against his personal representative after his death, within five years from the time of his qualification, is barred by the statute of limitations. The operation of the statute will not be prevented by a scire facias sued out within the five years, on which the plaintiff suffered a nonsuit. Peyton *v.* Carr, 1 Rand. 435.

January, 1869, to March, 1871.—In computing the time within which a scire facias may be sued out under § 3577 of the Code, to revive a judgment, the time which elapsed between the first day of January, 1869; and the twenty-ninth day of March, 1871, is to be included, though the same period, by the terms of that section, is excluded as to writs of fieri facias. Fadeley *v.* Williams, 96 Va. 397, 31 S. E. 515.

The right to file a bill in equity to enforce a judgment lien is coextensive, as to time, with the right to issue execution thereon; and under Va. Code, § 3577, which prescribes the limitation of proceedings to enforce a judgment, in computing time there shall, as to a writ of scire facias, be omitted the time elapsed between January 1, 1869, and March 29, 1871. Hence the limitation to a suit in equity to enforce a judgment obtained June 3, 1870, commenced to run, March 29, 1871. James *v.* Life, 92 Va. 702, 24 S. E. 275.

Execution on Final Decree.—No execution having been issued on a final decree within a year after its rendition, and no proceeding had to revive it within ten years thereafter; held, the decree was barred when the suit was brought, in 1887, to revive it. Code, 1873, ch. 182, §§ 12, 13. Serles *v.* Cromer, 88 Va. 426, 13 S. E. 859.

d. Particular Judgments Considered.

(1) Judgments Quando Acciderint.

Revised Va. Code, ch. 128, § 5, p. 489, provided as follows: "Judgments in any court of record within this commonwealth, where execution hath not issued, may be revived by scire facias, or an action of debt brought thereon, within ten years next after the date of such judgmtnt, and not after; or where execution hath issued and no return made thereon, the party in whose favor the same was issued, shall and may obtain other executions, or move against any sheriff or other officer, or his or their security or securities, for not returning the same, for the term of ten years from the date of such judgment, and not after."

A judgment quando acciderint does not come within the operation of the statute of limitations in relation to judgments, 1 Rev. Code, ch. 128, § 5, p. 487. By two judges in a court of three. Smith *v.* Charlton, 7 Gratt. 425, overruling Braxton *v.* Wood, 4 Gratt. 25.

(2) Judgments in Favor of Commonwealth.

The English maxim, that "nullum tempus occurrit regi," has been adopted in Virginia, in relation to the commonwealth; on which principle it has been held, that the acts of limitations do not extend to the commonwealth, in civil suits, not founded on any penal act expressly limiting the commencement of the action. No length of time can bar the commonwealth from execution on a judgment in its favor, nor even render it necessary to sue out a scire facias to entitle it to such execution. Nimmo *v.* Com., 4 Hen. & M. 57.

"The first error, suggested in the petition for a supersedeas to this judgment, is, that the commonwealth is bound by the statute of limitation; and therefore the scire facias was forever barred, after ten years. Whether the acts of limitations extend to the commonwealth, or not, was fully argued and considered in the case of Kemp v. Com., (a) in which the plea of the act of limitations was the sole defense relied on. And this court, consisting at that time of three judges, Judge Lyons, Judge Carrington and myself, two of whom are not present, unanimously agreed that they did not, in civil suits, not founded upon any penal act." Nimmo v. Com., 4 Hen. & M. 57.

e. Issuance of Writ on Judgment Prima Facie Barred.

Even in a case where no execution issued on judgment within the year, and which is prima facie barred, the practice is for clerk to issue scire facias, and for court to give judgment according to the writ, leaving defendant to plead the statute or not, at his own option, and plaintiff to reply the exceptions as far as applicable. Acts, 1874, ch. 144, § 6. Smith v. Hutchinson, 78 Va. 683.

Gee v. Hamilton, 6 Munf. 32, is cited in Smith v. Hutchinson, 78 Va. 683, 687, as illustrating the principle that where in a case in which no execution issued on a judgment within a year after it was obtained, and which prima facie is barred, the practice is for the clerk to issue a scire facias and leave the defendant to plead the statute, and the plaintiff to reply the exceptions, so far as they may be applicable to his case. This case is also cited in Mercer v. Beale, 4 Leigh 189, 204.

f. Pleading the Statute.

Although a scire facias is prima facie barred by the recitals therein, it is not demurrable; the statute of limitations must be pleaded so as to allow the plaintiff to reply the exceptions, if any are applicable to his case, or some other matter. And it must be pleaded by the defendant, the court can not of its own motion interpose the bar of the statute. Smith v. Hutchinson, 78 Va. 683.

The defense of the statute of limitations is a personal privilege, and to be made availing must be pleaded by the defendant. Thus, in a case in which no execution issued on a judgment within the year, and which prima facie is barred, the practice is for the clerk to issue the scire facias, and leave defendant to plead the statute, and the plaintiff to reply the exceptions, so far as they may be applicable to his case. As an illustration of this principle, Gee v. Hamilton, 6 Munf. 32, and Peyton v. Carr, 1 Rand. 435, 436, are cited in Smith v. Hutchinson, 78 Va. 683, 687.

Court of Its Own Motion.—The court can not of its own motion plead this statute. Gee v. Hamilton, 6 Munf. 32; Smith v. Hutchinson, 78 Va. 683, 687; Humphrey v. Spencer, 36 W. Va. 11, 14 S. E. 411, 413.

Where service of a writ of scire facias has been duly acknowledged, and the writ returned on the first day of the next term, and at the succeeding term, none of the defendants appeared, demurred or pleaded to such writ, it is the duty of the court to give judgment for the plaintiff, it can not of its own motion, interpose the bar of statute, even though the writ is prima facie barred. Smith v. Hutchinson, 78 Va. 683.

g. Revival by Collusion after Judgment Barred.

After a judgment is barred, if it be revived by scire facias through collusion between creditor and debtor, a court of equity, in a suit to enforce the liens against the debtor's estate, will not give effect to the revival so as to affect the rights of other lien creditors of the said debtor, though it be effectual against himself. Ayre v. Burke, 82 Va. 338.

h. Retrospective Operation of Statute.

The act of 1792, for limiting the time within which a scire facias may be issued on a judgment (Rev. Code, vol. 1, ch. 76, § 5, p. 108), did not apply to a scire facias, previously sued out, by leave of the court, to revive a judgment which was more than ten years old when such leave was given. Lyons *v.* Gregory, 3 Hen. & M. 237; Day *v.* Pickett, 4 Munf. 104.

To the point that the fifth section of the statute of limitations has no retroactive operation and does not embrace judgments previously obtained, Day *v.* Pickett, 4 Munf. 104, is cited in Mercer *v.* Beale, 4 Leigh 189, 203. To the same effect, see Day *v.* Pickett, 4 Munf. 104, cited in Shepherd *v.* Larue, 6 Munf. 529, 531. To the point that statutes of limitation are no exception to the rule that statutes are prima facie future in operation, Day *v.* Pickett, 4 Munf. 104, is cited in State *v.* Mines, 38 W. Va. 125, 134, 18 S. E. 470, 473.

12. Judgment.
a. Validity.

Judgment on a writ of scire facias, returnable on its face not within ninety days, can only be treated as a judgment rendered without service of process, because rendered on a void process, and is therefore void. Lavell *v.* McCurdy, 77 Va. 763.

Direct and Collateral Attack.—The utmost extent of the jurisdiction in the court upon a writ of scire facias, reciting a judgment for money, and notifying the defendants to appear and show why the plaintiffs should not have an execution against them for the debt, interest and costs of said judgment, is to render judgment that the plaintiffs in the writ of scire facias have execution of the judgment in the writ set forth. A judgment on such writ of scire facias (even where the writ is valid) for money, and not merely for award of execution, is in excess of the jurisdiction of the court, and is absolutely void, and may be so declared either in a direct or collateral proceeding. Lavell *v.* McCurdy, 77 Va. 763.

b. Conformity with Original Judgment.

Nothing is better settled than that the judgment upon the scire facias must pursue strictly the original judgment. The form and the nature of the writ shows this. It is but a mode of obtaining execution upon the original judgment, either against the same party, or against some other party, who has become bound for the same debt. The jury have only to inquire whether the alleged cause why such execution should not be taken out, exists or not. They can not, in any form, give damages for the detention of the debt, or look behind, or vary from the original judgment. Lavell *v.* McCurdy, 77 Va. 763; Bowyer *v.* Hewitt, 2 Gratt. 193; Zumbro *v.* Stump, 38 W. Va. 325, 18 S. E. 443, 446; Maxwell *v.* Leeson, 50 W. Va. 361, 40 S. E. 420.

The utmost extent of the jurisdiction in the court upon a writ of scire facias, reciting a judgment for money, and notifying the defendants to appear and show why the plaintiffs should not have an execution against them for the debt, interest and costs of said judgment, is to render judgment that the plaintiffs in the writ of scire facias have execution of the judgment in the writ set forth. Lavell *v.* McCurdy, 77 Va. 763.

"The scire facias must pursue the terms of the judgment, and a variance from it is error, as if it mistakes the sum." And Barton, in his Law Practice (vol. 2, p. 1016), says: "The function of these cases of the scire facias is not to render a new judgment, but it only awards an execution on the judgment originally rendered." Zumbro *v.* Stump, 38 W. Va. 325, 18 S. E. 443, 446.

Surplusage.—In Maxwell *v.* Leeson, 50 W. Va. 361, 40 S. E. 420, Brannon, P., was of opinion that, though the writ under an original judgment on a scire facias, instead of merely awarding execution, if it also awarded judgment, such judgment would not be void, but merely surplusage as to the excess beyond the award of execution and would still have the effect of keeping the original judgment alive. See also, Crumlish *v.* Central Imp. Co., 38 W. Va. 390, 18 S. E. 456.

Illustrative Cases.—An order on a

scire facias to the effect that "it is ordered that said decree be revived in the name of W. Brent Maxwell, administrator of Franklin Maxwell, deceased, against the said Leroy Leeson, for $910.50, the unpaid balance of the decree, with interest thereon, from the twenty-first day of March, 1895, and the costs of the original decree and the costs of the revival, except an attorney's fee, and that the plaintiff has leave to sue out execution for the same, "is not obnoxious to the objection that it is an original decree and not mere revival and award of execution. Maxwell v. Leeson, 50 W. Va. 361, 40 S. E. 420.

A judgment on a writ of scire facias, awarding an execution in favor of different parties, for a different sum of money than that recited in the scire facias, will be set aside by the court on motion made at the same term at which it is rendered, and a new trial will be awarded. Zumbro v. Stump, 38 W. Va. 325, 18 S. E. 443.

An objection that the judgment on a scire facias, awarding execution, is in favor of a certain person as administrator when it should have been in favor of the plaintiffs on the record, is merely formal, for while it might be more regular, for it to have been in favor of the plaintiffs on the record, for the use or benefit of the administration, as the judgment is to be understood with reference to the scire facias on which it is founded, and as that goes for award of execution according to the original judgment, it may be regarded in effect as an award of execution to be sued out in their names, for the use of such party or administrator according to the suggestion contained in the scire facias. Richardson v. Prince George Justices, 11 Gratt. 190.

c. **Amount.**

Upon a scire facias to revive a judgment, in debt, for a penal sum, to be discharged by principal and interest; if the defendant confess judgment according to the scire facias, the plaintiff is not entitled to a writ of enquiry of damages, to recover more than the penal sum (the principal and interest accruing by lapse of time, amounting to more); but must take execution upon the original judgment, with the addition, only, of the costs upon the scire facias. Cosby v. Bell, 6 Munf. 282.

An order reviving a judgment and awarding execution for money in the name of a personal representative of a deceased party for a less sum than the original recovery by reason of partial payments since the judgment, is not void as a new judgment or because of variance in amount from the original judgment. Maxwell v. Leeson, 50 W. Va. 361, 362, 40 S. E. 420.

If a clerk of a court issues a writ of scire facias for too little, and the plaintiff obtains judgment and issues execution for the sum in the scire facias, he shall recover against the clerk in a subsequent action, the difference between the true sum for which the scire facias ought to have issued, and that for which it did issue; nor will it make any difference whether the special verdict finds special damage sustained by the plaintiff or not. Russell v. Clayton, 3 Call 41.

Interest on Aggregate of First Judgment.—Upon a scire facias against bail, it is error to give a judgment for the aggregate amount of principal, interest, and costs of the first judgment, with interest thereon. Bowyer v. Hewitt, 2 Gratt. 193.

d. **Revival against Joint Parties.**

Upon a scire facias to revive a judgment against two persons jointly, it is error to enter final judgment against one, until the plaintiff has matured the case against the other also, so that a joint judgment may be entered against both, or has proceeded against the other as far as the law authorizes or enables him to proceed. Early v. Clarkson, 7 Leigh 83.

Upon a scire facias against heirs and

devisees, to revive a judgment in ejectment, if one of the defendants confess
the plaintiff's right to revive the judgment in the scire facias mentioned;
and thereupon judgment be entered
against him, that the plaintiff have execution for the whole tract of land in
question, there is no error in such
judgment, of which he can take advantage. Jones v. Doe, 6 Munf. 105.

e. Judgment by Default.

Now, by § 6, ch. 170, Va. Code, 1860,
no judgment by default on a scire
facias or summons shall be valid, if it
becomes final within one month after
the service of the process. Bolanz v.
Com., 24 Gratt. 31.

f. Judgment in Ejectment.

Upon a scire facias against heirs and
devisees, to revive a judgment in ejectment, if one of the defendants confess
the plaintiff's right to revive the judgment in the scire facias mentioned;
and thereupon judgment be entered
against him, that the plaintiff have execution for the whole tract of land in
question; there is no error in such
judgment, of which he can take advantage. Jones v. Doe, 6 Munf. 105.

"The following was the opinion of
this court, pronounced by Judge
Roane: The appellant in this case having admitted that he could not gainsay
the appellee's right to revive the judgment mentioned in the scire facias, the
court is of opinion that there is no error in the said judgment; at least, of
which he can complain. Nor would
the case be different, could we restrict
the acknowledgment to apply to his
own portion of the land merely. In
that case, the judgment, so far as it exceeded that portion, would not be injurious to him, nor could he complain
of it. Judgment affirmed." Jones v.
Doe, 6 Munf. 105.

**g. Judgment on Bond for Payment of
    Debt by Installments.**

A judgment on a bond, for payment
of a debt by installments, should be,
"for the debt in the declaration men-

tioned, to be discharged by the sum
due at the time of institution of the
suit; reserving liberty to the plaintiff
to resort to a scire facias to recover
such other damages as might thereafter arise under the condition of the
bond." Thatcher v. Taylor, 3 Munf.
249.

h. Lien of Judgment.

A judgment on a scire facias awarding execution does not constitute a lien
on real estate, hence of course a void
judgment for money, in such case, is
no lien. Lavell v. McCurdy, 77 Va.
763.

i. Inquiry of Damages.

See the title INQUEST AND IN-
QUIRIES.

Upon a scire facias to revive a judgment, in debt, for a penal sum, to be
discharged by principal and interest;
if the defendant confess judgment according to the scire facias, the plaintiff
is not entitled to a writ of inquiry of
damages, to recover more than the
penal sum (the principal and interest
accruing by lapse of time, amounting
to more); but must take execution
upon the original judgment, with the
addition, only, of the costs upon the
scire facias. Cosby v. Bell, 6 Munf.
282. See Saunders v. Gaines, 3 Munf.
225.

13. Revival as Matter of Course.

Upon the scire facias being properly
served, and returned, the judgment or
decree will be revived as a matter of
course, unless good cause be shown
against it. Garrison v. Myers, 12 W.
Va. 330; Beale v. Botetourt Justices, 10
Gratt. 278.

14. Jurisdiction.

"It is deemed unnecessary to inquire
here whether a justice of the peace has
jurisdiction to revive a judgment upon
a scire facias, under the provision of
§§ 10 and 11 of ch. 139, of the Code."
Meighen v. Williams, 50 W. Va. 65,
67, 40 S. E. 332.

15. New Trials.

In a proceeding to revive a judgment

by scire facias the scire facias must pursue the terms of the judgment, and a judgment on a writ of scire facias, awarding an execution in favor of different parties, for a different sum of money than that recited in the scire facias, will be set aside by the court on motion made at the same term at which it is rendered, and a new trial will be awarded. Zumbro v. Stump, 38 W. Va. 325, 18 S. E. 443.

16. Appeal and Error.

Presumptions on Appeal.—Upon a plea of nul tiel record to a scire facias, as the court below has the whole record before it, in the absence of the record in the appellate court, it will be presumed, that the part of the record recited in the scire facias was before the court below, and that the order reviving the decree is correct. Garrison v. Myers, 12 W. Va. 330. See Buchanan v. King, 22 Gratt. 414.

B. BY SUBPŒNA IN NATURE OF SCIRE FACIAS AND BILL.

It was the old practice, when a suit becomes abated after a decree signed and enrolled, to revive the decree by a subpœna in the nature of a scire facias, upon the returning of which the party, to whom it was directed, might show cause against the reviving of the decree, by insisting that he was not bound by the decree, and showing why; or that for other reason it ought not to be enforced against him; or that the person suing out the subpœna was not entitled to the benefit of the decree. If he opposed the reviving of the decree on the ground of facts, which were disputed, he was examined upon interrogatories, to which he might answer or plead; and, issue being joined and witnesses examined, the matter was finally heard and determined by the court. But if there had been any proceedings subsequent to the decree, this process was ineffectual, as it revived the decree only, and the subsequent proceedings could not be revived except by bill. The enroll-ment of decrees being much disused it became the practice to revive in all cases indiscriminately by bill. Story, Eq. Pleading, § 366. Garrison v. Myers, 12 W. Va. 330, 334.

C. BY ACTION.

And from the earliest times, the action of debt has been provided as a concurrent remedy with debt to revive a judgment. Smith v. Charlton, 7 Gratt. 425.

An action upon the judgment has the effect of reviving it. At common law, an action of debt upon a judgment was the only method of reviving known until the statute of Westminister 2, 13 Ed. 1, gave for that purpose the writ of scire facias. 3 Blk. 421. The right to sue upon the judgment was not taken away by the granting of that writ. It still exists and a judgment may form the basis of a civil action before a justice of the peace under ch. 50 of the Code. Section 49 of that chapter declares that the forms of action now existing shall not apply to justice's courts and that there shall hereafter be but one form of action in such courts, which shall be denominated a civil action. Section 8 gives the justice jurisdiction as to all civil actions for the recovery of money or the possession of property, including actions in which damages are claimed as compensation for an injury or a wrong, in which the amount of money or damages or the value of property claimed does not exceed three hundred dollars, subject to a few exceptions contained in said chapter. Section 52 specifically mentions in action founded on judgment as being cognizable in justice's courts. It is not denied by counsel for the defendant in error that such an action may be maintained in a justice's court, but he denies that the justice has jurisdiction to revive a judgment by scire facias and insists that the purpose of this action as disclosed by the summons is to revive the judgment, and not to recover a new judgment upon the old one. Meighen v. Williams, 50 W. Va. 65, 67, 40 S. E. 332.

D. BY MOTION ON NOTICE.

In Fawkes v. Davison, 8 Leigh 554, 559, President Tucker was of opinion that the remedy by motion on notice is equivalent to and may be resorted to in lieu of the scire facias.

XV. Actions on Judgments.

A. NATURE OF ACTION.

An action on a judgment can not be ranged among actions ex delicto, and there is then no place for it except among actions ex contractu. Marstiller v. Ward, 52 W. Va. 74, 82, 43 S. E. 178, followed in Hutton v. Holt, 52 W. Va. 672, 44 S. E. 164.

B. JUDGMENT AS CAUSE OF ACTION.

A judgment is a debt, for the recovery of which the creditor is entitled to all the remedies applicable to other debts. Watkins v. Wortman, 19 W. Va. 78, cited in Livey v. Winton, 30 W. Va. 554, 4 S. E. 451.

A judgment may form the basis and subject matter of a civil action before a justice of the peace, and such summons having all the requisites of a summons in such case, after striking out the words, "To show cause why said judgment should not revive and be re-entered and execution issue thereon," is amendable in that respect, and if the plaintiff files a complaint showing the object of the action to be the obtaining of a judgment and not the revival of the former judgment, such summons is thereby amended, that part of the summons which purports to set forth the cause of action being regarded as pleading in the action to that extent. Meighen v. Williams, 50 W. Va. 65, 40 S. E. 332.

C. ACTIONABLE JUDGMENTS.

1. Judgments by Default.

Where a judgment by default for money has become final, an action of debt will lie on it. Marstiller v. Ward, 52 W. Va. 74, 43 S. E. 178, followed in Hutton v. Holt, 52 W. Va. 672, 44 S. E. 164.

In Shadrack v. Woolfolk, 32 Gratt. 707, 715, it is said: "In the case of Digges v. Dunn, 1 Munf. 56, an action was brought on the judgment, and although the clerk had not entered it up upon his order book, it was nevertheless treated as a valid judgment, as of the last day of the court, under the statute. The court considered the omission as a mere clerical misprision, which could not prejudice the party, and that the judgment was equally valid, as though the clerk had performed his duty in the premises."

Affidavit.—The words, "for the recovery of money arising out of contract," in § 46, ch. 125, W. Va. Code, 1899, include all actions in form ex contractu, but not those ex delicto, and thus includes an action or scire facias upon a judgment, and therefore the plaintiff may, in such action or scire facias upon a judgment, file the affidavit of the amount due him prescribed in that section. "Counsel for Ward presents the point that § 46 only allows the plaintiff to get judgment on affidavits in actions 'for the recovery of money arising out of contract,' and this action being one on a judgment is not one for recovery of money arising out of contract, as a judgment is not a 'contract,' and therefore the plaintiff had no right to file any affidavit, or ask judgment by force of it. Like the words 'final judgment' mentioned above, that depends upon the sense in which, or the purpose for which, the statute uses the word 'contract.' Sometimes the word 'contract' would include a judgment, sometimes not. Generally, it does not include a judgment." Marstiller v. Ward, 52 W. Va. 74, 82, 43 S. E. 178, followed in Hutton v. Holt, 52 W. Va. 672, 44 S. E. 164.

Variance.—In an action of debt on an office judgment, if the judgment be declared upon as of a quarterly term, and the transcript produced be of a judgment at rules, which ought to have been entered at such quarterly term, the variance is immaterial. Digges *v.* Dunn, 1 Munf. 56.

2. Foreign Judgments.

See the title FOREIGN JUDGMENTS, vol. 6, p. 227.

3. Effect of Pending Appeal.

D. recovered judgment against N. from which N., complaining of error, regularly took an appeal; but before this appeal was or could be prosecuted, the office of the clerk of the court, and with it the record of the judgment, were destroyed by fire, and therefore the appeal was never prosecuted; then D. brought debt on the judgment whereof the record was so destroyed. Held, he was entitled to recover, notwithstanding the appeal taken from the judgment, and the circumstances which prevented the prosecution thereof. Newcomb *v.* Drummond, 4 Leigh 57.

4. Judgments in Favor of State.

A judgment in the name of the commonwealth, for W., treasurer of C. county, founded on a notice in the name of the commonwealth proceeding by W., late treasurer of C., against F., the collector of township M., and his sureties, upon his official bond, is a judgment in favor of the commonwealth. On such a judgment the commonwealth at the relation of T., auditor of accounts, may maintain a suit against F. and his sureties. The judgment having been recovered in C. county, the suit may be brought in that county. Except in cases where it is otherwise specially provided, the commonwealth may prosecute her suits in any of the courts in which other parties may prosecute suits of like character. And this case is not embraced in the statute, Va. Code, 1873, ch. 166. Com. *v.* Ford, 29 Gratt. 683.

D. THE PLEADINGS AND DEFENSES.

This question has been fully considered elsewhere in this series. See the title DEBT, THE ACTION OF, vol. 4, p. 269.

Defenses.—In a suit upon a judgment, the questions whether it was an illegal contract on which the judgment was recovered, or whether the agent who made the contract was authorized to make it, are concluded by the judgment. Fisher *v.* March, 26 Gratt. 765.

E. LIMITATION OF THE ACTION.

Early Statutes.—"Our statute of limitations, 1 Rev. Va. Code, ch. 128, § 5, p. 489, provides that judgments in any court of record within this commonwealth, where execution hath not issued, may be revived by scire facias, or an action of debt brought thereon, within ten years after the date, of such judgment and not after." Braxton *v.* Wood, 4 Gratt. 25.

"There is no limitation, by statute, to an action of debt or scire facias upon a judgment, except only in the case of a judgment on which no execution has been taken out; and in cases of executors and administrators, upon a judgment against their testator or intestate. In all other cases, these remedies are left as at the common law; and at common law, there was nothing like a limitation upon them, except the presumption of satisfaction, arising from a delay to proceed upon the judgment for twenty years, which might be repelled by circumstances." Randolph *v.* Randolph, 3 Rand. 490, cited in Smith *v.* Charlton, 7 Gratt. 425, 450.

"In Randolph *v.* Randolph, 3 Rand. 490, Judge Green remarked, that there is no limitation by statute to an action of debt or scire facias upon a judgment, except only in the case of judgment on which no execution has been taken out, and in case of executors, etc. The correctness of this observation, as to a scire facias where an execution has been taken out and not returned, came under the consideration of this court in Fleming *v.* Dunlop, 4 Leigh 338. There an execution had been sued out within the year, and another at a subsequent period, but neither returned; and to a scire facias sued out more than ten years after the judgment, the statute was held to be a bar. But Judge Tucker concurred with Judge Green in the opinion that debt would not be barred. At common law there was no limitation to the action of debt; nothing but the presumption of payment or satisfaction, arising from a delay to proceed upon the judgment for twenty years. This being the law, the statute provided that judgments, where execution hath not issued, may be revived by scire facias of an action of debt brought thereon within ten years next after the date of such judgment, and not after. No other reference is made to the action of debt. At common law, if no execution was issued within the year, a presumption of satisfaction or release was raised, and the plaintiff was driven to his action of the judgment. To this the statute of Westminster the 2d superadded a scire facias, to give the plaintiff the benefit of the original judgment. And the first provision in the 5th section of our statute limits the remedy to ten years. Where an execution had issued but was not returned, the execution could not be kept alive for want of continuances on the roll, and the party was driven to his scire facias or action. 4 Leigh 343. The second clause of the 5th section was designed to relieve the plaintiff from this inconvenience, and does so by authorizing him to obtain other executions within ten years without a scire facias. But unless he procures a return on the execution within the ten years, the act is a bar to obtaining any other execution on the judgment. But nothing is said as to the action of debt." Herrington *v.* Harkins, 1 Rob. 591.

Action of Debt.—The statute, 1 Rev. Code, 1819, p. 489, § 5, declaring that where execution hath issued and no return is made thereon, the party in whose favor the same was issued may obtain other executions for ten years from the date of the judgment and not after, does not bar such party from maintaining an action of debt on the judgment after ten years. Herrington *v.* Harkins, 1 Rob. 591.

"In construing the statute its aim and purpose must be looked to, and its language ought to have a fair and reasonable interpretation. The limitations imposed on the right of the plaintiff to maintain an action on his judgment, have reference to and grow out of his conduct in respect to the execution, and necessarily presuppose that the plaintiff had at some time the right to sue out execution which he has failed to exercise. That this is so, is, I think, made still more apparent by looking to the second clause of the section of the statute, now under consideration, which provides that 'where execution had issued and no return is made thereon, the party in whose favor the same was issued, shall and may obtain other executions, or move against any sheriff or other officer or their security or securities for not returning the same, for the term of ten years from the date of such judgment, and not after.' This court held in the case of Herrington *v.* Harkins, 1 Rob. 591, that whilst the right to sue out other executions on a judgment where an execution had been before issued but not returned, was, by this clause, expressly limited to ten years, an action of debt was not embraced in the words or meaning of the clause; and that in all cases where the plaintiff had sued out execution there was no limitation to the period within which an action of debt might be brought on the judgment." Smith *v.* Charlton, 7 Gratt. 425, 450.

A judgment quando acciderint did not come within the operation of the statute of limitations in relation to judgments, quoted above, 1 Rev. Code, ch. 128, § 5. Smith v. Charlton, 7 Gratt. 425, overruling Braxton v. Wood, 4 Gratt. 25.

Present Statutory Provisions.—The Virginia statute provides that on a judgment, execution may be issued within a year, and a scire facias or an action may be brought within ten years after the date of the judgment; and where execution issues within the year, other executions may be issued, or a scire facias or an action may be brought within ten years from the return day of an execution on which there is no return by an officer, or within twenty years from the return day of an execution on which there is such return; except that where the scire facias or action is against the personal representative of a decedent, it shall be brought within five years from the qualification of such representative; and in computing time under this section, there shall, as to writs of fieri facias, be omitted from such computation the time elapsed between the first day of January, eighteen hundred and sixty-nine, and the twenty-ninth day of March, eighteen hundred and seventy-one. Any return by an officer on an execution showing that the same has not been satisfied, shall be a sufficient return within the meaning of this section. (1870-71, p. 341.) Va. Code, 1904, § 3577.

The West Virginia Code provides that an action or suit may be brought upon a judgment on which no execution issues within two years after the date thereof, or where there has been a change of parties by death or otherwise, at any time within ten years next after the date of the judgment. But if such action or suit be against a personal representative of a decedent it shall be brought within five years from the qualification of such representative. W. Va. Code, 1899, ch. 139, § 4150.

These statutes have been fully considered elsewhere in this title. See ante, "Judgment Liens," VI; "Revival of Judgments," XIV.

Sufficiency of Return.—See the title EXECUTIONS, vol. 5, p. 462.

An execution returned with the endorsement by the attorneys for the plaintiff as follows: "The sheriff is hereby directed to return this execution without levying it," is a sufficient return under the Virginia statute to extend the right of action to twenty years. Rowe v. Hardy, 97 Va. 674, 34 S. E. 625.

Action on a judgment rendered by a justice. Sections 10, 11, ch. 139, W. Va. Code, are applicable to judgments rendered by a justice, so far as to provide that upon such a judgment, on which no execution within two years from the date of its rendition has issued, an action may be brought at any time within ten years after the date of the judgment; but if such action be against a personal representative of a decedent, it shall be brought within five years from the qualification of such representative. Handy v. Smith, 30 W. Va. 195, 3 S. E. 604; Livesay v. Dunn, 33 W. Va. 453, 10 S. E. 808.

Section 10 of this chapter (139) provides: "And an action, suit, or scire facias may be brought upon a judgment on which no execution issued within the said two years, * * * at any time within ten years next after the date of the judgment." Code, 1887, ch. 866, § 10. As all the other provisions in reference to limiting actions for money apply to the jurisdiction of a justice, it is quite clear that this § 10, and also 11, of this chapter (139) were intended to fix the standard of limitation by lapse of time, when the action is before a justice on a judgment. Livesay v. Dunn, 33 W. Va. 453, 10 S. E. 808, 809.

When Statute Begins to Run.—A personal judgment upon any cause of action merges and ends that cause of action, and thereafter the statute of limitations runs against the judgment.

"No matter what the cause of action on which that judgment rested, as the law is well settled that whatever that cause of action was, it is merged, closed and drowned in that personal judgment; for when a personal judgment is rendered upon any cause of action, that cause can not be again made the subject of a suit, and the judgment is thereafter the sole test of the rights of the parties, constitutes a new debt of the highest dignity, closing the statute of limitation on the original cause of action. Such is the general law. 13 Am. & Eng. Ency. L. 336; Freeman on Judgments, §§ 215, 216, 217. By the judgment the debt is 'changed into a matter of record and merged in the judgment, and the plaintiff's remedy is upon the latter security while it remains in force.' 'The original claim has, by being sued upon and merged in the judgment, lost its vitality and expended its force and effect.' Black on Judgments, § 674." Fisher v. Hartley, 48 W. Va. 339, 37 S. E. 578. See the title MERGER.

Suspension or Interruption of Statute.—See ante, "Judgment Liens," VI; "Revival of Judgments," XIV.

If a defendant, once a resident of the state, departs and resides out of it before a personal judgment against him, the time of his residence abroad will not excuse the judgment from the statute of limitations, though he was a resident when the cause of action on which the judgment rests arose or accrued. Fisher v. Hartley, 48 W. Va. 339, 37 S. E. 578.

Pleading the Statute.—Where an action of debt is brought on a judgment after ten years from the date thereof, and the defendant wishes to avail himself of the statute of limitations, it is necessary that he should do so by plea. A demurrer to the declaration is not the proper mode to take advantage of the statute. Herrington v. Harkins, 1 Rob. 591.

F. EVIDENCE.

Best Evidence.—In an action of debt on a judgment at common law the original record must have been produced wherever the cause was in the same court, a copy, however, authenticated, being under no circumstances admissible, unless the original were lost. 4 Min. Inst. (4th Ed.) 881, citing Burk v. Tregg, 2 Wash. 216; Anderson v. Dudley, 5 Call 529.

But the statutes now provide that a copy of any record or paper in the clerk's office of any court or in the office of the secretary of state, treasurer or auditor, or surveyor of lands in any county, attested by the officer in whose office the same is, may be admitted as evidence in lieu of the original. W. Va. Code, ch. 130, § 5; Va. Code, 1887, ch. 164; §§ 3334, 3335. See Baker v. Preston, Gilmer 235; Ben v. Peete, 2 Rand. 539; Rowletts v. Daniel, 4 Munf. 473; Pollard v. Lively, 4 Gratt. 73; Hinchman v. Ballard, 7 W. Va. 152, 153; Ott v. McHenry, 2 W. Va. 73; Anderson v. Nagle, 12 W. Va. 98; Dickinson v. Railroad Co., 7 W. Va. 390; Peterson v. Ankron, 25 W. Va. 56.

And it is believed that this statutory rule would apply even though the suit be in the same court where the judgment was rendered. See Anderson v. Dudley, 5 Call 529.

It must be observed, however, that the original order book of a county court is competent evidence wherever a certified copy would be evidence; the copy being received only on the ground of convenience, to obviate the necessity of removing the original record from place to place, and not because it is better evidence than the original. Ballard v. Thomas, 19 Gratt. 14.

Proceedings to Enforce Lien.—As to proof of the judgment in proceedings to enforce the lien, see ante, "Judgment Liens," VI.

G. VARIANCE.

See the title VARIANCE.

H. VENUE.

See the title VENUE.

Judgments by Confession.

See the title CONFESSION OF JUDGMENTS, vol. 3, p. 64.

JUDICIAL.—See MINISTERIAL. And see the title PUBLIC OFFICERS. As to mandamus to compel performance of a judicial act, see the title MANDAMUS.

Judicial Act.—An act done in the exercise of judicial power—an act performed by a court touching the rights of parties or property brought before it by voluntary appearance or by prior action of ministerial officers—is a judicial act. Arkle v. Board of Com'rs, 41 W. Va. 471, 23 S. E. 804.

Judicial Day.—See DAY, vol. 4, p. 224.

Judicial Proceedings.—See ADMINISTRATIVE PROCEEDINGS, vol. 1, p. 182.

In State v. South Penn Oil Co., 42 W. Va. 80, 24 S. E. 688, it is said: "A proceeding by writ of certiorari is a judicial proceeding, in the technical sense, as distinguished from a 'quasi judicial' one; and apart from its ancillary use, its main purpose and its commonest use is to supervise, control, review, and correct the proceedings of quasi judicial tribunals, or where such proceedings are different from the course of the common law. 2 Bac. Ab. 163; Harris Certiorari, § 1, et seq.; 2 Spell. Extr. Relief, § 1890, et seq." See also, the title CERTIORARI, vol. 2, p. 736.

A county court acting under the statute authorizing county courts to purchase salt, is not exercising a judicial power. Chesterfield County v. Hall, 80 Va. 321, 324; Pulaski Co. v. Stuart, 28 Gratt. 872.

The execution of a bond is not a judicial proceeding. Dinwiddie Co. v. Stuart, 28 Gratt. 526; Chesterfield County v. Hall, 80 Va. 324.

Judicial Power.—See the title CONSTITUTIONAL LAW, vol. 3, p. 166.

In Wise v. Bigger, 79 Va. 269, 274, it is said: "In Wolfe v. McCaull, 76 Va. 876, Judge Christian, in delivering the opinion of this court, says: 'To enact laws or to declare what the law shall be, is legislative power; to interpret law—to declare what law is or has been—is judicial power. The power to declare what is the law of the state, is delegated to the courts. The power to declare what the law is. of necessity involves the power to declare what acts of the legislature are, and what acts of the legislature are not laws.'"

Judicial Admissions.

See the title DECLARATIONS AND ADMISSIONS, vol. 4, p. 326, and references given.

Judicial Confessions.

See the title CONFESSIONS, vol. 3, p. 95.

JUDICIAL DISCRETION.—See DISCRETION, vol. 4, p. 682.

Judicial Department.

See the title CONSTITUTIONAL LAW, vol. 3, p. 180.

Judicial Guardians.

See the title GUARDIAN AND WARD, vol. 6, p. 789.

JUDICIAL NOTICE.

VIII. Sources of Information, 647.

I. Statement of General Rule.

It is not necessary either to allege or prove matters of which the courts take judicial notice, and this rule applies to pleadings at law and in equity, and to the indictment in a criminal proceeding. Richmond, etc., R. Co. v. Richmond, etc., R. Co., 96 Va. 670, 32 S. E. 787; Stribbling v. Bank, 5 Rand. 132; Hays v. Northwestern Bank, 9 Gratt. 127; Bayly v. Chubb, 16 Gratt. 284; Bird v. Com., 21 Gratt. 800; Savage v. Com., 84 Va. 582, 5 S. E. 563; Thomas v. Com., 90 Va. 92, 17 S. E. 788; Blankenship v. Chesapeake, etc., R. Co., 94 Va. 449, 27 S. E. 20; Hargraves v. Com., 2 Va. Dec. 139; Moundsville v. Velton, 35 W. Va. 217, 13 S. E. 373; State v. Gould, 26 W. Va. 258; Abell v. Penn Mutual Life Ins. Co., 18 W. Va. 400, 402; Hart v. Baltimore, etc., R. Co., 6 W. Va. 336, 338.

It is a general principle in pleading that it is not necessary to allege in the declaration more than it is necessary to prove at the trial, except so far as may be necessary for a right understanding of allegations that are required to be proved. Hart v. Baltimore, etc., R. Co., 6 W. Va. 336.

It is unnecessary to prove before the court matters of law or fact of which it may take judicial notice. Hart v. Baltimore, etc., R. Co., 6 W. Va. 336.

In an action against a railroad company, it is not necessary to aver in the declaration that it is a corporation, nor is it necessary to prove on the trial that the defendant is a corporation, unless with the plea there is filed an affidavit denying that it is. The court will ex officio take notice of the fact. Baltimore, etc., R. Co. v. Sherman, 30 Gratt. 602, followed in Douglass v. Kanawha, etc., R. Co., 44 W. Va. 267, 28 S. E. 705.

II. Matters of Common Knowledge.

A. IN GENERAL.

Facts which are so generally known that every well-informed person knows them or ought to know them, will be judicially recognized without proof. Richmond, etc., R. Co. v. Richmond, etc., R. Co., 96 Va. 670, 32 S. E. 787; Hart v. Baltimore, etc., R. R. Co., 6 W. Va. 336.

B. ANIMALS.

See the title CRUELTY TO ANIMALS, vol. 4, p. 145.

In an indictment under the West Virginia statute making it a misdemeanor to treat cruelly or kill any domestic animal, it is unnecessary to allege that a mule is a domestic animal as the court will take judicial notice that all mules in this state are domestic animals. State *v.* Gould, 26 W. Va. 258.

C. VALUE.

A declaration in an action on a contract, based on a promise by the plaintiff to deliver to the defendant dead cattle, is not demurrable as setting forth no consideration for the promise. "The court could not judicially know, that the dead bodies of these beeves were valueless except for their skins, and therefore the circuit court did not err in overruling the demurrer to this second count as well as to the first count." Davisson *v.* Ford, 23 W. Va. 617, 631.

D. EXPECTATION OF LIFE AS SHOWN BY MORTALITY TABLES.

Courts may take judicial notice of mortality tables, though not offered in evidence. Abell *v.* Penn Mutual Life Ins. Co., 18 W. Va. 400, 402.

E. DEVICES USED BY RAILROADS TO PROMOTE SAFETY.

Gates and Flagman at Crossings.—It is a matter of common knowledge, of which courts will take judicial notice, that the maintenance of gates and gatekeepers at grade crossings of railroads tends to promote safety. Courts have the right to take judicial notice of the result of the general experience of society as shown by adjudged cases, and the treatises of text writers. Richmond, etc., R. Co. *v.* Richmond, etc., R. Co., 96 Va. 670, 32 S. E. 787.

Bells are used on locomotives to lessen the danger to travelers on a street or highway of a collision with an engine crossing the same, and courts will take judicial notice of this fact, but they are not intended or useful in warning persons to keep at such distance from the track of the company as will prevent their horses from becoming frightened at a passing engine. Southern R. Co. *v.* Cooper, 98 Va. 299, 36 S. E. 388, citing Richmond, etc., R. Co. *v.* Richmond, etc., R. Co., 96 Va. 670, 673, 32 S. E. 787.

F. INTOXICATING LIQUORS.

See the title INTOXICATING LIQUORS, ante, p. 1.

That apple brandy is intoxicating is a matter of common knowledge of which the court will take judicial notice. 1 Greenl. Ev. (14th Ed.), § 5, note (b), p. 10; Thomas *v.* Com., 90 Va. 92, 95, 17 S. E. 788.

Ginger.—The court can not know, in the absence of proof, that "ginger" is intoxicating. Savage *v.* Com., 83 Va. 582, 5 S. E. 563.

Essence of Cinnamon.—The court can not judicially know whether or not the essence of cinnamon will produce intoxication. State *v.* Muncey, 28 W. Va. 494.

G. TIME, DATES AND DAYS.

The court will not take judicial notice of the fact that the next day after protest, or receipt of notice thereof, is not a mail day; or of the time it requires for a letter to go by mail between any two places. Such matters, if material, must be proved. Early *v.* Preston, 1 Pat. & H. 228.

H. USAGES AND CUSTOMS.

See the title USAGES AND CUSTOMS.

"There is some conflict among the authorities as to the necessity of pleading a custom or usage of trade. See 12 Cyc. 1097 and notes; 22 Am. & Eng. Ency. Pl. & Pr. 405, etc., and cases cited. But whenever the question has been raised in this court, except in the case of Hansbrough *v.* Neal, 94 Va. 722, 27 S. E. 593, which was thought to be an exception to the general rule, it has been considered necessary for the party relying on such custom or usage to set it up in his pleadings. Jackson *v.* Henderson, 3 Leigh 196; Governor *v.* Withers, 5 Gratt. 24, 50 Am. Dec. 95. And this view would seem to be the better one, since such customs or usages are generally regarded as facts, and like other material facts should be averred and proved. The court can not take judicial notice of them." Oriental Lumber Co. v. Blades Lumber Co., 103 Va. 730, 741, 50 S. E. 270.

Custom of Merchants.—A custom of merchants, when first brought into court, is a matter of fact, and merchants are examined to prove what it is, but when legal decisions are once made upon it, it becomes the law of the land, of which all parties and courts are to take notice without stating it. Branch v. Burnley, 1 Call 147.

I. CUSTOMARY WARRANTIES IN SALES.

See the title WARRANTY.

"From these authorities it appears that there are warranties which an agent to sell may make as one of the incidents of that employment, and of the power to make which the court will take judicial notice. They are such warranties as are usual. For example, a general agent to sell horses may warrant the soundness of a horse, for this is the warranty usually given in such transactions; but where the warranty is of an unusual character, the agent, having no express authority to warrant, can not bind his principal unless it shall appear that by the custom of trade in the market in which he is transacting business it is usual for such agents to make the warranty in question. If there be evidence tending to prove that it is usual, it then becomes a question to be submitted to the jury the particular case the agent was clothed with the requisite authority." Reese v. Bates, 94 Va. 321, 328, 26 S. E. 865.

J. CONDEMNATION OF LAND.

The court will not take judicial notice that a railroad company under its charter condemned or acquired title to any particular land or strip of land, upon which it locates its road; such a thing is not of that public notoriety, that every intelligent man is presumed to know it. Chapman v. Pittsburg, etc., R. Co., 18 W. Va. 184, 196.

K. MEANING OF WORDS AND PHRASES.

"Without deciding whether or not we can take judicial notice of the ingredients or constituents which compose the 'essence of cinnamon,' we certainly can take such notice of the meaning of the words used in the English language, and therefore we judicially know the meanings and definitions of the words 'essence' and 'cinnamon.'" State v. Muncey, 28 W. Va. 494, 495.

L. MUNICIPAL AID TO RAILROADS.

See the title MUNICIPAL AID.

"How can it be said that a period of over fourteen years of failure to do the work, making scarcely a commencement, ought not to debar the company from asking a court of equity to compel Harrison county to keep open its offer, even if time were not of the essence of the contract: First, from the very nature of the work; second, from the forfeiture clause in the contract? Perhaps time had changed things. How many of those voting for that subscription, parties to it, who expected to reap benefit from the railroad proposed, had gone to their graves? We may, from judicial cognizance, say that another railroad, now nearly completed, renders that subscription inadvisable." West Virginia, etc., R. Co. v. Harrison County Court, 47 W. Va. 273, 34 S. E. 786, 790.

M. KNOWLEDGE OF JURORS.

Matters of general history must be given in evidence, as well as all other facts; and the jury are not to be left to their own information, as to such things. Gregory v. Baugh, 4 Rand. 611.

III. Geographical Facts.

A. IN GENERAL.

"The objects sometimes called for

are so connected with the general history or geography of the country, or its legislation, that they will be taken notice of by the courts and deemed of general notoriety, and sufficiently identified without further proof. Such are rivers used as public highways, or thoroughfares between different parts of the country, or which are referred to in general laws and designated as boundaries of the counties or other districts of country. Mountains and points on the same may possess this character. And an entry calling for such objects may be supported without proof of notoriety or identity. Such was the entry in Watts v. Lindsey, 7 Wheat. R. 158. There the 'Ohio river' and 'Little Miami river' were regarded as sufficiently notorious and identified without further proof. So the notoriety of the 'Lower Blue Licks' was presumed. Hart v. Bodley, Hardin's R. 98. In Speed v. Severe, 2 Bibb's R. 131, 'Salt river' was regarded as a stream sufficiently notorious to be taken notice of without proof of its course or locality. So of 'Licking river,' Bowman v. Melton, Ibid. 151. So the 'Blue Licks,' from their connection with the general history of the country, were deemed notorious, and sufficiently identified without further proof. McKee v. Bodley, Ibid. 481. So of the 'Kentucky river,' Winslow v. Holders' Heirs, 2 Litt. R. 34." McNeel v. Herold, 11 Gratt. 309, 315.

B. TERRITORIAL EXTENT OF COURT'S JURISDICTION.

In General.—Courts take judicial notice of the territorial extent of the jurisdiction and sovereignty exercised, de facto by their own government, as that a particular county at a particular time was de facto within or without its jurisdiction. Simmons v. Trumbo, 9 W. Va. 358, citing 1 Greenl. on Ev., pt. 1, ch. 2, § 6.

Mercer and Richmond Counties.—Courts will take judicial notice of the fact that the jurisdiction of West Vir-

ginia was never during the war extended over Mercer county, but that it remained under the jurisdiction of the government of Virginia at Richmond. Kent v. Chapman, 18 W. Va. 485, citing Simmons v. Trumbo, 9 W. Va. 358.

In a chancery suit brought by K. of Richmond against A. B. & C. of Mercer county in this state to enforce the lien of a judgment obtained before the war against A. B. & C. as partners on an accepted order known to the partners to include the amount due from the partnership to K. and also an individual debt due from C. to K.; held, there should be no abatement of the interest on the judgment during the war, Richmond and Mercer county being judicially known to the court not to be in territories, which were hostile to one another during the war. Kent v. Chapman, 18 W. Va. 485, citing Simmons v. Trumbo, 9 W. Va. 358.

Greenbrier County.—The court will take judicial notice of the fact that Greenbrier county was all the time during the war within the confederate lines. Hix v. Hix, 25 W. Va. 481, citing Simmons v. Trumbo, 9 W. Va. 358; Kent v. Chapman, 18 W. Va. 485, 500.

The government of West Virginia, it is well known as a historical fact, never extended her laws over the county of Greenbrier until after the close of said war. And the restored government of Virginia never did extend its jurisdiction over the county of Greenbrier, nor did it extend its jurisdiction over the county of Bedford until after the close of the war. Smith v. Henning, 10 W. Va. 596, 617.

Kanawha County.—The court will take judicial notice, that the county of Kanawha in January, 1865, and for a long time before was under the jurisdiction of West Virginia, and within the lines of the federal army. Dryden v. Stephens, 19 W. Va. 1, 14.

C. PLACES WITHIN COUNTY.

When in any judicial proceeding it

becomes material to inquire within what county a certain city, town or village is situated, the court, judge or justice before whom the same is pending, will take judicial notice of the county within which the same is situated. Beasley *v.* Beckley, 28 W. Va. 81.

The supreme court of West Virginia will take judicial notice that the city of Wheeling is the county seat of, and is within, Ohio county. Seibright *v.* State, 2 W. Va. 591.

Particular Localities or Unincorporated Hamlets.—All crimes are local, and are to be tried in the court having jurisdiction of the locality where they are committed. The burden on the commonwealth to prove that the offense was committed within the jurisdiction of the trial court is just as great as it is to prove the commission of the offense itself. The court will not take judicial notice of the fact that a particular locality or an unincorporated hamlet is in a particular county. Anderson *v.* Com., 100 Va. 860, 42 S. E. 865.

An indictment charges that the murder, for which the plaintiff in error was tried and convicted, took place in the county of Campbell, but there is not the slightest proof in the record that such is a fact. The only proof as to the location of the crime is that it took place at "Anderson's Store," about a quarter of a mile or more from "Lynch's" or "Lynch's Station," but neither "Lynch's Station" nor "Anderson's Store" is shown to be located in Campbell county. "It is contended, however, that the court should take judicial notice that 'Lynch's Station' is in Campbell county, and deduce from that fact that 'Anderson's Store' is also in that county. 'When a crime is committed in an incorporated town, the court will notice in what county the town is situated.' State *v.* Reader, 60 Iowa 527. It was, therefore, held in Sullivan *v.* People, 122 Ills. 385, 13 N. E. 248, that proof that a crime was committed in Chicago is proof that it was committed in Cook county, judicial notice being taken that Chicago is in Cook county. But courts will not take judicial notice that a particular locality is within a county; nor of the local situation and distances in a county. Note to Oliver *v.* State of Alabama, 4 L. R. A. 33, and authorities cited. We have been cited no authority, and we have been unable to find any, for taking judicial cognizance of the fact that a point a given distance from Lynch's Station, an unincorporated hamlet or village, is in the county of Campbell." Anderson *v.* Com., 100 Va. 860, 863, 42 S. E. 865.

D. DISTANCE.

In an early case, the court took judicial notice of the fact that Beverly in the county of Randolph was at that time but three or four days' easy journey at the utmost from the Ohio river. Moore *v.* Holt, 10 Gratt. 284, 290.

E. STATE CAPITALS.

It is judicially known to the courts in West Virginia that the city of Richmond is the capital of the state of Virginia. Calwell *v.* Prindle, 19 W. Va. 604, 605.

F. POPULATION.

Judicial notice will be taken of the population of a county as established by the last United States census. Welch *v.* County Court, 29 W. Va. 63, 1 S. E. 337; People *v.* Williams, 64 Cal. 87.

G. PUBLIC LANDS.

The objects called for are sometimes so connected with the general history or geography of the country or its legislation, that the courts will take notice of them; and they will be deemed of general notoriety, and sufficiently identified without further proof. And an entry calling for such objects may be supported without proof of notoriety or identity. McNeel *v.* Herold, 11 Gratt. 309.

In a caveat, where the objects called

for in the entry are not of such public notoriety as that the courts will take notice of them, a special verdict must find that the objects called for have a real existence, and are such as is required to make it a valid entry; and a finding defective in these respects will not be remedied by finding that the survey was made in conformity with the entry. McNeel v. Herold, 11 Gratt. 309.

IV. Historical Facts.

A. BY THE COURT.

1. In General.

Courts can take judicial notice of such facts as are matters of general history, affecting the whole people, and where generally known to the people of the United States. Simmons v. Trumbo, 9 W. Va. 358. See ante, "In General," III, A.

2. History of Red Men's Act.

"The Red Men's act is made a part of chapter one hundred and forty-eight of our Code, which chapter is entitled 'Offenses against the Peace.' Its public history and the exigencies which led to its enactment are matters of judicial cognizance. Greenl. Ev., §§ 5 and 6; Taylor v. Barclay, 2 Sim. 221; Embry v. Com., 79 Ky. 439. It is well known, that at the time of and previous to the passage of this act there were in certain counties of the state lawless bands of men, known as 'Red Men,' and 'Regulators,' 'Vigilance Committees,' etc., who were in the habit of inflicting punishment and bodily injury upon peaceful citizens, and injuring, carrying away and destroying their property and committing other acts of trespass of the most violent and outrageous character. It was to punish and suppress such combinations and conspiracies that the act was passed. That such was its object is shown by its very terms, by the title of the chapter of which it is made a part and by the meaning and import of the offenses designated in it." State v. Porter, 25 W. Va. 685, 689.

3. Division of Virginia.

The courts will take judicial notice of such facts as the division of the state of Virginia and the formation of the new state of West Virginia. Darrah v. Watson, 36 Iowa 116, citing 1 Greenl. Ev., § 456; Northwestern Bank v. Machir, 18 W. Va. 271.

4. The Original Colonies.

The courts will take judicial notice of the fact that Maryland embraces a part of the territory of the original English colonies of America, and, in the absence of the evidence to the contrary, it will be presumed that the common law obtains there. Nelson v. Chesapeake, etc., R. Co., 88 Va. 971, 976, 14 S. E. 838, 15 L. R. A. 583; Stewart v. Conrad, 100 Va. 128, 40 S. E. 624; Bowers v. Bristol Gas, etc., Co., 100 Va. 533, 42 S. E. 296.

5. Power of Public Officers.

"It is said that the practice of making these purchases for the poor farm and of providing for such necessary supplies by the members of the county court acting as individuals is so common and universal as to be matter of public history, of which the courts will take judicial notice. If so, they would also take notice that such contracts are very generally, if not always, understood to be subject to the ratification of the county court as to the prices to be paid." Goshorn v. County Court, 42 W. Va. 735, 26 S. E. 452, 455.

6. Safety of Persons.

But the court should not take judicial notice of such facts as are not matters of general history, such as that a person entertaining certain political views was not safe in his person or property, in some particular county at a particular time. Simmons v. Trumbo, 9 W. Va. 358, 359.

7. Historical Facts Connected with the Civil War.

In General.—"It is an historical fact, that the recognized lawful state government, at the time, had its capital at the city of Wheeling. It had its troops in the field, aiding the federal forces, to maintain, not only the federal, but its own authority over its territory; but, nevertheless, the confederate troops held the county of Greenbrier by paramount force, and thus maintained over it the state organization and authority which adhered to the confederate cause and held its capital at Richmond." Henning *v.* Fisher, 6 W. Va. 338, 247.

Time of Civil War.—Courts can take judicial notice of such historical facts, as the pendency at a particular time, of the late civil war. Simmons *v.* Trumbo, 9 W. Va. 358.

Pecuniary Condition of Persons after the War.—It is known judicially that a large number of persons, solvent, when the war commenced, were rendered insolvent by the war. Estill *v.* McClintic, 11 W. Va. 399, 417.

History of Libby Prison and Castle Thunder.—The West Virginia court took judicial notice of the fact that Libby Prison and Castle Thunder were full of "loyal citizens whose only crime was loyalty to the constitution and union." Mann *v.* Lewis, 3 W. Va. 215.

Facts Concerning Confederate Currency.

In General.—Courts should take judicial notice of such facts as are matters of general history, affecting the whole people; as that confederate notes were issued early in the war by the confederate government, and these notes in a short time became almost the exclusive currency of the confederate states, that during the first year of the war these notes were but slightly depreciated and were then received throughout the confederate states in the payment of debts and all the channels of trade, without doubt or question; but these notes were never made a legal tender in the payment of debts, by an act of confederate congress. Simmons *v.* Trumbo, 9 W. Va. 358, overruling Mann *v.* Lewis, 3 W. Va.

215; Mann *v.* McVey, 3 W. Va. 232; Hix *v.* Hix, 25 W. Va. 481; Hale *v.* Wall, 22 Gratt. 424, 428.

That It Was the Exclusive Currency of the Confederacy.—Courts take judicial notice of such historical facts, as that confederate notes were issued early in the war by the confederate government, and that these notes in a short time became almost exclusively the currency of the confederate states. Simmons *v.* Trumbo, 9 W. Va. 358, citing Thorington *v.* Smith, 8 Wall. 7.

The court will take judicial notice of the fact that confederate money during the war was the general currency in circulation in Greenbrier county. Hix *v.* Hix, 25 W. Va. 481, citing Simmons *v.* Trumbo, 9 W. Va. 358; Kent *v.* Chapman, 18 W. Va. 485.

The fact that confederate states treasury notes was the only currency in circulation in Virginia in March, 1863, is so notorious, that it may be taken notice of judicially by the courts, as a matter of current public history. Walker *v.* Page, 21 Gratt. 636; Crockett *v.* Sexton, 29 Gratt. 47, 57.

In August, 1860, D., as commissioner, sold land to M. on a credit of one, two and three years. In October, 1861, on the application of M., the court authorized him to deposit in the B. Bank the amount of his first and second bonds; which M. does. D. afterwards collects the third bond and deposits in the same bank, and reports it to the court; and his report is afterwards confirmed. The court must be presumed to have known, when the reports were confirmed, that the deposits were made in confederate money, and neither M. nor D. are liable to repay the money they so deposited. "We say, judicially, because, when the court, by its order of October 4th, 1862, allowed Mead to pay the amount of his two first bonds into the Bedford Savings Bank, it knew judicially that confederate states treasury notes constituted not only the general, but almost the only, currency in Virginia." Mead *v.* Jones, 24 Gratt. 347, 360.

That It Was Made Legal Tender.— Mann *v.* McVey, 3 W. Va. 232, 238, in so far it was held, that the court could not take judicial notice of the fact that confederate notes were never made a legal tender in the payment of debts by any act of the confederate congress, was overruled in Simmons *v.* Trumbo, 9 W. Va. 358, 365.

That It Was Scaled in 1864.—It is a matter of history, whereof judicial cognizance is taken, that all confederate currency was in 1864 called in and scaled at two-thirds of its value, and administrator should be allowed credit accordingly. Dromgoole *v.* Smith, 78 Va. 665.

Depreciation of the Currency.— Courts take judicial notice of such matters of general history, as that during the first year of the war confederate notes were but slightly depreciated, and were then received throughout the confederate states in payment of debts, and in all the channels of trade without doubt or question. Simmons *v.* Trumbo, 9 W. Va. 358, citing Myers *v.* Zetelle, 21 Gratt. 733, 753.

Legality of Confederate Contracts.— It was judicially known to the West Virginia courts that a plea of illegality to a bond payable in confederate states treasury notes was held good in that state. Griffie *v.* McCoy, 8 W. Va. 201.

Military Occupation.—The court will take judicial notice of the fact, that Greenbrier county was within the confederate lines during the war, and that confederate money was the currency of the county. Hix *v.* Hix, 25 W. Va. 481.

And that the county of Kanawha in January, 1865, was within the lines of the federal army. Dryden *v.* Stephens, 19 W. Va. 1, 2.

Also, Richmond and Mercer county are judicially known to the court not to be in territories, which were hostile to each other during the war. Kent *v.* Chapman, 18 W. Va. 485.

B. BY THE JURY.

It is error to instruct the jury that they may consider facts connected with the history of the country, as if formally proved to them. Gregory *v* Baugh, 4 Rand. 611.

V. Courts and Court Records.

Courts.

Courts of Sister States.—The supreme court of West Virginia will take judicial notice that the corporation court of Lynchburg, Va., is a court of record, and will consult the Virginia Code or other law book to impart to it information, under § 4, ch. 13, W. Va. Code. Heffernan *v.* Harvey, 41 W. Va. 766, 24 S. E. 592.

Sources of Information.—See post, "Sources of Information," VIII.

"Another alleged defect in the certificate of the clerk of the corporation court of the city of Lynchburg verifying the certificate of the notary signing the affidavit to the mechanic's lien is that it does not certify that the court is one of record. Section 4, ch. 13, Code, allows us to inquire of books as to this. We see by the Virginia Code and Barton's Law Practice (page 8) that various cities in that state, among them Lynchburg, by the constitution and Code, have corporation courts, with judge, clerk record of proceedings, and the same jurisdiction within the cities, criminal and civil, as circuit and county courts; and we must say it is a court of record, by judicial notice, without the clerk's so certifying." Heffernan *v.* Harvey, 41 W. Va. 766, 24 S. E. 592.

British Vice Admiralty Courts.—The character of the British vice admiralty courts, and of their decisions, are known to the courts judicially, as a matter of general history. Bourke *v.* Granberry, Gilm. 16, 23.

Judges of Particular Courts.—"In addition to the facts appearing by the record in this cause, there are others of which this court will take judicial notice, which are necessary to the full understanding of this case. At the institution of this suit, and when it was decided, Wood county constituted a portion of the ninth judicial circuit, of which Judge Stewart was the judge, and Thomas W. Harrison, who really decided this cause, was the judge of the fourth judicial circuit. Judge Harrison, it appears by the record, held the January term of the circuit court of Ritchie county, instead of Judge Stewart, the judge of that court." Johnson v. Young, 11 W. Va. 673, 679.

Terms of Court.—Although the notice that an award would be recommitted for correction was that the motion would be made at the November term, 1872, this court, if there is nothing to show the contrary, will take judicial notice that the June term, 1873, was the first term actually holden after the notice had been served, by virtue of ch. 114, § 11, and acts 1872-73, ch. 9, § 11. (Wootten v. Bragg, 1 Gratt. 1.) Henley v. Menefee, 10 W. Va. 771, 780.

Clerk of Court.—And a court will take official notice of who is its clerk. Cent. Land. Co. v. Calhoun, 16 W. Va. 361, 362; Dyer v. Last, 51 Ill. 179.

Therefore if he fail to sign officially, will recognize his endorsement. Central Land Co. v. Calhoun, 16 W. Va. 361, 362.

Court Records.—See the title RECORDS.

The usual mode of proving the record of another court is by the production of a certified copy. But the copy is not produced in such cases, because it is better evidence than the original. It is received only on the ground of convenience, as a substitute for the original record. The reception of a copy avoids the inconvenience of removing the original record from place to place; and as one court will not take judicial notice of the records of another, the certificate supplies the

necessary authentication. But the original, if properly authenticated, is equally admissible, and is, in its nature, the highest evidence. Ballard v. Thomas, 19 Gratt. 14.

Order tnd Decree.

Effect of Orders.—The court can not know judicially what effect an order declaring a summons void as an alias summons, but good as an original summons, may have upon the ultimate determination of the rights of the parties. Rogers v. Bertha Zinz Co., 1 Va. Dec. 827.

Orders or Decrees of Foreign Courts.—Where a court of competent jurisdiction in one of the United States has by its final order or decree passed upon and confirmed the accounts of an executor, administrator, or other fiduciary, the courts of West Virginia will take judicial notice of the effect of such order or decree in any judicial proceeding in that state affecting the validity of the same. Shriver v. Garrison, 30 W. Va. 456, 4 S. E. 660.

VI. Seals and Signatures.

In General.—The statutes in Virginia and West Virginia provide that all courts and officers shall take notice of the signature of any of the judges, or of the governor of the state, to any judicial or official documents. Va. Code, 1904, § 3332; W. Va. Code, 1899, ch. 130, § 3924.

"It is a rule of evidence universally recognized, that the courts of a state take judicial notice of its seals and of the signatures of the heads of departments; nor will it be supposed, without proof, that any particular seal is counterfeit or irregularly impressed. The law assumes that the seal of the state is known to all her judicial officers; and there is nothing in the statute requiring the production of the bonds, in a proceeding like the present, which affects this rule of the common law." Com. v. Dunlop, 89 Va. 431, 16 S. E. 273.

Judicial Notice of Foreign Seals.—
The courts of Virginia take judicial
notice of the great seal of foreign
government or foreign sovereigns.
Hadfield *v.* Jameson, 2 Munf. 53.

Signing Orders.—Somerville *v.* Wimbish, 7 Gratt. 205, is cited in James
River, etc., Co. *v.* Littlejohn, 18 Gratt.
76,· where it is held, that the bill having alleged that the order was drawn
by one of the defendants, § 38, ch.
171, Va. Code, 1860, applies, and no
proof of the signature is necessary.

VII. Laws and Statutes.

See the title STATUTES.

A. IN GENERAL.

Private Laws.—Formerly the courts
would not take judicial notice of private laws or acts of the legislature,
but it was necessary that they be
proven when in issue. Hart *v.* Baltimore, etc., R. Co., 6 W. Va. 336, 338;
Stribbling *v.* Bank, 5 Rand. 132, 155,
171; Goodloe *v.* Dudley, Jeff. 59.

Though private acts of the Virginia
assembly may be given in evidence,
without being specially pleaded, they
are not to be taken notice of judicially,
by the court, as public acts are, but
must be exhibited, as documents, if
not admitted by consent of parties.
Legrand *v.* Hampton Sidney College,
5 Munf. 324.

Public Laws.

Former Rule.—The courts always
took judicial notice of all public laws
or acts of the legislature of the state,
without proof. Hart *v.* Baltimore, etc.,
R. Co., 6 W. Va. 336, 338; Blankenship *v.* Chesapeake, etc., R. Co., 94
Va. 449, 27 S. E. 20; Hamtranck *v.*
Selden, 12 Gratt. 28.

**Definitions of Public and Private
Laws.—**A private law is one which relates to private matters which do not
concern the public at large, and a public law is one which affects the public,
either generally or in some classes.
Hart *v.* Baltimore, etc., R. Co., 6 W.
Va. 336.

Present Rule.—But the statutes in
Virginia and West Virginia now provide that acts and resolutions of the
legislature though local and private,
may be given in evidence without being specially pleaded. Va. Code, 1904,
§ 3328; W. Va. Code, 1899, ch. 130, §
3922.

In ch. 176, § 1 of the Code of Virginia of 1860 there are these provisions: "Acts and resolutions of the general assembly, though local or private,
may be given in evidence without being specially pleaded; and an appellate
court shall take judicial notice of such
as appear to have been relied on in
the court below." Hart *v.* Baltimore,
etc., R. Co., 6 W. Va. 336, 350.

B. PENAL STATUTES.

See the title PENALTIES AND
FORFEITURES.

The courts will take judicial notice
of public penal statutes. Hamtranck *v.*
Selden, 12 Gratt. 28, 32.

C. ACTS OF CONGRESS.

The courts of the several states
take judicial notice of all public acts
of congress, including those which relate exclusively to the District of Columbia, without any formal proof.
Bayly *v.* Chubb, 16 Gratt. 284; Bird
v. Com., 21 Gratt. 800.

Greenleaf in his first volume upon
Evidence, § 490, says: "The reciprocal
relations between the national government and the several states are
not foreign, but domestic. Hence the
courts of the United States take judicial notice of all the public laws of the
respective states, whenever ,they are
called upon to consider and apply
them. And, in like manner, the courts
of the several states take judicial notice of all public acts of congress."
Dickinson *v.* Railroad Co., 7 W. Va.
390, 417.

The act of congress continues the
laws of Maryland in force in that part
of the District of Columbia ceded by
Maryland. The Maryland law thereby
became the law of congress in said

district, and is to be taken notice of by state courts, without proof. *Bird v. Com.*, 21 Gratt. 800.

"The acts of congress in relation to the District of Columbia must be taken notice of by the state courts, without proof, as all other public acts of congress are taken notice of. In 1 Greenl. on Ev., § 490, the author states that, because of the reciprocal relations between the national government and the several states, the courts of the United States take judicial notice of all the public laws of the respective states, whenever they are called upon to consider and apply them; and in like manner the courts of the several states take judicial notice of all public acts of congress, including those which relate exclusively to the District of Columbia, without any formal proof. I have been unable to find any case in which the latter member of the foregoing proposition, so far as it relates to the District of Columbia, has been in terms judicially announced by the supreme court of any one of the states, though it seems to me that it must be as the author has stated it." *Bayly v. Chubb*, 16 Gratt. 284, 287.

D. CONSTITUTIONAL PROVISIONS.

The supreme court may take judicial notice of the fact that a board of supervisors, which is a party to an appeal pending in that court, has, since the taking of the appeal, been extinguished by the adoption of a new constitution. *Stuart v. Livesay*, 6 W. Va. 45.

E. COMMON LAW.

See the title COMMON LAW, vol. 3, p. 17.

F. FOREIGN LAWS.

See the title FOREIGN LAWS, vol. 6, p. 239.

1. Rule in West Virginia.

a. Former Rule.

Formerly in West Virginia the general rule prevailed that the law, written or unwritten, of a foreign state or country, had to be proven as a fact, notwithstanding a dictum to the contrary in *Dickinson v. Railroad Co.*, 7 W. Va. 390, 417. See *Lockhead v. Berkeley Springs Waterworks, etc., Co.*, 40 W. Va. 553, 21 S. E. 1031.

Usury Laws of Another State.—For example, the courts of one state are not bound to take judicial cognizance of the usury laws of another state; and one who sets up the usurious, and therefore void, nature of a contract made in another state must also show what are the usury laws of such other state. *Klinck v. Price*, 4 W. Va. 4, 6 Am. Rep. 268.

b. Present Rule.

But under ch. 13, § 4, of the West Virginia Code, courts take judicial notice, without proof, of the law of another state, and in so doing may consult any book purporting to contain, state, or explain the same, and consider any testimony, information, or argument offered on the subject. *Wilson v. Phœnix Powder Mfg. Co.*, 40 W. Va. 413, 21 S. E. 1035; *Singer Mfg. Co. v. Bennett*, 28 W. Va. 16; *State v. Goodrich*, 14 W. Va. 834, 842; *Lockhead v. Berkeley Springs Waterworks, etc., Co.*, 40 W. Va. 553, 21 S. E. 1031.

Authority to Administer Oath.—See the title OATH.

The court will take judicial notice of what officers have the authority to administer an oath under the foreign law. *Lockhead v. Berkeley Springs Waterworks, etc., Co.*, 40 W. Va. 553, 21 S. E. 1031.

"At this important stage of the court, with its widespread judicial knowledge or notice of the facts of foreign law, has no concern in the matter. It is a notice, and is not intended by the lawmaker to answer the purposes of deciding subsequent demurrers. But the parties whom it does concern are not required to take judicial notice of the law of the District of Columbia saying who may administer an oath, but of the statute creating the lien, and there they find prescribed a method. So that, unfortunately for the argument, the judicial notice of foreign laws, and the concern in the validity of the lien, play somewhat at cross purposes; and for his purpose, when their coming together is important, they are not together, and when they do so come together, as to him, by the aid of the judicial notice of foreign laws as facts, his misplaced confidence in the record is past recall." Lockhead v. Berkeley Springs Waterworks, etc., Co., 40 W. Va. 553, 21 S. E. 1031, 1034.

2. Rule in Virginia.

On the other hand the rule in Virginia still is that foreign laws are facts to be proved as other facts; the courts will not take judicial notice thereof. See the title FOREIGN LAWS, vol. 6, p. 239.

In an action by indorsee against drawer of a bill of exchange, it is found by special verdict, that the bill was drawn in Maryland on a person in Virginia, and no law of Maryland found, declaring such a bill an inland bill. Held, the court can not take judicial notice of any law of Maryland to that effect, unless it be expressly found; and such bill being a foreign bill of exchange, according to the general law merchant, it must be so regarded. Brown v. Ferguson, 4 Leigh 37.

G. MUNICIPAL CHARTERS.

See generally, the title MUNICIPAL CORPORATIONS.

The courts take judicial notice of the charters of municipal corporations. 1 Dill. Mun. Corp., § 83; 4 Minor Inst. 1210, 1211; Code, § 3328; 1 Greenl. Ev., § 4, note 3; Duncan v. Lynchburg, 2 Va. Dec. 700, 706, 48 L. R. A. 331.

"Whether or not the work in which city officials were engaged when a nuisance, complained of, was created, was within the powers of the city, may be raised by demurrer to the declaration, as judicial notice will be taken of its

charter." Duncan v. Lynchburg, 2 Va. Dec. 700, 48 L. R. A. 331.

H. ORDINANCES.

See the title ORDINANCES.

Municipal Courts.—Courts of a municipal corporation will take judicial notice of its ordinances without allegation or proof of their existence. Moundsville v. Velton, 35 W. Va. 217, 13 S. E. 373; Wheeling v. Black, 25 W. Va. 266.

Where an ordinance, of which an amendment is a part, is pleaded, the court will take judicial notice of the amendment. "But the ordinance of which this amendment was a part, having been pleaded, the amendment itself was sufficiently pleaded, because it was part and parcel of the ordinance pleaded." Wheeling v. Black, 25 W. Va. 266, 281.

State Courts.—On the other hand, it is well settled that state courts do not notice judicially the ordinance of a municipal corporation unless directed by charter or statute to do so, but they must be pleaded and proven as facts. 1 Dill. Mun. Corp., § 413; Moundsville v. Velton, 35 W. Va. 217, 13 S. E. 373.

Where, upon conviction of a violation of an ordinance of a municipal corporation before its mayor, an appeal is taken to the circuit court, under § 230, ch. 50, and § 39, ch. 47, Code, 1887, on the trial of such appeal the circuit court will take judicial notice of such ordinance. "Why not? Because the case started in the municipal court. If the papers do not, and need not, allege the existence of the ordinance, why require proof of it? If the law excuses the absence of an allegation of such ordinance, why will it not excuse evidence of it? Again, shall it be said that when we are in the municipal court we need not prove the ordinance, but that when the case is transferred to the circuit court such proof must be given, though it is only a retrial of identically the same matter? This, it seems to me, would be an unreasonable anomaly. I think the rule of reason and common sense is that, as the law does not require such allegation or proof of the ordinance in the municipal court, neither does it require it on appeal to the circuit court; that the circuit court is only substituted for the municipal court in this case. And so it was held in City of Solomon v. Hughes, 24 Kan. 211." Moundsville v. Velton, 35 W. Va. 217, 13 S. E. 373, 374.

I. PARTICULAR ACTS CONSIDERED.

1. Incorporating Acts.

a. In General.

"In England, and in some states of this country, the rule seems to be, that when a body corporate institutes legal proceedings on a contract or to recover real property, it must at the trial, under the general issue, prove the fact of incorporation, unless the act of incorporation be a public act, which the courts are bound to notice ex officio. Angel and Ames on Corporations, page 698, § 632, and the various cases there cited in note 3 and note 1, p. 699. It is, however, generally admitted, that a corporation may declare in its corporate name, without setting forth in the declaration the act of incorporation, if the act be private; same author, p. 699, and the many cases there cited in note 2. In many of the states, on the other hand, the rule is well established, that if in a suit brought by a corporation the defendant pleads the general issue, it is an admission of the corporate existence of the plaintiff which dispenses with all proof on that point, same author, p. 700, § 633, and note 1, and the many cases there cited. See against and for this doctrine 5 Robinson's Practice, ch. 32, §§ 1, 2, and notes, pp. 315, 316, 317. In Virginia in the cases of Grays v T. P. Co., 4 Rand. 578; Rees v. Conococheague Bank, 5 Rand. 326; Taylor v. Bank of Alexandria, 5 Leigh 471; Jackson v. Bank of Marietta, 9 Leigh 240, it ap-

pears to have been held, that in case of private corporations the incorporation must be proved." Hart v. Baltimore, etc., R. Co., 6 W. Va. 336, 349.

b. Banking Institutions.

In General.—It has been held, in several cases, that acts of the legislature incorporating banks are public acts, of which the courts will take judicial notice; and in an action by the bank it is not required to prove its incorporation. Stribbling v. Bank, 5 Rand. 132; Hays v. Northwestern Bank, 9 Gratt. 127; Farmers' Bank v. Willis, 7 W. Va. 31; Northwestern Bank v. Machir, 18 W. Va. 271; Mason v. Farmers' Bank, 12 Leigh 84, 87; Hart v. Baltimore, etc., R. Co., 6 W. Va. 336, 356.

The act incorporating the Northwestern Bank of Virginia is a public act, of which the courts will judicially take notice; and, in an action by the bank, it is not required to prove its incorporation. Hays v. Northwestern Bank, 9 Gratt. 127.

That the incorporation of the Northwestern Bank of Virginia is a public act of which the courts take judicial notice, see Hays v. Northwestern Bank, 9 Gratt. 127, cited and approved in the following cases: Hart v. Baltimore, etc., R. Co., 6 W. Va. 336, 356; Farmers' Bank v. Willis, 7 W. Va. 31, 42; Northwestern Bank v. Machir, 18 W. Va. 271.

The act incorporating the Northwestern Bank of Virginia by the legislature of Virginia was a public act, of which the courts will take judicial notice; and in an action by the bank it is not required to prove its incorporation. This corporation existing under the laws of Virginia prior to the foundation of the state of West Virginia, its existence was preserved by art. 11, § 8, of the constitution of 1863, and art. 8, § 36, of the constitution of 1872. Northwestern Bank v. Machir, 18 W. Va. 271, following Hays v. Northwestern Bank, 9 Gratt. 127.

Farmers' Bank.—The court may judicially recognize or inform itself as to the charter of the Farmers' Bank of Virginia, or other like bank, and as to its organization and acceptance of a provision for the extension of its existence. Farmers' Bank v. Willis, 7 W. Va. 31.

c. Fire Insurance Companies.

See the title FIRE INSURANCE, vol. 6, p. 60.

In Bon Aqua Imp. Co. v. Standard Fire Ins. Co., 34 W. Va. 764, 12 S. E. 771, 774, the court, without deciding the point, seemed to think that it could take judicial notice of such private corporations created under the law, as that fire insurance companies are corporations.

d. Railroad Corporations.

It has been held, that the statutes of a state, creating railroad corporations, or licensing and authorizing them to exercise their franchises within the state, are public acts, of which the courts of the state will take judicial notice, without proof. Hart v. Baltimore, etc., R. R. Co., 6 W. Va. 336, 338; State v. Baltimore, etc., R. R. Co., 15 W. Va. 362, 363; Douglass v. Kanawha, etc., R. Co., 44 W. Va. 267, 28 S. E. 705; Baltimore, etc., R. R. Co. v. Sherman, 30 Gratt. 602.

In the case of Hart v. Baltimore, etc., R. Co., 6 W. Va. 336, it was held, by this court, as follows: "15· The acts of the legislature conferring corporate powers and privileges upon the Baltimore & Ohio Railroad Company are such public acts as the court should notice ex officio. 16. The court ex officio knows that the Baltimore & Ohio Railroad Company is an incorporated railroad company within the boundaries of this state, etc. 23. It is unnecessary to prove before the court matters of law or fact of which it may take judicial notice. Mahany v. Kephart, 15 W. Va. 609, 624.

The acts of the legislature conferring corporate powers and privileges upon the Baltimore and Ohio Railroad Company are such public acts as the court should notice ex officio. Hart v. Baltimore, etc., R. Co., 6 W. Va. 336; State v. Baltimore, etc., R. Co., 15 W. Va. 362, 36 Am. Rep. 803.

The court ex officio knows that the Baltimore and Ohio Railroad Company is an incorporated railroad company within the boundaries of this state, and was when ch. 61 of the Virginia Code of 1860 took effect, and was before and at the time said chapter took effect, governed by the act passed by the legislature of Virginia on the 11th day of March, 1837, prescribing general regulations for the incorporation of railroad companies so far as the same can apply. Hart v. Baltimore, etc., R. Co., 6 W. Va. 336.

All Charter Provisions.—It was left a quære in Chapman v. Pittsburg, etc., R. Co., 18 W. Va. 184, 196, whether a court will take judicial notice not only that a railroad is a domestic corporation, but of every provision in its charter.

Railroad Rates.—"It was not necessary to allege in the declaration in this case that the rates prescribed by § 19 of ch. 61 of Code of 1860, applied to the road of defendant, nor that different rates had not been prescribed by law." Hart v. Baltimore, etc., R. Co., 6 W. Va. 336.

Sunday Laws.—In an indictment against a railroad company for being found laboring at its trade and calling on a certain Sabbath day, it is not necessary to allege or prove that the railroad company is a corporation, because the court will take judicial notice of that fact. State v. Baltimore, etc., R. Co., 15 W. Va. 362, 36 Am. Rep. 803, citing Hart v. Baltimore, etc., R. Co., 6 W. Va. 336.

Removal of Causes.—"The Baltimore and Ohio Railroad Company is a domestic corporation of this state and liable to be sued here; and the court will take judicial cognizance of that fact. Hart *v.* Baltimore, etc., R. Co., 6 W. Va. 336. When such company is sued in the courts of this state by a citizen thereof, such suit can not be removed into the circuit court of the United States for the district of West Virginia; in such case said 639th section of said Revised Stautes does not apply to or embrace the said company." Henen *v.* Baltimore, etc., R. Co. 17 W. Va. 881.

Sworn Plea Denying Incorporation. —In an action against a railroad company, it is not necessary to aver in the declaration, nor is it necessary to prove on the trial, that the defendant is a corporation, unless with the plea there is filed an affidavit denying that it is. The court will ex officio take notice of the fact. Douglass *v.* Kanawha, etc., R. Co., 44 W. Va. 267, 28 S. E. 705, following Baltimore, etc., R. Co. *v.* Sherman, 30 Gratt. 602.

In an action of assumpsit the writ and declaration was in the name of a plaintiff which indicated that the plaintiff was a corporation but it was not stated to be a corporation. The defendant pleaded nonassumpsit, but did not file an affidavit that the plaintiff was not a corporation. Held, under the statute, Va. Code, 1887, § 3280, it was not necessary that the plaintiff should prove that it was a corporation. See also, Crews *v.* Bank, 31 Gratt. 348; Douglass *v.* Kanawha, etc., R. Co., 44 W. Va. 267, 28 S. E. 705. Baltimore, etc., R. Co. *v.* Sherman, 30 Gratt. 602.

e. Incorporation of Cities, Towns and Villages.

It was held, in Beasley *v.* Beckley, 28 W. Va. 81, that when in any judicial proceeding in West Virginia it becomes material to inquire whether a certain city, town or village has been incorporated, the court, judge or justice, before whom the same is pending, will take judicial notice of the acts of the legislature incorporating the same.

f. Powers of Municipal Corporations.

"The general law of this state (see Code, ch. 47, § 14) declares, that all the corporate powers of a municipal corporation shall be exercised by its council, and that the mayor, recorder and councilmen shall be the body politic and corporate, and the 13th section declares, that the mayor, recorder and councilmen constitute this council. The courts, of course, take judicial notice of this law, and when by the general law a power exists in certain parties to do a certain act, it is unnecessary to allege in pleading the existence of such power." Fisher *v.* Charleston, 17 W. Va. 595, 618.

2. Privilege of Assemblymen.

See the title PRIVILEGE.

It was held, in an early case, that the privilege of a member of the legislature, though prescribed by statute, a public law, could not be noticed by the courts ex officio; that it could only be claimed upon plea or motion tendered or made at the period proper for the consideration thereof by the court whose proceedings are sought to be abated or suspended. Prentis *v.* Com., 5 Rand. 697, 16 Am. Dec. 782, cited and approved in Turnbull *v.* Thompson, 27 Gratt. 306, 310.

And the privileges accorded members of the assembly are now embodied in §§ 198, 199 201, of the Virginia Code of 1904.

3. Statutes Prohibiting Office Farming.

See the title ILLEGAL CONTRACTS, vol. 7, p. 253.

It was held, in an early case, that 23 H. 6, prohibiting sheriffs to let their counties to farm, is a private act of which the judges can not take notice, unless it be pleaded. Goodloe *v.* Dudley, Jeff. 59.

But, as has been stated, the courts now take judicial notice of private as well as public laws. See ante, "In General," VII, A.

4. Local Option Laws.

See the title INTOXICATING LIQUORS, ante, p. 1.

An indictment for violation of a statute forbidding the sale of intoxicating liquors within any magisterial district voting against license, need not allege that the magisterial district in which the offense occurred had voted against license, since the court will take judicial notice of such a vote. Savage's Case, 84 Va. 582, 5 S. E. 563; Thomas v. Com., 90 Va. 92, 17 S. E. 788; Hargraves v. Com., 2 Va. Dec. 139.

5. Eminent Domain.

When the sovereign power attaches conditions to the exercise of the right of eminent domain, the inquiry, whether the conditions have been observed, is a matter for judicial cognizance. Baltimore, etc., R. Co. v. Pittsburg, etc., R. Co., 17 W. Va. 812.

But the court will not take judicial notice, that a railroad company, under its charter, condemned or acquired title to any particular land, or strip of land. Chapman v. Pittsburg, etc., R. Co., 18 W. Va. 184, 185.

6. Military Orders.

The court can not take judicial notice of the military orders extending the time for a stay of execution on judgments. "They are not acts or proceedings of which this court will take judicial notice, but ought to have been proved as other facts in the cause. Burke v. Miltenberger, 19 Wall. U. S. R. 519." Johnston v. Wilson, 29 Gratt. 379, 382.

7. Arrest in Civil Cases.

See the title EXECUTIONS AGAINST THE BODY AND ARREST IN CIVIL CASES, vol. 5, p. 474.

"By the act of 1748, ch. 6, incorporated in the late revisal, it is declared that it shall not be lawful for any sheriff or his officer or deputy, to take any obligation of or from any person or persons in his custody, for or concerning any matter relating to his office, otherwise payable, than to himself, as sheriff, and dischargeable upon the prisoner's appearance, etc. And every obligation by any sheriff taken, in other manner or form by color of his office, shall be null and void; except, in any special case, any other obligation is, or shall be by law, particularly and expressly directed. This clause was framed on the purview of stat. 23, Hen. 6, ch. 10, concerning which great doubts were formerly entertained, whether the judges must take notice of it, ex officio, or whether it must be pleaded, but that doubt has been lately overruled in England; and there is the same or greater reason for overruling it in this country, where special pleading is so seldom practiced, and where the law permits private acts to be given in evidence without pleading." Syme v. Griffin, 4 Hen. & M. 277, 281.

J. APPELLATE COURTS.

The statutes in Virginia and West Virginia provide that an appellate court shall take judicial notice of such acts and resolutions of the legislature, though local or private, as appear to have been relied on in the court below. Va. Code, 1904, § 3328; W. Va. Code, 1899, ch. 130, § 3922; Somerville v. Wimbish, 7 Gratt. 205; Hart v. Baltimore, etc., R. Co., 6 W. Va. 336 338; Groves v. County Court, 42 W. Va. 587, 26 S. E. 460.

The Code, ch. 51, § 1, p. 660, provides that an appellate court shall take judicial notice of private or local acts, that appear to have been relied on in the court below. The judicial notice to be taken of such a law is the same that is to be given to the laws of a general or public nature, and has reference to the hearing of the cause in the appellate forum, whether decided in the courts below, before or after the commencement of the revised statute. Somerville v. Wimbish, 7 Gratt. 205.

In Groves v. County Court, 42 W. Va. 587, 26 S. E. 460, 461, it is said: "The acts of 1872 show that the county seat of no other county was relocated during the period from the 1st day of January, 1872, to the 22d day of August, 1872, the day when the constitution went into effect. The act of 1872, and all acts of the legislature from the 1st day of January, 1872, to the 4th day of February, 1895, were relied on in the court below as showing that no county seat save that of Grant county was relocated by special act of the legislature, and therefore this court must take judicial notice thereof. See § 1 of ch. 130 of the Code. This act took effect for the first time on the 1st day of July, 1850. See Code, 1849, tit. 51, p. 660, § 1. See effect thereof as shown in Somerville *v.* Wimbish, 7 Gratt. 205, 226; Hart *v.* Baltimore, etc., R. Co., 6 W. Va. 336, 350; State *v.* Baltimore, etc., R. Co., 15 W. Va. 362, 392; Beasley *v.* Beckley, 28 W. Va. 81; Ross *v.* Austill, 2 Cal. 183. Therefore we judicially know that when the act of 14th day of February, 1895, now in question, was passed, Grant county stood alone as the one county having this peculiarity in its history, and no other county could have it when the act of 1895 was enacted." See, in accord, citing Somerville *v.* Wimbish, 7 Gratt. 205; Hart *v.* Baltimore, etc., R. Co., 6 W. Va. 336, 350.

Formerly the rule was otherwise. Legrand *v.* Hampton Sidney College, 5 Munf. 324.

VIII. Sources and Information.

In General.—It is not necessary that the courts should have actual knowledge of the subjects of which they may take judicial notice, but the judge may, where his knowledge is lacking or his memory indistinct, consult any person, even experts, or such works of reference, as judicial decisions and treatises of text writers, as the court may select. Richmond, etc., R. Co. *v.* Richmond, etc., R. Co., 96 Va. 670, 32 S. E. 787.

"This cognizance may extend far beyond the actual knowledge or even the memory of judges, who may therefore resort to such documents of reference, or other authoritive sources of information, as may be at hand, and may be deemed worthy of confidence. The rule has been held in many instances to embrace information derived informally by inquiry from experts." Richmond, etc., R. Co. *v.* Richmond, etc., R. Co., 96 Va. 670, 673, 32 S. E. 787.

Proof of Foreign Laws.—The West Virginia Code provides that "Whenever it becomes material to ascertain what the law statutory or otherwise of another state or country or of the United States is or was at any time, the court, judge or magistrate shall take judicial notice thereof and may consult any printed books purporting to contain, state or explain the same and consider any testimony, information or argument that is offered on the subject. (Code, ch. 15, § 4.) Singer Mfg. Co. *v.* Bennett, 28 W. Va. 16.

Under § 4, ch. 13, Code, courts take judicial notice, without proof, of the law of another state, and in so doing may consult any book purporting to contain, state, or explain the same, and consider any testimony, information, or argument offered on the subject. Wilson *v.* Phœnix Powder Mfg. Co., 40 W. Va. 413, 21 S. E. 1035, 52 Am. St. Rep. 890.

Foreign Courts.—A certificate of the clerk of the corporation court of the city of Lynchburg verifying the certificate of the notary signing the affidavit to the mechanic's lien, is not defective in West Virginia in that it does not certify that the court is one of record. Because under § 4, ch. 13, of the West Virginia Code, the court will take judicial notice that the corporation court of Lynchburg, Va., is a court of record, and the court will consult such books as the Virginia Code and Barton's Law Practice to inform itself that various cities in Virginia, among them Lynchburg, by the constitution and the Virginia Code, have corporation courts, with judge, clerk, record of proceedings, and the same jurisdiction within the cities, criminal and civil, as circuit and county courts. Heffernan *v.* Harvey, 41 W. Va. 766, 24 S. E. 592.

Adjudged Cases.—The court may with propriety look to the vast number of adjudged cases on the subject of railroad crossings, to ascertain that gates and gatekeepers at crossings tend to promote safety, and are regarded as useful and beneficial contrivances. Richmond, etc., R. Co. *v.* Richmond, etc., R. Co., 96 Va. 670, 32 S. E. 787.

Treatises of Text Writers.—And the courts may, with propriety, look to the treatises of text writers to ascertain that gates at crossings are resorted to to prevent accidents, and are regarded as useful and beneficial contrivances. Richmond, etc., R. Co. *v.* Richmond, etc., R. Co., 96 Va. 670, 32 S. E. 787.

Experts.—This rule as to judicial notice embraces information derived informally by inquiry from experts. Richmond, etc., R. Co. *v.* Richmond, etc., R. Co., 96 Va. 670, 32 S. E. 787.

Judicial Opinions.

See the title OPINION OF COURTS.

JUDICIAL SALES AND RENTINGS.

X. Setting Aside Sale after Confirmation, 751.

XVI. Collateral Impeachment, 841.

CROSS REFERENCES.

See the titles ACTIONS, vol. 1, p. 122; ADVERSE POSSESSION, vol. 1, p. 199; AFFIDAVITS, vol. 1, p. 227; APPEAL AND ERROR, vol. 1, p. 418; ASSIGNMENTS FOR THE BENEFIT OF CREDITORS, vol. 1, p. 799; ATTACHMENT AND GARNISHMENT, vol. 2, p. 70; AUCTIONS AND AUCTIONEERS, vol. 2, p. 174; BANKRUPTCY AND INSOLVENCY, vol. 2. p. 232; BILL OF REVIEW, vol. 2, p. 383; CLERKS OF COURT, vol. 2, p. 834; CONTEMPT, vol. 3, p. 236; CONTRACTS, vol. 3, p. 307; COSTS, vol. 3, p. 604; COURTS, vol. 3, p. 696; CREDITORS' SUITS, vol. 3, p. 780; DEEDS, vol. 4, p. 364; DEPOSIT, vol. 4, p. 548; DOCUMENTARY EVIDENCE, vol. 4, p. 756; EJECTMENT, vol. 4, p. 871; EVIDENCE, vol. 5, p. 295; EXECUTIONS, vol. 5, p. 416; EXECUTORS AND ADMINISTRATORS, vol. 5, p. 483; FOREIGN JUDGMENTS, vol. 6, p. 208; FRAUD AND DECEIT, vol. 6, p. 448; FRAUDS, STATUTE OF, vol. 6, p. 516; FRAUDULENT AND VOLUNTARY CONVEYANCES, vol. 6, p. 540; GUARDIAN AND WARD, vol. 6, p. 782; INFANTS, vol. 7, p. 461; INJUNCTIONS, vol. 7, p. 512; INTEREST, vol. 7, p. 819; JUDGMENTS AND DECREES, ante, p. 161; JURISDICTION; LARCENY; LIENS; MARSHALING ASSETS AND SECURITIES; MORTGAGES AND DEEDS OF TRUST; NOTICE; ORDERS OF COURT; PARTIES; PARTITION; PAYMENT; PENALTIES AND FORFEITURES; POSSESSION, WRIT OF; RECEIVERS; REMAINDERS, REVERSIONS AND EXECUTORY INTERESTS; RESTITUTION; SHERIFFS' SALES; TRUSTS AND TRUSTEES; VENDITIONI EXPONAS; WARRANTY.

As to execution or sheriffs' sales, see the title SHERIFFS' SALES. As to sales under writ of venditioni exponas, see the title VENDITIONI EXPONAS. As to sales by executors and administrators under orders of court, see the title EXECUTORS AND ADMINISTRATORS, vol. 5, p. 483. As to sales of infant's lands, see the titles GUARDIAN AND WARD, vol. 6, p. 782; INFANTS, vol. 7, p. 461. As to sales by trustees, see the title TRUSTS AND TRUSTEES. As to partition sales, see the title PARTITION. As to sales by receivers, see the title RECEIVERS. As to sales for taxes, including sales of forfeited lands by commissioner of school lands for the benefit of the school fund, see the title TAXATION. As to sales under trust deeds and power of sale mortgages and sales by order of court in proceedings to foreclose mortgages, see the title MORTGAGES AND DEEDS OF TRUST. As to sales of lands of insane persons, see the title INSANITY, vol. 7, p. 668. As to sales in proceedings to subject the separate estate of married women, see the title SEPARATE ESTATE OF MARRIED WOMEN. As to sales by widow of heirs' fee simple to get money in lieu of dower, see the titles DOWER, vol. 4, p. 818; INFANTS, vol. 7, p. 461. As to sales under decree of court in proceedings to enforce mechanics' liens, see the title MECHANICS' LIENS. As to sales under decree of court in proceedings to enforce vendor's lien, see the title VENDOR'S LIEN. As to the sale of property held under deed or will subject to a limitation contingent upon the dying of any person without heir or heirs of the body, etc., see the title REMAINDERS, REVERSIONS AND EXECUTORY INTERESTS. As to sales in attachment proceedings, see the title ATTACHMENT AND GARNISHMENT, vol. 2, p. 70. As to sales by assignee for the benefit of creditors, see the title ASSIGNMENTS FOR THE BENEFIT OF CREDITORS, vol. 1, p. 799. As to sales by assignee in bankruptcy, see the title BANKRUPTCY AND INSOLVENCY, vol. 2, p. 232. As to sales ordered in proceedings to set aside fraudulent and voluntary conveyances, see the title FRAUDULENT AND VOLUNTARY CONVEYANCES, vol. 6, p. 540. As to the effect of a judicial sale of land as converting it into personalty, see the title CONVERSION AND RECONVERSION, vol. 3, p. 503. As to judicial sales as constituting breach of condition in fire insurance policy, see the title FIRE INSURANCE. vol. 6, p. 84. As to matters of appeal relating to judicial sales, see the title APPEAL AND ERROR, vol. 1, p. 418.

I. Scope of Title.

It is the purpose of this article to treat generally of the principles applicable to all judicial sales, and specifically of sales made under decrees of court in suits to enforce judgment liens, leaving all matters relating to the various other kinds of sales which may be denominated judicial, to be discussed in their appropriate places elsewhere in this work. For particular reference to the titles where the various kinds of judicial sales are treated, see the table of cross references at the beginning of this article. This article also treats of rentings made under decrees of court instead of sales, where the rents and profits will pay off the liens upon the land within the time prescribed by the statute.

II. Definitions and Distinctions.

A. DEFINITIONS.

A judicial sale is one which is made by a court of competent jurisdiction in a pending suit, through its authorized agent. It must be made in a pending suit. Barton's Ch. Pr.; Rorer on Judicial Sales (2d Ed.), § 1. Alexander v. Howe, 85 Va. 198, 7 S. E. 248; Terry v. Coles, 80 Va. 695; McAllister v. Harman, 101 Va. 17, 42 S. E. 920; Christian v. Cabell, 22 Gratt. 82.

Bouvier defines a judicial sale to be a sale made by some competent tribunal, by an officer authorized by law for the purpose. Terry v. Coles, 80 Va. 695.

A judicial sale is one made under an order or decree of a chancery court, or subject to its confirmation and control. Atkinson v. Washington, etc., College, 54 W. Va. 32, 46 S. E. 253.

A judicial sale is the act of the court and not of the commissioner who offers the property and receives the bids. Arnold v. Casner, 22 W. Va. 444.

Rorer on Judicial Sales, at pages 1 and 2, § 1, says: "As a judicial act is one supposed to be clearly pendente lite of some sort or other, so a judicial sale is, in contemplation of law, a sale made pendente lite; a sale in court, and the court is the vendor. It matters not to the contrary, that it is made through the instrumentality of a master, commissioner, or other functionary appointed thereto by the court; it is not valid or binding, and confers no right to the property sought to be sold, until confirmed by the court. By such confirmation it is judicially made the act of the court, and is therefore a judicial sale. The master, or commissioner, in conducting it, acts by authority of, and as the instrument or agent of the court." Hyman v. Smith, 13 W. Va. 744.

Again, at page 7, § 12, he says: "In a legal sense the sale is made by the court itself in enforcement of its own orders and decrees, wherein is described the property to be sold. The person who conducts the same is merely the instrument, or means, used by the court to bring about such executory agreement as the court chooses, if satisfied therewith, by final act of confirmation, which makes the court the vendor. Such sale is unlike a sheriff's sale on an ordinary common-law, or statutory, execution, which is ministerial, and not a judicial act; and in making which the law regards the officer, and not the court, as the vendor." Hyman v. Smith, 13 W. Va. 744.

A sale made under a decree of the court is judicial, although it was not made at public auction, but was made by a party who had been appointed commissioner of the court; was reported to the court and confirmed as a sale made by the court. It is no less a judicial sale because made privately, and not at public auction. In either event it only becomes a sale at all when confirmed by the court. It is the confirmation by the court, and not the bidding or propositions to buy that constitutes such sale a judicial sale. Hess *v.* Rader, 26 Gratt. 746; Klapneck *v.* Keltz, 50 W. Va. 331, 40 S. E. 570; Core *v.* Strickler, 24 W. Va. 689; Blair *v.* Core, 20 W. Va. 265; Kable *v.* Mitchell, 9 W. Va. 492.

Sale made by order of a court of competent jurisdiction, pendente lite, is a judicial sale. An executor having authority under the will to sell land, declines to exercise his authority, but applies to the court for instructions and directions, and is ordered to make sale and report it to the court for confirmation; whereupon, he makes and reports the sale to the court as ordered. Such sale is a judicial sale. Terry *v.* Coles, 80 Va. 695.

Trustee advertises land for sale under trust deed. Owner enjoins sale on the ground of usury and the pendency of suit to partition the tract whereof this was an undivided part. Circuit court perpetuated injunction as to the usury, and dissolved it as to residue of the debt, and decreed that trustee proceed to sell the land and report to court. Trustee, ascertaining that there were several liens on the land, sold it "free of liens," and reported that fact to the court, and asked that an account of liens be taken before the proceeds of the sale were disbursed. Held, the sale was a judicial sale. Alexander *v.* Howe, 85 Va. 198, 7 S. E. 248; Schultz *v.* Hansbrough, 33 Gratt. 576.

A judicial sale is one made by a court of competent jurisdiction in a pending cause, through its authorized agent. In the case in judgment, a suit was pending, having for its object, amongst other things, the partition of a tract of land, and a sale of a moiety thereof to pay the debts of the owner, who was dead. Pending this suit, and before any partition was made, the plaintiff therein, who, as trustee, held the legal title to decedent's moiety, and the owner of the other moiety, united in giving an option to a third party to purchase the land as a whole, at a given price, which option was subsequently accepted and closed, but not until after the partition had been made and confirmed. The court neither made nor authorized the sale, and had no power under the pleadings to sell one moiety of the land. The sale did not purport to be a judicial sale, but a sale by the parties, although it was reported to and confirmed by the court, and the general receiver of the court directed to collect the purchase money, the vendor consenting thereto. The decree confirming the sale refers to the sale as made by the vendors mentioned in the contract, naming them. Held, this was not a judicial sale. McAllister *v.* Harman, 101 Va. 17, 42 S. E. 920.

Quasi Judicial Sales.—Some of the courts view sales by trustees, administrators and other persons, standing in a representative relation as quasi judicial sales. Atkinson *v.* Washington, etc., College, 54 W. Va. 32, 46 S. E. 253. See the table of cross references at the beginning of this article.

Conditional Sales.—All sales made by commissioners under decrees of court are conditional. They are merely accepted offers which the court may or may not approve and confirm. National Bank *v.* Jarvis, 28 W. Va. 805; Kable *v.* Mitchell, 9 W. Va. 492. See post, "Confirmation," IX.

B. DISTINCTIONS.

1. Distinguished from Execution Sales.

"A judicial sale is made pendente lite, whereas an execution sale is made after litigation in the case is ended, for, as we have before seen, a judicial act is something done during the pendency of a suit. The suit does not end with a decree of sale; the proceeding still continues until final confirmation." Ror. Jud. Sales, §§ 1, 18. Alexander *v.* Howe, 85 Va. 198, 7 S. E. 248; Terry *v.* Coles, 80 Va. 695. See the title SHERIFFS' SALES.

A judicial sale is unlike a sheriff's sale on an ordinary common-law or statutory execution, which is ministerial and not a judicial act; and in making which the law regards the officer, and not the court, as the vendor. Rorer on Judicial Sales, p. 7, § 12. Hyman v. Smith, 13 W. Va. 744.

2. Distinguished from Ordinary Auction Sales and Sales by Private Agreement.

There is a difference between judicial sales, and ordinary auction sales, and sales by private agreement. In the latter, says Daniel, in his Chancery Practice: "The contract is complete when the agreement is signed; but a different rule prevails in sales before a master. In such cases the purchaser is not considered as entitled to the benefit of his contract, till the master's report of the purchaser's bidding is absolutely confirmed." Such is the rule whether the sale be by a master, commissioner, or other person or functionary authorized by the court to conduct the sale. The bargain is not ordinarily considered as complete, until the sale is confirmed, and the conveyance made. Hyman v. Smith, 13 W. Va. 744; Terry v. Coles, 80 Va. 695; Brock v. Rice, 27 Gratt. 812; Carr v. Carr, 88 Va. 735, 14 S. E. 368; Todd v. Gallego Mills Mfg. Co., 84 Va. 586, 5 S. E. 676. See the title AUCTIONS AND AUCTIONEERS, vol. 2, p. 174. See post, "Confirmation," IX.

After decree in pending suit, to sell land to pay debts, debtor sells the land by written contract, undertaking to make vendee "sufficient title," takes for the purchase money vendee's bonds payable to commissioners named in the decree, and a trust deed on the land to secure them. The sale is confirmed by the court, and its receiver ordered to collect the bonds when due, and apply the proceeds to the debts. Such sale is not a judicial, but a private sale. Ware v. Starkey, 80 Va. 191; Christian v. Cabell, 22 Gratt. 82.

M. conveys a house and lot to W. in trust for B. for life, remainder to her children. On the 30th of June, 1870,

B. contracts in writing with C., to sell to him his property for ten thousand dollars, on the terms of two thousand dollars when he received a good deed for the property, and the balance in five years equal annual payments; possession to be delivered on the 15th of July, B. to procure the approval of the contract by the proper court without cost to C. On the 9th of July, W. filed a bill against B. and her children to have the contract approved, and by a decree on the same day the contract is approved, and W. is directed to convey the house and lot to C. with special warranty. On the same day, W. executes the deed and hands it to C. It was held, that this was a private and not a judicial sale. The court said: "It is impossible to regard this in any other like than a private contract of sale and purchase. The court was not asked or expected to make, but to confirm a sale already made. Its aid was invoked to ratify what had already been done, to sanction terms already agreed by parties." Christian v. Cabell, 22 Gratt. 82.

3. Sales by Commissioners and Trustees Distinguished.

"The nature of the contract between the trustee and the purchaser has been determined by this court in the case of Fleming v. Holt, 12 W. Va. 143, where Judge Green, delivering the opinion of the court, said: 'A sale by a trustee, like a sale by a commissioner, is without warranty; but there is this obvious difference between the two; the contract of purchase at a sale by the commissioner is incomplete, till his bid is accepted by the court, who is the real seller of the property, the commissioner of sale being the mere agent of the court. The bid is accepted by the court by the confirmation of the sale; after that, though the purchaser before the deed is made to him, finds out that the title to the land is defective, he is nevertheless bound to receive it, and pay the purchase money.

In a sale by a trustee, the court does not accept the bid of the purchaser, but it is accepted by the auctioneer, when he knocks the land down, and on the making by him of a memorandum of the sale and its terms, signed by the auctioneer, the contract for the sale is as complete as the contract for the sale made by a commissioner is when the court accepts the bid by confirming the sale. After such knocking down of the land by the auctioneer and the making of such memorandum, the purchaser must accept the deed and pay the purchase money, though he does find the title defective. He must, if he wishes to do so, investigate the title in this case, as in the other, while the contract is incomplete, that is, in the last case, before land is knocked down to him.'" Atkinson v. Washington, etc., College, 54 W. Va. 32, 46 S. E. 253. See the title MORTGAGES AND DEEDS OF TRUST; TRUSTS AND TRUSTEES.

III. Renting or Selling.

A. DETERMINATION AS TO PROPRIETY OF RENTING OR SELLING.

1. Equity Rule Prior to Statutes.

In General.—Under the common equity rule prevailing before the enactment of the statutes on the subject, a debtor's land could be rented instead of sold, if the liens thereon could have been satisfied out of the rents and profits within a reasonable time. Manns v. Flinn, 10 Leigh 93; McClung v. Beirne, 10 Leigh 394; Tennent v. Patton, 6 Leigh 196; Duncan v. Custard, 24 W. Va. 730; Hill v. Morehead, 20 W. Va. 429; Rose v. Brown, 11 W. Va. 122; Brengle v. Richardson, 78 Va. 406.

It was the well-established practice for many years in Virginia that when a proceeding was pending in a chancery court to enforce a judgment lien upon real estate, if the debtor or others interested asked it, they were entitled to have the fact ascertained, whether the rents and profits of the real estate, against which the proceeding was had, would not discharge the lien in a reasonable time, but if such rents and profits would so discharge the lien, not to decree a sale of the land, but to rent it to pay the debt charged upon it. And this was the established practice in Virginia, when the Code of 1849 was adopted, containing a provision concerning the renting and sale of land, in § 9 of ch. 186. Rose v. Brown, 11 W. Va. 122. For present statutes, see Va. Code, 1904, § 3571; W. Va. Code, 1899, ch. 139, § 7. See post, "Statutory Provisions." III, A, 2.

Upon a bill to enforce a judgment lien, the court may decree a sale of the land; but it is not bound, and ought not to decree such sale, if the rents and profits of the land will satisfy the liens charged upon it in a reasonable time. Hill v. Morehead, 20 W. Va. 429; Rose v. Brown, 11 W. Va. 122; Tennent v. Patton, 6 Leigh 196.

If consent to sale be made, the court ought to decree such sale, although the rents and profits of the land will satisfy the liens charged upon it in a reasonable time. Hill v. Morehead, 20 W. Va. 429; Rose v. Brown, 11 W. Va. 122.

Waiver of Inquiry.—If none of the parties ask an inquiry to ascertain whether the rents and profits will pay the debt in a reasonable time, they are presumed to have waived it, and there may be a decree for the sale of the property. McClung v. Beirne, 10 Leigh 394; Brengle v. Richardson, 78 Va. 406. See post, "Waiver of Inquiry," III, A, 2, e, (2), (d), cc.

What Is Reasonable Time.—What is a reasonable time, within which the rents and profits of the land will satisfy the liens charged thereon, is a matter of discretion by the court. The discretion to be exercised is not an arbitrary one, but a sound discretion in the interest of fairness and prudence towards all parties. Hill v. Morehead,

20 W. Va. **429**; Rose *v.* Brown, 11 W. Va. 122.

Not Matter of Right.—Prior to the statutory provisions relating to the enforcement of judgment liens, the right to have his land rented rather than sold was a privilege accorded to the judgment debtor and others interested when asked by them, and not a matter of right demandable at any time. Newlon *v.* Wade, 43 W. Va. 283, 27 S. E. 244; Arnold *v.* Casner, 22 W. Va. 444; Hill *v.* Morehead, 20 W. Va. 429; Rose *v.* Brown, 11 W. Va. 122.

Privilege Must Be Exercised with Reasonable Diligence.—To have real estate rented rather than sold, under the law of this state prior to the act of March 26, 1882, was a privilege accorded to the debtor and not an absolute right. And therefore, to entitle him to the benefit of this privilege, he must exercise reasonable diligence in claiming it, and where he has not done so and shows no sufficient excuse for his neglect, he can not be permitted at the last moment to have the cause sent to a commissioner or otherwise delayed to ascertain whether or not the rents and profits of land will pay the debts in a reasonable time. Arnold *v.* Casner, 22 W. Va. 444; Hill *v.* Morehead, 20 W. Va. **429**; Rose *v.* Brown, 11 W. Va. 122.

Privilege Must Be Exercised in Lower Court.—To have the real estate rented rather than sold, being a privilege accorded to the debtor and others interested, they must exercise it in the inferior court; and the decree must show that they asked a rental of the property, and it was refused, before the decree for that reason, will be reviewed in the appellate court. The inferior court must be called on to say, whether in a reasonable time the rents and profits of the real estate will pay the liens charged upon it; and this discretion must first be exercised by the court below before the supreme court will review the decree of said court; and upon such review, the supreme

court will not reverse it unless it appear that the court erred in the exercise of that discretion. Hill *v.* Morehead, 20 W. Va. 429; Rose *v.* Brown, 11 W. Va. 122; Hughes *v.* Hamilton, 19 W. Va. 366, 396.

While it is true that to have the real estate rented is a privilege accorded to the debtor under circumstances, still to entitle the debtor to have the benefit of such privilege he must exercise reasonable diligence in claiming it in the court below, and he must ask the rental of the property, before the decree of sale is entered, unless he shows to the court below good and sufficient reason, why he did not ask it, before the decree of sale was entered. Hill *v.* Morehead, 20 W. Va. 429; Rose *v.* Brown, 11 W. Va. 122.

An interlocutory decree directs a sale of lands to satisfy a debt, in a case where it might have been proper to decree satisfaction out of the rents and profits; but this was not a point controverted in the court below, or in any way brought to the notice of the court, and though the party had ample opportunity to apply to the court to alter the decree in that particular, he did not apply for such alteration, and upon appeal to this court, held, the decree shall not be reversed for such cause, but affirmed and the cause remanded with direction to alter the decree and direct satisfaction out of the rents and profits, if such alteration be asked, and if the debt can be satisfied out of the rents and profits within a reasonable time. Manns *v.* Flinn, 10 Leigh 93; McClung *v.* Beirne, 10 Leigh 394; Brengle *v.* Richardson, 78 Va. 406; Johnson *v.* Wagner, 76 Va. 587.

When, however, the cause is remanded, the appellate court may give the debtor, or other party interested, a right to apply to the court below, to have the inquiry made, whether the rents and profits will satisfy the liens on the real estate in a reasonable time, and to have the judgment of such court thereon. Rose v. Brown, 11 W. Va. 122.

2. Statutory Provisions.

a. In General.

If it appear to the court that the rents and profits of the real estate subject to the lien will not satisfy the judgment in five years, the court may decree the said estate, or any part thereof, to be sold, and the proceeds applied to the discharge of the judgment. Va. Code, 1904, § 3571; Va. Code, 1849, 1860; Va. Code, 1873, ch. 132, § 9; W. Va. Code, 1899, ch. 139, § 7. Dunfee v. Childs, 45 W. Va. 155, 30 S. E. 102; Ewart v. Saunders, 25 Gratt. 203; Neff v. Wooding, 83 Va. 432, 2 S. E. 731; Muse v. Friedenwald, 77 Va. 57; Horton v. Bond, 28 Gratt. 815; Cooper v. Daugherty, 85 Va. 343, 7 S. E. 387; Newlon v. Wade, 43 W. Va. 283, 27 S. E. 244; Coal River, etc., Co. v. Webb, 3 W. Va. 438; Compton v. Tabor, 32 Gratt. 121; Handly v. Sydenstricker, 4 W. Va. 605; Conaway v. Odbert, 2 W. Va. 25; Kane v. Mann, 93 Va. 239, 24 S. E. 938; Kyger v. Sipe, 89 Va. 507, 16 S. E. 627; Kennerly v. Swartz, 88 Va. 704, 3 S. E. 348; Brengle v. Richardson, 78 Va. 406; McAllister v. Bodkin, 76 Va. 809; Johnson v. Wagner, 76 W. Va. 587; Price v. Thrash, 30 Gratt. 515.

b. Construction and Effect of Statutes.

The effect of the statutory provisions is to take away from the courts the discretion of saying what would be a reasonable time; and the statute fixes it at five years. Rose v. Brown, 11 W. Va. 122.

Under the statute, if it appears that the rents and profits of the estate will not discharge the lien in five years, it is made the duty of the court to order a sale of the realty; but if such rents and profits will discharge the lien within five years, then it is the duty of the court to refuse to decree a sale of the realty, and decree that it be rented. Rose v. Brown, 11 W. Va.

122; Compton v. Tabor, 32 Gratt. 121; Dunfee v. Childs, 45 W. Va. 155, 30 S. E. 102.

The statutory requirement applies only to suits to enforce the lien of a judgment. Neff v. Wooding, 83 Va. 432, 2 S. E. 731.

A suit to enforce a lien reserved in favor of a grantor in his conveyance of land, as provided for by § 1, ch. 115, Va. Code, 1873, is not a suit to enforce a judgment lien and therefore the provisions of the Virginia Code, 1904, § 3571, do not apply, and the court may decree a sale of the land to satisfy the lien reserved on the face of the conveyance, without any previous account of rents and profits. Neff v. Wooding, 83 Va. 432, 2 S. E. 731.

c. Status of Provision under the Several Codes.

This provision was in the Codes of Virginia of 1849 and 1860, but was dropped from the Code of West Virginia of 1868, and reinserted in the acts of 1882, ch. 126. Newlon v. Wade, 43 W. Va. 283, 27 S. E. 244; Dunfee v. Childs, 45 W. Va. 155, 30 S. E. 102; Rose v. Brown, 11 W. Va. 122.

d. Effect of Repeal of Provision of West Virginia Code, 1860.

By the repealing act of the Code of 1868, ch. 166, § 1, the latter part of the section as it stood in the Code of 1860 was repealed. The latter part of the section, was omitted leaving only the first clause of the section, "The lien of a judgment may always be enforced in a court of equity." Concerning the effect of this repeal, the court said as follows: "What was the effect of such repeal? Was it to declare, that in no case can a court of chancery while enforcing the lien of a judgment, decree that the real estate shall be rented to pay the judgment? That in every case a sale must be ordered? By the practice in Virginia, as it existed prior to the Code of 1849, while enforcing judgment liens on land, the courts uniformly held, that it would be improper to decree the sale of real estate, when the debtor asked that it might be rented, and it appeared that the rents and profits of the estate would pay the lien in a reasonable time; and what was reasonable time was left to the sound legal discretion of the courts, which discretion was of course reviewable by the appellate court. If this was the practice of the chancery courts of Virginia, as we think it undoubtedly was, what was the effect of repealing the provision above referred to? It was to restore that practice." Rose v. Brown, 11 W. Va. 122.

Generally, as to the effect of the repeal of statutes, see the title STATUTES.

e. Proof of Insufficiency of Rents and Profits.

(1) Necessity.

Before a sale of realty can be decreed to pay judgment liens, the court must, in some way, be convinced that the rents and profits will not, in five years satisfy those liens. Muse v. Friedenwald, 77 Va. 57; Johnson v. Wagner, 76 Va. 587; Horton v. Bond, 28 Gratt. 815; Ewart v. Saunders, 25 Gratt. 203; Dillard v. Krise, 86 Va. 410, 10 S. E. 430; Etter v. Scott, 90 Va. 762, 19 S. E. 776; Conaway v. Odbert, 2 W. Va. 25; Newlon v. Wade, 43 W. Va. 283, 27 S. E. 244; Dunfee v. Childs, 45 W. Va. 155, 30 S. E. 102, 103; Effinger v. Kenney, 79 Va. 551; Cooper v. Daugherty, 85 Va. 343, 7 S. E. 387; Calvert v. Ash, 47 W. Va. 480, 35 S. E. 887; Coal River, etc., Co. v. Webb, 3 W. Va. 438; Preston v. Aston, 85 Va. 104, 7 S. E. 344; Kennerly v. Swartz, 83 Va. 704, 3 S. E. 348; Price v. Thrash, 30 Gratt. 515; Brengle v. Richardson, 78 Va. 406; Laidley v. Hinchman, 3 W. Va. 423; Daingerfield v. Smith, 83 Va. 81, 1 S. E. 599; Compton v. Tabor, 32 Gratt. 121; Mustain v. Pannill, 86 Va. 33, 9 S. E. 419; Kane v. Mann, 93 Va. 239, 24 S. E. 938; Ky-

ger v. Sipe, 89 Va. 507, 16 S. E. 627; Neff v. Wooding, 83 Va. 432, 2 S. E. 731; Barr v. White, 30 Gratt. 531; Crawford v. Weller, 23 Gratt. 835; McClung v. Beirne, 10 Leigh 394.

The insufficiency of the rents and profits to satisfy the judgment with the statutory period, is a fact preliminary to the exercise by the court of a jurisdiction to order a sale. Horton v. Bond, 28 Gratt. 815.

In Dunfee v. Childs, 45 W. Va. 155, 30 S. E. 102, the court said: "There is nowhere a showing that the rents would not satisfy the debts in five years. Code, 1891, ch. 139, § 7, declares that it must somehow appear that they will not do so before a sale can be had. There is error in the decree in this respect. This has been the law since the act of 1882, if not before."

Under the statute which authorizes the sale of a judgment debtor's land to satisfy the judgment only in case the rents and profits thereof will not satisfy the debt and costs in five years, it is entirely competent for the court to ascertain whether they will or not, to cause the same to be offered for rent. Compton v. Tabor, 32 Gratt. 121.

It appearing that none of the decrees for renting the land had been executed, and that the real estate would not in five years rent for enough to discharge the liens, a decree annulling them and ordering the sale of so much of the property as may be necessary, is proper. Preston v. Aston, 85 Va. 104, 7 S. E. 344; Kennerly v. Swartz, 83 Va. 704, 3 S. E. 348.

Although under the statute and the decisions of this court it is, as a general rule, improper to decree a sale of real estate without first ascertaining that the rents and profits will not pay off the debt in five years, it does not necessarily follow that the failure to make the proper inquiry in that respect will result in a reversal of the decree of sale. Johnson v. Wagner, 76 Va. 587.

(2) Manner of Proving.
(a) In General.

The statute prescribes no particular mode by which it shall be made to appear that the rents and profits will not pay the judgment in five years. Ewart v. Saunders, 25 Gratt. 203; Muse v. Friedenwald, 77 Va. 57; Horton v. Bond, 28 Gratt. 815; Neff v. Wooding, 83 Va. 432, 2 S. E. 731; Brengle v. Richardson, 78 Va. 406.

(b) Pleadings.
aa. In General.

The fact that the rents and profits of the lands in five years, will not discharge the judgment, may be shown by the pleadings. Horton v. Bond, 28 Gratt. 815; Newlon v. Wade, 43 W. Va. 283, 27 S. E. 244; Etter v. Scott, 90 Va. 762, 19 S. E. 776; Effinger v. Kenney, 79 Va. 551; Ewart v. Saunders, 25 Gratt. 203; Price v. Thrash, 30 Gratt. 515; Brengle v. Richardson, 78 Va. 406; Laidley v. Hinchman, 3 W. Va. 423; Neff v. Wooding, 83 Va. 432, 2 S. E. 731; Barr v. White, 30 Gratt. 531.

bb. Allegations in Bill or Answer.

In General.—The plaintiff may allege in his bill or the defendant in his answer that the rents and profits from the land, will be insufficient to discharge the liens in five years. Etter v. Scott, 90 Va. 762, 19 S. E. 776; Coal River, etc., Co. v. Webb, 3 W. Va. 438; Price v. Thrash, 30 Gratt. 515; Ewart v. Saunders, 25 Gratt. 203; Brengle v. Richardson, 78 Va. 406; Newlon v. Wade, 43 W. Va. 283, 27 S. E. 244; Muse v. Friedenwald, 77 Va. 57; Horton v. Bond, 28 Gratt. 815; Barr v. White, 30 Gratt. 531.

Where Defendant Alleges Sufficiency.—In Newlon v. Wade, 43 W. Va. 283, 27 S. E. 244, the plaintiff did not in his bill allege the insufficiency of the rents and profits, but the defendant in his answer affirmatively alleged the sufficiency. It was held, under the circumstances shown by the pleadings and proofs, that the lower court erred in decreeing a sale and

not recommitting the case for the purpose of ascertaining the true rental value of the property, the court being misled by the decisions in the cases of Duncan v. Custard, 24 W. Va. 730; Hill v. Morehead, 20 W. Va. 429; Rose v. Brown, 11 W. Va. 122; Manns v. Flinn, 10 Leigh 93; McClung v. Beirne, 10 Leigh 394; these cases being decided under the common-equity rule prevailing before the enactment of the statutes.

Necessity of Allegation.—In a bill to enforce a judgment lien, it would seem unnecessary to aver that the rents and profits will not pay the debt in five years, under the West Virginia Code of 1868. Handly v. Sydenstricker, 4 W. Va. 605. .

Nor in a suit by the state to set aside a fraudulent conveyance made by its judgment creditor, and to subject the land to the payment of such judgment, is it necessary to allege and show that the rents, issues and profits of the land will not pay the debt in five years. State v. Bowen, 38 W. Va 91, 18 S. E. 375.

Insufficiency Alleged without Denial.—Where the insufficiency of the rents and profits is alleged and not denied, there need be no inquiry. Muse v. Friedenwald, 77 Va. 57; Ewart v. Saunders, 25 Gratt. 203; Horton v. Bond, 28 Gratt. 815; Johnson v. Wagner, 76 Va. 587; Barr v. White, 30 Gratt. 531.

In Ewart v. Saunders, 25 Gratt. 203, while the bill alleged that the rents and profits of the land would not pay the judgment in five years, this allegation was not responded to in the answer of the defendant. The only defense set up in the answer was, that the debt was paid, and whether or not it was paid, was the whole matter of contention in the court below. It was held, that a decree directing a sale of the land without inquiry was not erroneous. Muse v. Friedenwald, 77 Va. 57.

Where the bill avers that the rents and profits will pay off the debt due the plaintiff in five years, and the answer of the defendant does not specifically deny this averment or make any allegation with respect to the rents and profits, but simply contains a general denial of all the statements of the bill not specially admitted, a decree for sale of such land before inquiry as to rents and profits, will not be reversed, as such form of denial was well calculated to mislead the court, and the opposing counsel more especially, as no inquiry was asked and no reference made in the court below, and the point was not even made in the petition for an appeal but was raised for the first time in argument in the appellate court. It was held, under the authority of the cases of Manns *v.* Flynn, 10 Leigh 93, and Ewart *v.* Saunders, 25 Gratt. 203, 209, that the appellant might still have an inquiry in the court below, touching the rental value of the land, if he desired it, and to that extent the decree would be modified by the appellate court. Johnson *v.* Wagner, 77 Va. 587.

Where the bill charged that the rents and profits of the land would not pay the debt in five years, and there was no answer filed by the defendant, the bill being taken for confessed, it was not error to decree a sale of the land without directing an inquiry whether the rents and profits would pay the debt in five years. Barr *v.* White, 30 Gratt. 531.

Insufficiency Not Alleged.—Where the insufficiency of the rents and profits is not alleged, there must be an inquiry before a sale can be decreed. Muse *v.* Friedenwald, 77 Va. 57; Ewart *v.* Saunders, 25 Gratt. 203; Horton *v.* Bond, 28 Gratt. 815; Etter *v.* Scott, 90 Va. 762, 19 S. E. 776; Coal River, etc., Co. *v.* Webb, 3 W. Va. 438; Price *v.* Thrash, 30 Gratt. 515; Brengle *v.* Richardson, 78 Va. 406.

Insufficiency Alleged and Denied.— Where the insufficiency of the rents and profits is alleged in the bill, and the allegation is denied, there must be an inquiry, and the court must ascertain the annual value of the rents and profits with reasonable certainty before decreeing a sale. Muse *v.* Friedenwald, 77 Va. 57; Ewart *v.* Saunders, 25 Gratt. 203; Horton *v.* Bond, 28 Gratt. 815; Dillard *v.*. Krise, 86 Va. 410, 10 S. E. 430; Newlon *v.* Wade, 43 W. Va. 283, 27 S. E. 244.

(c) Admissions of Parties.

The insufficiency of the rents and profits to discharge the liens within the prescribed time, may also be shown by the admissions of the parties. Horton *v.* Bond, 28 Gratt. 815; Newlon *v.* Wade, 43 W. Va. 283, 27 S. E. 244; Etter *v.* Scott, 90 Va. 762, 19 S. E. 776; Effinger *v.* Kenney, 79 Va. 551; Ewart *v.* Saunders, 25 Gratt. 203; Price *v.* Thrash, 30 Gratt. 515; Brengle *v.* Richardson, 78 Va. 406; Neff *v.* Wooding, 83 Va. 432, 2 S. E. 731.

(d) Inquiry by Commissioner.
aa. In General.

The insufficiency of the rents and profits to satisfy the judgment within the statutory period may be shown by the report of a commissioner on inquiry ordered. Horton *v.* Bond, 28 Gratt. 815.

When there is a doubt whether or not the rents and profits will pay the judgments in five years, or an inquiry is demanded by either of the parties, the court will generally direct one of its commissioners to ascertain and report the annual rents and profits of the land. But this is not necessary in every case. Muse *v.* Friedenwald, 77 Va. 57; Ewart *v.* Saunders, 25 Gratt. 203; Cooper *v.* Daugherty, 85 Va. 343, 7 S. E. 387; Calvert *v.* Ash, 47 W. Va. 480, 35 S. E. 887; Newlon *v.* Wade, 43 W. Va. 283, 27 S. E. 244; Horton *v.* Bond, 28 Gratt. 815; Mustain *v.* Pannill, 86 Va. 33, 9 S. E. 419; Neff *v.* Wooding, 83 Va. 432, 2 S. E. 731; Brengle *v.* Richardson, 78 Va. 406.

Where there is no allegation in the

bill or answer and no admission, evidence, information or proof that the rents and profits will not satisfy the liens in five years, it is erroneous to decree a sale of the land, without first ordering an inquiry to ascertain whether the rents and profits are sufficient to discharge the liens within the prescribed time. Coal River, etc., Co. v. Webb, 3 W. Va. 438; Etter v. Scott, 90 Va. 762, 19 S. E. 776; Price v. Thrash, 30 Gratt. 515; Ewart v. Saunders, 25 Gratt. 203; Brengle v. Richardson, 78 Va. 406; Laidley v. Hinchman, 3 W. Va. 423; Newlon v. Wade, 43 W. Va. 283, 27 S. E. 244.

The fact of the insufficiency of the rents and profits to satisfy the judgment within the prescribed period should be made to appear before any sale is made, and if the defendant desires it, he may have an inquiry to determine that fact. But the failure to ask or order such inquiry is no cause for reversing the decree of sale; the decree being interlocutory may be amended in that respect. Price v. Thrash, 30 Gratt. 515. See post, "Waiver of Inquiry," III, A, 2, e, (2), (d), cc.

It is not error to hold that the rents and profits will not pay the liens in five years, and to direct a sale of the land, where the master so reported and based his opinion on the testimony of four witnesses, one of whom was the appellant, who estimated the annual rental value at more than four times as much as it was estimated at by the highest disinterested witness, and where the average of the estimates of the four was only $246, a sum plainly inadequate to pay off liens amounting to nearly $2500, with the accruing interest, the costs of the suit, and the expenses of renting. Cooper v. Daugherty, 85 Va. 343, 7 S. E. 387.

Ineffectual Attempt to Rent. — Where, it appearing from the report of the commissioner to whom the case was referred, from the testimony before him, that the liens resting on the lands could be paid off from the rents and profits of the land in five years, a decree to rent is entered, and an ineffectual effort to rent is made, it is error to decree a sale of the land, where the report shows that the land was exposed for renting at periods in the year when it was almost impossible to rent land at all, and that the land was exposed for renting at a distance from the premises. Mustain v. Pannill, 86 Va. 33, 9 S. E. 419.

Deed of Trust or Vendor's Lien. — In a suit to enforce a deed of trust or a vendor's lien, it is not error to decree a sale of the land without inquiry into the rents and profits. And this is true even though the vendor has a judgment for the amount of his lien. Kyger v. Sipe, 89 Va. 507, 16 S. E. 627; Neff v. Wooding, 83 Va. 432, 2 S. E. 731; Kane v. Mann, 93 Va. 239, 24 S. E. 938; Coles v. Withers, 33 Gratt. 186; Armentrout v. Gibbons, 30 Gratt. 632. See generally, the titles MORTGAGES AND DEEDS OF TRUST; VENDOR'S LIEN.

bb. Trial Renting.

Upon a bill filed by a judgment creditor to subject the land of his debtor to satisfy his debt, the court, in order to ascertain whether the rents and profits of the land will pay the debt in five years, should generally offer the land for rent, first for one year, and if it did not rent for enough to pay the debt, then to offer it for two years, and if it did not yield enough, then to offer it for three years; and so on until it was offered for five years, if necessary to raise enough to pay the debt—and to rent for no longer period than was necessary for that purpose. If it rents for enough to pay the debt in five years or less, then the commissioner should close the contract of renting. If not, he should report the fact to the court, to the end that the cause might be further proceeded with. Compton v. Tabor, 32 Gratt. 121; Daingerfield v. Smith, 83 Va. 81, 1 S. E. 599.

cc. Waiver of Inquiry.

If none of the parties ask an inquiry to ascertain the annual rents and profits of the land, they may be presumed to have waived it, and there may, in a proper case, be a decree for a sale without it. Ewart v. Saunders, 25 Gratt. 203; Brengle v. Richardson, 78 Va. 406; McClung v. Beirne, 10 Leigh 394; Manns v. Flinn, 10 Leigh 93, 97; Muse v. Friedenwald, 77 Va. 57; Horton v. Bond, 28 Gratt. 815.

The exception that the commissioner ought to have ascertained the rents and profits should not have been sustained, because he reports, that no evidence was brought before him on the subject. If the debtor and his wife, who were more interested in that matter than anybody else, did not choose to present evidence of that fact, the commissioner could not be expected to hunt up evidence thereof. Duncan v. Custard, 24 W. Va. 730, 739.

Where the bill does not allege the insufficiency of the rents and profits to satisfy the liens within the period of five years, and where there has been no inquiry, but where the decree of the court below sets forth that it appears that the lands without the improvements when sold would not more than pay the liens, the party entitled to the inquiry may be presumed to have waived it, and the decree of sale will not be set aside on account of the omission of such inquiry; but it will be amended, and that party be allowed to have the inquiry if he chooses, and so amended the decree will be affirmed. Brengle v. Richardson, 78 Va. 406. See also, Ewart v. Saunders, 25 Gratt. 203; Price v. Thrash, 30 Gratt. 515.

f. Party Seeking Sale Must Show Insufficiency.

Under the provisions of the Code, before the court can decree a sale of a judgment debtor's property to pay the judgment liens thereon, it must appear to the court that the rents and profits thereof will not pay the judg-ments within five years. Nor does it devolve upon the judgment debtor to show such to be the case, but it is the duty of those seeking a sale of the land to show the necessity therefor. Newlon v. Wade, 43 W. Va. 283, 27 S. E. 244.

If the plaintiff alleges in his bill that the rental value of the real estate is insufficient to satisfy the judgment liens in five years, the defendant can controvert the same by a mere denial, which will cast the burden on the plaintiff of sustaining the controverted allegation. Newlon v. Wade, 43 W. Va. 283, 27 S. E. 244.

The mere fact that the plaintiff omits from his bill the allegation of the insufficiency of the rents and profits, and the defendant affirmatively alleges the contrary in his answer, does not shift the burden to the defendant, for the plaintiff must make it appear to the satisfaction of the court that the rents and profits of all the defendant's real estate, liable to the judgments will not satisfy such liens within five years, before he can demand a sale thereof. Newlon v. Wade, 43 W. Va. 283, 27 S. E. 244.

Statute Changes Equity Rule.—The cases of Duncan v. Custard, 24 W. Va. 730; Hill v. Morehead, 20 W. Va. 429, and Rose v. Brown, 11 W. Va. 122, are not authorities for the proposition that the judgment debtor must show that the rents and profits of the land are sufficient to pay the liens thereon in five years. These cases were all decided under the common-equity rule prevailing before the enactment of the Code of 1849 as determined by the Virginia court of appeals in the cases of Manns v. Flinn, 10 Leigh 93, and McClung v. Beirne, 10 Leigh 394, and they were all prior to the adoption into the Code of West Virginia of the provision governing the sale or renting of real estate to satisfy judgment liens. Newlon v. Wade, 43 W. Va. 283, 27 S. E. 244. See ante, "Equity Rule Prior to Statutes," III, A, 1.

g. What Lands Considered in Estimate to Ascertain Sufficiency of Rents and Profits.

Upon a creditor's bill to subject lands of a debtor to the payment of the liens of judgments thereon, the debtor can not, by any agreement with his wife, who is in no wise bound for said judgments, and not a party to the suit, have the rents and profits of her land considered in an estimate to ascertain whether the rents and profits of his lands for five years will pay and satisfy such judgments. Kane *v.* Mann, 93 Va. 239, 24 S. E. 938.

B. ASCERTAINMENT OF LIABILITY OF LAND AS PREREQUISITE TO DECREE OF RENTING.

Until the circuit court has first ascertained or determined by its decree that there is a lien or liability upon the land of the defendants, or upon its rents and profits, for the payment of some debt or liability, the court has no right to rent their land without their consent. Hollingsworth *v.* Brooks, 7 W. Va. 559.

The supreme court of appeals decided, in this case, that the circuit court had no right to make a decree to rent the land of the defendants, without their consent, for the year 1871—the circuit court not having first determined, by its decree, that there was a lien or liability upon the said land, or the rents and profits thereof, for the payment of some debt or liability. Held, as the legitimate effect of said decision, that a similar order, directing the land to be rented for the previous year of 1870, is, for the same reason, erroneous, and when coming in conflict with the rights of said defendants, as subsequently settled by said decision of the supreme court of appeals, must be regarded as of no validity. That it also follows, as a legitimate consequence of said decision, that the circuit court may properly make an order directing the rents, or the notes or bonds taken for the same, for the year 1870, to be paid or delivered to the parties entitled to the rightful possession of said property or land during that year—said order being based upon their petition filed in court. Hollingsworth *v.* Brooks, 7 W. Va. 559.

C. DETERMINATION OF AMOUNTS AND PRIORITIES OF LIENS AS PREREQUISITE TO DECREE OF RENTING.

It is not necessary before a decree is rendered for the renting of the land to discharge a lien thereon, to have the amounts and priorities of all the liens thereon ascertained and fixed. Douglass *v.* McCoy, 24 W. Va. 722.

"It is also assigned as error, that the decree fails to ascertain the several liens with their amounts and priorities other than that of the plaintiff; and that the state and condition of the title to said lands were not ascertained. This was wholly unnecessary in a cause like this. It has been repeatedly held in this state and Virginia, that it is error to decree the sale of land to pay the liens charged thereon without first ascertaining said liens and fixing their amounts and priorities. We said in Scott *v.* Ludington, 14 W. Va. 387, 395, that the reason for this rule is, that it is necessary in order to make the land bring a better price, and to save the debtor from being harassed with a multiplicity of suits and heavy costs. There is no such reason for requiring, that the liens should be ascertained and their amounts and priorities fixed when the land is rented as when the land is sold. It is to the interest of the debtor that this should not be so. The creditors not pressing might be entirely willing to indulge the debtor for a time, until by a rental of the property the pressing creditor is satisfied; because he does not lose his right to have the land subjected to the payment of his debt; but if the land is to be sold at the instance of the pressing creditors, all the creditors must attend to their interest or their debts will be lost. It is not therefore necessary, before a decree is rendered for the rental of the land, to pay a lien thereon, that the amounts and priorities of all the liens thereon shall be ascertained and fixed." Douglass *v.* McCoy, 24 W. Va. 722.

D. DECREE OF RENTING.

Simultaneous Decree for Renting and Sale.—It is improper to decree simultaneously for a renting and sale of the land, dependent upon a contingency, and to be determined by the sequel, e. g., if the rents prove insufficient, then to sell the land. The court should decree, first for renting; and, if the rents should prove insufficient, the commissioner should report to the court for further proceedings to be had before sale. Daingerfield *v.* Smith, 83 Va. 81, 1 S. E. 599; Compton *v.* Tabor, 32. Gratt. 121.

Setting Aside Decree of Renting and Ordering Sale.—Where, after renting of land has been decreed at a previous term, it appears to the court that the rents and profits will not, in five years, pay all the liens proven before the commissioner, the decree of renting may be set aside, and an order of sale entered in its stead, the liens on the land, and their respective priorities, having been first ascertained. Kennerly *v.* Swartz, 83 Va. 704, 3 S. E. 348.

E. PROPERTY SUBJECT TO RENTING.

The statute (Va. Code, 1904, § 3571), which is the only authority for renting out real estate of the judgment debtor, can not be construed so as to authorize the renting of the real estate of the judgment debtor's wife to satisfy the liens on her husband's property, where she was not a party to the suit, and the liens asserted are in no sense a lien upon her real estate and could not be made so by any agreement be-

tween her and her husband. Kane *v.* Mann, 93 Va. 239, 247, 24 S. E. 938.

F. TERMS OF RENTING.
1. In General.

The statute does not prescribe the terms of renting, and it would not be practicable or judicious for the court to prescribe any inflexible rule. Compton *v.* Tabor, 32 Gratt. 121.

2. In Discretion of Court.

The terms of renting whether the rents shall be payable annually or at shorter periods, must be determined by the court before whom the cause is depending, in the exercise of a sound discretion, under all the circumstances, as to the character of the property, its locality, and the usage of the country, etc. Compton *v.* Tabor, 32 Gratt. 121.

3. Dependent upon Species or Locality of Property, etc.

In General.—For some species of property, and in some localities, the rents may be payable, monthly, or quarterly or semiannually. For other species, or in other localities, the usage may be to pay annually. Compton *v.* Tabor, 32 Gratt. 121.

Land.—Where land, for instance, is decreed to be rented, as it yields its products, for the most part, annually, the rent would probably be directed to be paid annually. Compton *v.* Tabor, 32 Gratt. 121.

Mill Property.—Where a mill property is decreed to be rented, it, unlike the soil yielding products annually, may be presumed to yield its returns semiannually, or oftener, and the terms of renting may be determined accordingly. Compton *v.* Tabor, 32 Gratt. 121.

IV. Prerequisites to Decree of Sale.

A. DETERMINATION OF AMOUNT OF DEBTOR'S PROPERTY OR FUND FOR PAYMENT OF DEBTS.

Before decreeing a sale of a debtor's real estate the court should ascertain and definitely determine the full extent of all the real estate owned by such debtor. Newlon *v.* Wade, 43 W. Va. 283, 27 S. E. 244; McCleary *v.* Grantham, 29 W. Va. 301, 11 S. E. 949; Anderson *v.* Nagle, 12 W. Va. 98; Schultz *v.* Hansbrough, 33 Gratt. 576.

Before a sale is decreed it is the proper procedure to ascertain the exact amount of the fund for payment of debts. Crawford *v.* Weller, 23 Gratt. 835.

The bill alleges that the defendant is the owner of a certain piece of real estate, but does not allege that it is all the real estate owned by him. The commissioner was directed to ascertain the real estate of the judgment debtor, but he does not show in his report that he discharged his duty in this respect. He follows the bill. The judgment debtor excepts for the reason that the commissioner failed to report all his real estate, and suggests that the records of the county so disclose. It is not right that a judgment debtor should be harassed by repeated sales of different portions of his real estate, and therefore the full extent should be ascertained, before a decree for rent or sale thereof is entered. Newlon *v.* Wade, 43 Va. 283, 27 S. E. 244.

It is not necessary to refer the cause to a commissioner to ascertain of what property the judgment debtor was possessed, and upon which certain judgments were liens, where the bill alleges (which allegation is not denied or controverted by the answer), that "the aforesaid real estate" (the lot in question) "is all the real estate that the said A. L. Peadro was then" (at the date of the judgments) "or is now seized of." Anderson *v.* Nagle, 12 W. Va. 98.

C., a judgment creditor of S., files his bill against S., to subject his lands, consisting of five small tracts, to satisfy his judgment. S. answers and says he has sold a part of his land to M., and a part to G., and a part was set-tled on his wife by marriage agreement. And since the filing of the bill he had been adjudged a bankrupt on his petition. C. amends his bill and makes G. the wife, and the assignee in bankruptcy, defendants. A commissioner reports the plaintiff's judgment $548.87, and other judgments, in all $1,284.02; all docketed before the marriage contract; the assessed value of all the lands $1,745.50; the annual rental of all $75; the lands sold M. and G. of one-fifth value of the whole. The assignee has sold 213 acres of the land, not including the wife's; which was not embraced in S.'s schedule. The court decrees sale of wife's land on a credit, and directs a personal security, the obligors to waive the homestead exemption. Held, the commissioner having reported that the lands sold M. and G. was one-fifth of the value of the land, there is no necessity for further inquiry as to the lands purchased by them, before the decree for a sale of the wife's land. It was not necessary to show the assessed value of the wife's land before decreeing the sale. It was not necessary to have a separate report of the number of acres held by the wife, as that sufficiently appears. Sively *v.* Campbell, 23 Gratt. 893.

B. DETERMINATION OF EXISTENCE, AMOUNTS AND PRIORITIES OF LIENS.

See post, "Removal of Cloud from Title," IV, D.

1. Necessity.

a. General Rule.

Where there are various liens on the land of a debtor, it is premature and erroneous to decree a sale of the land to satisfy such liens, without first ascertaining all the liens existing against such land, and determining and definitely fixing their respective amounts and priorities. Barton's Chy. Pr. 1062; Scott *v.* Ludington, 14 W. Va. 387; Marling *v.* Robrecht, 13 W. Va. 440; McClaskey *v.* O'Brien, 16 W. Va. 791;

Parsons *v.* Thornburg, 17 W. Va. 356; Calvert *v.* Ash, 47 W. Va. 480, 35 S. E. 887; Beaty *v.* Veon, 18 W. Va. 291; Tavenner *v.* Barrett, 21 W. Va. 656; Hill *v.* Morehead, 20 W. Va. 429; Beard *v.* Arbuckle, 19 W. Va. 135; Payne *v.* Webb, 23 W. Va. 558; Wiley *v.* Mahood, 10 W. Va. 206; Cralle *v.* Meem, 8 Gratt. 496, 530; Alexander *v.* Howe, 85 Va. 198, 7 S. E. 248; Lipscombe *v.* Rogers, 20 Gratt. 658; Kendrick *v.* Whitney, 28 Gratt. 646; Anderson *v.* Nagle, 12 W. Va. 98, 113; Bock *v.* Bock, 24 W. Va. 586; Buster *v.* Holland, 27 W. Va. 510; McCleary *v.* Grantham, 29 W. Va. 301, 11 S. E. 949; Hutton *v.* Lockridge, 22 W. Va. 159; Hull *v.* Hull, 35 W. Va. 155, 13 S. E. 49; Keck *v.* Allender, 37 W. Va. 201, 16 S. E. 520; Lough *v.* Michael, 37 W. Va. 679, 17 S. E. 181; Lehman *v.* Hinton, 44 W. Va. 1, 29 S. E. 984; Schultz *v.* Hansbrough, 33 Gratt. 576; Daingerfield *v.* Smith, 83· Va. 81, 1 S. E. 599; Moran *v.* Brent, 25 Gratt. 164; Simmons *v.* Lyles, 27 Gratt. 922; Buchanan *v.* Clark, 10 Gratt. 164; Livesay *v.* Jarrett, 3 W. Va. 283; Murdock *v.* Welles, 9 W. Va. 552; Fidelity Loan Co. *v.* Dennis, 93 Va. 504, 25 S. E. 546; Horton *v.* Bond, 28 Gratt. 815; Effinger *v.* Kenney, 79 Va. 551; Adkins *v.* Edwards, 83 Va. 300, 2 S. E. 435; Trimble *v.* Herold, 20 W. Va. 602; Rohrer *v.* Travers, 11 W. Va. 146, 147; Cole *v.* McRae, 6 Rand. 644; Hoge *v.* Junkin, 79 Va. 220; Iæge *v.* Bossieux, 15 Gratt. 84; Smith *v.* Flint, 6 Gratt. 40; Strayer *v.* Long, 83 Va. 715, 3 S. E. 372; Houck *v.* Dunham, 92 Va. 211, 23 S. E. 238; New *v.* Bass, 92 Va. 383, 23 S. E. 747; Laidley *v.* Hinchman, 3 W. Va. 423; Pecks *v.* Chambers, 8 W. Va. 210; Bristol Iron, etc., Co. *v.* Caldwell, 95 Va. 47, 27 S. E. 838, 3 Va. Law Reg. 460; Sims *v.* Tyrer, 96 Va. 14, 30 S. E. 443, 4 Va. Law Reg. 377; Etter *v.* Scott, 90 Va. 762, 19 S. E. 776; Schmertz *v.* Hammond, 51 W. Va. 408, 41 S. E. 184; White *v.* Drew, 9 W. Va. 695; Artrip *v.* Rasnake, 96 Va. 277, 31 S. E. 4; Max Meadow Land, etc., Co. *v.* Mc-

Gavock, 96 Va. 131, 30 S. E. 460; Karn *v.* Rorer Iron Co., 86 Va. 754, 11 S. E. 431; Dillard *v.* Krise, 86 Va. 410, 10 S. E. 430; Utterbach *v.* Mehlenger, 86 Va. 62, 9 S. E. 479; Kennerly.*v.* Swartz, 83 Va. 704, 3 S. E. 348; Redd *v.* Dyer, 83 Va. 331, 2 S. E. 283; Hartman *v.* Evans, 38 W. Va. 669, 18 S. E. 802; Muller *v.* Stone, 84 Va. 834, 6 S. E. 223; Wallace *v.* Treakle, 27 Gratt. 479; White *v.* Mechanical, etc., Ass'n, 22 Gratt. 233; Crawford *v.* Weller, 23 Gratt. 835; Washington, etc., R. Co. *v.* Alexandria, etc., R. Co., 19 Gratt. 592, 617.

There is no better settled rule of equity practice in Virginia than that which declares it to be premature and erroneous to decree a sale of land to satisfy encumbrances thereon, before ascertaining the liens binding the land, and their amounts and priorities. Bristol Iron, etc., Co. *v.* Caldwell, 95 Va. 47, 27 S. E. 838.

Where there are judgment liens and trust liens against real estate and a bill is filed by a judgment creditor to enjoin a sale of the land by a trustee, and impeaching as fraudulent certain of the trust deeds, purporting to be made by the debtor for the benefit of other creditors, it is error to decree a sale before ascertaining the amounts of the several liens, and their respective priorities, and the validity of the respective trust deeds. Livesay *v.* Jarrett, 3 W. Va. 283.

In creditors' suit it is error to decree sale of debtors' lands before ascertaining the amount of the debts, and this can not be done until sums in receiver's hands, and sums realized by sale under execution of debtors' personalty, have been ascertained and credited. Strayer *v.* Long, 83 Va. 715, 3 S. E. 372.

Decree to sell share of an heir in his ancestor's lands, to pay heir's debts, without first ascertaining the amount of such share by an account taken of the ancestor's debts, and of the advancements, if any, to the several heirs, is premature and erroneous. Hoge *v.* Junkin, 79 Va. 220; Ryan *v.* McLeod, 32 Gratt. 367.

It is a settled rule that in suits to sell real estate to satisfy liens by judgments or deeds of trust, it is premature and erroneous to decree sale before account is taken of the liens and of their priorities. Horton *v.* Bond, 28 Gratt. 815. Quære: Does this rule apply where the subject of the suit is to enforce a vendor's lien. Effinger *v.* Kenney, 79 Va. 551.

The judgment debtor having been the owner of a large tract of land, charged with a lien of one thousand dollars in favor of his children payable at his death; and having at different times aliened the same to three different vendees, and to indemnify his second alienee against any loss by reason of said lien upon the portion of said land; having conveyed to a trustee another tract of land; and the commissioner to whom the cause was referred, having failed to report the amount of said lien, and whether the said three several parcels of said land are chargeable rateably with said lien, or whether same will be first chargeable upon the parcel last aliened, or whether any part thereof will be chargeable on the land conveyed in trust to indemnify said second alienee; and the court having thereupon decreed that the said land so conveyed in trust "be sold subject to the lien created thereon by said deed of trust; held, that it was error in the said circuit court to decree that the said land so conveyed in trust, should be sold subject to the lien created thereon by said deed of trust without first ascertaining the amount of said lien chargeable on said several parcels, and fixing the priorities thereof. Hutton *v.* Lockridge, 22 W. Va. 159.

Illustrations.—A vendor of land, who has retained the title, files a bill against the widow and infant children of the vendee, for a sale of the land to satisfy his debt. The widow answers,

claiming dower in the land subject to the vendor's lien. Judgment creditors of the vendee may make themselves parties to the cause, and have the land, subject to the vendor's lien and the widow's dower, applied to the payment of their debts. In such case the debt of the vendor is ascertained, and a commissioner is appointed to sell the land. He reports that a friend of the widow and children of the vendee has paid to the vendor his debt, and therefore he did not sell the land. The vendor then ceases to be interested in the case, and it becomes the suit of the creditors of the vendee. In such a case a commissioner is directed to settle the account of the administrator of the vendee, to take an account of the vendee's debts and their priorities, and before the commissioner makes report the court decrees a sale of the land. Held, it was premature to decree a sale of land before the debts of the vendee and their priorities were ascertained, and a settlement of the administration account was made. Simmons *v.* Lyles, 27 Gratt. 922.

R. is entitled to a decree for a sale of real estate to pay a debt due to him, secured by a deed of trust upon the property; but before the decree is made, T., by petition in the cause, alleges that he holds a prior lien upon the property to secure a debt due him; and he exhibits his bond and deed of trust. It is error to decree a sale of the property, and that the proceeds of sale be brought in court, before passing upon the claim of T. and ascertaining whether or not it is a valid prior lien, and the amount thereof. Lipscombe *v.* Rogers, 20 Gratt. 658.

Complaint on Appeal.—Although it is generally error to decree a sale of the debtor's property before the liens are ascertained and stated, yet in a case where the creditors have not appealed, and it does not appear that they, or any of them, object to the decree of sale for any cause, the debtor has no right to complain in that respect, upon appeal, when the record shows that the sale of part of his lands had been made at his own instance and with his consent, and where also it was necessary to sell all of the debtor's land to meet his liabilities, he is not prejudiced by the manner in which the debts and liabilities have been stated by the commissioner. White v. Drew, 9 W. Va. 695.

b. Reason for Rule.

It has been again and again held by the court of appeals of Virginia and West Virginia, that real estate should not be sold until the liens thereon and their priorities are fixed and determined. This is because it is necessary to thus make the land bring a better price; and also to prevent the debtor from being harassed with a multiplicity of suits and consequent costs. It would be hard indeed upon the debtor, if every judgment creditor could involve him in costs, and by selling his property subject to prior liens, sacrifice it; and it would be equally unjust to subsequent lienors, because they would be compelled to either purchase the property, or lose their liens. Scott v. Ludington, 14 W. Va. 387; Douglass v. McCoy, 24 W. Va. 722.

In the case of Marling v. Robrecht, 13 W. Va. 440, this court held, that "When there are various liens on lands of a judgment debtor, it is error to decree a sale of the lands without first ascertaining the amounts of the liens and their priorities, for the reason that to decree such sale before ascertaining the amount of the several liens and their respective priorities has a tendency to sacrifice the property, by discouraging the creditors from bidding, as they probably would, if their right to satisfaction of their debts, and the order in which they were to be paid out of the property, had been previously ascertained." McClaskey v. O'Brien, 16 W. Va. 791; Beaty v. Veon, 18 W. Va. 291; Keck v. Allender, 37 W.

Va. 201, 16 S. E. 520; Cole v. McRae, 6 Rand. 644; Livesay v. Jarrett, 3 W. Va. 283; Bristol Iron, etc., Co. v. Caldwell, 95 Va. 47, 27 S. E. 838; Alexander v. Howe, 85 Va. 198, 7 S. E. 248; Adkins v. Edwards, 83 Va. 300, 2 S. E. 435; Hoge v. Junkin, 79 Va. 220; Horton v. Bond, 28 Gratt. 815; Smith v. Flint, 6 Gratt. 40; Buchanan v. Clark, 10 Gratt. 16; Iaege v. Bossieux, 15 Gratt. 83; Lipscombe v. Rogers, 20 Gratt. 658; White v. Mechanical, etc., Ass'n, 22 Gratt. 233; Moran v. Brent, 25 Gratt. 104; Schultz v. Hansbrough, 33 Gratt. 576.

The theory upon which courts of equity require generally that lands should not be sold until accounts of liens are taken is, that the creditors are interested in bidding for the land and making it bring its full value, and may not be sacrificed. Wallace v. Treakle, 27 Gratt. 479.

The object of the rule is to secure a good sale of the property by promoting competition at the sale. Crawford v. Weller, 23 Gratt. 835.

It is the right of the defendant to have definitely ascertained the amounts of the liens upon his land, to the end that the court might not only know with certainty the amount of indebtedness, and thus be able to decree for the amounts actually due, but that the commissioner of sale might be informed, as far as practicable by the decree, as to the quantity of land necessary to be sold for its satisfaction. Without having fixed, by a decree of court, the amount and the priorities of the several liens, is to sell under circumstances calculated to suppress competition in the bidding rather than promote it among the several lien holders. Rohrer v. Travers, 11 W. Va. 146.

c. Waiver of Compliance with Rule.

While the general rule as laid down by this court requires, that when the court directs the sale of real property, it shall first ascertain the amounts of the lien debts, and their respective priorities, and give a day for payment in the decree, still this rule is not so fundamental in its requirements as to prevent the parties to the cause who may be interested in its enforcement, from dispensing therewith or waiving a compliance therewith by their consent. Parsons v. Thornburg, 17 W. Va. 356. And that the debtor may waive this right, see Crawford v. Weller, 23 Gratt. 835.

Though there was a decree for a sale of land, and a sale thereunder before an account of the liens was taken, yet an objection cannot be made on this point by some of the creditors who came in after the decree, made years after the sale, when it is obvious that the land would not sell for as much as it had sold for before. Wallace v. Treakle, 27 Gratt. 479.

d. Necessity of Ascertaining Balance after Partial Payment.

When once a decree has been made fixing the amount of a lien decreed upon land, and its place as a lien, a partial payment does not call for an ascertainment by the court of the balance before a sale under the decree. Schmertz v. Hammond, 51 W. Va. 408, 41 S. E. 184.

Thus where a decree of sale provides for the payment to a creditor, allowed a debt by it of money in the hands of a receiver of another court, and provides that when paid it should operate as a partial payment, there is no error in failing to ascertain the amount of such money in the decree, especially where before sale the amount of said money appears in the record of the case. Schmertz v. Hammond, 51 W. Va. 408, 41 S. E. 184.

e. Determination of Amount of Particular Debt.

It is error to direct a sale of land, although unquestionably chargeable in equity, for the payment of a debt, until the amount of the debt is ascer-

tained. Rohrer v. Travers, 11 W. Va. 146; Smith v. Flint, 6 Gratt. 40.

f. Necessity for Determining Liens before Resale.

Although a decree of sale is entered, which from the facts then appearing is proper, and a sale is made thereunder, it will still be error for the court by a subsequent decree, which sets aside such sale, to order a resale of the land, if the facts, then appearing in the cause, show the existence of liens, the amounts and priorities of which have not been ascertained and fixed. In such case the court should set aside the former decree of sale and refer the cause to a commissioner or otherwise determine the amounts and priorities of the liens before ordering a resale. Payne v. Webb, 23 W. Va. 558.

2. Manner of Determination.

a. By Decree.

Where it appears by the pleadings or evidence that all the liens on the land are set forth in the bill and proceedings, the amounts and priorities of the liens may be ascertained and determined by decree without an order of reference. Barton's Chy. Pr. 1062; Alexander v. Howe, 85 Va. 198, 7 S. E. 248. See also, Lipscombe v. Rogers, 20 Gratt. 658; Kendrick v. Whitney, 28 Gratt. 646; Anderson v. Nagle, 12 W. Va. 98, 113; Schmertz v. Hammond, 51 W. Va. 408, 41 S. E. 184; Lehman v. Hinton, 44 W. Va. 1, 29 S. E. 984; Bock v. Bock, 24 W. Va. 586.

It is not necessary to refer the cause to a commissioner to ascertain the liens, and fix their priorities, where the bill alleges that the two judgments set up therein are all the liens on the lot sought to be charged, as there would be no difficulty from the bill and exhibits for the court to fix their priorities. Anderson v. Nagle, 12 W. Va. 98.

b. By Making Lienors Parties.

In every suit in equity to enforce

a judgment lien by a sale of the judgment debtor's property, all persons having liens on the real estate sought to be subjected by judgment or otherwise, shall be made parties, plaintiff or defendant, or if the number of such persons exceed ten, the suit may be brought by any one or more of them, for the benefit of himself and such other lien holders as will come in and contribute to the expenses of the suit. W. Va. Code, 1899, ch. 139, § 7; Lough v. Michael, 37 W. Va. 679, 17 S. E. 181. See also, Calvert v. Ash, 47 W. Va. 480, 35 S. E. 887; Long v. Perine, 41 W. Va. 314, 23 S. E. 611. See the title CREDITORS' SUITS, vol. 3, p. 794.

In a suit brought by a judgment creditor to enforce his judgment lien, he should make formal defendants to the suit all creditors who have obtained judgments against the debtor in the courts of record in the county wherein the lands lie, which he seeks to subject, and if he fails to do so, he should in the order of reference in the cause provide for calling in all judgment creditors of the debtor by publication; and if this be not done, this court in such a case will reverse an order of the court confirming the commissioner's report and ordering a sale of debtor's lands. Livesay v. Feamster, 21 W. Va. 83.

e. By Lienors Coming in by Petition.

"Every such lien holder, whether he be named as a party to the suit or not, or whether he be served with process therein or not, may present, prove and have allowed any claim he may have against the judgment debtor, which is a lien on such real estate, or any part thereof, and from and after the time he presents any such claim, he shall be deemed a party plaintiff in such suit." W. Va. Code, 1899, ch. 139, § 7; Calvert v. Ash, 47 W. Va. 480, 35 S. E. 887; Lough v. Michael, 37 W. Va. 679, 17 S. E. 181. See also, Long v. Perine, 41 W. Va. 314, 23 S. E. 611.

In Calvert v. Ash, 47 W. Va. 480, 35 S. E. 887, English, J., after quoting the statute providing that every lien holder may present, prove and have allowed any claim, etc., said: "My interpretation of this statute is that he must present and prove his claim, which is ordinarily done by petition. How the commissioner ascertained these liens does not appear. It may have been done by reference to the record, but there is nothing to show that the lienors presented them to the commissioner in any manner; and the statute does not intend that the act of the commissioner in searching the record and thus reporting the liens shall make the lienors parties to the suit. The statute says 'parties plaintiff,' and so they would be if they filed petitions, presented their claims, and prayed that they be given their proper priority as lienors; and, for aught that appears in this case, these judgments may be entitled to credits. Neither of these lienors can be considered in any sense as parties plaintiff to this suit."

d. By Taking Account of Liens by Commissioner.

(1) In General.

Where it does not appear by the pleadings or evidence that all the liens are set forth in the bill and proceedings, and therefore can not be ascertained and determined by decree without an order of reference to a commissioner, is has been settled by repeated decisions that it is error to decree a sale of land before taking an account of liens thereon. Barton's Chy., 189, 859, 1155, 1156, 1062; Alexander v. Howe, 85 Va. 198, 7 S. E. 248; Lipscombe v. Rogers, 20 Gratt. 658; Kendrick v. Whitney, 28 Gratt. 646; Anderson v. Nagle, 12 W. Va. 98, 113; Etter v. Scott, 90 Va. 762, 19 S. E. 776; Calvert v. Ash, 47 W. Va. 480, 35 S. E. 887; Schultz v. Hansbrough, 33 Gratt. 576, and note; Daingerfield v. Smith, 83 Va. 81, 1 S. E. 599; Marling v. Robrecht, 13 W. Va. 440; Moran *v.* Brent, 25 Gratt. 104; Simmons *v.* Lyles, 27 Gratt. 922; Wiley *v.* Mahood, 10 W. Va. 206; Cralle *v.* Meem, 8 Gratt. 496, 530; Buchanan *v.* Clark, 10 Gratt. 164; Livesay *v.* Jarrett, 3 W. Va. 283; Murdock *v.* Welles, 9 W. Va. 552; Fidelity Loan Co. *v.* Dennis, 93 Va. 504, 25 S. E. 546; Hutton *v.* Lockridge, 22 W. Va. 159, 160; Horton *v.* Bond, 28 Gratt. 815, and note; Effinger *v.* Kenney, 79 Va. 551; Adkins *v.* Edwards, 83 Va. 300, 2 S. E. 435; McClaskey *v.* O'Brien, 16 W. Va. 791, 793; Scott *v.* Ludington, 14 W. Va. 387; Hill *v.* Morehead, 20 W. Va. 429; Trimble *v.* Herold, 20 W. Va. 602; Rohrer *v.* Travers, 11 W. Va. 146, 147; Cole *v.* McRae, 6 Rand. 644; Payne *v.* Webb, 23 W. Va. 558; Hoge *v.* Junkin, 79 Va. 220; Iaege *v.* Bossieux, 15 Gratt. 83, 84; Smith *v.* Flint, 6 Gratt. 40; Strayer *v.* Long, 83 Va. 715, 3 S. E. 372; Houck *v.* Dunham, 92 Va. 211, 23 S. E. 238; New *v.* Bass, 92 Va. 383, 23 S. E. 747; Laidley *v.* Hinchman, 3 W. Va. 423; Pecks *v.* Chambers, 8 W. Va. 210; Bristol Iron, etc., Co. *v.* Caldwell, 95 Va. 47, 27 S. E. 838, 3 Va. Law Reg. 460; Sims *v.* Tyrer, 96 Va. 14, 30 S. E. 443, 4 Va. Law Reg. 377; Beaty *v.* Veon, 18 W. Va. 291.

When judgment creditors file their petitions in a suit for the sale of their debtor's land, it is error to enter a decree of sale in their favor, before referring the cause to a commissioner, so that the judgment debtor may have an opportunity of showing any payments made, or set-offs to which he may be entitled. Kendrick *v.* Whitney, 28 Gratt. 646, 655; Marling *v.* Robrecht, 13 W. Va. 440.

Unless the record shows that there are other liens upon the land sought to be charged in addition to those appearing in the bill, the cause will not be referred to a commissioner to ascertain the liens thereon. Bock *v.* Bock, 24 W. Va. 586.

An order of reference is not to be awarded to enable a plaintiff to make out his case. It should not be made for the purpose of furnishing evidence in support of the allegations of the bill, nor until he has the right to demand it. 2 Barton's Ch. Pr. (2d Ed.) 680; Millhiser *v.* McKinley, 98 Va. 207, 35 S. E. 446; Baltimore, etc., Co. *v.* Williams, 94 Va. 422, 425, 26 S. E. 841; Lee County *v.* Fulkerson, 21 Gratt. 182; Sadler *v.* Whitehurst, 83 Va. 46, 1 S. E. 410.

(2) Who May Take Account.

When it is necesssary to take an account of liens before decreeing a sale of land, it is usual for the court to refer the matter to one of its commissioners to ascertain the amounts and proprieties of the liens. Kendrick *v.* Whitney, 28 Gratt. 646; Calvert *v.* Ash, 47 W. Va. 480, 35 S. E. 887.

A commissioner, who is a creditor and a party to a suit brought to subject a debtor's lands to pay his lien debts, is incompetent to take an account of lien ordered therein. Dillard *v.* Krise, 86 Va. 410, 10 S. E. 430; Simmons *v.* Lyles, 27 Gratt. 922, 928.

A commissioner taking an account of liens is a quasi judicial character, and if the law does not, in terms, disqualify him to take and report an account of liens in a cause wherein he is a party, the spirit of it does. Dillard *v.* Krise, 86 Va. 410, 10 S. E. 430.

(3) Commissioner Must Follow Directions Strictly.

It is generally true that the commissioner should follow strictly the directions contained in the order of reference, and if he is directed to settle the liens and their priorities on each parcel of the debtor's land, and he fail to do so, the report should be recommitted. White *v.* Drew, 9 W. Va. 695.

(4) Convention of Lienors.
(a) In General.

It is plainly the purpose of our present law to give purchasers at judicial sales good titles as far as may be, especially that the lands shall be free from incumbrance. To this end, § 7, ch. 139, of the Code, requires the lien holders to be convened; and if convened, it is, of course, for the purpose of ascertaining the amounts and priorities of their liens, so that the amount to be raised by sale may be known, and how much and in what order the proceeds will be going to the lien holders. There may be cases where this course is to some extent properly departed from, but such cases are exceptional, and the reasons for them ought to clearly appear. Lough v. Michael, 37 W. Va. 679, 17 S. E. 181.

The court should not render a decree for sale of land, without first bringing the lienors before the court, and thus ascertaining the existence, amount and priorities of the liens upon the land. Hoge v. Junkin, 79 Va. 220.

In a suit brought by a judgment creditor to enforce his judgment lien, if he fails to make formal defendants in the suit, all creditors who have obtained judgments against the debtor in the court of record in the county wherein the lands lie, which he seeks to subject, he should in the order of reference in the cause provide for calling in all judgment creditors of the debtor by publication; and if this be not done, the appellate court in such case will reverse an order of the court confirming the commissioner's report and ordering a sale of the debtor's lands. Livesay v. Feamster, 21 W. Va. 83.

In a suit to enforce a purchase money lien on land, no convention of the lienors of the debtor is necessary, as in a suit on judgment. Long v. Perine, 41 W. Va. 314, 23 S. E. 611; Cunningham v. Hederick, 23 W. Va. 579; Hull v. Hull, 26 W. Va. 1, 17; Armentrout v. Gibbons, 30 Gratt. 632.

The appellate court will reverse any decree ordering the sale of land or the distribution of the proceeds of such sale where all the judgment creditors are not made parties to the suit either formally or informally, which fact is disclosed by the record. But if all the judgment creditors are made parties to such a suit informally by having been summoned by publication before a commissioner to present their judgments, the appellate court will not reverse the decree ordering the sale of lands of the debtor merely because the record disclosed that some of the judgment creditors had not been made formal defendants, who ought to have been so made, unless it appears that the objection was made to the rendering of such decree on this account in the court below, before such decree was entered. Neely v. Jones, 16 W. Va. 625.

(b) After Decree for General Account All Other Creditors May Come in and Prove Debts.

After a decree for a general account in a creditor's suit (and this may be so considered, Newell v. Little, 79 Va. 141), all the other creditors may come in under the decree and prove their debts before the commissioner to whom the cause is referred. Simmons v. Lyles, 27 Gratt. 922, 929; Piedmont, etc., Ins. Co. v. Maury, 75 Va. 508; Beverly v. Rhodes, 86 Va. 415, 10 S. E. 572; 1 Barton's Ch. Pr. (2d Ed.) 286, etc. But the administrator has no right to have the commissioner to report debts against his decedent's estate. It is his duty to represent the estate, and not those having adverse interests. The creditor, or some one who is authorized to represent him, should lay his claim before the commissioner, in order that it may be reported. Conrad v. Fuller, 98 Va. 16, 34 S. E. 893.

(c) Notice to Lien Holders.
aa. Necessity.

No decree for the distribution of the proceeds of the sale of real estate to enforce a judgment lien, shall be made until a notice to all persons holding liens on the real estate of the judgment debtor be posted and published, under a decree of the court, as provided by statute. W. Va. Code, 1899, ch. 139, § 7. McNeel v. Auldridge, 34 W. Va. 478, 12 S. E. 851; Lough v. Michael, 37 W. Va. 679, 17 S. E. 181.

"The third assignment of error is that the notice to lien holders prescribed by statute was never published previous to said decree. When a plaintiff is proceeding in equity to enforce a judgment lien, as I understand it, the statute provides (page 863, ch. 139, § 7, of the Code), that 'no decree for the distribution of the proceeds of such real estate shall be made until a notice to all persons holding liens on the real estate of the judgment debtor, be posted and published under a decree of the court, as thereinafter provided;' giving the form of the notice. This notice I do not understand to be required to be published before a decree can be made directing a sale, but it must be done before a distribution of the proceeds of such real estate; and I do not think the court erred in directing a sale of defendant's lands before publishing said notice." McNeel v. Auldridge, 34 W. Va. 478, 12 S. E. 851. But see Lough v. Michael, 37 W. Va. 679, 17 S. E. 181.

bb. Form and Contents.

As to the form of the notice required to be given lien holders, see W. Va. Code, 1899, ch. 139, § 7; McNeel v. Auldridge, 34 W. Va. 748, 12 S. E. 851.

Although the commissioner's notice of the time and place of taking the account of liens, states that the decree of reference would be executed on a certain day, "if fair, if not, the next fair day thereafter, Sundays excepted," is a substantial compliance with the requirements of the statute (but it is not advisable to insert such a proviso in a notice of the kind); and as the commissioner did take the account on that day, and the appellant does not show that he was, in conse-

quence thereof, injured by its having been taken at that time, it is not sufficient ground to refuse confirmation of the report. White v. Drew, 9 W. Va. 695.

cc. Time and Place of Publication.

Such notice shall be published once in each week for four successive weeks, in some newspaper printed in the county, or if none be printed therein, in some newspaper of general circulation in the county, and posted at the front door of the courthouse of such county at least four weeks before the day mentioned in the notice. W. Va. Code, 1899, ch. 139, § 7.

The court, or the judge thereof in vacation, ordering an account to be taken, may direct that notice of the time and place of taking it be published once a week for four successive weeks in some convenient newspaper. Va. Code, 1904, § 3321; Dillard v. Krise, 86 Va. 410, 10 S. E. 430.

The publication in a newspaper is a substitute for personal service of the notice, and it must be strictly made. The commissioner executing the order of the court must comply in the precise manner directed. If he can change the mode or alter the terms of the decree in any particular, he can virtually and practically abrogate it. Dillard v. Krise, 86 Va. 410, 10 S. E. 430.

When notice of taking an account of liens is ordered to be given by publication in a newspaper under the Virginia Code, 1904, § 3321, there must be at least twenty eight days between the first insertion and the days of taking the account. Dillard v. Krise, 86 Va. 410, 10 S. E. 430.

Where it appears that the commissioner dated his notice 16th of May and fixed the day for taking the account of liens the 20th of June, but the editor's certificate is that its first insertion in the newspaper was in the issue of the 25th of May, which makes six days in May and twenty in June, or only twenty-six of actual publication, this was held not to be due notice, for on the 27th or 28th day, some one interested in or affected by the proceedings might see the notice. Dillard v. Krise, 86 Va. 410, 10 S. E. 430.

Virginia Code, 1887, § 5, says: "Where a statute requires a notice to be given, or any other act to be done a certain time before any motion or proceeding, there must be that time exclusive of the day for such motion or proceeding." Dillard v. Krise, 86 Va. 410, 10 S. E. 430.

dd. Publication Equivalent to Personal Service.

The publishing and posting of such notice as prescribed by the Code, shall be equivalent to the personal service thereof on all persons holding liens on any such real estate, unless the court shall in the decree directing such notice to be published and posted, otherwise order. W. Va. Code, 1899, ch. 139, § 7.

The court, or the judge thereof in vacation, ordering an account to be taken, may direct that the publication of the notice as required by the statute, shall be equivalent to personal service of such notice on the parties, or any of them. Va. Code, 1904, § 3321. Dillard v. Krise, 86 Va. 410, 10 S. E. 430.

(d) Hearing and Determination by Commissioner.

In General.—In a suit to enforce the lien of a judgment, the commissioner to whom the case is referred by the decree shall, as soon as possible after notice to the lien holders is published and posted as prescribed by the statute, or served in such manner as the court may order, proceed to ascertain all the liens on the real estate or any part thereof of the judgment debtor, the holders of such liens, the amount due to each, the priorities thereof, and such other matters and things as the court by its decree may direct. W. Va. Code, 1899, ch. 139, § 7.

A mere statement to a bank clerk, unsworn to, that "a note of five hundred dollars had been placed in the hands of the bank's attorney for suit," is not evidence of the claim, and the commissioner should not allow it without proof of its existence, and the court should in such a case recommit the report for proof. White v. Drew, 9 W. Va. 695.

Extension of Time to Prove Payments before Commissioner.

—It is not error for a court to refuse to extend the time for a debtor to prove payments before a commissioner, when the record shows no good reason for such extension of time. Beard v. Arbuckle, 19 W. Va. 135.

(e) Report of Commissioner.

aa. Necessity.

When the commissioner to whom the matter has been referred has ascertained the liens and their respective amounts and priorities, and such other matter and things as the court by its decree directed, it is the duty of the commissioner to report the same to the court. W. Va. Code, 1889, ch. 139, § 7.

Where a debt is presented before a commissioner taking an account of debts or liens, and his report is silent as to it, and no decree is made upon the report, though the creditor did not except for the failure to report his debt, he is not barred from afterwards asserting it. King v. Burdett, 44 W. Va. 561, 29 S. E. 1010.

Presumption as to Correctness of Report.

—In a suit brought by judgment creditors against the judgment debtor and other judgment and trust creditors, to obtain satisfaction of their several judgments by a sale of the lands owned by said debtor, and the cause has been properly referred to a commissioner to ascertain and report the several liens thereon, and their respective priorities, and also to ascertain and report the lands owned by said debtor, chargeable therewith, and where such commissioner has made and returned such report and no error appears upon the face thereof, it will be presumed by the court, that the character, amounts and priorities of the several liens, as well as the lands owned by the judgment debtor chargeable therewith, are correctly set forth therein "except in so far only, as and as to such parts thereof, as may be objected to by proper exceptions taken thereto before the hearing" of the cause. Hutton v. Lockridge, 22 W. Va. 159.

bb. Return of Report Condition Precedent to Order of Sale.

The sale should not be ordered, until the commissioner's report is returned, and the amounts as well as the priorities of the lien definitely ascertained and fixed. Beard v. Arbuckle, 19 W. Va. 135.

cc. Proceedings on Report.

(aa) In General.

The same proceedings shall be had on such report as in other suits in chancery. W. Va. Code, 1899, ch. 139, § 7.

(bb) Confirmation.

When the report of the commissioner is confirmed, if the claims therein reported (if any) be not paid, the court shall decree that the real estate of the judgment debtor subject to such lien or liens, so far as may be necessary, shall be rented or sold. W. Va. Code, 1899, ch. 132, § 7.

The judgment debtor having excepted to the commissioner's report, because it failed to set off the amount of a demand claimed by him against the estate of a decedent for the benefit of whose children and widow, one of said judgment creditors had assigned a large judgment against him of one thousand, three hundred and fifty-four dollars and twenty-one cents recovered against him to satisfy the indebtedness of said judgment creditor to the estate of said decedent, and there being no evidence in the cause showing the amount or justice of his said demand against said decedent, or his right to have same set off against the said judgment against him. His said exception was properly overruled, and the said commissioner's report in regard thereto was properly confirmed. Hutton v. Lockridge, 22 W. Va. 159.

(cc) Recommitting Report.

It is error to decree the sale of lands to pay liens charged thereon and in the same decree to recommit the report ascertaining the liens and their priorities with leave to the debtor to prove further credits. Beard v. Arbucke, 19 W. Va. 135.

It was error also to leave the amounts of the liens in uncertainty before the sale by recommitting the report to the commissioner with leave to the debtor within sixty days to reduce the amounts of any of the liens by proving payments. Scott v. Ludington, 14 W. Va. 387. If there was any good reason for recommitting the report to the commissioner with leave to the debtor to prove further payments, if he could, it should have been done, before the sale was ordered, and the sale should not have been ordered, until the report was returned, and the amounts as well as the priorities of the liens definitely ascertained and fixed. Beard v. Arbucke, 19 W. Va. 135.

If the commissioner is directed to settle the liens and their priorities on each parcel of the debtor's land, and fails to do so, the report should be recommitted. White v. Drew, 9 W. Va. 695.

If a report be made showing the liens on a debtor's land and their priorities, which the bill asks may be sold, and afterwards a demurrer to the bill is sustained, and an amended bill filed making a large number of lienors parties, who were not parties to the suit originally, such commissioner's report ought not to be confirmed, but a new order of reference should be made by the court to ascertain the liens. Tavenner v. Barrett, 21 W. Va. 656.

If the commissioner's report fails to state the debts, their priority and the amounts, and if it shows a debt to be a lien on the land of a surety, but fails to show the liabilities and assets of the principal, it should be recommitted. Dillard v. Krise, 86 Va. 410, 10 S. E. 430.

The commissioner who was directed to take an account of the debts of S. and their priorities, and of the lands of S. and to whom and when aliened, after stating certain judgments, and debts secured by specific liens, reports that the debts secured by the deed to L. were not presented before him, and he does not report them. Held, the report should be recommitted to the commissioner to take an account of said debts; and it was error to make a decree for the sale of the lands of S. before this account was taken. Schultz v. Hansbrough, 33 Gratt. 576.

(dd) Order of Further Account after Confirmation of Report.

Report of liens was returned and confirmed without exception, and sale decreed. Then, further account of liens was ordered. Sale was afterwards made at an unusually high price, and, without exception from any creditor, confirmed, but no distribution was directed. It was not claimed by judgment debtor that a higher price could be got at a second sale. Amount of liens greatly exceeded the price obtained. Held, sale was properly confirmed, though the further account of liens remained untaken. Utterbach v. Mehlenger, 86 Va. 62, 9 S. E. 479.

3. Effect of Error in Ascertaining Priorities.

When it appears upon the face of the decree of sale, that the court below ascertained the several liens on the land and the respective amounts thereof and their priorities, but it otherwise appears in the cause, that the court may have erred to some extent in ascertaining such priorities, the appellant is not prejudiced thereby, and the appellate court will not reverse the decree of sale for this cause at the instance of the judgment debtor, if none of the judgment creditors complain in the appellate court of such error but ask the affirmation of the decree. Hill v. Morehead, 20 W. Va. 429.

C. MAKING NECESSARY PARTIES.

See the title CREDITORS' SUITS, vol. 3, p. 794.

Persons Beneficially Interested.—All persons beneficially interested in the object of a suit for the sale of real estate under decree of court ought to be made parties, so that all questions arising may be fully and finally settled. Yost v. Porter, 80 Va. 855.

When it is uncertain whether or not certain persons have an interest in land, it is error to decree the sale of such land without making such persons parties to the suit. Donahue v. Fackler, 21 W. Va. 124; Hitchcox v. Hitchcox, 39 W. Va. 607, 20 S. E. 595.

The court of appeals having reversed a decree of the court below for the sale of land and another confirming the sale and distributing the proceeds, in the absence of the owners of one-half of the land, and having sent the case back, that they may be made parties and have an opportunity to defend their interests; though the decree is in other respects confirmed, these absent owners, when made parties have a right to except to the sale and its confirmation, and are not precluded by the affirmation of the decree in other respects than those on which it is reversed. Crockett v. Sexton, 29 Gratt. 46.

Lienors.—See ante, "By Making Lienors Parties," IV, B, 2, b; "By Lienors Coming in by Petition," IV, B, 2, c.

Trustee and Beneficiary in Deed of Trust.—The trustee and the beneficiary in a deed of trust on real estate of a decedent are necessary parties to a suit for the sale of such real estate, and it is error to decree a sale thereof until they are made parties. Conrad *v.* Fuller, 98 Va. 16, 34 S. E. 893.

The legal title to the land levied on in this case being in the trustees it was error in the court below to decree the sale of the land to pay the debt before the trustees were made parties to the cause. Baker *v.* Oil Tract Co., 7 W. Va. 454, 458.

Reversioners and Remaindermen.—Owners of vested estates in reversion and remainder, whether by legal or equitable title, are indispensable parties to a chancery suit to sell the fee; and the presence as parties of a tenant for life, or of the trustee holding for them, does not make them parties by representation, and a sale under the decree will not affect or pass their right in the land. Williamson *v.* Jones, 43 W. Va. 562, 27 S. E. 411.

Heirs.—In a suit by creditors for the sale of the land of their debtors, a decree is made with their consent for the sale, but the sale made is set aside, and the land rented out. After this, one of the debtors dies intestate, leaving heirs. Then another decree is made, reviving the suit against his administrator, and directing a scire facias against the heirs; and with the consent of the parties before the court, commissioners are directed to execute the previous decree of sale. They sell and the sale is confirmed, and the purchase money being paid a conveyance is ordered and made, and this is confirmed. These decrees and the sale having been made when the heirs were not before the court, the decrees are erroneous, and these and the sale must be set aside. Sexton *v.* Crockett, 23 Gratt. 857.

Lessees.—When proceedings are had to sell the fee in land, it is generally not necessary to make the lessee of the land a party to the suit. Chapman *v.* Pittsburgh, etc., R. Co., 18 W. Va. 184.

Pendente Lite Purchaser.—Pendente lite purchasers need not be made parties. Where judgments are docketed or deeds of trust recorded, or liens otherwise acquired, and a chancery suit to enforce same is pending, there need be no notice of the pendency of such chancery suit, under § 13, ch. 139, W. Va. Code, 1891, to bind purchasers purchasing after the docketing of such judgment or recordation of such deeds of trust or lien. They are pendente lite purchasers, under the common-law rule. Shumate *v.* Crockett, 43 W. Va. 491, 27 S. E. 240.

Whilst suit is pending the purchaser conveys the property in trust to secure a debt. The cestuis que trust are pendente lite purchasers, and are not necessary parties. Goddin *v.* Vaughn, 14 Gratt. 102, 103.

D. REMOVAL OF CLOUD FROM TITLE.

See ante, "Determination of Existence, Amounts and Priorities of Liens," IV, B.

1. Necessity.

The general rule undoubtedly is, that before a sale is decreed, any cloud on the title, or any impediment of any kind to a fair sale, ought to be removed, as far as practicable to do so, in order that the land may be sold to the best advantage. Thomas *v.* Farmers' Nat. Bank, 86 Va. 291, 9 S. E. 1122; Horton *v.* Bond, 28 Gratt. 815; Rossett *v.* Fisher, 11 Gratt. 492; Terry *v.* Fitzgerald, 32 Gratt. 843; Brown *v.* Lawson, 86 Va. 284, 9 S. E. 1014; Alexander *v.* Howe, 85 Va. 198, 7 S. E. 248; Schultz *v.* Hansbrough, 33 Gratt. 576; Lane *v.* Tidball, Gilm. 130; Hoge *v.* Junkin, 79 Va. 220; Peers *v.* Barnett, 12 Gratt. 410, 416; Gay *v.* Hancock, 1 Rand. 72; Miller *v.* Argyle. 5 Leigh 460. See the title QUIETING TITLE.

A decree of sale without first removing a cloud from the title, and adjusting and settling rights in dispute, tends to a sacrifice of the property, as to creditors, by discouraging them from bidding, when they probably would have bid for the protection of their own interest, if the rights of all parties had been previously ascertained, and fixed with reasonable certainty. Schultz v. Hansbrough, 33 Gratt. 576; Hoge v. Junkin, 79 Va. 220.

2. What Constitutes Cloud or Impediment.

a. In General.

What is such a cloud or impediment as ought to be removed before the decree of sale, must be determined upon the circumstances of each particular case. Thomas v. Farmers' Nat. Bank, 86 Va. 291, 9 S. E. 1122.

b. Undivided Interest.

In General.—Because the sale of an undivided interest in one case would result in a sacrifice, it does not follow that such must necessarily be the result in every similar case, and, therefore, no inflexible rule on the subject can be laid down. Thomas v. Farmers' Nat. Bank, 86 Va. 291, 9 S. E. 1122.

There is no absolute rule which forbids a sale of undivided interest in land in a suit brought to subject such land to the payment of judgment liens, before partition is made. The court, however, must exercise in every such case a sound discretion, having a due regard to the interests of all concerned. Thomas v. Farmers' Nat. Bank, 86 Va. 291, 9 S. E. 1122.

Sale was made of an undivided interest in land before partition, such sale was held not to be erroneous where no objection was made to the decree of sale when the decree was entered, or at any time before the sale was made, and where there is nothing to show that the appellant was prejudiced by the sale. Thomas v. Farmers' Nat. Bank, 86 Va. 291, 9 S. E. 1122.

Heir's Interest in Ancestor's Land before Settlement of Administrator.— It is error to decree a sale of an heir's interest in his ancestor's land, before a settlement has been made of the ad-ministrator's accounts. Where there are several heirs, the failure to direct such an account is contrary to the established rule in such cases. Bowden v. Parrish, 86 Va. 67, 9 S. E. 616; Hoge v. Junkin, 79 Va. 220.

c. Unlawful Detainer Pending to Determine Claim against Property.

In a suit to sell certain lands to satisfy judgment liens, answer is filed and treated as a petition whereby it was averred that a portion of the land was in the possession of H.; that unlawful detainer was pending against him to recover said portion; that the claim of H. constituted a cloud upon the title to a portion of the land, and, therefore, no sale could be ordered until the action of unlawful detainer, which was brought to remove this cloud, had been decided; and that the debtor was in a condition to effect a desirable private sale. It was held, that such case was not affected by the rule that a court of chancery ought not to make a sale of land to pay debts, before the title is cleared up, as far as it is practicable to do so, for independently of the principle that a judgment in an action of unlawful detainer settles nothing, even as between the parties, in regard to the title, the vague allegations of the petition filed in the court below show no ground for delaying the sale, and that therefore the unlawful detainer, seeming to be a mere contrivance for delay, the court will not stay the sale. Brown v. Lawson, 36 W. Va. 284, 9 S. E. 1014.

d. Mere Equitable Title.

As a general rule, the sale of mere equitable titles ought not to be decreed, since such sales lead to sacrifices, as bidders must purchase in a state of doubt and uncertainty, altogether unpropitious to a fair and advantageous sale. Goare v. Beuhring, 6 Leigh 585.

If a decree for sale of the land be proper, a court of equity should first direct the legal title to be perfected and then decree a sale of that. Goare v. Beuhring, 6 Leigh 585.

3. Inquiry as to Condition of Title.

a. English Practice.

According to the English practice, either party may have the report of a commissioner upon the title, and there is great advantage in this practice, because there the commissioners are men learned in the law and thoroughly conversant with such questions. Thomas v. Davidson, 76 Va. 338.

b. Virginia Rule.

But in Virginia the rule is not universal, and a reference to a commissioner is often refused where the facts are all before the court, and the only effect would be to burden the parties with unnecessary costs. There is no settled rule of practice in this state on the subject. A reference to a commissioner may be very proper, and is often had where the title is doubtful and obscure, or depending upon matters in pais. But when the court is in full possession of all the evidence, no possible advantage can result from an enquiry by a commissioner. Thomas v. Davidson, 76 Va. 338; Goddin v. Vaughn, 14 Gratt. 102, 128.

The discretion of the chancery court in allowing parties time to perfect their titles by curing defects and removing incumbrances is constantly exercised where no unusual delay ensues or loss to the purchaser occurs. And this is more especially true where the sale is made under the sanction of the court itself. The principles which govern in this class of cases are fully discussed in Young v. McClung, 9 Gratt. 336, and in Daniel v. Leitch, 13 Gratt. 195, and in other decisions of this court. Thomas v. Davidson, 76 Va. 338.

"In the case before us, it is not suggested that any further information could have been obtained by further inquiry. All the evidence, which was almost exclusively documentary, was before the court. Upon this evidence, the court was certainly as competent to adjudicate the question of title as any commissioner would be, who might have been appointed. A report adverse to the title, it is fair to presume, would not have brought the learned judge to a different conclusion. A report favorable to it would only have subjected the parties to additional costs without any corresponding advantage. These considerations are sufficient to show that the court committed no error in refusing to refer the question of title to a commissioner." Thomas v. Davidson, 76 Va. 338.

E. ASSIGNMENT OF DOWER.

See the title DOWER, vol. 4, pp. 782, 819.

The dower right of the widow must be settled before decreeing sale of the real estate. Wilson v. Branch, 77 Va. 65.

Unless it is impossible to assign to a widow her dower in real estate in specie, a court of equity has no power, under its general jurisdiction, against her will, to decree a sale of the real estate and to provide her a compensation in money in lieu of her dower. White v. White, 16 Gratt. 264.

It is error to decree a sale of the land before the widow's dower is assigned to her in kind, or it is ascertained that it can not be so assigned, or a moneyed compensation to her in lieu of her dower has been ascertained. Simmons v. Lyles, 27 Gratt. 922.

A widow is entitled, as against creditors of her husband, by lien created since her marriage, to have her dower in his real estate assigned in kind, if it can be done, without regard to its effect upon the interest of his creditors. If from the nature of the property, or of the husband's interest in it, the dower can not be assigned in kind, the court may sell the whole property, and make to her a moneyed compensation. Simmons v. Lyles, 27 Gratt. 922.

An infant feme covert, and her husband, in 1845, granted her "maiden land"—half of "Cedar Lawn"—to G., who next day conveyed it to the husband, who owned the other half. In 1876 he and she conveyed the whole in trust to secure his debt. He died in October, 1877. His will was probated in December, 1878. In March, 1879, B. and others filed a creditor's bill to settle his estate and subject his lands to pay his debts. In April, 1879, she answered, renouncing her husband's will, demanding dower in his lands, disaffirming her deed of 1845 as void by reason of her then infancy, and denying she had ever in any way ratified it. An account showed that the trust debt, amounting to $1,532.89 was the only debt paramount to dower. The fee simple value of "Cedar Lawn" was $2,750. The court below decreed that she had ratified the deed of 1845, when free from the disability of infancy, and without assigning dower, but reserving right to make all orders to protect the right of dower, decreed the sale of the whole tract to pay her husband's debts. On appeal here, held, the decree of sale without previous assignment of dower in kind, if practicable, or if impracticable, by compensation, was premature and erroneous. Wilson v. Branch, 77 Va. 65.

F. INQUIRY INTO AND PROVISION FOR PROTECTION OF INTEREST OF TENANT.

Decree for sale of land to satisfy judgment, without inquiring into and protecting the interest of tenant in possession under a lease made prior to the judgment, is erroneous. Moore v. Bruce, 85 Va. 139, 7 S. E. 195.

V. Decree or Order of Sale.

A. NECESSITY.

A decree or order of court is absolutely necessary to the validity of a judicial sale. Rorer on Judicial Sales, § 489. First Nat. Bank v. Hyer, 46 W. Va. 13, 32 S. E. 1000; Estill v. McClintic, 11 W. Va. 399.

"A sale without order of court is not a mere irregularity, which must be objected to by some proceeding in the court where the decree ought to have been sought and granted, and which, if not so objected to, is waived or ratified. It is a proceeding without any legal support. A conveyance in pursuance of it has no force whatever. It may be shown to be void when collaterally attacked. In fact, no attack, collateral or otherwise, may be made." Ror. on Judicial Sales, § 489. First Nat. Bank v. Hyer, 46 W. Va. 13, 32 S. E. 1000.

B. JURISDICTION TO DECREE SALE.

1. Court May Decree Sale of Property in Any Part of State.

A court, in a suit pending properly therein, may make a decree or order for the sale of property in any part of the state. Va. Code, 1904, § 3397; W. Va. Code, 1899, ch. 132, § 1; Sommerville v. Sommerville, 26 W. Va. 484; Rohrer v. Travers, 11 W. Va. 146; Dickinson v. Clement, 87 Va. 41, 12 S. E. 105.

2. Jurisdiction of Court to Decree Sale of Land in Another State.

"A Virginia court has no jurisdiction over land in another state, and can not fly by its order of sale or decree, or by deed of commissioners (merely as such) pass the title to such land. McLaurin v. Salmons, 11 B. Monroe, 96. The court of one state has no power over land in another, except through the person of its owner; it can not act for him in making a conveyance through a mere commissioner but it may compel the owner himself to convey the land, and such conveyance will be effectual in another state as if made at his own mere will." 1 Rob. Prac. 342; Wilson v. Braden, 48 W. Va. 196, 36 S. E. 367. See the titles CONFLICT OF LAWS, vol. 3, p. 100; FOREIGN JUDGMENTS, vol. 6, p. 308.

Even if a foreign court had the land and parties before it, that court could not itself sell, or by a commissioner, trustee or other agent sell, land in Virginia, as no state can give its laws force outside of its territory, nor can the decree of its courts operate upon land outside of it. Wilson *v.* Braden, 48 W. Va. 196, 36 S. E. 367; Pennoyer *v.* Neff, 95 U. S. 714, 722.

It is well settled that the courts of this state are without jurisdiction to sell and convey land situated beyond the limits of the state. Gibson *v.* Burgess, 82 Va. 650; Poindexter *v.* Burwell, 82 Va. 507; Wimer *v.* Wimer, 82 Va. 890, 5 S. E. 536.

"Lands lying in one state can not be reached or sold under an order, license, or decree of a court of another and different state. The jurisdiction is local. The lex loci rei sitæ governs." Rorer on Judicial Sales, § 39. Poindexter *v.* Burwell, 82 Va. 507, 514.

C. MUST CONFORM TO SALE PRAYED FOR IN PETITION.

The decree of the chancellor must be construed to conform to the sale prayed for in the petition, and a sale beyond that is not rendered valid by final ratification. Freem. Jud. Sales, § 9. Shriver *v.* Lynn, 2 How. 43. More so where the decree prohibits the sale. First Nat. Bank *v.* Hyer, 46 W. Va. 13, 32 S. E. 1000.

D. FACTS NECESSARY TO WARRANT DECREE FOR SALE.

In General.—It is not necessary that the facts necessary to warrant a decree for sale should appear from the report of commissioners or by the depositions of witnesses. It is sufficient if the facts appearing in the record reasonably warrant the decree of sale; and this especially when the proceeding is to defeat the title of an innocent purchaser. Zirkle *v.* McCue, 26 Gratt. 517.

Necessity That Plaintiff Retain Claim till Rendition of Decree.—Where a sale is made by the court in the exercise of its general jurisdiction in a creditor's suit, it makes no difference that when the decree of sale is entered, the plaintiff by whom the suit was brought has parted with his claims against the defendant, and is no longer interested in the suit, for when a general account is ordered in a creditor's suit, it is for the benefit of all the creditors, and the case thereupon ceases to be under the control of the party who instituted it. Karn *v.* Rorer Iron Co., 86 Va. 754, 11 S. E. 431; Simmons *v.* Lyles, 27 Gratt. 922; Piedmont, etc., Life Ins. Co. *v.* Maury, 75 Va. 508.

E. DECREE OF SALE NOT NULLIFIED BY SUBSEQUENT ORDER TO RENT.

In November, 1860, M. was appointed a commissioner to sell infant's land, on a credit of six, twelve, eighteen and twenty-four months. M. reports, that after three trials he had failed to sell, and suggests that it be rented out for the present; and in June, 1861, there is an order that M. be authorized to rent out the land for such time, and on such terms as he might think judicious; and he rents it out for that and the next year. In March, 1863, M. reports that he in that month sold the land on the terms of the decree, to S. and D. and the report is confirmed; and he is directed to collect the purchase money as it falls due, and pay it to the receiver of the court, if the parties entitled decline to receive it. Held, the decree of November, 1860, for the sale of the land, continued in force, notwithstanding the order of June, 1861, for renting it, and the commissioner had authority to sell in March, 1863. Dixon *v.* McCue, 21 Gratt. 373.

F. ORDER OF SALE IN DECREE ENTERING UP AWARD.

It is error for the court to order the sale of real estate in a decree entering up an award as the decree of the court, when the same was not provided for or directed by the award. Stevenson *v.* Walker, 5 W. Va. 427. See the title ARBITRATION AND AWARD, vol. 1, p. 687.

G. NECESSITY THAT DECREE FIX AMOUNT AND PRIORITY OF LIENS, ETC.

1. Amount and Priority.

After the commissioner makes his report as to the liens and their respective amounts and priorities, the court should do more than merely confirm such report. It should by its decree definitely fix, and show on its face the liens, their amounts, their priorities, and thus make these matters legally certain. Hull v. Hull, 35 W. Va. 155, 13 S. E. 49; Bank v. Wilson, 25 W. Va. 242; McCleary v. Grantham, 29 W. Va. 301, 11 S. E. 949; Marling v. Robrecht, 13 W. Va. 440.

The decree itself must fix and show upon its face the amounts and priorities of the liens before a sale of the property is ordered. Anderson v. Nagle, 12 W. Va. 98; Rohrer v. Travers, 11 W. Va. 146.

Although the commissioner ascertains the amounts and legal priorities of the liens in his report, and the court in its decree of sale confirm that report, thus perhaps sufficiently declaring the amount of these liens and their respective priorities, yet it is best and safest to declare on the face of the decree the amounts and respective priorities of the several judgments, or other liens, reported by the commissioner; so that, if the report of the commissioner should become lost or destroyed, the amount of the lien, debts, and their respective priorities, as determined by the court, may still be seen and known by the record. Marling v. Robrecht, 13 W. Va. 440.

A decree in a suit brought by a judgment creditor should upon its face show the amount and priority of every debt against the land of the judgment debtor. Kanawha Valley Bank v. Wilson, 25 W. Va. 242.

It is a well-settled rule that where there are conflicting claims to priority of payment out of the proceeds of land about to be sold to satisfy the liens upon it, the court in order to prevent the danger of sacrificing the property by discouraging the creditors from bidding as they probably might if their right to satisfaction of their debts and the order in which they were to be paid out of the property, were previously ascertained, should declare the order of payment before it decrees sale to be made. Cole v. McRae, 6 Rand. 644; Buchanan v. Clark, 10 Gratt. 164. It is therefore not sufficient that the court should direct the fund to be paid into court and should declare the priorities afterwards. The purpose for which it is done requires that it should precede the sale. Iaege v. Bossieux, 15 Gratt. 83.

A decree in a suit brought by a judgment creditor, that the judgment debtor (naming him) "do pay to the complainant and other judgment and trust creditors of said debtor the several sums ascertained to be due them respectively by the report of the commissioner contained on pages 33 and 34 of his report," is erroneous. Kanawha Valley Bank v. Wilson, 25 W. Va. 242; Hull v. Hull, 35 W. Va. 155, 13 S. E. 49; Hart v. Hart, 31 W. Va. 688, 8 S. E. 562.

Thus a decree which simply confirms a commissioner's report of debts, and directs a sale of lands therefor in default of payment, though that report specifies the debts and priorities, is erroneous, because the decree does not itself adjudicate and declare what debts are to be paid, and fix their order and priority as to the lands to be sold therefor. Hull v. Hull, 35 W. Va. 155, 13 S. E. 49.

If in a suit to enforce liens there has been a commissioner's report, showing the lands owned by the debtor, the nature, amounts, and priorities of the liens thereon, which has been confirmed, there is entered a decree "that unless the debts therein audited are paid within sixty days from the rising of the court by the debtor (naming him) then the lands of said debtor, in said report named, shall all be severally sold to pay the liens on the same in the order of their priority, as set out in said report," without any further statement or declaration therein, specifying the sums to be paid to the several creditors, the parcels of land on which they are chargeable, and the order of priority in which the proceeds of the sales of the several parcels of land shall be applied, such decree is erroneous, and for that cause will be reversed, unless the same from the commissioner's report and the face of the decree can be safely amended; in which case, it will be so amended in the appellate court, and when so amended, will be affirmed. McCleary v. Grantham, 29 W. Va. 301, 11 S. E. 949.

Where there are conflicting claims to priority of payment out of proceeds of land about to be sold to satisfy the liens upon it, the court, in order to prevent the danger of sacrificing the property by discouraging creditors from bidding, as they probably might if their right to satisfaction of their debts and the order in which they were to be paid out of the property were not previously ascertained, should declare the order of payment before it decrees the sale to be made. Reusens v. Lawson, 96 Va. 285, 31 S. E. 528; Iaege v. Bossieux, 15 Gratt. 83, 103.

2. What Debts to Be Paid.

The decree should declare on its face what particular debts shall be paid. Hull v. Hull, 35 W. Va. 155, 13 S. E. 49; McCleary v. Grantham, 29 W. Va. 301, 11 S. E. 949.

Thus, a decree which does not declare on its face what particular debts shall be paid or fix their order, but simply decrees that, "unless the defendants, the administrator and heirs of the late F. H. Hull, deceased, or some one for them, shall within sixty days from the raising of this court, pay to the special receiver in these causes the several debts reported by Commissioner Warwick, against the estate of F. H. Hull, deceased, the lands should be sold," is erroneous under the case of Kanawha Valley Bank v. Wilson, 25 W. Va. 242. Hull v. Hull, 35 W. Va. 155, 13 S. E. 49.

As Judge Wood very properly said in the opinion in the case of Kanawha Valley Bank v. Wilson, 25 W. Va. 242: "Upon its face it (the decree) neither ascertains the amount or priority of any debt, or the person to whom the same is to be paid;" "and as he said in that case I say in this, that while the decree does refer to the report for the debts to be paid, that leaves every creditor to determine for himself, at his peril, the amount decreed him. I add that this report' is complicated. A given debt is a specific lien on certain lands, and a general charge on others; another debt is a specific lien on certain lands and a general charge on others; and other debts general charges. The special commissioner and parties are to construe this report for themselves, at their peril, and fix the amounts of liens, their order, and what lands they bind; whereas, the decree should make these matters legally certain. Hull v. Hull, 35 W. Va. 155, 13 S. E. 49.

3. Person to Whom Payable.

A decree in a suit brought by a judgment debtor should not only show upon its face the amount and priority of every debt against the land of the judgment debtor, but should also show the person to whom the same is payable. Kanawha Valley Bank v. Wilson, 25 W. Va. 242; Hull v. Hull, 35 W. Va. 155, 13 S. E. 49; Hart v. Hart, 31 W. Va. 688, 8 S. E. 562; McCleary v. Grantham, 29 W. Va. 301, 11 S. E. 949.

4. Out of What Fund Payable.

The decree should also show upon its face in addition to the amount and priority of every debt against the land of the judgment debtor, the fund out of which each debt is entitled to be paid. i. e., what lands are bound. Kanawha Valley Bank v. Wilson, 25 W. Va. 242;

Hull *v.* Hull, 35 W. Va. 155, 13 S. E. 49; Hart *v.* Hart, 31 W. Va. 688, 8 S. E. 562; McCleary *v.* Grantham, 29 W. Va. 301, 11 S. E. 949.

If in a suit to enforce liens it clearly appears that one of the tracts of land charged with the liens of the several judgments against such debtor is also charged with a specific lien exceeding in amount the value thereof, having priority over all other liens thereon, the court may properly decree the sale of other lands of the debtor, without decreeing a sale of the tract charged with such specific lien. McCleary *v.* Grantham, 29 W. Va. 301, 11 S. E. 949.

H. DEBTS MUST BE DECREED TO CREDITORS.

The court must decree to the several creditors the debts ascertained by the commissioner's report to be due to them, respectively. Having ascertained the debts due to each creditor, it is error where there is nothing decreed to be paid to any of them. Hart *v.* Hart, 31 W. Va. 688, 8 S. E. 562; McCleary *v.* Grantham, 29 W. Va. 301, 11 S. E. 949.

"In like manner it wholly fails to decree to the several creditors of the decedent the debts ascertained by the commissioner's report to be due to them, respectively. Having ascertained the debts to each, there is nothing decreed to be paid to any of them. In Bank *v.* Wilson, 25 W. Va. 242, the commissioner's report, as in this case, ascertained and reported the amount and priority of the several liens on the land of the defendant. The decree concluded as follows: 'It is further adjudged, ordered, and decreed that unless the defendant, A. H. Wilson, or some one for him, do, within ninety days from this date, pay to the complainant, and other judgment or trust creditors of said Wilson, the several sums ascertained to be due them, respectively, by the report of said (commissioner) Gallaher, and contained on pages 33 and 34 of said report, and the

costs of this suit, then,' etc. In that case this court said that 'such a decree leaves every creditor to determine for himself, at his peril, the amount intended to be decreed to him. As this decree must for other errors therein be reversed, it is not necessary to decide whether this error in the decree would of itself be sufficient to reverse the same; but we are of opinion that the decree should upon the face thereof show the amount and priority of the several debts against Wilson, the person to whom each is payable, and the property or fund out of which the debt is entitled to be paid;' and accordingly this court held 'that a decree that the judgment debtor (naming him) do pay to the complainant, and other judgment and trust creditors of the said debtor, the several sums ascertained to be due to them, respectively, by the report of the commissioner contained on pages 33 and 34 of his report, is erroneous.' In the case in judgment the decree falls far short of the accuracy and precision of the terms of the decree in Kanawha Valley Bank *v.* Wilson, 25 W. Va. 242; and as we held in that case such decree was erroneous, so, for much stronger reasons, we must hold the said decree in this case, and sufficient to reverse the same, if there was no other error in the record." Hart *v.* Hart, 31 W. Va. 688, 8 S. E. 562.

I. PARTICULAR DIRECTIONS IN DECREE.

1. As to Time to Redeem.

It is error to decree a sale of land to satisfy a debt, without giving the debtor some time in which to redeem it by paying the amount charged upon it before sale. King *v.* Burdett, 44 W. Va. 561, 562, 29 S. E. 1010; Rohrer *v.* Travers, 11 W. Va. 146; Rose *v.* Brown, 11 W. Va. 122, 123; Harkins *v.* Forsyth, 11 Leigh 294; Pecks *v.* Chambers, 8 W. Va. 210; Wiley *v.* Mahood, 10 W. Va. 206; Gross *v* Pearcy, 2 Pat. & H. 493; Kyles *v.* Tait, 6 Gratt. 44; Speidel *v.*

Schlosser, 13 W. Va. 686, 702; Crawford v. Weller, 23 Gratt. 835, 836; Long v. Weller, 29 Gratt. 347; Hart v. Hart, 31 W. Va. 688, 8 S. E. 562; McDearman v. Robertson, Va. Law. J. 1879, p. 175; Parsons v. Thornburg, 17 W. Va. 356; Whitehead v. Bradley, 87 Va. 676, 13 S. E. 195; Blair v. Core, 20 W. Va. 265; Strayer v. Long, 89 Va. 471, 16 S. E. 357; Buster v. Holland, 27 W. Va. 510. See the title MORTGAGES AND DEEDS OF TRUST.

It is error to decree a sale of land for debt without giving a reasonable time for payment before sale. The length of time is within the sound discretion of the court. King v. Burdett, 44 W. Va. 561, 29 S. E. 1010.

The answer to the objection, that the time (twenty days) given by the decree for the redemption of the property from the lien is too short, is, that this is a matter resting in the sound discretion of the court under all the circumstances, and this court will presume that the discretion has been properly exercised, where, as in this case, no objection was made in the court below, and no extension asked for of the time allowed for redemption. Pairo v. Bethell, 75 Va. 825; Tucker, J., in Harkins v. Forsyth, 11 Leigh 294, 300; Standard, J., in Manns v. Flinn, 10 Leigh 93, 109; Green's Appendix to Wythe's Reports, 414, note 4, and cases there cited.

A decree in a creditor's suit, which directs a sale of land, but fails to give the defendant a day in which to pay the sums decreed against him, will not be set aside for that reason, where the decree has been suspended for sixty days at the instance of the defendant, in order to enable him to apply for an appeal to the supreme court of appeals. He has had a day in which he could have paid, if he desired, although it was not specially designated for that purpose. Ashworth v. Tramwell, 102 Va. 852, 47 S. E. 1011.

"Appellants complain that no day was given before sale to redeem the land from sale. As an original question, I would think that, as the debt was long past due, it would be no error not to give further time for payment before sale; but we must bow to authority holding such a provision in a decree necessary. Rohrer v. Travers, 11 W. Va. 146. I would think that, as the decree required four weeks' publication before sale, that would be a reasonable day; but Rose v. Brown, 11 W. Va. 122, 123, holds that not sufficient, but that there must be an additional indulgence given. The time of indulgence given is within the sound discretion of the court. Harkins v. Forsyth, 11 Leigh 294. It seems a violation of the rights of the creditor, but courts of equity have long followed this practice." King v. Burdett, 44 W. Va. 561, 29 S. E. 1010.

It is error to decree a sale of real estate without giving the defendant a day to redeem the property by paying the amount charged therein; and it is not giving a day to redeem to postpone the time in the decree for the property to be advertised and sold. Rose v. Brown, 11 W. Va. 122.

It is not per se error to decree a sale of land to enforce judgment liens without giving the debtor time to redeem, as in the foreclosure of mortgages, though such a practice ought in general to be pursued, but if the debtor does not show he has sustained any damage by the failure to do it, it is not ground for setting aside the sale. Crawford v. Weller, 23 Gratt. 835, 836.

The cases in which the heirs and devisees should have a day to pay the amount decreed against the testator's estate before a decree of sale is made of the real estate, are cases where the property is covered by a lien, such as a mortgage or a deed of trust, or other security for a debt. McDearman v. Robertson, Va. Law J. 1879, p. 175; Long v. Weller, 29 Gratt. 347; Hart v. Hart, 31 W. Va. 688, 8 S. E. 562. But where there is no lien of any kind but the suit to subject the lands of the decedent to the payment of a fiduciary debt, the personal estate being exhausted, it was not necessary to give the heirs and devisees a day to pay in the decree. McDearman v. Robertson, Va. Law J. 1879, p. 175.

Where land is resold for the failure of the purchaser to pay the purchase money, it is error to decree such resale without giving the purchaser a day to redeem. Long v. Weller, 29 Gratt. 347; Whitehead v. Bradley, 87 Va. 676, 13 S. E. 195.

While it is the general rule, that when the court directs the sale of land, it shall first ascertain the amounts of the lien debts, and their respective priorities and give a day for payment in the decree, still this rule is not so fundamental in its requirements as to prevent the parties to the suit who are interested in its enforcement from dispensing therewith by consent. Parsons v. Thornburg, 17 W. Va. 356.

Where the decree allows ninety days for redemption, and the commissioners advertise before the expiration of that period, but one hundred and three days elapsed before the sale, and neither the debtor nor his creditors could have been benefited by further delay, it was held, that this was a sufficient compliance with the decree. Strayer v. Long, 89 Va. 471, 16 S. E. 357.

As to time to redeem, when suit is brought to foreclose a mortgage lien, or to sell land under a deed of trust, see the title MORTGAGES AND DEEDS OF TRUST.

2. As to Property to Be Sold.

The decree should direct what land is to be sold. First Nat. Bank v. Hyer, 46 W. Va. 13, 32 S. E. 1000; Barger v. Buckland, 28 Gratt. 850.

Only such property can be sold at a judicial sale, as is directed by the decree or order to be sold. Rorer on Judicial Sales, § 489. First Nat. Bank v. Hyer, 46 W. Va. 13, 32 S. E. 1000.

A sale of a parcel of land in addition to that described in the decree is void. First Nat. Bank v. Hyer, 46 W. Va. 13, 32 S. E. 1000.

A court, having jurisdiction to sell land, reserves from sale a sawmill thereon. Though there is nothing in the record to warrant the reservation, it is not void, but voidable only by appeal, and can not be collaterally assailed. First Nat. Bank v. Hyer, 46 W. Va. 13, 32 S. E. 1000.

The decree directed the sale of the land in the bill and proceedings mentioned, or so much thereof as might suffice to satisfy the purposes of the decree. It was alleged that the court erred in said decree, because it did not specify in exact terms the land to be sold, but used such vague and indefinite terms with regard to it, that it was within the power or caprice of the commissioners to sell all the lands mentioned in the trust deed. The court held, that said decree was not erroneous; that the land was described with sufficient certainty in the bills, and the decree could be made certain by reference to the bills under the maxim, "that is certain which may be made certain." Barger v. Buckland, 28 Gratt. 850.

3. As to Order of Subjecting Property to Sale.

See W. Va. Code, 1899, ch. 139, § 8.

As to subjecting land in the inverse order of alienation, see the title MARSHALING ASSETS AND SECURITIES.

Circuit courts are bound to obey the decrees of this court in all cases. Where, on appeal, this court prescribes the order in which properties must be sold when decree for sale is made, the circuit court, in its decree of sale, must conform to that prescription; otherwise its decree will be reversed for such nonconformance. Strayer v. Long, 83 Va. 715, 3 S. E. 372.

H. files his bill to enforce his and the liens of other judgment creditors on the lands of S. An account of the liens and lands is taken. Report shows numerous liens and parcels of land. H.'s judgment was a lien on all the lands, and a vendor's lien on the parcel first aliened by S., viz., to R. There were, also, three deeds of trust of different dates; the first and third securing each one debt on one parcel; and the second securing on all the lands numerous debts, as well judgments as debts not reduced to judgments. But this second trust deed was not enforceable until May 3d, 1882. Besides H.'s, there was no lien on R.'s parcel. Exceptions to report being overruled, the circuit court decreed that, unless within sixty days, S. paid the costs of the suit, the judgment of H. and the other judgments appearing from the report to be chargeable on the lands of S., then commissioners, should sell so much of the lands of S., described in the report, as might be necessary to pay said costs and judgments, but should sell first so much of the land conveyed by S. to R. as might be necessary to pay said costs and the judgment of H.; and then sell so much of the other lands of S. as might be necessary to pay the balance (if any) of the judgment of H. and the other judgments chargeable thereon as set forth in the report. On appeal by defendants, held: By the plain meaning of the language of the decree, R. could only prevent the sale of his land under it by the payment of all the judgments reported by the master and all the costs of the suit. Under the circumstances of this case, any decree requiring and directing the sale of R.'s land, unless he paid the costs of the suit and all of the judgments, would be erroneous. Shultz *v.* Hansbrough, 76 Va. 817.

4. As to Advertisement.

See post, "Advertisement or Notice of Sale," VI.

5. As to Time of Sale.

See post, "Time," VII, A, 1.

6. As to Place of Sale.

See post, "Place," VII, A, 2.

7. As to Execution of Bond by Commissioner before Sale.

See post, "Decree Must Direct Bond to Be Given," VII, B, 2, g, (2), (b).

8. As to Terms of Sale.

See post, "Terms," VII, D.

9. As to Manner of Sale.

See post, "Manner of Sale," VII, C.

VI. Advertisement or Notice of Sale.

A. UNDER PROVISIONS OF VIRGINIA CODE.

See Va. Code, 1904, §§ 3398, 3399.

As to requirement that clerk's certificate of execution of commissioner's bond shall be appended to the advertisement, see post, "Certificate or Copy Appended to Advertisement," VII, B, 2, g, (1), (d), cc.

B. UNDER PROVISIONS OF WEST VIRGINIA CODE.

1. Necessity.

Where Real Estate Valued at Five Hundred Dollars or More.—Section 1, ch. 151, the acts of West Virginia, 1872-73, requires "that whenever a court shall hereafter decree the sale of real estate, if it appear to the court, that such real estate is of the value of five hundred dollars or more, it shall prescribe in the decree, that such sale, shall be advertised in a newspaper by the commissioner or person appointed to make the sale." W. Va. Code, 1899, ch. 132, § 1. Duncan *v.* Custard, 24 W. Va. 730.

The statute is mandatory, and it is error not to require the land to be so advertised, if it appears to the court that its value was over $500. Duncan *v.* Custard, 24 W. Va. 730.

It was held, to be error for the court in its decree not to direct the commissioner to advertise the sale at all, where it appeared from the record that the court only ordered one tract of land to be sold to pay about $2,000 of debts. Duncan *v.* Custard, 24 W. Va. 730.

If the debtor wishes to avoid the expense of advertising in a newspaper, he should by affidavit or otherwise satisfy the court that the property is not worth $500. Duncan *v.* Custard, 24 W. Va. 730.

Where Value of Real Estate Less than Five Hundred Dollars.—Section 1, ch. 132, W. Va. Code, 1899, provides that nothing therein shall be construed to limit the power of the court to direct sales of lands to be advertised in newspapers where the value may be less than five hundred dollars.

2. Presumption of Advertisement.

When a report of a judicial sale states that the sale was made "after advertising the sale in the manner and for the time required by the said order," it will be taken that the publication and posting of notice of sale required by the court's order were made, unless the contrary appear. Laidley *v.* Jasper, 49 W. Va. 526, 39 S. E. 169.

3. Manner of Advertisement.
a. In General.

The decree should direct on its face how the sale should be advertised. Beaty *v.* Veon, 18 W. Va. 291.

Thus, it is not sufficient, where the decree declared that, "said sale shall be at the courthouse of this county, on some courtday after being advertised according to law." Beaty *v.* Veon, 18 W. Va. 291.

b. Newspaper.
(1) In General.

See ante, "Necessity," VI, B, 1.

(2) Particular Newspaper.

Newspaper Published in County Where Real Estate Situated.—The sale shall always be advertised in a newspaper published in the county, if one be published therein, where the real estate to be sold is situated. W. Va. Code, 1899, ch. 132, § 1; Duncan *v.* Custard, 24 W. Va. 730.

Newspaper Having General Circulation in County.—Section 1, ch. 132, W. Va. Code, 1899, provides that nothing therein shall be construed to limit the power of the court to advertise the sale in some newspaper having a general circulation in the county, where no newspaper is published in the county where the real estate to be sold is situated.

Newspaper in Judicial Circuit.—If the newspaper published in the county refuse to do the work at the price prescribed by statute, then it shall be lawful to publish the advertisement in any newspaper in the judicial circuit. W. Va. Code, 1899, ch. 132, § 1.

c. Front Door of Courthouse and Other Public Places.

Where no paper in the judicial circuit will publish the advertisement at the price prescribed by statute, it shall be lawful to publish the same at the front door of the courthouse of the county and in three other places near the land to be sold. W. Va. Code, 1899, ch. 132, § 1.

4. Duration of Advertisement.

The decree should direct on its face, the time for which the sale should be advertised or published. Beaty *v.* Veon, 18 W. Va. 291.

5. Contents of Advertisement.

In the advertisement the commissioner shall state the time, terms and place of sale, together with a description of the property to be sold. W. Va. Code, 1899, ch. 132, § 1a. Maxwell *v.* Burbridge, 44 W. Va. 248, 28 S. E. 702.

West Virginia Code, 1899, ch. 132, § 1a, provides that a commissioner appointed by a decree to sell shall, in his advertisement, state the time, terms, and place of sale, together with a description of the property to be sold; and it is not necessary to place such requirement in the decree. Maxwell *v.* Burbridge, 44 W. Va. 248, 28 S. E. 702.

6. Appending Certificate of Execution of Commissioner's Bond to Advertisement.

See post, "Certificate as to Execution of Bond," VII, B, 2, g, (1), (d).

7. Effect of Clerical Error in Notice.

A mere clerical error, self-corrective,

in a notice of a judicial sale, will not affect it. Long *v.* Perine, 44 W. Va. 243, 28 S. E. 701.

Thus, where the sale notice fixed the day of sale for the 9th of January, 1996, it is a mere clerical error, which any court would correct. No one would suppose that the sale was intended to be postponed a century, and would know that 1896 was meant. Long *v.* Perine, 44 W. Va. 243, 28 S. E. 701.

8. Cost of Advertisement.

No more than five dollars shall be paid for any advertisement that does not exceed two inches square of space for the four consecutive insertions. W. Va. Code, 1899, ch. 132, § 1.

VII. The Sale.

A. TIME AND PLACE.

1. Time.

a. In General.

Where the court directs the time of sale, the directions must be adhered to. Long *v.* Perine, 41 W. Va. 314, 23 S. E. 611; Talley *v.* Starke, 6 Gratt. 339.

If the decree does not fix the time for sale, it is left to the sound discretion of the commissioner or officer making it. Rorer on Judicial Sales, § 38. Long *v.* Perine, 41 W. Va. 314, 23 S. E. 611.

However usual for a court in its decree for the sale of land to direct a sale on a courtday, or however proper, the failure to do so is not error, for there is no statute or other authority requiring such a provision. Long *v.* Perine, 41 W. Va. 314, 23 S. E. 611.

It is not proper in a decree of sale of land to direct that such sale shall be made "on some day fixed by law for judicial sales," there being no day fixed by law for judicial sales. But perhaps this may not be fatal to the decree. McClaskey *v.* O'Brien, 16 W. Va. 791.

b. Postponement.

It is the right of every party concerned or having all interest in property, when about to be sold at public auction, to have it offered for sale under such circumstances as afford an opportunity for fair competition amongst all who may be disposed to buy. Doubts about the identity or title of the subject to be sold may prevent prudent men from offering to buy, and are therefore enough to justify any one charged with the duty of making a sale, in postponing the sale until such doubts may be removed and the danger of sacrifice be avoided. See Rossett *v.* Fisher, 11 Gratt. 492; Goare *v.* Beuhring, 6 Leigh 585; 1 Lom. Dig. 425, top, 323 marg. Roberts *v.* Roberts, 13 Gratt. 639, 640.

Thus a sale of a tract of land should not be made by a commissioner under a decree of the chancery court, on a day so inclement that persons intending to be present and bid for a part of the land, are deterred from attending. Roberts *v.* Roberts, 13 Gratt. 639.

2. Place.

Where the court directs the place of sale, such directions must be adhered to. Long *v.* Perine, 41 W. Va. 314, 23 S. E. 611; Talley *v.* Starke, 6 Gratt. 339.

The decree directing the sale to be made upon the premises, the commissioner acts irregularly in making it at a different place; especially after advertising that it would be made on the premises. He should report to the court that it could not be made there for want of bidders, and obtain instructions for his future action. Talley *v.* Starke, 6 Gratt. 339.

A sale having been thus irregularly made, as the purchasers could not enforce their contracts, if resisted by the parties in the cause, they ought not to be compelled to perfect them if they object. Talley *v.* Starke, 6 Gratt. 339.

B. WHO MAY SELL.

1. Agent or Officer of Court.

A judicial sale being a sale made in a pending suit by order of and under the direction of the court, can only be conducted by some authorized agent or officer of the court. Terry v. Coles, 80 Va. 695; Alexander v. Howe, 85 Va. 198, 7 S. E. 248.

2. Special Commissioner.

a. In General.

The court may appoint a special commissioner to make a judicial sale. Va. Code, 1904, § 3397; W. Va. Code, 1899, ch. 132, § 1; Sommerville v. Sommerville, 26 W. Va. 484; Whitehead v. Bradley, 87 Va. 676, 13 S. E. 195; Hess v. Rader, 26 Gratt. 746; Tyler v. Toms, 75 Va. 116; Lloyd v. Erwin, 29 Gratt. 598; Martin v. Kester, 49 W. Va. 647, 39 S. E. 599; Washington Nat. Bldg., etc., Ass'n v. Westfall, 55 W. Va. 305, 47 S. E. 74; Klapneck v. Keltz, 50 W. Va. 331, 40 S. E. 570; Lehman v. Hinton, 44 W. Va. 1, 29 S. E. 984; Rohrer v. Travers, 11 W. Va. 146; Hall v. Hall, 12 W. Va. 1; Springston v. Morris, 47 W. Va. 50, 34 S. E. 766; Teel v. Yancey, 23 Gratt. 691.

In Virginia and West Virginia, a judicial sale is usually conducted by a special commissioner acting by and under the direction of the court. Terry v. Coles, 80 Va. 695; Brock v. Rice, 27 Gratt. 812; Stout v. Philippi Mfg., etc., Co., 41 W. Va. 339, 23 S. E. 571.

When two commissioners are appointed by a decree of a court of equity to sell land, a sale by one only is irregular. Gross v. Pearcy, 2 Pat. & H. 483.

On creditor's bill to enforce judgment and trust liens, sale is decreed to be made by three commissioners substituted for original sole trustee; no day is given debtor for redemption; a sale is made by two of the three, but in these respects not excepted to below. Held, the objections to the sale on those grounds are not well taken. Hansucker v. Walker, 76 Va. 753.

Where special commissioners are appointed under a decree of court to make sale of lands, and an unusual delay occurs on the part of such commissioners in carrying out said decree, and making their report, the court will ordinarily award a rule against such commissioners, requiring them to account for the delay, before removing them and appointing other commissioners to execute the decree. Connell v. Wilhelm, 36 W. Va. 598, 15 S. E. 245.

b. Necessity for Reappointment after Formation of State of West Virginia.

Special commissioners appointed by a court to make sale of property under a decree, not being public officers, it is not necessary that they should be reappointed after the formation of the state of West Virginia, before they were authorized to proceed to execute a decree in force at the formation of said state. Touching this point, the court, in delivering the opinion, said: "I have no knowledge of its having been done in any instance. The commissioners have been, and still are subject to the control and direction of the circuit court of Greenbrier county, in the cause in which they were appointed commissioners. By its order or decree in the cause, the court can remove them or restrict their powers or do whatever is necessary and proper for the purposes of the suit." Shields v. McClung, 6 W. Va. 79.

c. Office of Special Commissioner.

The office of a special commissioner under the statutes and rules of chancery practice of this state is the same in many cases as that of a receiver under the general chancery practice in England and in many of the states. Excluding that class of commissioners known as commissioners in chancery, whose duties are to take, state and report accounts, the only difference in the practice in this state seems to be, that in cases of sales the officer appointed to execute the orders of the court is designated a special commissioner, while in cases, where the duties are more general and comprehensive, he is designated receiver either general or special; the former being merely a species of the latter. Blair *v.* Core, 20 W. Va. 265.

d. Status of Court and Commissioner Selling.

Court Real Vendor.—In Virginia and West Virginia, the court and not the commissioner or other officer conducting the sale is the real seller at a judicial sale. Barton's Ch. Pr. 1070. Terry *v.* Coles, 80 Va. 695; Carr *v.* Carr, 88 Va. 735, 14 S. E. 368; Strayer *v.* Long, 83 Va. 715, 3 S. E. 372; Fleming *v.* Holt, 12 W. Va. 143; Atkinson *v.* Washington, etc., College, 54 W. Va. 32, 46 S. E. 253; Stout *v.* Philippi Mfg., etc., Co., 41 W. Va. 339, 23 S. E. 571; Coles *v.* Coles, 83 Va. 525, 5 S. E. 673; Springston *v.* Morris, 47 W. Va. 50, 34 S. E. 766; Arnold *v.* Casner, 22 W. Va. 444; Williams *v.* Blakey, 76 Va. 254; Davis *v.* Snead, 33 Gratt. 705; Crockett *v.* Sexton, 29 Gratt. 46; Teel *v.* Yancey, 23 Gratt. 691; Hyman *v.* Smith, 13 W. Va. 744, 779; Core *v.* Strickler, 24 W. Va. 689; Blair *v.* Core, 20 W. Va. 265.

In all judicial sales the court is regarded as the vendor and contracting party, on the one hand, and the purchaser on the other. Davis *v.* Snead, 33 Gratt. 705.

Commissioner Agent of Court.—And the commissioner or other officer conducting the sale is merely the ministerial agent of the court, the medium through which the bidder makes an offer of purchase to the court. Terry *v.* Coles, 80 Va. 695; Brock *v.* Rice, 27 Gratt. 812. Coles *v.* Coles, 83 Va. 525, 5 S. E. 673; Fleming *v.* Holt, 12 W. Va. 143; Atkinson *v.* Washington, etc., College, 54 W. Va. 32, 46 S. E. 253; Stout *v.* Philippi Mfg., etc., Co., 41 W. Va. 339, 23 S. E. 571; Springston *v.* Morris, 47 W. Va. 50, 34 S. E. 766; Alexander *v.* Howe, 85 Va. 198, 7 S. E. 248; Williams *v.* Blakey, 76 Va. 254; Crockett *v.* Sexton, 29 Gratt. 46; Teel *v.* Yancey, 23 Gratt. 691; Tyler *v.* Toms, 75 Va. 116; Hyman *v.* Smith, 13 W. Va. 744; Core *v.* Strickler, 24 W. Va. 689; Blair *v.* Core, 20 W. Va. 265.

Commissioner's Powers and Duties Conferred Solely by Decrees of Court.—A commissioner appointed by a decree of court to make sale of property, being an officer and special agent of the court, his powers and duties are conferred and imposed solely by the decrees and orders under which he acts. Crockett *v.* Sexton, 29 Gratt. 46.

The commissioner conducting the sale is regarded merely as the agent or servant of the court, and his proceedings are necessarily subject to its discretion, supervision and control, and his acts, when sanctioned, become the acts of the court. Terry *v.* Coles, 80 Va. 695; Brock *v.* Rice, 27 Gratt. 812; Teel *v.* Yancey, 23 Gratt. 691; Tyler *v.* Toms, 75 Va. 116; Dixon *v.* McCue, 21 Gratt. 373.

Effect of Sale Made by Commissioner without Previous Authority.—Where a sale of real estate is made under a decree of court and confirmed without exception, such sale is not void because made by a commissioner not previously authorized to make it. Core *v.* Strickler, 24 W. Va. 689.

Commissioner Clothed with Naked Authority.—A commissioner making sales under a decree of the chancery court is clothed with a mere naked authority. Walton *v.* Hale, 9 Gratt. 194, 197; Ronk *v.* Higginbotham, 54 W. Va. 137, 46 S. E. 128.

Not Public Officer.—Special commissioners appointed by a court to make sale of property over a decree, are not public officers. Shields *v.* McClung, 6 W. Va. 79.

e. Who May Be Appointed Special Commissioner.

(1) In Discretion of Court.

The rights of all parties being submitted to the court, it is a matter of its sound discretion as to the appointment of a proper special commissioner to execute its decree in making sale of the property decreed to be sold. Martin *v.* Kester, 49 W. Va. 647, 39 S. E. 599.

(2) Parties.

(a) Plaintiff.

"Under the English practice in chancery proceedings, the conduct of the sales is usually given to the plaintiff, or other party having the charge of the general proceedings. (See 2 Dan. Ch. Pr. 1267.) Nor is there anything in the rules of chancery practice in our courts, which forbids such appointment. The commissioner is the officer of the court, and acts under its supervision. His errors, when brought to the notice of the court, or when appearing on the face of the proceedings, will be corrected." Teel v. Yancey, 23 Gratt. 691, 697.

It is not error to appoint, as commissioner to make a second sale, one who was a party plaintiff in the suit, in his own right and as administrator de bonis non of his father, as trustee of one of the other parties interested, and as next friend of certain infants. There is nothing in these relations which disqualifies him as a commissioner to do the behests of the court. The fact that the commissioner was one of the plaintiffs does not affect the validity of the sale. Teel v. Yancey, 23 Gratt. 691.

"It is nowhere proved, or even charged, that the conduct of the commissioner was not perfectly fair and impartial. No objection was made to the commissioner in the court below, nor was the court asked to substitute another; nor was the sale objected to on account of the commissioner being a party to the suit. The objection is made for the first time in this court, and comes too late, even if it could have availed the party in the court below." Teel v. Yancey, 23 Gratt. 691, 697. See Goddin v. Vaughn, 14 Gratt. 102; Roberts v. Roberts, 13 Gratt. 639.

(b) Defendant Trustee.

The court will exercise a sound discretion in the appointment of a special commissioner, whether it be the defendant trustee or another person.

Martin v. Kester, 49 W. Va. 647, 39 S. E. 599.

(3) Counsel for Parties.

In General.—There is no impropriety in the court appointing the counsel for the parties special commissioners to sell land or in their accepting such appointment and acting in that capacity. It is usual for the courts to appoint the attorneys of parties, whose interest it is to get the highest price for the land, the commissioners to sell it; and there is no reason why this practice on the part of the courts should be changed. The commissioners when so appointed, have, as it were, a double motive to the just and full performance of their duty. Their individual interest accords with the interest of their clients; and both are promoted by the sale of the property at the highest possible price. Newcomb v. Brooks, 16 W. Va. 32.

Counsel for Plaintiff.—It is the constant practice of courts to name the counsel prosecuting a claim to a decree for the sale of property as the commissioner. If there be no objection personally, to the counsel named, there can be no impropriety in such appointment, especially as the whole matter is under the control of the court, whose duty it is to see that its commissioner acts with perfect fairness and impartiality, and to correct, and if necessary, punish any deviation from the line of duty. Goddin v. Vaughn, 14 Gratt. 102; Thomson v. Brooke, 76 Va. 160.

Counsel for Defendant.—In Goddin v. Vaughn, 14 Gratt. 102, the court in considering the allegation that it was error to refuse to associate the counsel for the defendant with the counsel for the plaintiff as commissioner for the purpose of making the sale, said: "Nor do I see any necessity or particular propriety in associating with him the counsel of the other party. If the former is liable to be biased in favor of his client, the latter is no less so in favor of his, and from this diversity of interests divided counsels might ensue not at all favorable to the prompt and harmonious execution of the decree of the court. At any rate it is a matter within the sound discretion of the court and I can not see or say that that discretion has been unduly exercised."

(4) Owner and Assignee of One-Half Judgment.

A person who is the assignee and owner of one-half of the judgment, to satisfy which the suit is brought to sell land, is incompetent to act as commissioner to sell the land, on account of his interest. Etter *v*. Scott, 90 Va. 762, 19 S. E. 776.

f. Qualification of Commissioner.

Every special commissioner appointed under § 1, ch. 132, W. Va. Code, 1899, shall be a resident of the state of West Virginia. W. Va. Code, 1899, ch. 132, § 1.

g. Bond Required of Commissioner before Sale.

(1) Under Provisions of Virginia Statute.

(a) Necessity.

No special commissioner appointed by a decree or order of court, or of a judge in vacation, to sell or rent any property, shall advertise the property for sale or renting, or sell or rent the same, until he shall have given bond as required by the statute. Acts of Va., 1883-84, p. 213; Virginia Code, 1904, § 3398; Tompkins *v*. Dyerle, 102 Va. 219, 46 S. E. 300; Pulliam *v*. Tompkins, 99 Va. 602, 39 S. E. 221; Southwest Virginia Min., etc., Co. *v*. Chase, 95 Va. 50, 27 S. E. 826; Whitehead *v*. Bradley, 87 Va. 676, 13 S. E. 195.

The provisions of § 3398 of the Virginia Code, 1904, requiring commissioners to give bond before selling property under a decree of court, applies to all judicial sales, whether original or resales. Tompkins *v*. Dyerle, 102 Va. 219, 46 S. E. 300.

The bond for the original sale may be made sufficiently broad to cover any resale. Tompkins *v*. Dyerle, 102 Va. 219, 46 S. E. 300.

A decree directed three commissioners to sell a debtor's real estate, and provided that those giving the bond might sell alone. One of said commissioners died previous to the sale. It was held, that a sale made by one of the surviving commissioners, who gave the bond, was valid, although said commissioner joined his co-commissioner with him in the advertisement and report made to the court. Strayer *v*. Long, 89 Va. 471, 16 S. E. 357.

Two commissioners were appointed to sell land, but were not to proceed to execute the decree until they jointly, or each of them separately, or such one of them as should act under the decree, should execute a bond in the penalty of one thousand dollars before the clerk of the court in his office, or in open court, conditioned according to law. The commissioners appeared in court and each of them executed a bond as commissioner under the decree with the other as his surety. It was held, that this was not a compliance with the decree or the statute requiring the execution of bond by special commissioners. Tyler *v*. Toms, 75 Va. 116.

(b) Before Whom Given.

The bond required by the statute (Va. Code, 1904, § 3398), to be given by commissioners directed to sell lands, can only be given before the court which requires the bond to be given, or before the judge thereof, or the clerk of the court in his office. It is plain from the provision of the statute that a decree which directs the commissioner to give bond before any other person or tribunal than those named in the statute is erroneous. By the terms of the statute the bond is required to be given before the court or before the judge of the court, or before the clerk of the court in his office—and the clerk of that court is required to certify that this has been done. Southwest Virginia Min., etc., Co. *v.* Chase, 95 Va. 50, 27 S. E. 826. See also, Tompkins *v.* Dyerle, 102 Va. 219, 46 S. E. 300; Pulliam *v.* Tompkins, 99 Va. 602, 39 S. E. 221.

It is error for the court to direct in the decree of sale that the bond should be taken before the clerk of the circuit court of a county, other than that which requires the bond to be given. Southwest Virginia Min., etc., Co. *v.* Chase, 95 Va. 50, 27 S. E. 826.

If the court fixes the penalty of the bond in the decree, and says nothing about the officer before whom it shall be executed, there can be no error in the decree, as the statute provides before whom this shall be done; but where the decree provides that he shall execute and acknowledge the bond before the clerk of the circuit court of another county, such direction is in plain violation of the express provision of the statute. Southwest Virginia Min., etc., Co. *v.* Chase, 95 Va. 50, 27 S. E. 826.

Although it is error to direct the clerk of the circuit court of any other county, to take the bond, yet if the decree directing the bond to be taken by some other court, is appealed from, the supreme court of appeals will correct the error, as the decree is simply interlocutory. Southwest Virginia Min., etc., Co. *v.* Chase, 95 Va. 50, 27 S. E. 826.

(c) Amount.

In General.—The bond shall be in a penalty, to be prescribed by the court or judge, sufficient to cover at least the probable amount of the whole purchase money or rent. Acts of Va., 1883-84, p. 213; Virginia Code, 1904, § 3398; Tompkins *v.* Dyerle, 102 Va. 219, 46 S. E. 300; Pulliam *v.* Tompkins, 99 Va. 602, 39 S. E. 221; Southwest Virginia Min., etc., Co. *v.* Chase, 95 Va. 50, 27 S. E. 826; Whitehead *v.* Bradley, 87 Va. 676, 13 S. E. 195.

May Be Made Sufficiently Broad to Cover Resale.—The court may require

a special commissioner appointed to make the original sale, to give bond sufficiently broad to cover not only the original sale, but any resale made by him. This is the practice in some of the circuits of the state. Tompkins *v.* Dyerle, 102 Va. 219, 46 S. E. 300.

(d) Certificate as to Execution of Bond.

aa. Necessity.

Section 3398, Va. Code, 1904, provides that the special commissioner appointed by decree or order of the court or by judge in vacation to sell or to rent any property, having given the bond required, shall before advertising the property for sale or renting, or renting or selling the same, obtain from the clerk of the court rendering the decree or making the order, a certificate that the bond required by law or by the decree or order has been given. Acts, 1883-84, p. 213; Tompkins *v.* Dyerle, 102 Va. 219, 46 S. E. 300; Pulliam *v.* Tompkins, 99 Va. 602, 39 S. E. 221; Southwest Virginia Min., etc., Co. *v.* Chase, 95 Va. 50, 27 S. E. 826; Whitehead *v.* Bradley, 87 Va. 676, 13 S. E. 195.

The provisions of § 3398 of the Virginia Code, 1904, requiring commissioners to give bond before selling property under a decree of the court and to append the certificate of the clerk to the advertisement showing that the bond has been given, applies to all judicial sales, whether original or resales. Tompkins *v.* Dyerle, 102 Va. 219, 46 S. E. 300.

Certificate Where Bond for Original Sale Covers Resale.—The court may require a special commissioner appointed to make the original sale, to give bond sufficiently broad to cover not only the original sale, but any resale made by him. This is the practice in some of the circuits of the state. If such bond be required and given under the original decree of sale, there would be no difficulty in the clerk making the required certificate and in the special commissioner appending it to his advertisement of resale. Tompkins v. Dyerle, 102 Va. 219, 46 S. E. 300.

bb. Time of Making Certificate.

The clerk shall make the certificate whenever the bond has been given and note the same in the proceedings in the cause. Va. Code, 1904, § 3398. Southwest Virginia Min., etc., Co. v. Chase, 95 Va. 50, 27 S. E. 826.

cc. Certificate or Copy Appended to Advertisement.

The certificate of the clerk that the bond required by law or by the decree or order has been given, or a copy thereof, shall be appended to the advertisement. Va. Code, 1904, § 3398. Acts, 1883-84, p. 213; Tompkins v. Dyerle, 102 Va. 219, 46 S. E. 300; Pulliam v. Tompkins, 99 Va. 602, 39 S. E. 221; Southwest Virginia Min., etc., Co. v. Chase, 95 Va. 50, 27 S. E. 826; Whitehead v. Bradley, 87 Va. 676, 13 S. E. 195. See ante, "Advertisement or Notice of Sale," VI.

dd. Return of Certificate.

The certificate or a copy thereof shall be returned with the report of the sale or renting. Va. Code, 1904, § 3398; Southwest Virginia Min., etc., Co. v. Chase, 95 Va. 50, 27 S. E. 826.

ee. Fee for Making Certificate.

The clerk shall receive for making the certificate a fee of twenty-five cents, to be taxed in the costs of the suit. Va. Code, 1904, § 3398; Southwest Virginia Min., etc., Co. v. Chase, 95 Va. 50, 27 S. E. 826.

ff. Liability of Clerk for False Certificate.

If any clerk make a certificate as to the bond, which is untrue, he and the sureties in his official bond shall be liable to any person injured thereby; and, if he issue such certificate, knowing it to be false, he shall, in addition to such liability, be fined not less than fifty nor more than five hundred dollars, and, upon conviction, be removed from his office. Acts of 1883-84, p.

213, Va. Code, 1904, § 3400; Whitehead v. Bradley, 87 Va. 676, 13 S. E. 195.

(2) Under Provisions of West Virginia Statute.

(a) Necessity.

aa. In General.

Every special commissioner appointed to make a sale of property under a decree or order of the court, shall receive no money under the decree or order until he gives a bond as prescribed by the statute. And no sale shall be made by such commissioner until such bond has been given. Acts, W. Va., 1882, ch. 142, § 1; W. Va. Code, 1899, ch. 132, § 1. Sommerville v. Sommerville, 26 W. Va. 484; Neeley v. Ruleys, 26 W. Va. 686; Park v. Valentine, 27 W. Va. 677; Baker v. Oil Tract Co., 7 W. Va. 454.

Section 1, ch. 132, W. Va. Code, before the amendment by the acts of 1882, ch. 142, § 1, provided that: No special commissioner appointed by a court to make a sale of property, should receive money under a decree or order until he give bond before the said court or its clerk. Sommerville v. Sommerville, 26 W. Va. 484; Lyttle v. Cozad, 21 W. Va. 183.

Section 1, ch. 142, acts, 1882, now latter part of § 1, ch. 132, W. Va. Code. 1899, amending original § 1, ch. 132, of the Code, provides, among other things, that "no sale shall be made b such commissioner until such bond and security has been given and approved by the clerk." Sommerville v. Sommerville, 26 W. Va. 484; Neeley v. Ruleys, 26 W. Va. 686.

In the case of a judicial sale under § 1, ch. 132, of the Code before the amendment by the acts of 1882, ch. 142, § 1, the failure of the commissioner to give bond before making the sale, does not authorize the court to declare the sale void for that reason, and to set it aside. Sommerville v. Sommerville, 26 W. Va. 484.

The law as provided in the acts of 1882, ch. 142, § 1, is much more stringent than the law under the original section of the Code, and the failure of the commissioner to give the bond required by the amendment would probably render the sale void. Sommerville v. Sommerville, 26 W. Va. 484.

It is irregular and dangerous in practice for the court to authorize its special commissioner, appointed for the purpose, to sell lands for cash in hand, in whole or in part, without requiring such commissioner in its decree to give bond with good personal security before receiving any money, in an adequate prescribed penalty conditioned according to law. McClaskey v. O'Brien, 16 W. Va. 791.

In Baker v. Oil Tract Co., 7 W. Va. 454, 458, it was assigned as error that the court decreed the sale of land for cash, and did not require the special commissioner to give bond with security, conditioned according to law, before making the sale. In delivering the opinion of the court upon this point, Haymond, P., said: "Under the statute, as it was at the date of the decree of sale, it was certainly not error to direct the sale of the land to be made for cash. But as the sale was directed to be made for cash, both of the real and personal property levied on, I think the court ought to have required the commissioner to give bond, with good personal security, in a penalty fixed by the court, conditioned according to law. It seems to me this is the better practice, and should be adhered to, especially as the law requires that such bond and security shall be given before the commissioner is authorized to receive any money upon the sale. While this might not be sufficient cause for reversing a decree of sale in all cases, still I think it is much the better practice where sales are decreed for cash in hand, to require the special commissioner, before he makes the sale, to execute and file the bond; and this would seem to be contemplated by the law."

bb. Statute Mandatory.

The statute is mandatory, not directory. It forbids the sale until the statute has been complied with, and if the sale is made without the bond being executed, it may be set aside. Neeley v. Ruleys, 26 W. Va. 686.

It would be very hazardous for a commissioner under a decree authorizing him to sell to receive any money before executing the bond. The first clauses is intended to prevent commissioners from receiving money under such decree, until the bond is executed, but the last clause forbids a sale under such decree until the bond is executed, and the certificate of the clerk that such bond has been given is appended to the notice of sale so that bidders may know that the law has been complied with in this important respect. Neeley v. Ruleys, 26 W. Va. 686.

Sometimes sales have been made by commissioners without executing bond, and much trouble and loss have been the result; now the statute affords the remedy by declaring no sale shall be made until bond is executed. Neeley v. Ruleys, 26 W. Va. 686.

cc. Waiver of Bond by Plaintiff.

As to the suggestion that the plaintiff could waive the bond, the court, in Neeley v. Ruleys, 26 W. Va. 686, says: "Such a thing is not contemplated by the statute. Of course, if all the parties to the suit, who were or might be interested in the giving of the bond, were to enter a consent decree that no bond should be executed, while it would be in violation of both the spirit and the letter of the statute, yet on well-settled principles, it being a consent decree, it could not be reviewed."

(b) Decree Must Direct Bond to Be Given.

The decree must expressly provide for the bond and direct it to be given. Neeley v. Ruleys, 26 W. Va. 686; Park v. Valentine, 27 W. Va. 677.

If the decree does not provide for the bond and fix the penalty thereof, it can not be executed before the clerk. The law requires a bond, and in accordance therewith it has been the practice for decrees to require one and to fix the penalty. Neeley v. Ruleys, 26 W. Va. 686.

A decree for a sale of land which does not provide for the giving of the bond by the commissioner, or in terms dispenses therewith, is necessarily erroneous and for such error the decree will be reversed. Neeley v. Ruleys, 26 W. Va. 686; Park v. Valentine, 27 W. Va. 677.

(c) Before Whom Given.

The bond shall be given before the court ordering the sale and appointing the commissioner, or before the clerk thereof. Acts, W. Va., 1882, ch. 142, § 1; W. Va. Code, 1899, ch. 132, § 1. Sommerville v. Sommerville, 26 W. Va. 484; Neeley v. Ruleys, 26 W. Va. 686; Park v. Valentine, 27 W. Va. 677; Baker v. Oil Tract Co., 7 W. Va. 454.

(d) Acknowledgment.

It is not necessary to the validity of such a bond, that it should be either acknowledged or proven before the clerk. Lyttle v. Cozad, 21 W. Va. 183. See the title ACKNOWLEDGMENTS, vol. 1, p. 104.

(e) Security.

Necessity.—The bond shall be given with good security. Acts, W. Va., 1882. ch. 142, § 1; W. Va. Code, 1899, ch. 132, § 1; Sommerville v. Sommerville, 26 W. Va. 484; Neeley v. Ruleys, 26 W. Va. 686; Park v. Valentine, 27 W. Va. 677; Baker v. Oil Tract Co., 7 W. Va. 454.

Sureties Approved by Clerk.—The bond must, as to the sufficiency of the sureties, be approved by the clerk. Lyttle v. Cozad, 21 W. Va. 183.

How Approval Shown.—But in order to make the bond valid, the clerk need not indorse his approval upon it. This approval is sufficiently shown by the fact, that the bond had been properly filed away by the clerk, and by the commissioner of sale proceeding to collect the money, which the giving of such bond authorized him to collect. Lyttle v. Cozad, 21 W. Va. 183.

(f) Penalty.

The court must, in its decree, fix the penalty of the commissioner's bond. Neeley v. Ruleys, 26 W. Va. 686.

(g) Conditional Delivery.

A bond of a special commissioner to make a sale in a chancery cause is delivered by the commissioner to the clerk of the court and on its face it appears to be a complete and perfect bond, which was executed by the sureties upon the condition that it should not be delivered to the clerk, till it was also executed by another person or surety, and when the clerk received the bond he was not informed of any such condition or of its being in any way conditioned. Held, this is a valid bond; and the sureties can not set up as a defense, when sued on it, this condition. Lyttle v. Cozad, 21 W. Va. 183.

(h) Certificate as to Execution of Bond.

Every notice of such sale made under decree or order of the court shall have appended to it the certificate of the clerk of the court that the bond and security has been given by the commissioner as required by law. Acts, W. Va., 1882, ch. 143, § 1; W. Va. Code, 1899, ch. 132, § 1. Sommerville v. Sommerville, 26 W. Va. 484; Neeley v. Ruleys, 26 W. Va. 686; Park v. Valentine, 27 W. Va. 677; Baker v. Oil Tract Co., 7 W. Va. 454.

The certificate of the clerk that such bond has been given is appended to the notice of sale so that the bidders may know that the law has been complied with in this important respect. Neeley v. Ruleys, 26 W. Va. 686.

(i) Liability of Clerk for Taking Bond with Insufficient Security.

If the clerk take bond with insufficient security, he and his sureties upon his official bond shall be responsible for any loss or damages sustained by any person injured thereby. W. Va. Code, 1899, ch. 132, § 1.

h. Bond Required of Commissioner before Receiving Money under Decree.

See post, "Bond Required of Commissioner before Receiving Money under Decree," XII, A, 2.

i. Nature of Conduct Required of Commissioner.

A special commissioner is the representative of the court, and should at all times deal honestly and openly with its litigants and the court itself, and not deceive either the one or the other by questionable practices. Springston v. Morris, 47 W. Va. 50, 34 S. E. 766.

3. Sheriff or Sergeant.

Where no special commissioner is appointed for the purpose, a decree or order of any court for the sale of property shall be executed by the sheriff or sergeant who attends such court, unless the place of sale be out of his county or corporation, in which case the sale shall be by the sheriff of the county wherein the place of sale is, or, if the place be in a corporation, by the sergeant thereof, or the sheriff of the county including such corporation, as the court may direct. Va. Code, 1904, § 3403.

Where no special commissioner is appointed for the purpose, a decree or order of court for the sale of property shall be executed by the sheriff who attends such court, unless the place of sale be out of his county, in which case the sale shall be by the sheriff of the county wherein the place of sale is. W. Va. Code, 1899, ch. 132, § 4.

4. Fee for Making Sale, Collecting and Paying over Proceeds.

Where Sale Made and Money Collected by Same Officer.—For the service of commissioners or other officers under any decree or order for a sale, including the collecting and paying over of the proceeds, there shall not be allowed any greater commission than five per centum on the first three hundred dollars received by them, and two per centum on all above that sum, unless the court otherwise order. W. Va. Code, 1899, ch. 132, § 4; W. Va. Code, 1904, § 3404; Va. Code, 1873, ch. 174, § 6; Womack v. Paxton, 84 Va. 9, 5 S. E. 550.

"The next assignment of error we shall notice is the action of the court in allowing W. A. Glasgow, the commissioner, commissions upon the whole $14,000, for which the 'Fork Farm' was sold at the first judicial sale, when only $1,400 thereof was ever collected, and its action also in allowing the same commissioner two sums, one of $50, and the other of $100, as extra compensation for his extraordinary efforts to sell this land. This objection is well taken, for however meritorious may have been the claims of the commissioner, we are concluded in this respect by the express terms of the statute which provides that for services of commissioners, or officers under any decree or order for a sale, including the collection and paying over the proceeds, there shall not be allowed any greater commission than five per centum of the first three hundred dollars received by them, and two per centum on all above that, and if a sale be made by one commissioner or officer, and the proceeds collected by another, or not collected at all, 'the court under whose decree or order they acted shall apportion the commission between them as may be just.' Code, 1873, ch. 174, § 6. As to the expenses for advertising, crier's fee, and surveying the land, they were all properly allowed." Womack v. Paxton, 84 Va. 9, 5 S. E. 550; Hogan v. Duke, 20 Gratt. 244.

Where but a part of price is ever collected, commissions should be allowed only on the part collected, and no extra compensation is allowable for extraordinary efforts to sell the land. Womack v. Paxton, 84 Va. 9, 5 S. E. 550.

The commissioners, appointed by this court to sell some of the lands of John Robinson, deceased, made their report, and claimed a commission of five per cent., which the court allowed. Lyons v. Bernard, 2 Hen. & M. 22.

Where Sale Made by One Officer and Proceeds Collected by Another.— If a sale be made by one commissioner or officer, and the proceeds be collected by another, the court under whose decree or order they acted, shall apportion the commission between them as may be just. W. Va. Code, 1899, ch. 132, § 4; Va. Code, 1904, § 3404; Va. Code, 1873, ch. 174, § 6; Womack v. Paxton, 84 Va. 9, 5 S. E. 550.

C. MANNER OF SALE.

1. In General.

Where the court directs the mode of sale, it must be adhered to. Long v. Perine, 41 W. Va. 314, 23 S. E. 611; Talley v. Starke, 6 Gratt. 339.

If the decree does not fix the manner of the sale, it is left to the sound discretion of the commissioner or officer making it. Rorer on Judicial Sales, § 83. Long v. Perine, 41 W. Va. 314, 23 S. E. 611; Rose v. Brown, 17 W. Va. 649.

2. Whether Public or Private.

It has been held, that a court could sell publicly or privately as the interests of the parties might require. 17 Am. & Eng. Ency. of Law, 2d Ed., 975; Rorer on Judicial Sales, p. 10, § 15. Klapneck v. Keltz, 50 W. Va. 331, 40 S. E. 570.

A direction to a commissioner, in a decree for the sale of real estate, to receive private offers and report them to the court to be acted upon in vacation, is within the discretion of the trial court, in order to obtain the best price for the land. Conrad v. Fuller, 98 Va. 16, 34 S. E. 893.

A sale is not necessarily private when not made at public auction. A sale is public where made by the court. All courts are open to the public in this country. Klapneck v. Keltz, 50 W. Va. 331, 40 S. E. 570.

Where a decree requires land to be sold at public sale, the commissioner has no authority to sell the land at private sale, and such a sale will not be confirmed by the court. The sale is void. Hutson v. Sadler, 31 W. Va. 358, 6 S. E. 920.

H. having consented to a private sale by the commissioners to R., at a certain price, and the commissioners having sold to M. at a higher price, he could not withdraw his consent to a private sale, so as to set aside the sale as made, as not made in pursuance of the decree. Hudgins v. Lanier, 23 Gratt. 494.

Notwithstanding the statute (W. Va. Code, 1899, ch. 132), there are circumstances under which for the purpose of doing equity and justice the court must have the power to make a sale of property without resort to public outcry. The object of advertisement and public outcry is to get bidders, and when this fails, and the court has a fair and adequate offer from purchasers made direct to it through its commissioners, there is no good reason to urge why such offer should not be accepted and the sale made, otherwise, the property might be eaten up with costs or so depreciated by delay that the debts secured thereon might be entirely lost. Klapneck v. Keltz, 50 W. Va. 331, 40 S. E. 570.

Where property had been advertised for sale and the bill for advertisement alone amounted to $112.90, and the court thereafter publicly in open court with the apparent acquiescence of all the parties, at least without any objections being made, accepted an offer in writing by a purchaser, and confirmed the sale to him, it was held, that the provisions of the statute as to advertising were more than complied with without bringing any result, and that the action of the court in accepting such offer privately, and confirming the sale, was proper. Klapneck v. Keltz, 50 W. Va. 331, 40 S. E. 570.

"The decree in this case provides for a private sale. This was proper, and indeed necessary, in view of the peculiar situation and character of the lunatic's interest in question. It consists of fractional parts of lots, and in such proportions and relations to the other interests of other owners in the same lots, that it would be most difficult, if not, indeed, impossible, to sell the said fractional part of these lots in which the lunatic is interested to any one other than to these joint owners of other fractional parts, who will be likely to give more for the lunatic's interest than any one else. Under such circumstances, the decree for a private sale is regular and proper. Hess v. Rader, 26 Gratt. 746, 749. The only object of putting up property at public sale is to give the public an opportunity of bidding; and this, not for the benefit of the public, but for the owner of the property. When, as in this case, the part owners are the only persons who are interested in bidding, and, therefore, no competition in bids can be hoped for, negotiation must take place of a public sale, to prevent the sacrifice of the property sold. The evidence in the record shows that a fair result has been reached in this case, and it would be mistaken kindness to reject it and take the hazard of a precarious auction." Palmer v. Garland, 81 Va. 444.

3. In Whole or in Parcels.

Whether the whole or only a part of the land should be sold, or whether as a whole or in parcels, must be referred to the discretion of the court, and its act will not be disturbed unless plainly erroneous. Long v. Weller, 29 Gratt. 347; Johnson v. Wagner, 76 Va. 587.

Where a decree directs property to be sold or rented, without direction whether it shall be offered in whole or in parcels, the commissioner must in the interest of the parties of the suit, in his discretion offer it for sale or rent in that manner, which will in his judgment bring the most money. Rose v. Brown, 17 W. Va. 649.

"In ordering a sale of property to satisfy a charge upon it, if partition be practicable and would not be injurious, and a sale of a part will produce means sufficient to satisfy the charge upon the whole, certainly such part only should be sold. But whether it be necessary to sell the whole subject, or a part only, and if a part, whether the cutting off that part will not materially impair the value of what remains, and of the whole, then whether it would be more advantageous to sell it altogether or in parcels, and if in parcels, what number there should be, how they should be laid off and in what order sold, are questions (and there are numerous others of a like character) which must of necessity be left for determination to the sound discretion of the chancellor who orders the sale. This court will supervise the exercise of this discretion by the chancellor, but will, in no case, reverse his action in the matter, unless plainly erroneous." Long v. Weller, 29 Gratt. 347.

In a proceeding by rule against a purchaser at a judicial sale to show cause why a resale of the property should not be had to satisfy the unpaid balance of the purchase money, it was alleged that the action of the court was erroneous in directing a sale of the whole property, instead of ordering a sale of so much only as might be necessary to discharge the unpaid balance of the purchase money. Touching this point, the court said: "There is nothing in the record which shows that the circuit court committed any error in ordering a sale of the entire property. Indeed, the contrary rather appears. The property consists of a parcel of land containing thirteen acres, with the buildings upon it. It was sold entire to the appellants. Three-fourths of the purchase money, with accrued interest, remain unpaid. Prima facie, it will take the whole property to discharge this unpaid balance. It is very improbable that the proceeds of the sale of the land detached from the mill seat and buildings on it would pay this balance. Nor has it been made to appear that it would be advantageous or judicious to sell in parcels. On the contrary, the appellants, in their answer to the rule, assert that the chief value of the property is in the mill seat and buildings, and that the land attached and sold with it, together with certain privileges, is 'necessary for the operation of the mill.' At all events, as the cause must be remanded, if in the further proceedings to be had in the circuit court, it be made to appear that it is necessary to sell only a part of the property, or that it would be more advantageous to sell the property in parcels than in one body, the circuit court can frame its decrees and orders accordingly." Long v. Weller, 29 Gratt. 347.

Complaint is also made that the court below decreed a sale of a tract of land worth $3,000 to satisfy a claim or debt not exceeding $400, when a sale of part only would have been sufficient. Here again we encounter the same difficulty that the whole matter was passed subsilentio in the court below. Not a word on the subject was said by anybody, and the circuit judge might well have presumed that all parties were willing to the sale of the entire tract, or he may have overlooked the question entirely. Upon this point all that is necessary is to refer to the case of Long v. Weller, 29 Gratt. 347, 358. In the opinion there delivered by Judge Burks it was held, that whether it be necessary to sell the whole subject, or proper to sell a part only, is a matter resting very much in the sound discretion of the lower court. And whilst that discretion is subject to the

supervision of the appellate court, the latter will not reverse unless the decree appears plainly erroneous. This court can not, therefore, reverse the decree in the present case. Inasmuch, however, as the case must be remanded on other grounds, the decree may be so modified as to direct a sale of part only of the tract, in the first instance; and, secondly, a sale of the whole, if such part prove to be insufficient to satisfy the debt and costs. Johnson v. Wagner, 76 Va. 587.

D. TERMS.

1. Discretionary with Court to Direct Sale for Cash or Credit.

The court may direct the sale to be for cash, or on such credit and terms as it may deem best. Va. Code, 1904, § 3397, Va. Code, 1873, ch. 174, § 1; W. Va. Code, 1899, ch. 132, § 1; Washington Nat. Bldg., etc., Ass'n v. Westfall, 55 W. Va. 305, 47 S. E. 74; Sommerville v. Sommerville, 26 W. Va. 484; Rohrer v. Travers, 11 W. Va. 146; Dickinson v. Clement, 87 Va. 41, 12 S. E. 105; Pairo v. Bethell, 75 Va. 825; Tennent v. Pattons, 6 Leigh 196; Langyher v. Patterson, 77 Va. 470; Yost v. Porter, 80 Va. 855.

This is substantially the same provision to be found in 1 Rev. Code, 1819, ch. 66, § 41, and has been repeatedly construed by this court. Pairo v. Bethell, 75 Va. 825; Brien v. Pittman, 12 Leigh 379.

In Washington Nat. Bldg., etc., Ass'n v. Westfall, 55 W. Va. 305, 47 S. E. 74, the court said: "The decree is further erroneous in that it does not direct the terms of the sale to be made, whether for cash or on credit, and terms, as provided in § 1, ch. 132, Code." In Baker v. Oil Tract Co., 7 W. Va. 454, it was assigned as error that court decreed the sale of the land for cash. Touching this point, the court said: "Under the statute, as it was at the date of the decree of sale, it was certainly not error to direct the sale of the land to be made for cash."

The discretion given to courts of chancery, by the statute, 1 Rev. Code, ch. 66, § 41, in decreeing sales of real estate, to direct the sales to be made on credit, should be exercised where the circumstances show that it ought to be; and the failure to exercise it, as a subject for examination in the appellate court. Tennent v. Pattons, 6 Leigh 196.

Decree requiring lands descended to heirs to be sold for cash, to satisfy a debt due from ancestor reversed, and sale directed to be made upon a credit of six, twelve and eighteen months. Haffey v. Birchetts, 11 Leigh 83.

Where the court acting under the statutory discretion decreed a sale of land by the commissioner, at public auction, before the courthouse door, "for one-third cash, one-third on a credit of twelve months, and the residue on a credit of two years from the day of sale, the credit installments to bear interest from the day of sale, taking from the purchaser or purchasers bonds for the deferred payments, secured by a deed of trust on the said realty," it was held, that the decree in respect to the terms of sale was within the statutory discretion of the court, and not erroneous. Rohrer v. Travers, 11 W. Va. 146.

At a sale under a decree of court, judgment debtor was the purchaser of his own land, and failed to pay the purchase money. On a resale to enforce the payment of the purchase money, it was held, not to be error, under the discretion given the court by the statute (Va. Code, 1904, § 3397) for the court to decree a sale on the following terms: "One-fourth of the purchase money in cash, and for the residue a credit of equal installments, at six, twelve, and eighteen months, with interest from the day of sale," instead of on the same terms and credit allowed by the first decree of one, two and three years for equal installments of the purchase money. If the terms of the resale of land, sold under a former

decree of the court to satisfy adjudged and admitted liens, and bought by the owner of the land, should be on the same terms of credit allowed by the first decree of one, two and three years for equal installments, then on successive resales for default of the purchaser, who was allowed to buy his own land, the time it would take to end the suit would be indefinite, and when and what the lien creditors would get in the end, would be uncertain. Dickinson v. Clement, 87 Va. 41, 12 S. E. 105.

The terms of sale being within the court's discretion, no complaint against them will be heard without evidence that the price would have been better had the terms been more liberal. Yost v. Porter, 80 Va. 855.

Under the Code of 1873, ch. 174, § 1, a court may direct the sale of property to be for cash, or on such credit and terms as it may deem best, but this rule does not apply to mortgages, deeds of trust, and other instruments, in which the terms of sale are agreed upon. In such cases the contract of the parties governs. Pairo v. Bethell, 75 Va. 825; Stimpson v. Bishop, 82 Va. 190; Hogan v. Duke, 20 Gratt. 244; Fultz v. Davis, 26 Gratt. 903; Wytheville Crystal Ice, etc., Co. v. Frick Co., 96 Va. 141, 146, 30 S. E. 491; Watterson v. Miller, 42 W. Va. 108, 109, 24 S. E. 578. See Code of 1887, § 3397. Wood v. Krebbs, 33 Gratt. 685. See the title MORTGAGES AND DEEDS OF TRUST.

The deed of trust provides for a sale for cash; but the court as supposed by consent, makes a decree for a sale on credit. The vendor of the purchaser in possession objects to the decree on a credit, and asks that the land shall be sold for cash. Held, the court should correct the decree and direct a sale for cash. Wood v. Krebbs, 33 Gratt. 685.

2. Better Rule to Sell on Reasonable Credit.

The general rule to be deduced

from the decisions is, that real property of value should be sold on a reasonable credit, unless under peculiar circumstances, and the circumstances to take the case out of general rule should appear by the record. Pairo *v.* Bethell, 75 Va. 825; Brien *v.* Pittman, 12 Leigh 379. See also, Tennent *v.* Pattons, 6 Leigh 196, 221; Haffey *v.* Birchetts, 11 Leigh 83, 90; Kyles *v.* Tait, 6 Gratt. 44, 49.

"The decree directs the sale of the property for cash sufficient to pay the complainant's claim, the cost of the proceeding and expenses of sale, and as to the residue of the purchase money on a credit of six and twelve months for equal installments. These terms are objected to by the appellant as unreasonable and inequitable, and we are of opinion that the objection is well founded. The complainant's claim allowed by the court, together with estimated costs and expenses, amounts to about $3,000 and it is quite probable that on the terms prescribed, the lot, with the buildings upon it, will not bring more than the amount of the claim, if so much." Pairo *v.* Bethell, 75 Va. 825.

3. Court May Change Terms Any Time before Confirmation.

So long as sale is unconfirmed, and the property and the sale remains under the power of the court, it has the power to change the terms of the sale. Tebbs *v.* Lee, 76 Va. 744.

"The second assignment of error is to the order made in Marshall against Lee, on the 31st of May, 1879, which directs that unless Mrs. Lee, who was the purchaser at the sale made, more than two years before, of the tract of about 165 acres of land owned by her husband and sold for his debts, shall, within fifteen days from the date of the order, comply with terms of the sale requiring the execution of bonds for the deferred payments, she having made the cash payment, the land shall be resold, but that the bonds shall bear date May, 1879, the date of this order, and bear interest from the date of the sale. The error assigned is that the bonds were not required to be dated, as of the sale. We are of opinion that the sale not having been confirmed, and the property and the sale being under the power of the court, it had the power to make the change in the terms of the sale, as to the date to be given to the bonds, with the assent of the purchaser, and it not appearing that the creditors were aggrieved by it, the bonds being required to bear interest from the day of sale, and it appearing in fact to be for the benefit of the creditors, that the first sale, which was fair and made under favorable circumstances, and to which no objection had been made, should stand, rather than that it should be set aside, and the risk of a new sale incurred, which is represented as the views of some of the creditors represented in this appeal, the court will not reverse the decree on that ground." Tebbs *v.* Lee, 76 Va. 744.

4. Payments Not to Fall Due More Rapidly than Installments of Debt.

It is error to decree the sale of land on terms, which make the payments fall due more rapidly than the installments of the debt, for which it is sold, become payable. Gates *v.* Cragg, 11 W. Va. 300.

5. Terms Must Be Adhered to When Directed by Court.

Where the court directs the terms of sale, they must be adhered to. Long *v.* Perine, 41 W. Va. 314, 23 S. E. 611; Talley *v.* Starke, 6 Gratt. 339.

6. Variance in Terms Cured by Confirmation.

Though a judicial sale be made on terms differing from those prescribed by the decree of sale, yet the confirmation of the report cures the irregularity and gives the sale the same validity and effect as if made upon the precise terms of the decree. Rohrer on Judicial Sales, §§ 122, 127. Robertson v. Smith, 94 Va. 250, 26 S. E. 579; Langyher v. Patterson, 77 Va. 470.

"There was no affidavit or deposition, or even a suggestion, that the price for which the land was sold was inadequate, and every step taken under the decree for sale was regular and strictly in conformity with the decree, except that the commissioner was directed to sell the property for one-fourth cash, and the balance in one, two and three years; and instead of so doing, sold for the costs cash, and the balance in one, two and three years. In his report of sale, he says: 'Your commissioner would further report, that by the terms of the decree he was required to sell the property for one-fourth cash; but your commissioner found it impossible to sell to any advantage on the terms set forth in the decree.' This slight variance in the terms of sale, as reported by the commissioner of sale, the court approved; and the confirmation of the sale, on these terms, made it equivalent to specifying them in the decree of sale, in the first instance, as by ch. 174 of the Code of Virginia, 1873, the court was fully empowered to do. In fact the majority of judicial sales in Virginia are made on these terms." Langyher v. Patterson, 77 Va. 470. Where special commissioner sells land on terms other than those prescribed in decree of sale, and without reporting his proceedings and obtaining confirmation, conveys the land to purchaser, though six months later the court does confirm the sale and deed; held, a bill will lie to cancel the deed as void ad initio. Miller v. Smoot, 86 Va. 1050, 11 S. E. 983. See post, "Confirmation as Ratification of Irregularities and Cure of Defects," IX, K.

E. BIDDING.

1. Nature and Effect of Bid.

In General.—A bid made at a sale under a decree of court is a mere offer to buy, which the court may accept or decline as it may seem best. Terry v. Coles, 80 Va. 695; Strayer v. Long, 83 Va. 715, 3 S. E. 372; Donahue v. Fackler, 21 W. Va. 124; Hildreth v. Turner, 89 Va. 858, 17 S. E. 471; Brock v. Rice, 27 Gratt. 812; Carr v. Carr, 88 Va. 735, 14 S. E. 368; Childs v. Hurd, 25 W. Va. 530; Cooper v. Daugherty, 85 Va. 343, 7 S. E. 387. See post, "Confirmation," IX; "Nature of Proceedings before Confirmation," IX, D; "Effect of Confirmation upon Rights and Title of Bidder," IX, L.

The court is not bound to accept every offer to buy land, but always has a right to decline it when it seems best to it. Cooper v. Daugherty, 85 Va. 343, 7 S. E. 387.

Confirmation as Acceptance of Bid. —See post, "Confirmation," IX.

Binding Effect of Bid.—A bid by a purchaser to a commissioner is a bid to the court, and if accepted he is bound by it. Terry v. Coles, 80 Va. 695. See post, "Confirmation," IX.

2. Bidders.

a. Distinction between Bidder and Purchaser.

There is a wide distinction between a bidder at a judicial sale and a purchaser. "Until confirmed by the court, the sale confers no rights. Until then it is a sale only in a popular and not in a judicial or legal sense." Rorer on Judicial Sales, p. 55, § 124. "By the purchase, the purchaser, at a judicial sale, becomes a party to the proceedings in which the sale is made." Id., p. 66, § 152. A bid at the commissioner's sale is a mere offer. 2 Barton's Chy. Pr. 1094. By his purchase, the purchaser becomes a quasi party to the suit. 2 Barton's Chy. Pr., § 353. Hildreth v. Turner, 89 Va. 858, 17 S. E. 471. See post, "Nature of Proceedings before Confirmation," IX, D; "Effect of Confirmation upon Rights and Title of Bidder," IX, L.

b. Who May Bid and Purchase.

(1) Person Concerned in Selling.

General Rule.—It is a general rule

that no person employed or concerned [1] in selling at a judicial sale is permitted to become a purchaser, or even to act as agent of a purchaser. Brock v. Rice, 27 Gratt. 812; Howery v. Helms, 20 Gratt. 1; Winans v. Winans, 22 W. Va. 678; Feamster v. Feamster, 35 W. Va. 1, 13 S. E. 53; Ayers v. Blair, 26 W. Va. 558; Newcomb v. Brooks, 16 W. Va. 32; Walker v. Ruffner, 32 W. Va. 297, 9 S. E. 215; Hilleary v. Thompson, 11 W. Va. 113.

Reason for Rule.—This rule rests upon the fact that it is impossible with good faith, to combine the inconsistent capacities of seller and buyer, crier and bidder, in one and the same transaction. If the commissioner or auctioneer faithfully discharges the duties, he will of course honestly obtain the best price he can for the property. On the other hand, if he undertakes to become purchaser for himself or another, his interest and his duty alike prompt him to obtain the property upon the most advantageous terms. There is an irreconcilable conflict between the two positions. And so the courts have always held. Rorer on Judicial Sales, 30. Brock v. Rice, 27 Gratt. 812.

In Minor's Institutes (vol. 2, p. 212, § 10), the author says: "As a general principle it is well settled that trustees, agents, auctioneers, and all persons acting in a confidential character, are disqualified from purchasing the subject committed to them. The functions of buyer and seller are incompatible, and can not be exercised by the same person without great danger of fraud. Such transactions are constructively fraudulent, and are therefore voidable at the instance of the beneficiary, although, if he chooses to recognize them, they are binding upon the trustees." etc. Feamster v. Feamster, 35 W. Va. 1, 13 S. E. 53, citing 1 Rob. Pr. (1st Ed.) 85; 1 Lom. Dig. 319; Carter v. Harris, 4 Rand. 199, 204; Seger v. Edwards, 11 Leigh 213; Buckles v. Lafferty, 2 Rob. 293, 300; Howery v. Helms, 20 Gratt. 1.

The principles thus declared are well sustained by the authorities, and are founded upon sound reason and morality. It is the duty of the seller to get the best possible price for the property sold, and is the right of the buyer to make the purchase at the lowest price. To allow a person to occupy the position of both buyer and seller is to subject him to a temptation which neither the law nor good morals can permit. The capacities in which he acts are inconsistent and in direct conflict with each other. The danger of the temptation to serve his own interest at the expense of those whom he represents, out of the mere necessity of the case, disqualifies a commissioner from having any interest in the purchase of property which he is directed to sell. The fact that he has undertaken the office of making the best possible sale for others, incapacitates him from acting on the other side; and consequently, any sale he may make while occupying such antagonistic position is, at least, voidable at the option of those interested in an advantageous sale of the property. Winans v. Winans, 22 W. Va. 678; Howery v. Helms, 20 Gratt. 1.

(2) Commissioner.

The law is well settled in this state that the same person can not occupy the antagonistic positions of seller and purchaser of the same subject. And if a person selling land as a commissioner of the court, becomes himself the purchaser, or has any understanding at the time of the sale that he is to have any interest in the purchase of the land sold by him, the sale will be held void and set aside at the election of any party interested in the land. Ayers v. Blair, 26 W. Va. 558; Winans v. Winans, 22 W. Va. 678; Newcomb v. Brooks, 16 W. Va. 32; Walker v. Ruffner, 32 W. Va. 297, 9 S. E. 215.

See Walker v. Ruffner, 32 W. Va. 297, 9 S. E. 215, the court said: "It is contended by counsel for the appellee that such a sale is not simply voidable, but absolutely void. I do not, however, consider that position to be in accord with the weight of authority either in the state of Virginia or in this state. In the case of Howery v. Helms, 20 Gratt. 1, the second point of the syllabus reads as follows: 'When the commissioner appointed by a decree in a partition suit to sell the land becomes himself the purchaser, the purchase is voidable at the election of any party interested in the land sold. And the law is the same where the purchase is made nominally by a third person, who is reported by the commissioner to the court as the purchaser, but who really purchased for the commissioner, and conveyed the land to him accordingly, after the purchase, as reported, had been confirmed.' Also, that 'the commissioner, by purchasing at his own sale, did an act which a court of equity treats as a fraud upon the parties interested." See also, Winans v. Winans, 22 W. Va. 678.

"The objection that at the time the appellant became the purchaser of the land he was the commissioner of the court to make the resale, can avail nothing, under the facts of the case. It is admitted to be the rule that ordinarily a commissioner to sell is not allowed to purchase the subject, either directly or indirectly. Such a purchase, however, is not absolutely void, but voidable only at the election of any party interested in the land. Howery v. Helms, 20 Gratt. 1. No objection or exception to the appellant's purchase was made or taken by any party, but, on the contrary, it was approved and ratified. Indeed, there could have been no good cause for any such objection." Hurt v. Jones, 75 Va. 341.

A release obtained, by a commissioner, who purchased the land at his own sale, from the person interested in the land, will not operate as a confirmation of such purchase, unless it clearly appears that such release was obtained without fraud or concealment and after a full disclosure of all the facts which rendered the sale voidable. Winans v. Winans, 22 W. Va. 678.

(3) Auctioneer or Crier.

An auctioneer or crier making a sale can not properly act for himself or any other person, in bidding for the property. Brock v. Rice, 27 Gratt. 812; Hilleary v. Thompson, 11 W. Va. 113. See the title AUCTIONS AND AUCTIONEERS, vol. 2, p. 174.

(4) Attorney.

In General.—Upon one point the English and all the American writers are agreed, that an attorney at law can not purchase property, real or personal, at a judicial sale, whether made by a commissioner of the court or by a sheriff, after a judgment has been obtained and an execution issued, when his client might sustain an inquiry by his being a purchaser. Newcomb v. Brooks, 16 W. Va. 32.

Quære: Can an attorney at law in any case, even with the consent of his client, purchase property sold for the benefit of his client at a judicial sale pending the suits, or on an execution after judgment? Newcomb v. Brooks, 16 W. Va. 32.

Without the consent of his client he can not purchase for his own benefit any property of the defendant sold under execution, unless he gives for it an amount equal to the whole of his client's judgment; and without such consent he can not purchase for his own benefit his client's property sold at a judicial sale. Newcomb v. Brooks, 16 W. Va. 32.

In most of these cases the application of the general principle that an attorney can not purchase property when his being the purchaser might prejudice his client's rights, have arisen when he purchased the property of the defendant on an execution issued by him for his client. The rule well established in such cases being, that he can not at a sale under an execution, whether of real or personal property, without the express consent of his client, purchase, unless he pays for the property a sum sufficient to pay off his client's whole debt, or if he has more than one client entitled to be paid out of the property sold, unless he pays for it a sum sufficient to pay off all his clients' debts, so as to render it certain that they can not suffer by his being a purchaser; and if he does not pay a sum sufficient to pay off all his clients' debts, the sale will be set aside at the instance of any client, though it may have been ever so fair, and an adequate price may have been paid for the property. Newcomb v. Brooks, 16 W. Va. 32.

"Although the commissioners are the agents of the court in making the sale, yet the attorney of the parties, at whose suit the property is to be sold, has a control in regard to it, that may in many instances be exercised either to the advantage or prejudice of his clients, as he pleases. It may be advisable for instance, on the part of the attorney, after the property has been advertised for sale, for some good reason to postpone the sale, in order to obtain a better price by offering it for sale at a particular time; or he, seeing at the time it is offered for sale, that the property was likely to be sold for a price greatly below its real value, might instead of countermanding it urge the commissioners to go on and make the sale, and he become the buyer for his own use." Newcomb v. Brooks, 16 W. Va. 32.

Where a tract of land was conveyed to a party ·to be held by him in trust for himself and numerous others, and he was appointed the agent of these equitable owners to manage the property and sell it at his pleasure, and one of the equitable owners brings a suit to have this property sold and to hold the trustee to an account for his agency, and the court renders a decree to sell the property with a view to a partition of the proceeds among the several owners, at a sale made by a commissioner under such decree the attorney for the trustee in the suit can not buy the property for his own benefit either with or without the consent of his client the trustee. And if he does purchase in the name of a third party, and the sale is confirmed by the court within two days after it is made, when the cestuis que trust were ignorant that the attorney of the trustee was the real purchaser, on an original bill brought by the cestui que trust, this decree of confirmation will be set aside, because the fact was not made known to the court, when the confirmation of the sale was asked, that the attorney for the trustee was the real purchaser, and the decree was therefore fraudulently procured by the suppression of this fact. And in such case the fact that the trustee does not desire the decree of confirmation set aside will make no difference, as the cestui que trust have a right to have it set aside without any inquiry as to the adequacy of the price. Newcomb v. Brooks, 16 W. Va. 32.

"Though no fraud is proven in this case, still it illustrates well the propriety of the rule of law, which we have seen the courts have adopted, or prohibiting as a matter of public policy an attorney from purchasing property at a judicial sale in which his client is interested without his client's consent whenever the purchase by him could possibly injuriously affect his client's interest. And the circumstances of this case tend strongly to countenance the propriety of the more stringent rule. which we have seen some of the courts countenance, which forbids an attorney to purchase at any judicial sale, though his client can not be prejudiced, or though done with his express consent, because even then such permission to a purchaser might tend to the injury of other parties to the suit and might induce the attorney to act oppressively and unjustly to them and deceitfully and unfaithfully to the court or its officers." Newcomb *v.* Brooks, 16 W. Va. 32.

Purchase of Land after Termination of Relation of Attorney and Client.— An attorney for client whose property is sold at judicial sale to satisfy liens and charge against it, who notified such client prior thereto of the time and terms of sale, and of the result thereof soon after the sale and confirmation, and no objection was made thereto by the client, the relation of attorney ceased between the parties as to the land itself, from the confirmation of the sale, and only continued so far as such attorney might have to do with the proceeds of the sale, and the moment such relations ceased he was at liberty to purchase the land or an interest in it. Williams *v.* Maxwell, 45 W. Va. 297, 31 S. E. 909. See the title ATTORNEY AND CLIENT, vol. 2, p. 145.

(5) Person Giving No Satisfactory Assurance of Ability to Comply with Bid.

The commissioners may decline to permit the auctioneer to announce the bids of persons who give no satisfactory assurances of their ability and willingness to comply, for bona fide bidders are entitled to that protection. 2 Bart. Ch'y Pr., p. 1079, § 340. Hildreth *v.* Turner, 89 Va. 858, 17 S. E. 471.

"So an insolvent purchaser at a judicial sale, who declares himself unable to give a bond that day for the payment of the price, can not, as a matter of right, demand time to procure the bond, where he gives no satisfactory assurance of his ability to do so, and resale may be had under such circumstances." U. S. Gen'l Digest, vol. 5, p. 1302, § 9. This doctrine is especially applicable in a case where the parties complaining have once baffled the commissioners, and openly proclaim their purpose to do so again. Hildreth *v.* Turner, 89 Va. 858, 17 S. E. 471.

(6) Person Who Refused to Comply with Terms of Former Sale.

Sale commissioners may decline to cry the bid of a person who refused to comply with the terms of a former sale, and who gives no satisfactory assurance of ability to comply with the terms of the second sale. Hildreth *v.* Turner, 89 Va. 858, 17 S. E. 471.

A person who bid at a judicial sale of land and refused to comply with the terms of sale, and, at a resale, attempted to bid through an agent, in disregard of the terms of sale; held, such person has no standing to appeal from a decree confirming the sale to another person. Hildreth *v.* Turner, 89 Va. 858, 17 S. E. 471.

A person who refuses to make good his bid, by complying with the terms of the sale, is not a bidder proper, much less a purchaser. Hildreth *v.* Turner, 89 Va. 858, 17 S. E. 471.

(7) Fiduciary of Trust Property Sold in Adverse Proceeding.

A fiduciary can not make a valid purchase of the trust property, though it be made at a public judicial sale under a decree made in an adverse proceeding. Any such purchase may be avoided at his option by any party to whom he holds such fiduciary relation. Newcomb *v.* Brooks, 16 W. Va. 32. See the title TRUSTS AND TRUSTEES.

In the case of Newcomb *v.* Brooks, 16 W. Va. 32, second point of syllabus, "a purchase by a fiduciary, while actually holding a fiduciary relation, of the trust property, either of himself, or of the party to whom he holds such fiduciary relation, is voidable at the option of the party to whom he stands in such a relation, although the fiduciary may have given an adequate price for the property, and gained no advantage whatever." Also, tenth point of syllabus: "But when such sales are sought to be avoided, the suit for the purpose must be brought in a reasonable time, though the property remains in the hands of the fiduciary."

Green, J., in delivering the opinion of the court in that case (page 69), says: "The general rule we have laid down, that a fiduciary will not be permitted to buy the trust property, even when the purchase is fair, and the price adequate, and that the cestui que trust, or person bearing a similar relation, may, at his option, set aside such a sale, applies as strongly to a public sale by a fiduciary as to a private sale; nor will the fact that the sale is made under an adverse proceeding, and at a judicial sale, make any difference. He can with no more propriety purchase at such a sale than at one made by himself" (quoting numerous authorities). "The reason of this is obvious, for if the purchaser bears such a relation to the person interested in the property to be sold as to impose on him the duty of making the property bring the highest price possible, this duty is as incumbent on him when the property is sold under an order of the court, or by any other person, or at any other sale, as it is when made by himself, either privately or publicly, and therefore he can not be permitted to put himself in a position in which it is his interest that the property should bring the least sum possible." Walker v. Ruffner, 32 W. Va. 297, 9 S. E. 215.

When there are several fiduciaries one can not purchase of the others, but such a purchase can be avoided at the option of the parties to whom such fiduciary relation is held; and the agent of such fiduciary or fiduciaries to sell the property is under a like disability to purchase. Any one of the persons, to whom such fiduciary relation is held, may avoid such a purchase so far as his interest is concerned, though all the others standing in the same relation to the fiduciaries are content that the sale shall stand. Newcomb v. Brooks, 16 W. Va. 32.

c. **Rights and Liabilities of Bidder before Confirmation.**

See post, "Confirmation," IX.

3. Selling Bid.

A purchaser at a judicial sale can not, before confirmation, sell his bargain to another at an advance price. Such a contract tends to prevent the property from bringing the best price, and is therefore contrary to public policy, and void. Camp v. Bruce, 96 Va. 521, 31 S. E. 901.

A court of equity will not, where the facts are known to it, confirm a sale where the bidder has sold his bid at an advance, unless the advance inures to the benefit of the parties to the suit. If the commissioner who made the sale knows of a resale by the bidder at an advance price, it is his duty to report it to the court. He is the mere agent of the court, and should give to it all information in his possession that can affect the confirmation of the sale. Camp v. Bruce, 96 Va. 521, 31 S. E. 901.

A court does not allow bidders to trade behind its back, and speculate in that way on property which it is selling. 2 Dan. Chy. Pl. & Pr. 1285 (2d Ed.); Hodder v. Ruffin, 1 Tamlyn 341. In order to prevent this, it became the practice of the English chancery courts, in the time of Lord Elden, it is said, to require the bidder who desired the court to substitute another in his stead, to file an affidavit that there was "no underhand bargain between them." Camp v. Bruce, 96 Va. 521, 31 S. E. 901.

The rule of the English chancery courts upon this subject is thus stated in 2 Daniel's Chancery Pleading & Practice, 1285 (5th Ed.): "If, after becoming the bidder for an estate, the purchaser is desirous of being discharged from his contract and of substituting another person in his stead, the court will, on motion, make an order to that effect; he must, however, support the motion by an affidavit that there is no underbargain, for the new purchaser may give the other a sum of money to stand in his place, and so deceive the court; and the rule appears to be, that if a purchaser resell behind the back of the court before the purchase is confirmed, the second purchaser is considered as a substituted purchaser, and must pay the additional price into court for the benefit of the estate. When the highest bidder at an auction induced the auctioneer to accept another person in his place, concealing the fact that he had sold his bargain at an advance, which he received and absconded, the property was ordered to be resold, reserving all questions of liability of the original or subpurchaser." Camp *v.* Bruce, 96 Va. 521, 31 S. E. 901.

The English rule of requiring affidavits, where one purchaser is asked to be substituted for another, is a wise one, and the agreement sought to be enforced shows the necessity for some safeguard in our practice. It might be well for our courts in all such cases, unless the parties consent to the substitution, to adopt the English practice. It is of the utmost consequence that judicial sales, and especially sales for partition where infants are generally interested, should be protected from practices and influences which may prevent the lands from bringing the best price. Camp *v.* Bruce, 96 Va. 521, 31 S. E. 901.

4. Upset Bids.

See post, "Opening Biddings on Upset Bids," XI.

5. Enforcing Bids.

See post, "Procedure upon Failure of Purchaser to Comply with Bid," XIV.

6. Sham Bidding and Puffing Bidding.

It is manifestly improper for the auctioneer to receive any but real bids. It may be said that the debtor can not complain of this, as he may receive a higher bid thereby. But this is not always true. If the bystanders see the auctioneer is conducting the sale for himself and bidder too; that he is crying bids that were not made; it would

not be likely that they would bid at all; the direct result of such a course would be to discourage bidding. When men attend a judicial sale, they expect fair and open competition; and if they discover that the bids are not of that character, they will be apt to refuse to bid at all; and that would surely be to the prejudice of the debtor. Hilleary *v.* Thompson, 11 W. Va. 113.

The second objection is that the auctioneer himself bid on the land; or that there was no competing bidding for several bids before the sale was made. The auctioneer in his affidavit, says: "There was no competing bidding for the said tract for several bids anterior to that at which the sale was made to the said Roberts at $26 per acre." If there was no competing bidding, there was "sham" bidding, either by the auctioneer himself, or some one with his knowledge. Hilleary *v.* Thompson, 11 W. Va. 113.

Whatever view might be held as to the propriety or impropriety of a special commissioner at a judicial sale procuring puffers at a sale he is directed to make as such by the court, or what effect puffers will have in invalidating a judicial sale, at the objection of a defrauded purchaser made before confirmation, is matter well understood in the chancery practices. Carr *v.* Carr, 88 Va. 735, 14 S. E. 368.

7. Stifling Bidding.

In General.—While there is no statute in Virginia declaring that contracts having a tendency to stifle bidding at a judicial sale are unlawful, yet under the principles of the common law, any contract which is made for the purpose of or whose necessary effect and tendency is to lessen competition and restrain bidding at judicial sales, is held to be illegal because opposed to public policy. The object in all such cases is to get the best price that can be fairly had for the property. The policy of the law, therefore, is to secure such sale from every kind of improper influence. Camp v. Bruce, 96 Va. 521, 31 S. E. 901; Nitro-Phosphate Syndicate v. Johnson, 100 Va. 774, 42 S. E. 995; Barnes v. Morrison, 97 Va. 382, 34 S. E. 93; Underwood v. McVeigh, 23 Gratt. 409, 428; Horn v. Star Foundry Co., 23 W. Va. 522; Ralphsnyder v. Shaw, 45 W. Va. 680, 31 S. E. 953. See the title ILLEGAL CONTRACTS, vol. 7, p. 246.

It is essential to the validity of judicial sales, not merely that they should be conducted in conformity to the requirement of law, but that they should be conducted with entire fairness. Perfect freedom from all influence likely to prevent competition in the sale should be strictly exacted. Underwood v. McVeigh, 23 Gratt. 409.

VIII. Report of Sale.

A. NECESSITY.

A commissioner for the sale of land is required to make report of his proceedings. Crockett v. Sexton, 29 Gratt. 46.

It is the universal practice for decrees to direct the commissioners to sell, and to report their proceedings to the court, so that the court, upon receiving the report, may approve and confirm the sale, or set it aside. Kable v. Mitchell, 9 W. Va. 492.

A commissioner appointed by decree of court to make sale of property, is an officer and special agent of the court, and his powers and duties are conferred and imposed solely by the decrees and orders under which he acts. He is required, among other things, to make report of his proceedings under the decree by which he is appointed to the court from which he derives his authority, as a basis for the further action of the court. Crockett v. Sexton, 29 Gratt. 46.

B. AMENDED, ADDITIONAL OR SUPPLEMENTAL REPORT.

If the report of sale by the commissioner be incomplete, insufficient, or in any way imperfect, he may be required to make a further report; and so, if, after he has made his report, and it has been received and accepted at any time before final action upon it, he discover any material mistake, or omission, or ambiguity in it, he may, by leave of the court, and it would be his duty to file an amended, additional or supplemental report, correcting the mistake, supplying the omission or explaining the ambiguity. Such is the common practice, and it seems convenient, conducive to justice, and free from objection. Crockett v. Sexton, 29 Gratt. 46.

C. REPORT FILED WITH PAPERS AND PART OF RECORD.

Commissioners' reports of sales are filed with the papers in the cause, become a part of the record, and are open to inspection, examination and exception by all of the parties. Crockett v. Sexton, 29 Gratt. 46.

D. SEPARATE REPORTS BY CO-COMMISSIONERS.

A sale by two commissioners and its validity can not be affected by the fact that one of them declined to join in the report, and made himself a separate report. Hildreth v. Turner, 89 Va. 858, 17 S. E. 471.

E. EXCEPTION TO REPORT.

Nature of Exception.—Exception to a commissioner's report has to be of the nature of a special demurrer; and if the report is erroneous, the party complaining of the report or excepting thereto must in his exceptions point out the errors with reasonable certainty, so as to direct the mind of the court to them; and when he does so, the parts not excepted to are admitted to be correct not only as regards the principals but as relates to the evidence, on which they are based. Crislip v. Cain, 19 W. Va. 438.

Grounds of Objection Must Be Specified with Reasonable Certainty.— The report may be excepted to. But in all cases where exceptions are necessary, they should specify with reasonable certainty, the particular grounds of objection, so as to enable the opposite party to see clearly what he is to meet, and the court what it is to decide. Crockett v. Sexton, 29 Gratt. 46; Robinett v. Robinett, 92 Va. 124, 128, 22 S. E. 856; Baldwin v. Baldwin, 76 Va. 345, 353; Simmons v. Simmons, 33 Gratt. 451.

Must Be Excepted to in Lower Court. —Where a commissioner's report has been confirmed without exception in the court below, it is too late for the first time in this court to except to such report, unless it be erroneous on its face. Hildreth v. Turner, 89 Va. 858, 17 S. E. 471.

Where sales-commmissioner's report shows that sale was made as decree prescribed and no exception was made below, none can be made here. Smith v. Henkel, 81 Va. 524.

A commissioner appointed to sell land, makes a report of his sale in 1863, and whilst he states the amount for which the land sold, he does not say anything of the kind of money for which it was sold. Some of the owners of the land not having been parties in the cause when the decrees for the sale and its confirmation were made, are afterwards made parties; and they except to the sale, if it was made for confederate currency. The commissioner then presents a supplemental report, stating that the land was sold for good money, and the report is not excepted to, but is received and acted on by the court. It can not be objected to in the appellate court. Crockett v. Sexton, 29 Gratt. 46.

From face of report usurious interest was paid; no exception when report was adopted; afterwards exception was endorsed, but attention of court not called thereto. Held, the decree can not be reversed on that ground, but on other grounds, being remanded, the court below can disallow the usurious interest and apply excess as a credit to the debt, in con-

formity with Moseley v. Brown, 76 Va. 419. Hansucker v. Walker, 76 Va. 753.

Immaterial Errors in Report Cured by Confirmation.—"After all this was done it was discovered by the plaintiff that an error of fact had crept into the report of sale made by the commissioner, in reporting the name of the security given by the purchaser at the sale, which I might say was not a material matter and especially after the confirmation by the court." McKinney v. Kirk, 9 W. Va. 26.

IX. Confirmation.

A. DEFINITION.

Confirmation is the judicial sanction of the court. Rorer on Judicial Sales, pp. 30, 55, 56, §§ 122, 124; 1 Sugd. on Vendors, p. 68; Brock v. Rice, 27 Gratt. 812; Terry v. Coles, 80 Va. 695; Langyher v. Patterson, 77 Va. 470, 473; Whitlock v. Johnson, 87 Va. 323, 12 S. E. 614; Carr v. Carr, 88 Va. 735, 14 S. E. 368.

Confirmation is final consent. Rorer on Judicial Sales, p. 56. Terry v. Coles, 80 Va. 695.

The bid is accepted by the court by the confirmation of the sale. Fleming v. Holt, 12 W. Va. 143; Atkinson v. Washington, etc., College, 54 W. Va. 32, 46 S. E. 253.

A sale is confirmed where both contracting parties concur in ratifying the inchoate purchase. Terry v. Coles, 80 Va. 695; Taylor v. Cooper, 10 Leigh 317.

A decree of confirmation is a judgment of the court, which determines the rights of the parties. Such a decree possesses the same force and effect of any other adjudication by a court of competent jurisdiction. Terry v. Coles, 80 Va. 695; Brock v. Rice, 27 Gratt. 812; Todd v. Gallego Mills Mfg. Co., 84 Va. 586, 5 S. E. 676; Coles v. Coles, 83 Va. 525, 5 S. E. 673; Allison v. Allison, 88 Va. 328, 13 S. E. 549; Berlin v. Melhorn, 75 Va. 636, 639; Hickson v. Rucker, 77 Va. 135.

It is the confirmation that makes a judicial sale, and nothing that happens prior thereto. Klapneck v. Keltz, 50 W. Va. 331, 40 S. E. 570.

It is not the advertising nor bids, private or public, that make a sale judicial. The decree of confirmation alone gives it character as such and places it beyond attack for errors or irregularities which might have been taken advantage of prior to such decree. Klapneck v. Keltz, 50 W. Va. 331, 40 S. E. 570.

B. NECESSITY.

In the case of a judicial sale, the court and not the commissioner or other officer, being the real seller or vendor, confirmation is essential to the validity of any sale that the commissioner or other officer of the court may make. Barton's Chy. Pr. 1070; Terry v. Coles, 80 Va. 695; Brock v. Rice, 27 Gratt. 812; Strayer v. Long, 83 Va. 715, 3 S. E. 372.

A sale by commissioners, made under a decree of a court of equity, is not an absolute sale, in Virginia, or in West Virginia, and it does not become absolute until the sale is confirmed by the court. Kable v. Mitchell, 9 W. Va. 492; Trimble v. Herold, 20 W. Va. 602; Hartley v. Roffe, 12 W. Va. 401; Childs v. Hurd, 25 W. Va. 530; Cocke v. Gilpin, 1 Rob. 20, 39; Crews v. Pendleton, 1 Leigh 297; Heywood v. Covington, 4 Leigh 373; Taylor v. Cooper, 10 Leigh 317; Hudgins v. Marchants, 28 Gratt. 177.

A bid by a purchaser to a commissioner is a bid to the court, and if accepted he is bound by it, but the court and not the commissioner is the seller, and the confirmation by the court, and its direction to convey, are essential to the validity of any sale that the commissioner may make. Barton's Chy. Pr. 1070; Terry v. Coles, 80 Va. 695; Thompson v. Cox, 42 W. Va. 566, 26 S. E. 189; Childs v. Hurd, 25 W. Va. 530.

A judicial sale is not conclusive and consummated until confirmed. Terry v. Coles, 80 Va. 695; Thompson v. Cox, 42 W. Va. 566, 26 S. E. 189.

C. DISCRETIONARY WITH COURT.

1. In General.

It lies within the discretion of the court ordering the sale, to determine whether it will accept the bid and confirm the sale, or set it aside. Rorer on Judicial Sales, pp. 30, 55, 56. Brock v. Rice, 27 Gratt. 812; Langyher v. Patterson, 77 Va. 470; Roudabush v. Miller, 32 Gratt. 454; Hansucker v. Walker, 76 Va. 753, 755; Terry v. Coles, 80 Va. 695; Taylor v. Cooper, 10 Leigh 317; Daniel v. Leitch, 13 Gratt. 195; Todd v. Gallego Mills Mfg. Co., 84 Va. 586, 5 S. E. 676; Berlin v. Melhorn, 75 Va. 636, 689; Effinger v. Kenney, 79 Va. 551, 553; Coles v. Coles, 83 Va. 525, 5 S. E. 673; Carr v. Carr, 88 Va. 735; 14 S. E. 368; Hartley v. Roffe, 12 W. Va. 401; Beaty v. Veon, 18 W. Va. 291; Thomas v. Farmers' Nat. Bank, 86 Va. 291, 9 S. E. 1122; Hickson v. Rucker, 77 Va. 135; Kable v. Mitchell, 9 W. Va. 492; Trimble v. Herold, 20 W. Va. 602; Hildreth v. Turner, 89 Va. 858, 17 S. E. 471; Roberts v. Roberts, 13 Gratt. 639; Moran v. Clark, 30 W. Va. 358, 4 S. E. 303; Bank v. Jarvis, 28 W. Va. 805; Childs v. Hurd, 25 W. Va. 530; Hughes v. Hamilton, 19 W. Va. 366; Hilleary v. Thompson, 11 W. Va. 113; Moore v. Triplett, 96 Va. 603, 32 S. E. 50; Hudgins v. Lanier, 23 Gratt. 494; Marling v. Robrecht, 13 W. Va. 440; Hyman v. Smith, 13 W. Va. 744.

The chancellor has a broad discretion in the approval or disapproval of judicial sales. Terry v. Coles, 80 Va. 695; Brock v. Rice, 27 Gratt. 812; Carr v. Carr, 88 Va. 735; 14 S. E. 368; Hyman v. Smith, 13 W. Va. 744.

The bid, made by the purchaser at the sale, must be considered as his offer to the court through its commissioners, and, in making it, he agrees to be bound thereby, if it is accepted and approved by the court; and it is discretionary with the court, whether it will accept the bid and confirm the sale, or set it aside. Marling v. Robrecht, 13 W. Va. 440; Kable v. Mitchell, 9 W. Va. 492.

2. Nature of Discretion to Be Exercised.

The court, in acting upon the report of the sale, does not exercise an arbitrary but a sound legal discretion in view of all the circumstances. It is to be exercised in the interest of fairness, prudence, and with a just regard to the rights of all concerned. Rorer on Judicial Sales, pp. 30, 55, 56. Brock v. Rice, 27 Gratt. 812; Terry v. Coles, 80 Va. 695; Taylor v. Cooper, 10 Leigh 317; Daniel v. Leitch, 13 Gratt. 195; Todd v. Gallego Mills Mfg. Co., 84 Va. 586, 5 S. E. 676; Berlin v. Melhorn, 75 Va. 636, 689; Hansucker v. Walker, 76 Va. 753, 755; Langyher v. Patterson, 77 Va. 470; Effinger v. Kenney, 79 Va. 551, 553; Coles v. Coles, 83 Va. 525, 5 S. E. 673; Roudabush v. Miller, 32 Gratt. 454; Carr v. Carr, 88 Va. 735, 14 S. E. 368; Hartley v. Roffe, 12 W. Va. 401; Beaty v. Veon, 18 W. Va. 291; Thomas v. Farmers' Nat. Bank, 86 Va. 291, 9 S. E. 1122; Hickson v. Rucker, 77 Va. 135; Kable v. Mitchell, 9 W. Va. 492; Trimble v. Herold, 20 W. Va. 602; Taylor v. Cooper, 10 Leigh 317; Roudabush v. Miller, 32 Gratt. 454; Childs v. Hurd, 25 W. Va. 530; Hughes v. Hamilton, 19 W. Va. 366; Hilleary v. Thompson, 11 W. Va. 113; Hudgins v. Lanier, 23 Gratt. 494; Marling v. Robrecht, 13 W. Va. 440.

The discretion which the court may exercise, in accepting a bid and confirming a sale or setting it aside, will not authorize it to set aside the sale in the absence of sufficient cause. Kable v. Mitchell, 9 W. Va. 492; Trimble v. Herold, 20 W. Va. 602; Hughes v. Hamilton, 19 W. Va. 366; Hyman v. Smith, 13 W. Va. 744.

One respectable authority goes so far as to declare that the court is clothed with an unlimited discretion to confirm a judicial sale, or not, as may seem wise and just. Confirmation is final consent and the court being the vendor, it may consent or not, at its discretion. Rorer on Judicial Sales, p. 56, cited by Judge Staples in Brock v. Rice, 27 Gratt. 812. Terry v. Coles, 80 Va. 695.

In the exercise of discretion allowed the court in affirming or refusing to confirm a judicial sale, a proper regard should be had to the interest of the parties and the stability of judicial sales. By sanctioning a sale, the courts make it their own. Terry v. Coles, 80 Va. 695; Brock v. Rice, 27 Gratt. 812; Carr v. Carr, 88 Va. 735, 14 S. E. 368; Coles v. Coles, 83 Va. 525, 5 S. E. 673; Hyman v. Smith, 13 W. Va. 744.

In Brock v. Rice, 27 Gratt. 812, Judge Staples, speaking for the whole court, said: "It has never been held that it is imperative upon the court to set aside the sale and reopen the bids. It is a question addressed to the sound discretion of the court, subject to the review of the appellate tribunal; and the propriety of its exercise depends upon the circumstances of each case, and can only be rightfully exercised, when it can be done with a due regard to the rights and interests of all concerned—the purchaser as well as others. This can not be done when no respect is had to the rights and interests of the purchaser. That is not the case, where the court seeks to extort every dollar it can get from the purchaser, and refuses to confirm a sale fairly made, because he has gotten a good bargain." Langyher v. Patterson, 77 Va. 470; Roudabush v. Miller, 32 Gratt. 454.

3. Appellate Review of Discretion.

In General.—The discretion of the court in confirming or setting aside a judicial sale, not being an arbitrary one, is liable to review by an appellate court in a proper case. Kable v.

Mitchell, 9 W. Va. 492. Trimble *v.* Herold, 20 W. Va. 602; Marling *v.* Robrecht, 13 W. Va. 440.

From refusal to confirm sale and order for resale, any party may appeal, and to refuse suspension of the decree is error, but this court will not reverse the decree for such error when it is right on its merits. Todd *v.* Gallego Mills Mfg. Co., 84 Va. 586, 5 S. E. 676.

When the circuit court has disapproved and set aside a sale made by its own commissioners, the appellate court should not disturb the action of the circuit court, unless it plainly appears, that there is error to the prejudice of the appellant. Kable *v.* Mitchell, 9 W. Va. 492; Hyman *v.* Smith, 13 W. Va. 744.

D. NATURE OF PROCEEDINGS BEFORE CONFIRMATION.

Before confirmation the whole proceeding is in fieri, and under the control of the court. Terry *v.* Coles, 80 Va. 695; Brock *v.* Rice, 27 Gratt. 812; Todd *v.* Gallego Mills Mfg. Co., 84 Va. 586, 5 S. E. 676; Coles *v.* Coles, 83 Va. 525, 5 S. E. 673; Thomas *v.* Farmers' Nat. Bank, 86 Va. 291, 9 S. E. 1122; Alexander *v.* Howe, 85 Va. 198, 7 S. E. 248; Hickson *v.* Rucker, 77 Va. 135; Berlin *v.* Melhorn, 75 Va. 636, 639; Hildreth *v.* Turner, 89 Va. 858, 17 S. E. 471; Virginia Fire, etc., Ins. Co. *v.* Cottrell, 85 Va. 857, 9 S. E. 132.

Until confirmation the bargain is incomplete. Until confirmed by the court, the sale confers no rights. Until then it is a sale only in a popular and not in a judicial or legal sense. Rorer on Judicial Sales, pp. 10, 30, 55, 56; Terry *v.* Coles, 80 Va. 695; Brock *v.* Rice, 27 Gratt. 812; Carr *v.* Carr, 88 Va. 735, 14 S. E. 268; Langyher *v.* Patterson, 77 Va. 470; Hildreth *v.* Turner, 89 Va. 858, 17 S. E. 471; Kable *v.* Mitchell, 9 W. Va. 492; Trimble *v.* Herold, 20 W. Va. 602; Thompson *v.* Cox, 42 W. Va. 566, 26 S. E. 189; Hyman *v.* Smith, 13 W. Va. 744.

Before confirmation the purchase is a mere offer to bid—a mere bid to the court never accepted. Strayer *v.* Long, 83 Va. 715, 3 S. E. 372.

The sale until confirmed is an incomplete contract, a mere offer to purchase. Donahue *v.* Fackler, 21 W. Va. 124.

Until the sale is confirmed, it is a mere inchoate sale, liable to be defeated, and the title remains in the former owner. Thompson *v.* Cox, 42 W. Va. 566, 26 S. E. 189.

E. JURISDICTION TO CONFIRM SALE MADE WITHOUT COURT'S AUTHORITY.

The court has power to confirm a sale previously made without its authority. Estill *v.* McClintic, 11 W. Va. 399. Examples of such sales being confirmed by the court may be found in the cases of Londons *v.* Echols, 17 Gratt. 15; Hughes *v.* Johnston, 12 Gratt. 479.

F. POWER OF PARTIES TO AGREE TO CONFIRMATION AT GIVEN PRICE.

Parties have no power to agree that the court shall confirm a sale at a given price. All sales made by commissioners under decrees of court are conditional; they are merely accepted offers which the court may or may not approve and confirm. The parties must necessarily contract with reference to the law. National Bank *v.* Jarvis, 28 W. Va. 805.

G. NOTICE BEFORE CONFIRMATION.

Where Report Acted on in Vacation. —On the motion of any party to a chancery cause pending in a circuit court on ten days' notice to the adverse party or his counsel, the judge of such court may, in vacation, make any interlocutory decree or order, or direct any proceedings therein preparatory to the hearing of the cause on the merits; and may, also, after like notice to the adverse party or his counsel, and to the purchaser or renter, make an order confirming or refusing to confirm a sale or renting made under a decree in any such case; and in case of a refusal to confirm a sale or renting, the judge may order a resale or rerenting, or release, as the nature of the case may require; and may also, after like notice to the purchaser or his assigns, order a resale of any real estate or other property made under a decree in any chancery cause, for default in the payment of the purchase money, or any part thereof, or the interest due thereon. In all cases of confirmation, rerenting, and resale, the judge shall have the authority to convene before him all necessary parties and to make all orders necessary to carry the same into effect, and any circuit or corporation court may at any time during vacation appoint a commissioner to convey title to any purchaser of a tract of land sold in any chancery proceedings, who shall have fully paid for the same; but in case of any such order made in vacation for such title, such order shall provide that the receiver or commissioner who has collected the purchase money for the same shall unite in said deed, acknowledging receipt of the purchase money for the said land in full. (1884, p. 57; 1893-4, p. 233; 1895-6, p. 178; 1897-8, p. 744; 1902-3-4, p. 633.) Va. Code, 1904, ch. 167, § 3426.

Where Great Delay in Executing Sale.—After a great delay in the execution of a decree of sale, the court should not confirm the sale, without notice to the parties interested in the sale. Ayers v. Blair, 26 W. Va. 558.

Thus where a decree of sale was made in 1868, and the sale was not reported to the court until 1882, more than thirteen years thereafter, it was held, to be error to confirm such sale without giving notice to the owner. Ayers v. Blair, 26 W. Va. 558.

A sale of slaves having been made by a commissioner of the court, but no report of said sale made and returned to the court until after a period of between four and five years thereafter, during which period the papers in the cause are absent from the clerk's office, precluding the purchasers from knowing what was done, or what it was proposed to do in the cause, and the order directing the sale not authorizing the delivery of the slaves to the purchasers, it was error to make an order confirming said sale, without notice to the purchasers. Boner v. Boner, 6 W. Va. 377.

By virtue of their purchase at the judicial sale, they acquired a relation to the cause; became subject to the orders of the court for the judgment of the purchase money; to a rule to show cause against it, and to an attachment for a failure to make payment, if the rule is made absolute. These liabilities entitle them to be heard, if they can properly get before the court. Boner v. Boner, 6 W. Va. 377.

H. PETITION TO POSTPONE CONFIRMATION.

A petition may be filed in a pending suit asking to postpone the confirmation of a sale of real estate, and to suspend the proceedings in the suit until the matters of controversy set up in the petition have been adjudicated. Upon the filing of such a petition, rules should be awarded against the parties named as defendants, and, if necessary, an opportunity given the parties to take depositions, or in a proper case the matter should be referred to a commissioner to take evidence and report. But if the parties have been proceeded to a hearing upon affidavits, without objection, the appellate court will not reverse the case for this reason only. In the case at bar the petition was rightly rejected, but it should have been without prejudice to the petitioner to litigate his rights in the pending suits. Houghton v. Mountain Lake Land Co., 93 Va. 149, 24 S. E. 920.

I. OBJECTIONS TO CONFIRMATION.

1. Necessity for Making Objection before Confirmation.

The time to make objections to a judicial sale by a party to a suit is before confirmation, and if he fails to do so, he can not afterwards be heard thereon unless he has been prevented from asserting his rights through fraud or other adventitious circumstance beyond his control. This rule is applied strictly when the purchasers are strangers to the suit and in no wise interested therein. Klapneck v. Keltz, 50 W. Va. 331, 40 S. E. 570; Dunfee v. Childs, 45 W. Va. 155, 30 S. E. 102; Hughes v. Hamilton, 19 W. Va. 366; Beard v. Arbucke, 19 W. Va. 135; Daniel v. Leitch, 13 Gratt. 195, 212.

General rule in Virginia is that objections by purchaser for defect of title should be made before sale is confirmed, and such objections, made afterward, come too late, except in cases of after-discovered mistake, fraud, and the like. Thomas v. Davidson, 76 Va. 338; Watson v. Hoy, 28 Gratt. 698.

In Virginia the maxim caveat emptor strictly applies to all judicial sales. Objections for defect in title must be made before confirmation of report of sale. Ordinarily, objections after confirmation come too late. Hickson v. Rucker, 77 Va. 135.

And it is too late after the sale has been confirmed by the court without objection on the part of the purchaser, for the purchaser to come in, in answer to the rule for a resale, and say he never assented to the terms of the sale. He assented to the terms by becoming a purchaser, and his mistake as to the terms, if such ever existed, was discovered on the day of sale, and therefore before the confirmation of the sale by the court. Hickson v. Rucker, 77 Va. 135.

"In this case fraud is not only not charged, but such charge is expressly disclaimed. The appellant in his answer says he brings no charge against the fairness of the sale. Was the mistake, or objection complained of by him, discovered after the confirmation of the sale? Such a conclusion is entirely excluded by the deposition of the appellant himself, for he shows that it was discovered on the day of sale, when the race track was sold as a whole. Upon the principles stated above, then it was his plain duty to have made his defense in the court before confirmation of the sale, and without unreasonable delay. As we have said, by becoming the purchaser of the land, he had selected his forum, he had chosen to come into that court in that case, and had by that act submitted himself to that court on all questions concerning that sale, and his purchase, and if objection be had, he should have made the same in that court before confirmation." Hickson v. Rucker, 77 Va. 135.

"In this case the purchaser had become a purchaser at a judicial sale. In making the purchase, he had submitted himself to the jurisdiction of the court in the cause, as to all matters connected with the sale, or relating to him as purchaser. See Clarkson v. Read, 15 Gratt. 288, 291; and if he had objection to make to the sale upon any ground whatever, he had his opportunity, and he should have availed himself of it to state his case in the court he had himself chosen. This he failed to do, and upon default made in complying with the terms of sale, the court having confirmed the sale without objection on his part, the court took the usual course according to the practice of awarding a rule against him, to show cause against a resale at his risk and costs of the land he had purchased. After the confirmation of the sale, he was, in equity, the owner of the land, subject to the lien retained for the purchase money, and he was allowed sixty days within which to comply with the terms of sale, after which, he still being in default, the land should be resold at his risk, and in this case, it was so decreed; and from this decree the appellant appealed to this court." Hickson v. Rucker, 77 Va. 135. See post, "Procedure upon Failure of Purchaser to Comply with bid," XIV.

"Another matter is alleged error in the confirmation of the sale. There were no exceptions to the sale, and we might dismiss this subject with this statement. The decree does say that plaintiff objected to confirmation 'because' of inadequacy of price, and for other reasons specified in writing.' There is no writing giving these reasons, and we can not consider them. The objection is too general." Schmertz v. Hammond, 51 W. Va. 408, 41 S. E. 184; Hartley v. Roffe, 12 W. Va. 401.

The 8th section of ch. 132 of the Code of this state, p. 630, provides, that "if a sale of property be made under a decree or order of a court, and such sale be confirmed, though such decree or order be afterwards reversed or set aside, the title of the purchaser at such sale shall not be affected thereby; but there may be restitution of the proceeds of sale to those entitled." A debtor can not have a decree reversed confirming a sale of real estate for an error in the decree ordering the sale, when he has not taken the proper steps in the court below before the confirmation to review said decree of sale, except perhaps in some cases where the purchaser is a party to the suit. Beard v. Arbucke, 19 W. Va. 135; Hughes v. Hamilton, 19 W. Va. 366; Klapneck v. Keltz, 50 W. Va. 331, 40 S. E. 570; Dunfee v. Childs, 45 W. Va. 155, 30 S. E. 102.

The same rule applies to motions to set aside and reverse a decree of sale in the court making the sale. If he waits until after sale is confirmed to strangers he can not have the decree of confirmation set aside because of errors in the decree of sale. Klap-

neck v. Keltz, 50 W. Va. 331, 40 S. E. 570.

Objections that could have been made before confirmation, come too late after the sale has been confirmed, without any excuse being offered why they were not made sooner. The W. Va. Code, § 8, ch. 132, bars such after objections in these words: "If a sale of property be made under a decree or order of a court and such sale be confirmed, though such decree or order afterwards be reversed or set aside, the title of the purchaser at such sale shall not be affected thereby." Klapneck v. Keltz, 50 W. Va. 331, 40 S. E. 570.

Whether the decree of sale was erroneous or whether the commissioner acted without authority in receiving private bids or in failing to advertise, are objections that could have and should have been made before confirmation. Klapneck v. Keltz, 50 W. Va. 331, 40 S. E. 570.

From what has been already said, it will be seen that nearly all the appellant's objections, here considered, are founded upon supposed irregularities in the court below. With respect to all such objections, it is the duty of the purchaser to bring them to the attention of the court before the confirmation of the sale, that the parties or the court may have an opportunity of correcting them. Thomas v. Davidson, 76 Va. 338.

After the confirmation, a complete contract has been made between the court and the purchaser, and the latter will not be heard to make objections founded upon the errors in the proceedings which might have been remedied by timely notice. This rule is constantly enforced in behalf of infant parties, where it appears that the sale is manifestly for their benefit. Thomas v. Davidson, 76 Va. 338; Cooper v. Hepburn, 15 Gratt. 551, 566; Watson v. Hoy, 28 Gratt. 698.

2. Who May Object.

Either Party.—Either party may ob-

ject to the report of the sale. Brock v. Rice, 27 Gratt. 812; Carr v. Carr, 88 Va. 735, 14 S. E. 368.

The court of appeals having reversed a decree of the court below for the sale of land, and another confirming the sale and distributing the proceeds, in the absence of the owners of one moiety of the land, and having sent the case back, that they may be made parties and have an opportunity to defend their interests; though the decree is in other respects confirmed, these absent owners, when made parties, have the right to except to the sale and its confirmation; and are not precluded by the affirmation of the decree in other respects than those on which it was reversed. Crockett v. Sexton, 29 Gratt. 46.

Purchaser.—The purchaser himself, who becomes a party to the sale, may appear before the court and have any mistake corrected. Brock v. Rice, 27 Gratt. 812; Carr v. Carr, 88 Va. 735, 14 S. E. 368.

Joint Principal in Debts for Which Land Sold.—A joint principal in some of the debts for which land is sold, the proceeds whereof are insufficient to pay all the debts, though owning no part of said land, may object to the confirmation of the sale. Thomas v. Farmers' Nat. Bank, 86 Va. 291, 9 S. E. 1122.

3. Form of Objection.

An exception to a report of sale of land by a commissioner, appointed by decree of a court of equity in these words: 2d. "For other reasons, apparent on the face of said report," is too general. An exception to the report of such commissioner "for defects on the face of report" ought to be so specific, as to direct the mind of the court and the parties in interest to the particular defect or omission, upon which the exception relies, unless the report be so substantially defective on its face, as to require the court of its own motion, in the absence of excep-

tions, to set aside the report. Hartley v. Roffe, 12 W. Va. 401.

4. Grounds for Setting Aside Sale before Confirmation or Withholding Confirmation.

a. In General.

When the court will confirm the sale, or set it aside, must in a great measure depend upon the circumstances of each particular case. It is difficult to lay down any rule applicable to all cases; nor is it possible to specify all the grounds which will justify the court in withholding its approval. Brock v. Rice, 27 Gratt. 812; Carr v. Carr, 88 Va. 735, 14 S. E. 368; Hartley v. Roffe, 12 W. Va. 401; Beaty v. Veon, 18 W. Va. 291; Hickson v. Rucker, 77 Va. 135; Berlin v. Melhorn, 75 Va. 636, 639; Moran v. Clark, 30 W. Va. 358, 4 S. E. 303; Childs v. Hurd, 25 W. Va. 530; Hansucker v. Walker, 76 Va. 753; Roudabush v. Miller, 32 Gratt. 454; Moore v. Triplett, 96 Va. 603, 32 S. E. 50; Marling v. Robrecht, 13 W. Va. 440.

The Virginia courts exercise a large discretion in refusing to confirm a report of sale, and in ordering a resale of property sold under a decree. Daniel v. Leitch, 13 Gratt. 195, 212.

The principles which control the court in setting aside or affirming judicial sale, have been subject to repeated adjudication by this court, and all that is necessary is to refer to some of the decisions bearing upon the subject. Brock v. Rice, 27 Gratt. 812; Roudabush v. Miller, 32 Gratt. 454; Berlin v. Melhorn, 75 Va. 636, 639. In most of the cases the controversy has been between the purchaser at the sale on the one hand, and parties interested in the land on the other. And the court has sometimes refused to interfere with the sale, unless upon a very substantial upset bid. Hansucker v. Walker, 76 Va. 753.

Whenever, in any proceedings held in any chancery court for the purpose of subjecting real estate to the payment of debts, or for the sale of real estate for any other purpose, it appears that the real estate can not be sold for enough to pay off the lien of taxes, levies, and assessments returned delinquent against it, and it appears that the purchase price offered is, in the opinion of the court, adequate and reasonable, the said sale shall be confirmed. Va. Code, 1904, § 3397b.

Whether a resale of property should be directed depends upon the circumstances of the particular case. If the sale was fairly made, and the terms of sale have been complied with by the purchaser, it ought not to be set aside, except upon the strongest grounds. The purchaser is frequently subjected to considerable inconvenience in making his arrangements to purchase, and has the right, after he has made the purchase at a fair price, and has complied with the terms of the sale, to expect the court to confirm the sale. The foregoing reasons assigned by the court for its ruling are, we think, in the main, sound. Roudabush v. Miller, 32 Gratt. 454.

Where it is shown that a judicial sale has been made by competent authority, was regular in all respects, and was fair, no fraud or unfairness being alleged or proved, the sale should be confirmed. Finney v. Edwards, 75 Va. 44.

Where it is not sought to set aside a judicial sale which has been absolutely confirmed by the court which ordered it, but the objection is to the confirmation, the rule is more liberal, and the court will refuse confirmation and set aside the sale on other grounds than fraud, mistake, surprise, or other cause for which equity will give like relief if the sale had been made by the parties in interest, instead of by the court. Berlin v. Melhorn, 75 Va. 636, 639; Coles v. Coles, 83 Va. 525, 5 S. E. 673; Brock v. Rice, 27 Gratt. 812; Allison v. Allison, 88 Va. 328, 13 S. E. 549; Patterson v. Eakin, 87 Va. 49, 12 S. E. 144; Karn v. Rorer Iron, etc., Co., 86

Va. 754, 11 S. E. 431; Virginia Fire, etc., Ins. Co. v. Cottrell, 85 Va. 857, 9 S. E. 132; Langyher v. Patterson, 77 Va. 470; Hickson v. Rucker, 77 Va. 135; Nitro-Phosphate Syndicate v. Johnson, 101 Va. 774, 42 S. E. 995.

b. Distinguished from Grounds for Setting Aside Sale after Confirmation.

The case where application is made to withhold confirmation stands upon different principles from those governing where motion is made to set aside a sale which had been confirmed. In the former case, the reasons for withholding confirmation need not be so strong or substantial as would be required to justify a court in setting aside a sale in the latter case. Todd v. Gallego Mills Mfg. Co., 84 Va. 586, 5 S. E. 676; Virginia Fire, etc., Ins. Co. v. Cottrell, 85 Va. 857, 9 S. E. 132.

All authorities agree that there is a wide distinction between an application to set aside a sale after it has been approved by the court, and an application to withhold a confirmation. For a decree of confirmation, like any other judgment of a court, determines the rights of the parties and renders the contract which up to that time was incomplete, complete. Coles v. Coles, 83 Va. 525, 5 S. E. 673; Brock v. Rice, 27 Gratt. 812, 816.

There is a great difference between the power of a court over the sale, before, and after confirmation. Trimble v. Herold, 20 W. Va. 602.

Where the objection is to the confirmation of the sale, the rule is more liberal than when application is made to set aside the sale after confirmation. Berlin v. Melhorn, 75 Va. 636, 639; Virginia Fire, etc., Ins. Co. v. Cottrell, 85 Va. 857, 9 S. E. 132.

Opening Biddings and Offer of Substantial Advance as Prerequisite to Right to Have Sale Set Aside.—According to the practice in Virginia, upon objection to a sale of land made by a commissioner, it is not necessary to ask that the biddings may be opened by the offer of a substantial advance upon the price reported. But the court will consider the objections to the sale, and confirm or set it aside as the merits of the case may require. Roberts *v.* Roberts, 13 Gratt. 639.

"It was said in the argument here that if the sale under consideration could be set aside at all, that it could only be done by opening the biddings by the offer of a substantial advance upon the price reported; that this practice of the English chancery courts should be followed here in cases like this; and that the exceptions to the commissioner's report in this case for this reason should be disregarded. This objection I think is not well taken. The commissioner is the officer of the court, and acts under its supervision. His errors, when brought to the notice of the court, or appearing on the face of his proceedings, may be corrected. Such has hitherto been the practice in Virginia without question as to its propriety; its convenience and justice are manifest, and it should not be disturbed. In Fairfax *v.* Muse, above cited, the chancery court, in a summary way, revised the action of its commissioners, and confirmed it; and this court upon appeal affirmed the decision of the chancery court." Roberts *v.* Roberts, 13 Gratt. 639, 642.

c. Particular Grounds.

(1) Grounds Justifying Setting Aside Sale after Confirmation.

Generally, whatever, and even less, is sufficient to set a sale aside after its consummation will of course, if known, cause confirmation to be denied. Rorer on Judicial Sales, p. 57, § 1; Hyman *v.* Smith, 13 W. Va. 744.

(2) Fraud or Mistake.

(a) In General.

If there is reason to believe that fraud or mistake has been committed to the detriment of the owner or purchaser, the court will withhold a confirmation. Rorer on Judicial Sales, 57; Brock *v.* Rice, 27 Gratt. 812; Carr *v.*

Carr, 88 Va. 735, 14 S. E. 368; Roudabush *v.* Miller, 32 Gratt. 454; Hilleary *v.* Thompson, 11 W. Va. 113; Hartley *v.* Roffe, 12 W. Va. 401.

(b) Mistake or Misunderstanding between Person Conducting Sale and Bidders.

aa. In General.

Any mistake or misunderstanding between the persons conducting the sale and intended bidders or parties in interest, and any accident, fraud, or other circumstance, by which interests are prejudiced, without the fault of the injured party or parties, will be deemed sufficient cause for refusing confirmation, and ordering a resale. Rorer on Judicial Sales, 57; Hilleary *v.* Thompson, 11 W. Va. 113; Hyman *v.* Smith, 13 W. Va. 744.

bb. Misunderstanding as to Whether Land Offered with Growing Crop.

An objection was made to the confirmation of a sale that different impressions existed at the sale as to what was really offered, whether the land alone, or the land with the growing crop thereon, no announcement being at the time made by the commissioners whether or not the landlord's share of the growing crop of corn on the land was or was not to be included in the sale. It is true, that when land is sold with a crop growing upon it, the purchaser takes the crop at the purchase, unless it is excepted. But the very fact that it may be excepted, makes it the duty of the commissioners who make the sale, to in some way indicate whether or not it will be sold with the land. In this case, as the decree shows, nothing was said by the commissioners, at the time of the sale or before, as to whether or not the growing crop would be reserved; and we may infer from the decree that the purchaser claimed that he bought it, as the court, before it confirmed the sale, required the purchaser to relinquish any claim to the growing crop. There seems to have been a misunderstanding at the sale, as to whether the growing crop was excepted; and that fact would directly tend to interfere with a proper competition among the bidders. Hilleary v. Thompson, 11 W. Va. 113.

At a judicial sale, R. became the purchaser of a tract of one hundred acres of land at $26 per acre; affidavits in the cause, which were uncontradicted, showed that the land was worth at least $40 per acre; there was a misunderstanding, as to whether or not the growing crop on the land was being sold with it; the auctioneer either bid himself, or received sham bids. Held, that under these circumstances the sale was invalid and ought not to have been confirmed. Hilleary v. Thompson, 11 W. Va. 113.

(3) Breach of Duty on Part of Officer Conducting Sale.

(a) In General.

Where it appears that the officer conducting the sale has been guilty of any wrong or breach of duty to the injury of the parties interested, the court will withhold a confirmation. Brock v. Rice, 27 Gratt. 812; Roudabush v. Miller, 32 Gratt. 454; Carr v. Carr, 88 Va. 735, 14 S. E. 368; Trimble v. Herold, 20 W. Va. 602; Roberts v. Roberts, 13 Gratt. 639; Hartley v. Roffe, 12 W. Va. 401.

If the commissioners are guilty of misconduct at the sale, by which the rights of the debtor are, materially, prejudiced by a fair price not being obtained, this would be sufficient to set aside the sale. Trimble v. Herold, 20 W. Va. 602.

Brock v. Rice, 27 Gratt. 812, was a case in which the court refused to enforce a sale against the purchaser on account of the misconduct of the life tenant and the auctioneer, though the conduct of the commissioner was unexceptionable.

The sale being set aside as to the life tenant, must be set aside in toto, though some of the remaindermen are infants. Brock v. Rice, 27 Gratt. 812.

(b) Conduct Preventing Fair Competition.

aa. In General

"Without going into an enumeration of the many causes for which public sales have been set aside, yet we see that many of them are founded on the principle that fair competition has been prevented, and sacrifice may have been incurred to the prejudice of those interested. This principle rules in cases of sales by auctioneers, executors, administrators, trustees, commissioners, and all others having authority to sell. 2 Rob. Prac. 65, old edition. Although the irregular action of the person making the sale may not always avoid it, still wherever the sale itself is allowed to stand, the delinquent in duty must make compensation to the party injured." Roberts v. Roberts, 13 Gratt. 639, 641; Teel v. Yancey, 23 Gratt. 691.

With respect to the objections made by the appellant to the manner of conducting, and circumstances attending, the sale of the land in question; while the court would discourage a limitation of time, prescribed to the bidders, which would prevent a fair sale of the property for the most it would bring at the time of auction; yet the limitation in this case having only been resorted to after the land had been cried for a considerable time, and even then repeatedly done away, and the sale again opened, the only effect thereof must have been to quicken and excite the bidders. In all other points of view, the conduct of the commissioners appears to have been equally unexceptionable, and is approved by this court; and, upon the whole, the decree of the court of chancery is affirmed. Under such circumstances, a sale of land by commissioners, in obedience to a decree in chancery, ought not to be set aside. Fairfax v. Muse, 4 Munf. 124.

A commissioner, selling land under a decree in chancery, ought not to permit the creditor's agent to force the sale, at an inadequate price, in the absence of other bidders. Quarles *v.* Lacy, 4 Munf. 251.

bb. Sale on Day So Inclement as to Deter Persons from Attending.

A sale of a tract of land made by a commissioner under a decree of the chancery court, on a day so inclement that persons intending to be present and to bid for a part of the land, are deterred from attending, and when there was but one bidder present, who lived at the place, will be set aside, without weighing the evidence, which is conflicting, as to the sufficiency of the price at which it was sold. Roberts *v.* Roberts, 13 Gratt. 639.

cc. Purchase by Commissioner.

A judicial sale of land is excepted to because one of the commissioners to sell was interested in the purchase of one-half of the land. This is a valid objection, and the sale will be set aside. Teel *v.* Yancey, 23 Gratt. 691.

(4) Errors in Decree Ordering Sale.
(a) In General.

Before confirmation, if exception be made to the report of sale, on the ground that the court erred in the decree ordering the sale in such a manner, as was calculated to affect the bidders at the sale, and consequently, the price, at which the lands would sell, and in support of such exception, the debtor would show, that he actually suffered material injury thereunder, in the land selling for materially less that it otherwise would, the court has power, and under such circumstances would exercise it, to refuse to confirm the sale and set it aside. Trimble *v.* Herold, 20 W. Va. 602.

If a decree directs the sale of real estate under circumstances which injure the sale, the parties injured should except to the report of the commissioner, and apply to the court to set aside the sale. A bill of review after a final decree is not the proper remedy. Vanmeter *v.* Vanmeters, 3 Gratt. 148, 149.

(b) Failure to Fix Amounts and Priorities of Liens.

If before the confirmation of a sale the report of sale be excepted to, on the ground that the decree ordering the sale failed to fix the amounts and priorities of the liens charged thereon, and it clearly appears to the court, that the debtor was materially prejudiced in the sale of the land thereby, the land on that account being actually sold for a price materially less· than it otherwise would have sold for, the court in the exercise of a sound discretion may for such reason refuse to confirm such sale, and set it aside. Trimble *v.* Herold, 20 W. Va. 602; Utterbach *v.* Mehlenger, 86 Va. 62, 9 S. E. 479.

In the case of Trimble *v.* Herold, 20 W. Va. 602, the court says: "But it is also insisted that the report of sale ought not to have been confirmed and that the sale should have been set aside, because the amount and priorities of the liens were not fixed when the sale was ordered. * * * There is nothing in this record to show that Herold was injured, in the slightest degree, by the error in the decree ordering the sale. There is no evidence that the property was sold for a dollar less than it otherwise would have sold for, if such error had not been committed." And the court affirmed the decision of the lower court confirming the sale. Utterbach *v.* Mehlenger, 86 Va. 62, 9 S. E. 479.

(c) Where Land Brought Less because of Error in Decree.

But § 8 of ch. 132 of the Code of West Virginia, p. 630, provides, that "if a sale of property be made under a decree or order of a court, and such sale be confirmed, though such decree or order be afterwards reversed or set aside, the title of the purchaser shall not be affected thereby; but there may be restitution of the proceeds of sale to those entitled." In construing the above statute this court has determined, that, if before the confirmation of a sale the report of sale be excepted to, on the ground that the decree ordering the sale is erroneous, and it clearly appears to the court, that the sale of the land was materially affected thereby, and that it brought materially less than it otherwise would have brought by reason of this error in the decree of sale, the court should refuse to confirm the sale; and if it be confirmed, the appellate court will reverse the decree confirming the sale as well as the decree ordering the sale. Tracey *v.* Shumate, 22 W. Va. 474, 500; Trimble *v.* Herold, 20 W. Va. 602.

The court would not refuse to confirm a sale and set it aside because of an error in the decree ordering the sale, unless such error did have the effect to bring the lands to a sale, under such circumstances, as in fact did cause them to be sold at a price materially less, than they would have brought, but for such error. Trimble *v.* Herold, 20 W. Va. 602; Hughes *v.* Hamilton, 19 W. Va. 366; Martin *v.* Smith, 25 W. Va. 579.

(5) Failure to Pursue Directions in Decree.

The courts exercise a large discretion in refusing a report of sale, and in ordering a resale of property sold under a decree. They will not confirm a report of sale and compel a purchaser to complete his purchase when the directions of the decree in regard to the sale have not been pursued, if either party object to such confirmation. Accordingly, in Talley *v.* Starke, 6 Gratt. 339, in which the land was not sold on the premises as directed by the decree, and the confirmation of the report was opposed by two of the purchasers on that ground; this court, for that and other reasons, reversed the decree of confirmation; saying that inasmuch as the purchasers could not have enforced their contracts, if resisted by the parties in the cause, they ought not to be compelled to perfect them. Daniel *v.* Leitch, 13 Gratt. 195, 212.

It is not just cause for vacating a judicial sale, that only a few bidders were present. The only inquiry for the court, is, whether the terms of the decree have been pursued and the property sold at an adequate price. Hudgins *v.* Lanier, 23 Gratt. 494.

(6) Laches.

See the title LACHES.

(a) By Purchaser in Complying with Terms of Sale.

A court of equity will not give a purchaser at a sale by its commissioners, the benefit of his purchase, when he neglects to comply with the terms of sale within a reasonable time, if a resale is deemed more beneficial to the parties interested in the proceeds of the sale. Hyman *v.* Smith, 13 W. Va. 744.

(b) By Court in Confirming Sale.

A court of equity will not compel the purchaser to take the land by confirming the sale, where by the action of the parties to the suit, action on the report of sale by the court in confirming the same has been delayed for such an unreasonable time, that confirmation of the sale would most probably cause him loss, if the purchaser is not in default, or guilty of laches or fraud or the like and has not acquiesced in such delay, and where it appears, that during the unreasonable time of delay, the property has depreciated in value. Hyman *v.* Smith, 13 W. Va. 744.

Ordinarily it is fair to presume, that all persons, who bid at sales of commissioners under decrees of court of equity, do so with the tacit understanding, at least, that the sale will be reported and approved or disapproved within a reasonable time, and that the highest bidder will not be kept in doubt, as to the result, and out of the use of money, he pays to the commissioners at the sale on his bid, for an unreasonable length of time thereafter. Hyman *v.* Smith, 13 W. Va. 744.

Justice to the bidder at such sales, and public policy in relation thereto, require and demand, that such sales be reported, and either approved or disapproved in a reasonable time after the sale, or the highest bidder, if he so desires, should be released from the obligation on his bid when the delay is not caused by his opposition to the confirmation of the sale, and it appears that during such unreasonable delay the property has depreciated in value for causes beyond his control. Hyman v. Smith, 13 W. Va. 744.

What is such unreasonable time of delay in the confirmation of the sale must of necessity depend, to some extent, upon the facts and surrounding circumstances in each case. And the court in determining the question must exercise a sound discretion in the interest of fairness, prudence and the rights of all concerned, in view of all such facts and surrounding circumstances. Hyman v. Smith, 13 W. Va. 744.

Hyman v. Smith, 13 W. Va. 744, was a case, where it is held proper by the appellate court to disapprove, and refuse to confirm, a sale made by commissioners under a decree of a court of equity, at the instance of the purchasers after more than three years from the day of sale.

"But it seems to me, that the court ought not to disapprove, and refuse to confirm the sale within a reasonable time after it is made by the commissioners, simply because the property has within that time depreciated in value. It may be that when the property, or a material part thereof, has been destroyed by fire or flood within such reasonable time after the sale by the commissioners, the court ought to decline to confirm such sale, if desired by the purchaser, or allow him proper deduction from the sale price for the destruction of the property; but as that question is not presented in this case, I do not express an opinion upon it." Hyman v. Smith, 13 W. Va. 744.

(7) Defect in Title.

In General.—The court in the exercise of its discretion in refusing to confirm a report of sale, and in ordering a resale of property sold under a decree, will not confirm a report of sale and compel a purchaser to complete his purchase when there is any defect of title of which he had no knowledge when the sale was made. Daniel v. Leitch, 13 Gratt. 195, 212.

If, therefore, there is any defect in the title which the purchaser could acquire under the decree, the court, on his motion, will refuse to confirm the report of sale, and discharge him from his purchase. Daniel v. Leitch, 13 Gratt. 195, 212.

The purchaser at a sale by a commissioner of the court has, to the time the sale is confirmed, the right to inquire into the title of the property, and if it is defective the court will let him off from his bid. Until such sale is confirmed by the court, the contract of the purchaser is incomplete. Fleming v. Holt, 12 W. Va. 143.

A purchaser of land at a judicial sale, can only obtain relief for defects in the title, or incumbrances on the property, by resisting the confirmation of the sale by the court, upon the return of the commissioner's report. And it is not competent for a court of equity to enjoin a judgment obtained against him for the purchase money, on the ground of defect of title to the property at the time of the purchase. Threlkelds v. Campbell, 2 Gratt. 198.

(8) Want of Memorandum.

A judicial sale of land is excepted to, because there was no memorandum. This is a valid objection, and the sale was properly set aside. Teel v. Yancey, 23 Gratt. 691.

(9) Mistake as to Nature of Ownership as Alleged in Original Bill.

T. D. and others file a bill, alleging that certain parties, therein named, were the owners of a tract of land, as the heirs at law of M. A. and pray that the same may be sold, as incapable of partition, and a sale is accordingly made. More than six years afterwards the same parties file an amended bill, alleging that the same parties own said land as the devisees of L. A. and not as heirs at law of M. A., as alleged in their original bill—the amounts of their interests being somewhat different—and pray that the sale may not be confirmed. The purchaser in the meantime, although the sale had not been reported or confirmed, had taken possession of said land, and made valuable improvements, and paid the whole or a large part of the purchase money. Held, that the fact, if such it be, that the same parties own the land as devisees, and not as heirs at law, in no sufficient objection to confirming the sale, there being no other objection made, or shown thereto, and as the proceeds of sale can be distributed among the parties in interest, in the proportion in which they hold said land as devisees. Donahoe v. Fackler, 8 W. Va. 249.

(10) Conditional Confirmation.

An objection is made that the confimation of the sale was made conditional upon the purchaser surrendering any claim to the landlord's share of the growing crop. If the sale had been in all other respects fair, this would be an error, of which Roberts could have made just complaint; but in that case, would not be an error to the prejudice of the debtor, as it would make the land bring more money. Hilleary v. Thompson, 11 W. Va. 113.

(11) Petition by Persons Not Parties Setting Up Vague and Indefinite Interest in Land.

After sale has been made and reported, a petition, filed by persons not parties to the suit and setting up a vague and indefinite interest in the land and praying that the sale be not confirmed, should not be entertained, but the petitioners should be left to litigate their rights in some other proceeding. Thomas v. Thomas, 81 Va. 17.

(12) Injunction Pending.

"The third exception to the sale was that Isbell, the purchaser, at the date of sale was a defendant in a suit in equity in the United States circuit court of Huntington v. Laidley and others, in which an injunction was in force at the date of the sale restraining Laidley from prosecuting the ejectment, and that the case had gone to the supreme court of the United States, and was still there pending. It does not appear by record what was the matter involved in the Huntington suit, or that the injunction operated upon this ejectment or this property, or that Isbell or Jasper was a party. We are asked to look at the case as reported in 176 U. S. 668. That is not a part of this record to show facts in this case. Even if it were, we can not there find legally the necessary facts to say that the injunction tied up this case. An injunction awarded by a federal court against a suit in a state court is contrary to U. S. Revised Statutes, § 720, and void. This is conceded by the opinion in the supreme court in the report referred to at page 678. Being void, the injunction could be lawfully disregarded. Ruhl v. Ruhl, 24 W. Va. 279; Hebb v. County Court, 48 W. Va. 279, 37 S. E. 676. Still, I am not prepared to say that upon the question of confirmation of a sale made while such an injunction is pending, it would not be ground for refusing confirmation by reason of its deterring bidders, promoting sacrifice and casting cloud over title." Laidley v. Jasper, 49 W. Va. 526, 39 S. E. 169.

(13) Upset Bid.

See post, "Opening Biddings on Upset Bids," XI.

Where a material advance is offered by a substantial bidder, the court may refuse to confirm the sale, and set it aside. Teel v. Yancey, 23 Gratt. 691.

(14) Inadequacy of Price.

(a) In General.

See post, "Inadequacy of Price," X, B, 4, n.

While the bidder at the sale may infer that if he is the highest and best bidder, and complies with the terms of sale, that the property is his, yet he is required to know that the court may, in the exercise of a sound discretion, approve or reject his bid for any sufficient cause, among others that the price is greatly inadequate. Kable *v.* Mitchell, 9 W. Va. 492; Hyman *v.* Smith, 13 W. Va. 744; Hughes *v.* Hamilton, 19 W. Va. 366.

But the sale for a price reported by the commissioners of sale and by the commissioner of account, and certified by three adjacent landowners, as much below the actual value of the land, and there being a well-secured upset bid of ten per cent.; held, the sale ought to have been set aside for inadequacy of price and a resale ordered. Hansucker *v.* Walker, 76 Va. 753.

It seems that it is necessary for the protection of the creditor and the oppressed debtor each, that the court should have and exercise a sound discretion in approving or setting aside sales of land made by its commissioners for cause such as greatly inadequate price, etc., especially when it is remembered that the sale is forced. It is equally necessary in the case of infants, insane persons, etc., and, in such cases, where the court below has disapproved a bid, or set aside such sale, this court should not disturb or reverse the action of the court below, unless it plainly appears that the court erred to the prejudice of the appellant. Kable *v.* Mitchell, 9 W. Va. 492.

The statute prescribes the inadequacy of price for which commissioners of judicial sales for debts contracted or liabilities incurred prior to the 10th of April, 1865, shall not sell the debtor's land. It provides that where the land does not bring, at the first and second exposure to sale, three-fourths of the last official assessment made for the purposes of taxation, it shall not be sold. Code of 1873, ch. 174, § 4, p. 1123. This act was passed in tenderness to the debtor. It may be regarded as a statutory prescription as to what shall be regarded inadequacy of price to avoid a judicial sale of real estate, and that only for the first and second exposure of the land to sale. After that, in deference to the rights of the creditor, the statute interposes no restriction, but allows the land to be sold for what it will bring. Curtis *v.* Thompson, 29 Gratt. 474.

A tract of land was fairly sold by commissioners, pursuant to a decree of court, to a purchaser for $27.50 per acre, subject to a contingent right of dower. The tract was assessed in 1870 at $30; and $30 per acre was the value fixed upon the land by a commissioner of the court, whose report had been confirmed without exception in the cause; in which valuation no allowance was made for the contingent right of dower. The owner of the land objected to a confirmation of the sale on the ground of inadequacy of price, and affidavits touching the value of the land were filed by both parties. The court below set the sale aside and ordered a resale; whereat the same party became the purchaser at the same price. In the meanwhile the assessment of the land had been reduced to $20 per acre. The owner of the land again objected to the confirmation of the sale on the same grounds as before; and the court again refused to confirm the sale, and again ordered a resale. Held, the first sale should have been confirmed; and the decree setting it aside and all the subsequent proceedings were erroneous. Curtis *v.* Thompson, 29 Gratt. 474.

(b) Mere Inadequacy.

From a review of the Virginia cases it may be seen that the Virginia supreme court of appeals is averse to refusing a confirmation of a sale merely on the ground of inadequacy of price. Coles *v.* Coles, 83 Va. 525, 5 S. E. 673; Effinger *v.* Ralston, 21 Gratt. 430, 433; Curtis *v.* Thompson, 29 Gratt. 474; Roudabush *v.* Miller, 32 Gratt. 454. See post, "Gross Inadequacy," IX, I,

4, c, (14), (c), for a review of Virginia cases touching this point.

In Effinger *v.* Ralston, 21 Gratt. 430, 436, Moncure, P., said: "To induce a court to set aside a sale fairly made in pursuance of a decree, merely upon the ground of inadequacy of price, there ought to be a decided preponderance of evidence of such inadequacy, even if it be conceded that mere inadequacy of price is in itself a sufficient ground for setting aside such a sale;" thus intimating that it was, in his opinion, doubtful whether inadequacy of price alone was a sufficient reason for setting aside a judicial sale, but declining to decide that it was not. Coles *v.* Coles, 83 Va. 525, 5 S. E. 673.

In the case of a judicial sale, where no advance bid has been made, and the objection to confirmation is grounded upon the inadequacy of price, supported only by parol evide ·e, the proof must be very clear. Atkinson *v.* Washington, etc., College, 54 W. Va. 32, 46 S. E. 253; Connell *v.* Wilhelm, 36 W. Va. 598, 15 S. E. 245.

Where a judicial sale has been sufficiently advertised, well attended, and fairly conducted, it should not be set aside for inadequacy of price merely because the bill, which was filed three years before the sale, charged that the property was worth a much larger sum than it brought at the judicial sale. Hazlewood *v.* Forrer, 94 Va. 703, 27 S. E. 507.

Public policy requires that purchasers at judicial sales should be entitled to certainty and security of their rights under their purchasers, and that they should not be refused confirmation, simply because they may have got a good bargain. Langyher *v.* Patterson, 77 Va. 470.

(c) Gross Inadequacy.

aa. Virginia Decisions.

From a review of the Virginia cases, it may be seen that while no test of inadequacy can be found which will apply to all cases, and while it is apparent that the Virginia supreme court of appeals is averse to refusing a confirmation of a sale merely on the ground of inadequacy of price, yet that it will always do so where the inadequacy of the sale will result in a sacrifice of the property. Coles *v.* Coles, 83 Va. 525, 5 S. E. 673; Terry *v.* Coles, 80 Va. 695.

In the case of Teel *v.* Yancey, 23 Gratt. 691, it was held, according to the syllabus, that where a judicial sale is excepted to, because the land was sacrificed, this is a valid objection and the sale was properly set aside. Cited in Kable *v.* Mitchell, 9 W. Va. 492.

In Effinger *v.* Ralston, 21 Gratt. 430, 436, objection was made to the confirmation of the sale because of the inadequacy of the price, when it was decreed that the sale should stand confirmed unless Effinger should file with the clerk of the court bond, with good security, in the penalty of $15,000 conditioned that at the next offer of the land for sale he would bid five per cent. more than the commissioner had sold the land for, including costs of said sale. In this case Moncure, P., said: "To induce a court to set aside a sale fairly made in pursuance of a decree, merely upon the ground of inadequacy of price, there ought to be a decided preponderance of evidence of such inadequacy, even if it be conceded that mere inadequacy of price is in itself a sufficient ground for setting aside such a sale;" thus intimating that it was, in his opinion, doubtful whether inadequacy of price alone was a sufficient reason for setting aside a judicial sale, but declining to decide that it was not. In that case, however, the court declared that the English practice of opening the biddings upon the offer of an upset bid substantially prevailed in this state. Cited in Coles *v.* Coles, 83 Va. 525, 5 S. E. 673; Curtis *v.* Thompson, 29 Gratt. 474; Kable *v.* Mitchell, 9 W. Va. 492.

In Hudgins *v.* Lanier, 23 Gratt. 494, there was an upset bid of $100 advance upon the price paid, which the court held was not a sufficient advance to justify a resale. But in that case Staples, J., who delivered the opinion of the court, while answering the objection that the court had erred in decreeing a sale before the difficulties in respect to the title were removed, said: "The legal title can at any time be obtained, and there is no reason to suppose that any sacrifice will result from a sale of the property without it. The whole subject is under the control of the circuit court, which will take care not to confirm a sale at a grossly inadequate price;" thus showing, that in his opinion, at least, gross inadequacy of price was a sufficient ground for refusing to confirm a judicial sale. Coles v. Coles, 83 Va. 525, 5 S. E. 673.

In Brock v. Rice, 27 Gratt. 812, 815, the doctrine is announced that in judicial sales the whole proceedings are in fieri before confirmation; that the action of the court must depend, in a large measure, upon the circumstances of the particular case, and that the discretion of the court must be exercised in the interest of fairness, prudence, and with a just regard to the rights of all concerned. But in that case no question of opening the biddings or of refusing to confirm for inadequacy of price arose. Coles v. Coles, 83 Va. 525, 5 S. E. 673.

In Curtis v. Thompson, 29 Gratt. 474, 477, Judge Anderson, with Christian, J., concurring, said: "I do not think that mere inadequacy of price is sufficient ground for setting aside a sale fairly made pursuant to a decree of the court." But note the reason, which can have no application to a case like the one in hand, when no creditor in a deed of trust is seeking to enforce his rights, but where the property is being sold for the purpose of distributing the proceeds as far as possible in accordance with the will of the testator. He says: "The creditor is entitled to his money and to a sale of the land to get it, according to contract. And all that the debtor can require is, that it shall be sold for as much as it will bring in market. After his default he is not entitled to hold the money and the land too, which he contracted should be sold to pay his debt, because, in the opinion of some of his neighbors, it is worth a great deal more than the price at which it is cried out." In this case Judges Staples and Burks, while concurring in the decree, declared that they "were not prepared to say that inadequacy of price was not sufficient to set aside a judicial sale." So, in this case, in which Judge Moncure did not sit, it is properly made a quære in the syllabus of the reporter, whether inadequacy of price alone is sufficient to set aside a judicial sale. Coles v. Coles, 83 Va. 525, 5 S. E. 673.

In Roudabush v. Miller, 32 Gratt. 454, 465, Judge Anderson, speaking for the court, after saying that it had never been decided how far the English practice had been adopted in this commonwealth, and that it had never been held that for mere inadequacy of price the court should set aside the sale, used this language: * * * "In a proper case, where it would be just to all the parties concerned, this court may be understood as having sanctioned a practice in the circuit courts, in the exercise of a sound discretion, of setting aside a sale made by commissioners under a decree, and reopening the biddings, upon the offer of an advanced bid of sufficient amount, deposited or well secured; and to that extent the former English practice has been allowed in this state." Coles v. Coles, 83 Va. 525, 5 S. E. 673.

Berlin v. Melhorn, 75 Va. 636, 642, was the case of an upset bid made by a defaulting purchaser at the same term, but after the confirmation of the sale. In this case is was not even alleged the price paid by Berlin was inadequate, and the court held, that the mere offer of a larger price by such a purchaser was not a good cause for setting aside the sale. Coles *v.* Coles, 83 Va. 525, 5 S. E. 673.

In the case of Hansucker *v.* Walker, 76 Va. 753, the court held that the sale ought to have been set aside for inadequacy of price and a resale ordered. In that case there was an upset bid of ten per cent. made by a responsible party, but the court seems to have attached no importance to that circumstance. And the opinion, after showing that the price offered was inadequate, and barely adverting to the fact that there was an upset bid, procéeds: "It is impossible to resist the conclusion that the property was sold at a grossly inadequate price, and that a resale is necessary in justice to the rights of the debtor and the junior creditors." Coles *v.* Coles, 83 Va. 525, 5 S. E. 673.

In Langyher *v.* Patterson, 77 Va. 470, 473, the court held, that it was error for the circuit court to set aside its decree of confirmation upon the mere offer of an advance bid of ten per cent., without notice to the purchaser or any of the parties to the suit, and without even a suggestion that the price for which the land sold was inadequate. Coles *v.* Coles, 83 Va. 525, 5 S. E. 673.

Where sale of land is decreed to pay specific legacies, and the residue to four residuary legatees, and the land is bid in by one of those legatees and the other legatees oppose the acceptance of the bid and the confirmation of the sale, and show by numerous witnesses well acquainted with the land, that though the sale was open and fair, yet the price bid was grossly inadequate, and that the land if divided and sold in parcels would, on the usual terms of payment in such cases, bring two or three times the price bid; there was no error in the court rejecting the bid, and refusing to confirm the sale and directing a resale. Terry *v.* Coles, 80 Va. 695.

bb. West Virginia Decisions.

It is well settled by repeated decisions of the West Virginia court, that gross inadequacy of price alone may be a sufficient ground for withholding confirmation and setting aside a judicial sale. Trimble *v.* Herold, 20 Va. 602; Kable *v.* Mitchell, 9 W. Va. 492; Moran *v.* Clark, 30 W. Va. 358, 4 S. E. 303; Hughes *v.* Hamilton, 19 W. Va. 366; Sinnett *v.* Cralle, 4 W. Va. 600; Tracy *v.* Shumate, 22 W. Va. 474.

It is clear from the authorities, that a sale by commissioners made under a decree of a court of equity, is not an absolute sale in Virginia and in West Virginia and it does not become absolute until the sale is confirmed by the court; the court may in the exercise of a sound discretion either affirm or set aside the sale, or direct the biddings to be reopened, where from the facts and evidence and circumstances before it, it appears clearly that the sale was made at a greatly inadequate price. Kable *v.* Mitchell, 9 W. Va. 492; Trimbel *v.* Herold, 20 W. Va. 602; Moran *v.* Clark, 30 W. Va. 358, 4 S. E. 303; Hughes *v.* Hamilton, 19 W. Va. 366; Beaty *v.* Veon, 18 W. Va. 291; Hartley *v.* Roffe, 12 W. Va. 401; Connell *v.* Wilhelm, 36 W. Va. 598, 15 S. E. 245; Hilleary *v.* Thompson, 11 W. Va. 113; Hyman *v.* Smith, 13 W. Va. 744.

The courts generally regard, as the value of a thing, the price it will bring. Value admits of no precise standard. This rule is especially applicable to public sales. When there are no ingredients in a case of suspicious character, and no peculiar relation of parties, mere inadequacy of price will not be considered by a court as any reason for setting aside a sale, unless where the inadequacy of price is so gross as of itself to prove fraud. But the case would have to be very strong to justify the court in holding a purchaser at a public auction, between whom and the vendor there had been no previous communication affecting the fairness of the sale, as chargeable with fraud, merely because the property has been knocked down to him at a small price. To set aside a sale for inadequacy of price under such circumstances the inequality must be so gross, that the mere stating of it must shock the conscience of a man of common sense and afford evidence of fraud. Bradford *v.* McConihay, 15 W. Va. 732.

In the absence of evidence tending to impeach the fairness of a sale, it can not be set aside for inadequacy of price, unless it be so inadequate as to justify the presumption of fraud and collusion, and, to justify such presumption from this inadequacy alone, it must be so strong and manifest an inadequacy as to shock the conscience and confound the judgment of any man of common sense. Bradford *v.* McConihay, 15 W. Va. 732; Atkinson *v.* Washington, etc., College, 54 W. Va. 32, 46 S. E. 253; Schmertz *v.* Hammond, 51 W. Va. 408, 41 S. E. 184; Connell *v.* Wilhelm, 36 W. Va. 598, 15 S. E. 245; Lallance *v.* Fisher, 29 W. Va. 512, 2 S. E. 775.

Half the estimated value of the property is not such inadequacy of price as to justify the setting aside of a judicial sale otherwise fairly conducted. Schmertz *v.* Hammond, 51 W. Va. 408, 41 S. E. 184; Bradford *v.* McConihay, 15 W. Va. 732; Connell *v.* Wilhelm, 36 W. Va. 598, 15 S. E. 245; Lallance *v.* Fisher, 29 W. Va. 512, 2 S. E. 775; Atkinson *v.* Washington, etc., College, 54 W. Va. 32, 46 S. E. 253.

And courts have frequently refused to set aside sales and other contracts, where there was a great inadequacy of price, and where the circumstances surrounding the case were to some extent suspicious. Bradford *v.* McConihay, 15 W. Va. 732.

Inadequacy of price must be very great to warrant the court in setting aside a sale. Atkinson *v.* Washington, etc., College, 54 W. Va. 32, 46 S. E. 253.

In the case of Sinnett *v.* Cralle, 4 W. Va. 600, it was held, that a sale of land made by commissioners under a decree of court, for the payment of judgment, which was a lien thereon, should be set aside for great inadequacy of price. Kable *v.* Mitchell, 9 W. Va. 492.

(d) Determination of Question of Inadequacy.

aa. Must Be Shown by Preponderance of Evidence.

To induce a court to set aside a sale fairly made in pursuance of a decree, merely upon the ground of inadequacy of price, there ought to be a decided preponderance of evidence of such inadequacy, even if it be conceded that mere inadequacy of price, is, in itself, a sufficient ground for setting aside such sale. Effinger *v.* Ralston, 21 Gratt. 430, 433; Kable *v.* Mitchell, 9 W. Va. 492; Curtis *v.* Thompson, 29 Gratt. 474; Coles *v.* Coles, 83 Va. 525, 5 S. E. 673.

A sale under the decree may be set aside before confirmation for gross inadequacy of price; but if it be attempted to establish this by parol evidence only, the proof must be very clear, especially if a great time has elapsed between the sale and its confirmation, and during this time no advanced bid has been made to the court. Tracey *v.* Shumate, 22 W. Va. 474; Connell *v.* Wilhelm, 36 W. Va. 598, 15 S. E. 245.

bb. Affidavits or Depositions.

The court may solve and determine the question as to whether the sale was made at a greatly inadequate price, upon affidavits or depositions in connection with the fact that a greatly larger price is offered to the court for the land, and secured, or offered to be secured. Kable *v.* Mitchell, 9 W. Va. 492; Moran *v.* Clark, 30 W. Va. 358, 4 S. E. 303; Hughes *v.* Hamilton, 19 W. Va. 366; Beaty *v.* Veon, 18 W. Va. 291; Hartley *v.* Roffe, 12 W. Va. 401; Connell *v.* Wilhelm, 36 W. Va. 598, 15 S. E. 245; Hilleary *v.* Thompson, 11 W. Va. 113; Hyman *v.* Smith, 13 W. Va. 744.

In the case of Schmertz *v.* Hammond, 51 W. Va. 408, 41 S. E. 184, Judge Brannon delivering the opinion of the court, said: "The affidavits of individual opinion of the worth of the land placed the property higher; but that is only opinion. There was no offer by anyone of greater price; no guaranty that on a third sale the land would fetch more." Atkinson *v.* Washington, etc., College, 54 W. Va. 32, 46 S. E. 253.

The demand constantly made of courts to destroy a purchaser's right, who has, in open auction, made the highest bid, on mere opinion of greater value, only estimated at best, and by those who, themselves, do not wish to buy and are not willing to guarantee more, should be discouraged as harassing to purchasers, prejudicial to the efficacy of judicial sales and contrary to settle law. Schmertz *v.* Hammond, 51 W. Va. 408, 41 S. E. 184.

Courts should be careful in setting aside the sale of realty made by their commissioners for mere inadequacy of price upon the simple opinions of men given in the shape of affidavits, especially where these opinions are materially in conflict. Hughes *v.* Hamilton, 19 W. Va. 366. "I am disposed and feel authorized under the circumstances in this cause to give reasonable force and weight to the said affidavits, and in doing so I feel authorized to conclude in the absence of other evidence and facts, that the said tract of land was sold at said sale by said commissioners at a greatly inadequate price." Beaty *v.* Veon, 18 W. Va. 291.

The case of Sinnett *v.* Cralle, 4 W. Va. 600, was decided upon the weight of conflicting affidavits, the court being of opinion from the weight of evidence, that the sale was for a greatly inadequate price, and the case was decided by the supreme court of West Virginia in 1871. Kable *v.* Mitchell, 9 W. Va. 492.

"Did the court err, in overruling his exceptions to the report of sale? His only ground was inadequacy of price. This is founded first on his own unsupported affidavit that 'the said real estate is in affiant's judgment and belief worth at least $40 per acre, and he believes it to be worth at least $50 per acre. While this court has held in Beaty *v.* Veon, 18 W. Va. 291, that the court may set aside a sale of lands made by a special commissioner under its decree of sale upon any evidence or facts before it, which clearly show that the land was sold at a greatly inadequate price; and further whether the court will confirm a sale by a commissioner made under its decree, must in a great measure depend upon the circumstances in each case, yet this court has never set aside a sale for such a poor reason as set forth in the defendant Stewart's affidavit. It is said it was not contradicted. It was not worthy of consideration. If he could get no stronger evidence than that to show that his land sold for a grossly inadequate price, it was not worth while for the plaintiff to procure counter affidavits at all. The affidavit is wholly insufficient to justify setting aside the sale." Stewart *v.* Stewart, 27 W. Va. 167.

The facts in the case of Tucker *v.* Tucker, 86 Va. 679, 10 S. E. 980, are as follows: "Pursuant to a consent decree entered in open court in this cause on the 11th day of June, 1888, a sale of one hundred and fifty-eight acres of land, lying in the county of Pittsylvania and belonging to the appellant, R. W. Tucker, was sold for the payment of a debt due from him to his brother, William Tucker. In October, 1888, the commissioner reported that the purchaser T. G. Anderson, had complied with the terms of sale. At November term, 1888, of the said court the appellant filed his petition in the cause, setting forth that the tract of land had been sold for an inadequate price, and that by reason of inclement weather a goodly number of bidders had been kept away; and, finally, one Creasy, who had engaged with him that he would put in an upset bid at that term, had been bought off by the purchaser for $50, and that he (Tucker) has thereby been prevented from having an upset bid filed in the cause, and praying that the purchaser (Anderson) might be summoned to show cause why said sale should not be set aside and a resale be had. Accordingly the purchaser (Anderson) having been ruled to show cause against a resale, and failing to appear, the court, on the 13th of December, 1888, entered a decree directing a resale, provided the defendant, or some one for him, should within forty days file with the clerk an upset bid of ten per cent. advance on the amount of the former sale, and from this decree the defendant has appealed." In delivering the opinion the court said: "But we see no merit in his application. There is no proof in the record worthy of consideration showing that any other probable bidder than Creasy was kept from the sale, and he, as we have seen, has been bought off. And as to the alleged inadequacy of price, we doubt if it can be said to exist. It is true that there are in the record some affidavits of the friends and neighbors, saying that in their opinion the property was sold for an inadequate price, but they give no reasons for their faith, and we do not think that mere opinions ought to outweigh the fact that the land sold for $150 per acre more than it was assessed for. The decree is right, and must be affirmed."

cc. Any Evidence of Facts Showing Inadequacy.

Or, the court may determine the question of inadequacy upon any evidence, or fact, or facts, before which, it clearly shows that the land sold at a greatly less price than it was worth. Kable v. Mitchell, 9 W. Va. 492; Hyman v. Smith, 13 W. Va. 744; Hughes

v. Hamilton, 19 W. Va. 366; Moran v. Clark, 30 W. Va. 358, 4 S. E. 303; Beaty v. Veon, 18 W. Va. 291; Hartley v. Roffe, 12 W. Va. 401; Connell v. Wilhelm, 36 W. Va. 598, 15 S. E. 245; Hilleary v. Thompson, 11 W. Va. 113; Sinnett v. Cralle, 4 W. Va. 600.

The decree of a circuit court setting aside a sale made by a trustee on the ground of inadequacy of price, where the evidence of unimpeached witnesses varied in their estimate of value from 500 to 600 to 650, to 700 to 725 and to 800 dollars, and where the highest bid at public auction was 605 dollars and 15 cents, and the property was actually sold at private sale for 650 dollars, is erroneous; no fraud being proven. Basnett v. Higgins, 2 W. Va. 485.

dd. Offer of Large Advance as Evidence of Inadequacy.

(aa) In General.

The offering to the court of a large amount, in advance of the price bid to be secured, either by the payment of the amount offered in court, or giving bond and security, is generally the very best evidence of the great inadequacy of price bid at the sale. Kable v. Michell, 9 W. Va. 492; Hyman v. Smith, 13 W. Va. 744; Schmertz v. Hammond, 51 W. Va. 408, 41 S. E. 184; Atkinson v. Washington, etc., College, 54 W. Va. 32, 44 S. E. 253.

(bb) Necessity for Upset Bid and Motion to Open Biddings.

See post, "Opening Biddings on Upset Bids," XI.

R. sold land to E., and retained the vendor's lien. E. sold parts of the land to F. and Q. E. not paying R., R. filed his bill against E., F. and Q. to enforce his lien. The court decrees a sale, of that in possession of E. first, and if that is not sufficient, then of that bought by F. and Q. The sale is made, and F. and Q. buy the parts they had before bought of E., at less than they were to give to E. The commissioner reports the sales good. E. objects to the confirmation of the sale, on the ground of the inadequacy of price, but he does not move to open the biddings, or offer an advance. Held, if E. objected to the sale for inadequacy of price, he should have moved the court to open the biddings, and have offered an advance on the price bid; his objection to the confirmation of the sale, without more, was no ground for refusing to confirm it. Effinger v. Ralston, 21 Gratt. 430.

Where a judicial sale has been regular, and there is an effort to defeat confirmation on the ground of inadequacy of price, there must be an upset bid, accompained by security. Atkinson v. Washington, etc., College, 54 W. Va. 32, 46 S. E. 253; Kable v. Mitchell, 9 W. Va. 492; Laidley v. Jasper, 49 W. Va. 526, 39 S. E. 169; Curtis v. Thompson, 29 Gratt. 474; Effinger v. Ralston, 21 Gratt. 430.

The constant application to annul fair court sales for mere smallness of price, without an upset bid or guaranty of material advance, finds no countenance in law. Schmertz v. Hammond, 51 W. Va. 408, 41 S. E. 184, 187.

When application is made to the court to set aside a judicial sale for mere inadequacy of price, there should be a guaranty that on a second sale, the property would bring more. Schmertz v. Hammond, 51 W. Va. 408, 41 S. E. 184.

Thus land had been sold a month before and the sale set aside because the price was too low. The second sale produced the same sum. Affidavit of individual opinion of the worth of the land placed the property higher; but that was only opinion. There was no offer by anyone of greater price; no guaranty that on a third sale the land should bring more. It was held that the sale should not be set aside without a guaranty of an advance, that the open auction on the two occasions was the better test as to the value of the property, and that it was useless to discuss the matter after two sales. Schmertz v. Hammond, 51 W. Va. 408, 41 S. E. 184. See, also, Moran v. Clark, 30 W. Va. 358, 359, 4 S. E. 303; Hughes v. Hamilton, 19 W. Va. 366.

It was said by this court in Effinger v. Kenney, 79 Va. 551, 553: "We are satisfied from the evidence, that the land was sold for a fair price; no advance bid was offered; no creditor is complaining; and there is nothing in the record to warrant the belief that, if the lands were again offered for sale, they would command a higher price." Utterbach v. Mehlenger, 86 Va. 62, 9 S. E. 479.

In a suit to subject lands of several debtors to the payment of the liens thereon, where it appears that an effort has been made, by offering the lands of the several debtors as a whole and in parcels, so to sell the lands as to obtain the best price therefor, and the sales have been made, and some of the lands have been resold on upset bids, an objection to the sale, unsupported by an upset bid, or a well-founded assurance that a greater price would be obtained if the lands were offered in some other way, should be overruled. Max Meadow Land, etc., Co. v. McGavock, 96 Va. 131, 30 S. E. 460.

The circuit court would not have been justified in setting aside the sales that had been made, and, by ordering a resale, in taking the risk of a less price being obtained, in the absence of an upset bid, or of a well-founded assurance that a greater price would be obtained, if, indeed, the difficulty of preserving or ascertaining the equities between the parties whose lands might be sold together, arising from the inequality in the value of the lands and the right of contribution, was not an insuperable objection to such a course. Max Meadow Land, etc., Co. v. McGavock, 96 Va. 131, 30 S. E. 460.

"As it is the right if the creditor to have the land sold for the best price it will bring in the open market for the payment of the debt, it would seem to follow, that to induce a court to set aside a fair sale made pursuant to its decree, it would not only be shown that the price for which it sold was clearly inadequate, but it should also appear that if exposed to sale again there was an assurance that it would bring materially more. Hence the English rule requiring the offer of an advance on the highest bid, and that, too, not an inconsiderable advance; some of the cases say, not less than ten per cent., and the money to be deposited or well secured. If the English practice is to be established in Virginia, this requirement, which is the best part of it, ought to be strictly carried out. I think if a judicial sale is to be set aside for inadequacy of price it should only be in a case where a higher price is offered and deposited or well secured. But I express no opinion upon the question, whether the practice where it obtains is founded in equity and justice of setting aside a sale for inadequacy of price and reopening the bids, notwithstanding that the property has been cried out to the highest bidder, and the sale was in all respects fairly conducted pursuant to the decree, and the purchaser is ready and offers to comply with the terms of sale. It is a question worthy of grave consideration, but is not involved in the decision of this cause." Curtis *v.* Thompson, 29 Gratt. 474.

It is not sufficient where in an amended bill there was a sort of an offer to pay more for the property, but it was not accompanied by any bid, or bond or guaranty of any kind, and it gave no assurance, that, if another sale should be allowed, a larger price would be obtained. Atkinson *v.* Washington, etc., College, 54 W. Va. 32, 46 S. E. 253.

Another exception to the sale is inadequacy of price. The jury valued the property at one thousand, nine hundred and fifty dollars. This is all that appears as to value. The property

may have somehow depreciated. No advance or upset bid was offered or guaranteed by Jasper. A property is worth what it brings. A court must see clearly a gross inadequacy, and a sale will not generally be set aside unless a guaranty of a better price be made. Hogg's Equity 405. Laidley *v.* Jasper, 49 W. Va. 526, 39 S. E. 169.

(cc) **Amount of Per Cent. Required to Be Offered in Advance.**

In General.—There can be no inflexible rule established, and no such rule exists in West Virginia, fixing any specific amount of per cent. required to be offered in advance of the last bid made at the sale, to justify or authorize the court to set aside the sale; the amount of per cent. that should be required must to a very great extent depend upon the amount bid at the sale. Each case should be determined according to its merits. For if a tract of land is sold for $10,000, an offer of ten per cent. made to the court, might be said to be an offer of a large advance in amount upon the price; which if the land sold for $100, an offer of ten per cent. could not properly be so considered. Kable *v.* Mitchell, 9 W. Va. 492; Hyman *v.* Smith, 13 W. Va. 744.

Where in a case there is conflicting evidence filed as to whether the land sold for its value or for greatly less than its value, a person comes before the court, and offers an advance of ten per cent. upon the price, which was over $11,000, the court must at once see that the advance offered is an increase of $11.52½ per acre, and over $1,100 in the aggregate, and that the sale made by the commissioners at the price bid was a greatly inadequate price, whatever doubts there may be upon the subject in the mind of the court from the affidavits and other facts in the cause. Kable *v.* Mitchell, 9 W. Va. 492.

The advance of $100 upon the price paid for the property, is no such substantial and material advance upon the price obtained by the commissioners, as would justify the court in annulling the sale, and ordering a new sale. Hudgins v. Lanier, 23 Gratt. 494.

Ten Per Cent.—The practice in the English courts of chancery is to open the biddings, and order a resale, whenever an advance of ten per cent. is offered with an indemnity to the purchaser by paying him his costs incurred by reason of his bidding. Kable v. Mitchell, 9 W. Va. 492.

ee. Highest Bid at Fair Auction Sale as Criterion of Value.

(aa) In General.

After full notice, an open sale fairly conducted, in the face of such competition as can be attracted, the highest bid which is made is a fair and just criterion of the value of the property at that time; and so, after stated opinions, affidavits of value, etc., are regarded with but little favor, and estimated as of little weight, in the presence of the fact established by the auction and its results. Nitro-Phosphate Syndicate v. Johnson, 100 Va. 774, 42 S. E. 995; Todd v. Gallego Mills Mfg. Co., 84 Va. 586, 5 S. E. 676.

"I do not mean to determine that a sale of land by a commissioner of court, made by virtue of a decree of sale, should in no case be set aside upon simple affidavits of the opinions of men, that the land sold for greatly less than its value, or ought to sell for or would sell for if reoffered. Each case must be determined on its merits as it arises. A sale made by a commissioner under a decree of a court of equity is not an absolute sale in this state, and does not become absolute until it is confirmed by the court. A greatly inadequate price is generally, when clearly shown, sufficient cause to authorize the court to set aside such sale." Hartley v. Roffe, 12 W. Va. 401; Kable v. Mitchell, 9 W. Va. 492.

"If this case stood simply upon the affidavits tending to prove, that the sale was for a greatly inadequate price, and the affidavits, which tend to prove that the sale was for a fair price, I should not, from these affidavits alone, taking them altogether, feel authorized, upon the principles adjudicated in the case of Kable v. Mitchell, 9 W. Va. 492, above cited, and the case of Hartley v. Roffe, 12 W. Va. 401, to interfere with said sale." Marling v. Robrecht, 13 W. Va. 440.

(bb) Repeated Sales as Test of Value.

The court will not set aside a sale of land made by a commissioner on the ground of inadequacy of price, where there had been four sales of the land, three of which had been set aside, the first for inadequacy of price, the second because of cloud on the title, and the third on an upset bid. Under such circumstances the repeated sales afford a better test of the value of the land, than mere affidavits that the land sold at an inadequate price. Trimble v. Herold, 20 W. Va. 602; Moran v. Clark, 30 W. Va. 358, 4 S. E. 303; Connell v. Wilhelm, 36 W. Va. 598, 15 S. E. 245.

The circuit court ought not to set aside a sale by a commissioner for inadequacy of price, when there has been two sales of the property previously, and the last sale was not made until after repeated adjournments by the commissioner of sale with a view to the getting of the highest possible price, merely because there was a slight apparent preponderance in the weight if the affidavits filed indicating that the price obtained was not the full value of the property. When there is a conflict of views as to the value of property, previous sales and attempted sales are entitled to more weight than the mere opinions of some persons as to its value. McMullen v. Eagan, 2 W. Va. 233.

Where there had been two sales of real property—one under a deed of trust, and the other at a judicial sale—made not far from each other in point of time, both sales at $2,000, and affidavits were filed, stating that the property was worth, at the time affidavits were taken, from $3,000 to $3,500, and "affiants believed that in the near future said property could be sold for an advance of from $500 to $1,000 over the price of $2,000 for which it sold, and another affidavit showed it sold for a fair price, this court refused, on the mere ground of inadequacy, to set aside the sale. Moran v. Clark, 30 W. Va. 358, 4 S. E. 303; Connell v. Wilhelm, 36 W. Va. 598, 15 S. E. 245.

"We do not undertake to say how many times a sale should be set aside for inadequacy of price. After a reasonable number of times having been exposed to a fair sale, we will not undertake to say that the failure to obtain a better price might outweigh other evidence as to the price of the land being inadequate." Hilleary v. Thompson, 11 W. Va. 113.

(e) Where Inadequacy Caused by Acts of Complainant.

A sale ought not to be set aside on the ground of smallness of price, if that was occasioned by the acts of the complainant. Forde v. Herron, 4 Munf. 316.

J. RELATION BACK OF CONFIRMATION.

When a judicial sale is confirmed by the court, such confirmation relates to and vests the title of the land in the purchaser from the date of the sale. Barton's Ch. Pr. 1094; Donahue v. Fackler, 21 W. Va. 124; Taylor v. Cooper, 10 Leigh 317; Evans v. Spurgin, 6 Gratt. 107; Hyman v. Smith, 13 W. Va. 744, 767; Terry v. Coles, 80 Va. 695; Stout v. Philippi Mfg., etc., Co., 41 W. Va. 339, 23 S. E. 571; Taylor v. Cooper, 10 Leigh 317, 319; Kable v. Mitchell, 9 W. Va. 492; Childs v. Hurd, 25 W. Va. 530; Hudgins v. Marchant, 28 Gratt. 177.

In the case of Taylor v. Cooper, 10 Leigh 317, 319, Judge Tucker, in delivering the unanimous opinion of the court, said: "The principles of the court, according to the English practice, I take to be these: * * * But, * * *, where the sale is confirmed, that is, where both contracting parties (the purchaser and the court) concur in ratifying the inchoate purchase, the confirmation relates back to the sale, and the purchaser is entitled to everything he would have been entitled to if the confirmation, and conveyance of title had been temporaneous with the sale. Anson v. Towgood, 1 Jac. and Walk. 647. In this manner, I think, the several authorities are easily reconciled; and if this be so in England, I think it may be safely affirmed to be yet more unquestionable under our practice." Kable v. Mitchell, 9 W. Va. 492; Hyman v. Smith, 13 W. Va. 744; Cale v. Shaw, 33 W. Va. 299, 10 S. E. 637.

On the 30th of October, 1834, a decree was made for the sale of a tract of land, on a credit of six, twelve and eighteen months. Before the decree, there had been a contract to rent the land, and pursuant to that contract, a lease was made for a year, commencing the 25th of December, 1834, and ending the 25th of December, 1835. During this year, to wit, on the 10th of January, 1835,. sale was made under the decree. That sale being confirmed and a conveyance executed to the purchaser, held, the purchaser must be considered complete owner from the date of the sale, and entitled to the rent which became due afterwards. Taylor v. Cooper, 10 Leigh 317.

In such case, if the rent has been paid to the representative of the former owner, the purchaser may recover it from him by an action of assumpsit for money had and received. Taylor v. Cooper, 10 Leigh 317.

"I have had much doubt, however, whether the remedy of Cooper was in the court of chancery, or at law. But upon much reflection, I think the action at law is maintainable. Before confirmation of the report, indeed, and while the cause is yet pending in the court of chancery, I am of opinion that to that tribunal alone can the purchaser resort for the adjustment of his rights and the enforcement of his claim. Such was the case of Crews v. Pendleton, 1 Leigh 297, and Heywood v. Covington, 4 Leigh 373. But where the chancery cause is ended, or where at least, by the confirmation of the report and the execution of the deed to him, the transactions with the purchaser in that court are closed and at an end, I apprehend it is competent to him to assert in this equitable action his title to the rent paid over wrongfully to the defendant." Taylor v. Cooper, 10 Leigh 317.

K. CONFIRMATION AS RATIFICATION OF IRREGULARITIES AND CURE OF DEFECTS.

The court, in confirming a sale, may ratify various iregularities in the proceeding of the commissioner of sale, even the changing of the terms of sale, and supply or cure all defects in the execution of its decree, except those founded in defect of jurisdiction, or in fraud. Rorer on Judicial Sales, § 122; Branch's Principia, 28; Freeman on Void Judicial Sales, § 42. Langyher v. Patterson, 77 Va. 470; Hyman v. Smith, 13 W. Va. 744.

Subsequent confirmation is equivalent to previous authority, cures departures from the terms prescribed, and supplies all defects in the execution of the decree, except those founded in lack of jurisdiction. It makes the sale the court's own act, and renders it no longer executory, but executed. Langyher v. Patterson, 77 Va. 470.

Confirmation cures voidable, not void, sales. If sale is void "because it included property not described in the decree of sale," an order confirming it is necessarily inoperative. Freem., Jud. Sales, § 44. First Nat. Bank v. Hyer, 46 W. Va. 13, 32 S. E. 1000.

"Every step taken under the decree for sale was regular and strictly in conformity with the decree, except that the commissioner was directed to sell the property for one-fourth cash, and the balance in one, two and three years; and instead of so doing, sold for the costs cash, and the balance in one, two and three years. In his report of sale, he says: 'Your commissioner would further report, that by the terms of the decree he was required to sell the property for one-fourth cash; but your commissioner found it impossible to sell to any advantage on the terms set forth in the decree.' This slight variance in the terms of sale, as reported by the commissioner of sale, the court approved; and the confirmation of the sale, on these terms, made it equivalent to specifying them in the decree of sale, in the first instance, as by chapter 174 of the Code of Virginia, 1873, the court was fully empowered to do. In fact, the majority of judicial sales in Virginia are made on these terms." Langyher v. Patterson, 77 Va. 470.

L. EFFECT OF CONFIRMATION UPON RIGHTS AND TITLE OF BIDDER.

See ante, "Relation Back of Confirmation," IX, J; post, "Purchasers—Title, Rights and Liabilities," XV.

1. Rights, etc., before Confirmation.
a. In General.

Until confirmation, the accepted bidder is not regarded as the purchaser. His contract is incomplete, and he acquires by his bid no independent right to have it perfected. Terry v. Coles, 80 Va. 695; Brock v. Rice, 27 Gratt. 812; Todd v. Gallego Mills Mfg. Co., 84 Va. 586, 5 S. E. 676; Coles v. Coles, 83 Va. 525, 5 S. E. 673; Thomas v. Farmers' Nat. Bank, 86 Va. 291, 9 S. E. 1122; Alexander v. Howe, 85 Va. 198, 7 S. E. 248; Hickson v. Rucker, 77 Va. 135; Berlin v. Melhorn, 75 Va. 636, 639; Childs v. Hurd, 25 W. Va. 530; Barr v. White, 30 Gratt. 531; Zirkle v. Mc-

Cue, 26 Gratt. 517; Zollman v. Moore, 21 Gratt. 313; Fleming v. Holt, 12 W. Va. 143; Hyman v. Smith, 13 W. Va. 744.

In Virginia Fire, etc., Ins. Co. v. Cottrell, 85 Va. 857, 9 S. E. 132, Lewis, P., says: "Until the sale has been confirmed, the proceeding is in fieri; the bidder is not considered as a purchaser, * * * nor is he compellable before confirmation to complete his purchase; but as soon as the sale is absolutely confirmed, then the contract becomes complete—the bidder, by the acceptance of his bid, becomes a purchaser, * * * and he may be compelled by the process of the court to comply with his contract." Hildreth v. Turner, 89 Va. 858, 17 S. E. 471.

The accepted bidder acquires by the acceptance of his bid, no independent right, as in the case of a purchaser at a sale under execution, to have his purchase completed, but is merely a preferred proposer, until confirmation by the court of the sale, as agreed by its ministerial agent. Terry v. Coles, 80 Va. 695; Brock v. Rice, 27 Gratt. 812; Carr v. Carr, 88 Va. 735, 14 S. E. 368; Childs v. Hurd, 25 W. Va. 530; Strayer v. Long, 83 Va. 715, 3 S. E. 372; Tyler v. Toms, 75 Va. 116; Barr v. White, 30 Gratt. 531; Hyman v. Smith, 13 W. Va. 744.

Until the sale is confirmed, the bidder is in no legal sense a purchaser of the property. As an accepted bidder, he is only a preferred purposer, to become a perfect purchaser. Rorer on Judicial Sales, § 106. Childs v. Hurd, 25 W. Va. 530; Hartley v. Roffe, 12 W. Va. 401.

"In the case of Cocke v. Gilpin, 1 Rob. 20, 39, Judge Baldwin, in delivering the opinion of the court, says: 'In truth, however, the purchaser acquires no right until a confirmation of the sale by the court, and until the order confirming the report, he is only inchoately, and not absolutely, a purchaser, having till then no fixed interest in the subject. That such is the

English doctrine is well settled. Sugd. on Vend. 50, 51, 52, 57.'" Kable v. Mitchell, 9 W. Va. 492. The same doctrine has been recognized in several cases. See Crews v. Pendleton, 1 Leigh 297; Heywood v. Covington, 4 Leigh 373; Taylor v. Cooper, 10 Leigh 317; Childs v. Hurd, 25 W. Va. 530; Hartley v. Roffe, 12 W. Va. 401; Hudgins v. Marchant, 28 Gratt. 177.

Until the sale is confirmed, the title remains in the former owner. Thompson v. Cox, 42 W. Va. 566, 26 S. E. 189.

Until confirmation, the purchaser is not compelled to complete his purchase, nor is he entitled to the possession of the estate. Brock v. Rice, 27 Gratt. 812; Strayer v. Long, 83 Va. 715, 3 S. E. 372.

Before confirmation of the report, and while the cause is yet pending in a court of chancery, to that tribunal alone can the purchaser resort for the adjustment of his rights, and the enforcement of his claim. Cocke v. Gilpin, 1 Rob. 20; Terry v. Coles, 80 Va. 695; Crews v. Pendleton, 1 Leigh 297; Heywood v. Covington, 4 Lea 373; Daniel v. Leitch, 13 Gratt. 195.

The purchaser's bid at a commissioner's sale is a mere offer, and although after confirmation his title relates back to the day of sale, yet he has until confirmation to examine into the matter, and to inquire if there be any defects in the title. Barton's Ch. Pr. 1094. Terry v. Coles, 80 Va. 695.

According to the English practice, the preferred bidder is never entitled to the benefit of his purchase until the master's report of the bidding is confirmed by the court. Brock v. Rice, 27 Gratt. 812.

b. Right to Compensation for Permanent Improvements.

A purchaser has no right to compensation for permanent improvements made on the land since his purchase, and before confirmation of the sale. Tyler v. Toms, 75 Va. 116.

Such a claim can not be asserted under the statute which authorizes a defendant against whom a decree or judgment is rendered to claim compensation for valuable improvements made under a title believed to be good. The statute has no application to a case of a purchaser at a judicial sale, against whom a claim for the purchase money is asserted, and in whose favor there has been no decree of confirmation. Such a purchaser is a mere preferred bidder without valuable rights in the property, and whatever improvements he may make upon the land are made subject to all the conditions attaching a purchaser before confirmation. If in any case a vendee can claim against his own vendor compensation for improvements as set-off against a demand for purchase money, a purchaser at a judicial sale which has not been confirmed can not do so; for in the nature of things he has no just cause to believe that his title is good. Tyler v. Toms.

"The appellant alleges, however, that since his purchase he has made permanent improvements on the land for which he claims compensation. This demand is asserted under the statute which authorizes a defendant against whom a decree or judgment is rendered to claim compensation for valuable improvements made under a title believed to be good. The statute, however, has no application to the case of a purchaser at a judicial sale, against whom a claim for the purchase money is asserted, and in whose favor there has been no decree of confirmation. Such a purchaser is a mere preferred bidder without vested rights in the property, and whatever improvements he may make upon the land are made subject to all the conditions attaching to a purchaser before confirmation. If in any case a vendee can claim against his own vendor compensation for improvements as set-off against a demand for purchase money, a purchaser at a judicial sale which has not been confirmed can not do so; for in the nature of things he has no just cause to believe that his title is good. We are, therefore, of opinion that the chancery court did not err in holding the land still bound for the purchase money, or in rejecting the claim for improvements." Tyler v. Toms, 75 Va. 116.

c. Right to Resell at Profit.

The highest bidder at a judicial sale is not considered as the purchaser until the report of sale is confirmed. Until then, according to the English practice, he has no right to resell at a profit, except for the benefit of the owner of the estate. Daniel v. Leitch, 13 Gratt. 195, 211; Heywood v. Covington, 4 Leigh 373; Taylor v. Cooper, 10 Leigh 317.

d. Right to Appreciation of Estate by Accidental Falling in of Lives, etc.

According to the English practice, the preferred bidder is not entitled to the benefit of any appreciation of the estate by the accidental falling in of lives or other means. Brock v. Rice, 27 Gratt. 812; Taylor v. Cooper, 10 Leigh 317; Daniel v. Leitch, 13 Gratt. 195, 211; Heywood v. Covington, 4 Leigh 373; Hyman v. Smith, 13 W. Va. 744; Kable v. Mitchell, 9 W. Va. 492.

In the case of Taylor v. Cooper, 10 Leigh 317, Judge Tucker, in delivering the unanimous opinion of the court, said: "The principles of the court, according to the English practice, I take to be these; * * * Where there is a sale by the master, and where the property appreciates by the accidental falling in of lives, or by other means, the court will only confirm the sale upon the terms of the purchasers making compensation. Davy v. Barber, 2 Atk. 490; Blount v. Blount, 3 Atk. 638. And in doing this, it but acts within the scope of its rights and powers for the sale is not conclusive until confirmed, and justice to the owner of the estate demands that when there has been a material appreciation before confirmation, a resale should be directed, unless the purchaser will make compensation." Kable *v.* Mitchell, 9 W. Va. 492; Hyman *v.* Smith, 13 W. Va. 744.

e. **Liability for Loss by Fire or Otherwise.**

According to the English practice, the preferred bidder is not liable to any loss by fire or otherwise, which may happen to the premises, until the report of the sale is confirmed. Brock *v.* Rice, 27 Gratt. 812; Taylor *v.* Cooper, 10 Leigh 317; Kable *v.* Mitchell, 9 W. Va. 492; Virginia Fire, etc., Ins. Co. *v.* Cottrell, 85 Va. 857, 9 S. E. 132; Daniel *v.* Leitch, 13 Gratt. 195, 211; Heywood *v.* Covington, 4 Leigh 373; Hyman *v.* Smith, 13 W. Va. 744. In the case of Taylor *v.* Cooper, 10 Leigh 317, Judge Tucker, in delivering the unanimous opinion of the court, said: "The principles of the court, according to the English practice, I take to be these; '* * * Where, after, the sale, and before confirmation (as in the cases of Ex parte Minor, 11 Ves. 559, and Heywood *v.* Covington, 4 Leigh 373), the property is destroyed, or materially injured, by flood, or fire, the loss must fall on the vendor; for, as in the case of appreciation, the vendee will be charged with compensation, so, in the case of depreciation by destruction of part of the estate, he has a fair claim to deduction. Until the sale is confirmed, he is considered, in England, as having no fixed interest in the subject of purchase. 11 Ves. 559. Before it is confirmed, he is always liable, there, to have the biddings opened, and, therefore, non constat that he is a purchaser. Anonymous, 2 Ves. Jun. 336. In case of loss, he is, therefore, allowed a deduction. The practice with us has gradually departed from that of the English courts, in some respects, which it is not necessary here to set forth." Kable *v.* Mitchell, 9 W. Va. 492; Hyman *v.* Smith, 13 W. Va. 744.

"If the mill and milldam were materially injured by freshets, after the sale and before the report of sale was confirmed, I should think, upon the authorities, that the loss should not fall upon the vendee, provided there was no fault in him. In Davy *v.* Barber, 2 Atk. 489; Blount *v.* Blount, 3 Atk. 636, 638, it was held, that a purchaser must pay for lives falling in; if so, he can not be charged with losses. And in Ex parte Minor, 11 Ves. 559, and Twigg *v.* Fifield, 13 Mes. 517, it was held, that the purchaser ought to be considered as having the purchase only from the time of the confirmation of the report of sale. But in Ansom *v.* Towgood, 1 Jac. & Walk. 619, Lord Eldon said the confirmation of the report related back, and thus settled the doctrine in Twigg *v.* Fifield. And see the course it behooves the purchaser to pursue to confirm his purchase, Sugd. Law Vend. 39, 40. So that it is possible the purchaser, in this case, may not be absolved. But the point can not now be determined; for the case is clearly coram non judice. The superior court of chancery could not entertain the bill, pending the suit in the county court." Heywood *v.* Covington, 4 Leigh 373.

f. **Liability for Rent Where Possession Taken before Confirmation.**

Before confirmation, the supposed purchase being a mere offer to bid, the purchasers, so called, have no right whatever to the possession of the lands; and having wrongfully taken and held the same and taken the profits to themselves, they must be held responsible and chargeable with a fair rental for the said lands, and must themselves bear the expenses they incurred in their own enterprise, for upon no just principle can they be paid a large salary for attending to their own business. Far less can they be allowed a credit for cash paid by them in commissions to their supposed vendors, which they paid in their own wrong. Strayer *v.* Long, 83 Va. 715, 3 S. E. 372.

2. Title, Rights, etc., after Confirmation.

In General.—By confirmation the court makes it a sale of its own, and the purchaser is entitled to the full benefit of his contract, which is no longer executory but executed, and which will be enforced against him and for him. Rorer on Judicial Sales, §§ 122, 124; 1 Sugd. on Vendor's p. 68; Langyher v. Patterson, 77 Va. 470, 473; Terry v. Coles, 80 Va. 695; Whitlock v. Johnson, 87 Va. 323, 12 S. E. 614.

Equitable Owner.—Upon confirmation of a judicial sale, the equitable title to the land passes to the purchaser. Virginia Fire, etc., Ins. Co. v. Cottrell, 85 Va. 857, 9 S. E. 132; Berlin v. Melhorn, 75 Va. 636, 639.

The equitable title passes to the purchaser at a judicial sale not by virtue of his compliance with the terms of the sale, but by the confirmation of the sale by the court; and while it is usual and proper to require compliance with the terms of sale before the report is acted on, yet if this is not required, and the sale is confirmed, the rights of the purchaser are the same as if the terms had been complied with, provided his conduct has been fair and not to the prejudice of any other party. Virginia Fire, etc., Ins. Co. v. Cottrell, 85 Va. 857, 9 S. E. 132.

In Hurt v. Jones, 75 Va. 341, 347, Judge Burks, in the opinion of the court, said: "As soon as the sale is confirmed by the court there is a complete contract; the bidder becomes a purchaser, and is thenceforth regarded and treated as the equitable owner of the land, with the right reserved to compel him to comply with his contract by payment of the purchase money." Langyher v. Patterson, 77 Va. 470.

Land Subject to Lien for Purchase Money.—Although after confirmation, the purchaser is the equitable owner of the land, yet the land is subject to the lien retained for the purchase money. Berlin v. Melhorn, 75 Va. 636, 639.

X. Setting Aside Sale after Confirmation.

A. DISCRETIONARY WITH COURT.

In General.—It is within the discretion of the court at any time during the term, to set aside the decree of confirmation and rescind the sale upon proper motion and notice to the purchaser and parties concerned, for good cause shown. Langyher v. Patterson, 77 Va. 470.

Nature of Discretion to Be Exercised.—Although it is within the discretion of the court at any time during the term, to set aside the decree of confirmation and rescind the sale, yet the court must exercise a sound legal discretion, and where it appears that the court did not exercise a sound but apparently arbitrary discretion, it is subject to correction by the appellate court. Langyher v. Patterson, 77 Va. 470.

B. GROUNDS.

1. In General.

If the report of the sale and order of confirmation is excepted to, and the record discloses, in support of such exceptions, sufficient reasons to show that the sale itself was improper and ought not to have been made, the decree or order of confirmation will be reversed and the sale set aside. Capehart v. Dowery, 10 W. Va. 130.

2. Distinguished from Grounds for Setting Aside Sale before Confirmation.

See ante, "Distinguished from Grounds for Setting Aside Sale after Confirmation," IX, I, 4, b.

3. Set Aside Only on Good Cause Shown.

After a judicial sale has been confirmed by the court, it will not be set aside except for good cause shown. Todd v. Gallego Mills Mfg., Co., 84

Va. 586, 5 S. E. 676; Langyher v. Patterson, 77 Va. 470; Berlin v. Melhorn, 75 Va. 636.

Courts in Virginia are but instrumentalities of the law; and public policy requires that purchasers at judicial sales, who are amenable to the coercion of the courts for the performance of their part of the contract of sale, should also be entitled to the certainty and security of their once vested rights under the contract. Langyher v. Patterson, 77 Va. 470.

While a purchaser at a judicial sale acquires by his bid and its acceptance no independent right to have his purchase completed, but is merely a preferred proposer until confirmation, yet after confirmation by the court, his condition is very materially changed. His contract is then executed, and he is regarded as a complete purchaser, with all the rights incident to that position. Against him the courts are never disposed to interfere, unless for very grave and substantial errors in the decrees and proceedings upon which his title is founded. Barr v. White, 30 Gratt. 531. See Zirkle v. McCue, 26 Gratt. 517, and cases there cited.

The action of the court in setting aside a sale once confirmed upon any but the most substantial reasons has been held in the supreme court to be error, for which the decree will be reversed. Todd v. Gallego Mills Mfg. Co., 84 Va. 586, 5 S. E. 676; Langyher v. Patterson, 77 Va. 470; Berlin v. Melhorn, 75 Va. 636.

4. Particular Grounds.

a. Grounds Which Would Vacate Any Other Executed Contract.

Previous to the decree of confirmation the purchaser has only an inchoate contract with the court; but after the confirmation, the purchase money paid and the deed executed, he has a complete and perfect contract, which can only be set aside upon grounds which would vacate any other executed contract. Zollman v. Moore, 21 Gratt. 313.

After confirmation, a purchaser at a judicial sale is as much entitled to the benefit of his purchase as a purchaser in pais, and the sale in the one case can be set aside only on such grounds as would be sufficient in the other. Virginia Fire, etc., Ins. Co. v. Cottrell, 85 Va. 857, 9 S. E. 132.

b. Fraud, Mistake, Surprise or Other Equitable Ground.

(1) In General.

It may be safely laid down as a general rule, deducible from the authorities, that after a judicial sale has been absolutely confirmed by the court which ordered it, it will not be set aside except for fraud, mistake, surprise, or other cause for which equity would give like relief, if the sale had been made by the parties in interest, instead of by the court. Berlin v. Melhorn, 75 Va. 636, 639; Coles v. Coles, 83 Va. 525, 5 S. E. 673; Brock v. Rice, 27 Gratt. 812; Allison v. Allison, 88 Va. 328, 13 S. E. 549; Patterson v. Eakin, 87 Va. 49, 12 S. E. 144; Karn v. Rorer Iron Co., 86 Va. 754, 11 S. E. 431; Virginia Fire, etc., Ins. Co. v. Cottrell, 85 Va. 857, 9 S. E. 132; Langyher v. Patterson, 77 Va. 470; Hickson v. Rucker, 77 Va. 135; Merchants' Bank v. Campbell, 75 Va. 455; McKay v. McKay, 28 W. Va. 514; Howery v. Helms, 20 Gratt. 1; Talley v. Starke, 6 Gratt. 339; Watson v. Hoy, 28 Gratt. 698; Nitro-Phosphate Syndicate v. Johnson, 100 Va. 774, 42 S. E. 995.

It is by no means, therefore, a matter of discretion with the court to rescind a sale which it has once confirmed; but some special ground must be laid, such as fraud, accident, mistake, or misconduct on the part of the purchaser or other person connected with the sale, which has worked injustice to the party complaining. Virginia Fire, etc., Ins. Co. v. Cottrell, 85 Va. 857, 9 S. E. 132.

This rule, which is an eminently just and salutary one, has been repeatedly recognized by the Virginia supreme court of appeals, and public policy, which looks to the stability of judicial sales, requires that it be adhered to. Virginia Fire, etc., Ins. Co. *v.* Cottrell, 85 Va. 857, 9 S. E. 132; Langyher *v.* Patterson, 77 Va. 470; Coles *v.* Coles, 83 Va. 525; Todd *v.* Gallego Mills Mfg. Co., 84 Va. 586, 5 S. E. 676.

If a purchaser is entitled to any relief after confirmation it must be on the ground of fraud, or mistake discovered after confirmation of sale. In such case the confirmation of the sale would not be insuperable barrier to relief in the absence of laches—acquiesence, waiver, or other circumstances rendering relief inequitable. Hickson *v.* Rucker, 77 Va. 135; Long *v.* Weller, 29 Gratt. 347, 351.

Even in England, the only ground on which a sale that has been confirmed by the court can be set aside, is fraud on the part of the purchaser. 1 Sugden on Vendors, 68; 2 Daniell's Ch. Pr. 1471 (Perkins' Ed.). Langyher *v.* Patterson, 77 Va. 470.

"The sale, which was sought to be set aside, was not confirmed conditionally, as the appellant contends it was, but absolutely. The unequivocal terms of the decree leave no room for doubt upon this point. And, unless there was mala fides on the part of the purchaser, the fact that the terms of sale had not been complied with when the sale was confirmed, does not affect the case. The equitable title passes to the purchaser at a judicial sale, not by virtue of his compliance with the terms of sale, but by the confirmation of the sale by the court; and while it is usual and proper to require compliance with the terms of sale before the report is acted upon, yet if this is not required, and the sale is confirmed, the rights of the purchaser are the same as if the terms had been complied with, provided his conduct has been fair and not to the injury of any party in interest. And so, reciprocally, he may be compelled to complete his purchase as fully in the one case as in the other." Vir-

ginia Fire, etc., Ins. Co. *v.* Cottrell, 85 Va. 857, 9 S. E. 132.

In the case of White *v.* Wilson, 14 Ves. 151, Lord Eldon said, "he could not do a thing more mischievous to the suitors than to relax further the binding nature of contracts in the master's office;" and he adhered to the rule stated in the case of Fergus *v.* Gore, (1 Schoales & Lefroy, 350), by Lord Redesdale, "that the biddings could not be opened after the report was absolutely confirmed, unless on the ground of fraud on the part of the purchaser." Langyher *v.* Patterson, 77 Va. 470.

The title having been obtained by a suit by the assignee of the purchase money, in which a conveyance was decreed; after the decree, but before the conveyance is made, a son of the vendor files a bill in another court, in which he falsely and fraudulently alleges that he had paid off the incumbrance on the land, and retained the lien, and with the fraudulent connivance of the vendor, who is insolvent, obtains a decree for the sale of the land to satisfy his pretended lien; and the land is sold and the sale confirmed; held, that the conveyance having been made in pursuance of a contract entered into long before the commencement of the suit by the son of the vendee, and in obedience to a decree made before the commencement of that suit, the deed had relation back to the date of the contract, or at least to the date of the decree directing it; and therefore the decree and sale in the son's suit is inoperative against the title of the vendee, and gives him no equity for an injunction and rescission of the contract. That the suit of the son having been commenced and prosecuted, and the decree obtained under circumstances of suggestion of falsehood and suppression of truth, of imposition practiced on the court in which it was rendered, and of confederacy and collusion with the father, the vendor, the decree may, and must, if necessary for the protection of the vendor and his assignee, be held to be wholly inoperative as to them. But the purchaser under the decree in the son's suit having been conusant of the proceedings in the suit by the vendee to enjoin the purchase money, and of the assignee to procure the title, and being in fact bound as surety for that purchase money, and having purchased and permitted the sale to be confirmed without objection, is not entitled to be relieved from his purchase, or from paying his purchase money, though he acquires no valid title to the land purchased by him. Young *v.* McClung, 9 Gratt. 336.

Fraud Must Be Distinctly Charged and Proved.—"Moreover, fraud or misconduct, when relied on as a ground for rescinding a contract, must not only be clearly proved, but it must be distinctly charged in the pleadings. And if not so charged, evidence to prove it is irrelevant, and ought to be suppressed as improperly taken, no matter how strong a case it may show. Thompson *v.* Jackson, 3 Rand. 504; Southall *v.* Farish, 85 Va. 403, 7 S. E. 534, and cases cited. The application of this rule is decisive here. The petition, as we will call it, which was filed by the plaintiffs in the court below, merely alleges the fact of the discovery of a valuable vein of coke by the purchaser on its own land since the confirmation of the sale, and that the plaintiffs believed that, in consequence of that discovery, an application would be made by the purchaser to the court to be allowed to complete its purchase. But this, at most, is only a vague and inferential charge, which falls far short of the requirements of the rule above mentioned; and, besides, we have been unable to discover any evidence in the record upon which fraud or bad faith can be imputed to the purchaser. Fraud, even when distinctly charged, must be clearly proved. Hickman *v.* Trout, 83 Va. 478. 'If the fraud is not strictly and clearly proved as it is al-

leged, although the party against whom relief is sought may not have been perfectly clear in his dealings, no relief can be had.' Hord *v.* Colbert, 28 Gratt. 49; Matthews *v.* Crockett, 82 Va. 394; Houghton *v.* Graybill, 82 Va. 573." Virginia Fire, etc., Ins. Co. *v.* Cottrell, 85 Va. 857, 9 S. E. 132.

(2) Fraudulent Concealment of Cave of Great Value.

In a creditor's suit there is a sale of a tract of land, and the sale is confirmed by the court; but before the purchase money is paid, creditors apply by petition to set aside the order confirming the sale, on the ground of the fraudulent concealment by the purchasers of a cave under it which gives great value to the tract. Held, in a judicial sale, if it should be made to appear either before or after the sale has been ratified, that there has been any injurious mistake, misrepresentation or fraud, the biddings will be opened, the reported sale rejected, or the order of ratification rescinded, and the property again sent into the market and resold. On the evidence in this case, the purchasers having discovered the cave, they used means to conceal it, and made false representations in relation to it; and upon this ground the order confirming the sale should be set aside. Merchants' Bank *v.* Campbell, 75 Va. 455. See Virginia Fire, etc., Ins. Co. *v.* Cottrell, 85 Va. 857, 9 S. E. 132, distinguishing Merchants' Bank *v.* Campbell, 75 Va. 455.

"Now in the case before us, it is not a case of vendor and vendee dealing at arm's length with each other and the mere concealment of a fact acquired by superior knowledge, but it is the case of a sale at public auction, and is a contract between a court of justice, administering for the benefit of creditors the real assets of the debtor on the one hand, and the purchaser at a judicial sale on the other. In such a case, the benefit of the interested parties for whom the court makes the sale is always and chiefly regarded. The highest price that can be had under all the circumstances should be obtained, and the sale should be, in all respects, a fair and honest one. These, and these only, are the ends in view. And I think it may be stated as the established law, both in England and in this country, that if it should be made to appear, either before or after the sale has been ratified that there has been any injurious mistake, misrepresentation or fraud, the biddings will be opened, the reported sale be rejected, or the order of ratification be rescinded, and the property again sent into the market and resold." Rorer on Judicial Sales, § 857, and note. Merchants' Bank v. Campbell, 75 Va. 455.

"It may be further conceded that mere silence on the part of the purchaser, or failure to disclose knowledge on his part of peculiar value of the property sold, would not be sufficient to set aside a sale fairly made without misrepresentation or fraud. But in the case before us, the facts show more than mere silence and witholding knowledge acquired by the purchasers. On the contrary, it is conclusively shown that they not only actively concealed from the public the knowledge acquired by them, but misrepresented the facts within their knowledge. Merchants' Bank v. Campbell, 75 Va. 455.

(3) Commissioner Purchasing at Own Sale.

Where it appears, from the evidence in the cause, that F. was the real purchaser of land, at the sale made by him as commissioner of the court, under the decree of that court, although J. was the nominal purchaser, and was by the said J. reported to the said county court as the real purchaser, such purchase by the said J. at his own sale, was fraudulent in contemplation of law; and any party interested was entitled to have the said sale set aside and annulled, as of course, without

proof of actual fraud, according to the principles recognized in the cases of Buckles v. Lafferty, 2 Rob. 293, and Bailey v. Robinson, 1 Gratt. 4. Howery v. Helms, 20 Gratt. 1.

(4) Confirmation without Notice to Owner Many Years after Decree of Sale.

A decree of sale was made in 1868, and a sale was not reported to the court until 1882, more than thirteen years thereafter, and then was confirmed without the knowledge of the owner. The court said: "It is very questionable whether this was not also ground for setting aside the sale. It would certainly have been so had this appeal been taken from the decree confirming the sale. After so great delay in the execution of a decree of sale, the court should not confirm the sale without notice to the parties interested in the sale. Ayers v. Blair, 26 W. Va. 558; Boner v. Boner, 6 W. Va. 377; Erwin v. Vint, 6 Munf. 267.

(5) Falsifying Commissioner's Report.

A decree of confirmation founded on a false report of sale made may be impeached by an interested party guiltless of culpable fraud or neglect. Springston v. Morris, 47 W. Va. 50, 34 S. E. 766.

"As in this case the plaintiffs allege that the land was sold on the 20th day of June, 1893, to Patton and Morris at the price of $510; that Commissioner Ayers made the report to this effect to the court; that on the 26th day of June plaintiffs indorsed exceptions thereon for inadequacy, and filed an upset bid, offering $700; with bond and security; that the bond was accepted in open court, and the judge made the announcement from the bench that the sale would be continued until the October term, and then stated the upset bid; that after the plaintiffs, laboring under the belief that the sale was continued, had left court and returned to their homes, the commissioner of sale made a new report to the court, that he had sold the land to the same purchasers at the price of $710 on the same day the other sale was made, to wit, the 20th day of June, and had a decree entered confirming such sale. These allegations attack the second report of the commissioner as being false and untrue, and made and procured by the commissioner and alleged purchasers in fraud of plaintiffs' rights, and that the decree formed thereon was invalid because thereof. These allegations are fully sustained by the proofs and the record other than the decree, and in fact they are not otherwise controverted by the defendants in their joint answer, but are virtually admitted. This is a practice that should be severely discountenanced by the circuit court, as without legal justification, and fraudulent as to parties who have no notice thereof and do not consent thereto. A special commissioner is the representative of the court, and should at all times deal honestly and openly with its litigants and the court itself, and not deceive either the one or the other by questionable practices." Springston v. Morris, 47 W. Va. 50, 34 S. E. 766.

"The dealings of a court, with a subject matter before it, should be open and public, without concealment or deception, or taking advantage of the absence of interested or innocent parties, whose absence is caused by prior oral and apparently final rulings of the court touching the same matter; and this always will be presumed in favor of the court unless the contrary is shown." Springston v. Morris, 47 W. Va. 50, 34 S. E. 766.

Unless plainly apparent, the court can not be held responsible for wrong conduct on the part of its officers. And it can not be presumed that if the court knew the fact it would permit a commissioner of sale to falsify his report, to the injury of an absent litigant. Springston v. Morris, 47 W. Va. 50, 34 S. E. 766.

The purchasers may be entirely free from blame in the matter; but, when it was brought to their attention by plaintiff's bill, they should have been prompt, eager, and willing to decline to be benefited by the unconscionable advantage they had obtained by reason of the confiding and innocent absence of the plaintiffs, instead of tenacious clinging thereto behind supposed legal barriers. This would have entirely freed them from the charge of collusion. Springston v. Morris, 47 W. Va. 50, 34 S. E. 766.

c. Want of Jurisdiction of Parties.

Want of jurisdiction of the parties and of the subject matter to the suit, or want of parties, are defects for which objection may be made after the sale has been confirmed. Daniel v. Leitch, 13 Gratt. 195; Hughes v. Hamilton, 19 W. Va. 366; Trimble v. Herold, 20 W. Va. 602. See the title CREDITORS' SUITS, vol. 3, pp. 794, 798.

If in a suit brought by a judgment creditor to subject the lands of his debtor to the payment of his judgment, and the land has been sold under a decree in the cause, and the sale has been confirmed, and it appears that the necessary parties were not formally or informally before the court, the decree ordering the sale to be made, as well as the decree confirming the sale made in pursuance thereof, will be reversed and the sale set aside. Pappenheimer v. Roberts, 24 W. Va. 702; Neely v. Jones, 16 W. Va. 625; Norris v. Bean, 17 W. Va. 655.

It is a general rule in equity that all persons interested in the subject matter involved in the suit, who are to be affected by the proceedings and result of the suit, should be made parties, however numerous they may be, and if they are not made parties, and their interest appears upon the face of the bill, the defect may be taken advantage of either by demurrer or upon the hearing; and if it appears on the face of the record that the proper parties are wanting, the decree will be reversed by the appellate court unless the objection was waived in the court below. Pappenheimer *v.* Roberts, 24 W. Va. 702; Hill *v.* Proctor, 10 W. Va. 59; Clark *v.* Long, 4 Rand. 451; Sheppard *v.* Starke, 3 Munf. 29; Barton's Chy. Pr., § 34; Story's Eq. Pl., § 76.

In a suit by creditors for the sale of the land of their debtors, a decree is made with consent, for the sale, but the sale made is set aside, and the land rented out. After this one of the debtors dies intestate, leaving heirs. Then another decree is made, reviving the suit against his administrator, and directing a scire facias against the heirs; and with the consent of the parties before the court, commissioners are directed to execute the previous decree of sale. They sell and the sale is confirmed, and the purchase money being paid, a conveyance is ordered and made, and this is confirmed. These decrees and the sale having been made when the heirs were not before the court, the decrees are erroneous, and these and the sale must be set aside. Sexton *v.* Crockett, 23 Gratt. 857.

If a court make an order to sell real estate when it had no jurisdiction to make such order, the owner of such real estate not having been summoned, or otherwise brought before the court, the appellate court will reverse such decree of sale in toto, as also the order confirming a sale made under such decree. Camden *v.* Haymond, 9 W. Va. 680.

A friendly suit is instituted in October, 1863, for the sale of land in which a number of persons are interested, in which there is a decree for a sale on a credit of six months, with the privilege to the purchasers to pay cash, and the commissioners are directed to give bond in the sum of $40,000. There is a sale, and the purchasers give their bonds for the purchase money, and afterwards pay part of the purchase money to the commissioner, who pays to several of the parties entitled their share of it, or a part of it. Upon a bill filed seven years afterwards, by the plaintiffs, to set aside the sale on the ground that they had not authorized the sut, and had not assented to the proceeding therein, and because one of the parties in interest, who joined as plaintiff in this suit, was not a party in that; held, it appearing that two of the parties in interest, acting for themselves and the other parties, had directed the institution of the suit; that many, if not all, the parties in interest were present in person or by their representatives, at the sale and made no objection to it, and that a number of the plaintiffs had received a part of the purchase money of the land; that the party who had been inadvertently omitted was so present; and after the long acquiescence in what had been done, the sale will be sustained as a valid sale. Finney *v.* Edwards, 75 Va. 44.

d. Errors in Decree Ordering Sale.

(1) In General.

After confirmation, no error of any kind, in the decree ordering the sale, not affecting the authority of the commissioners to make it, can disturb the sale or affect the purchasers' rights thereunder. Trimble *v.* Herold, 20 W. Va. 602.

A court of equity will not interfere to give relief to a purchaser under a decree of a court having jurisdiction of the subject, or to his sureties, for errors in the decree, or the proceedings under it, where the report of the commissioners has been confirmed. Worsham *v.* Hardaway, 5 Gratt. 60.

A motion to set aside a decree confirming a sale should show errors therein to the prejudice of the party complaining as against purchasers who are strangers to the suit and in no wise interested in the result thereof. Klapneck *v.* Keltz, 50 W. Va. 331, 40 S. E. 570.

When the court has jurisdiction of

the parties and the subject matter of the suits, the debtor can not have a decree confirming a sale of real estate reversed for errors merely in the decree ordering the sale of such realty, where the purchaser is a stranger. Hughes v. Hamilton, 19 W. Va. 366.

In Parker v. McCoy, 10 Gratt. 594, 605, Judge Lee, in delivering the opinion of the court, said: "There are strong authorities to show that a purchaser * * * is not bound to go through all the proceedings and to look into all the circumstances, and see that the decree is right in all its parts, and that it can not be altered in any respect. He can not, of course, be protected against a title not in issue in the cause, nor against the claims of persons not parties to the cause, and therefore not bound by the decree; but it should seem that he has the right to presume the court has taken the necessary steps to investigate the rights of parties, and upon such investigation has properly decreed a sale." Zirkle v. McCue, 26 Gratt. 517.

"As we have seen, the court below had jurisdiction of the parties and of the subject matter of the suit, and the decree of sale though erroneous in the respects, which I have indicated, was not void because of such errors. The decree of sale was valid and binding until superseded or set aside, reversed and annulled in whole or in part by a court having jurisdiction and authority so to do because of such errors. At the time, when all the rules in this case were made by the commissioners, and at the time of the confirmation thereof by the court below, the said decree of sale, under which the said real and personal property was sold, had not been superseded, set aside, reversed or annulled. In fact, the appellants did not apply for and perfect this appeal, until some time after the said decree confirming said sale was rendered. If the appellant had desired to prevent a sale of her said real and personal property by reason of

the errors in said decree of sale, she should not only have obtained from this court, under the circumstances, an appeal and supersedeas to said decree, but should have perfected the same, before the sale was made, or at farthest, perhaps, before the sale was confirmed by the court below. But this, as we have seen, she failed and neglected to do; and under these circumstances it is now beyond the power of this court under the law to set aside said sales because merely of said errors in said decree of sale." Hughes v. Hamilton, 19 W. Va. 366.

A decree confirming a sale of real estate will not be reversed for an error in the decree ordering the sale, when no steps have been taken in the court below before the confirmation to reverse said decree. Charleston Lumber, etc., Co. v. Brockmyer, 18 W. Va. 586; Beard v. Arbuckle, 19 W. Va. 135. In some cases, whether generally or not, is not now decided, this rule will apply to a party to the suit, who is a purchaser of lands sold under a decree, as well as to a stranger. Dick v. Robinson, 19 W. Va. 159.

(2) Decree Prematurely Made.

In Cralle v. Meem, 8 Gratt. 496, the court held: "Though such decree for a sale of land has been prematurely made, yet if the sale is made and confirmed, the court will not set the sale aside on the petition of the purchasers, if upon the hearing it appears that the sale is beneficial to the infants." Ammons v. Ammons, 50 W. Va. 390, 40 S. E. 490.

"In the case of Cralle v. Meem, 8 Gratt. 496, land in which infants were interested was sold under a decree prematurely made, and the report of sale was confirmed. It was held, that although it was competent for the court, the proceedings being interlocutory, to set them aside in the further progress of the cause, upon its appearing that they were prejudicial to the interests of the infants; yet, on the other hand, it appearing to be beneficial to them, there could be no good reason for disturbing them in behalf of any other party. This court was of opinion that the sale should be established or set aside, according as the circuit court should consider it to be advantageous to the infant heirs. I can see little or no difference, in principle, between that case and this. There, as here, infants were interested in the land decreed to be sold, and the report of sale was confirmed before any objection was made by the purchaser. There, as here, the purchaser contended that he was not bound because the infants were not bound. But the court in that case held, as I think it ought in this, that as the ground of objection to the title might be removed by a further decree of the court, the sale should be established and the purchaser compelled to complete his purchase if the interest of the infants required it." Daniel *v.* Leitch, 13 Gratt. 195, 214, 215.

The court having made the decree for a sale of the real estate, on the petition of the adult heirs, and with the assent of the creditors, it is erroneous to proceed to sequestrate the rents of the other real estate in the hands of the heirs for the payment of the debts, before deciding upon the claim of the purchasers to have the sale set aside. Cralle *v.* Meem, 9 Gratt. 496.

(3) Decree Authorizing Commissioner to Take Offers in Writing.

Where there is no error in the decree of confirmation, it is erroneous for the court to set aside such decree for the sole reason· that the decree of sale authorized the commissioners to sell after abortive attempts at public sale to take private offers in writing and report them to the court. Klapneck *v.* Keltz, 50 W. Va. 331, 40 S. E. 570.

Upon a bill for the sale of real estate, the court decrees a sale, and directs the commissioner to sell at private sale; and he advertised for sealed proposals, which are to be opened at a certain day in the presence of the court. Proposals are put in, and the court accepts one of them, and forthwith confirms the sale, and directs the party to execute it according to its terms. Such a purchaser stands upon the same footing as any other purchaser at a judicial sale; and is not entitled to any other or further relief. Cooper *v.* Hepburn, 15 Gratt. 551.

"This review of his conduct, instead of showing him entitled to any exemption from the rules applicable to the case of a purchaser, at a judicial sale made in the usual mode, seeking, after a confirmation of the sale, to be excused from his purchase, exhibits such a degree of laches on his part as justly subjects his case to the most vigorous application of those rules. He was not in a position to ask that the sale should be set aside and he discharged from his contract. The most that he could, in accordance with principles repeatedly announced by this court, properly ask, under the circumstances, was, that he should be protected against any future assertion of claim by the infant over fourteen years of age. See Cralle *v.* Meem, 8 Gratt. 496; Daniel *v.* Leitch, 13 Gratt. 195; Goddin *v.* Vaughn, 14 Gratt. 102. If the result of the proceedings is to afford such protection, there was no error to his prejudice in dismissing the petition; and such I think, is the case." Cooper *v.* Hepburn, 15 Gratt. 551.

(4) Where Land Sells for Materially Less on Account of Error.

Where land has been sold under and confirmed by decrees of court, the sale may be set aside for error in the decree ordering the sale, if it clearly appears that the land, on account of such error, sold for materially less than it otherwise would have done, especially if the purchaser was a party to the suit. Martin *v.* Smith, 25 W. Va. 579;

Hughes v. Hamilton, 19 W. Va. 366, 368; Trimble v. Herold, 20 W. Va. 602; Tracey v. Shumate, 22 W. Va. 474, 500.

e. Error in Decree of Confirmation.

If the name of the purchaser at a sale be by mistake not named in the decree confirming such sale, but by mistake the name of some other person is inserted in the decree as the purchaser, such mistake is no ground for reversing the decree in the appellate court, if no motion to correct it has been made in the court below. Mc-Mullen v. Eagan, 21 W. Va. 233.

f. Errors and Mistakes Disclosed by Record.

A judicial sale after confirmation, can not be set aside and annulled for errors or mistakes not disclosed by the record. Let it once be established that judicial sales may be annulled at any length of time for errors or mistakes not disclosed by the record, and the laws authorizing such sales will become a dead letter upon the statute book. Who would venture to purchase under such circumstances, except at ruinous losses to the owner, or to improve property so acquired? Who would incur the hazard of buying from a purchaser at such sale; for, if the original purchaser is not protected, neither is his vendee. Under the rule asserted, into whatever hands the property may pass, it is still subject to the equity of the original owner. Zollman v. Moore, 21 Gratt. 313.

g. Mistake of Law.

In March, 1863, M., the widow, and R. and others, adult children of S., deceased, file their bill against the infant heirs of S., for the sale of land. The bill says the land was conveyed by W., the father of M., to S. and M.; that M. is entitled to one-half of the land, and the other plaintiffs and the defendants are entitled to the other half. There is a decree for the sale, a sale for confederate money, to Z., the report confirmed, and a decree appointing a receiver to collect the money, and dis-

tribute it, and convey the land to Z. This is done and report confirmed. Afterwards M. files a bill of review, and claims that under the deed from W., she having survived her husband, S., is entitled to the whole of the land, and asks that the sale may be set aside, and the land 'restored to her. Held, the mistake of M. as to her rights was a mistake of law, and a court of equity will afford no relief in such case. Zollman v. Moore, 21 Gratt. 313.

h. Upset Bid.

The offer of a higher bid has been held not to be one of the substantial reasons for which a sale will be set aside after it has been confirmed. Todd v. Gallego Mills Mfg. Co., 84 Va. 586, 5 S. E. 676; Langyher v. Patterson, 77 Va. 470. See also, Berlin v. Melhorn, 75 Va. 636; Yost v. Porter, 80 Va. 855. See post, "Time of Putting in Bid," XI, E.

"It is also assigned as error that the court, in its decree, required the debtor to give a bond of $200, before the sale could be set aside. The decree provided: 'But if the plaintiff, or someone for him, shall, within twenty days from this date, give to the special commissioner a bond with good security in the penalty of $200, with a condition that, on a resale of said property, it shall sell for $2,750, or the parties to the bond will pay $200, then the said commissioner shall resell said property on the same terms, and after the same advertisement as before; otherwise, the said sale shall stand confirmed to the purchaser at the price of $2,500.' Of course, this was all irregular; no advanced bid had been made by the debtor, and a bond could not be properly executed payable to the commissioner. The manner in which a sale can be set aside on an advance bid is shown in Stewart v. Stewart, 27 W. Va. 167. This provision should not have been inserted, and the decree must be corrected by striking out said provision; and, as the error was not to the prejudice of the appellant, when it is thus corrected, both decrees appealed from are affirmed with costs." Moran *v.* Clark, 30 W. Va. 358, 4 S. E. 303.

i. Sale Made without Previous Authority.

If, without previous authority, a commissioner sells a particular tract of land, and this sale is confirmed without exception, the court should permit any party interested to file his petition for a rehearing of the decree confirming such sale; and, after the purchaser has been summoned to answer this petition, and it has been heard on its merits, the court should set aside said decree and sale, or refuse so to do, as on its merits, as shown by the evidence, justice to the parties requires. Estill *v.* McClintic, 11 W. Va. 399.

A decree opening a sale of land made by an unauthorized person, though confirmed by the court without objection at the time, should be made more readily than a decree opening such sale after confirmation, where the sale had been previously authorized. Estill *v.* McClintic, 11 W. Va. 399.

When an unauthorized sale is thus confirmed by the court, creditors and others may not have had notice that any such sale had been made, the record furnishing no information that any such sale of the land was to be made. They can not, therefore, be estopped from objecting to such a sale after the confirmation to the extent that they would be, if the sale had been made by a commissioner authorized to sell the land; for in such case it would have been the duty of the parties interested to ascertain what sales had been made, and if they were improper, to have objected to the commissioner's report of such sales and to their confirmation. Estill *v.* McClintic, 11 W. Va. 399.

j. Failure to Revive Suit after Defendant's Bankruptcy.

C. files his bill in the circuit court

of R. to subject the real estate of D. to satisfy a judgment for $199.80 with interest from the 20th of April, 1860, and costs ($6.96), which C. had recovered against D. The bill charges that the rents and profits will not discharge the debt in five years. The bill is taken for confessed, and there is a decree that A. appoint a commissioner, sell the land or so much as may be necessary to satisfy the judgment and the costs of this suit, upon credits stated. A. sells the whole tract for $2,000 to W., who complies with the terms of the sale; and A. reports the sale to the court, and it is confirmed. After the sale, but before it is confirmed, D. is declared a bankrupt; and without taking any step in the state court, he applies to the United States district court, and there obtains a decree setting aside the sale, which decree is reversed by the United States circuit court, and the assignee in bankruptcy of D. directed to proceed in the case in the state court to obtain such relief as he may be entitled to. Held, W., being a bona fide purchaser of the land, and his purchase confirmed by the court, it is for D. or his assignee, if they would set aside the sale, to show that the price was inadequate or that only a part of the land should have been sold to pay the plaintiff's debt; and this they failed to do. Barr *v.* White, 30 Gratt. 531.

"The ground mainly relied on in the bill of review for vacating the sale, is that upon Duff's becoming a bankrupt the suit of Cecil, the creditor, abated, and no further proceedings could be lawfully had therein affecting his rights or the rights of his creditors, until the suit was properly revived against the assignee in bankruptcy. Now it will be seen that the bill does not charge that White, the purchaser, either at the time of the sale or of its confirmation, had any notice of the bankruptcy. He is not charged with fraud or improper conduct in any respect, and there is no reason for attributing to him anything of the kind. The decree for the sale was rendered before the adjudication in bankruptcy, and the sale was made before the assignee was appointed. No suggestion of the bankruptcy was made on the record, nor was the matter brought in any manner to the attention of the court, although there was ample time to do so before the sale was confirmed. If the assignee failed in his duty in this particular the purchaser can not be affected by his neglect or misconduct in the absence of all proof showing that injustice was done. The mere fact of the bankruptcy of the debtor could not of itself prevent the sale or its confirmation. It might render proper the introduction of a new party on the record, when properly suggested to the court, but it could not prevent or in any manner interfere with the execution of a valid decree. Upon this point the case of Eyster v. Graff, decided by the supreme court of the United States (1 Otto U. S. R. 521) is a direct authority. In that case, Mr. Justice Miller, delivering the opinion of the court, said: 'At the time the suit was commenced the mortgagor, McClure, was vested with the title, and was the proper and necessary defendant. But for the bankruptcy of McClure there can be no doubt that the sale under the foreclosure decree and the deed of the master would have vested the title in the purchaser, and that this would have related back to the date of the mortgage. Nor can there be any question that the suit having been commenced against McClure when the title or equity of redemption was in him, any person who bought of him or took his title or any interest he had, pending the suit, would have been bound by the proceedings and their rights foreclosed by the decree and sale. These are elementary principles. Is there anything in the bankrupt law, or in the nature of proceedings in bankruptcy, which takes the interest in the mortgaged property acquired by the as-

signee out of this rule?'" Barr v. White, 30 Gratt. 531.

k. Failure to Take Account of Debts before Sale.

Though there was a decree for the sale of the land and a sale before an account of the debts was taken, the sale of the land will not be set aside upon the objection of some of the creditors who came in after the decree, made years after the sale, when it is obvious the land would not sell for as much as it had sold for before, and which was more than some of these creditors had expressed their willingness to take for it. Wallace v. Treakle, 27 Gratt. 479.

"I am further of opinion that the said circuit court did not err in refusing to order a resale of the land upon the ground assigned in the petition of appeal, that it was sold before any account was taken of the debts and liabilities of William Henderson. The theory upon which courts of equity require generally that land shall not be sold until such accounts are taken is, that the creditors are interested in bidding for the land and making it bring its full value, and may not be sacrificed; but in this case it abundantly appears that the land brought its full value, indeed a much larger price than it was sold for by Henderson, and for which two of the petitioners for appeal in this case were willing it should be sold. After the lapse of ten years, and when the rights of purchasers have intervened, and when the appellants acquiesced in said sale for four years, it would be to the last degree inequitable to set aside said sale, when a resale would inevitably result in a sacrifice of the property, consequent upon the general depreciation of real estate, especially in that portion of the state where this land is situate." Wallace v. Treakle, 27 Gratt. 479.

In a suit brought in 1858, by judgment creditors of W. for the sale of his lands for the payment of their debts, he answers and consents to a sale before an account is taken of the priority of the debts, but an account is ordered at the same time the land is decreed to be sold. The land is sold, and though W. excepts because the price is inadequate, it is confirmed. The account is taken, showing debts much more than sufficient to absorb the fund; but the report is recommitted to inquire for other debts. W. then removes to a distant county. Subsequently, by the death of a son, W. becomes entitled to another tract of land, and in 1863 the plaintiffs file their petition, asking that this land may be sold for payment of their debts. Of this petition W. had no actual notice, and does not then seem to have had counsel in the cause. The land is sold without giving W. a day to pay the debts, and purchased by C., who pays the purchase money, and obtains a conveyance. W. afterwards applies by petitions and cross bills to have the sale set aside. Held, W. having consented to the first sale, before an account of his debts and their priorities was taken, and not having withdrawn that consent, and the account taken, though not confirmed, showing that the proceeds of both sales are not sufficient to pay the debts of ·W., and he not in his petition showing errors in that report, or that he has been injured by the sale of the last tract sold, the failure to have an account of his debts and their priorities before that sale, is not good ground for setting it aside, as against the purchasers. Crawford v. Weller, 23 Gratt. 835.

l. Failure to Give Party Notice of Confirmation.

Testator, owning a storehouse whereon was a vendor's lien, and a farm, devised the latter to his wife and children. Storehouse and lot, in a suit to enforce the lien, were sold for enough to pay the lien. By an account in that suit, it was ascertained that the only other debt was an unsecured one, which, with the lien, had been assigned to the purchaser. Later, in suit by the devisees to sell the farm, and after paying the debts, to distribute the proceeds, sale of the farm was decreed, and the ˙causes consolidated. Sale was made and confirmed in vacation without notice to the creditor. Held, the creditor as purchaser became party to the first suit, and by the consolidation, also to the last suit, and as such party, was, under Code, § 3426, entitled to notice of the confirmation of the sale made in vacation; but the confirmation will not be set aside unless he was prejudiced by want of notice. Patterson v. Eakin, 87 Va. 49, 12 S. E. 144.

Attorney for landowner died about two weeks before sale was confirmed, and notice of motion to be made on 27th of September, for confirmation, was served on 25th of same month on owner. Held, these facts are insufficient to warrant setting aside the decree confirming the sale. Allison v. Allison, 88 Va. 328, 13 S. E. 549.

m. Confirmation of Report at Special Term.

A decree was entered at a special term confirming a report of sale filed before the commencement of the preceding regular term, and which could have been acted on at that term. Held, no error. Va. Code, § 3060. Harmon v. Copenhaver, 89 Va. 836, 17 S. E. 482.

n. Inadequacy of Price.

See ante, "Inadequacy of Price," IX, I, 4, c, (14).

A judicial sale which has once been confirmed can not be rescinded and set aside for mere inadequacy of price, or for an increase of price alone. Virginia Fire, etc., Ins. Co. v. Cottrell, 85 Va. 857, 9 S. E. 132.

It did appear, however, that the land had been sold at an inadequate price. This was shown by the best possible evidence and in the most conclusive manner by the upset bid for an advance price of more than twenty per cent. This was of itself sufficient to set aside the confirmation and order a resale. National Bank v. Jarvis, 28 W. Va. 805; Kable v. Mitchell, 9 W. Va. 493.

Where a sale is confirmed without objection, it is presumed that the property brought its full value. Karn v. Rorer Iron Co., 86 Va. 754, 11 S. E. 431.

If inadequacy of price was ground for setting aside decree of confirmation, a sale of land at $4,000, which had at two prior sales, within the period of two years, sold at $1,550 and $2,650, respectively, could not be deemed inadequate. Allison v. Allison, 88 Va. 328, 13 S. E. 549.

o. Defect in Title.

In General. — After confirmation, though the purchaser before the deed is made to him, finds out that the title to the land is defective, he is nevertheless bound to receive it, and pay the purchase money. A sale by a commissioner is without warranty. Fleming v. Holt, 12 W. Va. 143.

Equity has jurisdiction to remove cloud over title to land by vacating a void judicial sale and a deed under it, the former owner being in actual possession. Waldron v. Harvey, 54 W. Va. 608, 46 S. E. 603.

Giving Time to Perfect Title. — After a sale of infant's land has been confirmed by the court, although the proceeding has been irregular, yet if the title of the purchaser can be made good, and it is for the interest of the infants to confirm the sale, the purchaser will not be released from his purchase; but if the interest of the infants is injured by the sale, it will be set aside. Daniel v. Leitch, 13 Gratt. 195, 196.

Courts of equity have at least as large a discretion in giving time to perfect the title in cases of sales under their decrees, as in cases of purchases by private contract. Daniel v. Leitch, 13 Gratt. 195, 196.

"There are certainly some defects to which objection may be made by a purchaser even after confirmation, here as well as in England. Such, for example, as a defect arising from a want of jurisdiction, or want of parties, which would prevent a purchaser from getting the title intended to be sold and conveyed to him. But there is this difference between such an objection made before and after confirmation; that in the former case, if the objection be well founded, the purchaser will be discharged peremptorily; whereas, in the latter, he will be discharged only if the defect be incurable, or be not cured in a reasonable time. A complete contract having, in the latter case, been made between the court and the purchaser, the court has the same right which any other vendor has to cure defects and perfect the title, provided it be done in a reasonable time, so as to occasion no injury to the purchaser. On a reference as to title in a suit for specific performance, the inquiry generally is, whether the vendor can, not whether he could, make a title at the time of entering into the agreement? If a good title can be shown at any time before the master's report, and even after the report, if the vendor can satisfy the court that he can make a good title by clearing up the objections reported by the master, the court will generally make a decree in his favor. See 2 Daniel's Ch. Pr. 1195, and notes." Daniel v. Leitch, 13 Gratt. 195, 213.

But after confirmation of a report of sale, without any objection on the part of the purchaser, his rights and obligations are very different. His inchoate contract is then perfected, and the court has a right to compel him to complete his purchase. He has still a right according to the English practice, to have an order to inquire whether a good title can be made to him. But he may waive that inquiry; and if he pay the purchase money and enter into possession of the property, he will generally be considered as having waived the inquiry and accepted the title. 1 Sugd. on Vend. 73. In Virginia it would seem that the proper time for making objections to the title, and for having on inquiry, if one is desired, is before the confirmation of the report. Daniels v. Leitch, 13 Gratt. 195, 212; Threlkelds v. Campbell, 2 Gratt. 198; Young v. McClung, 9 Gratt. 336.

"I have no doubt of the correctness of the decision of that case, in which it seems a good title could not have made until an infant heir became of age. But I can not see why the same rule which applies to ordinary cases, should not apply to a judicial sale in this respect. The court considers itself to have greater power over the contract of sale when it is made under a decree, than when it is made between party and party. 2 Daniel's Ch. Pr. 1465. And it may, therefore, exercise at least as much discretion in affording parties an opportunity of perfecting the title in the former as in the latter case." Daniel v. Leitch, 13 Gratt. 195, 214.

"In the subsequent case of Chamberlain v. Lee, 10 Sim. R. 444, 16 Eng. Ch. R. 445, the case of Lechmere v. Brasier was not considered as making a judicial sale an exception to the general rule; but it being discovered after the sale of an estate under a decree, and after the confirmation of the report of sale, that a small portion of the estate was the property of another person, the court would not discharge the purchaser from his contract without giving the vendor an opportunity of acquiring a title to that portion." Daniel v. Leitch, 13 Gratt. 195, 214.

C. RIGHT OF PURCHASER TO HEARING UPON QUESTION OF SETTING ASIDE SALE.

In General.—In sales made by commissioners under decrees and orders of a court of equity, the purchasers, who have bid off the property and paid their deposits in good faith, are considered as having inchoate rights, which entitle them to a hearing upon the question, whether the sale shall be set aside. Hughes v. Hamilton, 19 W. Va. 366; Kable v. Mitchell, 9 W. Va. 492; Connell v. Wilhelm, 36 W. Va. 598, 15 S. E. 245; Hyman v. Smith, 13 W. Va. 744.

It was said by Joynes, Judge, in Londons v. Echols, 17 Gratt. 15, 19, that "it would be contrary to natural justice, and to the practice which has prevailed in like cases, to conclude the purchaser, whose purchase has been confirmed and consummated by a conveyance of the title, by a decision of these questions (whether the sale should stand or be set aside), before he has been brought before the court." Estill v. McClintic, 11 W. Va. 399.

In a suit for the sale of lands, a sale having been made and confirmed, and a conveyance made to the purchaser; he must be brought before the court as a party, before the court will inquire into the validity of the sale. Londons v. Echols, 17 Gratt. 15.

If in such a case an appeal is allowed before the purchaser is made a party in the cause, it will be dismissed as improvidently awarded, and the cause sent back for further proceedings. Londons v. Echols, 17 Gratt. 15.

"The court is of opinion that this case is ruled by that of Hughes v. Johnston, 12 Gratt. 479. The interests of all parties will be best promoted by remanding the case to the circuit court, to be there further proceeded in, after the purchaser of the 'Soldier's Joy' estate, and those claiming under him, if any, and all other parties interested, shall have been brought before the court. Then the alleged irregularities of the proceedings can be investigated upon the evidence now. in the cause, and such other as any of the parties may produce, and may be corrected, if they admit of correction; defective proof may be supplied, as far as may be proper; any accounts may be taken which may be necessary to do justice between the parties. And the court, with all the facts and all the parties interested before it, can determine, without the risk of injustice, whether the sale, which is the main subject of controversy, should stand or be set aside." Londons *v.* Echols, 17 Gratt. 15.

How Purchaser Brought before Court.—The purchaser was brought before the court by supplemental proceedings in Pierce *v.* Trigg, 10 Leigh 406, and in Parker *v.* McCoy, 10 Gratt. 594, as well as in Hughes *v.* Johnston, 12 Gratt. 479; while, in Huston *v.* Cantril, 11 Leight 136; Cocke *v.* Gilpin, 1 Rob. 20, 26, and Buchanan *v.* Clark, 10 Gratt. 164, there was no necessity to resort to supplemental proceedings, because the purchaser was already a party in the cause. Londons *v.* Echols, 17 Gratt. 15.

Right to Appeal from Decision Setting Aside Sale.—And if the court errs, by setting aside the sale improperly, the purchasers have the right to carry the question by appeal to a higher tribunal. Kable *v.* Mitchell, 9 W. Va. 492; Hyman *v.* Smith, 13 W. Va. 744. See the title APPEAL AND ERROR, vol. 1, p. 418.

D. PROCEDURE.

1. Petition for Rehearing.

a. In General.

After sale has been ratified and confirmed by the court, the decree of confirmation can not be set aside and the sale itself rescinded, except upon petition for rehearing filed in proper time, or upon proper motion. Langyher *v.* Patterson, 77 Va. 470.

A proceeding to rescind and set aside a judicial sale which has been absolutely confirmed, ought to be by a petition filed in the cause for a rehearing of the decree confirming such sale. Virginia Fire, etc., Ins. Co. *v.* Cottrell, 95 Va. 857, 9 S. E. 132; Ammons *v.* Ammons, 50 W. Va. 390, 40 S. E. 490; Cralle *v.* Meem, 8 Gratt. 496; Estill *v.* McClintic, 11 W. Va. 399.

In Virginia, the method of setting

aside a sale after confirmation by the court, was considered in Taylor *v.* Palmer, decided by the special court of appeals, 1873, and published in the July number, 1882, Virginia Law Journal. The court held: "Where a judicial sale has been confirmed, it can only be properly set aside by a rehearing, on petition; of the decree of confirmation, filed in proper time, and not by sustaining exception to the sale filed after such decree of confirmation." Langyher *v.* Patterson, 77 Va. 470.

b. Sufficiency.

Written Application.—"In the present case, however, according to the liberal practice which prevails with us in courts of equity, the written application, as it is termed in the record, which was filed by the plaintiff in the court below, praying that the property be again offered for sale, may be treated as a petition, and we will therefore consider the case upon its merits." Virginia Fire, etc., Ins. Co. *v.* Cottrell, 85 Va. 857, 9 S. E. 132.

Bill to Enjoin Collection of Purchase Money.—Athough the application of purchasers to have the sale set aside should be by petition in the cause, yet if they proceed by bill to enjoin the collection of the purchase money, and to have the sale set aside, the bill should be treated as a petition in the cause, and be brought to a hearing with it. Ammons *v.* Ammons, 50 W. Va. 390, 40 S. E. 490; Cralle *v.* Meem, 8 Gratt. 496.

Must Set Forth Grounds.—A petition filed in the cause to rescind a judicial sale which has been absolutely confirmed, should set forth distinctly the grounds upon which the application is based, in order that the purchaser or other adverse party to the proceeding, may see clearly, what they have to meet. Virginia Fire, etc., Ins. Co. *v.* Cottrell, 85 Va. 857, 9 S. E. 132.

c. Summons or Notice to Answer Petition.

When a petition for rehearing has

been filed by a party interested, the purchaser must be summoned to answer this petition. Estill *v.* McClintic, 11 W. Va. 399.

A judicial sale can not be set aside after confirmation, without proper notice being given to the purchaser and the parties to the cause. Langyher *v.* Patterson, 77 Va. 470.

d. Hearing.

After the purchaser has been summoned to answer the petition, the case should be heard on its merits. Estill *v.* McClintic, 11 W. Va. 399.

e. Evidence.

All the evidence bearing on the justice or propriety of the sales should be heard, including evidence as to the value of said lands when sold, and what improvements on them had been made by the purchasers, and what taxes paid by them, as also what rents and profits had been received from them; and the court should then, with all the facts and parties before it, do justice by setting aside the sale on such terms as are right, or by refusing to set it aside. Estill *v.* McClintic, 11 W. Va. 399. This was the course pursued in Londons *v.* Echols, 17 Gratt. 15; Hughes *v.* Johnston, 12 Gratt. 479. See also, as indicating that this is the proper course to be pursued, Pierce *v.* Trigg, 10 Leigh 406.

f. Decree.

After the purchaser has been summoned to answer the petition, and it has been heard on its merits, the court should set aside the decree and sale, or refuse to do so, as on its merits, as shown by the evidence, justice to the party requires. Estill *v.* McClintic, 11 W. Va. 399.

2. Rule to Show Cause.

A summary rule to show cause is not sufficient, where it is sought to rescind a judicial sale which has been absolutely confirmed. Virginia Fire, etc., Ins. Co. *v.* Cottrell, 85 Va. 857, 9 S. E. 132.

3. Bill of Review.

See the title BILL OF REVIEW, vol. 2, p. 382.

A bill of review may be filed by the parties interested, and injured by a judicial sale, to have such sale set aside. Zollman *v.* Moore, 21 Gratt. 313.

4. Separate Suit in Chancery.

In General.—A separate suit in chancery may be brought to set aside a sale made under a decree in another cause which is ended. McKay *v.* McKay, 28 W. Va. 514.

Sufficiency of Bill.—A bill in chancery by proper allegations should show on its face that proper parties are made to the suit; and if it claims to have set aside a sale made under a decree in another chancery cause which is ended, for fraud or for other reasons, and that a resale should be made of the land, and the proceeds should be distributed among the parties entitled to such proceeds, so much of the substance of such chancery cause and the decrees in it, as will fully show the character of such suit and its objects, and especially as will show the parties interested in such suit and sale and the disposition of the proceeds, if made by the court, should be set out, so as to give the court definite information as to these matters. McKay *v.* McKay, 28 W. Va. 514.

5. Effect of Laches in Making Application.

See the title LACHES.

To set aside a sale for fraud and conspiracy, suit must be brought within a reasonable time after the discovery of such fraud. One who delays three years after knowledge of all the facts attending a sale before bringing such suit is guilty of such laches as will debar him from relief. Williams *v.* Maxwell, 45 W. Va. 297, 31 S. E. 909.

XI. Opening Biddings on Upset Bids.

A. NATURE OF UPSET BIDS.

A substantial upset bid, well secured and safe, put in before confirmation, is as much a valid bid as if made at the auction. Todd v. Gallego Mills Mfg. Co., 84 Va. 586, 5 S. E. 676; Ewald v. Crockett, 85 Va. 299, 7 S. E. 386; Moore v. Triplett, 96 Va. 603, 32 S. E. 50.

Upset bids are not unusual but frequently occur and are recognized by the courts, and by all others having concern with judicial sales, having often been the subject of judicial consideration. Todd v. Gallego Mills Mfg. Co., 84 Va. 586, 5 S. E. 676.

B. UPSET BID DISTINGUISHED FROM MOTION TO REFUSE CONFIRMATION FOR MERE INADEQUACY.

A motion to the court to refuse a confirmation of a sale because of a material advance in the shape of an upset bid stands upon a different and stronger footing than an application to the court to refuse confirmation for mere inadequacy of consideration, and this difference seems not always to have been kept in view in the adjudged cases. Coles v. Coles, 83 Va. 525, 5 S. E. 673.

C. RIGHT TO OPEN BIDDINGS.
1. In General.

In a proper case, where it would be just to all the parties concerned, the Virginia supreme court of appeals may be understood as having sanctioned a practice in the circuit courts, of setting aside a sale made by commissioners under a decree, and reopening the biddings upon the offer of an advance bid of sufficient amount deposited or well secured; and to that extent the former English practice has been allowed in this state. Roudabush v. Miller, 32 Gratt. 454; Berlin v. Melhorn, 75 Va. 636, 639; Hansucker v. Walker, 76 Va. 753.

"From a long experience, the English government became so well satisfied of the evils resulting from this practice, that it has been abolished by an act of the British parliament during the present reign. 30 and 31 Vict. c. 48, cited 1 Snyd. Vendors, p. 161 note (a). Chancellor Kent says: 'The English practice of opening biddings, on a sale of mortgaged premises under a decree, does not prevail, to any very great extent in this country.' (4 Kent. Com., pp. 191, 192.) Judge Lomax says: 'We are not warranted by any reported decision of the highest tribunal in Virginia, to pronounce positively what is the course of practice in this particular in this commonwealth.' And he cites the opinion of Chief Justice Marshall, in Ross v. Taylor, to the effect that it is not a doctrine of equity, but a practice established by particular courts. But in Virginia he says, 'the courts have established a different practice. The purchaser is entitled to his purchase, and can not recede from it. The benefit or loss is largely his, and it requires some impropriety, which vitiates the transaction, to set it aside.' Since the above was written by Judge Lomax there has been some expression of opinion in this court on the subject. In Effinger v. Ralston, 21 Gratt. 430, Judge Moncure, after stating what were some of the rules of the English practice on this subject, expresses the opinion that the same practice and rules substantially exist in this state, though not in all the states of the union. But he said they did not apply to that case. The question was not involved in that case, and was not decided." Roudabush v. Miller, 32 Gratt. 454.

The propriety of setting aside a sale and reopening the bids depends upon the circumstances of each case, and can only be rightly done, when it can be done, with a due regard to the rights and interests of all concerned, the purchaser as well as others. Where the sale has been fair and for a fair price, it should never be set aside, when there is good reason to believe that the upset price has been offered to gratify ill will or malice towards the purchaser. Roudabush v. Miller, 32 Gratt. 454; Berlin v. Melhorn, 75 Va. 636, 639.

2. Discretionary with Court.

It has never been held, that it is imperative upon the courts to set aside the sale, and reopen the biddings. It is a question addressed to the sound discretion of the courts, subject to the review of the appellate tribunal. Roudabush v. Miller, 32 Gratt. 454; Berlin v. Melhorn, 75 Va. 636, 639.

The English practice of—as a matter of course—opening the biddings of a sale made by the master under a decree of the court, upon the offer of a reasonable advance bid, has not been adopted in Virginia. Roudabush v. Miller, 32 Gratt. 454.

In Todd v. Gallego Mills Mfg. Co., 84 Va. 586, 5 S. E. 676, it is said: "All the cases agree that the court must sell at the best price obtainable and when a substantial upset bid, well secured and safe, for ten per cent. advance, is put in before confirmation, it is as much a valid bid as if made at the auction. This is the settled law of this court, and will doubtless so remain until the legislature shall (otherwise) provide by law as has been done by the English parliament." This same language was quoted with approval in Ewald v. Crockett, 85 Va. 299, 7 S. E. 386; Moore v. Triplett, 96 Va. 603, 32 S. E. 50.

The above statement of law was construed by the counsel of the appellants to be a departure from the previous cases and the former practice in Virginia, and to mean that "a substantial upset bid, well secured and safe, for ten per cent. advance, put in before confirmation, was always to be accepted, without regard to the circumstances of the case, and that the court had no discretion in the matter.

Such a construction is a misapprehension of the import of that decision. The court in that case found no equitable circumstances, which, in the exercise of a sound legal discretion, called for a rejection of the upset bid. It was in amount a larger advance on the price obtained at the sale, and in that view substantial. It was well secured and safe. The creditors whom it benefited desired its acceptance, and the purchaser, as the court took pains to show at length, had no just ground of complaint. We understand the decision in that case to mean simply that a substantial and well-secured upset bid should be accepted, unless there are circumstances going to show that injustice would be done to the purchaser or other person. That such was the purport of that decision, and the understanding of the judge who delivered the opinion of the court in that case, and also in Ewald v. Crockett, 85 Va. 299, 7 S. E. 386, is clearly manifested in the subsequent case of Carr v. Carr, 88 Va. 735, 14 S. E. 368, where he enunciates the long and well-established rule in Virginia that 'the court in acting upon the matter, was called upon to act in the exercise of a sound legal discretion in view of all the circumstances. It is to be exercised in the interest of fairness, prudence, and with a just regard to the rights of all concerned.'" And he refers to the case decided long before Todd v. Gallego Mills Mfg. Co., 84 Va. 586, 5 S. E. 676, to sustain his declaration of the practice and the law on the subject. Moore v. Triplett, 96 Va. 603, 32 S. E. 50.

Considering the circumstances of the case at bar, and applying the rule prevailing in this state, our conclusion is that the circuit court did not err in rejecting the upset bids and confirming the report of sale of the parcels of land in question. The sale took place under favorable circumstances, was fairly made, and there is not a suggestion of misconduct or impropriety on the part of any one. There is no evidence or complaint even that the land did not sell for a fair price, and bring its market value. The commissioners state in their report that it brought a good price, and recommend the confirmation of the sale. Moore v. Triplett, 96 Va. 603, 32 S. E. 50.

Judicial sales are constantly taking place, and it must continue to be so as long as there are debts to be collected, and liens to be enforced. Great care should be observed that the practice of the court in acting upon a report of sale should not be such as to deter or discourage bidders, but such as to induce possible purchasers to attend such sales, to encourage fair, open and competitive bidding in order that the highest possible price be obtained, and to inspire confidence in the stability of judicial sales. This is due not merely to the purchaser but also to creditors, debtors, and the owners of property which has to be sold by the court. Moore v. Triplett, 96 Va. 603, 32 S. E. 50.

"In Langyher v. Patterson, 77 Va. 470, after the sale had been confirmed, the decree of confirmation was set aside and a resale ordered upon the offer of an advanced bid. Upon appeal by the purchaser to this court, the action of the circuit court was reversed, Judge Fauntleroy, in delivering the opinion of the court, after reviewing the authorities, said: "We think there was error * * * in setting aside the decree of confirmation * * * in this case * * * for though it was within the discretion of the court, at any time during the term, to set aside the decree and rescind the sale upon proper motion and notice to the purchaser and parties concerned, and for good cause shown, such, for instance, as a sacrifice of the property, yet it was in this case, so far as the record shows, not a sound, but apparently an arbitrary discretion, which calls for appellate correction by this court." Yost v. Porter, 80 Va. 855.

3. Principles on Which Upset Bids Allowed.

a. Upset Bid as Valid as Original Bid.

A substantial upset bid put in before confirmation, being as much a valid bid as if made at the auction, can not be disregarded, and the court as vendor is bound, in justice to all, to consider such upset bid. Todd v. Gallego Mills Mfg. Co., 84 Va. 586, 5 S. E. 676; Ewald v. Crockett, 85 Va. 299, 7 S. E. 386.

The English practice, before the act known as "The Sale of Land by Auction Act," passed in 1867 (30 & 31 Vict., ch. 48, § 7) in making judicial sales, was to open the biddings, and to allow a person to offer a larger price than the reported highest bid, and upon such offer being made, and a proportionate deposit paid in, to direct a resale of the property; and this was allowed upon an advance of price, even after confirmation of the sale reported. Ten per cent. upon small sums, and less upon large sums, was considered a sufficient advance to open the biddings. As is set forth by Lord Eldon in Andrews v. Emerson, 7 Ves. 420, and in White v. Wilson, 14 Ves. 151, and in Brooks v. Smith, 3 Ves. & B. 144, he opened the biddings upon an advance of 5 per cent. As was said by Judge Moncure, in Effinger v. Ralston, 21 Gratt. 430: "Such are some of the rules of the English practice on this subject; and the same practice and rules, substantially, exist in this state." Todd v. Gallego Mills Mfg. Co., 84 Va. 586, 5 S. E. 676; Coles v. Coles, 83 Va. 525, 5 S. E. 673.

b. Duty of Court to Obtain Best Possible Price.

The court selling to satisfy debts has always proceeded upon the principle that it was just to cause the property to bring as much as possible for the benefit of all concerned—the creditor, to the extent of his claim; the debtor, to the extent of his liability, so far as the property would go.

Todd *v.* Gallego Mills Mfg. Co., 84 Va. 586, 5 S. E. 676; Ewald *v.* Crockett, 85 Va. 299, 7 S. E. 386.

In case an upset bid is put in, it is the duty of the court to get the best price obtainable for the property, rather than to aid the first bidder in getting a good bargain. Property is again exposed to public sale, and the first bidder is afforded an opportunity to purchase if he is willing to give more for the property than anybody else, and he can not reasonably ask more. Ewald *v.* Crockett, 85 Va. 299, 7 S. E. 386.

As the chief aim of the court is to obtain as great a price for the estate as possible, it is in the habit, under certain regulations, of opening the biddings. 1 Sugd. on Vend. 84. It is unnecessary to inquire how far the English practice in these respects has been departed from in Virginia. Daniel *v.* Leitch, 13 Gratt. 195, 211.

All the cases agree that the court must sell at the best price obtainable; and when a substantial upset bid, well secured and safe, for ten per cent. advance, is put in before confirmation, it is as much a valid bid as if made at the auction. This is the settled law of this court, and will doubtless so remain until the legislature shall provide by law, as has been done by the English parliament, that "the highest bona fide bidder at a sale by auction of land under an order of the court, provided he has bid a sum equal to or higher than the reserved price, if any, will be declared or allowed the purchaser," unless in a case of fraud or improper management of the sale, etc. Todd *v.* Gallego Mills Mfg. Co., 84 Va. 586, 5 S. E. 676; Ewald *v.* Crockett, 85 Va. 299, 7 S. E. 386; Moore *v.* Triplett, 96 Va. 603, 32 S. E. 50.

A fair and just price alone could justify a court in disposing of the property within its jurisdiction—a fair and just price, all things considered; that is, all the attendant circumstances having been duly regarded. It may be said that after full notice, an open sale fairly conducted, in the face of such competition as can be attracted, the highest bid which is made is a fair and just criterion of the value of the property at the time; and such after-stated opinions, affidavits of under value, etc., are regarded with but little favor, and estimated as of light weight, in the presence of the fact established by the auction and its results. Todd *v.* Gallego Mills Mfg. Co., 85 Va. 586, 5 S. E. 676.

D. WHO MAY PUT IN UPSET BID.

The main upset bid was put in by one who had an agent at the sale, who bid for him. It has been generally understood by the profession, and enforced by the courts, that one who was a bidder at the sale, by himself or by an agent, which is the same thing, or was present and had the opportunity to bid, would not, as a general rule, be permitted to put in an upset bid. He must bid at the sale in open competition with all others what he is willing to give for the property. A different rule would have a pernicious effect upon judicial sales of property. Moore *v.* Triplett, 96 Va. 603, 32 S. E. 50.

E. TIME OF PUTTING IN BID.

General Rule.—An upset bid must, as a general rule, be put in before the sale is confirmed. Todd *v.* Gallego Mills Mfg. Co., 84 Va. 586, 5 S. E. 676; Coles *v.* Coles, 83 Va. 525, 5 S. E. 673; Yost *v.* Porter, 80 Va. 855; Ewald *v.* Crockett, 85 Va. 299, 7 S. E. 386; Roudabush *v.* Miller, 32 Gratt. 454; Berlin *v.* Melhorn, 75 Va. 636, 639.

The determinations on the subject of opening biddings assume a very different aspect, when the report is absolutely confirmed. Biddings are, in general, not to be opened after confirmation of the report. Sugden on Vendors, p. 67. Effinger *v.* Ralston, 21

Gratt. 430; Kable *v.* Mitchell, 9 W. Va. 492.

Increase of price alone, however large, is not sufficient to justify the court in opening the bidding after confirmation of the report, although it is a strong auxiliary argument where there are other grounds. Sugden on Vendors, p. 67. Effinger *v.* Ralston, 21 Gratt. 430; Kable *v.* Mitchell, 9 W. Va. 492.

Commissioners empowered to sell mill property for one-fourth cash and balance in one, two and three years, reported sale of same to L. at $1,000, receiving cash, $56.50, and purchaser's notes for balance payable in three annual installments, and that he had found it impossible to sell to any advantage on terms of decree. No exception. On hearing, sale confirmed. During same term, two days later, upset bid of ten per cent. offered. No money or security tendered. No affidavit or suggestion that the price was inadequate. Without notice to purchaser, who had left court, decree was entered rescinding confirmation, ordering the property to be set up on the terms ordered and started at $1,000. On appeal, held, the decree of rescission or confirmation of the sale was erroneous. Langyher *v.* Patterson, 77 Va. 470.

The case of Berlin *v.* Melhorn, 75 Va. 636, 639, was a judicial sale at which Berlin was the purchaser, and the commissioner conducting the sale made report of the fact to the court, and the court confirmed the report. Afterwards, and during the term at which the order of confirmation was made, Melhorn offered an advance on Berlin's purchase; and thereupon the court, without assigning any reason, by its decree set aside the order of confirmation and directed the land to be again exposed to sale at the price offered by Melhorn as an unjust bid. Berlin, on appeal allowed him, complains of this decree. "We are of opinion," said Judge Burks for the whole

court, "that he has just ground of complaint," and the decree was reversed. Langyher *v.* Patterson, 77 Va. 470; Virginia Fire, etc., Ins. Co. *v.* Cottrell, 85 Va. 857, 9 S. E. 132.

Under the English practice, before the act known as "The Sale of Land by Auction Act," passed in 1867 (30 and 31 Vict., ch. 48, § 7) a bid would be opened, and a resale ordered upon an advance of price, even after confirmation of the report of sale. Todd *v.* Gallego Mills Mfg. Co., 84 Va. 586, 5 S. E. 676.

Bid Put in after Confirmation with Consent of Purchaser.—Although there is no right on the part of any person to demand a resale of the property, upon the mere offer of an upset bid, after the sale has been confirmed, nevertheless, if, with the consent of the purchaser, the privilege of a resale is accorded, it can be enjoyed only on the terms which the court in its discretion may see fit to impose. These terms it is optional with the upset bidder to accept or not as he chooses. Yost *v.* Porter, 80 Va. 855.

Where, after a sale, fairly made for adequate price, has been confirmed, an upset bid is offered, and the sale is set aside upon condition that said bid be made good by a certain time, when the resale should take place upon terms which would not extend the deferred payments beyond the time at which the bonds taken at the previous sale were to become due, and no complaint of said terms was made below, and no proof offered that upset bidder could have complied with his bid had the terms been more liberal, there is no ground on this account for complaint in the appellate court. Yost *v.* Porter, 80 Va. 855; Langyher *v.* Patterson, 77 Va. 470.

The appellant's principal objection relates to the decree in respect to the upset bid which was offered in the case. That bid was offered after the sale had been confirmed, and the decree provides as follows: "That if the said Henry Simmerman shall, within thirty days from this date, pay into the hands of commissioners Terry and Crockett, the sum of $280, and the further sum of $700, with interest from 10th of November, 1884, and shall deposit with said commissioners his bond with security to be approved by them, and to secure the residue of the purchase money for which said house and lot was sold, on the 10th of November, 1884, and to make good his upset bid, then said commissioners shall proceed to resell the said house and lot according to the terms of the former decree of sale in this cause, except that the deferred payments therein provided for shall be so made in the resale as not to extend said deferred payments beyond the period provided for in the said decree of sale heretofore entered in this cause." Thus, by the terms of this decree, the credit allowed, in the event that the upset bidder made good his bid, and a resale was made, was not to extend beyond the time at which the bonds for the deferred payments taken at the sale which had been confirmed were to become due. And in consequence of these terms, which, in the petition for appeal are characterized as harsh and unprecedented, it is alleged by the appellant that the party desiring to make good his upset bid was rendered unable to do so. Of this, however, there is not a particle of proof in the record, and non constat that he could have complied with any terms, however reasonable or liberal. Yost v. Porter, 80 Va. 855.

Where, in such case of upset bid and conditional setting aside of sale and suspension of decree of sale to a certain period in order to give upset bidder opportunity to comply with the conditions of resale, he applies to the judge in vacation for an extension of such suspension in order to give time to apply for appeal and supersedeas, and the judge delays acting on such application till after the period within which compliance was permissible,

such action of the judge could not be corrected by the appellate court. Yost v. Porter, 80 Va. 855.

Under a decree of the court, a commissioner is directed to sell three tracts of land; on the day of sale the land is bid off to A., the debtor, and he being unable to comply with the terms of sale, makes a parol agreement with D. by which it is agreed he shall be reported as the purchaser instead of A., and the latter, as an inducement to D. to purchase, agrees to get his wife to release her contingent dower in the lands, which the wife afterwards refuses to do; the commissioner reports D. as the purchaser, and the court confirms the sale without objection; on a subsequent day of the same term, N., a creditor of A., offers for one of said tracts an upset bid of twenty per cent. advance on the price of said tract, and the court sets aside the confirmation as to the said one tract; at a subsequent term D. moves the court to confirm the sale to him of said tract, and A. moves to have the same set aside and a resale ordered; the court set aside the sale and ordered a resale on the basis of the upset bid, the resale is made and N. becomes the purchaser at his upset bid; this sale is confirmed, and D. appeals to this court. Held, the court properly set aside the order confirming said first sale. N. had the right to ask the court to set aside said order of confirmation and sale, although it was demonstrable that A. had ample other real estate to pay his debts. The said parol agreement could not be specifically enforced; nor could it operate as an estoppel or conclude the right of A. to resist the confirmation of the sale. National Bank v. Jarvis, 28 W. Va. 805.

F. AMOUNT OF ADVANCE.

In General.—The court will stipulate for the price, and not permit the biddings to be opened upon a small advance. Sugden on Vendors, p. 66. Effinger v. Ralston, 21 Gratt. 430; Kable v. Mitchell, 9 W. Va. 492.

Mere advance of price, if the report of the purchaser being the best bidder is not absolutely confirmed, is sufficient to open the biddings. Sugden on Vendors, p. 66. Effinger v. Ralston, 21 Gratt. 430; Kable v. Mitchell, 9 W. Va. 492.

The chancery court did not err in refusing to confirm a sale to the purchaser directing a resale on the basis of an upset bid, where, the said upset bid was a substantial advance of ten per cent., or, $12,000, on the real property alone. That the course pursued by the chancellor was the usual course, and was in accordance with the unbroken line of authorities in this state, is or must be conceded. There is no case to be found, in this state certainly, where this practice has been overruled by this court. Todd v. Gallego Mills Mfg. Co., 84 Va. 586, 5 S. E. 676.

Where a creditor's bill is filed to subject lands of defendant to the payment of debts and a decree rendered and the property sold thereunder, and reported to the court on the same day as sold to the highest bidder for $10,000, and a third person asked to be permitted to put in an upset bid of ten per cent. advance on the reported bid, the upset bid should be allowed and the bidding opened again to all. Ewald v. Crockett, 85 Va. 299, 7 S. E. 386.

Total debts secured by trust deed on the Gallego Mills property amounted to $542,146.34. Assessed value of trust property was about $208,000. First and second liens aggregated $248,610.78. A portion of creditors representing the latter liens agreed with T. that he could have the property at $120,000, unless a higher bid came from another quarter. The property was knocked down to T. at that price. Before report of sale was acted upon by the court below, a well-secured upset bid of ten per cent. was put in. That court refused to confirm the sale, and ordered a resale. Held, this was not error. Todd v.

Gallego Mills Mfg. Co., 84 Va. 586, 5 S. E. 676.

"These principles are decisive of this case; for, waiving all questions as to the adequacy or inadequacy of the price bid, it is perfectly clear that the offer of so large an advance bid as thirty per cent. at the price for which the land sold, made a resale necessary in justice to Mrs. Powell and Mrs. Withers, whose legacies will otherwise be entirely lost to them." Coles v. Coles, 83 Va. 525, 5 S. E. 673.

Although an advance of ten per cent. was formerly generally considered sufficient on a large sum, yet no such rule now prevails; but in the case of a sale under a creditor's suit, the court permitted the biddings to be opened upon an advance of five per cent. on one thousand pounds. Sugden on Vendors, p. 66. Effinger v. Ralston, 21 Gratt. 430; Kable v. Mitchell, 9 W. Va. 492.

An advance of 350 pounds upon 5300 pounds was refused, and it was said that the former cases only establish, that where an advance as large as 500 pounds is offered, the court will act upon it, though it be less than ten per cent. Sugden on Vendors, p. 66. Effinger v. Ralston, 21 Gratt. 430; Kable v. Mitchell, 9 W. Va. 492.

Where sixty-six acres of land were sold by a commissioner in a suit for $1,961, and the defendant showed an offer of an advance-bid of $5 per acre, the bidder offering to comply with such terms as the court might impose, it was the duty of the court to accept the bid, and if such terms were complied with, to set aside the sale and order a resale of the property. Stewart v. Stewart, 27 W. Va. 167.

It is not error to refuse a petition offering less than the value of the land, viz.: $800, of which $125 had been paid cash, and the balance was payable in one, two, and three years, without interest, where the master reported its value to be $900, and it cost $1,200 without improvements, and where the petitioner was no party to the suit, and had no interest whatever in it. Cooper v. Daugherty, 85 Va. 343, 7 S. E. 387.

"Should the court have set aside the sale because of the advance bid? This court in Kable v. Mitchell, 9 W. Va. 492, decided, that the offering to the court of a large amount in advance of the price bid, to be secured either by the advance offered being paid into court or by bond with good security, as was done in that case, is generally the very best evidence of the great inadequacy of price bid at the sale, and the offer in that case of $11.52 ½ per acre in advance of the bid was regarded as sufficiently large to justify the court in setting aside the sale made by the commissioner, the tract of land containing about 101 acres. It does not here appear why the court refused to receive the upset bid. The land sold was about sixty-six acres, and the advance bid would amount to about $330.00 or over sixteen per cent. on the former bid. We think this was sufficient to require the court on its terms being complied with to set aside the sale; and the court erred to the prejudice of the defendant, Samuel Stuart, in not receiving the bid, and if its terms were complied with, in not setting aside the sale and ordering a resale. There is no evidence in the record, that the offer of the advance bid was not made in good faith. The court must have rejected it, on the ground that the bid was not sufficient. For this error the decree confirming the sale must be set aside, and the cause remanded with instruction to accept the advance bid of five dollars per acre, if the said Caroline Shepherd will comply with such reasonable terms as may be imposed by the court, and in case she does, to put the purchaser in statu quo and order a resale of the property, and if she declines to comply with such terms to confirm said sale." Stewart v. Stewart, 27 W. Va. 167.

In Hudgins v. Lanier, 23 Gratt. 494, an advance bid was tendered. But the circuit court declined it, and confirmed the sale, and the decree was affirmed by this court. Judge Staples, delivering the opinion of the court, said: "It is obvious that this is no such substantial and material advance upon the price obtained by the commissioners as would justify the court in annulling the sale already made, and exposing the creditors to all the delays and hazards attending a resale. There is no doubt the property was sold at a very advantageous price; the sale was fairly conducted, and the terms of the decree fully complied with. * * * It would be a bad precedent, leading to most pernicious consequences, to vacate a sale made under such circumstances, because the owner may be able to find some one willing to advance a small sum in excess of the commissioner's sale. Such has not been the practice in Virginia." It has never been decided by this court how far the English practice has been held, that the commissioner of sale is the agent of the court, and that his proceedings are subject to revision and control, and whether the court will confirm the sale will depend upon the circumstances of the particular case. It has never been held, that for mere inadequacy of price the court should set aside the sale. That question has not been decided by a full court. Curtis v. Thompson, 29 Gratt. 474; Roudabush v. Miller, 32 Gratt. 454.

English Practice.—Under the English practice, before the act known as "The Sale of Land by Auction Act," passed in 1867 (30 and 31 Vict., ch. 48, § 7), ten per cent. upon small sums, and less upon large sums, was considered a sufficient advance to open the biddings. As is set forth by Lord Eldon in Andrews v. Emerson, 7 Ves. 420, in White v. Wilson, 14 Ves. 151 and in Brooks v. Smith, 3 Ves. & B. 144, he opened the biddings upon an advance of five per cent. Todd v.

Gallego Mills Mfg. Co., 84 Va. 586, 5
S. E. 676.

G. DEPOSIT OF AND SECURITY FOR AMOUNT OF ADVANCE BID.

1. In General.

Upon reopening the biddings upon
the offer of an advance bid, the amount
of such bid shall be deposited or else
secured. Such is the former English
practice, which has been adopted in
Virginia. Roudabush *v.* Miller, 32
Gratt. 454; Berlin *v.* Melhorn, 75 Va.
636, 639.

2. Time of Deposit.

Where the biddings are opened, the
advance should be ordered to be deposited immediately. Sugd. on Vendors, p. 69; Effinger *v.* Ralston, 21 Gratt.
430; Kable *v.* Mitchell, 9 W. Va. 492.

H. EFFECT OF UPSET BID UPON RIGHTS OF PURCHASER OF PART OF LAND.

Where land has been sold in parcels, and one person has become the
purchaser of two or more parcels to
be used together, and the purchase of
one parcel was the inducement to become the purchaser of the other, if by
reason of an upset bid, the purchaser
loses one parcel, a court of equity
ought not to compel him to take the
other against his consent, especially
if the terms of the upset bid preclude
a resale of the tract in the same manner as before. Moore *v.* Triplett, 96
Va. 603, 32 S. E. 50.

I. PROCEDURE.

1. Application by Motion.

When a person is desirous of opening a bidding, he must, at his own expense, apply to the court by motion
for that purpose, stating the advance
offered. If the court approve of the
sum offered, the application will be
granted, and a new sale ordered. Sugden on Vendors, p. 66. Effinger *v.*
Ralston, 21 Gratt. 430; Kable *v.* Mitchell, 9 W. Va. 492; Langyher *v.* Patterson, 77 Va. 470.

Judge Moncure, delivering the opinion of the court in Effinger *v.* Ralston,
21 Gratt. 430, 437, after reciting this
rule, among others, says: "Such are
some of the rules of the English practice on this subject, and the same
rules and practice substantially exist
in this state." Langyher *v.* Patterson,
77 Va. 470.

In the case of Effinger *v.* Ralston,
21 Gratt. 430, it is stated in the second
division of the syllabus, that it was
held: "If E. objected to the sale for
inadequacy of price, he should have
moved the court to open the biddings,
and have offered an advance on the
price bid; his objection to the confirmation of the sale, without more, was
no ground for refusing to confirm it."
In this case, on pp. 436, 437, Judge
Moncure, who delivered the opinion of
the court, said: "He made no motion
to open the biddings. If he had done
so, and pursued the proper course in
such cases, the court would have ordered them to be opened on proper
terms." Kable *v.* Mitchell, 9 W. Va.
492.

2. Notice of Motion to Open Biddings.

Notice of the motion to open a bidding must be given to the person reported the purchaser of the land, and
to the parties in the cause. Sugden
on Vendors, p. 66; Effinger *v.* Ralston,
21 Gratt. 430; Kable *v.* Mitchell, 9 W.
Va. 492; Langyher *v.* Patterson, 77 Va.
470.

3. Time Allowed for Perfecting Bid.

Where an upset bid has been put in
and accepted, it is not error to allow
the bidder twenty days to perfect his
bid by depositing his money and executing bond, etc., where the first bidder did not ask to be allowed to withdraw his bid, and, the sale being made
and reported to the court on the same
day, the court was called upon to act
definitely on the question in five days.
It is not an unreasonable delay under
the circumstances, and it is the duty of
the court to get the best price obtain-

able for the property, rather than aid the first bidder in getting a good bargain. The property is again exposed to public sale, and the first bidder is afforded an opportunity to purchase if he is willing to give more for the property than anybody else, and he can not reasonably ask more. Ewald v. Crockett, 85 Va. 299, 7 S. E. 386.

4. Resale.

Where an upset bid is put in, and accepted and received by the court, the court should order a resale of the property, upon the basis of the upset bid. Todd v. Gallego Mills Mfg. Co., 84 Va. 586, 5 S. E. 676; Ewald v. Crockett, 85 Va. 299, 7 S. E. 386.

5. Costs of Purchaser.

Where the biddings are opened, the costs of the purchaser shall be paid by the person opening the biddings. Sugden on Vendors, p. 69; Effinger v. Ralston, 21 Gratt. 430; Kable v. Mitchell, 9 W. Va. 492.

XII. Payment, Collection and Distribution of Purchase Money.

See the title PAYMENT.

A. PAYMENT AND COLLECTION.

See ante, "Notice to Lienholders," IV, B, 2, d, (4), (e); post, "Procedure upon Failure of Purchaser to Comply with Bid," XIV.

1. Who May Receive and Collect Purchase Money.

a. Virginia Rule.

(1) Commissioner Making Sale.

In General.—A commissioner, appointed for the purpose, who made the sale or renting, shall receive and collect all the purchase money or rent, unless by decree or order, some other person may be appointed to collect the same. Va. Code, 1904, § 3401, acts, 1883-84, p. 214; Tompkins v. Dyerle, 102 Va. 219, 46 S. E. 300; Pulliam v. Tompkins, 99 Va. 602, 39 S. E. 221.

Where a decree appoints commissioners to sell land for cash as to so much as will pay the costs and charges of the sale, and the balance on a credit of four, eight and twelve months, each for the same amount with bonds and good securities, carrying interest from date of sale; the title to be retained, etc., but said commissioners were not authorized to collect these installments, and no decree was ever entered in the cause empowering them to make such collections, a collection by such commissioners was unauthorized and void. Tyler v. Toms, 75 Va. 116.

A commissioner who is directed to file the bonds with his report has no authority to collect them. Omohundro v. Omohundro, 27 Gratt. 824.

Commissioner Not Creditor within Code, 1873, ch. 143, §§ 4, 5.—A person appointed by a court of equity in a pending cause a receiver to collect the purchase money of lands sold by him as commissioner under a previous decree in the cause, and for which he had taken a bond with surety to himself as commissioner, is not a creditor in the sense of the statute, Code of 1873, ch. 143, §§ 4, 5, to whom a surety on the bond may give the notice to bring suit upon it. Davis v. Snead, 33 Gratt. 705; Blair v. Core, 20 W. Va. 265.

If the receiver was such a creditor, he could only have authority to sue after giving the security required of him in the decree appointing him receiver; and in the absence of clear and satisfactory proof that he had given the security required, the notice to him is not sufficient to release the surety. Davis v. Snead, 33 Gratt. 705.

In all judicial sales the court is regarded as the vendor and contracting party, on the one hand, and the purchaser on the other. If the bond is payable to a commissioner or receiver, it is only so from the necessity of the case, because the court can act, only through the instrumentality of its officers and agents, and because there

must be some one who, in behalf of
the court, may if need be bring the action at law. Davis *v.* Snead, 33 Gratt.
705; Blair *v.* Core, 20 W. Va. 265.

**Implied Authority to Receive Pay-
ment.**—A friendly suit is instituted in
October, 1863, for the sale of land in
which a number of persons are interested, in which there is a decree for
a sale on a credit of six months, with
the privilege to the purchasers to pay
cash, and the commissioners are directed to give bond in the sum of
$40,000. There is a sale, and the pur-
chasers give their bonds for the purchase money, and afterwards pay part
of the purchase money to the commissioner, who pays to several of the parties entitled their share of it, or a
part of it. Upon a bill filed seven
years afterwards, by the plaintiffs, to
set aside the sale on the ground that
they had not authorized the suit, and
had not assented to the proceedings
therein, and because one of the parties in interest, who joined as plaintiff in this suit, was not a party in
that; held, under the terms of the decree in the case, and the condition of
things at the time, and looking to the
amount in which the commissioners
were required to give security before
acting, their authority to receive the
purchase money may be implied. Finney *v.* Edwards, 75 Va. 44.

**Effect of Payment to Commissioner
or Officer Unauthorized to Collect.**—
Where a purchaser at a judicial sale
pays the purchase money to a commissioner or other officer, believing the
commissioner or officer authorized to
collect the purchase money, and it
turns out that such commissioner or
officer was not authorized to collect
the money, and the purchase money
was subsequently lost before coming
under the control of the court, the purchaser is bound to pay the purchase
money again. Tyler *v.* Toms, 75 Va.
116.

The sale of the land is to be on a
credit, and bonds to be taken for the

several deferred payments, and the title
to be retained. The sale is made, the
bonds taken, the sale reported to the
court; but there does not appear to
have been a decree confirming the sale.
As the bonds fall due the purchaser
pays the money to one of the commissioners, and he deposits it as collected
in a bank to his credit as commissioner,
not using it or mingling it with his
own, but it is lost by the failure of
the bank. Held, the purchaser is
bound to pay the purchase money of
the land again. The commissioner
having received the money without authority to receive it, is liable to the
purchaser for the amount so paid. The
commissioner may be proceeded against
by rule in the cause, and an execution
of fieri facias may be sued out against
him for the money. Tyler *v.* Toms,
75 Va. 116.

"The question arises, however, how
is that liability to be enforced? Is a
separate suit necessary, or may the
object be effected by a rule? The latter
course was pursued by the chancery
court, and a rule was awarded against
Col. Richardson to show cause why a
decree should not be rendered against
him in favor of the appellant for the
sum of money erroneously and improperly paid him on account of the
purchase made by the appellant. We
are of opinion that there was nothing
irregular or improper in this mode of
proceeding. A commissioner or receiver is an officer of the court, subject to its supervision and control.
Whenever complaint is made against
him for loss or injury sustained by
reason of negligence or improper conduct, the court which appointed the
receiver may take cognizance of the
complaint, or it may permit the person aggrieved to bring an action against
him. When a party to a cause, or
even a third person, is interested in a
fund in a receiver's hands, he may
apply to the court for relief; and the
court may make whatever order is necessary for the restitution or proper ap-

propriation of the fund, and if disobeyed, the order may be enforced by process of contempt. Kerr on Receivers, p. 203-212; High on Receivers, §§ 255-286. Whether according to the English practice an order made against a receiver upon a rule for the payment of money is enforceable by execution, as well as by process of contempt, the books do not clearly show. In Foster v. Morton, 9 Eq. Cas. (Law Rep.) 171, it was held, that where a receiver makes default in payment of a balance due by him, payment may be enforced by committal. It was made a question, however, whether an attachment might be had, because it was said an attachment could not issue against a person not a party to the suit; but it was held, that a writ of fieri facias issued by the special leave of the court. Our statutes have removed all difficulties on this point; for with us every order for the payment of money has the force of a judgment, and may be enforced by execution. Code of 1873, ch. 182, § 172." Tyler v. Toms, 75 Va. 116.

(2) Other Person Appointed by Decree or Order.

In General.—Although it is usual for the commissioner who makes the sale or renting to receive and collect all the purchase money or rent, yet some other person may by a decree or order be appointed to collect the same. Va. Code, 1904, § 3401; Acts, 1883-84, p. 214. Tompkins v. Dyerle, 102 Va. 219, 46 S. E. 300; Pulliam v. Tompkins, 99 Va. 602, 39 S. E. 221.

Bond.—Where some person, other than the commissioner selling, is appointed to receive and collect the purchase money or rent, the court shall require of such person a bond in such penalty as to it may seem fit. Va. Code, 1904, § 3401. See post, "Bond Required of Commissioner before Receiving Money under Decree," XII, A, 2.

No payment shall be made to the person so appointed, until he shall have given bond required by the decree or order. Va. Code, 1904, § 3401.

Notice to Purchaser or Lessee of Appointment.—When an appointment is made of some other person than the commissioner, it shall be the duty of the clerk to give notice thereof, in writing, to the purchaser or lessee, to be served as other notices are required by law to be served. Va. Code, 1904, § 3401; acts, 1883-84, p. 214. Tompkins v. Dyerle, 102 Va. 219, 46 S. E. 300; Pulliam v. Tompkins, 99 Va. 602, 39 S. E. 221.

Liability Where Payment Made before Notice.—However, if, before the purchaser or lessee has received notice of such appointment, he shall have made any payment, on account of the purchase money or rent to the special commissioner, or any person appointed for the purpose, who made the sale or renting, such special commissioner, or other person, who made the sale or renting, and the sureties in his bond, shall be responsible for the money so paid, and the purchaser or lessee, who made the payment, shall not be responsible therefor. Va. Code, 1904, § 3401; acts, 1883-84, p. 214. Tompkins v. Dyerle, 102 Va. 219, 40 S. E. 300; Pulliam v. Tompkins, 99 Va. 602, 39 S. E. 221.

Liability of Clerk for Failure to Give Notice.—If any clerk fail to give the notice required to be given by him, he and the sureties on his official bond shall be liable to any person injured by such failure; and he shall, moreover, be fined not less than ten dollars or more than one hundred dollars. Va. Code, 1904, § 3401.

b. West Virginia Rule.

(1) Commissioner or Other Officer Expressly Authorized.

Only a special commissioner or other officer appointed by the court and expressly authorized to do so may receive payment and collect the purchase money arising from a judicial sale. Blair v. Core, 20 W. Va. 265; Blair v. Core, 29 W. Va. 477, 2 S. E. 326; Clark v. Shanklin, 24 W. Va. 30.

The authority of the commissioner to collect should not be inferential but express. The power is special and qualified, and unless it is directly conferred, it can have no existence. Blair v. Core, 20 W. Va. 265.

Where the penalty of the bond of the commissioner in the decree directing the sale in this cause is one thousand dollars, only, while the gross amount of the sales amounted to over three thousand and nine hundred dollars, it is not reasonable to suppose that the court in taking this bond intended that the commissioner should collect the whole of this purchase money. Blair v. Core, 20 W. Va. 265.

(2) **Appointment to Make Sale No Authority to Collect Purchase Money.** The appointment of a commissioner to make a sale under an order or decree of court, does not authorize him to receive payment of or to collect the purchase money, in the absence of express authority, authorizing him to do so. Blair v. Core, 20 W. Va. 265.

A person, who, appointed by a decree of court special commissioner to make sale of lands under such decree and take bonds for deferred payments on said lands, and who makes such sale and takes bonds payable to himself as such commissioner, when said sale is reported to court and confirmed, has no authority to collect said sale bonds unless the decree conferring the appointment or some subsequent decree or order of court gives him authority to do so. Blair v. Core, 20 W. Va. 265.

2. **Bond Required of Commissioner, before Receiving Money under Decree.**

See ante. "Bond Required of Commissioner before Sale," VII, B, 2, g.

a. **Necessity.**

Statutory Provisions.—No special commissioner appointed by a court shall receive money under a decree or

order, until he gives bond, before said court or its clerk in a penalty to be prescribed by the court. Va. Code, 1904, § 3397; Va. Code, 1873, ch. 174, § 1; Whitehead v. Bradley, 87 Va. 676, 13 S. E. 195; Tyler v. Toms, 75 Va. 116; Hess v. Rader, 26 Gratt. 746; Lloyd v. Erwin, 29 Gratt. 598; McAllister v. Bodkin, 76 Va. 809; Eggleton v. Dinsmore, 84 Va. 858, 6 S. E. 146; Eggleton v. Whittle, 84 Va. 163, 4 S. E. 222; Duffy v. Figgat, 80 Va. 664; Lamar v. Hale, 79 Va. 147, 163; Boisseau v. Boisseau, 79 Va. 73; Lee v. Swepson, 76 Va. 173; Thomson v. Brooke, 76 Va! 160; Davis v. Snead, 33 Gratt. 705; Dixon v. McCue, 21 Gratt. 373; Jones v. Tatum, 19 Gratt. 720.

Section 1, ch. 132, W. Va. Code, 1899, acts, 1882, ch. 142, § 1, provides that a special commissioner appointed by the court shall receive no money under a decree or order until he gives a bond with good security before the said court or its clerk. Neeley v. Ruleys, 26 W. Va. 686; Blair v. Core, 20 W. Va. 265; Hall v. Lowther, 22 W. Va. 570; Baker v. Oil Tract Co., 7 W. Va. 454; Park v. Valentine, 27 W. Va. 677; Flesher v. Hassler, 29 W. Va. 404, 1 S. E. 580, 581; Donahue v. Fackler, 21 W. Va. 124.

If the commissioners have not in fact given the bond, it is clear they have no right to recover a judgment, or to collect the money, until such bond should be given. Flesher v. Hassler, 29 W. Va. 404, 1 S. E. 580; Hess v. Rader, 26 Gratt. 746, 747; Blair v. Core, 20 W. Va. 265; Lloyd v. Erwin, 29 Gratt. 598; Davis v. Snead, 33 Gratt. 705; Tyler v. Toms, 75 Va. 116; Donahue v. Fackler, 21 W. Va. 124; Clarke v. Shanklin, 24 W. Va. 30.

Provision of Statute Useful and Salutary.—The provision of the statute referred to, Va. Code, 1873, ch. 174, § 1, is one most useful and salutary. It was intended as a shield of protection to all parties, whose property had to be disposed of, and proceeds administered by the court of chancery. These parties are most frequently persons under disability, such as infants, insane, and others not sui juris. The legislature in its wisdom has determined not to leave the matter to the chance of a court's requiring a bond for the faithful performance of the duties of its commissioner, or to the chance of the appointment of an insolvent commissioner; but has declared as the law of every case, that "no special commissioner appointed by any court shall receive money under a decree or order until he gives bond before said court or its clerk." Hess v. Rader, 26 Gratt. 746.

No case of individual hardship should influence the courts in weakening in any degree the force of this wise and salutary law; but it ought to be constantly maintained and enforced, as one which affords a wholesome and safe protection to all parties, whose property is sold under proceedings of a court of chancery. Hess v. Rader, 26 Gratt. 746.

Statute for Benefit of Parties, Not Third Persons.—The provisions of the statute requiring bonds of commissioners with sureties are for the benefit of parties interested in the funds, and not of third persons. If a commissioner collects money without having given such bond, and the parties choose to ratify the act, and to look to him alone for payment, no one has the right to complain or insist that such a proceeding raises up an equity in his favor. Lee v. Swepson, 76 Va. 173.

Commissioner made sale under decree, and received one-third of purchase money, without giving bond as required; sale reported and confirmed and decree entered directing him, out of funds reported in his hands, to pay certain creditors, therein mentioned, which he failed to do. The decree was docketed, and five days later he conveyed in trust his own real estate to secure his creditor, L. On bill by creditors, in the decree mentioned, to enforce it against that real estate, he having become insolvent; held, under Va. Code, 1873, ch. 182, §§ 1, 2, the decree against commissioner had effect of a judgment, and being docketed, L. was affected with notice of same, though purchaser paid commissioner in his own wrong. L. has no claim to be subrogated to the rights of the creditors against the purchaser, having no equity superior to that of the latter. Lee v. Swepson, 76 Va. 173.

Provision in Decree as to Bond.— When the commissioner is authorized by the court to collect the purchase money, it will be proper to provide in the decree that he shall give bond and security before he proceeds to collect or receive any money under the decree. McAllister v. Bodkin, 76 Va. 809.

But it is not error that the decree does not require the commissioner of sale to give bond and security; the statute requires that he shall, before he collects any money. McAllister v. Bodkin, 76 Va. 809; Cooper v. Daugherty, 85 Va. 343, 7 S. E. 387.

It is not necessary that the decree should require the commissioner of sale to give bond and security, where the decree does not authorize the commissioner to receive the proceeds of the sale, except the costs of suit and expenses of the sale. McAllister v. Bodkin, 76 Va. 809.

"And, among numerous other objections, it is said that the circuit court erred in not requiring the commissioners of sale to give security on their bond. The statute, acts, 1883-84, p. 213, says: 'The commissioner shall give bond and personal security, to be approved by the clerk of the court.' The decree of the March term, 1888, fixed the penalty of the bond which it directed the commissioners to give. And this court, in McAllister v. Bodkin, 76 Va. 809, held, that it is not a reversible error for a decree to fail to provide that the commissioner of sale shall give bond and security." Cooper *v.* Daugherty, 85 Va. 343, 7 S. E. 387.

"As to the objection that the decree does not require the commissioner of sale to give bond and security, before he collects the money, it is sufficient to say that when he is authorized to collect the purchase money, it will be proper to provide in the decree that he shall give such before he receives any money under the decree." Boisseau *v.* Boisseau, 79 Va. 73.

Giving of Bond Condition Precedent to Right to Receive Payment.—Where the decree directs the commissioner to give bond before collecting purchase money, the giving of the bond is a condition precedent to his right to receive any part of said purchase money. Donahue *v.* Fackler, 21 W. Va. 124.

b. Security.

In General. — The statute (acts 1883-84, p. 213) says: "The commissioner shall give bond and personal security, to be approved by the clerk of the court." Cooper *v.* Daugherty, 85 Va. 343, 7 S. E. 387; McAllister *v.* Bodkin, 76 Va. 809.

Failure to require security is not error where the decree ordering a sale of land directs the commissioner to give bond and fixes the penalty of the bond, although the statute (acts, 1883-84, p. 213) provides that the commissioner shall give bond and personal security to be approved by the clerk. Cooper *v.* Daugherty, 85 Va. 343, 7 S. E. 387; McAllister *v.* Bodkin, 76 Va. 809.

"Again it is claimed, that the securities are not as reported by the commissioner and decided by the circuit court bound for the amount of the first bond of the purchaser, which it is claimed was paid before October 7, 1870, at which time the bond of the commissioner of sale and his sureties is dated. Many authorities are cited to show that these sureties can not be bound for moneys collected by the commissioner of sale before the execution of his bond. And these among other authorities are referred to as sustaining this position." Lyttle *v.* Cozad, 21 W. Va. 183.

Sufficiency of Sureties Must Be Approved by Clerk.—The bond given by a special commissioner before receiving or collecting money under a decree, must, as to the sufficiency of the sureties, be approved by the clerk, but in order to make the bond valid, he need not endorse his approval upon it. This approval is sufficiently shown by the fact, that the bond had been properly filed away by the clerk, and by the commissioner of sale proceeding to collect the money, which the giving of such bond authorized him to collect. Lyttle *v.* Cozad, 21 W. Va. 183.

c. Acknowledgment and Proof before Clerk.

It is not necessary to the validity of a bond required of a special commissioner, before receiving the purchase money from a sale made under a decree of court, that it should be either acknowledged or proven before the clerk. Lyttle *v.* Cozad, 21 W. Va. 183.

"There can be no question, on the authorities we have cited, that this bond is valid against him unless it be a bond, which the law requires to be signed in the clerk's office in the presence of the clerk, as is claimed by the appellant in this case. Section 1 of ch. 132, Code of West Virginia, p. 629, provides, that 'no special commissioner appointed by a court to make a sale of property, should receive money under such decree until he gives bond before the said court or its clerk.' And § 1 of ch. 10 of Code of West Virginia, p. 79 (acts of 1872-1873, ch. 42, § 1), provides, that 'every bond required by law to be taken, or approved by, or given before any court, board or officer, shall unless otherwise provided, be made payable to the state of West

Virginia, with one or more securities deemed sufficient by such court, board or other officer, and be proved or acknowledged before such court, board or officer.' Now this § 1, last quoted, applies to two very different kinds of bonds. It applies to bonds of permanent public officers, such as clerks, sheriffs, state officers and other public officers, whose bonds are required to be filed in the particular offices named in the statutes. All such official bonds by § 20 of ch. 10 of Code of West Virginia, and § 17, ch. 42, of the acts of 1872-1873, are required to be recorded in a well-bound book. This § 1 of ch. 10 of Code of West Virginia, applies also to a very different class of bonds such as injunction bonds, appeal bonds, etc., which are private bonds but are required to be taken before some public officer, and are not required to be filed in a public office nor required to be recorded. To this second class really belongs the bonds executed by commissioners of sale appointed by chancery courts. These bonds, which taken before the clerk of the court and those included in this first section, ch. 10, of the Code of West Virginia, are not required to be filed in any public office and are not included in § 20, ch. 40, of the Code and are therefore not to be recorded. Now § 2 of ch. 73 of Code of West Virginia, p. 469, provides, that 'where any writing is to be recorded, the recorder, now clerk, shall admit the same to record in his office as to any person whose name is signed thereto, when it shall be acknowledged by him or proved by two witnesses as to him before such recorder, now clerk.' And the 5th section provides, that such writing shall also be admitted to record, when proven by certain acknowledgments certified to by certain officers, the forms of such acknowledgments for recordation being given. When, therefore, a bond is required to be taken before any clerk or officer, and it is a bond, which this statute law requires to be recorded, there must be such an acknowledgment or proof before such clerk or officer, of the execution of the writing, and it must be formally certified on the bond in order to comply with these recording statutes. Otherwise it could not be recorded." Lyttle v. Cozad, 21 W. Va. 183.

"Therefore, when the first section of ch. 10 of Code of West Virginia, p. 79, speaks of a bond required by law to be taken or approved by, or given before any officer and directs that it shall have the sureties approved as sufficient by such officer and further directs, that such bond is to be proved or acknowledged before such officer, this language must be construed with reference to the objects with which such proof or acknowledgment is required. If it be an official bond required to be recorded, there must be it seems to me, a preservation by endorsement on the bond of the proof or acknowledgment of it, that such proof or acknowledgment may be recorded with the bond. But if the bond be a private bond or one not required to be recorded, as for instance, the bond of a special commissioner of sale appointed by a chancery court in a particular suit, then there seems to be no such necessity for the formal endorsement on the bond of the acknowledgment of it by the obligors, or of the proof of their signatures, as it is not to be recorded and therefore an attested copy of it can not be received in evidence in the courts as the original. In such case, such acknowledgment or proof is required it seems to me, for the protection of the officer, who is required to approve the bond, and he need make no endorsement of such acknowledgment or proof on the bond; as it would in no manner protect or serve any purpose, so far as third persons interested in the bond are concerned, where it is not to be recorded. As it seems therefore, that when the bond is in the nature of a private bond and is not required to be recorded, the acknowledgment or proof of it before the clerk or other officer, is only required for his protection and justification in accepting and approving such bond. He waives his right to require such proof or acknowledgment, if he be satisfied that the signatures are genuine, and if he fails to require any formal proof or acknowledgment of such signature; but his failure to do so would not vitiate the bond. For in such case no endorsement of such proof or acknowledgment is required, and therefore no evidence of it is preserved. It seems to me clear, that the obligors can not, if they really signed the bond, object to its validity because they did not formally acknowledge it. Had they done so no record of their formal acknowledgment would have been kept. And therefore it seems to me, that the validity of the bond can not depend upon such an acknowledgment. If it did the statute law would have required the written evidence of such acknowledgment to have been officially endorsed on the bond so that all would know that it was or was not valid." Lyttle v. Cozad, 21 W. Va. 183.

"My conclusion is, that the bond of a commissioner of sale, appointed by a chancery court will be valid, though it was neither executed in the clerk's office before the clerk nor proven before him provided, that the clerk accepted the bond officially and approved of the sufficiency of the sureties on such bond. It is certainly however, a very careless thing in a clerk to accept such a bond without its being acknowledged or proven before him. For if it should turn out, that the signatures were forgeries or for any reason the bond was not binding on the sureties, doubtless the clerk and his securities would become responsible for any loss sustained by anyone, because of such carelessness of the clerk. He is authorized for his own protection to take such acknowledgment or proof, and he ought as a prudent person to endorse the fact of such acknowledgment on the bond. It would also be, in most cases, prudent to endorse on the bond, that the sureties had made oath to their sufficiency as such sureties. But the failure of the clerk to do these things, which he has a right to do for his own protection, in no manner affects the validity of the bond." Lyttle v. Cozad, 21 W. Va. 183.

"We regard, therefore, the provision in § 1 of ch. 10 of Code of West Virginia, p. 79, which provides, that every bond required by law to be given before the clerk of a circuit court in cases, in which the bond is not required to be recorded, is mandatory, so far and so far only as it requires such bond to be executed with one or more sureties deemed sufficient by such clerk, and therefore that the bond of a special commissioner of sale need not, in order to be valid, be either acknowledged or proven before such clerk if it be shown that the signatures are genuine. In this case the genuineness of the signatures are not disputed, and the securities were deemed sufficient by the clerk and the bond approved by him. This would be sufficiently proven by the simple fact, that it was filed away among the papers of the proper cause without any evidence accompanying it, that it was rejected; and the commissioner of sale has proceeded to collect the moneys to secure which the bond was given. This and more than this appears in this case." Lyttle v. Cozad, 21 W. Va. 183.

d. Liability of Purchaser Where Payment Made to Unbonded Commissioner.

(1) Where Bond Not Executed.

In General.—It is well settled by repeated decisions that a commissioner who has not executed the bond required by the statute or by the decree of the court, has no authority to collect the purchase money for the property which he is directed to sell, and the payment to such commissioner is unauthorized, and does not discharge the purchaser of his obligation to pay the purchase money to the person or persons authorized to receive it. Whitehead v. Bradley, 87 Va. 676, 13 S. E. 195; Hess v. Rader, 26 Gratt. 746; Lloyd v. Erwin, 29 Gratt. 598; Tyler v. Toms, 75 Va. 116; Woods v. Ellis, 85 Va. 471, 7 S. E. 852; Donahue v. Fackler, 21 W. Va. 124; Blair v. Core, 20 W. Va. 265; Hall v. Lowther, 22 W. Va. 570; Eggleton v. Dinsmore, 84 Va. 858, 6 S. E. 146; Eggleton v. Whittle, 84 Va. 163, 4 S. E. 222; Duffy v. Figgat, 80 Va. 664; Lee v. Swepson, 76 Va. 173; Lamar v. Hale, 79 Va. 147.

W. is appointed a commissioner to sell land at public auction, but he is not to act under the decree until he gives bond, etc., faithfully to perform this and any future decrees made in the cause. He does not execute the bond, but he sells the land at private sale to H. which he reports to the court. The court confirms the sale, and directs him to collect the money and invest it; and H. pays him the whole purchase money; only a part of which he invests, and dies insolvent. Held, W. not having given the bond as required, had no authority to receive the purchase money; and H. is responsible to the party who is entitled to the proceeds, for so much as has not been properly invested by W., and can not be made out of W.'s estate. Hess v. Rader, 26 Gratt. 746.

Decree to sell decedent's land in 1858. The two commissioners directed to make the sale were required to give the usual bond. One gave it. Sale made and confirmed, and commissioners ordered to collect and distribute the money. Bonded commissioner died in 1860. The other commissioner was also administrator of the decedent and counsel for the heirs. He collected in 1861 a large amount of the money and placed it to his individual credit in a solvent bank, where it perished by the war. Proceedings were instituted to hold the purchaser and the land bound for money paid to a commissioner who had given no bond, and also to hold the commissioner responsible for the funds collected and lost. Held, the case of Hess v. Rader, 26 Gratt. 746, 750, has no application to this case. Purchaser paid the money into hands legally entitled to receive it. On face of decree the commissioner is stated to be the counsel of the heirs of the decedent, and had the right to receive the money. Under the circumstances, neither payer nor receiver is responsible, and the loss must fall on the heirs. Thomson v. Brooke, 76 Va. 160.

In November, 1860, M. was appointed a commissioner to sell infant's land, on a credit of six, twelve, eighteen and twenty-four months. M. reports, that after three trials he had failed to sell, and suggests that it be rented out for the present; and in June, 1861, there is an order that M. be authorized to rent out the land for such time, and on such terms as he might think judicious; and he rents it out for that and the next year. In March, 1863, M. reports that he in that month sold the land on the terms of the decree, to S. and D.; and the report is confirmed; and he is directed to collect the purchase money as it falls due, and pay it to the receiver of the court, if the parties entitled decline to receive it. M. without giving bond as required by the statute, but which was not directed by the decree, collects the first three payments as they fall due, and pays the money into a bank which has been appointed receiver of the court. The last payment was not made by S. and D., one of them being in the army, and the other a prisoner. After the war they propose to pay the last payment; and the parties entitled object to the sale, and also to the payments made; which were in confederate currency. Held, the payments made to M., and his payments to the receiver of the court, were valid payments; though M. had not given the bond required by the statute; and the purchasers and M. are not liable for this part of the purchase money. Dixon v. McCue, 21 Gratt. 373.

Although no bond was given by the commissioner, before he proceeded to collect the purchase money for the land, yet, inasmuch as he was authorized by the decree to collect said money as it fell due, and to pay it to the receiver of the court, in the event of the refusal of the parties to receive it, and the money having been paid by the purchasers and deposited by said commissioner in bank acting as receiver, to the credit of the cause, in consequence of such refusal of the parties interested, and said fund having been lost without the default of said commissioner; the purchasers can not be in any manner prejudiced by his failure to execute the bond required by law. Dixon v. McCue, 21 Gratt. 373.

. **Statute Imperative.** — The statute, Code of 1873, ch. 174, § 1, is imperative, that a bond shall be given, and it is the duty of a purchaser at a judicial sale to see that the bond has been given before he pays his money to the commissioner or he does it at his own risk. Hess v. Rader, 26 Gratt. 746.

"Much was said in the argument, about the hardship of requiring parties to pay their money twice in the same transaction, when it had been once paid to a commissioner of the court. It may be answered to this, 1st, the hardship arises out of the negligence of the parties; and 2d, they have not paid it to a commissioner of the court authorized to receive it; because the very authority to receive the money is the execution of the bond required by law." Hess v. Rader, 26 Gratt. 746.

Incumbent on Purchaser to Make Inquiry.—Where not only the statute but the decree of sale provides that

no money under it shall be collected by the commissioner without first giving bond, it is incumbent on the purchaser before paying the money to the commissioner, to inquire whether the requirements of the decree and of the statute have been complied with, and, if they have not been complied with, payment to the commissioner is unauthorized and invalid. Whitehead v. Bradley, 87 Va. 676, 13 S. E. 195; Hess v. Rader, 26 Gratt. 746; Lloyd v. Erwin, 29 Gratt. 598; Tyler v. Toms, 75 Va. 116; Woods v. Ellis, 85 Va. 471, 7 S. E. 852; Donahue v. Fackler, 21 W. Va. 124; Lamar v. Hale, 79 Va. 147.

But besides the express directions of the decree, the statute law, which every party acting under it must be presumed to know, informed these appellants that "no special commissioner appointed by a court shall receive money under a decree or order until he gives bond before the said court or its clerk." Before they paid any part of the purchase money they should have inquired if the bond required by law had been given. Otherwise they might be paying to one who had no authority to receive it. They might as well have paid it to a stranger. Both the decree under which they purchased, and the law governing such decrees, declared that the giving a bond was a condition precedent to any authority of the commissioner in the premises. Hess v. Rader, 26 Gratt. 746.

The case of Whitehead v. Bradley, 87 Va. 676, 13 S. E. 195, differs from Thompson v. Brooke, 76 Va. 160, for in the latter case the commissioner was the counsel of the parties entitled to the money, and at their solicitation the money was collected. Hence, it was held, that the purchaser, having paid the money into a hand legally entitled to receive it—i. e., to the counsel of the parties—was not responsible, the case being analogous in principle to Dixon v. McCue, 21 Gratt. 373.

Purchasers at a judicial sale are

bound to take notice of the decrees and other material proceedings, under authority of which the land was sold, and must be presumed to know the law which governs such sales. Hess *v.* Rader, 26 Gratt. 746.

Thus, a decree directing a sale, and appointing a commissioner for that purpose, upon its face expressly provides, that "the said commissioner shall not act under this decree until he executes and files with the clerk of the court bond with security, to be approved by said clerk, payable to the commonwealth of Virginia in the sum of seven thousand dollars, and conditioned fairly to perform the requirement of this and every future order of the court within this cause." The bond not being executed as required, the very decree in which the purchasers purchased informed them that the party with whom they were dealing was not authorized to act until he had given the bond required. It was easy for them to have made the inquiry if the bond had been given; and it was their own culpable negligence in not making such inquiry; and if loss occurred to them it was in consequence of their own want of diligence and negligence in not seeing to it, that the party with whom they were dealing was clothed with proper authority. Hess *v.* Rader, 26 Gratt. 746.

Bond Executed but Disapproved by Clerk.—A purchaser at a judicial sale of land pays the purchase money to the commissioner; but the commissioner has not executed the bond required by the decree, or the bond executed by him is disapproved by the clerk. The purchaser has paid in his own wrong, and the land is liable for the purchase money received by the commissioner and misapplied, though the land has been conveyed by the commissioner to the purchaser, as the decree directed to be done when the purchase money was paid. Lloyd *v.* Erwin, 29 Gratt. 598.

In such a case, the parties to the fund are not bound to proceed against the commissioner and his sureties in the bond he executed, but which the clerk disapproved before proceeding against the land, to have it subjected to the payment of the purchase money misapplied by the commissioner. Lloyd *v.* Erwin, 29 Gratt. 598.

The court is of opinion that the decision of this case is controlled by the authority of Hess *v.* Rader, 26 Gratt. 746. In each case the commissioner collected the purchase money from the purchaser of land at a judicial sale without giving the bond required by the statute and the decree under which he acted, and then made default. The attempt is made to withdraw this case from the controlling influence of Hess *v.* Rader, as authority, upon the pretension that in making payment the purchaser acted, after due inquiry, on information furnished him by the clerk of the court, that the commissioner had given the bond required by the decree. Some evidence was taken as to that matter on both sides, and is more or less conflicting. It is immaterial, however, in this case, whether such information was given or not, or whether, if given, it induced the payment to the commissioner. The fact remains· that no bond was given and therefore the commissioner had no authority to collect. There was a bond filed among the papers in the cause, but whatever the clerk may have said to the purchaser about it, it is certain that the bond was never approved and accepted by the clerk, and his refusal to accept it was endorsed upon it at the time it was tendered and filed. Whatever remedy, if any, the purchaser may have against the clerk, his payment to the commissioner was a payment in his own wrong, and he continues personally bound for so much of the purchase money collected by the commissioner as was not accounted for by him. Lloyd *v.* Erwin, 29 Gratt. 598.

"The court is further of opinion, that

the complainant in the court below and the other parties in this cause were not, nor were any, nor was either of them, bound to resort to any remedy they may have had either against the defaulting commissioner separately or against him and his sureties on the bond aforesaid filed in this cause, before proceeding to subject the land purchased by the appellant for the balance of purchase money not accounted for as aforesaid. The bond, as before stated, was never approved and accepted as a bond authorized by the court, and it is recited in the decree complained of that the commissioner is insolvent, and such is doubtless the fact, or this controversy would never have arisen. But whether the commissioner be insolvent or not, the appellant is himself in default; and as to those entitled to the purchase money for which he is bound, he is the primary if not only debtor." Lloyd *v.* Erwin, 29 Gratt. 598.

The 11th section of ch. 174, Code of 1873, relied on by the appellant in his answer to the rule against him, has no application to a case like this. The decree under which the appellant purchased has never been reversed or set aside, nor has there been any attempt to reverse it or set it aside. On the contrary the proceeding against him was to enforce the decree and compel him to complete his purchase by payment of the purchase money remaining unpaid. Lloyd *v.* Erwin, 29 Gratt. 598.

Purchaser Paying Second Time Substituted to Creditor's Rights.—If purchaser should have to pay a second time, he would be substituted to the creditor's rights under a decree requiring the commissioner to pay them. Lee *v.* Swepson, 76 Va. 173.

It is clear that if the purchaser, in consequence of the default of the commissioner, is required to make good the loss, he would be entitled to a decree over against the commissioner for his indemnity. And there is no doubt that

in the present case, if the purchaser of the land, had been compelled to pay the second time, the court would have decreed in his favor against the commissioner—a practice sanctioned by this court in Tyler *v.* Toms, 75 Va. 116. Lee *v.* Swepson, 76 Va. 173.

Purchaser's Right of Appeal on Paying Second Time.—See the title APPEAL AND ERROR, vol. 1, p. 418.

Where purchasers at judicial sale are compelled to pay a second time a part of purchase money, by means of the special commissioner's failure to give required bond, and his default in paying over money collected of them, the jurisdiction of this court to hear their appeal, depends on the amount of the defalcation, and not on the amount of his official bond. Duffy *v.* Figgat, 80 Va. 664.

Sale under Trust Deed to Indemnify Purchaser.—Commissioner sold land under decree, and received the price without giving bond, or accounting for it. Purchaser had to pay it over, and the land was resold for that purpose. Commissioner gave a trust deed to indemnify purchaser. In creditor's suit trust subject was sold. Held, purchaser was entitled only to the amount he paid, with interest and costs of the resale. Eggleton *v.* Dinsmore, 84 Va. 858, 6 S. E. 146.

Commissioner sold land and received the money without giving bond or accounting. Purchaser was required to pay it again. Receiver got judgment against him and surety. Execution was returned, "no effects." Before the return, commissioner executed trust deed to secure purchaser. Receiver filed in pending creditor's suit against commissioner, his petition to enforce his execution lien against fund secured to purchaser. Latter resisted on the ground, (1), that he claimed the fund as his homestead, and, (2), that he had assigned it. Receiver then brought suit to enforce his judgment lien against lands of purchaser and surety. Held, receiver was entitled to maintain his suit to enforce said judgment on said lands. Code, 1873, ch. 182, § 9, p. 1167. Eggleton v. Whittle, 84 Va. 163, 4 S. E. 222.

(2) Where Certificate of Clerk as to Execution of Bond Appended to Advertisement.

· In General.—See ante, "Advertisement or Notice of Sale," VI.

When the certificate of the clerk that the bond required by law or by the decree or order has been given, shall have been published with an advertisement of the sale or renting of property, or when such bonds shall have been given prior to a sale or renting not publicly advertised, any person purchasing or renting such property in pursuance of such advertisement, or in pursuance of the decree or order of sale or renting, shall be relieved of all liability for the purchase money or rent, or any part thereof, which he may pay to any special commissioner, as to whom the proper certificate shall have been appended to such advertisement, or who shall have given the bond aforesaid. Acts of 1883-84, p. 213; Va. Code, 1904, § 3399. Whitehead v. Bradley, 87 Va. 676, 13 S. E. 195; Tompkins v. Dyerle, 102 Va. 219, 46 S. E. 300; Pulliam v. Tompkins, 99 Va. 602, 39 S. E. 221.

Construction of Statute.—The statute (Va. Code, 1904, § 3398) is a wise one, passed to protect purchasers at judicial sales, and to prevent them from being compelled to pay the purchase price of land a second time, as they were frequently compelled to do prior to its enactment, and should be carefully upheld and enforced by the courts. Southwest Virginia Min., etc., Co. v. Chase, 95 Va. 50, 27 S. E. 826.

The act of February 25, 1884 (Va. Code, 1904, §§ 3398-3402), was not intended to protect, and does not protect, purchasers of lands at judicial sales in their payments of purchase money to persons not authorized to receive it and who fail properly to account for it, unless the facts exist upon which this protection is by the act made to depend. Tompkins v. Dyerle, 102 Va. 219, 46 S. E. 300.

Purchaser Must Make Inquiry as to Execution of Bond, or Appending of Certificate.—The purchaser of land at a judicial sale made by a special commissioner, whether it be an original sale or a resale, must ascertain before paying the purchase money to such special commissioner, either that the special commissioner has actually given bond required by law or that he appended to his advertisement of sale the clerk's certificate that such bond had been given. If the purchaser can show that either of these facts exist, then he is fully protected in paying to such special commissioner until he has notice that some other person has been appointed to collect the same. Tompkins v. Dyerle, 102 Va. 219, 46 S. E. 300.

Under the provisions of the act of February 25, 1884 (acts, 1883-84, p. 213), a purchaser at a judicial sale who has paid his purchase money to one of the special commissioners who made the sale will be protected, although the money was never accounted for by the commissioner, where it appears that the bond directed by the decree of sale was given; that the required certificate was obtained from the clerk, appended to and published with the advertisement; that the land was sold in pursuance of the advertisement; and that no notice of another person having been appointed to collect the purchase money was ever issued or served upon the purchaser. Pulliam v. Tompkins, 99 Va. 602, 39 S. E. 221.

Statute Applicable to Resales as Well as Original Sales.—The language of the act of February 25, 1884 (Va. Code, 1904, § 3398), applies to all judicial sales made by special commissioners, appointed by decree or order of court to sell land. That is, it is just as applicable to resales as to original sales. It is just as important that the parties in interest should be protected by a proper bond on a resale as on an original sale, unless the bond for the original sale is sufficiently broad to cover the resale. Tompkins v. Dyerle, 102 Va. 219, 46 S. E. 300.

The provisions of § 3398 of the Virginia Code, 1904, requiring commissioners, to give bond before selling property under a decree of court and to append the certificate of the clerk to the advertisement showing that the bond has been given applies to all judicial sales, whether original or resales, and a purchaser who seeks to avail himself of the protection afforded by § 3399 of Code must show either that the commissioner to whom payments were made actually gave the bond required of him, or that the clerk's certificate that such bond had been given was appended to the advertisement. The commissioner is not authorized to collect the purchase money where another has been appointed for that purpose, though the purchaser is protected if the proper certificate of the clerk is appended to the advertisement of the sale, and he has no notice of the subsequent appointment of another. Tompkins v. Dyerle, 102 Va. 219, 46 S. E. 300.

A purchaser of land at a resale made in a judicial proceeding is not entitled to credit for payments made to a commissioner who has failed to account for the same, where it appears that the commissioner was not required to give any bond as commissioner to resell, and he neither gave any such bond nor appended to the advertisement of resale the clerk's certificate that such bond was given. The fact that a bond was required of and given by the same commissioner before making the original sale, and that the surety of the purchaser at the original sale became the purchaser at the resale can not change the result. The resale, though a means of enforcing the collection of the balance due on the first sale, was not such a collection of the bond given at the first sale as would be protected by the publication of the clerk's certificate annexed to the advertisement of the first sale. Tompkins v. Dyerle, 102 Va. 219, 46 S. E. 300.

If it were true that a special commissioner to sell has the right to resell the land without giving bond to cover such resale, because he has authority to "receive and collect" the original purchase price, it would follow that if at the resale the land did not bring a sufficient sum to pay the original purchase price, and it became necessary to get judgment for the deficiency and to sell other lands of the purchaser or his sureties to pay such deficiency the special commissioner could sell that land and collect the purchase price without giving a new bond, and thus bind his sureties on the original bond for any default which he might make. Tompkins v. Dyerle, 102 Va. 219, 46 S. E. 300.

The headnote in Whitehead v. Bradley, 87 Va. 676, 13 S. E. 195, states the law as follows: "Where purchaser, at sale made under decree of court, pays the purchase money to sale commissioner who has not given the bond required by law, such payment is invalid, unless certificate of clerk that such bond has been given was published with advertisement of sale. Code, 1887, §§ 3397, 3399." See, for very similar cases, Woods v. Ellis, 85 Va. 471, 7 S. E. 852; Lee v. Swepson, 76 Va. 173; Tyler v. Toms, 75 Va. 116. See also, Brown v. Taylor, 32 Gratt. 135, where the principal case is cited for the proposition that the mere possession of a bond is not such evidence of property as will justify a payment to the holder, without authority express or implied, for the owner to collect the same. Lloyd v. Erwin, 29 Gratt. 598; Thornton v. Fairfax, 29 Gratt. 669; Donahue v. Fackler, 21 W. Va. 124, 130; Flesher v. Hassler, 29 W. Va. 404, 405, 1 S. E. 580, 581.

e. Liability of Commissioner for Receiving Money without Executing Bond.

Where a commissioner is appointed to make a sale of land under a decree of court, and he fails to execute the bond required by the statute, or decree or order of court as a condition precedent to receiving the purchase money, he has no authority to receive the purchase money or any part thereof, and is liable to the purchaser for any amount paid him, with interest from the time of payment. Donahue v. Fackler, 21 W. Va. 124; Hess v. Rader, 26 Gratt. 746; Lee v. Swepson, 76 Va. 173; Tyler v. Toms, 76 Va. 116.

Commissioners are appointed to make sale of land under a decree of court, requiring them to give bond before proceeding to act. The sale is directed to be made for part cash and the residue on credit, and the sale is made as directed, the cash payment made to the commissioners and bonds executed by the purchaser to the commissioners for the deferred payments. The commissioners failed to give bond as required, and before the sale is reported by them or any order made for the collection of the sale bonds, the purchaser pays said bonds to the commissioners, who were also the counsel who had instituted and prosecuted the suit for the owners of the land sold and among whom the proceeds were to be distributed, but the purchase money was never paid over to said distributees. Held, that the commissioners, having received the money without authority, are liable to the purchaser for the amount so paid them, or either of them, with interest thereon from the time it was paid to them. Donahue v. Fackler, 21 W. Va. 124.

Where a commissioner sells and receives the purchase money without executing the bond required, he and his estate is liable for any money that may be paid to him by the purchaser, although unauthorized. Hess v. Rader, 26 Gratt. 746.

It would seem, however, to be very clear that if the commissioner, who has collected money without giving the proper bond, is before the court, is solvent and able to pay, the court would not hesitate to decree against him before resorting to the purchaser, and still less would it hesitate where the parties interested are content with that course of proceeding. Lee v. Swepson, 76 Va. 173.

In Lloyd v. Erwin, 29 Gratt. 598, it was casually said by the judge delivering the opinion of the court, "that as to the parties entitled to the purchase money, the purchaser at the sale under the decree was the primary, if not the only, debtor." The remark does not, of course, admit of general application. In that case it was perhaps held correct, for there the commissioner was insolvent and was not even before the court. He had never given any bond, and the only recourse of the parties interested was against the purchaser who had paid in his own wrong. Lee v. Swepson, 76 Va. 173.

f. Criminal Responsibility of Commissioner for Collecting Money without Giving Bond.

Guilty of Larceny.—If any special commissioner appointed by any court or judge to collect money as required by law, or decree or order of the court or judge, to give bond before collecting the same, shall collect said money, or any part thereof without such bond and fail properly to account for the same, he shall be deemed guilty of larceny of the money so collected and not so accounted for. Va. Code, 1904, § 3402. See the title LARCENY.

Guilty of Contempt of Court.—Any special commissioner violating the provision of the statute, by receiving money before executing bond as required, shall be deemed guilty of contempt of court and shall be punished by fine and imprisonment, or either, at the discretion of the court. W. Va. Code, 1899, ch. 132, § 1. See the title CONTEMPT, vol. 3, p. 236. Neeley v. Ruleys, 26 W. Va. 686.

3. When Payment Receivable on Bonds for Purchase Money.

Express power may be given by the decree to commissioners to receive payment of a bond for the purchase money, before such bond becomes due. Finney v. Edwards, 75 Va. 44.

4. Medium of Payment.

a. Money.

Part owners and lienors of the springs property agreed, as a joint stock company, to buy it, and to pay off the claims on it in the stock and bonds of the company. They so bought it, and the agreement was returned to the court with the report of the sale—certain other creditors, not parties to the agreement, assenting to it. Held, the purchaser's liability was to pay money, and it can not be discharged in any other thing, quoad any party in interest, against his wishes. Frazier v. Hendren, 80 Va. 265.

b. Confederate Currency.

See the titles CONFEDERATE STATES, vol. 3, p. 53; PAYMENT.

In March, 1863, M., the widow, and R. and others, adult children of S., deceased, file their bill against the infant heirs of S. for the sale of land. The bill says the land was conveyed by W., the father of M., to S. and M.; that M. is entitled to one-half the land, and the other plaintiffs and the defendants are entitled to the other half. There is a decree for the sale, a sale for confederate money, to Z., the report confirmed, and a decree appointing a receiver to collect the money, and distribute it, and convey the land to Z. This is done and report confirmed. Afterwards M. files a bill of review, and claims that under the deed from W., she having survived her husband, S., is entitled to the whole of the land, and asks that the sale may be set aside, and the land restored to her. Held, under the circumstances of this case it is to be presumed that the intention of the decree was that the sale should be for confederate money. Zollman v. Moore, 21 Gratt. 313.

When the sale was confirmed in March, 1863, the court must have understood and intended that the sale was for confederate currency, and the purchase money was to be paid in such currency. Dixon v. McCue, 21 Gratt. 373.

That the courts of this commonwealth, during the war, had the authority to decree sales for confederate money, and to make investments of funds under their control in confederate securities, is no longer an open question. Transactions in confederate currency during the war, and investments in confederate securities (when properly made), must now be held to be as valid and binding as if made in time of peace in a sound currency. Walker v. Page, 21 Gratt. 636.

In March, 1863, the fact, that confederate states treasury notes was the only currency in circulation in this state, is so notorious that it may be taken notice of judicially by the courts, as a matter of current public history. And all decrees made for the sale of property at as late a period of the war as 1863, and all judicial sales made under such decrees, must be taken as made for this currency; unless such decree in plain terms directed otherwise. Walker v. Page, 21 Gratt. 636.

At a judicial sale made in August, 1859, D. became the purchaser of a tract of land in the county of Franklin, and gave his bonds, payable in one, two and three years. The sale was confirmed, and the general receiver of the court was directed to collect the money—in advance—if the purchaser chose to pay it, deducting interest. D. paid the first bond, and a part of the second before it was due, in his lifetime. Soon after his death D.'s administrator, in January and February,

1863, paid to the receiver in confederate money the amount due upon the two last bonds, and took them in. October, 1863, the receiver reported the payment of the bonds, and his report was confirmed and the receiver directed to convey the land to D.'s heirs; was done. It appearing that at the time which of the payments and confirmation of the sale, confederate money was little depreciated in Franklin, and was generally received in payment of debts; held, the payments by D.'s administrator were valid payments, and the bonds of D. are fully discharged. Dickinson v. Helms, 29 Gratt. 462.

M. buys land at a judicial sale in 1859, and gives his bonds payable annually down to 1863. He pays all but the last bond, and pays on that $2,000 in confederate money; and a few days afterwards offers to pay the balance to the commissioner in confederate money, who refuses to receive it. M. then files his petition in the cause, stating that he owes this balance, and that the commissioner refused to receive it; that he is ready to pay it, and asking that he may be authorized to pay it, and that a commissioner may be directed to convey the land to him. The court decrees that M. be authorized to pay to the general receiver the balance due, stating the amount, and upon its payment a commissioner named should convey the land to M. Held, the decree being a proper decree upon its face, it could not have been altered on appeal. The decree did not authorize M. to pay in confederate money, and a payment to the receiver in that money was not a discharge of M.'s debt. Myers v. Nelson, 26 Gratt. 729.

R., a commissioner selling land in 1860 under a decree, is guilty of a breach of trust in receiving confederate currency from the purchaser in payment of his bonds, in 1863. Omohundro v. Omohundro, 27 Gratt. 824.

S., a brother of the commissioner, who as one of the parties entitled to the land and its proceeds, induces R. to collect the purchase money of the land sold, and to sell the balance, both to be received in confederate currency, and to lend it to him. S. is a party to the breach of trust by R., the commissioner, and is responsible for it. Omohundro v. Omohundro, 27 Gratt. 824.

It is no ground of complaint on the part of W. that the court decreed a sale of the land for confederate money. If the creditors were willing to receive such money in payment of debts due before the war, it was to the advantage of W., that it be so sold. And the creditors allowing the property to be sold for this money without objection, it is not for them afterwards to object to receive it in payment of their debts. Crawford v. Weller, 23 Gratt. 835.

In May, 1863, there is a decree for the sale of land, and in August, 1863, there is a sale by the commissioners, who announce publicly the terms of sale to be, on a credit of one, two and four years; the purchase money to be paid in the currency which may be in use when the respective payments fall due; but with the privilege to the purchaser to pay one-half of the purchase money upon the confirmation of the sale by the court. The land, which was worth in gold eighty dollars per acre, sold for one hundred and forty-two dollars per acre; and the sale being confirmed, the purchasers paid one-half the purchase money with confederate currency, executing their bonds for the other half, which fell due in August, 1865, and 1867. They must pay off these bonds in the currency of the United States, that being the currency in use when they fell due. Tell v. Yancey, 23 Gratt. 691.

In August, 1860, D., as commissioner, sold land to M. on a credit of one, two and three years. In October, 1861, on the application of M., the court authorized him to deposit in the B. bank the amount of his first and second bonds; which M. does. D.

afterwards collects the third bond and deposits in the same bank, and reports it to the court; and his report is afterwards confirmed. The court must be presumed to have known, when the reports were confirmed, that the deposits were made in confederate money, and neither M. nor D. are liable to repay the money they so deposited. Mead v. Jones, 24 Gratt. 347.

On the 15th of April, 1863, a decree is made appointing commissioners to sell land on the terms of cash for costs of suit and expenses of sale, and balance on a credit of six, twelve and eighteen months. On the day of sale, it is proposed to the commissioners to sell for confederate money; but they decline to do it, and say they sell according to the decree. Four of the heirs, representing six shares out of twelve, enter into a written declaration that they will take confederate money for their shares, and this is read to the assembly by the crier, who at the same time expresses the opinion that all the heirs will take the money. The land, worth then $15,000 in good money, sells for $50,301. The cash is paid in confederate money, the bonds given and the sale is reported to the court and confirmed; and S., receiver of the court, is directed to withdraw the bonds, and collect the money as it falls due. S. receives confederate money in payment of the first bond, upon the purchaser, P., undertaking to take· it back if the persons entitled will not receive it. When the second bond comes due P. offers to S. to give him a check on the bank of R., for the amount, which S. declines to receive; and so when the third bond fell due. S. says he declined to receive it because he knew it would be paid in confederate money. He did not doubt that P. had the money in bank, though there was no evidence of that fact, but P.'s statement to S. Held, the sale was a sale with reference to confederate treasury notes as the standard of value. The offer of P. to give S. a check for the money, was not a good and valid tender: First, because there was no evidence that P. had the money in the bank at the time; and, second, because a good and valid tender could not be made to the receiver of the court. P. allowed his option to take the land at its value in good money, to be credited with the true value of the money he had paid; or to surrender the land and account for the rents and profits, and be credited for the value of the money he paid. Poague v. Greenlee, 22 Gratt. 724.

J., by his will gave to his widow, H., for her life, a tract of land, and directed that at her death it should be sold, and two-thirds of the money be given to his brother, W., and the rest to other relations. In 1857, in a friendly suit in which the widow, H., and W. were plaintiffs and the other parties interested were defendants, there was a decree for the sale of the land, on a credit, except for the expenses of the sale, of one, two and three years, with interest from the day of sale. The sale was made by R. as commissioner, and W. became the purchaser at $4,000. At the October term, 1859, the report of the sale was confirmed, and the court, being of opinion that it was unnecessary to dispose of the principal of the proceeds of sale, appointed R. a commissioner to collect the interest then due on the bonds and thereafter as it became due, and pay the same to H. In May, 1863, without any notice to H., W. obtained a decree in the cause appointing U. a commissioner to collect the bonds of W. for the purchase money of the land, and invest the same in interest bearing bonds of the confederate states, or the state of Virginia, the investment to be made in the name of U. as commissioner, the interest to be paid to H. during her life; and upon payment of the bonds to convey the land to the purchaser. U. collected the bonds, and after deducting expenses invested the money in a confederate bond of $3,700. The commissioner made his report, and on the 27th of October, the court made a decree confirming it, and directing U. to deliver the bond to H., upon her giving bond and security to account for it to the parties entitled on her death, and to report his proceedings to the court. The commisssioner reported that H. refused to receive the bond. In May, 1866, H. presented her petition for a rehearing of the decree of May and October, 1863, alleging that the decrees were made without her knowledge; and she filed with her petition the affidavit of R. who had been the counsel of all parties in obtaining the sale, which went to show that the decree of May, 1863, was obtained by U., as the counsel of N., and without notice to H. The court allowed the petition to be filed, but in October, 1873, dismissed the petition with costs. Held: (1). The decree of May and October, 1863, were interlocutory decrees, and may be reheard upon petition. (2). It was error to make the decrees without notice to H. (3). It was error to authorize the investment of the purchase money of the land in confederate securities. (4). The affidavit of R. having been filed with the petition for a rehearing, and not having been objected to in the court below, can not be objected to in the appellate court. Purdie v. Jones, 32 Gratt. 827.

A friendly suit is instituted in October, 1863, for the sale of land in which a number of persons are interested, in which there is a decree for a sale on a credit of six months, with the privilege to the purchasers to pay cash, and the commissioners are directed to give bond in the sum of $40,000. There is a sale, and the purchasers give their bonds for the purchase money, and afterwards pay part of the purchase money to the commissioner, who pays to several of the parties entitled their share of it, or a part of it. Upon a bill filed seven years afterwards, by the plaintiffs, to set aside the sale on

the ground that they had not authorized the suit, and had not assented to the proceedings therein, and because one of the parties in interest, who joined as plaintiff in this suit, was not a party in that; held, the payment made by the purchaser to the commissioner was a valid payment; but a check for the balance due upon a party who admitted his indebtedness to the drawer, but did not pay it, of which the purchaser had notice, is not a valid payment, and he must account for that balance, at the scaled value thereof at the day of the sale, with interest from the end of the six months' credit. Finney v. Edwards, 75 Va. 44.

In November, 1860, M. was appointed a commissioner to sell infant's land, on a credit of six, twelve, eighteen and twenty-four months. M. reports, that after three trials he had failed to sell, and suggests that it be rented out for the present; and in June, 1861, there is an order that M. be authorized to rent out the land for such time, and on such terms as he might think judicious; and he rents it out for that and the next year. In March, 1863, M. reports that he in that month sold the land on the terms of the decree, to S. and D.; and the report is confirmed; and he is directed to collect the purchase money as it falls due, and pay it to the receiver of the court, if the parties entitled decline to receive it. M., without giving bond as required by the statute, but which was not directed by the decree, collects the first three payments as they fall due, and pays the money into a bank which has been appointed receiver of the court. The last payment was not made by S. and D., one of them being in the army, and the other a prisoner. After the war they propose to pay the last payment; and the parties entitled object to the sale, and also to the payments made; which were in confederate currency. Held, S. and D. were, under the circumstances, excused for the nonpayment of their fourth bonds as they fell due; and upon their paying these bonds are entitled to have the land conveyed to them. Dixon v. McCue, 21 Gratt. 373.

5. Validity of Payment Made before Confirmation.

As a conclusion from the fact that a judicial sale when confirmed relates to and vests the title of the land in the purchaser from the date of sale, any payment made by the purchaser between the day of sale and the day of confirmation, which would have been valid when made, if the sale had been confirmed, is made just as valid by the subsequent confirmation. Donahue v. Fackler, 21 W. Va. 124.

But this conclusion has no apppli-cation, where the commissioner who made the sale had no authority to collect purchase money, because not having executed the bond as required by the decree. In such case his act in this regard would be just as much unauthorized if the sale were confirmed as it was when it was not confirmed. Donahue v. Fackler, 21 W. Va. 124.

6. Application to Payment of Purchase Money of Claims Assigned Commissioner as Attorney.

Purchaser at judicial sale executed to S., as receiver, her bonds. To him, as her attorney, she also assigned certain claims to collect and pay on her bonds. Part of the collections he applied as directed; the balance he did not apply. There was nothing to show that he had charged himself, as such receiver, with said balance. Held, as S. collected the money as purchaser's attorney, she was not entitled to have it credited on her bonds until he had so applied it. Paxton v. Steele, 86 Va. 311, 10 S. E. 1.

7. Liability in Case of Loss of Money by Defalcation of Collecting Officer, etc., after Collection.

As between debtor, creditor, and purchaser in a judicial proceeding to subject land to the payment of liens thereon, the loss resulting from the defalcation of a receiver of the court must fall on the creditor; and, as between different classes of creditors, it must be borne in the inverse order of their respective priorities. Patterson v. Crawford, 97 Va. 661, 34 S. E. 458.

If, in a suit to subject a debtor's lands to the payment of the liens thereon, the proceeds of the sale of a part of the land be lost in consequence of the defalcation of the receiver of the court, the proceeds of the residue of the lands will be appropriated to the senior creditors in preference to the junior, in the absence of fault on the part of the senior creditors, although the lost fund was sufficient to pay the senior creditors, and the junior creditors were the purchasers of the residue of the land, and it was the purpose of the court to credit their purchase on their debt if the money realized from the other lands was sufficient to pay the senior creditors. No part of the fund could be appropriated to the payment of the junior creditors until the senior creditors had been paid in full. Patterson v. Crawford, 97 Va. 661, 34 S. E. 458.

It is plain that the debtor is absolved from making good the loss, even if he has the means of doing so. His lands were sold, and the proceeds of sale of certain parcels thereof collected by the commissioner sufficient to pay the creditors, who, by virtue of their liens, were entitled thereto. He has been deprived of his property for the express purpose of paying his creditors. The proceeds of sale were received by the representative of the court, and lost without the fault of the debtor. His estate having once borne the burden, it can not be made to do so again. He can not be made to pay his debts twice. 2 Spences Eq. Jur. mar., p. 344; Rigge v. Bowater, 3 Bro. Ch. Cas. 365; Omrod v. Hardman, 5 Vesey, 736; and Walker v. Commonwealth, 18 Gratt. 45, 47. Nor can the loss be thrown upon the purchasers whose money was misappropriated. They paid it as required by the court and to the person appointed by the court to collect it. It follows, therefore, that the loss must be borne by the creditors. Inasmuch, however, as the debtor, in conveying his real and personal estate by deed of trust for the payment of his debts, created preference among his creditors, arranging them in several classes, the manner in which the loss must be borne or upon which class of creditors it must fall is a vital question, and one of much practical importance. Patterson *v.* Crawford, 97 Va. 661, 34 S. E. 458.

Where property is subjected to the payment of liens thereon, the liens are transferred from the property to the proceeds of sale, and in the administration thereof the respective priorities are duly preserved. The cost of converting the property into money for the payment of the liens, and the expense of administering the fund, must be borne by the lienors in the inverse order of the priorities of their respective liens, if the fund be not sufficient to pay such cost and expense as well as all the liens. This results necessarily from the priority of one lien over another. And so, for the same reason, if the proceeds of sale of the property, or of any part thereof, fail, from any cause, to be realized, or, after it has been collected by the officer or representative of the court, is subsequently misappropriated by him or otherwise lost, the loss must be borne by the fund, and the lienors suffer to that extent in the order above stated. This is well understood to be the general rule. Patterson *v.* Crawford, 97 Va. 661, 34 S. E. 458.

Where purchaser at judicial sale buys in all the liens save one, and is allowed credit therefor, and then to prevent resale, pays into bank, with approval of the court, the amount of the said lien, which the court recognizes as appropriated to the owners of the said lien, and which is later lost by the bank's failure, the loss will fall wholly on the owners of the said lien. Had there remained more than one unsatisfied lien, the loss would then have fallen on the general fund, and been borne by the lienors in the inverse order of the priority of their liens. Gill *v.* Barbour, 80 Va. 11.

8. Fee for Collecting Purchase Money.

See ante, "Fee for Making Sale, Collecting and Paying over Proceeds," VII, B, 4.

9. Enjoining Collection of Purchase Money.

See the title INJUNCTIONS, vol. 7, p. 512.

The commissioners in selling the land were only acting as agents of the court, and so in collecting the purchase money for the purposes of the suit. A court of equity will not grant an injunction to stay the collection of the purchase money for land sold by its commissioners in obedience to its decree, upon allegations that the title is not in the commissioners. Shields *v.* McClung, 6 W. Va. 79.

B. DISTRIBUTION.

1. In General.

The proper rule for the court in directing a sale of real estate is to direct, in the decree ordering the sale, that the cash payment shall be retained by the commissioner making the sale, or be paid into bank to the credit of the suit, subject to the future order of the court. The money being thus under the control of the court, will, upon the confirmation of the report or upon setting aside the sale, be disposed of in the way that shall then seem proper. Arnold *v.* Casner, 22 W. Va. 444.

"On this question, I concur in the view of the counsel for the plaintiffs, that when the order of the court was made that the commissioner should pay these claims they became thereby prima facie satisfied so far as the estate of

Daniel Zane was concerned. The payment was ordered to be made out of the proceedings of the plaintiff's real estate. The creditors could no longer pursue Zane's estate. If the commissioner, the officer of the court, did not pay these debts out of the funds in his hands dedicated to that purpose, the creditors could require him to do so and this would be their only resort. Brandt on S. & G., § 194; Brown v. Kidd, 34 Miss. 291. The order directing the payment of the debts out of the proceeds of the plaintiffs' property, being prima facie evidence of such payment, completed the right of the plaintiffs to demand reimbursement, and placed the burden of rebutting the prima facie payment upon the appellant." Cranmer v. McSwords, 26 W. Va. 412.

"A party to a suit who has a lien against land which is sought to be subjected, who has had notice of the time and place of ascertaining the liens against the same and the amounts and priorities thereof, who fails to attend before said commissioner at the time of settling said account, or to except to the same after it is stated, after the report of the commissioner has been confirmed and a sale decreed, reported, and confirmed, and the proceeds directed to be distributed in accordance with the priorities so ascertained, will not be allowed to have the order of said priorities changed on petition in the nature of a bill of review, unless the error complained of in ascertaining said priorities appears on the face of the decree, or he sufficiently accounts for his laches." Keck v. Allender, 37 W. Va. 201, 16 S. E. 520.

This court held, in the case of Wyatt v. Thompson, 10 W. Va. 645, that "where defendants have had ample time to make a particular defense to a suit, and have not done so, and show no reason why they have not before made such defense, they can not be permitted to come in at the last moment and raise such defense, and have the cause sent back to a commissioner or otherwise delayed; but the answer raising such defense may be filed, although under such circumstances it can not delay the hearing of the cause." Keck v. Allender, 37 W. Va. 201, 16 S. E. 520.

When a sale is made and reported, the court below, if it confirms the sale, when it makes distribution of the proceeds of the sale, may determine any question as to right of priority, should it arise. M'Allister v. Bodkin, 76 Va. 809.

In a suit for the sale of land to satisfy liens upon it, there was an order for an account of the liens and their priorities, and in 1860 the account was returned arranging the debts in twenty-four classes, of which the 2d, 3d and 13th were debts reported to be due to S. In 1866, the report was confirmed, and there was a decree for the sale of the land, one-tenth cash and the balance at one and two years. The sale was made to J. and confirmed, and J. directed to pay the money to the receiver. In 1870, T. filed his petition in the cause, claiming that the debts mentioned in said 2d, 3d and 13th classes were his, acquired in 1864, and asking that the receiver might be required to report how much of the purchase money he had received, and what he had done with it; and if it had not been paid, for a resale of the land. The case was referred to the commissioner, and J. appeared before him, claiming that said debts were his, and contesting the claim of T. S. did not claim them. Held, that it was competent for T. though not a party to the suit, but who had acquired subsequently the liens of one who was a party, by petition or motion to require a report from the receiver showing the amount of the purchase money in his hands, and to have it applied to the satisfaction of the liens according to their priorities, and to direct a resale of the land for the balance of the purchase money due, pursuant to the decree of sale. It was not necessary that he should have proceeded by bill for that purpose, or to have made the purchaser a party defendant to his petition, or to have required him to answer. If S. had disputed the claim of T. then it would have been proper for T. to have asserted his claim by supplemental bill, or by an original bill in the nature of a supplemental bill. Thornton *v.* Fairfax, 29 Gratt. 669.

W. sold land to M., retaining the title, for $4,000, cash, $1,000, and three bonds payable January 1st, 1858, 1859, and 1860. The first was paid to W. He transferred the bond due January 1st, 1860, to S. in May, 1859, who assigned it to H. W. died in possession of the bond due January 1859. His administrators sued M. in equity, to subject the land to pay the bond held by W. at his death, without making S. or H. a party, and the land was sold by a commissioner to J. for $2,000, and the sale was confirmed, and the commissioner was directed to collect the money and pay the plaintiffs. H., upon his petition, is made a defendant in the suit, and files his answer, claiming that his bond is still unpaid, and that he is entitled to priority of payment out of the land. The administrators file an answer, insisting that H. had lost his right to subject the land by his laches in not suing M., who had in the meantime become insolvent. The decree gives priority to the plaintiffs over H., and he appeals. Held, the bond held by H. having been transferred by W. in his lifetime, though due after the bond retained by him, is to be first paid out of the proceeds of the sale of the land. H. was a necessary party to the suit, and it was error to decree a sale of land without first having him made a party, and the question of priority settled between him and the plaintiffs. The purchaser at the sale, made under the decree of the court, is interested in the decision of the question of priority between the plaintiffs and H., and ought to be heard in opposi-

tion to any order affecting his interest. And a rule, if desired by the plaintiffs, should be awarded by the court below against said purchaser, to show cause why said sale should not be set aside. But in no event is said sale to be set aside and a resale ordered, unless the plaintiffs, or some one for them, shall give bond with proper security before said court for a substantial advance upon the price for which the property heretofore sold. If no resale is made, the fund arising from the sale already made, being the proceeds of the sale of the land, is to be applied, or so much of it as may be necessary, to the satisfaction of H.'s debt, and the residue, if any, to that of the plaintiffs. McClintic *v.* Wise, 25 Gratt. 448.

2. When Distribution May Be Made.

It is generally improper to direct the distribution of the proceeds of a sale, before the sale is confirmed, but this irregularity in this cause is not to the prejudice of the appellant. Beard *v.* Arbuckle, 19 W. Va. 135.

It is irregular to direct payment of the money to the creditor, in the decree for sale. Before such direction is given, a report of the sale should be made, to enable the parties interested to show cause against it, and that the court may see that its decree has been properly executed. Payment of the proceeds to the creditor should be decreed only after the confirmation of the report of sale. Brien *v.* Pittman, 12 Leigh 379, 380.

A judicial sale is the act of the court and not of the commissioner who offers the property and receives the bids. The sale is not complete until a report of the bidding has been made and confirmed by the court. And, therefore, it would be irregular, though not sufficient ground, perhaps, to reverse the decree, for the court, by its decree ordering the sale, to direct the disbursement of the cash payment before the confirmation of the sale. Anderson *v.* Davies, 6 Munf. 484, 486. The proper rule in such sales is, to direct in the decree ordering the sale that the cash payment shall be retained by the commissioners making the sale, or. be paid into bank to the credit of the suit, subject to the future order of the court. The purchase money being thus under the control of the court, will, upon the confirmation of the report or upon setting aside the sale, be disposed of in the way that shall then seem proper. 2 Rob. (old) Pr. 388. Arnold *v.* Casner, 22 W. Va. 444.

3. Officer to Distribute as Court May Order.

a. In General.

Any sheriff, sergeant, or other officer, receiving money under any order or decree, shall pay the same as the court may order. Va. Code, 1904, § 3403.

Any sheriff or other officer, receiving money under any order or decree, shall pay the same as the court may order. W. Va. Code, 1899, ch. 132, § 4.

b. Effect of Distribution without Order of Court.

As to the exception to the report of said commissioners because they attempted to disburse a part of the proceeds of sale without any order of court, and without the consent of the appellant, this is a matter for which said commissioners must account to the court, and which would be covered by the bond required by statute for the faithful performance of their duty. Connell *v.* Wilhelm, 36 W. Va. 598, 15 S. E. 245.

c. Liability for Failure to Pay as Court May Order.

Where any sheriff, sergeant or other officer, receiving money under any order or decree, shall fail to pay the same as the court may order, he and the sureties in his official bond shall be liable therefor. Va. Code, 1904, § 3403.

If the sheriff or other officer receiving money under any order or decree shall fail to pay the same as the court may order, he and the sureties in his

official bond shall be liable therefor. W. Va. Code, 1899, ch. 132, § 4.

4. Costs, Taxes, Levies and Assessments to Be Paid First.

Whenever, in any proceedings held in any chancery court for the purpose of subjecting real estate to the payment of debts, or for the sale of real estate for any other purpose, it appears that the real estate can not be sold for enough to·pay off the lien of taxes, levies, and assessments returned delinquent against it, and it appears that the purchase price offered is, in the opinion of the court, adequate and reasonable, the said sale shall be confirmed, and the court shall further order and decree the payment and distribution of the proceeds of said sale pro rata to the taxes, levies, and assessments due the said state, county, and corporation, after having first deducted the cost of said proceedings in court. Va. Code, 1904, § 3397b. See the titles SPECIAL ASSESSMENTS; TAXATION.

Whenever it appears in any chancery proceedings heretofore had that the proceeds of any sale of land have been applied to the payment of taxes, levies, and assessments, and the same was not sufficient to fully satisfy the said taxes, levies, and assessments, it shall be the duty of the clerks of the said counties and cities to cause the said liens to be marked satisfied, and a certificate from the clerk of said chancery court of the facts shall be sufficient authority for the same (1899-00, p. 397; 1901-2, p. 731). Va. Code, 1904, § 3397b.

When property is sold under decree of court to satisfy liens thereon, out of the proceeds must be paid the taxed costs, but not more than the legal fee to the plaintiff's counsel. If an allowance beyond the usual fee, for counsel representing the creditors, be proper, and it be paid out of the proceeds, it should be credited rateably on the liens, so as not to tax the debtor with it. Citizens' Nat. Bank *v.* Manoni, 76 Va. 802.

Taxes on lands accruing while the land is being rented out under an order of the court, should be paid out of the rent. Camden *v.* Haymond, 9 W. Va. 680.

5. Dower.

As to wife's right to dower out of proceeds of sale of husband's land under decree of court, see the title DOWER, vol. 4, p. 782.

6. Purchaser Not Responsible for Proper Distribution of Purchase Money.

When the purchaser has paid the money, in obedience to the decree, to the commissioner of the court, who was authorized to receive it, and who had given bond with good security for its faithful application, he thereby discharged himself from all further liability for this money, and the proper application of it devolved upon the court. It is settled that a purchaser at such a sale is not answerable for any disposition which the court may make of the purchase money. Jones *v.* Tatum, 19 Gratt. 720; Daniel *v.* Leitch, 13 Gratt. 195, 211.

"One thing would seem, however, to be very clear, that the land is not liable in the hands of the purchaser, nor is he bound to see to the application of the purchase money." Holden *v.* Boggess, 20 W. Va. 62; Robinson *v.* Shacklett, 29 Gratt. 99, 107.

Ordinarily a purchaser at a judicial sale has no concern with the disposition of the purchase money. It is always so when the decree is free from error. But where there is not only a misapplication or wrongful disposition of the purchase money, but a positive, open and bald violation of the statute in decreeing the sale, that is a much more serious matter and a more wrongful disposition of the proceeds of a sale properly made, and if the purchaser has notice of it before he pays the purchase money, it may be possible that such error was affecting his title. Ammons *v.* Ammons, 50 W. Va. 390, 40 S. E. 490.

8 Va—51

On this question of the application of purchase money, it has been said, that "A purchaser under a decree can have no concern with the disposition which the court may make of the purchase money, nor can his right as a purchaser be in any manner affected by any irregularity in the case or misapplication of the purchase money. When he pays the whole of the stipulated amount, he is entitled to an absolute conveyance of the whole right of the parties to the suit, whatever that may be, and is not bound to look to anything beyond the express terms of his contract with the court, as reported by the trustee employed to make the sale." Coombs *v.* Jordan, 22 Am. Dec. 236, 277. In that case the court lays it down as a well-settled principle of law that "The only cases in which the purchaser is bound to see to the application of the purchase money, are where a trust has been raised by deed or will for the sale of the estate for the payment of debts and the like, and the trust so raised is of a defined and limited nature." Citing Sug. Ven. Pur., 366. In Woodbine *v.* Woodrun, 19 W. Va. 67, Judge Green discusses the several instances in which a purchaser is required to see to the application of the purchase money, and it is clear from what he says that the principle does not extend further than is stated in Coombs *v.* Jordan. Ammons *v.* Ammons, 50 W. Va. 390, 40 S. E. 490.

7. Offset Where Purchaser Creditor of Estate.

When a commissioner is directed by a decree in a creditor's suit to sell lands of the deceased debtor, and sells the lands, and the sale is confirmed, and he is ordered to collect the bonds and disburse the money, and the purchaser at the sale, who has executed his bonds, is a creditor, and the commissioner has been ordered to pay him a debt greater than the amount of the purchase money, the commissioner may offset pro tanto the indebtedness for purchase money on the debt due

the purchaser from the estate. Ellett
v. Reid, 25 W. Va. 550.

Whether under such circumstances
the commissioner may thus offset the
indebtedness after notice of assignment
of the debt due the purchaser, can not
properly be decided in the absence of
the sureties on the purchase money
bonds, who are directly interested in
the question; and no opinion with
reference thereto is here expressed.
Ellett v. Reid, 25 W. Va. 550.

**8. Recovery of Money Paid under
Void Decree.**

Where money from the sale of property has, by order of the court, been
paid, and the decree ordering its payment was void, the party whose property was sold to raise the money may
recover the same from the party to
whom it was illegally paid. Sturm v.
Fleming, 31 W. Va. 701, 8 S. E. 263.

XIII. Deed of Conveyance.

See the title DEEDS, vol. 4, p. 364.

A. NECESSITY.

Whether the sale be by a master commissioner, or other functionary authorized by the court to conduct the
sale, the bargain is not ordinarily considered as complete until the sale is
confirmed and the conveyance is made.
Terry v. Coles, 80 Va. 695; Brock v.
Rice, 27 Gratt. 812.

A judicial sale is not consummated
and conclusive until a decree of confirmation transferring or directing the
transfer of the legal title by proper
conveyance. Thompson v. Cox, 42 W.
Va. 566, 26 S. E. 189; Childs v. Hurd,
25 W. Va. 530.

B. REQUISITES AND VALIDITY.
1. In General.

The court can not by a mere affirmance, make a paper, which in fact and
in law is a nullity, a deed competent
to convey the fee simple title out of
the debtor, to the purchaser. Miller
v. Smoot, 86 Va. 1050, 11 S. E. 983.

2. Order to Convey.

In a judicial sale, the court and not
the officer being the real seller, after
confirmation by the court, an order directing the officer to convey, is essential to the validity of any sale that
the commissioner or other officer may
make. Barton's Ch. Pr. 1070. Terry
v. Coles, 80 Va. 695; Hughes v. Hamilton, 19 W. Va. 366; Hurt v. Jones, 75
Va. 341; Cales v. Miller, 8 Gratt. 6;
McKinney v. Kirk, 9 W. Va. 26.

It is irregular to direct the execution
of a deed to the purchaser, in the decree for sale. Before such direction is
given, a report of the sale should be
made, to enable the parties interested
to show cause against it, and that the
court may see that its decree has been
properly executed. The execution of
a deed to the purchaser should be decreed only after the confirmation of
the report of sale. Brien v. Pittman,
12 Leigh 379, 380.

The commissioner does not own the
land. He has a mere naked authority
uncoupled with any personal interest.
He has no authority to make a deed
of conveyance until such authority be
given by the decree. Wilson v. Braden, 48 W. Va. 196, 36 S. E. 367; Ronk
v. Higginbotham, 54 W. Va. 137, 46 S.
E. 128; Waggoner v. Wolf, 28 W. Va.
820.

A commissioner making sales under
a decree of the chancery court, is
clothed with a mere naked authority.
Having no interest in the land conveyed, the deed of the commissioner
can avail nothing where his authority
to make it does not appear, unless
there had been such a long acquiescence and possession under the deed
as to justify a presumption in favor of
the deed, as was the case in Robinett
v. Preston, 4 Gratt. 141, 144. Walton
v. Hale, 9 Gratt. 194, 197; Ronk v. Higginbotham, 54 W. Va. 137, 46 S. E.
128.

It has never been the rule of practice of courts of equity of Virginia, or
of West Virginia, in decreeing the sale

of lands, and appointing commissioners to make the sale, to direct and empower the commissioners to both sell and convey. The decrees universally direct the commissioners to sell, and report their proceedings to the court, and the court, upon the report of sale, either approves and confirms the sale, or sets it aside. Kable *v.* Mitchell, 9 W. Va. 492. ·

But on one occasion, in the case of Evans *v.* Spurgin, 6 Gratt. 107, commissioners appointed in 1807, to sell land to satisfy a debt which was a lien thereon, sold the land the same year, and conveyed it to the purchaser; and they collected the purchase money and paid it to the plaintiff in part discharge of the debt, but did not report their proceedings to the court until 1835, and in 1836, the court confirmed the sale, and ratified and confirmed the deed. Afterwards the devisee of the purchaser at the sale, brought a writ of right to recover the land, and the court held, in that action, that the confirmation gave full effect and validity to said deed, and related back to the time of its date, so as to invest the purchaser with the legal title of the original owner to the land. In this case, Judge Allen, in delivering the opinion of the court, says: "Yet as commissioners, appointed by the chancery court to make sale of property, act subject to the supervision and control of the court, their acts, when sanctioned and approved by the court, become the acts of the court." Kable *v.* Mitchell, 9 W. Va. 492.

It can not be doubted that a decree or order of the court at some stage of the cause is necessary to enable the purchaser to obtain the title; and if that decree or order be made subsequently to the sale, it is the final decree or order in the cause, and consequently the decree for sale interlocutory. It would derogate much from the power and dignity of that court to treat the purchaser as having acquired a right to the property, and at the same time turn him round to a new suit for the purpose of obtaining a conveyance. In truth, however, the purchaser acquires no right until a confirmation of the sale by the court; and until the order confirming the report, he is only inchoately and not absolutely a purchaser, having till then no fixed interest in the subject. That such is the English doctrine is well settled. Sugd. on Vend. 50, 51, 52, 57. Ex parte Minor, 11 Ves. 559. Twigg *v.* Fifield, 13 Ves. 517; Anson *v.* Towgood, 1 Jac. & Walk. 619. The same doctrine has been recognized by this court in several cases: Crews *v.* Pendleton, 1 Leigh 297; Heywood *v.* Covington, 4 Leigh 373; Taylor *v.* Cooper, 10 Leigh 317, from the first of which it will be seen that before the confirmation of the report and conveyance of the title, the purchaser must resort to that tribunal in which the proceedings were had, for the adjustment and enforcement of his claims. Cocke *v.* Gilpin, 1 Rob. 20.

"If it should be supposed that purchasers under such a decree as the one we are considering would be liable to mischief by treating it as interlocutory instead of final, I would remark that the mischief, in my apprehension, lies the other way; for though the lapse of five years protects the decree, if final, from being reversed by appeal or bill of review, yet within that period it is infallibly liable to such reversal, because fatally erroneous from its very finality; and if so reversed, the purchaser's claim must, for the same reason, necessarily fall; whereas if the decree be interlocutory, the purchaser has nothing to do but to obtain a confirmation of the report and conveyance of the title, in which aspect there is no error nor irregularity in the proceeding, and he is then protected against all other irregularities in the cause, if the proper parties having title to the subject be before the court; the rule being, that a purchaser has a right to presume that the court has taken the steps necessary to investigate the rights of the parties, and on that investigation has properly decreed a sale. 2 Smith's Ch. Pract. 198; Bennet v. Harrell, 2 Sch. & Lef. 566. In fine, I can not· perceive the propriety of construing a decree to be final, and thereby rendering it erroneous, when the regarding it as interlocutory relieves it from the imputed error." Cocke v. Gilpin, 1 Rob. 20.

"Besides, the marshal is directed 'to expose to sale,' not to convey the land. To 'expose to sale' is one thing; to transfer and convey the title is another. The former may safely be confided to the marshal; the latter should be directed by the court, after it has affirmed the sale. And such, I believe, has been the general if not the universal practice, except perhaps in a single case, which will be hereafter noticed. Even in England, a decree for the sale of land is not regarded as final until the confirmation of the sale by the court; as is abundantly shown by the authorities which my brother Baldwin has referred to, and which I need not repeat. I am therefore of opinion that this part of the decree also (as to the sale of the land) is interlocutory." Cocke v. Gilpin, 1 Rob. 20.

"It is said to be a grave error in the decree that it contains no provision that a deed shall be made or tendered to the appellant, and a precedent found in the excellent treatise of Mr. Sands (Sands' Suit in Equity, p. 471, 472), is cited as giving the usual and proper form of such a decree. That this may be a very correct and safe precedent, I am not disposed to question, but so far as I have observed it has not been generally adopted. On the contrary, the more usual practice has been in cases of this kind where a sale is directed to withhold by express provision a conveyance of the title till after the coming in of the report. And the court can as effectually transfer the title by a subsequent order as by a provision in the decree. At the most, I can not think it so material as to render necessary the reversal of the decree." Goddin v. Vaughn, 14 Gratt. 102.

3. Who May Convey.

Officer Appointed by Court.—When land is sold at a judicial sale, the title is in the court, and can be conveyed only by the deed of such an officer of the court, as it shall appoint to transfer the title. Miller v. Smoot, 86 Va. 1050, 11 S. E. 983.

Courts of equity under whose decrees lands are sold by their commissioners, direct who shall make deeds. Shields v. McClung, 6 W. Va. 79.

Commissioner.—A court of equity, in a suit wherein it is proper to decree or order the execution of any deed or writing, may .appoint a commissioner to execute the sale. Va. Code, 1904, § 3418.

A court of law or equity, in a suit in which it is proper to decree or order the execution of any deed or writing, may appoint a commissioner to execute the same. W. Va. Code, 1899, ch. 132, § 4.

Commissioner Making Sale.—It is the usual and proper practice for the court to appoint the commissioner or commissioners making a judicial sale, to execute a deed of conveyance of the land to the purchaser thereunder. Hurt v. Jones, 75 Va. 341; Terry v. Coles, 80 Va. 695; Wilson v. Braden, 48 W. Va. 196, 36 S. E. 367; Ronk v. Higginbotham, 54 W. Va. 137, 46 S. E. 128; Waggoner v. Wolf, 28 W. Va. 820; Mullan v. Carper, 35 W. Va. 215, 16 S. E. 527; Hughes v. Hamilton, 19 W. Va. 366; Cales v. Miller, 8 Gratt. 6; McKinney v. Kirk, 9 W. Va. 26.

While the court may appoint the commissioner, who makes the sale, to transfer the title, yet such commissioner is not necessarily the only person whom the court may appoint to convey the title and make the deed to the purchaser. Miller v. Smoot, 86 Va. 1050, 11 S. E. 983.

4. To Whom Conveyance May Be Made.

According to the authorities and upon principle, a commissioner, appointed by a chancery court, with directions to make a deed for lands to the purchaser, can properly and legitimately make the deed to the purchaser, or his assignee by deed. Rhorer on Judicial Sales, ch. 370, p. 145, §§ 764, 765, 767; Hall v. Hall, 12 W. Va. 1.

5. When Conveyance Made.

It is usual and proper for the court to order a deed of conveyance to be made to the purchaser after the sale has been reported to the court, confirmed, and the purchase money paid. Mullan v. Carper, 37 W. Va. 215, 16 S. E. 527.

Courts of equity under whose decrees lands are sold by their commissioners, direct when deeds shall be made. Ordinarily, deeds in such cases are not made, and frequently not directed to be made until the purchase money is paid. And when the purchase money is paid the courts will always on the application of the purchaser direct proper deeds to be made. Shields v. McClung, 6 W. Va. 79.

By the eighth section of the act of March 30, 1837, it is the duty of the court to direct the commissioner to convey to the purchasers upon the payment of the purchase money. Walton v. Hale, 9 Gratt. 194, 197, cited in Ronk v. Higginbotham, 54 W. Va. 137, 46 S. E. 128.

The ninth section of the act of the 15th of March, 1838, declares that the purchaser shall, on application to the commissioner, be entitled to his deed upon the payment of the purchase money. Walton v. Hale, 9 Gratt. 194, 197, cited in Ronk v. Higginbotham, 54 W. Va. 137, 46 S. E. 128.

The court can appoint an officer to convey, and direct a conveyance of the title by deed to the purchaser, only after the sale has been duly reported and confirmed. Miller v. Smoot, 86 Va. 1050, 11 S. E. 983.

But it is bad practice upon the confirmation of a sale of land to order a commissioner to convey the legal title to the purchaser; the title should be retained until the purchase money is all paid. Glenn v. Blackford, 23 W. Va. 182.

"The court is further of opinion, that the land purchased by the appellant under the decree of the court also continues bound for the purchase money collected and not accounted for by the commissioner, notwithstanding the deed of conveyance made by the commissioners. The title was retained by the decree ordering sale as a security for the payment of the purchase money, and the commissioners were not empowered by the decree to convey until payment was completed; and as no valid payment was ever made, the deed of the commissioners passed no valid title." Lloyd v. Erwin, 29 Gratt. 598.

The purchaser can not become entitled to a deed until the purchase money is validly paid. A deed made before the purchaser becomes entitled thereto has no validity, unless subsequently validated by confirmation of the court. Lamar v. Hale, 79 Va. 147.

6. Form of Deed.

See W. Va. Code, 1899, ch. 72, § 9.

7. Covenants of Title.

See the title COVENANTS, vol. 3, p. 741.

On a contract for the sale of land the vendee is entitled to a general warranty deed, where the vendor is seized of the land in his own right, unless the contrary is agreed upon; but if the vendor be an executor, trustee or commissioner of the court, the vendee is entitled to a deed with special warranty only. Tavenner v. Barrett, 21 W. Va. 656. See also, Hughes v. Hamilton, 19 W. Va. 366; Londons v. Echols, 17 Gratt. 15, 20.

Where a party purchases land of a special commissioner of the court, and his purchase is confirmed, but before a deed is made to him, he executes a power of attorney to the special commissioner authorizing him to sell this land for him, and the special commissioner does so and signs a written contract agreeing to convey this land to the purchaser on the payment of the whole of the purchase money, signing the contract as special commissioner and attorney in fact of the first purchaser; held, the true meaning of such contract is, that the subpurchaser takes a deed from the special commissioner with the assent of the first purchaser, and therefore he is in such case only entitled to a deed with special warranty of title. Tavenner v. Barrett, 21 W. Va. 656.

But where the estate is sold by trustees under a will, a purchaser is not entitled to covenents for the title. And the same rule applies where an estate is sold under an order of a court of equity. See Wakeman v. The Dutchess of Rutland, 3 Ves. jr. 505, 506. In both cases, the purchaser is entitled to a covenant from the vendors, that they have done no act to encumber the estate, a special warranty substantially. Tavenner v. Barrett, 21 W. Va. 656.

8. Confirmation of Deed.

Where a commissioner of court is directed to sell a tract of land and on compliance with the terms of sale to convey the same to the purchaser, and he makes such sale and conveyance, and reports the same to the court which confirms the report, this is a sufficient confirmation of the deed, though no deed or copy thereof is returned with the report. Virginia, etc., Coal, etc., Co. v. Fields, 94 Va. 102, 26 S. E. 426.

Quære, whether a deed to a purchaser, at a sale directed by a decree, conveys any title, without a subsequent decree confirming the sale? Lovell v. Arnold, 2 Munf. 167.

A decree was made in 1807, directing certain commissioners to sell a tract of land in order to satisfy a debt which was a lien thereon. The commissioners, in the same year, sold the land, and conveyed it to the purchaser; and they collected the purchase money and paid it to the plaintiff, in part discharge of his debt; but they did not report their proceeding to the court until 1835; and in the meantime the original owner of land, or those claiming under him, remained in possession. In 1836, when the defendant had been dead many years, though no suggestion of his death had been made upon the record, the court confirmed the report of the commissioners. And then the devisee of the purchaser brought a writ of right to recover the land, against the parties in possession holding under the original owner. Held, that although the decree of 1807, directing the commissioners to sell the land, did not authorize them to execute a deed to the purchaser, yet as they did execute the deed and the court by, its final decree of 1836 ratified and confirmed it, this order of confirmation gave full effect and validity to said deed, and related back to the time of its date, so as to invest the purchaser with the legal title of the original owner to the land. The death of the defendant not having been suggested on the record, the validity of the decree of 1836 can not be impeached by evidence of his death before the decree, given in another collateral action. The error in proceeding to decree after the death of the defendant, should be shown in some proceeding by the proper parties to set aside said decree for that cause. The possession of the original owner, and of those claiming under him, from the time of the sale by the commissioners until the final decree, was not an adverse possession to the purchaser and those claiming under him. Evans v. Spurgin, 6 Gratt. 107.

That the court having jurisdiction over the subject, has the power either to ratify and confirm a previous deed made by the commissioners, or to direct the execution of a new one; and the correctness of any order so made by the court, where it has jurisdiction over the subject, can only be inquired into by proper proceedings instituted to set aside or reverse the order or decree; but the same can not be impeached in a collateral proceeding. Evans v. Spurgin, 6 Gratt. 107.

The court is of opinion, that although the interlocutory decree of the Staunton chancery district court, pronounced on the 20th day of July, 1807, in the suit of John Staley against Daniel Lantz, did not direct the commissioners thereby appointed, to make sale of the land in controversy, to convey the same to the purchaser; yet as commissioners appointed by the chancery court to make sale of property, act subject to the supervision and control of the court, their acts, when sanctioned and approved by the court, become the acts of the court. Evans v. Spurgin, 6 Gratt. 107.

C. EXECUTION OF DEED AS PREREQUISITE TO COLLECTION OF PURCHASE MONEY.
It is not essential that a deed should be made or filed as an escrow before the commissioners can collect the bond. Shields v. McClung, 6 W. Va. 79.

D. EFFECT OF DEED.
1. As Passing Title of Parties to Suit.
The execution of a deed by a commissioner appointed in a decree or order to execute the same, shall be as valid to pass, release, or extinguish the right, title, and interest of the parties on whose behalf it is executed, as if such parties had been at the time capable in law of executing the same, and had executed it. Virginia Code, 1873, ch. 178, § 4; Va. Code, 1904, § 3418; W. Va. Code, 1899, ch. 132, § 4; Hurt v. Jones, 75 Va. 341.

According to settled principles, as soon as the sale to the purchaser is confirmed by the court, he becomes in equity the owner of the land with a lien resting upon it for the purchase money. He has an equitable es-

tate, and if he proceeds to comply with his engagement by paying the purchase money into court, or into the hands of a receiver authorized to collect, he acquires a complete equitable title to the land; that is the right to call for the legal title, without condition of the parties to the suit; and a deed to him by a special commissioner appointed and empowered by the court to convey under the statute (Code of 1873, ch. 174, § 7), will pass the title of all the parties. Hurt v. Jones, 75 Va. 341.

We apprehend that it was competent for the court to have ordered such conveyance by a commissioner under the provisions of the statute (Code of 1873, ch. 174, § 7), and that such conveyance would have effectually passed the wife's title. Although, however, no deed was ordered or made, the right was definitely settled and such determination is equivalent in equity for most purposes to a conveyance. Hurt v. Jones, 75 Va. 341.

2. As Passing Title to Purchaser as against Judgment Lien.
Where land is sold, under a decree of court having jurisdiction of the subject, to pay a deed of trust debt, and a judgment debt, which are liens on the land in full force, the deed of trust and judgment as liens, also, the decree of sale made in the cause, being prior in date to a judgment, which was obtained after such decree of sale, and also, docketed on the proper judgment lien docket before a sale was made by the special commissioner appointed to make said sale in the decree of sale, a sale made after the recovery and docketing of such judgment by said special commissioner, and the deed made to the purchaser at such sale, for the land purchased, by such special commissioner appointed in and by the decree of the court confirming such sale, is valid, and passes the title to the purchaser as against the judgment and any lien thereof, al-

though such sale, the decree of the court confirming the same, and such deed of such special commissioner to the purchaser for the land, were made subsequent to the recovery and docketing of said judgment, unless something is alleged and shown in proper form and manner against said sale, decree and deed, other than the mere fact that the sale, decree of confirmation thereof, and such deed were made subsequent to the recovery and docketing of the judgment. Davis v. Landcraft, 10 W. Va. 718.

3. As Evidence of Title.

a. In General.

When a conveyance of land made by a special commissioner under a sale under a decree of a court is offered in evidence to pass title, it must be accompanied by either the whole record of the cause, or enough to show that the parties holding title affected by the deed, and also the land itself, were before the court, and that it was decreed to be sold, and was sold, and the sale confirmed by the court, and that authority was given by the decree to the commissioner to make the conveyance. The recital in the deed of these important facts is no evidence of them, against strangers to the deed, contesting its effect. Wilson v. Braden, 48 W. Va. 196, 36 S. E. 367; Ronk v. Higginbotham, 54 W. Va. 137, 46 S. E. 128; Cales v. Miller, 8 Gratt. 6; Waggoner v. Wolf, 28 W. Va. 820; Walton v. Hale, 9 Gratt. 194, 197; Robinett v. Preston, 4 Gratt. 141.

Where a deed made under a decree by a commissioner or other authority is offered in evidence as a connecting link in the plaintiff's chain of title to land, it is necessary to introduce with it so much of the record of the suit in which such decree was made as will satisfactorily show that the person having the legal title to the land conveyed was a party to the suit, and as will identify the land conveyed with the land decreed. McDodrill v. Pardee

& Curtin Lumber Co., 40 W. Va. 564, 21 S. E. 878; Waggoner v. Wolf, 28 W. Va. 820.

As against a party who claims against the deed and is a stranger thereto, the recital of such facts therein, without more, is not evidence thereof, and the deed does not prove the transfer of the title to the land it purports to convey. McDodrill v. Pardee & Curtin Lumber Co., 40 W. Va. 564, 21 S. E. 878.

In the case of Walton v. Hale, 9 Gratt. 194, 198, the court said: "But in this case it seems to me the caveator has utterly failed in connecting himself with the Ruston v. Blanchard title. The commissioner to make sales under the delinquent land laws, under which these proceedings were had, has no interest in the subject of sale. He acts like a commissioner to make sales under a decree of the chancery court, and is clothed with a mere naked authority. Having no interest in the land conveyed, the deed of the commissioner could avail nothing where his authority to make it did not appear, unless there had been such a long acquiescence and possession under the deed as to justify a presumption in favor of the deed, as was the case in Robinett v. Preston, 4 Gratt. 141. In this case no such presumption can be raised. The caveator has rested his right upon the deed and the proceedings which led to it. In such a case, and as against a stranger setting up an adverse claim to the title asserted, the recitals in the deed are no evidence. Garver v. Jackson, 4 Peter's 1, 83; Wiley v. Givens, 6 Gratt. 277. In the case of Masters v. Varner, 5 Gratt. 168, a decree of the chancery court and the marshal's deed were offered in evidence. The decree did not describe specific land directed to be conveyed; but it was described with sufficient certainty in the deed. The court held that the recitals in the marshal's deed were no evidence as against a third person asserting an adverse claim, of the authority of the marshal to convey the specific tract; and that as the decree left it uncertain, it was necessary to produce the whole record, or so much thereof as, would show that the land conveyed was the land embraced in the suit, before the deed could be used as evidence. In the case under consideration, the report of sales set out that Raper, Graham and Allison were the purchasers. By the eighth section of the act of March 30, 1837, it was the duty of the court to direct the commissioner to convey to the purchasers upon the payment of the purchase money; and the ninth section of the act of March 15th, 1838, declares that the purchaser shall on application to the commissioner, be entitled to his deed upon the payment of the purchase money. By each act the authority of the commissioner is limited to a conveyance to the purchasers. The deed in this case is to a stranger, if regard be had to the record of the proceedings, which are relied on as authorizing the commissioner to convey. The name of Walton nowhere appears as purchaser, or as having any interest in the subject." Ronk *v.* Higginbotham, 54 W. Va. 137, 46 S. E. 128.

"The deed of said commissioners, purporting to convey said four thousand, two hundred acres to Shrewsberry is not accompanied by any of the reports, decretal orders, or other proceedings, or with the plat and report stated to have been filed with, and made part of, said proceeding, which are referred to in said deed, except the decretal order of October 24, 1840, hereinbefore mentioned. It will be observed that the decree of the 17th of May, 1841, confirming the sale of ten thousand acres, sold by said commissioners, was made and entered twelve days after said deed was made to Shrewsberry. This deed having been acknowledged by said commissioners on the 7th day of May, 1841, and admitted to record the same day,

as the certificate of the clerk of the county court of said county, appended thereto shows, could not have been and was not authorized by said decretal order of May 17, 1841, which order does not mention Shrewsberry or any other person by name as purchaser of said four thousand, two hundred acres. There is no other decree in the record conferring authority to execute said deed." Ronk *v.* Higginbotham, 54 W. Va. 137, 46 S. E. 128.

b. As Evidence in Action of Ejectment.

See the title EJECTMENT, vol. 4, p. 871.

A commissioner's deed of real estate, and the decrees of courts of competent jurisdiction under which the deed was made, are always admissible in an action of ejectment against a stranger to the suit, and can not be attacked because of irregularities or error in the cause in which they are made. Turnbull *v.* Mann, 99 Va. 41, 37 S. E. 288.

c. Sale Made under Void Decree.

A deed for land to a purchaser under a judicial sale, though the decree is without jurisdiction and void, is color of title for adverse possession, and actual possession under it is adverse to the owner of the land. Waldron *v.* Harvey, 54 W. Va. 608, 46 S. E. 603.

A court of equity without jurisdiction pronounces a decree for the sale of a certain parcel of land, and appoints commissioners, with directions to make the sale. They sell the land; the court confirms the sale, and appoints the commissioners to convey the land to the purchaser on payment of the purchase money. The purchase money is paid, and the commissioners make to the purchaser a deed purporting to convey the land in fee. Such deed being proved constitutes color of title. Mullan *v.* Carper, 37 W. Va. 215, 16 S. E. 527.

Under such deed the purchaser and

those claiming under him held the house and lot in question in actual, visible and exclusive possession continuously for more than ten years before the bringing of the suit, claiming it in fee as their own, subject only to the wife's contingent right of dower. Held, the remedy of the original owner and of those claiming under him is barred, and their right to the possession extinguished. Mullan v. Carper, 37 W. Va. 215, 16 S. E. 527.

E. COLLATERAL IMPEACHMENT.

Where there is a valid attachment and levy of the same, a decree of a court of competent jurisdiction, an order or decree of sale, and a sale by a commissioner appointed by the court, and confirmation thereof, with directions to the commissioner to make a deed to the purchaser, and commissioner's deed made to the purchaser, or his assignee by deed, the proceeding can not be held void when introduced collaterally in another suit; nor can such deed of the commissioner be held void in such other suit, because not made to the purchaser, but, to his assignee by deed, in which the said commissioner was directed by the purchaser to make the deed for the realty to such assignee, if the execution and delivery of such deed of assignment of the purchaser be properly proved, when such deed of the commissioner to such assignee is offered in evidence at the trial, in connection with a copy of the proceedings had in the chancery cause, in which said realty was decreed to be sold, sale made and confirmed, etc. In such case, said deed of the commissioner to such assignee should be admitted as evidence tending to show title in such assignee. Hall v. Hall, 12 W. Va. 1.

Such deed, made by such commissioner to such assignee by deed, passes the whole title and interest in the realty, sold and conveyed, that was vested in the debtor from whence the same was sold by the proceedings in chancery, to such assignee. And especially should it so be held in an action of ejectment, brought by such debtor against such assignee to recover the property so conveyed. Hall v. Hall, 12 W. Va. 1.

There seems to be no doubt that a deed made to a person other than the purchaser, after confirmation of the sale in pursuance to an order of the court, in which the case is pending, made after the confirmation of the sale, is valid and passes the legal title, and will be so considered and held in any collateral proceeding in which the validity of such deed is brought into question. Rorer on Judicial Sales, § 369, page 145. Hall v. Hall, 12 W. Va. 1; Hitchcock v. Rawson, 14 Gratt. 526.

"Under the authorities above cited, and upon principle, I am unable to see satisfactory reasons why a commissioner, appointed by a chancery court, with directions to make a deed for lands to the purchaser, can not properly and legitimately make the deed to the purchaser, or his assignee by deed. As before stated, it seems to me to do so is but carrying out the true spirit, intent and meaning of the decree, and such practice would save great and useless expenditure of money, time and trouble in many cases. I think, however, the most prudent course for the grantee would be to procure his title in the ordinary way, so that all papers necessary to establish his title may be recorded and not merely rest and depend upon oral testimony and the preservation or loss of an essential paper. Rorer on Judicial Sales, § 370. p. 145, §§ 765, 766, 767." Hall v. Hall, 12 W. Va. 1.

XIV. Procedure upon Failure of Purchaser to Comply with Bid.

A. LIABILITY OF PURCHASER TO HAVE CONTRACT ENFORCED.

In General.—When one becomes a

purchaser at a judicial sale by having the property knocked off to him, he incurs a liability for the price he agreed to pay, though he does not comply with the terms of sale under the decree, as by giving bonds with security, or other terms, provided proper steps be taken to enforce this liability. Stout *v*. Philippi Mfg., etc., Co., 41 W. Va. 339, 23 S. E. 571.

A purchaser of land under a decree of a court of equity, after the sale is confirmed, is the equitable owner of the land, subject to be compelled to comply with his contract by payment of the purchase money. Hurt *v*. Jones, 75 Va. 341.

By bidding, the purchaser subjects himself to the jurisdiction of the court, and in effect becomes a party to the proceedings in which the sale is made, and may be compelled to complete his purchase by the process of the court. Robertson *v*. Smith, 94 Va. 250, 26 S. E. 579; Brent *v*. Green, 6 Leigh. 16; 2 Lomax's Dig. 43 (side page 33); 2 Minor's Inst. 857 (4th Ed.).

When and as soon as a valid contract is made for the sale of land, equity, which looks upon things agreed to be done as actually performed, considers and treats the vendor as a trustee for the purchaser of the estate sold, and the purchaser as a trustee of the purchase money for the vendor. 1 Sugden on Vendors, 191 (bottom). The purchaser is deemed and treated as the equitable owner of the land; and subject to the lien for the unpaid purchase money, the title being retained, the equitable estate of the purchaser is alienable, devisable, and descendible in like manner as real estate held by legal title. 1 Story's Eq. Ju., §§ 789, 790; 2 Story's Eq. Ju., §§ 1212, 1217; Lewis *v*. Hawkins, 23 Wall. U. S. R. 119, 125, and authorities there cited. A contract for sale under a decree in chancery is governed by the same principles. As soon as the sale is confirmed by the court, there is a complete contract,

the bidder becomes a purchaser, and is thenceforth regarded and treated as the equitable owner of the land, with the right reserved to compel him to comply with his contract by payment of the purchase money. Hurt *v*. Jones, 75 Va. 341.

Purchasers under decree should not be required to take or pay for the property where it had been thrice sold without an account of liens and the title is uncertain. Etter *v*. Scott, 90 Va. 762, 19 S. E. 776.

Purchasers at such sale should not be compelled to complete their purchase where the land has been previously sold in another suit, and neither the sale nor the decree therefor has been set aside. Etter *v*. Scott, 90 Va. 762, 19 S. E. 776.

It is clear that if after sale, and before confirmation, the property is destroyed or injured, the purchaser will not be compelled to comply with his purchase, if without fault, as confirmation relates back to the moment of purchase, and the purchaser is entitled to it in its then condition. Stout *v*. Philippi Mfg., etc., Co., 41 W. Va. 339, 23 S. E. 571; Taylor *v*. Cooper, 10 Leigh 317; Hyman *v*. Smith, 13 W. Va. 744.

As a general rule the purchaser at a judicial sale is required to pay the consideration for the estate, although it be destroyed or taken from him by superior title before a conveyance is executed. Christian *v*. Cabell, 22 Gratt. 82.

Confirmation as Prerequisite to Liability of Bidder.—See ante, "Confirmation," IX.

When one has caused property to be knocked down to him, the court must, in some way, in order to hold him responsible, in such case, act on his bid, because the court is the seller, the commissioner only its agent. The bid must be accepted by the court before the bidder can be held liable. 2 Daniell's Ch. Prac. 1281, speaking of steps to compel an unwilling purchaser to complete his purchase, lays it down plainly, that the sale must be confirmed as a prerequisite, as well as where the purchaser claims the property. Stout v. Philippi Mfg., etc., Co., 41 W. Va. 339, 23 S. E. 571.

B. RESALE BY COMMISSIONER BEFORE REPORTING TO COURT.

When the purchaser fails to comply with the terms, a commissioner may ignore his bid, if the price is worth less, or for other reason he does not care to insist on it, and go on and make another sale at once. But he does so at his peril, where there is danger of loss to the parties, instead of reporting to the court. If he does this, the purchaser is not liable for his bid. Stout v. Philippi Mfg., etc., Co., 41 W. Va. 339, 23 S. E. 571.

C. PROCEDURE AFTER REPORT OF SALE TO COURT.

1. Setting Aside Sale and Ordering Resale.

In General.—If the purchaser fails to comply with the terms of the sale, the sale may be reported to the court, and then several courses are open. The court may set aside the sale, release the purchaser, and order a resale. Stout v. Philippi Mfg., etc., Co., 41 W. Va. 339, 23 S. E. 571.

If the purchaser is worthless, an order to discharge him and resell is proper. Stout v. Philippi Mfg., etc., Co., 41 W. Va. 339, 23 S. E. 571.

In the second volume of Daniell's Ch. Pr., 1460-62, it is stated that after the report of a sale by a master is confirmed, according to the English practice, if it appears that the purchase has been made to a person unable to perform his contract, the parties interested in the sale, may, upon motion, obtain an order simply discharging the purchaser from his purchase, and directing the estate to be resold. Clarkson v. Read, 15 Gratt. 288; Gross v. Pearcy, 2 Pat. & H. 483.

When Proper.—This would be proper where fire or other destruction of the property rendered it proper to release the purchaser. Stout v. Philippi Mfg., etc., Co., 41 W. Va. 339, 23 S. E. 571.

"In this case, before any report of the first sale to the court, the parties, by counsel, agreed that a resale take place without advertisement; and ten days after the first sale it was again sold to Douglass, but at a less price, and the sale confirmed, with a reservation of the right to creditors to look to him for the discrepancy in price between the two sales. Douglass gave to the commissioners, as his reason for not complying with his purchase, the act of God in working a damage to the property on the night of the day of sale, by a rise in Valley river, which inundated the property. Now, had this first sale been reported to the court, and notice given Douglass of an intention to hold him to his purchase, he could have shown the facts, and asked the court to release him, and not force upon him a ruined property or the court might have made an abatement, which I think it had power to do. Taylor v. Cooper, 10 Leigh 317, 319, cited in Hyman v. Smith, 13 W. Va. 744, 767. But without report of this bid, or its acceptance by the court, or intimation of a purpose to hold him to his bid, the property is resold, by mere act of the attorneys of the parties, without advertisement. As all parties consented to a resale, Douglass could fairly infer that they recognized the injustice of confirming the sale, and agreed to disregard it." Stout v. Philippi Mfg. Co., 41 W. Va. 339, 23 S. E. 571.

2. Proceedings by Attachment and Contempt after Confirmation.

See the title CONTEMPT, vol. 3, p. 236.

The court may confirm the sale, and compel the purchaser to comply with the terms of sale by paying money into court, in whole or in part, as required by the prior decree, and conform in other respects to it, and enforce its order by attachment and commitment after a rule, because the purchaser is in contempt. Stout *v.* Philippi Mfg., etc., Co., 41 W. Va. 339, 23 S. E. 571.

This course is rarely resorted to, but is clearly within the court's power. Stout *v.* Philippi Mfg., etc., Co., 41 W. Va. 339, 23 S. E. 571.

In the second volume of Daniell's Ch. Pr., 1460-62, it is stated that after a report of the sale by the master is confirmed, according to the English practice, if the purchaser is responsible, the court will, if required, make an order that he shall within a given time pay the money into court; and if the purchaser, on being served with the order, fails to obey it, his submission to it may be enforced by attachment. Clarkson *v.* Read, 15 Gratt. 288; Gross *v.* Pearcy, 2 Pat. & H. 483.

In Gross *v.* Pearcy, 2 Pat. & H. 483, it is held, that a purchaser of land sold under a decree of a court of chancery may be compelled to comply with the terms of the sale and complete the purchase by paying cash, if it be a cash sale, or by giving bond and security, if the sale be on time, by process of contempt. Glenn *v.* Blackford, 23 W. Va. 182.

Where there is no decree in the cause ordering the purchaser to pay in the purchase money, he can not strictly be treated as in contempt. Clarkson *v.* Read, 15 Gratt. 288.

3. Resale at Purchaser's Risk after Confirmation.

a. In General.

The court may order a resale, with the provision that the purchaser shall be held responsible, in case upon resale the property shall bring less than his bid. Stout *v.* Philippi Mfg., etc., Co., 41 W. Va. 339, 23 S. E. 571; Redd *v.* Dyer, 83 Va. 331, 2 S. E. 283; Mosby *v.* Withers, 80 Va. 82.

It is now the more usual and eligible course under the English practice, to obtain an order, not that the purchaser be discharged, but that the estate be resold, and that he may pay the expense arising from his noncompletion of the purchase, the expenses of the application to the court and of the resale, and any deficiency in price on the resale. Gross *v.* Pearcy, 2 Pat. & H. 483.

Nature of Proceedings to Resell.— In judicial sales the court in some sense is regarded as the vendor, making sale by a commissioner as its agent, and the contract is treated as a contract substantially between the purchaser on one side and the court as vendor on the other. Where the title is retained, the proceeding for resale, whether by bill or in the more summary way, by rule, is a proceeding substantially by the court, as vendor, to enforce the collection of the purchase money by enforcing the lien incident to the title retained as a security, and must be governed by the same rules and principles which control proceedings of a like nature in a like case by any other vendor. See authorities cited by Judge Daniel in Clarkson *v.* Read, 15 Gratt. 288, 295, and among the rest, the case of Harding *v.* Harding, 18 Eng. Ch. R. 514, in which Lord Cottenham said, "that there was no reason why a person purchasing under a decree of the court should not be held to his contract as much as a person purchasing in the ordinary way; that the court might enforce the vendor's lien against the estate, and that an order to hold the purchaser to his contract and to resell the estate in the meantime, was in strict analogy to the course the court takes against the purchaser in the ordinary way." Long *v.* Weller, 29 Gratt. 347.

b. Rule against Purchaser to Show Cause Why Land Shall Not Be Resold.

(1) In General.

Before resale, there ought to be a

rule upon the purchaser to comply with the terms of sale, or show cause why the property shall not be resold. Stout v. Philippi Mfg., etc., Co., 41 W. Va. 339, 23 S. E. 571.

Upon failure of the purchaser to comply with the terms of his purchase or bid by payment of the purchase money, it is the usual and proper practice for the court to issue a rule against such purchaser to show cause why the property shall be resold for the payment of such purchase money. Clarkson v. Read, 15 Gratt. 288; Gross v. Pearcy, 2 Pat. & H. 483; Glenn v. Blackford, 23 W. Va. 182; Long v. Weller, 29 Gratt. 347; Crislip v. Cain, 19 W. Va. 438; Robertson v. Smith, 94 Va. 250, 26 S. E. 579; Boyce v. Strother, 76 Va. 862; Kable v. Mitchell, 9 W. Va. 492, 517; Thornton v. Fairfax, 29 Gratt. 669; Hurt v. Jones, 75 Va. 341; Yancey v. Mauck, 15 Gratt. 300, 306; Williams v. Blakey, 76 Va. 254; Gilmer v. Baker, 24 W. Va. 72, 84; Berlin v. Melhorn, 75 Va. 636, 642; Hickson v. Rucker, 77 Va. 135; Ogden v. Davidson, 81 Va. 757, 761; Anthony v. Kasey, 83 Va. 338, 5 S. E. 176; Thurman v. Morgan, 79 Va. 367; Virginia Fire, etc., Ins. Co. v. Cottrell, 85 Va. 857, 9 S. E. 132; Whitehead v. Bradley, 87 Va. 676, 13 S. E. 195.

Where the purchaser at a judicial sale is in default, in that he has paid the purchase money to a person unauthorized to receive it, and refuses to pay the purchase money to a person entitled legally to receive it, he may be compelled to complete his purchase by a rule to show cause why the property should not be resold. Whitehead v. Bradley, 87 Va. 676, 13 S. E. 195.

In Gross v. Pearcy, 2 Pat. & H. 483. it was held, that a purchaser of land sold under a decree of a court of chancery may be compelled to comply with the terms of the sale and complete the purchase by paying cash, if it be a cash sale, or by giving bond and security, if the sale be on time by a rule to show cause why the land should not be re-

sold. In this case the legal title was retained. Glenn v. Blackford, 23 W. Va. 182.

Any purchaser who buys property embraced in a suit, and subject to the control of the court, becomes a quasi party to the cause, and is amendable to the orders of the court, and where such purchaser is in default, a rule against him to show cause why there should not be a resale is the regular practice. Ogden v. Davidson, 81 Va. 757; Clarkson v. Read, 15 Gratt. 288.

In delivering the opinion of the court in Gross v. Pearcy, 2 Pat. & H. 483, Thompson, J., said: "I confess, the question raised in the first assignment of error, as to the power of a court of equity to proceed in a summary way by rule to show cause to resell the land of a purchaser who has complied with the terms of sale, by making the cash payment, given bond and security for the deferred payments, whose purchase has been confirmed and he put into possession, is to me a novel one. I have met with no such case in my practice at the bar or my experience on the bench. It is certainly true, that the ordinary means of compelling performance of decrees and orders of a court of chancery are process of contempt, sequestration and execution as upon judgments at law; but these are not the only means: Cases may and do often occur where a resort to such a proceeding as this would be proper. Suppose a purchaser fails and refuses to comply with the terms of sale by paying cash, if it be a sale for cash, or by giving bond and security, if it be a sale upon time with the requisition of bond and security, and the fact of failure and refusal be reported to the court by the commissioner of sale. The court may either proceed by attachment, or by a rule, to show cause why the land should not be resold at the peril of the purchaser, holding him responsible for the deficiency."

"I am not prepared to say that there might not be cases, where bond and security had been given, the legal title being retained by the court as ultimate security in which a summary proceeding like this would not be justifiable. As for instance, where the exigencies of the case required a speedy collection of the proceeds of sale, where the purchaser and his sureties had been prosecuted at law to insolvency, or in the absence of any suit were proved to be notoriously insolvent. In such a case, I can see no good reason why the court should not have power to proceed by rule against the purchaser and his sureties to decree a resale, rather than to resort to the more tardy and tedious proceeding of an original bill to enforce the lien by foreclosure and sale. I must, however confess, no matter how reasonable such a practice may seem to me in the case supposed, its propriety is at least very questionable and doubtful, tested by the usages and practice of courts of equity in Virginia." Gross v. Pearcy, 2 Pat. & H. 483.

Quære, whether where the purchaser has complied with the terms of sale, by paying the cash required and giving bond and security for the credit payments, and the sale has been confirmed and the purchaser placed in possession of the property, the title being retained to secure the payment of the purchase money, the payment of the bonds can be enforced by a rule against the purchaser to show cause why there should not be a resale of the property? Gross v. Pearcy, 2 Pat. & H. 483.

But it is clearly erroneous, to decree a resale under such a rule, where the purchaser has complied with the terms of the sale, and there is no necessity for a speedy collection of the purchase money, no proof of any default in the payment of the bonds, and no suggestion or proof of the insolvency of the purchaser or his sureties. Gross v. Pearcy, 2 Pat. & H. 483.

Where the object of the rule is not to set aside the sale or the decree of sale, but to compel the purchasers to comply with their contracts by paying the purchase money to persons entitled legally to receive it, the case does not come within Va. Code, 1887, § 3425. Whitehead v. Bradley, 87 Va. 676, 13 S. E. 195.

The proper proceeding to obtain the resale in the case here was by rule to show cause against it. Whitehead v. Bradley, 87 Va. 676, 13 S. E. 195.

(2) Nature of Proceeding.

Summary Proceeding.—The proceeding against the purchaser to enforce payment of the purchase money by rule, is a summary proceeding. 2 Daniell's Ch. Pr. 1275, 1282; Hurt v. Jones, 75 Va. 341; Clarkson v. Read, 15 Gratt. 288; Gross v. Pearcy, 2 Pat. & H. 483; Virginia Fire, etc., Ins. Co. v. Cottrell, 85 Va. 857, 9 S. E. 132.

Proceeding for Specific Performance.—The proceeding to enforce payment of the purchase money by rule, is substantially a proceeding for the specific performance of a contract. 2 Daniell's Ch. Pr. 1275, 1282; Hurt v. Jones, 75 Va. 341; Clarkson v. Read, 15 Gratt. 288.

(3) For Whose Benefit Rule May Be Issued.

If no deed has been executed to the purchaser by the commissioners, it is competent for the court to proceed by rule, for their benefit, to enforce the collection of the unpaid purchase money. Clearly, if the commissioners, under the misrepresentation of the purchaser, have improperly charged themselves with money never collected, the purchaser still owes it, and the court may compel him to complete his purchase, whether it be for the benefit of the commissioners or of creditors or others interested in the funds. Williams v. Blakey, 76 Va. 254.

In judicial sale, the court is regarded, in a certain sense, as owner and principal, and the commissioner as agent and officer. When the commissioner has accounted for the money without having received it, upon the most ordinary principles of justice the court ought to substitute him to its rights and remedies against the purchaser. Williams *v.* Blakey, 76 Va. 254.

(4) Against Whom Rule May Issue.

Even in the case of a purchaser the proceeding by rule is against him in his capacity of purchaser, and so as a party to the suit, and not upon the bond, which is a mere legal security for the payment of the purchase money, enforceable only in a legal forum according to the established mode of procedure in that forum. This is clearly shown by the case of Clarkson *v.* Read, 15 Gratt. 288. This reason is wanting in the case of the surety, and we can perceive none other to justify such a summary proceeding against him. Anthony *v.* Kasey, 83 Va. 338, 5 S. E. 176.

Where purchaser at judicial sale fails to pay his bonds, and upon rule against him and his surety, a personal decree is rendered against the surety, such decree is extrajudicial and void. Anthony *v.* Kasey, 83 Va. 338, 5 S. E. 176.

In Clarkson *v.* Read, 15 Gratt. 288, this court held that the purchaser was a party to the suit as to all matters appertaining to the purchase, and might therefore be proceeded against by rule in case of default. But no such reason exists in our opinion for such a summary procedure against a surety. He does not deal directly with the court, and so become a party to the suit. His undertaking is collateral to the contract of purchase. It is that of a mere surety, and can not be extended by construction in any respect. And to use the language of this court in Thurman *v.* Morgan, 79 Va. 367: "Their liability, if any, grows out of their undertaking as sureties on the bond, and can be ascertained and enforced only by suit on the bond in a common-law court, where full oppor-

tunity for making defense and the constitutional right of trial by jury can be had." Anthony *v.* Kasey, 83 Va. 338, 5 S. E. 176.

The sureties are not parties to the suit, nor officers of the court and hence can not be proceeded against by a rule; their liability, as sureties can only be enforced by an action on their bond in a common-law court, where they can make defense on trial by a jury, and the decree for the payment of said sum of money, so obtained upon a rule, is a departure from established modes of procedure, and was void. Ogden *v.* Davidson, 81 Va. 757; Thurman *v.* Morgan, 79 Va. 367.

And so in Thurman *v.* Morgan, 79 Va. 367, a case not unlike the present, the circuit court had jurisdiction of the subject, and the parties against whom the decree was rendered were brought before the court, yet the decree was declared by this court to be void. Why? Because, though the sureties of the receiver may have been liable for his default, the circuit court has no power under the law to proceed against them in that cause according to the method adopted. They were not parties to the cause, and the procedure by rule to bring them in and subject them for liability as sureties on the bond of the receiver, though he was an officer of the court, was against every sound principle of jurisprudence and without any recognized precedent. It seems difficult to distinguish this last-mentioned case from the one at bar. In each of them the proceeding was against sureties, who were not parties to the suit in which the proceedings was had, unless made so by being on the bonds, and in both cases the proceeding was by rule. Yet in that case this court held, that the proceeding by rule was such a departure from the established mode of procedure as to render the decree not only erroneous but void. Anthony *v.* Kasey, 83 Va. 338, 5 S. E. 176.

Ward filed bill against guardian for

settlement. Guardian had loaned ward's money to W., secured by trust deed on Pedlar Mill. By consent decree, trust deed was transferred to ward, and commissioner appointed to collect loan and pay over to ward. Trustee made sale under trust deed to O., who paid part and gave bonds for residue, and made default. Sale was reported to court. Two days afterwards a rule was issued and served on O., to show cause next day why Pedlar Mills should not be resold. Next day a decree of resale was entered. Held, neither trustee nor purchaser being parties to the suit, and the sale not being judicial, the decree is a nullity quoad those persons. Ogden v. Davidson, 81 Va. 757.

(5) Necessity That Court Retain Legal Title.

The usual and better practice is for the court always to retain the legal title in confirming a judicial sale, so that should the purchaser fail to pay the deferred bonds, a rule might speedily issue against him, the amount of the balance ascertained, and a resale ordered. Glenn v. Blackford, 23 W. Va. 182.

(6) Propriety of Proceeding by Rule Rather than Bill.

See post, "Original or Supplemental Bill," XIV, C, 3, c.

In the case of Clarkson v. Read, 15 Gratt. 288, Daniel, J., entered into a discussion of the question, whether in a case like that, where the legal title was retained, an original or supplemental bill would have to be filed, or whether a rule was sufficient. On page 298, he says: "I do not mean to say that in all cases of the kind the proceeding should be by a rule, rather than by a bill. It is not difficult to conceive of cases in which there might grow up or be developed, between the direct parties to the cause and the purchaser, equities of a character, such as to require that they should be discussed and considered upon regular and formal pleadings original or supplemental. It is, however, but reasonable to believe, that in a majority of cases little else would be attained by requiring the parties to go through the steps of a regular suit instead of proceeding by a rule, except delay; delay which, whilst furthering no just end or object of the purchaser, would work inconvenience and injustice to those entitled to receive the proceeds of the sale." Glenn v. Blackford, 23 W. Va. 182.

A rule in such a case apprises the purchaser of the nature of the demand against him as fully as a bill could do. And the only additional office that a bill could perform, would be to recite, in a more formal manner, matters which he already knows; or which the law presumes that he already knows. If he has any cause to resist the demand, he can set it forth as fully in an answer to the rule as in an answer to a bill. And if in his answer to the rule he should show any reason why there should be no resale of the property, it would be just as incumbent upon the court to allow him an opportunity to bring forward his proofs as it would have been, had the same matter been averred in an answer to a bill. Clarkson v. Read, 15 Gratt. 288.

In proceedings by rule, the costs are less, and the end more speedily reached, than where an original or supplemental bill is filed. Glenn v. Blackford, 23 W. Va. 182.

(7) Rule Proper Proceeding Where Land Sold on Credit.

In Clarkson v. Read, 15 Gratt. 288, there was a judicial sale of land partly on credit and the purchaser paid the cash payment and executed his bonds for the deferred payments, and the sale was confirmed by the court, and the title was retained. When the bonds fell due, he failed to pay them. It was held, that the purchaser might be proceeded against by a rule made upon him to show cause why the land might not be resold for the payment of the purchase money, and upon that proceeding a decree may be made for the sale of the land. Glenn v. Blackford, 23 W. Va. 182.

"And if the court, in the case of a failure, by the purchaser at a cash sale, to pay in the money, may, without requiring the parties to the cause to file a bill, proceed, by rules and orders, to sell the land, and hold the purchaser accountable for the balance due, after applying the proceeds of sale to the discharge of the purchase money, it is difficult to see why the like proceeding may not be resorted to in the case of a sale for credit, when the credit has expired and the purchase money remains unpaid. Such rules and orders would have the same foundation to rest upon in the one case as in the other." Clarkson v. Read, 15 Gratt. 288.

(8) Property Sold as Property of Purchaser.

When a resale is ordered, upon default of the purchaser to comply with his contract by paying the purchase money, the former sale is not set aside, but the property is sold as the property of the purchaser and at his risk. Whitehead v. Bradley, 87 Va. 676, 13 S. E. 195; Tyler v. Toms, 75 Va. 116; Virginia Fire, etc., Ins. Co. v. Cottrell, 85 Va. 857, 9 S. E. 132; Hurt v. Jones, 75 Va. 341; Clarkson v. Read, 15 Gratt. 288.

(9) Liability of Purchaser for Deficiency on Resale.

The purchaser is responsible for any difference between the sum at which he agreed to buy, i. e., the unpaid purchase money of the former sale together with the costs and expenses of the resale, and the amount which the property brings on resale. Stout v. Philippi Mfg., etc., Co., 41 W. Va. 339, 23 S. E. 571; Whitehead v. Bradley, 87 Va. 676, 13 S. E. 195; Tyler v. Toms, 75 Va. 116; Virginia Fire, etc., Ins. Co. v. Cottrell, 85 Va. 857, 9 S. E. 132;

Clarkson v. Read, 15 Gratt. 288; Hurt v. Jones, 75 Va. 341; Gross v. Pearcy, 2 Pat. & H. 483.

"What is the proper mode of holding a bidder liable when he has failed to complete his purchase, necessitating a resale, which has brought a less price? This question has been anticipated in what is said above, as it is there answered. It may be by rule in the same case, proceeded in as above indicated." Stout v. Philippi Mfg., etc., Co., 41 W. Va. 339, 23 S. E. 571.

(10) Right of Purchaser to Surplus on Resale.

If, upon a resale of the property to compel the purchaser to comply with his contract, the property brings more than the debt, he is entitled to the surplus. Whithead v. Bradley, 87 Va. 676, 13 S. E. 195; Tyler v. Toms, 75 Va. 116; Virginia Fire, etc., Ins. Co. v. Cottrell, 85 Va. 857, 9 S. E. 132; Hurt v. Jones, 75 Va. 341.

(11) Defenses.

Commissioner having been induced to execute deed conveying the property to the purchaser, by the latter's fraud or willful misrepresentation upon an honest mistake of fact as to the payment of the purchase money, purchaser can not rely on the deed as an estoppel, but may be proceeded against by rule to have the deed annulled and the property subjected to sale. Williams v. Blakey, 76 Va. 254.

"The only question is, whether the deed executed by the commissioner is an obstacle in the way of a proceeding by rule. A single consideration is sufficient to solve that question. If, as charged by the appellee, the deed was procured by a fraud or willful misrepresentation, or by misrepresentation upon an honest mistake of fact as to the payment of the purchase money, the appellant could not rely upon it as an estoppel. Every difficulty with respect to the remedy by rule is removed as soon as it is made to appear that the execution of the deed was due to a misrepresentation of the facts produced by the appellant himself. The court will place the parties in the same situation, that they were before the deed was executed. Any other rule would give to the appellant an undue advantage, derived from his own misconduct. My opinion, therefore, is, that the court has jurisdiction in this case to afford such relief to the appellees as they may be justly entitled to under the evidence." Williams v. Blakey, 76 Va. 254.

Statute of Frauds as Defense.—See the title FRAUDS, STATUTE OF, vol. 6, p. 523.

(12) Procedure.

(a) Court Must Be Able to Act in Summary Manner.

Upon a rule against a purchaser or bidder at a judicial sale to show cause why he shall not be required to comply with the terms of his purchase or bid, courts of equity must be able to act in a summary manner. Robertson v. Smith, 94 Va. 250, 26 S. E. 579; Boyce v. Strother, 76 Va. 862; Kable v. Mitchell, 9 W. Va. 492.

(b) Service of Rule.

In General.—Before there can be a decree of resale it is proper and necessary that the purchaser should have notice of the proceeding. The practice which has received the sanction of this court is to proceed by the service of a rule on the purchaser to show cause why the lands should not be resold. Thornton v. Fairfax, 29 Gratt. 669.

Voluntary Appearance as Waiver of Necessity for Service of Rule.—And upon the filing of petition and the report of the receiver, showing that the purchase money had not all been paid, the court might have directed the rule. That does not appear to have been done, but the purchaser had notice of the proceeding, and came forward to show cause in his own chosen way. There was no need, therefore, for a rule. Thornton v. Fairfax, 29 Gratt. 669.

(c) Return of Rule.

Where the purchaser is in default in paying the purchase money, and a rule is awarded requiring him to show cause why there should not be a resale of the land, the objection that the rule is returnable to the same term at which it is issued, is without force, provided sufficient time is given to answer the rule. Boyce v. Strother, 76 Va. 862.

(d) Answer.

If the purchaser has any cause to resist the demand for the purchase money, he can set it forth in his answer to the rule. Clarkson v. Read, 15 Gratt. 288.

(e) Evidence.

In General.—If in his answer to the rule, the purchaser shows any reason why there should be no resale of the property, it is incumbent upon the court to allow him an opportunity to bring forward his proofs. Clarkson v. Read, 15 Gratt. 288.

Affidavits.—Upon a rule against a purchaser or bidder to show cause why he shall not be required to comply with the terms of his purchase or bid, it is the usual practice to allow ex parte affidavits to be read by either party. Robertson v. Smith, 94 Va. 250, 26 S. E. 579; Boyce v. Strother, 76 Va. 862; Kable v. Mitchell, 9 W. Va. 492, 517.

Depositions.—Although it is ordinarily the proper practice upon a rule against a purchaser or bidder at a judicial sale to allow ex parte affidavits, yet the trial court, in the exercise of a just discretion, may require depositions to be taken in whole or in part instead of ex parte affidavits, so that an opportunity for cross-examination may be had. Robertson v. Smith, 94 Va. 250, 26 S. E. 579; Boyce v. Strother, 76 Va. 862; Kable v. Mitchell, 9 W. Va. 492, 517.

Reference to Commissioner.—Upon a rule against the purchaser or bidder at a judicial sale to show cause why he shall not be required to comply with the terms of his purchase or bid, the court may, instead of allowing ex parte affidavits to be read, or requiring depositions to be taken, refer the matter to one of its commissioners where there is a necessity for it. Robertson v. Smith, 94 Va. 250, 26 S. E. 579; Boyce v. Strother, 76 Va. 862; Kable v. Mitchell, 9 W. Va. 492, 517.

(f) Prerequisites to Decree for Resale. Ascertainment of Amount of Purchase Money Due.—Where a judicial sale of land is made upon a credit, and the title retained as a security, upon a rule against the purchaser to show cause why the land should not be resold for his failure to pay the purchase money before making a decree for the sale, the court should ascertain how much of the purchase money is due. Long v. Weller, 29 Gratt. 347; Glenn v. Blackford, 23 W. Va. 182.

Time to Redeem.—Where a judicial sale of land is made upon a credit, and the title retained as a security, upon a rule against the purchaser to show cause why the land should not be resold for his failure to pay the purchase money before making a decree for the sale, the court should in the decree give a day in which to pay it, and if not paid in that time, the commissioner to sell. Long v. Weller, 29 Gratt. 347; Glenn v. Blackford, 23 W. Va. 182.

At judicial sale title is retained, bonds with personal security are taken, and, as additional security, collaterals are assigned by purchaser to commissioner. It is not error, in such case for the court, without first exhausting the bonds and collaterals, to decree a resale of the land unless within a prescribed period the purchase money in arrears shall be paid; especially where the commissioner has reported that the collaterals can not be made available without a chancery suit. Mosby v. Withers, 80 Va. 82.

(g) Decree for Resale.

In General.—Upon a proceeding by rule against purchaser to show cause why the land might not be resold for the payment of the purchase money, a decree may be made for the sale of the land. Clarkson v. Read, 15 Gratt. 288; Glenn v. Blackford, 23 W. Va. 182.

Jurisdiction to Render Decree.—If in a chancery cause land has been sold, and a sale confirmed, and a rule issued against the purchaser to show why the land should not be resold, to which rule the purchaser answers, and the evidence to overrule and support his answer is all taken, and the plaintiff in the original cause then dies, and the court, the original cause not having been revived, enters a decree on the proceedings under the rule; held, the court had jurisdiction to render such decree. Crislip v. Cain, 19 W. Va. 438.

(h) Terms of Resale.

Where judgment debtor bought his own land at sale under decree in creditors' suit against him, and failed to pay the purchase money; held, a resale on terms of one-fourth cash and balance in one, two and three years is not inequitable under Va. Code, § 3397. Dickinson v. Clement, 87 Va. 41, 12 S. E. 105.

c. Original or Supplemental Bill.

(1) Where Legal Title Conveyed and Lien Retained for Purchase Money.

(a) Original Bill.

Sometimes the court confirms the sale and orders the legal title to be conveyed to the purchaser retaining a lien for the residue of the purchase money. Where this is done, and the purchaser fails to pay the purchase money bonds as they fall due. it is the practice to file an original bill to enforce the lien for the purchase money. Glenn v. Blackford, 23 W. Va. 182; Clarkson v. Read, 15 Gratt. 288; Hurt v. Jones, 75 Va. 341.

Where a judicial sale is confirmed. and the court directs the commissioner to convey the land to the purchaser. retaining in the deed a lien for the purchase money, and such conveyance is made, and the purchaser sells the land and conveys it to a third party, and such third party sells and conveys to others, and the purchaser from the commissioner fails to pay the balance of the purchase money, the lien should be enforced by original bill, if the original cause is ended. Glenn v. Blackford, 23 W. Va. 182.

(b) Supplemental Bill.

If the original suit be still pending in court for any purpose, in a case where the legal title has been conveyed to the purchaser, a lien being retained for the purchase money, the same result obtained by filing an original bill, may be obtained by filing a supplemental bill in that case. Glenn v. Blackford, 23 W. Va. 182.

Where a judicial sale is confirmed, and the court directs the commissioner to convey the land to the purchaser, retaining in the deed a lien for the purchase money, and such conveyance is made, and the purchaser sells the land and conveys it to a third party, and such third party sells and conveys to others, and the purchaser from the commissioner fails to pay the balance of the purchase money, the lien should be enforced, if the original cause is still pending for any purpose, by supplemental bill filed in such cause. Glenn v. Blackford, 23 W. Va. 182.

(c) Nature of Proceeding by Bill.

The proceeding by bill to enforce the payment of the purchase money is substantially a proceeding for the specific performance of a contract. 2 Daniell's Ch. Pr. 1275, 1282; Hurt v. Jones, 75 Va. 341; Clarkson v. Read, 15 Gratt. 288.

(d) Necessary Parties Defendant.

When an original bill is filed to enforce the lien for the purchase money, it is of course necessary to make defendants all the parties interested in that proceeding, the purchaser and his immediate and remote vendees, if he has sold the land or any part thereof.

Glenn v. Blackford, 23 W. Va. 182; McClintic v. Wise, 25 Gratt. 448.

When a supplemental bill is filed, it is necessary to make defendants thereto, the purchaser and his vendees, if any. Glenn v. Blackford, 23 W. Va. 182.

(e) Pleading.

aa. In General.

Upon proceedings by original or supplemental bill, the equities between the parties are discussed and considered upon regular and formal pleadings. Clarkson v. Read, 15 Gratt. 288.

bb. Answer.

If the purchaser has any cause to resist the demand for the payment of the purchase money, he can set it forth in an answer to the bill. Clarkson v. Read, 15 Gratt. 288.

(f) Evidence.

If in his answer to the bill, a purchaser avers any matter why there should be no resale of the property, the court should allow him an opportunity to bring forward his proofs. Clarkson v. Read, 15 Gratt. 288.

(g) Decree for Sale.

The equities being settled between the purchaser and his vendees, if he had sold the land or any part thereof, the land will be decreed to be sold according to the equities between the parties. Glenn v. Blackford, 23 W. Va. 182; McClintic v. Wise, 25 Gratt. 448.

(h) Conveyance of Legal Title to Purchaser.

In a proceeding by an original bill to enforce the lien for the purchase money, after sale under decree in such proceeding, the court can then order the legal title to be made to the purchaser at said sale. Glenn v. Blackford, 23 W. Va. 182.

(2) Where Legal Title Retained as Security.

Where the court, in confirming a judicial sale, retains the legal title as security, no original or supplemental bill is necessary, the proceeding in such case being by rule. Glenn *v.* Blackford, 23 W. Va. 182. See ante, "Rule against Purchaser to Show Cause Why Land Shall Not Be Resold," XIV, C, 3, b.

4. Action to Enforce Payment of Purchase Money Bonds.

In General.—Upon failure of the purchaser to complete his contract, suit may be brought upon the purchase money bonds to enforce payment thereof. Blair *v.* Core, 29 W. Va. 477, 2 S. E. 326; Blair *v.* Core, 20 W. Va. 265; Davis *v.* Snead, 33 Gratt. 705.

The court as vendor has the right to sue upon the purchase money bond, and thus compel the purchaser to complete his purchase. Clarkson *v.* Read, 15 Gratt. 288.

The proper course is to order the collection of the bonds by suit, if not paid without. Gross *v.* Pearcy, 2 Pat. & H. 483.

Action on Bond Not Exclusive of Other Remedies.—By the execution of bonds the purchaser has placed it in the power of the court to cause the collection of the purchase money by a suit upon the bonds at law. The jurisdiction of a court of law in respect to the bond is not in exclusion of the jurisdiction of a court of equity to compel a complete performance of the contract in all of its parts. The bond is but an additional security for the purchase money; and the power of the court to sue on the bond is in aid of and not in conflict with its other powers to compel the execution of the contract. Such, clearly, is the law as between two parties occupying strictly the relations to each other of vendor and vendee, and there is no reason why the same rule should not hold between the court and the purchaser at a judicial sale. Clarkson *v.* Read, 15 Gratt. 288.

Averments in Bill.—A special commissioner appointed to make sale of lands by a decree, who makes the sale and takes bonds payable to himself as commissioner, has no authority to collect or sue on said bonds unless specially appointed, or directed, by the court to do so. And when he is so authorized and brings a suit to enforce the payment of such bonds he must aver in his bill that he has been so appointed and authorized to sue and collect said bonds. If he fails to make such averment and show such right to sue, his bill will be dismissed on demurrer. Clarke *v.* Shanklin, 24 W. Va. 30; Blair *v.* Core, 20 W. Va. 265; Blair *v.* Core, 29 W. Va. 477, 2 S. E. 326.

Where a commissioner who made sale of land under a decree of the court brings suit, and avers in his bill that the sale had been confirmed, and that he had been appointed commissioner to collect the sale bonds, and exhibits with his bill a decree, which, by fair and reasonable construction and strong implication, though not in express terms, authorizes him to collect the sale bonds, both the bill and the decree offered to prove its allegations will be treated as sufficient to sustain the suit. Blair *v.* Core, 29 W. Va. 477, 2 S. E. 326.

When the commissioner sues on the bonds given for the purchase money it being necessary for him to aver in his bill his authority to sue or at least, to collect the money, he must exhibit therewith the decree conferring the authority. Where this is not done, the court should sustain a demurrer to the bill. Blair *v.* Core, 20 W. Va. 265.

Action to Enforce Judgment on Bond.—There was a judgment for balance on bonds executed by U. as principal and W. as surety, for price of land purchased by U. at judicial sale. At resale property brought less than judgment. Payments made by U. on bonds and proceeds of resale were applied to the purchase money under the court's supervision, and with U.'s assent. Held, in action to enforce the judgment on land owned by W. at its date, purchasers from W., with notice of the judgment, could not claim that said payments and proceeds were misapplied. Wells v. Hughes, 89 Va. 543, 16 S. E. 689.

XV. Purchasers—Title, Rights and Liabilities.

A. STATUS OF PURCHASER.

1. Upon Submission to Jurisdiction.

By buying at a judicial sale the purchaser selects his forum, comes into the case and submits himself to the court as to all questions concerning the sale and his purchase. Hickson v. Rucker, 77 Va. 135.

He becomes a party to the suit from the time of his purchase, and subjects himself to the orders of the court in all subsequent proceedings connected with the sale, or relating to him in the character of purchaser. Haymond v. Camden, 22 W. Va. 180; Kable v. Mitchell, 9 W. Va. 492, 507; State v. Irwin, 51 W. Va. 192, 41 S. E. 124; Marling v. Robrecht, 13 W. Va. 440; Hughes v. Hamilton, 19 W. Va. 366; Tally v. Starke, 6 Gratt. 339; Curtis v. Thompson, 29 Gratt. 474; Berlin v. Melhorn, 75 Va. 636, 639; Hickson v. Rucker, 77 Va. 135; Crawford v. Weller, 23 Gratt. 835; Hudgins v. Marchant, 28 Gratt. 177; Clarkson v. Read, 15 Gratt. 288; Williams v. Blakey, 76 Va. 254.

Such purchaser seems to be universally regarded as a party to the suit, and being such, is liable to be bound both by the terms of the decree under which he purchased, and by the subsequent decree of confirmation, or other orders touching the disposition of the property, or the purchaser's liability for the purchase money. Turnbull v. Mann, 99 Va. 41, 37 S. E. 288.

He, in like manner, acquires rights in regard to the subject matter of litigation which the court is bound to respect. Haymond v. Camden, 22 W. Va. 180; Kable v. Mitchell, 9 W. Va. 492, 507.

A purchaser at a judicial sale becomes a quasi party to the suit. Shirley v. Rice, 79 Va. 442; Turnbull v. Mann, 99 Va. 41, 37 S. E. 288.

When a person purchases at a judicial sale, he thereby becomes in a certain sense a party to the cause, and submits himself to the jurisdiction of the court. Christian v. Cabell, 22 Gratt. 82.

A purchaser is so far a party to the suit that he may appeal from an order confirming or refusing to confirm the commissioner's sale. Todd v. Gallego Mills Mfg. Co., 84 Va. 586, 5 S. E. 676; Ewald v. Crockett, 85 Va. 299, 7 S. E. 386; Turnbull v. Mann, 99 Va. 41, 37 S. E. 288.

He is obliged to pay his purchase money as the court directs, and will be protected in so doing. Turnbull v. Mann, 99 Va. 41, 37 S. E. 288.

Sale of Forfeited Land.—A person who buys the title of the state to forfeited lands at a judicial sale, is bound by the final decrees entered in the suit in which such sale is had, prior to the confirmation thereof, as though he were a party to such suit. State v. Irwin, 51 W. Va. 192, 41 S. E. 124. See the title TAXATION.

2. As Trustee.

See generally, the title TRUSTS AND TRUSTEES.

One who buys at a judicial sale under oral agreement for the benefit of another will be held a trustee. The fact that it is a judicial sale makes no difference. Currence v. Ward, 43 W. Va. 367, 27 S. E. 329.

3. As Receiver.

See generally, the title RECEIVERS.

Where, after an appeal allowed, commissioners sold the lands decreed to be sold, and the sale never was confirmed, but the decree afterwards annulled, and the so-called purchasers took possession, appropriated the profits, claimed to be treated as receivers and allowed the commissions paid in cash and compensation for expenses and services in managing the lands, it was held, that they were mere intruders, with no claim to compensation in any way, but were accountable for a fair rental. Strayer v. Long, 83 Va. 715, 3 S. E. 372.

B. PERFECTING TITLE.

Courts of equity have at least as large a discretion in giving time to perfect the title in cases of sales under their decrees, as in cases of purchasers by private contract. Daniel v. Leitch, 13 Gratt. 195; Ammons v. Ammons, 50 W. Va. 390, 40 S. E. 490; Cralle v. Meem, 8 Gratt. 496.

C. TITLE, RIGHTS AND INTERESTS CONVEYED.

1. General Rule.

The purchaser at a judicial sale perfectly understands that the court does not undertake to convey a good title, and that it is his duty to make all necessary inquiry in regard to the estate he is purchasing. Christian v. Cabell, 22 Gratt. 82.

He can only expect to get the special title which was in contemplation of the parties at the time. Goddin v. Vaughn, 14 Gratt. 102.

It is a well-established principle that, in adversary proceedings in a court of equity for the sale of land, nothing but the title which is vested in the parties to the proceedings can be sold, and a deed made under a decree in such proceedings carries with it only the title of the parties to the suit. Adams v. Alkire, 20 W. Va. 480.

The court undertakes to sell only the title, such as it is, of the parties to the suit, and it is the duty of the purchaser to ascertain for himself whether the title of these parties may not be impeached or superseded by some other and paramount title; and if he have just grounds of objection for want or defect of title, he should present them to the court before the confirmation of the report of sale. Ordinarily, objections after confirmation comes too late. Long v.

Weller, 29 Gratt. 347; Young v. McClung, 9 Gratt. 336, 358; Threlkelds v. Campbell, 2 Gratt. 198; Daniel v. Leitch, 13 Gratt. 195, 212, 213; Watson v. Hoy, 28 Gratt. 698.

"The title to the easement is necessarily connected with the title to the land to which it is appurtenant; and whatever the purchasers believed, they must be taken to know that they could acquire by their purchase only the title that the court sold, which was the title, whatever it might be, of the parties to the suit. They purchased at their own risk, and can not be heard to object for want or defect of title, at least after confirmation of the sale." Long v. Weller, 29 Gratt. 347.

2. Warranties.

See generally, the title WARRANTY.

The rule seems well settled that a purchaser at a judicial sale is not entitled to demand covenants of general warranty. Goddin v. Vaughn, 14 Gratt. 102; Ware v. Starkey, 80 Va. 191.

The court never undertakes, to warrant title to land sold under its decrees. The court sells only such title as is lodged in it by operation of law, and only warrants specially. Ware v. Starkey, 80 Va. 191.

A sale by a commissioner is without warranty. Fleming v. Holt, 12 W. Va. 143; Atkinson v. Washington, etc., College, 54 W. Va. 32, 46 S. E. 253.

3. Seisin of Purchaser.

See generally, the titles CURTESY, vol. 4, p. 148; DOWER, vol. 4, p. 782.

By virtue of a decree of confirmation of a judicial sale of vacant and unoccupied lots or lands, the purchaser has, by construction of law, such possession as amounts to such seisin in fact as will entitle the husband of such purchaser to curtesy in such lots or land. Seim v. O'Grady, 42 W. Va. 77, 24 S. E. 994.

4. Investigation of Title after Property Cried Off.

A person to whom, at a commissioners' sale, property is cried off, is not entitled to any time to investigate the title before complying with the terms. Hildreth *v.* Turner, 89 Va. 858, 17 S. E. 471.

And in the case of Hildreth *v.* Turner, 89 Va. 858, 17 S. E. 471, it was held, in the particular case, that if the person, so claiming, did have such rights, ample time had elapsed in which to assert.

The proper time for a purchaser to inquire into the title and satisfy himself about it, is while the contract of sale remains executory. A purchaser at a judicial sale, ought to make such inquiry before the confirmation of the sale by the court; and a purchaser at a private sale, ought to make it before he receives possession of the property and a deed from the vendor. In neither case will the purchaser be compelled to accept a bad or doubtful title, unless he has agreed to do so. But having accepted the title, and received the deed, he will generally have to look only to the covenants contained in the deed, for his indemnity and protection against any defects which may be in the title. Faulkner *v.* Davis, 18 Gratt. 651.

5. Irregularities in Complying with Terms as Affecting.

Failure of a purchaser to take a deed from the commissioner and to give a trust deed for deferred payments, is irregular, but not such as to vitiate his title. Whitlock *v.* Johnson, 87 Va. 323, 12 S. E. 614.

6. Regularity of Proceedings as Affecting.

When the legal title is transferred by judicial proceedings, those proceedings must be regular, and free from fraud. If fraudulent they have no operation, and a deed under them, fraudulently made, or for property made at a fraudulent sale, conveys nothing, and will be treated in every court where this can be shown, as a nullity. This is the plain result of all the author-ities. Underwood *v.* McVeigh, 23 Gratt. 409.

7. Confirmation as Affecting Title.

See ante, "Confirmation," IX.

8. Mill on Land.

In a suit to sell land for its purchase money, on which is located a sawmill that is part of the freehold, and the decree to sell provides that the sale shall not include the mill, a sale of the land does not pass the mill to the purchaser. First Nat. Bank *v.* Hyer, 46 W. Va. 13, 32 S. E. 1000.

9. Time of Offering Objections.

General Rule.—An objection to the title of land by a purchaser at a judicial sale, must be made before the sale is confirmed by the court. Ordinarily an objection after confirmation comes too late. Long *v.* Weller, 29 Gratt. 347; Hickson *v.* Rucker, 77 Va. 135, 139; Redd *v.* Dyer, 83 Va. 331, 2 S. E. 283; Watson *v.* Hoy, 28 Gratt. 698; Young *v.* McClung, 9 Gratt. 336; Daniel *v.* Leitch, 13 Gratt. 195; Threlkelds *v.* Campbell, 2 Gratt. 198.

The English rule is different. The reason of the difference would seem to be, that in England the courts undertake to sell a good title, while in Virginia they sell such title only as the parties to the suit have. Hence, in such cases here the rule of caveat emptor applies. But even here the rule is subject to exceptions. Watson *v.* Hoy, 28 Gratt. 698. "There are certainly some defects," says Judge Moncure, in Daniel *v.* Leitch, 13 Gratt. 195, "to which objection may be made by a purchaser even after confirmation, here as well as in England—such, for example, as a defect arising from a want of jurisdiction, or want of parties, which would prevent a purchaser from getting the title intended to be sold and conveyed to him."

The title to an easement on the land to which it is appurtenant is necessarily connected with the title to the land, and an objection referring to such easement must be governed by the same rules. Long *v.* Weller, 29 Gratt. 347.

An objection of the kind should be made to the court as soon as it is discovered by the purchaser. Long *v.* Weller, 29 Gratt. 347.

Thus an objection by a purchaser, after the sale has been confirmed, that owing to his misinformation as to the boundaries of the land, he does not get certain water privileges which he would have had if he had been correctly informed as to the said boundaries, can only be sustained on the ground of fraud or mistake; and, if mistake is relied on, it must be the mistake of both parties. Long *v.* Weller, 29 Gratt. 347.

After-Discovered Fraud or Mistake. —See generally, the titles FRAUD AND DECEIT, vol. 6, p. 448; MISTAKE AND ACCIDENT.

This rule does not apply to the equity of a purchaser arising from after-discovered mistake, fraud, or from other like manner. Watson *v.* Hoy, 28 Gratt. 698; Long *v.* Weller, 29 Gratt. 347. See also, Redd *v.* Dyer, 83 Va. 331, 2 S. E. 283.

10. Statute of Limitations as Affecting Rights.

See generally, the titles LACHES; LIMITATION OF ACTIONS.

Where a sale of land under decree is made and confirmed, the purchase money paid, but no deed executed, and the former owner's heirs remain in possession, the statute of limitations does not begin to run against the purchaser until the heirs make distinct disavowal of his title, and their assertion of adverse claim is brought home to him. Whitlock *v.* Johnson, 87 Va. 323, 12 S. E. 614; Creekmur *v.* Creekmur, 75 Va. 430, 436.

11. Estoppel of Owner to Deny Title.

A person who causes his land to be sold for some purpose of his own, under a judicial proceeding which turns out to be void, and receives and retains the proceeds of sale, can not aft-

erwards be heard to question its validity. He has made his election.· If such person afterwards stands by and sees the purchaser expend large sums in developing oil on the property, he may not afterwards set up such defect in the purchaser's title; he is estopped. Williamson *v.* Jones, 39 W. Va. 231, 19 S. E. 436. See also, Wandling *v.* Straw, 25 W. Va. 692.

12. Collateral Impeachment.

See post, "Collateral Impeachment," XVI.

D. INNOCENT OR BONA FIDE PURCHASERS PROTECTED.

1. General Consideration.

A bona fide purchaser for value and without notice, is a great favorite with a court of equity, and that court will not disarm such a purchaser of a legal advantage. Lamar *v.* Hale, 79 Va. 147; Woods *v.* Krebbs, 30 Gratt. 708, 715; Zollman *v.* Moore, 21 Gratt. 313.

Purchasers can not be held responsible for the errors of the court, nor can they be required to look beyond the proceedings in the cause to find authority for the court to act. If it were otherwise, such sales would be snares for honest men. Marrow *v.* Brinkley, 85 Va. 55, 6 S. E. 605; Hess *v.* Rader, 26 Gratt. 746; Wilcher *v.* Robertson, 78 Va. 602, 616.

The decision of the courts, as a system of equity, founded upon an enlightened public policy to give sanction to judicial sales, and security and repose to judicial titles, establish the rule that a purchaser at a judicial sale, without notice, under proceedings regular upon the face of the record of a court of competent jurisdiction will be protected as against the mere errors of the court, and secret vices in the proceedings, which can only be made to appear by the proof of extrinsic facts not appearing on the face of the record. Marrow *v.* Brinkley, 85 Va. 55, 6 S. E. 605.

In Daniel *v.* Leitch, 13 Gratt. 195, 210, Judge Moncure, also speaking for the other judges, said: "The purchaser at a judicial sale will not be affected by error in the decree, such as not giving a day to show cause in cases in which a day ought to be given, or in decreeing a sale of lands to satisfy judgment debts without an account of the personal estate. A fortiori, he will not be affected by any imperfection in the frame of the bill if it contain sufficient matter to show the propriety of the decree." Zirkle v. McCue, 26 Gratt. 517.

"These extracts, and others that might be given, show that while this court has never gone as far as the courts of other states in favor of purchasers at judicial sales, it has, on all occasions, manifested a very strong disinclination to interfere with the rights of such purchasers, unless upon palpable and substantial errors in the proceedings and decrees under which such titles are acquired." Zirkle v. McCue, 26 Gratt. 517.

Thus, to admit a party to a suit, the record of which solemnly vouches him to be such, to recover against a purchaser at a judicial sale made under that record, by swearing that no service was actually made on him and that there was no authorized appearance for him, as in this case, many years after the event, and after the death of the officers of the court and the distinguished and honorable counsel who had knowledge and could prove the facts vouched in the record of the proceedings, would open the door, most invitingly, to perjury, injustice and fraud, destroy all confidence in and efficiency of judicial sales, unsettle titles, and produce untold misery, mischief and confusion throughout the commonwealth. Marrow v. Brinkley, 85 Va. 55, 6 S. E. 605.

But whatever conflict of authority there may be as to how far a bona fide purchaser at a judicial sale will be protected against error in the proceedings, it is well settled, that when the purchaser combines with others to prevent competition, and thus gets the property at a sacrifice, he is not a bona fide purchaser, and he can not hold the property obtained by his own fraud. Kerr on Fraud 224, and cases there cited. The law does not tolerate any influence likely to prevent competition at judicial sales, and it accords to every debtor the chance for a fair sale and full price. Underwood v. McVeigh, 23 Gratt. 409.

Purchasers at a judicial sale should be protected when their conduct is free from fault and above suspicion Klapneck v. Keltz, 50 W. Va. 331, 40 S. E. 570; Frederick v. Cox, 47 W. Va. 14, 34 S. E. 958.

In order that property sold at judicial sales should bring a fair price, it is necessary that the title of purchasers at such sales should be protected. Capehart v. Dowery, 10 W. Va. 130.

Errors in Sale of Infant's Lands.— The errors for which a judicial sale of an infant's land may be set aside must be substantial errors. A fair purchase is not bound to go through all the proceedings and to look into all the circumstances and see that the decree is right in all its parts. He has the right to presume the court has taken the necessary steps to investigate the rights of parties, and upon such investigation has properly decreed a sale. He will not be affected by any imperfection in the frame of the bill if it contain sufficient matter to show the propriety of the decree. The propriety of the sale must be tested, and its validity determined by the circumstances then existing, and the surrounding circumstances. The only matter for inquiry is, Did the court have jurisdiction of the subject matter? Were the proper parties before it? Were the proceedings regular? Was the sale proper under all the circumstances then surrounding the parties? If so, the title of an innocent purchaser is not to be disturbed, because, from subsequent events, the sale has proved unfortunate for the infants. Zirkle v. McCue, 26 Gratt. 517.

Subrogation.—H., of foreign birth, died in 1867, seized and possessed of real estate in R., intestate and without any known heirs. The real estate of which he died seized vested in possession in the state without office found, or other proceedings at law. After the death of H., G. sued his curator, S., for a large debt, alleged to be due from H., and there was a judgment by default. G. then sued S., the curator, in equity, to subject the real estate of which H. died seized for the payment of the judgment. There was a decree for a sale, and a sale in pursuance of the decree, when J. became the purchaser of a part of the property. Held, the estate not having been a party to the suit, the decree and sale are a nullity as to her, and gave J. no title to the property purchased by him. If J. was a bona fide purchaser, he is entitled to be substituted to the rights of the creditor, G.; and upon showing that the claim of G. is just to have the real estate subjected to its payment. Sands v. Lynham, 27 Gratt. 291.

2. What Constitutes a Bona Fide Purchaser.

Purchaser Using Unfair Means.—It has been held, in numerous cases, that a purchaser who used unfair means to prevent competition, can not hold the property. When a purchaser at a judicial sale combines and confederates with the officer and others to conduct the sale as secretly as possible to prevent competition, and represents to the party interested in such sale, that it had been postponed, with intention to deceive such party, to the end that he shall not be present to compete for the purchase of such property at such sale, such party is not a bona fide purchaser, and will not be protected against errors in the proceedings. Underwood v. McVeigh, 23 Gratt. 409.

Vendee of Purchaser under Void Decree.—A purchaser from a purchaser in a decree void for want of jurisdiction is not a bona fide purchaser without notice. He is bound to know the want of jurisdiction in the case. He is bound to know defects in papers showing his claim of title. Waldron v. Harvey, 54 W. Va. 608, 46 S. E. 603; Hoback v. Miller, 44 W. Va. 635, 29 S. E. 1014; Wood v. Krebbs, 30 Gratt. 708; Williamson v. Jones, 43 W. Va. 562, 27 S. E. 411.

3. Sufficiency of Notice to Put Purchaser on Inquiry.

See post, "Rule of Caveat Emptor," XV, E.

However, other persons are entitled to the protection and favor of a court of equity as well as purchasers. Purchasers are bound to use a due degree of caution in making their purchase, or they will not be entitled to protection. Caveat emptor is one of the best-settled maxims of the law, and applies exclusively to a purchaser. He must take care to make due inquiries, or he may not be a bona fide purchaser. He is bound not only by actual, but also by constructive notice. He must look to the title papers under which he buys, and is charged with notice of all the facts appearing upon their face, or to the knowledge of which anything there appearing will conduct him. He has no right to shut his eyes or his ears to the inlet of information, and then say that he is a bona fide purchaser without notice. Lamar v. Hale, 9 Va. 147; Wood v. Krebbs, 30 Gratt. 703, 715.

A purchaser at a judicial sale is conclusively held as having notice of all facts touching the rights of others in the property sold, disclosed by the record of the case. Williamson v. Jones, 43 W. Va. 562, 27 S. E. 411.

A purchaser at a judicial sale of a city lot can not, after his purchase, make the objection that a street encroaches on the lines of the lot, where it appears that before the sale a plat was made of the lot distinctly showing the encroachment, which plat was referred to in the advertisement of the property as being at the auctioneer's room, where it could be seen by any one interested in the sale; and where it further appears that the plat was exhibited at the sale, examined by the bidders, and the encroachment discussed in an open and general way. His ignorance of the facts disclosed by the plat is no excuse. He was put upon inquiry and is chargeable with knowledge of all facts to which this inquiry would have led him, if diligently pursued. In the case at bar there would seem to be no encroachment. Acts, 1883-84, page 494. Carneal v. Lynch, 91 Va. 114, 20 S. E. 959.

Purchasers at judicial sales may well presume that all things in the cause have been rightly conducted; but purchasers in pais are negligent if they fail to examine their chains of title. Effinger v. Hall, 81 Va. 94. Doubted in Williamson v. Jones, 43 W. Va. 562, 27 S. E. 411. See also, to the contrary, Hall v. Hall, 30 W. Va. 779, 5 S. E. 260. And see Harner v. Price, 17 W. Va. 523.

Where Plat Filed.—With the report of a sale was filed a plat of the land sold. Deeds for same, to intermediate purchasers, mentioned that plat. Deed to defendant refers to those deeds. Defendant's agent to examine the title, by the deeds, was referred to the plat and the report of sale, and inspection thereof must have given him notice of the plaintiff's rights therein. Held, that the defendant is affected with constructive notice of the outstanding title of the plaintiff. Whitlock v. Johnson, 87 Va. 323, 12 S. E. 614.

Judgment in Another County.—A purchaser of land under a decree in a county wherein it lies, is not affected by constructive notice of judgment in another county which is not docketed in former county until after sale is confirmed and purchase money paid though title is retained. Logan v. Pannill, 90 Va. 11, 17 S. E. 744.

4. Within Protection of Recording Acts.

Where, prior to 1850, a vendor of real estate took a deed of trust to secure the purchase price, he can not afterwards rely on the implied vendor's lien then recognized, although the deed of trust is void as to subsequent purchasers for want of due registry. This rule applies to judicial sales as well as to sales between private individuals. Hunton v. Wood, 101 Va. 54, 43 S. E. 186.

Purchasers at a judicial sale are entitled to the same protection against an unrecorded deed of trust as a purchaser from a private individual. Hunton v. Wood, 101 Va. 54, 43 S. E. 185.

"A purchaser under a judicial sale, made in behalf of a creditor, holds the rights and occupies the place of the creditor, in a controversy with a purchaser from the debtor under an unrecorded conveyance. The notice of the unrecorded deed which might affect him as a purchaser in ordinary cases, will not affect him, because he occupies the place of the creditor, who was not by the statute affected by notice. If it were otherwise the rights of a creditor would be of no avail." Lomax's Digest, vol. 2, p. 367, 368. Houston v. McCluney, 8 W. Va. 135.

E. RULE OF CAVEAT EMPTOR.

See generally, the title VENDOR AND PURCHASER. And see ante, "Innocent or Bona Fide Purchasers Protected," XV, D.

1. General Doctrine.

There is perhaps no principle in our jurisprudence more firmly established by repeated decisions of the Virginia and West Virginia courts, than that the maxim caveat emptor strictly applies to all judicial sales. Hickson v. Rucker, 77 Va. 135; Watson v. Hoy, 28 Gratt. 698; Boyce v. Strother, 76 Va. 862; Zollman v. Moore, 21 Gratt. 313;

Hoge v. Currin, 3 Gratt. 201; Capehart v. Dowery, 10 W. Va. 130; Young v. McClung, 9 Gratt. 336; Cooper v. Hepburn, 15 G.att. 551; Threlkelds v. Campbell, 2 Gratt. 198; Worsham v. Hardaway, 5 Gratt. 60; Peirce v. Graham, 85 Va. 227, 7 S. E. 189; Lamar v. Hale, 79 Va. 147; Long v. Weller, 29 Gratt. 347; Smith v. Wortham, 82 Va. 937, 1 S. E. 331; Redd v. Dyer, 83 Va. 331, 2 S. E. 283; Flanary v. Kane, 102 Va. 547, 46 S. E. 312; March v. Chambers, 30 Gratt. 299; Wissler v. Craig, 80 Va. 22; Wood v. Krebbs, 30 Gratt. 708; Burwell v. Fauber, 21 Gratt. 446; Holden v. Boggess, 20 W. Va. 62; Williamson v. Jones, 43 W. Va. 562, 27 S. E. 411; Stout v. Philippi Mfg., etc., Co., 41 W. Va. 339, 23 S. E. 571; Shields v. McClung, 6 W. Va. 79.

The purchaser is charged with knowledge of want of authority in the commissioner to convey. He is held to know the contents of the decree under which the sale is made, and to know what property or estate he is to acquire. Thornton v. Fairfax, 29 Gratt. 669; Hess v. Rader, 26 Gratt. 746; Lloyd v. Erwin, 29 Gratt. 598; Calvert v. Ash, 47 W. Va. 480, 35 S. E. 887; Hoback v. Miller, 44 W. Va. 635, 29 S. E. 1014; Williamson v. Jones, 43 W. Va. 563, 27 S. E. 411; First Nat. Bank v. Hyer, 46 W. Va. 13, 32 S. E. 1000.

He is held to perfectly understand that the court does not undertake to convey a good title, and that it is his duty to make all necessary inquiries in regard to the estate he is purchasing. Christian v. Cabell, 22 Gratt. 82.

In Long v. Weller, 29 Gratt. 347, it is said: "The court undertakes to sell only the title, such as it is, of the parties to the suit, and it is the duty of the purchaser to ascertain for himself whether the title of these parties may not be impeached or superseded by some other and paramount title; and if he have just grounds of objection for want or defect of title he should present them to the court before the

confirmation of the report of sale." The court, in that case, referred to numerous cases to the same effect, to which may be added the case of Hickson v. Rucker, 77 Va. 135, 138, and other later cases. Redd v. Dyer, 83 Va. 331, 2 S. E. 283

"Purchasers are bound to use a due degree of caution in making their purchases, or they will not be entitled to protection. Caveat emptor is one of the best-settled maxims of the law, and applies exclusively to a purchaser. He must make due inquiry, or he may not be a bona fide purchaser. He is bound not only by actual but also by constructive notice, which is the same in effect as actual notice." Burwell v. Fauber, 21 Gratt. 446. And in Cardover v. Hood, 17 Wall. 1, it is said: "Means of knowledge, with the duty of using them, are in equity, equivalent to knowledge itself." Wissler v. Craig, 80 Va. 22.

And although after confirmation of the sale he finds that the title he will receive will be worthless, yet he can not be relieved from the payment of the purchase money. Capehart v. Dowery, 10 W. Va. 130; Shields v. McClung, 6 W. Va. 79; Young v. McClung, 9 Gratt. 336; Cooper v. Hepburn, 15 Gratt. 551.

But complete purchasers for value without notice under a decree of a court of competent jurisdiction over the subject matter, with all parties in interest before it, are not responsible for any error in the subsequent proceedings. Crawford v. Weller, 23 Gratt. 835. The purchaser is not bound to look back further than the order of the court. Allan v. Hoffman, 83 Va. 129, 2 S. E. 602.

And the doctrine of caveat emptor is, of course, subject to the qualification that the purchaser at a judicial sale is entitled to relief on the ground of after-discovered mistake of material facts, or fraud. But the mistake must be mutual; for the mistake of one of the parties occasioned by his own culpable negligence does not entitle him to relief as against the other, who is free from negligence. Long v. Weller, 29 Gratt. 347. And it is scarcely necessary to say that where fraud or mistake is relied on by a purchaser, after the sale has been confirmed, it must be clearly and distinctly charged and proved. Redd v. Dyer, 83 Va. 331, 2 S. E. 283; Hord v. Colbert, 28 Gratt. 49; Gregory v. Peoples, 80 Va. 355.

And while it is true that in Virginia the maxim caveat emptor strongly applies, in judicial sales, it only applies as between the purchaser and third persons who are not parties to the suit. Their interests are not affected by any proceedings that may be had, and the purchaser must always incur the risk of losing the estate by some superior title. But the court does undertake to sell the title of the parties to the suit. Whaever that may be, the purchaser acquires it. He must take care that the sale is made in accordance with the decree but he is not bound to see to the proper application of the purchase money; nor is he responsible for any error the court may commit in any of the subsequent proceedings. These are matters over which he has no control, and as to which he can not be heard. He has the right to suppose that the court, under whose sanction the sale is made, will distribute the funds according to the respective interests of those entitled; and if an error is committed in this respect the remedy is not against him; but by an appeal to a higher court to correct the distribution. Zollman v. Moore, 21 Gratt. 313.

2. Notice May Be Actual or Constructive of Charges on Property.

Notice to affect purchasers for value with charges on property purchased, may be actual or constructive. Whatever suffices to put purchaser on an inquiry which should lead to discovery of charge, is constructive notice. Lamar v. Hale, 79 Va. 147; Wood v. Krebbs, 30 Gratt. 708, 715.

Under doctrine of caveat emptor purchasers are as much affected by implied as by express charges on the purchased property. Lamar v. Hale, 79 Va. 147.

F. WHEN POSSESSION OF PURCHASER ADVERSE.

See the title ADVERSE POSSESSION, vol. 1, pp. 199, 215.

The possession of a purchaser at a judicial sale is adverse to the judgment debtor. And this is true though the sale be void. Waldron v. Harvey, 54 W. Va. 608, 46 S. E. 603.

G. SALES UNDER VOID OR VOIDABLE JUDGMENTS AND DECREES.

1. Void Judgment or Decrees.

a. General Rule.

A decree being void, not merely voidable, a sale under it, and a title vested under it, fall with the decree. Hoback v. Miller, 44 W. Va. 635, 29 S. E. 1014; Hall v. Hall, 12 W. Va. 1; Haymond v. Camden, 22 W. Va. 180; Grinnan v. Edwards, 21 W. Va. 347.

The West Virginia Code, ch. 132, § 8, does not protect a sale under a totally void decree. Title falls with its vacation. The title was never for a moment good; never existed. Waldron v. Harvey, 54 W. Va. 608, 46 S. E. 603.

A sale, under a decree of property which it does not authorize to be·sold, or excepts from sale, passes no title to such property, and is void. First Nat. Bank v. Hyer, 46 W. Va. 13, 32 S. E. 1000.

b. Relief Afforded.

Upon the disaffirmance of a void judicial sale the purchaser should be placed in statu quo. To do this where no improvements have been put on the property, he must receive back his purchase money with interest, and be charged with the reasonable rents and profits of the property while in his possession less the taxes paid by him. Charleston, L., etc., Co. v. Brockmeyer, 23 W. Va. 635.

Right of Subrogation.—See generally, the title SUBROGATION.

A purchaser of land under a void decree, whose money has been applied upon liens on the land valid against the owner of the land, will be entitled to charge such money upon such land by substitution to the right of the creditor, upon disaffirmance of the sale. Hull v. Hull, 35 W. Va. 155, 13 S. E. 49.

"The position of appellant's counsel, that in Haymond v. Camden [22 W. Va. 180] substitution was allowed only because Camden and Andrews asked that the debt might be ascertained, is untenable. The court gave that as a reason why though the proceeding was void for want of jurisdiction as to them, substitution could be made in that proceeding; holding that they thereby waived objection to jurisdiction, save in those respects they excepted to it and submitted to the jurisdiction. The court, however, held the general proposition in a separate point that a purchaser under a void decree was entitled to be substituted to the debts his money pays. Principles of justice demand this, and courts of equity have raised up this principle, a being of their creation, called 'substitution,' unknown to common-law forums, to accomplish the ends of justice; and I know of no more signal instance to exemplify the disposition, as well as the power, of equity to adopt means to accomplish right, than this of substitution, accorded purchasers under void proceedings, whose money has gone to satisfy liens good against the debtor." Hull v. Hull, 35 W. Va. 155, 13 S. E. 49.

Nature of Proceeding to Obtain Relief.—Such purchaser may maintain a bill to enforce such right, and as incident to his relief make his bill a creditor's bill. Hull v. Hull, 35 W. Va. 155, 13 S. E. 49.

2. Voidable Judgments or Decrees.
a. Rule in the Absence of Statute.

Most of the courts elsewhere than in this jurisdiction have held that an innocent purchaser's title does not fall with the reversal of the decree of sale. These cases assert the doctrine that a right acquired under a judicial sale while the judgment or decree is enforced will be protected, notwithstanding its reversal afterwards; that it is sufficient for the buyer to know that the court had jurisdiction; and that he had nothing to do with the court's errors. But the Virginia courts hold otherwise, and refuse to recognize this doctrine. While the decisions are not settled, the leaning has been strongly against the doctrine. Zirkle v. McCue, 26 Gratt. 517, 528; White v. Jones, 1 Wash. 116; Wilson v. Stevenson, 2 Call 213; Rucker v. Harrison, 6 Munf. 181; Newcomb v. Drummond, 4 Leigh 57; Spencer v. Pilcher, 10 Leigh 490; Jones v. Tatum, 19 Gratt. 720; Hudgins v. Marchant, 28 Gratt. 177; Hull v. Hull, 26 W. Va. 1; Underwood v. Pack, 23 W. Va. 704; Newcomb v. Brooks, 16 W. Va. 32, 77; Turk v. Skiles, 38 W. Va. 404, 18 S. E. 561, 563; Capehart v. Dowery, 10 W. Va. 130, 142; Pappenheimer v. Roberts, 24 W. Va. 702, 712; McNeel v. Auldridge, 25 W. Va. 113, 118; Frederick v. Cox, 47 W. Va. 14, 34 S. E. 958; Durrett v. Davis, 24 Gratt. 302, 317; Daniel v. Leitch, 13 Gratt. 195; Cocke v. Gilpin, 1 Rob. 20; Parker v. McCoy, 10 Gratt. 594; Dunfee v. Childs, 45 W. Va. 155, 30 S. E. 102; Ammons v. Ammons, 50 W. Va. 390, 40 S. E. 490.

b. Under Statutory Provisions.
(1) Statement of Provisions.

Va. Code (1904), § 3425.—If a sale of property be made under a decree or order of the court, after six months from the date thereof, and such sale be confirmed, though such decree or order be afterwards reversed or set aside, the title of the purchaser at such sale shall be affected thereby; but there may be restitution of the proceeds of sale to those entitled. Va. Code, 1904, § 3425; Va. Code, 1860, ch. 178, § 8; Va. Code, 1873, ch. 174, § 11; Whitehead v. Bradley, 87 Va. 676, 13 S. E.

195; Peirce *v.* Graham, 85 Va. 227, 7 S.
E. 189; Frazier *v.* Frazier, 77 Va. 775;
Quesenberry *v.* Barbour, 31 Gratt. 491;
Cooper *v.* Hepburn, 15 Gratt. 551;
Dixon *v.* McCue, 21 Gratt. 373; Lancaster *v.* Barton, 92 Va. 615, 24 S. E.
251; Garland *v.* Pamplin, 32 Gratt. 305;
Lloyd *v.* Erwin, 29 Gratt. 598; Taylor
v. Cooper, 10 Leigh 317; Marling *v.*
Robrecht, 13 W. Va. 440.

W. Va. Code (1899), Ch. 132, § 8.—
If a sale of property be made under a
decree or order of a court, and such
sale be confirmed, though such decree
or order be afterwards reversed or set
aside, the title of the purchaser at
such sale shall not be affected thereby;
but there may be restitution of the proceeds of sale to those entitled. W. Va.
Code, 1899, ch. 132, § 8. Waldron *v.*
Harvey, 54 W. Va. 608, 46 S. E. 603;
Stewart *v.* Tennant, 52 W. Va. 559, 44
S. E. 223; Klapneck *v.* Keltz, 50 W. Va.
331, 40 S. E. 570; Ammons *v.* Ammons,
50 W. Va. 390, 40 S. E. 490; Martin *v.*
Smith, 25 W. Va. 579; Dunfee *v.* Childs,
45 W. Va. 155, 30 S. E. 102; Sinnett *v.*
Cralle, 4 W. Va. 600; Calvert *v.* Ash,
47 W. Va. 480, 35 S. E. 887; Underwood *v.* Pack, 23 W. Va. 704; Pappenheimer *v.* Roberts, 24 W. Va. 702, 712;
Frederick *v.* Cox, 47 W. Va. 14, 34 S.
E. 958; Capehart *v.* Dowery, 10 W. Va.
130; Turk *v.* Skiles, 38 W. Va. 404, 18
S. E. 561; Hoback *v.* Miller, 44 W. Va.
635, 29 S. E. 1014; Peck *v.* Chambers,
44 W. Va. 270, 28 S. E. 706; Hull *v.*
Hull, 26 W. Va. 1; Park *v.* Petroleum
Co., 25 W. Va. 108; Beard *v.* Arbuckle,
19 W. Va. 135; Estill *v.* McClintick, 11
W. Va. 399; Tracey *v.* Shumate, 22 W.
Va. 474; Hughes *v.* Hamilton, 19 W.
Va. 366; Neely *v.* Jones, 16 W. Va. 625;
Newcomb *v.* Brooks, 16 W. Va. 32, 76;
Marling *v.* Robrecht, 13 W. Va. 440;
Hitchcox *v.* Hitchcox, 39 W. Va. 607,
20 S. E. 595; Cooper *v.* Hepburn, 15
Gratt. 551, 569; Buchanan *v.* Clark, 10
Gratt. 164.

(2) Scope and General Application.
(a) General Consideration.
While the courts of Virginia and

West Virginia have never gone as far
as the courts of other states in favor
of purchasers at judicial sales, they
have on all occasions, manifested a
very strong disinclination to interfere
with the rights of such purchasers, unless upon palpable and substantial errors in the proceedings and decrees
under which such titles are acquired.
Hull *v.* Hull, 26 W. Va. 1; Zirkle *v.*
McCue, 26 Gratt. 517, 529.

Jurisdiction Essential.—All the decisions agree, that in order to protect
a purchaser at a judicial sale, which
has been confirmed, the court making
the decree of sale must have competent
jurisdiction not only over the parties
whose lands are to be sold but also
over the subject matter; that is, shall
have power to render a decree of sale.
Hull *v.* Hull, 26 W. Va. 1.

**(b) Sale and Confirmation Free from
Fraud.**
Of course it must be understood that
the decree of sale, the sale itself, and
the confirmation of the sale are free
from fraud. Underwood *v.* Pack, 23
W. Va. 704; Capehart *v.* Dowery, 10
W. Va. 130.

**(c) Confined to Sales Made under
Previous Order of Court.**
Section 8, ch. 132, of the West Virginia Code, is confined to sales made
under a previous order of the court.
Hence, if without previous authority a
commissioner sells a particular tract
of land, and the sale is confirmed without exception, the court should permit
any party interested to file his petition for a rehearing of the decree confirming the sale; and after the purchaser has been summoned to answer
upon the petition, and it has been heard
upon its merits, the court should set
aside such decree and sale or refuse
to do so, as on its merits justice to the
parties requires. If set aside, the purchaser at such sale can not have his
purchaser protected against further disturbance after confirmation under the
provisions of § 8. ch. 132 of the Code.

Marling v. Robrecht, 13 W. Va. 440; Estill v. McClintic, 11 W. Va. 399.

Therefore, a purchaser at a sale made without the authority of the court, although such sale be subsequently confirmed, can not have his purchase protected against future disturbance after confirmation by the provisions of the West Virginia Code, ch. 132, § 8. Estill v. McClintic, 11 W. Va. 399.

(d) Does Not Refer to Order Confirming Sale.

The language of the statute does not refer to the order made confirming the sale, but to the decree or order under which the sale was made, and the purchaser can not be protected by it in such case. Sinnett v. Cralle, 6 W. Va. 600.

(e) Purchasers Protected.
aa. Strangers to Suit.

The reversal of a decree under which land is sold will not affect the title of the purchaser, if he is not a party to the suit. Dunfee v. Childs, 45 W. Va. 155, 30 S. E. 102.

The reversal of a decree of sale ever so erroneous can not affect the title of purchasers at a judicial sale, strangers to the suit. Klapneck v. Keltz, 50 W. Va. 331, 40 S. E. 570.

bb. Party to Suit.
(aa) Without Interest.

If the purchaser is a party, but has no interest in the debt or cause for which the land is sold, it seems that his title will not be affected by a reversal of the decree. Dunfee v. Childs, 45 W. Va. 155, 30 S. E. 102; Stewart v. Tenant, 52 W. Va. 559, 44 S. E. 223; Martin v. Smith, 25 W. Va. 579; Dunfee v. Childs, 45 W. Va. 155, 30 S. E. 102; Buchanan v. Clark, 10 Gratt. 164.

(bb) Interested in Cause.

But, if the purchaser is a party with interest in the debt or cause for which the land is sold, his title will fall with a reversal of the decree. Dunfee v. Childs, 45 W. Va. 155, 30 S. E. 102.

cc. When Fact of Being a Party Immaterial.

Error in Decree.—If a decree confirming a sale be reversed for error in it, the purchaser's title falls whether he be a party or not. Dunfee v. Childs, 45 W. Va. 155, 30 S. E. 102.

(f) Effect of Failure to Make Proper Parties.

See generally, the title PARTIES.

aa. In General.

The purchaser at a judicial sale can get no title, unless the parties interested in the land so sold are before the court. Underwood v. Underwood, 22 W. Va. 303. Where necessary parties, having title, are not before the court, the purchaser's title falls with the reversal of the decree of sale. Dunfee v. Childs, 45 W. Va. 155, 30 S. E. 102; Underwood v. Pack, 23 W. Va. 704; Peck v. Chambers, 44 W. Va. 270, 28 S. E. 706; Turk v. Skiles, 38 W. Va. 404, 18 S. E. 561; Newcomb v. Brooks, 16 W. Va. 32; Calvert v. Ash, 47 W. Va. 480, 35 S. E. 887; Hull v. Hull, 26 W. Va. 1; Pappenheimer v. Roberts, 24 W. Va. 702, 712; Capehart v. Dowery, 10 W. Va. 130.

It is the business of a purchaser at a judicial sale to see, that all the persons, who are necessary to convey the title, are before the court, and that the sale is made according to the decree. Holden v. Boggess, 20 W. Va. 62; Daniel v. Leitch, 13 Gratt. 195.

This is no hardship on the purchaser; for by examining the records of the suit he can ascertain whether necessary parties are plaintiffs or defendants to such suit. Neither is it any hardship upon the creditor; for he is in law and duty bound, before he can subject the land of his debtor to the payment of his debt, to make those interested in the land parties to the suit. Underwood v. Pack, 23 W. Va. 704.

bb. Formal Defendants.

If the persons whom it was necessary to make formal defendants to the suit, were not parties either formally or informally, and were not before the court, the purchaser would not be protected in his purchase under § 8, ch. 132. Underwood *v.* Pack, 23 W. Va. 704.

cc. Owner of Property.

There is no doubt that a purchaser could get no title and would not be protected by § 8, ch. 132, if the owner of the property was not before the court. Underwood *v.* Pack, 23 W. Va. 704.

dd. Lienors.

It is also clear, that the purchaser would not be protected under § 8, ch. 132, if the parties, who, the record of the suit shows, were necessary, being interested in such property by having liens thereon, were not before the court. Underwood *v.* Pack, 23 W. Va. 704; Turk *v.* Skiles, 38 W. Va. 404, 18 S. E. 561; Calvert *v.* Ash, 47 W. Va. 480, 35 S. E. 887.

ee. Trustees.

So when a trustee holding the legal title to the land is not a party, a purchaser at a judicial sale is not protected upon reversal of the decree under § 8, ch. 132, of the Code. Underwood *v.* Pack, 23 W. Va. 704; Turk *v.* Skiles, 38 W. Va. 404, 18 S. E. 561.

ff. Reversioners and Remaindermen.

Owners of vested estates in reversion and remainder, whether by legal or equitable title, are indispensible parties to a chancery suit to sell the fee; and the presence as parties of a tenant for life; or of the trustee holding for them, does not make them parties by representation, and a sale under the decree will not affect or pass their right in the land. Williamson *v.* Jones, 43 W. Va. 562, 27 S. E. 411.

(g) Where Object of Proceedings to Compel Compliance with Contract.

The statute does not apply where the object of the proceeding is, not to set aside the decree of sale, or the sales made under it, but to compel purchasers by the process of the court to comply with their respective contracts. Thus, the purchasers being in default, they were compellable to complete their respective purchases by a rule upon each to show the cause why the property should not be resold. And in such case, when a resale is ordered, the former sale is not set aside, but the property is sold as the property of the purchasers. Whitehead *v.* Bradley, 8 Va. 677, 13 S. E. 195.

(h) Exceptions to Facts Negativing Confirmation.

If there were reasons why the sale should not be confirmed, and exceptions made to the report of sale and the confirmation thereof, and these reasons show that the sale was improper and should not be confirmed, then the title of the purchasers would be affected by these facts. Sinnett *v.* Cralle, 4 W. Va. 600, 603.

Sale Confirmed without Report or Objection to Confirmation.—But if the sale is confirmed without exception to the report, or objection to its confirmation, then such title as the purchaser acquired by the sale, is not affected by reversal or setting aside of the order or decree under which the sale was made. Sinnett *v.* Cralle, 4 W. Va. 600, 603; Capehart *v.* Dowery, 10 W. Va. 130.

Such sale is, of course, in a case where the parties interested in the property are before the court, and the decree of sale, the sale itself and the confirmation of the sale are free from fraud. Fraud vitiates everything. Capehart *v.* Dowery, 10 W. Va. 130.

(i) Sale of Infants' Lands.

Section 3425 of the Code, with reference to judicial sales made after six months from the date of the decree therefor, and which have been confirmed, applies to sales of lands of infants made in suits properly brought for that purpose. Lancaster *v.* Barton, 92 Va. 615, 24 S. E. 251; Quesenberry *v.* Barbour, 31 Gratt. 491; Cooper *v.* Hepburn, 15 Gratt. 551.

There is no decision of the supreme court of West Virginia holding that § 8, ch. 132, of the Code of 1899, applies to the sale of infants' lands. In Ammons v. Ammons, 50 W. Va. 390, 40 S. E. 490, the court says: "It can not be doubted that said section was intended so to apply. See Rev. Rep. 1849, p. 878, note. The revivors, after stating that it had been decided that the title of a purchaser at judicial sale might be overthrown by subsequent proceedings in a suit in which he was not a party, after twenty years or more had elapsed, and that where infants were in the case his title might be impeached after a greater length of time, say: 'We think this evil ought to be guarded against. If it be deemed proper, it may be required that when the lands of infants are sold the court shall require bonds to refund, in case the decree of sale should be reversed or set aside on rehearing or review.'"

(j) Lapse of Time from Date of Decree.

The Virginia statute makes provision for cases where there is a sale of property under a decree or order of the court after six months from the date thereof. Va. Code, 1860, ch. 178, § 8; Va. Code, 1873, ch. 174, § 11; Va. Code, 1904, § 3524.

If the sale has been made under a decree, and after six months from the date of the decree, and such sale has been confirmed, the rights of the parties are fixed by the statute. Garland v. Pamplin, 32 Gratt. 305.

Section 8 of ch. 175 of the Code of Virginia, 1860, was in force in West Virginia until the Code of 1868 took effect, consequently the provisions of the Virginia Code that "after six months from the date thereof" was at one time in force in this state, though it is now omitted in § 8, ch. 132, W. Va. Code, 1899-1906. Marling v. Robrecht, 13 W. Va. 440.

Computation of Time.—Under the statute (Va. Code, 1904, § 3425) forbidding a judicial sale to be set aside when made more than six months after the date of the decree of sale, that period must be computed from the date the decree becomes operative, where a day of redemption is given, and not from the date of decree. Frazier v. Frazier, 77 Va. 775.

Where Sale Made More than Six Months after Decree.—Where the sale is made more than six months after decree for sale, and has been confirmed, it can not be set aside as to purchasers. Dixon v. McCue, 21 Gratt. 373.

(k) Does Not Protect Sale under Void Decree.

Chapter 132, § 8, of the West Virginia Code, does not protect a sale under a totally void decree. Waldron v. Harvey, 54 W. Va. 608, 46 S. E. 603.

(3) Restitution.

Right in General.—Where a sale has been made under a decree or order of the court and the sale is confirmed, and the decree or order is afterwards reversed or set aside, there may be a restitution of the proceeds of the sale to those entitled. W. Va. Code, 1906, ch. 132; Va. Code, 1904, § 3425; Waldron v. Harvey, 54 W. Va. 608, 46 S. E. 603; Stewart v. Tennant, 52 W. Va. 559, 44 S. E. 223; Klapneck v. Keltz, 50 W. Va. 331, 40 S. E. 570; Ammons v. Ammons, 50 W. Va. 390, 40 S. E. 490; Martin v. Smith, 25 W. Va. 579; Dunfee v. Childs, 45 W. Va. 155, 30 S. E. 102; Sinnett v. Cralle, 4 W. Va. 600; Calvert v. Ash, 47 W. Va. 480, 35 S. E. 887; Underwood v. Pack, 23 W. Va. 704; Pappenheimer v. Roberts, 24 W. Va. 702, 712; Frederick v. Cox, 47 W. Va. 14, 34 S. E. 958; Capehart v. Dowery, 10 W. Va. 130; Turk v. Skiles, 38 W. Va. 404, 18 S. E. 561; Hoback v. Miller, 44 W. Va. 635, 29 S. E. 1014; Peck v. Chambers, 44 W. Va. 270, 28 S. E. 706; Hull v. Hull, 26 W. Va. 1; Park v. Petroleum Co., 25 W. Va. 108; Beard v. Arbuckle, 19 W. Va. 135; Estill v. McClintic, 11 W. Va. 399; Tracey v. Shumate, 22 W.

Va. 474; Hughes *v.* Hamilton, 19 W. Va. 366; Neely *v.* Jones, 16 W. Va. 625; Newcomb *v.* Brooks, 16 W. Va. 32, 76; Marling *v.* Robrecht, 13 W. Va. 440; Hitchcox *v.* Hitchcox, 39 W. Va. 607, 20 S. E. 595; Buchanan *v.* Clark, 10 Gratt. 164; Cooper *v.* Hepburn, 15 Gratt. 551, 569.

When the title of the purchaser fails as the result of the reversal of the decree, and the judicial sale is set aside, the parties are to be put in statu quo. Stewart *v.* Tennant, 52 W. Va. 559, 44 S. E. 223; Hull *v.* Hull, 26 W. Va. 1; Williamson *v.* Jones, 43 W. Va. 562, 27 S. E. 411; Charleston L., etc., Co. *v.* Brockmeyer, 23 W. Va. 635.

Restoration in Specie—The Thing Itself, Not Value.—Where a man recovers land in a real action, and takes possession or acquires title to land or goods by sale under execution, and the judgment is afterwards reversed, so far as he is concerned, his title is at an end, and the land or goods must be restored in specie; not the value of them but the things themselves. There is an exception where the sale is to a stranger bona fide, or where a third person has bona fide acquired some collateral right before reversal. Dunfee *v.* Childs, 45 W. Va. 155, 30 S. E. 102.

Exception—Sale to Stranger Bona Fide.—There is an exception where the sale is to a stranger bona fide, or where a third person has bona fide acquired some collateral right before reversed. Dunfee *v.* Childs, 45 W. Va. 155, 30 S. E. 102.

Rents and Profits.—The rents and profits less the taxes received by the purchaser, whilst in possession of the land, should be deducted from the amount for which he is entitled to charge it, and he should have a decree charging the land for the balance. Charleston L., etc., Co. *v.* Brockmeyer, 23 W. Va. 635; Haymond *v.* Camden, 22 W. Va. 180; Hudgin *v.* Hudgin, 6 Gratt. 320.

"She should be charged reasonable rents and profits, less taxes paid by her for the time she had the house and lot in her possession. If the rents and profits should be less than the money paid by her, and interest thereon, she would have the right to charge the house and lot for any balance; if, however, the rents and profits should exceed the money paid with interest for such balance, after crediting her with such payment and interest, a personal decree should be had against her. This is not only what equity requires, but it is sustained by the authorities." Charleston L., etc., Co. *v.* Brockmeyer, 23 W. Va. 635.

Subrogation.—See generally, the title SUBROGATION.

A purchaser having purchased land under a void decree, is entitled upon the disaffirmance of the sale to be substituted to the rights of the creditor, and charge the land with the amount of the debt paid by him. Haymond *v.* Camden, 23 W. Va. 180; Charleston L., etc., Co. *v.* Brockmeyer, 23 W. Va. 635.

H. LIABILITY TO COMPLETE PURCHASE.

Where Title Defective.—After the bid is accepted by the court by the confirmation of the sale, though the purchaser before the deed is made to him, finds out that the title to the land is defective, he is nevertheless bound to receive it, and pay the purchase money. Fleming *v.* Holt, 12 W. Va. 143; Atkinson *v.* Washington, etc., College, 54 W. Va. 32, 46 S. E. 253.

In the case of Goddin *v.* Vaughn, 14 Gratt. 102, the purchaser having discovered a defect in the title declined to pay the purchase money, and the court compelled him to do so but it also perfected his title clearly as could be done. In that way the error and defect were corrected at the suit and at the instance of the purchaser. See also, Ammons *v.* Ammons, 50 W. Va. 390, 40 S. E. 490.

Where Land Sold in Another Suit.—Purchasers at a judicial sale should not be compelled to complete their purchase where the land has been sold in another suit, and neither the sale nor the decree therefor has been set aside. Etter v. Scott, 90 Va. 762, 19 S. E. 776.

Where Sold without Account of Liens.—Purchasers under decree should not be required to take or pay for the property where it had been thrice sold without an account of liens and the title is uncertain. Etter v. Scott, 90 Va. 762, 19 S. E. 776.

I. LIABILITY WHERE PURCHASE MONEY PAID TO PERSON UNAUTHORIZED TO COLLECT.

See ante, "Payment, Collection and Distribution of Purchase Money," XII.

J. LIABILITY TO DOMINANT TENEMENT.

See generally, the title EASEMENTS, vol. 4, p. 851.

One of two adjoining lots owned by the same parties was sold at auction under the decree of the court. At the time of the sale nothing was said of an easement running from the unsold lot through the one sold, for carrying the water from the former to a culvert in the street; and such easement was not to be seen on the lot sold, and was not known to the purchaser. Held, that the purchaser was entitled to have his lot free of the easement. Scott v. Beutel, 23 Gratt. 1.

K. DETERIORATION OR APPRECIATION IN VALUE BETWEEN DATE OF SALE AND PAYMENT OF PURCHASE MONEY.

See generally, the title VENDOR AND PURCHASER.

Where Estate Destroyed or Lost by Title Paramount.—As a general rule the purchaser at a judicial sale is required to pay the consideration for the estate, although it be destroyed or taken from him by superior title before a conveyance is executed. Christian v. Cabell, 22 Gratt. 82.

Abatement of Purchase Price on Account of Defect in Title.—It is well set-

tled that a purchaser at a judicial sale, with full knowledge of all the facts connected with the title, will not, after the sale has been confirmed, be entitled to any abatement of the purchase money, or any suspension of its collection on account of any defect in the title. Boyce v. Strother, 76 Va. 862.

Abatement of Purchase Price for Deficiency in Quantity of Land.—If lands be sold under direction of a court of chancery by certain metes and bounds by a widow as guardian of her infant children, who own the land subject to the widow's right of dower therein, and she conveys their interest as well as her own designating the boundaries of the land and warranting the title, and she having shown to the purchaser before the sale the tract offered to be sold, and he is put in possession and enjoys without controversy all the land so shown him, the title thereto being perfect, but it turns out, that the boundaries set out in the deed include land not shown to the purchaser, and never held or claimed by the vendor, or those under whom she claims, the court by a rule in said cause may properly require the purchaser to pay the whole of the purchase money without allowing him any abatement for t'e land, which was not shown him, but which is within the boundaries specified in his deed, and to which his title is worthless. Crislip v. Cain, 19 W. Va. 438.

Fraud or Mutual Mistake as to Quantity of Land.—See generally, the titles FRAUD AND DECEIT, vol. 6, p. 448; MISTAKE AND ACCIDENT.

In Virginia the general rule would seem to be that objections by purchasers at judicial sales for defect of title must be made before the sale is confirmed by the court, and objections afterwards come too late. This rule, however, does not apply to the equity of a purchaser, arising from after-discovered mistake, fraud or the like matter. Courts of equity are always ready to relieve innocent, injured parties in such cases, unless by reason of acquiescence, laches or other special circumstances. Watson *v.* Hoy, 28 Gratt. 698; Hyman *v.* Smith, 13 W. Va. 744.

Hence, where there has been a mutual mistake as to the quantity of land in a tract, the purchaser is not precluded by confirmation of the sale from obtaining relief. Watson *v.* Hoy, 28 Gratt. 698.

L. RIGHT TO POSSESSION.

1. General Rule.

When property is sold under a decree of a court of chancery and the report of the sale is confirmed by the court, the purchaser is entitled to the possession of the property from the time of such confirmation, unless there be something in the decree to the contrary, even though there be in the decree no express direction for the delivery of such possession to the purchaser. Childs *v.* Hurd, 25 W. Va. 530; Seim *v.* O'Grady, 42 W. Va. 77, 24 S. E. 994; Taylor *v.* Cooper, 10 Leigh 317; Hudgins *v.* Marchant, 28 Gratt. 177; Evans *v.* Spurgin, 6 Gratt. 107.

By the decree of confirmation, the law says to the purchaser: "There is your property. It is entirely unoccupied. No one claims it, and from this time it will be regarded as constructively in your possession. The question of occupation is with you. The question of seizin in fact is settled for you." Seim *v.* O'Grady, 42 W. Va. 77, 24 S. E. 994.

2. Where Appeal Obtained.

a. Perfected before Possession.

If an appeal in the case has been obtained and perfected before possession of the property is obtained by the purchaser, he is not entitled to have possession. Hudgins *v.* Marchant, 28 Gratt. 177.

b. Possession before Appeal.

But if possession is obtained before the appeal is perfected, the purchaser is entitled to retain it until the case is decided in the appellate court. Hudgins *v.* Marchant, 28 Gratt. 177.

But where a decree was rendered for the sale of a tract of land at public sale, and there was but one judgment lien upon it at the time, and, by the consent of the judgment creditor and the debtor, the land was, by the commissioner, sold to the wife of the debtor, and, out of her own separate estate, she, without fraud, paid for the land, by paying the said judgment and costs of the suit, and afterwards another judgment was recovered against the debtor, while the wife is not entitled to hold the land under her purchase, yet she is entitled to be subrogated to the rights of the creditors in the said judgment which she discharged. Hutson *v.* Sadler, 31 W. Va. 358, 6 S. E. 920.

3. Enforcement of Possession.

a. Equity Jurisdiction.

See generally, the title JURISDICTION.

A court of equity always has jurisdiction to carry into effect its own decrees. The court of chancery is not functus officio until the decree is executed by the delivery of possession. Newman *v.* Chapman, 2 Rand. 93; Paxton *v.* Rucker, 15 W. Va. 547.

b. Writ of Possession.

On the confirmation of the sale the purchaser is immediately entitled to a writ of possession to place him in possession of the land, as against any one adversely holding the same. Seim *v.* O'Grady, 42 W. Va. 77, 24 S. E. 994.

The usual course of the court has been to make a rule upon the person in possession, where he is not a party to the suit; and, unless, he shows a paramount right in himself, to order the property to be delivered to the commissioners acting under the decree; and, if necessary to enforce such order by an attachment. Paxton *v.* Rucker, 15 W. Va. 547; Com. *v.* Ragsdale, 2 Hen. & M. 8.

If the land is in the possession of a

person who is not a party to the suit, the court should issue a rule against the person to show cause why he should not surrender possession of the land before issuing an habere facias possessionem directing the sheriff to put the purchaser in possession. Williamson v. Russell, 18 W. Va. 612.

But if the court should issue such writ requiring the sheriff to remove such person from the land and put the purchaser in possession without having issued such rule, the sheriff would not be liable to be mulcted in damages for executing such writ. Williamson v. Russell, 18 W. Va. 612.

Upon the hearing of a rule against a person to show cause why he should not give up possession of a certain tract of land which had been sold to another under a decree of the court, the court made a decree which showed that the court heard the cause upon the rule, the answer thereto, "and upon the deposition taken upon the rule, and the evidence of the witnesses adduced in open court." But the record did not show what "the evidence of the witness adduced in open court" was. Held, that a rule might be awarded against a person not a party to the suit, in possession of the land sold under the decree of the court to another person, to show cause why he should not surrender possession to the purchaser. Paxton v. Rucker, 15 W. Va. 547; Trimble v. Patton, 5 W. Va. 432.

When Writ Unnecessary.—But where the land is lying open to the commons, and no one has or is in any manner disputing the possession thereof, such writ is entirely unnecessary, as the land is wholly at the purchaser's command. Such being the condition of the land, he is, on the confirmation of the sale, by construction of law, in actual possession thereof, although not in personal or actual occupancy, for there is none his right to dispute. Vacant lots, while not fenced, are not in the actual occupancy of the undisputed owner; but they are in his constructive posses-

sion, or seisin in fact, for the law raises around them an invisible fence, which renders every one a trespasser thereon, entering without his consent, express or implied. In other words, he has all the possession, undisputed, which the law can give, without, by his own action, he in some manner personally occupies the lots. Seim v. O'Grady, 42 W. Va. 77, 24 S. E. 994.

Finality of Decree Where Issue Joined.—See generally, the title JUDGMENTS AND DECREES, ante, p. 161.

When in a suit, in chancery a purchaser at a judicial sale moves the court for a rule against the former owner to show cause why the purchaser should not be awarded a writ of possession, and the former owner files an elaborate answer to the rule in the nature of a cross bill, claiming a right to the possession upon equitable grounds bearing upon the conscience of the purchaser, and fully set out, and the purchaser files a special replication, and the issue between these parties thus made up as to their mutual rights is fairly tried by the court upon extensive proofs on either side, and a decree is rendered of an appealable character, such decree is final between the parties so long as it remains unreversed, and the issue thus decided can not be reopened by an original suit instituted by the losing party. Burner v. Hevener, 34 W. Va. 774, 12 S. E. 861. See also, McKinney v. Kirk, 9 W. Va. 26; Vanmeter v. Vanmeters, 3 Gratt. 148; Crim v. Davisson, 6 W. Va. 465.

c. Action for Trespass.

See generally, the title TRESPASS.

Where a count alleges that before a judicial sale and before its confirmation a party cut and destroyed timber on the land purchased, the purchaser so alleging such matter shows no right of action. Newlon v. Reitz, 31 W. Va. 483, 7 S. E. 411.

d. Ejectment.

See generally, the title EJECTMENT, vol. 4, p. 871.

e. Unlawful Entry and Detainer.

See the title FORCIBLE ENTRY AND DETAINER, vol. 6, p. 156.

M. VENDEE OR ASSIGNEE OF ORIGINAL PURCHASER.

A party enters into a verbal contract for the purchase of land from a commissioner of the court, who is authorized to make a private sale of land subject to the confirmation of the court, and enters upon the land and improves it, but the sale is not reported to the court or any part of the purchase money paid, and he then by a written contract, without warranty, sells his claim and improvement in and upon the land to a third person, stating therein that the title to the land is outstanding, but makes no reference to his verbal purchase. More than ten years after the sale of his claim he buys the same land from the commissioner by a written contract, and thereafter the assignee of the person to whom he sold his claim purchases from the commissioner a part of said land with full notice of the written contract of purchase by said party and obtains from the commissioner a deed for such part, neither of said sales having been confirmed by the court. Held, that the last purchase by said party was valid and he was entitled to the land as against said assignee of the person to whom he sold his claim, and his purchase should be confirmed by the court. Kent v. Watson, 22 W. Va. 561.

XVI. Collateral Impeachment.

If a court make an order to sell real estate when it had no jurisdiction to make such order, the owner of such real estate not having been summoned, or otherwise brought before the court, the appellate court will reverse such decree of sale in toto, as also the order confirming a sale made under such decree. Such a decree, and such order confirming such sale, should be treated as nullities, even in a collateral controversy. Camden v. Haymond, 9 W.

Va. 680. See generally, the title JUDGMENTS AND DECREES, ante, p. 161.

Title acquired under proceedings of courts of competent jurisdiction must be deemed inviolable in collateral actions, or none can know what is his own. Wilcher v. Robertson, 78 Va. 602; Lancaster v. Wilson, 27 Gratt. 624; Hughes v. Hamilton, 19 W. Va. 366; Allan v. Hoffman, 83 Va. 129, 2 S. E. 602; Crawford v. Weller, 23 Gratt. 835.

It is a well-settled principle of law, that the decree or judgment of a court, which has jurisdiction of the person and subject matter, is binding until reversed, and can not be collaterally attacked. The court may have mistaken the law or misjudged the facts, but its adjudication when made concludes all the world until set aside by the proper appellate tribunal. And although the judgment or decree may be reversed, yet all rights acquired at a judicial sale, while the decree or judgment was in full force, and which they authorized, will be protected. It is sufficient for the buyer to know, that the court had jurisdiction and exercised it, and that the order, on the faith of which he purchased, was made and authorized the sale. With the errors of the court he had no concern. These principles have so often received the sanction of this court, that it would not have been deemed necessary again to reaffirm them, had not the extent of the doctrine been questioned at the bar. Hughes v. Hamilton, 19 W. Va. 366.

Purchasers at a judicial sale made in a suit to which they were not parties, for value, and without notice, in which the record showed all the necessary and proper parties, and perfectly regular proceedings, are entitled to the protection of a court of equity against any question or attack upon their title in another suit, and a collateral proceeding. Allan v. Hoffman, 83 Va. 129, 2 S. E. 602; Crawford v. Weller, 23 Gratt. 835.

Judicial Separation.

See the title DIVORCE, vol. 4, p. 734.

Judiciary. Powers of.

See the title CONSTITUTIONAL LAW, vol. 3, p. 180.

Jurat.

See the title AFFIDAVITS, vol. 1, p. 227, and references given.

JURISDICTION.

CROSS REFERENCES.

See the titles ABATEMENT, REVIVAL AND SURVIVAL, vol. 1, p. 2; ADMIRALTY, vol. 1, p. 182; APPEAL AND ERROR, vol. 1, p. 418; APPEARANCES, vol. 1, p. 667; BANKRUPTCY AND INSOLVENCY, vol. 2, p. 232; CERTIORARI, vol. 2, p. 734; CHAMBERS AND VACATION, vol. 2, p. 767; CHANGE OF VENUE, vol. 2, p. 780; COMMON LAW, vol. 3, p. 18; CONFLICT OF LAWS, vol. 3, p. 100; CONSOLIDATION OF ACTIONS, vol. 3, p. 125; CORPORATIONS, vol. 3, p. 510; COURTS, vol. 3, p. 696; CRIMINAL LAW, vol. 4, p. 1; CROSS BILLS, vol. 4, p. 100; DISMISSAL, DISCONTINUANCE AND NONSUIT, vol. 4, p. 683; EXCEPTIONS, BILL OF, vol. 5, p. 357; FOREIGN JUDGMENTS, vol. 6, p. 208; FORMER ADJUDICATION OR RES ADJUDICATA, vol. 6, p. 261; FRAUD AND DECEIT, vol. 6, p. 448; INJUNCTIONS, vol. 7, p. 512; JUDGES, ante, p. 150; JUDGMENTS AND DECREES, ante, p. 161; JUSTICES OF THE PEACE; LACHES; MAXIMS; .MISTAKE AND ACCIDENT; MULTIPLICITY OF SUITS; NEW TRIALS; ORDERS OF COURT; PARTIES; PLEADING; QUESTIONS OF LAW AND FACT; REMOVAL OF CAUSES; SERVICE OF PROCESS; STATE; SUMMONS AND PROCESS; VENUE; WILLS.

As to the jurisdiction over various subject matters and in the different proceedings, see the specific titles in this work.

I. Definition, Nature and General Consideration.

A. DEFINITION, NATURE AND ESSENTIALS.

Definition and Nature.—"The power to hear and determine a cause is jurisdiction." Lemmon v. Herbert, 92 Va. 653.

"Jurisdiction is defined by both Bouvier and Burrill as follows: 'Jurisdiction is a power constitutionally conferred upon a court, a single judge or a magistrate to take cognizance of and decide causes according to law and to carry their sentence into execution;' and by the latter in a more general sense 'power or right to exercise authority.' " Craft v. Com., 24 Gratt. 602.

"The substance of practically all the definitions of jurisdiction, found in the law books, is the power of a court or other judicial tribunal to hear and determine a cause." Sperry v. Sanders, 50 W. Va. 70, 40 S. E. 327.

"There are numerous definitions of jurisdiction, the substance of all of which is the power to hear and determine a cause. U. S. v. Arredondo, 6 Pet. 691; Freeman on Judg., § 118; State of R. I. v. State of Mass., 12 Pet. 718; Works on Courts and their Jurisdiction 16; Quarl v. Abbott, 102 Ind. 239. That definition probably covers the full meaning of the term, for it may be elaborated in various ways and still retain the same meaning. Power or authority to hear and determine a cause implies the existence of a tribunal to exercise such power, and such tribunal can not exist except by authority of law. There must be a court or tribunal with judicial power. This feature has not been overlooked in the many definitions given. Jurisdiction in courts is the power and authority to declare the law. The very word, in its origin, imports as much; it is derived from juris and dico—I speak by the law. And that sentence ought to be inscribed in living light on every tribunal of criminal power. It is the right of administering justice through the laws, by the means which the law has provided for that purpose. * * * Mills v. Commonwealth, 13 Penn. State 630." Johnston v. Hunter, 50 W. Va. 52, 40 S. E. 448.

When the jurisdiction of a court is asserted over a cause of action, it embraces everything in the case and every question arising which can be determined in it; and, until thus exhausted, or in some way relinquished, the jurisdiction is exclusive and can not be encroached upon by any other tribunal. State v. Fredlock, 52 W. Va. 232, 43 S. E. 153.

By jurisdiction over the subject matter is meant the nature of the cause of action and of the relief sought. Stewart v. Northern Assur. Co., 45 W. Va. 734, 32 S. E. 218; Hall v. Hall, 12 W. Va. 1.

Essentials of Jurisdiction.—"In Munday v. Vail, 34 N. J. Law 418, it is said, 'Jurisdiction may be defined to be the right to adjudicate concerning the subject matter in the given case. To constitute this there are three essentials: First. The court must have cognizance of the class of cases to which the one to be adjudged belongs. Second. The proper parties must be present. And, third. The point decided must be, in substance and effect, within the issue.' This was quoted with approval in Reynolds v. Stockton, 140 U. S. 254, 268, the court saying: 'We regard the views suggested in the quotation from the opinion as correct, and as properly indicating the limits in respect to which the conclusiveness of a judgment may be invoked in a subsequent suit inter partes.' " St. Lawrence, etc., Co. v. Holt, 51 W. Va. 352, 41 S. E. 351.

The existence and legal constitution of a court is an inseparable part of its jurisdiction, and it has no power to hear and determine causes except at times and places authorized by law. Johnston v. Hunter, 50 W. Va. 52, 40 S. E. 448.

"The existence and legal constitution of a court as an inseparable part of jurisdiction is recognized in the following, taken from Hawes on Jur. of Courts, § 1: 'From its origin, a hearing and a determination of rights seem to be implied; and in natural sequence the proper presentation of the claim, upon which an adjudication is asked, to a proper tribunal; and power in that tribunal to decide upon and determine the rights thus presented.'" Johnston v. Hunter, 50 W. Va. 52, 40 S. E. 448.

"That the existence of a court is implied in the very nature of jurisdiction and its exercise, clearly appears in the definition of a court, which Blackstone says is 'A place wherein justice is judicially administered.' 3 Blk. Com. 23; 4 Am. & Eng. Ency. Law 447, says a court is 'A body in the government, organized for the public administration of justice at the time and place prescribed by law.' Courts or tribunals in the nature of courts are the only agencies of the law by which a cause can be heard and determined, they are the only depositaries of judicial power. Without them it lies dormant and inactive in the sovereignty of the state. Its active and potent existence is inseparable from that of a court. It is not only necessary to the existence of judicial power that can be exercised that it be vested in a court or other tribunal, but there can be no court vested with such power unless and until all the requirements of law, necessary to constitute such court, are complied with. The election and qualification of a judge or a justice of the peace does not constitute a court. The holding of a commission as judge by an individual does not authorize him to hear and determine causes until all other requirements of law, necessary to the transaction of judicial business,

are fulfilled. 'To constitute a court, the judge or judges must be in the discharge of judicial duties at the time and in the place prescribed by law for the sitting of the court.' Works on Courts and their Jur. 1. 'The times and places at which courts shall sit are usually fixed by statute, and in order that a court may exercise its jurisdiction, these statutory provisions must be observed. The proceedings of a court at a time or place other than that prescribed by law are coram non judice, and, therefore, void. It is not only void; it is not the act of a court at all.' Works on Courts and their Jur. 81." Johnston v. Hunter, 50 W. Va. 52, 40 S. E. 448. See the title COURTS, vol. 3, p. 701.

Jurisdiction Matter of Law—Venue Matter of Fact.—An indictment which charges that an offense was committed "within the jurisdiction of the court," but does not state where the offense was committed is bad on demurrer. Jurisdiction is matter of law. The place where an offense is committed is a matter of fact. It is necessary to aver and prove the place where the offense is alleged to have been committed. Early v. Com., 93 Va. 765, 24 S. E. 936. See the titles INDICTMENTS, INFORMATIONS AND PRESENTMENTS, vol. 7, p. 371; VENUE.

Jurisdiction at Chambers.—See the title CHAMBERS AND VACATION, vol. 2, p. 768.

B. ESSENTIAL TO VALID JUDGMENT OR DECREE.

1. In General.

Jurisdiction of Parties and Subject Matter Essential.—To render a judgment or decree binding, the court rendering the same must have jurisdiction both of the parties and of the subject matter. Seamster v. Blackstock, 83 Va. 232, 2 S. E. 36; Wade v. Hancock, 76 Va. 620; Lavell v. McCurdy, 77 Va. 763; Dillard v. Central, etc., Co., 82 Va. 734, 735, 1 S. E. 124; Anthony v. Kasey, 83 Va. 338, 5 S. E. 176; Richardson v. Seever, 84 Va. 259, 4 S. E. 712; Gresham v. Ewell, 85 Va. 1, 6 S. E. 700; Blanton v. Carroll, 86 Va. 539, 10 S. E. 329; Dorr v. Rohr, 82 Va. 359; Staunton, etc., Co. v. Haden, 92 Va. 201, 23 S. E. 285; Underwood v. McVeigh, 23 Gratt. 409, 418; Gray v. Stuart, 33 Gratt. 351; Cox v. Thomas, 9 Gratt. 323, 326; Withers v. Fuller, 30 Gratt. 547; Hartigan v. Board of Regents, 49 W. Va. 14, 38 S. E. 698; Mayer v. Adams, 27 W. Va. 244; Chapman v. Maitland, 22 W. Va. 329; St. Lawrence, etc., Co. v. Holt, 51 W. Va. 352, 363, 41 S. E. 351, 357; Houston v. McCluney, 8 W. Va. 135; Fowler v. Lewis, 36 W. Va. 112, 14 S. E. 447; Hoback v. Miller, 44 W. Va. 635, 29 S. E. 1014; Haymond v. Camden, 22 W. Va. 180; Hopkirk v. Bridges, 4 Hen. & M. 413. See the titles CONSTITUTIONAL LAW, vol. 3, p. 209; JUDGMENTS AND DECREES, ante, p. 161. Generally, as to the manner of acquiring jurisdiction, and the invalidity of judgments rendered without due notice, see post, "How Acquired," III.

"The power to render the decree or judgment which the court may undertake to make in the particular cause, depends upon the nature and extent of the authority vested in it by law, in regard to the subject matter of the cause." Hall v. Hall, 12 W. Va. 1.

"It is an elementary principle in our jurisprudence, that jurisdiction of the subject matter and the parties is essential to the conclusiveness of a judgment or decree." Seamster v. Blackstock, 83 Va. 232, 2 S. E. 36.

"I take it to be a fundamental principle of law, requiring no citation of authorities to sustain it, that in order for the decrees of a court, of either special or general jurisdiction, to be binding (unless in pure proceedings in rem) two things are necessary: It must have jurisdiction of the person and of the subject matter. The rule is founded upon principles of reason and justice, and the instances in which it has been violated have met with the unqualified disapproval and condemnation of the courts." Moorman v. Arthur, 90 Va. 455, 18 S. E. 869.

When a statute confers on a court power to be exercised ex parte over a subject, upon the existence of certain facts, the action of the court, if the facts do not exist, is void. Twiggs v. Chevallie, 4 W. Va. 463.

"Without jurisdiction over his person, a personal judgment or decree against him, would be a nullity; without such jurisdiction, or a seizure of the subject matter of the suit, such decree or judgment against the thing will be a nullity, and with such jurisdiction of the person of said defendant, there may be either a decree in personam or in rem, or both at the election of the plaintiff." Chapman v. Maitland, 22 W. Va. 329.

The rendition of a judgment against a party not before the court in any way will be as utterly void as though the court had undertaken to act when the subject matter was not within its cognizance. This rule has reference to all courts, with this difference, that the jurisdiction of a superior court will be presumed until the contrary appears, whereas that of an inferior court must be shown. Blanton v. Carroll, 86 Va. 539, 10 S. E. 329; Underwood v. McVeigh, 23 Gratt. 409. See also, Lancaster v. Wilson, 27 Gratt. 624; Fairfax v. Alexandria, 28 Gratt. 16; Connolly v. Connolly, 32 Gratt. 657; Gray v. Stuart, 33 Gratt. 351.

Acts without Jurisdiction Coram Non Judice.—"'Acts done by a court which has no jurisdiction either over the person, the cause, or the process, are said to be coram non judice.' Bouvier's Law Dic. 'Where an action is brought and determined in a court which has no jurisdiction over the matter, it is said to be coram non judice.' 7 Am

& Eng. Ency. Law (2d Ed.) 596."
St. Lawrence, etc., Co. *v.* Holt, 51 W.
Va. 352, 363, 41 S. E. 351.

When a court transcends its jurisdiction its unauthorized judgment or
decree is void. Twiggs *v.* Chevallie, 4
W. Va. 463. See also, Adams *v.* Jennings, 103 Va. 579, 49 S. E. 982.

A judgment may be valid to the extent of the jurisdiction, and invalid beyond. Wade *v.* Hancock, 76 Va. 620.

A court may rightfully obtain jurisdiction, and its decrees may be void.
because, in the progress of the cause,
it has exceeded its jurisdiction. In
such cases the decrees may be attacked
directly or collaterally. Wade *v.* Hancock, 76 Va. 620; Seamster *v.* Blackstock, 83 Va. 232, 2 S. E. 36.

"The adjudged cases furnish numerous examples of this kind. Thus,
where a bill is filed to sell a certain
lot, and a decree is entered for the
sale of another and different lot, not
named in the bill, and to which the
bill has no relation, such decree, as respects the last-mentioned lot, is a
nullity. This principle is illustrated by
the case of Wade *v.* Hancock, 76 Va.
620. In that case it was held, that in
summary proceedings under the ninth
section of chapter 76 of the Code of
1873, the circuit court of the state have
jurisdiction to appoint, change, and remove church trustees, but not to determine how they shall administer their
trust; and accordingly, the judgment
complained of was held void, because
in pronouncing it the court had exceeded its jurisdiction. In delivering
the opinion of the court, Burks, J.,
cites with approbation, the case of Ex
parte Lange, 18 Wall. 163, in which
this question is discussed with much
learning and ability by Mr. Justice
Miller, in delivering the opinion of the
supreme court of the United States.
See also, 7 Rob. Pr. 107, et seq., where
numerous cases to the same effect are
referred to." Seamster *v.* Blackstock,
83 Va. 232, 2 S. E. 36.

·8 Va—54

2. Want of Jurisdiction as Ground for Collateral Attack.

General Rule.—If a court does not
have jurisdiction, it is a matter of no
importance, however correct its proceedings and decisions may be; its
judgments are nullities, and may not
only be set aside in the same court,
but may be declared void by every
court in which they are called in question. Staunton, etc., Co. *v.* Haden, 92
Va. 201, 23 S. E. 285; Blanton *v.* Carroll, 86 Va. 539, 10 S. E. 329; Gresham
v. Ewell, 85 Va. 1, 6 S. E. 700; Anthony *v.* Kasey, 83 Va. 338, 5 S. E.
176; Seamster *v.* Blackstock, 83 Va.
232, 2 S. E. 36; Dillard *v.* Central, etc.,
Co., 82 Va. 734, 735, 1 S. E. 124; Lavell *v.* McCurdy, 77 Va. 763; Gray *v.*
Stuart, 33 Gratt. 351; Withers *v.* Fuller, 30 Gratt. 547; Underwood *v.* McVeigh, 23 Gratt. 409, 418; Hoback *v.*
Miller, 44 W. Va. 635, 29 S. E. 1014;
Fowler *v.* Lewis, 36 W. Va. 112, 14 S.
E. 447; Houston *v.* McCluney, 8 W.
Va. 135.

Jurisdiction of the person and of
the subject matter are prerequisites
and must exist before a court can render a valid judgment or decree, and a
judgment, which appears upon the face
of the record to have been rendered
without jurisdiction of the subject matter or person, is absolutely void, whenever it is called in question. Blanton
v. Carroll, 86 Va. 539, 10 S. E. 329;
Seamster *v.* Blackstock, 83 Va. 232, 2
S. E. 36; Dorr *v.* Rohr, 82 Va. 359;
Wade *v.* Hancock, 76 Va. 620; Mayer
v. Adams, 27 W. Va. 244; Haymond *v.*
Camden, 22 W. Va. 180.

"It is true that a court or tribunal
passing judgment or resolution must
have both power to pass on the particular matter and over the person by a
notice to him, where notice is required
by law in the case, and in the absence
of either its action is void, whenever
its validity comes up." Hartigan *v.*
Board of Regents, 49 W. Va. 14, 38
S. E. 698.

Want of jurisdiction makes the judgment a nullity, and it may be so treated by any court in any proceeding, direct or collateral. Wade *v.* Hancock, 76 Va. 620.

For a full treatment of the question of collateral and direct attack upon judgments and decrees, see the title JUDGMENTS AND DECREES, ante, p. 161.

Application to Courts of General Jurisdiction.—Want of jurisdiction affirmatively appearing on the face of the proceedings makes the judgment even of courts of general jurisdiction null; and they may be so treated by any court in any proceeding, direct or collateral. Wade *v.* Hancock, 76 Va. 620; Dillard *v.* Central, etc., Co., 82 Va. 734, 1 S. E. 124. See post, "Presumption Only Arises Where Record Silent or Not Inconsistent," IV, A, 1, b.

Query as to Application Where Court Decides That It Has Jurisdiction. —"'Acts done by a court which has no jurisdiction either over the person, the cause, or the process, are said to be coram non judice.' Bouvier's Law Dic. 'Where an action is brought and determined in a court which has no jurisdiction over the matter, it is said to be coram non judice.' 7 Am. & Eng. Ency. Law (2d Ed.) 595. That such judgment or decree could not stand for a moment, if attacked in a direct proceeding by motion in proper time in the court below, or by appeal, or writ of error, or bill of review, there is not the slightest doubt, but if it is merely erroneous and not absolutely void, it is binding until reversed, and, if never reversed by a direct proceeding, it is binding forever or until it expires by limitation. It can never be attacked in any collateral proceeding and all matters settled by it are res judicata in every court so long as it remains unreversed. But where a court erroneously pronounces a decree in respect to a matter which is not cognizable in that court, but belongs to the jurisdiction of another court, but deciding that it has jurisdiction when it has not, is the decree absolutely void? If so, it may be ignored by all courts and is worthless for any purpose. There are a number of cases which hold that such a judgment or decree is coram non judice, but they all appear to have been judgments of inferior courts, in respect to which jurisdiction is never presumed, but must always be affirmatively shown, or judgments in special proceedings." St. Lawrence, etc., Co. *v.* Holt, 51 W. Va. 352, 363, 41 S. E. 351.

Collateral Attack for Excess of Jurisdiction.—See ante, "In General," I B, 1.

3. Effect of Erroneous Proceedings by Courts Having Jurisdiction.

Error Immaterial on Collateral Attack.—While a judgment may be directly attacked for irregularity, this can only be done in a direct proceeding in the same court, or in an appellate court; if a court has jurisdiction, it is immaterial how erroneous its proceedings are, when its judgment is collaterally called in question. Pennybacker *v.* Switzer, 75 Va. 671; Neale *v.* Utz, 75 Va. 480, 487; Woodhouse *v.* Fillbates, 77 Va. 317; Wimbish *v.* Breeden, 77 Va. 324; Hill *v.* Woodward, 78 Va. 765; Wilcher *v.* Robertson, 78 Va. 602; Brengle *v.* Richardson, 78 Va. 406; Perkins *v.* Lane, 82 Va. 59; Allan *v.* Hoffman, 83 Va. 129, 2 S. E. 602; Lawson *v.* Moorman, 85 Va. 880, 9 S. E. 150; Gresham *v.* Ewell, 85 Va. 1, 5, 6 S. E. 700; Pugh *v.* McCue, 86 Va. 475, 10 S. E. 715; Marshall *v.* Cheatham, 88 Va. 31, 13 S. E. 308; Grigg *v.* Dalsheimer, 88 Va. 508, 13 S. E. 993; Lemmon *v.* Herbert, 92 Va. 653, 24 S. E. 249; Preston *v.* Kindrick, 94 Va. 760, 27 S. E. 588; Harman *v.* Stearns, 95 Va. 58, 27 S. E. 601; Building, etc., Co. *v.* Fray, 96 Va. 559, 32 S. E. 58; Adams *v.* Jennings, 103 Va. 579, 49 S. E. 982; Fisher *v.* Bassett, 9 Leigh 119;

Burnley *v.* Duke, 2 Rob. 102; Cox *v.* Thomas, 9 Gratt. 323; Schultz *v.* Schultz, 10 Gratt. 358, 379; Hutcheson *v.* Priddy, 12 Gratt. 85; Andrews *v.* Avory, 14 Gratt. 229; Devaughn *v.* Devaughn, 19 Gratt. 556; Ballard *v.* Thomas, 19 Gratt. 14; Cline *v.* Catron, 22 Gratt. 378; Durrett *v.* Davis, 24 Gratt. 302; Shelton *v.* Jones, 26 Gratt. 891; Lancaster *v.* Wilson, 27 Gratt. 624; Spilman *v.* Johnson, 27 Gratt. 33; Pulaski Co. *v.* Stuart, 28 Gratt. 872, 879; Withers *v.* Fuller, 30 Gratt. 547; Quesenberry *v.* Barbour, 31 Gratt. 491; Smith *v.* Henning, 10 W. Va. 596; Hall *v.* Hall, 12 W. Va. 1; Patton *v.* Merchant's Bank, 12 W. Va. 587; Keystone Bridge Co. *v.* Summers, 13 W. Va. 476; Davis *v.* Point Pleasant, 32 W. Va. 289, 9 S. E. 228; Northwestern Bank *v.* Hays, 37 W. Va. 475, 16 S. E. 561; Withrow *v.* Smithson, 37 W. Va. 757, 17 S. E. 316; First Nat. Bank *v.* Hyer, 46 W. Va. 13, 32 S. E. 1000; Starr *v.* Sampselle, 55 W. Va. 442, 47 S. E. 255. See the title JUDGMENTS AND DECREES, ante p. 161.

It is an axiom of law "that when a judgment of a court is offered in evidence collaterally in another suit, its validity can not be questioned for errors which do not affect the jurisdiction of the court which rendered it." Cooper *v.* Reynolds, 10 Wall. (U. S.) 308; Miller *v.* White, 46 W. Va. 67, 33 S. E. 332.

There is an obvious distinction between a case where the court has no jurisdiction to enter the judgment complained of, and a case where the court having a general jurisdiction over the subject matter has erroneously exercised it. In the latter case the judgment can not be questioned in any collateral proceeding, and if not appealed from, is final; but where the court is without jurisdiction, its judgment must be treated as a mere nullity, and all proceedings under it, or dependent on it, are void. Withers *v.* Fuller, 30 Gratt. 547.

A decree entered in a cause, in which all interested parties are before the court, and upon a bill upon which such decree would have been proper, under certain conditions which might have been shown by proof, upon the allegations· of the bill, to exist, is not void for want of jurisdiction, however erroneous it may be. Stewart *v.* Tennant, 52 W. Va. 580, 44 S. E. 223.

Judgment or Decree Conclusive until Reversed or Set Aside.—Where a court has jurisdiction, both of the parties and the subject matter of litigation, its decree, though erroneous, is conclusive until reversed or set aside. Rhea *v.* Shields, 103 Va. 305, 49 S. E. 70; St. Lawrence, etc., Co. *v.* Holt, 51 W. Va. 352, 363, 41 S. E. 351; Baltimore, etc., R. Co. *v.* Pittsburg, etc., R. Co., 17 W. Va. 812; Peirce *v.* Graham, 85 Va. 227, 7 S. E. 189.

As was said in Howison *v.* Weeden, 77 Va. 704, 710: "It is a well-established principle, that the judgment of a court of record, having jurisdiction of the cause and of the parties, is binding and conclusive upon parties and privies in every other court until it is regularly reversed by some court having jurisdiction for that purpose. Notwithstanding the proceedings may be erroneous, yet, as between the parties, the judgment must stand until regularly vacated or reversed. Where a court has jurisdiction, it has a right to decide every question which arises in the cause, and whether its decision be correct or otherwise, its judgment, until reversed, is regarded as binding in every other court. In no collateral way can the parties question the correctness of a judgment which has been rendered between them in a court having jurisdiction of them and of the subject matter."

It was said in Connolly *v.* Connolly, 32 Gratt. 657, that the then state of the law of probate was in Virginia, that a sentence pronounced by a court having jurisdiction, whether admitting or excluding the paper, as long as it remains in force, binds conclusively not only the immediate parties, but all other persons, and all other courts.

As to direct attack on judgments or decrees for errors or irregularities therein, see the title JUDGMENTS AND DECREES, ante, p. 161.

As to presumptions in favor of jurisdiction, see post, "Presumptions as to Jurisdiction," IV.

Erroneous Exercise of Judgment Not Ground for Writ of Prohibition.— In a chancery suit brought to enforce the lien of a judgment upon real estate, a circuit court has jurisdiction to determine whether or not such judgment is valid, although it may be void upon its face, and the writ of prohibition does not lie to restrain the judge of such court from proceeding in such cause. Sperry *v.* Sanders, 50 W. Va. 70, 40 S. E. 327.

"The proceeding sought to be restrained is a suit in chancery, brought to enforce the alleged lien of a judgment, alleged to be void, against the real estate of the petitioner, and to have the same sold for the purpose of paying off and satisfying said judgment. Such a cause of action clearly belongs to the chancery jurisdiction of the circuit court. The court has power and jurisdiction to hear and determine all cases of that class. It may consider whether the judgment is valid and determine the question in this case as well as in any other. Having the right to consider that question and to hear and determine it, its jurisdiction of the cause is complete and prohibition does not lie to prevent it from so proceeding even if it should err in the determination of the question to the extent of holding a judgment good and valid which is clearly void upon its face. Such error would not amount to an act in excess of the court's legitimate powers nor to an abuse of its jurisdiction. Should the court decide the question wrong, the defendant's

remedy, if any, would be by appeal, as in any other chancery cause in which the court has jurisdiction and an erroneous decree is entered. Prohibition does not lie for the correction of errors and it can not take the place of any of the ordinary proceedings for the correction of errors." Sperry *v.* Sanders, 50 W. Va. 70, 40 S. E. 327.

"The office of the writ of prohibition, we need hardly say, is not the correction of mere errors. The writ lies only to restrain an inferior court from acting in a matter of which it has no jurisdiction, or from exceeding the bounds of its jurisdiction. Hence, if the inferior court has jurisdiction of the subject matter of the controversy, and the parties are before it, or have had notice and an opportunity to be heard, a mistaken exercise of that jurisdiction does not render its judgment void, or justify a resort to the extraordinary remedy by prohibition. Or, as it has been tersely expressed, the writ of prohibition does not lie to prevent a subordinate court from deciding erroneously, or from enforcing an erroneous judgment, in a case in which it has a right to adjudicate. High, Extr. Rem., § 772; Hogan *v.* Guigon, 29 Gratt. 705; Nelms *v.* Vaughan, 84 Va. 696, 5 S. E. 704." Grigg *v.* Dalsheimer, 88 Va. 508, 13 S. E. 993. See the title PROHIBITION.

C. CLASSIFICATION OF COURTS ACCORDING TO JURISDICTION.

Courts of General and Courts of Special and Limited Jurisdiction.— "Some courts are of general jurisdiction, by which is meant that their authority extends to a great variety of matters; while others are only of special and limited jurisdiction, by which it is understood that they have authority extending only to certain special cases." Fausler *v.* Parsons, 6 W. Va. 486, citing Cooley Const. Lim., p. 405, et seq., etc., notes.

As to presumptions of jurisdiction in the case of the two classes of courts, see post, "Presumptions as to Jurisdiction," IV.

As to the nature of the jurisdiction of particular courts, see post, "Jurisdiction of Particular Courts," VIII.

Courts of Appellate Jurisdiction.— "The true criterion of distinction between our superior and inferior courts, seems to be appellate jurisdiction; placing the district courts and all above them, in the first class; and in the latter the county and corporation courts; coupled together in principal; and referred to, as in the same predicament, in the laws allowing appeals, which sometimes use the expressions 'from the county and corporation courts' at other times 'the county and other inferior courts.'" Thornton v. Smith, 1 Wash. 81, 85. See the title APPEAL AND ERROR, vol. 1, p. 418.

D. TERRITORIAL LIMITATION OF JURISDICTION.

Laws Have No Extraterritorial Force.—It is a principle universally recognized that laws have no extraterritorial force. Their authority is limited to the territorial jurisdiction of the state or country that enacts them, so far as their right or power of enforcement or claim to obedience is concerned. Stevens v. Brown, 20 W. Va. 450; Pennsylvania R. Co. v. Rogers, 52 W. Va. 450, 44 S. E. 300. See generally, the titles CONFLICT OF LAWS, vol. 3, p. 100; CRIMINAL LAW, vol. 4, p. 26; FOREIGN JUDGMENTS, vol. 6, p. 208.

As to jurisdiction of suits against foreign executors and administrators, see the title EXECUTORS AND ADMINISTRATORS, vol. 5, p. 747.

Nonresidents without Property within Jurisdiction.—A court of chancery has no jurisdiction of a bill to perpetuate testimony, or for any other purpose, against a defendant who is absent from, or residing out of, the state, and has no property, and claims title to none, in the commonwealth. Miller v. Sharp, 3 Rand. 41.

A bill against a defendant, not an inhabitant of this country, and having no property therein, can not be sustained. Hopkirk v. Bridges, 4 Hen. & M. 413.

So a court of chancery has no jurisdiction against an officer as an absent defendant, who resides out of the state at the time the claim is asserted here, which arises out of his official neglect. Dunlop v. Keith, 1 Leigh 430, 19 Am. Dec. 755.

A court of equity has no jurisdiction of a resident of another state, without his consent to compel him to acknowledge the trust character of his holding of real property in another state. Solenberger v. Herr, 2 Va. Dec. 550.

Power of Court Having Jurisdiction in Personam to Control Defendant's Acts beyond Territorial Jurisdiction.— A court having jurisdiction in personam may require the defendant to do, or refrain from doing, beyond its territorial jurisdiction, anything which it has power to require him to do or omit within the limits of its territory. State v. Fredlock, 52 W. Va. 232, 233, 43 S. E. 153.

A court having jurisdiction in personam may restrain a party from prosecuting a subsequent suit in another county, the effect of which will be to withdraw, from the court first acquiring jurisdiction, a part of the subject matter of the suit, and disobedience of the injunction order is an act of contempt which may be summarily punished. State v. Fredlock, 52 W. Va. 232, 233, 43 S. E. 153.

Jurisdiction of Actions Affecting Realty in Other States.—The well-settled general rule is that the court of one state has no jurisdiction to make a decree which will directly affect either the legal or equitable title to land situated in another state. The doctrine is, that if the person to do the act decreed is within the jurisdiction of the court, and the act may be done without the exercise of any authority operating territorially within the foreign jurisdiction, the court may act in personam, and oblige the party to convey, or otherwise comply with its decree. But it is not competent to the court to decree touching a foreign subject, when the act to be done can be accomplished and perfected only by an authority operating territorially. Thus a conveyance may be decreed of lands abroad, if the defendant is within the jurisdiction of the court, but not a partition of lands, as between joint tenants, tenants in common or coparceners. Poindexter v. Burwell, 82 Va. 507, 513; Farley v. Shippen, Wythe 254; Guerrant v. Fowler, 1 Hen. & M. 5; Aldridge v. Giles, 3 Hen. & M. 136, 142; Humphrey v. McClenachan, 1 Munf. 493, 500; Dickinson v. Hoomes, 8 Gratt. 353, 416; Wimer v. Wimer, 82 Va. 890, 901, 5 S. E. 536.

A court of chancery has no authority to decree an allotment of a widow's dower as to lands lying in another state, outside the jurisdiction of the court, but it is otherwise as to lands lying within this state. Blunt v. Gee, 5 Call 481.

A court of equity in Virginia may subject heirs living here, upon the covenants of the ancestor binding the heirs, to the extent of the value of land descended to them in another state. Dickinson v. Hoomes, 8 Gratt. 353.

Jurisdiction to Require Execution of Conveyance of Land in Another County.—A decree of the court of a county requiring a defendant residing within its limits to execute a conveyance for land lying in another county, can be enforced upon the person only of such defendant, and does not of itself vest any legal title in the complainant. Aldridge v. Giles, 3 Hen. & M. 136. See the title CONFLICT OF LAWS, vol. 3, p. 105.

Clearing Title to Land in Foreign State.—A court of equity having jurisdiction of the parties has the power to compel the defendant to release and discharge an apparent cloud upon the title to land situated in another state. Vaught v. Meador, 99 Va. 569, 39 S. E. 225.

Fraudulent Title Affecting Foreign Land—Vacation of.—If a title or power affecting lands in another state was obtained by duress or fraud, and a court of equity has jurisdiction of the parties, upon proper averments it may enter a personal decree vacating such title or power. Vaught v. Meador, 99 Va. 569, 39 S. E. 225.

Accounting by Party Converting Such Land.—Where one acting under a fraudulent title or power converts lands in a foreign state into money, he can be compelled to account either at law or in equity if the court has jurisdiction of the person. Vaught v. Meador, 99 Va. 569, 39 S. E. 225.

Jurisdiction of State Courts over Navigable Waters of State.—Courts have jurisdiction of cases of attachments against the owners of steamboats navigating in the waters of a state, and levy can be made on such boats. Com. v. Fry, 4 W. Va. 721.

Over Offences in Ohio River.—The jurisdiction of West Virginia is coextensive with the water of the Ohio river while confined within its banks, and in the proper county the state has jurisdiction of offenses committed on a boat, which is afloat on the river, whether fastened to the bank or not. State v. Plants, 25 W. Va. 119.

In a prosecution for aiding in the escape of slaves from the state of Virginia, it appeared that defendants, citizens of the state of Ohio, after the canoe in which the slaves crossed the Ohio river to the Ohio shore was run upon the shore, stepped into the water above low-water mark, and aided the slaves in the removal of their effects from the canoe. It was held that the offense was not committed in the jurisdiction of Virginia. Com. *v.* Garner, 3 Gratt. 655.

Over Potomac River—Offense by Citizen of Maryland.—Under the compact between Virginia and Maryland (see pp. 110 and 111 of the Va. Code of 1873), providing that all laws necessary for the preservation of fish in the Potomac river shall be made with mutual consent of both states, a citizen of Maryland is liable to prosecution and conviction for the violation of §§ 18, 20, ch. 100, Code, 1873, of Virginia, which were enacted with the consent of Maryland, relative to fishing in the Potomac river. Hendricks *v.* Com., 75 Va. 935.

State Can Not Interfere with Interstate Commerce.— The navigable waters of the state and the soil under them within its territorial limits, are the property of the state, for the benefit of its people, and it has the right to control them as it sees proper, provided it does not interfere with the authority granted the United States to regulate commerce, and navigation. Morgan *v.* Com., 98 Va. 812, 35 S. E. 448. See McCready *v.* Com., 27 Gratt. 985, 94 U. S. 391. See the title INTERSTATE COMMERCE, vol. 7, p. 864.

As to the limitation of jurisdiction of particular courts to their respective counties, districts, etc., see post, "Jurisdiction of Particular Courts," VIII.

As to jurisdiction over government property situated within a state, see post, "Relative Jurisdiction of State and Federal Courts," XI.

E. HOW JURISDICTION DETERMINED.

As to the power of a court to pass upon the question of its jurisdiction, the effect of such decision, etc., see post, "Conclusiveness of Determination as to Jurisdiction," IV, A, 1, c.

As to decision on plea to jurisdiction in criminal causes, see post, "De-termination of Question on Plea to Jurisdiction," XII, D.

As to jurisdiction as dependent on amount involved, see post, "Original Jurisdiction," I, F, 1.

F. AMOUNT IN CONTROVERSY AS CONTROLLING JURISDICTION.

1. Original Jurisdiction.

Definition.—The amount in controversy in an action or suit, so far as the plaintiff is concerned, is the amount really claimed by him, which amount is to be ascertained according to the circumstances of each case from the pleadings, the evidence before the court or jury, or from affidavits. Marion Machine Works *v.* Craig, 18 W. Va. 559.

Where the principal sum demanded, together, with the interest, is of sufficient amount to give jurisdiction, a court may hold cognizance of the case. Stratton *v.* Mutual Assur. Society, 6 Rand. 22.

Insertion of Penalty to Give Jurisdiction.—An action of debt was brought on a penal bill for $100, conditioned to pay $47, the defendant moved the court to stay the proceedings, because the penalty was inserted for the purpose of giving the court jurisdiction. It was decided that the motion would not be sustained. Heath *v.* Blaker, 2 Va. Cas. 215.

Waiver of Portion of Amount.—"It is very well settled that one may waive a portion of the amount in controversy where it is greater than the court's jurisdiction, in order to confer jurisdiction, if it is done without fraudulent intent. 1 Ency. Pl. & Prac. 707. That is a release of the balance of the debt." Ward *v.* Evans, 49 W. Va. 184, 38 S. E. 524.

Division of Single Matter into Several Suits.—" 'It is to be observed, with reference to inferior courts, which are limited by law to the decision of controversies where the amount involved falls within a specified sum, as in justices' courts, and other petty tribunals, that they will not be allowed to manufacture a jurisdiction for themselves by dividing a single matter into several suits, so as to bring them within the limits fixed by law, when the whole amount in controversy is sufficient to bring it within the jurisdiction of a higher court. Thus, where a plaintiff brings several distinct actions before a justice of the peace upon promissory notes, against one and the same defendant, each of the notes being for an amount within the jurisdiction of the justice, but the aggregate amount being beyond his jurisdiction, prohibition lies to restrain the justice from proceeding, even after judgment rendered, but before the money has been paid." Bodley v. Archibald, 33 W. Va. 229, 10 S. E. 392, quoting High on Extraordinary Legal Remedies.

As to the amount in controversy fixing the jurisdiction of particular courts. —See post, "Jurisdiction of Particular Courts," VIII.

As to the amount in case of justices' courts, see the title JUSTICES OF THE PEACE.

Splitting Cause by Consent.—While a writ of prohibition will be awarded to prevent a justice of the peace from taking jurisdiction of a debt in excess of one hundred dollars which has been split up into notes, each less than one hundred dollars, all of which are due, and for which separate warrants are being prosecuted before him, yet where such warrants have proceeded to judgment before the justice, with the consent or acquiescence of the defendant, such judgments can not be thereafter collaterally assailed by third persons. This result does not in any degree impinge upon the maxim that consent can not give jurisdiction, as the justice had jurisdiction over the amount represented in each judgment. Adams v. Jennings, 103 Va. 579, 49 S. E. 982. See ante, "Effect of Erroneous Proceedings by Courts Having Jurisdiction," I, B, 3.

2. Appellate Jurisdiction.

As to appellate jurisdiction as dependent on the amount in controversy, see the title APPEAL AND ERROR, vol. 1, pp. 475, 656, 662.

II. Derivation, Regulation and Divestiture.

A. CONSTITUTIONAL AND STATUTORY PROVISIONS CONFERRING AND REGULATING.

In General.—As to the constitutional provisions vesting the judicial power of the state, in the various courts, and providing that the jurisdiction of these tribunals and the judges thereof, except so far as conferred by the constitution shall be regulated by law, see the title COURTS, vol. 3, p. 699.

"In Virginia we have no courts deriving their origin from prescription or charter. They are all created by the legislative acts, defining their powers, and their jurisdictions." Thornton v. Smith, 1 Wash. 84.

"By jurisdiction over the subject matter is meant the nature of the cause of action and of the relief sought; and this is conferred by the sovereign authority which organizes the court, and is to be sought for in the general nature of its powers or in authority specially conferred." Hall v. Hall, 12 W. Va. 1.

"The regulation by law of the jurisdiction of the several courts of the commonwealth, embraces the distribution of the judicial power amongst them; in regard to which, there is no limitation, except such as arises out of the distinctive character of the tribunals, so far as designated by the constitution. The jurisdiction of the supreme court is to be appellate, or of that nature in a liberal sense; that of the other courts may be either original or appellate—the jurisdiction of all may be either civil or criminal. There can be no appeal from the supreme court to the superior courts, nor from the latter to the county courts; but, on the other hand, there is no constitutional right of appeal from the county to the superior courts, nor from the latter to the supreme court. The legislative department has authority to terminate litigation where it pleases, but can not protract it beyond the supreme court of appeals." Sharpe v. Robertson, 5 Gratt. 518.

"There is no such thing as a lien upon the jurisdiction of a court, obtained by the institution or prosecution therein, of an action or suit, whether original or appellate. So far as the legislature may constitutionally distribute the judicial power amongst the several courts of the commonwealth, to the same extent they may afterwards reapportion it, in the whole or in part, both prospectively and retrospectively; and no suitor has a right to complain that his cause is thereby transferrd from the cognizance of one tribunal of justice to that of another." Sharpe v. Robertson, 5 Gratt. 518. See the titles APPEAL AND ERROR, vol. 1, p. 476; CONSTITUTIONAL LAW, vol. 3, p. 140; COURTS, vol. 3, p. 696.

As to the constitutional and statutory provisions as to the jurisdiction of the various courts, see post, "Jurisdiction of Particular Courts," VIII.

To Be Exercised at Times and Places Authorized by Law.—The existence and legal constitution of a court being an inseparable part of its jurisdiction, it has no power to hear and determine causes except at times and places authorized by law. Johnston v. Hunter, 50 W. Va. 52, 40 S. E. 448.

Constitutional Limitations upon Power of Legislature.—If the constitution absolutely separated the common-law and chancery jurisdictions, the legislature could not unite them in the same courts, directly or indirectly. Kamper v. Kawkins, 1 Va. Cas. 19.

As to the constitutional right to trial by jury in certain matters, as limiting the power of the legislature to give

equity jurisdiction over such matters, see post, "Scope and Limitation of Jurisdiction," VII, E.

Usurpation of Power by Illegal Extension of Jurisdiction—Remedy.—The jurisdiction of inferior tribunals is fixed by law, and for such a tribunal, even though in good faith, to extend its jurisdiction beyond the . limitations of law, is to make it guilty of usurpation and abuse of power. Norfolk, etc., R. Co. v. Pinnacle Coal Co., 44 W. Va. 574, 30 S. E. 196.

Under pretense of determining its jurisdiction, an inferior tribunal can not usurp a jurisdiction which is denied to it, nor, having jurisdiction of the subject matter in controversy, abuse or exceed its legitimate powers. Norfolk, etc., R. Co. v. Pinnacle Coal Co., 44 W. Va. 574, 30 S. E. 196.

In all cases of usurpation and abuse of power, when the inferior court has no jurisdiction of the subject matter in controversy, or, having such jurisdiction, exceeds its legitimate powers, prohibition now lies as a matter of right, and not as a matter of sound judicial discretion. Norfolk, etc., R. Co. v. Pinnacle Coal Co., 44 W. Va. 574, 30 S. E. 196. See the title PROHIBITION, WRIT OF.

B. DIVESTITURE OF JURISDICTION.

1. Effect of Repeal of Statute Conferring.

Whenever a court is deprived of jurisdiction over any class of cases, by the repeal of a statute which gives the jurisdiction, and there is no provision made for the transfer of such cases to some other court which has or is given jurisdiction, and no reservation is made for the trial of pending cases in such courts, all such cases fall with the repealed statute. Dulin v. Lillard, 91 Va. 718, 20 S. E. 821.

Where a bill was filed in a county court for the sale of a ward's real estate, when that court had jurisdiction of such cases, the repeal of the statute giving it jurisdiction while the cause is pending, will not affect the validity of its decree entered after the repeal of the statute. Pennnybacker v. Switzer, 75 Va. 671.

Where an enactment of the legislature which authorized certain causes of action has been repealed, the jurisdiction of the justice of the peace over the same is repealed therewith, and he can not, under the pretense of deciding whether such enactment. has been repealed or not, take jurisdiction of such causes of action, and, if he does so, he is guilty of exceeding his legitimate powers subjecting him to restraint by prohibition. Norfolk, etc., R. Co. v. Pinnacle Coal Co., 44 W. Va. 574, 30 S. E. 196. See the title STATUTES.

2. Effect upon General Jurisdiction of Statute Conferring Powers in Special Enumerated Cases.

"As a general rule a statute conferring power upon a court in special, enumerated cases, is ˙not to be construed as divesting a general jurisdiction in cases of an analogous nature not enumerated." Durrett v. Davis, 24 Gratt. 302.

3. Subsequent Disability of Defendant.

Where a court has fairly acquired jurisdiction of a cause and the parties, that jurisdiction continues notwithing the subsequent disability of the defendant, as where process was served upon a defendant prior to his conviction of a felony, and judgment by default was obtained against him while confined in the penitentiary. Neale v. Utz, 75 Va. 480.

4. Recession of Territory.

A cause pending in the supreme court of the United States at the time the county of Alexandria was receded to the state of Virginia was properly heard by that court after that time, and it was proper for its decision to be sent down to the circuit superior court for that county, and is to be enforced by that court. McLaughlin v. Bank, 7 Gratt. 68.

III. How Acquired.

A. SERVICE OF PROCESS OR APPEARANCE.

In General.—Jurisdiction is acquired by the issuance and service of process. Spiller v. Wells, 96 Va. 598, 32 S. E. 46; Craig v. Hoge, 95 Va. 275, 28 S. E. 317.

Besides having jurisdiction of the class of causes to which a given cause of action belongs, a court must obtain cognizance of the particular cause by requisite process, before it can hear and determine it. Moore v. Holt, 55 W. Va. 507, 508, 48 S. E. 251; Pennsylvania R. Co. v. Rogers, 52 W. Va. 450, 44 S. E. 300; Railway Co. v. Wright, 50 W. Va. 653, 41 S. E. 147; Ensign Mfg. Co. v. McGinnis, 30 W. Va. 532, 4 S. E. 782; Craig v. Hoge, 95 Va. 275, 28 S. E. 317.

Generally, as to the necessity, form and sufficiency of process and the service thereof, see the titles SERVICE OF PROCESS; SUMMONS AND PROCESS.

Notice and opportunity to be heard are essential to the jurisdiction of all courts, even in proceedings in rem, and judgment without jurisdiction is a nullity. Dorr v. Rohr, 82 Va. 359. See the titles JUDGMENTS AND DECREES, ante, p. 276; SERVICE OF PROCESS.

Appearance as Conferring Jurisdiction.—Where there has been no actual or implied notice to a party, and he has not consented to the jurisdiction of the court over him, it may still be acquired by his appearance in the cause, and if a party appear for any purpose other than to object to the legality of the process or its service, it dispenses with service of process. Frank v. Zeigler, 46 W. Va. 614, 33 S. E. 761.

Generally, as to appearance as conferring jurisdiction, see the title APPEARANCES, vol. 1, p. 674.

Jurisdiction of the res is obtained by a seizure under process of the court, whereby it is held to abide such order as the court may make concerning it. Hall *v.* Hall, 12 W. Va. 1.

When a party out of the jurisdiction of the court has property within the jurisdiction, it may be subjected to a claim against the party, although he can not be served with personal process. O'Brien *v.* Stephens, 11 Gratt. 610; Fowler *v.* Lewis, 36 W. Va. 112, 14 S. E. 447, 451; Barrett *v.* McAllister, 33 W. Va. 720, 11 S. E. 220, 228; Coleman *v.* Waters, 13 W. Va. 278, 311; Mahany *v.* Kephart, 15 W. Va. 609, 619; Taylor *v.* Cox, 32 W. Va. 148, 9 S. E. 70, 75; Wetherill *v.* McCloskey, 28 W. Va. 195, 198.

In an attachment proceeding the jurisdiction acquired by the seizure of the property attached, is not to pass absolutely upon the rights of the parties, but to pass upon those rights after opportunity has been afforded its owner to appear and be heard. To this end the notice by publication prescribed by statute is indispensable, and a decree entered without such publication is void. Haymond *v.* Camden, 22 W. Va. 180. See the title ATTACHMENT AND GARNISHMENT, vol. 2' p. 70.

Issuance of Writ as Commencement of Suit.—See the title ACTIONS, vol. 1, p. 133, and cross references there found.

B. HOW ACQUIRED AS TO NON-RESIDENTS.

Notice by Publication.—See generally, the titles SERVICE OF PROCESS; SUMMONS AND PROCESS.

Attachment against Foreign Corporations and Nonresident Debtors.—See the titles ATTACHMENT AND GARNISHMENT, vol. 2, p. 70; FOREIGN CORPORATIONS, vol. 6. p. 190.

C. NECESSITY FOR PLEADINGS INVOKING ACTION OF COURT.

In General.—The court in order to sustain its action must obtain actual cognizance of the cause both by the requisite process and pleadings. Moore *v.* Holt, 55 W. Va. 507, 47 S. E. 251. See the title PLEADING.

Effect of Want of Allegation against Defendant.—Where a person by a decree in a cause on the defendant's motion was made a party defendant, but there was no allegation in the bill, nor was there any decree prayed against him, and he was not named in the bill, he was not in any sense of the term a defendant, and the court had no jurisdiction to render a decree against him, and if it did so it would be a mere nullity. McCoy *v.* Allen, 16 W. Va. 724; Moseley *v.* Cocke, 7 Leigh 224, 226; Newman *v.* Mollohan, 10 W. Va. 488, 503.

An answer to a bill in chancery shows that a third party should have been made defendant. Such third party then tendered his answer, waiving service of process. The original bill was not amended and in it there were no allegations against this third person, no relief prayed against him, and no allusion whatever to him. Evidence was taken which showed the interest of this party in the suit, but the court had no jurisdiction over him, as he was no proper party to the suit, and a decree affecting him was a mere nullity as to him. Shaffer *v.* Fetty, 30 W. Va. 248, 4 S. E. 278.

Nonresidence of Defendant.—A bill against an absent debtor or defendant, in order to give the court jurisdiction, under the statute concerning attachments and suits against absent defendants, 1 Rev. Code, ch. 123, must distinctly aver the nonresidence of the debtor, and if his nonresidence be not distinctly averred the court has no jurisdiction. Kelso *v.* Blackburn, 3 Leigh 299.

If the home defendants, to a bill in chancery filed against them and an absent defendant or debtor, alleging them to have in possession lands of the debtor by a voluntary or fraudulent conveyance, answer that the debtor is a resident, the plaintiff to sustain the jurisdiction of the court under 1 Rev. Code, ch. 123, must prove the fact of the debtor's residence abroad. Kelso v. Blackburn, 3 Leigh 299.

Allegation of Cause of Action within Jurisdiction—Laying Venue.—Generally, as to the necessity and sufficiency of laying venue, see the titles INDICTMENTS, INFORMATIONS AND PRESENTMENTS, vol. 7, p. 371; PLEADING; VENUE.

In an action of assumpsit in the superior court of a county, the declarations laying the venue in a different county, and omitting to state that the cause of action arose within the jurisdiction of the court, is not error sufficient in arrest of judgment. Buster v. Ruffner, 5 Munf. 27.

The declaration in an action of debt to recover the value of a ship, insured in case of its being captured and condemned, should show where, when, and by whom she was captured, and that the court which condemned her had jurisdiction. Stone v. Patterson, 6 Call 71.

Actions may be brought in the courts of this state upon contracts entered into, or personal injuries committed, anywhere. It is not necessary as a general rule to state in the declaration where the contract arose or the injury was committed. But this is sometimes necessary and then the plaintiff is permitted by a fiction to state under a videlicet, that the place is within the jurisdiction of the court in which the suit is brought; which fiction can not be traversed. Shaver v. White, 6 Munf. 110.

Where a suit is brought in a corporation court, the declaration must lay the cause of action to have arisen within the jurisdiction of the court. Thornton v. Smith, 1 Wash. 81. See Turberville v. Long, 3 Hen. & M. 309.

In Turberville v. Long, 3 Hen. & M. 309, it was held not to be necessary in actions in the district court to aver in the declaration that the cause of action arose within the jurisdiction of the court; but that it seemed that such averment was necessary only in actions in the corporation courts.

It is not necessary to give jurisdiction that the declaration contains an averment of the facts authorizing the plaintiff to sue in the county where the action may be brought; jurisdiction will be presumed unless questioned by plea in abatement interposed in proper time. Where circuit courts, being courts of general jurisdiction, take cognizance of causes, every intendment is in favor of their jurisdiction, and rightfully to exercise it. Empire Coal, etc., Co. v. Hull Coal, etc., Co., 51 W. Va. 474, 41 S. E. 917.

D. EFFECT OF CONSENT OR WAIVER OF OBJECTION.

1. Jurisdiction of the Subject Matter.

In General.—When the court has not jurisdiction of the subject matter, the consent of parties can not give it. McCall v. Peachy, 1 Call 55; McCarthy v. Gibson, 5 Gratt. 308, 329; Clarke v. Conn, 1 Munf. 160, 161; McCall v. Peachy, 3 Munf. 285, 296; Alexander v. Coleman, 6 Munf. 328, 350; Freer v. Davis, 52 W. Va. 1, 2, 43 S. E. 164; Yates v. Taylor Co. Court, 47 W. Va. 376, 35 S. E. 24; Bogle v. Fitzhugh, 2 Wash. 213; Beckley v. Palmer, 11 Gratt. 625; Litterall v. Jackson, 80 Va. 604; Stuart v. Coalter, 4 Rand. 74, 79; Adams v. Jennings, 103 Va. 579, 49 S. E. 982; McCall v. Peachy, 1 Call 55; Mayo v. Murchie, 3 Munf. 358.

The law alone can give jurisdiction over the subject matter; therefore it can not be given by consent. Ohio River R. Co. v. Gibbens, 35 W. Va. 517, 12 S. E. 1093.

Consent of parties can not confer upon a court jurisdiction which the law does not confer, or confers upon some other court, although the parties may by consent submit themselves to the jurisdiction of the court. In other words, consent can not confer jurisdiction of subject matter. Yates *v.* Taylor Co. Court, 47 W. Va. 376, 35 S. E. 24; Bogle *v.* Fitzhugh, 2 Wash. 213.

As consent can not confer jurisdiction, a plaintiff upon whose bill there is a final decree and ad.udication against him, upon matters set up in the bill, is not estopped to assert, upon appeal, that the court to which he resorted had no jurisdiction of the subject matter. In such case, although the decree will be reversed at t'1e instance of the plaintiff, the costs in the appellate court will be awarded aga'nst him. Freer *v.* Davis, 52 W. Va. 1, 2, 43 S. E. 164; Sprinkle *v.* Duty, 54 W. Va. 559, 563, 46 S. E. 557.

"Though the admission of a party in a suit, is conclusive as to matters of fact, or may deprive him of the benefit of a privilege, which, if insisted on, would exempt him from the jurisdiction of the court; yet, no admission of parties can change the law, or give jurisdiction to a court, of a cause, of which it hath no jurisdict'on. Agreeably hereto, the established and universal practice of courts of equity is to dismiss the plaintiff's bill, if it appears to be grounded on a title merely legal, and not cognizable by them; notwithstanding the defendant hath answered the bill, and insisted on matters of title; and it can make no difference whether the legal title be insisted on by the answer, or by the plea; that nothing hath a greater tendency to introduce uncertainty in the law, than the giving way to new exceptions to general, settled and known rules of practice in courts of justice; and therefore, no such exceptions ought to be allowed, but upon the clearest grounds." Stuart *v.* Coalter, 4 Rand. 74, 79. See the title DISMISSAL, DISCONTINUANCE AND NONSUIT, vol. 4, p. 683.

Jurisdiction in Vacation.—Consent of parties can not give jurisdiction to the circuit court to render in vacation any decree or judgment not authorized by statute. Tyson *v.* Glaize, 23 Gratt. 799. See the title CHAMBERS AND VACATION, vol. 2, p. 767.

Consent to Equity Jurisdiction as Dispensing with Strictness of Form.—Although consent of parties can not give a court of equity jurisdiction, or supply the total absence of other necessary parties, yet such consent may dispense with strictness of form, and enable the court to decide a cause in relation to parties who are in fact, though irregularly before it. Mayo *v.* Murchie, 3 Munf. 358.

Exercise of Equity Jurisdiction at Defendant's Instance.—Where a court of equity at the instance of the defendant, and without any objection to its jurisdiction took possession of slaves and directed them to be sold, and having since held and controlled the proceeds, it was too late for the defendants to object to the jurisdiction of the court. Henley *v.* Perkins, 6 Gratt. 615.

2. Jurisdiction of the Person.

In General.—While consent of the parties can not confer upon a court jurisdiction of the subject matter, it may confer jurisdiction of the person. Yates *v.* Taylor Co. Court, 47 W. Va. 376, 35 S. E. 24; Bogle *v.* Fitzhugh, 2 Wash. 213.

All Parties Must Consent.—The consent of two of the parties can not give jurisdiction where the objection appears on the face of the bill, and there are many other parties. Randolph *v.* Kinney, 3 Rand. 394.

At Special Term of Court.—Section 3062, of the Virginia Code of 1887, provides that at a special term of a court, any cause then ready for hearing, although not ready at the previous term, may with consent of parties, be heard. But without such consent the court can not hear a demurrer to a bill at such special term, and dissolve an injunction. Fowler *v.* Mosher, 85 Va. 421, 7 S. E. 542.

Effect of Taking Continuance.—If the parties consent that a suit shall be docketed and proceeded in to a final decree in a court which had general jurisdiction of the class of cases to which the case belonged, they waived all right to object to the jurisdiction of the court. The fact of taking and agreeing to a continuance is evidence of being made parties to the record, and of having recognized the case as in court. Bell *v.* Farmville, etc., R. Co., 91 Va. 99, 20 S. E. 942.

Pleadings Made and Cause Docketed —No Objection after Trial and Judgment.—Parties may, by consent, make up the pleadings in a case, and have it docketed and tried in any court having jurisdiction, and if they appear and make no objection to its regularity, such court may exercise jurisdiction, and no objection can be made after the trial and judgment. Hunter *v.* Stewart, 23 W. Va. 549.

As to waiver by appearance and failure to object, see the title APPEARANCES, vol. 1, p. 667.

As to time and manner of raising objections to jurisdiction of the person, see post, "Raising and Waiving Objections to Jurisdiction," XII.

3. Application of Rules to Proceedings in Error or on Appeal.

Jurisdiction of Court of Appeals.— Neither consent nor long acquiescence of parties can give the court of appeals jurisdiction. Clarke *v.* Conn, 1 Munf. 160. See the title APPEAL AND ERROR, vol. 1, p. 476.

But in Bogle *v.* Fitzhugh, 2 Wash. 213, it is said: "Consent of parties can not give jurisdiction where the court has it not. But this rule is only applicable to a case of original jurisdiction."

Jurisdiction of County Court.—"It was further objected for the defendants in error, that the plaintiff in error by appealing from the judgment of the justice to the county court of Ohio county, thereby submitted himself to its jurisdiction; and having invoked its aid could not afterwards be heard to question its judgment in the premises. In reply to this objection it was alleged for the plaintiff in error, that if the county court of Ohio had not jurisdiction by law, it could not be conferred by the consent of plaintiff. The correctness of this is too well settled to require comment." Ingersoll *v.* Buchanan, 1 W. Va. 181.

E. EFFECT OF FRAUD.

Can Not Confer or Take Away Jurisdiction.—If a claim is merely colorable in order to give a court jurisdiction, and that fact was made to appear, jurisdiction will be declined, for jurisdiction can no more be conferred than it can be taken away by improper devices of parties. Cox *v.* Carr, 79 Va. 28; Fink *v.* Denny, 75 Va. 663, 667.

As to colorable allegations by which it is sought to give jurisdiction to a court of equity, see post, "Manner of Acquiring," VII, B, 1.

As to fraud in obtaining service of process, see the title SERVICE OF PROCESS.

IV. Presumptions as to Jurisdiction.

A. OF COURTS OF GENERAL JURISDICTION.

1. Where Proceeding within Scope of General Powers.

a. General Rule.

Jurisdiction Presumed till Contrary Shown.—In the case of courts of general jurisdiction proceeding within the scope of their general powers, every presumption, not inconsistent with the record, is to be indulged in favor of the jurisdiction. Devaughn *v.* Devaughn, 19 Gratt. 556; Wade *v.* Hancock, 76 Va. 620; Woodhouse *v.* Fillbates, 77 Va. 317; Hill *v.* Woodward, 78 Va. 765; Lamar *v.* Hale, 79 Va. 147; Richardson *v.* Seever, 84 Va. 259, 4 S. E. 712; Shenandoah, etc., R. Co. *v.* Ashby, 86 Va. 232, 9 S. E. 1003; Lemmon *v.* Herbert, 92 Va. 653, 24 S. E.

249; Preston *v.* Kindrick, 94 Va. 760, 27 S. E. 588; Chesapeake, etc., R. Co. *v.* Washington, etc., R. Co., 99 Va. 715, '40 S. E. 202; Turner *v.* Burraud, 102 Va. 324, 46 S. E. 318; Fausler *v.* Parsons, 6 W. Va. 486; Chesapeake, etc., R. Co. *v.* Pack, 6 W. Va. 397; Hall *v.* Hall, 12 W. Va. 1; Mayer *v.* Adams, 27 W. Va. 244; Yates *v.* Taylor Co. Court, 47 W. Va. 376, 35 S. E. 24; Empire Coal, etc., Co. *v.* Hull Coal, etc., Co., 51 W. Va. 474, 41 S. E. 917; St. Lawrence, etc., Co. *v.* Holt, 51 W. Va. 352, 360, 41 S. E. 351; Starr *v.* Sampselle, 55 W. Va. 442, 450, 47 S. E. 255.

"All judgments and decrees of courts which do not belong to that class called inferior courts and courts of limited jurisdiction, are conclusive in themselves, unless clearly beyond the jurisdiction of the tribunals from whence they emanate. 1 Herman Est. & Res., § 346." St. Lawrence, etc., Co. *v.* Holt, 51 W. Va. 352, 360, 41 S. E. 351.

"A court of general jurisdiction, proceeding within the general scope of its powers, is presumed to have jurisdiction to give the judgment it renders until the contrary appears." Yates *v.* Taylor County Court, 47 W. Va. 376, 35 S. E. 24, quoting Galpin *v.* Page, 18 Wall. (U. S.) 350, 21 L. Ed. 959.

"Superior courts of general jurisdiction are presumed to have jurisdiction of every particular case which comes before them; and if the contrary is alleged, it must be proven." Mayer *v.* Adams, 27 W. Va. 244.

"'When a court of general jurisdiction pronounces judgment, the presumption is in favor of its jurisdiction, and it is not incumbent upon one who bases a right upon such judgment to aver facts essential to the existence of jurisdiction. And whatever is upon the records of such court is presumed to be rightfully there.' Black on Judg., § 270." St. Lawrence, etc., Co. *v.* Holt, 51 W. Va. 352, 361, 41 S. E. 351.

"Where a court of general jurisdic-

tion acts within the scope of its general powers, its judgment will be presumed to be in accordance with its jurisdiction, and can not be collaterally impeached." Pulaski Co. *v.* Stuart, 28 Gratt. 872.

Unless the want of jurisdiction appears on the face of the record, the validity of a judgment of a court of record can not be collaterally attacked on that ground. Wandling *v.* Straw, 25 W. Va. 692. See Poole *v.* Dilworth, 26 W. Va. 583.

"The presumption that the powers committed to judicial tribunals of general jurisdiction have been properly exercised is essential to the repose and safety of society, and the inconvenience of allowing it to be met and overcome by parol evidence is greater than any benefit that could be derived from a different course. Public safety demands that when such a tribunal of general jurisdiction has pronounced judgment its adjudication on that subject shall be as conclusive on the question whether the defendant was duly notified as on any other point essential to the determination of the cause. 1 Smith's Lead Cas. 1119, 1127, etc." Preston *v.* Kindrick, 94 Va. 760, 27 S. E. 588.

As to the rule that mere erroneous exercise of jurisdiction will not render a judgment or decree void and liable to collateral attack, see ante, "Effect of Erroneous Proceedings by Court Having Jurisdiction," I, B, 3. And see the title JUDGMENTS AND DECREES, ante, p. 161.

Presumption Extends to Both Parties and Subject Matter.—Such courts are presumed to have jurisdiction of both the subject matter and the parties to causes in which they render judgments. Turner *v.* Burraud, 102 Va. 324, 46 S. E. 318.

"This presumption embraces jurisdiction not only of the cause or subject matter of the action in which the judgment is given but of the parties also." Yates *v.* Taylor County Court, 47 W. Va. 376, 35 S. E. 24, quoting Galpin *v.* Page, 18 Wall. (U. S.) 350, 21 L. Ed. 959.

Principle Applies to Every Judgment or Decree in Various Stages of Proceeding.—"There is no principle of law better settled, than that every act of a court of competent jurisdiction shall be presumed to have been rightly done till the contrary appears; the rule applies as well to every judgment or decree, rendered in the various stages of its proceedings from the initiation to their completion, as to their adjudication that the plaintiff has a right of action. Every matter adjudicated becomes a part of its record, which thenceforth proves itself, without referring to the evidence on which it has been adjudicated." Hall *v.* Hall, 12 W. Va. 1.

Presumptions on Appeal.—Generally, as to presumptions on appeal, burden of proof to show error, etc., see the title APPEAL AND ERROR, vol. 1, p. 609, et seq.

If several grounds are apparent from the record, whereon the court might have acted, it is presumed to have acted on that ground which gave it jurisdiction, and not upon the others. Woodhouse *v.* Fillbates, 77 Va. 317; Lamar *v.* Hale, 79 Va. 147.

This presumption is especially applicable when from loss of any part of the record it is difficult to ascertain the ground whereon jurisdiction was taken in the particular case, and there is danger of injustice. Woodhouse *v.* Fillbates, 77 Va. 317.

It not appearing in the record whether the term of the county court at which the award was entered as the judgment of the court, was a quarterly or monthly term, it must be presumed by the appellate court, that it was a term at which the court had jurisdiction to enter the judgment. Forrer *v.* Coffman, 23 Gratt. 871.

In Steenrod *v.* Wheeling, etc., R.

Co., 27 W. Va. 1, 12, it is said: "The decree of June 5, 1880, states that the cause came on to be heard, among other things, upon the order of publication against the nonresident defendants 'duly executed.' This according to the settled law is conclusive as to the due publication of the order, so far as the appellate court is concerned. Hunter *v.* Spotswood. 1 Wash. 145; Gibson *v.* White, 3 Munf. 94; Moore *v.* Holt, 10 Gratt. 284."

b. Presumption Only Arises Where Record Silent or Not Inconsistent.

In General.—This presumption in favor of jurisdiction only arises as to jurisdictional facts concerning which the record is silent. Turner *v.* Burraud, 102 Va. 324, 46 S. E. 318.

There is no place for presumption when the want of jurisdiction appears affirmatively on the face of the proceedings. In such case the judgments and decrees of a court of general jurisdiction are of no greater force than those of inferior courts of limited jurisdiction acting beyond their powers. Wade *v.* Hancock, 76 Va. 620; Dillard *v.* Central, etc., Co., 82 Va. 734, 1 S. E. 124.

Want of jurisdiction makes such judgments null; and they may be so treated by any court in any proceeding, direct or collateral. Wade *v.* Hancock, 76 Va. 620; Dillard *v.* Central, etc., Co., 82 Va. 734, 1 S. E. 124.

"The presumptions which the law implies in support of the judgments of superior courts of general jurisdiction only arise with respect to jurisdictional facts, concerning which the record is silent. Presumptions are only indulged to supply the absence of evidence or averments respecting the facts presumed. They have no place for consideration when the evidence is disclosed, or the averment is made. When, therefore, the record states the evidence, or makes an averment with reference to a jurisdictional fact, it will be understood to speak the truth on that point, and it will not be presumed that there was other or different evidence respecting the fact, or that the fact was otherwise than as averred. If, for example, it appears from the return of the officer, or the proof of service contained in the record, that the summons was served at a particular place, and there is no averment of any other service, it will not be presumed that service was also made at another and different place; or, if it appears in like manner that the service was made upon a person other than the defendant, it will not be presumed, in the silence of the record, that it was made upon the defendant also. Were not this so, it would never be possible to attack collaterally the judgment of a superior court, although a want of jurisdiction might be apparent upon its face. The answer to the attack would always be that, notwithstanding the evidence or the averment, the necessary facts to support the judgment are presumed." Turner v. Burraud, 102 Va. 324, 46 S. E. 318, quoting Galpin v. Page, 18 Wall. (U. S.) 350, 21 L. Ed. 959.

The presumption that a court of general jurisdiction within its authority acts rightly and has jurisdiction to render its judgment until contrary appears, applies only to matters as to which the record is silent, and can not operate to supply jurisdictional facts, which the returns must show affirmatively. Shenandoah, etc., R. Co. v. Ashby, 86 Va. 232, 9 S. E. 1003.

If the record discloses a particular method of service of process and none other is alleged, none other will be presumed. Turner v. Burraud, 102 Va. 324, 46 S. E. 318.

When the record shows want of jurisdiction over a given person, the judgment or decree affects not such person. Lamar v. Hale, 79 Va. 147.

No presumption lies in favor of court of competent jurisdiction that all parties in interest were before it, unless the record shows that all such parties had notice. Pitzer v. Logan, 85 Va. 374, 7 S. E. 385.

When the record shows in any court, whether superior or inferior, that the court has proceeded without notice, any presumption in its favor is at an end, and it may not only be reversed as erroneous, but be impeached and set aside collaterally as void, the rendition of a judgment against a party not before the court in any way being as utterly void as though the court had undertaken to act when the subject matter was not within its cognizance. Thus, where the original process, and the return thereon, showed the defendant was not included in either, a judgment against her was held to be void, as the presumption of jurisdiction was overcome. Blanton v. Carroll, 86 Va. 539, 10 S. E. 329; Fairfax v. Alexandria, 28 Gratt. 16, and note; Lawson v. Moorman, 85 Va. 880, 9 S. E. 150.

c. Conclusiveness of Determination as to Jurisdiction.

"The question of the sufficiency of service, or whether property attached was subject to seizure is one of jurisdiction. A judicial determination of jurisdiction is binding upon the parties until set aside or reversed in a direct proceeding. The judgment of a court of superior jurisdiction may be collaterally attacked upon the ground that the court rendering such judgment had not jurisdiction of the action. But such facts or circumstances only can be shown or relied on, in support of such attack, as affirmatively appear on the face of the record, or what, under the law as it read at the date of the judgment, constituted the judgment roll. Where a judgment recites the fact that the defendant has been duly served with process, this is a direct adjudication by the court upon the point, and is as conclusive on the parties as any other fact decided in the cause, provided it does not affirmatively appear from other portions of the record constituting the judgment-roll, that the recital is untrue. * * * The record of a court of superior jurisdiction imports absolute verity; it can not be collaterally attached by proof aliunde. If the court has jurisdiction of the subject matter and the parties, it is altogether immaterial how grossly irregular or manifestly erroneous its proceedings may have been; its final order can not be regarded as a nullity, and can not, therefore, be collaterally impeached. And this even where the judgment would without question be reversed on appeal." St. Lawrence, etc., Co. v. Holt, 51 W. Va. 352, 360, 41 S. E. 351. See the title JUDGMENTS AND DECREES, ante, p. 551.

"Vanfleet on Col. Attack, § 1, says: 'And as no one would think of holding a judgment of the court of last resort void if its jurisdiction were debatable or even colorable, the same rule must be applied to the judgments of all judicial tribunals. This is the true theory of judicial action when viewed collaterally. If any jurisdictional question is debatable or colorable, the tribunals must decide it; and an erroneous conclusion can only be corrected by some proceeding provided by law for so doing, commonly called a direct attack.' These considerations and authorities lead to the conclusion that in a case in which it is questionable or debatable whether a court has jurisdiction, and it erroneously decides that it does have, its judgment or decree is erroneous and voidable only, and subject to correction only by proper proceedings in the court which rendered it or by an appellate court, and is not void or open to collateral attack." St. Lawrence, etc., Co. v. Holt, 51 W. Va. 352, 371, 41 S. E. 351.

"The rule that a court has power to determine its own jurisdiction when the question is debatable at all applies in ascertaining whether it has juris-diction of the person. 'The rule is, that if the notice is defective or irregular, but not to the extent of being substantially worthless, a judgment by default entered thereon will be regular and liable to be corrected or set aside on motion, or reversed above, but not absolutely void, and hence not open to collateral attack.' " Black on Judg., § 83." St. Lawrence, etc., Co. v. Holt, 51 W. Va. 352, 370, 41 S. E. 351.

Generally, as to the conclusiveness of judicial records, see the title RECORDS.

Where an inferior court has general jurisdiction of the subject matter, it must exercise its own judgment as to the sufficiency of the process by which it acquires jurisdiction of the special subject or person in any particular case, and an erroneous judgment in that regard is no ground for a writ of prohibition, but is the subject of a writ of error. But this general rule is subject to this modification, that where, the inferior courts having a general jurisdiction of the subject matter in controversy, it clearly appears that in the conduct of the trial they have exceeded their legitimate powers, for which there is no adequate remedy in the ordinary course of proceedings, the writ of prohibition will lie in such cases under the West Virginia statute and under the general principles of law. McConiha v. Guthrie, 21 W. Va. 134; Board of Supervisors v. Gorrell, 20 Gratt. 484; Swinburn v. Smith, 15 W. Va. 483.

2. Where Exercising Special Statutory Jurisdiction.

Courts of general jurisdiction stand upon the same footing with courts of limited powers, when not acting within the scope of statutory authority. Richardson v. Seever, 84 Va. 259, 4 S. E. 712.

"Even though a court be a superior court of general jurisdiction, still when the particular proceedings are not according to the course of common law but under a statute giving a summary remedy, the record on its face should generally show, that the particular case comes within the statute and that the statute has been followed." Mayer *v.* Adams, 27 W. Va. 244.

Where a court of general jurisdiction has conferred upon it special powers by special statutes, which are only exercised ministerially, and not judicially, no presumption of jurisdiction will attend its judgments, and the facts essential to the exercise of the special jurisdiction must appear on the face of the record. Pulaski County *v.* Stuart, 28 Gratt. 872; Dinwiddie County *v.* Stuart, 28 Gratt. 526, 531; Chesterfield County *v.* Hall, 80 Va. 321.

A county court acting under the statute authorizing county courts to purchase salt, is exercising a special authority, and it must appear from the record that the justices were summoned, or that a majority were present, when a bond was executed for salt purchased, or the bond will be held to be null and void. Dinwiddie County *v.* Stuart, 28 Gratt. 526; Chesterfield County *v.* Hall, 80 Va. 321.

B. OF COURTS OF SPECIAL OR LIMITED JURISDICTION.

1. General Rule.

Jurisdiction Must Affirmatively Appear of Record.—The rule stated above as to presumptions as to jurisdiction of courts of general jurisdiction is different with respect to courts of special or limited authority. Their jurisdiction must affirmatively appear by sufficient evidence or proper averment in the record or their judgments will be deemed void on their face. Yates *v.* Taylor County Court, 47 W. Va. 376, 35 S. E. 24; Richardson *v.* Seever, 84 Va. 259, 4 S. E. 712; Cox *v.* Thomas, 9 Gratt. 323; Fausler *v.* Parsons, 6 W. Va. 486; Rutter *v.* Sullivan, 25 W. Va. 427; Hamilton *v.* Tucker County Court, 38 W. Va. 71, 18 S. E. 8; Shank *v.* Ravenswood, 43 W. Va. 242, 27 S. E. 223.

"Inferior courts of limited jurisdiction are not presumed to have jurisdiction of the particular case on which they have acted. It must be made to appear affirmatively that the case falls within the defined limits of their jurisdiction." Mayer *v.* Adams, 27 W. Va. 244.

The jurisdictional facts necessary to give a court of special and limited jurisdiction a right to act must appear in the record of its proceedings, or such proceedings will be regarded as had without any jurisdiction and therefore as absolute nullities. Mayer *v.* Adams, 27 W. Va. 244.

"Judge Cooley, with his usual correctness in eliminating authorities, in his most excellent work on Constitutional Limitations, p. 405, et seq. and notes, says: 'Some courts are of general jurisdiction, by which is meant that their authority extends to a great variety of matters; while others are only of special and limited jurisdiction, by which it is understood that they have authority extending only to certain special cases. The want of jurisdiction is equally fatal in the proceedings of each; but different rules prevail in showing it. It is not to be assumed that a court of general jurisdiction has in any case proceeded to adjudge upon matters over which it had no authority; and its jurisdiction is to be presumed, whether there are recitals in its records to show it or not. On the other hand, no such intendment is made in favor of the judgment of a court of limited jurisdiction, but the recitals contained in the minutes of proceedings must be sufficient to show that the case was one which the law permitted the court to take cognizance of, and that the parties were subjected to its jurisdiction by proper process. There is also another difference between these two classes of tribunals in this, that the jurisdiction of the one may be disproved under circumstances where it would not be allowed in the case of the other. A record is not commonly suffered to be contradicted by parol evidence; but wherever a fact showing want of jurisdiction in a court of general jurisdiction can be proved without contradicting its recitals, it is allowable to do so, and thus defeat its effect. But in the case of a court of special and limited authority, it is permitted to go still further, and to show a want of jurisdiction even in opposition to the recitals contained in the record.'" Fausler v. Parsons, 6 W. Va. 486.

The jurisdiction must be averred, in courts of limited authority, as well in real as in transitory actions. Hill v. Pride, 4 Call 107.

Legislature May Change Rule.— While the general rule is that the jurisdiction of a court of limited jurisdiction must appear by the record, yet it is in the power of the legislature to change the rule and declare that it shall be presumed, until the contrary appears. Rutter v. Sullivan, 25 W. Va. 427.

Appl'cation to Special Session of County Court.—"Mayer v. Adams, 27 W. Va. 244, holds that, to give a special session of the county court any jurisdiction in any matter, it must appear, not only that notice of it was posted, but 'it must also appear from such entry on its record book what were the purposes for which the special session was to be held as stated in said notice, and that, if such entry is not made in the record book, everything done at such special session must be held an absolute nullity,' for want of jurisdiction, because jurisdictional facts in courts of limited and special jurisdiction must appear on its record." Hamilton v. Tucker County Court, 38 W. Va. 71, 18 S. E. 8, 10'

In the case of suits before a justice the record must show jurisdictional facts giving the justice a right to act. Yates v. Taylor County Court, 47 W. Va. 376, 35 S. E. 24. See the title JUSTICES OF THE PEACE.

The district court of the United States is a court of limited jurisdiction, and it is necessary to give validity to its decrees and orders, that its jurisdiction of the case should be shown by the record. And where this is not shown a decree is null and void. Mason v. Tuttle, 75 Va. 105.

2. Effect of Recital in Record of Jurisdictional Facts.

While in the case of an inferior court, board, or body, required to keep a record, the facts essential to give it jurisdiction must appear in its proceedings, else its action will be void and open to attack collaterally; yet, if its record state such facts, its jurisdiction will not be open to attack, nor can such facts be disproven in a collateral proceeding, nor will any error appearing therein affect its action. Shank v. Ravenswood, 43 W. Va. 242, 27 S. E. 223.

In the case of an inferior court, if the record shows that facts necessary to give it jurisdiction existed, its jurisdiction will not be open to attack, in a collateral proceeding. It is presumed that the courts ascertained that the facts giving it jurisdiction existed. Cecil v. Clark, 44 W. Va. 659, 30 S. E. 216.

"It seems settled that, where the facts essential to give jurisdiction to an inferior or special tribunal of limited authority are shown by its record, the same presumption prevails in favor of its jurisdiction as prevails in favor of the jurisdiction of superior courts of general jurisdiction, and the statement of jurisdictional facts can not be denied upon a collateral attack, nor will its plain errors affect it. 12 Am. & Eng. Ency. Law, p. 274; Bigelow Estop. 66; 1 Herm. Estop. Res. Jmd. 405; Van Fleet. Coll. Attack. 538; Morrow v. Weed. 66 Am. Dec. 122; 1 Black, Judgm., § 287. Can not attack collaterally proceedings of city to annex territory. City of Terre Haute v. Beach, 96 Ind. 143; Kuhn v. City of Port Townsend

(Wash.), 41 Prac. 923. An inferior court or tribunal of limited jurisdiction must decide on its jurisdiction, or power to act in the matter; and, when its jurisdiction depends on a fact which it is required to ascertain before acting, the decision is held conclusive, if that fact appears in its record. Wells, Jur., § 61. Facts necessary to be shown of record by an inferior tribunal are those facts only without which it has no power to act. 12 Am. & Eng. Ency. Law, p. 274, note 2." Shank v. Ravenswood, 43 W. Va. 242, 27 S. E. 223, 224.

"If certain facts are required to be proven in order to give a court or judge special or limited jurisdiction, as for instance the posting of such a notice as we have named to give the county court jurisdiction at a special session, its action would be an absolute nullity, if there be a total defect of proof tending to establish such facts. But when there is some proof tending to establish these jurisdictional facts, though it be slight and inconclusive, if the court regard such jurisdictional facts as thereby sufficiently proven and assumes jurisdiction, its action can not be a nullity; for the court tried to decide whether the facts were proven on which its jurisdiction depended." Mayer v. Adams, 27 W. Va. 244.

V. Disposal of Cause Where Want of Jurisdiction Appears.

Generally, as to dismissal for want of jurisdiction, see the title DISMISSAL, DISCONTINUANCE AND NONSUIT, vol. 4, p. 695.

As to dismissal of appeal for want of jurisdiction, see the title APPEAL AND ERROR, vol. 1, p. 418.

VI. Concurrent Jurisdiction.

A. OF LAW AND EQUITY.

Equity Jurisdiction Not Ousted by Subsequent Legal Remedy.—"Courts of equity having once acquired jurisdiction never lose it because jurisdiction of the same matter is given to courts of law, unless the statute conferring such jurisdiction uses restrictive or prohibitory words. Filler v. Tyler, 91 Va. 458, 22 S. E. 235; Kelly v. Lehigh Mining, etc., Co., 98 Va. 405, 36 S. E. 511, 81 Am. St. Rep. 763; Steinman v. Vicars, 99 Va. 595, 39 S. E. 227." Johnson v. Black, 103 Va. 477, 49 S. E. 633. See the title ADEQUATE REMEDY AT LAW, vol. 1, p. 164.

As to concurrent jurisdiction of law and equity in certain cases, see post, "As to Particular Grounds and Subject Matters," VII, E, 3; "As to Remedies," VII, E, 4.

B. RETENTION BY COURT FIRST ACQUIRING.

1. General Rule.

In case of conflict of jurisdiction between two courts having concurrent jurisdiction the general rule is that the court which first acquires cognizance of the controversy, or obtains possession of the property in dispute, is entitled to retain it until the end of the litigation, and should decide all questions which legitimately flow out of the controversy. Until then, all proceedings in the second suit should be stayed. Craig v. Hoge, 95 Va. 275, 28 S. E. 317; Spiller v. Wells, 96 Va. 598, 32 S. E. 46; Griffin v. Birkhead, 84 Va. 612, 5 S. E. 685; Parsons v. Snider, 42 W. Va. 517, 26 S. E. 285; Davis v. Morris, 76 Va. 21.

When the object of a suit requires the control and dominion of the property involved in the litigation, the court which first acquires possession, or that dominion which is equivalent to possession, becomes vested with the exclusive right to dispose of it for the purpose of its jurisdiction. State v. Fredlock, 52 W. Va. 232, 43 S. E. 153.

As was said in Griffin v. Birkhead, 84 Va. 612, 5 S. E. 685. "Two courts, at one and the same time, can not entertain suits over the same subject matter and adjudicate the rights of the same persons thereto, contrary to the rule that there must not be a double investigation of the same matter."

Application to Concurrent Jurisdiction of Law and Equity.—The doctrine that courts of equity, once having acquired jurisdiction of a subject matter because there was no remedy at law, or because the remedy at law was inadequate, do not, as a rule, lose their jurisdiction merely because courts of law afterwards give the same or similar relief, is applied in those cases where equity has first obtained jurisdiction, and the defendant seeks to oust its control of the case on the ground that the remedy at law is complete and adequate. It has no application to a case where the two courts have concurrent jurisdiction and the litigant has been first impleaded in a court of law, and the machinery of that court is adequate to give as full and as complete relief as could be given in equity. Hoge *v.* Fidelity, etc., Co., 103 Va. 1, 48 S. E. 494.

"The learned counsel for the appellant has invoked with great earnestness the doctrine that equity once having jurisdiction of a subject matter, because there was no remedy at law, or because the remedy at law was inadequate, does not lose such jurisdiction merely from the fact that courts of law afterwards give the same or similar relief, and that this original jurisdiction to grant relief by courts of equity is neither impaired by the assumption of the same powers by courts of law, nor by the extension to those courts of such powers by the legislature, unless the statute conferring such jurisdiction uses restrictive or prohibitory words. The doctrine contended for is as well established as that we have been discussing. Pom. Eq. Juris. (1st Ed.), vol. 1, § 182; Barton's Ch. Prac., vol. 1, § 16, p. 60; Steinman *v.* Vicars, 99 Va. 595, 39 S. E. 227; Kelly *v.* Lehigh Mining, etc., Co., 98 Va. 405, 36 S. E. 511, 81 Am. St. Rep. 763; Hull *v.* Watts, 95 Va. 10, 27 S. E. 829; Filler

v. Tyler, 91 Va. 458, 22 S. E. 235. But it has no application to a case where the jurisdiction of the court of law and the court of equity is concurrent, and where the litigant has been first impleaded in a court of law, and the machinery of that court is as adequate to afford the defendant a full and unembarrassed defense as a court of equity would be. In such a case, as already seen, he must make his defense in the court of law, and his failure to do so does not entitle him to relief in a court of equity." Hoge *v.* Fidelity, etc., Co., 103 Va. 1, 48 S. E. 494.

"In Long *v.* Colston, 1 Hen. & M. 110, where a defendant at law exhibited his bill of injunction, it was decided, that although on a specific agreement either party has a right to resort to equity to compel a specific performance, yet if one of them elects to sue for damages for an alleged breach of the covenant, the other party has no right to carry him into equity, to compel him to abandon his common-law remedy, and to hold him to his remedy for specific performance. In this case, the two courts had a concurrent jurisdiction; the defense at law might have been as full and ample as the ground of complaint in equity, and to whichever tribunal the right to decide first attached, the other ought not to have intercepted its action." Harvey *v.* Fox, 5 Leigh 444.

Date of Services as Determining Priority of Jurisdiction.—Jurisdiction on a court is acquired by the issue and service of process, and, in case of conflict between courts of concurrent jurisdiction, the date of service of the process determines the priority of the jurisdiction. Craig *v.* Hoge, 95 Va. 275, 28 S. E. 317; Spiller *v.* Wells, 96 Va. 598, 32 S. E. 46.

2. Qualification of and Exceptions to Rule.

First Suit Must Afford Opportunity for Adjudication of Rights.—In order that the rule just stated may apply, the first suit must afford the plaintiff in the second an adequate and complete opportunity for the adjudication of his rights. Spiller *v.* Wells, 96 Va. 598, 32 S. E. 46.

"The rule established is necessary to the orderly and decent administration of justice. Nothing can be more unseemly than a struggle for jurisdiction between courts; but a rule which rests for its support upon consideration of convenience however great, and of decency, order, and priority however exacting, must yield to the higher principle which accords to every citizen the right to have a hearing before some court. An essential condition, therefore, of the application of the rule insisted upon as to priority of jurisdiction, is that the first suit shall afford the plaintiff in the second as adequate and complete opportunity for the adjudication of his rights." Spiller *v.* Wells, 96 Va. 598, 32 S. E. 46.

Even among courts of concurrent jurisdiction, the rule that the court which first obtains jurisdiction has the right to decide every question in the case, is subject to limitations, and is confined to suits between the same parties seeking the same remedy, and to such questions as properly arise in the progress of the suit first brought, and does not extend to all matters which may possibly become involved. Davis *v.* Morriss, 76 Va. 21.

Exception in Case of Technical Creditor's Bills.—Technical creditor's bills are exceptions to the general rule which pertains to a conflict of jurisdiction between courts of concurrent jurisdiction, but a bill which assails one of several debts secured in a deed of trust, and seeks to obtain its place in the distribution of the trust fund, is not such a bill as excepts it from the general rule, and must await the termination of a prior suit brought by the trustee for the purpose of administering the trust fund. Craig *v.* Hoge, 95 Va. 275, 28 S. E. 317; Spiller *v.* Wells,

96 Va. 598, 32 S. E. 46. See the title CREDITORS' SUITS, vol. 3, p. 793.

VII. Equity Jurisdiction.

A. OBJECT, NATURE AND REQUISITES.

The great objects of a court of equity are, to do complete justice by setting the rights of all persons interested in the subject of the suit, to make the performance of the orders of the court perfectly safe, and to prevent further litigation and multiplicity of suits. King *v.* Ashley, 5 Leigh 408.

To Supply Want of or Defective Legal Remedy.—"'The most general description of a court of equity is, that it has jurisdiction in cases where a plain, adequate, and complete remedy can not be had at law.' Robinson's old practice, 2 vol. page 1." Vanbibber *v.* Beirne, 6 W. Va. 168.

The jurisdiction of equity purports in all cases to come in aid of and supply some defects in the law. Bowyer *v.* Creigh, 3 Rand. 26.

"A court of chancery should, to be really useful to the people, confine itself to those cases where a party is without remedy, or relief, at law, unless, from circumstances (which, if true, could not be controlled), he was unable to make his defense at law; because it is obvious to my mind, and must be to all those who know anything about the mode of proof, and of trial, in the two courts, that the difference is greatly in favor of a common-law trial; for there, justice can scarcely ever fail; because, the parties, the witnesses, the jury, and a disinterested court are, or may be, looking at each other, at the same time; and the smallest deviation in a witness is often of more importance, than to hear him; for his looks sometimes conduct our senses to a conclusion, which his words would not; but, in this court, the parties and their witnesses are only known upon paper; and injustice, more or less, on that account, must be in almost every sentence." Alderson v. Biggars, 4 Hen. & M. 471.

"Our system of jurisprudence seems not so defective as to suffer a right to redress for any injury to be without a remedy; the common law delights, if the prosopopœia may be allowed, in redressing injuries, by whatever causes produced. In some instances, it is restrained from granting any redress, and in others, the redress which it can grant is inadequate, being either too much, or too little, or not early enough. In such instances, the court of equity, supplying or proportioning the remedy, or applying it in time, exerciseth the functions which were objects of its institution. In proceeding thus, the court of equity maintains a perfect harmony with the court of common law, or is not at variance with it, aiding the party to assert, or to assert in the most convenient form, those rights which the common law either recognized or doth not reprobate and giving remedies which that law reluctantly withholds, and thereby contributing its part towards accomplishing the main design of both, which is the attainment of justice." Dandridge v. Lyon, Wythe 122, 127.

"There is no more frequent or better settled ground of demurrer to bills, than that there is a complete remedy at law. See 3 Atk. 740; 3 Bro. Parl. Cas. 525. Mitford, 111, says, 'In general, where a plaintiff can have as effectual and complete remedy in a court of law, as in a court of equity, and that remedy is clear and certain, a demurrer, which is, in truth, a demurrer to the jurisdiction of the court, will lie.' Many cases in the modern reporters might be referred to, but the doctrine is too well settled to require it." Bowyer v. Creigh, 3 Rand. 26.

In a case of grave doubt equity will not grant relief, but will leave the parties to their legal remedies. Ohio River R. Co. v. Johnson, 50 W. Va. 499, 40 S. E. 407.

The fact that a person, if left to his legal remedies, will lose his debt if the statute of limitations be pleaded, is no ground of relief in equity. Courts should adjust the rights of parties according to the law, and leave the consequences to take care of themselves. See Moncure, P., in Dobson v. Culpepper, 23 Gratt. 352, 359. Pendleton v. Taylor, 77 Va 580.

For a full treatment of the effect of the existence of or want of an adequate legal remedy, as affecting the jurisdiction of equity, see the title ADEQUATE REMEDY AT LAW, vol. 1, p. 161. See also, the titles DEMURRERS, vol. 4, p. 475; DISMISSAL, DISCONTINUANCE AND NONSUIT, vol. 4, p. 695.

Jurisdiction of Person and Subject Matter Essential to Valid Decree.—A court of chancery has no power over a person not a party to the suit, nor as a general rule are its decrees binding on the subject matter if it is not within the territorial limits of the court. Preston v. Kindrick, 94 Va. 760, 27 S. E. 588. See ante, "In General," I, B, 1.

As to dismissal for want of jurisdiction, see the title DISMISSAL, DISCONTINUANCE AND NONSUIT, vol. 4, p. 695.

As to the territorial limitation of equity jurisdiction, see ante, "Territorial Limitation of Jurisdiction," I, D.

B. ACQUISITION AND RETENTION.

1. Manner of Acquiring.

Generally, as to the manner of acquiring jurisdiction, see ante, "How Acquired," III.

Allegations Showing Ground for Equitable Relief.—As to the necessity for the bill to set out facts entitling the plaintiff to the intervention of court of equity, the form and sufficiency of such allegations, etc., see the title EQUITY, vol. 5, p. 127.

False, Colorable or Vague Allegations in Bill.—Where a bill alleges proper matter for the jurisdiction of a court of equity, if it appears on the hearing that the allegations are false, the result is the same as if it had not been alleged; the bill will be dismissed for want of jurisdiction. Jones *v.* Bradshaw, 16 Gratt. 355.

The jurisdiction of a court of equity to make partition of land can not be defeated by the mere allegation of the defendants that they hold adverse possession, when in point of fact they do not, for it could be defeated at any time by such false allegations, if this were so. Hudson *v.* Putney, 14 W. Va. 561.

Averments and allegations giving equitable jurisdiction, which are shown to be merely colorable, will not do so, if the real cause of action is one for which there is an adequate and full remedy at law. Laidley *v.* Laidley, 25 W. Va. 525; Thompson *v.* Whitaker Iron Co., 41 W. Va. 574, 23 S. E. 795.

Where a bill shows that the relief sought may be obtained in a court of law, the simple fact that it contains vague and general statements of grounds for equitable relief will not support the jurisdiction of equity. These statements will be considered as colorable and as pretexts to give jurisdiction to equity when it does not properly belong to it, and the jurisdiction will be declined. Grafton *v.* Reed, 26 W. Va. 437. See Lefever *v.* Billmyer, 5 W. Va. 33; Bass *v.* Bass, 4 Hen. & M. 479.

Where fraud is alleged and proved, courts of equity have jurisdiction and will give relief; yet, if the allegations are not sustained by proof, the bill will be dismissed. Jones *v.* White, Wythe 111.

Generally, as to dismissal for failure of bill to show facts giving equity jurisdiction, see the title DISMISSAL, DISCONTINUANCE AND NONSUIT, vol. 4, p. 695.

2. Retention of Jurisdiction Once Acquired.

Jurisdiction Not Ousted by Subsequent Legal Remedy.—See ante, this catchline, under, "Of Law and Equity," VI, A.

Jurisdiction Once Acquired Not Ousted by Subsequent Acts of Defendant.—Where the court has once acquired jurisdiction upon equitable grounds, no subsequent act of the defendants can oust that jurisdiction. Grubb *v.* Starkey, 90 Va. 831, 20 S. E. 784.

Jurisdiction of Subject Matter Not Dependent on Good Cause of Action.—The principle is almost universal that jurisdiction of the subject matter does not depend upon the ultimate existence of a good cause of action in the particular case. Being once properly and lawfully acquired, no subsequent fact can defeat that jurisdiction. But this rule can have no application where it is manifest that the object is by false pretence to transfer the controversy from a legal to an equitable forum. Walters *v.* Farmers' Bank, 76 Va. 12.

Retention for Complete Relief.—No question is better settled than that where a court of chancery has jurisdiction for one purpose it will not send the parties back to a court of law, but will retain the jurisdiction for all purposes, and do complete justice between the parties, unless some good reason appears for not doing so. See the title ADEQUATE REMEDY AT LAW, vol. 1, p. 171, for a full treatment or this question.

When a court of equity has once acquired jurisdiction, it may go on to a complete adjudication, even to the extent of establishing legal rights and granting legal remedies, which would otherwise be beyond the scope of its authority. Walters *v.* Farmers' Bank, 76 Va. 12; Grubb *v.* Starkey, 90 Va. 831, 20 S. E. 784.

As to the application of this rule in

allowing damages, see post, "Compensation or Damages," VII, E, 4, f.

C. CONCURRENT JURISDICTION OF LAW AND EQUITY.

Generally, as to the concurrent jurisdiction of law and equity, the rule as to retention by court first acquiring, etc., see ante, "Concurrent Jurisdiction," VI.

D. EQUITY JURISDICTION OF PARTICULAR COURTS.

See post, "Jurisdiction of Particular Courts," VIII.

E. SCOPE AND LIMITATIONS OF JURISDICTION.

1. In General.

The familar grounds of equitable jurisdiction may be stated as follows: Accidents, mistakes, relief against penalties, accounts, fraud, discovery, trust, specific performance, injunctions, avoiding illegal transactions, contribution, substitution, want of adequate remedy at law, and jurisdiction conferred by statute. Neff *v.* Baker, 82 Va. 401, 4 S. E. 620.

"Courts of equity exercise jurisdiction: 1. Over those cases where the principles of law, governing the ordinary courts, give a right, but from accident, fraud or defect in their mode of proceedings, they either afford no remedy or an incomplete one. To this class, belong cases of relief, where instruments have been lost, suppressed, or destroyed; cases of enlarging the remedies of the ordinary courts, or of affording remedies where none exist, or those previously existing are lost or incomplete; cases of specific performance, of partition, dower, account, etc. 2. Where by fraud, accident, or otherwise, a party has an advantage in proceeding in a court of law, which would render such court an instrument of injustice, courts of equity will restrain the party from using such advantage. On this principle, equity interferes with respect to fraudulent deeds, or deeds, by fraud, accident or mistake, framed contrary to the intention of the parties. To this class belong also, cases of accident, oppression, improper contracts, as marriage brokage bonds, etc. 3. In those cases where, according to the principles of natural and universal justice, there are rights, but the law has provided no remedy, courts of equity provide a remedy. Of this kind are matters of trust and confidence. 4. Where there are impediments to the fair decision of a question in other courts, equity exercises an ancillary jurisdiction, to remove those impediments. 5. Where pending a litigation, the property in dispute is in danger of being lost, and the powers of the court, in which the controversy depends, are insufficient for the purpose, equity will interpose to preserve it. 6. Equity exercises a jurisdiction to prevent the assertion of a doubtful right, in a manner productive of irreparable injury; such are cases of waste, the invasion of copyrights and patents. 7. Where two or more claim the same thing by different titles, and another is in danger of injury from ignorance of the real title, equity will compel the claimants to interplead. 8. Equity exercises a jurisdiction to put an end to the oppression of repeated litigations, after satisfactory determinations of the question, upon the principle interest reipublicæ ut sit finis litium. This enumeration is carefully abstracted from the books, and especially from that admirable treatise of Lord Redesdale's on Pleading, which is so well established as to have the authority of a text book. The heads of equity here stated, with a few others not at all relating to the case before us, will be found to comprehend nearly all the subjects of equitable jurisdiction. They all purport to come in aid of, and supply some defects in, the law. Even in those cases where equity exercises concurrent jurisdiction, as dower, partition, account, it was assumed to avoid the difficulties raised by the numerous and

nice technicalities of the common law."·
Bowyer *v.* Creigh, 3 Rand. 25. See
ante, "Object, Nature and Requisites,"
VII, A.

It is the advantage of a court of
equity that it can modify the demands
of parties according to justice; and
it may refuse its decree, unless the
party will take a decree upon condition of doing or relinquishing certain
things. West Virginia, etc., Co. *v.*
Vinal, 14 W. Va. 637.

Ancillary Jurisdiction.—A court of
equity, ancillary to its jurisdiction to
set aside a fraudulent transfer of property, may take the necessary steps to
preserve the property involved during
the pendency of the litigation. Keneweg Co. *v.* Schilansky, 47 W. Va. 287,
34 S. E. 773.

A court of equity will take jurisdiction of a case when in so doing it
will avoid a multiplicity of suits, and
as ancillary will enjoin the prosecution of the several claims at law. St.
Lawrence Boom, etc., Co. *v.* Price, 49
W. Va. 432, 38 S. E. 526.

Equity will not entertain a suit to
settle title and boundaries to land, but
in· an urgent case the property will
be protected by injunction, until the
question of right can be settled at law.
Callaway *v.* Webster, 98 Va. 790, 37 S.
E. 276; Manchester Cotton Mills *v.*
Manchester, 25 Gratt. 825. See the
titles INJUNCTIONS, vol. 7, p. 512;
MULTIPLICITY OF SUITS.

The aid of the court of equity is
necessary and proper in assisting process of execution levied on tobacco in
public warehouses. Ogg *v.* Randolph,
4 Hen. & M. 445.

As to suits in equity in aid of execution, see the title EXECUTIONS,
vol. 5, p. 468.

As to the ancillary jurisdiction of
equity to award damages, see the title
SPECIFIC PERFORMANCE. And
see post, "Compensation or Damages,"
VII, E, 4, f.

Limited to Civil Matters.—A prose-

cution for having contracted a marriage within the prohibited decrees contrary to statute is a criminal proceeding, and hence the provision in the
act giving the court of chancery jurisdiction of such prosecution is repugnant to the constitutional provision
limiting the jurisdiction of the court of
chancery to civil matters. Attorney
General *v.* Broaddus, 6 Munf. 116. See
the titles CRIMINAL LAW, vol. 4, p.
25; INJUNCTIONS, vol. 7, p. 512.

"Criminal cases are never cognizable
by courts of equity. Under no circumstances could that court take jurisdiction of them." St. Lawrence, etc., Co.
v. Holt, 51 W. Va. 352, 369, 41 S. E.
351.

Equity Can Not Extend over Matters Entitled to Jury Trial.—See the
title· JURY.

Defense of Set-Off Does Not Enlarge.—Sections 5 and 6 of ch. 126 of
the Code of 1868 of West Virginia, allowing defendants by plea to defend
action on contract by way of set-off,
which could not be done in a court of
law, were held in Black *v.* Smith, 13
W. Va. 780, not to enlarge the jurisdiction of courts of equity.

Will Not Interfere with Legislative
Department.—It is not within the
province of a court of equity to relieve property from taxation charged
thereon according to the value of the
property prior to the rebellion, where it
is greatly depreciated in value by acts
resulting from the war. Such should
be addressed to the legislative department of the government. White Sul-
phur Springs Co. *v.* Robinson, 3 W.
Va. 542.

2. Principles and Maxims Determining
and Controlling.

Generally, as to equitable principles
and maxims, and instances of their application, see the title MAXIMS.

Necessity for Want of Adequate
Legal Remedy.—As to the general
principle that equitable jurisdiction is
in aid of and to supply defects in the

law, and will not attach where there is an adequate legal remedy, see ante, "Object, Nature and Requisites," VII, A. And see the title ADEQUATE REMEDY AT LAW, vol. 1, p. 161.

Effect of Laches.—It is a familar doctrine of courts of equity that nothing can call forth these courts into activity but conscience, good faith and reasonable diligence. Where these are wanting, the court is passive. Staples, J., in Harrison v. Gibson, 23 Gratt. 212, 223; Hill v. Umberger, 77 Va. 653.

A court of equity will not take jurisdiction of an equitable claim where the party delays until there can be no longer a safe determination of the controversy, and his adversary is exposed to the danger of injustice from loss of information and evidence occasioned by death, insolvency and other untoward circumstances. Smith v. Thompson, 7 Gratt. 112, 54 Am. Dec. 126; West v. Thornton, 7 Gratt. 177, 54 Am. Dec. 134. See the title LACHES, and other titles involving the exercise of equitable jurisdiction.

Case Must Be Brought under Acknowledged Head of Equity Jurisdiction.—As to the rule that a party seeking equitable relief must, by his bill and proofs, make a case for the cognizance of a court of equity, see the title EQUITY, vol. 5, p. 127. And see the specific titles involving equitable relief, as INJUNCTIONS, vol. 7, p. 512, etc.

3. As to Particular Grounds and Subject Matters.

a. Acts of Public Officers.

See the titles INJUNCTIONS, vol. 7, p. 512; PUBLIC OFFICERS.

Chancery has jurisdiction to enjoin illegal acts of an officer attempted colore officii. Blanton v. Southern, etc., Co., 77 Va. 335.

b. Administration of Decedent's Estates.

See the titles DESCENT AND DISTRIBUTION, vol. 4, p. 588; EXE-

CUTIONS, vol. 5, p. 416; INJUNCTIONS, vol. 7, p. 512; MARSHALING ASSETS AND SECURITIES; RECEIVERS.

c. Assignment of Dower.

See the title DOWER, vol. 4, p. 818.

d. Boundaries.

See the title BOUNDARIES, vol. 2, p. 610.

e. Charitable Bequests and Trusts.

See the title CHARITIES, vol 2, p. 790.

f. Contribution.

See the title CONTRIBUTION AND EXONERATION, vol. 3, p. 461.

The jurisdiction now assumed by courts of law to enforce contribution in some cases, does not affect the jurisdiction originally belonging to a court of equity. Wayland v. Tucker, 4 Gratt. 267, 50 Am. Dec. 76.

g. Conversion and Reconversion.

See the title CONVERSION AND RECONVERSION, vol. 3, p. 498.

h. Corporations.

As to equity jurisdiction in the matter of the winding up and dissolution of corporations, see the title CORPORATIONS, vol. 3, p. 588.

As to the jurisdiction of equity to restrain by injunction the acts of corporations, see the title INJUNCTIONS, vol. 7, p. 512.

i. Criminal Cases.

As to the rule that criminal cases are never cognizable by courts of equity, see ante, "In General," VII, E, 1. And see the title CRIMINAL LAW, vol. 4, p. 25.

j. Duress and Undue Influence.

See generally, the titles DURESS, vol. 4, p. 841; FRAUD AND DECEIT, vol. 6, p. 448; WILLS.

"Equity grants relief wherever influence is acquired and abused, or confidence reposed and betrayed. Lord Kingsdowne, in Smith v. Kay, 7 H. L. Cases 750. 'Equity is especially jealous to guard the welfare of the weaker party in all contracts between parent and child, guardian and ward, attorney and client, trustee and cestui que trust, and, indeed, in all persons standing in fiduciary relations to each other. It is especially active and searching in dealing with gifts, voluntary conveyances and deeds without due consideration, though its range is so wide as to cover all possible dealings between persons holding such relations, or any relations in which dominion, whether physical, intellectual, moral, religious, domestic, or of any sort, may be exercised by one party over the other; or in which the parties contracting are not at arm's length.' White & Tudor's Leading Cases in Equity, 1184, Ed. 1887. In the case of Dent v. Bennett, 4 My. & Cr., 269, Lord Chancellor Cottenham said: 'I will not narrow the rule, or run the risk of, in any degree, fettering the exercise of the beneficial jurisdiction of this court by any enumeration of the description of persons against whom it ought to be most freely used.' In the famous case of Huguenin v. Basely, 14 Vesey 273. Lord Eldon said: 'The question is not whether she knew what she was doing, had done or proposed to do, but how that intention was produced; whether all that care and providence was placed around her, as against those who advised her, which, from their situation and relation with respect to her, they were bound to exert in her behalf.' Among the relations, the mere existence of which casts suspicion on all business transactions between parties holding them, the one which most excites the jealous watchfulness of a court of equity is that of parent and child—especially where (as in the case at bar) it is the parent who is the beneficiary of the child's bounty, and when that bounty is large and entirely disproportionate to the means of the donor." Davis v. Strange, 86 Va. 793, 11 S. E. 406.

Where daughter, in situation of sudden suprise, without advice, of friend or counsel, and when rendered unable to exercise a consenting mind, by the undue influence of her father and of his attorney, who pressed her with importunity and strong persuasions, and assurances that she would be otherwise provided for and compensated, and that it would be best to convey the property back to her father, as it was threatened to be burned, hastily and inconsiderately executed a deed granting the property to him without any consideration whatever; held, a case for equitable relief. Davis v. Strange, 86 Va. 793, 11 S. E. 406.

k. Fiduciary Relations, Trusts and Powers.

See the titles ASSIGNMENTS FOR THE BENEFIT OF CREDITORS, vol. 1, p. 830; EXECUTORS AND ADMINISTRATORS, vol 5, p. 483; GUARDIAN AND WARD, vol. 6, p. 782; POWERS; TRUSTS AND TRUSTEES.

"Speaking of matters of account, Chief Justice Marshall, in Fowle v. Lawrason, 5 Peters 495, remarked, that 'in all cases in which an action of account would be the proper remedy at law, and in all cases where a trustee is a party, the jurisdiction of a court of equity is undoubted. It is the appropriate tribunal.' It is upon the principle of trust mainly, that equity takes jurisdiction at the instance of the principal to compel his agent to account. Simmons v. Simmons, 33 Gratt. 451, 456; Zetelle v. Myers, 19 Gratt. 62; Coffman v. Sangston, 21 Gratt. 263; Thornton v. Thornton, 31 Gratt. 212. And if in the settlement of a joint administration, one executor or administrator gets credit with the estate for what another is entitled to receive, what he gets or is allowed him he holds as trustee for the latter and may in equity be required to account for it." Huff v. Thrash, 75 Va. 546.

l. Fraud, Accident or Mistake.

See the titles FRAUD AND DECEIT, vol. 6, p. 448; FRAUDULENT AND VOLUNTARY CONVEY-

ANCES, vol. 6, p. 540; MISTAKE AND ACCIDENT; RESCISSION, CANCELLATION AND REFORMATION.

Jurisdiction Sustained Wherever Person Found.—In cases of fraud, trusts, or of contract, the jurisdiction of a court of equity is sustainable wherever the person can be found, although lands not within the jurisdiction of the court may be affected by its decree. Davis v. Morriss, 76 Va. 21.

m. Liens and Charges on Property.

See the titles CREDITORS' SUITS, vol. 3, p. 780; JUDGMENTS AND DECREES, ante, p. 161; LIENS.

n. Lost Instruments and Records.

In case of lost instruments, courts of law and equity exercise concurrent jurisdiction. Equity assumed jurisdiction originally because there was no remedy at law, and where the law courts subsequently took jurisdiction of these cases the equity jurisdiction was not ousted. Lyttle v. Cozad, 21 W. Va. 183; Hickman v. Painter, 11 W. Va. 386; Mitchell v. Chancellor, 14 W. Va. 22; Shields v. Com., 4 Rand. 541; Harrison v. Field, 2 Wash. 136; Hall v. Wilkinson, 35 W. Va. 167, 12 S. E. 1118.

See the title LOST INSTRUMENTS AND RECORDS.

o. Multiplicity of Suits.

See the title MULTIPLICITY OF SUITS.

Probable delay, expenses and circuity of action may properly be anticipated and avoided by resorting at once to a court of equity, where all the questions arising, and all the rights involved in the controversy, can be determined and adjusted in one proceeding. Roberts v. King, 10 Gratt. 184.

Suit Must Be against Same Person. —As a ground of equity jurisdiction the prevention of a multiplicity of suits can only be invoked where such suits are against the same person, and it will not lie when a bank seeks to enjoin separate suits against its stockholders for the collection of taxes levied on their shares. People's Nat. Bank v. Marye (U. S. Cir. Ct.), 7 Va. Law Reg. 47.

p. Nuisances.

See generally, the titles INJUNCTIONS, vol. 7, p. 512; NUISANCES.

q. Penalties and Forfeitures.

See the title PENALTIES AND FORFEITURES.

r. Rights of Parties under Insurance Policies.

See the titles FIRE INSURANCE, vol. 6, p. 60; INSURANCE, vol. 7, p. 746; LIFE INSURANCE; MARINE INSURANCE; MUTUAL INSURANCE.

Where it is a question whether insurance money for buildings destroyed by fire should be treated as real or personal assets and disposed of as one or the other, a court of equity has jurisdiction of the question. Portsmouth Ins. Co. v. Reynolds, 32 Gratt. 613.

s. Separate Estates of Married Women.

See the title SEPARATE ESTATES OF MARRIED WOMEN.

t. Waste.

See the titles INJUNCTIONS, vol. 7, p. 512; WASTE.

u. Wills.

See the title WILLS.

"A suit can never be entertained for the sole purpose of construing a will. There must be an actual litigation in respect to matters which are proper subjects of equity jurisdiction, such as relief on behalf of an executor, trustee, cestui que trust, or legatee. It is a special and limited jurisdiction incident to general equity jurisdiction over trusts and administrations. Pom. Eq. Jur., §§ 1156, 1157." Martin v. Martin, 52 W. Va. 391, 394, 44 S. E. 198.

Issue of Devisavit Vel Non—Limited Jurisdiction.—Where an issue of devisavit vel non is directed, a court of equity does not proceed under its general jurisdiction, but can exercise only the special limited powers conferred upon it by the statute; it acts as a court of probate with the single object to ascertain by a jury trial whether the paper in question is or is not the will of the decedent; it can perform no other act, and can grant no further relief. It has no jurisdiction of the estate of the decedent and can make no order respecting it. Kirby v. Kirby, 84 Va. 627, 5 S. E. 539; Coalter v. Bryan, 1 Gratt. 18; Hartman v. Strickler, 82 Va. 225, 233.

4. As to Remedies.

a. Accounts and Accounting.

"For the assertion, that account is a head of equity, authority may be found in several elementary writers, and books of practice. But, the position is not to be taken in that large and comprehensive sense, given to the word account in common parlance." Smith v. Marks, 2 Rand. 449.

No precise rule can be laid down defining the extent and limits of the concurrent jurisdiction, which courts of equity will exercise with courts of law in matters of account. In such matters courts of equity reserve to themselves a large discretion, in the exercise of which they will pay due regard to the nature of the case and the situation and conduct of the parties. Grafton v. Reed, 26 W. Va. 437.

"Although the line may not be drawn with absolute precision, yet it may be safely affirmed that a court of equity can not draw to itself every transaction between individuals in which accounts between the parties are to be adjusted. In all cases in which an action of account would be a proper remedy at law, and in all cases involving trusts or confidential relations resulting in transactions which can not be adequately adjusted at law, the jurisdiction of a court of equity is undoubted. But in transactions not of this peculiar character, some difficulty at law should interfere, or some discovery should be necessary to the relief sought, in order to confer jurisdiction upon a court of equity. Fowle v. Lawrason, 5 Pet. 495; Petty v. Fogle, 16 W. Va. 497; Merchants' Bank v. Jeffries, 21 W. Va. 504." Grafton v. Reed, 26 W. Va. 437. See the title ACCOUNTS AND ACCOUNTING, vol. 1, p. 88.

b. Bills of Peace.

See the title BILL OF PEACE, vol. 2, p. 383.

c. Bills Quia Timet.

See the title QUIETING TITLE.

d. Bills of Revivor.

See the title ABATEMENT, REVIVAL AND SURVIVAL, vol. 1, p. 48.

e. Creditors' Suits.

See the title CREDITORS' SUITS, vol. 3, p. 780.

f. Compensation or Damages.

See generally, the titles CONTRACTS, vol. 3, p. 307; DAMAGES, vol. 4, p. 162.

(1) General Rule Stated and Applied. Claims for Damages Not Subject for Equity Jurisdiction.—As a general proposition courts of equity do not entertain jurisdiction to give redress by way of compensation or damages for breaches of contracts and other wrongs cognizable at law. This relief is only given in equity as incidental to other relief. Laidley v. Laidley, 25 W. Va. 525; Meze v. Mayse, 6 Rand. 658; Anthony v. Leftwich, 3 Rand. 238; Ewing v. Litchfield, 91 Va. 575, 22 S. E. 362; Witz v. Mullin, 90 Va. 805, 20 S. E. 783; Robertson v. Hogsheads, 3 Leigh 667; Gilliat v. Lynch, 2 Leigh 493, 505. See generally, the title ADEQUATE REMEDY AT LAW, vol. 1, p. 161.

A bill in equity does not lie to recover damages for a breach of contract merely sounding in damages. Meze v. Mayse, 6 Rand. 658.

A claim for damages for a breach of

contract to do some collateral thing, is not a fit subject for the jurisdiction of a court of equity. Witz v. Mullin, 90 Va. 805, 20 S. E. 783.

A court of equity can give damages in no case where the party has a clear remedy at law; nor even when he has no such remedy, unless, perhaps, under very peculiar circumstances. Anthony v. Leftwich, 3 Rand. 238; Meze v. Mayse, 6 Rand. 658, 660.

Liquidated Damages No Exception to Rule.—So far from liquidated damages constituting an exception to the rule that courts of equity will not entertain suits for damages for breach of contract, it seems that if the damages for the breach of a contract have been liquidated by the parties to the contract (that is, ascertained and agreed upon), that fact, so far from inviting the assistance of a court of equity, is sufficient to repel it. Ewing v. Litchfield, 91 Va. 575, 581, 22 S. E. 362. See the title DAMAGES, vol. 4, p. 171.

Unliquidated Damages.—A suit for unliquidated damages can not be entertained by a court of equity unless there is an allegation of insolvency which is established. Bunting v. Cochran, 99 Va. 558, 39 S. E. 229, 7 Va. Law Reg. 327.

A bill in any form claiming damages for breach of a contract can not be entertained in equity, neither can unliquidated damages be set off in equity. Robertson v. Hogsheads, 3 Leigh 667.

Bill for Rescission and for General Relief.—Upon a bill in chancery by vendee against vendor of land, after the contract fully executed by conveyance of the land and securities given for the purchase money, alleging fraud practised by vendor's agent on the vendee, in the original agreement, and praying that the contract may be rescinded for the fraud, and general relief; the court having held, that plaintiff, under the circumstances of the case, was not entitled to a rescission of the contract, held further, that he was not entitled to ask that the damages he had sustained by reason of the alleged fraud, should be ascertained by the court of chancery, and decreed to him, in abatement from the purchase money. Robertson v. Hogsheads, 3 Leigh 667, cited on this proposition in Campbell v. Rust, 85 Va. 653, 668, 8 S. E. 664; Cleaver v. Mathews, 83 Va. 801, 804, 3 S. E. 439; Rice v. Hartman, 84 Va. 251, 253, 4 S. E. 621; Koger v. Kane, 5 Leigh 606, 608; Miller v. Argyle, 5 Leigh 460; Morgan v. Carson, 7 Leigh 238, 241; Nagle v. Newton, 22 Gratt. 814, 823; Rosenberger v. Keller, 33 Gratt. 489, 494; Crislip v. Cain, 19 W. Va. 438, 520; Kelly v. Riley, 22 W. Va. 247, 249; Laidley v. Laidley, 25 W. Va. 525, 528. See the title RESCISSION, CANCELLATION AND REFORMATION.

Where suit is brought to enforce a deed of trust whereby are secured "all the debts and liabilities of certain firms and of the individuals composing them;" held, no claim merely sounding in damages for breach of contract to deliver shares of stock, ought to be taken cognizance of by a court of equity, but the claimants should be left to their remedy at law. Witz v. Mullin, 90 Va. 805, 20 S. E. 783.

(2) Where Ancillary to Relief Prayed for.

In General.—It seems to be now well settled that where a court of equity clearly had jurisdiction of the subject of the controversy, jurisdiction for compensation or damages will always attach where it is ancillary to the relief prayed for. Nagle v. Newton, 22 Gratt. 814.

In a suit to rescind or enforce specific execution of a contract for the sale of land, if a proper case is made out for specific execution, the court has jurisdiction, as ancillary thereto, to decree compensation to the defendant for damages which he has sustained by the improper acts of the plaintiff and his agents. Nagle v. Newton, 22 Gratt.

814; Campbell *v.* Rust, 85 Va. 653, 8 S. E. 664; Grubb *v.* Starkey, 90 Va. 831, 834, 20 S. E. 784. See Witz *v.* Mullin, 90 Va. 805, 806, 20 S. E. 783. See the titles RESCISSION, CANCELLATION AND REFORMATION; SPECIFIC PERFORMANCE.

Equity may enforce specific performance of a contract to do on plaintiff's property definite work, wherein he had a material interest, and there can not be adequate compensation in damages; and may also, as ancillary, award damages for a breach of the contract. Grubb *v.* Starkey, 90 Va. 831, 20 S. E. 783.

A court of equity, even where specific performance of a contract for the sale of land is refused, will decree compensation for damages, where there is no adequate remedy at law, where some peculiar equity intervenes; it will do so to prevent a multiplicity of suits, and where it has obtained jurisdiction of the case on other grounds. Where a bill asks alternative relief, if it can not execute the contract, a court of equity will decree repayment of purchase money. Stearns *v.* Beckham, 31 Gratt. 379.

g. Discovery.

See the title DISCOVERY, vol. 4, p. 658.

h. Injunctions.

See the title INJUNCTIONS, vol. 7, p. 512.

i. Marshaling Assets and Securities.

The equitable principle of marshaling assets will be sufficient to give a court of equity jurisdiction of a case. Henley *v* Perkins, 6 Gratt. 615. See the title MARSHALING ASSETS AND SECURITIES.

j. Partition.

See the title PARTITION.

k. Quieting Title.

See the title QUIETING TITLE.

l. Receivers.

See the title RECEIVERS.

8 Va—56

m. Relief against Judgments and Decrees.

See the titles INJUNCTIONS, vol. 7, p. 512; JUDGMENTS AND DECREES, ante, p. 161.

n. Rescission, Cancellation and Reformation.

See the title RESCISSION, CANCELLATION AND REFORMATION, and cross references there found.

o. Set-Off, Recoupment and Counterclaim.

See the title SET-OFF, RECOUPMENT AND COUNTERCLAIM.

p. Specific Performance.

See the title SPECIFIC PERFORMANCE, and cross references there found.

q. Subrogation.

See the title SUBROGATION.

r. Suits by Paupers for Freedom.

Courts of equity, as well as courts of law, have jurisdiction of suits by paupers for freedom, and in a case proper for a court of equity, it will appoint counsel for the pauper. Dempsey *v.* Lawrence, Gilmer 333. See the title SLAVES.

s. Suits for Alimony or Divorce.

Alimony.—A court of chancery has jurisdiction in cases of alimony. Purcell *v.* Purcell, 4 Hen. & M. 507. See the title ALIMONY, vol. 1, p. 297.

Divorce.—See the title DIVORCE, vol. 4, p. 747.

5. On Proceedings in Review, or Appeal.

See the title APPEAL AND ERROR, vol. 1, p. 418.

F. ENFORCEMENT OF ORDER OR DECREE.

It is well established that a court of equity always has jurisdiction to carry into effect its own decrees. Patton. 5 W. Va. 432; Newman *v.* Chapman. 2 Rand. 93. 14 Am. Dec. 766; Paxton *v.* Rucker, 15 W. Va. 547. "A court of equity has jurisdiction to entertain a bill to give effect to a decree of a court of equity." Hobson *v.* Yancey, 2 Gratt. 73. See the titles CONTEMPT, vol. 3, p. 236; EXECUTIONS, vol. 5, p. 416; INJUNCTIONS, vol. 7, p. 512; JUDGMENTS AND DECREES, ante, p. 161.

VIII. Jurisdiction of Particular Courts.

Generally, as to the establishment, organization, terms and sessions, powers and duties, etc., of courts, see the title COURTS, vol. 3, p. 696. Generally, as to appellate jurisdiction, see the title APPEAL AND ERROR, vol. 1, p. 427.

A. GENERAL COURT.

1. As Dependent on Amount in Controversy.

In Tutt *v.* Freeman, Jeff. 24, it was held, that the jurisdiction of the general court did not depend upon the amount of the judgment given, but upon the amount of damages laid in the declaration, if it was for as much as ten pounds sterling.

2. Jurisdiction in Particular Instances.

Ecclesiastical Jurisdiction.—The general court was held in Godwin *v.* Lunan, Jeff. 96, to be possessed of ecclesiastical jurisdiction in general, and as an ecclesiastical court it had the power to censure or deprive a minister of the gospel of his office if there should be sufficient cause.

Jurisdiction to Decide Questions of Law from Superior Court.—The general court has no jurisdiction to consider matters of law certified to it for opinion by the higher court of chancery. Com. *v.* Hening, 1 Va. Cas. 324.

If a superior court decides upon a question at law in a criminal court, and afterwards refers it to the general court for its opinion, the general court has no jurisdiction to consider the question. Com. *v.* Hening, 1 Va. Cas. 324, 325. But see M'Caul's Case, 1 Va. Cas. 271.

Constitutional and Legislative Provisions as to Final Jurisdiction of Impeachment, Felonies and Misdemeanors.—"The sense of the convention, who formed the constitution, was not, that the court of appeals should have jurisdiction in all cases. The constitution has deposited with the general court the final jurisdiction on impeachment. The judgment in such cases to be given against the highest officers of the government, may not only be of perpetual disability to hold any office, but to suffer such pains or penalties as the law shall direct. This, then, is a high authority excluding the jurisdiction of the court of appeals, in a very penal and important case. A nearly cotemporaneous legislature (in 1777), pursuing this same principle, deposited with the same court the final jurisdiction (as it is on all hands confessed), in treasons and felonies. It is remarkable also, that the original act constituting the general court (as well as the subsequent ones), after declaring its jurisdiction to be 'general over all persons and in all cases, matters and things, at common law,' deemed it necessary to confer a jurisdiction by express words in all 'treasons, murders, felonies, and other crimes and misdemeanors;' thereby clearly implying, that the jurisdiction over the latter subjects was not conveyed under the former general and extensive expressions." Bedinger *v.* Com., 3 Call 461.

Concurrent Jurisdiction with Circuit Court to Admit to Bail in Murder Case.—It was held, in Com. *v.* Semmes, 11 Leigh 665, that the general court had original concurrent jurisdiction with the circuit superior court to admit a prisoner to bail for good cause, where he is confined in jail upon an indictment for murder.

Habeas Corpus Proceedings.—A prisoner confined in the penitentiary under the judgment of a court of oyer and terminer, for an offense which said court had no jurisdiction to try, may be discharged by the general court upon a writ of habeas corpus. Cropper v. Com., 2 Rob. 842.

Felonies Committed beyond Territorial Limits.—By cl. 1, § 7, act, 1 Rev. Code 1792, ch. 136, all treasons, etc., and other offenses against the commonwealth, except piracies and felonies on the high seas, though committed beyond the territorial limits of the state, are indictable and punishable in the general court. Com. v. Gaines, 2 Va. Cas. 172.

Felonies Committed on Bays, Rivers, Creeks, etc.—The federal courts of admiralty established under the articles of confederation, had power to try piracies and felonies on the high seas only; the Virginia court of admiralty was excluded from the jurisdiction in all capital cases, and hence it also follows that the general court as one of common law had jurisdiction in 1786, to try all felonies committed on the bay, rivers, creeks, etc. Com. v. Gaines, 2 Va. Cas. 172.

Prior to the revolution, the commissioners of admiralty appointed under the great seal of England, had jurisdiction to try all treasons, felonies, and piracies committed, not only on the high seas, but on the bays and rivers. Those powers ceased with the revolution. By the act of 1777, the general court was vested with the power of trying those offenses within the limits of the commonwealth, on the bay and rivers, as well as on the land. Com. v. Gaines, 2 Va. Cas. 172.

Larceny in District of Columbia.—Under act, 1 Rev. Code 1792, ch. 136, § 7, if a citizen of Virginia steal a horse from another citizen in the District of Columbia, he may under said law be indicted, tried, convicted and sentenced in the general court. Com. v. Gaines, 2 Va. Cas. 172.

B. SUPREME COURT OF APPEALS.

Original Jurisdiction.

Former Rule.—In Mayo v. Clarke, 2 Call 389, it was held, that the court of appeals had no original jurisdiction, and could not decide the merits of any case, until they had been passed upon by the district court.

Original Jurisdiction in Cases of Habeas Corpus, Mandamus, and Prohibition.—As to the original jurisdiction of the supreme court in these proceedings, see the titles HABEAS CORPUS, vol. 7, p. 15; MANDAMUS; PROHIBITION.

Appellate Jurisdiction.—See the title APPEAL AND ERROR, vol. 1, p. 475.

C. SPECIAL COURT OF APPEALS.

The proper cases to be decided by the special court of appeals are all cases on the docket of the court of appeals, not involving a constitutional question, and not decided in the lower court by one of the judges of the special court. It is the duty of the judges of the court of appeals to select the cases to be tried by the special court. Bolling v. Lersner, 26 Gratt. 36. See the title COURTS, vol. 3, p. 714.

D. DISTRICT AND SUPERIOR COURTS.

As to the origin and history of district and superior courts of law, see the title COURTS, vol. 3, p. 715.

1. District Courts.

Jurisdictional Amount.—A judgment in a district court in an action of assumpsit was arrested upon a verdict for less than $100 because the record did not show that the plaintiff's demand was reduced below $100 by a set-off offered at the trial on the part of the defendant. Maitland v. M'Dearman, 1 Va. Cas. 131.

The special counts in an action of assumpsit claimed less than $100, but the general count claimed $200, and the damages were laid at $500. The jury being unable to agree the case was submitted to arbitration, the award to be the judgment of the court. The award was for less than $100.

Held, that the district court had jurisdiction. Neff *v.* Talbot, 1 Va. Cas. 140.

Jurisdiction to Issue Writs of Mandamus and Prohibition.—The third section of the act regulating the jurisdiction of the district courts and court of appeals, passed June 5th, 1853, sess. acts, p. 53, provides that each district court shall have jurisdiction to issue writs of mandamus and prohibition to a circuit court held within the district. Barnett *v.* Meredith, 10 Gratt. 650. See the titles MANDAMUS; PROHIBITION.

Transfer of Admiral Jurisdiction to District Court.—See title ADMIRALTY, vol. 1, p. 182.

Writs Can Not Issue into Another District.—A writ can not issue from one district court into another district, although against joint defendants. McCall *v.* Turner, 1 Call 133.

2. Superior Courts of Law and Chancery.

In General.—"In the county and corporation courts, whilst those courts were at once courts of law and courts of equity, yet the two jurisdictions were by no means blended, nor in any wise confounded. The same justices would decline, as composing a court of common law, a jurisdiction which they would assert as constituting a court of equity. But in the superior courts, the two jurisdictions were lodged in the hands of different judges, sitting at different times and places. At first, in imitation of the English system, there existed but one superior court of chancery in the state, which held its sessions in Richmond, and was known as the high court of chancery. * * * In 1802, the commonwealth was divided into three districts, and a chancery court provided for each, to sit respectively at Richmond, Williamsburg, and Staunton. * * * Subsequently, four chancellors were created for the whole state, two for the territory east, and two for that west of the Blue Ridge, who held in

their respective districts as many in the aggregate as nine chancery courts, namely, at Richmond, Williamsburg, Norfolk, Fredricksburg, Lynchburg, Wytheville, Staunton, Winchester, and Clarksburg, and during the latter period of the system, at Lewisburg. This system continued until 1831, when it yielded to that which has ever since been in force." 4 Minor's Inst., pt. 1, p. 270.

Territorial Limits.—The several superior courts of chancery have jurisdiction in cases where their process is served upon the defendant within their respective districts, though his place of residence, and also the land in controversy be in a different district. Hughes *v.* Hall, 5 Munf. 431. See ante, "Territorial Limitation of Jurisdiction," I, D.

Can Not Enjoin Courts of Law Outside Their Districts.—The several superior courts of chancery have power to grant injunctions to the judgments of all courts of common law within their respective districts, and not otherwise; the place where the court of law is held, and not the residence of the parties, furnishing the rule of jurisdiction in such cases. Cocke *v.* Pollok, 1 Hen. & M. 499.

Jurisdictional Amount.—It was formerly the rule that a superior court of chancery had jurisdiction only where the subject in controversy exceeded $150. But when a bill was brought for relief against usury, it had jurisdiction, although the usury was for less than that sum, as it and the principal exceeded it. Stone *v.* Ware, 6 Munf. 541

Where a debt is reduced by payments below one hundred dollars, the superior court has not jurisdiction to render judgment on the verdict. Larowe *v.* Binns, 2 Va. Cas. 203.

Debt for a sum more than one hundred dollars, reduced to a sum below it, by a set-off. The superior court has jurisdiction to render judgment on the verdict. Ferguson *v.* Highley, 2 Va. Cas. 255.

Where the damages for breach of contract were uncertain, and therefore unknown until ascertained by verdict, the superior court had jurisdiction although the verdict is for less than $100. Newsum *v.* Pendred, 2 Va. Cas. 93.

The defendant, in an action upon a penal bill for $100, conditioned to pay $47.77, moved for a stay in the proceedings, because the penalty was inserted for the purpose of giving the court jurisdiction not passed by law. It was held that the court had jurisdiction. Heath *v.* Blaker, 2 Va. Cas. 215. See Newell *v.* Wood, 1 Munf. 555, which holds that the penalty decides the jurisdiction.

Jurisdiction over Indictments for Building Fence across Public Road.— An indictment lies against a person for making a fence across a public road. If the obstruction is permitted to continue for so many days as will raise the penalty to the sum of five dollars, the superior court of law has jurisdiction to try the indictment. Justice *v.* Com., 2 Va. Cas. 171.

E. CIRCUIT COURTS.

1. Jurisdiction of Circuit Court Generally.

Generally, as to the origin of circuit courts and their powers and duties as successors of the district and superior courts, see the title COURTS, vol. 3, p. 715, et seq.

a. Nature of Jurisdiction.

Courts of General Original Jurisdiction.—The circuit court is a court of general jurisdiction, taking cognizance of all actions at law between individuals, with authority to pronounce judgments and to issue execution for their enforcement. Cox *v.* Thomas, 9 Gratt. 323.

"Under the late constitution and legislation of this state, the circuit courts had not only the highest and most general, but the only general original jurisdiction exercised by any court in the state. Under the present constitution the circuit courts have the highest gen-

eral original jurisdiction." Chesapeake, etc., R. Co. *v.* Pack, 6 W. Va. 397.

b. Scope and Extent of Jurisdiction.

(1) Constitutional and Statutory Provisions.

For the provisions of the Virginia Code as to the jurisdiction of circuit courts, see § 3058 of the Virginia Code of 1904.

West Virginia Constitution and Code.—"The circuit court shall have the supervision and control of all proceedings before justices and other inferior tribunals, by mandamus, prohibition and certiorari. They shall except in cases confined exclusively by the constitution to some other tribunal, have original and general jurisdiction of all matters at law, where the amount in controversy, exclusive of interest, exceeds fifty dollars; of all cases of habeas corpus, mandamus, quo warranto and prohibition; and of all cases in equity and of all crimes and misdemeanors. They shall have appellate jurisdiction in all cases, civil and criminal, where an appeal, writ of error or supersedeas may be allowed to the judgment or proceedings of any inferior tribunal. They shall also have such other jurisdiction, whether supervisory, original, appellate or concurrent, as is or may be prescribed by law." Const., W. Va., art. 8, § 12, W. Va. Code, 1899, ch. 112, § 2. State *v.* Kyle, 8 W. Va. 711.

Statutory Restrictions.—Where the circuit court of a county is without jurisdiction under any of the clauses of § 1, ch. 123, W. Va. Code, amended by ch. 46, acts, 1897, it can not obtain jurisdiction by reason of service of process in any other county, except as against a railroad, canal, turnpike, telegraph, or insurance company. Rorer *v.* People's, etc., Ass'n, 47 W. Va. 1, 34 S. E. 758.

As to the appellate jurisdiction of circuit courts, see the title APPEAL AND ERROR, vol. 1, p. 654, et seq.

(2) Jurisdiction of Civil Proceedings. The Granting of Administrations.— Under 1 Rev. Code, Va., ch. 104, §§ 12, 32, the circuit courts have jurisdiction to grant administrations within certain limits. The place of the intestate's residence gives jurisdiction to the local courts. If he has no known place of residence, then the place of his death, or the place where his estate lies, gives jurisdiction. Ex parte Barker, 2 Leigh 719.

Concurrent Jurisdiction with County Court in Probate Matters, Appointment of Personal Representatives, etc.— "The circuit court shall have concurrent jurisdiction with the county courts in all matters of probate of wills, the appointment and qualification of personal representatives, guardians, committees and curators and the settlement of their accounts." W. Va. Code, ch. 112, § 2a, 1. See the titles EXECUTORS AND ADMINISTRATORS, vol. 5, p. 483; GUARDIAN AND WARD, vol. 6, p. 782; WILLS.

Concurrent Jurisdiction to Appoint Committees—Question of Insanity.— By §§ 1697, 1698, 1700, of the Virginia Code, 1887, circuit courts are given concurrent jurisdiction with county and corporation courts to appoint committees for lunatics, after they have been adjudged insane by three justices, or by the county or corporation court of the county or corporation of which they are inhabitants. The circuit courts are nowhere given the power to try the question of insanity, and the power to appoint a committee does not include such power. Harrison v. Garnett, 86 Va. 763, 11 S. E. 123.

Incorporation of Cities, Towns and Villages.— Chapter 47 of the W. Va. Code, 1899, in relation to the incorporation of cities, towns, and villages, in so far as it confers on the circuit court functions in their nature judicial and administrative, although in furtherance of the legislative department of the state government, is constitutional and valid. The circuit court, in the discharge of such functions, acts as a subordinate branch or tribunal of the legislative, not of the judicial, department, and is not subject to the appellate jurisdiction of the supreme court of appeals of this state. Bloxton v. McWhorter, 46 W. Va. 32, 32 S. E. 1004; In re Town of Union Mines, 39 W. Va. 179, 19 S. E. 398. See the titles COURTS, vol. 3, p. 705; MUNICIPAL CORPORATIONS.

Over Church Trustees.— While the circuit courts have general powers as courts of law and chancery, their jurisdiction in a summary proceeding under § 9, ch. 76, Code, 1873, is special, and limited to the appointment and removal of church trustees, but it does not extend to the regulation of their conduct of administration of the trust under the instrument creating it. Wade v. Hancock, 76 Va. 620.

To Sell Real Estate Devised.— Under § 20, ch. 112, Code, 1873, the circuit courts have jurisdiction to sell real estate devised by a testator to his two children for life, with remainder to their issue, if any be living at the time of their deaths; and if either should die without issue living, then to go to the issue of the other. Troth v. Robertson, 78 Va. 46.

To Grant License for Retail of Ardent Spirits.— The statute, acts, 1879-80, p. 148, in regard to license for retail of ardent spirits, provides that the county court "shall grant the license" if the one applying therefor shall bring himself within its requirements, and that the circuit court "may grant the license." The latter words mean that the circuit court shall have jurisdiction to grant the license, and must grant it if the applicant conforms to its requirements. Leigton v. Maury, 76 Va. 865.

Recovery of Money by Motion.— Section 3211, Va. Code, authorizes a remedy by motion in the circuit court in those cases in which the plaintiff is entitled to recover money by action on contract, and where the proceeding is founded upon a tort, it has no jurisdiction of the case. West. Union Tel. Co. v. Bright, 90 Va. 778, 20 S. E. 146; West. Union Tel. Co. v. Pettyjohn, 88 Va. 296, 13 S. E. 431. See material changes in procedure to recover money by motion, in the amendment of § 3211, by Acts 1895-96, p. 140.

Bastardy Cases — Maintenance of Child.—When the act of December 9, 1873, entitled "An act to amend and re-enact ch. 80 of the Code, concerning the maintenance of illegitimate children," went into operation, it did not oust the jurisdiction of the circuit courts to hear and determine cases of bastardy, where recognizance had theretofore been given, requiring the defendant to appear at the next term of the circuit court and answer the charge. After the passage of this act proceedings in the circuit court should conform as far as practicable to its requirements. Tennant v. Brookover, 12 W. Va. 337.

Mandamus, Prohibition and Certiorari.—Section 12, art. 8, W. Va. Const., 1872, giving to circuit courts the jurisdiction over all inferior tribunals, by mandamus, prohibition and certiorari, is restrained and limited by § 29 of the same article, which provides that in certain cases the county courts shall have jurisdiction of all appeals from justices, and their decision shall be final. Poe v. Machine Works, 24 W. Va. 517.

Generally, as to jurisdiction by mandamus, prohibition and certiorari, see the titles CERTIORARI, vol. 2, p. 752; MANDAMUS; PROHIBITION.

Injunctions.—See generally, the title INJUNCTIONS, vol. 7, p. 512.

Quo Warranto.—Held in Bland and Giles County Judge Case, 33 Gratt. 443, that the writ of quo warranto was not abolished in Virginia, and that the circuit courts had jurisdiction of the same. See the title QUO WARRANTO.

Causes Removed from County Court. —All civil causes of which the circuit court has either original or appellate jurisdiction, may be removed from the county to the circuit court, upon motion, after they have been pending in the county court for one year. Harrison v. Middleton, 11 Gratt. 527; Hale v. Burwell, 2 Pat. & H. 608, 610; Kincheloe v. Tracewells, 11 Gratt. 587, 598; Gas Co. v. Wheeling, 7 W. Va. 22, 25.

Under the act, ch. 174, § 1, Code of 1860, the case of a railroad company asking the county court to ascertain the compensation to a landowner for the land proposed to be taken for its purposes, which has remained in the court for more than one year without being determined, may be removed to the circuit court. Virginia, etc., R. Co. v. Campbell, 22 Gratt. 437.

Where commissioners are appointed under § 1, ch. 174, Va. Code, 1860, for the purpose of ascertaining compensation to landowners for land proposed to be taken by a railroad company, which cause has been removed to the circuit court, if it is set aside by the court, it should not send the case back to the county court; but should take jurisdiction of the case, and proceed in it with the same powers that are vested in the county court by the statute. Virginia, etc., R. Co. v. Campbell, 22 Gratt. 437.

Causes Transferred from District Court of Appeals.—Acts, 1869-70, p. 227, in relation to the transfer by the court of appeals of cases pending in the district court of appeals to the circuit court, to be heard there as by an appellate court, are constitutional. Cowan v. Fulton, 23 Gratt. 579.

When the court of appeals, in pursuance of § 5, ch. 171, act, 1869-70, sends a cause to a circuit court, which had been pending in a district court of appeals, that act was constitutional, and the circuit court has jurisdiction to rehear and decide the case. Cowan v. Doddridge, 23 Gratt. 458; Kent v. Dickinson, 25 Gratt. 817; Cowan v. Fulton. 23 Gratt. 579.

(3) Criminal Jurisdiction.

In General.—"The circuit courts except where otherwise provided, shall have exclusive original jurisdiction for the trial of all presentments, indictments, and informations for offenses committed within the counties and within the cities which may not have corporation courts, of their respective circuits, and also of all presentments, indictments and informations pending in the county courts on the first day of February, nineteen hundred and four." Va. Code, 1904, § 4016.

Section 3058 of the Virginia Code, 1904, provides that "no circuit court shall have any original or appellate jurisdiction in criminal cases arising within the territorial limits of any city wherein there is established by law a corporation or hustings court." See post, "Jurisdiction of Such Courts Generally," VIII, G, 2, a.

The former constitution of West Virginia conferred upon the circuit courts of the various counties original and general jurisdiction of all crimes and misdemeanors, by the sixth section of the sixth article thereof. The present constitution, in the twelfth section of the eighth article thereof, confers upon the circuit courts original, and general jurisdiction of all felonies and misdemeanors. The circuit courts under the constitution are the highest courts of general jurisdiction in the state. The third section of the act of the legislature, passed December 21, 1872, also confers upon the circuit courts original and general jurisdiction of all felonies and misdemeanors. Buskirk v. Judge, 7 W. Va. 91.

"The power and authority of the circuit courts of the state in a criminal case—their jurisdiction—extends to and embraces the power and duty of summoning, under circumstances, an impartial and duly qualified jury from beyond the limits of the county or corporation." Craft v. Com., 24 Gratt. 602.

Jurisdiction upon Election of Prisoner Arraigned in County Court.— Formerly under § 4016, of the Virginia Code of 1887, a person charged with a felony might, in certain instances when called to the bar to answer the indictment, elect to be tried in the circuit court. By the amendment of this section (acts. 1893, 1894, p. 270), the prisoner was deprived of the right of election.

For a discussion of this question, and citation of the cases construing and applying the law as it stood, before the amendment, see the title CRIMINAL LAW, vol. 4, p. 38.

Disturbance of Religious Worship.— The circuit superior courts have jurisdiction to try offenses against the statute, 1 Rev. Code, ch. 141, forbidding the disturbance of congregations assembled for the purpose of religious worship. Com. v. Jennings, 3 Gratt. 624.

Violation of Revenue Laws.—The act of February 27th, 1871, in relation to the municipal court of Wheeling, is unconstitutional so far as it attempts to confer sole jurisdiction on that court for the trial of cases involving a violation of the revenue laws by selling ardent spirits on the Sabbath; where the party charged had given bond according to the provisions of chapter 32 of the Code. The sixth section of the act purports to repeal all acts and parts of acts, inconsistent with it, but it does not take away any jurisdiction from the circuit court in such cases. Part of an act may be inoperative and void, and part of it operative, but this can only be when the parts are not connected. If they are so connected with each other as to warrant the belief that the legislature intended them as a whole, and if all could not be carried into effect, the legislature could not pass the residue independently; then if some parts are unconstitutional, all the provisions which are thus connected must fall with them. Any act that would seek to take away from the circuit court jurisdiction to try such cases as the one under consideration, would be in violation of the 6th section of article 6 of the constitution, which provides that the circuit court shall have original jurisdiction of all crimes and misdemeanors. Eckhart *v.* State, 5 W. Va. 515.

Homicide by Free Negroes and Mulattoes.—Under the construction of § 11, ch. 22, acts, 1831-32, free negroes and mulattoes are still to be tried by jury in the circuit superior courts for homicide and such crimes as were punishable with death before the statute. Com. *v.* Weldon, 4 Leigh 652.

(4) Invested with Jurisdiction and Powers of Former County Courts.

(a) In General.

By § 3058b of the Virginia Code, 1904, it is provided that "the jurisdiction and powers which vested in the county courts and the judges and officers thereof, respectively, on the thirty-first day of January, nineteen hundred and four, by the laws of this state, or under any will or other instrument of writing, shall be vested in, exercised by and imposed upon the circuit courts and the judges and officers thereof, except when otherwise specially provided."

(b) Transfer of Causes Pending in County Courts.

"All causes at law, and all presentments, informations, and indictments for felonies or misdemeanors pending in the county courts of the commonwealth on the thirty-first day of January, nineteen hundred and four, shall be removed to the circuit court of the respective counties, and the clerk of the county court is hereby directed to deliver to the circuit court for such county the original papers, complete, of all such causes, and all presentments, informations, and indictments for misdemeanors or felonies so removed, with the copies of all rules and orders made, not contained in the original papers, and shall enter on the order book of the county court the disposition made of such causes, and the clerk of the circuit court is hereby di-rected to receive and file in the office of his said court the papers so removed, and the said causes, indictments, and presentments shall stand in all respects as they stood in the county court, and like proceedings shall be had and process issued as if said causes, presentments, and indictments had been originally commenced in the circuit court. The cost of such removals shall be borne by the commonwealth." Va. Code, 1904, ch. 148, § 3058c.

Section 4016 of the Virginia Code, 1904, provides that the circuit court shall have jurisdiction "of all presentments, indictments and informations pending in the county court on the first day of February, nineteen hundred and four."

"All actions, suits and proceedings not embraced in the next preceding section, pending in a county court when article eight of the constitution, as amended, took effect, together with the records and papers pertaining thereto, as well as all records and papers pertaining to such actions, suits and proceedings as have been disposed of by said courts, shall be transmitted to and filed with the clerk of the circuit court of the county, and said clerk shall have the same power, and shall perform the same duties in relation to such records, papers and proceedings as were vested in and required of the clerk of the county court, on the day before said article took effect. All such actions, suits and proceedings so pending, as aforesaid, shall be docketed, proceeded in, tried, heard and determined in all respects by the circuit court, as if said suits and proceedings had originated in said court. And it shall be the duty of the clerk of the county court of each county, as soon as possible after the passage of this chapter, to transmit all such actions, suits and proceedings, together with such records and papers, to the clerk of the circuit court of such county, who shall receive and file the same in his office." W. Va. Code, 1899, ch. 39, p. 300.

An award of arbitrators was returned to a county court before the adoption of the amendments of the West Virginia constitution taking from the county court the right to try civil suits and transferring suits then pending in such courts to the circuit courts; and the county court made an order directing the parties to be summoned to appear before the court at its next trial term to show cause, if any they can, why said award should not be entered up as the judgment of the court; but before the next county court was held, this amendment of the constitution was adopted, and the clerk of the circuit court issued the summons, which the county court had ordered, returnable to the first day of the next circuit court. This summons was issued prior to the passage of any statute law to carry into effect this amendment of the constitution. The parties appeared in answer to the summons, and exceptions were filed to the award, and the case was heard on its merits, though no formal entry was made docketing the case in the circuit court. But no objections were made by the parties to the jurisdiction of the court. On a writ of error to the judgment of the circuit court, it was held, that the appellate court will not reverse the judgment of the circuit court, on the ground that it had not jurisdiction of the case. State v. Rawson, 25 W. Va. 23.

c. Jurisdiction as Dependent on Amount in Controversy.

In **Virginia** it is provided that the circuit court shall have jurisdiction of all cases in chancery and civil cases at law, except cases at law to recover personal property or money, not of greater value than twenty dollars, exclusive of interest, except such cases as are assigned to some other tribunal. Where a motion to recover money is allowed in said courts other than under section thirty-two hundred and eleven they may hear and determine the same although it be to recover less than twenty dollars. Va. Code, 1904, § 3058.

In **West Virginia**, the circuit courts "shall, except in cases confined by this constitution exclusively to some other tribunal, have original and general jurisdiction of all matters of law where the amount in controversy, exclusive of interest, exceeds fifty dollars." W. Va. Constitution, art. 8, § 12. State v. Kyles, 8 W. Va. 711.

2. Jurisdiction of Richmond Circuit Court.

Code Provisions Stated and Construed.—By § 3069 of the Virginia Code, 1904, "the said circuit court shall, within the corporate limits of the city of Richmond, have original jurisdiction of all such causes, motions, matters, and things, whether now pending or hereafter brought therein, as are cognizable by law in other circuit courts of the commonwealth, and the jurisdiction whereof is not vested exclusively in the said chancery court or the said hustings court. The said circuit court, and judge thereof, respectively, shall also have jurisdiction of all such suits, motions, prosecutions, and matters and things as are specially cognizable by the said court or judge under chapters thirty, thirty-one, thirty-two, one hundred and fifty-seven, and two hundred and four, and section thirty-four hundred and thirty-two, or any other section of this Code."

"The Code of Virginia, 1873, ch. 44, § 7, provides, 'there shall be brought and prosecuted in the circuit court of the city of Richmond all suits in which it may be necessary or proper to make any of the following public officers a party defendant as representing the commonwealth, to wit: The governor, attorney general, treasurer, register of the land office, or either auditor.' And by § 8: 'If any such suit be now depending or be hereafter brought in any other court, such court shall, by its order made therein, transfer such suit, together with all the papers and proceedings therein, to such court as is designated in the preceding section, there to be proceeded in to a final decision. And if such suit be not so transferred, but be proceeded in to judgment or decree in the court wherein it may have been so depending or brought, such judgment or decree, so far as it is against any of the said public officers of public corporations, or against the commonwealth, shall be void.'" Taylor v. Williams, 78 Va. 422; Universal Life Ins. Co. v. Cogbill, 30 Gratt. 72.

Virginia Code, 1873, ch. 44, §§ 7, 8, is mandatory, and ousts all jurisdiction in suits against the state officers (including treasurer) enumerated from every other court, and confers it upon the circuit court of the city of Richmond. Ragland v. Broadnax, 29 Gratt. 401, 414; Taylor v. Williams, 78 Va. 422.

A foreign insurance company has deposited bonds with the treasurer of the state in pursuance of the statute, and fails. A policy holder may sue the company in the circuit court of the city of Richmond, and make the treasurer a party defendant to subject the bonds in his possession to satisfy the premiums he has paid upon the policy. See act of April 4, 1877, amending § 32, ch. 36, Code, 1873, p. 368. In such case the treasurer represents the commonwealth as a public officer, and the case is embraced in the statute, Code of 1873, ch. 44, § 7, giving to the circuit court of the city of Richmond exclusive jurisdiction in cases in which certain state officers named are necessary or proper parties. Universal Life Ins. Co. v. Cogbill, 30 Gratt. 72.

By § 4, ch. 155, Va. Code, 1873, the circuit court of the city of Richmond has no chancery jurisdiction, except in suits in which it may be necessary or proper to make certain enumerated officers or public corporations parties defendant. The commissioner of agriculture is not within the exception. Blanton v. Southern, etc., Co., 77 Va. 335; Ragland v. Broadnax, 29 Gratt. 401.

"The circuit court of the city of Richmond is different from the other circuit courts of the state—a court of limited jurisdiction. It has no chancery jurisdiction (there being created by statute a separate chancery court for the city of Richmond), except 'in suits in which it may be necessary or proper to make any of the following public officers a party defendant as representing the commonwealth, to wit: The governor, attorney general, treasurer, register of the land office, or either auditor; or in which it may be necessary or proper to make any of the following public corporations parties defendant, to wit: The board of the literary fund, board of education, board of public works, or any other public corporations composed of officers of government, of the funds and property of which the commonwealth is sole owner, or in which it shall be attempted to enjoin or otherwise suspend or affect any judgment or decree in behalf of the commonwealth, or any execution issued on such judgment or decree.' Sess. acts, 1869-70, pp. 42, 43." Ragland v. Broadnax, 29 Gratt. 401.

Suit to Enjoin or Affect Judgments in Behalf of Commonwealth.—Under § 1, ch. 165, Va. Code, 1873, the circuit court of the city of Richmond alone. has jurisdiction of any suit to enjoin or affect any judgment or decree in behalf of the commonwealth, and no such suit can be maintained in any other court of the state. Com. v. Latham, 85 Va. 632, 8 S. E. 488.

Administration—Claim against State. —A resident of Kentucky dies intestate there, having no estate in Virginia but a claim on this commonwealth for money. It was held, that the circuit court of Henrico county, wherein is the seat of government, has jurisdiction to grant administration of such decedent's estate. Com. *v.* Hudgin, 2 Leigh 248.

Jurisdiction of Convicts.—In Ruffin *v.* Com., 21 Gratt. 790, a penitentiary convict was hired to work on a railroad, and in Bath county, in attempting to escape, he killed his guard. It was held, that he may be tried for the offense before the circuit court of the city of Richmond, and by a jury summoned from that city.

Court of Richmond Has No Jurisdiction of Offense in Essex.—The circuit court of Richmond issues a capias against a person then indicted for felony, which is directed to the sheriff of Essex, and by him served, and in Essex he willfully permits the prisoner to escape. In such case a criminal prosecution against the sheriff can not be maintained in the circuit superior court of Richmond, for this official malfeasance committed in Essex. Com. *v.* Lewis, 4 Leigh 664.

F. COUNTY COURTS.

1. In General.

Generally, as to the establishment, organization, powers and duties of county courts, see the title COURTS, vol. 3, p. 723.

As to the abolition of county courts in Virginia, see the title COURTS, vol. 3, p. 727.

2. Nature of Jurisdiction.

In Virginia, before their abolition, county courts, with respect to purely judicial powers, were held to be courts of general jurisdiction, and their judgments were presumed to be right, and could not be attacked collaterally, however erroneous they might be. Chesapeake, etc., R. Co. *v.* Washington, etc., R. Co., 99 Va. 715, 40 S. E. 202; Devaughn *v.* Devaughn, 19 Gratt. 556; Woodhouse *v.* Fillbates, 77 Va. 317; Shelton *v.* Jones, 26 Gratt. 891.

Until the enactment of §§ 2, 3, ch. 124, Va. Code, 1873, the county court was a court of general and concurrent jurisdiction with the circuit court, except in respect to suits for the sale or partition of the lands of infants, or for the sale of the lands of insane persons, as to which the law gave exclusive jurisdiction to the circuit courts. Litterall *v.* Jackson, 80 Va. 604.

The county courts in West Virginia were formerly courts of general jurisdiction. Mayer *v.* Adams, 27 W. Va. 244.

The character of these courts in this state was, however, essentially changed by the amendment of the constitution made in 1880. They are now inferior courts of limited jurisdiction. Their character and jurisdiction are prescribed in § 24, art. 8, of the West Virginia constitution. Mayer *v.* Adams, 27 W. Va. 244.

Generally, as to the presumption in favor of the jurisdiction of courts of general jurisdiction, see ante, "Presumptions as to Jurisdiction," IV.

These tribunals were local; bounded in their general jurisdiction by the limits of their county. Gholson *v.* Kendall, 4 Leigh 612.

3. Scope and Extent of Jurisdiction.

a. Constitutional and Statutory Provisions.

(1) Provisions of Virginia Code.

For an account of the origin and powers of county courts in Virginia, and a summary of the provisions of the various acts of the legislature relating to the jurisdiction of such courts, see the case of Devaughn *v.* Devaughn, 19 Gratt. 556.

In the revision of 1748, ch. 7, § 5, 5 Hen. Stat. at Large, p. 491, the jurisdiction of the county courts is thus expressed: "The justices of every county court, or any four of them as aforesaid, shall and may take cognizance of, and are hereby declared to have power, authority and jurisdiction, to hear and determine all causes whatsoever, at common law, or in chancery, within their respective counties;" and these precise words we find used in all the laws since. In some of the latter revisions are added, "and all such other matters as by any particular statute is or shall be made cognizable therein." Gholson v. Kendall, 4 Leigh 612.

In § 16 of ch. 157, Va. Code, 1860; also, in 1 Rev. Code, p. 249, ch. 71, § 7; it is provided that: "The court of a county or corporation shall have jurisdiction to hear and determine all causes at law or in chancery within such county or corporation which are now pending, or may hereafter be brought in said court," except certain cases therein enumerated. Litterall v. Jackson, 80 Va. 604.

By the act of 1870, ch. 38, § 4, it was provided that the county courts should "have exclusive original jurisdiction for the trial of all presentments, informations and indictments, for offenses committed within their respective counties," except as therein mentioned. Marshall v. Com., 20 Gratt. 845.

By the Virginia Code of 1887, § 3046, it was provided that "the county courts (concurrently with the circuit courts) shall have jurisdiction of writs of mandamus in all matters or proceedings arising from or appertaining to the actions of the boards of supervisors of the counties for which the said courts are respectively held. They shall have original jurisdiction of all presentments, informations, and indictments for felonies and misdemeanors, and the proceedings thereon, and appellate jurisdiction in such cases as are allowed by law to be brought before them on appeal. They shall also have jurisdiction of all causes, motions and other matters and things made cognizable therein by law." Hancock v. Whitehall, etc., Co., 100 Va. 443, 41 S. E. 860.

Section 4016 of the Code was amended by acts, 1893-94, p. 270, and the provision, under which indictments for felonies punishable by death, which had theretofore been removed upon motion of the prisoner to the circuit court, was omitted, and the county courts were clothed, except where otherwise provided, with exclusive original jurisdiction for the trial of all presentments, indictments, and information for offenses committed in their respective counties. Gilligan v. Com., 99 Va. 816, 37 S. E. 962, 7 Va. Law Reg. 178. See the title CRIMINAL LAW, vol. 4, p. 38. And see ante, "Criminal Jurisdiction," VIII, E, 1, b, (3).

(2) Provisions of West Virginia Constitution.

The jurisdiction of county courts in West Virginia is prescribed in § 24, art. 8, of the West Virginia constitution, 1899. Their jurisdiction now extends only to all matters of probate, the appointment and qualification of personal representatives, guardians, committees, curators and the settlement of their accounts, and to all matters relating to apprentices, and to the superintendence and administration of the internal police and fiscal affairs of their counties including the establishment of roads, ways, bridges, public landings, ferries, mills with authority to levy and disburse the county levy and in all cases of contest to judge of the election, qualification and returns of their own members and of all county and district officers, subject to such regulations by appeal or otherwise, as may be prescribed by law. Mayer v. Adams, 27 W. Va. 244; Fowler v. Thompson, 22 W. Va. 106; Arkle v. Board of Comm'rs, 41 W. Va. 471, 23 S. E. 804; Lance v. McCoy, 34 W. Va. 416, 12 S. E. 728.

b. Jurisdiction at Quarterly and Monthly Terms.

The county or corporation courts at quarterly terms, may, in their discretion, receive the probate of deeds, or wills, or decide on controversies concerning mills, etc., or indeed transact any business embraced by the general jurisdiction of such courts; but at a monthly session they can not take jurisdiction of any case expressly and exclusively assigned to a quarterly term. Wilkinson *v.* Mayo, 3 Hen. & M. 565.

"Now, it is well settled, both by the statute law and the decisions of this court, that at a monthly term of the county court, no judgment against a debtor upon action at law for the recovery of money can be had, but such judgment can only be had at the quarterly term of such court. Code, 1873, ch. 154, § 3 and § 12; see also, Wynn *v.* Scott, 7 Leigh 63, and Claflin & Co. *v.* Steenbock & Co., 18 Gratt. 842. In this case the judgment was at a monthly term and it is plain the court had no jurisdiction." Withers *v.* Fuller, 30 Gratt. 547.

Where an attachment has been sued out under § 2, ch. 151, Va. Code, 1860, in a · suit pending in a county court, though the defendant has given a forthcoming bond, the court has jurisdiction at a monthly term to abate the attachment. Claflin *v.* Steenbock, 18 Gratt. 842. See Withers *v.* Fuller, 30 Gratt. 547, 552. See the title ATTACHMENT AND GARNISHMENT, vol. 2, p. 70.

c. Civil Jurisdiction.

Assignment of Dower.—The county courts are courts of general jurisdiction, and in proceeding under the act, ch. 110, § 9, Va. Code, 1860, for the assignment of dower, it is to be presumed, in the absence of proof to the contrary, that the court had jurisdiction of the case, and proceeded regularly in it. Devaughn *v.* Devaughn, 19 Gratt. 556. See the title DOWER, vol. 4, p. 818.

Appointment of Additional Justices. —Va. Code, § 97, authorizing county courts to appoint additional justices to the number specified in the constitution when the public service requires it; held, not violative of §§ 2, 4, art. 7, of the constitution, and not an unwar-

ranted delegation of legislative power. Ex parte Bassitt, 90 Va. 679, 19 S. E. 453.

Condemnation Proceedings by Railroad.—It was held in Chesapeake, etc., R. Co. *v.* Hoard, 16 W. Va. 270, that the provisions in ch. 88, acts 1872-73, in reference to the condemnation of land by railroad companies was not repealed nor abrogated by ch. 114, acts, 1875, and ch. 8, acts, 1879, amending the same, and that therefore the circuit court has no jurisdiction in a case where a railroad company seeks to condemn lands, the jurisdiction in such cases being confined to the county court, as decided in Chesapeake, etc., R. Co. *v.* Patton, 9 W. Va. 648. See the title EMINENT DOMAIN, vol. 5, p. 101.

Elections.—As to the jurisdiction of county courts in matters pertaining to elections, see the title ELECTIONS. vol. 5, p. 1.

Matters of Probate, Appointment of Personal Representatives, etc.—The grant of jurisdiction to the county court in chapter 39, § 9, W. Va. Code, 1899, is only in the general language used in the constitution (art. 8, § 24), namely: "They shall have jurisdiction in all matters of probate, the appointment and qualification of personal representatives, guardians, committees, curators." Lance *v.* McCoy, 34 W. Va. 416, 12 S. E. 728.

Grant of Administration.—Under 1 Rev. Va. Code, ch. 104, §§ 12, 32, the county courts have jurisdiction to grant administrations within certain limits. The place of the intestate's residence gives jurisdiction to the local courts. If he had no known place of residence, then the place of his death, or the place where his estate lies, gives jurisdiction. Ex parte Barker, 2 Leigh 719.

After administration has been granted to a sheriff, on application of a distributee to be given the administration, the county court may exercise its discretion in the matter. Hutcheson v. Priddy, 12 Gratt. 85.

After a county court has granted administration of an estate to the sheriff, it can not grant it to a distributee, without notice to the sheriff. Hutcheson v. Priddy, 12 Gratt. 85. See the title EXECUTORS AND ADMINISTRATORS, vol. 5, p. 506; GUARDIAN AND WARD, vol. 6, p. 782; WILLS.

Injunctions.—By the Virginia Code, 1873, ch. 175, § 6, authority is given to every judge of a county court to award injunctions where the act or proceeding to be enjoined, is apprehended, or is to be done, or is doing, in his county or district. Rosenberger v. Bowen, 84 Va. 660, 5 S. E. 697. See the title INJUNCTIONS, vol. 7, p. 512.

Investment of Fiduciary Money.—Under § 34, Va. Code, 1860, a county court is not authorized to make any order for investing or loaning out the money or fund referred to in that chapter, unless the commissioner who settles the accounts of the fiduciary has previously conformed to the provisions of § 16 of that chapter. And if the county acts without the report, the county court has jurisdiction on the motion of the parties whose money is invested upon notice to the other parties to annul the order. Whitehead v. Whitehead, 23 Gratt. 376.

Motion on Sheriffs' Bonds.—It was held in Carr v. Meade, 77 Va. 142, that § 5, ch. 173, Va. Code, 1873, providing remedy by motion on the bonds of sheriffs, etc., was not repealed by § 9, ch. 395, acts, 1872, 1873, and that motions were properly cognizable in the county court in such cases, in 1879. See the title SHERIFFS AND CONSTABLES.

Prohibition.—The county courts have no power to grant writs of prohibition; if they exceed their jurisdiction by granting them, the superior courts of law may restrain the exercise of such jurisdiction by prohibition. Jackson v. Maxwell, 5 Rand. 636. See the title PROHIBITION.

Removal of Executor.—The county courts in which an executor has qualified, in the exercise of the power vested in it by statute (Code, 1873, ch. 128, § 18), may remove him from office. Reynolds v. Zink, 27 Gratt. 29; Snavely v. Harkrader, 29 Gratt. 112, 128; Lance v. McCoy, 34 W. Va. 416, 420, 12 S. E. 728. See the title EXECUTORS AND ADMINISTRATORS, vol. 5, p. 515.

Sale of Decedent's Land—Partitions When Shares Exceed $300.—The county courts had jurisdiction in 1860, to sell real estate of a decedent for the purpose of paying the debts of the ancestor from whom it descended, and being a court of general jurisdiction for this purpose, every presumption must be made in favor of its proceedings when collaterally attacked. They did not have, however, jurisdiction of suits brought by guardians to sell the real estate of infants, nor of suits brought for the purpose of making partition where the shares of such infants exceed in value the sum of $300. Woodhouse v. Fillbates, 77 Va. 317; Wimbish v. Breeden, 77 Va. 324. See Seamster v. Blackstock, 83 Va. 232, 2 S. E. 36. See also, Va. Code, 1860, p. 581, § 3. And see the titles EXECUTORS AND ADMINISTRATORS, vol. 5, p. 561; GUARDIAN AND WARD, vol. 6, p. 782; INFANTS, vol. 7, p. 461; JUDICIAL SALES AND RENTINGS, ante, p. 648; PARTITION.

Wills.—Although a will has been admitted to record in a district court, a county court in chancery has jurisdiction to try its validity, and may direct an issue to be tried on the common-law side of the same court. Ford v. Gardner, 1 Hen. & M. 72. See the title WILLS.

As to powers of county courts as county officers, see the title COUNTIES, vol. 3, p. 636.

d. Criminal Jurisdiction.

No Jurisdiction of Felonies in 1860.
—An indictment for petit larceny which
charges that the person indicted had
been previously convicted of another
petit larceny, is an indictment for a
felony, and a county court has no jurisdiction to try the prisoner. Rider v.
Com., 16 Gratt. 499.

**Constitutional Provisions Giving
County Court Jurisdiction of Felonies.**
—Section 27, art. 8, of the constitution,
which provides that the county courts
shall have jurisdiction of all criminal
cases beneath the grade of a felony, is
not an implied prohibition against the
legislature giving the county court jurisdiction in cases of feleny; hence, an
act giving county courts jurisdiction
to examine persons charged with felonies, is not in violation of this provision. State v. Strauder, 8 W. Va.
686.

**Felonies by Free Negroes and Mulat-
toes—Exceptions—Statute of 1831-32.**—
Under the construction of the statute
of 1831-32, ch. 22, § 11, free negroes
and mulattoes are to be tried by the
county courts of oyer and terminer, in
the same manner in which slaves are
tried, in all cases of felony, except
homicide and such crimes as were punishable with death before the statute.
Com. v. Weldon, 4 Leigh 652.

Recognizance to Keep the Peace.—
A county court has authority to require
a party to enter into a recognizance to
keep the peace; certainly where the
proceeding was commenced before the
acts, 1847-48, ch. 14. Welling's Case,
6 Gratt. 670.

**Concurrent Jurisdiction in Case of
Violations of Revenue Law.**—By the
acts of 1897-98, ch. 264, pp. 289, 290, it
is provided that the county and corporation courts, police justices, and
justices of the peace shall have concurrent jurisdiction, among other
things, of all violations of the revenue
laws of this state. Catching and taking fish in the waters of the commonwealth without first having obtained a
license and paid the required tax (acts,
1897-98, p. 864), is a violation of the
revenue laws, and a county court has
jurisdiction to indict and try persons
for violation of this law. Morgan v.
Com., 98 Va. 812, 35 S. E. 448. See
the title REVENUE LAWS.

4. Jurisdiction as Dependent on Amount in Controversy.

In Virginia.—Under Rev. Code, 1860,
p. 663, authorizing county courts to
hear and determine all cases involving
more than $20, except certain crimi-
nal cases, a county court is a court of
general jurisdiction. Shelton v. Jones,
26 Gratt. 891.

A county court has no jurisdiction
at a monthly term in any suit at law
where the value in controversy exceeds $20, and therefore a confession
of judgment for a debt of a larger
amount, entered at a monthly term of
a county court, is of no effect whatever. Wynn v. Scott, 7 Leigh 63.

Forfeited forthcoming bonds taken
on distress warrants issued for rent by
justices of the peace of a county are
returnable to the county courts, and
when motion is made for judgment in
such courts, the tenant may make any
defense which shows that the rent is
not due in whole or in part. The tenant has the right to rely upon set-offs
in said courts to the extent to which
it is necessary to make complete defense to the landlord's demand, regardless of the amount of such set-off.
There is no pecuniary limit to the
jurisdiction of said courts in this respect. Code, §§ 2787, 3004, 900, 3046.
Hancock v. Whitehall, etc., Co., 100
Va. 443, 41 S. E. 860.

In West Virginia.—By art. 8, § 27,
of the West Virginia constitution and
§ 13 of the acts of 1872-73, p. 35, it is
provided that the county court shall
have original jurisdiction in all actions
at law, where the amount in controversy exceeds $20. Marion Machine
Works v. Craig, 18 W. Va. 559.

5. Transfer of Jurisdiction to Circuit Courts.

As to the provision of the Virginia Code, 1904, vesting in the circuit court the jurisdiction and powers of the former county court, and the provisions of the Codes of Virginia and West Virginia for the transfer to the circuit court of cases pending in the county courts, see ante, "Invested with Jurisdiction and Powers of Former County Courts," VIII, E, 1, b, (4).

G. MUNICIPAL, HUSTINGS AND CORPORATION COURTS.

1. Municipal Courts.

a. Courts of Limited Jurisdiction Established under West Virginia Constitution, Art. 8, § 19.

As to the establishment of such courts, see the title COURTS, vol. 3, p. 727.

Code Provisions as to Jurisdiction.— For the provisions of the West Virginia Code as to jurisdiction of courts of limited jurisdiction established in incorporated towns or cities, see the West Virginia Code of 1899, pp. 1110, 1111.

Jurisdiction of Municipal Court of Huntington.—The municipal court of Huntington created by the act of March 4, 1879, is a court of limited jurisdiction. Rutter v. Sullivan, 25 W. Va. 427.

Municipal Court of Wheeling—Recovery of Taxes.—Section 12, ch. 51, acts, 1865, establishing the municipal court of Wheeling, grants that court jurisdiction of cases, in which the city seeks to recover taxes due it. Wheeling v. Hawley, 18 W. Va. 472.

Municipal Court of Wheeling—Violation of Revenue Laws—Constitutional Law.—An act relative to the municipal court of Wheeling was unconstitutional where it attempted to confer sole jurisdiction on that court of cases involving a violation of the revenue laws by selling spirituous liquors on the Sabbath. It did not take

away the jurisdiction of the circuit court in such cases, and is in violation of § 6, art. 6, of the constitution, which prov'des that the circuit court shall have original jurisdiction of all crimes and misdemeanors. Eckhart v. State, 5 W. Va. 515.

Transfer of Causes to Circuit Court Where Judge Can Not Preside.—"If a judge of any court of limited jurisdiction, established in any town or city in this state, can not properly preside at the hearing or trial of any cause pending therein, on motion of any party thereto, the cause shall be certified to, and the original papers, with a copy of the orders of the court, shall be filed in the circuit court of the county, and the cause shall be docketed therein and proceeded with as though the cause had been originally brought, and the prior proceedings had in the circuit court to which it was transferred." W. Va. Code, 1899, p. 1111.

b. Mayor's, Recorder's and Police Courts.

As to the jurisdiction of these courts, see the title MUNICIPAL CORPORATIONS.

2. Hustings and Corporation Courts.

a. Jurisdiction of Such Courts Generally.

(1) Constitutional and Statutory Provisions.

Co-Ordinate with Circuit Courts.—"The power and jurisdiction of corporation courts generally, as at present organized, are nowhere prescribed and defined in detail by separate express legislation. The jurisdiction of these courts has been generally conferred, both in the constitution of the state and in the acts of assembly under that constitution, by reference to the jurisdiction of other courts, and chiefly of the circuit courts, without stating in the grant of jurisdiction, otherwise than by reference as aforesaid, what that jurisdiction is, except in some special cases. * * * When, therefore, in a criminal case, we wish to ascertain what are the powers and duties of a corporation court (other than that of the city of Richmond), we are referred by the constitution and the laws to the jurisdiction of the circuit courts; to the powers and duties of those tribunals in such case; and the same jurisdiction precisely is conferred on the corporation courts." Craft *v.* Com., 24 Gratt. 602. See also, Jordan *v.* Com., 25 Gratt. 943; Chahoon's Case, 21 Gratt. 822.

By virtue of § 14, art. 6, of the constitution of Virginia, corporation and hustings courts are vested with similar jurisdiction to the circuit courts, and are of co-ordinate dignity with them; and any act of the legislature so far as it undertakes to confer appellate power on a circuit court to review an action of a corporation or hustings court is unconstitutional and void. Watson *v.* Blackstone, 98 Va. 618, 38 S. E. 939.

Jurisdiction Enlarged—Felony Cases. —Section 14, art. 6, of the constitution of Virginia, which provides that corporation courts shall have similar jurisdiction which may be given by law to the circuit courts of the state, was not intended to restrict, but to enlarge, the jurisdiction of these courts, and to elevate them to the grade and dignity of circuit courts. And it was competent, therefore, for the legislature to give to the corporation courts jurisdiction to try cases of felony, though the jurisdiction in such cases was taken away from the circuit courts. Chahoon *v.* Com., 21 Gratt. 822; Watson *v.* Blackstone, 98 Va. 618, 38 S. E. 939.

For the provisions of the present Virginia Code as to the jurisdiction of ·corporation or hustings court, see the Virginia Code, 1904, § 3055.

(2) Jurisdiction at Quarterly and Monthly Terms.

The corporation courts at a quarterly term may in their discretion, receive the probate of deeds or wills or decide controversies concerning mills, etc., but at a monthly session, they can not take jurisdiction of any case expressly and exclusively assigned to a quarterly term. Wilkinson *v.* Mayo, 3 Hen. & M. 565.

Where an attachment has been sued out under § 2, ch. 151, Va. Code, 1860, in a suit pending in a corporation court, though the defendant has given a forthcoming bond, the court has jurisdiction at a monthly term to abate the attachment. Claflin *v.* Steenbock, 18 Gratt. 842. See Withers *v.* Fuller, 30 Gratt. 547, 552.

(3) Jurisdiction in Particular Instances.
(a) Civil Jurisdiction.

Removal of Judge of Election.—The corporation courts have authority to remove a judge of election for malfeasance in office or gross neglect of duty, though he has not been convicted by the verdict of a jury for any offense. McDougal *v.* Guigon, 27 Gratt. 133; Lewis *v.* Whittle, 77 Va. 415, 423; Nelms *v.* Vaughan, 84 Va. 696, 698, 5 S. E. 704.

Vacating an Election.—Under § 69, acts, 1870, p. 97, which provides for the general election, the corporation courts have jurisdiction to vacate an election. Ex parte Ellyson, 20 Gratt. 10. See the title ELECTIONS, vol. 5, p. 1.

Condemnation of Land in Incorporated Town for County Clerk's Office. —The condemnation of land for a county clerk's office in an incorporated town, does not create a conflict of jurisdiction between the city and county courts, as the city court has jurisdiction of the locality and the county court does not acquire the same by the condemnation proceedings. Board of Supervisors *v.* Cox, 98 Va. 270, 36 S. E. 380.

(b) Criminal Jurisdiction.

Similar Jurisdiction to Circuit and County Courts.—Under the act of April 2, 1870, ch. 38, §§ 6, 7, sess. acts, 1869-70, corporation courts in cities and towns having a population of more than five thousand have the same jurisdiction to try offenses committed within their respective limits as circuit and county courts had; and the act of April 2, 1873, to regulate and define the jurisdiction of the county and circuit courts does not apply to or affect the jurisdiction of said corporation courts. Tremaine v. Com., 25 Gratt. 987.

"The power and authority of the circuit courts of the state in a criminal case—their jurisdiction—extends to and embraces the power and duty of summoning, under circumstances, an impartial and duly qualified jury from beyond the limits of the county or corporation; and this being a most important and valuable safeguard to an impartial trial, as well on the part of the prisoner as of the commonwealth, we can see no reason in favor of its exercise by a circuit court which would not apply a fortiori to the corporation courts when exercising the grave functions of a criminal tribunal. We say a fortiori, because, from the necessarily contracted limits of such corporations, the necessity for the exercise of this wholesome power must more readily and frequently arise in a corporation than in counties." Craft v. Com., 24 Gratt. 602.

Creating City and Corporation Court —Offenses Prior to Act.—An act incorporating a city, and creating a court therein, will not be presumed to give, by implication, that court jurisdiction of an offense committed before the passage of the act. Ryan v. Com., 80 Va. 385.

No Jurisdiction of Felonies in 1860. —An indictment for petit larceny which charges that the person indicted had been previously indicted, tried and sentenced for another petit larceny, is an indictment for felony, and a corporation court has no jurisdiction to try the case. Rider v. Com., 16 Gratt. 499.

Removal from County Court.—An indictment for a felony was found against the prisoner in the county court of Alexandria, and it was removed to the corporation court of Alexandria. The corporation court had no jurisdiction to try it. See § 4, ch. 38, acts 1868-70; Marshall v. Com., 20 Gratt. 845.

Proceedings against Master for Allowing Slave to Hire Himself Out.— By the provisions of 1 Rev. Va. Code, ch. 111, § 81, the court of hustings has jurisdiction to proceed against the master who permits a slave to go at large and hire himself out contrary to the provisions of the above act. Abrahams v. Com., 1 Rob. 675.

b. Jurisdiction of Particular Courts.

(1) Hustings Court of Richmond.

For the statutory provisions as to the jurisdiction of the hustings court of Richmond, see § 3072 of the Virginia Code, 1904.

Territorial Extent.—The criminal jurisdiction of the hustings court of Richmond extends one mile beyond the city limits on the north side of the James river. Jordan v. Com., 25 Gratt. 943; Chahoon v. Com., 20 Gratt. 733.

When Judge Can Act for Chancery Court.—By the act of 1869-70, p. 427, the judge of the hustings court of the city of Richmond 'is authorized in certain cases to perform the duties of the judge of the chancery court. Where cause pending in the chancery court was by consent submitted to its judge in vacation, and a decree was entered by the judge of the hustings court acting for the judge of the chancery court, it was held, that under § 53, ch. 167, Code, 1873, the decree was valid. Morriss v. Virginia Ins. Co., 85 Va. 588, 8 S. E. 383.

Jurisdiction of Felony Cases.—In Chahoon's Case, 21 Gratt. 822, 825, the point was made by counsel, that under the constitution in force at that time the hustings court of Richmond could not be given jurisdiction to try cases of felony. The court said since the case of Boswell v. Com., 20 Gratt. 860, Bird's Case, 21 Gratt. 800, and Smith's Case, 21 Gratt. 809, all proceed upon the tacit admission of the existing jurisdiction of the corporation courts to try such cases, the court was of opinion that the hustings court of the city of Richmond had jurisdiction over the case. Boswell v. Com., 20 Gratt. 860.

Though a suit at law was brought in the county court of Henrico upon a forged note and judgment recovered, and a suit in equity to enforce this judgment was brought in the circuit court of Henrico, yet as both these courts were held in the limits of the city of Richmond where the prisoner lived, the hustings court of the city had jurisdiction to try him for the offense. Chahoon v. Com., 20 Gratt. 733; Sands v. Com., 20 Gratt. 800.

(2) Hustings Court of Roanoke.

Prior to the incorporation of Roanoke, act January 31, 1884, and to the creation of the hustings court of that city, act February 25, 1884, the county court of Roanoke county had jurisdiction of all cases committed in what afterwards became the city limits. The hustings court had no jurisdiction of a murder committed there January 27, 1884. Ryan v. Com., 80 Va. 385.

H. CHANCERY COURT OF RICHMOND.

For the statutory provisions as to the jurisdiction of the chancery court of Richmond, see § 3070 of the Virginia Code, 1904.

Extent beyond Corporate Limits.— The jurisdiction of the chancery court of Richmond extends one mile beyond the corporate limits. Boston v. Chesapeake, etc., R. Co., 76 Va. 180.

I. JUSTICE'S COURTS.

See the title JUSTICES OF THE PEACE.

J. EXAMINING COURTS.

See the title COMMITMENTS AND PRELIMINARY EXAMINATION OF ACCUSED, vol. 3, p. 1.

K. SPECIAL COURTS TO DETERMINE ELECTION CONTESTS.

See the title ELECTIONS, vol. 5, p. 32.

IX. Jurisdiction of State Courts Where State Interested.

See generally, the titles PUBLIC OFFICERS; STATE.

Suits by Commonwealth.— Except when it is otherwise specially provided, any of the courts have jurisdiction over suits by the commonwealth, in cases in which other parties may prosecute like suits. See ch. 166, Va. Code, 1873; Com. v. Ford, 29 Gratt. 683.

Suit against State.— It is an established principle that a sovereign state can not be sued in its own courts, or in any other, without its consent and permission, and in the manner and in the tribunals expressly provided. And this principle, except so far as modified by the United States constitution, art. 3, § 2, cl. 1, applies as well to the states of the union as to the government of the United States. Board of Public Works v. Gannt, 76 Va. 455; McCandlish v. Com., 76 Va. 1002.

Suits against Agents of Government. —The true owner of property, found in possession of agents or officers of the government under a void title, may bring an action against such agents and officers for its recovery, and it is no answer to say that the state has an interest in or claim to the property. In such cases jurisdiction is neither given nor ousted by the relative situation of the parties concerned in interest, but by the relative situation of the parties named on the record. Board of Public Works v. Gannt, 76 Va. 455.

As to the jurisdiction of the Richmond circuit court in certain cases, see ante, "Jurisdiction of Richmond Circuit Court." VIII, E, 2.

X. Jurisdiction of Constitutional Questions.

See the title CONSTITUTIONAL LAW, vol. 3, p. 153.

XI. Relative Jurisdiction of State and Federal Courts.

Exercise of Judicial Powers of United States.—By the constitution, the judicial power of the United States is vested in the supreme court, and inferior courts to be ordained and established by congress. Therefore state courts have no right to exercise that judicial power. Jackson v. Rose, 2 Va. Cas. 34.

State Court May Not Enjoin Execution of Decree of Federal Court.—A state court has no jurisdiction to enjoin the execution of a decree of a federal court. Dorr v. Rohr, 82 Va. 359.

Jurisdiction of Offenses Created by Act of Congress.—The courts of this commonwealth have no jurisdiction to try offenses created by acts of congress. Com. v. Feely, 1 Va. Cas. 321.

Thus a state court has no jurisdiction to try a defendant charged with feloniously stealing from the mails of the United States, as that is an offense created by an act of congress. Com. v. Feely, 1 Va. Cas. 321.

The penal laws of congress can not be enforced in the state courts, as they do not have any of the judicial powers of the United States. Jackson v. Rose, 2 Va. Cas. 34.

Jurisdiction over Land Ceded to Federal Government. — Where the United States purchases land from a state with the consent of its legislature, it acquires under the federal constitution jurisdiction over the ceded lands, and they are no longer a part of that state and are not subject to the jurisdiction of its courts. The reservation in the act of cession of concurrent jurisdiction with the United States over the land, so that the courts and officers of the state may take such cognizance, execute such process and discharge such legal functions within the same as may not be incompatible with the consent given, is subject to the provisions of the first article and eighth section of the federal constitution, that is, as may not be incompatible with the exclusive jurisdiction of the United States, and which may operate to authorize the service by the officers of the state of the civil and criminal process of the state courts, with reference to acts done within the acknowledged territory of the state outside of the ceded lands. This reservation is valid and is intended to prevent such places from becoming harbors of refuge for debtors and criminals. Foley v. Shriver, 81 Va. 568.

Concurrent Jurisdiction Where Act an Offense by State and Federal Laws. —A state court has jurisdiction to punish an act made an offense by the laws of the state, although the same act was made an offense against the United States by an act of congress. Jett v. Com., 18 Gratt. 933.

Thus, although a counterfeiter be indictable in the courts of the United States for an offense against the laws of the United States, he is also indictable in the courts of Virginia for the offense against the laws of the state. Hendrick v. Com., 5 Leigh 707.

And a state court has jurisdiction to punish the offense of attempting to pass a forged note purporting to be a note of one of the national banks of the United States. Jett v. Com., 18 Gratt. 933.

Question Involving Patents and Patent Rights.—The state courts have jurisdiction over questions arising out of contracts made concerning patent rights, where the validity of the patent arises collaterally, and is not directly involved. Hotchkiss v. Fitzgerald, etc., Plaster Co., 41 W. Va. 357, 23 S. E. 576; Maurice v. Devol, 23 W. Va. 247. See the title PATENTS AND TRADE MARKS.

Effect of Bankruptcy on Jurisdiction of State Courts.—See the title BANKRUPTCY AND INSOLVENCY, vol. 2, p. 234.

In Admiralty Proceedings.—See the title ADMIRALTY, vol. 1, p. 182.

Habeas Corpus.—See the title HABEAS CORPUS, vol. 7, p. 1.

Interstate Commerce.—See the title INTERSTATE COMMERCE, vol. 7, p. 864.

Maritime Liens.—See the title MARITIME LIENS.

Receivers.—See the title RECEIVERS.

Ships and Shipping.—See the title SHIPS AND SHIPPING.

As to removal of causes to the federal courts, see the title REMOVAL OF CAUSES.

XII. Raising and Waiving Objections to Jurisdiction.

A TIME OF RAISING.

Must Be Taken at Early Stages of Cause.—When want of jurisdiction arises from formal defects in the process, or when the want of jurisdiction is over the person, it must be taken advantage of in the early stages of a cause. Western Union Tel. Co. *v.* Pettyjohn, 88 Va. 296, 13 S. E. 431.

Objections Should Be Made before Pleas in Bar.—Objections to the jurisdiction of a court must be taken by plea in abatement, before the defendants plead in bar. Code, 1849, ch. 171, § 19; Washington, etc., Tel. Co. *v.* Hobson, 15 Gratt. 122.

Objection by Plea or Motion before Jury Sworn.—In a suit for freedom though the detention of the plaintiff where the suit was brought is necessary to give the court jurisdiction, yet where the court has general jurisdiction over the subject matter of controversy, the objection to the exercise of jurisdiction in the particular case is a matter in abatement and should be so pleaded, or brought to the notice of the court by rule or motion before the

jury is sworn. Hunter *v.* Humphreys, 14 Gratt. 287. See also, Ratcliff *v.* Polly, 12 Gratt. 528.

No Objection after Joinder of Issue.—It is too late after issue is joined, to object to the jurisdiction of the court, on the ground of the nonresidence of the defendant. Monroe *v.* Redman, 2 Munf. 240.

As to the right to object to any stage of the proceedings for want of jurisdiction of subject matter, see post, "Jurisdiction of the Subject Matter," XII, C, 2.

B. MANNER OF RAISING.

1. In Civil Cases.

By Plea.—Generally, as to pleas in abatement for want of jurisdiction, see the title ABATEMENT, REVIVAL AND SURVIVAL, vol. 1, p. 12. "An objection to the jurisdiction, where the declaration shows jurisdiction on its face, can not be raised by mere motion. 'Where the declaration or bill shows on its face proper matter for the jurisdiction of the court, no exception for the want of such jurisdiction shall be allowed, unless it be taken by plea in abatement.' Code, ch. 125, § 16. The defendant can not allow the action to proceed through trial and verdict to judgment and then complain that the cause of action did not arise in the county in which the venue is laid. If he proposes to contest the jurisdiction of the court on that ground, he must give notice of it by plea in abatement. In Osborne *v.* Taylor, 12 Gratt. 120, the jurisdiction depended upon a question of fact to be decided by the court, namely, whether certain slaves, necessary parties to the bill, had been emancipated. No plea of the jurisdiction had been filed, and the court held that the statute applied and prevented the making of the objection to the jurisdiction for the first time in the appellate court. In Washington, etc., Tel. Co. *v.* Hobson Co., 15 Gratt. 122, it appeared on the trial that some of the defendants resided out of the state and it was held, under statute, that, even if this were good ground for objection to the jurisdiction of the court, it was no excuse for arresting the judgment, as, to be available, it must have been set up by plea in abatement. In Beckley *v.* Palmer, 11 Gratt. 625, and Hudson *v.* Kline, 9 Gratt. 379, where objections to the jurisdiction in equity were sustained at the hearing, the reasoning of the court indicates that they were sustained simply because the bills on their faces showed want of jurisdiction. Had it been otherwise, the statute would have applied. For further illustration of the application of the statute in analogous cases, see Bank *v.* Gettinger, 3 W. Va. 309; Middleton *v.* White, 5 W. Va. 572; Quarrier *v.* Peabody Ins. Co., 10 W. Va. 507." Snyder *v.* Philadelphia Co., 54 W. Va. 149, 46 S. E. 366.

As to pleas to the jurisdiction by corporations, see the title CORPORATIONS, vol. 3, p. 582.

Demurrer and Reply Can Not Be Made to Plea.—A plaintiff can not both demur and reply to a plea to the jurisdiction. Chesapeake, etc., R. Co. *v.* American Exch. Bank, 92 Va. 495, 23 S. E. 935.

By Demurrer.—The question of jurisdiction may always be raised by demurrer, and though no objection has been so taken, the court will dismiss at the hearing if it does not state a case proper for relief. Poindexter *v.* Burwell, 82 Va. 507; Green *v.* Massie, 21 Gratt. 356; Salamone *v.* Keiley, 80 Va. 86.

Generally, as to demurrers for want of jurisdiction, see the title DEMURRERS, vol. 4, p. 475.

By Motion to Dismiss.—A motion to dismiss for want of jurisdiction is the proper and only mode of procedure where the defendant has not been summoned, and has not waived the summons. One not before the court can not be required to plead. A plea in abatement is proper only when the defendant has been summoned, or by appearance has waived the summons. Where the matter relied upon to abate an action is a fact not appearing on the record, or the return of an officer, it must be pleaded in abatement so as to give the other party an opportunity to traverse and try it, but where all the facts relied upon in abatement appear by the record, including the return of the officer, of which the court will take judicial notice without plea, there the action may be dismissed on motion. Hilton *v.* Consumer's Can Co., 103 Va. 255, 48 S. E. 899.

Generally, as to dismissal for want of jurisdiction, see the title DISMISSAL, DISCONTINUANCE AND NONSUIT, vol. 4, p. 695.

By Motion in Arrest.—See the title JUDGMENTS AND DECREES, ante, p. 161.

2. In Criminal Prosecutions.

Questions of jurisdiction may be appropriately raised by a motion for instruction, by demurrer, by motion in arrest of judgment on general issue, or by writ of error. Ryan *v.* Com., 80 Va. 385; Philips' Case, 19 Gratt. 485, 519.

In prosecutions for felonies and other serious offenses, the court will not on motion of the prisoner quash the indictment, unless where the court has no jurisdiction, where no indictable offense is charged, or where there is some other material and substantial defect. Bell *v.* Com., 8 Gratt. 600.

The absolute want of jurisdiction in any form or upon any condition is confessedly good cause of arrest of judgment. Philips *v.* Com., 19 Gratt. 485. See the titles ABATEMENT, REVIVAL AND SURVIVAL, vol. 1, p. 24, et seq.; CRIMINAL LAW, vol. 4, p. 40; INDICTMENTS, INFORMATIONS AND PRESENTMENTS, vol. 7, p. 370; JUDGMENTS AND DECREES, ante, p. 161; NEW TRIALS; SENTENCE AND PUNISHMENT.

C. WAIVER OF OBJECTION.
1. Jurisdiction of the Person.

Generally, as to the power to confer jurisdiction of the person by consent or failure to object, see ante, "Jurisdiction of the Person," III, D, 2, and cross references.

Bill Answered and Merits Contested.
--If the defendant answers the bill without objection to the jurisdiction, and contests the merits of the case, the court will entertain the bill if it be a proper one for equitable cognizance. But if the subject matter is not cognizable in equity, it will dismiss the bill. Hickman v. Stout, 2 Leigh 6; Cresap v. Kemble, 26 W. Va. 603; Mayo v. Murchie, 3 Munf. 358. See the title ADEQUATE REMEDY AT LAW, vol. 1, p. 174.

2. Jurisdiction of the Subject Matter.

Can Not Be Waived.—The objection that a court has no lawful power to act by reason of lack of jurisdiction of the subject matter, can not be waived; it is fatal to the proceedings at any time. Poindexter v. Burwell, 82 W. Va. 507; Beckley v. Palmer, 11 Gratt. 625.

Generally, as to the rule that consent can not give jurisdiction of the subject matter, see ante, "Jurisdiction of the Subject Matter," III, D, 1.

Objection May Be Raised at Any Stage of Proceedings.—"When the court has no lawful power to act by reason of the fact that such power is not conferred, or is expressly withheld, with regard to the subject matter of the suit, the parties thereto can not be said to have waived their objection to the want of power because it is not made at the proper time. Such objection can not be waived, and is fatal at any stage of the proceedings." Yates v. Taylor County Court, 47 W. Va. 376, 35 S. E. 24, quoting 12 Ency. Pl. & Prac., pp. 188, 189.

A bill will be dismissed which does not state a proper case for equitable relief, although no objection is taken to the jurisdiction in the pleadings. Objection on that ground may be taken at any stage of the proceedings. Buffalo v. Pocahontas, 85 Va. 222, 7 S. E. 238.

Subject Matter Not Cognizable in Equity — Dismissal on Hearing. — Where a bill does not state a case proper for relief in equity, or if it is brought in the wrong jurisdiction, the court will dismiss it at the hearing, though no objection has been taken by the defendant in his pleadings. Trout v. Trout, 86 Va. 295, 9 S. E. 1121; Graveley v. Graveley, 84 Va. 145, 151, 4 S. E. 218; Salamone v. Keiley, 80 Va. 86; Boston Blower Co. v. Carman Lumber Co., 94 Va. 94, 26 S. E. 390; Green v. Massie, 21 Gratt. 356, 362; Jones v. Bradshaw, 16 Gratt. 355, 361; Beckley v. Palmer, 11 Gratt. 625; Hudson v. Kline, 9 Gratt. 379; Pollard v. Patterson, 3 Hen. & M. 67. See the title DISMISSAL, DISCONTINUANCE AND NONSUIT, vol. 4, p. 695.

Objection for the First Time on Appeal.—As to the rule that objection may be made to the jurisdiction for the first time on appeal where the want of jurisdiction appears on the face of the record, see the title APPEAL AND ERROR, vol. 1, p. 548.

If a bill is without equity, although it was not demurred to in the lower court, the objection may be taken for the first time in the appellate court, and may be enforced by the court sua sponte, though not raised by the pleading nor suggested by counsel. Boston Blower Co. v. Carman Lumber Co., 94 Va. 94, 26 S. E. 390; Collins v. Sutton, 94 Va. 127, 26 S. E. 415.

3. Jurisdiction of Court in Criminal Prosecutions.

The objection that the county court, at which the indictment was found, did not consist of at least four justices, as required by Const. art. 6, § 5, goes to the jurisdiction of the court, and hence is not waived by pleading to the indictment and going to trial thereon. Jackson *v.* Com., 13 Gratt. 795. See the title INDICTMENTS, INFORMATIONS AND PRESENT-MENTS, vol. 7, p. 371.

D. DETERMINATION OF QUES-TION ON PLEA TO JURIS-DICTION.

Although a plea to the jurisdiction of the court tendered by a prisoner was informal and properly rejected, yet, the objection being a mere question of law, however made, whether by suggestion or motion ore tenus, should be considered and decided by the court. Philips *v.* Com., 19 Gratt. 485.

JURISDICTION IN REM.—See the title JURISDICTION, ante, p. 842. And see PROCEEDINGS IN REM AND IN PERSONAM.

8 Va—58

Lightning Source UK Ltd.
Milton Keynes UK
UKHW012345080219
336872UK00005B/474/P